KT-503-081

POLAND

SILESIA

HOLY ROMAN EMPIRE

Elbe

Weser

Aachen
Liege
Cologne

ABANT

Rhine

Limburg

Fulda

Glogau

Oder

Trier

Mainz

Prague

Craco

Metz

Nuremberg

BOHEMIA

Regensburg

Brno

Constance

Munich

Vienna

Danube

St. Gall

Einsiedeln

HUNGARY

Drava

Milan

Ivrea

Verona

Venice

Po

Mantua

Padua

Sava

Turin

Piacenza

BOSNIA

Ferrara

ROVENCE

Bologna

Rimini

Florence

Pesaro

Vallombrosa

Arezzo

PAPAL STATES

CORSICA

Rome

NAPLES

Naples

£10

The Concise Oxford History of Music

THE
CONCISE OXFORD
HISTORY OF MUSIC

Gerald Abraham

London

Oxford University Press

New York   Melbourne

1979

Oxford University Press, Walton Street, Oxford OX2 6DP

OXFORD LONDON GLASGOW NEW YORK
TORONTO MELBOURNE WELLINGTON CAPE TOWN
IBADAN NAIROBI DAR ES SALAAM TOKYO
KUALA LUMPUR SINGAPORE JAKARTA HONG KONG
DELHI BOMBAY CALCUTTA MADRAS KARACHI

© Gerald Abraham 1979

ISBN 0 19 311319 8

British Library Cataloguing in Publication Data

Abraham, Gerald
  1. The concise Oxford history of music.
  1. Music – History and criticism
  I. Title
  780'.9   ML160   79-40540
  ISBN 0-19-311319-8

Maps drawn by Mike Strickland

Filmset in Monophoto Ehrhardt 11/12pt by
BAS Printers Limited, Over Wallop, Hampshire
Printed and bound by
The Pitman Press Limited, Bath

Preface

It has long been generally agreed that large-scale histories of music by single authors are things of the past. Nevertheless it has seemed to me that a chronological synoptic survey of the whole field in tolerably readable quasi-narrative form, a survey by one man who has for years been occupied in scrutinizing the work of specialists, might still be useful to the intelligent layman and non-specialist. It might even perhaps be useful to a specialist who, finding himself 'knowing more and more about less and less', might wish to stand back and consider the whole continuum of musical history.

It is the reality of this continuum that concerns me: music itself in so far as and when we can grasp it. Not composers except as producers of it, not instruments except as they help to make it; there are plenty of other books which give that kind of information. Instead of attempting a general valuation of X, I have tried to show what X contributed to the course, and perhaps the evolution, of church music, of orchestral music, of opera. If his creative career falls partly in one period, partly in another, I wish to show each part of his output in the context of that of his contemporaries rather than in that of what he himself had already achieved or was to achieve later.

Far from being a condensation of the *New Oxford History of Music*, which would be impossible, this book is not even based on it. The *New Oxford History* employs the microscope, the *Concise* the telescope. Through the telescope one sees the broad lines and can also pick out details that reveal life and reality – though not, unfortunately, the details which would fill out and qualify simplified accounts of complex matters. In far distant time past the telescope is useless; one sees mostly haze and mirage. In the recent and immediate past it is again useless. One sees all too many figures close at hand – some of them personal friends and acquaintances – among whom it is not easy to pick out the really significant. Yet one must try to do so if the account is not to degenerate into a meaningless list of names. Even with the telescope there is a famous precedent for the use of the blind eye.

The choice is necessarily arbitrary, as many other decisions must be arbitrary – choice of music examples (I have tried to avoid the familiar), bibliographical references, and so on – though I have always had reasons for my decisions. Some omissions have no doubt been accidental; but the thinning out of references to bibliographical help and to complete editions after the eighteenth century has been deliberate, not merely because the bibliography is impossibly large and the complete editions are less necessary to the probable reader – the intelligent layman or student, not the mature musicologist – but because the probable reader is likely to be much better informed about music in the normal repertory. For the same reason I have modified my general approach, giving over-familiar music of the nineteenth century perhaps over-much space in order to avoid annotated lists of great names and works, but at the same time drawing attention to the music of secondary and tertiary masters so as to correct any impression that great names make up the whole picture.

Since the area I have swept with my telescope is practically boundless, I have directed it principally to what I conceive to be the main stream of Western music which flowed initially from Western Asia and the East Mediterranean lands. And not improperly, for in the long run it has spread and flooded the greater part of the world. It is true that the serious musicologist no longer regards 'music' as Euro-centred; he recognizes that the vast majority of the world's inhabitants have their own musics – some of them 'high' cultures of great antiquity and sophistication. Even the widest Euro-American musical public is aware of their existence and sometimes enjoys superficially the musics of India, the Islamic world, and Eastern Asia, although these can hardly convey to Western listeners what they convey to natives of their own lands. All the same, Western music has developed more richly than any other and when it has come into contact with these others it has, regrettably, often tended to absorb or contaminate them without being more than occasionally and superficially influenced in return. Writing for the Western reader, I have tried to give at least brief *aperçus* of some outstandingly important non-Western musical systems, interrupting my main account at those points in history where the West became intelligently conscious of them.

The relationship between 'high art' Western music and anonymous-popular music presents another kind of difficulty. The relationship has been mutually beneficial and the gap that began to open between them during the nineteenth century has been harmful to both. But here again I have generally had to bypass the music of the 'folk' as I have the 'high art' of some peripheral Western countries.

Even so, the areas I have tried to cover are so extensive that, in contrast to the specialist, I have found that I know less and less about more and more and have called upon kindly experts to save me from grievous error: in particular Professor Denis Arnold and Mrs. Arnold, Dr. E. J. Borthwick, Dr. John Caldwell, Mr. W. V. Davies, Mr. T. C. Mitchell, Mr. Jeremy Noble, Dr. Laurence Picken, Dr. Richard Widdess, and Mr. Owen Wright. I am infinitely grateful to them and, last but far from least, to Mr. Anthony Mulgan of the Oxford University Press for his constant encouragement and helpful advice.

Contents

Part I *The Rise of West Asian and East Mediterranean Music*

Introduction   2

1. MESOPOTAMIA AND EGYPT 7

Pre-history	7	Egypt: the New Kingdom	14
Sumer	7	Egypt in decline	17
Post-Sumerian music	10	The Assyrian empire	18
Egypt: the Old Kingdom	12	Nebuchadnezzar's alleged orchestra	21
Egypt: the Middle Kingdom	13	Mathematical theory	21

2. THE GREEK CONTRIBUTION 22

Homeric music	22	Music in the age of tragedy	30
From phorminx to kithara	24	Plato on music	31
The aulos	25	Aristotle	33
The importance of *Mousike* in Greek life	26	The *Harmonics* of Aristoxenus	33
		Greek notation	34
Pythagoras and early music theory	27		

3. THE HELLENISTIC–ROMAN WORLD 37

The process of internationalization	37	Music under the Empire	47
Music in the Old Testament	37	Musicians' guilds	48
Hebrew music under Hellenistic pressure	39	Monster concerts and choral *concentus*	49
Etruscan influence on Rome	40	The Alexandrian theorists	50
Roman festivals and Roman theatre	42	The earliest Christian music	50
Origin of the organ	44	The early Christian hymn	51

4. MUSIC IN THE CHRISTIAN WORLD 53

Music of the barbarians	53	'Old Roman' and 'Gregorian' chant	59
Music of the Eastern Church	54	The evidence of notation	61
The church-fathers and the psalms	54	Neumes	62
Development of the Christian hymn	55	The eight church modes	64
The Offices and the Mass	56	The division of the Church	65
The role of Gregory the Great	57	The isolation of conservative Orthodoxy	66
Choral music under the Frankish monarchs	58		

Part II *The Ascendancy of Western Europe*

Introduction 70

5. THE BEGINNINGS OF POLYPHONY 75

The writings of Hucbald	75	St. Martial and Santiago polyphony	86
Musica Enchiriadis and early organum	77	Trope and sequence	88
Developments in notation	80	Liturgical drama	91
The embryonic staff	84	Secular song	93
Guido d'Arezzo and the hexachord	84	Vernacular song	93
Notation of note-values	85	The earliest troubadours	94

6. MUSIC OF THE PROTO-RENAISSANCE 97

The spread of courtly song in France and Germany	97	From clausula to motet	108
Cantigas, Laudi, and English song	98	The Montpellier Codex	109
Courtly song: its types, forms, and performance	100	Developments in the motet	110
		The instrumental motet	111
Mensuration of note-values	102	Interrelation of upper parts	112
The Notre Dame organa	103	Secular tenors	113
Three and four-part harmony	106	Franconian notation	114
Conductus	108	Adam de la Hale	115

7. THE 'NEW ART' OF THE FOURTEENTH CENTURY 117

Ars Nova	117	Early Italian polyphony	128
The *Roman de Fauvel*	118	The trecento madrigal	129
The Robertsbridge Codex	119	Francesco Landini	131
Political and ceremonial motets	122	Fourteenth-century English music	133
Machaut's secular music	123	The French mannerists	135
Chace and *Caccia*	124	Italy at the turn of the century	136
Machaut and the polyphonic Mass	125		

8. THE EUROPEAN SYNTHESIS 138

French and Walloon musicians in Italy	138	Dufay's successors	149
Italian influence on Ciconia	140	English songs and carols	149
Dunstable and the 'Old Hall' composers	141	The Burgundian chanson	151
		Binchois and the last Burgundians	152
English conductus-style and fauxbourdon	142	The beginnings of German polyphony	153
Dufay and the 'cyclic' Mass	144	Early fifteenth-century keyboard music	156
Proportional notation	146		
Dufay's last compositions	148	Paumann and the Buxheim tablature	158

9. THE IMPACT OF THE RENAISSANCE 161

Dominance of the Netherlanders	161	Laudi and carnival songs	171
Ockeghem the master	162	The frottola	173
Interrelationship of the Netherlanders	164	Josquin des Prez	174
Technical ingenuities	165	Josquin's French contemporaries	177
Pierre de La Rue	167	Spanish composers	179
Jacob Obrecht	169	Music in Eastern Europe	180
Words in polyphony	169	German polyphony	180
Netherland composers in Italy	170	Heinrich Isaac	181

German and Italian instrumental tablatures	183	English keyboard music 186
		English musical insularism 186

Interlude

10. MUSIC IN THE ISLAMIC WORLD 190

The origins of Islamic music	190	Ṣafī al-Dīn and the melodic modes 196
Music under the earlier caliphates	191	Muslim music in Spain and North
Classical practice and theory	191	Africa 197
Byzantine influence	192	Contemporary practice 197
Music under the divided caliphates	195	

Part III *The Ascendancy of Italy*

Introduction 202

11. MUSIC DURING THE REFORMATION 207

Verbal intelligibility in church music	207	New forms of secular polyphony 226
Church music of Josquin's followers	207	The earlier sixteenth-century
New paraphrase techniques in the		madrigal 228
Masses	211	The church music of Willaert and his
The French chanson	213	circle 232
The chanson after Attaingnant	216	Cipriano de Rore and the madrigal 233
Parisian church music	219	Venetian instrumental music 234
Vernacular religious song: Calvinist		Spanish church music 236
psalters	219	Instrumental music in Spain 236
Lutheran hymns	222	The lute in other countries 239
German secular song	224	English organ music 239
German and Polish keyboard		Church music under Henry VIII and
tablatures	225	Mary 241

12. MUSIC DURING THE COUNTER- REFORMATION 244

The Tridentine reform	244	The religious music of Lassus 254
The Oratorian movement and		Vernacular psalm settings 256
'Gregorian' reform	246	Lutheran *Geistliche Lieder* 257
The perfection of the Roman style	247	German Passion music 258
Venice and the *stile concertato*	248	Venetian influence and the Lutheran
Spartitura and *basso continuo*	251	hymn-motet 259
Monteverdi's church music	253	Religious music in England 261
The end of the Netherland tradition	254	

13. SECULAR SONG AND INSTRUMENTAL MUSIC (*c.* 1560–*c.* 1610) 264

Netherland composers of madrigal		Morley's canzonets and balletts 276
and chanson	264	Weelkes, Wilbye, and their
The Italian madrigalists	265	contemporaries 277
The revival of monody	268	The English ayre 278
The Florentine intermedii	269	Italian vocal forms in Germany 280
The earliest operas	271	The madrigal in the European
Cavalieri's *Rappresentazione* and		periphery 283
Caccini's *Nuove musiche*	273	Madrigalian influence and *musique*
Monteverdi's *Orfeo* and *Arianna*	274	*mesurée* in the chanson 283
The madrigal in England	275	

The international repertories for lute and keyboard	284	English music for consort and virginals	290
Venetian instrumental music	286	The keyboard music of Sweelinck and	
Dance music in Germany	289	Praetorius	294

14. SECULAR SONG (*c.* 1610–60) 295

The transformation of the madrigal	295	The north German and Saxon	
Cantade and *arie*	297	composers	304
The cantata in Rome	299	The French *air de cour*	306
Italian influence on German song	303	English song	308

15. THE EARLY GROWTH OF OPERA (*c.* 1610–60) 311

The entertainment of princes	311	Italian opera in Paris	322
Opera in Rome	313	French *pastorales* and *comédies-ballets*	324
The first public opera-houses	316	Opera in Germany and Spain	325
Monteverdi's lost operas	317	The English masque	325
Francesco Cavalli	319	The spread of public opera	326
Cesti in Venice and Vienna	320		

16. INSTRUMENTAL MUSIC (*c.* 1610–60) 328

The basic problem of instrumental composition	328	German dances and *Symphonien*	334
Instrumental monody	329	Organ treatment of Lutheran *Choräle*	337
The mid-seventeenth-century sonata	330	The keyboard music of Frescobaldi	338
English music for viols	332	Organ music in Iberia and France	340
French ensemble music	333	French lutenists and *clavecinistes*	340
		Froberger's international summation	342

17 RELIGIOUS MUSIC (*c.* 1610–60) 344

A cappella style and *concertato* style	344	Lutheran bible *Historiae*	353
Dramatic dialogue and oratorio	346	German Passion music	354
Concertato church music in Venice	347	Conservatism in France and England	355
Venetian influence in Germany	350	Vernacular psalms	356

18. THE DIFFUSION OF OPERA (*c.* 1660–*c.* 1725) 358

Popularization in Venetian opera	358	Purcell's music for the stage	369
Court opera at Naples and Vienna	359	Italian opera in London	370
'Aria Opera'	361	The general triumph of Italy	372
Italian opera in Germany	365	The beginnings of French opera	372
The Hamburg Opera	366	Quinault, Lully, and *tragédie en*	
Handel in Italy	368	*musique*	373
Opera in Restoration England	369	Lully's heirs and the *opéra-ballet*	376

19. SECULAR VOCAL MUSIC (*c.* 1660–*c.* 1725) 379

The Italian chamber cantata	379	The French *air*	387
Scarlatti's cantata model	381	The *cantate française*	387
Handel's Italian cantatas and duets	382	Public concerts in London	390
Marcello's reaction against *bel canto*	383	The English ode	390
The German secular *Arie*	385	Purcell's chamber cantatas	391
Italian influence on the German cantata	385	English theatre songs and cantatas	392
The *dramme per musica* of Telemann and Bach	386	The Russian *kant*	393

20. RELIGIOUS MUSIC (*c.* 1660–*c.* 1725) 395

Operatic influence on oratorio	395	Cantata elements in other church	
Italian *oratorio volgare*	395	music	409
Oratorio in Vienna	398	Survival of the 'Palestrina style'	410
The Roman oratorios of Scarlatti	399	Motets for solo voices	410
The German oratorio Passion	400	Spanish conservatism	411
Passion-oratorio at Hamburg	402	Church music of the Western Slavs	411
Bach's Passions	403	Royal taste in French church music	412
Sacred dialogues and *Kirchenstücke*	403	Italianate elements in French oratorio	
The Lutheran church cantata	405	and motet	413
Recitative, aria, and hymn in Bach's		Composers of the English Chapel	
cantatas	407	Royal	415
Telemann's cantata cycles	408	The anthems of Blow and Purcell	416
		Handel's early Anglican music	417

21. INSTRUMENTAL MUSIC (*c.* 1660–*c.* 1725) 419

Tonal organization of instrumental		Telemann's eclecticism	432
forms	419	The German keyboard suite	434
The opera *sinfonia*	420	French music for clavecin	435
The concerto grosso	423	French organ music	436
The trio sonata	424	Italian keyboard music	438
The influence of Corelli's style	425	Kuhnau and the harpsichord sonata	439
German experimentalism	426	Survival of older keyboard forms	440
Torelli's ritornello form	427	The Lutheran organ composers	441
Vivaldi and his followers	428	Bach's earlier keyboard works	443
Bach at Cöthen	430		

22. CHANGES IN OPERA (*c.* 1725–90) 445

The challenge to *opera seria*	445	Gluck in Vienna	464
Metastasian opera	445	Gluck's regeneration of Italian opera	465
Dialect comedy and comic intermezzi	448	Gluck's French operas	466
English ballad opera	450	Mozart's *opere serie*	469
The precursors of *opéra comique*	450	Opera in Paris before the Revolution	469
Italian opera of the mid-century	451	Serious elements in *opera buffa*	471
Rameau as the heir of Lully	454	The development of *Singspiel*	473
The *Querelle des bouffons*	456	Mozart's operatic masterpieces	475
The return to nature	457	Opera in Spain	477
Opéra comique	459	The English *pasticci*	477
The rejuvenation of Italian opera	459	Opera in Poland	478
Sentiment in *opéra comique*	463	The birth of Russian opera	478

23. ORCHESTRAL AND CHAMBER MUSIC (*c.* 1725–90) 482

Varieties of concerto	482	Haydn and string-quartet style	495
The concert sinfonia	483	The *symphonie concertante*	496
The new instrumental idiom	484	Mozart's development as instrumental	
Embryonic sonata-form	485	composer	497
The concerto in mid-century	487	The Bach brothers and Haydn	499
The symphony at Paris	487	Haydn, Mozart, and string quartet	
Stamitz and the younger symphonists	489	texture	500
Diversity of instrumental forms	491	Mozart and the piano concerto	502
Haydn's early symphonies	492	Mozart's last instrumental works	504
The piano concertos and symphonies		The symphony during the 1780s	505
of J. C. Bach	494		

24. MUSIC FOR OR WITH KEYBOARD (*c.* 1725–90) 509

The later clavier music of Bach,
  Handel, and their German
  contemporaries 509
Domenico Scarlatti and the
  harpsichord sonata 511
'The Scarlatti sect in London' 512
Italian harpsichord composers 514
The decline of organ music in
  Germany 516
German keyboard music for amateurs 517
Keyboard music with optional
  accompaniment 517

The solo sonatas of J. C. Bach and
  the young Haydn 520
Mozart and the pianoforte 521
Clementi and some contemporaries 522
C. P. E. Bach's influence on Haydn 524
The accompanied keyboard sonatas of
  Haydn and Mozart 526
Mozart's piano quartets and trios 527
The 'keyboard song' 528
German domestic song 529
North German ode settings 529
Lyrical song and narrative ballad 531
Mozart's *Deutsche Arien* 532

25. RELIGIOUS MUSIC (*c.* 1725–90) 534

The decline of church music 534
Bach's last cantatas and *Matthew
  Passion* 534
The 'B minor Mass' 535
The church cantata in decline 538
Passion and oratorio in the age of
  sensibility 539
Handel's English oratorios 542
English composers of oratorio 544
Liturgical music in France 545

Oratorio in Italy 546
Liturgical music in Italy 547
Hasse at Dresden 549
Religious music at Vienna 550
Haydn at Eszterház 551
Church music at Salzburg 552
The reform of church music by
  Joseph II 553
Mozart's last religious compositions 554

Interlude

26. THE MUSIC OF INDIA 558

The beginnings of Indian music 558
The musical system 559

Differences of North and South 561

27. THE MUSIC OF EASTERN ASIA 564

Early Chinese music 564
Foreign influences on Chinese music 565
Music under the T'ang, Sung, and
  Yüan emperors 567
The Ming period 568

The Manchus and 'Peking Opera' 568
Chinese influence on Japan 569
Japanese music under the *Shōguns* 570
The impact of the West 571
The music of Indonesia 572

Part IV *The Ascendancy of Germany*

Introduction 574

28. OPERA (1790–1830) 577

Operas of the French Revolution 577
The *Léonores* of Gaveaux and
  Beethoven 581
Spontini and 'Empire classicism' 582
Parisian *grand opéra* 583
Romantic *opéra comique* 584
Simon Mayr and Ferdinando Paer 585
Rossini's conquest of Europe 586

The romantic melancholy of Bellini 587
German opera after Mozart 588
The dawn of German romantic opera 590
Spohr and Weber 591
Continuous texture and reminiscence
  themes 592
Marschner and 'horror opera' 593

National opera in peripheral
European countries 594

Opera in New York and London 595

29. ORCHESTRAL MUSIC (1790–1830) 596

Haydn's last symphonies 596
Refugee composers in London 597
Popularity of the concerto 598
Beethoven's years of symphonic
composition 600
Piano concertos by Beethoven's
contemporaries 603

Innovations in overture and
symphony 605
Schubert's early orchestral music 609
The symphony in the 1820s 610
New trends 612
The piano concerto in the 1820s 613

30. CHAMBER MUSIC (1790–1830) 617

Haydn's last chamber works 617
Beethoven's early chamber music 618
Dussek and Louis Ferdinand 620
Beethoven's middle-period chamber
music 621

Varied concepts of chamber music 622
Chamber compositions of Schubert's
youth 624
Chamber music during the 1920s 625
Beethoven's last quartets 626

31. PIANO MUSIC (1790–1830) 629

The piano sonata: 1794–1805 629
New piano textures 631
The poetic miniature 632

Dance music for piano 634
The piano sonata: 1816–26 635
The new generation 640

32. SOLO SONG (1790–1830) 642

Haydn's canzonets and folk-song
accompaniments 642
The romance in France 642
The Lied in the 1790s 643
The inspiration of Goethe 644

Cycles and collections of Lieder 645
The gradual revealing of Schubert 647
The German narrative ballad 649
The art-songs of the Western Slavs 651
Birth of Russian art-song 652

33. CHORAL MUSIC (1790–1830) 654

The open-air festivals of the French
Revolution 654
Haydn's symphonic Masses 656
The Mass in provincial Austria 657
Cherubini's first Masses 658

Haydn's oratorios 660
Oratorio after Haydn 662
Catholic music in the post-war period 662
'Missa Solemnis' 664
Secular music 665

34. ORCHESTRAL MUSIC (1830–93) 667

The symphonies of Berlioz 667
Spohr and the programme-symphony 669
Mendelssohn's orchestral forms 671
Concert overtures of the 1830s 672
Changes in the orchestral brass 675
Schumann and the symphony 675
The romantic concerto 677
'Tone-pictures', 'overtures', and 'tone-
poems' 680
Innovations in concerto and
symphony 683
The 'New German School' 684

Defections from the Liszt camp 685
Symphonic music in the 1860s 686
Liszt's international protégés 688
Renaissance in France after 1871 691
The advent of Brahms 693
The symphonies of Bruckner 695
Dvořák: heir of Schubert 696
Russian orchestral music: 1876–93 698
Orchestral composition in the West 699
The young Strauss and his
contemporaries 702

35. OPERA (1830–93) 705

The golden age of *grand opéra*	705	Wagnerian music-drama	722
Italian romantic opera	709	The last phase of *grand opéra*	727
German romantic opera	711	Russian opera	728
The novel elements in Wagner	713	Polish and Czech opera	733
National opera in Eastern Europe	717	Diversity of non-Wagnerian opera	739
Irish and English composers	720	Wagner's influence in French opera	741
Opera during the 1850s	720	Late Verdi and *verismo*	743

36. CHORAL MUSIC (1830–93) 746

Oratorio in Germany	746	Liszt's Masses and oratorios	754
The 'sacred concert' in France	748	Oratorio in decline	756
Influence of the plainsong revival	749	The 'oratorio of sentiment'	756
Secular oratorios	750	Liturgical music in Germany and	
Religious music in England	751	Russia	758
Liturgical music in Bavaria and		The choral works of Brahms	759
Austria	752	The narrative ballad	760

37. THE DOMINANCE OF THE PIANO (1830–93) 761

The Parisian pianist-composers	761	The piano miniature	775
Schumann's piano music	763	French chamber music	778
Romantic piano music: 1830–50	764	Chamber music in Russia	779
Piano-dominated chamber music	765	The chamber music of Dvořák	780
The French *mélodie*	767	Czech song	781
Solo song in the Slav lands	768	Solo song in Russia	783
The spate of romantic *Lieder*	770	The *mélodie*: 1855–93	786
Organ music in mid-century	772	The late nineteenth-century *Lied*	788
Problems of large-scale instrumental		Solo song in Scandinavia	791
form	772	English song	792

38. THE DECLINE AND FALL OF ROMANTICISM (1893–1918) 794

Central European music at the turn of		Cross-currents in French music	803
the century	794	Individual eclectics	804
The influence of Bach	796	Hybridization of forms and media	806
Schoenberg's change of course	797	The crisis of 'expressionism'	807
Belated Wagnerism	798	Artificial harmonic construction	808
The Wagnerian sunset in the Latin		Influence of the Dyagilev Ballet	809
lands	801	The retreat from romantic excess	809
The landmark of *Pelléas*	802		

Interlude

39. THE MUSIC OF BLACK AFRICA AND AMERICA 812

General characteristics	812	Negro music in North America	816
African instruments	813	Cakewalk, ragtime, and blues	817
Contact with Western music	815	Jazz	817

Part V The Fragmentation of Tradition

Introduction 820

40. MUSIC BETWEEN THE WARS (1919–45) 823

Musical prosperity in America	823	The twelve-note row	834
Contemporary idioms in Britain	824	Hindemith and *Gebrauchsmusik*	835
The main stream in Paris	825	Czech opera	837
Satie and *Les Six*	827	East European masters	838
Ondes Martenot and quarter-tone		Music in Russia after the Revolution	840
music	831	The concept of 'Socialist realism'	842
The contemporary spirit in Italy	831	Music during the Second World War	844

41. CROSS-CURRENTS AFTER 1945 846

The eclectic language	846	International disciples of Stockhausen	853
Messiaen's grand synthesis	847	Modified serialism	855
The Darmstadt *Ferienkurse*	848	The post-war symphony	856
Total serialization	849	Twelve-note music in the U.S.S.R.	857
Electronically-produced sound	851	Post-war opera	858
Indeterminacy	852	Stravinsky: the last years	859
The avant-garde in America	853		

FURTHER READING AND RECOMMENDED EDITIONS 864

PART I *The Rise of West Asian and East Mediterranean Music* 865

PART II *The Ascendancy of Western Europe* 869

INTERLUDE *Music in the Islamic World* 876

PART III *The Ascendancy of Italy* 877

INTERLUDE *The Music of India* 892

INTERLUDE *The Music of Eastern Asia* 894

PART IV *The Ascendancy of Germany* 897

INTERLUDE *The Music of Black Africa and America* 907

PART V *The Fragmentation of Tradition* 910

Index 913

Plates

Page

1   Sumerian harp-players of *c.* 2650 B.C., represented on a vase from Bismaya *(Oriental Institute of Chicago University)*.   8

2   Harp with bull-headed soundbox on an inlaid panel from Ur (*c.* 2600 B.C.) *(London, British Musum)*.   9

3   Vertical angled harp on a clay plaque (2000–1800 B.C.) from Ishchali *(Musée du Louvre, Paris)*.   11

4   Babylonian terracotta plaque (early 2nd millennium B.C.) showing a long-necked 'lute' *(London, British Museum)*.   11

5   Bedouin lyre-player: from the tomb of Khnum-hotep (12th Dynasty) at Beni Hasan.   14

6   Egyptian angle-harp with vertical soundbox, and lyre with curved arms, from Tomb 22 at Thebes (18th Dynasty).   15

7   Musicians in a wall-painting at Thebes (Tomb 38) playing harp, 'lute', possibly small castanets, double reed-pipes, and curved-arm lyre.   16

8   Fragment of an ivory unguent box, probably made in Phoenicia, possibly in north Syria, found in Ashurnasirpal II's palace at Nimrud. Women musicians are playing a zither (or xylophone), frame-drum, and double reed-pipes *(London, British Museum)*.   19

9   Ninevite lyre-players of the Sennacherib period, possibly prisoners guarded by an Assyrian soldier *(from a relief in the British Museum)*.   19

10   Elamite court-singer squeezing her larynx, from Nineveh *(London, British Museum 124802)*.   20

11   Apollo, accompanied by two Muses (?), plays a seven-stringed lyre with a plectrum, after his arrival on Delos. From a late 7th-century B.C. amphora from Melos *(Athens, National Archaeological Museum)*.   23

12   Players of barbiton, phorminx, krotala, and aulos: on the Mosaon amphora *(Staatliche Antikensammlung, Munich)*.   25

13   Troops marching to the aulos: from a 7th-century black-figure pot *(Rome, Villa Giulia)*.   26

14   Procession of auloi and kitharas from the north frieze of the Parthenon (*17th-century drawing by James Carey. Paris, Bibliothèque Nationale*).   27

15   First of two hymns to Apollo on the wall of the Treasury of the Athenians at Delphi (*c.* 138 B.C.)   36

16   Cup-bearer, *tibicen*, and lyra-player *(fresco in the 'Tomb of the Leopards'*, c. 480–70 B.C., *Tarquinia)*.   40

17   Etruscan musicians, wearing the long robes of their guild, in a relief on a 5th-century B.C. sarcophagus from Caere *(Rome, Museo Etrusco Gregoriano)*.   41

18   Relief on a 1st-century B.C. Roman sarcophagus from Amiternum *(Museo Civico, Aquileia)* showing two *cornicines*, a *liticen*, and four *tibicines* taking part in a funeral procession.   41

19   (a) Pipes of the 3rd-century organ at Aquincum near Budapest, (b) sliders admitting wind to the pipes, and (c) the sliders in position.   46

20   Papyrus of the 2nd century A.D. from Contrapollinopolis in the Thebaid: a paean to Apollo and a funeral song for a hero, with instrumental interludes (indented), in notation denoting note-values and rests (*Berlin, Staatliche Museen*).   49

21   Gloria in a St. Amand manuscript of *c.* 871, with transliterated Greek text and Latin translation in parallel columns (*Paris, Bibliothèque Nationale, ms. lat. 2291*).   62

22   Two details from Hucbald, *De Institutione Harmonica* (*Brussels, Bibl. Royale Belgique, Codex Bruxell. 10078–95, fo. 87*).   75

23   Two-part composition on the melody 'Benedicta sit' (*Paris, Bibliothèque Nationale, lat. 7202, fo. 56*).   79

24   Neumes written at varying heights above the words in the Laon Gradual of *c.* 930 (*Laon, Ms. 239, fo. 12*).   81

25   *Vox principalis* (i) and *vox organalis* (ii) of a Gloria in the 11th-century Winchester troper (*Cambridge, Corpus Christi 473, fo. 64 and fo. 142*).   83

26   'Boethian' letter-notation used to clarify pitch of neumes in an 11th-century *Antiphonarium* from the abbey of St. Bénigne, Dijon (*Montpellier, Bibl. de l'École de Médecine, fo. 30*).   83

27   Two-part setting of 'Ut tuo propitiatus' (11th-century), notated in letters only (*Oxford, Bodleian Library, Bodl. 572*).   83

28   The earliest source of 'Per partum virginis' (*c.* 1150) (*Paris, Bibliothèque Nationale lat. 3719, fo. 64*).   86

29   Miniatures in the *Cantigas de Santa Maria* of Alfonso X of Castile, showing players of *guitarra morisca*, *rabāb* and lute, pipe and tabor, and tuned bells (*Biblioteca del Monastirio del El Escorial*).   99

30   Ballade with instrumental accompaniment in the Chansonnier Cangé (*Paris, Bibliothèque Nationale, fr. 846*).   101

31(i)   (*a*) Triplum, (*b*) *motetus*, and (*c*) tenor of Philippe de Vitry's *Fauvel* motet 'Firmissime/Adesto, sancta trinitas/Alleluya, Benedictus' (*Paris, Bibliothèque Nationale, fr. 146, fos. 43–45*).   120

31(ii)   Detail from the Robertsbridge Codex, the earliest known collection of keyboard music, showing the end of an instrumental piece and the beginning of a transcription of the Fauvel motet (*London, British Library, Add. 28550, fo. 43v*).   120

32(i)   Landini's ballata 'Questa fanciulla' in the Squarcialupi Codex. (*Florence, Biblioteca Medicea-Laurenziana, Pal. 87, fo. 138*).

(ii)   Keyboard transcription in the Codex Reina (*Paris, Bibliothèque Nationale, nouv. acq. fr. 6771, fo. 85*).   132

33   Players of slide trumpet and two shawms in 'The Hunt of Philip the Good': 16th-century copy of a painting (destroyed in 1608) by a follower of Jan van Eyck (*Paris, Musée de Versailles*).   150

34   Part of an organ composition of the Kyrie 'Cunctipotens genitor Deus' (played by the left hand) in the Faenza Codex of *c.* 1420. (*Faenza, Biblioteca Comunale*).   157

35   Two of the earliest known examples of free preludial composition for keyboard: *praeambula* in the tablature compiled in 1448 by Adam Ileborgh of Stendal in Brandenburg (*Philadelphia, Curtis Institute of Music*).   158

36   Florentine carnival singers: woodcut from *Canzone per andare in maschera per carnesciale* (Florence, 1485), a collection of song-texts without music (*Florence, Biblioteca Nazionale Centrale*).   172

37(i)   '*Ūd* (lute) in an early fourteenth-century copy of the *Kitāb al-adwār* (Book of Modes) of the Baghdad musician Ṣafī al-Dīn (*Oxford, Bodleian Library, Ms. Marsh 521, fo. 157v*).   196

37(ii)   The big 64-stringed *qānūn* (psaltery), invented by Ṣafī – who called it *nuzha* (*from the same manuscript, fo. 158*).   196

38   Three ladies painted by the so-called 'Master of the female half-lengths', a
     Franco-Fleming of the early 16th century, about to play Sermisy's 'Jouyssance
     vous donneray'.   214

39   *Romance*, 'Toda mi vida', for voice with vihuela accompaniment, from Luis
     Milan's *Libro de musica de vihuela de mano, intitulado El Maestro* (Valencia, 1535
     or 1536).   238

40   The title-page of Marbeck's *The Booke of Common Praier noted* (1550).   262

41   Bernardo Buontalenti's design for 'La gara fra Muse e Pieridi', the second of the
     intermedii performed in Florence in 1589 at the wedding of Ferdinando de'
     Medici and Cristina of Lorraine. (*Crown copyright, Victoria and Albert Museum*). 270

42   Dowland's 'Awake sweet love' in his *First Booke of Songs or Ayres of foure partes*
     (London, 1597).   279

43   The standard Elizabethan mixed consort, shown in a detail from the Unton
     memorial painting of *c*. 1596 (*London, National Portrait Gallery*).   291

44   One of Giacomo Torelli's stage-sets for Luigi Rossi's *Orfeo*, performed in the
     Palais-Royal, Paris, during the carnival of 1647.   323

45   The Oratorio del Santissimo Crocifisso, Rome, for which Carissimi composed
     his oratorios.   348

46   Renaud escapes from Armide's toils in the Fifth Act of Lully's opera (*after the
     engraving by Jean Bérain*)   375

47   The opening of Purcell's solo cantata 'Bess of Bedlam', published in the first
     volume of *Orpheus Britannicus* (second edition, 1706), with 'through-bass . . .
     figur'd for the *Organ, Harpsichord*, or *Theorbo-Lute*'.   392

48   Pelham's Humfrey's 'Like as the Hart' in the hand of the 18-year-old Purcell
     (*Cambridge, Fitzwilliam Museum Ms 88, fo. 7*).   417

49   Justine Favart as Bastienne in *Les Amours de Bastien et Bastienne* (1753), after a
     portrait by Charles-André Vanloo. She made theatrical history by dressing as a
     real peasant girl.   458

50   First of the four title-pages of Bach's so-called 'B minor Mass' (*Berlin,
     Staatsbibliothek Preussischer Kulturbesitz, Musikabteilung*).   536

51   (i) the *sārangī* has three strings played with a bow and forty to fifty sympathetic
     strings
     (ii) North Indian ensemble with (left to right) *sitar, sārod, tambura*, and *tāblā*
     (Jodhpur, Rajasthan) (*photo Deben Bhattacharya*).   561

52   Players of hand-drum and *biwa*. At the feet of the blind *biwa* player lie a pitchpipe
     and a small recorder. Illustration by Tosa Mitsunobu from the *Shokunin Zukushi
     Uta-awase* (1744).   571

53   Title-page of Le Sueur's opera *La Caverne* (1793) (*London, British Library*).   578

54   Haydn (seated in the foreground) being honoured with a fanfare of trumpets and
     drums before the performance of *Die Schöpfung* in the Aula of the Old University,
     Vienna, on 27 March 1808.   661

55   Opening of the 'Bluminen-Kapitel' (flower chapter), after Jean Paul's *Siebenkäs*,
     which was originally the second movement of Mahler's First Symphony but later
     discarded, in autograph score (*Yale, University Library, and Theodore Presser
     Company*).   704

56   Coronation scene in Act IV of Meyerbeer's *Prophète*: the first London performance
     at Covent Garden (24 July 1849) with Mario as John of Leyden and Pauline
     Viardot as Fidès (*Illustrated London News*).   708

57   Wotan and Fricka, followed by Froh, Freia, and Donner, cross the rainbow-
     bridge to Valhalla while Loge calls to the lamenting Rhine-maidens in the valley
     below: last scene of the first production of *Das Rheingold*, staged separately at
     Munich on 22 September 1869.   726

58   Liszt conducting the first performance of his *Legende von der heiligen Elisabeth* in the Redoute at Pest on 15 August 1865 to commemorate the 25th anniversary of the Pest Conservatoire (*after a drawing by Bertalen Székely*).   755

59   V. A. Hartmann's project of 1869 for a city gate and bell-tower at Kiev, surmounted by suggestions of a traditional woman's head-dress and an old Slavonic helmet. It was shown in the posthumous exhibition of his sketches, water-colours, and designs at the Petersburg Academy of Arts in March 1874 and inspired the last of Musorgsky's *Pictures from an Exhibition*.   777

60   Composition sketch for the opening of Act v of Debussy's *Pelléas et Mélisande*; the curtain rises on a room in the castle where Mélisande lies dying (*François Meyer and Editions Minkoff*).   803

61   Ewe ensemble (Ghana) consisting of three drums – *atsimevu* (master-drum), *sogo*, and *kidi* – flanked by players of *axatse* (calabash rattles) and *gankogui* (double bell).   814

62   Fate Marable's jazz-band on a Mississippi steamboat (*c.* 1918). The trumpeter (fourth from the left) is Louis Armstrong.   817

63   Fernand Léger's maquette for the décor for the original production of Milhaud's ballet *La Création du monde* at the Théâtre des Champs-Élysées, Paris, on 25 October 1923 (*Stockholm, Dance Museum*).   829

64   No. 12 of the cycle of seventeen 'periods' of Stockhausen's *Zyklus für einen Schlagzeuger* (Universal Edition).   856

Maps

Western Asia and the Eastern Mediterranean   4–5

The Umayyad Caliphate, AD 750   192–3

Eastern Asia   566

Western Europe, *c.* 1350   *front endpaper*

Central Europe, *c.* 1760   *rear endpaper*

Designation of notes by letters

Abbreviations

AfMF	*Archiv für Musikforschung*
AfMW	*Archiv für Musikwissenschaft*
CEKM	*Corpus of Early Keyboard Music*
BWV	*Thematisch-Systematisches Verzeichnis der Werke J. S. Bachs*
CMM	*Corpus Musicae Mensurabilis*
ChW	*Das Chorwerk*
DDT	*Denkmäler deutscher Tonkunst*
DTB	*Denkmäler der Tonkunst in Bayern*
DTÖ	*Denkmäler der Tonkunst in Österreich*
EDM	*Das Erbe deutscher Musik*
EECM	*Early English Church Music*
HAM	*Historical Anthology of Music*
JAMS	*Journal of the American Musicological Society*
MB	*Musica Britannica*
MF	*Die Musikforschung*
MGG	*Die Musik in Geschichte und Gegenwart*
M&L	*Music & Letters*
MQ	*Musical Quarterly*
NOHM	*New Oxford History of Music*
OAM(M)	*Oxford Anthology of Music (Medieval Music)*
PRMA	*Proceedings of the Royal Musical Association*
SIMG	*Sammelbände der internationalen Musikgesellschaft*
StMW	*Studien zur Musikwissenschaft*
TCM	*Tudor Church Music*
VfMW	*Vierteljahrsschrift für Musikwissenschaft*
ZfMW	*Zeitschrift für Musikwissenschaft*
ZIMG	*Zeitschrift der internationalen Musikgesellschaft*

Acknowledgements

Grateful thanks are due to the institutions named in the List of Plates, their trustees and directors, for permission to reproduce illustrations under their control. In addition acknowledgements are due to the following for photographic prints or other services: Fratelli Alinari (Plates 13, 16, 17, and 18), Bibliothèque de la Ville de Laon (Plate 24), the Mansell Collection (Plate 38), Robin Langley (Plate 47), the Mary Evans Picture Library (Plate 56), the Institute of African Studies, University of Ghana, Legon (Plate 61), and the William Ransom Hogan Jazz Archive, Tulane University, New Orleans (Plate 62).

Grateful thanks are also due to the following for permission to quote from the works indicated: Boosey & Hawkes Music Publishers Ltd (Stravinsky's Cantata, Symphony of Psalms, and *The Rake's Progress*), Durand et Cie, Paris and United Music Publishers (Messiaen's *Turangalîla* Symphony), Editions Max Eschig (Satie's *La Mort de Socrate*), Editions Salabert (Honegger's First Symphony), Schott and Co. Ltd (Nono's *Canto sospeso* and Henze's *Prince of Homburg*), Universal Edition (London) (Boulez's *Structures* and Stockhausen's *Zyklus* and *Klavierstück II*), and Universal Edition (Alfred A. Kalmus Ltd) (Berg's *Wozzeck*).

Part I
The Rise of West Asian and East
Mediterranean Music

Introduction

One wonders how many of the multitude who have helped to wear out Walter Scott's story of a *Hamlet* without the Prince have ever bothered to consider seriously what that would be. All the other characters talk about him or to him so that we can make a host of surmises about him, but he is not *there*. He remains more immaterial than his father's ghost. So it is with the music of the pre-Christian era. From a very early age we have instruments and representations of instruments, actual instruments fragmented but capable of reconstruction, and the names of instruments which cannot always be confidently attached to the right instrument. We have examples of what is almost certainly notation which scholars have sometimes claimed, never quite convincingly, to be able to decipher. We know how professional musicians were trained. We know that the Babylonians and Chinese very early arrived at scientific theories of music. Cultures and empires rise and are superseded: Sumer, Babylon, Egypt, Assyria, Chaldaea, Persia, Crete, Athens, Rome. In Egypt thirty dynasties pass. Troy and Carthage fall. Alexander conquers. Rome bestrides the Western world. But despite all our knowledge of these people's instruments and practices, how they employed music and what they thought about it, the substance itself escapes us. And just as the tragedy of Hamlet would not move us if he were not present, we remain unmoved by descriptions of instruments and accounts of theory. It does not help, it is only tantalizing, to read of the emotional excitement that could be aroused by the sound of the Greek *aulos* and how Sacadas of Argos at Delphi in 586 B.C. was able to depict Apollo's fight with the dragon in an *aulos* composition in several 'movements', or how David's playing on the *kinnôr* expelled Saul's 'evil spirit'. We cannot re-create these sounds, feel the emotional excitement, or even faintly imagine what Sacadas's piece or David's harp-playing really sounded like. The historian can only tell 'the story of the play' with the hero left out.

The story is itself hideously complicated. One can only outline the main plot, following – for the sake of clarity as well as of concision – a line that leads blindly and with varying degrees of distinctness – from Sumer around 3000 B.C. and the succeeding Mesopotamian cultures, through Egypt to the Eastern Mediterranean lands generally. Some types of instrument and some practices – lyres and harps, the double-pipe, responsorial and antiphonal chanting – are documented from the earliest historic times. Lyres and harps and double-pipes were known in Sumer, in Egypt from the Old Kingdom onward, in Crete and probably Mycenae, indeed Greece generally, centuries before Homer, in Assyria and Babylon. (The Romans appear to have acquired the double-pipe from the Etruscans.) Percussion instruments, of various kinds but mainly drums and rattles, are of course universal but trumpets were merely signal instruments rather than genuinely musical ones. The spread of instruments of the lute family is less well documented but Mesopotamia – actually Larsa – had them *c.* 2000 and Egypt a few centuries later. Responsorial and antiphonal singing in temples was practised in Sumer, known in Egypt, and probably continued little changed when the Hebrews adopted it for psalm-singing. Curiously the panpipes seem to have been relatively late comers to the East Mediterranean scene; we do not hear of them until Homer mentions *syringoi* in the *Iliad*, though the Chinese had them much earlier – and may have levitated them across the Pacific to Peru during the first millennium B.C. However when the first mechanical improvement of wind-instruments was made – the invention of bags or chests for maintaining constant wind-pressure – the panpipes turned out to be the ancestor of the organ while the double-pipe begat only the humbler bagpipe, one of the most popular and widely diffused of folk-instruments but with nothing like the potentiality of the organ.

This is a basic distinction. The music of history is for a very long time largely the music of kings and priests, poets or philosophers; the music of common folk has left few records in almost every age. The organ has accumulated a great literature; the bagpipe has not. The earliest music of which we know, Mesopotamian and Egyptian, was the music of the temple and the palace – not so very different when kings were also gods or priests. We hear later of the music of entertainers, of the Greek drama and the Roman circus, of wedding-songs and vintage-songs and shepherds playing pipes to their flocks or to each other, but these are very much 'noises off'. The first important injection of popular music into the mainstream was Christian song.

The psalm-singing of the early Church derived directly from the practices of the Jewish Temple and the synagogues. But hymn-singing by untrained congregations in various musical and linguistic dialects seems to have been a novelty. It was popular music, popular in two senses, although the great and memorable new hymn-poems – whether to new or traditional melodies we do not know – were written in the fourth century by learned men, St. Chrysostom in Greek, St. Ambrose in Latin. When Christianity became the official religion of the Empire the music of the Church became the most important form of music throughout the imperial dominions. In the confusion of the barbarian invasions and downfall of the Western Empire the liturgy and music of the Latin-speaking part of the Church were freed from the rigorous guidance of Byzantium. They went their own ways, diverging ever further from those of the East and in effect laying the foundations of Western music – which was long mainly ecclesiastical. Fortunately they were not papally dominated as those of the Eastern Church were imperially dominated, especially after Justinian. When cycles of liturgical chant were instituted for the Roman use they were disregarded in the Gallican, Celtic, Mozarabic, and even Milanese liturgies while any monastery was liable to do as it liked.

Attempted uniformity in the eighth century was brought about by a political accident: the misfortunes of the Papacy and the ambitions of the Frankish monarchs, Pepin the Short and his son Charlemagne. The first musical consequence of this Papal–Frankish alliance was the establishment of *scholae cantorum* first at Metz and then in other cities of Charlemagne's

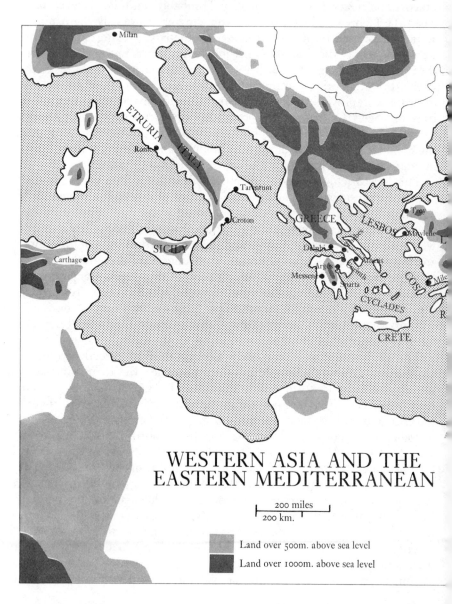

WESTERN ASIA AND THE EASTERN MEDITERRANEAN

200 miles
200 km.

Land over 500m. above sea level
Land over 1000m. above sea level

domains; the second was Charlemagne's determined drive to establish uniform adoption of the Roman chants – for which his musical advisers, with little or no foundation, invoked the name and authority of Gregory the Great who had lived two centuries earlier. The attempted romanization was bitterly resisted but the antagonists still had no satisfactory musical notation as a weapon of argument. For although the Greeks had had notation of a sort since about *c.* 320 B.C., the key to it was not provided till six centuries later and centuries more were to pass before knowledge of notational devices percolated to the West. The first West European to write about them was a

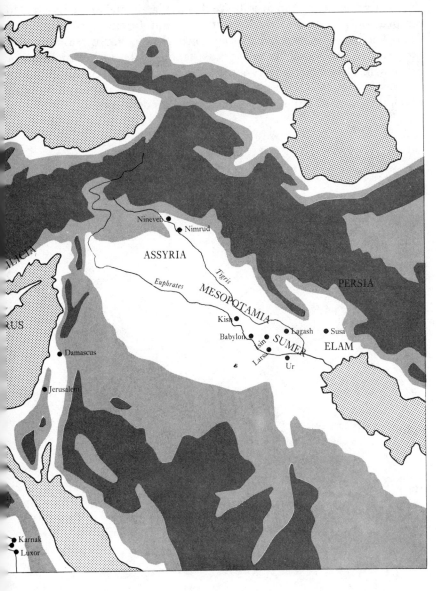

ninth-century West Frankish Benedictine and they were soon employed in a number of Frankish centres, mostly in what is now north-eastern France, but hardly at all in Italy – one indication among many that the hegemony of living church music had passed not merely from Byzantium but from Rome to the 'French' lands of the Carolingian dynasty – more particularly to their north-eastern part plus St. Gall and a few other centres.

The change was of fundamental importance, not only because it marked the beginning of that ascendancy of Western European music which was to last almost unchallenged until the end of the fifteenth century. It saved Western music from the near stagnation which paralysed that of the Eastern church. Orthodoxy spread to embrace the Slav lands, and in the East had to compete only with the relatively insignificant Coptic, Armenian, and Ethiopian churches which had their own chants, but it was intensely conservative. Above all its music was hampered by its renunciation of instruments, based on the fears of the Early Fathers, while the Latin church accepted the organ and with its aid laid the foundations of polyphony from which the entire tradition of Western music has developed.

I

Mesopotamia and Egypt

PRE-HISTORY

It may well be that the exceedingly primitive music of the modern pygmies of Africa and Malaysia, the Bushmen, the Vedda of Ceylon, and the natives of Tierra del Fuego, can throw light on the very beginnings of the art. But it is an uncertain light. Primitive music is a vast and fascinating field of study for its own sake but it belongs to the province of the ethnomusicologist, not that of the musical historian; remembering that culture can retrogress as well as progress, the historian should listen to his colleague's arguments with respectful scepticism. The prehistorian is a more welcome helper, for he can bring such tangible and approximately datable evidence as Neolithic bone flutes with finger-holes, but we must not welcome him too eagerly. At least we must not be more eager than he is. There is, for instance, a famous engraved drawing[1] in the Magdalenian cave of Les Trois Frères (Ariège) dating from c. 13,500 B.C., which includes a figure half-bison, half-man, whom Jacquetta Hawkes thinks may possibly be a disguised hunter, though 'on the whole he seems more likely to be taking part in a ritual'.[2] Sandars comments that 'the bow-shaped object, apparently suspended from the bison-man's nose, but actually superimposed on nose and forearm' does not necessarily belong to him.[3] But one eminent musicologist has been much less cautious; 'a magician', he declares, 'is playing on the type of bow that has survived among many African peoples, including Bushmen, as the musical bow'; it is 'both a shooting and music-making bow, which is fastened to the mask and struck with the right arm'. Another has taken the 'bow-shaped object' to be a flute. Genuine history of music begins not with such debatable specimens of Palaeolithic art or with the primitive music of the most primitive peoples of the twentieth century, but with what we know – it is little enough – of the music of the most ancient civilizations.

SUMER

It is generally agreed that the earliest cradle of civilization lay between the Tigris and Euphrates in the fourth millennium B.C. and that similar

---

[1] Reproduced in N. K. Sandars, *Prehistoric Art in Europe* (Harmondsworth, 1968), pl. 74.
[2] Jacquetta Hawkes and Leonard Woolley, *Prehistory and the Beginnings of Civilization* (London, 1963), p. 163.
[3] Op. cit., p. 72.

revolutions in human culture took place very quickly by the Nile and Indus and, later, the Huang-ho. Geographical conditions dictated that the civilizations of India and China should develop more independently than those of Mesopotamia and Egypt, and that these latter should become the bases of a Near Eastern or East Mediterranean civilization from which were ultimately to develop both the Greek and the Jewish, and hence Early Christian music and art. It is convenient, therefore, to consider them first, leaving the musics of India and China for discussion at a later point.

It is certainly in Mesopotamia that we find the earliest representations of the instruments and musical performance of a 'high culture', the earliest remains of actual instruments, and the earliest written accounts of the use of music. The earliest representations of all appear as phonograms or ideograms on Sumerian writing-tablets of *c.* 3000 B.C.: semi-elliptical harps with three strings and a slight thickening of the lower end which may indicate a soundboard. (Graphic representation of instruments has throughout the ages the disadvantage that the artist's standard of accuracy is unknown.) Exactly similar instruments appear on a number of seals of the rather later period known as Early Dynastic I; and from the Early Dynastic III period (*c.* 2600) we have a number of limestone plaques with figures in relief which in several cases include players on bow-shaped harps, less

Pl. 1   Sumerian harp-players of *c.* 2650 B.C., represented on a vase in the Oriental Institute of Chicago University.

drastically curved than the earlier ones and with six or seven strings; they vary in size (in relation to the player) and appear to be held or slung against the man's left side and played with his right hand.[4] A steatite vase from Bismaya, of uncertain date but probably *c.* 2650, shows two men holding

[4] One such plaque from Khafaje is illustrated in Henri Frankfort, *The Art and Architecture of the Ancient Orient* (Harmondsworth, 1954), pl. 33(a), two others in *MGG*, xii, pl. 80. For further information, see Max Wegner, *Die Musikinstrumente des Alten Orients* (Münster, 1950), pp. 22 ff. and Wilhelm Stauder, *Die Harfen und Leiern der Sumerer* (Frankfurt, 1957); Stauder's article 'Sumerisch-babylonische Musik' in *MGG*, xii, corrects or supersedes the writings of Galpin, Sachs, and other earlier scholars.

harps horizontally; the strings are continued beyond the neck and dangle quasi-ornamentally (see pl. 1). Very much more sophisticated is the famous 'harp of Queen Pu-abi' (formerly read as 'Shub-ad') (*c*. 2500) from the royal tombs at Ur, in the British Museum;[5] the neck is straight and the soundbox enlarged, so that the original bow-shape begins to approach an angle, and the number of strings is increased to eleven. (This instrument was twice faultily reconstructed with the soundbox of another instrument, a lyre.) The lyre, which differs from the harp in that the strings are stretched between the soundbox and a crossbar supported by arms, had also been known to the Sumerians as early as the Early Dynastic II period. It is represented on seals and other reliefs, in the earliest of which the soundbox is shaped like a bull, no doubt with religious significance (and the sound is said to have resembled

Pl. 2   Harp with bull-headed soundbox on an inlaid panel from Ur (*c*. 2600 B.C.)

the bellowing of a bull). The animal's legs provide a stand on which the large and heavy instrument could be placed on the ground, though players are also shown carrying it. Later the body becomes more stylized but the bull's head remains as an ornament to the soundbox, as shown on the inlaid panel depicting a victory banquet and known as the 'standard' of Ur (see pl. 2) and in the actual instruments found in the royal tombs at Ur, now in the British Museum and the University Museum at Philadelphia.[6] The inlay on the soundbox of the Philadelphia instrument[7] shows a seated ass playing just such another lyre, which is supported by a bear – animal musicians appear in

[5] Joan Rimmer, *Ancient Musical Instruments of Western Asia in the British Museum* (London, 1969), p. 16, but now reconstructed somewhat differently on the basis of representations on the seals and limestone plaques referred to above.
[6] See Rimmer, cover, and Frankfort, pl. 27(b). Of the two in the British Museum, one was part of the wrongly made up instrument mentioned above; it lacks all the upper structure (now restored in modern materials).
[7] Frankfort, pl. 38.

other examples of Sumerian art – while a small animal sits at the bear's feet beating a small frame-drum or tambourine and shaking a species of sistrum. Pairs of copper clappers have been found at Kish and Ur, and are represented on seals. The harp, the lyre, and two or three kinds of simple percussion were apparently the only instruments employed in the earliest 'high culture'. The paucity of wind instruments at this period is astonishing, and the extremely few graphic representations may not be of musical instruments at all, though a fragment from Khafaje[8] and the Bismaya vase show men playing long conical tubes which may be trumpets. All we actually have is a silver double-pipe, about nine inches long, one pipe pierced with four finger-holes, the other with one, presumably, a reed instrument, found in the Ur tombs and now at Philadelphia. Nor is it possible to identify with certainty these instruments with the names which appear in the literary texts,[9] and we should be equally cautious in speculating about the music these instruments produced and what was sung by the figures sometimes shown beside the players.[10] On the other hand, we do know quite a lot about professional musicians, their training and their functions. We even know the name of one musician from the early part of the Early Dynastic III period: Pa-Pab-Bi-gagir-gal – *gal* meaning 'great'. Until the beginning of the second millennium B.C., when certain musicians are named as royal servants, all served in the temples; from the earliest times music had been strongly associated with magic and religion. They were divided into two groups, *gala* and *nar*, whose functions are given widely different and sometimes diametrically opposed explanations by the best modern authorities, and each group was divided into three grades. The literary remains of what they sang or cantillated have come down to us in vast quantities: in earliest times only simple psalms or hymns, but later much elaborated liturgically. It is also clear from the texts that instruments were employed and that there were both responsorial and antiphonal chanting of paired verses of a type that survived in the Hebrew psalms. But while Sumerian civilization was centred on religion and hence its music on the temple service, music was also a feature of feasts, military triumphs, burials, and other rites.

POST-SUMERIAN MUSIC

After *c.* 2370 the Sumerians suffered conquest by the Semitic Akkadians, who united the city-states of the plain under a single monarch, and then by the Guti, barbarians from the mountains. But the Akkadians adopted Sumerian culture and even in the Guti period one city, Lagash (Telloh),

---

[8] Rimmer, p. 30.

[9] The identifications suggested by Galpin and H. G. Farmer, *NOHM*, i. pp. 240 ff., cannot be relied on. See H. Hartmann's dissertation, *Die Musik der sumerischen Kultur* (Frankfurt, 1960), pp. 48 ff.

[10] Several tablets preserve the names of harp strings and intervals: see David Wulstan, 'The Tuning of the Babylonian Harp', *Iraq*, 30 (1968), p. 215, O. R. Gurney, 'An Old Babylonian Treatise on the Tuning of the Harp', ibid., p. 229, and A. D. Kilmer, 'The Discovery of an Ancient Mesopotamian Theory of Music', *Proceedings of the American Philosophical Society*, cxv (1971), p. 131. But readable notation of actual music is another matter.

under its ruler Gudea remained an island of remarkable artistic accomplishment. Contemporary texts tell us of the music that accompanied Gudea's greatest achievement, the rebuilding of Eninnu, the temple of the city-god Ningirsu: for instance, the king instructs the chief musician of the temple 'to cultivate diligently pipe-playing and to fill the forecourt of Eninnu with joy'.[11] They also mention a bull's horn trumpet. A stele from Lagash, now

Pl. 3   Vertical angled harp on a clay plaque (2000–1800 B.C.) from Ishchali (Musée du Louvre, Paris).

Pl. 4   Babylonian terracotta plaque (early 2nd millennium B.C.) in the British Museum, showing a long-necked 'lute'.

in the Louvre, shows a seated man playing a very large lyre – the cross-bar comes to the top of his head – which is very like the lyres from the Ur tombs, except that, instead of a bull's head, a model of a complete bull stands on the end of the soundbox and one of the arms rises from it.[12] Another stele from Lagash and one from Ur show huge frame-drums standing as high as a man's shoulder from the ground.

A restored Sumerian kingdom under the Third Dynasty of Ur was overthrown by Elamites and Amorites, and another period of city-states ended in the early second millennium B.C. with the successive domination of dynasties based on Isin, Larsa, and Babylon. The kings of the Babylonian dynasty, of whom the best known was Hammurabi, were Amorites, a west Semitic people who had been settling in Mesopotamia over a considerable period, and the new types of instrument that now appeared are rightly or wrongly regarded as West Semitic. They included a new type of lyre: much

[11] Hawkes and Woolley, p. 793.   [12] Wegner, pl. 6b.

smaller and lighter, held at an angle or even horizontally with the soundbox against the player's body, and played with a plectrum while the fingers of the left hand appear to touch the strings too. The harp is no longer bow-shaped, the neck being set nearly at a right angle to the soundbox, which may be held vertically against the player's body and played with the hand, as in a terracotta relief from Ishchali now in the Musée du Louvre, Paris (see pl. 3), or horizontally and played with a plectrum. A long-necked instrument of the lute type has been found on a relief at Lagash from the time of the ascendance of Larsa and similar lutes are also shown in the Babylonian time (see pl. 4), while a relief from Larsa itself, now in the British Museum, shows a large pedestal drum very like a modern kettledrum, which the player is beating with both fists while a seated figure appears to be clashing cymbals.[13]

After the First Babylonian Dynasty there is a gap of many centuries in our knowledge of Mesopotamian music, a gap which can only be attributed to the incursion of new peoples: Hittites, Kassites, and Hurrians. The Hittites – who sacked Babylon *c.* 1585 – established a powerful, widespread state, but their literary remains tell us only that they had a wooden instrument, perhaps a lute, associated with the goddess Ishtar and their graphic art shows no more than instruments – double-pipes, small lyres, lutes, drums – already known to the peoples with whom they came in contact, the Mesopotamians and Egyptians.

The same must be said of another culture of this period, the Aegean. The only Cycladic evidence consists of marble statuettes from Amorgos showing what appears to be a species of triangle-framed harp[14] and a double-pipe, held in both hands V-wise. From Crete itself we have a Middle Minoan seal[15] showing both a lyre and what seems to be a double-harp, but the curious shape of the instruments is obviously conditioned by the need to fit them into the circle of the seal. A vase from Hagia Triada shows a man leading a singing procession of harvesters and shaking on high a horseshoe-shaped sistrum exactly like the Egyptian ones,[16] and also from Hagia Triada, from the last period before the catastrophe of *c.* 1400, we have paintings of a double-pipe and a large lyre on a sarcophagus and another fragmentary painting of a lyre from the 'villa', one played by a woman, the other by a priest. Both finger and plectrum techniques are shown; there are seven strings; and the strongly curved arms into which the soundbox is extended are not so very different from a type found in Egypt rather earlier.

EGYPT: THE OLD KINGDOM

It is indeed to Egypt that we must turn to get a coherent idea of the development of musical instruments – and the employment of music

---

[13] Rimmer, pl. V(b).
[14] *MGG*, v, col. 1540; Germain Bazin, *A Concise History of Art* (London, 1958), p. 83.
[15] A. J. Evans, *The Palace of Minos*, i (London, 1921), fig. 205, and Wegner, p. 45.
[16] Wegner, pl. 15(b).

generally[17] – during the second millennium B.C. The beginnings of Egyptian music are, of course, earlier than that, though not so early as those of Mesopotamia. Numerous reliefs of the Fifth Dynasty, which was roughly contemporary with the royal tombs at Ur, show instruments related to those of Mesopotamia. (More primitive ones, clappers and rattles, are depicted earlier, but the 'trumpets' shown in early pictures of funerary boats probably represent instruments to disguise the human voice rather than sound-generating instruments.) Although hardly any actual instruments from the Old Kingdom (*c.* 2635–2155 B.C.) have survived, the reliefs and paintings are generally more precise than the Mesopotamian ones and it is possible to be more confident in the use of names. Reliefs in the tombs of Ti and Mereruka at Sakkara, paintings in the mastaba (tomb superstructure) of Kaiemankh at Giza, show the bow-shaped harp (*bint*), usually with five to seven strings, of the earlier Mesopotamian type but with a more developed sound-chest, sometimes decorated with the eye of Horus; very long flutes often without finger-holes which have to be held diagonally across the body; shorter double-pipes bound together which – because later specimens have proved to have single reeds – have been rather unhappily styled 'double clarinets'; fork-shaped clappers; and frame-drums. Groups of musicians, usually seated, generally include at least one harp, sometimes two, and one long flute – perhaps merely a drone – while each instrumentalist is faced by a singer who puts his left hand to his left ear, making conventional signs with the other in what is perhaps a mnemonic code[18] and strikingly resemble the hand-signs used in Coptic liturgical singing today. Sometimes, as also in some Mesopotamian pictures (e.g. pl. 10 below), the singer pinches his larynx. If there are dancers they clap their hands or use wooden or ivory clappers; but the – sometimes pantomimic – dances appear to be restrained.

EGYPT: THE MIDDLE KINGDOM

The same instruments were played during the Middle Kingdom (*c.* 2134–1650) and new ones appeared, notably a smaller, portable shoulder-harp in which, as in some of the larger ones, the soundbox was much enlarged and the neck correspondingly shortened. The cylindrical drum (*teben*) was now known and two new types of sistrum, with stirrup-shaped frame of pottery, wood, or metal (*sekhem*), or in the shape of a little house or shrine (*sesheshet*, or *naos*-sistrum as it is sometimes called);[19] in both types part of the handle is formed by the head of Hathor, goddess of love and joy, in whose cult an important part was played by dancing to sistra. The sistrum was always a temple-implement, as much a religious symbol as a musical instrument. Under the Semitic Hyksos kings, who ruled a large part of Egypt from *c.* 1650 B.C. to *c.* 1550, foreign elements were

---

[17] The most reliable authority is Hans Hickmann: see his numerous monographs and, above all, his *Musique et vie musicale sous les Pharaons*, three vols. (Paris, 1956), and for iconography his *Ägypten* (Leipzig, 1961) in the series *Musikgeschichte in Bildern*.
[18] E.g. Wegner, p. 9.   [19] See *MGG*, xii, pl. 34.

introduced, though the Hyksos themselves left no literature or graphic art. And even before this a painting in a tomb at Beni Hasan, dating from *c.* 1890, showing Bedouin coming to visit the governor of the Oryx nome, includes a man playing a lyre (see pl. 5) of exactly the same 'new' type that was brought to Mesopotamia at roughly the same time, also by a Semitic people.

Pl. 5   Bedouin lyre-player: from the tomb of Khnum-hotep (12th Dynasty) at Beni Hasan.

EGYPT: THE NEW KINGDOM

After the expulsion of the Hyksos, under the Eighteenth Dynasty – the first of the new Kingdom (*c.* 1550–1080 B.C.) – the country entered upon its most brilliant period of artistic development, a period that has been not unjustly compared with that of the Italian Renaissance. It was the period of the temples at Karnak and Luxor, the period of the heretical, monolatrous Akhenaten and his queen Nefertiti at Amarna, and of Tutankhamun, restorer of the old religion, at Thebes; and even those religious upheavals stimulated artistic production first to promote the new faith, then to re-establish the old in greater magnificence. International contacts were lively. It has been suggested that Mycenaean workmen helped to decorate the new capital at Amarna and there were plentiful contacts in peace and war with the Mitannians, Kassites, and Hittites. Music shared in this cultural explosion; musicians with new instruments and elaborations of older types appear in profusion in wall-paintings and reliefs; sometimes we have the instruments themselves.

The large bowed harp remained extremely popular and a new, more decidedly bowed type was introduced, with a support at the lower end to keep the soundbox from touching the ground. Another new variety of the bowed harp was smaller, with only three or at most four strings, and carried on the shoulder. During the reign of Amenophis II another kind of harp became known: portable, with vertical soundbox and the neck fastened at a right angle to its lower end.[20] The angle-harp (see pl. 6) was never as

Pl. 6   Egyptian angle-harp with vertical sound-box, and lyre with curved arms, from Tomb 22 at Thebes (18th Dynasty).

popular as the bowed harp, though it came to influence the shape of the latter, resulting in slightly bowed harps which curve sharply into straight, horizontal necks at the upper end of the soundbox as with the two great six-foot-high instruments depicted in the tomb of Ramesses III (*c.* 1151: Twentieth Dynasty) at Thebes. These appear to have eleven and thirteen strings respectively. The – usually seven-stringed – lyre also took a striking new form with gracefully curved arms of different length, so that the cross-bar is not quite parallel with the soundbox (see pl. 6 and 7): it was not completely naturalized, although even in Akhenaten's time the girls playing it with plectrum or fingers appear to be Syrians and its earliest distinctive name (*c.* 1200), *kenanawr*, seems to be Semitic (cf. the Hebrew *kinnôr*). At this later period the arms are equal in length and topped with graceful animal heads.[21] The Mesopotamian lute also became naturalized *c.* 1500. There are actual instruments from this period, one now in the Metropolitan Museum, New York, and one – from the tomb of a musician named Harmosis – in the Cairo Museum. After this numerous examples are shown

[20] The one in pl. 6 has nine strings. A wooden figurine in the British Museum shows a girl playing one with six strings; see R. D. Anderson, *Catalogue of Egyptian Antiquities in the British Museum*, iii (*Musical Instruments*) (London, 1976), pp. 2–3, fig. 3.   [21] Wegner, pl. 3(b) and 7(b).

15

in paintings. The soundbox, of various shapes, is always small with a belly usually of skin or parchment; the neck is very long and the usual two strings – Harmosis's instrument has three – were played with a plectrum. Fairly large lutes seem to have been favourite instruments of male professional musicians, but slave-girls – often naked – are shown playing a smaller variety. (It may be significant that in a well-known wall-painting from the tomb of Nakht at Thebes, of the time of Amenophis II, the lute-player is naked while her companions, playing the double-pipe and harp, are clothed.)

Pl. 7   Musicians in a wall-painting at Thebes (Tomb 38) playing harp, 'lute', possibly small castanets, double reed-pipes, and curved-arm lyre.

The girl in the tomb of Nakht is, characteristically for this period, blowing two separate pipes held divergently; the older parallel pipes, tied together, disappeared soon after the beginning of the Eighteenth Dynasty and the long single pipe became much rarer. While pipes were always played by women, the trumpet was naturally a man's instrument. Under the New Kingdom its representation is unmistakable in military and other processions; it is no longer the doubtful instrument of earlier times and the tomb of Tutankhamun contained two superb instruments now in the Cairo Museum, one of bronze and gold, the other silver, with funnel-shaped bells though without true mouthpieces; instead the end of the tube is turned over a metal ring which provides sufficient embouchure.[22] In 1933 Percival Kirby was able to obtain two notes from each, the fourth overtone (which was dull in quality) and the tenth (which was brilliant), a♭–c″ on the silver instrument, a tone higher on the other. But the trumpet was essentially a signal instrument and remained so for nearly three millennia. Percussion instruments under the New Kingdom often became works of fine craftsmanship; clappers, for instance, were sometimes of ivory and often carved in the form of little hands. The tomb of Tutankhamun contained

[22] See Lise Manniche, *Musical Instruments from the Tomb of Tut'ankhamūn* (Tut'ankhamun's Tomb Series, vi, Griffith Institute, Oxford, 1976), pp. 7–13, pls. v–xii.

particularly fine examples: sistra of gilded wood and bronze, ivory castanets. In the time of Tuthmosis III a curious rectangular drum or tambourine begins to be represented; it is nearly always played by women in conjunction with other instruments. From nearly the same period representations of the annual festival of Amun at the height of the flood season, when the god with his consort and son was taken by water from Karnak to Opet (Luxor), show barrel-shaped drums.

Graphic art tells us a great deal about performance as well as instruments: the great number of women-musicians (not only the slave-girls of the great households but the temple-musicians), the blind male singers and harpists, the surely significant fact that players are no longer faced by singers making cheironomic signs. Yet the representations raise almost as many questions as they give us facts. The influx of foreign slave-girls, bringing their lutes and divergent double-pipes, was undoubtedly a consequence of military triumphs, but why the blind musicians? And what is indicated by the disappearance of cheironomic signs? Possibly the invention of some system of written notation, but so far no completely convincing evidence of any such system – other than scattered mnemonic signs – has been produced.[23] Nor, despite the careful measuring of numerous surviving pipes and their finger-holes and the counting of harp-strings and examination of hand-positions in pictures, has any convincing system of tuning been established although many theories have been put forward. We may be confident that the Egyptians, like the Sumerians, employed a drone-bass; if the second tube of a double-pipe was pierced with a finger-hole or holes this was simply to enable the pitch of the drone to be altered by the finger or with wax. But what intervals were played by the melody-pipe, or the harp or lyre, it is impossible to determine – except that they were not as small as a semitone; the Asiatic lute was of course capable of producing small and variable intervals. Still less do we know anything of the patterns in which the intervals were arranged. When lyre and pipes played together or when the lute joined them, we have no idea how differently they played the same melody.

The numerous literary texts confirm what paintings and reliefs tell us about the general employment of music: in the home and at feasts, in processions and funeral ceremonies, and in the temples. But their greatest value to us lies in the refrains and responsorial structure of liturgical texts, hymns, and lamentations, like those of the Sumerians, which must have been reflected in the music to which they were sung or chanted and thus imposed a pattern on it. And religious song and chant appear to have been generally accompanied by instruments.

EGYPT IN DECLINE

After the Eighteenth Dynasty a general artistic stagnation seems to have set in, though it is difficult to decide whether there was less practice of music or

---

[23] The best study is Hickmann, *Le problème de la notation musicale dans l'Égypte ancienne* (Cairo, 1955).

only less representation of it. The causes were probably political in origin; the relative peace and prosperity in which the arts can flourish was succeeded by weakening of royal authority, division and sub-division of the kingdom, external pressures by land and sea – the 'sea-peoples' beaten off by Ramesses III included Danu, who were probably Danaoi (Greeks), and Peleset, who were certainly Philistines and perhaps the people Herodotus called Pelasgians (fugitive Mycenaeans?) – and finally foreign conquest by the Assyrians in the seventh century, by the Persians in the sixth and again in the fourth, and then immediately after that by Alexander the Great in 332 B.C. Throughout this long period Egyptian culture – despite periods of renaissance, as under the Twenty-fifth and Twenty-sixth Dynasties (eighth–sixth centuries B.C.) – was permeated more and more by foreign influences and dissolved into the general Eastern Mediterranean culture. It is reasonable to suppose that Egyptian music was the dominant element in Eastern Mediterranean music and that types of instrument were less affected by change than musical idiom and practice were; indeed, forms of ancient instruments survive in popular forms to this day, the long flutes as the *nāy*, the 'double-clarinets' as *zummârah*, and old Egyptian types of lyre in Ethiopia and the Sudan. But for a clearer picture of musical instruments and musical performance during the ninth–seventh centuries before Christ we must turn again in the first place to Mesopotamia.

THE ASSYRIAN EMPIRE

By the beginning of the first millennium B.C. the warlike and aggressive Assyrians had become the dominant people of Mesopotamia. In religion and culture they were the heirs of Babylonia, but their art was devoted to the glorification of their kings, their hunting prowess and their ferocious military triumphs, rather than to the service of the gods, so since our knowledge of their music is derived almost entirely from stone and bronze reliefs our view of it may be slightly strabismic; music in Assyria must have been heard in many different circumstances but all we see is associated with the king's war-prisoners, the king pouring libations over the animals he has killed, the king taking his ease in a garden with his queen (with the head of the unfortunate king of Susa hanging from a tree), or musicians going to meet men bearing severed heads in each hand. From the reign of Ashurnasirpal II (883–859) to that of Ashurbanipal (668–626), particularly from the ninth and seventh centuries, we have a considerable number of such representations. Ashurnasirpal II was the first Assyrian monarch to reach the Mediterranean and his booty from the West in the south-east palace at his new capital, Nimrud, includes an ivory box with figures of women musicians (see pl. 8). According to R. D. Barnett, this shows on its edge 'remains of Phoenician or Aramaean letters'; two of the musicians are playing frame-drum and double-pipes but behind them come two more playing rectangular instruments which are clearly delineated yet have been variously interpreted as a species of zither and a species of xylophone.

(Wegner, the proponent of the xylophone, regards a not altogether dissimilar instrument half visible in a relief from Nineveh of Sennacherib's time[24] as a species of lyre.) More typically Assyrian is a relief from Nimrud, in the British Museum,[25] showing two men playing harps with plectra and a third with a small drum; the nine-stringed harps have long soundboxes held horizontally and the short necks, each ending in a carved hand, rise at a right angle from the ends farthest from the players. Except that they are angled instead of bowed,

Pl. 8   Fragment of an ivory unguent box, probably made in Phoenicia, possibly in north Syria, found in Ashurnasirpal II's palace at Nimrud. Women musicians are playing a zither (or xylophone), frame-drum, and double reed-pipes.

Pl. 9   Ninevite lyre-players of the Sennacherib period, possibly prisoners guarded by an Assyrian soldier (from a relief in the British Museum).

they might be those of the Bismaya vase of eighteen centuries earlier and the similarity is still more marked in later representations of horizontal harps which show more clearly the strings dangling beyond the neck, which is decorated with a small carved hand at the end. The lute type of instrument appears very rarely in Assyrian art of any period. As for Assyrian percussion, the British Museum has a large collection of bronze cymbals and bells – the latter seemingly for attachment to horse-harness or priestly vestments and therefore not strictly musical – and shell castanets.

The reliefs of Shalmaneser III and the immediately succeeding reigns show nothing new, though a figurine from Elamite Susa, of the time of Tiglathpileser III, has what appears to be a crooked double-pipe. But from the Sennacherib period we have pictures of lyres both with straight but unequal arms[26] and with curved arms as in the already mentioned relief with the mysterious 'zither/xylophone' (which also shows a frame-drum and

[24] Wegner, pl. 8(b).
[25] Rimmer, pl. IX.

cymbals). A particularly interesting relief in the British Museum[27] shows two trumpeters, one sounding his trumpet as a signal to men moving a giant statue, the other holding his instrument – long conical tubes of the type represented on the Khafaje fragment and Bismaya vase mentioned on p. 8 and quite unlike the Egyptian trumpets. It is, however, from the reign of Ashurbanipal that we have the richest iconography, though the most famous piece represents not actual Assyrians but Elamite musicians: the court musicians of the vanquished Teumman, king of Susa, coming from the city to greet the new king imposed on them by the victor. This has often been reproduced in whole or part.[28] Seven vertical harps with about twenty strings are being played with fingers by men and women; the 'string-continuations' dangling from the now horizontal necks, appear to be thicker and are perhaps long ornamental tassels rather than continuations of the strings. But the one horizontal harp has tassels at the end of normal string-continuations. One man and one woman play double-pipes and another woman plays a drum. This is the largest instrumental ensemble shown in Mesopotamian art and behind the players comes a choir of six women, one of whom squeezes her larynx (see pl. 10),[29] and nine children. Vertical harps

Pl. 10   Elamite court-singer squeezing her larynx (from Nineveh, B.M. 124802).

(with normal string-continuation) and horizontal harps are shown in other reliefs of this period, but only two examples of lyres[30] and these have boldly curved yokes and curved arms reminiscent of those depicted on bronze and silver bowls of rather earlier date from Idalion and Kurion in Cyprus. Another rarity is the long-necked lute, although it was a very old Mesopotamian instrument; it may well have been popular with the masses who left no graphic records.

[26] See pl. 9.
[27] Rimmer, pl. XI.
[28] E.g. Rimmer, pl. XIII–XIV; Frankfort, pl. 103; *NOHM*, i, pl. VIII(c).
[29] A technique employed to this day in Sicily: see Nanie Bridgman, *La vie musicale en quattrocento* (Paris, 1964), p. 228.
[30] Rimmer, pl. XI and XV.

NEBUCHADNEZZAR'S ALLEGED ORCHESTRA

The Assyrian dynasty at Nineveh was overthrown in 612 B.C. and for some seventy years Chaldaean kings, of whom the most famous was Nebuchadnezzar, reigned in Babylon until they in turn were overthrown by Cyrus the Great in 539 and Mesopotamia became part of the Persian empire. This 'Neo-Babylonian' period has left no graphic remains depicting musicians and what evidence we have of its music – such as the Hellenistic terracotta figurines of a rather later date found at Babylon, showing players of double-pipes and drum, vertical harp and cymbals[31] – does not suggest that there were innovations. As for the famous band that played at the dedication of Nebuchadnezzar's golden image, we may understand the Aramaic names of the instruments listed three times in the third chapter of the Book of Daniel more accurately than King James's translators, although the only two we can be absolutely sure about are the *qaytērōs* (kithara, lyre, not harp) and *qeren* (horn rather than cornet). But the Book of Daniel was written in the second century B.C. and has no more historical value than would Shakespeare's account, had he written one, of the instruments that played at the coronation of King John. All the same, if we assume with most modern authorities that the 'flute' was a double-pipe and the alleged 'sackbut' and 'psaltery' were respectively a horizontal and a vertical harp – all we know about the *sûmpōněyâ* is that it was not a 'dulcimer' – Nebuchadnezzar's orchestra would have been identical with that of Teumman, king of Susa, less than a century earlier. It may well have been the kind of ensemble familiar to a Hellenized Jew four hundred years later, perhaps heard when Antiochus IV temporarily established the worship of Zeus in the Temple of Jerusalem in 168 B.C., another 'golden image'.

MATHEMATICAL THEORY

Similarly, although the stories of Pythagoras studying in Babylon in the latter part of the sixth century B.C. originate with Iamblichos many centuries later, there is – from what we know of the advanced state of Mesopotamian astronomy and mathematics – nothing inherently improbable in his having learned from them the relationships between pitch and length of string, between the mathematical ratios $1:2$, $2:3$, $3:4$ and the intervals of octave, fifth, and fourth, even the conception of a universe constructed according to such ratios. We may be fairly confident that the Sumerian-Babylonian musical system, whatever it was, had a scientific basis based on a cosmic theory and we may well suspect, from what we know of the Egyptians,[32] that their musical system, whatever it was, was arrived at empirically. Both systems, like their systems of practical notation, remain open fields for ingenious speculation.

---

[31] Ibid., pl. XXIII and XXIV(a).
[32] Hawkes and Woolley, op. cit., pp. 668–76.

2

The Greek Contribution

HOMERIC MUSIC

The previous chapter has shown a number of relationships between the musical instruments of Mesopotamia and Egypt and those of what may be loosely called 'the early Greek world': the Cyclades, Crete. To these we may add a few Mycenaean examples such as the fragments of two ivory lyres, their crossbars pierced for eight strings, from the tholos at Menidi in Attica.[1] It is idle to argue about priorities in such matters yet the slight evidence we have favours the theory that the Greek world got the lyre from the Egyptians and Phoenicians; the earliest form of the Greek instrument, shown on vases of the so-called Geometric Period (eighth century) from the tombs near the Dipylon in Athens,[2] is a simplified version – small and round-based, with only four parallel strings – of the Mycenaean and Phoenician lyres; a late eighth-century bronze statuette from Heraklion is of a player with an exactly similar instrument. From the same period, *c.* 725, have survived late Hittite reliefs from Karatepe in Cilicia.[3] One shows two lyres, of which that on the right is very like the Greek *phorminx* though with six strings, while another shows double-pipes and a lyre resembling a rather later Greek pattern.[4] Tantalizingly, the Phoenician version of a bilingual inscription on one of the stone slabs which alternate with the reliefs refers to the king as 'king of the *Dnnym*', not impossibly Homer's *Danaoi* – Greeks.[5]

The 'black-figure' pottery of a century later shows lyres with seven strings played with a plectrum (see pl. 11). This is the instrument, with four or seven strings, which Homer – whose name, if a fiction, is a convenient fiction – calls *phorminx*. It is a phorminx that Apollo plays at the end of the First Book of the *Iliad*. (We need not accept Herodotus's downright identification of Horus with Apollo in order to find some significance in the parallel between the association of the lyre with Apollo and the association of the harp with Horus.) When Odysseus and his companions visited Achilles in his tent, they found him singing to the accompaniment of a beautifully fashioned phorminx with a silver cross-bar; Phemius in the First Book of the *Odyssey* and the blind Demodocus in the Eighth sing to the phorminx. One of the pictures on the shield of Achilles showed youths dancing to the sound of *auloi* and phorminxes, one of the earliest literary references to the

---

[1] See *MGG*, v, col. 866.
[2] Max Wegner, *Das Musikleben der Griechen* (Berlin, 1949), pl. 1(a) and (b).
[3] Frankfort, *The Art and Architecture of the Ancient Orient*, pl. 165(a).
[4] O. R. Gurney, *The Hittites* (Harmondsworth, 1952), pl. 29.   [5] Ibid., pp. 42–3.

aulos, the double-pipe, though, as we have seen,[6] it was known to the Greek world seven or eight centuries before Homer's time. Homer only once uses the word *kitharis* – never *kithara* – unambiguously for an actual instrument: Phemius's (*Odyssey*, i, 153), as a synonym for *phorminx*. But he uses it several times for the act of playing one.[7] Hector tells Paris his *kitharis* will not help him when he meets Menelaus (*Iliad*, iii), and in the Thirteenth

Pl. 11   Apollo, accompanied by two Muses (?), plays a seven-stringed lyre with a plectrum, after his arrival on Delos. From a late 7th-century B.C. amphora from Melos, now in the National Museum at Athens.

Book Polydamas speaks of one man having the gift of dancing, 'another *kitharis* and singing'. Again on the shield of Achilles Hephaestus depicted a boy 'kitharizing on his phorminx' as he sang 'the song of Linus', a lament for Linus/Adonis traditionally sung at harvest or vintage time, not only in Greece but under other names in Egypt and Phoenicia (as Herodotus tells us, ii, 79), Babylonia, and perhaps (judging from *Ezekiel* viii, 14) Israel.

Another instrument shown on the shield was the *syrinx* or panpipes: the two ambushed herdsmen were playing syrinxes. And the sleepless Agamemnon at the beginning of *Iliad*, x, heard the Trojans playing auloi and syrinxes. But the earliest actual representations of the syrinx that we have are post-Homeric; probably the earliest of all is the one with nine pipes of equal length played by Calliope on a vase in the Museo Archeologico at Florence.[8] This was a new type of instrument, seemingly Greek in origin and always with pastoral associations. The equally long pipes of the earliest instruments were internally shortened with wax. (Incidentally, the word *syrinx* seems also to have been used for a hole near the mouthpiece of the aulos.) The only other Homeric instrument was the *salpinx*, the trumpet, used as a simile for a loud noise: Achilles's shout (*Iliad*, xviii) was like a salpinx and when the gods quarrelled (xxi) great heaven rang as with a

[6] See p. 12.
[7] The verb *citharizare* appears in Latin with Cornelius Nepos (first century B.C.) and survived into the Middle Ages with the sense of playing any stringed instrument.
[8] Wegner, op. cit., pl. 2(a).

salpinx. The vase representations, which are later in date, show it as a long, very narrow tube with bell.

The phorminx was evidently first and foremost an accompanying instrument, particularly for solo song. But although we know that Achilles and the bards in the *Odyssey* sang of the deeds of heroes, and the boy on the shield sang his 'Linus song' to which his companions danced, and although we read of choral dirges and bridal songs, we know nothing of the nature of the music they may be supposed to have made. Yet we may venture a conjecture or two about the music of the bards, the music to which the *Iliad* and *Odyssey* were themselves chanted. Since Homer's language is interwoven with a vast number of ready-made phrases – 'bright-toned phorminx', 'the goddess, grey-eyed Athena', and the rest – it is not unreasonable to suppose that the melodic line to which it was sung also embodied a great number of ready-made formulae not necessarily associated with specific verbal formulae. These would have been of small compass, readily supported by the four nearly equal strings of the early phorminx which look as if they must have sounded the adjacent notes of a scale: a tetrachord. These suppositions are supported, though not of course confirmed, by the facts that composition by melodic formulae was an exceedingly common practice in Mediterranean and Western Asian musics at a much later period and that very limited compass characterizes the music of sung epics which have survived into modern times, such as the Russian *bïlïnï*.

FROM PHORMINX TO KITHARA

Hesiod, and Pindar in the fifth century, uses the word *phorminx* for Orpheus's instrument; after that it soon dies out or is used only to give an archaic tinge. With the passage of time the lyre acquired not only more strings but new shapes which were given new names. The seven-stringed phorminx of the late sixth and the fifth century had longer arms and the strings are carried over a bridge and sometimes fastened to the soundbox by a species of tailpiece; it is represented occasionally on black-figure pottery (see pl. 12) but mainly on red-figure. From this evolved the large classical *kithara*, which makes its literary appearance in Epicharmus of Cos and Euripides, with its flat-based, nearly rectangular soundbox and stout arms projecting some distance above the thin cross-bar; it was played with fingers or plectrum and was essentially a man's instrument.

Two lighter instruments had appeared rather earlier: the *barbiton* or *barbitos* (also shown in pl. 12), and the *lyra*, sometimes called the *chelys* because the soundbox was made of tortoise-shell or wood carved to look like it. Both had slim arms, those of the lyra curved like an animal's horns, those of the barbiton long, divergent, and straight until near the top where they curve suddenly inward to be connected by a very short cross-bar. The barbiton had a very small soundbox and, like the lyra, was played with the fingers of the left hand and a plectrum held by the right. This was the instrument of Sappho,

Alcaeus, and Anacreon, who also mention a Lydian instrument called the *pektis* which was probably a harp. Another Lydian harp of this time, the *magadis*, had ten strings with ten more simultaneously sounding an octave higher. But the harp, depicted in various shapes and known by various names, was never a favourite instrument of the Greeks and was usually played by women. For that matter the barbiton also was a favourite feminine

Pl. 12   Players of barbiton, phorminx, krotala and aulos: on the Mosaon amphora (Staatliche Antikensammlung, Munich).

instrument, though by no means exclusively feminine, while the big kithara was more often played by men. Both were largely supplanted by the lyra after the fifth century.

THE AULOS

The aulos, on the other hand, seems to have been disliked by women perhaps for the reason ascribed to Athena in the legend: that playing it distorted the features. However, it was played by women sometimes, and not only by courtesans. The black-figure vases show auloi which are simply the familiar divergent double-pipes with four finger-holes of the Near East; later double mouthpieces are shown on red-figure pottery; but another innovation, the phorbeia, a leather mouth-band tied round the lips and cheeks to support the wind-pressure, appears already on a Corinthian pyxis of the early sixth century. The aulos was considered a Phrygian – Asiatic – instrument, perhaps imported into mainland Greece as late as 700, and like the percussion (*krotala*, clappers; *kymbala*, small cymbals) was specially associated with the cults of Dionysus and Cybele and with the orgiastic generally; in Athens Boeotians were reputed to be the best players. All the same, from *c*. 700 onward it was as ubiquitous as the human voice, being used for other religious purposes, in teaching the young, to accompany feasts, processions, dancing and dramatic choruses – in fact, because of its piercing sound-quality, for every kind of outdoor music-making. Troops marching to an aulos played by a boy are shown on a seventh-century black-figure pot (see pl. 13) and centuries later Thucydides tells us that at the

Pl. 13 Troops marching to the aulos. From a 7th-century black-figure pot at the Villa Giulia, Rome.

battle of Mantinea in 418 B.C. the Spartans advanced slowly to the music of many aulos-players, 'a regular institution in their army, that has nothing to do with religion but is meant to make them advance evenly, keeping in step'. The aulos was essentially a solo instrument, and the faulty intonation of which it was often accused must have mainly kept it so, though it was improved by Pronomus of Thebes late in the fifth century. The Spartan military bands and the ensemble of four auloi and four kitharas taking part in the Panathenaic procession on the north frieze of the Parthenon (see pl. 14), from nearly the same time, are exceptional and come from a relatively late period: we know nothing in Greek music comparable with the seventh-century Elamite orchestra described in the previous chapter. But vase-paintings often show solo auloi playing with a barbiton or kithara or accompanying a solo singer.

THE IMPORTANCE OF *MOUSIKE* IN GREEK LIFE

The Greek contribution to the tradition of Western music went very far beyond the development of instruments. However important music had been in early Mesopotamia and Egypt in religious ceremonies and for entertainment, there is no evidence that it dominated life as it did in Greece – to such an extent that by Plato's time it could be considered the most important factor in the shaping and control of morals and institutions. (It is true that by *mousike* the Greeks meant not only music in our sense but poetry and dancing, but to their minds this was a natural synthesis which had existed before its elements were separated.) The ethical and therapeutic powers of music were traditionally associated in the first place with the semi-legendary figures of the Phrygian aulos-player Olympus (*c.* 700) and his Cretan pupil Thaletas (*c.* 665), who settled at Sparta, and they occupied an

Pl. 14   Ensemble of auloi and kitharas from the north frieze of the Parthenon (17th-century drawing by James Carey, before the partial destruction of the frieze).

important place in the teaching of Pythagoras and his followers. Unfortunately, all we know of these characters comes from three hundred years or more later and tradition ascribes to them and to their near contemporary, Terpander of Lesbos (*c.* 645), various inventions and innovations which may or may not have been theirs but which appeared in their time. For instance, if Terpander was not certainly the originator of the seven-stringed phorminx, at any rate its earliest known representation, on the already-mentioned amphora from Melos (pl. 11), dates it from his supposed lifetime.

The names of both Terpander and Olympus are connected with the invention of the *nomos*, a word which in its early, musical sense remains unsatisfactorily defined; there were *nomoi* for a singer with kithara accompaniment, and *nomoi* for aulos alone – like the one 'depicting' Apollo's victory over the Python with which Sacadas of Argos created a sensation at the Pythian Games in 586. (According to Pausanias, *Description of Greece*, IV, xxvii, 7, the melodies of Sacadas were still being played, in rivalry with those of Pronomus – the Argives played Sacadas, the Boeotians Pronomus – two hundred years later when Epaminondas founded Messene in 369.) Possibly the word *nomos* means only 'custom' or 'convention', something like the 'orders' of architecture, or possibly a composition on a given melodic formula. It seems at first to have been specially connected with the cult of Apollo, a solo form of the choral *paian* which we first encounter in the First

Book of the *Iliad* when the Greeks sing one to appease Apollo and induce him to stop the plague. (But when Achilles calls on the Greeks to sing a paean after the killing of Hector, it is a simple song of victory not directed to the god.) Later it became a song of praise in general. The dithyramb was the Dionysian counterpart of the Apollonian paean; the earliest mention of the word is by Archilochus. There are thus plenty of indications of the cultivation of *mousike* during the seventh century, above all of lyrical song of the kind initiated by Archilochus, personal and subjective, convivial and satirical. In him we have at last a solid historical figure with one probable date, 648, when he saw an eclipse of the sun; we know from his fragments various biographical details, that he attached particular importance to *rhythmos* (measured structure, 'the rhythm that keeps men within bounds') and perfected iambics and trochaics, that he preferred being accompanied by an aulos-player to accompanying himself on the lyre. So did his younger contemporary Alcman, a Lydian who settled in Sparta. But Sappho and Alcaeus, who flourished later, at the turn of the century, metrical innovators writing in their own Aeolian dialect since they came from Lesbos, preferred the lyre – it is thought the barbiton.

Their lyric *mousike*, like the work of Alcman who composed antiphonal choral dances, was naturally word-dominated and of course we have numerous fragmentary remains of their poems – but not the slightest remnant of their *melos*. Centuries were to pass before the Greeks had a musical notation and we can only surmise, for instance, that lyric strophes encouraged a more 'melodious' style, with regular rhythmic patterns, than the near-recitative which probably sufficed for the Homeric epics. Archilochus was later credited with the introduction of heterophony, the very free doubling of the vocal line by the accompanying instrument which was all, except the drone, that the Greeks knew of what we call harmony – though it is not improbable that famous virtuosi of the aulos, such as Sacadas and his successors, gave the drone considerable mobility.

PYTHAGORAS AND EARLY MUSIC THEORY

Before the end of the sixth century, however, epoch-making innovations in thinking about music were introduced by the teachings of Pythagoras of Samos, who settled at Croton in southern Italy about 530: the mathematical bases not only of music but of the universe (coinciding in that conception of 'the music of the spheres', distorted echoes of which were to haunt men's minds as late as Sir Thomas Browne and Schopenhauer) and once again the ethical influence of music on man. So far as his theories affected practical music, they must be treated with the utmost caution for he left no writings and we first hear about them from writers of the fourth century. Pythagoras may have learned of the connection between mathematical ratios and musical intervals from the Babylonians and is credited with knowledge of the monochord. But the first use of the monochord to demonstrate the connection is reported by Euclid (*c.* 300) in his *Katatome kanonos* (Division of the Monochord); he was probably drawing on Archytas of Tarentum (*c.* 375), an acquaintance of Plato. Nevertheless, by ignoring the later wild excesses of Greek musical theory and considering its primitive foundations in the light of what we know of the instruments, together with a few terms employed in the seventh and sixth centuries, we may make some reasonable conjectures.

The early phorminx was literally *tetrachordos*, four-stringed, and the tetrachord always remained the basis of Greek music; we shall never know whether the compass of the oldest phorminxes was a perfect fourth or how the intermediate strings were tuned, but it is quite possible that at least by the beginning of the seventh century the tetrachord was firmly defined by the perfect fourth, a *symphonos* (consonant) interval easily mastered by the human voice without the help of a monochord. Soon, if not at once, the strings were tuned to give intervals: two tones (the Pythagorean tone being the ratio 8:9) and a *leimma* (the 'remainder' of the fourth after the subtraction of two tones: a 'semitone'). In what seems to be the oldest forms, the Aeolian and Dorian which, judging from Pindar, may have been more or less identical, the semitone came at the bottom of the tetrachord: e′ f′ g′ a′ (though not, of course, at any such definite pitch). The tetrachords in which the semitone was differently placed were significantly associated with Asia Minor: when it came in the middle the tuning was Phrygian, when it was uppermost it was Lydian. The addition of three strings made possible a second tetrachord with identical interval-structure. Its lowest string was the highest of the first tetrachord, and it was called *mese*, the middle note. The other string-names refer to distance from the player, so that *nete* (meaning lowest string) is the highest in pitch and *hypate* (highest string) the lowest; the other names mean next to lowest (*paranete*), third string (*trite*), forefinger (*lichanos*), and next to highest (*parhypate*). They did not, to the Greek mind, constitute a 'scale'; they were 'conjunct tetrachords' in which *nete*, *mese*, and *hypate* were the fixed points within whose limits his *melos* moved. Thus there were three *harmoniai* or systems (using the modern letter names for convenience):

Lydian	*Phrygian*	*Aeolian*	
bb′	c″	d″	NETE
a′	bb′	c″	paranete
g′	a′	bb′	trite
f′	g′	a′	MESE
e′	f′	g′	lichanos
d′	e′	f′	parhypate
c′	d′	e′	HYPATE

To these we should perhaps add a fourth: Théodore Reinach,[9] basing his assertion on what Aristotle in the fourth century seems to say about Terpander in the seventh, affirms that, unlike the Aeolians, the people of

---

[9] *La musique grecque* (Paris, 1926), p. 11. I have followed him in naming the *harmoniai*; on the total confusion of nomenclature at a later period, see Aristoxenus, *Harmonics*, 37.

Dorian origin 'separated the two tetrachords by a disjunctive note', later called *paramese*, so that their upper tetrachord lay between b♮' and e". As only three strings were available the *trite* (c") or perhaps *paranete* (d") had to be omitted. When more strings became available, on instruments of the harp rather than the lyre family, the Aeolians obtained the octave by adding a string (*hyperhypate* = d') to the lower of two conjunct tetrachords. But later the conjunct tetrachords were largely superseded in all systems by the disjunct: *hypate* to *mese* and *paramese* to *nete*. An octave scale on the white notes of a modern keyboard instrument consists precisely of two such disjunct diatonic tetrachords.

These were the diatonic *harmoniai* which always remained the real basis of Greek music. Sappho and Alcaeus sang in the Aeolian style. Yet already in the sixth century a certain Lysander of Sicyon is said to have introduced a modification in which the *lichanos* was tuned down, producing a 'crowding' or 'compression' of intervals (*pyknon*), two semitones, at the bottom of the tetrachord. At a later period it seems to have been mixed with the diatonic, the upper of two tetrachords being chromatic, the lower diatonic. All systems of tuning were based on the lyre for, as a number of literary references make clear, the intonation of the aulos was liable to be inaccurate. The aulos is often referred to as a Phrygian instrument, though the specifically so called 'Phrygian pipes' were a much later instrument, and it is reasonable to assume that, up to the classical period, it usually employed the Phrygian system or, rather, four or five notes of the conjunct or disjunct Phrygian tetrachords with *hypate* as the usual drone.

MUSIC IN THE AGE OF TRAGEDY

About 530 B.C., when Pythagoras was settling in Italy, the Dionysian dithyramb began in Athens to evolve into a ritual action and so into the tragedy of Phrynichus and Aeschylus. First the purely choral performance was 'interpreted' by a soloist (*hypokrites*) and then the narration of a legend was superseded by the enactment of it. Aeschylus introduced a second actor and Sophocles a third. Early tragedy was a work of total *mousike* – poetry, dance, music – and, both on account of its Dionysian associations and of its performance in the open air, we may be confident that the instruments employed were auloi. The music must still have been word-dominated but we know hardly anything about it. Indeed we know astonishingly little about Greek music in the ensuing fifth century, the golden age of Greek culture. We do not gather much from Sophocles but it is clear that great changes in the music of tragedy were wrought by Euripides; the chorus became much less important, the soloists much more so.

Another tuning, known later as 'enharmonic', became fashionable; in it the *lichanos* was tuned two whole tones lower than *mese*, leaving a *pyknon* of only a semitone which could itself be subdivided. It could, as Reinach has suggested, have originated in an aulos-tuning of disjunct tetrachords in the Dorian *harmonia*, with certain notes omitted. Then, assimilating Asiatic melodic influences, players would divide the semitone by partial stopping of the sound-hole. It is certainly probable that the microtones of the enharmonic tuning were arrived at empirically, not by the mathematical theorists.

In the latter half of the fifth century Pronomus of Thebes improved the aulos so that all the *harmoniai* could be played on the same instrument: metal rings were used to close or half-close holes, and the number of holes was increased to as many as fifteen. (Pitch could also be altered by pinching the reed between the lips or by 'drawing down' the hole called *syrinx*). And, according to Athenaeus in the second century A.D., quoting Aristoxenus, auloi were made in five registers: *parthenioi, paidikoi, kitharisterioi, teleioi*, and *hyperteleioi*, the 'virginal', the 'juvenile', the 'kitharistic', the 'perfect', and the 'pluperfect'.

These innovations of tuning, improved auloi, and the possibility of easily mixing *harmoniai*, may well have been associated with – perhaps led to – the new style of music cultivated towards the end of the fifth century by Phrynis of Mitylene and Melanippides (d. before 413), Philoxenus of Cythera, and Phrynis's pupil Timotheus of Miletus. The new style was manifest in the kithara-accompanied *nomoi* of Phrynis and the dithyrambs of Melanippides and Philoxenus; indeed it mixed the two genres of *nomos* and dithyramb. It was attacked as over-sophisticated, tortured, spineless, florid, destructive of the fine old classical style; it was ridiculed by Pherecrates in the surviving fragment of his *Cheiron* (*c.* 430) and by Aristophanes in the *Thesmophoriazusae* and elsewhere; it was attacked by Plato (427–347) in the *Republic* and *Laws*; by the time of Aristoxenus of Tarentum (born *c.* 354) its excesses had been softened and conventionalized. Its most lasting effect was its partial liberation of music, in the modern sense, from the domination of words.

PLATO ON MUSIC

It is to Plato and to Aristotle's disciple, Aristoxenus, a generation or so later, that we turn not only for information about Greek music in the fourth century but for the most influential thinking about music in general. Greek music is lost, except for a few fragments, but the pronouncements of Plato and the theoretical writings of Aristoxenus were echoed and re-echoed for many centuries. Plato inherited from the Pythagoreans and from Pericles' teacher, Damon of Oa, the conceptions of the mathematical basis of music and its ethical importance; and it is his writings, above all the passages in the *Republic* and in the work of his old age, the *Laws*, which have familiarized us with the Greek view of the ethical power and hence the importance of music and its role in education. Music and words are in complementary relationship: words are rational, sound is emotional. Through the customarily associated words the different *harmoniai* have acquired their own emotional connotations and should not be mixed, any more than the styles of hymns and dirges, paeans and dithyrambs, should be mixed. In both the

Republic and the *Laws* he concedes that such mixing is 'most pleasant' and popular with children and the crowd, but it is anarchic, symptomatic of the folly and degeneracy of modern *mousike*. In any case, the criterion is not the mere giving of pleasure. Plato goes further: in the ideal state he really wants only two *harmoniai*. Since music consists of three elements, the word, the *harmonia*, and the rhythm (or metre), and these must be congruent, if we want to do away with wailings and lamentations we must also do away with the 'wailing' *harmoniai*, such as the Mixolydian and Syntonolydian. (What Plato understood by 'mixed' and 'stretched' or 'high-pitched' Lydian remains, like other Greek technical terms, open to debate.) Even the ordinary Lydian and the Ionian must be rejected as effeminate and relaxing, very bad for fighting men; only the heroic Dorian and the persuasive Phrygian are left. *Rhythmos* is important, too; but Plato confesses his inability to tell 'which species imitates one kind of life, which another'. As for instruments, the lyra and kithara should suffice; the many-stringed pektis and *trigonon* (triangular harp), capable of many *harmoniai*, are 'imitations of the aulos' (an odd remark) – and Plato has nothing but contempt for 'the instruments of Marsyas', i.e. auloi. However, the syrinx is well enough for shepherds.

When Plato stops laying down the law and airing conservative prejudices, he sometimes throws invaluable light on practical music: for instance, on the nature of *heterophonia*. In teaching singing, one should use the lyre – not the aulos (as is shown in a number of vase-paintings of music lessons) – for the sake of its clear, precise sounds,

player and pupil producing note for note in unison. Heterophony and embroidery by the lyre – the strings throwing out melodic lines different to the *melodia* which the poet composed; crowded notes where his are sparse, quick time to his slow, high pitch to his low, whether together or in answer, and similarly all sorts of rhythmic complications of the lyre against the voice – none of this should be employed in dealing with pupils who have to absorb quickly a practical knowledge of music in three years.[10]

The lyre-player performed not another part but a very free and florid version of the same melody; heterophony anticipated ornamental variation, not counterpoint.

A three-year course in practical musicianship was sufficient for the ordinary young man, but the study of *mousike*, the union of music and poetry, was fundamental: 'children in their earliest play' should be 'imbued with the spirit of law and order through their music'. Or as he puts it in the *Protagoras* (326b), through becoming familiar with *harmoniai* and *rhythmoi* children learn *euharmostia* (good temper) and *eurhythmia* (gracefulness). Yet this must always be paired with gymnastic education, not because *mousike* is good for the soul, physical exercise for the body, as most people imagine, but because these two aspects of education are complementary and mutually corrective; cultivation of the one without the other leads to

[10] *Laws*, 812d. Translation from *NOHM*, i, p. 338, with modifications.

effeminacy or to crude intractability. But 'he who best blends gymnastics with music and applies them most suitably to the soul is the man whom we should most rightly pronounce to be the most perfect and harmonious musician'; such are the men one needs as guardians of the state.[11]

ARISTOTLE

As a pupil of Plato, Aristotle (*c.* 384–322) also recognizes the ethical power of music and its importance in education (*Politics*, viii). But he is prepared to accept purely instrumental music, since the ethical effect of music does not depend on words; it appeals directly to the emotions. He agrees that the ethical influence of music is more important than its power to give pleasure. And while the layman should have a certain amount of musical training, he should not try to achieve professional standards; the professional will always be better and there is much to be said for passive listening. The layman should not try to learn the aulos: for one thing it is an instrument for virtuosi, for another the amateur, who will be primarily a singer, will need to accompany himself – preferably on the simple lyra rather than the kithara, which is likewise an instrument for professionals. But Aristotle is not contemptuous of aulos-music, as Plato is; it is orgiastic and therefore, on the homoeopathic principle, cathartic.

THE *HARMONICS* OF ARISTOXENUS

Aristotle's disciple Aristoxenus was as many-sided as his teacher but far more concerned with music. It is with the light thrown by his incomplete *Elements of Harmonics* (*c.* 320),[12] surviving fragments of his *Elements of Rhythm*, and alleged – but sometimes obviously spurious – quotations from his lost works in writings of five hundred years later, that we try to clarify our understanding of earlier periods of Greek music and to find support for hypotheses about them. The son of a good professional musician, Aristoxenus was eminently practical. While Aristotle had doubted the possibility of measuring the enharmonic microtones and Plato (*Republic*, 531) mocked it in his gibe at the learned musicians who talk about the microtones of the *pyknon*[13] and, straining their ears, claim to hear differences where their colleagues assert there is no difference, Aristoxenus says flatly that it is impossible to sing more than two microtones consecutively; to employ a third-tone is a very different matter from dividing a tone into three parts and singing all three; 'we must not follow the harmonic theorists in their dense diagrams which show as consecutive notes those which are separated by the smallest intervals' but 'try to find what intervals the voice is by nature able to place in succession in a melody'.[14] 'The first and oldest *genos* is the diatonic which men hit upon naturally, the second the chromatic, the third and most

[11] *Republic*, Paul Shorey's translation (Loeb Classical Library), i, p. 293, and ii, p. 149.
[12] Edited and translated by Henry S. Macran (Oxford, 1902). Macran's own views are out-dated.
[13] Which Shorey, op. cit., ii, p. 191, translates as 'minims'!
[14] *Harmonics*, 46 and 28.

recent the enharmonic to which one accustoms oneself only after much hard work',[15] but which is nevertheless 'almost the most beautiful'. Exactly measured microtones were merely theoretical. And a serious flaw in Pythagoras's system – that six 'whole tones' calculated by the harmonic proportion 8:9 amount to slightly more than an octave was disposed of by defining a tone as 'the difference between the fifth and the fourth: the fourth consists of two tones and a half',[16] consequently the fifth of three tones and a half, and the octave was thus divided into twelve equal semitones. This cleared the way for a system of *tonoi* or double-octave scales (two disjunct tetrachords,[17] extended by conjunct tetrachords above and below, and an 'additional' note, *proslambanomenos*) which could be transposed to begin on any note of the diatonic system.

Aristoxenus considered two octaves and a fifth the utmost compass for practical purposes,[18] though he admitted that the difference between the highest note of a *parthenios aulos* and the lowest of a *hyperteleios* might be more than three octaves. The *tonoi* could of course be of any *genos* – diatonic, chromatic, or enharmonic – and *metabole* (modulation) was possible, though it is not crystal clear what Aristoxenus meant by it. Unfortunately he was the last 'classical' Greek theorist; the next Greek writing about music dates from the first and second centuries A.D., when the 'harmonists' were mathematicians unconcerned with practical music though willing enough to claim the authority of Aristoxenus for their statements, even when they contradict his known views. Unfortunately too it is from their 'dense diagrams' and still more dense technicalities that many people derive their impressions of 'Greek music'.

GREEK NOTATION

Aristoxenus was also acquainted with notation, though he was surprisingly contemptuous about it. It indicated only intervals, not their position in the tetrachord, and understanding of it was no more the be-all and end-all of musical science than was understanding of aulos-playing – which, one gathers, he rated fairly low. He tells us nothing about the system of notation; unfortunately for us, he took it for granted that his readers would know anything so elementary. Still more unfortunately, we have no notation from his time. Probably the earliest fragment of Greek notation we possess, a tiny mutilated fragment, is preserved on a papyrus in the Archduke Rainer's collection in Vienna: a few broken lines from a chorus in the *Orestes* of Euripides,[19] though not, we may be sure, the music of the original performance of 408 B.C. It is customary to read it with the aid of the tables in the *Introduction to Music* (c. A.D. 350) of Alypius. Alypius actually gives

---

[15] Ibid., 19.   [16] Ibid., 46.
[17] In the Perfect System. There was also a Lesser Perfect System consisting of three conjunct tetrachords (plus *proslambanomenos*), the highest of which was called *synemmenon*, the 'hooked' tetrachord (see p. 76)   [18] *Harmonics*, 20.
[19] Facsimile in *The Oxford History of Music: Introductory Volume* (London, 1929), p. 22; transcription in Reinach, op. cit., pp. 175–6.

two systems of notation, which were in practice used indiscriminately except when it was necessary to distinguish song from instrumental music.

The 'instrumental' system, whose characters are only partially recognizable as alphabetic, is obviously the older and may well have been the one known to Aristoxenus. Its essential part consists of signs for a two-octave diatonic scale:

Ex. 1

Six higher notes are indicated by adding a ' to the second to seventh notes of this series, and extra signs give two lower notes. A character is turned on its back to indicate sharpening by a microtone and reversed mirrorwise to indicate sharpening by two microtones. It was perhaps originally a *kithara* notation, possibly extended and elaborated from that of the pair of conjunct tetrachords marked in Ex. 1.

The so-called 'vocal' notation on the other hand was evidently developed from a basic octave scale, with all the microtonal possibilities as an integral part of the system, and smacks of 'the harmonists'. This central diatonic octave with its microtonal alterations is shown by the twenty-four letters of the Greek alphabet: *alpha* – the highest note raised by two microtones, *beta* – the same raised by one microtone, *gamma* – the note unaltered, *delta* – the second highest note twice sharpened, and so on. An upward extension was obtained by adding a ' to the first fifteen letters and inverting the last six, the problems of inverting *chi* being solved with an asterisk: downward extension was managed by further inversion or fragmentation of letters and borrowings from the 'instrumental' notation. But what was the theoretical 'pitch' of the basic octave? Modern writers, following the late Hellenistic theorists, show it as what we should call f'–f, but Isobel Henderson[20] has put forward very strong arguments for considering that it was originally a'–a, thus (using a 'half-sharp' for the first microtonal sharpening):

Ex. 2

The Greeks had no notation indicating rhythm as distinct from metre; with the poetic-metrical basis of their music, they did not need one. But the sign and letter notations enable us to read approximately the *Orestes* fragment, such as it is, in the 'vocal' notation, and the two late-second-century hymns to Apollo inscribed on the walls of the Treasury of the Athenians at Delphi (see pl. 15), the first in 'vocal', the second in

[20] *NOHM*, i, pp. 359–60.

'instrumental' notation. Thus the lines about the 'glorious great city of Attica dwelling in an inviolate plain, thanks to Athena's prayers' sounded something like this:

Ex. 3

κλυτὰ   με-γα - λό - πο-λις Ἀθ-θὶς εὐχαῖεῖ-σι   φε - ρό - πλοι-ο ναί - ου - σα

Τρι-τω-ω - νί - δος δά-πε-δον   ἄ - θραυστον·

But this was music of 'Hellenistic' Greece; the first Delphic hymn probably dates from *c*. 138 B.C. and the second from ten years later – it ends with a prayer for the Roman empire. The essentially Greek contribution to the mainstream of musical tradition had been completed. As we have seen, it was very great – the conception of the mathematical basis of music, recognition of it as something more than ancillary to worship and entertainment, the diatonic system, notation. But we now have to consider the later music of the Greeks in a wider international context.

Pl. 15   First of two hymns to Apollo on the wall of the Treasury of the Athenians at Delphi (*c*. 138 B.C.) The lines marked are transcribed in Ex. 3.

3

The Hellenistic-Roman World

THE PROCESS OF INTERNATIONALIZATION

The downfall of the Achaemenids in Persia, which by that time included Mesopotamia and Egypt, and the accession (toward the end of the fourth century) of Macedonian rulers – Seleucid and Ptolemaic – established a Hellenized Near East. Not long after, from the second century B.C., the expanding Roman world in the Western Mediterranean became gradually, and before long rapidly, Hellenized as well. There had already been a great deal of cultural exchange between the peoples of all these lands; we have already seen how many types of musical instrument they had in common. Certainly throughout the later Roman Republic and the heyday of the Empire there existed an 'international' music comparable with that of the Western hemisphere in much later times, no doubt with dialects differing as German, Italian, and French musics did in the eighteenth and nineteenth centuries. It is reasonable to call it Hellenistic-Roman though, as it happens, the most important strand in it from a historical point of view – to contemporaries probably too insignificant to be noticeable at all – was neither Hellenistic nor Roman.

Before examining this essentially Hellenistic music we should reckon up what we know of the peripheral musical cultures during the preceding centuries. It is not very much. We know little or nothing about music in Persia under the Achaemenids beyond what Herodotus[1] noticed at sacrificial ceremonies: the absence of auloi (together with libations and garlands) and the presence of a magus who sang a *theogonia* or genealogy of the gods. All the representations of instruments from the area of Phoenician culture belong to the common East Mediterranean stock, but in the Western Mediterranean the destruction of Carthage totally obliterated everything connected with its music. As for the Hebrews, the poetic texts and the descriptions of the use of music in the Old Testament suggest that both were strikingly similar to those of the Sumerians and Babylonians.

MUSIC IN THE OLD TESTAMENT

When Miriam and her women (Exodus xv: 20), the women welcoming David (1 Samuel xviii: 7), and Jephthah's daughter (Judges xi: 34) sang

[1] *Histories*, i, 132.

their songs of victory and danced *tôph* in hand, they were following the practice of their age, not of their race – and we may be more confident than in the case of some instruments mentioned in the Bible that a *tôph* was some sort of small hand-drum. As for the others, the *nēbel* was possibly a harp, the *kinnôr* a lyre; both are said to have been made of sandal-wood and to have had ten and eight strings respectively; the kinnôr was small enough to be hung on a willow-tree. The *shōphār* and *qeren* were animal horns, signal instruments[2] rather than genuinely musical ones, and whatever the *'ûgāb* and *ḥālîl* may have been, we can be fairly confident that they were instruments known by other names to the Mesopotamians and Egyptians – *ḥālîl* means 'made of hollow reed' but appears only in the singular or plural, never in the dual, so it cannot have been a double-pipe. No remains of instruments nor even representations of them have survived from the pre-Hellenistic ages; the religious objection to pictures or images of human beings makes it improbable that there ever were any; the double-pipe player on a bronze tripod found at Megiddo, said to be of Solomon's time (*c*. 950), must have been the work of a foreign craftsman.

With the return from the Babylonian captivity, *c*. 530, and the consequent rebuilding of the Temple in Jerusalem, we get from the more or less contemporary author of the Book of Chronicles clear indications of the importance of both vocal and instrumental music in the Temple services not only on feast-days but in the daily order of worship. How far he can be relied on for his account of the Levites being 'set over the service of song in the house of the Lord' (1 Chronicles vi: 31) by David more than four hundred years earlier, before even the first Temple was built, with the names of those who were to play the *nĕbhālîm* and who the *kinnōrôth* (xv: 20–1), one can only speculate. But there is no reason to doubt what he says of the constitution of what might be called family guilds of professional musicians (e.g. 'the sons of Korah') who presumably performed both at the royal court and in the Temple. We have the words of their repertory in the book of Psalms, some of which may indeed date from the time of David or even much earlier, though most are from after the exile. We can deduce from the verse-structure that they were probably sung to short melodic patterns many times repeated with the necessary variation, that some were antiphonal or responsorial; and it is clear that the singing was instrumentally supported. The headings of a number of psalms show that they were sung to traditional melodies: for instance, Psalms lvii–lix and lxxv are marked to be sung to 'Al-taschith' ('Destroy not') which has been identified with a vintage-song quoted in Isaiah lxv: 8. However much these sixth-century practices owed to earlier tradition it seems likely that they were also directly influenced by those of the Mesopotamian lands of the captivity – with which they were in any case related.

It is generally agreed that after the captivity music played an even more important part in the Temple worship than before, possibly because there

[2] On the signals see David Wulstan, 'The Sounding of the Shofar', *Galpin Society Journal*, xxvi (1973), p. 29.

was no longer a royal court making demands on the musicians' time. Something like a liturgical calendar emerged: thus Ps. xxiv was sung on the first day of the week, xlviii on the second, lxxxii on the third, xciv on the fourth, lxxxi on the fifth, xciii on the sixth, and xcii on the Sabbath. Psalm xxx was sung annually on the anniversary of 'the dedication of the House of David'.

HEBREW MUSIC UNDER HELLENISTIC PRESSURE

If we can only speculate on the actual music of the Temple, the position is even worse in the field of Hebrew secular music. We know what we hardly need to be told – that they had harvest songs, vintage songs, workers' songs of other kinds, and love-songs; but beyond a few fragmentary quotations we do not even know the words, except the amorous lyrical poetry of the third-century Song of Songs. But by that time Jewish music had been drawn into the Hellenic world and in the second century we find the author of the Book of Daniel talking about instruments with Greek names: the *qaytěrōs* (kithara), *pěsantěrîn* (psalterion), and *sŭmpōněyă* (symphonia). The Jews no doubt exercised their customary ability to preserve their traditions and resist cultural absorption with particular success in everything connected with the Temple worship and their religion generally, but the pressure of the Hellenic world is manifest in their resistance to it. For instance, the religious use of instruments, so long an important feature of the Temple worship, was not prohibited after the destruction of the Temple in A.D. 70 in token of mourning, as was long believed, but discouraged before then in order to safeguard the purity of religious music 'against the musical and orgiastic mystery cults in which Syrian and Mesopotamian Jews not infrequently participated'.[3] It was equally disapproved of by the Hellenistic-Judaic philosopher Philo of Alexandria, who wrote in the early years of the Christian era and was opposed to any kind of music in worship, and in the early Christian communities – whose interdiction of instrumental participation in service-music has been maintained to this day by the Eastern Church.

There can be little doubt that after the fall of the Temple its practices, including its musical tradition, were continued on the one hand in the synagogues, on the other in the gatherings of that originally Jewish sect, the Christians. (It is significant that both Jews and Christians employed Greek words, *synagoge* and *ekklesia*, both meaning 'assembly'.) Philo 'Judaeus' is a valuable witness on other points besides the ban on instruments in liturgical use. His accounts of psalm-singing by a solo cantor, with congregational responses, and of antiphonal hymn-singing by choirs of men and of women – he is talking in *De vita contemplativa* of the sect of Therapeutae who also inherited orthodox Jewish practices – have often been quoted, first of all by the church historian Eusebius of Caesarea (*c.* 260–*c.* 340) who tells us that

[3] *NOHM*, i, p. 315.

39

Philo's description applies equally to Christian practice.[4]

It is this thread of tradition irrefragably connecting Jewish practices and Jewish music with those of the Christian church and thus ultimately with the 'high culture' music of the West in general which gives Jewish music its peculiar historical importance. In its contemporary context it cannot have seemed important; it may not even have seemed peculiar, for, with all the differences of religious belief and practice, we do not know how and how much – if at all – the actual musical language differed from that of the Hellenistic-Roman world generally.

ETRUSCAN INFLUENCE ON ROME

It has been said that 'three main influences affected the Romans; the first was from the Etruscans, the second from the Greeks, and the third from the East'.[5] But although this has the appearance of making sense chronologically, the three influences were closely interrelated, perhaps nearly identical. We have already seen how Greek music was related to that of the East, and the Etruscans (probably immigrants from Asia Minor and linguistically connected with the Lydians) were heavily indebted to Greek culture. What

Pl. 16   Cup-bearer, *tibicen*, and lyra-player (fresco in the 'Tomb of the Leopards', *c.* 480–70 B.C., Tarquinia). The pipes of the *tibia* (double reed-pipes) are slightly flared and the position of the player's left hand suggests that he could supply a movable drone.

we know of Etruscan music is almost entirely derived from pictorial representations, mainly funerary and possibly by Greek artists, and from scattered references in Greek and Roman literature. Representations of kithara and lyra[6] are like those of Greek instruments of the pre-classical age,

[4] *Historia ecclesiastica*, ii, 17.   [5] *NOHM*, i, p. 404.
[6] See Günter Fleischhauer, *Etrurien und Rom* (Leipzig, n.d.) in the series *Musikgeschichte in Bildern*, pl. 1–4, 10, 12, 13, 15, 16.

and the Etruscans knew not only the Greek *krotala* but the Egyptian clappers. But it was in wind-music that they excelled. They cultivated the aulos (see pl. 16), traditionally of Asian origin,[7] to such an extent that after the

Pl. 17   Etruscan musicians, wearing the long robes of their guild, in a relief on a 5th-century B.C. sarcophagus from Caere (Museo Etrusco Gregoriano, Rome). The two on the left are playing *tibia* and kithara; the man in the middle is presumably a herald; on the right are players of *lituus* (end-curved trumpet) and *cornu* (horn).

Pl. 18   Relief on a 1st-century B.C. Roman sarcophagus from Amiternum (Museo Civico, Aquileia) showing two *cornicines*, a *liticen*, and four *tibicines* taking part in a funeral procession.

Roman conquest the music at public festivals and so on in Rome was provided by Etruscan *subulones* – the Romans significantly used the Etruscan word as well as the Latin *tibicines* – as in Athens by Boeotian aulos-players. They also played the transverse flute.[8]

---

[7] See p. 25.   [8] Fleischhauer, pl. 20.

But their only innovations, so far as we can tell, were in the trumpet family; they presumably knew the straight trumpet – the *salpinx* or Roman *tuba* – but the sarcophagi and tomb-paintings show one with a bell less flared than that of the *tuba* but bent round[9] (the Roman *lituus*), and the nearly circular, narrow-bored instrument which the Romans called *cornu* (see pl. 17).[10] It is perhaps one of these instruments that Aeschylus, Sophocles, and Euripides mean when they refer to the 'Etruscan trumpet' (*Tyrsenike salpinx*), though the adjective may have no more meaning than in 'French horn' or 'cor anglais'. The *bucina*, a less powerful relative of the *cornu* and often confused with it, seems to have been a Roman invention; surprisingly, no reliable representation of it has survived. Instruments of the trumpet and horn family were always in the first place military signal instruments or sounded at religious ceremonies, and it is never easy to determine when or how they were first employed in 'art' music. When they are represented on sarcophagi as apparently being played in consort with *tibiae* (see pl. 18), they may actually have been sounded alternately. But Appianus tells us that when the body of Sulla was brought to Rome in 78 B.C. the trumpeters sounded 'mournful melodies',[11] which suggests full use of the available overtones; indeed *aeneatores* (players of bronze or copper instruments) were commonly engaged for funerals and formed *collegia* for that purpose.

ROMAN FESTIVALS AND ROMAN THEATRE

Roman militarism, has, however, led to a very false impression of Roman music. Although their instruments and their use of music were common to those of the Mediterranean peoples generally, there is nothing to suggest that the Romans were less musical than their neighbours. On the contrary, there is abounding evidence of their introduction of song into every phase of social activity: at work, in recreation, in worship, festive songs, satirical songs, love-songs, drinking songs. According to tradition, both the Salii – the college of priests of Mars Gradivus who sang and danced through the streets of Rome annually on the Kalends of March – and the first guild of tibia-players date from the reign of the semi-legendary Numa Pompilius in the seventh century B.C. The Arvales, who perambulated the fields or city boundary before the harvest, also sang, and there are indications that both they and the Salii sang responsorially or antiphonally. Such annual celebrations and religious and other innovations give us our firmest landmarks in the chronology of Roman musical history. For instance, Livy (vii, 2ff.) chronicles pantomimic performances in 364 B.C. by visiting Etruscan actors, dancing to tibia-music but without song of any kind (*sine carmine ullo . . . ad tibicinis modos saltantes*); these were imitated by the

---

[9] Ibid., pl. 15, 18, 19. The last is a photograph of an actual bronze instrument, 1.60 metres long and giving the second to eighth overtones; the sound is said to be 'sharp and shrill'.
[10] A bronze Etruscan *cornu* is preserved in the museum of the Villa Giulia, Rome.
[11] *Bell. civ.*, I, 105.

Roman youth and gradually led to the establishment of a professional class of actors and singers. Then about 240 a Greek prisoner, Livius Andronicus, 'actor of his songs', composer and musical teacher, introduced notions of Greek drama which superseded the rude dramatic and satirical dialogues. And the second-century adaptors of Greek comedy introduced music where their originals had had none. Plautus turned passages of dialogue into passages with music, either sung or spoken to tibia accompaniment, only the iambic trimeters being left without music; he also intercalated songs of various kinds, though not for chorus. In Terence the musical passages were fewer but the text of his *Hecyra* (The Mother-in-law) in the tenth-century Codex Victorianus has one iambic octonarian for the *cantor* Bacchis Meretrix with Greek 'instrumental' notation above the accented syllables (Act V, sc. 4, v. 861). This source is, of course, much too late to carry any conviction that we have here a fragment of the original music. But we do know the names of some of the composers, for instance Flaccus 'the slave of Claudius' who 'made the tunes' for Terence's *Andria* (The Woman of Andros) and *Phormio*. There was music before the prologue and between the acts; 'in the mean time the *tibia* player will entertain you here', says the hero of Plautus's *Pseudolus* as he makes his exit at the end of Act I.

Claudius's Flaccus composed his *Andria* music for *tibiae pares*, 'equal pipes', that for *Phormio* for *tibiae impares*, 'unequal pipes', the inequality consisting in the fact that one pipe, supplying a movable drone, had a large curved bell rather like that of the *lituus*. Probably this bell was originally a cow horn and the instrument was the prototype of that still surviving and widely diffused folk-instrument, the hornpipe. These *tibiae impares*, more powerful than the older types, seem to have reached Rome about 204 B.C., with various kinds of drums, cymbals, and rattles, when the orgiastic cult of Cybele, the Great Mother of the gods, was officially recognized. The bent pipe, and hence the pair, was also referred to as *curva tibia*, *Idaea buxus* (from the goddess's other name and the boxwood of which the instrument was made), and *tibia Berecynthia* (from the mountain in Phrygia Major that was sacred to her). And although the Greeks had, as we have seen, always considered auloi to be Phrygian in origin, the Romans now specifically called the *tibiae impares* – which were considerably more powerful than the normal pipes – *tibiae Phrygiae* and the normal type 'Lydian'. Like the later cult of the Egyptian Isis, the worship of Cybele was disliked by respectable Romans under the republic though encouraged by the influx of foreigners from the East, and became privileged only after two centuries during the reign of Claudius; the well-known relief of a priest of Cybele, with tibiae, a tympanum, and a pair of little cymbala, in the Palazzo dei Conservatori in Rome[12] dates from still later. At the other end of the scale of respectability the cithara retained not only its Greek name but its Greek place as the finest solo and accompanying instrument. It naturally assumed new shapes with the passage of time, as did the type of lute known as *pandura*, imported from the East by way of Greece.

[12] *NOHM*, i, pl. XI(a), and Fleischhauer, op. cit., pl. 47.

3. The Hellenistic-Roman World

ORIGIN OF THE ORGAN

At some time before the beginning of the Christian era, Hellenistic ingenuity produced an epoch-making change in the hitherto very simple mechanism of wind instruments, a change which was to provide the Rome of the emperors with one of its favourite instruments. The maintenance of wind-pressure had always been one of the problems of the aulos and the only known solution from the early sixth century onward had been the leather 'halter' – the Greek *phorbeia*, the Roman *capistrum* – tied across the player's mouth. Two passages in Aristophanes[13] could be taken to mean that squeezed bladders were sometimes used as wind-reservoirs and an Alexandrian terra-cotta of the first century B.C. shows a 'one-man band':[14] the player holds large panpipes in his left hand, squeezes with his left arm a bag from which projects a pipe (obviously only a drone) which he holds with his right hand, and manipulates a *scabellum*, a hinged wooden clapper, with his foot. If he were playing a *monaulos* also supplied with wind from the bag, instead of an independently blown syrinx, we should have a fully developed bagpipe. Nothing more than this is known of the origin of the bagpipe, afterwards one of the most widely diffused and popular of folk-instruments; but it always was a folk-instrument and in Roman times its place was in the tavern, not the palace – although Suetonius[15] says Nero had ambitions as an *utricularius* (bagpiper). It never won acceptance in sophisticated music. Yet its basic principle was brilliantly developed by Alexandrian science to produce an instrument which in the fourth century A.D. came to be called *organon* – *tout court* – 'the instrument' *par excellence*. All the same, the origins of the organ are almost as unclear as those of the bagpipe.

Tradition, summed up in the second century A.D. by that pleasant gossip Athenaeus,[16] attributes the invention of the *organon hydraulikon* or *hydraulos*, the 'water-aulos',[17] to Ctesibius of Alexandria, an engineer of the mid-third century B.C. who made various machines exploiting the power of compressed air, particularly air compressed by weight of water. According to Athenaeus again,[18] an Alexandrian poet described a *rhyton*, a drinking vessel, placed in a temple of Arsinoë II, which gave forth a sound like a trumpet when water was poured; this invention, which presumably produced only one note, he attributed to Ctesibius. An Arabic treatise cited by H. G. Farmer[19] credits Archimedes, contemporary with Ctesibius, with the construction of a statuette of an aulos-player which worked in precisely the same way, by air forced through the instrument by water pressure, and Tertullian[20] actually refers to Archimedes as the inventor of the hydraulus. Philo of Byzantium, who is supposed to have lived in Alexandria, rather later in the third century B.C., talks about Ctesibius's cylinder pumps in his

[13] *Lysistrata*, 1242; *Acharnians*, 862. See Anthony Baines, *Bagpipes* (Oxford, 1960), p. 63.
[14] *NOHM*, i, p. 414; illustration in Baines, op. cit., p. 65.
[15] *Nero*, liv.   [16] *Deipnosophistæ*, iv, 174.
[17] Also spelled *hydraulis* and latinized as *hydraulus*.   [18] Ibid., xi, 97.
[19] *The Organ of the Ancients from Eastern Sources* (London, 1931), p. 80.   [20] *De Anima*, xiv.

Mechanike Syntaxis and then goes on to say that their practicality is demonstrated by 'the syrinx which is played with the hands and is known as the *hydraulis*' in which 'the wind mechanism . . . forces the air into a *pnigeus* [literally, 'oven'] of brass placed in the water'.[21] A mechanically activated syrinx 'played with the hands' would certainly be a prototypal organ, though Philo does not actually say that Ctesibius invented it. It was a notable advance on the salpinx- or aulos-playing automata, and his testimony shows that it existed in early Hellenistic times.

The several pipes of the syrinx, sounded by air maintained at a fairly stable pressure by weight of water, could obviously be stopped or unstopped by some further mechanical device more easily than the holes of the *monaulos*. The first step must have been a row of slides pulled out and pushed in, the next – a considerable one – the moving of the slides by pressing on keys returned to the original stopping position by springs. How soon this was thought of, we do not know; we hear of it first in the *Pneumatics* of Hero of Alexandria in the first century A.D.,[22] who incidentally refers to the pipes as *auloi*, reed-pipes, and the *De Architectura* of his (possibly older) contemporary Vitruvius, who describes a more complicated instrument[23] with double pumps and four, six, or eight *canales* each admitting or denying wind to a separate rank of pipes – more probably differing in *harmonia* or *genos* than in tone-colour or pitch. The numerous representations of the hydraulis, of which the earliest we have is an Alexandrian terracotta[24] of probably the same date and nearly the same size as the one that gives us our earliest representation of the bagpipe, nearly always show the front of the instrument, with the player looking over the top. The earliest sight of keys is given by a seven-inch high terracotta model of an organ with its player, dating from the early second century A.D. and found at Carthage (now in the Lavigerie Museum there); it has eighteen broad keys which play three ranks each of eighteen pipes, of which at any rate two ranks are visibly flue-pipes (i.e. on the flute principle, not reeds).[25] No doubt the player used both hands and his left hand would have been freer than the larger pipe of a pair of tibiae. He may have used it for nothing more agile than an occasionally changing drone, but Seneca in the first century A.D. makes an unequivocal reference to consonance, in the modern sense, on stringed instruments, 'quomodo inter se acutae ac graves voces consonent, quomodo nervorum disparem reddentium sonum fiat concordia' (how high and low voices may agree with each other, how concord may be made from strings giving a different sound) (*Epistulae*, LXXXVIII). Still this should not be taken to indicate anything more than the simultaneity of different sounds in heterophony.

One curious circumstance in the early history of the organ is that the obvious hybrid link between the bagpipe and the hydraulos – a smaller

[21] Quoted in Jean Perrot, *The Organ from its Invention in the Hellenistic Period to the end of the Thirteenth Century* (Paris, 1965; English translation by Norma Deane, London, 1971), p. 24.
[22] Perrot gives Hero's description of the mechanism in great detail, pp. 27ff., and reproduces the diagram from the thirteenth-century copy of his treatise, the earliest surviving one, pl. XXIII.
[23] See ibid., pp. 34ff.   [24] Ibid., pl. V.   [25] Ibid., pp. 96–8 and pl. XI (3 and 6) XII.

organ blown by ordinary bellows and with a leather bag, compressed by weights, for a wind-chest – is first referred to by Julius Pollux as late as the second century A.D. As with the bagpipe itself, it is difficult to believe that it had not existed long before its existence was documented; and like the bagpipe it was essentially a 'popular' instrument. It was the technical ingenuity of the hydraulos that led people like Philo and Hero and Vitruvius to write about it, and even the hydraulos withdraws from the daylight of history for a century or two after Philo.

In the year 90 B.C. a player on the hydraulos scored a sensational success at Delphi. This was at a time when Hellenistic musical and theatrical influences were making themselves more and more strongly felt in southern Italy, as they did before long in Rome itself, and the organ seems to have reached the capital about the middle of the century. During the Imperial period it was played in the theatre and at gladiatorial contests, sometimes – perhaps often – with cornua and a tuba, as shown in the mosaics of the first and second centuries A.D. in the Tripoli Museum and at Nennig on the upper Mosel.[26] It was also a domestic instrument and, since music was practised more and more by amateurs under the Empire, it was played by Nero himself – who also justly fancied himself as a singer and composer and

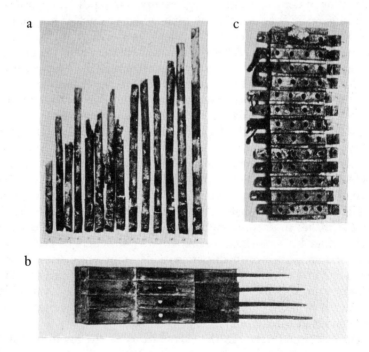

Pl. 19   (a) Pipes of the 3rd-century organ at Aquincum near Budapest, (b) sliders admitting wind to the pipes, and (c) the sliders in position.

[26] Ibid., pl. II and I.

performed on the cithara, tibia, and (as we have seen) the bagpipes – and in the third century by Heliogabalus and Alexander Severus. From the latter's reign dates the earliest partially surviving organ, the instrument found at Aquincum near Budapest, presented to the Guild of Weavers by their prefect in A.D. 228; it is a very small domestic organ with four ranks of thirteen flue-pipes, three ranks stopped, one open, and consequently thirteen sliders with keys,[27] each rank being for a different *harmonia*. The largest pipe is only about thirteen inches long.

MUSIC UNDER THE EMPIRE

The popularity of the organ was coeval with the most flourishing period of Roman music which in turn coincided with that period of the Empire from the time when Egypt became a Roman province (30 B.C.) till the transference of the capital to Byzantium in A.D. 328. We have a bewildering amount of literary information and representational evidence of the cultivation of music under the Empire but only a few fragments of notated music: all associated with Greek texts and none found in Italy. The most important are the often transcribed tombstone 'epitaph of Seikilos'[28] (perhaps first century A.D., from Aidin, the ancient Lydian Tralles), the Contrapollinopolis papyrus (mid-second century, from the Thebaid) (see pl. 20), and the Oxyrhynchus papyrus (late third century, from Egypt). All the same it is possible to extract from the evidence a good idea of general conditions and tendencies. There was, for instance, a persistent conservative and moralistic strain based on the preservation of the old Roman musical institutions of religious music and the use of military music. The centuries-old Salii and Arvales were drawn into the worship of the emperor – an Arval *acclamatio* was noted in A.D. 213 and the words of an ancient *carmen arvale* are preserved in an inscription of 218. On the other hand, the Eastern cults and the instruments associated with them, which reached the capital in ever increasing quantity under the Empire and became naturalized and popular, were regarded as decadent by upholders of the old Roman ethos. Seneca[29] had already deplored the growing taste for effeminate music and Quintilian followed him. The association of music with the theatre – particularly in the often licentious mime and in pantomime (originally a solo dramatic dance) – with vulgar spectacle in the arena, and with orgiastic banquets, made its more widespread cultivation seem all the more deplorable. It was not music and dancing in themselves that were objectionable, although Cicero held that Greece had been depraved by music,[30] but their nature and the mania for them. The ancient Romans had dined to the sound of strings and tibia

---

[27] The remains, with a dubious reconstruction, may be seen in the Aquincum Museum (see pl. 19). Detailed description in Perrot, op. cit., pp. 109ff., but his interpretation of the nature of the ranks is refuted in Werner Walcker-Mayer, *Die römische Orgel von Aquincum* (Stuttgart, 1970).
[28] Photograph in *MGG*, v, col. 847, and Curt Sachs, *The Rise of Music in the Ancient World* (New York, 1943), pl. 8. Both date it much earlier.
[29] *De Ira*, iii, 35.   [30] *De legibus*, ii, 15.

provided by slave professionals and Marcus Aurelius in his youth had led the songs and dances of the Salii; but orgiastic music, and aristocrats – even emperors – publicly competing with professionals in singing to the cithara, were different matters.

MUSICIANS' GUILDS

The old idea of organizing professional musicians in guilds had been adopted by the early Romans far back in the seventh century B.C. with Numa's *collegium tibicinum Romanorum*, which in 311 B.C. successfully went on strike for the restoration of withdrawn privileges. When Augustus in 12 B.C. assumed the title of *pontifex maximus*, becoming the religious as well as the military and civil head of the state, he lost little time in establishing a *collegium symphoniacorum*, a guild of religious and official musicians in Rome. In A.D. 43 we hear of a 'world union of artists in the service of Dionysus': poets and actors as well as all kinds of musician connected with the theatre. The centre was in Rome, with local branches, and its privileges were renewed at least three times in the early third century. Septimius Severus allowed the military musicians to form *collegia*, with an entrance payment of 750 *denarii*, savings fund, and pension fund. Even the players of the humble *scabellum*, the foot clapper, had their guild in the late second century. The spectacular emergence of a virtuoso *citharoedus* and composer such as Menecrates, to whom Nero gave a palace, or Mesomedes of Crete, to whom compositions of a much later time have been attributed, a freedman of the Emperor Hadrian who rewarded him extravagantly, was rather exceptional. But the coincidence of virtuoso-worship with aristocratic or plutocratic amateurism is a common enough phenomenon; Hadrian himself was proud of his singing and cithara playing. (The *citharoedus* was still, as in classical Greece, the highest type of musician.)

MONSTER CONCERTS AND CHORAL *CONCENTUS*

Another symptom of decadence, in the eyes of the stern moralists, was the cult of the monster concert, an Alexandrian importation. We need not take literally Seneca's assertion that there were now more singers at concerts than there used to be spectators in the theatres and his description of gangways blocked with singers, the seats (*cavea*) surrounded by *aeneatores* (brass-players), and every sort of tibiae and other instruments sounding from the platform.[31] But two centuries later the outstanding event of the brief reign of the profligate Carinus (A.D. 284) was a concert in which a hundred trumpeters, a hundred horn-players, and two hundred *tibicines* gathered in Rome from all the provinces, took part.

Seneca admits that all these different voices – high, deep, medium, of men, women, and tibiae – make concord (*fit concentus ex dissonis*), as of

[31] *Epistulae*, LXXXIV.   [32] Ibid.

course they must have done. The single voices disappear, he says; one hears the total effect (*singulorum illic latent voces, omnium apparent*).[32] But what was this *concentus* and how was it achieved? The most probable answer is that, as with the Greeks of an earlier age, it was some kind of heterophony: the simultaneous performance of different elaborations or simplifications of the same melody. And despite Ptolemy of Alexandria, Cleonides, Gaudentius, Aristides Quintilianus (perhaps a freedman of the more celebrated Quintilian), and the other Alexandrian musico-mathematical theorists of the second century A.D. who have done so much to confuse our notions of ancient Greek music, the melody was almost certainly diatonic; the surviving fragments of notation mentioned above show no traces of enharmonic tuning and very little of chromaticism. Furthermore, the same fragments show that musicians were now using signs indicating five different note-values: ∪ for the smallest unit (*chronos protos*) and ˷ , ˻ , ˻˻ ˻˻ for the equivalent of two, three, four, or five *chronoi*, with the corresponding rests for the first four: ʌ ᴛ ᴛ˒ ˈᴛ˒ as well as the old pitch-notations. Musical rhythm could now be indicated independently of poetic metre. And, incidentally, time was now literally beaten – with the foot: describing a *citharoedus* performing, Quintilian says his right hand

Pl. 20   Papyrus of the 2nd century A.D. from Contrapollinopolis in the Thebaid: a paean to Apollo and a funeral song for a hero, with instrumental interludes (indented) in notation denoting note-values and rests. Albert Thierfelder, 'Ein neuaufgefundener Papyrus mit griechischen Noten', *ZfMW*, 1 (1918–19), p. 217, reads line 13, the first instrumental line, as:

Ex. 4

strikes the strings (that is, with a plectrum), the left plucks them, 'nor is even the foot idle, marking the fixed rule of the quantities' (*ne pes quidem otiosus certam legem temporum servat*).[34]

THE ALEXANDRIAN THEORISTS

Broadly speaking, the Latin sources of the period tell us when and how music was employed, the Greek ones what philosophers thought about it. The Romans were practical; the Alexandrians – including those who, like Plotinus, settled in Rome – were theorists, students of the classical past and rather out of touch with contemporary reality. Even such a worldling as Athenaeus, the second or third-century recorder of table-talk (as he pretends), was much more interested in the past than in the present. The Alexandrians leaned heavily on the Greek thinkers of the great age, Pythagoras, Plato, Aristotle, Aristoxenus, elaborating their ideas with typical Hellenistic ingenuity and causing their dissemination down the centuries in sophisticated forms which often obscure rather than throw light on the original. Thus Nicomachus of Gerasa elaborated Pythagoras's theories of music and numbers in a fantastic system of number-symbolism. More important was the teaching of the neo-Platonists: above all, Plotinus (205–70), his pupil Porphyry (233–304) who was also a biographer of Pythagoras, and Porphyry's pupil Iamblichus (d. *c.* 330). Plotinus laid great stress on the moral power of music, not so much to mould good citizens as to purify the souls of men, to lead them by its magic power to surrender to the beautiful and then to the good. Porphyry, a pagan ascetic, on the other hand emphasized the sensual dangers of music particularly in its association with mime and dance; supreme divinity was not to be approached through any medium as sensuous as music, though intermediary spirits – good as well as evil – could be. And Iamblichus developed still further this conception of approach to spirits and inferior deities through the medium of music. These ideas, particularly those of Porphyry despite his bitter anti-Christianity, certainly exercised considerable influence on early Christian attitudes to music.

THE EARLIEST CHRISTIAN MUSIC

Throughout this period Christianity had been subtly permeating the Hellenistic-Roman world, first as a Jewish sect – though about the year 80 the Christian Jews were formally anathematized by the orthodox – then making proselytes even in the imperial family at a very early period, gaining toleration and taking part in the normal life of the community, until at last in 325 a Christian emperor, Constantine, summoned the first oecumenical council at Nicaea. We have already seen[35] that Constantine's friend Eusebius was aware, from the writings of Philo of Alexandria, of the extent

---

[34] *Institutio oratoria*, i, 12.   [35] See pp. 39–40.

to which Jewish musical practices in worship had persisted in those of the Christian church. Philo himself, a Hellenized Jew and a follower of Pythagoras and Aristotle, regarded music as one of the scientific handmaids of philosophy but held that in worship 'praises and hymns should not be in actual sounds but sung in our minds'.[36] This is not quite what St. Paul seems to mean by 'singing in your hearts' (Ephesians v: 19 and Colossians iii: 16): that is, singing *from* the heart, not merely for pleasure.

Paul's twice-employed categories of 'psalms and hymns and spiritual songs' can be taken literally. His *odai pneumatikai* are problematic but were almost certainly melismatic 'Alleluias and other chants of a jubilant or ecstatic character, richly ornamented'.[37] As for psalms and hymns, we have Philo's already mentioned account of the different ways they were performed and the psalms would, of course, be the Jewish ones, cantillated in the Jewish manner. The Jews had also sung hymns and vocalized Alleluias. (The very word is Jewish: *halelû-yâh*, praise to Yah, Jehovah.) How, if at all, the substance of such music was peculiar to the Jews we shall never know. The manner of performance was not; the *Odyssey* and *Iliad* may have been cantillated, indeed as late as Quintilian Graeco-Roman oratory was more or less cantillated. Neither hymns nor jubilant wordless songs were Jewish inventions: they evoked the god and induced ecstasy in his worshippers in Babylon and Egypt, Greece and Rome. Nor was responsorial or antiphonal singing in worship. As we have seen, there is evidence that both were practised by the Sumerians at the beginning of human history and by the Arvales and Salii at the beginning of Roman history. The actual music was probably no more than a dialect of the music practised throughout the Hellenistic-Roman world. If so, it was the dialect first used by Christians, however – and however quickly – it was modified as the faith spread among the Gentiles.

THE EARLY CHRISTIAN HYMN

It was almost certainly the early Christian psalm that adhered most faithfully to the music of the Jewish psalm; even at a much later period there remained marked similarities between Jewish and Christian psalm-tones.[38] The Christian hymn took a more independent course, particularly in Syria and among the heretical sects. With one notable exception, we have only the literary texts but they are significant. In the original Greek, Philippians, ii: 6–11 reveals itself as five three-line stanzas, each line having three beats[39] in the oriental manner. But a century or so later Clement of Alexandria (*c.* 150–*c.* 220) ended his *Paedagogus* with a hymn to Christ in quantitative metre, though as Wellesz says[40] 'his style becomes more and more ecstatic and turns from Greek to Semitic diction. . . . It is the metre of the Hellenistic poets imbued with Oriental thought.' Aramaic hymns were

---

[36] *De plantat.* ii, 158, 14ff.   [37] *NOHM*, ii, p. 2.   [38] *NOHM*, i, p. 319.
[39] Ibid., p. 308.
[40] *Byzantine Music and Hymnography* (Oxford, 1949), p. 123.

translated into Greek and the Greek texts of pagan hymns – for instance those of the cult of Aesculapius – were adapted for Christian or Gnostic use, no doubt preserving the associated music. The 'Hymn of Jesus' from the apocryphal Acts of St. John, familiar from Gustav Holst's setting:

> Divine Grace is dancing:
> Fain would I pipe for you [literally: play the aulos].
> Dance ye all!
> > Amen
> The Holy Twelve dance with us;
> All things join in the dance!
> Ye who dance not, know not what we are knowing.
> > Amen.

suggests adaptation from such a pagan original and reminds one of the paintings of Orpheus as Christ, or Christ as Orpheus, in the catacombs and the parallel between Christ and Orpheus drawn by Clement of Alexandria. It also illustrates that association of dancing and instrumental music with paganism and heresy which so worried the Fathers of the Church and presented them with the difficult problem of explaining away the religious practices of King David.

As it happens, we possess a fragment[41] from Oxyrhynchus in Egypt giving not only the words but the music, in both pitch-notation and rhythmic notation, of the end of a Christian hymn of the late third century:[42]

Ex. 5

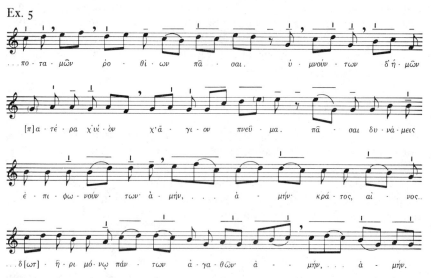

diatonic, melismatic, and marked by the recurrence of certain melodic formulae.

---

[41] *Oxyrhynchus Papyri*, xv, ed. A. S. Hunt (London, 1922), No. 1786. Notation and transcription in Wellesz, op. cit., pp. 125ff; photograph of papyrus with varying transcriptions by six scholars, including Wellesz, in *MGG*, iv, cols. 1052–6.
[42] Wellesz's transcription.

4

Music in the Christian World

MUSIC OF THE BARBARIANS

Official recognition of Christianity coincided with the establishment of a new cultural centre of gravity in Byzantium. Even before this, the boundaries of Hellenistic-Roman culture had begun to contract. In Persia during the late second century a reaction against it had set in which was completed under the Sassanians after about 226. In the West, the barbarian peoples, enemies or military auxiliaries, whose music is so contemptuously alluded to by Tacitus and others – the Germans with their war-song *barditus* or *barritus* (*carmina quem 'barditum' vocant*),[1] the Iberians beating on their shields as they sang, the Picts with their 'singing and bawling in barbarous fashion and dissonant cries' (*barbari moris cantu et fremitu clamoribusque dissonis*)[2] – these and still more powerful and dangerous peoples constricted and assailed the Empire during the century and a half after Constantine the Great and finally overthrew the Western Empire, replacing it by the 'dark age' kingdoms of the Visigoths and Ostrogoths, Franks and Vandals. We know nothing specific about their music. Nor do we know very much about the music of the far more highly cultivated Persians except that it flourished under the Sassanian kings, particularly Bahrām Gūr (420–38) who was himself a talented musician and imported great numbers of singers and dancers from India. There is graphic and literary evidence that in Persia the old familiar West Asian instruments were always in use; indeed, we hear of an 'improved' type of lute in the third century; but when Aramaic supplanted Greek as the language of Persian officialdom some instruments acquired Aramaic names – for instance, the trumpet became *shaipūr* (cf. the Hebrew *shōphār*).

We may be sure that in the West the newcomers adopted and no doubt modified the music of the Roman world as they did its laws, its architecture, and ultimately its language and religion. The music of Christianity, particularly that of the Church in the West, now played a uniquely important historic role; it was preserved and transmitted by jealous tradition and enriched and developed by the ecclesiastics who were the saviours of Western civilization and who with the passage of time evolved a method of recording their music in written sources. To what extent, if at all, it enriched or was enriched by secular music we cannot even guess for the

---

[1] Tacitus, *Germania* III.   [2] idem, *Agricola*, XXXIII.

secular music has all disappeared into the darkness behind history. What were the songs celebrating the victories of Attila which, according to Priscus, the Imperial ambassador, were sung by two men after a feast? What sort of performance did Caedmon, the monk of Whitby, avoid giving when (as Bede tells us) he dodged his turn of singing to the harp? Perhaps music not very different from that to which the Homeric epics were sung. It was techniques which seem first to have been applied in church music in the West which made possible the later evolution of European music, other than folk-music, sacred and secular alike.

MUSIC OF THE EASTERN CHURCH

The historic role of the Church in the East was different. For reasons which will have to be examined, its music became static, took no part in the great European efflorescence, and, although not sterile, failed to develop any remotely comparable efflorescence of its own. But in the early centuries of Byzantium, Christian music was still essentially an Eastern, Judaic, dialect of Hellenistic-Roman. Or rather, more probably, it embraced a number of such dialects. For the various races – not all subjects of the Empire – together with the multiplication of heresies, must have originated varieties of liturgical practice and music. We get occasional glimpses of these at later periods – Syrian ekphonetic notation (signs indicating patterns of pitch) about 900, Armenian neumes in the twelfth century, Ethiopian neumes and hymns in the sixteenth – which presumably survive, with whatever changes produced by many centuries of oral transmission, in the music of the Syrian, Armenian, Coptic, and Ethiopian churches today. It was the accession of Justinian in 527, with his rigorous suppression of heresy and his passion for systematizing and codifying, which finally established the supremacy of the 'Orthodox' church of the imperial capital, its liturgy and the splendour of its ceremonial, in both of which music played a more important part than ever before. The Church at Rome, however, using Latin from the middle of the fourth century onward instead of the Greek 'common tongue' of early Christianity and disengaged from the State through the crumbling of the Western Empire, had long followed the spiritual leadership of Rome and Milan and tended to develop different liturgical practices.

THE CHURCH-FATHERS AND THE PSALMS

The writings of the late fourth-century Fathers, St. Jerome (330–420) and St. Augustine (354–430), St. Ambrose (340–97) and St. John Chrysostom (345–407), show no essential change from the attitude to music of their predecessors. They all recognize its power. Augustine, above all, not only acknowledged it in famous passages of his *Confessions* (Books IX and X), but tells us again and again in his *Enarrationes* of the psalms that the melismatic *jubilatio* or *jubilus* at the end of the Alleluia is wordless because words cannot express what the heart sings (e.g. *Quid est in jubilatione canere? Intelligere verbis explicare non posse quod canitur corde*: commentary on Psalm xxxii). On the other hand he refers with approval to the practice of Athanasius of Alexandria (d. 313) who had the psalms executed with such limited modulation of the voice that the delivery was nearer speech than song (*Tam modico flexu vocis faciebat sonare lectorem psalmi, ut pronunciati vicinior esset quam canenti*: *Confessions*, x, 33). In fact, as he admits, he was hopelessly torn between fear of sensual pleasure and recognition of music's power for good. Because of its power, the Fathers were the more fearful of instrumental music, associated with paganism and the theatre, even in private life, though Augustine, Basil (*c.* 330–79), and others tried to defend the ten-stringed psaltery, for instance, as a symbol of the body of Christ or of the ten commandments.

Psalm-singing was universal 'not only among the Greeks but also among the barbarians', Eusebius had said; the whole congregation sang, including the women, particularly at night in the celebration of the Vigils. The originally eastern practices of antiphonal and responsorial psalm-singing were introduced at Byzantium by St. John Chrysostom and at Milan by St. Ambrose. About the same time, however, a Spanish nun, Etheria, who made a pilgrimage to Jerusalem in the 380s, seems in her *Peregrinatio* to make a distinction between *psalmi* and *antiphonae*. The people respond to a precentor (*psalmi responduntur*) and a boys' choir replies to a litany with 'Kyrie eleison' – not, she notes, the usual 'Amen'. But elsewhere she speaks of *psalmi et antiphonae* (xxiv, 12) and *psalmi vel antiphonae* (xxv, 5) as if the 'antiphon' were beginning to be recognized as something distinct from the psalm proper. It was presumably a refrain of repeated Alleluias or a verse from the psalm with which the antiphon was associated, though not, of course, in its much later sense as an independent votive or processional song. In any case, antiphonal – as distinct from responsorial – singing would have been easier in monasteries where all would be trained to participate than in churches with their untrained congregations.

DEVELOPMENT OF THE CHRISTIAN HYMN

The other main category of Christian music, the hymn, also underwent considerable changes at this time. Again the innovation came from the East. As we have already seen,[3] Christians, both orthodox and heterodox, had not been slow to enrich their services with newly written and newly composed hymns. These became so popular and thus so efficacious in the dissemination of false doctrine that the Council of Laodicea (360–81) forbade the singing of all non-biblical texts in the liturgy. Nevertheless a Syrian, Ephraem (306–73), was able to establish a new and even more popular type of hymn, based on Syriac poetry and music, in which quantitative verse was replaced by isosyllabic verse with a regular pattern of accentuated syllables. This made possible not only the singing of all the stanzas of a hymn to the

[3] See p. 51.

same melody, with slight adjustments, but the use of a popular melody for more than one hymn-poem. It seems likely that Ephraem himself wrote his poems to the melodies of the third-century Syrian Gnostic hymn-writers Bardesanes and his son Harmonios.

This Syrian form was quickly taken up in Greek and later became the model for the Byzantine *kontakion*.[4] It was also practised in Latin by St. Hilary of Poitiers (d. 366) and, with much greater success, by St. Ambrose at Milan to whom his pupil Augustine ascribes the words of four famous hymns: 'Aeterne rerum conditor', 'Deus creator omnium', 'Jam surgit hora tertia', and 'Veni redemptor gentium'. At least ten other 'Ambrosian' hymns, including 'Splendor paternae gloriae' and 'Aeterna Christi munera', are unquestionably by the saint himself. (The adjective 'Ambrosian' is commonly applied not only to later hymns modelled on those of Ambrose – eight four-line strophes, each line of four iambic feet – but also to other forms of chant in the Milanese use.) Whether the melodies long associated with these texts were also Ambrose's or of popular origin, even whether they date from his time, is much more problematic; the earliest sources in which they are found are seven or more centuries later. But Ewald Jammers[5] has argued persuasively from the largely tetrachordal structure of the music, that they are, if dubious later melismata are removed, genuine fourth-century melodies. If we accept that Augustine's *tempora* in his discussion of 'Deus creator omnium' (*De Musica*, iv, 2) – three *tempora* to an iambic foot – were musical as well as metrical, as he seems to mean, we can reconstruct the melody thus:

Ex. 6

De - us   cre - a - tor   o - mni - um,   Po - li - que rec - tor ve - sti - ens

Di - em   de - co - ro   lu - mi - ne   Noc - tem   so - po - ris gra - ti - a.

A rather later hymnographer, the Spaniard Aurelius Prudentius (d. *c.* 405), left two collections of hymns, a *Kathemerinon* (for every day) and a *Peristephanon* (in honour of martyrs), from which at least three, 'Salvete flores Martyrum', 'Quicumque Christum', and 'O sola magnarum', are still in common use. But the strophic hymn never played such an important liturgical role in the West as it did in the East.

THE OFFICES AND THE MASS

Hymns and psalms were from the first particularly important in the celebration of the Vigils, the earliest of the daily Offices of the Church to

---

[4] See below, pp. 65 and 91.
[5] 'Rhythmische und tonale Studien zur Musik der Antike und des Mittelalters-II', *AfMF*, viii (1943), p. 27.

come into existence. The nun Etheria tells of the celebration of other Offices at Jerusalem – Matins, Sext, None, Vespers – as well as the Sunday Mass, and celebrations of the Nativity (of which her account is lost), Epiphany, Holy Week, Easter, Ascension, Whitsun, and the finding of the Cross. These also had their hymns and antiphons 'proper to the day'. The liturgical patterns of the Church's day and the Church's year, with the appropriate music, were thus already well developed at Jerusalem. They were, in fact, the models for the organization of the Latin liturgy at Rome about 382–4 by Pope Damasus and his secretary, St. Jerome, an acknowledged expert on Eastern liturgy. And it was precisely at this period, the 380s, that the word *missa* – from the formula of dismissal, 'Ite missa est', at the end of the service – was first used, both by Etheria and by St. Ambrose in his Letter 33, as a technical term though an imprecise one: Ambrose applies it to the eucharist and the preliminary readings, Etheria to the Office Hours. Indeed, readings from the Testaments and the singing of responsorial psalms were common to both Mass and Offices; it was only later that responsorial singing was largely replaced by antiphonal in the Offices and after 422 in the Roman Mass. Neither the Mass as we think of it nor the full number of Offices had yet been evolved. But the Church in the West had at least begun to assemble the great frame on which was to be woven the tapestry of the most durable part of European music for the next thousand years.

THE ROLE OF GREGORY THE GREAT

According to one much later and rather doubtful authority, a late eighth-century Frankish monk known to us only as the author of a treatise on Roman monastic meals (*Anonymus de prandiis monachorum*),[6] Leo I, Pope from 440 to 461, established an *annalis cantus*, a cycle of chants for the liturgical year, and enforced its use by threat of excommunication. The same author, who can only have been reporting centuries-old tradition, says that Gelasius and several later Popes during the period 492–532 also instituted similar cycles; he ends his list with Gregory I (590–604), Martin (649–53), and three seventh-century Roman abbots. These cycles of liturgical chant, of which the actual music could still have been transmitted only orally, were for the Roman use alone. The Gallican, Celtic, Visigothic Spanish (known after the Moorish conquest in the early eighth century as 'Mozarabic'), and Milanese liturgies developed independently, and everywhere the monasteries, free from episcopal jurisdiction, were even more individual. The student of monastic meals attributes no special importance in this respect to Gregory the Great, beyond remarking that his cycle was 'renowned' (*nobilis*). Yet before long – though centuries after Gregory's death – a myth emerged according to which the great Pope not merely instituted a musical-liturgical order but actually composed the corpus of what came to be known as 'Gregorian melodies'. He was depicted by illuminators of medieval manuscripts as inspired by the Holy Ghost in the

[6] J. P. Migne, *Patrologiae Cursus Completus: Series Latina*, 221 vols. (Paris, 1844–55), CXXXVIII.

form of a dove at his ear – and sometimes with the help of a monochord – dictating (notation having been invented by that time) to a scribe.

Gregory's own writings seldom touch on music at all. Indeed, a decree of 595 makes it clear that music existed only as the vehicle of the text, that it was not the concern of the higher clergy, and that even deacons should not be chosen for their musical ability.[7] An often referred to letter of three years later, in which he defends himself against the charge of following such Greek practices as having Alleluia sung at Mass out of the season of Eastertime, and says he has 'restored our old practices or established new and useful ones', is not concerned with music as such. The earliest evidence which can be construed as referring to Gregory's musical activity consists of passages in Bede's *Historia Ecclesiastica* (iv, 2 and v, 20), dating from 731, which tell us that Putta, Bishop of Rochester (d. 688), was 'particularly skilled in singing in church in the manner of the Romans, which he had learned from the *discipuli* of the blessed Pope Gregory', and that a cantor named Maban was taught singing by the 'successors' of these *discipuli* in Kent. The *discipuli*, however, were not Gregory's musical 'pupils' but Augustine the Less and his band of missionaries – who had, incidentally, been impressed during their journey by the Gallican uses and were expressly authorized by the Pope to borrow from them in England if they thought fit. Bede's insistence here and elsewhere on the Roman provenance of English church music is probably due to his anxiety to show that it owed nothing to the Celtic church; within twelve years of his death, the Council of Cloveshoe (Glasgow?) (747) marked the final victory of the Roman practice over the Celtic. Two *Antiphonales*, actually a Gradual (containing the chants of the Mass) from Mont-Blandin near Ghent and a *cantatorium* from Monza near Milan, of the late eighth century[8] – that is, more or less contemporary with the treatise *De prandiis monachorum* – have prefatory words mentioning 'Gregory' and making it clear that there is no question of one of the later popes of that name. The Mont-Blandin codex claims only to be the Antiphonary ordained (*ordinatus*) by him *per circulum anni*, but the one from Monza says he actually 'put together this little book of music of the song-school' (*Tum composuit hunc libellum musicae artis scolae cantorum*). Needless to say, the *libellus musicae artis* is void of musical notation.

CHURCH MUSIC UNDER THE FRANKISH MONARCHS

By this time political events had occurred which were to exercise a decisive influence on the course of liturgical and hence musical history. The Frankish king Pepin the Short (741–68) in the process of rescuing the Papacy from the Lombards had sent Chrodegang, Bishop of Metz, as one of his envoys to Rome where he became interested in Roman church music. The following year, 754, the grateful Pope Stephen II came to Saint-Denis to anoint his rescuer and there was a confrontation of Roman with Gallican

---

[7] Amédée Gastoué, *Les Origines du chant romain* (Paris, 1907), App. A.
[8] R.-J. Hesbert, *Antiphonale missarum sextuplex* (Brussels, 1935).

rites and music, with the result that Pepin was either genuinely impressed by the Roman practice or conscious of the political advantages of adopting it. (Another consequence of these events was that the Byzantine Emperor, Constantine V, as part of his attempts to reassert imperial influence in the West, presented Pepin in 757 with an organ, an instrument forgotten in the West since Roman times.) About 760 a singing teacher who had studied in Rome was brought to Metz to establish a *schola cantorum*, and the *secundus* of the Roman *schola* was despatched to Rouen, where one of the king's brothers was bishop, to do the same there; the Pope sent Pepin a so-called *Antiphonale* and *Responsale* containing the chants of the Mass and Office respectively.

This process of Romanization was carried on with equal vigour by Pepin's son Charlemagne who in 774 styled himself 'King of the Franks and Lombards and Patrician of the Romans' and in 800 found himself – beyond his expectation – crowned by Leo III as 'Emperor of the Romans'. A new Western Empire had come into being, albeit a temporary one, and Charlemagne already, without the Pope's unasked-for help, regarded himself as a theocrat, 'King and Priest, Leader and Guide of all Christians'. Unity of faith and ritual was basic to his conception of empire. There was naturally strong and prolonged resistance to the abandonment of Gallican practices and Gallican chant, and in his *Admonitio generalis* of 789 Charlemagne had to insist that all clergy should learn and employ the *cantus romanus*, while the synod of Aix-la-Chapelle in 803 reminded the bishops of their duties in this respect and ordered them to establish *scholae cantorum*.

'OLD ROMAN' AND 'GREGORIAN' CHANT

It is easy to see why the Carolingian Romanizers, like Bede in England, took every opportunity to invoke the name and authority of Gregory the Great; the Mont-Blandin and Monza *Antiphonales* are perhaps the earliest instances. Amalar of Metz (*c.* 780–*c.* 850), pupil of Charlemagne's friend and adviser Alcuin, believed 'the blessed Pope Gregory' to be the *auctor* (which may mean author or merely originator) of a Missal. And Johannes Hymmonides, author of a *Vita Sancti Grigorii* written about 872[9] – who incidentally takes an opportunity for a swipe at the raucous voices of the Germani and Galli which prevent their catching the sweetness of the Gregorian chants – claims that Gregory not only compiled an Antiphonary but founded a *schola cantorum*. (Earlier popes, Leo I and Gelasius, have also been credited with the establishment of such *scholae*.) The name and authority of Gregory were thus invoked, but on behalf of what? The problem is one of the most puzzling in musical history.

It was apparently Amalar who first realized that a problem existed, as he relates in the preface to his *De ordine Antiphonarii*.[10] Puzzled by apparent defects in the Office books at Metz, regarded as the special repository of the

[9] Migne, op. cit., LXXV.　　[10] Migne, op. cit., CV.

Roman tradition since Chrodegang's time, he went to Rome in 831–2 to study the sources and asked Gregory IV for an authentic Antiphonary which he might take home. The Pope was unable to oblige but suggested that he should consult four volumes of Offices given a few years before to the Abbot of Corbie, near Amiens. Amalar did so and was astonished to find that the order and words often differed from those in use at Metz, that there were many new antiphons and responsories, and that, according to an entry in one volume, all this was the result of a revision undertaken by or under Hadrian I (772–95). Realizing that there was no single authoritative version as he had supposed, Amalar set about the compilation of a new Antiphonary for use at Metz, drawing on the old Metz versions, the Corbie version, and things taught him by Alcuin in his youth at Tours.

Modern scholarship has distinguished two bodies of chant: that is, of written liturgical texts – the music was still only orally transmitted with more or less accuracy, for at this period Western music was only on the brink of the discovery or rediscovery of a system of notation. One body, to which the (lost) Corbie Offices can be shown from Amalar's account to belong has been called 'Old Roman' and supposed to be older than the so-called 'Gregorian' and even dated as early as the time of Gregory I himself. Alternatively it has been argued that 'Old Roman' and 'Gregorian' were coeval but used in different places or in monasteries on one hand and churches on the other. It is certainly true that the oldest 'Old Roman' manuscripts with musical notation are Roman in the narrowest sense: a Gradual from the monastic church of St. Cecilia in Trastevere (1071) and a Gradual in the Vatican Library (lat. 5319) supposed to have been used at the Lateran. And there is no reason why the supposedly Old Roman Corbie volumes should not have been what they claim to be: a revision from the very end of the eighth century.

What then was 'Gregorian' chant? One view is that it stemmed from a special chant developed by the papal *schola* from that used in the city churches of Rome; but the earliest written sources were not compiled in Rome; they originated in the West and East Frankish states into which the Carolingian empire was divided. And in these lands the acknowledged model was that of Metz. As an anonymous monk of St. Gall wrote in his *De Carolo Magno*[11] (*c.* 883), one said simply 'cantilena Metensis' for 'ecclesiastica cantilena'; he also emphasized the 'excessive difference' (*nimia dissimilitudo*) between 'our *cantilena* and that of the Romans', perhaps meaning 'Old Roman'. As late as the first half of the twelfth century, St. Bernard (d. 1153) based his reform of the Cistercian chant-books on the Metz tradition. And it has been suggested[12] that during the tenth century, with the revival of the Western Empire under Otto the Great and his subjection of the Papacy, this Frankish tradition actually established itself in Rome itself.

[11] Migne, op. cit., XCVIII.
[12] A. Jungmann, *Missarum Sollemnia* (Freiburg i. Br., fourth ed. 1958), i.

THE EVIDENCE OF NOTATION

All this enables us to see the actual music of Western chant 'as in a glass darkly': the invisible yet deducible reflection of liturgical texts. For we may assume that the melodies were at least essentially the same as those to which the texts were sung when the unclear beginnings of notation come to our help. And these unclear beginnings are clarified when, as often, later notation gives us what is obviously the same melody in notes of definite pitch. We also have some help from theoretical writings. Both theory and notation came from the East.

At the risk of vastly oversimplifying a vastly complicated and obscure subject, it may be said that during the first Christian millennium the old letter notations passed out of practical use into the hands of the theorists, while another system of signs, developed from accent signs which originally regulated the 'pronouncing aloud' (*ekphonesis*) of texts, were the roots from which grew the practical notation of the West. Theodoric's great minister Boethius (*c.* 480–524), to whom – with his contemporary Cassiodorus (*c.* 485–*c.* 580) – early medieval scholars were mainly indebted for their somewhat muddled knowledge of ancient Greek and Hellenistic attitudes to music and theorizing about it, was familiar with the old Greek letter notations. But he also used Roman letters in his *De Institutione Musica* (though confusingly in different ways in different chapters) as a shorthand for the longwinded Greek names of the tetrachords and the note-positions within the tetrachords (*quoniam earum nomina longum fuit adscribere*).[13] Thus one could call *hypate meson* (*hypate* of the middle tetrachord) simply D, *parhypate meson*, E, and so on. To add to the confusion, Boethius uses A as the lowest note whereas in Greek 'vocal' notation *alpha* represents the highest note.[14]

Letter notation indicated the pitch of each note and consequently, thanks to the system of tetrachords, its intervallic relationship to its neighbours; ekphonetic notation, an empirical device for marking correct accent, inflection, and punctuation, did neither. The ekphonetic signs, derived from the Hellenistic prosodic signs, when first employed in a pitch sense could indicate no more than indeterminate relationships within the tiniest melodic particles. They are thought to have been used in Byzantine lectionaries before the end of the fourth century and a system of fifteen signs[15] appears in the manuscripts of the eighth century. Probably originating in directions for manner of performance, some at any rate acquired a relative-pitch sense: for instance, the *oxeia* (the ancient Greek or modern French acute accent) indicating a rise, the *bareia* (grave) a fall, the *syrmatike* (circumflex, written ∼) a rise and fall. They are concerned with a method of enunciation which, like the declamation of Greek tragedy, the

---

[13] *De Institutione*, iv, 5.
[14] See p. 35 above. On the whole question of Boethius and notation, see Martin Vogel, 'Boetius und die Herkunft der modernen Tonbuchstaben', *Kirchenmusikalisches Jahrbuch*, Jg. 46 (1962), p. 1.
[15] See *NOHM*, ii, pp. 36–7, for the list, and Wellesz, *Byzantine Music and Hymnography* (Oxford, 1949), pl. II and III for ninth and tenth-century manuscripts.

cantillation of Hebrew psalms, recitative, and *Sprechgesang*, lay between normal speech and true song.

Knowledge of these devices spread only gradually to the West. Cassiodorus says nothing about notation of any kind and Isidore of Seville (*c.* 560–636), who leans heavily on him, says flatly (*Etymologiae*, iii, 15) that if sounds are not preserved in the memory they are lost, for they cannot be written down (*Nisi enim ab homine memoria teneantur, soni pereunt, quia scribi non possunt*). The early punctuation signs in the Latin lectionaries are simply that and have no musical significance. Alcuin, who also depends on Cassiodorus, never mentions notation in his *De Musica*, and there is none in the *Antiphonales* from Mont-Blandin and Monza already referred to. Nor is there in some important later ones of the ninth century – not even in a Gradual from Corbie where, as we have seen, they were particularly interested in 'Roman' chant.

NEUMES

It is just at this time, the middle of the ninth century, that Latin neumes – so called from the Greek *neuma*, a sign or nod – unmistakably appear. (Claims for earlier examples are to be treated with caution; neumes were sometimes added to older texts.) They are clearly related to, though not identical with, the older Byzantine neumes; and it is perhaps significant that one of the earliest examples, in a manuscript from St. Amand in the diocese of Tournai of *c.* 871 (Paris, Bibl. nat., ms. lat. 2291), has the neumes set above the Greek

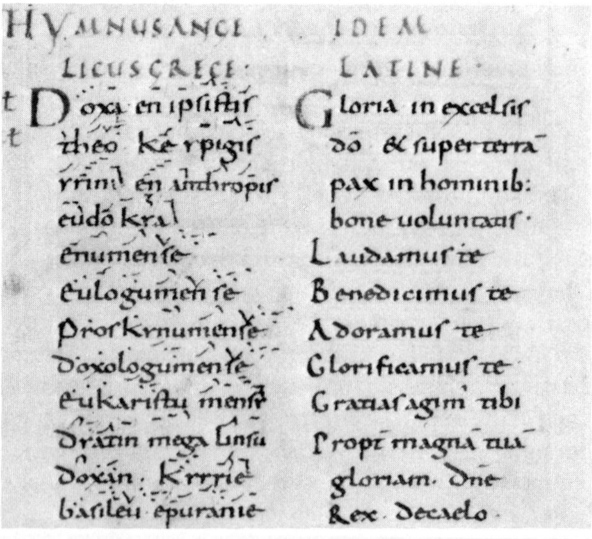

Pl. 21   Gloria in a St Amand manuscript of *c.* 871, with transliterated Greek text and Latin translation in parallel columns (Paris, Bibl. Nat. ms. lat. 2291). Only the Greek text has musical notation.

text, transliterated in Roman characters, of the Gloria (*Hymnus angelius grece*) while the Latin version in the parallel column has none (see pl. 21).[16] During the tenth century neumes appear all over the place: above all in what is now France – St. Amand, Lyons, Paris, Rheims, Corbie, Metz, Laon, Noyon – but also at St. Gall, Regensburg, Essen (where there was a Frankish mission), and Winchester in a famous troper which will be discussed later.[17] But as yet they occur hardly anywhere in Italy, except for a curious and dubious fragment of song, 'O tu qui servas armis ista moenia' in the Chapter Library at Modena, and some specimens at Como which show the influence of Metz. For there were local varieties of shape, and before long one can distinguish regional species of neumes: North French, Metz, St. Gall, Aquitanian (Southern French), Nonantolan, Beneventan, and others. But despite calligraphic differences and the development of different potentialities of meaning (ornamentation and so on), the original basic shapes were the same.

The earliest Western to write about them, Aurelianus Reomensis (Aurelian of Réomé) whose *Musica disciplina* dates from the middle of the ninth century, simply translates some of the Greek names: thus he calls the sign for two notes rising, *acutus* (it was later known as *podatus* or *pes* and written ⌡), for two notes falling, *gravis* (later *clivis* or *flexa*, written ⌐), while his *circumflexus* is presumably the *syrmatike*. Another ninth- or tenth-century writer, the South German Anonymus Vaticanus,[18] reveals that neumes could also indicate rhythm:

The modulation of the voice is shown by the accents of the note and by the syllabic feet. From the accents of the note, in fact, in the *acutus, gravis,* and *circumflexus*; from the syllabic feet in *brevis* and *longa*. Out of the accents has come the figure known as *neuma*. If this is simple and a *brevis*, it forms a *punctum*; if a *longa*, it is protracted (*producta*). But this *punctum* is manifest in three ways, in *brevis* and *gravis* and *subpositus*. The *longa* is likewise manifest in three ways: in the protracted form, the *acutus*, and the *circumflexa* (*sic*). Moreover they can be joined in a rise or descent of two notes [or figures], or three or four or five or six, up to the seventh or eighth degree, as in the Alleluia, *Beatus vir sanctus Martinus*. . . . A *brevis* and a *longa* often come together . . . or a *brevis* and *liquida* [presumably a 'liquescent' neume indicating perhaps a light *portamento*]; sometimes a *gravis* and a *longa*, sometimes *gravis* and *producta* or *circumflexa*. The figure called *tremula* consists of three degrees, that is, of two *breves* and an *acutus*. And another figure, called *coagulata*, consists of three accents: two acutes and a *subpositus*. . . .

This may not be crystal clear and some of his technical terms are not those of a later period, but it is evident that his neumes indicate rise and fall, length (a *longa* presumably approximately twice as long as a *brevis*), and could be joined to indicate little melodic formulae. That plainsong was performed rhythmically at this period is confirmed by verses in a poem by Alcuin which

---

[16] Jacques Handschin, 'Eine alte Neumenschrift', *Acta Musicologica*, xxii (1950), p. 69.
[17] See below, p. 81.
[18] So called from his treatise in the Vatican Library, Cod. lat. palat. 235, quoted by Peter Wagner, *Einführung in die gregorianischen Melodien*, ii (second edition, Leipzig, 1912), pp. 355–6.

indicate that rhythm was based on poetic quantity,[19] by the rhythmic signs in some manuscripts, and by the reports of bone-clappers being used to mark the rhythm of the singing.

THE EIGHT CHURCH MODES

The West derived from Byzantium not only the beginnings of its notation but the beginnings of its tonal system. Whereas Alexandrian and Byzantine theory took over Greek metaphysical and mathematical thinking and terminology, and threw them into ever greater confusion, the practical Byzantine system was infinitely simpler. Briefly, it was based on the conception of eight modes each consisting of two disjunct diatonic tetrachords.[20] Four of these modes were 'authentic', the first on D, the second on E, the third on F, the fourth on G, indicated by the letter-figures of the Greek alphabet, $\acute{\alpha}$, β, $\acute{\gamma}$, $\acute{\delta}$, prefixed to the line of neumes. The other four were 'plagal' (oblique), indicated by the letters $\pi\lambda$, and based on 'starting-notes' a fourth lower than the corresponding authentic mode. But the modes were differentiated not only by the different position of the semitone in the tetrachord but by melodic formulae indicated by neumes:

Byzantine melody . . . is a sort of mosaic in which conventional melodic formulas are combined, now in one order, now in another, producing designs which, despite their general similarity, are never twice the same. These conventional melodic formulas are of two sorts. On the one hand are what we may call the patterns . . . these are ideal melodic forms; their actual shape, as a function of the momentary text, varies from use to use. On the other hand are the ornaments and melismas . . . these are set figures; as pure vocalizations they tolerate no essential change. The patterns are restricted in principle to a single mode or pair of modes and are thus a significant factor in modal individualization. The ornaments and melismas, though for the most part free from this restriction, tend nevertheless to attach themselves to fixed points within the tonal system.[21]

The principle of melodic composition by formulae was, of course, extremely old and seems to have been common to all Mediterranean and near-Mediterranean musics, and not only the principle but sometimes actual Byzantine formulae were taken over in Western, particularly Milanese, religious music. What was seemingly peculiar to the Byzantine church was the systematic use of modes through the liturgical year,[22] which orginated in the Syrian church early in the sixth century and was adopted by St. John of Damascus (*c.* 700–760): the *Oktoechos* or eight-week cycle of hymns – a week of hymns in the first mode at Easter, followed by a week of hymns in the second mode, and so on until it was time to start in the first mode again. In the West the first mentions of church modes occur in

---

[19] Ibid., p. 354.
[20] See p. 30 above.
[21] Oliver Strunk, 'The Tonal System of Byzantine Music', *MQ*, xxviii (1942), p. 196. This, with *NOHM*, ii, pp. 41–5, is the clearest account.
[22] A system not without similarity to the very much older Chinese practice of 'ritual transposition' (see p. 565).

Alcuin who gives them Latinized Greek names – *protus, deuterus, tritus*, and (oddly) *tetrachius* – and in Aurelian of Réomé who knows all about the different melodic types, particularly the opening formulae. Clear teaching on the modes is to be found in the *Epistola de harmonica institutione* of Regino of Prüm (d. 915), who still uses the Greek names – *authenticus protus, plaga proti*, and so on – and denounces as *degeneres* and *non legitimae* those antiphons 'which begin in one *tonus*, go into another in the middle, and end in a third'. Significantly, Regino was probably the compiler of one of the earliest known *tonaria* (collections of liturgical songs classified by mode, and – in the case of antiphons – within each mode by cadence-formula). A still earlier complete Office *tonarium* is one compiled at Metz between 840 and 869[23] – that is, during Amalar's lifetime and just after; unfortunately it has only a few neumes.

THE DIVISION OF THE CHURCH

This much of the Byzantine legacy came to the West. But the Eastern and Western Churches had been drifting wide apart for centuries before the final break in 1054. Justinian I's reorganization of the Church in the East in 528, with his rigorous attempts to stamp out the remains of paganism and the numerous heresies that had flourished in the Empire, his brutal bullying of Pope Vigilius, his establishment of a powerful and rigid church structure in which Constantinople was supreme, his numerous measures to enhance the church's prestige and artistic splendour, such as the building of St. Sophia – all this acted divisively. Hymns, always particularly important in the Eastern Church, now played an even greater part in the Matins and Vespers which became musically more important than the mainly responsorial Mass. Hymnology was enriched by new poetic forms; to the older *troparion* were added the many-stanzaed *kontakion*[24] of St. Romanus (late fifth-early sixth century) and his followers, and the *kanon* (a set of nine odes, all differing in metre and melody) first devised by St. Andrew of Crete (*c.* 660–*c.* 740). All these were peculiar to the Orthodox Church. The Office, rather than the Mass, was the principal daily service.

The Catholic Mass had by no means reached its definitive form, but it already tended to take notice of the feasts and saints' days, which were excluded from the Orthodox Liturgy of St. John Chrysostom. The Kyrie, even with its Greek invocation, was retained from the pre-Damasian days when Greek was still the language of the Church in Rome (though the Christe was a later, Roman innovation), and both Churches shared the 'thrice holy': the Trisagion which follows the Little Entrance of the Orthodox liturgy, and the threefold Sanctus of the Roman Mass. But the Cherubic Hymn of the Great Entrance, introduced in the East in 574, had no counterpart in the West. Yet despite these differences of liturgical-musical practice, Orthodox and Catholic could have remained in com-

[23] Published by Walther Lipphardt, *Der Karolingische Tonar von Metz* (Münster, Westphalia, 1965).
[24] See p. 56.

munion and continued to exercise some mutual influence, had it not been for the deepening rifts caused by the Iconoclastic controversy in the Eastern Empire, the Photian heresy, and of course the final schism.

THE ISOLATION OF CONSERVATIVE ORTHODOXY

The cleavage had fateful consequences for the music of Eastern Europe. The long ascendancy of the Mediterranean and Near Eastern lands was passing; the cultural centre of gravity of Christian music lay not even in Italy but rather in the Frankish lands: the kingdom of France and the Ottonian Empire. It was there that bold developments were taking place: in notation, fresh melodic invention, polyphony. Byzantium continued rigidly in its old groove, monophonic and without instrumental support, though its musical notation did develop. The liturgy hardly changed after the schism of 1054. But at about that time appeared what is now known as Middle Byzantine notation, a more elaborate system of neumes capable of indicating the size of intervals, rhythm, and even dynamics,[25] and about half a century before the fall of Constantinople in 1453 additional red-ink signs were employed. These were improvements on the old; what the West needed, and consequently found, was something new.

The conservatism of the Byzantines was unfortunate not only for themselves but for their Christian converts, who continued to suffer the consequences for a quarter of a millennium after the collapse of the Empire. Despite the temporary conversion of the Central European Slavs – Czechs, Moravians, and Slovaks – to Orthodox Christianity, they were cut off from Byzantium around 900 by the Magyar invasion and ultimately adopted Roman Catholicism and the Roman alphabet. The pagan Poles adopted Catholicism straight away, and the Southern Slavs near the Adriatic – Slovenes and Croats – likewise fell to Rome. On the other hand, the Bulgarians and Russians adopted the religion and culture of Byzantium, including the Cyrillic adaptation of the Greek alphabet. After long hesitation, Boris I of Bulgaria opted for the Eastern rather than the Western form of Christianity in 865, and it was Bulgarian missionaries who took the Orthodox faith and a liturgy in Bulgarian (not Greek, though Greek and Bulgarian were sometimes used side by side) to Kievan Russia when in 989 Vladimir the Great, after similar hesitation between Catholicism, Orthodoxy, and Islam, forced mass conversion on his subjects. With the liturgy came the music, although – just as in the West – the imprecision of ekphonetic neumes permitted the development of 'dialects'. This process was probably assisted by the difference of language, and still further as Russian began in the thirteenth and fourteenth centuries to modify Old Bulgarian. Not only did the melodic lines so unclearly transmitted by the neumes develop dialects, but the shapes of the neumes themselves did likewise. However, in the twelfth century there was still a demonstrable

---

[25] See *NOHM*, ii, pp. 38–41.

relationship between the latest form of Old Byzantine notation, the 'Coislin' neumes (so called from the manuscript, Paris, Bibl. nat., Fonds Coislin 220), and the neumes of the early Russian *znamenny raspev* (sign chant).[26] And the very last innovation of Byzantine notation – the red signs of the early fifteenth century – was echoed in the red cinnabar letter-signs introduced by the Novgorod musician and theorist Ivan Shaydurov in the late sixteenth century to indicate precise pitch. Culturally isolated by the Mongols who held them in submission for two centuries and by the Turks who had flooded all south-eastern Europe, the Russians were musically still at a stage of development reached by the Franks five hundred years earlier. By a strange trick of history, the last relics of the purely Mediterranean tradition survived in Moscow and Novgorod.

[26] See Miloš M. Velimirović, *Byzantine Elements in Early Slavic Chant* (Copenhagen, 1960), particularly pp. 94ff.

Part II
The Ascendancy of Western Europe

Introduction

The renewal of Western culture after the Dark Ages was of course a continuous, imperceptibly slow process, yet historians have discerned three notable waves in the incoming tide: the Carolingian renaissance, the so-called proto-Renaissance of the twelfth century, and what we may call the Renaissance proper. Each had a musical correlative. During the first, ecclesiastical chant began to be the basis of elementary polyphony – an evolutionary step by which Western music quickly differentiated itself from all others – and the clearer methods of notation necessitated by polyphony began to evolve. The second was marked by the inclusion of secular elements and the consequent emergence of a music free from ecclesiastical leading-strings. The third saw the consolidation of a pan-European music in which French, Walloon, Italian, English, and finally German and other peoples participated.

Though illiterate himself, Charlemagne admired learning as much as he adored the Roman ritual. Guided by his counsellors, Alcuin of York – who wrote a treatise on music and is said to have composed a sequence[1] dedicated to his master – and Alcuin's successor Einhard, he gathered scholars around him, established a *scriptorium* for the copying and translation of manuscripts, and founded monastic and diocesan schools throughout his dominions. The building of cathedrals and monasteries, which before long all had their *scholae cantorum*, went on apace. And despite the division of his empire after his death in 814 and the consequent political disorders, cultural activity continued unabated in the successor states, and the monasteries and cathedral schools grew in importance as centres of learning, islands of peace amid military strife.

Admittedly the Carolingian and post-Carolingian world was laggardly in picking up the intellectual heritage of the old Empire. It was not until the last quarter of the tenth century that the treatises of Boethius and his translations from the Greek began to be generally studied in Western Europe. Yet long before then Aurelian of Réomé and Hucbald of St. Amand had based their musical writings on his *De Institutione musica*. They, and the anonymous author of *Musica enchiriadis* (see p. 77), transmitted the ancient theories of music, however garbled, to the new Europe that was emerging. They struggled with the problems of notation and described the working of that early polyphony which was just being encouraged, perhaps

---

[1] On 'sequence', see p. 89.

inspired, by the introduction of the organ; the vaulting of the new cathedrals and abbey churches provided resonance for the deployment of the new musical technique. Boethius's conception of music as a branch of mathematics was for centuries very much alive in practice as in theory; his dictum that 'geometry makes visual the musical consonances' controlled the proportions of the third church (*c.* 1086) at that outstanding centre of religious music, Cluny, under the great abbot Hugh. With remarkable speed Cluniac chant and Cluniac architecture spread over a large area of Western Europe.

Naturally there were considerable idiomatic varieties in both music and architecture. The different usages – for instance the Ambrosian chant of the Milanese rite – modified the idiom, and minor differences were brought to light when greater precision of notation revealed that German clergy at Trier and elsewhere were singing slightly wider intervals than the French and Italians. Italian Romanesque architecture – San Miniato at Florence, San Ambrogio at Milan – is markedly different from Cluniac.

The great corpus of religious music that had been accumulating since the early years of the Western Church and was now being documented with increasing clarity was to be the real melodic basis of Western music in general. The popular music of the time was ephemeral; church music survived. Indeed the only people capable of preserving music in notation were churchmen, and the secular music they composed and preserved – settings of Horatian odes and passages from Virgil, laments for dead monarchs – was certainly not 'popular'; it was in fact, so far as it is decipherable, very like ecclesiastical melody. A secular flavour is first perceptible in the words of the songs of the goliards, wandering students in minor orders; scansion by accent gets the upper hand over scansion by quantity. But the music has not survived. As it happens, the oldest preserved vernacular music we have is not secular but a tenth-century Provençal Passion narrative. The great secular narratives in vernacular have lost their music; the *Chanson de Roland*, as we have it, it as musicless as the *Iliad* and the *Odyssey*. Nor is the more modest vernacular song at first by any means 'popular'. We have practically nothing of the music of the *jongleurs*, the travelling entertainers. No doubt something of it was adopted by the first notable non-churchmen musicians, the courtly troubadours who flourished in the wonderful twelfth-century flowering of culture in Languedoc and Provence – but they also adopted many melodic formulae from church music.[2]

Troubadour song and its emulation in France and Germany by the *trouvères* and *Minnesänger* was the most obvious manifestation of the proto-Renaissance: the age of early Gothic architecture in England and France, of the deeper rediscovery of Greek learning (mostly, thanks to the Crusades, by way of Arabic translations), and of the embryos of universities at Bologna and Oxford and Paris, the age of Abelard and of Chrétien de Troyes. But

[2] See p. 95.

so far as music was concerned the more important if less spectacular development was not a birth or rebirth but a growth, particularly from the middle of the century onward (as was also the case with architecture). The new French cathedrals – above all Notre Dame at Paris, of which the building was begun in 1163 and the high altar consecrated in 1182 – fostered a more ambitious kind of polyphony well adapted to their vast spaces. And the new polyphony was in the next century to provide a technical framework for a new musical form of central importance. Just as the corpus of ecclesiastical chant may be said to have expanded horizontally through the insertion of trope and sequence,[3] it had now expanded vertically in the harmony produced by organal polyphony. For a long time polyphony had opened out slowly as a flower, always treating the plainsong with devout respect as a sacred object to be adorned, just as an illuminator might elaborate Christ's halo in a Gospel illustration. But this attitude was ultimately to be changed imperceptibly by the setting first of troped words to the counterpoint, then of vernacular and secular texts; and thus a new musical form, a typically medieval symbiosis of sacred and secular, came into existence during the thirteenth century: the motet.

The new juncture is fully apparent in the motets inserted in the early fourteenth-century *Roman de Fauvel*. And the composer of five of these motets, Philippe de Vitry – poet, musician, ecclesiastic, statesman, and friend of Petrarch – soon afterwards, *c*. 1320, was also the author of a treatise describing new principles of notation and construction which has appropriately thrown the cloak of its name over the entire period: *Ars nova*. (Another theorist had anticipated Vitry with an *Ars novae musicae*.)

Ars nova is the first full manifestation of pure musical art, freed from the service of religion or poetry and constructed according to its own laws: and as the second of the Avignon Popes, John XXII, bitterly complained in his Bull 'Docta Sanctorum', words were now treated as mere pretexts for music.

This new attitude to music is reflected also by the writers of the fourteenth century. . . . The influence of Aristotelian thought, the growth of empiricism, the need for 'imitation of nature', make themselves felt in music as in the other arts and fields of European thought. Giotto points the new way in painting, and the musicians imitate nature most vividly in the *chaces* and *cacce* that are the musical counterparts of characteristic pages of Chaucer and Boccaccio.[4]

As the last great master of *ars nova* (and 'last of the *trouvères*', as he has been called), Guillaume de Machaut, poet, composer, ecclesiastic and diplomat, put it in the *Prologue* written near the end of his life:

> Et musique est une science
> Qui vuet qu'on rie et chant et dance.

However, although his own music is mostly concerned with laughter, song, and dance and his secular motets greatly outnumber his sacred ones, Machaut did give the world the first complete polyphonic composition of

[3] See pp. 88–9.   [4] *NOHM*, iii, pp. xvii–xviii.

the Ordinary of the Mass. It had been preceded by anonymous centos or mere pairs of movements – even compilations of complete plainsong cycles were fairly novel – and some time still was to elapse before the Mass as a musical entity was to become the principal form of church composition.

During the last quarter of the fourteenth century, after Machaut's death, extreme rhythmical and notational ingenuity was cultivated to the point of mannerism – even graphically as when one composer notated two *chansons* in the forms of circle and heart. Yet French music was for a time more than ever paramount. Italian polyphony had been slow in developing and like English was following a somewhat independent course, though both caught winds from France – not mannerist airs – during that last quarter-century. Even the Papal Chapel exiled at Avignon numbered French-speaking singers from Liège among its members, and a more important Walloon, Johannes Ciconia, spent the first decade of the next century at Padua. The return of the Papacy to Rome intensified the process, for Martin V recruited a number of French or Walloon musicians for his chapel. But it was not a one-way traffic. Ciconia himself was influenced by Italian music and in the next generation a Walloon from the other prince-bishopric, Cambrai, Guillaume Dufay, was to become the archetype of a West European musician. At the Papal court he was infected by Italian cantilena, at that of Philip the Good, Duke of Burgundy, by the 'frisque concordance' of the English musicians – above all Dunstable – in the service of Philip's ally and brother-in-law Bedford, the English Regent in temporarily conquered France.

The fall of Constantinople in 1453 does not mark the beginning of the Renaissance; nothing does. But Philip the Good's Feast of the Oath of the Pheasant for which Dufay composed music, intended as the prelude to a crusade for its recapture, was the last grand futile flourish of medieval chivalry; while the Italian streak in Dufay as in Ciconia enables one to speak of Renaissance elements in Netherland music. (Similar give-and-take occurred in painting; Ghirlandaio was influenced by Flemish painters, Dürer by Giovanni Bellini and Leonardo.) Political as well as cultural events did much to alter the pattern of European music. The English invasion of France had helped to make English composers – Bedingham and Leonel Power and others besides Dunstable – famous as far as northern Italy; the expulsion led to isolation and the cultivation of another English style independent of the Continent. The marriage of Mary, heiress of Burgundy, to Maximilian of Austria (later emperor as Maximilian I), carried Netherland musical influence to Innsbruck and assisted in drawing the German-speaking lands into the European concert.

Hitherto German music had been conservative, the polyphony comparatively rudimentary. The *Minnesänger* often leaned on *trouvère* models. But it is significant that Western polyphony is first importantly documented in the German lands in the form of keyboard music. The Bavarian court organist Conrad Paumann had already played to Philip the Good in 1454 and it was presumably he who, as a result of this foray, included in the Buxheim organ-book a number of transcriptions of pieces from the Anglo–Burgundian area. The fingers of German keyboard performers were later to play a very important part in the history of Western music.

But the type-figure of the European composer of the late fifteenth century was a Fleming, Henricus Isaac, who served Lorenzo de' Medici and his son for nearly twenty years, was then appointed court composer to Maximilian I, and composed Netherlandish church music, Italian *frottole* and carnival songs, French *chansons*, and square-cut German *Lieder* with equal mastery. He was a true Renaissance figure comparable with Dürer – who also paid extended visits to Italy and entered Maximilian's service. The diffusion of Isaac's music was promoted by that most powerful instrument of the rebirth of learning, the printing-press. When Ottaviano dei Petrucci set up his press in Venice his first great collection, the *Harmonice Musices Odhecaton A* of 1501, included five pieces by Isaac – nearly all the rest are by Netherlanders too – and in 1506 he published a volume of five *Misse henrici Izac*, four of them based not on plainsong *cantus firmi* but, like so many Masses from Dufay onward, on secular *chansons*. No composer, except Josquin des Prez, was a happier synthesis of Northerner and Italian.

Isaac was not the last of the great French-speaking Netherlanders. They continued to hold dominating posts in Venice and Florence and Rome until the middle of the next century, maintaining a Flemish-Italian axis which tilted more and more in the direction of Italy. It was a time of sweeping changes in other fields than music and painting. New learning had led to new thinking, and printing disseminated both with unprecedented speed. Politically a new Europe was coming into shape. France was consolidated under Louis XI, England delivered from her chivalrous and pugnacious nobility under Henry VII, and the Holy Roman Empire of the German Nation vastly expanded under a Flemish emperor, Charles V, who acquired Naples, Spain, and the New World across the Atlantic by inheritance from his mother. It was in the matrix of this new Europe that the music of the sixteenth century was to be cast.

5

The Beginnings of Polyphony

THE WRITINGS OF HUCBALD

The earliest unmistakable mention of Western polyphony, something a little more sophisticated than heterophony or than melody accompanied by a fixed or moveable drone, occurs in a treatise *De Institutione Harmonica*[1] by Hucbald (*c.* 840–930), a monk of St. Amand in the diocese of Tournai. When Cassiodorus and Isidore of Seville and Aurelian of Réomé write of *symphonia*, they mean the agreement of successive, not simultaneous sounds; but Hucbald leaves us in no doubt that he means simultaneous sounds:

Consonantia . . . is a prescribed and harmonious mixing together of two sounds, which will come about only if two different notes coincide at the same time in one *modulatio* as when a man's voice and a boy's sing at the same time; or also in what people commonly call *organizatio* (*sic*).[2]

Two points strike one here: the word *organizatio* for a polyphonic practice involving instruments (*organa*), and the need for a notation of pitch more precise than neumes if *consonantia* – which Hucbald defines as fourths, fifths, and octaves, each of which may be compounded with a further octave – are to be really 'prescribed' (*rata*). And, sure enough, he gives a diagram showing how a scrap of melody, not polyphony, can be notated so as to indicate the precise consecutive intervals. He draws six parallel lines corresponding to the strings of the cythara, puts letters in the margin to show the interval between them (T for *tonus*, S for *semitonus*), and writes each syllable closely above the relevant pitch-line (pl. 22(i) is from fo. 87 of the Brussels manuscript: see n.1):

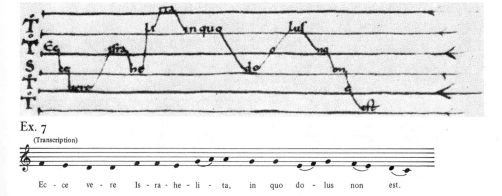

Ex. 7
(Transcription)

Ec - ce ve - re Is - ra - he - li - ta, in quo do - lus non est.

75

This hexachord was to play an important part in medieval practice, but Hucbald's diagram was not a basis for a general system of notation: it was too cumbersome and he himself uses neumes elsewhere in his treatise, because they can indicate slowing and quickening and *tremula* of the voice and so on. The diagram is a textbook illustration to his discussion of musical

Pl. 22(ii)   From fo. 87 of the Brussels manuscript, showing Hucbald's system of two identical octaves.

theory which he professes to derive from Boethius and might indeed be described as Boethius-simplified-and-brought-up-to-date, though in fact it looks back to Aristoxenus.[3] His system, expounded with the help of diagrams of tones and semitones, and descriptions of the ways it can be constructed from STT tetrachords, consists essentially of two identical 'conjunct' octaves: $_{\text{TSTTSTT}}^{\text{TSTTSTT}}$

Ex. 8

DIEZEUGMENON
(disjunct tetrachord)

SYNEMMENON
(conjunct tetrachord)

(He tells the pupil, assumed to be a singer, that a whole tone is the interval between the first two strings of an instrument, when properly tuned, or between the first two pipes of a hydraulus.) As the two-octave scale gives only fifteen notes, Hucbald adds the old Greek *proslambanomenos*[4] at the bottom – thus, in practice, G – and, as indeed the Greeks had done, borrows an auxiliary tetrachord (*synemmenon*) joined conjunctly with the second tetrachord (giving a b♭ c′ d′) in place of the disjunct one (*diezeugmenon*), in order to provide a semitone that often occurs in the authentic and plagal forms of the *tonus tritus*, the modes with F as the final. However this note is lacking on the organ, as are the two lowest notes of his system, A and B; on the other hand organs have more than fifteen or sixteen pipes to facilitate playing in different modes. The 'instrumental' scale thus beginning on c is identical with the modern major scale, as Hucbald shows

---

[1] The best and only complete text is in Brussels, Bibl. Royale, Codex Brüxell. 10078-95. See Rembert Weakland, 'Hucbald as Musician and Theorist', MQ xlii (1956) p. 66.
[2] Original text in *NOHM*, ii, p. 277.
[3] See pp. 34–5.
[4] See p. 34.

by one of his diagrams (vertical and wrongly aligned in the original), though the letter notation beside which the intervals are indicated, the falsely so-called 'Boethian notation', runs from A to P:

A B C D E F G H I K L M N O P
   T T S T T T S T T S T   T T S

Hucbald, it should be added, was not only a very practical theorist but a composer. He is known to have composed Offices of St. Peter, St. Andrew, and St. Theodoric, and *laudes* beginning with the words 'Quem vere pia laus' which, as Rembert Weakland has pointed out,[5] must be the popular Gloria trope found in a number of sources from the late tenth century onward.

In addition to *De Institutione Harmonica* a number of treatises were once ascribed to Hucbald but have long been recognized as probably or certainly not by him, though he may have had a hand in their compilation. One of them, *Alia Musica*, is concerned with the church modes and enjoys the deplorable distinction of having led the way in misapplying to them the names of the Greek *harmoniai*: *Dorius* for the *protus autentus* with D as final, *Phrygius* for the *deuterus*, *Lydius* for the *tritus*, *Mixolydius* for the *tetrachius*. And it should be noted that, as with Hucbald, the author or authors consider the final note as determining the mode – the melody may begin on any note within a fifth above or fourth below the *finalis* – whereas earlier theorists, such as Regino of Prüm, regard the opening as the determinant.

MUSICA ENCHIRIADIS AND EARLY ORGANUM

Another treatise, the famous *Musica Enchiriadis* with its 'notes', the *Scholia Enchiriadis*, preserved in more than forty varying manuscripts embodying errors which must have crept in at a very early stage, also mentions the Greek names for the modes, but is important above all for its attempt to indicate polyphony by a notation resembling Hucbald's in Pl. 22(i). The author's lost original may well have been identical with Hucbald's except that it must have had more lines than the six corresponding to the strings of the *cythara*; in the copies the text is sometimes still written very close to the line. But generally the significance of lines and spaces is reversed; it is the space that indicates the note, and the text is written in the middle of it. The marginal T and S signs are placed against the lines, not the spaces, and – except where a scribe has transposed a T and S at the very top of the scale – the result is identical with Hucbald's system. Unfortunately the whole thing is thrown into confusion by the addition of 'daseian' signs (so called from the Greek *daseia prosodia*, a 'rough' aspirate mark) against the spaces: a garbled

[5] Op. cit., p. 69.

derivation from Greek 'instrumental' notation (cf. Ex. 1). Four signs are employed for each TST tetrachord, in normal position for d e f g, reversed for the tetrachord below, inverted for the one above, reversed and inverted for the highest. The tetrachords are all disjunct and the result sometimes contradicts the T and S marks, producing a scale unknown to any other medieval theorist. The B near the bottom of the scale has to be flattened, despite the clear T mark below it and S mark above, in order to make it fit the rigid tetrachord pattern; perhaps the transposition of T and S near the top is a desperate effort to do the same there, though it produces F sharps in the original melody (which has the correct F naturals an octave lower).

Despite the inconsistencies of this system of notation, it enabled the author of *Musica Enchiriadis* to illustrate with perfect clarity the kinds of polyphony he was explaining: that in which the original melody, *vox principalis*, is accompanied in parallel fourths by a lower *vox organalis* (whether the *principalis* was played as well as sung, or the *organalis* sung as well as played, we do not know); that in which the *principalis* is doubled an octave lower and the *organalis* an octave higher; and that in which the *organalis* is a fifth instead of a fourth below the *principalis* and again both are doubled at the octave. The normal organal practice was the first method: organum in parallel fourths. Actually, as the author recognizes, rigid parallel fourths are often impossible, since the third note of every tetrachord will always be dissonant with the second one of the tetrachord above (*a symphonia deficit*) because the interval exceeds a fourth, amounting to *tribus integris tonis* (three whole tones, the tritone, 'the devil in music' as later theorists called it) (Cap. XVII). To avoid this dissonance, the *organalis* should never go below the fourth note of the tetrachord – a procedure which the author tries to demonstrate with a fragment from the 'Te Deum' sung in all four authentic modes:

Ex. 9

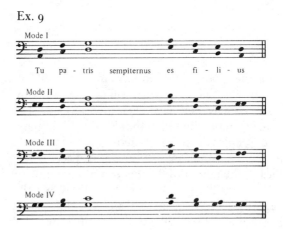

Here again there is inconsistency. In mode I the organal voice begins and ends below the fourth note of the tetrachord, and there is no reason why it should not; parallel fourths are possible throughout. In mode II there is, after all, a tritone at 'es' and, remembering Hucbald's *synemmenon* tetrachord, one wonders whether in practice the singers would not have substituted B flat. In mode III, the author says, a proper organal part to the

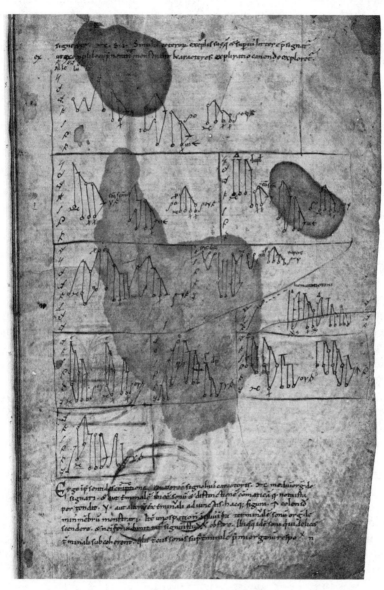

Pl. 23   Two-part composition on the melody 'Benedicta sit' (Paris, Bibl. Nat. lat. 7202, fo. 56). See p. 80.

repeated Bs is really impossible, although here again, remembering Hucbald's remark about the currency of B flats in the *tonus tritus*, it is odd that the author does not suggest flattening these Bs to remove the difficulty.

The G suggested here is accommodatingly permitted by the little treatise *De organo*[6] which also figures among the Hucbaldian apocrypha: 'owing to lack of space we may set down improper organum (*abusivum organum*) in thirds and seconds'. The mode IV passage exemplifies this more fully. *De organo* furthermore tells us that in the majority of cases the voices come together at intermediate or final cadences on the *finalis* or the note above or below, and that when the melody falls to one of these notes the organum should not descend lower than the note below the *finalis*, a rule ignored in the mode II and III excerpts of Ex. 9. A later version of *De organo*[7] includes a complete two-part composition on the sequence melody 'Benedicta sit',[8] in notation derived from Hucbald's (see pl. 23); it has one section in which the *organalis* is higher than the *principalis*:

Ex. 10

Vox organalis

Vox principalis

DEVELOPMENTS IN NOTATION

Such were the theoretical beginnings of something that was to distinguish Western music not only from that of the Eastern Mediterranean lands but from all the other musics of the world, the basis of the entire Western European musical tradition. The practical beginnings must have been earlier; indeed, it is difficult to speak of a 'beginning' when all that happened was a slight and gradual sophistication of heterophony. What makes the writings of Hucbald and the pseudo-Hucbalds so important is that they record and codify the practices, and do so in connection with the most important form of Western music: that of the Church. It can hardly be mere coincidence that *organizatio* and organum began to be recognized at the very time when the organ, 'the instrument' *par excellence*, having in Western Europe finally shed the last trace of its pagan associations, was at last tolerated in church not only for the training of singers but actually, at least by the tenth century, allowed to participate in the service. Instrumental support must have been of great help in primitive polyphony, if not essential to it; much further complication is hardly conceivable without it – or without a practical method of indicating accurate pitch. Hucbald's diagrams were not a practical notation and did not lead to one although, as we shall see, they were used occasionally until the twelfth century. His lines and spaces were not a precursor of the staff, although they look like it. The solution was to make the neumes more precise.

The neumes themselves developed local varieties of shape, the most important being the types of Northern France and Metz, to which those of

[6] Cologne, Dombibl. 52.   [7] The latter part of Paris, Bibl. nat. lat. 7202.
[8] Willi Apel, 'The earliest polyphonic composition and its theoretical background', *Revue belge de musicologie*, x (1956), pp. 135–6.

England, the German-speaking lands, and Northern Italy were more or less closely related. The later 'Aquitanian' neumes of Southern France and the 'Beneventan' neumes of Southern Italy developed ever more marked divergencies, while in Spain and Catalonia the Mozarabic rite preserved its own notation nearly until it was superseded by the Roman rite in the eleventh century. The writing of neumes at varying heights above the words was a first step in the right direction; it was first taken about the middle of the tenth century (see pl. 24). But its inadequacy as a pitch-notation, especially

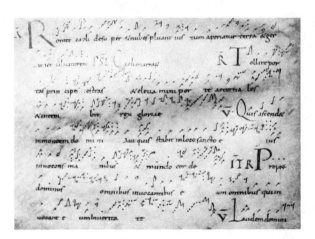

Pl. 24   Neumes written at varying heights above the words in the Laon Gradual of *c.* 930 (Laon, MS. 239, fo. 12).

for the notation of polyphony, is demonstrated by one of two eleventh-century tropers from Winchester[9] (Cambridge, Corpus Christi 473), a collection of Kyries, Tracts, Alleluias, Responds, etc., which is indeed written only partly in diastematic (heighted) neumes (see pl. 25). The liturgical melodies can be partially read with the help of later versions, but the organal parts – written in a different part of the manuscript – were long considered impossible to read with confidence. Nevertheless Andreas Holschneider has proposed acceptable solutions.[10]

It must not be thought that the diastematic writing of neumes, sometimes with the aid of a ruled line scratched on the parchment, or any of the later innovations, was adopted generally and quickly; there exists a Czech missal of *c.* 1300 with notation still in nondiastematic neumes,[11] and St. Gall began

---

[9] Where at some time between 984 and 994 a famous organ had been built, probably in the New Minster adjacent to the Old.
[10] *Die Organa von Winchester* (Hildesheim, 1968); facsimile, with Holschneider's transcription in Heinrich Besseler and Peter Gülke, *Schriftbild der mehrstimmigen Musik* (*Musikgeschichte in Bildern*, III/5) (Leipzig, 1973), pl. 4(a). Another example is reproduced from Holschneider in *OAM(M)*, no. 38. For evidence of instrumental participation, see Holschneider, 'Instrumental Titles to the Sequentiae of the Winchester Troper', *Essays on Opera and English Music* (ed. F. W. Sternfeld, Nigel Fortune, and Edward Olleson) (Oxford, 1975), p. 8. See also Alejandro Planchart, *The Repertory of Tropes at Winchester* (Princeton, 1977).

to use lines only in the fifteenth century.[12] During the eleventh century letter-notations were used to supplement the neumes or even instead of neumes. The so-called 'Romanus' letters (named after a semi-mythical papal singer), which are first explained by the St. Gall Benedictine Notker 'Balbulus' (the stutterer) (840–912), are really directions for performance rather than notation: *a* (alacriter), *c* (cito, celeriter), *e* (equaliter), *t* (trahere vel tenere), and so on. Thus the Gospel for Palm Sunday, with its title 'Passio Domini nostri Jesu Christi secundum Matthaeum. In illo tempore: Dixit Jesus discipulis suis', is prefixed with a *c* for quick recitation but Christ's words 'Quid molesti estis huic mulieri?' with a *t* for sustained utterance. But as Johannes Cotto (*fl.c.* 1100), probably an Englishman,[13] pointed out, these were as indefinite as the neumes themselves, while a later system of letters and symbols indicating intervals precisely, devised by another Benedictine, Hermannus Contractus (1013–54), was out of date when it was conceived. Yet another letter notation of the early eleventh century was employed by the anonymous Italian author of a *Dialogus de musica* long ascribed to Odo of Cluny.[14] This begins with a Greek *gamma* for *proslambanomenos* (the note G) and repeats the alphabet after the first octave, using smaller Roman letters for the second octave and Greek ones for the third, which is very nearly the letter system we still use. A classic source for the use of Boethian notation to clarify neumes is the fine eleventh-century *Antiphonarium Tonale Missarum* from the abbey of St. Bénigne, Dijon (Montpellier, H.159) (see pl. 26), and it was used without neumes in a famous fragment of two-part polyphony, 'Ut tuo propitiatus', in a manuscript at Oxford (see pl. 27).[15] Here the two rows of letters make the mainly contrary motion perfectly clear, in contrast to the dimly perceptible contrary motion of the Winchester troper or even that of the Easter, Ascensiontide, and Whitsun Alleluias in Chartres 109,[16] although in this case scholars are nearly in agreement about the transcription of the two rows of diastematic neumes. It is worth noting that in the Chartres codex only the polyphonic passages are shown, not the monophonic music – sung by the choir in unison – needed to complete the text. Polyphony was only for highly trained soloists.

---

[11] Brno, Moravské museum A7115; facs. in Jan Racek, *Středověká hudba* (Brno, 1946), pl. 1, and *Česká hudba* (Prague, 1958), pl. 4.

[12] Peter Wagner, *Einführung in die gregorianischen Melodien*, ii (Leipzig, 1912), p. 285.

[13] Cotto in his *De musica cum tonario* and the contemporary anonymous author of a treatise *Ad organum faciendum* (Milan, Bibl. Ambrosiana 17), were the earliest theorists to discuss contrary motion and the crossing of parts. Examples from *Ad organum faciendum* are given in *HAM*, i, No. 25(*a*), and *OAM(M)*, No. 39.

[14] Michel Huglo, *Les Tonaires* (Paris, 1971), pp. 166 and 182.

[15] Transcription, *HAM*, i, No. 26(b).

[16] Facs. in Marius Schneider, *Geschichte der Mehrstimmigkeit*, ii (Berlin, 1935), appendix, p. 53. Complete transcription in *NOHM*, ii, pp. 282–4; partial transcriptions in *HAM*, i, No. 26(c), and Guido Adler, *Handbuch der Musikgeschichte*, i (Berlin 1930), p. 175.

(i)

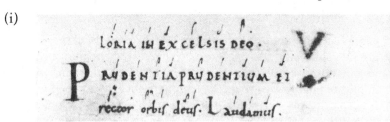

(ii)

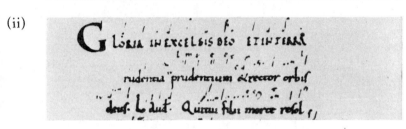

Pl. 25   *Vox principalis* (i) and *vox organalis* (ii) of a Gloria in the 11th-century Winchester troper (Cambridge, Corpus Christi 473, fos. 64 and 142).

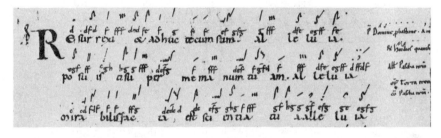

Pl. 26   'Boethian' letter-notation used to clarify pitch of neumes in an 11th-century *Antiphonarium* from the abbey of St. Bénigne, Dijon (Montpellier, Bibl. de l'École de Médecine, fo. 30).

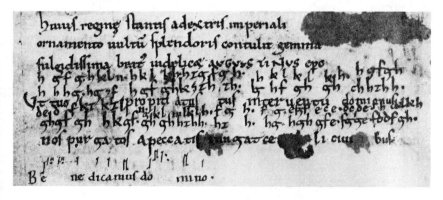

Pl. 27   Two-part setting of 'Ut tuo propitiatus' (11th-century), notated in letters only (Oxford, Bodl. 572).

THE EMBRYONIC STAFF

With the gradual adoption of the embryonic staff, something more than a mere alignment line either scratched or coloured red, neumes became a more and more satisfactory means of notating pitch. (At the same time the more complicated neumatic groupings tentatively began in the Aquitanian script to be written in separate notes, although 'ligatures', more clearly defined note-groupings later evolved from them, were an unconscionable time – some four hundred years – dying). The first step was the determination of the red line as F by prefixing that letter, which survives to this day as the F clef 𝄢:, the second was the addition of a C line coloured yellow, F and C presumably being chosen as fixed points because these were the notes with semitones beneath them. At first any additional lines were still only drawn with a dry point but the decision to use both lines and spaces, instead of lines only or spaces only, was another important step. All this is most clearly explained (and to make doubly sure the letters of the alphabet are written on the lines and spaces) in a treatise *Micrologus de Musica*, its versified form *Regulae Rhythmicae*, and a *Prologus in Antiphonarium*, which must have been written between 1025 and 1033 by a Benedictine named Guido who taught the choir-school of the cathedral at Arezzo during those years.[18]

GUIDO D'AREZZO AND THE HEXACHORD

Guido was not a theorist but a practical pedagogue and his method, the basis of all medieval teaching, embraced much more than an advanced system of notation. It was based on the Hucbaldian conception of the TTSTT hexachord, of which he conceived three positions: the *hexachordum naturale*, c d e f g a; the *hexachordum durum*, G A B c d e; and the *hexachordum molle*, f g a b♭ c′ d′. 'Mutation' from one hexachord to another was effected by pivoting on a note or notes common to both. And Guido employed both mnemonic and cheironomic aids. He borrowed the melody of a setting, in Montpellier MS 425, of the Horatian ode (IV, 11) in which the poet invites Phyllis to share a jar of nine-year-old Alban wine; changed the first seven notes (to 'Est mihi nonum') which did not suit his purpose; and fitted the melody to the words of a well-known hymn to St. John. He thus produced a setting in which each line began one note higher in the hexachord than its predecessor, and he named the notes after the first syllable of each line:

> *Ut* queant laxis
> *Re*sonare fibris
> *Mi*ra gestorum
> *Fa*muli tuorum
> *So*lve polluti
> *La*bi reatum,
> Sancte Johannes.

(It will be noticed that, with his names for the 'hard' and 'soft' hexachords, Guido was the originator of a number of modern French and German technical terms although their sense has changed: e.g. the French *ut* is always C, whereas Guido's could be C, G, or F, according to the position of the hexachord. Later the initials of 'Sancte Johannes' – S.I. – conveniently provided *si*.) His cheironomic device was equally ingenious; adapting a means first employed by the ancient Egyptians,[19] he showed how the teacher could indicate the notes by pointing to positions on his left hand: G, the tip of the thumb; A, the thumb joint; B, the root of the thumb; c, d, e, and f the roots of the four fingers, and so on.

Toward the end of his life Guido is said to have joined the Camaldolians, not yet a separate order, so it is not surprising that the earliest known examples of his staff notation are found in codices from such Camaldolian monasteries as Struma and Vallombrosa;[20] in the course of the twelfth century it was generally adopted throughout Italy, France, England, and Spain. Germany was a little slower; Einsiedeln, for instance, rewrote its choirbooks in staff notation only at the beginning of the fourteenth century. And the introduction of precise notations of intervals, the Guidonian staff or the symbols of Hermannus Contractus, reveals that German monks had got into the habit of singing thirds in melodies where French and Italians sang tones or semitones (e.g. ac′a instead of ab (or b♭)a).[21]

NOTATION OF NOTE-VALUES

Western music had acquired a reasonably satisfactory means of indicating intervals, but polyphony also needed a satisfactory means of indicating note-values. The Anonymous Vaticanus quoted on p. 63 talks about *breves* and *longae* associated with syllabic feet in the text; the 'Romanus' letters *c* and *t* of Notker Balbulus have been claimed as indications of short and long notes rather than of speed; and one of the manuscripts of the *Scholia Enchiriadis* says that 'we put points and *virgulae* to distinguish between short sounds and long'. And the relationship is exact: two shorts equal a long. the *punctum* was a . , the *virga* or *virgula* was a diagonal line /, like the *acutus*, or horizontal (when it was called a *virgula jacens* and sometimes interpreted as a *brevis*). One or two of the compound neume-forms could indicate, say, two shorts and a long note. But in practice things were neither systematic nor unambiguous, and sometimes this equation of *punctum* and *virga* with short and long leads to manifest absurdities. In another passage the same writer describes 'rhythmical singing' (*numerose canere*) as the congruence of his mathematically precise shorts and longs with the short and long syllables of the text. But he is only talking about monophonic song;

[18] *Micrologus*, ed. Smits van Waesberghe, *Corpus Scriptorum de Musica* iv (American Institute of Musicology, 1955).
[19] See p. 13.   [20] Florence, Bibl. Laur. 158 and 247.
[21] See the examples in Peter Wagner, op. cit. pp. 445–7, and Robert Haas, *Aufführungspraxis der Musik* (Potsdam, 1934), p. 43.

he says organum is performed so slowly that it is hardly possible to pay attention to rhythm.[22] Indeed, the earliest note-against-note organum must have been performed very cautiously, and perhaps slowed down by the relatively clumsy mechanism of the organ.

ST. MARTIAL AND SANTIAGO POLYPHONY

The principal melody must have been slowed down even more by the florid nature of the organal parts we find first in such twelfth-century sources as the manuscripts commonly associated with the Abbey of St. Martial at Limoges (Paris, Bibl. Nat. lat. 1139, 3549, and 3719, and London, Brit. Lib. Add. 36881), though their true provenance is uncertain, and in the Codex Calixtinus allegedly from Santiago de Compostela,[23] a pious fraud concocted in central France soon after 1130, probably in part at

Pl. 28   The earliest source of 'Per partum virginis' (*c.* 1150) (Paris, Bibl. Nat. lat. 3719, fo. 64).

---

[22] Another anonymous treatise of the same period, *Commemoratio brevis de tonis et psalmis modulandis* (reprinted, with German translation, in Wagner, op. cit., pp. 359–63), gives fascinating directions for performance: generally pace and values of shorts and longs must be strictly maintained throughout a piece, except that at the end (and sometimes at the beginning) of a quick melody the note-values may be doubled and at the end of a slow melody they may be halved; the first syllable of a psalm and the last syllables of each verse should be prolonged; the antiphon between verses should be repeated at the same pace as the verse, but the final repetition should be at half speed; the psalms and other melodies should be sung at different pitches according to the occasion (e.g. higher at Lauds than at Vespers, the Gospel Canticles higher and slower); series of psalms with antiphons should be sung at the same pitch or at successively higher pitches.

[23] Published complete in three vols. (facsimile, transcription, and notes) by W. M. Whitehill and Germán Prado (Compostela, 1944).

Cluny.[24] Together these manuscripts form a closely related corpus of early twelfth-century polyphony (together with a great deal of monophony) and some pieces occur in more than one of them. Thus the strophic song 'Per partum virginis', though not in Bibl. Nat. 1139, *c.* 1100, the earliest of these sources, occurs in both the other Bibl. Nat. codices of half a century later, and in the British Library manuscript of a still later date.[25] Transcription of the Bibl. Nat. 3719 version (see pl. 28):

Ex. 11

(Square brackets indicate note-groupings)

Per   par -   tum   vir - gi -   -   -   nis

shows the nature of the problem; the most eminent scholars have suggested in such cases (a) even note-values for the principal part, with variable values for the *organalis*, (b) even note-values for the *organalis*, with variable ones for the principal. But even the vertical alignment is (as usual) unclear, and differs from that in 3549. The British Library version is more definite and helped by vertical lines like modern bar-lines, which are usually immediately preceded, and often followed, by consonances: unisons, fourths, octaves. The neumes, late Aquitanian, are now 'square' – really miniature rectangles – in the form notation was generally adopting, though the staff-lines are still scratched with a dry point. But the question of note-values remains unsolved.[26]

Ex. 12

Per   par -   tum   vir -   -   gi - nis

[24] It was the Cluniac Order which provided in part the link between St. Martial and Santiago. In 1072, six years before the foundation of the cathedral of Santiago – the shrine of St. James had already been a popular pilgrimage-goal for two centuries – the Cluniacs had persuaded Alfonso VI to replace the Mozarabic by the Roman rite throughout Castile and León; their own new abbey at Limoges (dedicated 1095) was one of the most important stations on the pilgrimage route, as were Moissac and Aurillac where other 'St. Martial' manuscripts are believed to have originated; and it is not impossible that the Codex Calixtinus was taken to Santiago by the ruler of the Limousin, William X of Aquitaine, on his pilgrimage in 1137.
[25] Facs. in *MGG*, xi, col. 1265, pl. 67, and col. 1269.
[26] Further easily accessible examples of florid organum are: from Bibl. Nat. 1139, the Benedicamus trope 'Jubilemus, exultemus', facs. in Carl Parrish, *The Notation of Medieval Music* (London, 1958), pl. XXII, and *MGG*, ii, cols. 1617–8; complete transcriptions in *ZfMW*, x (1927–8), pp. 13–14; from Codex Calixtinus, the Kyrie trope, 'Cunctipotens genitor', facs. in Apel, *Notation*, end of fac. 45; transcription in *HAM*, i, No. 27(b).

However in a number of these 'St. Martial' pieces both parts move abreast, note against note with passing decorations, so that scholars have been tempted, especially in the case of hymns, to transcribe metrically on the lines of Ex. 6.[27] In one of the Calixtinus hymns, 'Congaudeant catholici', a slightly later hand has added a third part – not much more than a simplified version of the original *organalis* – note-against-note with the lower part, thus producing one of the earliest known examples of three-part music.[28] The ascription to 'Magister Albertus Parisiensis', like that of an Alleluia 'Vocavit Jhesus' to 'Magister Coslenus episcopus Suessionis' (i.e. 'of Soissons'), and other alleged composers – mostly French bishops – in the same manuscript, to say nothing of the notabilities whose authority is claimed in the non-musical part of the Codex, has been regarded as bogus; but there was an undoubted Albertus, cantor of Notre Dame in Paris, who died about 1180 and bequeathed to the church a Missal, Lectionary, Gradual, and 'Psalterium cum hymnis'. Sometimes both florid and note-against-note polyphony are found in the same piece, as in the Christmas gradual trope, 'Viderunt Hemanuel', in Bibl. Nat. 3549.[29] Here the first two lines are sung in the florid style, each ending with note-against-note melismata, and the third and fourth in fairly strict note-against-note style, also ending with melismata. After that the chorus comes in, unison, with the final words of the actual liturgical text, 'omnes fines terrae salutare Dei nostri; jubilate Deo omnis terra'.

TROPE AND SEQUENCE

'Viderunt Hemanuel' illustrates very conveniently not only types of composition which figure prominently in the St. Martial-Calixtine manuscripts, *versus* and *tropus*, hymn and trope – sometimes identical, as here – but also the nature of troping, a practice well established by *c*. 900. In late Latin *tropare* meant to sing and a *tropus* was a melody;[30] more specifically it was an addition of music or text or, much more commonly, both to an 'official' liturgical passage. Significantly the practice became widespread at the very time when the Church was trying to establish liturgical and musical uniformity. The earliest form of trope was the wordless *jubilus* of the Alleluia which St. Augustine talks about[31] and is doubtless much older, and Amalar of Metz seems to mean just that when he speaks of 'this *jubilatio* which they call

---

[27] For instance, Bruno Stäblein's version of the final melismas on 'termino' and 'domino' of the fifth strophe of the hymn 'Noster coetus psallat laetus' in the Brit. Lib. 36881 version, in *MGG*, xi, facing col. 1265, ex. 10, and his 'Modale Rhythmen im Saint-Martial Repertoire?', *Festschrift Friedrich Blume* (Kassel, 1963), particularly pp. 346–8. Cf. also 'Mira lege, miro modo' from Bibl. Nat. 1139 (facs. in Coussemaker, *Histoire de l'harmonie au moyen âge* (Paris, 1852), pl. XXIII, and often transcribed, e.g. in *Oxford History of Music*, i (1901), pp. 95–6).
[28] Facs. in Parrish, op. cit., pl. XXIII, with transcriptions by the author and three other scholars on pp. 69–71.
[29] Facs. in Apel, op. cit., p. 211, and differing transcriptions in *HAM*, i, No. 27(a), and Adler, *Handbuch*, i, pp. 179–80.
[30] Cf. the Byzantine *troparion*: see above, p. 65.
[31] See above, p. 54.

sequentia';[32] but very soon after Amalar we find Hucbald, Notker Balbulus, and the author of *Musica Enchiriadis* all describing or illustrating a new way of treating the *sequentia*. Notker in the *Prooemium*, written *c.* 885, to his *Liber Hymnorum*, gives an often quoted account of how a monk fleeing from the monastery of Jumièges near Rouen, when it was destroyed by the Normans, brought to St. Gall an Antiphonar, in which verses had been set to the previously wordless *sequentiae*.[33] Notker felt he could do better and his *Liber*, preserved in a number of manuscripts of the tenth and eleventh centuries, contains forty such sequences, some to existing melodies, others to new ones.[34] The author or copyist of one of the manuscripts of *Musica Enchiriadis* quotes words and music of the sequence 'Rex caeli' to illustrate organum:[35]

Ex. 13

Vox organalis
1. Rex cae - li, Do - mi - ne ma - ris un - di - so - ni, 3. Te hu - mi - les fa - mu - li mo - du - lis
2. Ti - ta - nis ni - ti - di squa - li - di - que so - li, 4. Se, ju - be - as, fla - gi - tant va - ri - is

ve - ne - ran - do pi - is.
li - be - ra - re ma - lis.

– the double-line strophes to the repeated melody, usually 'framed' by independent opening and closing strophes, are characteristic of the sequence. Hucbald not only refers to a sequence, 'Stans a longe', in *De Institutione Harmonica*, but as we have already seen[36] was the composer of *laudes* inserted in the Gloria, that is to say a Gloria trope. Actually, as Richard Crocker has pointed out,[37] the singing of the Gloria had until recently been the prerogative of bishops – and according to Peter Wagner[38] 'the oldest Gloria melodies had the character of a syllabic recitation ... more a declamation than a song' – while the Agnus Dei is first documented as part of the order of the Mass by Aurelian of Réomé (and, for that matter, the Credo was still not a part of it). Thus a great number of Gloria and other melodies may be no older than those to the interpolated words. The important point is that there was, particularly in the 'Frankish' lands during the tenth and eleventh centuries, a great outpouring of new composition: hymns and antiphons, tropes and sequences.

---

[32] Migne, *Patrologia Latina*, CV: '*sequentia*' because it followed the part with text.
[33] The oldest surviving specimen of German neumes, in Munich, Staatsbibl. Ms clm 9543, shows such an underlay of text, 'Psalle modulamina', to the Alleluia 'Christus resurgens' written by the monk Engyldeo of Regensburg half a century before Notker. Facs. in *MGG*, ix, col. 1625; trans. (also with facs.) in J. Smits van Waesberghe, 'Zur ursprünglichen Vortragsweise der Prosulen, Sequenzen und Organa', *IGM Kongressbericht: Köln 1958*, p. 252.
[34] An example is given in *HAM*, i, No. 16(a).
[35] From Handschin, 'Über Estampie und Sequenz I', *ZfMW*, xii (1929–30), p. 19.
[36] See above, p. 77.
[37] 'The Troping Hypothesis', *MQ*, lii (1966), p. 183. See also Crocker's *The Early Medieval Sequence* (Berkeley, 1977).   [38] Op. cit., i, p. 78.

5. The Beginnings of Polyphony

As we have noted in passing, many tropes were polyphonic – and the polyphonic trope was to lead to developments of inestimable importance to Western music generally. But the monophonic tropes and sequences in, for instance, what we may loosely call the St. Martial repertory vastly outnumber them. There are a score of codices, mostly from the eleventh century, containing no polyphonic pieces and even the four later ones already mentioned which do contain them have nearly as many monophonic pieces as polyphonic. But the proportion changes: the earliest of the four, Bibl. Nat. 1139, has 38 monophonic pieces compared with 13 in two parts, the later 3549 and 3719 have 47 as against 52, and the latest of the four, Brit. Lib. 36881, has only seven as compared with 30 polyphonic pieces. A large proportion are tropes of 'Benedicamus Domino', the priest's dismissal which concludes the Office, and also the Mass during Lent; the already mentioned 'Jubilemus, exultemus' is one of these. Even the 'polyphonic' pieces, particularly the hymns, are often mixtures of monophony and polyphony: for instance, monophonic rhymed strophes with a two-part rhymed refrain, as in the New Year hymn from 1139 quoted by Stäblein.[39] Here the five strophes decline 'Annus novus' ('Anni novi principium . . .', 'Anno novo in cantica . . .' and so on) and the refrain forcibly suggests an iambic rhythmical interpretation on which the final melismata impose a ritenuto:

Ex. 14

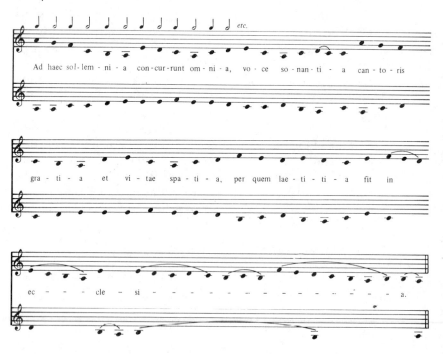

---

[39] *MGG*, xi, facing col. 1264, ex. 7.

LITURGICAL DRAMA

The earliest of the monophonic St. Martial codices, Bibl. Nat. lat. 1240, *c*. 900, and one of those probably compiled at Limoges, contains an Easter Mass trope of quite outstanding importance, 'Quem queritis in sepulchro, O Christicole?',[40] a dialogue between the angel at the empty sepulchre and the three Marys:

> Whom do you seek in the sepulchre, O followers of Christ?
> > *Jesus of Nazareth who was crucified, O heavenly one.*
> He is not here, he is risen as he foretold; go and tell that he is risen, saying:
> > *Alleluia, the Lord is risen today, the strong lion, Christ*
> > *the son of God. Thanks be to God, sing 'eia'.*
> Come and see the place where the Lord was laid. Alleluia, alleluia.
> > Go quickly and tell the disciples that the Lord is risen.
> > > > Alleluia, alleluia.
> > *The Lord is risen from the sepulchre, who hung for us on the cross.*
> > > > > *Alleluia.*

Then follows the cue, 'Resurrexi . . .' for the Mass Introit, 'Resurrexi, et adhuc tecum sum'. No doubt the trope itself was sung antiphonally. There were Byzantine precedents for such dialogue versions of Gospel events in the Nativity *kontakion* of Romanus (*c*. 500) and the Nativity *troparia* of Sophronius, a seventh-century Patriarch of Jerusalem, perhaps even earlier in the hymnody of the Syrian church,[41] but 'Quem queritis' quickly won enormous popularity – and with very good reason. Within half a century it was moved from its place before the Mass Introit to the end of Matins and there not merely sung but represented dramatically.[42] This seems to have been done first at Fleury-sur-Loire and Ghent, whence it was taken over at Winchester and we are so fortunate as to have not only the Winchester text and music in one of the two famous tropers (Oxford, Bodl. 775) (*c*. 1000) but also the Winchester 'stage-directions' in the *Concordia Regularis* issued *c*. 970 by Ethelwold, Bishop of Winchester, who explains that the purpose of this custom was 'to fortify the unlearned people in their faith'. One monk, dressed in white and carrying a palm, is to enter unobtrusively during the third lesson and sit by the 'sepulchre'; during the third respond three others, in copes and bearing censers, appearing to search for something, will enter and approach the 'angel'. The dialogue now begins. When the 'angel' sings 'Venite et videte locum', he will show the 'women' the cloths in which the cross had been wrapped (on Good Friday) and they in turn, putting down their censers, will show the empty cloths to the other clergy. Next they sing 'Surrexit Dominus' and lay the cloths upon the altar, upon which the prior begins the 'Te Deum laudamus' and 'all the bells chime out

[40] Transcription in *NOHM*, ii, p. 179.
[41] See *NOHM*, ii, pp. 9, 20, and 21–2.
[42] A different theory has been put forward by Timothy McGee, 'The Liturgical Placements of the *Quem quaeritis Dialogue*', *JAMS*, Spring 1976.

together'.[43] In the course of the next two or three centuries 'Quem queritis' spread all over Europe, naturally with all sorts of variants and accretions but with the same essential text and music. The stage-directions were sometimes inserted as rubrics as in the eleventh or twelfth-century Piacenza, Bibl. Capit. 65;[44] the Marys sing as they approach the tomb; the women go off to tell the apostles ('Dicunt nunc Judei') as in Einsiedeln 367 (c. 1100);[45] at a still later period there are scenes with the risen Christ. Sometimes independent compositions are introduced, a special favourite being the sequence 'Victimae paschali laudes' by the Imperial Chaplain, Wipo (c. 995–c. 1050), one of those melodies that have gone on sounding through the ages, still sung by Catholics in the Easter Mass and by Protestants who know it best in Bach's versions as 'Christ lag in Todesbanden'.

The idea of the Easter play was quickly adapted to other events in the Church's year. In fact, two of the eleventh-century 'St. Martial' codices, Bibl. Nat. lat. 903 and 1084,[46] have tropes beginning 'Quem queritis in presepe pastores?' ('Whom do you seek in the manger, shepherds?') which in turn led to Epiphany plays and hence to plays with an ever larger element of true drama centred on Herod.[47] The general tendency to employ other subjects resulted in such plays being taken outside the church itself, making the drama no longer liturgical but generally religious, and introducing popular, vernacular elements. Again it is a 'St. Martial' codex, Bibl. Nat. lat. 1139 (c. 1100), that supplies the earliest example of vernacular words: a *Sponsus* (Bridegroom) play on the parable of the ten virgins, with a mixed text, partly Latin, partly Angoulême dialect.[48]

At almost exactly the same time we hear of another kind of religious play, that acted by students in monastery schools sometimes in honour of patron saints, sometimes on Old Testament subjects. Such a play in honour of St. Catharine of Alexandria was performed at Dunstable in 1110, and a little later we have in Bibl. Nat. lat. 11331 three short plays by a *goliard*, or wandering scholar, named Hilarius, a pupil of Abelard: *Suscitatio Lazari* (The Raising of Lazarus), *Ludus super Iconia Sancti Nicolai* (The Ikon of St. Nicholas), which has a certain amount of French text, and a *Historia de Daniel Representanda*. They were certainly sung but unfortunately the music was not written down. For a complete school drama with preserved music we have to wait another century (c. 1230) for the famous *Ludus Danielis* of Beauvais, in Brit. Lib. Egerton 2615.[49]

---

[43] A complete translation of the Latin text from E. K. Chambers, *The Mediaeval Stage* (London, 1903), ii, p. 6, is quoted in Gustave Reese, *Music in the Middle Ages* (London, 1941), p. 194.
[44] Facs. in *NOHM*, ii, facing p. 178.
[45] Transcription in Arnold Schering, *Geschichte der Musik in Beispielen* (Leipzig, 1931), No. 8.
[46] Facs. in *MGG*, ix, pl. 90(3), and viii, col. 1027.
[47] See the complete twelfth-century Herod play in *OAM(M)*, No. 12.
[48] Examples in *NOHM*, ii, pp. 212–3. For an excerpt from a late fourteenth-century Easter play with partly Latin, partly Czech words, see Jaroslav Pohanka, *Dějiny české hudby v příkladech* (Prague, 1958), No. 7.
[49] See ibid., pp. 214–9.

SECULAR SONG

The gradual contrivance of feasible means of notation had already allowed secular song to appear from the darkness that had hitherto concealed its real nature, though we may be a little sceptical about the lament for Charlemagne ('A solis ortu usque ad occidua') and other songs about early ninth-century happenings in the 'St. Martial' codex Bibl. Nat. lat. 1154 which gives the music in indefinite though diastematic neumes of a century or two later; the compass of 'A solis ortu' seems to be limited to a tetrachord. A Spanish manuscript of the same period (Madrid, Bibl. Nac. 10029)[50] preserves similar *planctus* for Visigothic rulers, as well as one of two popular 'nightingale' songs, 'Sum noctis socia, sum dulcis amica' (found also in Berne 36). The other nightingale song, 'Philomela demus laudes', appears in various sources even as late as the fifteenth century.[51] There are also settings of Horace – five odes besides the one mentioned on p. 84 – Juvenal (part of the eighth satire), Virgil (passages from the *Aeneid*), and Boethius,[52] perhaps the work of goliards. The music, in so far as it is readable, seems to be not unlike that of ecclesiastical melody – as is shown by the ease with which Guido adapted 'Est mihi nonum'. Similarly Abelard's *planctus* for Jephthah's daughter,

> Ad festas choreas celibes
> Ex more venite virgines

is set to diastematic neumes in Rome, Bibl. Vat. reg. 288, which show the identity of the tune with that of a *Lai des Puceles* in Paris, Bibl. Nat. fr. 12615.[53] But one goliard song is decidedly different in character; it appears in Cambridge, Univ. Lib. Gg. v 35, with the words 'O admirable Veneris ydolum' and the melody in staffless neumes; in Vatican 3327 with the same words and those of a pilgrim song in the same metre, 'O Roma nobilis' and the melody in diastematic neumes; and in Monte Cassino, Q 318 with the 'Roma' text only and the melody notated in Guido's manner, with letters on a staff (and a drawing of a 'Guidonian hand' into the bargain).[54] Even amid the ecclesiastical propriety of Bibl. Nat. lat. 3719 nestles a sad love-lyric:

> De ramis cadunt folia,
> Nam viror totus periit.[55]

VERNACULAR SONG

The earliest known vernacular song is probably a tenth-century Provençal –

[50] Facs. in Higini Anglès, *El Còdex musical de Las Huelgas* (Barcelona, 1931), i, p. 26.
[51] One version, from Florence, Bibl. naz. Conv. s.F. 3.565, is transcribed in Adler, *Handbuch*, i, p. 162.
[52] Complete list in Adler, *Handbuch*, i, p. 160.
[53] See Bruno Stäblein, 'Die Schwanenklage. Zum Problem Lai-Planctus-Sequenz', *Festschrift Karl Gustav Fellerer* (Regensburg, 1962), pp. 491–2.
[54] Facs. in *NOHM*, ii, facing p. 221.
[55] Quoted in Heinrich Besseler, *Musik des Mittelalters und der Renaissance* (Potsdam, 1937), p. 106.

or French-garbled-by-a-Provençal-copyist – account of the Passion (Clermont-Ferrand 189):

> Hora uos dic uera raizun
> de jesu x̄p̄i passiun.
> (Now I will tell you the true narrative of Jesus Christ's Passion)

It runs to 149 four-line strophes; unfortunately the music, notated partly in *puncta*, partly in 'hooked' neumes of the Metz type, is unreadable. But the narrative *chansons de geste* ('songs of deeds'), the eleventh-century *Chancun de Guillelme, Gormont et Isembart*, the great *Chanson de Roland*, and the rest have come down to us without even unreadable musical notation. However we learn from a later source, the *De Musica* (*c.* 1300)[56] of the Parisian Johannes de Grocheo that the *Cantus gestualis* was made up of a number of little verses usually ending in the same rhyme and that the same *cantus* must be repeated for every verse: probably the age-old epic technique and certainly the technique of the narrative Russian *bilini* as they survived in the nineteenth century. One such *cantus* that has survived is that for a *Bataille d'Annezin* in Brit. Lib. Royal 20 A XVII:[57]

Ex. 15

Thu - ma   de   Bail -   loel   físt   ce   bien   prés   de   Se - clin.

Incidentally Johannes de Grocheo mentions that *chansons de geste* should be sung to the old and to workers and ordinary citizens when they rest from their labours so that, hearing of the miseries and calamities of others, they will the more easily bear their own and return to work the more cheerfully. Like liturgical drama – and like the mural paintings in churches and the sculpture on their portals, which may well be related to the dramas – the *chansons de geste* were art for the unlearned, art for the people but not of the people.

THE EARLIEST TROUBADOURS

Very different was the corpus of vernacular song, mainly in the Limousin dialect of the *langue d'oc*, that began to be built up under William IX (1071–1127), Duke of Aquitaine. William himself was a *trobador*[58] and when he came back from the First Crusade in 1102 he delighted in entertaining

---

[56] Text with German translations ed. Johannes Wolf, *SIMG*, i, pp. 69 ff., and E. Rohloff, *Der Musiktraktat des Johannes de Grocheo* (Leipzig, 1943).
[57] Friedrich Gennrich's transcription (from *MGG*, ii, col. 1082).
[58] Perhaps from the Latin *tropator*, a maker of melodies; the derivation from *trobar*, to find, like the French form *trouvère*, seems to be an etymological detour.

noble audiences with *chansons de geste*, humorous accounts of his military misfortunes.[59] A few of his poems, fairly scabrous, have survived but only one scrap of his music – preserved accidentally in a fourteenth-century *Jeu de sainte Agnès*. Yet this scrap,[60] for a poem of farewell, is fascinating, for it is nearly identical with the opening of the melody of the 'St. Martial' 'Annus novus in gaudio' mentioned above; the whole of Guillaume's poem could be sung to the St. Martial melody. Affinities with ecclesiastical music are also shown in the four surviving melodies of Marcabru[61] who enjoyed the patronage of William's son, William X, until the latter's death in 1137, although the affinities are obscured in modern transcriptions (based on theories which will be explained in the next chapter).

Neither William IX nor Marcabru supports that just emerging cult of 'courtly love' for unattainable mistresses which was to become so important in later troubadour verse; in fact, Marcabru actually attacks it in his 'Dirai vos senes duptansa' (I shall tell you without delay).[62] It was under William X's remarkable daughter, Eleanor, who became queen of France, then of England, and mother of Richard Lionheart, that *amour courtois* first flourished and was first sung by Jaufré Rudel 'de Blaia', who like Eleanor went on the Second Crusade (1147–8); Jaufré's 'Lanquan li jorn son lonc en mai' (When the days are long in May)[63] is a classic expression of 'L'amor de lonh' (love from afar). It is also melodically sophisticated; the music of lines 1 and 2 of each strophe is repeated for 3 and 4, transposed a fifth higher for 5, and returns through 6 to the original pitch for 7. Technical ingenuity and subtlety were, from the first, characteristic of troubadour poetry and music, which reached a much fuller flowering during the latter part of the twelfth century. It was the art of a closed, aristocratic society.

The troubadours frequently sang their own songs but there is a strange lack of evidence that they accompanied their songs or played instruments at all. But the low-class wandering professional entertainers disapproved of by the Church, of whom we first hear about the ninth century, the *joculatores* or *jongleurs* who were known all over Europe – as *Gaukler* in Germany, as *skomorokhi* in Russia (already in 1068 according to Nestor's Chronicle) – and who performed everywhere, from court and castle to village inn, were both singers and players on all sorts of instruments, often the bowed *vielle*, as well as jugglers and bear-leaders. Some settled in the service of aristocrats and may have accompanied their masters' songs, though how they did so is another completely open question; there is no evidence earlier than the thirteenth century.[64] And no doubt they not only performed the *chansons de*

---

[59] On which see Steven Runciman, *A History of the Crusades* (Harmondsworth, 1965), ii, pp. 27–33.
[60] See Alfred Jeanroy, *Le jeu de sainte Agnès* (Paris, 1931), p. 72, for a transcription by Théodore Gérold.
[61] All four transcribed in Gennrich, *Lo Gai Saber* (Darmstadt, 1959), pp. 1–5; other transcriptions of his lament for William X in *NOHM*, ii, p. 229, and *HAM*, i, No. 18(a).
[62] *Gai Saber*, p. 2; another transcription in Adler, *Handbuch*, i, p. 189.
[63] Transcriptions of the version in Bibl. Nat. fr. 22543 in *Gai Saber*, p. 6, and Gérold, *Histoire de la Musique des origines à la fin du XIVe siècle* (Paris, 1936), p. 275; of the version in Bibl. Nat. fr. 20050 in *MGG*, vi, col. 1783.
[64] See below, p. 101.

geste but also gave wider circulation to some of the aristocratic songs they picked up in the course of their wanderings.

6

Music of the Proto-Renaissance

Cultural historians have long familiarized us with the notion of a 'twelfth-century renaissance'. When they consider music they think at once of the great flowering of troubadour song which reflected and perhaps stimulated the concept of 'chivalry' in the same way that the contemporary Arthurian romances did, while the musician lays more emphasis on the music fostered by the new French cathedrals. Yet while we know the mere names and very little else of only two French masters of cathedral music, we not only know the names and often the precise dates and other biographical details of a great number of the poet-composers, but we have their works in almost overwhelming quantity.[1]

The troubadours – Bernart de Ventadorn (*c*. 1125–95) and the rather younger Peire Vidal, Raïmbaut de Vaqueiras, and Giraut de Borneill (to take only a few outstanding names) – flourished until the horrors of the Albigensian Crusade of 1209–29 ferociously extinguished the high culture of Provence and Languedoc. But their art had already spread north, thanks in part to the influence of Eleanor of Aquitaine, who in the course of her matrimonial adventures took Bernart de Ventadorn with her, first to the French court, then to England (in 1154–5). Her own son, Richard Lion-heart, was a trouvère, a troubadour employing French instead of Provençal – a song made in captivity at Dürrenstein is preserved in the Chansonnier Cangé (Bibl. Nat. fr. 846). So was his legendary rescuer, Blondel de Nesle.[2] To the same generation belong Conon de Béthune, the 'Chastelain de Couci', and the immensely prolific Gace Brulé. Colin Muset and Moniot de'Arras strike a more popular note, while at the other end of the social scale was the activity of Thibaut de Champagne, later King of Navarre, and Henry III of Brabant, in the first half of the following century.

Nor was the influence of such poetry and music limited to France. Dynastic marriages alone would have sufficed to promote a unity of European culture and the ideas, poetry, and music of *l'amour courtois* quickly became naturalized in the German-speaking lands as *Minne*. When Frederick Barbarossa's sons were admitted to the order of knighthood at Mainz in

---

[1] There are plenty of easily accessible transcriptions, e.g. in *NOHM*, ii, pp. 229ff., *HAM*, i, Nos. 18ff., *OAM(M)*, Nos. 14ff., and Friedrich Gennrich, *Troubadours, Trouvères, Minne- und Meistergesang* (in the series *Das Musikwerk*) (Cologne, 1951).
[2] His final captor, the emperor Henry VI, was a *Minnesänger*.

1184, French and German knights competed in the festivities and those present included the trouvère Guiot de Provins and the earliest of the great German singers of *Minne*, Friedrich von Husen (d. 1190). Friedrich's song 'Iche denke under wîlen' is based on the melody of Guiot's 'Ma joie premeraine' and in four other cases he took songs by Bernart de Ventadorn, Folquet de Marseilles, Conon de Béthune, and an anonymous composer as his models. Quite a number of *Minnelieder* are similarly based on melodies of French or Provençal origin and sometimes freely adapt the sense of the words as well. Even the most famous of all the *Minnesänger*, Walther von der Vogelweide (*c.* 1170–*c.* 1230), a 'wandering singer', made such contrafacta of Jaufré Rudel's 'Lanquan li jorn', mentioned in the last chapter, and songs by Bernart de Ventadorn and Blondel.[3] Walther's younger contemporary, Neidhart von Reuental, and the considerably later Heinrich von Meissen (nicknamed 'Frauenlob', praiser of women) (d. 1318) do not appear to have employed this practice. But there is nothing surprising about these German contrafacta, for the French themselves interchanged Provençal and French texts or added Latin ones[4] to favourite melodies. Bernart de Ventadorn's 'Quan vei l'aloete',[5] one of the most popular of all medieval songs, exists not only with melodic variants but with a different Provençal text and two French texts, one of which is a translation of a well-known 'contest between heart and eyes', 'Quisquis cordis et oculi', also set to Bernart's melody, by Philippe, chancellor of the Paris churches from 1218 to 1236.[6]

CANTIGAS, LAUDI, AND ENGLISH SONG

Provençal song also survived in the south, despite the crusade against the Albigensian heretics, at the courts of Castile and Aragon; for instance, the last of the famous troubadours, Guiraut Riquier (*c.* 1239–*c.* 1300), enjoyed the patronage of the half-German Alfonso X 'el Sabio' (the learned), King of Castile and Leon from 1252 to 1284. Alfonso himself was responsible for the collection and probably to some extent for the composition of some thirty secular *Cantigas de Amore e de Maldizer* and more than four hundred *Cantigas de Santa Maria* devoted to the miracles, and praise, of the Virgin, preserved in superbly illuminated manuscripts with miniatures depicting players of every conceivable medieval instrument: the bowed rabāb (of Moorish origin) and somewhat similar rebec, the vielle, guitar- and lute-like instruments, double-shawms, bladder-pipes, trumpets, tuned bells, and so on, in rich variety (see pl. 29).[7] There is no demonstrable trace of Moorish influence in the music, as distinct from the instruments; the melodic affinities are with *chanson courtois* (courtly song) and church music, and there are a few

---

[3] See Gennrich, *Mittelhochdeutsche Liedkunst* (Darmstadt, 1954), pp. xviii–xx; for another of his *contrafacta* see *OAM(M)*, No. 31.
[4] See Gennrich, *Lateinische Liedkontrafaktur* (Darmstadt, 1956).
[5] Quoted in *NOHM*, ii, p. 236; another version in *OAM(M)*, No. 62.
[6] See Gennrich in *ZfMW*, vii (1924–5), p. 68, and xi (1928–9), p. 322, for tabular comparisons.
[7] Complete edition of the *Cantigas* by Higini Anglès in three vols. (facsimile, transcription, and notes) (Barcelona, 1943–51); examples of *cantigas* in *NOHM*, ii, pp. 262–6 and *OAM(M)*, Nos. 28 and 29.

contrafacta from those sources, but there is an occasional whiff of Spanish popular music as in 'Como poden per sas culpas'.[8] More decidedly popular are the contemporary Italian *laudi spirituali*, a product of the Franciscan movement, closer in spirit to the jongleurs than to *chanson courtois*: St. Francis himself suggested that his followers should be 'joculatores Dei'.

Pl. 29   Miniatures in the *Cantigas de Santa Maria* of Alfonso X of Castile, showing players of the *guitarra morisca*, *rabāb* and lute, pipe and tabor, and tuned bells.

As for English song, the literary 'vernacular' up to the middle of the thirteenth century was Norman French. Although it includes an attractive love-song 'Bryd one brere'[9] and one piece, 'Worldes blis',[10] the deeply felt pessimism of which contrasts strongly with the mostly artificial despair of courtly song, the quantity of written down and preserved early Middle English song is pitifully small. One should perhaps qualify this by saying 'written down with music'; even in that celebrated late-thirteenth-century anthology of international song collected at the monastery of

[8] Quoted in *NOHM*, ii, p. 263.
[9] Gennrich, *Aus der Formenwelt de Mittelalters* (Darmstadt, 1953), p. 26.
[10] *NOHM*, ii, p. 251.

Benediktbeuren, the *Carmina Burana* – satires, songs to be danced to, songs of love and drinking, songs of goliards and trouvères and *Minnesänger*, some named but mostly anonymous, generally Latin but some in a Bavarian dialect – only a small proportion have their melodies, though these can sometimes be provided from concordances in other sources.[11]

COURTLY SONG: ITS TYPES, FORMS, AND PERFORMANCE

The same types recur in the courtly song of Provence, northern France, and German: not only perennial types like the *canso* (love-song) and *planh* (plaint), but such peculiar ones as the *sirventès* (literally, 'of service') or German *Spruch*, with a political or moral content; the *tenso* and *jeu parti*, both forms of dialogue but the latter specifically concerned with love; the *alba*, *aube*, or *Tagelied*, a dialogue between a lover and the friend who keeps watch for him. Some of the musico-poetic forms, however, were to survive for some time longer. Leaving aside those which are set to a *vers* (continuous melody), not really forms at all, we find a number of forms: that later known as the *ballade* or German *Bar*, basically *AAB* (two *pedes* and a *cauda*), or *AABA* or *AABB*, in which the first *pes* may be *vert* (open), the second *clos* (closed); the similar but much less common *rotrouenge*, which may have an internal refrain; and the German *Leich*, with repeated versicles – often more than two – on the lines of the ecclesiastical sequence.[12] And, as Jacques Handschin was the first to point out,[13] this same form of sequence or lai was also employed without words in the *estampie*, of which the earliest known example has been preserved by the chance that when two French *joglares* played it at the court of Boniface II of Montferrat, the marquis's sister begged Raïmbaut de Vaqueiras, who was in love with her, to set words to it. He sang the well-known 'Kalenda maya' (Neither the first of May, nor the leaf of the beech, nor birdsong . . .)[14] and, says his biographer, 'aquesta 'stampida fo facha a las notas de la 'stampida quel joglar fasion en las violas' (this '*stampida* was made on the tune the *joglars* played on the viols). Thus the estampie could be a purely instrumental piece and, like the virelai, it could be danced to. All these musico-poetic forms were naturally susceptible to an almost infinite variety of modifications.

The actual melodic material of courtly song, like the melodies of church music, makes a great deal of use of formulae that recur in a number of songs; indeed, the formulae are often identical with those of church music.[15] The notation shows the melodic outlines clearly enough but, except in one of the latest important collections of trouvère songs, the already-mentioned

[11] See Hans Spanke, 'Der Codex Buranus als Liederbuch', *ZfMW*, xiii (1930–1), p. 241.
[12] See above, p. 89. A new type of rhymed sequence was devised between *c.* 1130 and *c.* 1180 by an Augustinian canon, Adam, of the Parisian Abbey of St. Victor.
[13] 'Über Estampie und Sequenz I', *ZfMW*, xii (1929–30), p. 1.
[14] Pierre Aubry, *Trouvères et Troubadours* (Paris, 1909), pp. 54ff., for the whole story. 'Kalenda maya' has often been printed, e.g. in *HAM*, i, No. 18(d).
[15] See the tabulated examples in Theodore Karp, 'Borrowed Material in Trouvère Music', *Acta Musicologica*, xxxiv (1962), p. 87.

Chansonnier Cangé (*c.* 1300),[16] the notation is not mensural. Even in the Cangé collection, which contains songs by Thibaut de Navarre, Gace Brulé, the 'Chastelain de Couci', and others, it is by no means unambiguous. The Chansonnier does, however, give us the first known example of what appears to be an instrumental accompaniment added to a melody (see pl. 30) – as distinct from a melody composed above a pre-existent cantus firmus – though this assumption could at once be upset by identification of the instrumental part with some ecclesiastical melody. The quotation shows only the *pedes* of the first stanza of the ballade:

Pl. 30

Ex. 16

Bien m'ont   a - mors   en - tre - - pris,   Je   crois
Car   la   nuit quant   voi dor - - mir,   Et   je

n'i   por - - ` rai du - - rer;
me   cuit   re - po - - ser;

etc.

[16] Published complete in two vols., facsimile and not altogether satisfactory transcription, by J.-B. Beck (Paris, 1927). The transcription in Ex. 16 is Handschin's, *Schweizerisches Jahrbuch für Musikwissenschaft*, ii (1927), p. 40.

6. Music of the Proto-Renaissance

It is now generally agreed that the songs of the troubadours and trouvères were probably sung in one or another of the 'rhythmic modes' (one of which has been suggested in Ex. 14), already perhaps long familiar but first described in a twelfth-century treatise, *Discantus positio vulgaris*,[17] where the six modes are shown as trochaic, iambic, dactylic, anapaestic, *longae* only, and *breves* only, though the author does not use the Greek metrical terms. But the fairly rigid application of modal rhythm to the trouvère melodies, first advocated independently but almost simultaneously by Pierre Aubry and J. B. Beck in 1908–9, is itself open to differing interpretations,[18] and has been modified by later scholars,[19] and it is questionable how far it should be applied to *Minnelieder* since German verse was measured by its stressed syllables, not by metrical feet.

MENSURATION OF NOTE-VALUES

The author of the *Discantus* gives us useful information on other points. For instance he still regards thirds as dissonant, whereas his probably very near contemporaries, the writer known as 'Anonymous VII' in his *De diversis manieribus in musica mensurabili*[20] and Johannes de Garlandia in his *De musica mensurabili positio*[21] (*c.* 1240), admit them as 'imperfect' consonances. But the crucial matter at this period was not liberalization of the conception of consonance but the measuring – or, rather, notation of the measuring – of note-values. There was now a distinction between *musica mensurabilis* and *musica plana* (music not definitely measured in *longae* and *breves*) though at first the notation was identical: Anonymous VII and the author of the *Discantus* agree that the 'square' notation of the late Aquitanian stylization of the old neume-forms[22] could indicate longae and breves. Thus in measured music the virga indicated a longa, the square punctum a brevis; the rising podatus or pes and falling clivis or flexa are both followed by longae; three-note ligatures are longa-brevis-longa unless (according to the author of the *Discantus*) preceded by a longa, in which case they are brevis-brevis-longa; four-note ligatures are all breves but Anonymous VII says the total value of a four- or five-note ligature is that of a three-note ligature, while the *Discantus* allows five-note ligatures to be outside the mensural pale altogether:

Ex. 17

[17] Included by a Paris Dominican, Hieronymus de Moravia (*c.* 1250), in his *Tractatus de musica* (ed. Simon Cserba, Regensburg, 1935).

But although both authors talk about ligatures and rhythmic modes they do not suggest using one to indicate the other. It is Johannes de Garlandia, perhaps a generation later, though he is obviously only codifying an established practice, who lays down the rules for that: the first and most usual mode will begin with a three-note ligature and proceed by two-note ligatures as far as a vertical dash indicating the *divisio modi* (rest or breathing space) and ending the first *ordo* of the mode, after which the second *ordo* begins, and so on. The second rhythmic mode will proceed in two-note ligatures but end with a three-note one with *values reversed*: brevis-longa-brevis. (Inconstancy bedevils medieval notation generally.) The remaining modes are notated similarly.

THE NOTRE DAME ORGANA

Ligatures were now used mainly for melismata or instrumental music. They are much employed in the works of Leoninus and Perotinus, the two outstanding masters of French cathedral music – 'Notre Dame polyphony' – during this period. We know little of these composers beyond their names, and that little from a treatise *De mensuris et discantu* (*c.* 1275) by an Englishman, Coussemaker's 'Anonymous IV',[23] who tells us that

Master Leoninus was an excellent *organista* who made a great book of organum for the Gradual and Antiphonary, for the augmentation of the divine service. And this was in use up to the time of the great Perotinus, who shortened it and made many better *clausulae* or *puncta*, for he was an excellent composer of *discantus* and better than Leoninus. . . . Indeed this Master Perotinus himself made excellent *quadrupla*, to wit 'Viderunt', 'Sederunt', with abundance of melodic figuration (*cum abundantia colorum*); furthermore, many very celebrated *tripla*, to wit 'Alleluia: Posui adjutorium', 'Nativitas', etc. He also made three-part *conductus* such as 'Salvatoris hodie'; two-part *conductus* such as 'Dum sigillum summi patris'; and simple conductus with many other things, such as 'Beata viscera', 'Justitia', etc. The book or books of Master Perotinus were in use up to the time of Master Robertus de Sabilone, and [especially?] in the choir of the major church of Paris, the Blessed Virgin Mary, and from his time up to the present day.

In the passage preceding this the writer indicates that 'Leo', as he calls him here, was familiar only with the rhythmic-modal notation just described, whereas Perotinus knew the freer form that can be called genuinely 'mensural'. Otherwise we know absolutely nothing about him, though we can make reasonable surmises. Perotinus and his very fine *quadrupla* (four-part organa) are mentioned by Johannes de Garlandia as well as Anonymous IV,

---

[18] See, for instance, *HAM*, i, No. 18(c), showing three readings of Giraut de Borneill's 'Reis glorios'.
[19] See *MGG*, ii, cols. 1143–4, where Aubry's strictly modal transcription of the Chastelain de Couci's famous 'Quant li rosignol jolis' (col. 1140) is compared with that by Gennrich. Beck's transcription in *NOHM*, ii, p. 240, though fairly close to Aubry's, was made from a different source.
[20] Ed. Alberto Gallo in *Corpus Scriptorum de Musica* (in preparation).
[21] Also included in Hieronymus de Moravia.   [22] See pp. 80–1.
[23] *Scriptores*, i, p. 327. Modern edition by Fritz Reckow, *Der Musiktraktat des Anonymus 4 (Beihefte zum AfMW*, iv/v) (Wiesbaden, 1967); English translation by Luther Dittmer (New York, 1959).

but he too is a ghostly figure for whom no fewer than five possible embodiments have been proposed.[24]

Yet we have the *Magnus liber organi* itself in four copies – none, unfortunately, with any claim to be the original:

> Wolfenbüttel, Herzogl. Bibl. 677, commonly known as *W1*.
> Florence, Bibl. Laur., plut. xxix, 1, commonly known as *F*.
> Madrid, Bibl. Nac. 20486.
> Wolfenbüttel, Herzogl. Bibl. 1206, or *W2*.[25]

The most important are *W1* and *F*. Although not the oldest copy, *W1* appears to give us Leoninus's *Magnus liber* most nearly in its original form of 1163–82. It contains two-part organal responds for Antiphonary and Gradual for Office and Mass; some three-part ones, including an 'Alleluia: Nativitas' which is probably the one Anonymous IV attributes to Perotinus; and the four-part 'Viderunt' and 'Sederunt' which are undoubtedly his and can be confidently dated 1198 and 1199 respectively. *W1* was almost certainly compiled in England, probably at Winchester or Ely.[26] In the nearly five hundred folios of the magnificent Florentine copy, probably of French origin, the *Magnus liber* (though considerably augmented) takes up only 82 folios. The Spanish copy is garbled and *W2* has a great many pieces in common with *F*. These four manuscripts are not the only ones containing parts of the *Magnus liber*, nor do they contain the whole body of polyphony preserved from the late twelfth century; some of it originated at Beauvais and Sens; but their importance establishes the central position of Paris so that everything else must be regarded as peripheral.

A brief quotation from the opening of the first duplum of the *Magnus liber*, the antiphon 'Judea et Jerusalem' which at that time was sung at Notre Dame at First Vespers on Christmas Day, will give an idea of the modal-rhythmic style in practice and also illustrate some technical points:

Ex. 18(i)

[24] See Jacques Chailley, *Histoire musicale du moyen age* (Paris, 1950), pp. 158–61.

[25] Facsimiles and transcriptions of *F*, Madrid, and *W2* have been published by Luther Dittmer, *Mediaeval Musical Manuscripts* (New York, 1957–72), x–xi, i, and ii respectively. *W1* was published in facsimile by J. H. Baxter, *An Old St. Andrews Music Book* (London, 1931), and its two-part music transcribed complete in William G. Waite, *The Rhythm of Twelfth-Century Polyphony* (Yale, 1954).
Heinrich Husmann's transcription of the three- and four-part organa is available in *Publikationen älterer Musik*, xi (Leipzig, 1940; reprinted Wiesbaden, 1967) and all the works ascribed to Perotinus by Anonymous IV are given in Ethel Thurston (ed.), *The Works of Perotin* (New York, 1970). There are numerous transcriptions of separate pieces.

[26] For the suggested dating of the *Liber* and its liturgical use, see Heinrich Husmann, 'The Origin and Destination of the *Magnus liber organi*', *MQ*, xlix (1963), p. 311, and on the provenance, idem, 'Zur Frage der Herkunft der Notre-Dame-Handschrift W1' in *Musa-Mens-Musici* (Vetter Festschrift) (Leipzig, 1969), p. 33.

(ii)

Ju-[dea]

(*a*) The regular alternation of breves and longae in modal rhythm led to the conception of the *perfectio*. This was the equivalent of the metrical foot, equal in time-value to brevis-plus-longa or three breves; consequently a single longa sometimes had the value of three breves to fill out a *perfectio* and was known as a *longa perfecta*. Such are the two longae at the beginning (from *W1*; in *F* they are replaced by a single *duplex longa* with a double-length head), indeed all those represented in the transcription by dotted crotchets. On the other hand the penultimate longa of the excerpt has to be shortened. (*b*) The one-flat key-signature is given to the upper part only, not to the lower one because the note B never occurs in it. (*c*) The vertical strokes indicating *divisio modi* were ancestors of the mensural rest and are twice interpreted as such here. (*d*) The first note of the last ligature has a *plica*, an ornament derived from the neumatic *quilisma* (portamento), now taking half the value of the main note; the rhomboid form of punctum was to be used half a century or so later as a semibrevis. (*e*) The sustained F on 'Ju-' in the lower part, the first note of the plainsong melody, is held for six more *perfectiones* (26 in all) before it moves to the second note (on '-de-'). It is difficult to believe that such very long-held notes were not sustained on the instrument most suited for such feats: the organ. The three words 'Judea et Jerusalem' are spread over eighteen notes. They are not all so prolonged, indeed 'et Jerusalem' is set almost syllabically, one note to a perfectio – and the solo section lasts for nearly 70 perfectiones. Only then does the unison chorus take over, singing to what we may now call plainsong, not strictly measured song, the words 'nolite timere: cras egrediemini, et Dominus erit vobiscum', which are, of course, omitted from the manuscript sources; after this the duplum is resumed with 'Constantes estote. Videbitis auxilium Domini super vos'.

Few examples of modal rhythm are as straightforward as 'Judea et Jerusalem' but even so alternative readings of the notation are possible; indeed the interpretation of modal rhythm has proved in modern times as debatable as the counting of angels on a needle-point.[27] But it should always be borne in mind that not only during the Middle Ages but for centuries after them the conception of a single 'correct' method of performance did

[27] For a conspectus, see H. H. Eggebrecht, 'Organum purum', *Musikalische Edition im Wandel des historischen Bewusstseins* (ed. T. G. Georgiades) (Kassel, 1971), p. 93.

not yet exist. There were obviously inadmissible ways but a choice of admissible ones. Thus Garlandia[28] mentions the use of instruments in Perotinus's quadrupla only casually – the parts sometimes lie too high or too low for the human voice, he observes – with no hint *how* they were used.

THREE- AND FOUR-PART HARMONY

The tripla and quadrupla also confront us with the earliest stage of three- and four-part harmony. Here again Garlandia and his more or less contemporary colleagues find difficulty in codifying composers' practice. The triplum – meaning here not a three-part composition but the 'third' voice, the treble – must be consonant with the first two voices within *duplex diapason* (within the second octave). (Franco of Cologne, a little later, says that when the treble is discordant with the descant it should be concordant with the tenor, and vice versa.) As for the fourth part, Garlandia observes that it is sometimes called *duplex discantus* because one perceives 'two alternately now with one, now with the other' voice (*quia duo invicem nunc cum uno nunc cum reliquo*). His 'first rule' for the fourth voice is that in the first mode all its longae must be consonant with all the longae of the three lower voices; his second is that it must rise or fall now with the treble, now with the descant.

In Perotinus's two great quadrupla, new not only in their resources but in their vast scale – lasting perhaps twenty minutes – the notes of the plainsong are often in fact reduced to mere bases for musical architecture, whatever the theory that the added parts were merely embellishments of a sacred object, the divinely inspired 'Gregorian' melody. And the embellishments themselves were organized with more artifice. Leoninus had already shown a sense of descant organization in advance of the wayward arabesques of St. Martial: e.g. a three-note motive repeated in descending steps or a repetition of a more extended pattern:[29]

Ex. 19

Di-[es]

These are nothing more than formulae but their employment in this way is none the less suggestive of a sense of organization. Multiplication of added parts opened up further possibilities: interchange of phrases between different parts, sometimes at different pitch, and that overlapping of interchange which was to lead to canonic imitation and fugue. Peter Wagner

[28] Coussemaker, op. cit., i, p. 116.
[29] 'Alleluia: Dies sanctificatus', in the transcription by Waite, op. cit., p. 74.

and Handschin found a monophonically written hymn, in the 'St. Martial' manuscript Bibl. Nat. lat. 1139 and other sources, capable of two-part performance with complete interchange for alternate lines of text;[30] and an easily accessible example of overlapping interchange occurs in the three-part 'Haec dies' in *W1*.[31] But Perotinus goes much farther in combining interchange with repetition of short motives, as in these two excerpts from the versus 'Notum fecit' of the four-part setting of the Nativity Gradual 'Viderunt omnes':[32]

Ex. 20

[30] *ZfMW*, xvi (1934), p. 119.   [31] *HAM*, i, No. 31.
[32] From Marius Schneider's transcription, 'Zur Satztechnik der Notre-Dame Schule', *ZfMW*, xiv (1932), p. 398.

CONDUCTUS

Perotinus's two great quadrupla are only the most imposing part of his contribution to the *Magnus liber*. Anonymous IV says he made 'many *clausulae* or *puncta*' and three-part, two-part, and 'simple' conductus. Conductus 'properly means a song for escorting: in particular, a song for a ceremonial procession. The occasion for it might arise in the liturgy whenever an official moved from one place to another to perform a liturgical function' but it 'came to signify generally a song with a text in verse form, used in the liturgy as a transition to a particular function or to precede the end of the service'.[33] By the 'Notre Dame' period it had also passed into secular use. Both verse and music were freely composed and strophic. The conductus first appeared about 1100 in the 'St. Martial' group of manuscripts and quickly became polyphonic. Although Perotinus clearly composed the two parts of his 'Dum sigillum' simultaneously, the lower part – or rather the lowest *written* part – was generally conceived first. Conceived or borrowed: for in a number of cases the basic part, or the only part of a monodic conductus, is a Latin contrafactum of a French or Provençal courtly or popular song, many of the Latin poems (including Perotinus's 'simple conductus' 'Beata viscera') being the work of the already mentioned Parisian Chancellor Philippe.[34] Essentially the added parts are note-against-note, though often slightly ornamented, and the syllabic passages – notated mainly in longae according to the convention of the period and probably meant to be sung in modal rhythm – sometimes alternate with melismatic ones which, if prolonged and textless, are what Anonymous IV calls *caudae*.[35]

FROM CLAUSULA TO MOTET

The clausulae with which Perotinus is credited originated in those passages of organum such as the setting of 'et Jerusalem' in 'Judea et Jerusalem' where the plainsong melody instead of being endlessly prolonged moves at a pace of one note to a perfection. Such passages in so-called 'descant' style broke up the polyphonic composition into sections which could be removed and new ones substituted; this is what Anonymous IV appears to say that Perotinus did with Leoninus's organa in the *Magnus liber*, generally with the descant sections but sometimes, as in 'Haec dies', with those originally set in *organum purum*.[36] But if clausulae originated as substitute passages, they

---

[33] *NOHM*, ii, p. 172.
[34] See above, p. 98. On the contrafacta, see Gennrich, *Lateinische Liedkontrafaktur* (21 conductus with secular originals, in 'diplomatic' notation), and his 'Internationale mittelalterliche Melodien', *ZfMW*, xi (1928–9), pp. 259 and 321.
[35] Examples of Notre Dame conductus are easily available in *HAM*, i: monophonic, Nos. 17(c) from *W2* – Perotinus's 'Beata viscera' – and (d) from *F*; two- and three-part, Nos. 38 and 39, from *W1*. Also in *OAM(M)*, Nos. 13 and 51. Others in two and three parts in Husmann, *Die mittelalterliche Mehrstimmigkeit (Das Musikwerk)*, (Cologne, n.d.), Nos. 8–11. A selection of *Thirty-five Conductus for two and three voices* has been edited by Janet Knapp (Yale, 1965).
[36] *HAM*, i, Nos. 28(c), (d), (e), and (h) ('Benedicamus Domino') and Nos. 29, 30 and 31 ('Haec dies'), all from *W1*. Further clausulae for 'Haec dies', from *F* and *W2*, in Husmann, *Mittelalterliche*

quickly established themselves as self-sufficient pieces inserted at suitable places in the church service very much as the sacred conductus were. And as such they quickly acquired a new dimension; at first vocalized on single syllables, they were given words of their own and thus became polyphonic tropes.[37]

Polyphonic tropes can be traced at least from the St. Martial period; the manuscript Bibl. Nat. lat. 1139 preserves Christmas tropes, 'Stirps Jesse' and 'Organa laetitiae', sung against the melody of 'Benedicamus Domino' in long note-values.[38] But the clausula with words, the motet, differed not only in musical style – for instance, the plainsong broken up in short repeated patterns based on one or other of the rhythmic modes – but in that the words were, at first, added to pre-existent music. Again, as with the conductus, a number of the Latin texts are known to have been supplied by the Chancellor Philippe. Indeed the two genres, clausula or early motet and conductus, were by no means unrelated. When in a clausula or early motet other parts were added as well as the duplum (or motetus), they were in the same rhythmic mode and, in the case of a motet, to the same words, just as in conductus. Six motets in manuscript *F* actually appear in *W1* as conductus; they have simply lost their tenors. For instance, *F* contains a two-part clausula 'Latus est' – from the Alleluia 'Pascha nostrum immo*latus est* Christus' – which elsewhere is given a third and fourth part and the words 'Latex silice mel petra profluit' (the identity or echo of the initial syllable being highly typical of motet-texts); *W1* gives duplum, triplum, and quadruplum only.[39] Conversely, cases are known of conductus with caudae which are in fact borrowed or specially composed clausulae.[40] And just as a conductus might be based on a vernacular song-tune, by the middle of the thirteenth century vernacular – and very secular – texts were written to clausulae.[41]

THE MONTPELLIER CODEX

The thirteenth-century motet is a remarkable synthesis of the ecclesiastical and secular music of the twelfth century, of outstanding consequence as the main medium through which polyphony passed into profane use. Its genealogy can be traced in popular anthologies[42] and its development in a

Mehrstimmigkeit, No. 4(b), pp. 22–3; the two-part 'bo[-nus]' clausula, (b)3, is practically identical with the two lower parts of the corresponding three-part clausula in *HAM*, i, No. 31.

[37] See above, p. 90. [38] See Amédée Gastoué, *Les Primitifs de la musique française* (Paris, 1922), p. 15, and *MGG*, xi, facing col. 1265, ex. 11.

[39] See Gennrich, *Aus der Frühzeit der Motette*, ii (Langen bei Frankfurt, 1963), pp. 20, 31, and 30.

[40] See Manfred Bukofzer, 'Interrelations between Conductus and Clausula', *Annales musicologiques*, i (Paris, 1953), p. 65.

[41] See the collection of 40 clausulae from the Abbey of St. Victor, with incipits of motet texts written in the margin, given in facsimile in Gennrich, *Sankt Viktor Clausulae und ihre Motetten* (Darmstadt, 1953). Eighteen of the actual motets appear in *W2*, and it is not impossible that these particular clausulae are motets stripped of their words, perhaps for instrumental performance, instead of vice versa.

[42] That from 'Benedicamus Domino' in *HAM*, i, No. 28, that from 'Haec dies', ibid. Nos. 29–32, and Husmann, *Mittelalterliche Mehrstimmigkeit*, No. 4; more exhaustively in Gennrich, *Perotinus Magnus: Das Organum 'Alleluja Nativitas gloriose virginis Marie' und seine Sippe* (Darmstadt, 1955), which gives both Leoninus and Perotinus versions, with contrafacta, clausulae, and motets in facsimile or diplomatic transcription.

number of important collections, of which the largest – Parisian in origin – is Montpellier, Faculté de Médecine, H 196 (generally known as *Mo*),[43] the first six fascicles of which date from *c.* 1280, the seventh from *c.* 1300 and eighth from *c.* 1310. The first fascicle includes six organa (two by Perotinus), a conductus, and three pieces in the curious *hoquetus* style – one part ejaculating single notes separated by rests, while another voice supplies complementary rests and notes – sometimes introduced near the end of Notre Dame clausulae and now employed through a whole piece. But the rest of the codex consists almost entirely of motets, more than two hundred in fascicles 2–6 alone. While fascicle 1 is written in score, the parts aligned above each other, the remaining fascicles are laid out as in other post Notre-Dame motet manuscripts: the upper parts in parallel columns, with the instrumental tenor at the bottom of the page, its free use of ligatures making it very economical of space. Clearly this was music for the diversion of solo performers, highly cultivated clerics or even laymen, members of the University of Paris. Some of the Latin motets, e.g. *Mo*, No. 64, 'Post partum virgo mansisti/Ave, regina glorie/Veritatem', for the Assumption of the Virgin, are church music but very many are not.

DEVELOPMENTS IN THE MOTET

Although none of the motet collections is arranged conveniently for us in rough chronological order, it is possible to trace developments. The 'conductus-motet' with motetus and triplum singing the same text in the same rhythm soon disappeared; as early as the Notre Dame codex *F* one finds a double-motet on the tenor 'Et gaudebit' over which the motetus sings the praises of the prelates while the triplum in different verse-metre and musical rhythm denounces the 'hypocritical pseudo-priests',[44] no doubt sung with relish. The next step was the introduction of vernacular texts, practically all French of course, though there are a few in Provençal, and the earliest English example 'Worldes blise have god day/Benedicamus Domino' appeared *c.* 1280.[45] Sometimes, as throughout fasc. 3 of *Mo*, Latin moteti have French tripla. In fasc. 5 in most cases both upper parts are in French and one actually has a French tenor (notated entirely in breves), a rare example of something that was to become not uncommon by the end of the century. In fasc. 2 there is, still more exceptionally, a motet in four parts all with French texts (the tenor notated entirely in longae). But interchange of language, particularly in the tripla, was common throughout the motet

[43] Published in facsimile, with transcription and commentary by Yvonne Rokseth, *Polyphonies du XIIIe siècle* (Paris, four vols., 1935–9). Other large collections of motets, containing numerous concordances with *Mo* and with each other, include La Clayette (Paris, Bibl. nat., nouv. acq. fr. 13521) (*c.* 1270: ed. Dittmer, *Mediaeval Musical Manuscripts*, iv (New York, 1959)); Bamberg, Staatsbibl. Ed. iv. 6 (*c.* 1300: ed. Aubry, *Cent Motets du XIIIe siècle* (Paris, three vols. 1908)); and Burgos (*c.* 1300: ed. Anglès, *El Còdex musical de Las Huelgas* (Barcelona, three vols., 1931).
[44] Husmann, *Mittelalterliche Mehrstimmigkeit*, No. 6(b), and *OAM(M)*, No. 44. The tenor comes from an Alleluia verse for the Sunday within the Octave of the Ascension: 'Vado, et venio ad vos, *et gaudebit cor vestrum*'.
[45] Printed by Manfred Bukofzer, *M & L*, xvii (1936), p. 232.

repertory: one finds Latin contrafacta of French texts and vice versa. It is not unusual to find tripla removed altogether, as well as added; the simple motetus was, of course, in effect a solo song with accompaniment and French motets of this kind were very popular during the first half of the thirteenth century; their Latin contrafacta perhaps represent a vain attempt (*c.* 1205–30) to 'stem the tide of secular composition that threatened to sunder the close connection that had hitherto existed between organum, clausula and motet composition and the liturgy'.[46]

The basis of 'Ypocrite/Velut stelle/Et gaudebit' is a clausula, also in *F*,[47] the duplum wordless, the tenor played twice as in the motet. *W2* has a version of this in which the duplum has become a motetus with a text beginning 'Virgo, virginum regina', and also a secular double-motet in which the motetus has Provençal words, a song of unhappy love, while the new triplum sings in French of happy love. Actually the commonest form of the piece has a motetus beginning 'O quam sancta', with or without the 'Ypocrite' triplum. In the St. Victor collection of clausulae it appears in two parts with the Provençal text written in the margin, and is immediately followed by a version with no suggested text, the tenor played only once but both parts then continuing quite differently from any motet version.

THE INSTRUMENTAL MOTET

It is not unreasonable to suppose that this last version of the motet on 'O quam sancta' was intended for purely instrumental performance, as indeed the whole St. Victor collection may have been; they are written in score. And there is supporting evidence. Of the favourite tenors, differently fragmented and rhythmized, which were used again and again for quite different motets, few occur more often than 'In saeculum' from the already-mentioned Easter Sunday gradual 'Haec dies' ('quoniam *in saeculum* misericordia ejus'). At the beginning of *Mo* there is a four-part piece on this tenor; the quadruplum has a French text while duplum and triplum are both textless and marked 'In seculum' although not based on the melody. But this is not a solo song with three-part instrumental accompaniment; in the Bamberg codex the 'accompaniment' appears without the quadruplum as 'In seculum breve'. This codex contains four more of these three-part wordless 'motets' on 'In saeculum' written in score unlike normal motets, one of which is actually styled 'In seculum viellatoris' – 'Vielle-player's In seculum':[48]

Ex. 21

In seculum

[46] Gordon A. Anderson, *M & L*, l (1969), p. 161.   [47] Husmann's No. 6(a).

The three textless pieces in Brit. Lib., Harley 978, the mid-thirteenth-century English manuscript which also preserves 'Sumer is icumen in', have their two parts marked 'Cantus superior' and 'Cantus inferior' and are almost certainly instrumental.[49] So possibly were the textless caudae of conductus. While it would be absurd to suggest that all textless music was instrumental, the notation of *musica sine littera* with its free employment of ligatures was the basis for the systematic mensural notation of Franco of Cologne, whose *Ars cantus mensurabilis*[50] seems to have been written before 1267.[51]

INTERRELATION OF UPPER PARTS

By the end of the twelfth century Perotinus had sensed the importance of the short motive in melodic line and the possibility of relating upper parts to each other by common motives and by interchanging melodic lines between voices (see Ex. 20). In the course of the thirteenth century these techniques were frequently employed, though the tenor of the motet was never involved in them. A hilarious example is the French double-motet in *W2* where, over the tenor 'Balaam [de quo vaticinans]' from an Epiphany sequence, motetus and triplum make fun of the 'goudaliers'[52] ('Lie en sont engliskeman') who have 'fait escoterie' before Arras. However the land of good ale also produced some striking examples of thirteenth-century polyphony, notably the third piece from the Harleian manuscript, an extended instrumental composition. The principal melody is in the form of an estampie:[53] pairs of 'four-bar' puncti – reckoning two perfectiones to a modern 6/8 bar – the first of the pair with an 'open', the second with a 'closed' ending. It is given first to the cantus inferior and repeated with a different counterpoint, then transposed up a fifth and given to the upper voice with a new counterpoint in the lower, repeated with a different counterpoint, and repeated again in a slightly ornamented form with yet another counterpoint. (The second piece is similar but less tightly organized and lacking the final pair of ornamented puncti.) Of special interest is the near identity of the opening of the first transposed punctus with Walter Odington's example of conductus,[54] which he also relates to the peculiarly English rondellus with its complete inter-changeability of all three parts, in his *De speculatione musicae* (probably *c.* 1316):

---

[48] Aubry, *Cent Motets*, ii, No. 105; No. 108 is also given in *HAM*, i, No. 32(e). The bar in Aubry's transcription is the equivalent of a perfectio. *HAM*, No. 32(d) is another 'In seculum' motet showing the curious practice of 'grafting' the verbal and musical refrains of trouvère songs on to the end of dupla and moteti; in No. 28(i) III only the motetus has the 'graft'.

[49] The first two are printed in *HAM*, i, No. 41(a) and (b); facs. in Apel, *Notation*, p. 247.

[50] *Scriptores*, i, p. 117; reproduced by Gennrich with two of Coussemaker's manuscript sources in facsimile (Darmstadt, 1957); see below, p. 114.

[51] *MGG*, iv, col. 693.

[52] *Godailleur* is still a colloquial word for tippler.

[53] See above, p. 100.

[54] Coussemaker, *Scriptores*, i, p. 247, and *Corpus Scriptorum de Musica* 14 (ed. F. F. Hammond); facs. in *Early English Harmony* (ed. H. E. Wooldridge) (London, 1897), pl. 41.

Ex. 22

(i) Harley 978

etc.

(ii) *De speculatione musicae*

Here we have something like an English musical dialect, manifest also in the rondellus-like 'Sumer is icumen in' – though in that the upper parts enter successively instead of simultaneously – which is at the same time a species of motet since, as Frank Harrison has pointed out, the lower part of the two-part *pes* is taken from the Marian antiphon, 'Regina caeli laetare'.

SECULAR TENORS

Actually the motet itself became less dependent on plainsong tenors toward the latter part of the thirteenth century; more than a quarter of the motets in the two later fascicles of *Mo*, 7 and 8, have secular tenors such as the often quoted cry of the Parisian seller of strawberries and blackberries – with motetus and triplum singing the other delights of the city.[55] A number of English motets in the so-called 'Worcester fragments' appear to have newly composed tenors and the previously quoted 'accompanied song' from the Chansonnier Cangé (Ex. 16), very nearly contemporary with *Mo*, fasc. 7, may well be another example of the same thing.

Musically more important was the development of the tripla; from a very early stage they had tended to be livelier than the moteti and the increasing use of secular texts encouraged this tendency with ornamentation, dance-like or irregular rhythms, and – owing to the nature of the French language – shorter note-values. For these the diamond-shaped puncta of the Notre Dame conjuncturae were employed as semibreves, fractions of the brevis though by no means necessarily halves. Groups of three or even more semibreves, usually at first descending scalewise like conjuncturae, had the value of one brevis.

[55] *HAM*, i, No. 33(b).

FRANCONIAN NOTATION

In the course of the thirteenth century rhythm became freer in that more and more liberties were taken with the six modes until there was little or no distinction between them and they merged into a general *modus perfectus*, our modern triple time. The introduction of smaller note-values also necessitated a slowing of the pulse, so that the 'beat' unit was no longer the perfectio of three tempora (breves) but the brevis itself. The *longa perfecta* of the *modus perfectus* was thus equal in value to three breves. But it was regarded as 'imperfected', though still notated in precisely the same way, by a brevis (or two semibreves) following or preceding it within the perfectio. This led to a modus in which *longae imperfectae*, equal to only two breves, were normal. Music began occasionally to be conceived in *modus imperfectus*, our modern duple time.

A great step forward in the systematization of notation was taken by Franco of Cologne in his already-mentioned *Ars cantus mensurabilis*. Still thinking in terms of *modus perfectus*, though he recognizes the obsolescence of the six modes, he explains how seemingly irregular successions of notes are to be sorted into perfectiones. If, for instance, a longa is followed by four breves, the first brevis will imperfect it and the three others will form a perfectio in themselves; if a longa is followed by five breves, the fifth imperfects the longa that follows it; in some circumstances a brevis may be doubled (*brevis altera*) to fill out a proportio. Franco also gives rules for the grouping of semibreves, pairs of which are in his system major and minor, 2/3 and 1/3 of a brevis, not 1/2 and 1/2. Most important of all, he codified the system of ligatures, which had already begun to undergo certain changes, to enable them to indicate patterns other than the simple brevis-longa and longa-brevis-longa shown in Ex. 17. These original forms were said to have *proprietas* and *perfectio*. Franco proposed systematic changes depriving the first note of its proprietas (making it a longa), or the last note of its perfectio (making it a brevis). Thus the initial note of the ascending ligature in Ex. 17(ii) could be given a stroke or the initial of the descending ligature deprived of its stroke. Either change would make it a longa. Similarly the final note of a ligature could be deprived of its perfectio by turning it to the right instead of left (ascending) or making it oblique (descending); this converted it to a brevis. Middle notes of three-note ligatures are breves. An upward stroke to the initial of a ligature makes the first and second notes semibreves. Other points in Franco's system are the use of a dot, the *punctus perfectionis*, where necessary to clarify the separation of *perfectiones*, and a methodical treatment of the old vertical dash indicating *divisio modi*[56] to show the length of rests. A dash extended over three spaces for the perfect-longa rest, over two for the imperfect, over one for the brevis, and still shorter ones marked major and minor semibreve rests.

It naturally took some time before Franconian notation was generally known and adopted, although some of its features had been in use before

[56] See p. 103.

him. It does not appear in *Mo* until the seventh and eighth fascicles, forty years after his treatise. The first two motets of fasc. 7, ascribed to one Petrus de Cruce – probably the Amiens *magister* who in 1298 was paid for composing an Office for St. Louis after the king's canonization – actually go further than Franco. Petrus introduces in the tripla of his motets groups of up to seven semibreves in the value of a brevis, marking them off by puncti, and using repeated notes in a quasi-parlando manner.[57] In performance this involved a slowing down, so that the brevis was now nearly as long as the former longa: the first step in a process which, repeated, led in the end to 'semibreve' surviving in British terminology as the name of the longest note in normal use, the German *ganze Note* or American whole-note.

ADAM DE LA HALE

Another name which appears in the later part of *Mo* is that of Adam de La Hale, a more substantial and, historical significance apart, a more important figure than Petrus de Cruce. Most of the few thirteenth-century composers whose names have survived are known to us only by one or two isolated, sometimes tantalizing facts: Tassin, who provided the tenor of a motet in *Mo* and is mentioned in 1288 as a *ministerallus* in the Court Chapel of Philip IV, Jehannot de L'Escurel, composer mainly of monodic ballades, rondeaux, and virelais preserved in the *Fauvel* manuscript,[58] who was hanged at Paris in 1303 for various 'ancis, raz et autres forfaiz' (murders of pregnant women, rape, etc.). As for the 'sweet English singers' mentioned by Anonymous IV, 'Johannes filius Dei, Makeblite of Winchester, Blaksmit, cantor at the court of the late King Henry [III]' (that is, some time between 1216 and 1272), we cannot identify a note of their music. One wishes one could credit them with those wild-flowers of thirteenth-century polyphony, 'Edi beo thu', 'Foweles in the frith',[59] and 'Jesu Christes milde moder', which reveal that love of thirds the Anonymous associates with the composers 'in patria quae dicitur Westcuntre'.

We know a great deal more about Adam de La Hale, born about 1237 of an Arras family nicknamed 'li Bossu' to distinguish them from other La Hales, educated at the Cistercian Abbey of Vaucelles and, after marriage in 1262, at the University of Paris. After various vicissitudes he entered the service of Count Robert II of Artois as a *menestrel* in 1271 and accompanied him when he was sent to Naples in 1283 with troops to reinforce his uncle, Charles of Anjou, after the disaster of the Sicilian Vespers. There Adam entered the service of King Charles and there he died in 1288. Adam was not a particularly distinguished musician, but he was also a lyric and epic poet and a dramatist. His compositions, which include 36 monodic songs, 18 *jeux partis*,[60] five three-part motets, and 16 three-part rondeaux, virelais and

[57] His 'Aucun/Lonc tans/Annun[-tiantes]' has often been quoted, e.g. in *HAM*, i, No. 34.
[58] See below, p. 118.
[59] Both in *NOHM*, ii, pp. 342–3; 'Edi beo thu' in *OAM(M)*, No. 57.
[60] See above, p. 100.

ballades in conductus style, had the unusual distinction of being collected in a single manuscript (Paris, Bibl. nat. fr. 25566) and have been published in a number of modern editions from the late nineteenth century onward.[61] His work very well exemplifies the *formes fixes* in which polyphonic secular song was commonly cast during the next two centuries: the old ballade (see p. 100), the danced virelai, which begins with a refrain, probably choral, repeated at the end of each stanza, and – most important of all – the rondeau, in which two strains of melody carry six or eight lines of verse. The poetic-musical form of the rondeau may be represented by the formula *aAabAB* or *ABaAabAB*, in which *A* represents a repetition of the first strain with the same words, *a* repetition of the music with different but rhyming words.

Adam's strongest claim to fame is *Li Gieus de Robin et de Marion*, a pastoral play with a great deal of earthy humour and a considerable number of short, simple songs. Nearly all are for Robin and Marion though a few are given to the knight who vainly pursues Marion and to Robin's cousin Gautier. No doubt the *Gieus* provided welcome entertainment for Charles and his dispirited French court. But Charles died in 1285 and Adam's last work was an unfinished epic dedicated to his memory, *Le Roi de Sezile*.

The airs of *Robin et Marion* are simple, as befits a bawdy country comedy, but to regard them as imitations of, or even borrowings from, popular music, begs an important question. Modal rhythms, particularly the first mode, had been deep rooted in the Western musical consciousness for many centuries before Adam de La Hale. They have survived in their simplicity to modern times in the folk-music of France and England because there they have not been overlaid by the innumerable sophistications of 'learned' music. We involuntarily, but unjustifiably, retroject this modern association of simple modal rhythm with folk-music even, and most absurdly, on to such a carefully wrought piece as 'Sumer is icumen in'. In the same way we are tempted, for instance, to invest a motet like 'A la clarté qi tout enlumina/[Surge] et illuminare' in *W2* with a subjective tenderness not inherent in the music of the textless clausula from which it was derived.

---

[61] *HAM*, i, No. 36, is a monodic ballade and two of the rondeaux, and *OAM(M)*, No. 56, is a rondeau.

7

The 'New Art' of the Fourteenth Century

ARS NOVA

Few historical labels are better justified than that of 'Ars nova' applied to French music of the early fourteenth century. So many innovations of spirit and technique coincided that musicians could hardly fail to be conscious they were practising a 'new art'. The Parisian theorist of the turn of the century, Johannes de Grocheo, says nothing about it in his treatise *De musica*,[1] but his approach is noticeably more empirical and practical than that of his predecessors; and he is very up-to-date. For instance, while Petrus de Cruce, in the contemporary seventh fascicle of the Montpellier Codex (*c.* 1300) with its fully Franconian notation, divides the brevis into as many as seven semibreves, Grocheo admits the possibility of division *ad infinitum* within practical limits. The 'new art' is, however, much less apparent in Petrus's motets than in the musical interpolations inserted in 1316 in one splendid manuscript of the *Roman de Fauvel*. Three years later an associate of one of the *Fauvel* composers, the Parisian mathematician and astronomer Johannes de Muris, completed a treatise actually entitled *Ars novae musicae*. And probably in 1320 his friend Philippe de Vitry (1291–1361), soon to be hailed by Petrarch as *poeta nunc unicus Galliarum* and by Jean Campion as *musicorum princeps egregius*, himself produced a short treatise, *Ars nova*.[2]

It was against the 'disciples of the new school' that the eighty-year-old John XXII, second of the Avignon popes, thundered in his bull 'Docta Sanctorum' (1324–5):[3] musicians who 'fuss with the measuring of the *tempora*, aim at new notes, prefer to invent their own music rather than sing the old; church music is sung in semibreves and minimae, pierced with these little notes. For they cut up melodies with hoquets, smoothe them with descants, sometimes force upon them vulgar tripla and moteti . . .' (*Sed nonnulli novellae Scholae discipuli dum temporibus mensurandis invigilant, novis notis intendunt fingere suas quam antiquas cantare malunt; in semibreves et minimas ecclesiastica cantantur, notulis percutiuntur. Nam melodias hoquetis intersecant, discantibus lubricant, triplis, et motectis vulgaribus nonnumquam*

---

[1] Published by Johannes Wolf in *SIMG*, i (1899–1900), p. 65, and Ernst Rohloff, *Der Musiktraktat des Johannes de Grocheo* (Leipzig, 1943), in both cases with German translation.
[2] Ed. Gilbert Reaney *et al.*, *Corpus Scriptorum de Musica* 8 (American Institute of Musicology) and in *Musica Disciplina*, x (1956), p. 13; French trans. ibid., xi (1957), p. 12.
[3] Full text printed by Fr. X. Haberl in *Vierteljahrsschrift für Musikwissenschaft*, iii (1887), p. 210.

inculcant.) At this very moment the greatest of all the 'disciples of the new school', Guillaume de Machaut (*c.* 1300–1377), made his début with a motet, 'Bone pastor Guillerme/Bone pastor, qui pastores/[Tenor un-identified]', for the installation of Guillaume de Trie as Archbishop of Rheims in 1324.

The first great source of the new music, however, is the Paris manuscript, Bibl. Nat. fr. 146, the sumptuous version of the *Roman de Fauvel* in which 'mesire Chaillou de Pesstain', *bailli d'Auvergne*, amused himself by inserting numerous literary and musical glosses. 'Prose and verse, Latin and French, liturgical and devotional, sacred and profane, monophonic and polyphonic, chant and chant-like, borrowed and newly composed, old and new: what the past produced and the present furnished is made to fit the original *Roman*'[4] of the beast F[latterie], A[varice], V[ilenie], V[anité] (or Variété), E[nvie], L[âcheté], which all men 'stroke'. There were thirteenth-century pre-cedents for the insertion of songs in narrative, for instance the famous 'chante-fable' *Aucassin et Nicolete*, but the 160 or so pieces in *Fauvel* are quite unusual. Particularly interesting are the motets. Some date from the first half of the previous century, e.g. 'Condicio nature defuit/O Nacio nephandi generis/Mane prima sabbati' is the first motet in fasc. 4 of Montpellier H 196, so that we get an interesting conspectus of the music still familiar to French courtiers in the second decade of the fourteenth century. But it is the motets in the new style, especially the five that can be confidently attributed to Philippe de Vitry, on which attention fastens.

Two technical features must be pointed out. One is the notation of smaller note-values: the *semibreves caudatae* (diamond-shaped semibreves with stems) or *minimae* in the third motet, 'Quare fremuerunt'. Vitry even recognizes the possibility of the *semiminima* (*minima* with a little 'flag', resembling a modern quaver or eighth-note), though he never employs it. *Ars nova* theory soon accepted not only modus perfectus (longa = three breves) and imperfectus (longa = two breves) and tempus perfectum (brevis = three semibreves) and imperfectum (longa = two semibreves), but also prolatio major (semibrevis = three minima) and minor (semibrevis = two minima). In one of the motets ascribed to Vitry, 'Garrit Gallus/In nova fert/Neuma',[5] temporary changes from modus perfectus to modus imperfectus in the tenor are indicated by red notation,[6] a procedure which he explains, with a reference to this very motet, in his treatise *Ars Nova*. The same motet illustrates the other important technical innovation, a constructional one known as isorhythm. This was an extension and elaboration of the repeated rhythmic patterns of modal tenors; a tenor

[4] Leo Schrade, p. 20 of commentary to *Polyphonic Music of the Fourteenth Century*, i (Monaco, 1956), which contains the 34 inserted motets.
[5] Schrade, op. cit., i, p. 68; opening only in *NOHM*, iii, p. 8.
[6] See fac. 67 in Apel, *The Notation of Polyphonic Music* (Cambridge, Mass., third edition, 1945).

would be broken into segments, each in the same arbitrary rhythmic pattern (called a *talea*), as in 'Garrit Gallus':

Ex. 23

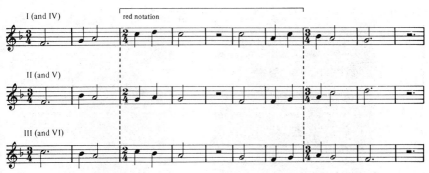

In this particular motet the same melody is then repeated after talea 3, so that taleae 4–6 are melodically as well as rhythmically the same as 1–3. But sometimes a longer stretch of melody is employed before repetition, so that melodic and rhythmic repeats do not coincide, in which case the melodic segment is called a *color*, a term in medieval rhetoric meaning 'repetition'. At first, isorhythm was employed only in tenors, which it must be remembered were only the bases for composition, comparable with the idea of sonata-form for later composers. But in one of Vitry's post-*Fauvel* motets, 'Vos qui admiramini/Gratissima virginis/Gaude gloriosa' (which also has a fourth part, a freely composed contratenor),[8] the tenor note-values are diminished in the second half of the piece and the hoquets in triplum and motetus are also treated isorhythmically.

THE ROBERTSBRIDGE CODEX

Two of Vitry's *Fauvel* motets, 'Firmissime/Adesto, Sancta Trinitas/ Alleluya, Benedictus' (see pl. 31(i)) and 'Tribum, quem non abhorruit/Quoniam secta latronum/Merito hec patimur', are noteworthy on another account. Transcriptions of them are included in the earliest known collection of keyboard music, Brit. Lib. Add. 28550, which is bound up with an old register of Robertsbridge Abbey in Sussex but of uncertain origin. It is possibly as old as 1325 and, if so, practically contemporary with the *Fauvel* manuscript itself. The Robertsbridge codex[9] includes the end of a purely instrumental piece in the estampie form of paired puncti with 'open' and 'closed' endings,[10] two complete pieces in this form, the second marked

---

[8] Schrade, op. cit., p. 76, and *OAM(M)*, No. 58.
[9] Complete facsimile in Wooldridge, *Early English Harmony* (London, 1897); complete transcription by Willi Apel, *CEKM* 1 (American Institute of Musicology, 1963). There are a number of partial facsimiles and transcriptions, e.g. facsimiles of the second complete instrumental piece in Apel, *Notation*, p. 38, and in Johannes Wolf, *Handbuch der Notationskunde*, ii (Leipzig, 1919), p. 9, which also shows the beginning of the 'Firmissime' transcription; transcription of the first, fourth, and fifth puncti of the same piece in *HAM*, i, No. 58; transcription of the first complete instrumental piece in *OAM(M)*, No. 84.
[10] See above pp. 100 and 112.

'Retroue', the two *Fauvel* transcriptions, and an incomplete transcription of a hymn, 'Flos vernalis'. These may have been meant to be played on a small organ; but only a little later, in 1360, Edward III presented his captive, John II of France, with an *eschiquier* (probably an ancestor of the harpsichord) and

(a)

(b)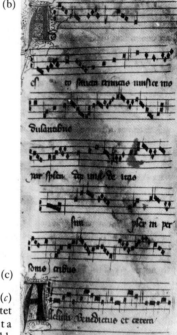

(c)

Pl. 31(i) Beginning of (*a*) *triplum*, (*b*) *motetus*, and (*c*) tenor of Philippe de Vitry's *Fauvel* motet 'Firmissime/Adesto, sancta trinitas/Alleluya, Benedictus' (Paris, Bibl. nat. fr. 146, fo. 43). For partial transcription, see Ex. 24(i).

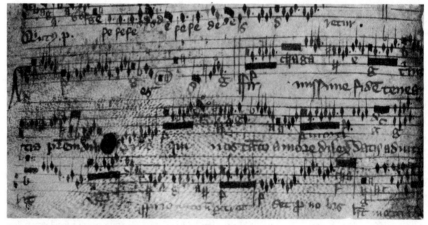

Pl. 31(ii) Detail from the Robertsbridge Codex, the earliest known collection of keyboard music (Brit. Lib. Add. 28550, fo. 43v), showing the end of an instrumental piece and beginning of a transcription of the Fauvel motet. For transcription see Ex. 24(ii).

Ex. 24[11]

(i)

Ad —

Alleluya, Benedictus [es, Domine]

(ii)

Ad   es

Fir — — — — — mis - si — me   fi — dem te - ne - a-

-es — — — to ,   sanc — ta   tri — ni — —

fir   missime   fi

(i)   -mus:

-tas,

(ii)

- dem teneamus

[11] (i) slightly adapted from Schrade, op. cit., p. 60, (ii) from Apel, *CEKM* 1, p. 3. In both cases the
original sources are of course unbarred.

Machaut refers twice in his non-musical works to *eschaquiers d'Engleterre*. Organ or eschiquier, the performer had to read and play simultaneous parts originally laid out separately across two pages. To enable him to do that, he had to 'intabulate' the parts immediately under each other in a condensed form. The method employed in the Robertsbridge manuscript, and in German organ tablatures a century and more later, was to write the highest part in ordinary notation on a stave, the other part or parts generally in letters of the alphabet (including the 'square B', resembling 'h', for B natural, and 's' for *sine*, i.e. a rest, and so on). But the highest part is never simply copied out; it is 'coloured' or provided with decorative figuration, a term which survives in the modern 'coloratura'. It will be noticed that in Ex. 24(ii) the transcriber has roughly cued in the text (mainly) of the triplum.

One or two other points in his work are noteworthy, particularly those which involve *musica ficta*, that practice of inserting 'implied' accidentals which has bedevilled the study of medieval and renaissance music. In the motet source only the tenor has a key-signature; but the motetus has an accidental B flat in 'bar' 4 and the triplum has one at the very last note of the quotation, and Schrade suggests flattening the Bs in bars 5 and 9 of the motetus, inserting flats above the notes in question, while Heinrich Besseler[12] leaves the B in bar 5 untouched but suggests flattening the Bs in both bars 8 and 9 of the motetus. But the Robertsbridge transcriber had other ideas; he dealt with the unpleasant diminished fifth in bar 9, not by flattening the B but by sharpening the F – and he made doubly sure by inserting unnecessary naturals before the Bs in bars 6 and 8. One must not say dogmatically that he was 'right' and the modern scholars 'wrong'; only that this is a practical contemporary musician's solution. His transcription of the other *Fauvel* motet is transposed up a tone, with a one-sharp key-signature for the right hand; he sprinkles accidentals freely, especially in the fragment at the beginning of what survives of his manuscript,[13] a fragment in which the oscillation of fifths in the right hand is a peculiarly keyboard effect; and he does not hesitate to insert an additional note where he feels the harmony sounds too thin.

POLITICAL AND CEREMONIAL MOTETS

It is even possible to surmise why the Robertsbridge transcriber's choice fell on these two particular motets. One was topical, the other in a special category. 'Tribum/Quoniam secta latronum/Merito', rejoices over the downfall of 'the fox who had devoured the *Galli* [cocks/Gauls – a nice pun] in the time when the blind lion was reigning', presumably meaning Philip the Fair's unpopular chancellor Enguerrand de Marigny, who had just been hanged. It was a favourite work and occurs in more additional sources than any other *Fauvel* motet. The other, 'Firmissime/Adesto/Alleluya', is unique in being non-polemical. Not only in *Fauvel* but in the half-dozen or so later motets ascribed to him, Vitry concentrates almost exclusively on religious or

---

[12] *AfMW*, viii (1927), p. 193.   [13] See *NOHM*, iii, pp. 421–2 and pl. IV(*a*).

political subjects: attacks on an unidentified, hypocritical Hugo or on some enemy of Robert of Anjou, King of Naples, a celebration of the election of Clement VI as Pope in 1352. We know only one amatory, French motet by him, though no doubt the lost, or unidentified, ballades, lais, and rondeaux he is said to have written were both French and concerned with love.

This tendency in the motet was not peculiar to Vitry. The motet was no longer so predominantly intimate solo music; the triplum was now commonly written at a higher pitch, a genuine *treble*, and several voices, even instruments, joined in both triplum and motetus. Motets were often composed for state occasions. Motets celebrating all the French kings of the fourteenth century have been preserved; Popes, bishops and noblemen were similarly honoured; and we have a splendid English example of the ceremonial isorhythmic motet in 'Sub Arturo plebs/Fons citharizantium/In omnem terram' by Johannes Alanus (supposedly John Aleyn, d. 1373 or 1374), perhaps marking a St. George's Day meeting of the Knights of the Garter at Windsor in 1358 or 1374.[14]

MACHAUT'S SECULAR MUSIC

Vitry's rather younger contemporary, Machaut, like himself a native of Champagne, was another ecclesiastical servant of kings, poet and composer, but more prolific and more widely travelled. Vitry was sent on royal missions to the Pope at Avignon, but Machaut as secretary to John of Luxembourg, King of Bohemia, from 1323 probably to 1337 was not only in Prague but in Poland and Lithuania. If he was not actually more prolific, as seems likely, his works – which include 19 monophonic or polyphonic lais, 42 ballades (practically all polyphonic), 22 polyphonic rondeaux, 33 monophonic or polyphonic virelais, 23 motets (the majority with French texts), a three-part textless and presumably instrumental piece entitled 'Hoquetus David', and a four-part setting of the complete Ordinary of the Mass, to say nothing of purely literary writings – were preserved by collection in manuscripts originally compiled under his own supervision.[15] A number of the secular pieces were, like the *Fauvel* music, insertions in long poems such as Machaut's own *Remède de Fortune* and *Veoir Dit*. It was this secular music, composed mostly between *c.* 1340 and *c.* 1370, that earned him the sobriquet 'last of the trouvères' although no trouvère was as many-sided or as intellectual. For among the ballades one finds not only

---

[14] (1) Facsimiles of the best source (Chantilly, Mus. Condé 1047) in Johannes Wolf, *Musikalische Schrifttafeln* (Bückeburg and Leipzig, 1923), pl. 30–1, and Gennrich, op. cit., Pl. XVIII *a* and *b*; transcriptions in *DTÖ*, Jg. xl, p. 9, and *CMM* 39, p. 49. See also Brian Trowell, 'A fourteenth-century ceremonial motet and its composer', *Acta Musicologica*, xxix (1957), p. 65, for the argument for the earlier date; Margaret Bent sounds a note of caution in 'The Transmission of English Music 1300–1500', *Studien zur Tradition in der Musik*, ed. Hans Heinrich Eggebrecht and Max Lütolf (Munich, 1973), p. 65.
[15] Paris, Bibl. Nat. fr. 22545–6, 1584 and 1585 (the last being a copy of the so-called de Vogüe manuscript, now in New York). There are complete editions by Friedrich Ludwig (Leipzig, 1926–43; reprinted Wiesbaden, 1954) and Schrade, *Polyphonic Music of the Fourteenth Century*, ii–iii (Monaco, 1956), and numerous editions of separate compositions, particularly of the Mass. *HAM*, i gives secular pieces, Nos. 44–6, and *OAM(M)*, Nos. 68–71.

purely delightful things like 'Je puys trop bien', a solo song with instrumental tenor and contratenor, but a three-part canon at the unison with triple text: 'Sanz cuer m'en vois/Amis, dolens/Dame, par vous'. But this is nothing compared with the intellectual feat of the rondeau 'Ma fin est mon commencement',[16] a setting of a moralizing motto with directions for performance:

> C'est teneure vraiement.
> Ma fin est mon commencement,
> Mes tiers chants trois fois seulement
> Se retrograde: et einsi fin . . . .

That is, the cantus sings the same notes as the triplum but in reverse order, while the tenor of the first strain[17] is exactly reversed in the second; in each case the part is written only once. Trouvère art was often 'artificial' in every sense; isorhythm is an intellectual basis for composition; but in this rondeau Machaut demonstrates unprecedented intellectuality in the act of composition itself while avoiding even a suspicion of the dry coolness of Vitry's music.

CHACE AND CACCIA

Extended canons at the unison, like 'Sanz cuer m'en vois', were a favoured fourteenth-century form. One of Machaut's lais, 'Le lay de confort', is built up of twelve such three-part canons; the preceding one in the sources, 'Le lay de la fonteinne', consists of six monophonic strophes alternating six three-part canons each marked 'chace'. Indeed such canons were commonly called 'chaces': for instance, the anonymous 'Chase de septem temporibus fugando et revertendo', 'Talent m'est pris', a spring song with cuckoo calls[18] preserved in a codex which probably originated c. 1360 at the Papal Court at Avignon and is now in the chapter library of Ivrea in Savoy. The Ivrea manuscript, though it consists mostly of Latin motets and church music including some by Vitry and Machaut, contains three other French chaces one of which, 'Se je chant' mains que ne suel',[19] describes an actual hunt, a hawking scene with the hunters' realistic cries set to hoquets. The chace seems to have passed into Italy as the 'caccia', though in the Italian variety only two parts are usually canonic over a free instrumental tenor as in one of the earliest known examples, 'Or qua compagni',[20] possibly by one Magister Piero who was in the service of the Visconti in Milan and the Scaligeri at Verona, c. 1330–50.

[16] Original notation in Johannes Wolf, *Geschichte der Mensural-Notation*, ii (Leipzig, 1904; reprinted Hildesheim, 1965), p. 40.   [17] See above, p. 116, on the rondeau form.
[18] Quoted in *NOHM*, iii, p. 136. The piece occurs in other sources, notably in a manuscript in the University Library at Innsbruck with German words by Oswald von Wolkenstein (1377–1445).
[19] A facsimile of the notation in another source, Paris, Bibl. Nat., Coll. de Pic. 67, is given in *MGG*, i, cols. 715–6. Another Ivrea chace is printed in *OAM(M)*, No. 72.
[20] In Rome, Vatican, Rossi 215, compiled about 1350. There is a facsimile in *MGG*, i, cols. 719–20, and transcriptions in Husmann, *Die mittelalterliche Mehrstimmigkeit* (Cologne, 1955), No. 15, *Polyphonic Music of the Fourteenth Century*, viii (ed. W. T. Marrocco), No. 31, and Nino Pirrotta, *Music in Fourteenth-Century Italy* (*CMM*, 8, iv, No. 28).

MACHAUT AND THE POLYPHONIC MASS CYCLE

Before turning to Italian secular polyphony of the mid-*trecento*, however, we must consider two church compositions by Machaut, one a curious throwback to an old form in a fresh guise, the other a great innovatory landmark of medieval music. The 'Hoquetus David'[21] is a 'Notre Dame clausula' in the idiom of a century-and-a-half later: two upper parts, marked 'hoquetus' and 'triplum', over an isorhythmic tenor formed from the final melisma ('. . . clara ex stirpe David') from the Alleluia verse, 'Solemnitas', for the Solemnity of the Most Holy Rosary.[22] We may imagine it played by such fairly recently introduced instruments as the strident double-reed shawm with its conical bore and wide bell, the *calamel* or *scalmuse* of the metrical romances, and the trumpet, perhaps with sliding mouthpiece, the *trompette des ménestrels* (as distinct from the military trumpet), both acquisitions of the later Crusades.

Isorhythm and hoqueting also play notable parts in the *Messe de Nostre Dame* but its outstanding importance, apart from the splendour of the music, is the fact that it is the earliest known setting of the Ordinary by one composer. The evolution of the liturgical Ordinary had been a slow process. The Credo became a normal part of the Mass only at the beginning of the eleventh century and it was at about the same time that the plainsong chants of the Ordinary, settings of the texts which (except for their tropes) were unchanged throughout the calendar, began to be written down with those of the Proper whose texts are special to each occasion. In the written sources, grouping of the Ordinary began with the placing together of a number of Kyries, a number of Glorias, and so on. The natural assembly of Kyrie-Gloria pairs because of their immediate juxtaposition in the Mass and, much less often, Sanctus with Agnus which are widely separated, did not begin until the twelfth century and so far as the plainsong melodies were concerned 'Mass-pairs' never died out during the Middle Ages. The eleventh-century Winchester tropers[23] contain troped Kyries and Glorias with organal parts and the Notre Dame repertory included polyphonic troped Sanctus and Agnus. But it was chiefly polyphonic setting of the Proper chants of Mass and Office that attracted composers until the fourteenth century.

During the heyday of the motet the composition of Mass movements of any kind was somewhat neglected. Then the Ordinary came into its own; in the early fourteenth century we find not only compilations of complete plainsong cycles at last but also more polyphonic settings of separate movements and even complete cycles of polyphonic (three-part) settings. Stylistically the earliest of these is the so-called 'Mass of Tournai'; later are the 'Toulouse' and 'Barcelona' Masses and the fragmentary 'Besançon' or 'Sorbonne' Mass. All these are named from the places where they were found, but there is reason to suppose that they – or the separate movements

[21] Transcriptions by Guillaume de Van (Paris, 1938) and Schrade, op. cit., iii, p. 65.
[22] *Liber Usualis*, p. 1676.   [23] See p. 81.

from which they were compiled – came from the vicinity of the Papal court at Avignon,[24] perhaps from Avignon itself where Benedict XII (1334–42) established a Papal chapel, the old *schola cantorum* having stayed behind in Rome. These Masses are demonstrably interrelated: a better text of the Credo of the Tournai Mass exists separately in a manuscript from Apt in Provence, not far from Avignon, related to – though a little later than – the Codex Ivrea; the final motet setting ('Laudemus Jhesum Christum') of the 'Ita missa est' in Toulouse is based on a troped Gloria in the Codex Ivrea itself, and the Credo of Toulouse, of which only part of the tenor survives, can easily be supplied from Ivrea and Apt where it appears complete but separately, and from the Barcelona Mass. (In these sources it is attributed to an unknown composer, Sert or Sortes.) Further: the Besançon Sanctus is closely related to a Sanctus in Ivrea and, much more remarkable, its Gloria is freely re-worked in an Ivrea Credo.[25]

These Mass compilations are very conservative in style, as one would expect of Avignon church music, with much note-against-note writing in all three parts relieved only by figuration in one or both upper parts. The Tournai Kyrie lacks even that relief and is actually in modal rhythm, as are Sanctus and Agnus Dei. There are brief and very discreet passages of hoquet in the 'Amen' of the Gloria, in the Sanctus and in the Agnus Dei. None of the tenors has been identified as a liturgical chant and none is isorhythmic. Pope John XXII would have found little to object to; but the final 'Ite missa est' – a passage soon omitted from polyphonic settings of the Ordinary – would have horrified him, not on musical grounds but because the triplum has the words of a French love-song. It is, in fact, a bilingual motet, 'Se grace n'est a mon maintien/Cum venerint/Ite missa est', on an isorhythmic instrumental tenor and appears as such in the Ivrea Codex; it is difficult to believe that it was used liturgically in this form. The parallel passage in the Toulouse Mass is also a motet, but with only one, perfectly respectable, Latin text; in this Mass also none of the tenors has been identified and none is treated isorhythmically.

In strongest contrast with these conservative Masses, written and compiled under the shadow of the bull 'Docta Sanctorum', is Machaut's masterpiece. It is also almost certainly later in date, though there is no documentary support for the tradition that associates it with the coronation of Charles V in 1364. The Kyrie sets the pattern, with a plainsong tenor – the Kyrie 'Cunctipotens', so called from its popular trope, 'Cunctipotens Genitor Deus' – treated isorhythmically, as is also the contratenor (bassus); hoquets are introduced near the end of each section. Sanctus,[26] Agnus, and 'Ite missa est' are also based on isorhythmic liturgical tenors. Gloria and Credo are in a free note-against-note style, the Gloria opening most

[24] The Tournai, Toulouse, and Barcelona Masses are published in Schrade, op. cit., i, the Besançon fragment (facsimile and transcription) by Jacques Chailley in *Annales musicologiques*, ii (1954), p. 93. All four are also published in *CMM* 29 (ed. Hanna Stäblein-Harder).
[25] See Schrade, 'A Fourteenth Century Parody Mass', *Acta Musicologica*, xxvii (1955), p. 13.
[26] Facsimile (Bibl. Nat. fr. 22546) in Parrish, *The Notation of Medieval Music* (London, 1958), pl. L and LI.

impressively (after the priest has intoned 'Gloria in excelsis Deo') with the words 'Et in terra pax' in long note-values. The words 'Jesu Christe' and, in the Credo, 'ex Maria virgine' are highlighted in the same way, and the device was borrowed by such later composers as Dufay. The 'Amen' which concludes the Credo can easily be described technically – three taleae isorhythmic in all four parts, the rhythmic patterns of tenor and contratenor being exchanged in the last talea, each talea ending with hoquets – but its ecstasy is indescribable and can be suggested only very imperfectly by quotation:[27]

Ex. 25

The final cadence of this 'Amen' may be quoted to illustrate a technical point by no means peculiar to Machaut but indicative of the changing tonal sense of the time. The Credo is in the D mode, so the contratenor falls to the final and the motetus rises to it; but Machaut sharpens the C from which it rises, making it what we should call a leading-note. Not only that: the penultimate G of the triplum is sharpened as well (and the same note in the tenor must be sharpened by musica ficta), thus producing a 'double leading-note' effect:

Ex. 26

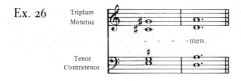

Kyrie and Gloria, also in the D mode, end with precisely the same cadence though the lay-out of the parts is different, e.g. in the Gloria the tenor falls to the final and the other parts rise. Sanctus, Agnus, and 'Ite missa est' are really in the C mode transposed to F with a plentiful sprinkling of accidental flats before the Bs, though not of course to the penultimate notes of the final cadences. Sometimes such transpositions to F were given one-flat key-signatures, as in Ex. 24(i) where the original plainsong of the tenor was in the G mode (popularly known as Mixolydian). The modes of C and D, embryonic ancestors of major and minor keys, were asserting themselves more and more.

EARLY ITALIAN POLYPHONY

When and how the influence of French ars nova generally, and of Machaut particularly, affected Italian polyphony 'though puzzling questions, are not beyond all conjecture'. Until the fourteenth century Italian polyphony was very modest in bulk, judging from what has come down to us, and in style too, as in this processional piece of *c.* 1300[28] from the Chapter Library at Padua, a particularly important musical centre throughout the *trecento*:

Ex. 27

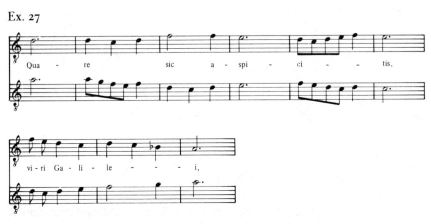

Even much later in the century Italian sacred music was not markedly different from secular. 'In the Agnus composed by Gherardello [de Florentia] about 1350 not only the style but also the formal structure is related to the madrigal. The first two Agnus sections correspond to some extent to two through-composed stanzas . . . while the third . . . corresponds to the *ritornello*. As in most of the madrigals the upper part seems to be the leading voice.'[29] And the Gloria Gratiosus de Padua[30] is in ballata

[27] From Schrade, *Polyphonic Music*, iii, p. 53.
[28] Ed. Giuseppe Vecchi, *Uffici drammatici padovani* (Florence, 1954), p. 106 (facs. CXIV–CXVI), and *Polyphonic Music of the Fourteenth Century*, xii (ed. Kurt von Fischer and Alberto Gallo), No. 31a.
[29] Fischer, 'The Sacred Polyphony of the Italian Trecento', *PRMA*, c (1973–4), p. 152. The Agnus is published in *Polyphonic Music*, xii, No. 20. On madrigal and ballata, see below, pp. 129 and 131.
[30] *Polyphonic Music*, xii, No. 6, and *OAM(M)*, No. 63.

style. One of the Paduan pieces, 'Iste formosus',[31] however, is marked by chromaticism, and the celebrated theorist Marchettus of Padua, whose principal treatises, the *Lucidarium* and *Pomerium*,[32] probably date from about 1318, expresses highly controversial views on chromaticism – his *semitonum chromaticum* is four-fifths of a tone – as well as explaining the differences between Italian notation and French.[33]

THE TRECENTO MADRIGAL

The earliest source containing secular Italian polyphony is the Vatican codex, Rossi 215, probably representing a Paduan repertory of *c.* 1330 and contains 29 anonymous compositions, one of which we know from a concordance to be by the already mentioned Magister Piero.[34] Three are by another composer contemporary with him and active in the same areas, Padua, Verona, Milan: Johannes de Florentia, also known as Giovanni da Cascia (which is very near Florence). A third musician, Jacopo da Bologna (Jacobus de Bononia), though not represented in the Rossi manuscript, unless anonymously, is known to have belonged to the same group and was indeed the most famous of the three.[35]

The great majority of the Rossi pieces – and of the total work of these three composers – consists of two-part madrigals. (The *trecento* madrigal of Petrarch and his contemporaries derived its name, *madriale* or *mandriale*, from the medieval Latin *matriale*, probably meaning a poem in the mother tongue. It consisted of two to five three-line stanzas, all set to the same music, followed by a two-line ritornello in a different rhythm, and was noted as a 'new' poetic form *c.* 1313.) The very earliest and most naïve examples, such as the anonymous 'Cum altre ucele':[36]

Ex. 28

[31] *Polyphonic Music*, xii, No. 31c.
[32] Modern edition of the *Pomerium*, ed. Vecchi, *Corpus Scriptorum de Musica* 6; excerpts translated in Oliver Strunk, *Source Readings in Music History* (London, 1952), p. 160. The treatise is dedicated to that Robert d'Anjou, King of Naples and Vicar of Tuscany and the Romagna for the Avignon popes, whom Philippe de Vitry had defended in a motet.
[33] Only one composition by Marchettus is known, the motet in *Polyphonic Music*, xii, No. 37.
[34] See p. 124.
[35] The collected works of Giovanni da Cascia have been edited by Nino Pirrotta in *CMM* 8, i; those of Piero and the unidentified pieces in the Rossi Codex, ibid., ii; those of Jacopo da Bologna, ibid., iv. The works of all three have also been edited by Frank Ll. Harrison, *Polyphonic Music of the Fourteenth Century*, vi. There are numerous separate editions and facsimiles.
[36] Husmann, op. cit., No. 14; Marrocco, *Polyphonic Music*, viii, No. 7; facs. in Gennrich, *Abriss der Mensuralnotation des XIV Jahrhunderts* (Nieder-Modau, 1948), pl. XXVI.

already show all the hallmarks of the musical style: the florid upper part with its prolonged exploitation of one vowel after another, the much more restrained lower one often moving in parallel or even unison, the avoidance of part-crossing. Nothing could be more essentially Italian; there is not the faintest trace of French influence. Sometimes the false promise of the opening of Ex. 28 is fulfilled as in Piero's 'Cavalcando',[37] in Florence, Bibl. Naz. Panciatichi 26,[38] and we get a canonic madrigal, though the ritornello is not canonic. Conversely his 'Si com' al canto' in the same manuscript is canonic only in the ritornello. The sole three-part piece in the Rossi Codex is the caccia 'Or qua compagni' already mentioned on p. 124. This is not exactly a canonic madrigal with an instrumental tenor, for there is no ritornello and the second voice participates in the florid passages with consequent crossing of parts, yet it is so like a canonic madrigal that this, rather than the French chace, has been claimed as the origin of the caccia. 'Or qua compagni' is also characteristic of the Italian variety[39] in that it is concerned with an actual hunt.

The real masters of the early madrigal were Giovanni, as in his 'Nel mezzo a sei paon', and Jacopo in his setting of Petrarch's 'Non al suo amante' and his beautiful 'Fenice fu'. Yet Giovanni never, and Jacopo only seldom, goes beyond two parts in his madrigals. Jacopo's three-part setting of 'Uselletto selvaggio' – he also made a two-part one – simply uses the caccia technique; the tenor comes to life only momentarily in the ritornello. Even in the technically more sophisticated tri-textual 'Aquil' altera/Creatura gentil/Uccel di dio',[40] the tenor (though more lively) shares only momentarily in the imitative and florid duetting of the upper parts. And this is a late work which we can date to 1355 since it seems to refer to the Emperor Charles IV's visit to Italy. So also is the three-part 'Lux purpurata/Diligite justiciam'[41] which looks like an attempt to imitate a French motet, even with a hoquet and a final cadence like Ex. 26, by a composer who failed to realize that the tenor was the initial basic part, not an additional one. Here, in fact, about the middle of the century, is the point where French influence began to tell in Italian polyphony. This is

---

[37] *CMM* 8, ii, No. 5 and *Polyphonic Music*, vi, No. 2.
[38] A manuscript in which a later hand has entered French compositions, including five by Machaut.
[39] Selection of twenty in Marrocco, *Fourteenth Century Italian Cacce* (Cambridge, Mass., 1942; revised edition, 1961). There are fourteenth-century Spanish religious canons styled *caça*, with Latin words, in the Montserrat *Llibre Vermell*: see Otto Ursprung's transcriptions in *ZfMW*, iv (1921–2), pp. 151–3.
[40] *CMM* 8, iv, No. 1; Husmann, op. cit., No. 20; *OAM(M)*, No. 76.
[41] *CMM* 8, iv, No. 34.

particularly noticeable in the work of such slightly younger men as Gherardellus de Florentia, Laurentius de Florentia, Donatus de Florentia (Donato da Cascia), and Niccolò da Perugia. There is more three-part writing, more crossing of parts, the influence of French notation, even occasional setting of French texts.

FRANCESCO LANDINI

French influence is yet more apparent in the work of the greatest master of the *trecento*, the blind Florentine organist Francesco Landini ('Franciscus caecus', 'Francesco degli organi') (*c.* 1335–1397).[42] The bulk of his work consists of polyphonic *ballate*, a form practically unknown before about 1360. The monodic ballata, the Italian version of the virelai, was no novelty; there are four examples by Piero in the Rossi Codex[43] and we have a few by Gherardellus and Niccolò; it was perhaps a descendant of troubadour song. But the polyphonic ballata is another matter, particularly in Landini's masterly hands. It is in two parts, the second either vocal or instrumental, or in three, sometimes entirely vocal but more often with instrumental tenor or contratenor or both. In those entirely vocal two-part ballate where the upper voice is much more florid than the lower (e.g. 'Per servar umiltà' and 'Donna l'animo tuo') and in his only caccia, 'Chosi pensoso', Landini is not so very far from the earlier *trecento* madrigal style, but he will also write one so simple, with nearly identical rhythm in both parts like 'Ecco la primavera', that it might be a real, not a stylized, dance.

Landini's masterpieces, however, are to be found among the three-part ballate, such as 'Gram piant' agli ochi' and 'Amar si glì alti tuo' gentil' costumi' and 'L'alma mia piange',[44] with their more 'modern' consonant sound. 'Amar' in particular is marked by a cadential mannerism not peculiar to him but such a favourite of his – the seventh degree of the scale falling (simply or decorated) to the sixth before rising to' the final – that it has become known as the 'Landini cadence'. One of the three-part ballate, 'Questa fanciulla', was transcribed for keyboard in the Codex Reina (Paris, Bibl. Nat. nouv. acq. fr. 6771) (*c.* 1400) (Pl. 32). Two others, 'Non arà ma' pietà' and 'Che pena questa', are transcribed – with pieces by Machaut, Jacopo da Bologna, and Bartolino da Padova – in the Codex Faenza (*c.* 1420).[45] Landini's almost complete neglect of the madrigal and caccia is striking: twelve madrigals, one canonic, as against 140 ballate. One of his two three-part madrigals, 'Si dolce non sono',[46] is remarkable in having an

---

[42] Complete works in Schrade, *Polyphonic Music*, iv; numerous modern editions of separate pieces. The early fifteenth-century Squarcialupi Codex includes a nearly complete edition, though not the best texts, of Landini headed by his portrait; unfortunately the posthumously published transcription of the Codex by Wolf (Lippstadt, 1955) is unsatisfactory.
[43] One quoted in *NOHM*, iii, p. 37; all four in *CMM* 8, ii, nos. 25–7 and 31.
[44] *OAM(M)*, No. 77.
[45] Parallel excerpts, original and transcription, from 'Non arà ma' pietà' and 'Questa fanciulla' are printed in *NOHM*, iii, pp. 80 and 423, Jacopo's 'Aquila altera' in *OAM(M)*, Nos. 76 and 85. Reina has been ed. Nigel Wilkins, *CMM* 36 and 37, Faenza by Dragan Plamenac, *CMM* 57.
[46] *HAM*, i, No. 54. Another madrigal in *OAM(M)*, No. 78.

(i)

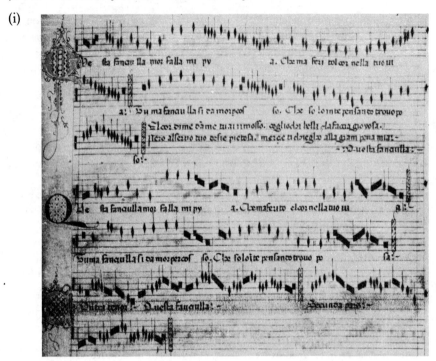

(ii)

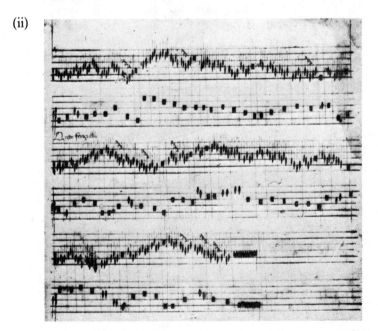

Pl. 32   (i) Landini's ballata 'Questa fanciulla' in the Squarcialupi Codex (Florence, Bibl. Med. Laur. Pal. 87) fo. 138, and (ii) a keyboard transcription of it in the Codex Reina (Paris, Bibl. Nat., nouv. acq. fr. 6771) fo. 85.

isorhythmic tenor as well as hints of isorhythm in the other parts; isorhythm is totally foreign to *trecento* music, which is no more *ars nova* than 'Italian Gothic' architecture is Gothic. Other signs of French influence are his frequent use of French notation and his three-part setting of a French virelai.

Less surprising is the total absence of church music. It must always be borne in mind that polyphonic liturgical music was still special and exceptional everywhere, even more so in Italy than in France or England. The only complete polyphonic Italian Mass is a composite affair – Gloria and Agnus by Gherardello, Credo by 'Frate Bartholino' (Bartholus de Florentia), Sanctus by Lorenzo da Firenze[47] – at the end of Bibl. Nat. ital. 568. It is in madrigal-like two-part style:

Ex. 29

though it is followed by a three-part 'Benedicamus Domino' by Paolo da Firenze in a later style with a plainsong tenor in long note-values, unique in *trecento* music, and some hoqueting in the upper parts. Here is further evidence of French penetration. Such two-part religious polyphony was the norm all over Europe from Spain to Poland in the lands peripheral to French musical culture. Sometimes it was even more primitive; a Prague manuscript[48] from the second half of the century contains a setting of the Nativity lesson 'Primo tempore' in bare organum fifths.

FOURTEENTH-CENTURY ENGLISH MUSIC

English music was much more closely related to French, and even used French secular tenors for sacred motets, as in 'Triumphat hodie/Trop avet fet/Amy', which has been pieced together from Oxford, New College 362 (an important source for early fourteenth-century English music) and Brit. Lib., Add. 24198. Two motets from New College 362 both use a virelai melody 'Mariounette douche' as tenor. One employs it instrumentally, with three higher parts (each having a different Latin text), the other as the middle voice with a fresh text 'Virgo mater' in a three-part piece of which

---

[47] Ed. Pirrotta, *CMM* 8, Gloria, i, p. 53; Credo, i. p. 1; Sanctus, iii, p. 1; Agnus, i, p. 55. Facs. of the third part of Bartholus's Credo (see Ex. 29) in Parrish, op. cit., pl. LVI and LVII.
[48] Univ. knih. VH 11. See Zdeněk Nejedlý, *Dějiny Husitského zpěvu*, i (new edition, Prague, 1954), p. 134.

the lowest part is instrumental and the nominal tenor yet obviously composed later.[49] Placing of the tenor cantus firmus in the middle instead of the lowest part was indeed a common English practice. These New College motets also illustrate other peculiarities of English technique which distinguish it from the mainstream of French music and enable us to speak of an English musical dialect. We have already seen[50] how Walter Odington relates the peculiarly English rondellus technique, with its complete interchange of parts, to the simultaneous rhythms of the conductus style, and how both are combined motet-wise over a liturgical tenor in 'Sumer is icumen in'. In 'Triumphat hodie' the tenor is interchanged between the two lower voices, who thus sing alternately the true tenor and its counterpoint – but the piece ends with thoroughly French hoquets. The four-part 'Mariounette douche' is conductus-like both in its simultaneity of rhythm and in its frequent employment of parallel thirds and sixths, imperfect concords resolving on the sixth and octave. This was the commonest English cadence of the period in other contexts as well:

Ex. 30

The parallel thirds and sixths are above all the hallmark of the English dialect, so commonplace that there was a practice of improvised 'descanting' at sight on a plainsong in this way. They are prominent also in a four-part motet from Bury St. Edmunds (Oxford, Bodl. E Mus. 7), 'Ave miles celestis/Ave rex gentis Anglorum',[51] which is a paradigm of the English rondellus-conductus-motet and also of a type of liturgical work which was becoming increasingly important in England, the votive antiphon. Not only do the two lower parts interchange the phrases of the tenor – an 'Ave Rex' in the Worcester and Sarum antiphonals, musically identical with the Roman antiphon 'Ave Regina caelorum' (*Liber Usualis*, p. 1864) – in rondellus style; at the same time the two upper voices similarly interchange phrases. On the other hand four motets in the later part of this same manuscript are French in notation and technique, with isorhythm; one of them, 'Domine quis habitabit/De veri cordis/Concupisco', actually appears in the Ivrea codex as 'Se paour d'umble astinance/Diex tan desir estre ames d'amour/Concupisco'. Like 'Sub Arturo',[52] they must be dated later than the middle of the century. Thus a fresh wave of French influence seems to have made itself felt in England at the same time as the impact of French influence on Italian music. Unfortunately, in striking contrast with France and Italy, we have hardly any secular polyphony or vernacular texts from

[49] Opening quoted in *NOHM*, iii, p. 86.   [50] See p. 112.
[51] Transcribed complete in Manfred Bukofzer, *Studies in Medieval and Renaissance Music* (London, 1951), p. 30, as an appendix to a study of 'Two Fourteenth-Century Motets on St. Edmund'.
[52] See p. 123.

this period, many of the sacred works survive only in fragments, and practically all are anonymous. None can be attached to the names in the roll-call of English musicians in the triplum of 'Sub Arturo', so that 'J. de Corbe', 'Ricardus Blich' and 'Blich G.' (Richard and perhaps William Blithe), 'Episwich J.' (John of Ipswich), and the rest remain figures as shadowy as the Makeblites and Blacksmits of Anonymous IV.[53] Only Alanus, who mentions himself in the contratenor text, can be tentatively identified with the 'Aleyn' whose 'Gloria' is included in the oldest part of the much later Old Hall manuscript.[54]

THE FRENCH MANNERISTS

It is perhaps because the English composers concentrated on church music that, despite its increased sophistication, English music never approached the extremes of rhythmic complexity reached by the French after Machaut. Religious music now tended everywhere to be simpler than secular. The composers who emerged from under Machaut's shadow – F. Andrieu and Magister Franciscus (who may have been the same man), Vaillant, Cuvelier, Susay – are naturally closest to him in style and cultivated the same forms: ballade, rondeau, and less often the virelai. But they delighted in more flowing cantilena, especially in the highest part; indeed the melodious upper part began to invade religious music as well. There are ten three-part hymns in the Apt Codex[55] in nine of which the liturgical melody, simple or lightly decorated, provides the top part; in the tenth it is in the middle.[56] But even before Machaut's death a very different tendency had set in. The same forms, ballade and so on, were complicated by division and subdivision of the shorter note-values and by subtleties of rhythm and cross-rhythm which necessitated equally intricate innovations in notation which Apel has aptly described as 'mannered': 'It is in this period that musical notation far exceeds its natural limitations as a servant to music, but rather becomes its master, a goal in itself and an arena for intellectual sophistries.'[57] This 'mannered' style was practised by composers many of whom served or dedicated works to such princes as Gaston Phébus, Count of Foix (d. 1391), the celebrated art-connoisseur John, Duke of Berry (d. 1416), and John I of Aragon (d. 1395). The last of these not only recruited musicians from Avignon but ordered from there in 1389 a book of 'xv.en..xx. motets' as well as 'ballades, rondells e virelays que sien la flor'[58] (for these are the best). Another patron was Pope Clement VII himself (d. 1394), for a very worldly and Frenchified papal court still remained at Avignon when the exile was followed by the Great Schism.

---

[53] See p. 115.   [54] See below, p. 141.
[55] *Le manuscrit de musique de Trésor d'Apt (XIVe–XVe siècle)*, ed. Amédée Gastoué (Paris, 1936).
[56] Two examples transcribed by Besseler in *ZfMW*, xi (1928–9), pp. 19 and 20.
[57] *The Notation of Polyphonic Music*, p. 403.
[58] Quoted from Gilbert Reaney, 'The Manuscript Chantilly, Musée Condé 1047', *Musica Disciplina*, viii (1954), p. 83, n. 84.

The French mannerist composers, with Machaut and his immediate disciples, are all represented in the magnificent Chantilly Codex, which may indeed be the very collection ordered by the King of Aragon, or a de luxe copy of it, since it answers closely to his prescription. Some of them – with French-influenced Italians – appear also in Modena, Bibl. Est. M.5.24 (*olim* lat. 568) and other sources.[59] Their art was intensely self-conscious, music for aristocratic connoisseurs. One of them, a certain Guido, even complains at being obliged to write 'contre nature'; the 'boin exemplaire' of 'Philipe' [de Vitry] goes for nothing nowadays: and each stanza of his ballade ends with the refrain 'Certes se n'est pas bien fayt'.[60] Guido was not one of the extremists. Nor was the Duke of Berry's Solage. Philippus (Filipoctus) de Caserta, who was at Avignon *c.* 1380, indulged in very complicated notation, but the most prominent of the real extremists was a French harper at the Aragonese court, variously known as Jacob de Senleches, Jacomi de Sentluch, and (in the Modena Codex) Jacopinus Selesses.[61] Even his tortured ingenuities were trumped by a 'Magister Zacharias' whose Latin ballade 'Sumite karissimi'[62] in the Modena manuscript has been described by Apel as 'the acme of rhythmic intricacy in the entire history of music'. Artifice not only in notation but in the lay-out of the notation is displayed in two rondeaux by Baude Cordier which open the Chantilly Codex, though added at a later date: the famous heart-shaped 'Belle, bonne, sage' and the canon notated in circular form 'Tout par compas'.[63] In one corner of the latter is a verse telling us that the composer comes from Rheims and that his music is known as far as Rome:

> De Reins dont est et jusqu'a Romme
> sa musique appert et a rode.

But the actual music of 'Belle, bonne, sage' is by no means as mannered as some of his work (for instance, 'Amans ames').[64] He was probably active in the early fifteenth century, when a reaction against mannerism had set in.

ITALY AT THE TURN OF THE CENTURY

Similar contrasts of intricate and much simpler pieces mark the work of the Italians around the turn of the century, Landini's younger and more strongly gallicized contemporaries. Of these the most important was Matteo da Perugia. Matteo is known to have been a singer and then the first *maestro*

---

[59] The Chantilly and Modena codices have been ed. Ursula Günther, *CMM* 39.

[60] Facsimile and transcription by Ursula Günther, *MF*, xvi (1963), p. 117.

[61] Compositions transcribed in Apel, *CMM* 53, i; one example, the ballade 'En attendant', in *HAM*, i, No. 47, and facsimile of the piece in Apel, *Notation*, p. 423.

[62] Notation in Wolf, *Geschichte*, ii, p. 127; transcription, ibid., iii, p. 168. Partial transcription in Apel, *Notation*, appendix No. 63.

[63] Both often reproduced in facsimile, e.g. in *MGG*, ii, pl. 55 (not showing coloured notation), in Gennrich, op. cit., pl. XIX and XX, 'Belle, bonne' in Apel, *Notation*, p. 427, 'Tout par compas' in Parrish, *Notation*, pl. LXII (not showing colour). 'Belle, bonne' transcribed in *HAM*, i, No. 48b; Cordier's complete works, ed. Reaney, in *CMM* 11, i.

[64] Transcribed, *HAM*, i, No. 48a; facs. *MGG*, ii, col. 1665. A less mannered example is 'Se cuer d'amant', *OAM(M)*, No. 98.

di cappella of Milan Cathedral[65] from 1402 to 1416, with an interlude during which he served the Milanese Pope Alexander V and perhaps his successor. His works, all in the Modena Codex, consist of five Glorias, an Agnus (and possibly some anonymous Mass-movements), and some two dozen secular pieces, rondeaux, virelais, and ballades to French words and completely in the French style.[66] Like Baude Cordier's, they are sometimes less complicated in sound than their notation would lead one to expect, e.g. the anonymous virelai 'Plus onques dame' plausibly attributed to him.[67] But one of his Glorias[68] is certainly a high point of Italian mannerism.

It is noteworthy that the motets at the end of the Chantilly Codex, nine in four parts, four in three, are rhythmically less complicated than the songs, although they are by no means all religious despite the Latin texts of all but three. The secular motet, long so important, was now a dying form. On the other hand the religious motet was just then being given a new life in Italy, where it had been practically unknown, by a composer whose name never appears in Chantilly but does appear modestly in its counterpart the Modena Codex beside the mannerists (and still Machaut) as the composer of a Latin canon and a virelai, 'Sus un fontayne'.[69] Here he is seen as a mannerist himself, weaving into his virelai the words and music of three ballades by Philippus de Caserta who must have been his friend or even master. This newcomer was a northerner, a Walloon from Liège, Johannes Ciconia (d. 1411), who spent at least the last nine years of his life at Padua.

He was not the only musician from the prince-bishopric who came to Italy at this time, nor were the Avignon popes the only ones who employed foreigners. The Roman Boniface IX had at least three Liègois singers in his chapel (1389–90): Henricus de Latunna, Egidius de Lens, and Henricus Tulpijn.[70] These were among the forerunners of an extraordinary invasion which was to transform Italian music, already conditioned to such a change by the contacts of the previous half-century. By far the most important of them was Ciconia.

[65] Begun only in 1386 and still the subject of bitter architectural controversy in 1401.
[66] Twenty-two secular compositions in Apel, *CMM* 53, i; twenty-nine pieces in Cesari and Fano, *La Cappella musicale del Duomo di Milano* (Milan, 1957).
[67] Apel, *CMM* 53, iii, p. 48.
[68] Ed. Cesari and Fano, op. cit., p. 235, and Guillaume de Van (Paris, 1938).
[69] *OAM(M)*, No. 73. [70] Haberl, op. cit., p. 214.

8

The European Synthesis

Hitherto European polyphony had developed almost exclusively in the hands of French-speaking musicians, or musicians in close and constant contact with them as the English were. As we have just seen, even the temporarily individual music of *trecento* Italy was gradually transformed by French influence. But the appearance of Ciconia at Padua and his compatriots in the Papal chapel marked a new development, the occupation of Italian posts by foreigners. This became particularly noticeable after the ending of the Papal Schism. The Council of Constance itself had brought together musicians from various countries; the Emperor Sigismund was accompanied by Oswald von Wolkenstein and the singers who accompanied the English delegation were particularly admired in Cologne on the way as well as at Constance.

When at last Martin V was elected in 1417 and made his tortoise-like journey to Rome, he recruited his chapel as he went, arriving with fifteen singers mostly bearing such names as Hanelle, Bruyant, Reyner, Dore and 'Guillermus magnus' (Guillaume Legrant). By Legrant, who was acquired at Mantua in 1419, we have a Gloria, two Credos, and three French virelais,[1] mostly in note-against-note style but with bold chromaticisms. Another eminent composer – but only of chansons – Pierre Fontaine ('Petr. de fonte') was recruited in Florence in March 1420, at the same time as Jehan Dore with whom he had been a choirboy at Rouen Cathedral and also from 1404 to 1419 a fellow-member of the Duke of Burgundy's chapel. To that chapel he returned in 1428 on leaving the Papal service, until his death *c.* 1450. In 1425 there was a more notable accession. Nicolaus Grenon had been at the Burgundian court as early as 1385, then held posts in Paris, at Laon, Cambrai, the Duke of Berry's chapel, back to the Burgundian court, Cambrai again. Now in June 1425 he turned up in Rome, bringing a group of boys (*cantores pueri et parvi*). When he went back to the north in 1427, he was succeeded by a close friend, a Walloon from Cambrai who was to become one of the greatest composers of the century, Guillaume Dufay. Dufay had already been in Italy during 1420–6 in the service of the Malatestas at Rimini and Pesaro. Before he too wandered away in 1433, he

---

[1] All ed. Gilbert Reaney in *CMM* 11, ii. One of the Credos, dated 1426, by which time Legrant had left the Papal service, is easily accessible in *HAM*, i, No. 56.

had saluted a new Pope, Eugenius IV, with one of his finest motets, 'Ecclesiae militantis'[2] and greeted three Liègois recruits to the chapel: Arnold and Hugo de Lantins, who had already been at Venice, and Johannes Brassart.[3] Like Dufay they did not stay long; from 1439 to 1443 Brassart was in the Court chapel of the first two Habsburg emperors, Albert II and Frederick III. As for Dufay, he went to Turin in 1434 for the marriage of Louis of Savoy to the daughter of the last Lusignan King of Jerusalem and Cyprus,[4] followed the Pope to Florence and Bologna when disorders drove him from Rome, left the Papal service for good in 1437, was at Turin till about 1444, and spent the last thirty years of his life – he died in 1474 – at Cambrai and Mons under the wing of the Dukes of Burgundy.

These restless wanderings tell their own story. The Walloons from the prince-bishoprics of Cambrai and Liège – and there were many besides those mentioned here – took service in Italy but never quite lost touch with their native land. Some, of course, never went south at all, or only briefly: Dufay's teacher, Richard Loqueville (d. 1418), Jacobus Vide who was at the Burgundian court during the 1420s, and, most famous of all, Gilles Binchois of Mons (c. 1400–1460). But there were enough invaders to swamp the native Italian disciples of Ciconia or the mannerists – such men as Antonius Romanus, by whom we have a motet commemorating the election of Tomaso Mocenigo as Doge of Venice in 1415,[5] Paolo da Firenze (d. c. 1419),[6] Antonius de Civitate, and Bartholomaeus de Bononia. This last was one of the pioneers of the technique which has unfortunately become known as 'parody', and would be better called 'paraphrase': the free remodelling usually of a secular work into a sacred one. His Gloria and Credo[7] are based respectively on his ballata 'Vince con lena' and virelai 'Que pena maior'. When Matteo da Perugia left Milan Cathedral in 1416, his successor after a nine-year break was not an Italian but an Avignonese, Beltrame or Bertrand Feragut, who had already been at Vicenza. Yet the ultimate result was easily predictable. Italy conquered her conquerors and the Walloons became Italianized. The process had begun with Ciconia himself.[8]

---

[2] Ed. Heinrich Besseler, *Dufay: Opera Omnia* (*CMM* 1), i, p. 46.
[3] *Opera Omnia*, ed. Keith E. Mixter, in *CMM* 35.
[4] Who is thought to have brought with her a vast footnote to French Crusader culture: a manuscript, Turin, Bibl. Naz. J II 9, containing Mass-movements, including a nearly complete Mass cycle, 41 motets, 103 ballades, and 64 rondeaux and virelais, all anonymous and none with concordances, ed. Richard H. Hoppin, *CMM* 21, from which an anonymous motet is reproduced in *OAM(M)*, No. 60.
[5] Printed by Schering, *Geschichte der Musik in Beispielen* (Leipzig, 1931), No. 30. There is a complete edition of Antonius's works ed. Alberto Gallo (Bologna, 1965).
[6] The opening of his famous madrigal, 'Godi, Firenze' (1405) is printed in *NOHM*, iii, pp. 31–2.
[7] Ed. Charles Van den Borren, *Polyphonia Sacra* (Burnham, 1932), pp. 37 and 44.
[8] The music of all these composers is preserved in numerous sources, of which three of the most important are Trent, Castel del Buon Consiglio, 87 and 92, probably representing the repertory of the court chapel of the Emperor Sigismund (ed. Guido Adler *et al.*, *DTÖ*, Jg. vii, xi(1), xix(1), xxvii(1), xxxi, and xl (vols. 14/15, 22, 38, 53, 61, and 76), Oxford, Bodl. Canonici misc. 213, probably of Venetian origin (ed. Van den Borren, op. cit., and Reaney, *CMM* 11), and Aosta, Seminario. They are interesting in that they are written on paper in *white* notation, that is to say breves, semibreves, and minims are only outlined (as they still are) instead of being filled in with ink. Semiminimae and fusae were generally black like their modern equivalents, the crotchet (quarter-note) and quaver (eighth-note). The change, made about the middle of the fourteenth century, was the result of difficulties in writing black notation on paper, which was made semi-transparent (or even eaten through) by ink, instead of parchment.

8. The European Synthesis

ITALIAN INFLUENCE ON CICONIA

That practically all Ciconia's secular works are settings of Italian poems is not surprising. But he also cultivated the ballata in two or three parts with plenty of coloratura in the upper parts[9] and took part in the brief revival of the madrigal which occurred at the turn of the century. On the other hand the three-part canon, 'Le ray au soleyl',[10] is a typical exercise of northern ingenuity and the mannerism of his Modena virelai, 'Sus un fontayne', has already been mentioned on p. 137. It is his motets, the most important part of his work though a form foreign to the Italians, which show how Italy began to fertilize the invaders. They can practically all be dated, by the persons and events to which they refer, to the period 1400–10. Two of them are for two voices only, both singing the same Latin text and stylistically indistinguishable from madrigals, though one of them, 'O Petre, Christi discipule', can be dated to 1409; two others are monotextual, with two equal voices duetting with free or canonic imitation over an instrumental tenor. The rest have two or in one case three texts as in the old type. But the melodic lines of the duetting voices are assimilated, instead of markedly differentiated like those of the *ars nova* motet, and fall into short phrases with a tendency to sequential treatment of motives.

Ciconia, like the trecento Italians, invents his own tenors and in the four cases where he employs isorhythmic patterns these are simple and obvious. When he introduces a contratenor as well, this is assimilated to the tenor and forms with it a quasi-harmonic basis with considerable emphasis on the final and fifth of the mode. Both tenor and contratenor were almost certainly for the most part conceived for instruments. So, evidently, was the fanfare-like introduction to 'Doctorum principem/Melodia suavissima', after which the texture perfectly illustrates what has just been said:[11]

Ex. 31

[9] For a two-part example see Wolf, *Geschichte der Mensural-Notation*, original notation of 'Dolce fortuna', ii, p. 50, and transcription, iii, No. 30. Most of Ciconia's compositions are transcribed, not altogether reliably, in Suzanne Clercx, *Johannes Ciconia* (Brussels, 1960), ii.
[10] See Richard Hoppin's solution in *MQ*, xlvii (1961), p. 419.
[11] See the more extended quotation in *NOHM*, iii, p. 154.

Ciconia understood better perhaps than any earlier musician how to crown a work with an effect of splendid sonority, witness the fanfares at the end of 'Venetia, mundi splendor/Michael', and the final 'Amen' of 'O virum/O lux/O beate Nicholae',[12] which should be compared with the less worldly but still impressive 'Amen' of a Gloria in the Canonici Codex.[13] This particular Gloria resembles Ciconia's motets, with its cantabile highest part and quasi-instrumental tenor and contratenor. But the one (with a 'Spiritus et alme' trope) which immediately precedes it in the manuscript shows an innovation found in yet another Gloria of Ciconia's and a Credo: the markings 'dui' and 'chorus' for the alternation of soloists with choir which confirm that by this time vocal polyphony was no longer for soloists only.[13a]

It is hazardous to attribute to the influence of one composer what may have been general tendencies, but it is clear that Ciconia enjoyed a considerable reputation, and when we find Dufay's earliest datable motet, the youthful, monotextual 'Vasilissa, ergo gaude' of 1421 with its duetting upper voices supported harmonically by isorhythmic but liturgical tenor and contratenor, and Guillaume Legrant's already mentioned Credo of 1426[14] with its alternation of two-part with three-part sections suggesting alternation of soloists and chorus, it is not unreasonable to suspect that Legrant and Dufay were familiar with Ciconia's practices. By that time, however, other forces had come into play: not only the Council of Constance with the consequent establishment of Rome as a musical focus, but the English conquest of Northern France, as a result of which Henry V's Chapel was in France in 1417–21, and an English Regent, the Duke of Bedford, ruled in Paris from 1422 to 1435. The Earl of Suffolk also maintained a musical household in Paris in the 1420s.

DUNSTABLE AND THE 'OLD HALL' COMPOSERS

By far the most important English source of this period, preserved at St. Edmund's College, Old Hall, Ware, was compiled *c*. 1410–20.[15] It contains isorhythmic motets by members of the Chapel Royal, Cooke (d. 1456), Sturgeon (d. 1454), and Damett (d. 1437), praying for and giving thanks for victory in the Agincourt year, 1415, while another – 'En Katerine/Virginalis/Sponsus amat sponsam' by Byttering – may well commemorate the King's wedding to the 'queen of all Katharines'. But these are surpassed in both technical skill and sheer beauty of sound by another motet added to Old Hall by a later hand: 'Veni sancte Spiritus/Veni creator/Mentes tuorum'[16] by John Dunstable (d. 1453). Frank Harrison suggests[17] that this may have been sung by the Chapel Royal or the Chapel

[12] Quoted in Heinrich Besseler, *Musik des Mittelalters und der Renaissance* (Potsdam, 1937), p. 204.
[13] Van den Borren, op. cit., p. 88; easily accessible in *HAM*, i, No. 55.
[13a] See further Howard M. Brown, 'Choral Music in the Renaissance', *Early Music*, vi (1978), p. 164.
[14] See n. 1.
[15] Ed. Andrew Hughes and Margaret Bent, *CMM* 46, i and ii (1969).
[16] Ed. Manfred Bukofzer, *John Dunstable: Complete Works* (*MB*, viii) (London, revised edition by Margaret and Ian Bent and Brian Trowell, 1970), p. 88.
[17] *Music in Medieval Britain* (London, 1958), p. 244.

of the Duke of Bedford at the coronation of the nine-year old Henry VI in Notre Dame in 1431. For Dunstable was in the service of Bedford, ally and brother-in-law of Philip, Duke of Burgundy, who numbered among his subjects many of the most gifted musicians of Europe. And it was Dunstable more than any other English composer – more even than the Canterbury Benedictine Leonel Power (d. 1445),[18] whose works are likewise preserved in more continental than English sources – who through the Burgundian masters injected the English strain into European music. It was Dunstable who was singled out not only by the Burgundian court poet, Martin le Franc (*Le Champion des dames, c.* 1440), as the man from whom 'G. Du Fay' and Binchois had acquired the 'nouvelle pratique De faire frisque concordance En haulte et en basse musique' (in public and in intimate music). And a generation later the Walloon theorist-composer Johannes Tinctoris (*Proportionale musices, c.* 1474) declared that 'the possibilities of our music have been so marvellously increased that there appears to be a new art . . . whose fount and origin is held to be among the English, of whom Dunstable stood forth as chief.[19] Even as late as 1508 Eloy d'Amerval in his *Livre de la Deablerie* coupled 'Dompstaple et du Fay' at the head of a list of 'grans musiciens'.

ENGLISH CONDUCTUS-STYLE AND FAUXBOURDON

What was the nature of this 'new way of making *frisque concordance*' which so transformed the art? It was not the cultivation of cantilena in the highest part of polyphony, freely invented or (in some church music) decorated plainsong (cf. Ex. 32 below), for as we have seen[20] this was favoured by the non-mannerist French composers of the post-Machaut period. It was almost certainly the full euphonious sound of the conductus-like writing in parallel thirds and sixths.[21] This was still expressly forbidden by the sonorously named Paduan theorist Prosdocimus de Beldemandis in his *Tractatus de Contrapuncto* (1412)[22] who accepted thirds and sixths as consonant and even allowed dissonances in ornamental passages where, owing to the speed, the ear does not feel them as such (*in cantu fractibili eo quod in ipso propter velocitatem vocum earum non sentiuntur dissonantiae*). But Prosdocimus objected to parallelism on the ground that it is contrary to the purpose of counterpoint 'which is that what one voice sings shall be different from what the other sings'. This medieval conception of absolute differentiation of parts had already been undermined in the later fourteenth century. There are many indications that the practice of purely horizontal composition – first the tenor, then a second part, and so on – was beginning to die out, although the tenor was long to remain the hard core of liturgical

---

[18] Complete works ed. Charles Hamm *CMM* 50, and see Hamm's study of the motets in *Studies in Music History* (ed. Harold Powers) (Princeton, 1968), p. 127.
[19] Trs. Oliver Strunk, *Source Readings in Music History* (London, 1952), p. 195.
[20] See p. 135.
[21] See p. 134 and Ex. 30.
[22] Published in Coussemaker, *Scriptorum*, iii, p. 193.

music. The specifically English practice of 'wandering' cantus firmus – a segment of plainsong in one part, the next in another, the next perhaps in the third, as in Byttering's antiphon 'Nesciens mater'[23] – depended on simultaneous instead of successive composition of the parts.

Old Hall does contain isorhythmic motets, pieces employing the Italian caccia technique, e.g. an anonymous Credo,[24] and even two essays in mannerist complication – a Gloria and Credo by Power.[25] But many of the Glorias, Credos, Sanctus, and Agnus which constitute the major part of the collection, usually with the plainsong (naturally in the Sarum forms used in England) in the middle part, are in this conductus-like style, each simple group in each category being followed by a more elaborate group. The opening of a Sanctus by Power[26]

Ex. 32

illustrates a slight elaboration of the conductus-style with an ornamented version of the plainsong (Sarum: Sanctus No. 2 marked with asterisks) in the highest part, and at the same time shows the careful handling of dissonance by suspension which was another sign of the times. The note-against-note conductus style, with only occasional elaboration in the highest part, is also that of the settings of the Passions according to Matthew (incomplete) and Luke in Brit. Lib., Egerton 3307, probably compiled in the 1430s. These are the earliest polyphonic Passions so far discovered.[27] The words of the crowd, Pilate, the centurion, and the two thieves are all set in three parts, without reference to any known plainsong or recitation tone though this must have been sung by Christ and the evangelist.

The main part of the Old Hall manuscript, which it must be remembered contains only part of the enormous English repertory of this period, must have been compiled before the death in 1422 of Henry V who may himself be represented in it by a Gloria and Sanctus.[28] The next decade of Anglo-Burgundian alliance is that in which we should expect to find English influence at its height on the Continent and, sure enough, the earliest known

[23] Hughes and Bent, No. 50.
[24] Ibid., No. 85.
[25] Ibid., Nos 22 and 81; the Credo is also given in *OAM(M)*, No. 66.
[26] Ibid., No. 116. Like Legrant's Credo (see pp. 138 and 141), it alternates two-part writing ('Pleni sunt coeli' and 'Qui venit') with three-part.
[27] See Bukofzer, *Studies in Medieval and Renaissance Music* (London, 1951), pp. 113ff.; for Bukofzer's transcription of the Luke Passion see *MQ*, xxxiii (1947), p. 43. Egerton 3307 has been published in entirety by Gwynn S. McPeek (London, 1963). Two tiny fragments from a St. John Passion from Füssen in southern Bavaria, published by Otto Kade, *Die ältere Passionskomposition* (Gütersloh, 1893), p. 115 (facsimile in *MGG*, x, col. 899), date from almost exactly the same time.
[28] Ibid., Nos. 16 and 94. Frank Harrison, op. cit., pp. 220–1, suggests that 'Roy Henry' was his father, Henry IV.

non-English examples of the style are to be found in a Piacenza manuscript of this period, Bologna, Liceo mus., Q 15 (*olim* 37). One is a Communion, '[Vos] qui secuti estis me', appended to a *Missa Sancti Jacobi* by Dufay, a work historically important in another respect. The other is a Marian antiphon, 'Regina caeli laetare', by his compatriot Johannes de Lymburgia. In both, the plainsong, ornamented as in Ex. 32, is in the upper part, and both are notated in two parts only. Dufay, however, provides a gloss instructing 'if a third part is required, take the notes of the highest part and sing them a fourth lower',[29] while the Limburg composer writes against his lower part 'Tenor letare faulx bourdon'.

This mysterious term 'fauxbourdon' has given rise to endless controversy concerning its origin (French or English), its etymology, its meaning, and its distinction from 'English descant', but it is perfectly clear that the intention is the same as in Dufay's 'Qui secuti':[30]

Ex. 33

'Fauxbourdon' may indeed be a misapprehension of an English term, 'faburdon'. This is used in an early fifteenth-century treatise quoted in the later manuscript Brit. Lib., Lansdowne 763, for a method of singing at sight a treble a fourth above a plainsong and a tenor a third below it; 'fauxbourdon' still consisted of parallel fourths between the upper parts, but now when the plainsong was commonly in the upper part the term was applied to the non-written lower one. But its meaning may not always have been understood. Whereas Dufay's hymn 'Tu lumen, tu splendor patris' (a verse of 'Christe, redemptor omnium, ex patre') appears in the Bologna manuscript and three other sources with the simple instruction 'Contra au fauxbourdon', in Modena, Bibl. Est. M. 5.24 (*olim* lat. 568) someone has composed an independent and somewhat awkward contratenor.[31]

DUFAY AND THE 'CYCLIC' MASS

English composers also played a leading role in the development of the so-called 'cyclic' Ordinary of the Mass, which during the second quarter of the century gradually replaced the isorhythmic motet as the most important form of liturgical composition. (Dufay's last datable isorhythmic motets were composed between 1436 – 'Nuper rosarum flores/Terribilis' for the consecration of the cathedral at Florence – and 1446.) More than half a

[29] See *MF*, i (1948), p. 109, and *Dufay: Opera Omnia* (ed. Heinrich Besseler), ii (*CMM* 1, ii), p. 44.
[30] Quoted from Besseler, *Bourdon und Fauxbourdon* (Leipzig, 1950), p. 18.
[31] See *Opera Omnia* (*CMM* 1), v, p. 40, and ed. Rudolf Gerber in *ChW*, xlix (Wolfenbüttel, 1937), p. 5.

century seems to have passed after Machaut's isolated masterpiece before another composer attempted a single-handed setting of the complete Ordinary. There is no complete Mass in Old Hall although, like other collections of the period, it contains probable or certain 'pairs'. One such is Power's Sanctus, No. 118, and Agnus, No. 141, each of which borrows its tenor from the corresponding plainsong of Mass XVII (*Liber Usualis*, p. 61), the same tenors (with variants) that Machaut had taken for the same movements. When the young Dufay composed what was probably his first complete Mass,[32] as distinct from his numerous single movements and pairs, he used no plainsong tenor but gave his setting a musical inter-relationship by opening Kyrie and Sanctus with identical superius and rather similar contratenor. In another early work, the *Missa Sancti Jacobi*, he introduces plainsong in tenor or upper part for Kyrie ('Cunctipotens Genitor', likewise following Machaut), Sanctus, and Agnus, as well as in the four movements for the Proper of St. James (concluding with the already mentioned fauxbourdon Communion) which he composed as well. Like Ciconia (see p. 141) he marks an alternation of 'duo' and 'chorus'. (Incidentally, the youthful Dufay was not above quoting other melodies than plainsong; a Gloria-Credo pair in the same codex as this Mass end respectively with a French popular tune, 'Tu m'a monté su la pance et riens n'a fait', and an Italian one, 'La villanella non è bella', and the words are written in so that the point shall not be missed.[33]) Bologna, Q 15, contains two other complete Masses besides Dufay's *Sancti Jacobi:* one by Johannes de Lymburgia, the other by Dufay's colleague in the Papal Chapel during 1431–2, Arnold de Lantins. Each is musically unified by a 'motto' or 'head-motive', each movement opening with a variant of the same basic melody in the highest part.[34]

At the same time English composers were beginning to employ another method of giving musical unity to settings of the complete Ordinary. This was the composition of all the movements on the same liturgical tenor, the so-called 'tenor Mass', and it was this method which became a standard one for centuries. The earliest known examples are one on the popular antiphon 'Alma Redemptoris Mater' by Leonel Power[35] and one on 'Rex saeculorum'[36] which is ascribed in Trent 92 to Power and in the Aosta Codex to Dunstable. An anonymous Englishman took a further step in the *Missa Caput*, formerly ascribed to Dufay, which employs both 'mottos', and a unifying tenor. (The latter is drawn from the English form of an antiphon for Maundy Thursday, the melisma on the word 'caput' when Peter pleads for the washing of 'not my feet only, but also my hands and my *head*'.[37])

[32] His Masses are published in the *Opera Omnia*, ii and iii.
[33] Ibid., iv, No. 4, pp. 24 and 30.
[34] The five Lymburgia incipits are printed in Besseler, *Musik des Mittelalters*, p. 200; Lantins' Mass has been edited by Charles Van den Borren from the version in Bodl. Canonici 213, op. cit., p. 1.
[35] Trent Codex 87 and Aosta, Seminario; ed. Laurence Feininger, *Documenta Polyphoniae Liturgicae*, series i, No. 2 (Rome, 1947).
[36] Ed. Bukofzer, *MB*, viii.
[37] See Bukofzer, *Studies in Medieval and Renaissance Music* (London, 1951), particularly pp. 230–1, 245, 257 ff., and 272.

8. The European Synthesis

Another anonymous Mass dubiously ascribed to Dufay – like 'Caput' it is included in the modern *Opera Omnia* – 'La mort de Saint Gothard', in the Modena Codex lat. 456, uses an obviously secular tenor for the third Agnus. Dufay was, however, indubitably the composer of the great Mass 'Se la face ay pale' (*c.* 1450)[38] based on the tenor of his own much earlier chanson which provides the tenor of every movement. Here, probably for the first time, was frank abandonment of the theory that polyphony was a decoration of a sacred object, the plainsong dictated to St. Gregory by the Holy Ghost, and recognition that the basic tenor was nothing more or less than a structural device for which a secular melody would serve as well as a sacred one.

PROPORTIONAL NOTATION

As in most of his motets, from the early 'Vasilissa, ergo gaude' onward, Dufay begins each movement of 'Se la face ay pale' except the Kyrie with duetting upper voices; tenor and 'tenor bassus' then also enter together. The tenor maintains the same rhythmic pattern as in the chanson but is modified from movement to movement, or within the movement, by 'proportional notation': the augmentation or diminution of note-values in arithmetical ratios indicated by time-signature and 'canon' (which in this context means nothing more than 'rule' or 'prescription'). Thus the canon at the head of the Gloria, 'Tenor ter dicitur. Primo quaelibet figura crescit in triplo, secundo in duplo, tertio ut jacet', indicates that the tenor is to be sung first ('Adoramus te') in note-values three times those of the other parts, the second time ('miserere nobis') in doubled note-values – although since the other parts are now in binary rhythm three of their bars now equal one of the tenor (rewritten in modern note values, $3 \times 2/4 = 1 \times 3/2$) – while at 'Cum sancto spiritu' the tenor is sung 'as it lies', in normal note-values. (Similarly in the tenor of Dunstable's motet 'Veni sancte Spiritus', mentioned on p. 141, the third and fourth of its isorhythmic taleae have only two-thirds the time-value of the first two, and the fifth and sixth only one third.)

In the music of the fifteenth century and some time after, such 'proportions' and the 'canons', often in riddle form, which indicate them, were a notable feature – perhaps an aftermath of fourteenth-century mannerism. It need hardly be said that these ingenuities are purely structural. Dufay does not even rely, as the English composers did, solely on an almost omnipresent tenor – it is silent in the Christe, Benedictus, and second Agnus – to give a sense of unity to his Mass. He also employs the device of the initial motive in the highest part, or, rather, in imitation between the two upper parts in their preliminary duetting:

[38] Ed. Besseler separately, *Capella*, ii (Kassel, 1951), as well as in *Opera Omnia*, iii.

Ex. 34

(i) Ky – – ri – – e

Contra

[Se   la   face   ay   pa –   le,
Tenor

Tenor bassus

la   cause et amer]

(ii) GLORIA

Et   in   ter – ra   pax   ho – mi – ni – – bus

Et   in   ter – ra   pax   ho – mi – ni – – bus

(iii) CREDO

Pa – – – – – – trem   o – – – mni – – –

Pa – – – – – – – trem   o – mni – po –

po – – – ten – – – tem,

– ten – – – – – – – tem,

The flowing cantabile lines and euphonious harmony overlaying the intellectual structure represent a perfect synthesis of Italian, English, and Walloon elements. But it would be premature to regard the harmony as 'tonal' for whereas the original chanson does indeed cadence on C, all the movements of the Mass and all but one of the internal sections cadence on F harmony, although the final of the tenor is always C and there is no feeling of 'Lydian' mode. The superius and contratenor of the chanson are ignored in the Mass except for the beginning of the – probably instrumental – coda to each stanza, which is reflected in the corresponding part of each movement. This is part of the already mentioned process later known as 'parodia'. In the 'Amen' of Gloria and Credo Dufay quotes rather than paraphrases:

Ex. 35

(i) CHANSON

(ii) GLORIA

DUFAY'S LAST COMPOSITIONS

Dufay employed a secular tenor in one more Mass (perhaps *c.* 1460), the most famous of all secular cantus firmi, probably borrowed from the tenor of the chanson, 'L'omme armé', by Robert Morton, an English member of the Burgundian ducal chapel from 1457 to 1475.[39] The final cadence of the third Agnus Dei[40] is identical in all four parts with that of Morton's piece. In his last two great Masses 'Ecce ancilla Domini' (1463) and 'Ave regina coelorum' (*c.* 1464) Dufay returned to liturgical tenors, Marian antiphons in both cases. All the main movements of both Masses, and most of the interval sections, end with the equivalent of 'dominant-tonic' harmonic cadences in C, although the tenors are in the plagal modes of G and F respectively. The 'Ave regina', every movement of which opens with a passage identical in all four parts, has at 'misererere nobis' in the second Agnus a passage completely

[39] The four-part version of Morton's chanson, with two others by him, ed. J. Marix, *Les Musiciens de la cour de Bourgogne (1420–1467)*, (Paris, 1937), p. 96; an earlier form lacking the contratenor bassus is preserved in the Mellon Chansonnier (Yale University). On the origin of the tune, and the innumerable Masses based on it, see Lewis Lockwood, 'Aspects of the "L'Homme armé" Tradition', PRMA, c (1973–4), p. 97.
[40] Easily accessible in *HAM*, i, No. 66*c*.

identical with the setting of the words 'Miserere supplicanti Dufay' in a remarkable four-part setting of the same antiphon (also 1464).[41] In this work, which the composer intended according to his will to be sung by his death-bed, he inserted dramatically impassioned tropes imploring the Virgin's intercession.

DUFAY'S SUCCESSORS

Younger composers were not slow in following the way pointed by Dufay in Mass-composition, even choosing the same subjects. His own *clerc* at Cambrai, Johannes Regis (*c.* 1430–*c.* 1485), wrote Masses in by no means slavish imitation on 'L'homme armé' (as early as 1462) and 'Ecce ancilla Domini'.[42] And a greater than Regis, Johannes Ockeghem (*c.* 1420–1497), leader and later *maistre* of the French royal chapel for more than forty years, composed a 'L'homme armé' and a 'Caput'. (His 'Ecce ancilla' is on a different melody.) The so-called 'tenor Mass' was to be the preferred form, but the diversity of styles continuing after the middle of the century is illustrated by the three Masses of Walter Frye,[43] an Englishman who was probably at the Burgundian court at about the same time as Morton: the three-part 'Nobilis et pulchra' is in the old English style with the liturgical melody mostly in the lowest part and (since he was not writing for the English use) a polyphonic troped Kyrie; the four-part 'Flos regalis' is a tenor Mass with a harmony-supporting contratenor bassus in Dufay's style; in the three-part 'Summe Trinitati' the tenor is isorhythmic in every movement. The movements of all three have motto openings – indeed Gloria and Credo of 'Summe Trinitati' open with paraphrases of Frye's motet 'Salve virgo'. However, Frye's most popular religious work was not a Mass but a little Marian antiphon, on no known liturgical melody, 'Ave Regina', which is preserved in thirteen sources plus three organ transcriptions; it provided the basis of a motet and Mass by Obrecht, and its superius and tenor are represented in a Netherland painting of the Madonna.[44] Hardly less popular was his three-part secular song 'So ys emprentid in my remembrance' which is found all over the Continent with such garblings of the text as 'Soyez aprantiz', with French texts, with a Latin text, and as a tenor in a motet and Mass.

ENGLISH SONGS AND CAROLS

The music of Frye and Morton, like Dunstable's and John Bedingham's, is preserved almost entirely in continental sources and they seem to have shown no special preference in their secular works for the setting of English words. On the other hand English secular song of the period is mostly anonymous. Much of it is unsophisticated yet sometimes deeply felt, as is

[41] Ed. Besseler, *Capella*, i, p. 10 (Kassel, 1950).
[42] In *Opera omnia Johannis Regis*, i (*CMM* 9(i)), ed. Cornelius Lindenburg.
[43] *Opera Omnia*, ed. Sylvia Kenney, in *CMM* 19.
[44] Reproduced in Besseler, *Musik des Mittelalters*, pl. XIII.

the two-part 'Alas departynge' in the Bodleian MS, Ashmole 191, to say nothing of the fine three-part 'Go hert hurt with adversite' in the same manuscript, sometimes roistering as in the three-part 'Tappster, dryngker' (in Bodleian, Selden B 26). The Selden manuscript and the already mentioned Egerton 3307 (see p. 143) preserve a great number of examples of that peculiarly English variety of song: the carol, which had English, Latin, or mixed texts, generally but not invariably religious. It seems likely that it was originally a round dance with the 'burden' or refrain sung by the group, who paused while the intermediate verses were sung by the leader rather as in the virelai (see p. 116); but in the polyphonic carol of the fifteenth century the verse is commonly in two parts and the burden may be in three. There may even be two different burdens, of which the second is sometimes marked 'chorus'. Hardly any composers' names appear and those few are unknown or obscure, yet they were gifted not only technically but creatively and their work covers a wide range, from the tender simplicity of 'There is no rose' to the exultant choral second burden of 'Alleluia: Now well may we mirthes make' and the proud patriotism of 'Deo gracias, Anglia', the song of thanksgiving for Agincourt.[45]

Pl. 33   A detail from 'The Hunt of Philip the Good': 16th-century copy of a painting (destroyed in 1608) by a follower of Jan van Eyck, in the Musée de Versailles, Paris. The instruments are a slide-trumpet, an undistinguishable wind-instrument, and two varieties of shawm.

THE BURGUNDIAN CHANSON

It would be an exaggeration to say that turning from the English carols to the chansons that were produced in quantities by the leading composers of Europe for the delectation of the sophisticated court of Philip the Good, Duke of Burgundy, is liking stepping from a cottage garden into a hothouse filled with exotic flowers. But it would hardly be an exaggeration if one were considering only the texts. For one thing, the carols are nearly all religious while the Burgundian chansons, though composed by clerics, are almost without exception concerned with love. Easily the favourite form was the rondeau, followed by the ballade, while the virelai was dying out.

It was the highest of the three parts that was composed first, as an anonymous English theorist of the times tells us: '. . . qui vult condere baladam, rotundellum, viriledum . . . fiat primo discantus'.[46] The tenor is often textless and the contratenor is almost always so, crossing and recrossing the tenor and providing with it a harmonic basis like that described on p. 140 in Ciconia's motets. The phrases are short, with clearly marked cadences, as in this charming little song[47] by Dufay's friend and predecessor in the Papal chapel, Nicolas Grenon:

Ex. 36

Indeed Dufay's master, Loqueville,[48] seems to have been the initiator of the fourteenth-century type of chanson. Dufay himself composed a dozen or so Italian songs when he was in the Malatesta or Papal service – and drew very near to Matteo da Perugia in his setting of Petrarch's 'Vergine bella'. Thereafter he produced chansons prolifically and with an infinite variety of method: solo song over instrumental tenor and contra ('Je languis en piteux martire' and, simpler, 'Las! Que feray?'), canonic duet for superius and

[45] Ed. John Stevens, *Mediaeval Carols* (*MB*, iv) (London, 1952), Nos. 14, 20, and 8.
[46] Quoted by Bukofzer, *MQ*, xxxviii (1952), p. 38, n. 25.
[47] In Codex Canonici 213; trans. J. F. R. and C. Stainer, *Dufay and his Contemporaries* (London, 1898), p. 162.
[48] Works, ed. Reaney, in *CMM* 11, iii.

tenor, with contra between ('Bon jour, bon mois'), freer imitation, with the contra sounding the initial phrase only ('Franc cœur gentil'), duet for superius and contra, over a tenor singing a different text ('Je ne puis plus'), all three parts texted in mainly note-against-note style ('J'attendray tant qu'il vous playra'), quasi-parlando ('La belle se siet').[49] Some have instrumental introductions or interludes or postludes – though absence of text does not in itself exclude vocal performance, while texted passages may well have been doubled by instruments: recorder, vielle, lute, or harp. Or the chansons may have been performed out of doors by instruments alone, a trio of shawm, pommer (alto shawm), and slide-trumpet such as we see on the left of a well-known painting of a festivity at the Burgundian court, *c.* 1430–1 (see pl. 33). (We know that Dufay's 'Je ne vis onques la pareille' was sung by a boy of twelve at the most famous of all Philip the Good's festivities, the banquet of the 'Vœux du Faisan' at Lille on 17 February 1454 when the Duke gathered his Knights of the Golden Fleece to take crusading vows against the Turks[50]). But it is the contratenor, with its often unvocal intervals, which is most often and most obviously instrumental. It is usually responsible for that stressing of the fifth and final of the mode referred to on p. 140 in connection with Ciconia which, occurring at cadences:

Ex. 37

(i) Las! que feray? (ii) Pour l'amour de ma doulce amye

no doubt formed the habit which was to become the familiar 'full close' of tonal harmony. (Intermediate cadences are commonly on to the fifth, less often on other degrees of the mode, as well as on the final.) But with Dufay and his contemporaries it was the fall of the tenor to the final of the mode which constituted the essence of the cadence. The characteristic octave leap of the contra was only quasi-harmonic filling in or support, and the 'under third' or 'Landini' cadence had not finally disappeared even in Josquin's day.

BINCHOIS AND THE LAST BURGUNDIANS

The composer whose name is most commonly mentioned beside Dufay's, and who is even depicted talking to him in the manuscript of Martin Le Franc's *Champion des Dames* (1440), is Binchois, for a time in the service of

---

[49] All the secular works are in *Opera Omnia*, vi; many of the chansons are also printed elsewhere, e.g. *HAM*, i, Nos. 67–8, *OAM(M)*, No. 99.

[50] For a full contemporary account of the banquet and its music, see Marix, *Histoire de la musique et des musiciens de la Cour de Bourgogne sous le règne de Philippe le Bon* (Strasbourg, 1939), p. 37ff.

the Earl of Suffolk, from 1430 a member of the Burgundian court chapel. Binchois was a more limited composer than Dufay. He wrote no complete Mass, only separate movements in the old way. His other church music, other than four Magnificats, consists mostly of short three-part hymns and antiphons, which may have the liturgical melody in the highest part (richly ornamented in the English manner) or in the tenor, or may dispense with it altogether; the third part may be simply 'fauxbourdon'.[52] But in the chanson, the secular solo with two instrumental parts, Binchois was arguably the superior even of Dufay.[53] The enchanting 'De plus en plus' has often been printed but such songs as 'Je loe amours' and the setting of Charles d'Orléans's 'Mon cuer chante' are in no way inferior in lyrical sweetness, while 'Ay! douloureux disant hélas!' and the settings of Alain Chartier's 'Tristre plaisir' and Christine de Pisan's 'Dueil angoisseux', particularly the last,[54] reflect the pessimism of the period and its pre-occupation with ideas of death.

Outstanding among the later, indeed the last, generation of Burgundian song-composers were Hayne van Ghizeghem, who seems to have died young in the 1470s,[55] and Antoine Busnois (d. *c.* 1492).[56] Hayne's rondeau 'De tous biens plaine'[57] was one of the most popular of all Burgundian chansons; Busnois borrowed the superius in his four-part setting of the words. Busnois was a more sophisticated composer, who lived on into a period when, as we shall see in the next chapter, imitation permeated the whole texture of music much more thoroughly than in Dufay or such pieces as Binchois's 'Files à marier'. His chansons are often marked by complex rhythm, occasionally by strict canon. In his four-part songs he sometimes, as in 'Acordes moi ce que je pensse' and 'Terrible dame',[58] contrives a dialogue – in the latter justified by the text – between the two lower voices and the two upper ones, each running overmuch in parallel sixths. Busnois's chansons, in fact, represent not so much the decadence of the 'Burgundian' species as a transition to a new style of secular polyphony.

THE BEGINNINGS OF GERMAN POLYPHONY

Historically Busnois was a transitional figure in more senses than one, for after being for a number of years the favourite musician of Charles the Bold, whose military follies brought about his own death and the decline of the romantic, fragmented Burgundian state, Busnois passed into the service of his daughter. In the hope of saving the situation, Mary of Burgundy

[52] The Magnificats, ten Mass-movements, and 17 liturgical pieces in Marix, *Les Musiciens*.
[53] Complete edition, ed. Wolfgang Rehm, *Die Chansons von Gilles de Binchois* (Mainz, 1957). There are numerous other reprints, including 36 chansons in Marix, ibid., and 16, ed. Wilibald Gurlitt, *ChW*, xxii.
[54] *OAM(M)*, No. 100.   [55] Sixteen songs in Marix, ibid.
[56] Ten songs, ed. Droz, Rokseth, and Thibault, in *Trois Chansonniers français du XVième siècle* (Paris, 1927).
[57] Ibid., i, p. 20 and *NOHM*, iii, p. 247.
[58] Printed respectively in Petrucci's *Harmonice Musices Odhecaton A* (Venice, 1501), p. 290 of Helen Hewitt's edition (Cambridge, Mass., 1946); and (incomplete) in André Pirro, *Histoire de la musique de la fin du XIVe siècle à la fin du XVIe* (Paris, 1940), p. 120.

promptly (in 1477) married the Archduke Maximilian, afterwards the Emperor Maximilian I, and under the music-loving emperor Netherland musical influence began to strike roots in the German lands where up to then polyphony had been conservative, not to say homespun. Thus, whereas the English after their heyday in the first half of the century had according to Tinctoris[59] failed to move with the times (although as we shall see, below, p. 186, they were moving quite successfully on their own isolated and conservative lines), Germany was about to produce such composers as Adam of Fulda, who in a treatise of 1490, specifically mentions Busnois as the 'würdigstes Muster nachzueifern' (the worthiest example to emulate).

Until then fifteenth-century German polyphony had been represented by little more than some of the love-songs (*c.* 1408–1438) of Oswald von Wolkenstein (d. 1445), 'the last of the Minnesinger'; the song-books owned by Wolflein von Lochamer (compiled *c.* 1452–1460), Hartmann Schedel, a humanist who had studied medicine in Italy (compiled *c.* 1461–1467), and the collegiate church at Glogau in Silesia (1470 or later); and by organ-tablatures. Most of Wolkenstein's songs[60] are monophonic and two-thirds of the rest are in two parts only. Despite the wide variety and general attractiveness of Wolkenstein's songs as such, he was a poor contrapuntist[61] and often fell back on contrafacta. His two-part 'Der may mit lieber zal'[62] is, for example, based on a three-part virelai by Jean Vaillant in the Chantilly Codex, 'Par maintes foys',[63] with its charming imitations of bird-song; his two-part 'Mein herz das ist versert'[64] borrows almost unaltered the cantus and tenor of Landini's popular ballata 'Questa fanciulla'.[65] But it is symptomatic that whereas the best source of the Landini (Florence, B.N. Panciatichi 26) has the text only in the cantus, Wolkenstein writes his words only under the tenor. So emerged the *Tenorlied*, its essential melody, anonymous and presumably popular, in the middle of the texture, and with accompanying parts for instruments – in the next century for voices. It was to be the basic type of German secular song until the middle of the sixteenth century.

The fifteenth-century song-books contain a number of such pieces, though many more monophonic songs. Most of the 45 pieces in the *Lochamer Liederbuch*[66] are monophonic; one is a very crude two-part composition; and of the six three-part songs two have the melody in the highest part, three in the tenor, and one is textless. One of the monophonic songs is the tenor of Wolkenstein's 'Wach auff, myn hort', here preceded – as are other songs in the

[59] In the dedication of his *Proportionale Musices* (*c.* 1476); the relevant passage is quoted in Strunk, *Source Readings*, p. 195.
[60] Complete edition, ed. Oswald Koller and Josef Schatz, in *DTÖ*, Jg ix(1) (vol. 18) (Vienna, 1902; reprinted Graz, 1959).
[61] Cf. his best-known song, 'Wach auff, myn hort', ibid., p. 200, also in Gustave Reese, *Music in the Middle Ages* (New York, 1940), p. 379, and Schering, op. cit., No. 46.
[62] Ibid., p. 179, and also *HAM*, i, No. 60. *CMM* 53, i, p. 222.
[64] Koller and Schatz, op. cit., p. 193.
[65] See Pl. 32(i) and Theodor Göllner, 'Landinis "Questafanciulla" bei Oswald von Wolkenstein', *MF*, xvii (1964), particularly p. 396 where both tenors are printed.
[66] Facsimile ed. Konrad Ameln (Berlin, 1925); the polyphonic pieces transcribed idem (Augsburg, 1925); complete edition, ed. Walter Salmen and Christoph Petzach, *DTB. Neue Folge* (Wiesbaden, 1972). See also Salmen, *Das Lochamer Liederbuch: eine musikgeschichtliche Studie* (Leipzig, 1951).

book – by a brief textless introduction which gives us an idea of fifteenth-century instrumental preluding. Another song with an instrumental prelude, marked off by a vertical line, is 'Des klaffers neyden' (The gossip's jealousy) which also appears as a *Tenorlied*, though without text, a few pages later:

Ex. 38

This may be compared with a contemporary piece of popular Italian polyphony, a setting of Giustiniani's 'Ayme sospiri'[67] (in the Escorial MS. IV.a.24), as an illustration of national differences:

Ex. 39

[67] From Walter Rubsamen's 'The Justiniane or Viniziane of the 15th Century', *Acta Musicologica*, xxix (1957), p. 180.

-pi - ri non tro - - - vo pa - ce.

Hartmann Schedel's *Liederbuch* is interesting for its evidence of his knowledge of foreign composers, for he has included compositions by Busnois, Walter Frye, Ockeghem, and others. The more important *Glogauer Liederbuch*,[68] one of the earliest known collections in separate part-books, also contains music by Dufay, Busnois, Hayne van Ghizeghem, Ockeghem, and Tinctoris among others, although anonymously in the manuscript. It is indeed much more than a 'song book' for it includes a great deal of church music, antiphons and so on, and more than sixty instrumental compositions, dances and nameless pieces of various kinds, some with the principal melody in the tenor, some with it in the descant.

EARLY FIFTEENTH-CENTURY KEYBOARD MUSIC

Seen in the perspective of musical history, the German song-books are overshadowed by the keyboard tablatures, for here the Germans were entering a field where they quickly showed special pre-eminence. Apart from the isolated Robertsbridge Codex and a few separate pieces such as the two in the Reina manuscript, the only earlier source of keyboard music is the Faenza Codex 117 mentioned in the previous chapter (see p. 131). The keyboard music in Faenza is written on two six-line staves with 'bar' – lines.[69] The left-hand stave bears the tenor of the original composition more or less exactly, though sometimes transposed; the right-hand stave has a florid part which is either completely free or a highly decorated form of the original cantus and employs recurrent formulae. The original contratenor (and triplum if there is one as in Machaut's 'De toutes fleurs') is ignored. In the very first piece, 'Biance flour', the broken figuration shared between both hands suggests that it was written for an instrument of the virginals type. But the codex also contains undoubted organ music for liturgical use: two Kyrie-Gloria pairs and a separate Kyrie, all on the favourite Mass IV plainchants (with the Kyrie, 'Cunctipotens Genitor Deus'). Again the plainsong is in the left hand, with a florid right-hand part (see pl. 34):

[68] Ed. Heribert Ringmann, *EDM*, iv and viii (Kassel, 1936–7); pieces in *HAM*, i, Nos. 82 and 83(*a*) and (*b*).
[69] See complete facsimile in *Musica Disciplina*, xiii–xv (1959–61), also published as No. 10 of the *Musicological Studies and Documents* of the American Institute of Musicology.

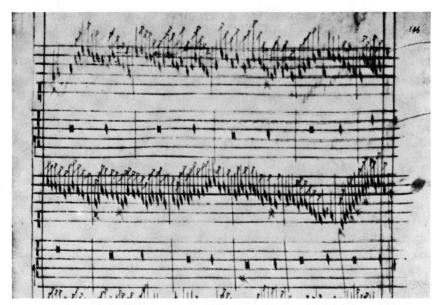

Pl. 34   Part of an organ composition on the Kyrie 'Cunctipotens genitor Deus', played by the
left hand, in the Faenza Codex of *c.* 1420. Ex. 40 is a partial transcription.

Ex. 40

These provide the earliest evidence we possess of the so-called 'alternatim'
practice: plainsong played on the organ alternating with sung plainsong in,
for instance, the invocations of the Kyrie, the odd or even verses of the
Magnificat and hymns.

The earliest German organ music – a fragment from the Augustinian monastery at Sagan in Silesia (*c.* 1425), another belonging to Ludolf Wilkin of Winsum (*c.* 1431), a third at Munich (before 1436)[70] – all slightly later than Faenza, consists mostly of such 'versets' for the Mass and one Magnificat. The Sagan music is closely related to Faenza, except that the left-hand part is notated in letters (as in Robertsbridge) instead of on a second stave. But in the Sanctus and fragment of Credo from Winsum[71] the right hand moves much more soberly on a basis of four notes (or their halves) to each one of the plainsong. The same source gives us the earliest of all the numerous keyboard pieces based on German song: 'Wol vp ghesellen'.[72]

A tablature compiled in 1448 by Adam Ileborgh[73] consists of five *praeambula* and three pieces 'on the tenor "frowe al myn hoffen" ': the first in triple time, the second in duple (*mensura duarum notarum*), the third in sextuple (*mensura sex notarum*). The 'preludes' (see pl. 35), crude and shapeless wanderings through they are, have special interest as the earliest known specimens of that peculiarly instrumental genre, uninfluenced even remotely by song or dance, in which the 'fingers wander idly Over the noisy keys' presumably in order to loosen them up. The first prelude is 'in C et potest variari in d, f, g, a'; written in the C mode it can be transposed to the others.

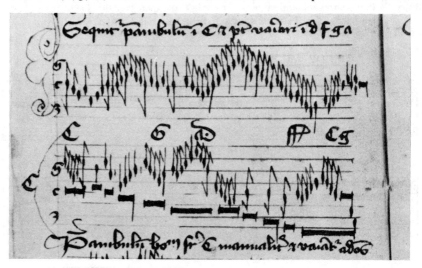

Pl. 35   Two of the earliest known examples of free preludial composition for keyboard: *praeambula* in the tablature compiled in 1448 by Adam Ileborgh of Stendal in Brandenburg.

Indeed all the preludes are transposable, though three of the five are written 'in d'. No. 3 is described as a 'good prelude for pedals or manual in d', the

---

[70] Breslau (Wrocław), Univ. I Qu 438, Berlin, Deutsche Bibl., theol. lat. quart. 290, and Munich, Staatsbibl., cod. lat. 5963; these are all transcribed in Apel, *CEKM* 1 (American Institute of Musicology).
[71] Transcriptions by Leo Schrade, *AfMF*, i (1936), pp. 150–2, and Apel, op. cit., pp. 16–17.
[72] Facsimile in Wolf, *Musikalische Schrifttafeln* (Bückeburg and Leipzig, 1923), pl. 32–3; transcription, Apel, p. 15.

earliest indication of the use of organ pedals. They must as yet have been limited to church organs. The contemporary portraits of Landini (in the Squarcialupi Codex) and the also blind Nuremberg organist Conrad Paumann (*c.* 1415–1473) (tomb-slab in the Munich Frauenkirche), show them playing portative organs for which or for the larger 'positive' instruments, with their light touch and sweet pure tone, most fifteenth-century organ music was obviously written.

PAUMANN AND THE BUXHEIM TABLATURE

The Berlin manuscript Deutsche Bibl. 40613 contains not only the *Lochamer Liederbuch* but the best known of Paumann's four *Fundamenta organisandi*. It was compiled in 1452, just after Paumann, master not only of the organ but 'in all musical instruments', had become court organist to the Duke of Bavaria at Munich. This *Fundamentum*[74] is in the first place a thesaurus of melodic formulae which can be applied in the writing of florid upper parts to long-note basses which ascend and descend first scalewise, then in thirds, fourths, fifths, and sixths, in cadences, and so on. Paumann then proceeds to give practical examples. The first is a composition on the sixth tone for the Magnificat, but most are on the tenors of German songs, e.g. Wolkenstein's 'Wach auff' and the anonymous 'Des klaffers neyden'. His version of the latter may be compared with Ex. 38(ii); only the tenor, marked here with crosses, is common to both and even that has been freely altered:

Ex. 41

At the end Paumann gives three praeambula, more shapely than Ileborgh's.

[73] Transcribed Apel, op. cit., praeambula Nos. 1 and 4 are easily accessible in *HAM*, i, No. 84(*a*) and (*b*).
[74] Facsimile, see n. 66 above, transcription in Apel, *CEKM* 1. Separate pieces in *HAM*, i, No. 81, *OAM(M)*, No. 104.

Paumann's influence is also very apparent in the great tablature from the monastery of Buxheim on the Iller (compiled between 1460 and 1470).[75] This not only contains two continuations of his *Fundamentum* but shows a number of musical relationships with the earlier collection. It is much larger – with more than 250 pieces – and the music is mostly in three parts as compared with the essentially two-part texture (cf. Ex. 41) of the 1452 volume. It could have been written under Paumann's direction during his last years at Munich. The third part was regarded as a contratenor and at the end of the manuscript there is a direction: 'when the contratenor is higher than the tenor then play the tenor lower on the pedals; but if the contratenor is placed lower then play the tenor above and the contratenor below'. Paumann – if it was Paumann who was responsible for the Buxheim book – probably derived his notions of the contratenor from the Burgundians. As we have noticed (see p. 73), he was well acquainted with their music for, side by side with the compositions on German song-tenors which naturally constitute the biggest group of works, the book includes a number of Anglo-Burgundian pieces: Dunstable's 'O rosa bella' (three transcriptions), 'Puisque m'amour', and 'Sub tuam protectionem' (two transcriptions),[76] three transcriptions of Frye's popular 'Ave regina',[77] two of Dufay's 'Se la face ay pale' and one of his 'Franc cueur gentil', no fewer than seven of Binchois's 'Je loe amours' (variously disguised as 'Geloymors' and 'Jeloemors'), and compositions by Arnold de Lantins, Franchois, Guillaume Legrant, Touront, and one or two Italians (Jacobus Viletti, Bartholomeo Brolo).

The technique of transcription is on the whole fairly uniform. The right-hand part, whether freely invented or based on the cantus of a chanson, is extremely florid even in the liturgical pieces (mostly Kyries), being based on the formulae proposed in the *Fundamenta*; the original melody becomes nearly or quite unrecognizable, although in both transcriptions of 'Se la face ay pale' the fanfare-like passage quoted as Ex. 35(i) is allowed to emerge with startling clarity. Sometimes the tenor is preserved faithfully – in 'Des klaffers nyd' more so than in the *Fundamentum* version (Ex. 41), though the right-hand part is much more highly decorated; sometimes it is elaborated, or conversely simplified in long note-values, out of all recognition. An example of the long note-value treatment is 'Mit gantzem willen', again an elaboration of the version in the *Fundamentum*, while inventiveness in variation is exemplified in the treatments of the tenor (and cantus and contratenor) in the Binchois song.[78] With its German, English, Burgundian, and even Italian repertory, the *Buxheimer Orgelbuch* is an outstanding monument of European music in the middle of the fifteenth century.

---

[75] Complete facsimile ed. Bertha Wallner, *Documenta Musicologica: Zweite Reihe*, i (Kassel, 1955) and complete transcription, idem., *EDM*, xxxvii–xxxix (1958–9).
[76] These are all printed in *MB*, viii.   [77] See p. 149.
[78] In his study 'Eine Chanson von Binchois im Buxheimer Orgel- und Locheimer Liederbuch', *Acta Musicologica*, v (1933), p. 3, Heinz Funck has tabulated the various forms of (a) tenor, (b) contratenor, (c) cantus in the original chanson (Codex Canonici 213: printed in Marix, *Les Musiciens*, p. 52) and in all seven Buxheim versions.

9

The Impact of the Renaissance

DOMINANCE OF THE NETHERLANDERS

Although our conception of 'the Renaissance' is a good deal wider and less clearly defined than that current at the beginning of the present century, the term is much too useful to be lightly abandoned. When we speak of 'Renaissance painting' everyone knows that we mean the work of Leonardo and Raphael, Botticelli and Giorgione, the Bellinis and Mantegna (and their successors rather than their predecessors). And it is significant that we do not, for one reason or another, think quite so readily of Dürer and the Holbeins and certainly not of Matthias Grünewald. The 're-birth' was Italian in origin. Musically its symptoms in the fifteenth century were insignificant compared with the masterpieces of painting, yet they spread none the less all over Europe. Insofar as it was 'Netherland', secular music was still medieval, just as the courts of Philip of Burgundy and Louis XI were medieval courts. In the music of the church isorhythm was dead, but the intellectual ingenuities of 'canon' and 'proportion' (see above, p. 146), musical counterparts of the verse of the *Rhétoriqueurs*, were still cultivated and by no one more brilliantly than the leading musician of the French royal chapel from 1452 until his death, Johannes Ockeghem (*c.* 1420–1497). And Ockeghem was the examplar, if not literally the teacher, of composers named in the *déplorations* written by two of the *Rhétoriqueurs* after his death. In one of these Guillaume Crétin calls upon Alexander Agricola (1446–1506), 'Verbonet' (also known as Johannes Ghiselin), Josquin des Prez (*c.* 1440–1521), 'Gaspar' (van Weerbeke) (*c.* 1440–*c.* 1515), Antoine Brumel (*c.* 1460–*c.* 1520), and Loyset Compère (*c.* 1450–1518) to lament their 'maistre et bon pere'. A second *déploration*, 'Nymphes des bois' by Jehan Molinet, set to music by Josquin, adds the name of 'Perchon' (Pierre de La Rue, perhaps really Van der Straeten, after 1460–1518) to those who have lost a 'bon pere'.

At the same time in Italy, where during the earlier part of the *quattrocento* the only native composers had been such minor figures as Antonius de Civitate, Bartolomeo Brolo, and Jacobus Viletti, there was a remarkable upsurge of popular polyphony, the forms and styles of which were soon practised – though only in minor works – by some of the so-called Flemish masters whose influence dominated all Europe, except England, from the Pyrenees to the Oder.

9. The Impact of the Renaissance

OCKEGHEM THE MASTER

Ockeghem himself was probably a genuine Fleming, not a Walloon, though unlike his younger contemporaries, Jacob Obrecht (*c.* 1450–1505) and Ghiselin/Verbonnet, he never set poems in his native language. His chansons are essentially Burgundian in style, as one would expect, but he was of the same generation as Busnois and like him (see above, p. 153) made innovations. He too preferred the rondeau form – soon to go out of fashion – although two of his most beautiful songs, 'Ma maistresse' with its long flowing melodic lines and 'Ma bouche rit',[1] are virelais. The latter, with the rondeau 'Maleur me bat', both marked by syllabic declamation, had the distinction of posthumous publication in Ottaviano Petrucci's epoch-making *Odhecaton* of 1501 (see Chapter 8, n. 58), the earliest volume of printed part-music. (Graduals and Missals with plainsong had been printed in the 1470s, and the *Musices opusculum* of Nicolo Burzio (Bologna, 1487) contains a three-part composition without text, printed from a wood-block.)[2] What distinguishes his chansons – indeed his music in general – from those of the Dufay-Binchois generation is their more closely woven, unbroken texture, bridging over cadences, and their greater use of imitation. His device of bringing in a new entry on the last note of a cadence in the other parts was later to be employed almost universally:

Ex. 42

In only one of his chansons does Ockeghem display the mathematical virtuosity that was long supposed to be his principal claim to fame; this is the rondeau 'Prenez sur moi vostre exemple, amoureux'.[3] Only the lowest part is written, the second voice enters a bar later and a fourth higher, beginning on D instead of A, the third enters at bar 3 and begins on G, and this is effortlessly sustained for more than thirty bars. This feat is far

[1] Printed in *HAM*, i, Nos. 74 and 75.
[2] Facsimile in *Grove* (fifth edition, 1954), vi, p. 929.
[3] Facsimile in *MGG*, ix, col. 1829; for various solutions see Joseph Levitan, 'Ockeghem's Clefless Compositions', *MQ*, xxiii (1937), p. 440.

surpassed, however, by the *Missa Prolationum*.[4] In this only superius and tenor are notated, in perfect time but respectively in minor and major prolation (see p. 118), while contratenor and bassus are to be deduced from them, singing the same notes in *imperfect* time and again in different prolation. Thus the two derived parts are in canon with the two written-out ones – at the unison in the Kyrie, at the fourth in the Gloria, fifth in the Credo, sixth in the Sanctus.

Ex. 43

GLORIA (Perfectum in subdiatessaron)

The only thing more astonishing than the feat itself is the grave beauty of the resultant music. And the same may be said of the *Missa Cujusvis toni*[5] which can be sung in the D, E, F, or G modes according to the clefs one adopts – Ockeghem gives none – and with the help of a one-flat signature. But these Masses are exceptional. The *Missa Mi-mi*,[6] Ockeghem's supreme master-piece, is freely composed and probably owes its name to the fact that every voice begins each movement with either E (*mi* in the 'natural hexachord') or B (*mi* in the 'hard hexachord').

The majority of his Masses – which were performed by voices only in accordance with what was now the general practice – are 'tenor Masses' with cantus firmus either liturgical ('Caput', and 'Ecce ancilla Domini') or borrowed from the melody or tenor of a chanson ('L'homme armé'). But the 'tenor' is often placed in the lowest part and styled 'tenorbassus' or 'bassus', and the other voice-parts of the chanson may be referred to. Thus the incomplete five-part Mass on Ockeghem's own 'Fors seulement' (see Ex.

[4] Ed. Dragan Plamenac in *Johannes Ockeghem: Collected Works*, ii (New York, 1947), p. 21.
[5] Ibid., i, p. 44.
[6] Ibid., ii, p. 1; also ed. Besseler, *ChW*, iv (second edition, Wolfenbüttel, 1950). The customary explanation of the title – that it derives from the descending fifth e–A – is unacceptable. A is not '*mi* in the soft hexachord' but *re* in the hard hexachord (see p. 84).

42) is based on the superius of the song which is actually placed in the bassus I of the Kyrie, while the tenor of the song, with its identical opening, begins the superius of the Kyrie. Such similarities between the openings of parts, which diverge later, contribute very much to the impression of all-pervading imitation. The Kyrie-Gloria pair on 'Ma maistresse' is another instance. The tenor of the chanson is moved to the bass but the openings of superius and tenor refer to it; in the Gloria the contratenor sings the superius of the chanson but now in a different relationship to the tenor. In the Mass 'De plus en plus' the elaborated tenor of Dufay's chanson occupies the normal 'tenor' position. So does the tenor of 'L'homme armé' except in the Credo and Agnus where it is moved to the lowest part. In 'L'homme armé' the final cadence of the last Agnus is, like Dufay's, identical in all parts with Morton's (see p. 148).[7] In Ockeghem's Requiem – one of the earliest – the basis is mostly plainsong but the treatment ranges from the hardly surpassable simplicity of the Tractus to the complexities of the Offertorium.

INTERRELATIONSHIP OF THE NETHERLANDERS

Nothing gives a more lively impression of the close contacts of the Netherlanders, all working mainly within a limited area, than the way in which they emulated each other in treating the same themes. 'L'homme armé' is very far from being an isolated case. 'Fors seulement', for instance, provided the basis for Masses by the smooth eclectic Obrecht[8] and the austere and learned Pierre de La Rue. And not only Masses but chansons based on Ockeghem's: by Obrecht (who puts the original superius into the second highest part and works the original tenor in close imitation in his three other parts),[9] by La Rue (in a superb five-part piece with original superius at the top, the tenor in close canon at the fifth, and two freer parts),[10] by Josquin des Prez, the greatest master of them all[11] – though this is attributed in another source to Johannes Ghiselin 'alias Verbonnet' – and by such lesser masters as Brumel, Alexander Agricola, Matthaeus Pipelare, Marbriano de Orto, and the same Ghiselin/Verbonnet (a different composition, under both his names). Various other songs underwent similar treatment, though none was as popular as 'Fors seulement'. 'L'homme armé' incited only La Rue and Josquin to song-compositions.

---

[7] The Kyrie and Agnus Dei III of 'L'homme armé' are published in *HAM*, i, No. 73 (*a*) and (*b*) as well as in the *Collected Works*, i.

[8] Obrecht's three-part Mass is published in *Jakob Obrecht: Werken* (ed. Johannes Wolf) (Leipzig and Amsterdam, 1908–21), *Missen* (deel V), p. 133.

[9] idem, *Wereldlijke Werken*, p. 14, and *Ein altes Spielbuch* (St. Gallen, Stiftsbibl. 461), ed. F. J. Giesbert (Mainz, 1936), p. 12.

[10] In O. J. Gombosi, *Jacob Obrecht* (Leipzig, 1925), musical app., p. 21.

[11] Gombosi, ibid., p. 18, and Giesbert, op. cit., p. 16; the 'Ghiselin/Verbonnet' setting in Gombosi, p. 16, and Giesbert, p. 10.

TECHNICAL INGENUITIES

Inevitably both also composed 'L'homme armé' Masses, indeed two each if La Rue's second one is authentic. Josquin's are entitled 'Sexti toni' and 'Super voces musicales',[12] the meaning of the latter being 'on the notes of the hexachord'. This is essentially a tenor-Mass, but the tenor begins each successive movement one note higher: Kyrie on C, Gloria on D, Credo on E, Sanctus on F, Agnus on G and A – while the surrounding texture always remains in the D mode. There are numerous ingenuities such as mensuration canons, the most ingenious of which is the second Agnus where only one part is notated but must be read in three different mensurations. La Rue goes literally one better in the third Agnus of his authentic 'L'homme armé',[13] deriving four parts from one; the Kyrie derives three parts from one, with a free discantus. (La Rue was capable of writing an entire six-part Mass, 'Ave sanctissima Maria',[14] in three parts – each with another in canon.) Besides these, we have from this period 'L'homme armé' Masses by Obrecht (who leans heavily on Busnois's), Brumel, Compère, Pipelare, de Orto, the theorists Tinctoris (*c.* 1436–1511) and his antagonist Gafurius – and others if one wished to compile a complete catalogue.

Such ingenuities were by no means confined to 'L'homme armé' Masses or to masters of the rank of Pierre de La Rue and Josquin des Prez. Even the clearest and least sophisticated of these composers, Gaspar van Weerbeke, indulges in mensural complexities in the tenor of his Mass 'O Venus banth'[15] (on a Flemish song which Petrucci in the *Odhecaton* ascribes to Josquin). But this aspect should be regarded as a relic of medieval scholasticism. Not so the continuance of Dufay's initial upper-part duetting, which survived and appeared in new forms in La Rue and Josquin. Indeed some of the Netherlanders of this period, those who had spent a considerable time in Italy, Josquin, Brumel, Weerbeke, Ghiselin/Verbonnet, seem closer in spirit – though not in technique – to Dufay than to Ockeghem. Technically, whatever the stylistic variety brought about by inclination and environment, all the Netherlanders generally followed their 'maistre et bon pere' in avoidance of symmetry and in the melodic concealment of harmonic cadences, in introducing imitative entries (as distinct from protracted canon) less haphazardly and more frequently. Thus, although it would be

---

[12] Both printed by Petrucci in his earliest publication of Masses, *Misse Josquin* (Venice, 1502); both in *Josquin des Prez: Werken*, ed. Albert Smijers *et al.* (Amsterdam, 1921–69), *Missen*, i, pp. 109 and 1 respectively; Agnus II of 'L'homme armé super voces musicales' in *HAM*, i, No. 89.

[13] Published by Petrucci in *Misse Petri de la Rue* (1503); ed. Nigel Davison, *ChW*, cxiv; Kyrie in *HAM*, i, No. 92, but incorrectly until the revised edition of 1954.

[14] Ed. Antonio Tirabassi in *P. de la Rue: Liber Missarum* (Milan, 1941). This volume consists entirely of Masses on liturgical themes.

[15] Printed by Petrucci, *Misse Gaspar* (1507), who thoughtfully provided a solution of the canon. Weerbeke was one of the composers whose Masses, with those of Josquin and La Rue, Petrucci considered worth bringing out in separate volumes during 1502–7, the others being Obrecht, Brumel, Ghiselin, Agricola, de Orto, and Isaac. Petrucci published a second volume of Josquin's Masses in 1505 (and a third in 1514 after his removal from Venice to Fossombrone).

premature to speak of all-pervading imitation, the way was being well
prepared for it.

The difference between the true 'Burgundian' style and the newer
technique is graphically illustrated by a comparison of the opening of Loyset
Compère's arrangement ('Venez regretz') of Hayne van Ghizeghem's very
popular 'Alles regrets' with the original; he removes Hayne's contra, puts
the superius below the tenor, and brings in a fresh imitative entry bridging
over the cadence:

Ex. 44

(i) HAYNE VAN GHIZEGHEM

(ii) LOYSET COMPÈRE

The opening of the four-part Kyrie of Compère's Mass 'Alles regrets' is a curious conflation of both versions.[16]

PIERRE DE LA RUE

So far as we know neither Ockeghem nor La Rue ever visited Italy, and Obrecht is generally believed to have done so only twice very briefly,[17] dying at Ferrara during the second visit. Whereas Ockeghem went to France, La Rue remained a faithful 'Burgundian', although the masters of Burgundy were now Habsburg archdukes. He served in their court chapel for twenty years from Maximilian (later Emperor) to Charles (afterwards Charles V). During 1502–3, with Agricola and Weerbeke among others, he accompanied the Archduke Philip – son-in-law of Ferdinand and Isabella – to Spain where the little *capilla flamenca* of fourteen singers and a few instrumentalists contrasted strongly with the unison singing of the large Spanish royal choir. There he must have met the Spanish composers Anchieta, Encina, Escobar, and Peñalosa who had learned something of Netherland polyphony probably from Johannes Urrede (or Wrede), a musician of Ferdinand of Aragon and composer of an extremely popular song, 'Nunca fué pena maior'. One result of the Spanish visit was a Mass on this song which appears beside 'L'homme armé' in Petrucci's volume of La Rue's Masses. (The song itself had been printed anonymously in the *Odhecaton*.) La Rue begins the superius of his Kyrie almost identically with that of the song, while his tenor has no more than a general resemblance to the tenor of the song:

Ex. 45

(i)

Nun - ca   fué   pe - - - na   ma - -

(ii)

----

[16] Hayne's chanson in *Odhecaton*, No. 57; Compère's, ibid., No. 53, and ed. Ludwig Finscher in *Loyset Compère: Opera Omnia* (CMM 15), v, p. 59; his Mass, ibid., i, p. 26, and also ed. Finscher, *ChW*, 55.
[17] However, Bain Murray in 'New Light on Jacob Obrecht's Development', *MQ*, xliii (1957), p. 500, argues that Obrecht was probably educated in Italy in his youth.

La Rue's greatest Mass is unquestionably the *Missa pro defunctis*,[18] perhaps for the obsequies of the Archduke Philip in 1507, as the motet 'Delicta juventutis' obviously was. Syllabic setting, even note-against-note declamation, plays an important part in the Requiem, as it also does in some of his motets (e.g. 'Vexilla regis/Passio domini' and 'Delicta juventutis') and chansons (e.g. 'Autant en emporte le vent', 'Cueurs desolez').[19] The Requiem, like some of La Rue's other works, is pitched remarkably low (cf. Ex. 47 by Josquin) – deepening its dark solemnity. Even La Rue's few chansons are shot through with melancholy. In two of them – 'Cueurs desolez' where the first bass sings 'Dies irae' in long note-values, and 'Plorés, gemiés, criés' where the two basses sing 'Requiem aeternam' in canon – he was writing for his young twice-widowed mistress, the Regent Margaret, who had now lost her brother. The words of his 'Cueurs desolez' are hers. (A motet-chanson attributed correctly to Compère, but more often

[18] Ed. Friedrich Blume, with 'Delicta juventutis' in *ChW*, xi.
[19] Both in *ChW*, iii.

to Obrecht,[20] in the *Album de Marguerite d' Autriche* (Brussels, Bibl. Roy. 28),[21] combines another sad poem of hers, 'O devotz cueurs', with the quotation from Jeremiah with which she ended her Latin epitaph on her brother, 'O vos omnes . . .'.)

JACOB OBRECHT

No such emotional groundswell troubles the smooth surface of Obrecht's music; nothing like the occasional roughness of La Rue's polyphony. His pellucid but always well-knit textures are produced by parallel movement, often in tenths between superius and bass, sequences and ostinato-like repetitions of short motives. Clear articulation is secured by literal repetition by two lower voices of a passage that has just been sung by two higher ones, a device also much favoured by Josquin. His Mass 'Ave Regina coelorum',[22] based on Frye's motet (the tenor of which he also borrowed for a motet of his own), exhibits all these characteristics. It also illustrates Obrecht's habit of literal quotation: the superius of his setting of the 'Qui propter nos homines' section of the Credo and the Benedictus both appropriate Frye's superius essentially unchanged, and he opens the Gloria of his 'Caput' Mass[23] with an eight-bar quotation from the Gloria of Dufay's. But his free treatment of tenors, distributing segments of the tenor among different voices, and drawing on other parts of the model as well as the tenor (as in 'Ave Regina'), is most noteworthy. Notable also is his employment of German melodies – 'Maria zart', 'Der Pfobenswanz' – as Mass-tenors.

WORDS IN POLYPHONY

Obrecht left only a handful of French songs, one song, 'La Tortorella', with Italian words, and a dozen or so settings of Dutch words,[24] perhaps arrangements of Dutch popular tunes. Their most striking feature is the amount of syllabic note-against-note word-setting. The age of Humanism attached great importance to words, which pure polyphony uses but absorbs and dissolves. The first motive of a late fifteenth-century contrapuntal line might be verbally inspired but its continuation was essentially musical, controlled by its relationship to other contrapuntal lines, not by relationship to the text which was fitted (or not fitted) to it quite haphazardly.[25] Even when verbal inspiration was carried further, the successive entries of voices and

---

[20] *Loyset Compère: Opera Omnia*, (CMM 15) v, p. 4.
[21] Edited by Martin Picker (Berkeley, 1965).
[22] *Werken* (ed. Wolf), *Missen* iii, p. 141.
[23] Ibid., iv, p. 189.
[24] Their authenticity has not been proved beyond all doubt. Two – 'T'saat een meskin' and 'T'Andernaken' – in the *Odhecaton*; ten (ed. Smijers) in *Van Ockeghem tot Sweelinck*, pp. 70 ff. (Amsterdam, 1941).
[25] See, for instance, Isabel Pope's study of the *Odhecaton* texts in Helen Hewitt's edition.

texts made the words unclear. To counter this, Dufay himself, when he supplies the words for all three voices of a chanson, sets them note-against-note, 'chordally', as in 'J'attendray tant qu'il vous playra' or takes other measures to keep them lucid. This 'chordal' conception of vocal music, together with the growing tendency to make the parts of a polyphonic texture equally important, was ultimately to make it possible for Zarlino in the middle of the next century to declare not only that 'four parts contain the full perfection of the harmony' but that 'un harmonia et un concerto de voci' was the highest form of music.[26]

Such music could be – whether or not it often was – sung without instrumental participation. Similarly, those polyphonic pieces which appear in the sources not merely without words – Petrucci's *Odhecaton* and its successors, the *Canti B* (1502)[27] and *Canti C* (1504), are mostly wordless – but obviously intended for instruments alone, like Ghiselin's 'La Alfonsina' in the *Odhecaton* and 'La Spagna' in a Florentine manuscript (Bibl. Naz. Panciatichi 27),[28] are more likely to have been played by instruments of the same family than by one of the heterogeneous ensembles of the past. And the favourite family was undoubtedly that 'quattro viole de arco', 'suavissima e artificiosa' as Castigliano calls it in his *Cortegiano* (written in 1514, though not published till 1528).

NETHERLAND COMPOSERS IN ITALY

Syllabic note-against-note word-setting is most noticeable in the Netherland composers who spent some considerable time in Italy: Weerbeke, Compère, Josquin, and Henricus Isaac 'de Flandria' (as he styled himself) (*c.* 1450–1517). Isaac is actually first heard of in 1484 at Florence where he was invited by Lorenzo the Magnificent.[29] Weerbeke also is first heard of in Italy; in 1472 he was put in charge of the Milanese court chapel by Galeazzo Maria Sforza, who sent him to Burgundy to recruit singers. Compère was one of them, and Josquin, who had already been a member of the Milan cathedral choir since 1459, was recruited by the court. During the 1480s – or perhaps earlier – Compère left for the French court, Josquin and Weerbeke for the Papal service. Weerbeke put in some time in the Burgundian court chapel later and then spent the last decade or so of his life once more at Rome, while Josquin served in turn the Cardinal Ascanio Sforza, Louis XII of France, Ercole I of Ferrara (at whose court Isaac was a visitor at the same

---

[26] *Istitutioni harmoniche* (Venice, 1558), p. 166.
[27] Ed. Hewitt (Chicago, 1967).
[28] Ed. Clytus Gorwald, *Ghiselin: Opera Omnia* (*CMM* 23), iv, pp. 36 and 32. The 'La Spagna' tenor is one of the most famous and frequently used of the long-note *cantus firmi* in black breves to which courtly basse-danses were danced, the tenor marking the actual steps.
[29] See Frank A. D'Accone, 'Heinrich Isaac in Florence: New and Unpublished Documents', *MQ*, xlix (1963), p. 464, which corrects earlier accounts of Isaac's activities in Florence.

time), and for the last fourteen years of his life the Regent Margaret in his homeland. Isaac became the court composer of Margaret's father, the Emperor Maximilian, but maintained a personal connection with Florence until he died there in 1517. Like their predecessors from Ciconia onward, they set Italian texts and allowed their music to become impregnated with the bland sweetness of Italian melody and the transparency of Italian textures. But there was now a fresh factor; they were brought into contact with a new type of popular polyphony which had grown up in Italy during the fifteenth century at a time when sophisticated composition was almost at a standstill.

LAUDI AND CARNIVAL SONGS

Early quattrocento Italy had been full of music. But its courtly music consisted of the monodies, mainly improvised, of intellectuals who chanted their poems to their own lute accompaniment: such men as the Venetian Leonardo Giustiniani (*c.* 1388–1446), who gave his name to a whole genre, the neo-Platonic humanist Marsilio Ficino (1433–1499), who sang his own Latin translations from the Greek while accompanying himself on his *lyra orphica*,[30] and Serafino d'Aquila (Aquilano) (1466–1500), who served Ascanio Sforza at the same time as Josquin. Their music is lost. So is that of the earliest polyphonic *laudi spirituali* (see p. 99) of which we hear: five three-part laudi by the Florentine cantor Andrea Stefani in 1400.[31] When we do find polyphonic laudi they are in two parts, often as primitive as very early organa of the type of Ex. 13 (p. 89), mostly syllabic, with only brief melismata in the highest part before cadences. Even in the later fifteenth century the typical three-part laude[32] is almost entirely syllabic and 'chordal' – 'triads in root position' as we should say – mildly enlivened only at the cadences (e.g. a 'Landini cadence' at the end). This exceedingly jejune kind of music served for the popular *frottole* and *strambotti* and Florentine *canzoni a ballo* and *canti carnascialeschi*, usually in four parts performable by voices only or voice (the descant) and instruments. These were written in quantities by the Italians, particularly the Florentines, as they began to recover from the fit of Latinity that had threatened for a time to swamp the *volgar lingua*. Lorenzo the Magnificent (1448–92) himself loved the Tuscan vernacular and, long before it was polished and codified as literary Italian, wrote in it both laudi spirituali and carnival songs. The genres were musically not very different, as Savonarola demonstrated by turning the one into the other, simply substituting religious for secular texts, e.g. 'Regina del paradiso' for 'Regina del cor mio'.

---

[30] See D. P. Walker, 'Le Chant orphique de Marsile Ficin' in *Musique et poésie au XVIe siècle* (ed. Jean Jacquot) (Paris, 1954), p. 17.
[31] See Jacques Handschin, *Musikgeschichte im Überblick* (Luzern, 1948), pp. 233–4.
[32] Cf. the example in *MGG*, viii, col. 317.

And, as might be expected, Lorenzo's favourite musician, Isaac, set them to music[33] though none have survived complete. We have, however, a May song of his, 'Or'e di Maggio', a strambotto, 'Morte che fai', and a quodlibet,

Pl. 36 Florentine carnival singers: woodcut from *Canzone per andare in maschera* (Florence, 1485), a collection of song-texts without music.

'Donna di dentro/Fortuna d'un gran tempo/Damme un pocho di quella maza chroca'.[34] In this last Isaac exercised considerable skill in welding together melodic and verbal scraps of three songs, the third and most persistent of which is – whatever its disputed literal meaning – undoubtedly obscene. This is typical of the Netherlanders when they amuse themselves in these genres; without spoiling the simplicity of the syllabic note-against-note style, they usually cannot suppress, though they can carefully conceal, their skill as craftsmen. Thus Josquin in his 'Scaramella' slips in a bit of clef-ingenuity comparable with that of his Mass 'L'homme armé super voces

[33] D'Accone, op. cit., p. 467.
[34] Respectively in *DTÖ*, Jg xvi (1) (vol. 32), p. 206, *Annales musicologiques*, i (1953), p. 280, and *ChW*, xliii, p. 4.

musicales', while Compère, setting the same comic text, scans the tenor first in duple, then in triple time though preserving the same note-values.[35]

THE FROTTOLA

Yet Josquin at times, as in his delicious 'El grillo',[36] can be as artless as the native Italians whose pieces constitute the bulk of the nine books of frottole that Petrucci brought out between 1504 and 1509. Chief among these were the three Veronese, Marchetto Cara, Michele Pesenti, and Bartolomeo Tromboncino, and the Venetian organist Francesco Anna (d'Ana).[37] (The same musicians appear also, with Innocentius Dammonis, as composers of polyphonic laudi in precisely the same style, though often incorporating a plainsong melody, in the two books Petrucci published in 1508.)[38] These composers were by no means as artless as their true frottole suggest. The middle section of Tromboncino's 'Se ben or' in Petrucci's First Book shows him aerating the texture with a point of imitation:

Ex. 46

etc.

[35] Josquin, *Werken: Wereldlijke Werken*, ii, p. 16, and Compère, *Opera Omnia*, v, p. 65. Howard M. Brown suggests that these two settings of a popular tune date from 1474–5 when both composers were working in Milan, *Report of the Ljubljana Congress 1967*, p. 92.

[36] *Werken*, ii, f. 14.

[37] Petrucci's first and fourth books have been reprinted by Rudolf Schwarz, *Publikationen älterer Musik*, viii (Leipzig, 1935), *Libri I, II e III* by R. Monterosso (Cremona, 1954); the *Libro tertio* of Petrucci's first rival, Andrea Antico, himself a composer of frottole and strambotti (Rome, 1517) has been edited by Alfred Einstein, *Smith College Music Archives*, iv (Northampton, Mass., 1941). Also in 1517 Antico published the first printed Italian organ tablature, *Frottole intabulate da sonare organi* (six complete pieces with vocal originals in Knud Jeppesen, *Die italienische Orgelmusik am Anfang des Cinquecento*, Copenhagen, 1943). A great number of frottole are easily accessible elsewhere and there is a useful small selection of canti carnascialeschi, ed. Kurt Westphal, in *ChW*, xliii.

[38] On the polyphonic laudi see Knud Jeppesen, *Die mehrstimmige italienische Laude um 1500* (Copenhagen and Leipzig, 1935), and on the conversion of frottole to laudi, Federico Ghisi, 'L'Aria di Maggio et le travestissement spirituel de la poésie musicale profane en Italie' in *Musique et poésie au XVIe siècle*.

When he sets a famous Petrarch sonnet, 'Hor che'l ciel et la terra'[39] – his setting was published in 1516 – it is as a solo song with lively instrumental parts.

As Einstein put it, the frottola ultimately disintegrated through the intrusion of quasi-Netherland polyphonic passages.[40] But, as a matter of fact, polyphony threatened quite early to take over the frottola: Pesenti's 'O dio che la brunetta mia', also in Petrucci's First Book of 1504, is completely polyphonic. This piece was known to the first madrigalists. When Verdelot (see below, p. 228) set the same text in his first book of six-part madrigals (Venice, 1541) he borrowed Pesenti's superius almost note for note, and Costanzo Festa passed off Pesenti's work as his own in his *Vero libro di madrigali a tre voci* (Venice, 1543), simply omitting one part.

However, the result of this cultural contact was not only the impact of Netherland polyphony on the frottolists, which was to lead to the sixteenth-century madrigal, but the permeation of Netherland polyphony by the spirit of the frottola and laude. It is not the actual frottole of Compère and Josquin that matter so much as the frottola or laude element in their other music. This is most obvious in their chansons – for instance, Compère's 'Vostre bergeronette' in the *Odhecaton*, and his 'Et dont revenes vous',[41] or – serious as it is – Josquin's 'Plaine de dueil'.[42] It penetrates their church music as well: Weerbeke's motets 'Virgo Maria' and 'Verbum caro factum est', and his *Lamentationes Jeremiae*[43] (all published by Petrucci), parts of Isaac's *Missa Carminum*,[44] Josquin's 'O Domine Jesu Christe' and 'Tu solus', and many pages of his Masses, including his supreme masterpiece, the Mass 'Pange lingua',[45] 'one of those works of art which shine like stars through all succeeding ages'.[46]

JOSQUIN DES PREZ

The frottolists were men of mediocre talent, Josquin one of the highest genius, 'the real discoverer of the word as inexhaustible source of musical inspiration. In the vocal music of his predecessors, in his own early works, words and music go loosely side by side', whereas in those of his maturity 'they form an intimately blended unity'.[47] As an example of loose association one might cite Josquin's beautiful setting of a famous passage from Dido's lament in the *Aeneid*, 'Dulces exuviae', a favourite with sixteenth-century composers – among other settings an anonymous frottola was published in 1519. An example of the later 'blended unity' is one of his

---

[39] Alfred Einstein, *The Italian Madrigal* (Princeton, 1949), iii, No. 11.
[40] Ibid., i, pp. 119ff.   [41] *Opera Omnia*, v, pp. 61 and 21.
[42] *Werken: Wereldlijke Werken*, i, p. 7 and *ChW*, iii, p. 9.
[43] Reprinted respectively in A. W. Ambros, *Geschichte der Musik*, v (Leipzig, 1889), p. 183, Smijers, *Van Ockeghem tot Sweelinck*, p. 174, and Schering, *Geschichte der Musik in Beispielen*, No. 58.
[44] Ed. Reinhold Heyden, *ChW*, vii.
[45] *Werken: Motetten*, i, p. 35 and 56, and *Missen*, iv, p. 1 (also ed. Blume, *ChW*, i).
[46] Ambros, op. cit., iii, p. 223.
[47] Eduard Lowinsky, 'Zur Frage der Deklamationsrhythmik in der a-cappella-Musik des 16. Jahrhunderts', *Acta Musicologica*, vii (1935), p. 62.

numerous psalm-motets (a genre in which Josquin seems to have been a pioneer), 'Dominus regnavit', with its consistent upward octave leaps on 'Ele*va*verunt' and *'ela*tiones', or, to take an extreme case, the 'descent into hell' at the end of one of his two motets on David's lament for Absalom, 'Absalon fili mi' :[48]

Ex. 47

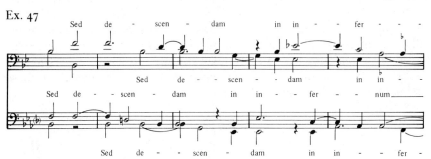

(The Db occurs only in the key-signature of the lowest part)

Here we have a striking example of what was later to be known as *musica reservata*, a term first used though not explained by a composer who claimed to be a pupil of Josquin's, Adrian Petit Coclico, in the preface to his *Compendium musices* (Nuremberg, 1552). It was clearly defined by the humanist Samuel Quickelberg in Pantaleon's *Prosopographia* (Basle, 1565–6) as music 'conforming to the whole text and to each word, expressing every emotion and putting things before the imagination as if actually happening' (*ad res et verba accommodando, singulorum affectuum vim exprimendo rem quasi actam ante oculos ponendo*).

Side by side with Josquin's increasing attention to detailed verbal expressiveness, certain purely musical characteristics of his style became more and more prominent in his later work: abandonment of rhythmic intricacies; symmetry of phrase often produced by a habit of writing for voices in pairs, one pair duetting antiphonally with the other as in 'Tribulatio et angustia' ;[49] systematic imitation; ever longer scale-passages

---

[48] Respectively in *Wereldlijke Werken*, ii, p. 4, and (ed. Osthoff), *ChW*, liv, p. 5; *Motetten*, iv, p. 33, and (ed. Blume), *ChW*, xxxiii, p. 4; and *Werken: Supplement*, p. 22.
[49] *Motetten*, iii, p. 95. The earliest source attributes this to Verdelot.

which impart a sense of flow and also act as binding agents almost as potent as the 'continuous imitation'; use of the C mode either frankly as in his 'Ave Maria'[50] or transposed as F mode with B♭. His diversity of style and means, even within his religious music, is vast. He parades his utmost learning in addressing the Lamb of God (second Agnus of 'L'homme armé super voces musicales'), but needs only the simplest imaginable means to express the rapt ecstasy of 'Ave verum corpus'.[51] The variety of his score or so of Masses is fascinating. The ingenuities of his two relatively early 'L'homme armé' Masses represent only one facet of his genius. Twice in early works[52] he bases the whole composition on the favourite saying of a patron (presumably Ascanio Sforza) or on solmization syllables with vowels equivalent to those in another patron's name:

(i)	Lascia	fa-re	mi	(ii)	Hercu-	les	du*x*	Ferra-*ri*-	ae
	la	sol	fa re mi			*re*	*ut re*	*ut*	re *fa* mi re
	A	G	F D E			D C D		C	D FE D
and	E	D	C A B						

These are cantus firmus Masses, sometimes with the cantus firmus in long note-values. So are some of the Masses on chansons – his own, Ockeghem's, Agricola's – which bulk largely in his output, and his 'Stabat Mater',[53] like La Rue's, is based on the tenor of Agricola's 'Comme femme desconfortée'. But in his Masses on the anonymous 'Fortuna desperata' from Petrucci's *Canti C* and on Ockeghem's 'Maleur me bat'[54] he makes free use of all the parts of the model – superius, tenor, and bass – and in the probably later Mass 'Mater Patris'[55] he draws on the general texture of his model, a motet by Brumel, so generously that he may be said to have arrived at the *missa parodia*. Yet in his last and greatest Masses, 'De beata Virgine' and 'Pange lingua',[56] he abandons both cantus firmus in the normal sense and 'parody'. Instead he freely develops the ordinary chants of Masses IX and IV in the former and the melody of the Corpus Christi hymn[57] in the latter, where it is fragmented and the fragments woven into four often equally important parts. Josquin's own thought flowers from these fragments so that from the final Alleluia of the hymn (i) comes the 'Amen' of the Credo (ii) which crystallizes into the all-pervading motive (iii) of the hypnotic 'Dona nobis pacem', 'the supreme manifestation of Flemish mysticism in music of Italian limpidity and sweetness':[58]

Ex. 48

(i)

[50] *Motetten*, i, p. 1; excerpts in *NOHM*, iii, p. 267.
[51] *Motetten*, i, p. 48, and (first part only) *NOHM*, iii, p. 263.
[52] *Missen*, i, p. 35, and ii, p. 19.   [53] *Motetten*, ii, p. 51.
[54] *Missen*, i, p. 81, and ii, p. 39.   [55] Ibid, iii, p. 1.
[56] Ibid., iii, p. 125, and iv, p. 1; *ChW*, xlii and i.
[57] In the form given on p. 957 of the *Liber Usualis* (1950 edition).
[58] The whole passage is quoted in *NOHM*, iii, p. 266.

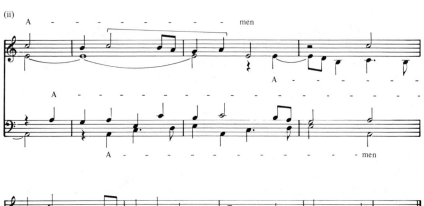

Few composers have exercised such widespread influence in their own day as Josquin, but his clear statement of words and lucidity of texture were most strikingly perpetuated in France by such composers as Brumel (already mentioned beside Josquin as a co-disciple of Ockeghem), Antoine de Fevin (*c.* 1470–*c.* 1512), described by the Swiss theorist Glareanus as the 'felix aemulator' of Josquin, Jean Mouton (*c.* 1459–1522), Elzéar Genet (also called Carpentras from his birthplace) (*c.* 1470–1548), and Antoine Longueval or Longaval whose one claim to fame is that he was the originator of the so-called 'motet-Passion': a four-part non-dramatic setting (*c.* 1507) of a pastiche of the Passion narrative compiled from all four Gospels.[59] All except Brumel, who held French cathedral posts, served in the chapel of Louis XII. Brumel and Genet also served the Medici pope, Leo X, at a later period – as did the Spanish composers Peñalosa and Encina.

Brumel is said (again by Glareanus) to have composed his *Missa de Beata*

---

[59] See Basil Smallman, *The Background of Passion Music* (enlarged edition, New York, 1970), pp. 26 and 136–9. The first edition (Wittenberg, 1538) attributed the work to Obrecht and Johannes Wolf published it in *Obrecht: Werken* (Lief. 28), but the attribution to Longueval is now generally accepted.

Virgine[60] in competition with Josquin – and acquitted himself very well. He also wrote a 'L'homme armé'[61] and a tour de force: a twelve-part Mass 'Et ecce terrae motus'.[62] But his Masses and motets are chiefly notable for their melodiousness and euphony. He often writes the simplest note-against-note counterpoint, above all in the enigmatically named *Missa de Dringhs*,[63] even two parts in parallel thirds and sixths in the 'Benedictus' of the same Mass and the 'Qui venit' of the Mass 'Je nay dueul'[64] (on Agricola's chanson). The 'Confiteor' in the Credo of 'L'homme armé' has been justly described as 'almost frottolesque', and the same might be said of the third Agnus of his Mass 'Mente tota'.[65]

Fevin's Masses were highly thought of in their day, for both Petrucci and Antico published them and a solo lute arrangement of his Mass 'Ave Maria' (on Josquin's motet) was printed in Venice in 1546. Indeed he occasionally shows complete mastery of the later Josquin style in fluent, transparent part-writing and exquisite euphony, witness his motet 'Descende in hortum meum'.[66] But his facile two-part writing, like Brumel's at his weakest, and often syllabic as well, enabled the Wittenberg publisher Georg Rhaw to rifle his Masses for sections which could be supplied with fresh words and printed as *Bicinia* (1545). His friend Mouton's work is another matter. He was capable of formidable canonic feats, as in his 'L'homme armé' Mass and the four-part mirror canon 'Salve matter'[67] which Glareanus printed in his *Dodecachordon* (Basle, 1547), but he does not obtrude his skill. Mouton[68] was indeed a much more successful 'emulator' of Josquin than Fevin was, though whether he was Josquin's actual pupil is doubtful. (But we have it on Zarlino's reliable authority that he was Willaert's teacher.) His themes tend to be more angular, his structures more sectional than Josquin's. And he has a 'popular', bucolic vein of his own which shows in the Christmas motet 'Noë noë psallite',[69] the gay six-part 'Gaude virgo Catharina', and the triple-time refrain with complete 'dominant-tonic full close' that concludes both sections of 'Non nobis Domine',[70] which celebrates the birth of a daughter to Louis XII in 1510:

---

[60] *Opera Omnia* (ed. Barton Hudson) (*CMM* 5), iv, p. 1.
[61] Ibid., i, p. 65.
[62] Ibid., iii, p. 1.
[63] Ibid., iv, p. 35.
[64] Ibid., i, p. 1.
[65] Complete Agnus Dei in *HAM*, i, No. 106.
[66] Reprinted in Ambros, op. cit., v, p. 208.
[67] Reprinted in Schering, *Geschichte der Musik in Beispielen* (Leipzig, 1931), No. 66.
[68] *Opera Omnia*, ed. Andrew Minor, in *CMM* 43. *Motets à 4 et 5 voix*, ed. Henry Expert *et al.* (Paris, 1971).
[69] In Smijers, *Treize livres de motets parus chez Pierre Attaingnant* (Paris, 1936), ii, p. 86.
[70] In *Jean Mouton: Fünf Motetten* (ed. Paul Kast), *ChW*, lxxvi, No. 1. No. 5, 'Exalta Regina Galliae', was one of ten compositions by Mouton included in the splendid collection of motets dedicated to the younger Lorenzo de' Medici, nephew of Pope Leo X, ed. Edward Lowinsky, *The Medici Codex of 1518* (Monuments of Renaissance Music, iii–v) (Chicago, 1968).
[71] First seven pieces in Ambros, op. cit., v, pp. 212ff.; another in *NOHM*, iii, p. 299. There is an edition of Genet's collected works, *CMM* 58, ed. Albert Seay.

Ex. 49

(i)

Er - go cla - me - mus in coe - lum vi - vat Rex in ae - ter - num

(ii) Final cadence

[Re] -gi - - - - na

The bipartite – or rather quadripartite – motet, in the form AB:CB, was favoured by Mouton and other composers of the early sixteenth century, though he was certainly not its originator. Genet/Carpentras was a lesser talent, remembered mostly for his *Lamentationes Jeremiae*.[71] These were originally commissioned by Leo X but so dissatisfied the composer when he heard them again after some years that he rewrote them for Clement VII.

SPANISH COMPOSERS

As we saw in a previous chapter (p. 135) the music of the Aragonese court had been closely linked with Avignon during the later Middle Ages. Aragon and Catalonia shared the common European musical culture and the court at Barcelona, like those of Italy, was mostly served by Netherland musicians. That of Castile was less so and it is noticeable that of the four outstanding Spanish composers who grew up under the dual reign of the 'Catholic Monarchs of the Spains', Ferdinand and Isabella, the least enterprising, Juan de Anchieta (1462–1523), was a Castilian. He was predominantly, though not exclusively, a church composer. But the other three, Pedro Escobar (d. 1514), Francisco de Peñalosa (*c.* 1470–1528) and, above all, Juan del Encina (1468–1529),[72] cultivated the Spanish counterpart of the frottola: the *villancico*.[73] Encina was also if not the earliest

---

[72] The music of all these composers is well represented in *La música en la Corte de los Reyes Católicos* (ed. Higini Anglès): *Polifonia religiosa*, i (Barcelona, 1941) and *Polifonia profana*, i and ii (Barcelona, 1947 and 1951) (= *Monumentos de la música española*, I, V, and X). *Antología musical* (ed. Elústiza and Hernández) (Barcelona, 1933) contains motets by Anchieta, Peñalosa, Escobar, and others; Office hymns by Escobar and Peñalosa are included in the *Spanisches Hymnar um 1500* (ed. Rudolf Gerber) (*ChW*, lx).

[73] The most important collection of villancicos is the *Cancionero de Palacio* (*Monumentos* V and X). Three examples by Encina in *HAM*, i, No. 98; another in *NOHM*, iii, p. 378, together with an example of 'Netherlandish' imitative writing. On the peculiarities of the villancico, see Isabel Pope, 'Musical and Metrical Form of the Villancico', *Annales musicologiques*, ii (Paris, 1954), p. 189.

Spanish dramatist at least the earliest significant one; his *eglogas*, said to have been first performed in 1492, end with villancicos sung and danced by all the characters.

MUSIC IN EASTERN EUROPE

At the other extremity of Europe, the still monophonic music of Russia was not yet written on a stave. In Sweden polyphony, 'discantus in nova mensura', was a novelty in 1489. Polish and Bohemian musicians at the beginning of the fifteenth century were writing rondelli and motets in styles long outdated in western Europe though Mikołaj z Radomia, probably clavicembalist to the Queen of Poland, who celebrated in a motet the birth of a prince in 1426, must have known the works of Ciconia and other western composers which appear in the same manuscript (Warsaw, Kras 52 Bibl. Narod.). There is also a Magnificat by him in which passages of the contratenor are formed by fauxbourdon.[74] But after Mikołaj Polish polyphony remained in the doldrums and the leading musician at the court of Cracow during the last decade of the fifteenth century and the first of the sixteenth was a German, Heinrich Finck (*c.* 1444–1527).

In Bohemia the development of the art was blighted by the religious wars, for while the Hussites were responsible for a great outpouring of vernacular monophony which was to influence not only later Czech music but Lutheran and even Catholic religious song, they denounced polyphony as frivolous. However the song-book compiled about 1505 for Jan Franus, a citizen of Hradec Králové, contains some very unsophisticated three-part pieces – one with a Hussite song as cantus firmus, another based on a popular Czech dance song.[75] Western musicians, such as the Liègois Johannes Stokhem, who appears to have replaced Josquin during the latter's absences from the papal chapel, were attracted to the brilliant court of Matthias Corvinus of Hungary and his Aragonese queen. The *magister capellae* of the last pre-Habsburg king of Hungary was a German, Thomas Stoltzer – a disciple, possibly a pupil, of Heinrich Finck – who is presumed to have died with his master after the battle of Mohács in 1526. We hear of no native Hungarian composers among their colleagues.

GERMAN POLYPHONY

Finck, Stoltzer, and the Emperor Maximilian's organist Paul Hofhaimer (1459–1537) were the three earliest German composers other than the Minnesänger to win international recognition. Finck has the additional distinction of being the earliest composer known to have employed a device popular as a method of treating German hymn tunes at least until Bach's day: the anticipation of the melody by imitations in much shorter note-

[74] Motet and Magnificat in *Muzyka w dawnym Krakowie* (ed. Zygmunt Szweykowski) (Cracow, 1964), pp. 10 and 22.
[75] *Dějiny české hudby v příkladech* (ed. Jaroslav Pohanka) (Prague, 1958), Nos. 57 and 58.

values, as in the opening of his Ascension hymn 'Festum nunc', an early work from the end of the fifteenth century:[76]

Ex. 50

Another hymn in the same source is bitextual, 'Veni, sancte spiritus/Veni, creator spiritus', with the initial imitation based on the second text. It is illuminating to compare this with the smoothly flowing, almost Josquin-esque setting of 'Veni, creator', obviously much later in date, which the Wittenberg publisher Rhaw published in 1542. Even when Finck adopts the device of initial imitation in these later works, such as 'Iste confessor', everything flows evenly in the latest Netherland style.[77] The difference between the obviously early three-part *Missa de Beata Virgine* and the impressive six-part Mass (seven parts in the Credo) dating probably from 1511,[78] is equally striking and not to be accounted for by simple maturing of a talent. The early works belong to the world of Busnois's admirer Adam of Fulda (*c.* 1445–1505), whose hymns[79] appear beside his own in the Apel Codex; the later ones to that of Josquin – and Isaac. And it is to the impact of Isaac that the transformation of German music at this time is commonly, and in all probability correctly, attributed.

HEINRICH ISAAC

The favourite composer first of Lorenzo the Magnificent, later of the Emperor Maximilian, Isaac was second only to Josquin in stature and perhaps not at all in influence on the next generation – though his influence

[76] In the Apel Codex (Leipzig, Univ. Bibl. 1494); published in *ChW*, xxxii (ed. Rudolf Gerber), p. 14. Gerber has also (with Ludwig Finscher and Wolfgang Dömling) edited the entire Apel Codex, *EDM*, xxxii–xxxiv (Kassel and Basle, 1956–75).
[77] Respectively in *ChW*, xxxii, p. 10 (also *HAM*, i, No. 80), and ibid., ix, pp. 10 and 22 (beginning of the latter also in *NOHM*, iii, p. 287).
[78] Respectively in Ambros, op. cit., v, p. 247, and (ed. Karl Hasse) *ChW*, xxi.
[79] E.g. his 'Veni, creator spiritus' (*EDM*, xxxii, p. 28; opening in *NOHM*, iii, p. 285) and 'Nuntius celso' (ibid., p. 8, and *ChW*, xxxii, p. 21).

was stronger on the German-speaking composers, Josquin's on the French-speaking ones. (We have an amusing comparison of the two men by the agents of Ercole I of Ferrara before he appointed Josquin as master of his chapel: Josquin composes better but he does it only when it suits him, not when others want him to, whereas Isaac is more easy-going and prolific – and moreover asks only 120 ducats while Josquin wants 200. When Isaac was appointed 'court composer' to Maximilian in 1497 he was paid 150 gulden a year, but seems to have had no duties in the Imperial Chapel as such.) Something has already been said of Isaac's Italian songs. His French ones, such as the delightful 'E qui la dira' (No. 11 in the *Odhecaton*) are comparably French in spirit; but it is his German songs that are the most important, the most individual, and the most beautiful. Even in this miniature genre he achieves great variety[80] despite the heavy preponderance of full four-part harmony and common time; most of them are *Tenorlieder* but with the other parts, particularly the highest, taking a share of the principal melody. In them Isaac found a perfect form of expression for the previously only imperfectly articulate German spirit in music. The most famous, 'Isbruck, ich muss dich lassen',[81] bequeathed its melody to the common stock of German music in the form of the Lutheran hymn, 'O Welt, ich muss dich lassen'. Another popular piece, in more normal Netherland style, 'Zwischen berg und tiefem tal',[82] formed the basis of a version by Isaac's Swiss pupil Ludwig Senfl (*c*. 1486–*c*. 1543), which supports the view that Isaac's piece is really a canonic duet for tenor and bass with instrumental upper parts;[83] another, a keyboard arrangement by the Constance organist Hans Buchner ('Hans von Constantz') (1483–1538), appears in Leonhard Kleber's tablature-book of 1524. The number of Isaac songs preserved without words – or even title[84] – has suggested that they were original instrumental compositions; and it is true that his 'Benedictus'[85] is wordless in all its nearly a score of sources and expressly marked *Absque verbis* in one of them. But we can be confident that Isaac specifically had instruments in mind only when, as in 'Der hundt',[86] he writes 'jagged' lines rather like Finck's in Ex. 50.

Not only Petrucci (*Misse henrici Izac*, 1506) but the German publishers later in the century were interested mainly in Isaac's chanson-Masses while a number of his most characteristic works, on plainsong cantus firmi, were allowed to lie for centuries in the libraries of Munich and Vienna. In his Masses as in his songs Isaac displays the widest variety of treatment, from

---

[80] Isaac's secular works are published, though not complete, in *DTÖ*, Jg. xiv (1) (vol. 28), ed. Johannes Wolf.

[81] *NOHM*, iii, p. 280; another treatment of the same melody, in canon for the two inside parts, provides the second 'Christe' in Isaac's *Missa Carminum*, partly based on other German song material, ed. Blume in *ChW*, vii.

[82] *DTÖ*, xiv (1), p. 26, and *HAM*, i, No. 87.

[83] See Helmuth Osthoff, 'Zu Isaacs und Senfls deutschen Liedern', *ZfMW*, xiv (1931–2), particularly p. 221 where the Isaac and Senfl versions are shown in parallel.

[84] E.g. *DTO*, xiv (1), p. 119; also in *HAM*, i, No. 88.

[85] No. 76 in Petrucci's *Odhecaton*; *DTÖ*, xiv (1), p. 112.

[86] *DTO*, xvi (1) (vol. 32), p. 225.

the tightly woven Mass 'O praeclara', on a four-note theme,[87] to the spacious six-part 'Virgo prudentissima', a very free paraphrase of his own six-part motet.[88] This diversity is fully displayed in the compilation known as the *Choralis Constantinus*, settings of the Proper for the entire year based on plainsong according to a Gradual in use at Constance or Passau, which was completed after his death by Senfl.[89] But the Netherland tours de force of such pieces as 'De radice Jesse', with each part in different mensuration,[90] are much less characteristic of the work as a whole than, for instance, the exquisitely simple Alleluia for the 16th Sunday after Pentecost:

Ex. 51

It was this simpler kind of counterpoint which influenced the later music of Finck, Adam Rener, and Senfl (whose work is discussed later: see pp. 223 and 225). It also influenced Stoltzer – as in the so-called 'Easter Mass', consisting of Kyrie, Gloria, and Sanctus only, and the psalm-motet 'Erzürne dich nicht',[91] which is probably the earliest setting of Luther's translation of the Bible – and, to a lesser extent, Hofhaimer, generally a rather conservative composer.[92]

GERMAN AND ITALIAN INSTRUMENTAL TABLATURES

One surprising thing about Hofhaimer is that, although he was the Imperial court organist, we have little authentic organ music by him – or, for that matter, by Isaac who was also an outstanding organist. Yvonne Rokseth's explanation may well be correct: that 'the greatest masters considered instrumental music . . . performed by a single player, a matter of improvisation; it was the less skilful organists, those unable to play without a book,

---

[87] See Peter Wagner, *Geschichte der Messe* (Leipzig, 1913), pp. 282–8. Wagner prints the complete Kyrie, as well as several other complete Mass-movements. Five of Isaac's Masses have been published by Louise Cuyler (Ann Arbor, 1956) and eight by Martin Staehelin (Mainz, 1970 and 1973), and four by Fabio Fano, *Archivium Musices Metropolitanum Mediolanense*, x (Milan, 1962).

[88] Kyrie, Wagner, p. 307; the motet in Ambros, op. cit., v. p. 314.

[89] It was printed only after Senfl's death (Nuremberg, 1550 and 1555). Parts 1 and 2 have been published in *DTÖ*, Jg, v (1) (vol. 10) (ed. Bezecny and Rabl) and xvi (1) (vol. 32) (ed. Anton von Webern), part 3, ed. Louise Cuyler (Ann Arbor, 1950).

[90] See the facsimile in Apel, *The Notation of Polyphonic Music* (Cambridge, Mass., 1945), p. 172, and the transcription, No. 24.

[91] Published respectively in *ChW*, lxxiv (ed. L. Hoffmann-Erbrecht) and vi (ed. Gombosi).

[92] The best known of his secular songs is 'Mein's traurens ist', printed in H. J. Moser, *91 Tonsätze des Kreises von Paul Hofhaimer* (originally published as an appendix to his book on the composer) (Stuttgart, 1929); *HAM*, i, No. 93; and elsewhere.

who were obliged to compile the tablatures which preserve for us today the art of the "Imperial" school'.[93] The first such tablature to be printed was the *Tabulaturen etlicher lobgesang und lidlein uff die orgeln un lauten* (Mainz, 1512)[94] of the blind Arnolt Schlick (*c.* 1460–*c.* 1521), who had already published a book on organ-building, *Spiegel der Orgelmacher und Organisten*[95] the year before. The *Tabulaturen* contain nine organ-pieces, twelve songs to the lute ('two voices to pluck and one to sing') and three lute-pieces ('with three voices to pluck'). Schlick was thus hard on the heels of Petrucci who had brought out in 1507 his first two books of *Intabulatura de Lauto*. These were largely transcriptions by Francesco Spinacino of polyphonic pieces Petrucci had already published, but also a number of non-thematic *ricercari* (lit. 'researches') on the lines of the German organ preludes. In 1509 and 1511 he brought out two books of *Tenori e contrabassi intabulati* ('two voices to pluck') *col soprano in canto figurato* ('one to sing') *per cantar e sonar col lauto*, mainly arrangements by 'Franciscus Bossinensis' from Petrucci's frottola books.[96] (Franciscus solved the problem of the fourth voice of the frottola, the altus, very simply – by omitting it.)

The histories of lute and keyboard music, both putting polyphony into the hands of a solo performer, remained closely allied for at least a century although the limitations of the lute, which could give no more than a sketchy impression of part-writing, must have been apparent from the first. It never had a literature comparable with that initiated with the German keyboard tablatures: Schlick's, those of Johannes ('Hans') Kotter (*c.* 1480–1541) and Leonhard Kleber (*c.* 1495–1556), and Buchner's *Fundamentbuch* with appended pieces, all liturgical.[97] Kotter and Buchner were Hofhaimer's pupils and Kleber may well have been. Kotter was one of the earliest Lutherans, hence his setting of Luther's 'Uss tieffer nodt'.[98] He compiled the greater part of his book in 1513 (though it was not finished till 1532)[99] for his friend, the celebrated Basle humanist Bonifacius Amerbach. Amerbach is known to have played the clavichord, so we may assume that the dances in particular were composed or 'tabulated' for that instrument though there is no difference in style. Unlike Kleber, Kotter sometimes acknowledges his own authorship of a piece; the other composers on whom he draws include

[93] *NOHM*, iii, p. 434.

[94] Modern edition by Gottlieb Harms (second edition, Hamburg, 1957). Two examples, the first verset (see p. 158) of an organ antiphon, 'Salve regina' (on a plainchant in German use) and a setting of the Marian hymn-tune 'Maria zart), with a certain amount of imitation, in *HAM*, i, Nos. 100 and 101.

[95] Version in modern German by E. Flade (second edition, Kassel, 1951).

[96] A number of the Spinacino pieces have been reprinted separately, e.g. a ricercare and transcription of Josquin's 'La Bernardina' in Schering, *Geschichte*, No. 63, a ricercare in *HAM*, i, No. 99*b*. The Bossinensis books have been reprinted complete by Benvenuto Disertori, *Istituzioni e monumenti dell'arte musicale italiana, Nuova serie III* (Milan, 1964). The Bossinensis version of Cara's 'Non è tempo' is in Schering, op. cit., No. 72.

[97] *Buchner: Sämtliche Orgelwerke EDM*, liii and liv (ed. H. Schmidt); one example in Schering, op. cit., No. 83.

[98] Schering, No. 82. The tune is the one printed in the *Deutsches Kirchenamt* (Strasbourg, 1525), not the familiar and equally old one used by Bach.

[99] Wilhelm Merian gives a thematic index to Kotter's tablature, with twenty complete pieces, in *Der Tanz in den deutschen Tabulaturbüchern* (Leipzig, 1927), pp. 37ff. Kotter compiled a second tablature *c.* 1525; both are published in *Schweizerische Musikdenkmäler*, vi.

Isaac, Josquin, Hofhaimer, and Buchner, while Kleber throws his net wider to include also Brumel, Adam of Fulda, Finck, Senfl – and Kotter. The repertory covers preludes, organ versets (particularly for the 'Salve regina', popular with German organists from the Buxheim book onward), French and German songs, and dances (including a number of 'Spanish dances' on the basse-danse tenor, 'La Spagna' (cf. p. 170, n.28)). The 'Imperial school' still relied heavily on 'coloration' but their figuration is less stereotyped, more flowing – indeed derived to some extent from the patterns of Netherland polyphony – and it is no longer more or less confined to the highest part. Kotter's version of Hofhaimer's 'Zucht, eer und lob' is compared here with the original as printed in Georg Forster's *Ein Ausszug guter alter und newer Teutscher liedlein* (Nuremberg, 1539):[100]

Ex. 52

---

[100] Hofhaimer's 'Nach willen din' is given, with Kotter's transcription and later versions for organ (anon., 1530) and lute (Newsidler, 1536), in Ernest T. Ferand, *Die Improvisation (Das Musikwerk)* (Cologne, 1956).

9. The Impact of the Renaissance

With the exception of a short setting of the Sarum Offertory 'Felix namque',[101] dating from around 1400, the earliest surviving English keyboard music is contemporary with Kotter and Kleber. (England can claim the possession, but only very dubiously the origination, of the much older Robertsbridge Codex.) It consists of a little collection of eleven pieces, all but two of them dances, obviously for the virginals – witness the left-hand part of 'My Lady Carey's dompe' – in the British Library manuscript, Royal App. 58.[102] By far the longest and the only one bearing a composer's name is a rather dull 'Hornepype' by Hugh Aston,[103] presumably the Hugo Haston who, 'after eight years' study and practice', supplicated for the degree of B. Mus. at Oxford on 20 November 1510. A Mass and antiphon of his were sung on his admission – possibly the thematically connected *Missa Te Deum* and votive antiphon 'Te Deum laudamus' of his in the Bodleian Library[104] – and incidentally the Mass shows a relationship to the 'Hornepype' in its quasi-ostinato technique. Neither Aston's church music nor the keyboard writing of Royal App. 58 has much, if anything, in common with contemporary Continental music. But he graduated just at the time, the beginning of the reign of Henry VIII, when England was about to end a period of musical insularism.

ENGLISH MUSICAL INSULARISM

The isolation, perhaps originating in the military expulsion from France followed by the disruption of the Wars of the Roses, had been by no means inglorious. For the English composers, though conservative in the eyes of the cosmopolitan Fleming Tinctoris in the 1470s (see p. 154), had not stood still. They clung to the cantus firmus principle and made only sporadic and unsystematic use of imitation, but they developed an extremely florid style of their own, seldom writing in fewer than five or six parts, sometimes more, in an intricate counterpoint of rhythms, which has been aptly compared with the equally idiosyncratic Perpendicular style of English architecture. 'Each was the final phase of the Gothic in its medium, and both expressed the late medieval trend towards the adornment of devotion by the most elaborate and decorative forms of art and craft.'[105] The music is preserved in a number of sources, of which the most important – the most splendid of all English musical manuscripts – is that compiled for the choir

---

[101] In Oxford, Douce 381; printed in *M & L*, xxxv (1954), p. 205. John Caldwell, introduction to *EECM*, vi (London, 1965), has suggested that this may be 'a simple piece of vocal descant' rather than organ music.

[102] Ten of the pieces have been published, not altogether satisfactorily, in *Schott's Anthology of Early Keyboard Music*, i (London, 1951). The Aston 'Hornepype' is also published in Johannes Wolf, *Sing-und Spielmusik* (Leipzig, second edition, 1931), No. 24, and Apel, *Musik aus früher Zeit*, ii, p. 5, 'Lady Carey's dompe' in *HAM*, i, No. 103.

[103] However, the French lutenist Guillaume Morlaye based on it a 'Hornepipe d'Angleterre'.

[104] Mus. Sch. e. 376–81, No. 7, and e. i–5, No. 5; printed in *TCM*, x, pp. 1 and 99. See Frank Ll. Harrison, *Music in Medieval Britain* (London, 1958), p. 335.

[105] Harrison, *NOHM*, iii, p. 303.

of Eton College, *c.* 1490–1502.[106] The composers who first developed this ornate style never became internationally known like their expatriate contemporaries Bedingham, Frye, and Morton, or the theorist John Hothby (d. 1487), happily settled in Italy till Henry VII summoned him home. By Henry Abyngdon, Master of the Children of the Chapel Royal during the Wars of the Roses, we have not even one composition. By his successor in 1478, Gilbert Banester (d. 1487), we have an antiphon 'O Maria et Elizabeth'[107] (probably datable 1486), some alternatim (even number) verses for the hymn 'Exsultet caelum laudibus', a two-part 'Allelui laudate', and a carol 'My feerful dreme',[108] the end of which suggests a keyboard postlude. These are old-fashioned works, with minimal use of imitation and only gentle flowering of line, but in the 'Salve Regina', alternatim (even verse) 'Magnificat', and incomplete 'Gaude Virgo, Mater Christi'[109] of William Horwood (d. 1484) the florid style is already well developed. It reached its highest point in the compositions of John Browne (*c.* 1426–98) and Walter Lambe (*c.* 1452–*c.* 1500), both well represented in the Eton Choirbook; for a supreme masterpiece of the style one need look no further than Browne's 'O Maria salvatoris mater'[110] which opens the book, while his song 'Margarit meek'[111] is a gem of sophisticated Court music. Another outstanding work in the Eton book is the *Passio Domini ... secundum Matthaeum*[112] of Richard Davy (*c.* 1467–*c.* 1516), the moving simplicity of which, and of much of his 'Stabat Mater', is in the strongest stylistic contrast with such antiphons as 'O Domine caeli terraeque' (said to have been composed in one day of 1491 or 1492) and 'Salve Jesu mater vera'.[113]

Two composers represented in the Eton book – Robert Fayrfax (*c.* 1464–1521)[114] and William Cornysh (*c.* 1468–1523)[115] – employ a rather less florid style exemplified by verse 2 of Fayrfax's puzzlingly named alternatim 'Regali' Magnificat[116] – puzzling because, unlike Fayrfax's Mass of the same name, it is not based on the plainsong antiphon 'Regali ex progenie'. The numerous little points of imitation in the Magnificat are significant too. But the puzzle-canons in 'King Henry VIII's Manuscript' (Brit. Lib., Add. 31922)[117] are relics of medievalism; at least two of them are by John Lloyd (or Fluyd) (d. 1523), composer of a Mass, 'O quam suavis',[118]

[106] Ed. Harrison, *MB*, x–xii.
[107] Ibid., xi, p. 117.
[108] *NOHM*, iii, p. 346, and *Early Tudor Songs and Carols* (*MB*, xxxvi), ed. John Stevens, p. 110.
[109] *MB*, x, p. 101, and xii, pp. 69 and 141.
[110] Ibid., x, p. 1.
[111] *Mb*, xxxvi, p. 121.
[112] *MB*, xii, p. 112.
[113] 'Stabat Mater' and antiphons in *MB*, xi, pp. 83, 62, and 73.
[114] *Collected Works* (ed. Edwin B. Warren), in *CMM* 17. See also Warren's 'Life and Works of Robert Fayrfax' and 'The Masses of Robert Fayrfax', *Musica Disciplina*, xi, p. 134, and xii, p. 145, and Anselm Hughes's 'Introduction to Fayrfax', ibid., vi, p. 83.
[115] Presumably 'William Cornyssh, Junior' as he is called in one source. There was another William Cornysh, perhaps his father, master of the choristers of Westminster Abbey (d. before 1502).
[116] *MB*, xii, p. 96, and *CMM* 17, ii.
[117] Ed. John Stevens as *Music at the Court of Henry VIII* (*MB*, xviii).
[118] Ed. H. B. Collins (London, 1927).

the tenor of which can be arrived at likewise only by the solution of Latin 'canons'. All three – Cornysh, Fayrfax, and Lloyd – were members of Henry VIII's Chapel Royal and it was Henry VIII, even more than his father, who put an end to English musical isolationism. He himself played both the 'clavychordes', and the lute (as did his brother-in-law James IV, who played a similar role in revitalizing the music of Scotland), and composed – though not very well, as we may see from the more than thirty pieces attributed to him in 'King Henry VIII's Manuscript'. He took his Chapel with him in 1513 to Lille where they met the Burgundian Chapel of Margaret of Austria, and in 1520 to the Field of the Cloth of Gold where they met the French Chapel of Francis I and on Trinity Sunday alternately sang the movements of a Mass. Already in 1516 Henry had recruited a Venetian Dionisio Memo, first organist of San Marco, though he employed more French and Flemish musicians – for instance 'Benet de Opicijs' (possibly Benedictus Ducis), organist at Bruges in 1516–17 – than Italians.

Whereas the so-called 'Fayrfax Book' (Brit. Lib., Add. 5465: *MB*, xxxvi), reflecting the repertoire of Henry's father's court, contains only English music – largely by the composers of the Eton book – Add. 31922 opens with Isaac's 'Benedictus' and also includes his 'La my' and compositions by Ghizeghem, Barbireau, Fevin, and Compère. No. 83 is a version of a laude published by Petrucci. Not only that: Cornysh has to show his paces not simply in the homely three-part songs that came naturally to him – and were no doubt written for the dramatic entertainments, 'disguisings' and masques, the arrangement of which was an important part of his duties – 'Adew adew my hartis lust', 'Blow thi horne hunter', 'Trolly lolly', and the like. He also had to write four-part settings of French words ('Adew mes amours') beginning with extended imitation.

All the same, the Netherland style never substantially affected English music, either religious or secular. The wind which was to do more than ruffle its surface blew from Italy and much later.

Interlude

IO

Music in the Islamic World[1]

THE ORIGINS OF ISLAMIC MUSIC

Throughout the Middle Ages the only non-European music with which that of Christendom had come into contact was Islamic. During the hundred years after the death of Muḥammad in 632 his Arab followers overran the whole Mediterranean coast from the Bosphorus to the Straits of Gibraltar, conquered Spain – sealing behind them in the province of Toledo the rites and music of the Visigothic church, hence known as Mozarabic – and threatened at the same time both the Frankish kings and the Byzantine emperors. The Islamic peoples never neglected the arts of war but – Arabs, Persians, Turks – they also cultivated literature and music, and when in the eleventh century the Christians embarked on the reconquest of Spain and the expulsion of the Muslims from the Holy Land they were opposed by peoples equal if not superior in culture to themselves. The centuries-long war ended in the West with the conquest of Granada by the Christian Monarchs in 1492, but in the East Constantinople had fallen half a century earlier, and when in 1526 Louis of Hungary (and his *magister capellae*, Stoltzer) died at Mohács all Eastern Europe lay open to the Turks. This is an appropriate place, therefore, to pause and consider Islamic music both for its own sake and because of its relations with European music.

Its roots, of course, were in that music common to all the Middle East until the Christians gradually evolved their own ritual dialects. The Persians, Arabs, and Kurds of the pre-Islamic period possessed the instruments of Western Mediterranean culture, often under essentially the same names; the Arab *kinnāra* (kithara) was the Hebrew *kinnôr*[2] and the pipe was a folk-instrument, still known to Muslims as *arghūl*. But secular music had originally no role in Islamic culture. Although the Koran says nothing against music the Prophet's puritanical followers, after his death, claimed that he had regarded it – particularly instrumental music – as a 'forbidden pleasure' and proceeded to ban the lute (*al'ūd*, literally 'the wood', an instrument derived from the Persian *barbât*), harp (*jank*), and flute (Persian *nāy*, Arabic *quṣṣāba*), all associated with frivolity and moral licence, although percussion instruments such as the tabor (*ṭabl*) and hand-drum (*duff*, no doubt the Hebrew *tôph*) of common social festivities were permitted. The call

---

[1] In this chapter, I have inevitably leaned heavily on the innumerable writings of H. G. Farmer and am much indebted to the helpful criticism of Owen Wright.
[2] See p. 38.

to prayer, the cantillation of the Koran (probably akin to Jewish cantillation of the psalms), the chanting of verses commemorating the birthday of the Prophet (*Mevlid*), prayers, praises, and hymns were a different matter; for Muslims they are not 'music'. They differ considerably in style. The hymn is syllabic, metrical, and undecorated; *Mevlid* is floridly melismatic; but there are no obligatory phrases or melodies attached to particular texts. Similarly, the muezzin's call to prayer is his own personal version, often in his chosen, recognizable *maqām* (see pp. 197–8).

MUSIC UNDER THE EARLIER CALIPHATES

This did not last long. The Umayyad caliphs (661–750), under whom the Maghrib (the West) and Spain were conquered, were lovers of music and imported from Khorasan singing girls who brought with them the long-necked Persian *tanbūr*, its two strings plucked with fingers or plectrum, and displayed their virtuosity in vocal and instrumental ornamentation. We also know from this period the names of male musicians, who now supplanted women in what had hitherto been a mainly female profession. The ʿAbbāsids, who in 768 made Baghdad their capital, were also enthusiasts for music, none more so than Hārun al-Rashīd who loved not only court music but the music of the people.

As for the court music, it seems likely that the form of concert later called *nauba*, Central Asian in origin and already known to the Chinese – a series of vocal and instrumental pieces of different types – began to be adopted under the early ʿAbbāsids; it is still the most important 'form' of Islamic music.

CLASSICAL PRACTICE AND THEORY

The basis of the classical system had already been established under the Umayyads. According to the *Kitāb al-aghāni al-kabīr* (Great book of songs) of Al-Iṣfahānī (897–967), it was Ibn Misjaḥ (d. *c.* 715) who first brought Persian song and its rhythmic accompaniment (*ḍarb*) to Mecca: 'He chose from the scales (*nagham*) of the [until recently Byzantine-governed] Syrians the most agreeable sounds, rejecting those which displeased him ... It was he who fixed the order of notes in Arab song and he was the first to make melodies from it.' And when in the early tenth century the system was defined by Ibn al-Munajjim (d. 912) in his *Risāla fi'l mūsīqī* (Treatise on music: he uses the Greek word, not the Arabic *ghina'*) it is based on the tuning of the lute in fourths. The 'second' string (*mathnā*) was tuned first: *mutlaq* (open string, say f'), *sabbāba* (first finger, g'), *wusṭā* (second finger, approximately a♭'), *binṣir* (third finger, approximately a♮') – *wusṭā* and *binṣir* were alternatives and could not be used in close proximity – and *khinṣir* (fourth finger, b♭'). From this the 'first' string, *zīr*, was tuned a fourth higher; to complete the octave, says Ibn al-Munajjim, one need only extend the little

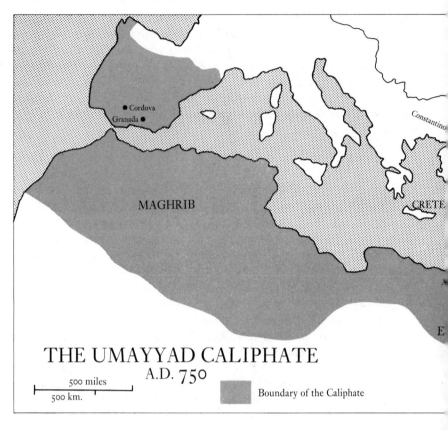

Cordova
Granada

Constantino[...]

MAGHRIB

CRETE

A

E

THE UMAYYAD CALIPHATE
A.D. 750

500 miles
500 km.

Boundary of the Caliphate

finger on *zīr*. The third and fourth strings, *mathlath* and *bamm*, were tuned each a fourth lower. Thus each string covered a tetrachord, with either *wusṭā* or *binṣir*. Unfortunately Ibn al-Munajjim 'fails to supply any definition of tunings and intervals'[3] though the strings were obviously tuned in perfect fourths and Owen Wright goes on, like H. G. Farmer,[4] to deduce a Pythagorean scale of tones and *leimma* (see p. 29) as indicated above.

BYZANTINE INFLUENCE

Thus Byzantine as well as Persian influence infiltrated into Arab music to form its original 'classical' style, practised at the court of Hārun al-Rashīd by two famous musicians, Ibrāhīm al-Mauṣilī (743–804?) and his even greater son, Isḥāq al-Mauṣilī (767–850). But Isḥāq had to contend with a royal rival, Hārun's brother Ibrāhīm (779–839), a singer with an extraordinary voice, who introduced fresh Persian influence and made unwarranted simplifications in the classical style. His sister, Princess ʿUlaiya, also a

[3] Owen Wright, 'Ibn al-Munajjim and the Early Arabian Modes', *The Galpin Society Journal*, xix (1966), p. 27.
[4] *NOHM*, i, p. 457.

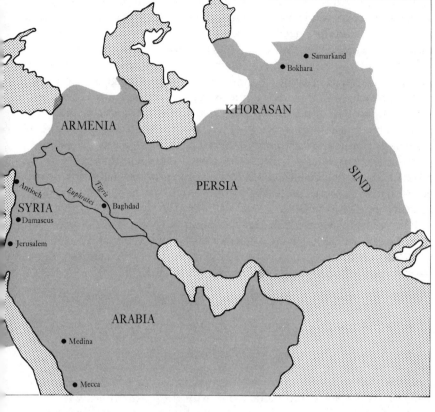

notable singer, had an *urġan rūmī*, a Roman (i.e. Byzantine) organ, though we do not know whether or how she played it.

In Ishāq al-Mauṣilī's time the caliph Al-Ma'mūn, nephew of these royal musicians, greatly encouraged cultural contacts with Byzantium. Byzantine scholars were invited to Baghdad and Greek treatises on music were translated into Arabic, so that cultivated Arab musicians knew not only the writings of Ptolemy of Alexandria (see p. 49) but those of his more practical predecessor Aristoxenus (see p. 31 and 33–4) indeed more than we do, for they had translations of works by Aristoxenus which have since been lost.[5] It is possible that Euclid's treatise on the division of the monochord, *Katatome kanonos* (see p. 28), translated as *Kitāb al-qānūn*, may have given its name, *qānūn*, to the Arab psaltery (a development of the monochord principle) which was to come back to Europe after the Sixth Crusade as the *canon* of Adenès li Roi's *Li Romauns de Cléomadès*. Intensive study of the Alexandrian and earlier Greek theorists naturally led to excessive preoccupation with mathematics, the precise measurement of micro-intervals, and so on, rather than with practical music which (like that of the Greeks) was much simpler; but the works of the neo-Platonist Ya'qūb ibn Ishāq al-Kindī

[5] *NOHM*, i, p. 458.

('Alkindus') (*c*. 790–*c*. 874) give us valuable information about actual Arab music of this period. He mentions that the lute was fretted and advocates a fifth string (as did the singer Ziryāb in Spain), and he describes a decorative device of sounding on the lute a fourth, fifth, octave, or other interval simultaneously with the melody note which has survived till today. He describes a system of eight rhythmic modes quite foreign to the Greeks[6] and, followed by Ibn al-Munajjim, uses nine letters in discussion of the notes possible within the octave – but not for the notation of actual music. (No Arabic music was written down, even alphabetically, before the thirteenth century; everything was transmitted orally and the essence of performing artistry lay – as it still does – in the subtleties of voice-production and the invention of literally 'arabesque' melismatic ornamentation, trills and grace-notes in vast profusion, to the long, highly organized, mostly conjunct melodies.)

For Al-Iṣfahānī and the Aristotelian polymath Al-Fārābī (*c*. 870–*c*. 950), a century later, the lute's four or five strings were all tuned in fourths in the Persian manner – g, c′, f′, b♮′ and if necessary e♭′ (though other tunings were in use) – thus giving the following tetrachords:

muṭlaq	*sabbāba*	*wusṭā/binṣir*	*khinṣir*
b♭′	c″	d♭′/d′	e♭″
f′	g′	a♭′/a♮′	b♭′
c′	d′	e♭′/e♮′	f′
g	a	b♭/b♮	c′

And Al-Isfahānī speaks of twice four modes: *muṭlaq fī majrā al-wusṭā* and *al-binṣir* (two open string modes, one with *wusṭā*, the other with *binṣir*), *sabbāba fī majrā al-wusṭā* and *al-binṣir* (two first-finger modes with *wusṭā* or *binṣir*), and so on. Al-Fārābī, who claimed to have clarified the utterances and corrected the errors of the Greek theorists, observed that the *sabbāba* and *binṣir* of the third string corresponded to the Greek *mese* and *paramese* and consequently the alternative *wusṭā* to the *trite synemmenon*.[7] He used letters of the Arabic alphabet for the 15 notes corresponding to the Greek Perfect System and transliterated the names of the modes (aeolian, dorian, and so on) from Greek to Arabic. Al-Fārābī also tells us, among other practical things, that the holes of the simple nine-holed pipe (*mizmār* or *zamr*) were placed in accordance with the *wusṭā* modes of the lute – and also that there were three ways of measuring *wusṭā*: the diatonic (proportion of *wusṭā* to *khinṣir* as 8 to 9), the 'Persian *wusṭā*' which exactly halved the whole tone *sabbāba-binṣir*, and 'Zalzal's *wusṭā*' which was half-way between the Persian *wusṭā* and *binṣir*. There were also microtonal 'neighbours of the *sabbāba*' used mainly as ornaments. Other microtones were played on the *ṭunbūr*, a species of lute with very long neck and small body which was then

---

[6] Ibid., p. 448; the version deduced from Al-Iṣfahānī and Al-Farabī in Lavignac and La Laurencie *Encyclopédie de la musique (Ière partie)* v (Paris, 1922), p. 2704, is markedly different and perhaps equally incorrect.

[7] See pp. 29, 30, and 76.

coming into favour as a solo instrument, no longer merely an accompanying one. Al-Fārābī distinguishes two types, the *ṭunbūr baghdādī* or *mīzānī* and the *ṭunbūr khurasānī*; both had two strings variously tuned, and fretted necks, the Baghdad, or 'measured', variety having an already obsolescent scale of microtones, the Khorasanian having frets giving *leimma, leimma, comma*.[8] But the fixed framework into which these microtones were fitted was always the perfect fourth (and hence octave and fifth).

MUSIC UNDER THE DIVIDED CALIPHATES

Arabic/Persian music of the golden age thus had a relationship with that of Greece, Byzantine/Alexandrian and even classical. It also had differences, perhaps more in practice than in theory; and these differences, notably the profusion of ornament – with the differences within the Islamic world – were later to be accentuated as Islamic culture became fragmented by religious division and foreign invasion.

A rival Fāṭimid caliphate was established in North Africa in 909 with its capital at Cairo from 969 and in Spain the Emir of Cordoba took the title of caliph in 929; Baghdad itself fell into the hands of the Seljuk Turks; and in the course of the Middle Ages the Berbers in the West and the Mamelukes in the East became the masters and went down in turn before the Mongols, who destroyed Baghdad in 1258, and the Ottoman Turks. But the Caliph of Baghdad remained the spiritual head of the Islamic world and the music of the Baghdad caliphate was paramount until the Mongol conquest. Its history, however, was uneventful. We get further information about theory and instruments in Persia from the treatise, *Al-shifā* (The Cure)[9] of Ibn Sīnā (Avicenna) (980–1037): for instance, that the number of modes had been increased and were now given non-technical names – 'Ushshāq' ('passion'), 'Nawā' ('melody' or 'sound'), 'Irāq', Iṣfahān', and so on – and that, probably as a result of foreign contacts, new forms of instrument were known. (Purely instrumental music now assumed much greater importance in the Islamic world.) Some of these instruments are unidentifiable; for instance the *salyāq* may or may not be a descendant of the Syrian *sambyke*, presumably a harp, and the *anqā* remains a mystery. The Persian plucked *rubāb*, a kind of lute, is not to be confused with the bowed *rabāb*, an ancestor of the viol. There were double-reed instruments – *mizmār, zamr* or *surnāy* – and the single-reed *dūnāy* ('double-pipe') and *arghūl* (melody-pipe and drone). And there were variously named types of drum, one of which – the pair of single-skin *naqqārāt* – was soon borrowed by the Crusaders, who were much impressed by the Mameluke military bands of reed-pipes, trumpets, and drums, as *nacaires* or nakers. One stringed instrument probably brought from Central Asia to Persia and Syria by the Seljuks was

---

[8] The Pythagorean comma is the difference between seven octaves and twelve perfect fifths. For a detailed account of these *ṭunbūr* scales, see Lavignac and La Laurencie, op. cit., pp. 2710–12; with all his mathematical pedantry, Al-Fārābī does tell us what most practical musicians of his day actually did.
[9] Complete French translation by Baron d'Erlanger, *La Musique arabe* (Paris, 1935), ii, p. 103.

the *kamāncha*: a type of viol with hemispherical belly supported on the ground by an iron spike, long neck, and commonly two strings tuned a fourth apart. But there were a number of varieties, including the larger *ghichak* which had eight additional strings that could vibrate 'sympathetically' or be occasionally plucked. The Turks also contributed a variety of *ṭunbūr* with hemispherical belly: *ṭunbūra-yi turkī*.

ṢAFĪ AL-DĪN AND THE MELODIC MODES

One outstanding musician and theorist, Ṣafī al-Dīn (*c.* 1230–1294), escaped from the sack of Baghdad and was taken into the service of the

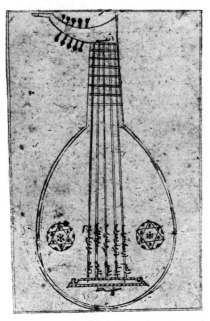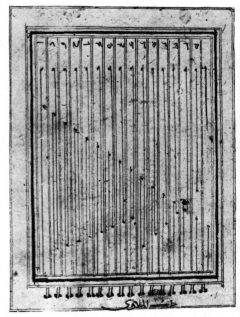

Pl. 37(i)   ʾŪd (lute) in an early fourteenth-century copy of the *Kitāb al-adwār* (Book of Modes) of the Baghdad musician Ṣafī al-Dīn. (Oxford, Bodl. Ms. Marsh 521, fo. 157v). The five double-strings are tuned in fourths.

Pl. 37(ii)   The big 64-string *qānūn* (psaltery), invented by Ṣafī – who called it *nuzha*. From the same manuscript, fo. 158.

conqueror, Hulāgū Khan, grandson of Jenghiz. Ṣafī al-Dīn was the author of two important treatises, *Risālat al-sharafiyya* (Treatise for Sharaf, his pupil) and *Kitāb al-adwār* (Book of modes),[10] and an inventor of instruments (including a bass-lute, *mughnī*, and a rectangular 64-stringed *qānūn*, *nuzha*).[11] He derived a scale from the *leimma-leimma-comma* tuning of the

---

[10] French translations in d'Erlanger, op. cit., iii, pp. 3 and 185.
[11] He gives examples in notation; see the two quotations from the *Kitāb al-adwār* in *NOHM*, i, pl. XIV, and transcriptions, pp. 454–5.

Khorasanian *ṭunbūr*[12] and his twelve primary modes became known as *maqāmāt*, a word that had not yet acquired its meaning of 'melodic patterns'; his recognition of 17 intervals within the octave does not, of course, imply that all could be used in the same melody. He also notes that there were six secondary modes, originally Persian, called *avāzāt*. The Mongols and Turks added more melodic modes, to say nothing of no less complicated rhythmic ones performed by percussion instruments accompanying, but quite independent of, the melody; and by the fifteenth century there were forty-eight melodic and twenty-one rhythmic modes.

MUSLIM MUSIC IN SPAIN AND NORTH AFRICA

In Muslim Spain the outstanding theorist seems to have been Ibn Bājja (Avenpace) (*c*. 1090–1139) but his *Kitāb al-mūsīqī* has not survived. Here in the far West the music of the Islamic world influenced that of the Christians, though probably only at the popular level. The music of the old Visigothic church – Mozarabic chant – was preserved under Moorish rule not only from supersession by Roman chant but also from Arabic contamination; the interesting theory that troubadour song was indebted to Arab influence remains unproven. But the folk-music of Andalusia, with its microtonal inflections and florid ornamentation, is unmistakably marked by traits of Eastern Mediterranean music – not only Arab but gypsy (so far as manner of performance is concerned) and even Jewish.[13] The illustrations to the *Cantigas de Santa Maria*[14] show Moorish musicians at the court of Alfonso X of Castile playing the same instruments as their Christian colleagues; the *guitarra morisca* became the *vihuela de mano*, the *rabāb*, the *rabel* (and hence *rabeca* and rebec). But there is little or no traceable converse influence. As the Moors withdrew from Spain after the reconquest in the thirteenth century of Seville (their chief musical centre) and Cordoba, of Granada in 1492, and a further expulsion in 1609, they took with them to the western Maghrib pure classical dialects, *andalusī* and *granaṭī*, of Arab music whereas the eastern Maghrib, like the Middle East generally, came under Turkish influence.

CONTEMPORARY PRACTICE

The music of the Maghrib today once more, after a long period of degeneration, probably represents the purest classical form of Muslim music

[12] Ibid., pp. 449–50 and 462.
[13] Later Islamic overlordship left even deeper marks on the folk-music of south-eastern Europe. The Turkish *aksak* (limping) rhythms occur in the folk-music of Greece, Macedonia, and Bulgaria. Both Greeks and Bulgars employ the *maqām* known as *ḥijāz*; indeed Bulgarian folk-music uses several *maqāmāt* (see Boris A. Kremenliev, *Bulgarian-Macedonian Folk Music* (Berkeley and Los Angeles, 1952), pp. 55–8). The Turkish bagpipe, *gayda*, is so-called in Serbia, Bulgaria, and Greece, the Serbs, Bulgars, Macedonians, and Greeks all speak of a *zurna* or *zurla*, and the long shepherd's pipe is *kaval* in Serbian, even sometimes *kaba kaval* (Turkish: 'big pipe') in Bulgarian.
[14] See p. 98 and pl. 29.

– thanks, ironically, to such European scholars as Salvador-Daniel and Jules Rouanet, director of the École de musique in Algiers and author of the monumental articles on Arab music in the Lavignac and La Laurencie *Encyclopédie* – while the Bedouins preserve one of the purest forms of Arab folk-song. For there is both a classical and a popular music, and there are Moroccan, Algerian, and Tunisian dialects. Egypt was naturally much more open to Turkish ideas, an influence which was actually strengthened in the late nineteenth century by the Khedive Ismail, and since the modern codification of Arabic music was initiated in Cairo by Darwīsh Muḥammad and Muḥammad Kamel el-Kholay at the beginning of the present century, Ṣafī al-Dīn's theoretical octave of 17 degrees has been superseded by one of 24 degrees favoured by the Turks.

The lute is tuned in fourths, plus one lower note, and Darwīsh Muḥammad explains how to stop the principal notes between: on *'ashirān* with the second finger you get *'irāq*, with the fourth you get *rast*; and so on:

jaga 'ashirān ('irāq rast) dūkāh (sīkāh jahārka) nawā (husenī auj) kardan[15]
g   a   -b c′   d′ -e′   f′   g′   a′ -b′   c″

The minus-signs indicate flattening by a microtone, the intervals *'irāq-rast*, *dūkāh-sīkāh*, *sīkāh-jahārka*, *husenī-auj*, and *auj-kardan* being each more than a semitone. And the system is extended upward to the octave above *jahārka*: f″. Moreover the intervening microtones are available, each with its name (e.g. *nam ḥiṣar*, *ḥiṣar*, and *taq ḥiṣar qaba* between *jahārka* and *'ashiran*).

There are twelve principal *maqāmāt* and a larger number of secondary ones, some only in local use; needless to say there are Persian, Turkish, and other variants and the *maqāmāt* have long been not simply 'modes', note-series, but 'matrices for composition' each distinguished by its treatment of the scale, by certain melodic patterns, and by association with particular moods and circumstances. Thus the *maqām rast*, which is named from the note itself (the 'direct' note), begins with this note and ends with it, keeps within the octave above it, and is quiet and restrained even in its ornamentation. *Bayātī*, the 'domestic' *maqām*, d′, -e′, f′, g′, a′, bb′, c″, d″, very popular in the Middle East, is associated with tenderness and may be used for religious or secular music. *Rehaw*, said to be the old name of the city of Edessa, has the same intervals but must begin on *nawā*, emphasize *dūkāh* in between, and end on *jahārka*. The Persian *bayāt-i kurd* also begins on g and has the same intervals (g, -a, bb, c′, d′, eb′, f′, g′), but the *bayāt-i Ispahān* begins the series on *rast* and makes the penultimate note -b′ instead of bb′. The Persian 'royal mode', *humāyūn*, differs from the *bayāt-i kurd* only in having b instead of bb.

Although Arab and Persian and Turkish melodies can now be written in European notation, with half-flats and half-sharps for the microtones, improvisation – not only of the ornaments – remains an essential feature of

---

[15] In the table drawn up by the Cairo Congress of Arabian Music in 1932 (see *MGG*, i, col. 595), the names are transposed down a fourth so that the scale g-g′ is named from *rast* to *kardan*.

Islamic music. In the *nauba*, that mixture of instrumental suite and vocal cantata in five to ten movements in different tempi[16] which is the principal form of musical performance in most Islamic countries, there is always provision for improvisation; in the Turkish field of influence it is the *taqsīm*, the opening piece in which the principal instrumentalist gives a display of improvised ornamentation, in Morocco the overture (*taushiya*) is preceded and followed by an instrumental *bughya* which again allows scope for improvisation. There is no polyphony, only the heterophony which results from the performance of the same melody simultaneously on different instruments and the counterpoint of rhythm produced by the independent patterns of a percussion instrument.

---

[16] On the *nauba* generally and the various groupings of movements in different countries, see *Grove's Dictionary* (fifth edition, London, 1954) vi, p. 32. Further east the Uzbeks confusingly called the *nauba* 'makom'; V. A. Uspensky noted down six of them in Bokhara and published them as *Shest' muzïkal'nïkh poem (Makomï)* (Bokhara, 1924).

Part III
The Ascendancy of Italy

Introduction

Although the musical ascendancy of Italy did not begin to assert itself immediately after the deaths of Josquin and Isaac and their great contemporaries, Pierre de La Rue and Loyset Compère, its foundations were already laid. And now that specifically Italian form, the madrigal, was born. (The tidy-minded may like to date it from Petrucci's publication of Bernardo Pisano's *Musica . . . sopra le canzone del petrarcha* which actually occurred in 1520.) So long as such men as Willaert, Verdelot, and Arcadelt held posts in Venice, Florence, and Rome – that is, until the mid-century or after – Italian music cannot be said to have emancipated itself from northern tutelage. Yet, when it did, it quickly established a leadership even more remarkable than that of north-western Europe during the Middle Ages and maintained that position until near the end of the eighteenth century. It may seem premature to date the 'ascendancy' so early. But the madrigal was not merely a new art form – it had nothing in common with the *trecento* madrigal except the name – but a landmark in a revolution of which we have already seen the beginnings in the frottole and laudi spirituali and occasional passages in the Italian-influenced northerners from Dufay onward.

The madrigal was polyphonic but not purely polyphonic. Its polyphony had to reckon with an element to which Humanism attached enormous importance: the words. Whereas the intellectual, 'mathematical' polyphony of the Middle Ages had, as John XXII complained, treated sacred texts as mere subjects for music, music was now often composed expressly to project words – especially secular ones. But 'the humanistic subordination of music to text, the insistence that music shall have meaning through carrying words or shall simply heighten the effect of words, is as evident in religious music as in frottola, madrigal, and chanson. And in the religious music both of the Catholics and of every variety of Protestant.'[1]

In so far as religious thinking was permeated by the spirit of Humanism, religious music also submitted to become the vehicle of the word while pure polyphony of the utmost technical refinement continued to serve the religion of pure unreasoning faith, 'the magic of sound matching the magic of faith'. As it happens, the supreme masters of 'golden age' polyphony toward the latter part of the century, when Italian innovators were making

[1] *NOHM*, iv, p. xxiii.

even bolder experiments with word-carrying music, were an Italian, Palestrina, an Italianized Spaniard, and – more affected by humanism – an Italianized Fleming, who are widely known by Italianized forms of their names, 'Vittoria' and 'Orlando di Lasso'.

While these were the two basic trends in European music, the general picture was much more complicated. The Church had ceased to be monolithic; the social structure of Europe had become more fluid. Hitherto, music – other than the anonymous, never written down and therefore lost music of the people – had been the affair of the Church or the court or great nobles. Now, an increasingly influential and literate middle class was sharing in making it and in the demand for it. It was able to do so more easily when large-scale music publication, including a high proportion of Italian music, spread from Italy to France (with Pierre Attaingnant in Paris from 1528 and Jacques Moderne at Lyons four years later), Germany (with Georg Rhaw at Wittenberg from 1538 and Montanus (Berg) and Neuber at Nuremberg from 1542), and the Netherlands (with Tylman Susato at Antwerp from 1543 and Pierre Phalèse at Louvain in 1545). Conversely, reputable composers became more interested in popular music, the tunes of which they preserved in keyboard or lute arrangements and as themes for instrumental variation or even for Masses.

Intimate music-making by amateurs must have been practised much earlier, but never on the scale made possible by the invention of printing. And publication also tells us what the amateur was considered likely to want. The frottola and madrigal were evidently good commercial lines – though there were also madrigals for ceremonial occasions. French publishers found a lively market for the polyphonic chanson and its instrumental arrangements; composers based Masses on it, even in its most scabrous forms; and even before the foundation in 1570 of the Académie de Poésie et de Musique on the initiative of Jean-Antoine de Baïf, French composers had developed an extreme form of Humanist song in *musique mesurée à l'antique*. This was music in which note-values were determined entirely by the prosodic quantities of the text, so that note-against-note setting was inevitable. But everywhere else – equally in the madrigal, chanson, and German polyphonic *Lied*, in the music of the Roman Church, Lutheran hymn, and Calvinist psalm – note-against-note writing, in chords rather than contrapuntal lines, met most fully the demand for verbal clarity. A different cause, the hand on the keyboard, produced a similar effect.

English music during the sixteenth century was prolific in every field and on the whole as remarkable in quality as in quantity. But it was insular and its diffusion was sadly retarded by the lack of English music-printers. The tradition of church music was confused by the peculiar nature of Henry VIII's semi-Reformation. The English part-song continued to flourish but few examples were printed before 1588. The real impact of the madrigal also dates from the same year, when Thomas East published *Musica Transalpina*, a collection of Italian madrigals with English translations together with one English madrigal by Byrd. It heralded a flood of Italian imitation such as might be expected of a period when English culture was particularly fascinated by everything Italian. Not only madrigals but *canzonette* and *balletti*, under anglicized names, were modelled – sometimes all too closely – on Italian originals and printing at last gave them to the public. English keyboard music had a tradition at least as old, was produced at least as copiously, and was later to influence through Sweelinck the German organ school from Samuel Scheidt onward. Yet it was not until 1612 that the little selection entitled *Parthenia* got into print.

Italian keyboard music never lacked publishers after the Roman, Andrea Antico, issued a collection of organ arrangements of frottole in 1517. But it was not instrumental music *per se* that gave Italy its centuries of primacy, though it contributed to the main form in which that primacy was manifested; it was the continuing drive to make music express poetic texts. The madrigal composers of the late cinquecento had striven by the introduction of chromaticism, tone-painting, tone-symbolism, and other means sometimes as dramatic as the work of the great contemporary 'mannerist' painters – El Greco, Caravaggio – to convey violent emotion and pictorial suggestion. In music for court entertainments, masques and dramatic *intermedii*, a group of Florentine musicians influenced by a learned Humanist, Girolamo Mei, who had come to the correct conclusion that ancient Greek music had been monodic, mixed madrigals with a new kind of monody in 'another way of singing than the usual' (*un altro modo di cantare che l'ordinario*). It was what we know as recitative and it became the staple of *opera in musica*. Yet from the first the doctrinaire employment of recitative was tempered by occasional songs, dances, and instrumental pieces; and in the first real masterpiece of the new genre, Monteverdi's *Orfeo* of 1607, the element of vocal melody – even virtuosity – bulked much more considerably. In France the same ingredients of spectacle, song, dance, and instrumental music were likewise compounded under the influence of a humanist 'academy', Baïf's, but in different proportions so that the result was not opera but *ballet de cour*. It is true that the *ballet de cour* exercised great influence on French opera when it emerged very much later, but French opera remained French and by that time Italian opera was well on the way to becoming European.

Opera was peculiarly suited to the Italian genius: its sense of drama, its intense musicality, its language rich in broad open vowels and liquid consonants. It is not surprising that as opera spread over Europe it tended to preserve its original language, resisting the various vernaculars. Indeed if one were obliged to single out Italy's basic contribution to the expressive vocabulary of Western music it would have to be the warm sensuous cantilena generated by her speech. Opera soon ceased to be a severely intellectual form of art and with the opening of the first public opera-house in Venice in 1637 it ceased to be an exclusively aristocratic one, though it seldom flourished without princely or aristocratic support. (The opera founded at Hamburg in the late seventeenth century was exceptional, a social portent.) Long before the century was out recitative was becoming more and more perfunctory, the interpolated arias more numerous, and the heyday of aria opera was reached with Alessandro Scarlatti and the numerous composers born or trained at Naples. It was now so cosmopolitan that Italian opera was composed by Handel, Hasse, Gluck (until he defected to French opera, of which the first great master, Lully, had been a native of Italy), Haydn and, greatest of all, Mozart.

Until vernacular opera made progress during the second half of the eighteenth century, 'opera' was almost synonymous with Italian opera from one end of Europe to the other. In Spain, which shared a monarch with Naples from 1735 onward, opera was almost entirely in the hands of Neapolitans and Parmesans who only occasionally set Spanish texts. Under the Vasa and Saxon kings opera in Poland was purely Italian. Araja took Italian opera to Russia in 1736 and Italians almost completely monopolized the imperial opera for nearly half a century while promising Russian musicians, such as Bortnyansky and Berezovsky, were sent to Italy to be trained – and had their operas produced there. In England Handel's most serious rival was a native Italian, G. B. Bononcini, and of the next generation the most successful London composer of *opere serie* in a city obsessed with *pasticci* and ballad-operas was the totally Italianized Johann Christian Bach. In France, the one country that had developed a strong tradition of vernacular opera with its own different aesthetic, it needed only a visit of an Italian company playing a repertoire of *opere buffe* to spark off one of the most celebrated of musical civil wars, the *querelle des bouffons*, a war which was renewed a quarter of a century later when the pro-Italian faction set up Piccinni in rivalry with the now gallicized Gluck.

It was not only in opera that Italy bestrode Europe like a Colossus. In the 1590s the Polish king, Sigismund III, invited Marenzio to Warsaw and for at least half a century the directors of the royal chapel were Italians. The greatest German composer of the seventeenth century, Heinrich Schütz, studied in Venice with Giovanni Gabrieli, composed Italian madrigals there, and returned twenty years later to sit at the feet of Monteverdi. Italy originated the oratorio and chamber cantata, the sonata, the concerto, and the *sinfonia*. It gave us the violin – an instrument which (it has been said) 'with its vibrato manner of performance, in distinction from the older viol family, emulates and even surpasses the human voice' – indeed the whole violin family with viola and cello. The finest makers were the Amati and Guarneri and Stradivari families and the finest idiosyncratic composers Corelli, Vivaldi, Tartini, Viotti. Purcell declared that in his first set of trio sonatas he had 'faithfully endeavour'd a just imitation of the most fam'd Italian Masters', and a few years later a French writer, Le Cerf de La Viéville, complained bitterly of 'cette fureur de composer des sonates à la manière italienne'. François Couperin, captivated by Corelli's sonatas, produced his own earliest ones under an Italian-sounding anagram of his own name and in later years paid homage to Corelli in a splendid *Apothéose*. Bach himself did not disdain to transcribe Vivaldi concertos for organ or harpsichord and to borrow fugue-subjects from Legrenzi and Corelli.

The ultimate weakening of this unique ascendancy was due not to lack of outstanding operatic composers to continue the tradition, though vernacular opera – sometimes consciously national and therefore to some extent anti-Italian – produced more and more gifted rivals. Nor was it mainly caused by the increasing importance of symphony and sonata, a field in which such fine musicians as Boccherini and Clementi could hardly rival their Germanic contemporaries. The yeast of romanticism was fermenting – and the Italian genius was not particularly sympathetic to romanticism. Operatic composers might take subjects from romantic literature. But intimate, self-centred poetry on the one hand and heaven-storming energy on the other conquered music north of the Alps and Italian music gradually ceased to be pan-European.

I I

Music during the Reformation

VERBAL INTELLIGIBILITY IN CHURCH MUSIC

The third decade of the sixteenth century was a real turning-point in musical history – and not only because the Reformation quickly called into existence a body of religious music which preferred the vernacular to Latin and served other liturgical needs than those of the Roman church. Latin was by no means totally banished from the Lutheran liturgy. Various linguistic alternatives were permitted but the Greek Kyrie and Latin Gloria were generally retained. Yet the preference for the vernacular was itself symptomatic. The Humanist stress on the importance of the word was not only redoubled but given a special orientation by the Reformation – which experienced its supreme crisis, the Diet of Worms, in 1521, four months before Josquin's death. It was desirable that the words of the liturgy should be understood by the congregation and that the congregation should take part in the singing. Indeed, a younger and more radical Reformer than Luther, Thomas Münzer (1491–1525), the real pioneer of 'German song' for the congregation, wished them to participate much more fully in a vernacular liturgy. This need for verbal intelligibility was recognized not only by the Reformers in the Lutheran hymns and Calvinist psalm-settings but by the semi-Reformers (Cranmer's view that the musical setting of his translation of the liturgy in 1544 should 'not be full of notes, but, as near as may be, for every syllable a note, so that it may be sung distinctly and devoutly') and the Counter-Reformers (the direction of the Council of Trent in 1562 that the words of the Mass 'should be uttered clearly and perfectly, and sink quietly into the ears and hearts of the hearers', not with music 'contrived for the empty delight of the ears').

CHURCH MUSIC OF JOSQUIN'S FOLLOWERS

Yet throughout these eventful years the tradition of Catholic imitative polyphony flowed on undisturbed, reaching even greater technical equability in the work of Josquin's presumed pupil Nicolas Gombert (c. 1500–c. 1556)[1] and Jacobus Clemens 'non Papa' (c. 1510–c. 1557),[2] with whom we may associate other natives of French Flanders: Thomas Crecquillon (d.c. 1557); Jean Richafort (c. 1480–c. 1547), an older pupil of Josquin's; two composers whose identities were confused even in their

---

[1] *Opera Omnia*, ed. J. Schmidt-Görg, *CMM* 6.   [2] *Opera Omnia*, ed. K. P. Bernet Kempers, *CMM* 4.

lifetime, Lupus Hellinck (*c.* 1495–1541) and Johannes Lupus or Lupi (Jean Leleu) (*c.* 1506–1539), the confusion being worse confounded by two less distinguished contemporaries named Johannes Lupus; Noel Bauldewyn (d. 1530), who was Richafort's successor at Malines Cathedral and composer of the *Missa Da Pacem* long attributed to Josquin;[3] and Pierre de Manchicourt (*c.* 1510–1564) who towards the end of his life became master of Philip II's *capilla flamenca*, in which both Gombert and Crecquillon had served under Philip's father, the Emperor Charles V.

Although traditionalists, the best of these were not mere epigones. They tightened the polyphonic weave, intensifying the element of imitation – plastic rather than strict – in which all voices, usually five, participate on equal terms, and concealing the cadential seams. (The Josquinian antiphony of paired parts was abandoned.) Gombert's linear sense – and sometimes Crecquillon's and Lupi's – was so strong that he cared nothing for the asperities of harsh suspensions or accented passing-notes, as in this passage from his motet, 'Ave sanctissima Maria':[4]

Ex. 53

[A] -ve san - ctis - si - ma

Clemens cultivated euphony. He will end with a third in the final chord, even when he omits the fifth, and both he and Crecquillon anticipate Palestrina in the climactic use of great descending scales – often in thirds, sixths, or tenths – as at the end of his 'Jerusalem surge':[5]

Ex. 54

[3] See Edgar H. Sparks, *The Music of Noel Bauldewin* (Philadelphia, 1973). 'Da Pacem' is published in Josquin, *Werken:* Missen, iv, p. 24, and *ChW*, xx.   [4] *CMM* 6, v, p. 77.   [5] *CMM* 4, xiii, p. 62.

or the end of Crecquillon's 'Ingemuit Susanna'.[6] Initial motives are often conditioned by the text, and the melodic lines, particularly with Gombert and Crecquillon, are generally more syllabic than melismatic; even the old practice of employing homorhythmic, 'chordal', music for special verbal emphasis is occasionally remembered. But emotional expressiveness like that of Clemens's famous 'Vox in Rama',[7] with its unforgettable opening motive, is rare. Rhythmic patterns tend to be sober and square-cut, and that liking for the C mode – as such, e.g. in Clemens's *Missa Misericorde*,[8] or transposed to F with a B flat key-signature – which we have already noticed in Josquin,[9] becomes very pronounced. The legitimatization of the C and A modes, 'Ionian' and 'Aeolian', by the Swiss theorist Heinrich Loris ('Glareanus') in his *Dodecachordon* (Basel, 1547) was a very belated admission of their existence. All the same, the *Missa Misericorde* is not 'in C major'; every section ends with a triad on C but the final cadences of Kyrie, Gloria, Credo, and Agnus are plagal. On the other hand, the chanson on which it is based[10] is really in C major with a number of V-I and I-V cadences (see Ex. 57).

Practically all the work of these composers lay in the fields of Mass, motet, and chanson. Gombert, Clemens, and Richafort wrote Magnificats. Clemens made a nearly complete three-part setting of the popular tunes of the Dutch metrical psalter, the *Souterliedekens* (Antwerp, 1556–7).[11] Crecquillon composed Lamentations and a few French psalms. But their favourite form was the motet, which offered a wide field for expressive symbolism and the suggestion of generalized emotions. Gombert composed 160, Clemens 230, Crecquillon 116, Richafort merely 35 (but his output in all fields was small). As for Hellinck and Lupi, their work is a chaos of dubious attributions but motets bulk largely in it. The variety underlying the superficial similarity of idiom is enormous, even within the work of a

---

[6] Quoted in *NOHM*, iv, p. 226.
[7] *CMM* 4, ix, p. 105, and *HAM*, i, No. 125. See Edward Lowinsky, *Secret Chromatic Art in the Netherlands Motet* (New York, 1946), particularly pp. 12 and 35, Ex. 15 and 34, for the way in which the unusually liberal, but defensible, application of *musica ficta* can heighten the pathos of this motet.
[8] *CMM* 4, i, p. 1.   [9] See p. 176.   [10] *CMM* 4, x, p. 140.   [11] *Opera Omnia*, ii.

single composer. Bernet Kempers has shown, for instance, that one can distinguish between Clemens's motets for solo voices and those which are genuinely choral.[12] They may be, indeed they usually are, based on freshly invented material or the composer may take a plainsong melody not as a cantus firmus but for plastic treatment through all the parts, as Gombert does in his 'Salve regina'.[13] The texture may be close and the effect massive, as in his six-part 'Quem dicunt homines',[14] or as light-handed as Clemens's 'Nobilis illa'.[15] Very many are cast in the AB:CB form employed by Mouton and the others of the previous generation (see p. 179). But here, the B section may be no more than a brief refrain like the 'Alleluias' which end both parts of Richafort's 'Quem dicunt homines'[16] or an extended section of more than forty bars as with the 'fera pessima devoravit filium meum Joseph' of Clemens's 'Tulerunt autem'[17] which is spliced with the ends of the preceding sections in a way that epitomizes the composer's technical skill:

Ex. 55

(i)

[12] K. P. Bernet Kempers, *Jacobus Clemens non Papa und seine Motetten* (Augsburg, 1928).
[13] *CMM* 6, vi, p. 48.
[14] Ibid., ix, p. 166, and ed. Lewis Lockwood, *Das Chorwerk*, 94, p. 18.
[15] *CMM* 4, xii, p. 49.
[16] *ChW*, 94, p. 1.
[17] *CMM* 4, iv, p. 36, and ed. Bernhard Meier, *ChW*, 72, p. 10.

NEW PARAPHRASE TECHNIQUES IN THE MASSES

The motets of these composers show their liturgical style in its purest form. In their Masses it is complicated – in some cases one is tempted to say 'contaminated' – by another factor: the *res facta*, the model, which was often secular. The *missa parodia* was, of course, nothing new but these composers devoted themselves to it almost exclusively and developed new techniques. Of Gombert's ten Masses, all but two – 'Da pacem' and the big *Missa Tempore paschali*[18] for six (in the Agnus twelve) voices – are *parodiae*. So are all Clemens's except his Requiem, and so are all but one of Crecquillon's sixteen, the exception in his case being a cantus firmus Mass on a German secular song. Their models are their own or each others' motets and chansons and the chansons of such Parisian colleagues as Claudin de Sermisy, and they make fuller use of the whole polyphonic complex of the model than their predecessors had done: how flexibly may be seen by comparing the opening of the Kyrie of Clemens's already mentioned Mass 'Misericorde':

---

[18] *CMM* 6, i, p. i, and iii, p. 53.

Ex. 56

with that of his chanson 'Misericorde au martir amoureulx':

Ex. 57

Bars 3–5 of the Kyrie are not the extraneous interpolation they seem to be; they come from bars 18–20 of the chanson:

Ex. 58

The repeated application of this technique of varied adaptation to each movement has led to the not unjust description of Clemens's Masses in particular as sets of variations. The Agnus is naturally the culminating variation; in 'Misericorde' the four parts are expanded for it to six.

Even when the highest part of a secular model was more obviously tuneful than that of 'Misericorde au martir amoureulx' – as we shall see, such songs were very fashionable in Paris at this time – and the composer took few pains to disguise it (e.g. Gombert's Mass 'Je suys déshéritée'[19] on a chanson attributed in the earliest source, Attaingnant's *Trente chansons musicales* (Paris, 1533) to Lupi, in later ones to Pierre Cadéac), the

[19] *CMM* 6, i, p. 81; Lupus's chanson, ed. Hans Albrecht, in *ChW*, 15, p. 6.

incongruence evidently did not disconcert contemporaries. Clemens was not content to borrow Pierre Sandrin's very popular 'Doulce memoire' (first published in the first book of Moderne's *Le Parangon des chansons* (Lyons, 1538)) for the 'Sicut erat' of his first *Magnificat Primi Toni*;[20] he based every section of his *Magnificat Octavi Toni*[21] on a chanson, actually drawing attention to their titles in his superius part:

Et exultavit	C'est une dure despartie
Quia fecit	Pour ung plaisir
Fecit potentiam	C'est a grant tort
Esurientes	Tous mes amis
Sicut locutus est	Tou partement
Sicut erat	Tant quen amours

The first five notes of Clemens's bass are indeed those of the plainsong eighth-tone Magnificat, but his superius is identical with that of Sermisy's 'C'est une dure despartie'[22] except that it does not follow Sermisy's repeat of the first two phrases and does repeat his last phrase. It is noteworthy that 'Fecit potentiam' follows Sermisy's version[23] of 'C'est a grant tort', not Clemens's own six-part setting.[24]

THE FRENCH CHANSON

Clemens, Gombert, Crecquillon, and their colleagues all cultivated the chanson with great success. The first two are represented in Attaingnant's collections – Clemens, it is true, by an anonymous and doubtfully authentic piece – as early as 1529 and by a trickle of songs during the next decade. But it was only when Susato began to publish at Antwerp in 1543 that their songs appeared in quantity and it was Susato who really launched Crecquillon with a book of 36 *chansons à 4 parties* in 1543, though he had published Crecquillon's greatest hit, 'Ung gay bergier', in a miscellaneous collection the year before. 'Ung gay bergier', a bawdy little anecdote for which the music is the simple, effective vehicle, with its opening note-repetition in ♩ ♩ ♩ rhythm, its mixture of imitative with note-against-note passages, and its loose form (AaBCc), is characteristic of the French chanson of the second quarter of the century. But the chanson was by no means always obscene. Clemens was a master of the frankly bawdy song and the song *à double entente* – witness his musically delicious 'Jaquin jaquet', his enormously popular 'Frisque et gaillard', and his 'Entre vous filles de XV ans' ('Tetin poignant, bouche riant, connin mouflant') which provided the model for the most scandalous of Lassus's Masses – but his 'Je prens en gre'

[20] *CMM* 4, iv, p. 8.   [21] Ibid., p. 110.
[22] From Attaingnant's *Trente et une chanson* (sic) (Paris, 1529); modern editions include one in *CMM* 20, ed. Albert Seay, p. 81, with the keyboard transcription published by Attaingnant the next year. There exist later settings of the melody by Lupi (*ChW*, 15, p. 22), and, for dancing, in Susato's *Het derde musyck boexken* (Antwerp, 1551), published by F. J. Giesbert (Mainz, 1936), a version which can be scanned in duple time or triple, as a *Nachtanz*.
[23] In *Trente et quatre chansons* (1528); *CMM* 20, p. 114. See Ex. 60(i).
[24] *Le 13e livre de chansons* (Antwerp, 1550); *Opera Omnia*, x, p. 135. See Ex. 60(ii).

(if it is his: one source attributes it to 'Jennequin') is a gravely beautiful love-song.[25] And despite the obvious connections between the Netherlanders and the Parisian composers, Clément Janequin (*c.* 1475–*c.* 1559), Claudin de Sermisy (*c.* 1495–1562), and their younger colleagues, there were notable stylistic differences.

Pl. 38   Three ladies painted by the so-called 'Master of the female half-lengths', a Franco-Fleming of the early 16th century, about to play Sermisy's 'Jouyssance vous donneray'. The flute-player seemingly doubles the voice while the lutenist plays the lower parts.

The four-part chansons which poured from Attaingnant's press from 1528 to 1550 – Clément Marot (1496–1544) his favourite poet, Sermisy his favourite composer (though he devoted one of his earliest volumes solely to Janequin) – still have so much in common with the frottola and kindred Italian popular forms, however much they sophisticated them, that their Italian ancestry hardly needs a birth-certificate. (Frottole were performed in France.)[26] They inherited the syllabic note-against-note style, dominated by the text and with a good many repeat notes, lightly relieved by melismas or imitation, and the clearly marked cadences. Even the ♩ ♩♩

[25] See *CMM* 4, x, pp. 5, 17, 75, and 14.
[26] See Daniel Heartz, 'Les Gouts Réunis', in *Chanson and Madrigal 1480–1530* (ed. James Haar) (Cambridge, Mass., 1964).

opening had already appeared in the Italian settings of Genet/Carpentras
(see p. 179),[27] a Frenchman who worked in Italy. Like the frottole they
were music for a wide public and, as with the frottole, the printing-presses
multiplied their popularity by producing them in alternative forms. In any
case, with their predominant highest parts, the lower parts could be played
instead of sung – as we see from contemporary pictures. Attaingnant lost no
time in following the examples of Petrucci and Antico by bringing out in
1529 a *Tres breue et familiere introduction pour entendre et apprendre . . . a
iouer toutes chansons reduictes en la tablature du Lutz*, containing among
other things seven of Claudin's songs from the *Chansons nouvelles . . . a
quatre parties* of the previous year, now arranged both for lute solo and for
voice with lute accompaniment.[28] And he published in 1531 three volumes
respectively of *Dixneuf, Vingt et cinq*, and *Vingt et six chansons musicales
reduictes en la tabulature des Orgues Espinettes Manichordions, et telz
semblables instrumentz.*[29]

Ex. 59

(i) CHANSONS NOUVELLES (1528)

(ii) TRES BREVE .... INTRODUCTION (1529)

(iii) VINGT ET SIX CHANSONS MUSICALES (1531)

[27] See the examples in Antico's Third Book of *Canzoni Sonetti Strambotti et Frottole* (Rome, 1517),
modern edition (ed. Alfred Einstein) in *Smith College Music Archives*, iv, Nos. 7 and 9.
[28] Modern edition, *Chansons au luth*, ed. L. de La Laurencie, A. Mairy, and G. Thibault (*Publications de
la Société française de musicologie*, Series I, iv–v, Paris, 1934).
[29] Modern edition of the three volumes, with the four-part originals, ed. Albert Seay, in *CMM* 20.

Janequin is popularly known by his imitative, or rather onomatopoeic, chansons – four of which, 'Le chant des oyseaux', 'La guerre' (celebrating Francis I's victory at Marignano in 1515), 'La chasse', and 'L'alouette', appeared in Attaingnant's *Chansons de maistre C. Janequin* of 1528.[30] But in fact his range was very much wider, from the Rabelaisian but musically brilliant 'Au joly jeu du pousse avant' (he was an almost exact contemporary of Rabelais) to the innocent sweetness of 'Au premier jour du joly moys de may' and the exquisite 'Petite Nymphe folastre', from the pure homophony of 'Ce moys de may' to the florid counterpoint of 'Si d'ung petit de vostre bien'.[31] He even published in 1540 an Italian madrigal. And beside Janequin and Sermisy Attaingnant brought out the songs of such younger men as the immensely prolific Pierre Certon and Sandrin, whose 'Doulce memoire' was transcribed for lute or keyboard all over Europe from Spain to Poland. Like Sandrin, Pierre Cadéac was a late arrival on the scene (1538) and he was published at Lyons, a more cosmopolitan musical centre than Paris, by Jacques Moderne who had as his musical adviser the composer François Layolle (*c.* 1475–*c.* 1540), friend of Benvenuto Cellini and Andrea del Sarto.

THE CHANSON AFTER ATTAINGNANT

The heyday of the Parisian chanson was over by 1550 when Attaingnant was succeeded by other publishers (Du Chemin, Le Roy, Ballard); the most important song-publishers were now Susato at Antwerp and Pierre Phalèse at Louvain. And it was presumably owing to their encouragement that in the 1540s Crecquillon began to compose chansons and Clemens and Gombert increased their production from a trickle to a flood. It was now that a more marked difference from the Parisians showed itself in their work, most obviously when they laid hands on Sermisy or Janequin for their own purposes. When Clemens and Crecquillon borrow respectively the superius of Sermisy's 'C'est a grant tort' and 'Dont vient cela', their own six- and five-part compositions make considerably more use of imitation and the cadence points are woven over. So with Gombert's and Crecquillon's compositions on the musically insignificant tenor of 'C'est a grant tort'. Most curious of all is Gombert's delightful re-composition of Janequin's famous 'Chant des oyseaux' in three parts yet with more closely knit polyphony and concealment of caesurae which Janequin had not attempted to disguise. Comparison of the Sermisy and Clemens settings of 'C'est a grant tort' vividly illustrates the difference between Parisian and Netherland chanson:

---

[30] Complete edition of Janequin's chansons, ed. A. Tillman Merritt and François Lesure (Monaco, 1965–71) i, pp. 5, 23, 54, and 106; numerous separate editions.
[31] Ibid., pp. i, p. 137; iv, p. 1; v, p. 196; i, p. 129; ii, p. 43.

Ex. 60

(i) SERMISY (Paris, 1528)

(ii) CLEMENS NON PAPA (Antwerp, 1550)

It remained for Susato to turn Ex. 60(i) into instrumental dance-music in *Het derde musyck boexken* in 1551, in ambiguous notation that can be read in either duple or triple time:[32]

Ex. 61

In this he followed Attaingnant, who had from his earliest days been printing *gaillardes et pavanes* for four instruments (1529), *basses danses garnies de recoupes* for the lute (1529), *basses dances, branles, pavennes* and *gaillardes*, nearly all in four instrumental parts (1530), and *gaillardes, pavennes, branles et basses dances* for keyboard (1531), at least some of which were based on polyphonic chansons.[33] Again at the end of his career Attaingnant, and after him his widow, published similar *Livres de danceries*

---

[32] Cf. the triple transcription of Sermisy's 'Dont vient cela' in Friedrich Blume, *Studien zur Vorgeschichte der Orchestersuite* (Leipzig, 1925), Anh. B, ex. 12a, with the duple in *Tielman Susato: Danserye* (ed. F. J. Giesbert) (Mainz, 1936), p. 4. Sermisy's chansons underwent many changes in later hands; 'Il me suffit' served not only as model for a Mass by Lassus, its superius became a basse-danse, a Dutch psalm-tune, and the Lutheran hymn 'Was mein Gott will, das g'scheh' allzeit'.

[33] The two books of four-part dances have been ed. Giesbert (Mainz, 1950), the *Quatorze Gaillardes* of 1531 by Heartz, *CEKM*, 8.

(1550–5) compiled by Claude Gervaise[34] – which may have suggested Francesco Bendusi's *Opera Nova de Balli a quatro* (Venice, 1553).

PARISIAN CHURCH MUSIC

Although Janequin and Sermisy, Certon and Sandrin, served in the chapels of Francis I and Henry II, their church music is unremarkable. Sandrin left none; Certon left a great deal but it is mostly frivolous or feeble.[35] Only two Masses by Janequin have survived – an early one 'La Bataille', on the non-onomatopoeic sections of 'La guerre', and a later one on his chanson 'L'aveuglé dieu' – and a single motet.[36] Sermisy's contribution was larger and more substantial. No French composer in the generation after Fevin and Brumel could disguise the secular flavour of his church music and sometimes Sermisy shows the cloven hoof of the chanson writer, but generally his Masses and motets are more 'Netherlandish'. (In his Mass 'Tota pulchra es',[37] for instance, he sets the Benedictus as a canon for tenor and bass.) And he is noteworthy also as the composer of one of the only two known French Passion-settings of the sixteenth century: a Matthew Passion published by Attaingnant in 1534 in his tenth volume of motets, where it is followed by an anonymous John Passion.[38] These were not 'motet Passions' like Longueval's, mentioned on p. 177, but 'dramatic' Passions in which the various persons are represented by two or more soloists (e.g. in both works Pilate is impersonated by two, three, or four voices, with no consistency). In both the polyphony is freely based on the traditional Passion tones. Sermisy was the only contemporary composer represented (by his 'Si bona suscepimus') in the *Treze Motetz musicaulx avec ung Prelude* transcribed for organ of 1531,[39] the others being older men: Obrecht ('Parce Domine'), Compère ('O vos omnes'), Fevin, Brumel, and Louis XII's *maître de chapelle* in 1507, Johannes Prioris (the 'Dulcis amica' mentioned in n. 35 below).

VERNACULAR RELIGIOUS SONG: CALVINIST PSALTERS

At the middle of the century both Janequin and Certon became involved in another form of religious, though not liturgical, composition. The Refor-

---

[34] A selection from these was published by Henry Expert, *Les Maitres musiciens de la Renaissance française*, xxiii (Paris, 1908); three examples in *HAM*, i, No. 137.
[35] Expert published the Mass 'Regnum mundi' in his *Répertoire populaire de la musique de la Renaissance*. Peter Wagner prints a dull but then popular motet 'Dulcis amica' by Johannes Prioris and the first Kyrie of the Mass Certon based on it in *Geschichte der Messe* (Leipzig, 1913), pp. 246–8.
[36] The *Missa super La Bataille* was republished by Expert (Paris, 1947); Wagner gives the first Kyrie and Benedictus of 'L'aveuglé dieu', op. cit., 242–4. The motet 'Congregati sunt' was published by François Lesure (Monaco, 1950).
[37] Ed. J. A. Bank (Amsterdam, 1950).
[38] There is a modern edition of Attaingnant's *Treze livres de motets*, ed. A. Smijers and A. Tillman Merritt (Monaco, 1934–62). These also contain Sermisy's *Lamentationes*, Magnificat, and nineteen motets, as well as compositions by another musician of the Sainte-Chapelle, Pierre Vermont, by Hesdin of Beauvais, Manchicourt, Guillaume Le Heurteur of Tours, and others.
[39] Modern edition (Paris, 1930) by Yvonne Rokseth, who also edited the two books of organ versets for the Mass, Magnificat, and Te Deum published by Attaingnant at the same time (Paris, 1925).

mation had quickly called into being a great quantity of vernacular religious song: hymns, 'spiritual songs' for domestic devotion, metrical translations of the Psalms. Numerous collections were published, some with tunes only, some for (usually) four voices, with melodies either original or adapted from plainsong or popular song. The most important early Lutheran ones include the four-part *Geystliche gesangk Buchleyn* (Wittenberg, 1524)[40] of Johann Walter (1496–1570), supervised by Luther himself, Valentin Babst's monophonic *Geystliche Lieder* for congregational singing (Leipzig, 1545), and Martin Bucer's also monophonic *Gesangbuch* (Strasbourg, 1541).[41] Strasbourg was also the birthplace of the modest first Calvinist psalter in 1539.[42] It contained 19 psalms (with other *cantiques*), 13 translated by Marot, six by Calvin himself, some of the melodies by a Strasbourg musician, Mathias Greiter (*c.* 1490–1550). Marot continued his translations but had produced only fifty when he died in 1544, so that the work had to be finished by Théodore de Bèze. But it was Marot's fifty which were 'mise en musique . . . à quatre parties à voix de contrepoinct égal consonante au verbe' by Loys Bourgeois and published at Lyons in 1547.[43] In this collection, not to be confused with *Le premier livre des Pseaulmes* of the same year in which he treats 24 of them more elaborately, Bourgeois nearly always puts the (usually borrowed) tune in the tenor with note-against-note counterpoint. It was 28 of these Marot translations which Janequin set (Paris, 1549), also in four parts and also with 'le chant ia usité' in the tenor, following these with 82 'by Marot and others' in 1559.[44] All 50 of Marot's were set by Certon (Paris, 1546) though only 13 of them have survived – in a transcription for voice and lute by Guillaume Morlaye published in 1555.[45] The Dutch *Souterliedekens* with tunes only were published at Antwerp in 1540 and in England during the same period Miles Coverdale brought out his *Goostly psalmes and spirituall songes*, also with tunes only (*c.* 1543), while Francis Seagar's selection of 19 *Certayne Psalmes* (London, 1553) are all accommodated to two four-part compositions. Owing to the Maryan interlude Thomas Sternhold's version, with a tune for each psalm, had to be first published at Geneva in 1556.

The most famous of the French psalm-composers, Claude Goudimel (*c.* 1514–1572), who also wrote chansons (notably settings of Ronsard), Horatian odes, Masses, and Latin motets, published in 1551 eight

---

[40] Reprinted at once and in several revised and enlarged editions, of which the most important is the sixth (1551); modern editions of the original by Otto Kade (*Publikationen der Gesellschaft für Musikforschung*, vii) (Leipzig, 1878) and of the 1551 version, ed. O. Schröder, in *Johann Walter: Sämtliche Werke* (Kassel, 1953–), i. Easily accessible examples of the 1524 edition in *HAM*, i, No. 111(a), and Schering, *Geschichte der Musik in Beispielen*, No. 80.

[41] Facsimile editions of Babst and Bucer by Konrad Ameln (Kassel, 1929, and Stuttgart, 1953, respectively).

[42] *Calvin's First Psalter*, ed. R. R. Terry (London, 1932).

[43] A selection of 37 has been ed. K. P. Bernet Kempers (Delft, 1937); one example in *HAM*, i, No. 132. On the Calvinist psalm-settings generally, see Pierre Pidoux, *Le Psautier Huguenot du XVIe siècle* (Kassel and Basel, 1962).

[44] See Maurice Cauchie, 'Les Psaumes de Janequin' in *Mélanges de musicologie offerts à M. Lionel de La Laurencie* (Paris, 1933).

[45] Modern edition by François Lesure and Richard de Morcourt (Paris, 1957).

compositions of Marot's psalms 'mis en musique au long (en forme des mottetz)' based on the Bourgeois melodies, for three, four, or five voices, and during the next fifteen years produced seven more books of 'motet' psalms.[46] About 1560 he became a Protestant, as Janequin and Certon never did, and made a four-part setting of the complete Marot-de Bèze Psalter in lightly ornamented note-against-note counterpoint with the melodies generally in the highest part (Paris, 1564). This was reissued in slightly different form at Geneva in 1580 after his death at Lyons in the Massacre of St. Bartholomew, but before this Goudimel had made another and even simpler complete setting, leaning heavily on Bourgeois's of 1547, with the tunes usually in the tenor (Geneva, 1565):

Ex. 62

(i) PSALM I (Tiers livre, 1557)

(ii) (1580)

(iii) (1565)

Qui au con - seil des ma - lins n'a e - sté, Qui n'est

These settings must have been intended for private use since Calvin objected to polyphony in church, but when the Lutherans adopted them, using Ambrosius Lobwasser's translation of Marot-de Bèze (Leipzig, 1573), their congregations undoubtedly sang the tunes.

LUTHERAN HYMNS

Despite the widespread diffusion, adaptation, and imitation of the Calvinist psalm-tunes throughout northern Europe, their ultimate contribution to Western music generally was less than that of the Lutheran hymns to which they were so closely related. Or they made their contribution *through* Lutheran forms, as happened in the famous case of Greiter's melody for Ps. 119, 'Es sind doch alle'. This was used by Bourgeois and Certon for Ps. 36 and Goudimel for Ps. 68, 'Que Dieu se montre seulement', but has come down through the centuries as a hymn to Sebaldus Heyden's words 'O Mensch bewein dein Sünde gross'. The psalm-settings certainly pointed the way for Lutheran unison congregational singing with organ or other instruments playing the accompanying parts. But political conditions favoured Lutheranism more than Calvinism and gave free scope to Lutheran composers to develop their church-music on the basis of hymnody, with such a publisher as Georg Rhaw, a former cantor of the Thomasschule at Leipzig, to encourage them. Rhaw's collection of *Newe deudsche geistliche Gesenge* (1544)[47] was not the earliest collection of polyphonic Lutheran hymn-compositions – Walter's *Gesangbüchlein* (see p. 220) reached its fifth edition in the same year and the *Concentus novi trium vocum*[48] of Hans Kugelmann (d. 1542) had appeared at Augsburg in 1540 – but it was by far the most important. Like Kugelmann's *Concentus*, it was

[46] The eight books of psalm motets are published in the first eight volumes of *Claude Goudimel: Oeuvres complètes*, ed. Henri Gagnebin *et al.* (Kassel and Basel, 1967–74); Ex. 62(i) is from the *Tiers livre* of 1557. The Masses, of which the most beautiful is the 'Audi filia', are in *Oeuvres complètes*, xii, the Magnificats and Latin motets, which include a superb twelve-part 'Salve Regina', ibid., xi, and the religious and secular *chansons*, ibid., xiii. There are numerous separate reprints in earlier editions.
[47] Modern edition ed. Johannes Wolf, *DDT*, xxxiv (Leipzig, 1908). Examples in *HAM*, i, Nos. 108, 110, and 111(b), and Schering, op. cit., Nos. 84, 108, and 110.
[48] Modern edition ed. Hans Engel, *Das Erbe deutscher Musik, Sonder-Reihe*, ii (Kassel, 1955). Kugelmann's five-part setting of his own melody to 'Nun lob' mein Seel den Herren' (cf. Bach's Cantata 28, No. 2) also in Schering, op. cit., No. 109.

intended 'für die gemeinen Schulen', for young and untrained singers. But Rhaw drew on all the leading German composers of the post-Isaac generation – Ludwig Senfl (*c.* 1486–*c.* 1543), Balthasar Resinarius (Harzer) (*c.* 1485–1544), Arnold von Bruck (*c.* 1490–1554), Sixt Dietrich (*c.* 1493–1548), Benedictus Ducis (d. 1544) (who is possibly the same man as Benedictus de Opitiis), Stephan Mahu (*c.* 1485–*c.* 1541) – as well as the long dead Stoltzer and one Fleming, Lupus Hellinck. And although the basic conception of song-treatment is generally the same as in Walter's collection (four or five parts, melody usually in the tenor) there is much more imitative polyphony and higher technical accomplishment. This is particularly true of the contributions by Senfl, by far the greatest of the group, such as his setting of 'Gelobet seist du'.[49] By no means all the composers were Protestants; Senfl, Arnold von Bruck, Mahu, and Hellinck were not, although they may have had secret leanings to Protestantism; but Rhaw also published Latin church music, while Catholics all over Europe enjoyed vernacular Calvinist psalms. Intolerance set in only with the Counter-Reformation. The stylistic difference was not so much between Lutheran and Catholic as between settings of German words and settings of Latin ones, even by the same composer: e.g. Senfl's 'Ewiger Gott', conditioned by the hymn-text, and his 'purely' musical, exquisite 'Ave rosa sine spinis'[50] based, like Josquin's 'Stabat mater', on the chanson tenor 'Comme femme'. The difference is still more striking when it occurs in the same work, e.g. Arnold von Bruck's 'O du armer Judas' (published by Hans Ott of Nuremberg in his collection of *121 newe Lieder*, 1534)[51] which ends with a Kyrie:

Ex. 63

(i)

---

[49] Rhaw's attribution of 'Da Jakob nun das Kleid ansah' to Senfl is incorrect.
[50] Easily available respectively in Schering, op. cit., No. 84, and *ChW*, lxii, p. 15.
[51] Ott's second collection, *115 guter newer Liedlein* (1544), has been ed. Eitner, *Publikationen der Gesellschaft für Musikforschung*, i–iii.

GERMAN SECULAR SONG

German secular songs of this period, like the religious ones, are preponderantly on tenor cantus firmi, the tenors usually being 'courtly songs'

(*Hofweisen*). But more popular tunes and words figure largely in the collections compiled, and partly composed, by the Nuremberg doctor Georg Forster (*c.* 1510–1568) and originally published during 1539–56.[52] Forster also includes student drinking-songs with the melody in the highest part and purely chordal support. His title-pages specify that his songs may not only be sung but also played 'on all sorts of instruments' (*auff allerley Instrumenten zu brauchen*); indeed the non-tenor parts are often obviously instrumental, as in Senfl's 'Wol kumpt der May'[53] in Ott's *121*. But broadly speaking the tendency around the middle of the century was toward a more motet-like treatment of the parts. In this field, as in those of religious song and Latin church music, Senfl was outstanding in variety of technique and subject: to take three examples from Ott's collections, the loose polyphony of 'Oho, so geb' der Mann ein Pfenning', the more tightly woven 'Es jagt ein Jäger', and the purely onomatopoeic bell-sounds of the six-part 'Das Gläut zu Speyr',[54] where polyphony and melody are both discarded. Some of his compositions are based on songs dating back to the mid-fifteenth century.[55] The youngest composers of this group were Caspar Othmayr (1515–53) whose songs began to appear in Ott's and Forster's collections from 1544 onward and to whom the Nuremberg publishers Berg (Montanus) and Neuber devoted an entire volume, *Reutterische und Jegerische Liedlein*,[56] in 1549, and Jobst vom Brandt (1517–70).[57] With these 'Heidelberg masters', not unworthy disciples of Senfl, the secular *Tenorlied* became more and more nearly a miniature motet.

GERMAN AND POLISH KEYBOARD TABLATURES

One looks in vain for any reflection of this outpouring of German song in keyboard tablatures. The organists of the 'Imperial' group (see pp. 180 and 183–5), to whom we may add Buchner's pupil, the St. Gall organist Fridolin Sicher (1490–1546), were still active through much of this period. But their tablatures had been completed around 1530 and cover an older repertory, plus a few pieces by Senfl, and then there is an almost complete gap until Ammerbach published his *Orgel oder Instrument Tabulatur* in 1571. The two chief Polish tablatures, that of 'Ioannis de Lyublyn' (Jan z Lublina) (1540)[58] and that from the Monastery of the Holy Ghost at Cracow

---

[52] Complete edition ed. Kurt Gudewill and W. Heiske (Wolfenbüttel and Berlin, 1942), and many separate editions.
[53] *Senfl: Sämtliche Werke*, ed. Arnold Geering and W. Altwegg (Wolfenbüttel, 1938–61), iv, p. 58.
[54] *Sämtliche Werke*, v, pp. 38 and 32; iv, p. 109.
[55] H. J. Moser, 'Hans Ott's erstes Liederbuch', *Acta Musicologica*, vii (1935), gives on pp. 11 ff. a tabulated comparison of Senfl's 'Mein hertz in hohen frewden' with the melody as it appears in the *Lochamer Liederbuch*, the Buxheim tablature, Hartmann Schedel's song-book (see above p. 154), and other sources.
[56] Ed. F. Piersig (Wolfenbüttel and Berlin, 1928 and 1933).
[57] Songs from Forster's collections by Othmayr and Brandt in *ChW*, lxiii (ed. Gudewill), and *Das Musikwerk* (*Das deutsche Chorlied*) ed. Helmuth Osthoff.
[58] Complete facsimile, with thematic index, *Monumenta Musicae in Polonia*, series B, i (Warsaw, 1964); complete transcription by John R. White, *CEKM*, 6 (American Institute of Musicology, 1967).

(1548),[59] are scarcely more aware of German song. They preserve a great number of preludes and dances (many by 'N.C.', supposedly Nicolaus Cracoviensis, 'Mikołaj z Krakowa'), organ service-music, transcriptions of Josquin and his contemporaries, chansons by Janequin ('La Guerre' of course), Sermisy, Sandrin, a little Senfl (including 'Ave rosa'), but only three or four German songs by minor composers – though the monk of Cracow does include a transcription of Mahu's 'Ein' feste Burg' which had appeared in Rhaw's *Newe deudsche geistliche Gesenge* only four years before. However, the gap in the German organ tablatures is to some extent filled by those for lute from Hans Judenkünig's (Vienna, 1523) onward. Beside the very numerous 'preambles' and dances – courtly and popular German, Italian, French, gypsy – and transcriptions of Netherland motets and Parisian chansons, there are plenty of German songs, both secular and sacred,[60] Senfl again being the most popular composer.

NEW FORMS OF SECULAR POLYPHONY

Like the Parisian chanson, the *Tenorlied* was a purely national form, as conservative as the contemporary Netherland polyphony. Its secular form began to die after the middle of the century and the *geistlicher Gesang* with tenor cantus firmus was supplanted, perhaps under the influence of the Calvinist psalms, by the so-called *Kantionalsatz* – melody in the highest part, the others note-against-note – to encourage congregational singing. But in Italy at the same time both foreign and native composers were developing forms of secular polyphony which later in the century were to spread over most of Europe and bring about a remarkable expansion of music's technical resources in the regions of harmony and tonality and in emotional and pictorial expressiveness. The madrigal and its cognate forms not only embodied the musical spirit of the age in southern Europe but ultimately provided the basic vocabulary of a new, Humanist type of monody, of opera, and even of independent instrumental music.

If one wished to sum up the 'spirit of the age' in early sixteenth-century Italy in a single word, that word would have to be 'neo-Petrarchan'. Mainly under the influence of Pietro Bembo, the codifier of the Tuscan speech as the literary language of Italy in his *Prose della Volgar Lingua* (1525), there had been an extraordinary revival of interest in Petrarch and the patrons of the frottola-composers, such as the Mantuan Duchess Isabella d'Este, asked them for settings of Petrarch's sonnets and strophic canzoni. Tromboncino's composition of the sonnet 'Hor che'l ciel et la terra' has been

[59] *Monumenta Musicae in Polonia* series B, ii.
[60] See, for example the collection of Austrian lute-music of the sixteenth century in *DTÖ*, Jg. xviii(2) (vol. 37), ed. Adolf Koczirc (Vienna, 1911). There is an easily accessible selection of lute-pieces, giving a good cross-section, from Munich, Staatsbibl. 1512 (from *c.* 1550), ed. Heinz Bischoff and Heinz Zirnbauer (Mainz, 1938); it includes, for example, on p. 8 a transcription of Senfl's 'Ich armes Käuzlein' from Ott's *115 Liedlein* (Eitner, op. cit., ii, p. 158, and *Sämtliche Werke*, v, p. 65) which omits the altus but is otherwise very faithful, and on p. 5 a transcription of tenor and bass only, leaving the descant to be sung, as with Petrucci's *Tenori e contrabassi intabulati* (see p. 184).

mentioned in Chapter 10 (p. 174). The poetic canzone was a strophic form, like the musical frottola in which the same music was commonly fitted to each quatrain or tercet, carrying the words very distinctly but without reflecting their specific sense. The frottola ultimately disintegrated not only 'through the intrusion of polyphonic passages' (loc. cit.) but under literary pressure. The 'madrigal' which succeeded it – a fourteenth-century term revived in 1530 for something quite different from the Florentine madrigal – was a fairly free poem of anything from six to sixteen lines, roughly equivalent to one stanza of a canzone. When a frottola is through-composed under textual pressure, and aerated and enlivened by polyphonic passages, it is indistinguishable in musical style from the earlier madrigal, particularly as the madrigal tended at first to cling to the note-against-note style with a melodically more important highest part. The distinction, if any, was in the less frivolous nature and superior literary quality of the madrigal texts.

The term 'frottola' died out during the 1520s; its substance may be seen at its most sophisticated in Antico's *Canzoni Sonetti Strambotti et Frottole, Libro Tertio* (Rome, 1517),[61] which includes beside a number of examples by Tromboncino some nearly madrigalian pieces by Genet/Carpentras[62] and Michele Vicentino. Three years later Petrucci brought out a collection of *Musica di messer Bernardo pisano sopra le Canzone del petrarcha* (Fossombrone, 1520). It was his last publication, but at the same time the first in which he printed secular music in part-books with full text to each separate part, in place of the choirbook lay-out. This innovation was quickly adopted and greatly facilitated the singing of all four parts (whether or not instrumentally supported). Pisano (1490–1548),[63] a protégé of the Medici pope, Leo X, friend of Andrea del Sarto in Florence and Michelangelo in Rome, approached even nearer to the madrigal, as in his setting of Petrarch's canzone 22, 'Che debb'io far?', the end of which:

Ex. 64

---

[61] Ed. Alfred Einstein, *Smith College Music Archives*, iv (Northampton, Mass., 1941).
[62] See pp. 177 and 179.
[63] Collected works ed. Frank D'Accone in *CMM* 32, i.

shows several highly characteristic features: free, irregular imitation, the melodic line of the superius in bars 5–4 from the end, the repetition of the last line of the text. On the other hand, the same music had to serve for six more stanzas – Pisano wrote fresh music for the short final one – and therefore could not reflect details of the text.

THE EARLIER SIXTEENTH-CENTURY MADRIGAL

All the same, Pisano's work is more truly 'madrigalian' than some of the earliest published madrigals actually so called, the *Madrigali de diversi musici libr. po. de la serena* (Rome, 1530). Of the seventeen pieces in this collection, which survives complete only in the second edition of 1533, no fewer than eight – only seven in the 1533 version – are by Philippe Verdelot (d. *c.* 1540),[64] a Frenchman who lived in Italy from a very early age, two (three in the second edition) are by an Italian, Costanzo Festa (*c.* 1495–1545),[65] one is by another Festa, Sebastiano, of whom we know nothing, one by a mysterious 'Maistre Jan' or Ihan who has only recently been identified as 'a French-born musician active at the court of Ferrara from 1512 to about 1543',[66] and the remainder by still more shadowy characters. This publication was a landmark only in its title; the 'madrigals' are still predominantly note-against-note pieces, as are the majority of Verdelot's later ones. Willaert (see below, p. 230) had no difficulty in arranging 22 of Verdelot's four-part madrigals for voice and lute (*Intavolatura de li madrigali*

[64] *Opera Omnia*, ed. Anne-Marie Bragard, *CMM* 28.
[65] *Opera Omnia*, ed. Alexander Main, *CMM* 25. On Costanzo Festa see *JAMS* xxviii (1975), pp. 102 ff. and xxx (1977), pp. 106 ff.
[66] By George Nugent of Syracuse University, to whom I am indebted for this and other information concerning the composers with whom he has been confused.

de Verdelotto, Venice, 1536)[67] as had been done with frottole and Parisian chansons.

Chanson and madrigal were still closely related to each other as well as to the frottola. (Both Verdelot and Festa composed chansons and the 1533 edition of the *Madrigali* included Sermisy's 'Languir me fais' and an anonymous 'Tous mes amys' from Attaingnant's *Trente deux chansons* of 1529.) What distinguishes them is the relationship to the text. The madrigal is nearly always 'through composed' even when, exceptionally, the text is strophic; the music of the chanson carries the text and is moulded by its symmetry while that of the madrigal more closely reflects the details of an often much freer text. Melismas tend to be expressive or symbolic rather than purely ornamental. Indeed fluidity – of both form and texture – is perhaps the chief characteristic of a type of music so free and richly varied that it defies definition. When phrases of the text are repeated or thrown from voice to voice, they may or may not be set to the same or similar melodic phrase; imitation is free and texturally loose; metrical symmetry is at a discount. A passage from Verdelot's 'Ogn'hor per voi sospiro'[68] (in his *Secondo libro de Madrigali*, 1537)[69] will illustrate typical early madrigal texture with an exchange of phrases obvious only to the singer (madrigals were seldom written with listeners in mind) (cantus, bars 2–4, and tenor 4–6; altus bars 2–4, and cantus 4–6), contrasts of four- and two-part, writing, highlighting of 'tacendo' and 'amando' with their semitonal sighs:

Ex. 65

[67] One example in Einstein, *The Italian Madrigal* (Princeton, 1949), iii, No. 95.
[68] After Einstein, op. cit., iii, No. 17.
[69] This also contains the earliest known works of Jachet Berchem, a Netherland madrigalist whose church music has often been confused with that of Jachet of Mantua.

In the late 1530s another Northerner, the Fleming Jakob Arcadelt (*c.* 1504–after 1567),[70] began to publish madrigals at Venice, including one of the most popular of all, 'Il bianco e dolce cigno'.[70a] Later he left the Papal service and in the 1550s accompanied the Cardinal Charles de Lorraine to France where he naturally preferred the chanson. Arcadelt was more successful than Verdelot in catching Italian *dolcezza e soavità*, particularly in such pieces as 'O felici occhi miei',[71] although of course less so than the native Italians: for instance, Festa in 'Cosi suav'è'l foco et dolce il nodo',[72] and Domenico Ferrabosco, earliest of a whole dynasty of musicians, in his very popular setting of Boccaccio's 'Io mi son giovinetta'.[73] Even this belongs to a type that one might call the 'declamatory madrigal' (cf. Verdelot's 'Divini occhi'[74] and Arcadelt's 'Ancidetemi'[75]). However all these composers are overshadowed in historical importance by a Flemish master of all-round achievement, Adrian Willaert (*c.* 1490–1562), pupil of Mouton in Paris, who served the court of Ferrara for several years from 1522 but went to Venice as *magister cappellae* at St. Mark's in 1527 and spent the rest of his life there.

As early as 1520 some Willaert motets and *chanzoni franciose a quatro sopra doi* (that is, double canonic chansons) had been published in Venice.[76] His madrigals began to be printed in 1536 when he was already a complete master of the Verdelot type of madrigal, as is demonstrated in 'Amor mi fa morire'. There the transition near the end to the recapitulated music (and words) of the opening is effected as subtly as any Wagnerian transition. He went on to exploit the complete range of types and styles from what is practically a secular 'Netherland' motet in two *partes*, corresponding here to the *ottava* and *sestina* of the sonnet text, to the completely Italianate lighter

[70] *Opera Omnia*, ed. Albert Seay in *CMM* 31; the madrigals are in ii–vii, the chansons in viii–ix.
[70a] Ibid, ii, f. 38.
[71] Ibid, ii, p. 82, and in *ChW*, v (ed. Walter Wiora), p. 19.
[72] Einstein, op. cit., iii, No. 21.
[73] Ibid., No. 30.
[74] *Die Kunst der Niederlander (Das Musikwerk)*, ed. R. B. Lenaerts (Cologne, 1962), p. 91.
[75] *CMM* 31, ii, p. 9.
[76] See Erich Hertzmann, *Adrian Willaert in der weltlichen Vokalmusik seiner Zeit* (Leipzig, 1931), pp. 10–14.

forms in the tradition of the simplest type of frottola such as the North Italian *villotte* and the *canzone villanesche alla napolitana* of which he published a collection in 1545.[77] Typical of his dramatic handling of words is this passage from 'Quanto piu m'arde' (published in 1540). Like 'Mentre che'l cor' it is in five parts, already the favourite combination of voices:

Ex. 66

As Einstein says, 'The singers seem to snatch the single words from one another's mouths'.[78]

---

[77] These two extremes are nicely contrasted in *ChW*, v, which prints the severely contrapuntal 'Mentre che'l cor' from his *Musica nova* (1559) (*CMM* 3, xiii) on p. 5, and the villanesca 'O bene mio', p. 12. *ChW*, viii (ed. Hertzmann) gives four other villanesche by Willaert and examples by his Italian contemporaries, of whom the most important in this field was Giovanni Domenico da Nola (*c*. 1510–1592), also a composer of motets and madrigals.

[78] Op. cit., i, p. 329. The madrigal was printed by Peter Wagner in *Vierteljahrsschrift für Musikwiss-enschaft*, viii (1892), p. 455.

THE CHURCH MUSIC OF WILLAERT AND HIS CIRCLE

Both Verdelot and Arcadelt wrote church music but are far more important as madrigalists. Festa was a much more considerable church composer and Willaert also did perhaps his greatest work in this field. His last publication, the *Musica nova* of 1559, contains 33 motets[79] as against 24 madrigalian settings of Petrarch sonnets and the proportion of motets (more than three hundred) to madrigals (sixty odd) in his total output is much greater. His handful of Masses, three of them 'parodies' of motets by his teacher Mouton, do not show him as an innovator.[80] Nor do a great many of his motets. What they do present, like those of Gombert or Clemens non Papa, is a superb display of Netherland polyphony of the post-Josquin period from the freest to the strictest, though sometimes more declamatory and expressive, more 'madrigalian', than theirs. Madrigalian also are the occasional chromaticisms, such as the F sharps in his four-part setting of 'Pater noster'.[81] But in the motets proper Willaert never employs the device of *cori spezzati*, 'broken' (i.e. antiphonal) choirs, which he used in eight psalm-settings[82] published in a collection of psalms by Jachet of Mantua, 'Maistre Jan', and others in 1550. This was a practice already known in Padua and its neighbourhood, notably to Ruffino d'Assisi (*c.* 1524) whose *salmi spezzati* anticipated the later Venetian double-choral style more closely than Willaert's.[83]

Willaert was one of those musicians, like Josquin and Isaac in the previous generation, whose influence was more than that of a great model for composition. His circle of friends and pupils, the younger of whom will have to be considered in the next chapter, was vast. Together with them he established the musical pre-eminence of Venice in composition and performance, as Petrucci had done half a century earlier in publishing. Two of them were fellow-countrymen, Cipriano di Rore (1516–65) and Jakob Buus (d. 1564), the rest Italians: to name only some outstanding ones, Marco Antonio Cavazzoni ('di Bologna') (*c.* 1490–*c.* 1559) and his son Girolamo, Alfonso della Viola (*c.* 1508–70),[84] one of a family of Ferrarese musicians, Andrea Gabrieli (*c.* 1515–86), Girolamo Parabosco (*c.* 1522–57), Annibale Padovano (1527–75), Costanzo Porta (*c.* 1529–1601), Baldissera Donato (*c.* 1530–1604), Gioseffo Guami (*c.* 1535–*c.* 1611), and two who were

---

[79] In *Opera Omnia* (*CMM* 3), ed. H. Zenck and Walter Gerstenberg, v; there is an easily accessible example in *HAM*, i, No. 113.
[80] See Hermann Beck, 'Adrian Willaerts Messen', *AfMW*, xvii (1960), p. 215.
[81] *CMM* 3, ii, p. 11. On the F sharps, see Lewis Lockwood, 'A Sample Problem of *Musica Ficta*; Willaert's *Pater noster*', *Studies in Music History* (ed. Harold Powers) (Princeton, 1968), particularly pp. 177 ff.
[82] *CMM* 3, viii.
[83] See *NOHM*, iv, pp. 277 ff., which gives further references, particularly pp. 278–9, which show parallel settings by Ruffino and Willaert, and Anthony F. Carver, 'The Psalms of Willaert and his North Italian contemporaries', *Acta Musicologica*, xlvii (1975), p. 270.
[84] Composer of music for the tragedies and pastoral plays produced at the court of Ferrara. An invocation for the priest of Pan with choral responses, and a four-part *canzone finale*, for Agostino Beccari's *Il sacrificio* (1554) have been preserved. See quotations in *NOHM*, iv, pp. 790–1.

notable also as theorists, Nicola Vicentino (1511–76) and Gioseffo Zarlino (1517–90).

CIPRIANO DE RORE AND THE MADRIGAL

Rore properly stands at the head of this roll-call, above all for his madrigals[85] which are both artistically and historically more important than his generally rather conservative Masses and motets. The latter are by no means all religious, e.g. the intensely dramatic setting of Dido's bitter reproach, 'Dissimulare etiam sperasti', in the Fourth Book of the *Aeneid*. This piece also illustrates profoundly important innovations of musical idiom. These, already adumbrated here and there by Willaert – for instance in the above-mentioned 'Pater noster' and in 'Amor mi fa morire' – are boldly developed in some of Rore's madrigals: the insertion of accidentals beyond those which simply confirm the procedures of musica ficta, accidentals related to points in the text which they underline. That which is possibly implicit in Clemens non Papa's 'Vox in Rama' (see p. 209 n. 7) is here explicit. In a passage such as this:

Ex. 67

'mode' crumbles in beautiful ruins but is not replaced by any sense of 'key'. At the words 'Porto de' ciechi e miseri mortali' in the madrigal 'O morte, eterno fin'[87] Rore writes what in modern terminology we should call a succession of C major, A major, B minor, G major, C major, and G minor chords. Setting another poem concerned with death, Petrarch's 'Crudele acerba

---

[85] In *Opera Omnia*, (*CMM*, 14), ed. Bernhard Meier, iii–v, and various separate modern editions.
[87] *CMM* 14, iv, p. 84; the relevant passage quoted in *NOHM*, iv, p. 49.

inexorabil morte',[88] he employs conflicting key-signatures to sharpen the 'bitterness'. Yet these kinds of 'chromaticism' were exceptional in Rore. The most popular of all his madrigals, 'Anchor che col partire',[89] contains no more than one or two F sharps and G sharps which are written-out musica ficta. And when Rore himself uses the term 'chromatic', as in the title of his *Primo libro de madregali cromatici a cinque voci* (1544), he means something quite different: the writing of *note negre*, 'black notes', modern crotchets, as the time unit (4/4) instead of the minim (4/2).[90] The black notation of the second and third *partes* of the Virgil motet, 'Dissimulare', produces an acceleration, perhaps a final change to triple scansion. This corresponds with the augmentation of voices: five in the *prima pars*, six in the second ('Quin etiam'), and seven in the third ('Mene fugis'). Rore also composed a *Missa a note negre*[91] on one of his own few chansons, 'Tout ce qu'on peut'.

VENETIAN INSTRUMENTAL MUSIC

Rore's instrumental compositions are negligible. But Willaert is well represented in *Musica nova accomodata per cantar et sonar sopra organi et altri strumenti* (Venice, 1540),[92] and we also have a number of his three-part ricercari, notably eight in a collection of *Fantasie et rechercari a tre voci accomodate da cantare et sonare per ogni instrumento* (Venice, 1549),[93] in which Rore is also represented. They are essentially wordless motets, each polyphonic section neatly dovetailed into the next. Neither Willaert nor Rore composed for the keyboard though their works were often published in lute or keyboard transcription. More surprisingly, Buus and Annibale Padovano, organists at St. Mark's, composed their ricercari originally for four solo instruments – Buus's two books in 1547 and 1549[94] and Annibale's in 1556[95] – and Buus's sole *Intabolatura d'Organo* (also 1549) contains only four pieces: ornamented transcriptions of four of the other ricercari obviously made for the use of the 'molto nobile e vertuoso giovane' to whom they are dedicated.[96] No doubt Buus played his other pieces from memory and improvised the ornamentation. As for Annibale's organ-works, three

[88] Ibid., iv, p. 80, and Einstein, op. cit., iii, No. 48.
[89] *CMM*, iv, p. 31, and Einstein, op. cit., iii, No. 47. On its popularity see E. T. Ferand, ' "Anchor che col partire": Die Schicksale eines berühmten Madrigals', *Festschrift Karl Gustav Fellerer* (Regensburg, 1962), p. 137.
[90] It is the modern practice, followed in the present volume, to transcribe the music of this period in these halved note-values. The 'modern practice' was initiated by Arcadelt, Rore, and others in Venice about 1540, though the innovation was of course not generally accepted for some time.
[91] *CMM* 14, vii, p. 91.
[92] Ed. Colin Slim, *Monuments of Renaissance Music*, i (Chicago, 1965).
[93] Ed. Hermann Zenck (Mainz, 1933) from the 1559 edition which includes a ninth piece.
[94] In 'The Ricercari of Jacques Buus', *MQ*, xxxi (1945), p. 448, Gordon Sutherland has shown how Buus's compositions do differ from motets, e.g. the greater range of individual parts, the stronger, even angular, profiles of the melodic ideas, the working of each idea until its possibilities are exhausted. The second ricercar from the 1547 book is printed in R. B. Lenaerts, *Die Kunst der Niederländer (Das Musikwerk)* (Cologne, 1962), p. 99.
[95] Ed. N. Pierront and J. P. Hennebains (Paris, 1934) who incorrectly describe them as 'for organ'.
[96] Otto Kinkeldey prints one example complete in *Orgel und Klavier in der Musik des 16. Jahrhunderts* (Leipzig, 1910), p. 245, with part of the original four-part form.

toccatas and two ricercari were published in 1604, long after he was dead;[97] they are probably late works. His 'toccatas' are essentially quasi-preludial and improvisatory affairs of passage-work but two of them have polyphonic sections. So far as we know, the real pioneer of the motet-type of organ ricercar was Girolamo Cavazzoni. His two books of *Intavolature* (Venice, 1542–3) contain four such ricercari (together with organ Masses, alternatim Magnificats, hymn-settings, and free re-workings of two chansons by Josquin and Passereau),[98] whereas the two examples in his father's publication[99] are of the same improvisatory nature as the German organ preludes and the early ricercari for lute.[100] Girolamo's are actually more instrumental than the ensemble ricercari of Willaert and Buus; the influence of hand on keyboard is apparent in more than ornamentation. It remained for Buus (e.g. in No. 4 of his First Book) to achieve the unification of a ricercare by deriving all its imitative sections from the same basic theme, which was, exceptionally, transposed to other degrees of the mode – not merely to the fifth or fourth. A parallel development occurred in the ricercari, or *fantasie* as they are often called, for lute: a development from those of the Capirola lute-manuscript of *c.* 1517, which have been compared with Marco Antonio Cavazzoni's,[101] to the fully imitative *fantasie* in the first and third *Intabolature* (Venice, 1546 and 1547) of Francesco da Milano (1497–1543),[102] or to the ricercari which Simon Gintzler, lutenist to the Cardinal of Trent, published with transcriptions of vocal works by Josquin, Willaert, Senfl, Verdelot, Arcadelt, and others, also at Venice in 1547.[103] Indeed during 1546–8 there was a remarkable amount of lute publication at Venice.

While genuinely instrumental styles had emerged in keyboard and lute music and were beginning to emerge in ensemble music, the problem of purely instrumental construction remained unsolved except in the short dance-forms. The successive musical ideas of the motet were given cohesion by the words; those of the ricercare merely follow each other. Willaert will immediately repeat a section (or a bass only) near the end of a piece but not an earlier section. Buus does in a few cases revert to earlier material or in one instance, as we have seen, achieve cohesion at the expense of monotony by basing a whole piece on a single idea. He also perceived that monotony could be relieved by transposition of material, a foreshadowing of the key-schemes

[97] They have been edited by Klaus Speer in *CEKM* 34. The toccatas are discussed in detail by Giacomo del Valle de Paz in *Annibale Padovano nella storia della musica del Cinquecento* (Turin, 1933), pp. 46 ff.
[98] Ed. Oscar Mischiati (Mainz, 1958); ricercare No. 4, *Missa Cunctipotens*, and Josquin transcription in *HAM*, i, Nos. 116–8.
[99] *Recerchari Motetti Canzoni composti per Marcoantonio di Bologna* (Venice, 1523), reprinted complete in Knud Jeppesen, *Die italienische Orgelmusik am Anfang des Cinquecento* (Copenhagen, 1943).
[100] See above, p. 184.
[101] By Otto Gombosi in the introduction (p. xxxiv) to his edition of Capirola's book (Paris, 1954).
[102] Complete works ed. Arthur J. Ness (*Harvard Publications in Music*, 3 and 4) (Cambridge, Mass., 1970); one example in Schering, *Geschichte der Musik in Beispielen* (Leipzig, 1931), No. 115. See also Gombosi's paper on Francesco in *La Musique instrumentale de la Renaissance*, ed. Jean Jacquot (Paris, 1955), p. 165.
[103] The ricercari and a Senfl transcription have been ed. Adolf Koczirz in *DTÖ*, Jg. xviii (2) (vol. 37), pp. 60 ff.

that would be possible when modality had given way to tonality. Meanwhile an alternative way of achieving variety within unity had been discovered in Spain.

SPANISH CHURCH MUSIC

Throughout this period Spanish church music was mainly in the pure Netherland tradition. Until his abdication in 1555 the king – the Emperor Charles V – kept his 'Flemish chapel', while the greatest native composer, Cristóbal Morales (*c.* 1500–1553), apart from ten years in the Papal service, spent his whole life not at court but in his native Andalusia. Morales, too, followed the Netherland tradition; of his 22 Masses, two are on 'L'homme armé' and others are modelled on motets by Gombert, Mouton, Richafort, Verdelot, and Josquin's 'Mille regretz', only two on Spanish villancicos. He is perhaps most Spanish in the mystical emotion at the heart of such motets as 'Emendemus in melius' and 'O crux, ave'.[104] However the king–emperor allowed his wife, Isabella of Portugal, in 1526 to have a chapel of Spanish and Portuguese musicians and it was among the instrumentalists of this body, which was taken over by Philip II when he became regent of Spain in 1543, that we find the innovators: the blind organist Antonio de Cabezón (*c.* 1500–1566), who was one of its original members, the clavichordist Francisco de Soto (*c.* 1500–1563), who joined soon after, and Luis de Narváez (d. after 1555), a player of the *vihuela de mano* (the Spanish lute)[105] who was recruited by Philip.

INSTRUMENTAL MUSIC IN SPAIN

Cabezón and Narváez were the pioneers of *diferencias*, sets of variations, and it is impossible to claim priority for either. For although Cabezón's compositions first appeared in print in Luys Venegas de Henestrosa's *Libro de cifra* (figure notation) *nueva para tecla* (keyboard), *harpa y vihuela* (Alcala, 1557),[106] and the rest of them only in the *Obras de música* published posthumously by his son (Madrid, 1578),[107] no doubt many had been written as early as the lute pieces in Narváez's *Delphin de música* (Valladolid, 1538).[108] The most obvious origin of their *diferencias* is the organ versets which alternated with the sung verses of a psalm or hymn, the plainsong – now in one part, now in another – being surrounded each time by fresh counterpoints. Cabezón wrote such *versos* or *versillos*[109] and it has been

---

[104] *Opera Omnia*, ed. Higini Anglès (Barcelona, 1952), viii, p. 73 and v, p. 103. 'Emendemus' is also printed in *HAM*, i, No. 128.

[105] The viol was called *vihuela de arco*.

[106] Ed. Anglès, *Monumentos de la música española*, ii (*La Música en la corte de Carlos V*) (Barcelona, 1944). This collection also contains pieces by the Barcelona organist Pedro Alberch Vila (1517–82) and Soto's only surviving compositions, two *tientos* (lit. 'touches': cf. the Italian *toccata*), with echo effects.

[107] Ed. Anglès, *Monumentos*, xxvii–xxix (Barcelona, 1966), and Charles Jacobs (New York, 1967–). Eight pieces ed. Santiago Kastner (Mainz, 1951); two in *HAM*, i, Nos. 133–4.

[108] Ed. Emilio Pujol, *Monumentos*, iii (Barcelona, 1945). One example in *HAM*, i, No. 122.

[109] E.g. those on the first and sixth psalm-tones, *Monumentos*, xxvii, pp. 31 and 42; the latter also in *HAM*, i, No. 133.

suggested[110] that he was stimulated by the example of Arnolt Schlick (see p. 184) who also composed what one might call suites of versets, notably those on 'Da pacem Domine' in the first part of his *Tabulaturen* (1512), without the choral alternation. It remained for the Spaniards to connect them in extended compositions and base them on secular songs as Cabezón did on the 'Canto del Caballero' and 'Guárdame las vacas'[111] or play them – as so many Mass-movements and motets were even more incongruously played – on the lute.[112] But the composers of *diferencias* went further. They combined variations on a melody with a similar technique originating in dance-music: composition on 'conventional' tenors or basses (see p. 170, n. 28), which, like the melodies, were elaborated with great freedom. In fact melody and bass together defined *harmonies* which were the real basis of variation. One extremely popular melody-and-bass was 'Guárdame las vacas'. This was varied not only by Narváez and Cabezón but by Venegas de Henestrosa in his *Libro de cifra* and the contemporary lute-composers Alonso de Mudarra[113] (who also calls it 'Romanesca' under which name the bass became one of the most popular of all 'conventional basses' in Italy as well), Enrique de Valderrábano,[114] and Diego Pisador:[115]

Ex. 68

Another famous conventional melody-and-bass, 'Ruggiero' (to which originally a stanza from Ariosto's *Orlando furioso*, xliv, 61, was sung), also made probably its first appearance in a Spanish source, the *Tratado de glosas*

---

[110] By Santiago Kastner, 'Rapports entre Schlick et Cabezón', *La Musique instrumentale de la Renaissance*, p. 217.
[111] Both in Kastner's selection, pp. 1 and 7; the former also in *HAM*, i, No. 134.
[112] E.g. Narváez's on 'O gloriosa domina', *HAM*, i, No. 122.
[113] *Tres libros de música* (Seville, 1546); ed. Pujol, *Monumentos*, vii (Barcelona, 1959).
[114] *Silva de Sirenas* (Valladolid, 1547), ed. idem., xxii–xxiii (Barcelona, 1965).
[115] *Libro de música de vihuela* (Salamanca, 1552).

(treatise on ornamental variation) (Rome, 1553)[116] of Diego Ortiz. This teaches players of the vihuela de arco how to make *glosas* on cadences and *recercadas* on a cantus firmus which the *cymbalo* will harmonize or on a single part of a chanson or madrigal, the other parts being played on the 'cymbalo' – with illustrations based on Sandrin's 'Doulce memoire' and Rore's 'O felice occhi miei'.

The vihuela tablatures contained villancicos and romances – with the melody in red figures, as in Luis Milan's *El Maestro* (Valencia, 1535 or 6),[117]

Pl. 39   *Romance*, 'Toda mi vida', for voice with vihuela accompaniment, from Luis Milan's *Libro de musica de vihuela de mano, intitulado El Maestro* (Valencia, 1535 or 1536). The lines of the tablature correspond to the strings of the *vihuela*, tuned: C, c, f, a, d′, g′. D represents an open string, the other fingers indicate the number of semitones above the open string: thus the first chord is e, g, b, e. Note values are shown above the tablature.

[116] Ed. Max Schneider (Berlin, 1913; second edition, Kassel, 1936).
[117] Ed. Leo Schrade, *Publikationen älterer Musik* (Leipzig, 1927); easily accessible examples of romance and villancico in Schering, op. cit., Nos. 96(*a*) and (*b*); a fantasia in *HAM*, i, No. 121.

so that it could easily be sung as well as played. They also included sets of diferencias and dances (e.g. Milan's beautiful pavanas), transcriptions of sacred and secular polyphony, and fantasías or tientos. These last show the same development of imitative polyphony as the Italian lute fantasias; indeed, those in Narváez's *Delphin* anticipate Francesco da Milano and Gintzler by several years, though Mudarra includes a few simply 'para desenboluer las manos'. Narváez's fantasías[118] also occasionally have echo-passages like those in Francisco de Soto's keyboard tientos (see p. 236, n. 106). In Miguel de Fuenllana's *Orphénica lyra* (Seville, 1554)[118a] the transcription of a vocal piece is often followed by a fantasía sometimes thematically related to it. (Both Spanish and Italian lute-composers used the terms 'tiento' and 'ricercare' for the more loosely constructed type of piece.)

THE LUTE IN OTHER COUNTRIES

The rest of Europe could at this time show little lute music comparable with that of the Spanish and Italian lutenists. The German Hans Neusidler (*c.* 1510–1563) and the Parisian Guillaume Morlaye (*c.* 1515–1560) were essentially transcribers and dance-composers, though skilled ones.[119] Perhaps only the Transylvanian Valentin Bakfark (Greff) (1507–76), lutenist at the Polish court, who not only made the customary transcriptions but composed ten extended fantasias packed with imitative polyphony,[120] can be ranked with Francisco de Milano, Gintzler, and the Spaniards. As for England, although the lute was played at the beginning of the century, the only music for it in any source earlier than *c.* 1540 consists of a few pieces in the British Library manuscript, Royal App. 58 (see p. 186), two of which bear titles showing that they were settings of songs by Sir Thomas Wyatt ('Hevyn and erth') and Henry Howard, Earl of Surrey ('In winter's just return').[121] Henry VII engaged as his court lutenist not an Englishman but a Brescian.

ENGLISH ORGAN MUSIC

English organ music began to flourish after the King's recruitment of two foreign organists, the Venetian Memo and Benedictus Opitiis, a Hofhaimer pupil, in 1516. Both stayed for five or six years. Not long after this time (*c.* 1530) we have a source, Royal App. 56, containing half-a-dozen anonymous

[118] E.g. No. 11, *Monumentos*, iii, p. 23, bars 69–76.   [118a] Ed. Charles Jacobs (Oxford, 1978).
[119] Hans's son Melchior (1531–*c.* 1590) was to cultivate the polyphonic lute ricercare in the second half of the century.
[120] Complete in appendix to Otto Gombosi, *Der Lautenist Valentin Bakfark* (Budapest, 1935); seven ed. Koczirz, op. cit., pp. 68 ff.; one complete example in Bence Szabolcsi, *A Concise History of Hungarian Music* (Budapest, English version 1964), p. 113.
[121] See Ivy L. Mumford's studies of the musical settings of Wyatt and Surrey respectively in *M & L*, xxxvii (1956), p. 315 and *English Miscellany*, viii (1957). Attaingnant's widow published 'Hevyn and erth' in the *Sixieme Livre de danceries* (1555) as a 'Pavane d'Angleterre' with the customary gaillarde transformation, by Claude Gervaise, ed. Expert, *Les Maîtres musiciens*, xxiii, p. 18, and a florid keyboard transcription is included in the Fitzwilliam Virginal Book (No. 105) (see p. 292).

liturgical pieces: a Kyrie and Christe, two 'Felix namque' and a Communion 'Beata viscera',[122] an antiphon, 'Miserere', and an unornamented transcription of a four-part hymn, 'A solis ortus cardine'.[123] The Kyrie-Christe is based on one of the set of conventional tenors employed at this period in English votive Masses of the Virgin, for instance those of Nicolas Ludford (*c.* 1485–*c.* 1557),[124] which are mysteriously called 'squares'. Indeed the Kyrie of Ludford's Lady-Mass for Tuesday[125] is based on the same square as the organ piece. The organ-writing is undistinguished, a florid, aimless counterpoint for right or left hand, while in the 'Felix namque' and 'Beata viscera' long-note cantus firmi are accompanied by two parts in loose and minimal imitation.

Another source of perhaps a decade later, Brit. Lib., Add. 15233, however, gives us seven pieces – mostly Office hymns – by a composer of different quality who knew how to make his texture cohere by sequences, short ostinato motives, and other devices. This was John Redford, vicar-choral and master of the choristers of St. Paul's Cathedral from at least as early as 1534 (when he signed the loyal declaration denying papal authority over the Church in England) till his death in 1547, playwright and poet. Brit. Lib., Add. 29996[126] preserves many more of his compositions, together with an alternatim organ Mass by another St. Paul's musician Philip ap Rhys, who succeeded him as organist, and a considerable number of organ works (including the Proper of a Mass for Easter Day and eight 'Felix namque' which might be regarded as a set of variations though they were not of course played as such) by Thomas Preston (d. *c.* 1564), organist of Magdalen College, Oxford, and later of the Chapel Royal at Windsor. Even more of Redford's music exists in the great repertory-book belonging to Thomas Mulliner, possibly also of St. Paul's and later at Oxford, more than half of which was probably copied between 1550 and 1560.[127]

Redford is much more richly represented in Mulliner's book than anyone else, with Thomas Tallis (*c.* 1505–1585) as the next and a younger man, William Blitheman (*c.* 1525–1591), third. Of the composers of Redford's own generation, two of the greatest – Christopher Tye (*c.* 1500–1573) and John Taverner (*c.* 1490–1545) – are represented by only one piece each, although Taverner's 'In nomine' was the progenitor of a whole species of English music for keyboard, lute, or instrumental ensemble during the next hundred years and more. This 'In nomine' of Taverner's is an almost exact

[122] Ed. Denis Stevens, *Early Tudor Organ Music . . . for the Mass* (*EECM*, x) (London, 1967), Nos. 2, 10, 11, and 29.
[123] Ed. John Caldwell, *Early Tudor Organ Music . . . for the Office* (ibid., vi) (London, 1965), No. 10 and p. 181.
[124] *Opera Omnia* (*CMM* 27), ed. John D. Bergsagel, i. See also Bergsagel, 'An Introduction to Ludford', *Musica Disciplina*, xiv (1960), particularly pp. 119 ff. on the 'squares'.
[125] *CMM* 27, i, p. 44.
[126] All these compositions are published in *EECM*, vi and x.
[127] The 'Mulliner Book' has been edited by Denis Stevens, *MB*, i (London, 1951), with a separately published commentary (1952) which includes as a supplement some pieces for cittern or gittern, at the end of the manuscript, composed on conventional Italian basses such as the *passamezzi antico* and *moderno* which would presumably have been played on a viol.

transcription of the section 'In nomine Domini' of the Benedictus of his Mass *Gloria tibi Trinitas* (on the Sarum version of a Vesper antiphon for Trinity Sunday),[128] and it was this segment of plainsong, sometimes with quotation of Taverner's other parts, which served generations of English composers as cantus firmus for contrapuntal 'fancies'. (Tye alone wrote more than twenty for viols, nearly all in five parts.) Two such 'In nomines' in Mulliner's book – by the Scottish religious refugee Robert Johnson (*c.* 1490–*c.* 1565) and Robert White (*c.* 1530–1574) – appear to be transcriptions of viol compositions. That by the otherwise almost unknown Nicholas Carleton, probably a pupil of Redford's, however, and the six by Blitheman, practically a set of variations all styled 'Gloria tibi Trinitas', are unmistakably keyboard compositions with showy and rhythmically complicated passage-work. Indeed Mulliner's collection contains an entire repertory: original keyboard pieces, some brilliant, some as sober as most of Redford's organ hymns, transcriptions of Latin motets, English anthems and unsophisticated secular part-songs, a few dances, and a 'fancy', probably originally for viols, by one Newman otherwise unknown.[129]

CHURCH MUSIC UNDER HENRY VIII AND MARY

What Mulliner's book does not represent adequately is English church music during the agonizing years 1534–58 which saw Henry VIII's pseudo-Reformation and dissolution of those musical strongholds, the monasteries; the Protestant triumph and English liturgy of 1549; the Catholic reaction and Mary's marriage to Philip of Spain (who brought with him during 1554–5 his 'Flemish chapel' including Philipp de Monte and his organist Cabezón); and the accession of Elizabeth I. Most of Taverner's church music was probably written before this period, during the years 1526–30 when he was organist and choirmaster of Cardinal College (now Christ Church), Oxford; it includes eight Masses, three Magnificats, as well as shorter pieces.[130] But he was already attracted to Lutheranism. He became a zealous agent of Thomas Cromwell in the Dissolution and, according to John Foxe,[131] 'repented him very muche that he had made Songes to Popish Ditties in the time of his blindnes' and seemingly abandoned composition. The rather clumsy adaptations of his Masses, *The Meane Mass* and *Small Devotion*,[132] to English words can hardly have been his own. Some of

---

[128] The Mass is published in *TCM*, i (London, 1923), p. 126.

[129] *MB*, i, p. 9. It is the earliest known piece so called; Willi Apel has shown ('English Organ Music of the Renaissance', *MQ*, xxxix (1953), pp. 389 ff.) that it is freely modelled on a 'Salve virgo' by the elder Cavazzoni (in Jeppesen, op. cit., p. 43*).

[130] The Masses are printed complete in *TCM*, i, the rest ibid., iii the six-part Masses, ed. Hugh Benham, also in EECM, xx.

[131] *Actes and Monuments* (popularly known as 'The Book of Martyrs'), edition of 1583, ii, p. 1032.

[132] A 'meane' was a voice lying between treble and alto; in the *Meane Mass* the highest part was a 'meane'. *Small Devotion* is partially a 'parody' on an antiphon of St. William of York, 'Christe Jesu pastor bone' (*TCM*, iii, p. 73), and Frank Ll. Harrison has suggested that the title of the Mass is a scribal misreading of 'S W[ilhelmi] devotio'. The English versions of these two Masses, preserved in the so-called 'Wanley part-books' at Oxford (Bodl. Mus. Sch. e. 420–2), a collection of music for the English liturgy compiled 1547–8, are published ibid., iii, pp. 143 and 169.

Tallis's Latin motets were turned into English anthems in the same dubious way, though the bulk of his music for the English rite is original.[133] So is Tye's and presumably that of John Sheppard, a turbulent and eccentric figure too little of whose music has been printed.[134] But the Anglicans, like the Lutherans, did not suddenly give up the composition of Latin texts. Their Scottish contemporary Robert Carver (1487–after 1546) never accepted the Reformation.[135]

The music of this last flowering of Latin church composition in Britain, with all its often masterly workmanship and sheer beauty of sound, has hardly anything in common with contemporary Continental music. Taverner's dense polyphony often flows in florid and rhythmically subtle lines in the tradition of the masters of the Eton Choirbook and his imitational practice is, if anything, nearer to Ockeghem's than to Gombert's or Clemens non Papa's. Only Sheppard, in his 'Frences Mass', shows any sign of foreign influence.[136] Tallis, greatest of the group, was capable of the most ingenious contrapuntal feats – as he demonstrates in his seven-part 'Miserere nostri'[137] where superius I and II are in canon at the unison while simultaneously the descant is in canon with (a) the contratenor in quadruple augmentation, (b) bassus I in inverted intervals and 16-fold augmentation, (c) bassus II inverted and in double augmentation – to say nothing of his famous 'Spem in alium' for eight five-part choirs[138] with its effects of mass rather than subtlety. But 'Miserere nostri' is medieval in technique as the lovely 'Ave rosa sine spinis'[139] is in feeling, and at his finest – as in the glorious antiphon 'Gaude gloriosa Dei mater'[140] – we hear him as the heir of the Eton composers, not of Josquin.

Taverner made one innovation in English music: the use of a secular cantus firmus, the tune of 'Westron wynde' very obviously in the highest part, throughout a Mass.[141] Tye and Sheppard also wrote 'Westron wynde' Masses[142] and these are almost the only big English masses after Taverner's (if we exclude Lady Masses and the three much later examples by Byrd). We have only two Masses by Tallis. English composers preferred the votive antiphon, hymn, and respond, and in Mary's reign there was an outburst of Latin psalm-settings by Tallis, Tye, Sheppard, White in particular and others.[143] By Tallis and White we also have particularly fine Lamen-

---

[133] Ed. Leonard Ellinwood (rev. Paul Doe), *EECM*, xii and xiii.

[134] Tye's Latin church music has been ed. John Sutterfield, *Recent Researches in the Music of the Renaissance*, i and ii, and his English sacred music by John Morehen, *EECM*, xix. Sheppard's responds are ed. David Chadd, *EECM*, xvii, and Masses ed. Nicholas Sandon, ibid., xviii.

[135] His Mass *L. homme armé* and the remarkable 19-part motet 'O bone Jesu' have been ed. Kenneth Elliott, *Music of Scotland (1500–1700)* (*MB*, xv) (London, 1957), pp. 30 and 37, and by Denis Stevens, *CMM* 16.

[136] See Nigel Davison, '*The Western Wind* Masses', *MQ*, lvii (1971), p. 442.

[137] *TCM*, vi, p. 207.

[138] Ibid., p. 299.

[139] Ibid., p. 169, with missing portions of tenor in *TCM Appendix* (London, 1948), pp. 49 ff.

[140] Ibid., vi, p. 123.

[141] Ibid., i, p. 3; Benedictus in *HAM*, i, No. 112.

[142] See Davison, loc. cit.

[143] Examples by Tallis, ibid., vi, pp. 246 and 266; Tye's 'Omnes gentes', ed. H. B. Collins (London, n.d.); the remarkable series by White, *TCM*, v, pp. 48–167.

tations.[144] But despite the generalized emotional expressiveness of such works, English composers achieved a true marriage of words and music only in the next generation.

[144] Ibid., vi, pp. 102 and 110, and v, pp. 14 and 35 respectively.

12

Music during the Counter-Reformation

Until the middle of the sixteenth century there was considerable hope, held by the Emperor Charles V among others, that the breach between Catholic and Protestant might yet be closed; the abortive visit of the Protestant envoys to the Council of Trent in 1551 showed once and for all that that hope was delusive. The second half of the century was a period of intolerance, of deepening division not only between Catholic and Protestant – though a Catholic emperor, Maximilian II, could still favour Lutherans and as late as 1583 a Catholic Archbishop of Cologne could contemplate marriage to a nun – but between Lutheran and Calvinist and even within the various religious camps. The religious divisions also hardened to a considerable extent into national ones; Catholicism not only held firm in southern Europe but extended itself northward, Lutheranism failed to root itself outside the Teutonic lands, while Calvinism spread in a long thin arc from Scotland, through France and the Netherlands to Poland and Hungary. These differences are clearly reflected in music. Even Catholic music suffered a crisis.

THE TRIDENTINE REFORM

There had for some time been complaints about the secular elements in Catholic church music, the exhibitionism of organists, the use of tropes, the obscuring of the sacred texts by polyphony, and so on. They came to a head in 1562 at the Council of Trent, reconvened after a ten-year break.[1] In September the Council formulated the general directive quoted in the previous chapter (see p. 207) and the next year, just before it broke up, two new members actually advocated the suppression of polyphonic church music altogether. But this aroused influential opposition notably from the Emperor, Ferdinand I, and the Bavarian Duke, Albrecht V. The Pope's *motu proprio* of 2 August 1564, which nominated eight cardinals to see to the carrying out of the Tridentine reforms generally, says nothing at all about music. However, the two cardinals who did take over the musical reforms – the Pope's young nephew Carlo Borromeo and Vitellozzo Vitellozzi – were men of intelligence and culture. They probably adopted as their standard of

---

[1] For a preliminary guide to the copious documentation, see *NOHM*, iv, p. 317, n. 4.

'homophonic polyphony' with clearly intelligible text the *Preces speciales*[2] of the Italianized Netherlander Jacobus de Kerle (*c.* 1532–1591) and his Mass 'Regina coeli'; the 'special prayers' for the Council's success had been commissioned by a German cardinal, Truchsess von Waldburg, in 1562 and were sung at Trent three times almost every week.

Ex. 69

No 1. *Pro Concilio*

The *Missa Papae Marcelli* of Giovanni Pierluigi da Palestrina (*c.* 1525-1594), then master of the chapel at St. Maria Maggiore at Rome, may well date from this time and have been accepted at once as an embodiment of the Tridentine ideal but there is no evidence that it was the unique exemplar of the legend. It was probably among the Masses performed at Vitellozzi's house on 27 April 1565. His Masses 'Benedicta es' (on Josquin's motet), 'De beata Virgine', and 'Ut re mi fa sol la' are also said to have been approved.[3] So, rather surprisingly, was a Mass on Rore's madrigal 'Qual donna attende' by Albrecht V's *magister capellae* Lassus ('Orlando di Lasso') (*c.* 1532–1594), though this grave work is admittedly very different from Lassus's flippant, not to say scandalous chanson-Masses like the one on Clemens non Papa's 'Entre vous filles' (cf. p. 213), which nevertheless is preserved in a post-Tridentine Munich copy. Palestrina himself composed Masses modelled on chansons and madrigals, e.g. the Lupus/Cadéac 'Je suys desheritée' (cf. p. 212) and Domenico Ferrabosco's 'Io mi son giovinetta' (cf. p. 230). But he took care to publish them as 'Sine nomine' or 'Missa primi toni' and when he issued his Second Book of

---

[2] Ed. Otto Ursprung, *DTB*, xxxiv (Jg. 26) (Augsburg, 1926).
[3] See K. G. Fellerer, 'Church Music and the Council of Trent', *MQ*, xxxix (1953), p. 588, n. 52.

Masses (Rome, 1567) he claimed that he had composed 'music of a new order in accordance with the views of the most serious and religious-minded persons in high places'. In the same year Giovanni Animuccia (*c.* 1500–1571), who succeeded Palestrina as master of the Cappella Giuliana in 1555 and was succeeded by him in 1571, described his First Book of Masses as composed 'seconda la forma del Concilio di Trento', and Vincenzo Ruffo (*c.* 1510–1587) of Milan Cathedral explained in the dedication of his book of Masses 'according to the Milan rite' (1570) that he had composed them on Borromeo's instructions 'ex sancti tridentini Concilii decreto'. In Ruffo's case this necessitated a striking change of style from his *Madrigali a notte negre* (Venice, 1545) and *Madrigali cromatici* of 1552. Other composers did not yet differentiate so sharply between secular and sacred idioms; even Palestrina introduced madrigalian elements – with beautiful effect – in his settings from the Song of Songs,[4] while Victoria toward the end of his life, in 1600, broke into a much more surprisingly secular vein in a *Missa pro victoria* with organ, modelled on Janequin's 'La guerre'.

THE ORATORIAN MOVEMENT AND 'GREGORIAN' REFORM

The Tridentine reforms were in practice essentially an Italian, even a Roman affair, except where they were enforced by the Jesuits, the 'soldiers of the Counter-Reformation'. In Rome itself there was another musical manifestation of the Counter-Reformation, associated with the Oratorian movement founded by St. Philip Neri for which Animuccia composed two volumes of laudi spirituali (1563 and 1570).[5] These were very much in the tradition of the older polyphonic laudi, but before long imitation and chromaticism appeared in Oratorian laudi and by the end of the century an element of dramatic dialogue which was to flower into the full-blown 'oratorio'. A more sophisticated form of vernacular religious music of the Counter-Reformation was the *madrigale spirituale* which began to flower in 1581 with the publication of the first book of *Madrigali spirituali a cinque voci*[6] by the Imperial *Kapellmeister* Philipp de Monte (1521–1603), another Italianized Fleming. The supreme masterpieces in this short-lived genre are Lassus's posthumously published *Lagrime di San Pietro*.[7]

One most unfortunate consequence of the Counter-Reformation must be mentioned. In 1577 Gregory XIII took it into his head that the 'Gregorian' chant itself needed reform and entrusted the task to Palestrina and a Papal contralto, Annibale Zoilo. They were frustrated by the intervention of a

---

[4] *Motettorum 5 vocibus, liber quartus* (Rome, 1584); complete in vol. iv of the old edition of *Palestrina: Werke* (ed. Haberl *et al.*) (Leipzig, 1862–1907) and vol. xi of Palestrina: *Le opere complete* (ed. Casimiri, Jeppesen *et al.*) (Rome, 1939–   ). There is a typical example in Schering, *Geschichte der Musik in Beispielen*, No. 122: the motet 'Adjuro vos', with a decidedly madrigalian effect ar 'quia amore langueo'.
[5] One example from the *Libro primo*, 'Ben venga, Amore', in Schering, op. cit., No. 120; this borrows the popular tune, the 'Maggiolata', to Angelo Poliziano's famous 'Ben venga maggio'.
[6] Ed. Piet Nuten, *De Madrigali Spirituali van F. de Monte* (Brussels, 1958).
[7] Ed. H. J. Therstappen, *ChW*, xxxiv, xxxvii, and xli.

Spanish composer, Fernando de las Infantas, but in 1582 Palestrina's pupil Giovanni Guidetti published a version giving the notes definite mensural values which his master warmly approved, and further attempts at 'reformation' led to the disastrous so-called 'Medici' edition of 1614.

THE PERFECTION OF THE ROMAN STYLE

The 'Roman style' was not, of course, created by the Council of Trent though the Council did give it a partial façade of quasi-homophonic simplicity. Essentially it is the ultimate perfection – a hostile critic might say 'emasculation' – of Netherland polyphony, its florid elements pruned, its dissonances disguised or mollified by preparation and other devices which so lend themselves to codification that 'the style of Palestrina' has become the ideal model for students of sixteenth-century composition. It was practised not only by Palestrina but by Animuccia, by the Mantuan court composer, the Netherlander Giaches de Wert (1535–96), by Marc Antonio Ingegneri of Cremona (after 1547–1592) and Giovanni Matteo Asola of Verona (c. 1524–1609), both probably pupils of Ruffo, by the Nanino brothers, Giovanni Maria (c. 1545–1607) and Giovanni Bernardino (c. 1560–1623), and by Palestrina's own pupils Francesco Soriano (c. 1549–1620) and Felice Anerio (1560–1614), who were responsible for the *Editio Medicaea* of the chant, and Felice's younger brother Giovanni Francesco (c. 1567–1630), although the music of these younger composers reveals the impression of new ideas. Far greater than any of these, second only to Palestrina himself, was Tomás Luis de Victoria (c. 1548–1611), who in 1565 came to Rome from Spain where Morales (see p. 236) and his pupil Francisco Guerrero (c. 1527–1599) had already arrived at a perfection of the Netherland style hardly distinguishable from the Roman.

Palestrina's more than a hundred Masses are of all the familiar types: Masses like 'Aeterna Christi munera', based on the plainsong Matins hymn, 'parodies' like 'Assumpta est Maria' based on his own six-part motet, freely composed ones like the *Missa Papae Marcelli* and *Missa brevis*, to mention only a few supremely fine examples. Victoria's output of Masses, and of motets, was much smaller – no more than a score – eight of them being modelled on his own motets, though he was much more selective than most of his contemporaries, borrowing only sparsely from the model[8] instead of treating it almost as the theme for a series of variations as Palestrina does with 'Assumpta est' and de Monte in most of his Masses. Both Palestrina and Victoria toward the end of their lives became aware of the festive possibilities of the Venetian double-choral effect, Palestrina in the Mass 'Laudate Dominum' and a number of motets, Victoria in the already mentioned *Missa pro victoria* and the three Marian Masses published with it (Madrid, 1600), all of which have organ accompaniment. But the great bulk of their music makes its effect exclusively by its singing lines, moving by step more often than leap,

[8] On this see Hans von May, *Die Kompositionstechnik T. L. de Victorias* (Berne, 1943), pp. 82–5.

and beautifully spaced harmonic euphony, producing a sense of timelessness by the absence of marked rhythm or the thrust of any but the gentlest dissonance. The spirit had been caught from time to time long before and by the same crossing of Italian sweetness with Netherland technique, for instance in Josquin's 'Pange lingua' Mass (see pp. 176–7), but in Palestrina and Victoria it is all-pervading, incantatory, the ideal music of mystical faith, totally purged of human emotion (except occasionally in their motets) and of human vanity – except the vanity of performers who (we learn with a shock from Giovanni Bassano's *Motetti, Madrigali et Canzoni Francese di diversi eccellentissimi Auttori . . . Diminuiti per sonar con ogni sorte di Stromenti & anco per cantar con semplice Voce*, published in 1591, when Palestrina was still living) ornamented the highest parts not only of madrigals and chansons but of motets. Here, for example, is Bassano's version of a few bars of the soprano part of Palestrina's 'Benedicta sit sancta Trinitas' :[9]

Ex. 70

VENICE AND THE *STILE CONCERTATO*

Bassano's book was published in Venice, however, and Venice – where 'music had her very own home' as Francesco Sansovino claimed in his *Venetia, citta nobilissima et singolare* (Venice, 1581) – was politically at odds with the papacy during the latter part of the century and was shortly afterwards able to defy successfully a papal interdict. The austere artistic ideals of Rome made little impression on the city of Veronese, who himself got into trouble with the Roman Inquisition for his secular treatment of a 'Last Supper'. Even one of the more conservative of Willaert's disciples, Andrea Gabrieli (*c.* 1515–1586), expressly mentions the use of instruments ('tum viva Voce, tum omnis generis Instrumentis') in his *Sacrae cantiones* (1565) and again in his Penitential Psalms (1583).[10] He makes it clear in the

---

[9] Quoted from Max Kuhn, *Die Verzierungs-Kunst in der Gesangs-Musik des XVI und XVII Jahrhunderts* (Leipzig, 1902), where the complete motet with Bassano's ornaments is printed, pp. 100 ff.
[10] There is a modern edition of the Psalms by Bruno Grusnick (Kassel, 1936).

dedication of the latter that voices and instruments were to be used now together, now separately ('per vocum et instrumentorum melodiam, tam conjuncte quam divisim') but not at all clear how this was to be done.[11] However it is evident that he intended something different from the simple *a cappella* doubling of voices by instruments, and this 'something different' became known as the 'concerted style' (*stile concertato*), a 'consort' of voices and instruments. Clearly this is what Andrea's nephew Giovanni (*c.* 1555–1612) had in mind when in 1587 he published a collection of motets, Mass-movements, and madrigals by his uncle and himself as *Concerti* (a very early use of the term) *per voci, & stromenti Musicali; a 6.7.8.10.12. & 16.* (The *stromenti musicali* available at San Marco at that time, besides the two organs, were cornetti and trombones plus one or two *violini*[12] – the only stringed instruments that could hold their own with the brass – engaged as extras.)[13] Whereas in his earlier four- and five-part motets Andrea had generally maintained a conservative style, the Penitential Psalms show his skill in what one may call choral orchestration, and in the *Concerti*[14] he developed polychoral writing far beyond the simple antiphony of the *salmi spezzati* of Ruffino and Willaert. He employed for instance three four-part groups differentiated by pitch (high, medium, and low) and probably by constitution (soli, tutti), by instrumental support or substitution, and positioning in the church – to produce those exciting contrasts which led Michael Praetorius thirty years later into the etymological error of deriving the term 'concerto' from the Latin *concertare*, to contend. A typical example is shown in Ex. 71, from the last concerto in the collection, 'Magnificat anima mea'[15] (see p. 250).

This is far indeed in both technique and spirit from the contemporary work of Palestrina and Victoria. Religious music in Venice, in particular at San Marco, was very often music for state occasions and Andrea Gabrieli was very much an official composer. He wrote the music for royal visits, for the carnival rejoicings after the battle of Lepanto, for the performance of *Edippo Tiranno*,[16] a translation of Sophocles which opened Palladio's Teatro Olimpico at Vicenza in 1585, and his church music was planned with much greater concern for splendid and effective sound than these secular compositions. One can trace the same development from conservative polyphony to polychoral music demanding instrumental co-operation for its full effect in the works of the other Venetians and Willaert pupils of the latter half of the century: Costanzo Porta (*c.* 1529–1601), Claudio Merulo

[11] On this problem see Denis Arnold, 'Andrea Gabrieli und die Entwicklung der "cori-spezzati" Technik', *MF*, xii (1959), p. 258 ff. – particularly pp. 263–6.
[12] See Eleanor Selfridge-Field 'Bassano and the orchestra of St. Mark's', *Early Music*, iv (1976), p. 153.
[13] The violin family, bowed overhand, the smaller members of which were held on the arm (*da braccio*), had not long achieved respectability and only very slowly began to supersede the viol family, bowed underhand and held on or between the legs (*da gamba*). The Venetian *violino* was what we should call a viola; the violin was then *violino piccolo*.
[14] Examples reprinted by Giovanni d'Alessi, *A. Gabrieli: Messe e mottetti da cinque a sedici voci (I classici musicali italiani*, v) (Milan, 1942), and Denis Arnold, *ChW*, 96 (Wolfenbüttel, 1965).
[15] d'Alessi, ibid., p. 48.
[16] The choruses have been ed. Leo Schrade (Paris, 1960).

Ex. 71

$(1533-1604)$,[17] Giovanni Croce (*c.* $1557-1609$), and above all Andrea's nephew Giovanni Gabrieli (*c.* $1555-1612$).[18] Of these the most conservative was Porta, who as late as 1578 could publish an old-fashioned cantus firmus Mass on the Josquin subject 'La sol fa re mi'[19] and who corresponded with Carlo Borromeo; on the other hand, his Magnificat for the Franciscan Chapter at Bologna was in 24 parts and we know that he frequently employed trombones, cornetts, violins, and portative organs as well as the large ones at San Antonio, Padua, where he spent the last six years of his life. Merulo, as one would expect of such a prolific instrumental composer,[20] included in his second book of motets (1593) *7 per concerti e per cantare*, and after his death were published two remarkable Masses, on Giaches de Wert's madrigal 'Cara la vita mia' for two choirs and on Andrea Gabrieli's 'Benedicam Dominum' – itself a three-choir work – for three.[21]

SPARTITURA AND *BASSO CONTINUO*

Croce published his earliest motets and Masses for two choirs in 1594 and 1596 respectively. They are works of peculiar historical interest since they are the earliest publications to include a special part – what the publisher, Giacomo Vincenti, called a *sparditura* or *partidura* – for the accompanying organist. It consists of the bass-parts for each choir, placed one above the other, with bar-lines but no text or figures to indicate how he was to fill out the bass, only an occasional flat or sharp above the notes; when in the Masses a movement begins in a higher part only, this is shown in the organ part; but when the higher voices sing without the bass, the organ part is marked 'tacet' or 'non est hic'. At the same time (1595) Vincenti published the eight-part *Concerti ecclesiastici* of another of the San Marco musicians, Adriano Banchieri ($1567-1634$), with a spartitura for the *choro primo* only. This gives both cantus and bass above each other, textless, with the indication 'a 8' where the *secondo choro* sings as well, and a note telling organists how quickly and easily they can make a 'spartitura di tutti due chori' for themselves if they need one. The usefulness of having voice-parts in score, so that they could be played on a keyboard instrument (as distinct from the highly embellished transcriptions) or used 'for the study of counterpoint', had been recognized at least as early as 1577, when Gardano published two such volumes, one of Rore's four-part madrigals, the other of miscellaneous pieces. And ten years later the Mantuan composer Alessandro Striggio (*c.* $1535-c.$ 1595), in order to hold together the forty parts of his four-choir motet 'Ecce beatam lucem', devised a *bassone* or 'general bass' 'extracted from the lowest voices, to be played in the middle of the circle [of performers] by a trombone for the sustaining of the harmony

---

[17] Sacred works, ed. James Bastian, *CMM* 51.
[18] *Opera Omnia*, ed. Denis Arnold, *CMM* 12, and numerous modern editions of individual works.
[19] Ed. Oscar Mischiati, *ChW*, xciii (1963).
[20] See p. 287.
[21] Ed. Bastian, op. cit., ii.

with organ, lute and *cembali* or viols'.[22] Porta's alleged pupil Ludovico
Viadana (*c.* 1560–1627) needed no such aid to the performance of his
Concerti ecclesiastici . . . Con il basso continuo per sonar nell' organo[23] (Book 1,
Venice, 1602), for the mainly solo voices never number more than four. The
Second Book of his *Concerti* (1607) actually contains a monodic 'Missa
Dominicalis' with continuo,[24] though his textures are often contrapuntal
and have no very close affinity, except in coloratura, with the secular
monody which was developing at this time.[25] Although the monodists were
already using figures to indicate the intervals to be played above the bass,
Viadana does not.[26] But in 1607 his friend Agostino Agazzari published the
first little treatise on continuo performance, *Del suonare sopra il basso con
tutti stromenti & uso loro nel conserto*,[27] which does explain the use of figures.
And in the same year as Agazzari, Giovanni Gabrieli's German pupil
Gregor Aichinger (1564–1628) published at Dillingen his *Cantiones
ecclesiasticae*, partly composed earlier in Rome in admitted emulation of
Viadana, with an appendix in German explaining the 'Bassus Generalis Et
Continuus'. Thus in a few years a mere convenience for keyboard players
had developed into a widely adopted performing practice which re-
volutionized musical textures and was to remain in use for two centuries.

The extent of the revolution is most strikingly illustrated by comparison
of Giovanni Gabrieli's two settings of 'O Jesu mi dulcissime': in his First
Book of *Sacrae Symphoniae* (1597) and in his Second Book (posthumously
published in 1615).[28] In his First Book Giovanni, like Croce in his *Sacrae
Cantilene Concertate* (also posthumous, 1610),[29] was following splendidly in
his uncle's footsteps. (Like Andrea, he and Croce were first and foremost
composers for state occasions, although Giovanni could also express intense
personal anguish in a smaller work, the six-part 'Timor et tremor'[30] with its
madrigalian symbolism from the literal 'tremor' motive at the beginning to
the descending chromatic line of 'non confundar' at the end.) Already in the
'O magnum mysterium'[31] of the 1587 volume of *Concerti*, he had revealed
his penchant for festive passages in triple time. But although instruments
were freely used they are not clearly differentiated from voices until the
Second Book of *Symphoniae*. Here, in the 'Surrexit Christus' (for three-part
choir, two violini, two cornetti, and four trombones) and 'In ecclesiis' (for

[22] See Max Schneider, *Die Anfänge des Basso continuo und seiner Bezifferung* (Leipzig, 1918), p. 67.
Schneider gives the beginning and end of the *bassone* in facsimile.
[23] *Opere di Lodovico Viadana (Monumenti musicali mantovani)*, Series I, No. 1 (ed. C. Gallico) (Mantua,
1964), and numerous separate reprints.
[24] Printed complete in Peter Wagner, *Geschichte der Messe* (Leipzig, 1913), p. 534.
[25] See Chapter 13, pp. 268ff.
[26] Viadana's *Concerti* and Croce's double-choral compositions with organ partitura seem to have provided
the models for the *Offertoria* and *Communiones* (Venice, 1611) of the Polish composer Mikołaj Zielénski
Opera omnia, i and ii (*Monumenta Musicae in Polonia*, series A), ed. Władysław Malinowski (Cracow, 1966
and 1974).
[27] Facsimile reprint (Milan, 1934) and translation in Oliver Strunk, *Source Readings in Music History*
(London, 1952), p. 424.
[28] *Opera Omnia (CMM* 12), i, p. 167, and iii, p. 30; the openings of both are quoted in *NOHM*, iv, p. 300.
[29] See Arnold, 'Giovanni Croce and the *Concertato* Style', *MQ*, xxxix (1953), p. 37.
[30] Ed. Bank (Amsterdam, 1950) and Noble (Pennsylvania, 1968).
[31] *CMM* 12, i, p. 10.

four soloists, four-part choir, violino, two cornetti, and four trombones),[32] the obbligato parts are not only independent but written in an unmistakably instrumental style while the florid or declamatory vocal solos are contrasted with the generally block-like – but at times harmonically startling – chords of the choir. Obbligato instruments were by this time also being used in much more modest works, such as the *Concerti Ecclesiastici* (Venice, 1608) of the Ferrarese Archangelo Crotti which actually include a 'Sonata sopra Sancta Maria' humbly anticipating the famous one in Monteverdi's Vespers.

MONTEVERDI'S CHURCH MUSIC

Claudio Monteverdi (1567–1643) was already famous as a madrigalist and composer of the operas *Orfeo* and *Arianna* but when he brought out his *Sanctissimae Virgini Missa senis vocibus . . . ac Vesperae* (Venice, 1610) he had published no church music since the juvenile *Cantiunculae Sacrae* of the 'pupil of the eminent Ingegneri' in 1582. He was still in the service of the Mantuan court and did not begin his three decades as *maestro di cappella* of San Marco till three years later. The Mass and Vespers nicely illustrate the stylistic dichotomy of church music which was to last for a very long time and which Monteverdi had already distinguished in the foreword to his Fifth Book of madrigals[33] as *prima* and *seconda pratica*. The Mass is an old-fashioned *a cappella* Mass – for the continuo is disposable – freely modelled on Gombert's motet 'In illo tempore';[34] the Vespers,[35] although 'composto sopra canti fermi', exhibit the most modern idioms of expressive de-clamation, showy coloratura, echo effects of forte and piano, and free use of instruments, but also double-choral passages *a cappella* (opening of the 'Ave maris stella'). The voice-parts of the opening 'Domine ad adjuvandum' are largely composed on to a transposed version of the preludial 'toccata' – a true Shakespearian 'tucket' – of *Orfeo*. The solo vocal coloratura of 'Audi caelum', echoed by an unspecified instrument, and the instrumental ritornelli of 'Ave maris stella' could equally well have originated in the opera. As an appendix to the Vespers, Monteverdi added two versions of what is essentially the same Magnificat, though one is for six voices and organ only, the other for seven voices and a considerable orchestra. So far had music come in the sixteen years since Palestrina's death. Monteverdi's Vespers were of course quite exceptional, yet common Venetian and North Italian practices were better adapted to the expression of human emotion than of transcendental faith. And the year after the Vespers Carlo Borromeo's nephew, the Neapolitan Carlo Gesualdo, Prince of Venosa (*c*.

[32] Ibid., iii, p. 193 and v, p. 32. There are several separate editions of 'In ecclesiis', the best of which is Frederick Hudson's (London, 1963).
[33] See below, p. 267.
[34] *Claudio Monteverdi: Tutte le opere* (ed. G. F. Malipiero) (Asolo, 1926–42), xiv, p. 57; there is a separate edition of Mass and motet together, ed. H. F. Redlich (London, 1963).
[35] *Tutte le opere*, xiv, p. 123. There are a number of 'practical' or 'performing' editions.

1562–1613), published a set of *Responsoria*[36] charged with chromatic emotionalism.

THE END OF THE NETHERLAND TRADITION

Nor was the successful Counter-Reformation beyond the Alps much affected by the spirit of Trent even in non-musical matters; the most firmly Catholic of rulers, the King of Spain and the prince-bishops of the Empire, were very jealous of Papal interference in their domains. The Emperors Ferdinand I and Maximilian II were tolerant and Rudolf II (1576–1612), though a fervent Catholic, was a mentally unstable recluse; their court chapel, stationed mostly at Prague particularly during Rudolf's reign, consisted almost entirely of Netherlanders. Philipp de Monte (1521–1603) was the outstanding character: the last surviving great master of the parody-Mass, composer of more than three hundred motets, and the most prolific madrigalist of his day.[37] With his compatriot colleagues – the already mentioned Kerle, Jacob Regnart (*c.* 1540–1599), Charles Luython (*c.* 1557–1620) – and other composers in Prague, Jacobus Handl, 'Gallus vocatus, Carniolanus' (1550–91) and the remarkable Czech amateur Kryštof Harant z Polžic (1564–1621), together with Giaches de Wert (1535–96) who settled in Italy, he represents the last flowering of the Netherland tradition in church music. Admittedly it was an Italianized flowering, and the pollination is particularly apparent in the Masses based on madrigals, e.g. on Verdelot's 'Ultimi miei sospiri', Rore's 'Ancor che col partire', and de Monte's own 'La dolce vista'[38] – the last a superb quasi-Venetian Mass for two four-part choirs. Another fine eight-part composition, the motet 'Super flumina Babylonis',[39] was in 1583 sent by de Monte to William Byrd whom he must have met thirty years earlier during his visit to England as a member of Philip II's chapel.

THE RELIGIOUS MUSIC OF LASSUS

A yet greater Netherlander, Lassus – much more versatile than de Monte in his church music alone, to say nothing of the secular field, and a much stronger and more complex creative personality – served the dukes of Bavaria from 1556 till his death in 1594. It was Bavaria that provided the Catholic leadership of the Counter-Reformation in Germany, yet as we have seen the young Lassus was capable of composing not only Masses approved by the reforming cardinals but others in flagrant disregard of everything that Trent stood for (see p. 245). While the *Psalmi Davidis penitentiales* were commissioned by Albrecht V, their textual expressiveness of the kind we have already noticed in Rore (p. 233) is so intense that one is tempted to

---

[36] Ed. Glenn E. Watkins, *Gesualdo di Venosa: Sämtliche Werke* (Hamburg, 1966).
[37] The edition of Monte's *Opera Omnia* by J. Van Nuffel *et al.* (Bruges, 1927–39) is incomplete and not very satisfactory. A new edition *Philippi de Monte opera*, ed. René Lenaerts *et al.* is in progress (1975–   ).
[38] *Opera Omnia*, v, viii, and xiv.
[39] Ibid., xv.

hear in them a note of personal anguish. The same note, perhaps struck from
him by Loyola's *Exercises*, is often heard in Lassus's motets – in 'Infelix ego'
and 'Timor et tremor',[40] both from the *Sacrae Cantiones* of 1566, to take
only two examples out of many – in the *Lamentationes* of 1585, and in his
very last composition, the already mentioned *Lagrime di San Pietro*. His
music in general reflects his character, which we know from his letters and
from the diagnosis of his friend, the Court doctor Thomas Mermann, to
have been manic-depressive; and comparable extremes are apparent even in
the vocabulary of his church music. He employs every technical device from
the archaism of fauxbourdon, as at 'descendit de coelis' in the Credo of the
Mass on Sandrin's 'Douce mémoire',[41] to the boldest harmonic progressions. He uses Josquin's paired imitation, as at the beginning of
'Exspectans exspectavi',[42] and achieves Josquin's pellucid serenity. He
employs Venetian double and triple choral effects.[43] (He was clearly
influenced by Andrea Gabrieli and influenced him in turn, as he did
Giovanni who served under him in the Munich choir from *c*. 1575 to 1579.)
Above all, he delights in madrigalian pictography and symbolism – to some
extent in the Masses, but very much more in the motets where they are
innumerable and infinitely varied. He juxtaposes dramatically contrasted
chords, as in 'Concupiscendo concupiscit':[44]

Ex. 72

and opens 'Non des mulieri potestatem'[45] with coloratura curiously instrumental in character. And as we shall see in the next chapter, his secular music was at least equally various.

VERNACULAR PSALM SETTINGS

Lassus's church music was extremely well known in France where his works were published from 1564 onward by Le Roy and Ballard. But religious music was composed in France largely by Huguenots and therefore limited to little other than psalms. Goudimel seems to have composed no more Latin church music after he embraced Protestantism *c.* 1560. Of the Latin church music of Jacques Mauduit (1557–1627), a Catholic, little survives except the end of his Requiem for Ronsard (1586),[46] an early and probably uncharacteristic work in the peculiar style of *musique mesurée à l'antique* which will be discussed in the next chapter (p. 284); we know that he employed instruments in his annual Holy Week concerts at the Abbaye Saint-Antoine and the St. Cecilia celebrations in Notre Dame. Another Requiem Mass[47] which enjoyed considerable popularity was that by Eustache Du Caurroy (1549–1609), a member of the Royal Chapel, whose motets for double choir are supposed to have introduced the 'Venetian' style in France.

Yet it was the vernacular psalms, whether for private or public devotion, which more faithfully reflected the mood of France during the years of the religious wars. Although Calvinist in origin, they were sung and fresh settings were composed by Catholics and Lutherans as well. The Marot-Bèze Psalter was set by Mauduit as well as by Claude Le Jeune (*c.* 1530–1600) and Pascal de L'Estocart (b. *c.* 1540); Le Jeune and Mauduit also published psalms (posthumously 1606, and 1623) in *musique mesurée* and Le Jeune furthermore composed elaborate motet settings, notably the *Dodecacorde contenant douze pseaumes de David* (La Rochelle, 1598),[48] each in one of Glareanus's twelve modes. Nor were they confined to France. Lobwasser's German translation of Marot-Bèze, with Goudimel's music adapted, was sung by Lutherans for nearly three centuries after its appearance in 1573 and there were less successful Lutheran and Catholic translations, some with fresh music. The treatment was as diverse as the

---

[40] *Orlando di Lasso: Sämmtliche Werke*, ed. F. X. Haberl and A. Sandberger (Leipzig, 1894–1927), xiii, p. 95, and xix, p. 6. The odd-numbered volumes of this incomplete edition contain the 516 motets which the composer's sons collected in rather unsatisfactory versions as his *Magnum Opus Musicum* (Munich, 1604); the even-numbered volumes consist of secular works. In 1956 Wolfgang Boetticher began the edition of a *Neue Reihe* of the complete works (Kassel and Basel).
[41] *Neue Reihe*, iv, p. 3.
[42] *Sämmtliche Werke*, iii, p. 72.
[43] Examples in ibid., xxi.
[44] Ibid., xvii, p. 145.
[45] Ibid., xv, p. 139.
[46] Ed. Julien Tiersot in *SIMG*, iv (1902), pp. 137 ff., after Mersenne's *Harmonie universelle* (1636).
[47] Ed. E. Martin and J. Burald (Paris, 1951).
[48] Ed. Henry Expert, *Les Maîtres musiciens de la Renaissance française*, xi, and Le Jeune's *Pseaumes en vers mesurez*, ibid., xx–xxii.

geographical distribution, from the simple four-part settings of the complete Psalter in Polish by Mikołaj Gomółka (Cracow, 1580),[49] employing tunes drawn from plainsong, Protestant song, and the popular music of Eastern Europe generally, to the astonishing collection of settings of Marot-Bèze published by the Dutch master Jan Pieterszoon Sweelinck (1562–1621) in four books (Amsterdam, 1604, 1613, 1614, and Haarlem, 1621).[50] Sweelinck set the Geneva tunes in styles which range from those of the motet and madrigal to the onomatopoeic French chanson; it is indeed strange that he ignored both words and tunes of his native *Souterliedekens*.[51]

LUTHERAN *GEISTLICHE LIEDER*

In the Lutheran lands the 'spiritual song' was cultivated with the same variety of treatment, often by the same composer. For instance the *Geistliche und Weltliche teutsche Geseng* (Wittenberg, 1566) of Johann Walter's successor as Dresden Court *Kapellmeister*, the Liègois Mattheus Le Maistre (*c*. 1505–1577), include both simple settings with the hymn-melody in the highest part[52] and elaborate canonic ones in the Netherland tradition.[53] In a second collection (1577) Le Maistre keeps generally to a simpler polyphonic style, while the enormously influential *Fünffzig Geistliche Lieder und Psalmen* (Nuremberg, 1586) of Lucas Osiander (1534–1604) were specifically 'set so that an entire Christian congregation can join in the singing throughout (*durchaus mitsingen*)', in four-part block harmony with the melody in the highest part and firmly marked tonal (V–I) cadences on what may surely be called 'dominant' and 'tonic':

Ex. 73

Ein fe - ste Burg ist un - ser Gott, Ein gu - te Wehr und Waf - - fen.

At the same time Lutheran music began to be exposed to foreign influences. While such German Catholics as Blasius Amon (*c*. 1560–90) and Gregor Aichinger (1564–1628) studied in Venice, came under the influence

[49] Ed. Mirosław Perz *et al.*, *Wydawnictwo dawnej muzyki polskiej*, xlvii–xlix (Cracow, 1963–6).
[50] Ed. Max Seiffert, *Werken van J. P. Sweelinck*, ii–v (Leipzig, 1897–8).
[51] See p. 220.
[52] Cf. 'Aus tiefer Not' in Schering, *Geschichte der Musik in Beispielen* (Leipzig, 1931), No. 123.
[53] Cf. 'Mensch, wiltu leben seliglich' and 'Christe der du bist Tag und Licht', ed. Helmuth Osthoff, *ChW*, xxx, pp. 7 and 10.

of Lassus, and introduced *cori spezzati* and the basso continuo in their native land, it was the contact of the same musical influences with Lutheran thought and the poetry and music of Lutheran song which proved more fruitful. In his *Sacrae cantiones* of 1573 Joachim a Burck (1546–1610) had employed chromaticism and the other devices of *musica reservata* to underline the sense of the Biblical texts, but when he began to set the very personal religious verse of Ludwig Helmbold – Latin odes and German *Liedlein* – the relationship between text and music became much closer, even madrigalian, and he himself claimed he had provided the *40 deutsche christl. Liedlein* of 1599 with 'suavibus harmoniis ad imitationem italicarum Villanescarum'. Another composer, friend of Burck and singer in the Munich choir under Lassus, who set Helmbold's poems on similar lines was Johann Eccard (1553–1611). He published *geistliche Lieder* in 1578 and 1589, though the finest of them, the *Preussische Festlieder*, appeared more than thirty years after his death. Yet after all, these original compositions had less historical importance than his *Geystliche Lieder, auff den Choral* (Königsberg, 1597),[54] the familiar melody in the highest part while the four lower ones move in ornamented harmony rather than true polyphony. Another Lassus pupil at Munich, Leonhard Lechner (*c*. 1553–1606), later a convert to Protestantism, began his career with Latin church music in his master's style, composed a great tri-choral, 24-part epithalamium, 'Quid chaos' (1582) in the Venetian manner, and bade farewell to life in an extraordinary set of fifteen *Sprüche von Leben und Tod* – the dramatic power and profound emotion of which, however, he had already anticipated in 'O Tod, du bist ein bittre Gallen', one of his *Newe teutsche Lieder* (Nuremberg, 1582).[55]

GERMAN PASSION MUSIC

Burck and Lechner also made significant contributions to German Passion music. Luther's musical adviser, Johann Walter (see p. 220) had composed 'dramatic' Passions after both St. Matthew and St. John[56] which exist in various forms, the earliest dating from 1545. Another Dresden Court musician, the Italian Lutheran convert Antonio Scandello (1517–80), had composed a John Passion in 1561. But Burck's *Deutsche Passion* was the earliest German motet-Passion and it had the distinction of getting into print, in 1568, before either of Walter's. It is to some extent modelled on the supposed 'Obrecht' Passion, which he mentions in his preface, though his text is entirely from St. John and he goes on to point out that he has been 'diligent so to set the words under the notes that almost every syllable has its

[54] Part I, ed. F. von Baussnern (Wolfenbüttel, 1928).
[55] The *Sprüche* have been ed. W. Lipphardt (Kassel, fourth ed., 1956), the 1582 *Lieder* by E. F. Schmid (Augsburg, 1926). A complete edition of Lechner is being ed. Konrad Ameln (Kassel, 1954).
[56] On the difference between 'dramatic' and 'motet' Passions, see p. 219. Walter's Passions have been ed. Werner Braun, *Johann Walter: Sämtliche Werke*, iv; their ascription to him is slightly dubious.

note, and the four voices sing the words at the same time so that the listeners may hear the words clearly'. However he does admit 'madrigalisms' such as the agonized chromatic harmonies in which the Evangelist tells of the crown of thorns. There are similar touches of word-painting in Lechner's *Das Leiden unsers Herren Jesu Christi* (Nuremberg, 1594),[57] a 'motet' setting of an early Lutheran 'Gospel-harmony' by Johann Bugenhagen; but this is an altogether finer work, based on the traditional 'Passion tone' from which Lechner sometimes spins most lovely and moving polyphony:

Ex. 74

VENETIAN INFLUENCE AND THE LUTHERAN HYMN-MOTET

Some of the rather younger Lutheran composers – Hieronymus Praetorius (1560–1629), Hans Leo Hassler (1564–1612), Christoph Demantius (1567–1643), and Michael Praetorius (*c.* 1571–1621) (unrelated to Hieronymus) – came under Venetian as well as Lassus's influence, although only one of them, Hassler, is known to have visited Venice (1585) and studied with Andrea Gabrieli. Hassler, a Protestant, was long in the service of the banking family of Fugger of Augsburg, who were strict Catholics, and was later – with his brothers Kaspar and Jakob, both notable musicians – ennobled by the Emperor Rudolf II. Consequently while his secular music (see the next chapter) was set to German words his church music consists mainly of Latin motets and Masses. Some of it – e.g. 'Ad Dominum, cum

---

[57] Ed. Ameln (Kassel and Basel, fourth ed., 1949).

tribularer'[58] from the *Sacri concentus* of 1601, with the five successive rising semitones of the opening phrase in each voice successively and the five falling ones at 'et a lingua dolosa' – remarkably 'modern'. Latin motets, particularly the shorter and simpler ones by Lassus and Gallus (Handl), were much used by the Lutheran church. Yet it was only toward the end of his life – in the *Psalmen und christliche Gesäng . . . auff die Melodeyen fugweiss componiert* (Nuremberg, 1607) and the *Kirchengesäng, Psalmen und geistliche Lieder, auff die gemeinen Melodeyen simpliciter gesetzt* (1608),[59] which paved the way to his connection with the Protestant court of Dresden – that Hassler turned to the Lutheran hymn. The 'simpliciter' collection is simple indeed – four parts, the highest carrying the melody – but the 'fugue-wise' ones treat the successive phrases of the hymn in motet style on lines that were to be followed throughout the seventeenth century and beyond. But in this field of the Lutheran hymn-motet Hassler was far surpassed in bulk and variety, if not in artistic achievement, by Michael Praetorius.

Almost the whole of Praetorius's enormous output[60] consists of compositions of the most diverse types, from the simplest to the most elaborate, on Lutheran hymns (and secondarily on the Latin portions of the Lutheran liturgy). The nine parts of his *Musae Sioniae*, published in various centres between 1605 and 1610 when he was in the service of the Brunswick court at Wolfenbüttel, are in themselves an astonishing monument of skill and industry. Parts I–IV consist of double-choral pieces for eight, but sometimes twelve, voices; with Part V he began a systematization according to category, with motet-settings of *Festlieder*, and went on to produce three volumes – 746 pieces to 458 different texts – of straightforward four-part settings for congregational use plus a few organ 'variations' in VII; in IX he again set the hymns of I–IV but for two or three voices – and even contemplated doing them yet again 'motet-wise in the style of Lassus', 'madrigal-wise in the style of Marenzio', and *per choros* in the style of Victoria. Next he turned his attention to the Latin pieces and finally, after a short period (1613–16) at the Dresden court with its greater resources, produced a group of publications of which the most important is the *Polyhymnia Caduceatrix et Panegyrica* (1619). In this he took as models all the most up-to-date Italian works with which he boasts his acquaintance: Monteverdi's Vespers, Giovanni Gabrieli's Second Book of *Sacrae Symphoniae*, the works of Viadana and Agazzari. At the same time he embarked on a great literary work, *Syntagma musicum*, in three volumes: I, historical, published at Wittenberg in 1615; II, 'concerning instruments', 1618 (with a supplementary volume of illustrations, *Theatrum Instrumentorum*, in 1620); and III, 1619, in which, as in the preface to *Polyhymnia*, he gives the most copious information as to the heterogeneous

---

[58] Ed. Blume, *ChW*, xiv, p. 21. The complete *Concentus* are ed. Joseph Auer, *DDT*, xxiv–xxv (Leipzig, 1906).
[59] The 1607 collection is ed. C. Russell Crosby in *Hassler: Sämtliche Werke*, vii (Wiesbaden, 1965), that of 1608 has been ed. Ralf von Saalfeld (Kassel, 1927) who has also edited selections from the 'fugue-wise' collection.
[60] *Gesamtausgabe* in 21 vols., ed. Blume *et al.* (Wolfenbüttel, 1928–60), and numerous separate editions.

ways in which these great Italian-mannered but profoundly German compositions may be performed – with or without continuo, with contrasting groups of instruments, voices soli or ripieni, and so on.[61]

RELIGIOUS MUSIC IN ENGLAND

The religious situation in Britain throughout this period was peculiar and, particularly in England, complicated. While in Scotland Calvinism was soon officially triumphant, in England it was on the whole successfully opposed by the compromise of Elizabethan Anglicanism upheld by the monarch and most of the Archbishops of Canterbury. Only during the regime of Edmund Grindal did the Puritan reformers stand any chance of success, but Grindal was quickly suspended and his successors, Whitgift and then Bancroft were intolerant of them. And all the time there was a powerful Catholic minority which included the greatest English composer of the age, William Byrd (1543–1623), and possibly also his pupil Thomas Morley (1557–1602) though the latter's politico-religious activities were mysterious and ambiguous.[62] Another notable Catholic, Peter Philips (*c.* 1560–1628), left England as a young man. Nevertheless the dividing line between the musicians who composed both Latin and English church music and those who composed only English music must be drawn not between Catholics and Protestants but between generations. Byrd and his master Tallis (see p. 242), Morley and William Mundy (*c.* 1529–*c.* 1591) composed both; the church music of William's son John (*c.* 1552–1630) is overwhelmingly English; and that of Byrd's pupil Thomas Tomkins (1572–1656), Thomas Weelkes (*c.* 1575–1623), and Orlando Gibbons (1583–1625) is entirely so.

The earliest essays in English service-music were on similar lines to early Lutheran ones: truncation of the Mass, and drastic simplification of plainsong as in the Cranmerian *Booke of Common praier noted* (1550) of John Marbeck (*c.* 1510–85).[63] The Anglican 'Service' as set by Tallis, Byrd, and the elder Mundy consists of Morning Prayers with responses, litany, 'Te Deum' and 'Benedictus', Kyrie and Creed for the Communion, and the Evening canticles 'Magnificat' and 'Nunc dimittis', or some portion of these (e.g. Byrd's second and third Services consist only of the evening canticles). Yet the demand 'for every syllable a note' was felt as a constraint and only when Byrd for some reason was able to resist it, in his Great Service,[64] does he rise to the heights of the four- and five-part Masses evidently intended for some great Catholic household,[65] and the finest of his motets, in which

---

[61] The *Syntagma musicum* has been ed. W. Gurlitt, *Documenta musicologica*, i (Kassel, 1958).
[62] See David Brown, 'Thomas Morley and the Catholics: Some Speculations', and Thurston Dart, 'Morley and the Catholics: Some Further Speculations', *Monthly Musical Record*, lxxxix (1959), pp. 53 and 89 respectively.
[63] See Robert Stevenson, 'John Marbeck's "Noted Booke" of 1550', *MQ*, xxxvii (1951), p. 220.
[64] *TCM*, ii, p. 190, and *The Collected Works of William Byrd*, ed. E. H. Fellowes (revised ed. by Thurston Dart *et al.*, London, 1962–75).
[65] *TCM*, ix, pp. 17 and 36, and *Collected Works*, i, pp. 30 and 68.

he reveals his mastery of freely imitative polyphony. However his second Service[66] is marked by a peculiarly English innovation: the introduction of

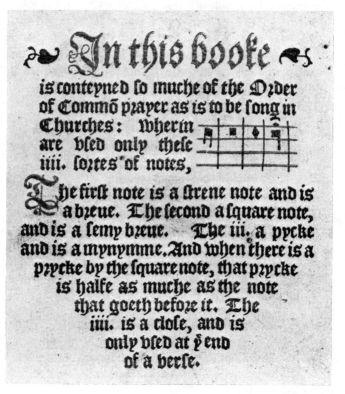

Pl. 40　The title-page of Marbeck's *The Booke of Common Praier noted* (1550)

passages for solo voice and organ, which plays not a continuo role but polyphony to which the voice doubles a part or supplies an otherwise missing one:

Ex. 75

Lord, now let-test Thou thy ser - vant de-part in peace,

Organ (Tenbury 791)

[66] *TCM*, ii, p. 99, and *Collected Works*, x, p. 108.

Byrd employs the same device in some of his anthems, a type later known as 'verse anthems'. But never in these and only exceptionally in his 'full anthems' (English motets) does he display the expressive power of his Latin motets. For Byrd's finest expression of religious emotion to English words we must turn to his *Psalmes, Sonets and songs of Sadnes and pietie* (1588), his *Songs of sundrie natures* (1589), and his *Psalmes, Songs and Sonnets* (1611), which include equivalents of the *geistlicher Gesang* and *madrigale spirituale* though often conceived with instrumental parts; for his greatest church music to his two hundred or so motets. The earliest of these were collected in a volume of *Cantiones* which he published in 1575 jointly with Tallis, thus marking Elizabeth I's grant to them of a twenty-one year monopoly of music printing;[67] others followed in two sets of *Cantiones sacrae* (1589 and 1591) and two of *Gradualia* (1605 and 1607),[68] a corpus of work almost as varied in technique and sometimes as 'madrigalian' in word-painting as that of Lassus – some of which Byrd may well have known – or of Alfonso Ferrabosco the elder (1543–88) who was his friend and colleague in the Queen's service for sixteen years and wrote not only 'madrigalian' motets but simple Latin hymn-settings[69] in a style very similar to Byrd's.

With Morley's dozen Latin works,[70] probably early and almost all intensely penitential, the motet in England came to a not undistinguished end. The motet was replaced by the two forms of anthem, the Mass by the Service. But the Service soon became less important, musically, than the anthem. Despite some fine passages in the Services of Tomkins and Weelkes, and the two specimens by Gibbons, it is their anthems – and some of those by their lesser contemporaries – which are the finest flowers of Anglican church music in this, its greatest, period.[71] Full anthems like Tomkins's 'When David heard', Weelkes's 'Gloria in excelsis: Sing, my soul' and 'Hosanna to the Son of David', Gibbons's setting of the latter text and his 'O clap your hands' are masterpieces of free and flexible polyphony. But the full anthem was gradually making way for the verse anthem, of which Gibbons was the outstanding master. His finest things in this form date from his later years – 'Behold thou has made my days' can be dated 1618 and 'Glorious and powerful God' was probably nearly contemporary – and the great 'O Lord, let me know mine end' of the long-lived though generally conservative Tomkins may be later still. Gibbons's verse anthems generally have accompaniments for viols as well as organ, while Tomkins's organ accompaniments are full and sometimes marked by florid ornament in strong contrast to the frequently sketchy organ parts of the previous generation.

---

[67] Tallis's contribution, which includes such masterpieces as 'O sacrum convivium', is published in *TCM*, vi, pp. 180 ff., Byrd's in *The Byrd Edition*, i, ed. Craig Moreon (London, 1977).
[68] *Collected Works*, ii–iii and iv–vii respectively; the two sets of *Gradualia* also in *TCM*, vii.
[69] See the quotations in *NOHM*, iv, pp. 491–5.
[70] Ed. Thurston Dart and H. K. Andrews (London, 1959).
[71] Most of Tomkins's church music was published very belatedly in *Musica Deo Sacra* (1668), of which there is a modern edition by Bernard Rose, *EECM*, v, ix, and xiv. Weelkes's collected anthems have been ed. David Brown, Walter Collins, and Peter Le Huray, *MB*, xxiii (London, 1966). Gibbons's church music is in *TCM*, iv and the verse anthems are also ed. David Wulstan, *EECM*, iii (London, 1963).

13

Secular Song and Instrumental Music
(c. 1560–c. 1610)

So long as religious music and sophisticated secular music shared the common techniques of imitative polyphony they naturally preserved a relationship the closeness of which is demonstrated by the numerous paraphrase Masses based on madrigals or chansons. But as new technical means evolved through the emergence of the keyboard and other instrumental idioms, the continual striving for closer relationship with texts (particularly the various vernacular texts), and the novel conceptions of space and contrast, so the role of imitative polyphony became less important – particularly in secular music. Even in church music its purest type reached ultimate perfection in the work of Palestrina and Victoria, and thereafter became the idiom of epigones. It was an exhausted technique and its exhaustion quickly weakened the relationship of religious and secular.

NETHERLAND COMPOSERS OF MADRIGAL AND CHANSON

The last great ambidexterous polyphonist was Lassus. Whereas Palestrina is almost negligible as a composer of secular music, Lassus was equally at home in the Italian madrigal and the more popular and homophonic villanella (successor of the frottola), the French chanson and German song, to say nothing of the secular Latin motet. His German compositions are the least numerous: less than a hundred (of which half are *geistliche Lieder*) as against nearly 140 chansons and about 180 madrigals and villanelle. Like the chansons they are permeated with the stylistic influence of the Italian forms and show delight in the bawdy, the roistering, and the comic, but unlike the chansons they lack poetry, elegance, and lightness. The chansons, mostly published between 1564 and 1576, vary in style from the mostly note-against-note of 'Margot labourez' and the setting of Ronsard's 'Bon jour, mon coeur' to the graceful polyphony of 'Le rossignol',[1] from three such different scherzi as 'Fuyons tous d'amour', 'Quand mon mary', and 'Sauter, danser' to the grave du Bellay settings 'O foible esprit', a pure madrigal, and 'La nuict froide et sombre'.[2] Lassus was no less versatile in his Italian pieces: such classic madrigals as his early Petrarch settings – 'Occhi

---

[1] All three transcribed by Peter Philips in the 'Fitzwilliam Virginal Book' (see p. 292).
[2] Lassus's secular songs are in the even-numbered volumes of the *Sämmtliche Werke*: Italian, ii–x, French, xii–xvi, German, xviii–xx. There are innumerable separate reprints.

piangete', 'Amor che ved' ogni pensier' – and the profoundly melancholy *Lagrime di San Pietro* of his last years, mentioned in the previous chapter (p. 246), and the delicious humour of the *Villanelle, Moresche et altre canzoni* (Paris, 1581) which include his best-known songs: the *Landsknecht*'s serenade in Germanic Italian, 'Matonna mia cara', and 'O la, o che bon eccho!' in which two quartets sing in close canon throughout.

With Lassus the last notable Netherland madrigalists – Sweelinck's four isolated examples hardly make him 'notable' – were de Monte, his pupil 'Giovanni' de Macque (1551–1614), and Giaches de Wert. De Monte published some Ronsard sonnet-settings in 1575, including a beautiful 'Le premier iour du moy de may', and a few other chansons,[3] but nothing German despite his long residence at the Imperial court in Vienna and Prague. But his output of madrigals between 1554 and 1603 – more than a thousand secular ones alone – is so overwhelming in bulk and seemingly so equable in accomplishment that even anthologists have generally recoiled from it although Alfred Einstein has published de Monte's greatest success in his own day, 'Verament' in amore' in his Fifth Book *a cinque voci* (Venice, 1574).[4] De Monte was a quiet, pious man who excelled in the *madrigale spirituale* which he also produced in great quantity, a celibate who never forgot he was an ecclesiastic; Wert's temperament was very different. He also had the advantage of employment at a much livelier court – that of Mantua where Tasso became his friend, with that of Ferrara and the celebrated three lady singers who ornamented it from *c.* 1580 onward near at hand. He became the lover of one of the ladies, Tarquinia Molza, and in his Eighth Book of five-part madrigals (Venice, 1586)[5] he published two examples of what have been described as forerunners of the *concerto da camera*, 'Vezzosi augelli' and 'Non è si denso velo'. In these pieces the three higher parts are clearly distinguished from the two lower and given showy coloratura. Declamation, not coloratura, distinguishes the three upper parts in 'O Primavera', the second of a set of pieces on Guarini's *Pastor fido* in his Eleventh Book.[6] It was perhaps the influence of the three ladies that brought about a re-casting of five-part writing: two sopranos, alto, tenor, and bass supplanting soprano, alto, two tenors, and bass.

THE ITALIAN MADRIGALISTS

Similar parts for the *tre nobilissime giovani Dame* (or a similar group at Mantua) were composed by a younger musician at the Mantuan court, Claudio Monteverdi, whose *Terzo Libro de Madrigali* (1592)[7] includes a number of such pieces exploiting their various skills. Alessando Striggio sent them his compositions from Florence where their master, the Duke of

---

[3] In *Opera Omnia*, ed. J. Van Nuffel *et al.* (Bruges, 1927–39), xx. The madrigals have been only partially published in this edition.
[4] In *The Golden Age of the Madrigal* (New York, 1942); it is also in *Opera Omnia*, xxv, p. 66.
[5] Ed. Carol MacClintock, *Giaches Wert: Opera Omnia* (CMM 24), viii.
[6] Ibid., xii, p. 3.
[7] *Tutte le opere di Claudio Monteverdi*, ed. G. F. Malipiero (Vienna, 1926–42), iii.

Ferrara, also allowed them to participate in masques. And the final tribute was paid them by the Ferrarese organist Luzzasco Luzzaschi (1545?–1607), a pupil of Rore, in his *Madrigali . . . per cantare et sonare a uno, e doi, e tre soprani* (Rome, 1601)[8] in which the lower parts of the madrigal were played on a harpsichord. More precisely: all four polyphonic parts were played, and the highest part or parts doubled, with elaborate coloratura of the type suggested by Bassano (see p. 248) and others, by the voice or voices. Perhaps the duets were those sung by one of the *giovani Dame* and her sister, accompanied by the composer at the gravicembalo, when the future Emperor Rudolf II passed through Brescello in 1571.

Even in his conventional madrigals – for instance, the Dante setting 'Quivi sospiri, pianti ed alti guai'[9] in his Second Book (Venice, 1576) and 'Dolorosi martir'[10] in his Fourth (Ferrara, 1594) – Luzzaschi indulged in that exaggerated, even agonized, expressiveness which it is so tempting to relate to 'mannerism' in painting. Mannerism had appeared in the madrigal at least twenty years earlier, with Rore (see p. 233), and still more with Wert who, like Luzzaschi, had studied with Rore. Wert's setting of 'Crudele acerba'[11] (pub. 1588) challenges comparison with his master's of thirty years before,[12] beginning less bitterly but with great chromatic intensification at 'Ma di menar tutta mia vita in pianto'. Another of his Petrarch settings, 'Solo e pensoso' (pub. 1581),[13] is decidedly more manneristic than Marenzio's famous one.[14]

Luca Marenzio (1553–99) has been justly hailed as 'the Schubert of the madrigal'.[15] Einstein[16] has traced in his work the conservative influences of Ingegneri, a melodious master of Palestrinian polyphony, and Andrea Gabrieli, who excelled in the lighter types of madrigal and villanella, the Venetian *gregesche* and *giustiniane*.[17] Unlike the Mantuan and Ferrarese madrigalists, Marenzio composed mainly for the pleasure of the performers themselves, not for courtly audiences listening to brilliant executants, though he did make some essays in the three-upper-part style associated with the Ferrarese ladies, notably the exquisite 'Hor chi Clori' in his Sixth five-part book (1594),[18] and he must have reckoned on good performers to

[8] Trio example in Einstein, *The Italian Madrigal*, iii, No. 92; duet example in Johannes Wolf, *Sing- und Spielmusik* (*Music of Earlier Times*) (New York, 1946), No. 48; solo example in Schering, *Musikgeschichte in Beispielen* (Leipzig, 1931), No. 166; numerous excepts in Otto Kinkeldey, 'Luzzasco Luzzaschi's Solo-Madrigale mit Klavierbegleitung', *SIMG*, ix (1907–8), p. 538, and two complete solo examples and one duet in his *Orgel und Klavier in der Musik des 16. Jahrhunderts* (Leipzig, 1910), pp. 286, 289, and 292.
[9] Ed. Einstein, *Golden Age*, p. 53.
[10] Ed. Einstein, *The Italian Madrigal*, iii, No. 81.
[11] *CMM* 24, ix, p. 38, and Einstein, *The Italian Madrigal*, iii, No. 65.
[12] Einstein, ibid., No. 48.
[13] *CMM* 24, vii, p. 32.
[14] Schering, op. cit., No. 165.
[15] Denis Arnold, *Marenzio* (London, 1965), p. i.   [16] *Italian Madrigal*, ii, p. 615.
[17] See the examples in ibid., iii, Nos. 60–64, and *Marenzio: Ten Madrigals*, ed. Denis Arnold (London, 1966).
[18] Einstein edited the first six books of five-part madrigals in *Publikationen älterer Musik*, iv and vi (Leipzig, 1929 and 1931) and 'Hor chi Clori' is in vi, p. 121. This edition of 'complete works' progressed no further but another complete edition of the madrigals has been begun, with the *Settimo libro de madrigali a cinque*, by John Steele (New York, 1975).

tackle the chromaticisms of 'O voi che sospirate' (Book II, 1581).[19] But his style was essentially diatonic, melodically and rhythmically inventive, exploiting all the sensuous charm of passages in thirds and tenths (for instance in 'Scaldava il sol' (Book III, 1582)[20] or in 'Vezzosi augelli' in Book I of four-part madrigals, 1587), and the all-pervading pictorial touches are seldom exaggerated. Marenzio's First Book appeared in 1580. Containing such things as 'Liquidi perle', 'Tirsi morir volea', and 'Dolorosi martir', it is no wonder that by 1588 it had been reprinted four times and that in the same year five of the madrigals – with 'Io partirò' from the Second Book – were published in London with English words. In later years the shadow of the Counter-Reformation overcast his work with a new seriousness which found its most impressive expression in the Sixth Book of six-part madrigals (1595) with 'Se quel dolor' and the Ninth Book of five-part madrigals (1599) with 'Solo e pensoso'.

The madrigals of Marenzio's younger contemporaries, Gesualdo, Prince of Venosa, and Claudio Monteverdi, take very different directions. Gesualdo,[21] after publishing four books of not particularly individual madrigals in the Rore-Wert tradition (1594–6), brought out two more in 1611 in which chromatic alteration simultaneously in several parts produces the most extraordinary effects of dislocation (often alternating with very commonplace diatonic passages). Monteverdi, an Ingegneri pupil like Marenzio, began by publishing three books of more or less conventional madrigals (1587–92),[22] though they include such a masterpiece of tone-painting as 'Ecco mormorar l'onde' in Book II and a striking increase in monotone declamation, particularly in three more Tasso settings (from *Gerusalemme liberata*), in Book III. He went on in Book IV (1603) to introduce free declamation on whole chords ('Sfogava con le stelle') and to heighten his norm of unconventional dissonance, thus provoking a famous attack by the conservative theorist Giovanni Artusi.[23] In his Fifth Book (1605) he introduced the continuo and – also in the three-part *Scherzi musicali* (1607) – instrumental sinfonie and ritornelli. Gesualdo's later madrigals, however fascinating their scent of decadence, are an evolutionary dead end; Monteverdi was taking part in the transformation of the madrigal into something quite different, though in view of his dramatic and pictorial ability it is strange that he neglected to produce one of those suites of madrigals popular at the time (*comedie armoniche*) realistically describing women gossiping at the wash (Striggio's *Cicalamento delle donne al bucato*, 1567), Venetian scenes (Croce's *Triaca musicale*, 1596), or a complete *commedia dell'arte* (the *Amfiparnaso*, 1597, of Orazio Vecchi (1550–1605),

[19] Ibid., iv, p. 89.
[20] Ibid., iv, p. 126.
[21] *Sämtliche Werke*, ed. Wilhelm Weismann and Glenn Watkins (Hamburg, 1957–63); the madrigals are in i–vi. There are numerous separate editions .
[22] *Tutte le opere*, i–iii.
[23] Artusi's *Della imperfettioni della musica moderna* (Venice, 1600) must have been based on manuscript copies. His 'second discourse' is translated in Oliver Strunk, *Source Readings in Music History* (London, 1952), p. 393, with Monteverdi's reply in the preface to his *Quinto libro* and his brother's *dicharazione* appended to the *Scherzi musicali* of 1607.

the outstanding masterpiece of this genre[24]), and a whole series of works by Banchieri.

THE REVIVAL OF MONODY

Already about 1580, when Marenzio was bringing out his earliest madrigals, secular vocal music had entered a period of crisis. The conception of *musica reservata* (see p. 175) might suffice for the relationship of music and words in church, where Zarlino's rules for verbal expression and underlaying words to music (in his *Istituzioni armoniche*, Venice, 1558)[25] were still valid. But in the madrigal it had led to heightened tone-painting of individual words and phrases, a practice which Zarlino's own pupil, the Florentine lutenist and singer Vincenzo Galilei (*c.* 1520–1591), father of the astronomer, ridiculed in his *Dialogo della musica antica e della moderna* (Venice, 1581).[26] Influenced by a learned correspondent, Girolamo Mei, a philologist and student of ancient Greek music and drama who rightly believed Greek music to have been monodic (but seemingly supplied Galilei with thirteenth-century Byzantine melodies to Mesomedes' hymns under the impression that they were ancient),[27] Galilei argued that the polyphonic 'music of today is not of great value for expressing the passions of the mind by means of words, but is of value merely for the wind and stringed instruments, from which the ear ... desires nothing but the sweet enjoyment of the variety of their harmonies ...'. Vocal music should be monodic, as simple as such popular tunes as the 'Romanesca' (see p. 237) or those of laudi and villanelle, with an accompaniment too simple to distract the listener. Galilei's own monodies with accompaniments by a consort of viols are lost. But such songs were no novelties even at court entertainments in Florence and we have the melody and bass of a song[28] composed by Piero Strozzi and sung by Giulio Caccini (*c.* 1550–1610) in a masque for the wedding of Francesco I[29] two years before the publication of Galilei's *Dialogo*, in which Strozzi was supposed to be one of the interlocutors. All three – Strozzi, Caccini, and Galilei – belonged to the *camerata* or salon of Count Giovanni de' Bardi, the deviser of the masque, a wealthy amateur who (*c.* 1580) addressed to Caccini a *Discorso . . . sopra la musica antica e'l cantar bene*[30] making points like those of the *Dialogo*.

THE FLORENTINE INTERMEDII

When the next Grand Duke, Ferdinando I, was married in 1589, the music for the dramatic *intermedii* (again devised by Bardi) was composed by a

---

[24] Ed. Cecil Adkins (Chapel Hill, N.C., 1977).
[25] Translated in Strunk, op. cit., pp. 255–61.
[26] Trans., ibid., pp. 315–7.
[27] See *NOHM*, i, pp. 372–3.
[28] Opening quoted in *NOHM*, iv, p. 149.
[29] The wedding music also included madrigals by Alessandro Striggio and Claudio Merulo.
[30] Trans. Strunk, op. cit., p. 290.

number of musicians including Cristoforo Malvezzi (1547–97), Marenzio, Caccini, Bardi himself, Emilio de Cavalieri (*c.* 1550–1602), and Malvezzi's pupil, Jacopo Peri (1561–1633). Ottavio Rinuccini, who had written verses for the ladies of Ferrara, was one of the poets. The music[31] consists largely of madrigals, though there is a good deal of purely chordal writing; the solos by Caccini, Cavalieri, and Peri have a great deal of coloratura, as in this 'Ecco con due risposte' by Peri in the fifth intermedio:

Ex. 76

The composer sang the principal part himself and the accompaniment was played on a chitarrone. But the accompanying instruments are constantly varied, and the groups which play introductory *sinfonie* to the intermedii or double the voices in the madrigals are impressive: Malvezzi's madrigal 'Noi

[31] Edited by D. P. Walker, *Les Fêtes du mariage de Ferdinand de Médicis et de Christine de Lorraine* (Paris, 1963).

che cantando' in the first intermedio is sung by two choirs, the first doubled by lyre, harp, large lute, and 'sotto Basso di Viola', the second by lyre, harp, chitarrone, and 'Basso di Viola', while in the six-part sinfonia which follows these instruments are joined by 6 lutes (three large and three small), psaltery, 'Basso di Viola' with three tenor viols, 4 trombones, cornetto, flauto traverso, *cetera* (cittern), mandola, and a 'Sopranino di Viola' (which was played by Striggio).[32]

Pl. 41   Bernardo Buontalenti's design for 'La gara fra Muse e Pieridi', the second of the *intermedii* performed in Florence in 1589 at the wedding of Ferdinando I and Cristina of Lorraine. Apollo, surrounded by hamadryads, is seated on Parnassus to judge the musical contest between the Muses and the daughters of Pierus.

These intermedii with their mixture of styles and resources, differing from earlier sixteenth-century dramatic or festive ones only in their lavishness, were not yet opera but they were the most important harbinger of opera, which just because of that mixture was gradually to supplant church music as the very heart of European music and hence establish Italian pre-eminence throughout the continent. And it was the composers of Bardi's circle who began it. The most important missing ingredient was supplied by Cavalieri, who had devised the extended final ballet of the intermedii and composed the music for it. The very next year (1590) he provided music for the pastoral interludes of Tasso's *Aminta* and two other

---

[32] See Howard M. Brown, *Sixteenth-century Instrumentation: the Music for the Florentine Intermedii* (American Institute of Musicology, 1973)). Robert L. Weaver has compiled a valuable set of tables showing the orchestra employed in Olympian, pastoral, infernal, and battle scenes in various intermedii throughout the sixteenth century, *MQ*, xlvii (1961), pp. 374–8.

pastorals which was in an 'altro modo di cantare che l'ordinario',[33] presumably some kind of recitative. The music is lost, but Cavalieri's contemporaries agree that it was he who, as Peri put it in the preface to his *Euridice* (1600), 'before anyone else made our music' (i.e. the 'nuova maniera di canto') 'heard on the stage'. Then Rinuccini wrote a *Dafne*[34] consisting of a prologue and six scenes. Another Florentine nobleman, Jacopo Corsi, who took over the role of patron of the *camerata* when Bardi left for Rome, composed two numbers for *Dafne*, a tiny *aria* for Apollo and a unison *coro finale*, which have survived,[35] but these are hardly in a *nuova maniera*. Nor are the six surviving fragments[36] of Peri's complete setting of *Dafne* which was produced at the Palazzo Corsi during the Carnival of 1597.

THE EARLIEST OPERAS

Rinuccini's next *favola* for music, a *Euridice* with a happy ending, was composed by Peri (but included some pieces by Caccini which are duly acknowledged in the preface) for the wedding of Maria de' Medici to Henry IV of France and performed in the Pitti Palace on 6 October 1600. Caccini also set the *Euridice* text at the same time and both works were published at once,[37] though Caccini's was not performed till 5 December 1602.

While these, the two earliest complete operas that we have, differ radically from the festive intermedii in their dramatic unity and the overall employment of the *nuova maniera di canto* over sustained bass notes, there was still a mixture of styles. Peri's prologue is a strophic solo with instrumental ritornello; scene 1 ends with a 12-bar 'madrigalian' chorus of nymphs and shepherds (composed by Caccini in both operas) which serves as refrain to brief solos by two nymphs and a shepherd, and the other scenes have similar finales, those to 2 and 4 also by Caccini. In scene 2 the shepherd Tirsi appears, playing a short *sinfonia* on a *triflauto* – the sinfonia being in two parts, mostly in thirds, over the bass – and sings two stanzas. (We learn from the preface that the orchestra included a chitarrone, a lira grande, a liuto grosso, and a gravicembalo on which the player was Jacopo Corsi.) After a few bars of dialogue between Orfeo and the shepherds, Dafne returns with her tragic news which she recites in strikingly contrasted tones:

---

[33] Angelo Solerti, *Gli albori di melodramma* (Milan, 1904), i, p. 51.
[34] Ibid., ii, p. 75.
[35] See *NOHM*, iv, p. 825.
[36] They are published in William V. Porter, 'Peri and Corsi's *Dafne*: some new discoveries and observations' *JAMS*, xviii (1965), p. 170.
[37] Both have been published in miniature score (Milan, n.d.), Peri's also in facsimile by E. M. Dufflocq (Rome, 1934). There are other editions and numerous excerpts. Both Peri and Caccini wrote very interesting prefaces to their operas, which are published in Solerti, op. cit., ii, pp. 108 and 111, and translated in Strunk, op. cit., pp. 373 and 370 respectively. Both draw attention to their attempted reconstruction of the supposedly ancient Greek musical declamation; both pay homage to the singer Vittoria Archilei, who had also played the leading part in the 1589 intermedii, and her new types of ornamentation (which Caccini claims were 'inventati da me'); Caccini talks about his *basso continovato* while Peri applies the word *continuato* to speechlike movement of the voice.

Ex. 77

The sixth and last scene opens with a more extended and shapely song, a miniature aria, for Orfeo:

Ex. 78

which is followed by recitative conversation between Euridice, Orfeo, Dafne, and the shepherds. The work ends with a more elaborate finale: two five-part stanzas (see Ex. 79) sung and danced by the whole chorus; an *aria a 3* sung by three women 'without dancing'; a short instrumental ritornello (melody and bass only given) 'repeated several times and danced by two soloists of the chorus'; two more stanzas of Ex. 79; another stanza of the *aria* but this time sung by three tenors; and a final pair of stanzas of Ex. 79. *Euridice* was already compounded of all the rudiments of true opera: solo recitative and song, chorus and dancing, orchestra, and organized act-finale.

Ex. 79

CAVALIERI'S *RAPPRESENTAZIONE* AND CACCINI'S *NUOVE MUSICHE*

Cavalieri also contributed a setting of Guarini's dialogue of Juno and Minerva to these wedding celebrations. Eight months before, his *Rappresentazione di Anima e di Corpo*[38] had been staged and published in Rome

---

[38] Facsimile of the first edition, ed. Francesco Mantica (Rome, 1912) and several modern editions; excerpts easily accessible in Schering, op. cit., No. 169, and Carl Parrish, *A Treasury of Early Music* (New York, 1958), p. 211.

– musically, it is arguable, a finer work than Peri's but not dramatic enough to be considered an opera; the allegorical personages were costumed, and there were dances, but the work was performed in the Oratorio della Vallicella and human interest and the sense of festivity, both indispensable to opera, were necessarily lacking. Nor does Caccini's *Euridice* represent an advance on Peri's. Caccini was always more interested in song as such and his most important work is not *Euridice* but his collection of solo songs, *Le nuove musiche* (Florence, 1602),[39] with figured bass – which he describes in his preface as 'bass for the chitarrone'. The songs are of different types, the most important being solo madrigals which Caccini says should be sung with 'una certa nobile sprezzatura' ('freedom' or what we understand as 'rubato'). But he also includes strophic arias, sometimes with varied strophes (e.g. 'Ard' il mio petto'), and *canzonette a ballo* in which the singer is to attend only to 'la vivezza del canto'. The solo madrigals lean now toward declamatory monody, now toward coloratura song, often fusing both as in 'Amarilli', and in his preface Caccini has much to say about the types of graces – *trilli* and *gruppi* – which can heighten expressiveness.

MONTEVERDI'S *ORFEO* AND *ARIANNA*

What puts Monteverdi's *Orfeo* (produced at Mantua, 1607)[40] in quite a different class from the operas of Peri and Caccini or the *Dafne* (1608) (again on Rinuccini's text) of a younger Florentine, Marco da Gagliano (*c.* 1575–1642), is quite simply that it is the work of an immeasurably more gifted musician. The backbone of his work is the new recitative but he uses it with a power quite beyond Peri's so that it is not merely 'expressive' but when necessary, as in Orfeo's lament in Act II, heart-breaking. And his librettist, Alessandro Striggio, son of the composer, provided him with many more opportunities than Rinuccini to break up the recitative with musically attractive relief: extended madrigalian choruses and strophic solos such as Orfeo's lilting 'Vi ricordo' in Act II (accompanied only by continuo instruments, but with ritornelli played by five viole da braccio, a contrabass, two harpsichords, and three chitarroni), his display piece 'Possente spirto' in Act III (accompanied by *organo di legno* and a chitarrone, but in the four stanzas competing with brilliant concertante parts for two violini, then two cornetti, a double-harp, and finally a string trio), and his swinging 'Qual honor' in Act IV (varied strophes for the voice over an ostinato bass). These are all justified by the dramatic context – Orpheus's happiness as he sings to the shepherds, his effort to impress Charon, his triumph as he marches off to fetch Eurydice – but they also gave the audience music to remember. And he uses a very large orchestra of 36

[39] Ed. H. Wiley Hitchcock (Madison, Wis., 1970). Facsimile ed. Francesco Vatielli (Rome, 1934); numerous editions of separate songs, e.g. Wolf, *Sing- und Spielmusik*, No. 49, Schering, op. cit., No. 173 (the extremely popular 'Amarilli'), Parrish and Ohl, *Masterpieces of Music before 1750* (New York, 1951), p. 122. Preface in Solerti, *Le origini del melodramma* (Turin, 1903), p. 55. Trans. Strunk, op. cit., p. 377.
[40] *Tutte le opere*, xi; facsimile of the first edition, ed. Adolf Sandberger (Augsburg, 1927); and a number of vocal scores have been published.

players[41] not only to play sinfonie and ritornelli more substantial than Peri's but for dramatic effect, as in the sudden change of tone-colour when Orpheus fatally looks backward.

For a ducal wedding in Mantua the following year Monteverdi wrote a second opera, *Arianna*, to a text by Rinuccini, and a dramatic ballet *Il Ballo dell' ingrate*, but nothing remains of *Arianna* except the heroine's justly famous lament which survives not only in its original form but in the composer's arrangements of it as a five-part madrigal in his Sixth Book (1614) and as a 'Pianto della Madonna' for solo voice and continuo in his *Selva Morale* (1640);[42] it set a remarkable and long-lasting fashion for *lamenti*. But Monteverdi's later operas, most of them lost, belong to another chapter.

THE MADRIGAL IN ENGLAND

The madrigal substantially appeared in England only in the 1580s when the English mania for the Italian reached its height – for instance, in the poetry of Spenser and Philip Sidney. It is true that manuscript collections of madrigals had reached England earlier[43] and that a minor conservative and non-dramatic madrigalist, Alfonso Ferrabosco the elder,[44] had been in Elizabeth I's service during the years 1562 to 1578. But English secular song continued the tradition of mainly note-against-note polyphony, as in the only printed collection of the period, the *Songes to three, fower, and five voyces* (1571) of Thomas Whythorne (1528–96), one of which, 'Buy new broom', is a solo accompanied by a consort of four viols. Such 'consort songs' began to proliferate during the second half of the century and still flourished during the first decade of the next;[45] the viol parts soon became more animated as in the masterly hands of William Byrd whose *Psalmes, Sonets, and songs of sadnes and pietie* (1588)[46] were 'originally made for Instruments to expresse the harmonie, and one voyce to pronounce the dittie [text]', though he now published them 'framed in all parts for voyces to sing the same'. These were not genuine madrigals though they show madrigalian traits, nor are most of his *Songs of sundrie natures* of the following year. But the 1588 volume does contain one tentative madrigal, a setting of Ariosto's 'La verginella', and a few months later appeared a collection which was a milestone in the naturalization of the madrigal in England. This was *Musica Transalpina*, compiled by Nicholas Yonge, a choirman of St. Paul's, who had been accustomed to entertain his guests with the singing of 'Italian songs' from books 'yeerely sent me out of Italy and other places'. His collection consists of 57 madrigals with anonymous

[41] See J. A. Westrup, 'Monteverdi and the Orchestra', *M&L*, xxi (1940), p. 230.

[42] *Tutte le opere*, xi, vi, and xv(2) respectively.

[43] One now in the Newberry Library, Chicago, another in the library of Winchester College. See Alfredo Obertello, *Madrigali italiani in Inghilterra* (Milan, 1949).

[44] See p. 263.

[45] See the anthology, mostly from manuscript sources, edited by Philip Brett in *MB*, xxii.

[46] Ed. Fellowes and Thurston Dart, *The English Madrigalists*, xiv and *Collected Works*, xii. The best edition of Byrd's choral songs is *The Byrd Edition*, xvi, ed. Philip Brett (London, 1976).

English texts, including 14 by Ferrabosco, ten by Marenzio, five by Palestrina, two chansons by Lassus ('Susanna fair' and 'The nightingale'), and an English version of Byrd's effort ('The fair young virgin'). Next, in 1590, came the *First Set of Italian Madrigals Englished, not to the sense of the original dittie, but after the affection of the Noate* by Thomas Watson, next to Spenser the earliest of the Elizabethan sonneteers; they are nearly all by Marenzio but also include two fine settings, *à* 4 and *à* 6, of Watson's own 'This sweet and merry month of May' by Byrd[47] 'composed after the Italian vaine' at the poet's request. Yonge also brought out a second *Musica Transalpina* in 1597[48] but by that time the English madrigal was well established and flourishing.

MORLEY'S CANZONETS AND BALLETTS

The lead was given both as composer and as publisher by Byrd's pupil Morley. It was he who first anglicized the word, as he did also with canzonetti and balletti; his *Canzonets. Or Little Short Songs to Three Voyces* (1593), *Madrigalls to Foure Voyces* (1594), *First Book of Balletts to five voyces* (1595),[49] and their successors are the most Italianate of all Elizabethan compositions. Morley unashamedly imitated both Italian texts and Italian music; indeed some of his balletts are modelled all too closely on the *Balletti a 5* (Venice, 1591) of Giovanni Giacomo Gastoldi (d. 1622).[50] Yet Morley was much more than an imitator; he was a more gifted melodist than Gastoldi. In his balletts he often breaks away from the Mantuan composer's genuinely dancelike and predominantly note-against-note style, keeping only the 'fa-la' refrain which is the hallmark of the balletto – but extending even that with great contrapuntal and rhythmic ingenuity. 'Sing we and chant it' is a true balletto, the opening of its second strain practically identical in every part with that of Gastoldi's 'A lieta vita' (which in Germany as early as 1598 was seized *in toto* and provided with sacred words, 'In dir ist Freude') yet, as Joseph Kerman has pointed out,[51] more sophisticated in its sense of dominant contrast. 'Fire, fire' however is really a madrigal with 'fa-las' and 'Leave alas this tormenting' is pure madrigal. In his madrigals actually so called, Morley's technical debt is mainly to Marenzio and in his canzonets to Felice Anerio. But he transforms whatever he touches; the English words alone would suffice to make the English madrigal different from the Italian, and the numerous monosyllables give a peculiar crispness to such genre-pictures as 'Ho! who comes here all along?' and the canzonet 'Arise, get up my dear'.

---

[47] *English Madrigalists*, xii, and *Collected Works*, xiv.
[48] For the originals of the two *Musica Transalpina* sets and *Italian Madrigals Englished*, see Joseph Kerman, *The Elizabethan Madrigal* (New York, 1962), pp. 53–5, 59, and 62–3.
[49] *English Madrigalists*, i, ii, and iv.
[50] There are numerous separate editions of Gastoldi balletti.
[51] Op. cit. The tables on pp. 65, 68–9, and 140 show Morley's Italian sources.

WEELKES, WILBYE, AND THEIR CONTEMPORARIES

Morley excelled in the lighter types of madrigal and kindred forms; the supreme masters of the English school were Weelkes, who published his first book in 1597,[52] and John Wilbye (1574–1638) who began the following year.[53] Even Wilbye did not disdain specific Italian models; his 'Lady, your words do spite me' takes off from Ferrabosco's 'Donna se voi m'odiate' which had appeared in *Musica Transalpina* as 'Lady, if you so spite me':

Ex. 80

(i) FERRABOSCO

(ii) WILBYE

and once more the English monosyllables leave their stamp on the music. Not even Weelkes maintained such a consistently high level as Wilbye in his two sets. Although best known for such delicious things as 'Sweet honeysucking bees', his greatest work is to be found in serious madrigals like 'All pleasure is of this condition' and 'Thou art but young'. Weelkes also covered a vast range, from the dancing ballet 'On the plains' to the great picturesque 'Thule, the period of cosmography', the piercing chromatic anguish of 'O Care, thou wilt despatch me' with its *ironic* 'fa-las', and the dazzling counterpoint of 'As Vesta was from Latmos hill descending'. 'Vesta' was his contribution to *The Triumphes of Oriana* (London, 1601),[54] a collection of madrigals by twenty-four composers compiled by Morley in emulation of the Italian *Trionfo di Dori* (Venice, 1592) to which Giovanni Gabrieli, Vecchi, Marenzio, de Monte, Croce, Striggio, Felice Anerio, Gastoldi, Palestrina, and others had contributed.

Morley, Weelkes, and Wilbye were the outstanding figures of the English madrigal school, but some fine things were also written by Bateson, Benet, Michael East, Kirbye, Francis Pilkington, Ward, and others – to say nothing of the Catholic exile, Peter Philips, who set Italian verse.[55] Orlando Gibbons published a masterly set remarkable for its general seriousness in 1612, and Tomkins a very fine book of what he preferred to call *Songs* in 1622, after which the English madrigal went into a rapid decline – as did the type of solo song which had flourished beside it, the ayre with lute accompaniment.

THE ENGLISH AYRE

French composers, notably Le Jeune, preferred in the 1590s to describe their chansons as 'airs'[56] and the lute ayre was as definitely French in origin

[52] *English Madrigalists*, ix. He published further collections in 1598, 1600 (the first set to be described as 'apt for the Viols and voices') and (*Ayres or Phantasticke Spirites*) 1608; ibid., x, xi/xii, and xiii.
[53] *English Madrigalists*, vi. His *Second Set of Madrigales* was published in 1609; ibid., vii.
[54] *English Madrigalists*, xxxii.
[55] A selection has been ed. John Steele, *MB*, xxix.

as the madrigal was Italian – and as completely anglicized by the different language. Its composers adopted the much older French practice of publishing in alternative forms: as part-songs and as solos with lute. When Morley brought out his *Canzonets or Little Short Aers to five and six Voices*[57] in 1597, he also provided most of them with a lute transcription of the lower voices. And in the same year the *First Booke of Songes or Ayres of foure partes*[58] of the greatest of all English lutenists, John Dowland (1563–1626), was printed 'with Tableture for the Lute: So made that all the parts together, or either of them severally may be song to the Lute, Orpherian [a species of cittern, tuned like a lute] or Viol de Gambo', a confused description which conceals the condition that the highest part *must* be sung. This First Book of Dowland's raises the problem of which was the original form; some were undoubtedly composed as part-songs, others (for instance, 'Sleep, wayward thoughts' and 'Awake, sweet love') probably originated as solos to the lute, while others again ('If my complaints', 'Can she excuse', 'Now, oh now I needs must part') seem to have been instrumental dances to

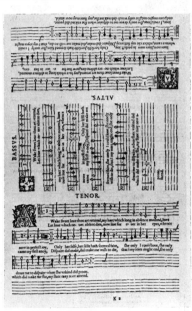

Pl. 42 Dowland's 'Awake sweet love' in his *First Booke of Songes or Ayres of foure partes* (London, 1597). The 'tableture for the lute' is printed below the cantus; altus, tenor and bass are laid out for singers seated at a table.

---

[56] The term *air de cour* seems to have originated with the *Livre d'airs de cour mis sur le luth* (1571) of the publisher-composer Adrian Le Roy (c. 1520–1598), friend of Lassus, Ronsard, and Baïf: 'jadis voix de ville, aujourd'hui aïrs de cour . . .' Le Roy's lute-books are published in the *Corpus des luthistes français* (Paris, 1970–).

[57] *English Madrigalists*, iii.

[58] The four-part versions of Dowland's ayres, transcribed by E. H. Fellowes and ed. Thurston Dart and Nigel Fortune are published in *MB*, vi.

which words were later added. On the other hand, Morley's *First Booke of Ayres, or little short Songs, to sing and play to the lute, with the bass viole* (1600),[59] which includes that marvel of flexible English word-setting 'Thyrsis and Milla', and 'It was a lover and his lass', has no part-song version. *As You Like It* was then a very new play and Morley's is not the only piece of theatre music preserved in these song-books. Some of Dowland's ayres almost certainly came from masques; the *Ayres* (1609)[60] of Alfonso Ferrabosco the younger (*c.* 1575–1628), the completely Anglicized son of 'the elder', include a number composed for Ben Jonson's earlier masques and one, 'Come my Celia', from his music to Jonson's *Volpone*; Thomas Campion (1567–1620), better poet than composer, was much concerned in the writing and production of masques; while Robert Jones and Philip Rosseter, masters of the lighter type of ayre, were also men of the theatre.

As with the madrigal, so with the ayre: a number of delightful things were produced by minor composers. But Dowland towers above them as Wilbye and Weelkes above the other madrigalists, particularly in some of his later songs. In 1610 his son Robert published a collection of foreign and English songs, *A Musicall Banquet*,[61] including two from Caccini's *Nuove Musiche*; and two of the three by his father – 'Far from triumphing court' and 'In darkness let me dwell' (Dowland's supreme masterpiece of emotional declamation) – reveal awareness of the new style. So also do some of the songs in Dowland's fourth book, *A Pilgrimes Solace* (1612), one of them actually to Italian words, 'Lasso, vita mia'. These and the religious pieces in the *Solace* are the swan-song of the English ayre; but for Campion's last two books (1617), there was little more to come.

Dowland was a European figure, lutenist to James I's brother-in-law, Christian IV of Denmark, from 1598 to 1606; he boasted of his European travels, his friendship with Marenzio and Giovanni Croce, and the fact that his compositions had been published in Paris, the Netherlands, and several German cities, for instance in Jean Baptiste Besard's famous collection of lute solos and songs, *Thesaurus harmonicus* (Cologne, 1603). But the English lute ayre, though not unknown on the continent, stimulated no imitation there. Nor did the *Nuove musiche*.

ITALIAN VOCAL FORMS IN GERMANY

In Germany solo song was neglected altogether and even the influences of villanella and madrigal penetrated only a few years earlier than in England, in the first place through Lassus and two Netherland protégés of his: Ivo de Vento (d. 1575) and Jacob Regnart (*c.* 1540–1599). Vento composed Italian

[59] Ed. Fellowes and Dart, *The English Lute-Songs*, xvi.
[60] *English Lute-Songs*, second series, xvi.
[61] Ed. Peter Stroud (London, 1968).

madrigals for the Bavarian duke, his master, but his collections of rather old-fashioned German songs include only one, the *Neue teutsche Lieder mit dreien Stimmen* (Munich, 1572), that shows Italian influence. On the other hand the titles of the Imperial Kapellmeister Regnart's two books of *Canzone italiane* (1574 and 1581) and three books of *Kurtzweilige teutsche Lieder zu drei Stimmen, nach Art der Neapolitanen oder welschen* [Italian] *Villanellen* (1576, 1577, and 1579) speak for themselves. The first native German to follow this path was Lechner (*c.* 1553–1606), who had studied with both Lassus and Vento. Encouraged by the three amateur musical societies which then flourished in Nuremberg, he published *Newe teutsche Lieder, zu drey Stimmen, Nach art der Welschen Villanellen* (1576 and 1577), *Newe Teutsche Lieder mit vier und fünff stimmen* (1577), and *Neue lustige Teutsche Lieder, nach art der Welschen Canzonen* (1586),[62] in which German polyphonic song, no longer exclusively *Tenorlied*, is crossed with an Italian strain; he also wrote a few Italian madrigals.[63] But he was surpassed both in Italianism and in quality of invention by another Nuremberg composer, Hassler (1564–1612), who studied for fifteen months in Venice (1584–5). Two of Hassler's earliest publications were settings of Italian texts, *Canzonette a quattro voci* (Nuremberg, 1590) and 33 *Madrigali* (1596);[64] sometimes they lean heavily on specific Italian models: thus his canzonetta, 'Io son ferito, Amore', borrows musically as well as textually from Palestrina's 'Io son ferito, ahi lasso'. But in the latter year he also published *Neue teütsche* [*sic*] *Gesang nach Art der welschen Madrigalien und Canzonetten*[65] in which the weight of German words naturally affects the music; when he sets translations of Italian texts he has also composed, the difference is startling:

Ex. 81

[62] *Leonhard Lechner-Werke* (general editor, Konrad Ameln) (Kassel, 1954–   ), ii, iii, and ix. There are various editions of separate pieces, e.g. one of the German villanelle in Wolf, *Music of Earlier Times* (New York, 1946), No. 42.
[63] *Werke*, v.
[64] Ed. Rudolf Schwartz, *Hans Leo Hassler: Sämtliche Werke*, ii and iii, and previously published as *DTB*, Jg. v(2) and xi(1).

The note-against-note style of the *Canzonetten* suggests the allemande, that 'heavie daunce', as Morley calls it,[66] 'fitly representing the nature of the people whose name it carrieth', though sometimes gravely beautiful, as 'Jungfraw dein schöne Gstalt' is. Nor are there any madrigalian extravagances in Hassler's madrigals; they make good use of antiphony between higher and lower voice-groups as in the openings of 'Ach Schatz, ich thu dir klagen' and 'Fahr hin, guts Liedelein'; but they lack rhythmic spring.

That element appears, however, in his last collection of secular, including instrumental, works, the *Lustgarten neuer teutscher Gesäng Balletti Galliarden und Intraden* (1601). Many of these were written under the direct, sometimes very direct, influence of Gastoldi's balletti, 'fa-la' refrains and all – 'Tantzen und springen', 'Unter all'n auf dieser Erden', 'All Lust und Freud' – while others such as 'Ihr Musici, frisch auf' are masterpieces of the

---

[65] Ibid., ii. There is an easily accessible example in *HAM*, i, No. 165.
[66] *A Plaine and Easie Introduction to Practicall Musicke* (London, 1597); p. 295 of the modern edition by R. Alec Harman (London 1952).

German madrigal. One song, 'Mein Gmüt ist mir verwirret', was soon given sacred words ('Herzlich tut mich verlangen' and, later, 'O Haupt voll Blut und Wunden'); indeed the *Lustgarten* sank deep into the consciousness of German musicians, both composers and amateurs. Its examples were followed in one way or another in the various collections of Christoph Demantius (1567–1643), Valentin Haussmann (d. *c.* 1612), Erasmus Widmann (1572–1634), Hassler's pupil Melchior Franck (*c.* 1580–1639), and others. A greater than these, or any earlier German composer, was to make his début with a *Primo libro de madrigali* (Venice, 1611), but this 26-year-old pupil of Giovanni Gabrieli, 'Henricus Sagittarius' (Henrich Schütz), was to work almost entirely in other fields and he belongs to a later age.

THE MADRIGAL IN THE EUROPEAN PERIPHERY

The madrigal reached the periphery of European musical culture but never struck root. Dowland's Danish patron, Christian IV, sent musicians to study in Italy and two Danes, Hans Nielsen (*c.* 1580–after 1620) and Mogens Pedersen (*c.* 1585–1623), worked in Venice with Giovanni Gabrieli and published books of five-part madrigals there in 1606 and 1608.[67] Sigismund III of Poland actually enticed Marenzio to his new capital at Warsaw for a short period in 1595–6 and employed a number of Italian musicians, one of whom, Asprilio Pacelli (1570–1623), published a book of madrigals (Venice, 1601); but that was all. There was little more in Spain. The *Libro de Madrigali* (Venice, 1568) of Mateo Flecha the younger (1530–1604) includes one with Spanish text, and Joan Brudieu (*c.* 1520–1591) published a collection of eleven Spanish and four Catalan madrigals (Barcelona, 1585),[68] while a few negligible composers set Italian texts. Even the native polyphonic villancico died out in the 1560s, as the solo form with vihuela did a decade or so later.

MADRIGALIAN INFLUENCE AND *MUSIQUE MESURÉE* IN THE CHANSON

In France the position was more complicated. There were no French madrigalists but, beginning in the 1560s, the native polyphonic chanson was given new life by the immensely popular example of Lassus, whose chansons are often shot through with madrigalian techniques. Thus in the *Musique* (1570)[69] of the finest master of the later sixteenth-century chanson, Guillaume Costeley (*c.* 1531–1606) one encounters madrigalian traits, for instance passages in 'Puisque ce beau mois' and in his masterpiece 'Mignonne, allons voir si la rose'. Still more Italianate are the three *Livres de*

---

[67] Three by Pedersen and three by Nielsen, ed. Rudolf Gerber, *ChW*, xxxv.
[68] New edition by Felipe Pedrell and Higini Anglès (Barcelona, 1921).
[69] Reprinted by Henry Expert, *Les Maîtres musiciens de la Renaissance française*, iii, xviii, and xix.

chansons (1576–8)[70] of Antoine de Bertrand (d. *c.* 1581), whose harmonic daring carried him beyond chromaticism to consider the ad libitum use of microtones.[71] (Costeley, also, in the preface to his *Musique*, confesses to having played with the idea of third-tones.) This was typical of the intellectual, experimental tendencies in French music at this time, the most important of which was *musique mesurée à l'antique* which owed its inception to a crackbrained idea of the poet Antoine de Baïf, an associate of Ronsard and Du Bellay in the *Pléiade*, who in 1570 persuaded Charles IX to establish an Académie de Poésie et de Musique. Baïf was a typical humanist and, like Girolamo Mei and Vincenzo Galilei, strove to probe into Greek poetry and music; for fourteen years the Académie propagated his ideas. In *Les Etrènes de poézie fransoêze an vers mezurés* (1574) – he was also a spelling-reformer – he published a collection of verse based on a conception quite foreign to the French language: that of quantitative metre. And during the next thirty years composers associated with the Académie set his poems, including a translation of the Psalms, to music in which, as Philip Sidney put it, 'every semibreif or mynom had its syllables matched accordingly with a long foote and a short foote',[72] not monodic but in harmony with each syllable sung simultaneously in all parts.[73] Within these doctrinaire limits the *Chansonettes mesurées à l'antique* (1586) of Mauduit, the posthumously published *Le Printemps* (1603) of Le Jeune, and the *Meslanges* (1610) of Du Caurroy[74] do contain a few delightful things. Both Le Jeune and Du Caurroy also composed chansons of the normal type.

To them also, and particularly to Du Caurroy, we owe almost all we know of French instrumental ensemble music of the period. It is disappointing. Du Caurroy's *Fantasies a III, IV, V et VI parties* (1610)[75] are so old-fashioned – instrumental motets, sometimes with long-note cantus firmus, on plainsong or Huguenot melodies – and so lacking in rhythmic vitality that one suspects they were composed long before their posthumous publication.

THE INTERNATIONAL REPERTORIES FOR LUTE AND KEYBOARD

Contemporary French lute composers such as Antoine Francisque (*c.* 1570–1605) also neglected the fantasia; Francisque's *Trésor d'Orphée* (1600) consists almost entirely of dances. Besard's *Thesaurus*, on the other hand, contains more than forty fantasias and nearly as many *praeludia*, as well as a great quantity of dances. But then the *Thesaurus* was an international collection which included beside 38 of his own compositions,

---

[70] Modern edition by Expert, *Monuments de la musique française au temps de la Renaissance* (Paris, 1926–7).   [71] See *NOHM*, iv, pp. 28–9.
[72] Quoted in Bruce Pattison, *Music and Poetry of the English Renaissance* (London, 1948), p. 64.
[73] Something similar had been attempted much earlier in the century in settings of Horatian odes by such Germans as Peter Tritonius, Hofhaimer, and Senfl: see the examples quoted by R. von Liliencron in *Vierteljahrsschrift für Musikwissenschaft*, iii (1887), pp. 49–91, from which one is reproduced in Schering, op. cit., No. 73.
[74] Reprinted by Expert, *Maîtres musiciens*, x, xii–xiv, and xvii.
[75] Five, with one of Le Jeune's fantasies, reprinted by Expert (Paris, 1910).

pieces by his teacher 'Laurencinus Romanus', Vincenzo Galilei, Ferrabosco the elder, Dowland, Diomedes Cato (a Venetian who settled at Cracow), two Polish religious refugees – Jakub Reys (Polak/Jacques Pollonois), lutenist at the French court, and Bakfark's pupil, Wojciech (Albert) Długoraj – and various others. Solo lute-music at this period of its highest popularity was quite international; among the most important of the numerous published lute-books – the manuscript collections are innumerable – are Sebastian Ochsenkun's *Tabulaturbuch* (Heidelberg, 1558), the four books of Giacomo Gorzanis (Venice, 1561–4), Galilei's (Rome, 1563),[76] the four published by Matthäus Waisselius (Frankfurt-on-Oder, 1573–92), William Barley's *A new Booke of Tabliture*, an instruction book for orpharion and bandora besides the lute (London, 1596), and Robert Dowland's *Varietie of Lute-lessons* (London, 1610)[77] containing 42 pieces by composers 'as well beyond the Seas as of our own country'. Most of the lute repertory consisted of dances – frequently pairs and sometimes groups of three (embryonic suites) – or arrangements of vocal compositions, though at the beginning of the seventeenth century Diomedes Cato and John Dowland were writing extended polyphonic fantasias, rich in elaborate imitation.[78]

Much the same might be said of the keyboard repertory, particularly in Germany. The German keyboard tablatures – Elias Ammerbach's (Leipzig, 1571 and 1575), those of Bernhard Schmid the elder (Strasbourg, 1577) and Jacob Paix (Lauingen, 1583), and the manuscript ones of Christoph Löffelholtz (Tübingen, Univ. Bibl., Mus. ms. 40034) and August Nörmiger (1598, idem, 40098) – consist almost exclusively of vocal transcriptions and dances of various nationalities. The specifically German element comes to the fore, however, in Lutheran hymn-settings as in the first part of Nörmiger's book and the 'Celler Tabulatur' of 1601.[79] The Imperial organist Luython composed ricercari for his instrument, but he was a Netherlander. German 'pure' contrapuntal keyboard music was at first always for organ, not harpsichord, and stylistically modelled on the Venetians, as may be seen in the two fantasies and two *canzoni francese* in Paix's book and the various organ works of Hassler and his successor at Augsburg, Christian Erbach (c. 1570–1635).[80] When Bernhard Schmid's son published *his Tabulatur Buch* (Strasbourg, 1607), the contents were overwhelmingly Italian and included the *intonazioni* (preludes on the different modes) of the two Gabrielis, toccatas by them and by Merulo and his pupil Girolamo Diruta (1561–after 1625), and twelve 'Fugen (oder wie es die Italianer

---

[76] Galilei also left a manuscript tablature (Florence, Bibl. Naz.) and other lute pieces illustrate his *Fronimo*, a treatise on 'the entabulation of music for the lute' (Venice, 1568). Three ricercari from *Fronimo* are reprinted by Kinkeldey, op. cit., pp. 283 ff.

[77] Keyboard transcription by Edgar Hunt (London, 1957).

[78] See Cato's, ed. Piotr Poźniak with facsimiles or original notation, in *Wydawnictwo dawnej muzyki polskiej*, xxiv and lxvii (Warsaw, 1970 and 1973), and Dowland's remarkable chromatic fantasies, 'Farewell' and 'Forlorne Hope', ed. David Lumsden, *An Anthology of English Lute Music* (London, 1954).

[79] Ed. Willi Apel, *CEKM*, 17.

[80] A selection of organ works by Hassler and Erbach is published in *DTB*, iv(2); Hassler's also in *Sämtliche Werke*, xii, and Erbach's, ed. Clare G. Rayner in *CEKM*, 36.

nennen) *Canzoni alla Francese*' by various Italians. Schmid took four of his six toccatas from the examples in Diruta's *Il Transilvano* (Venice, 1597), a *dialogo* on the playing of organs and harpsichords – including the method of making ornamented transcriptions for them.

VENETIAN INSTRUMENTAL MUSIC

It was the Venetians who led the way in extended instrumental composition independent of dance-forms and vocal models. The keyboard and ensemble ricercari and the *canzoni alla francese* for 'istromenti da tasti' of Andrea Gabrieli[81] were nearly all published posthumously when they were probably thirty or forty years old, that is to say not much more modern than the ricercari of Buus and Annibale Padovano (see p. 234). His short *intonazioni* and longer toccatas are quasi-improvisatory preludes, two of the toccatas having imitative polyphonic middle sections. Conversely Andrea will sometimes diversify his ricercari with sections in triple time: thus the ricercar *primo tono* of his *Libro secondo* ends with a short triple-time section on a version of the opening theme:

Ex. 82

One of the ensemble ricercari *del secondo tono* is planned similarly but rounded off with a brief reference to the opening theme, while the ensemble ricercar *del duodecimo tono*[82] is twice interrupted by identical (but

---

[81] Complete keyboard works ed. Pierre Pidoux (Kassel and Basel, 1941–52); one eight-part ricercar and seven four-part ones ed. Giacomo Benvenuti, *Istituzioni e Monumenti dell'arte musicale italiana*, i (Milan, 1931).
[82] Benvenuti, p. 86, and *HAM*, i, No. 136.

thematically fresh) 17-bar passages in triple metre. At the same time, by frequently basing an entire ricercar on only one or two themes – inverted, diminished, augmented, drawn together in stretti, sometimes paired with a regular counter-subject – he contrived to give an extended piece musical cohesion replacing the mainly verbal cohesion of a motet. Andrea's ricercari on chansons by Crecquillon, Janequin, and their contemporaries differ markedly from his actually so called *canzoni alla francese* on the same songs; these are ordinary ornamented transcriptions whereas the ricercari are free compositions on the successive phrases of the melody.

Merulo's *Canzoni . . . fatte alla Francese* (1592, 1606, and 1611)[83] treat their originals, so far as one can trace them,[84] with great freedom of keyboard texture. His keyboard ricercari are early works (1567), mostly 'instrumental motets', but in his two books of toccatas (1598 and 1604)[85] he developed further the alternation of quasi-improvisatory and ricercar-like passages and treated the material more plastically so that the two elements cohere instead of being sharply juxtaposed. Both he and the elder Gabrieli followed in Cavazzoni's wake also by composing organ Masses.

The ensemble canzon soon ceased to lean on specific chansons and developed a style of its own, uncluttered by the ornamentation of the keyboard canzon or the contrapuntal science of the ricercar, a style which Praetorius characterized in his *Syntagma* as 'fresh, gay and quick' (*frisch, frölich und geschwinde*). It may be illustrated by the opening of Merulo's 'La Zerata' (transcribed as 'La Gratiosa' in the 1592 book):

Ex. 83

---

[83] *Libro primo*, ed. Pidoux (Kassel, 1941).
[84] Four of them are based on ensemble canzoni by Merulo himself (Verona, Bibl. Cap. MCXXVIII; ed. Benvenuto Disertori, Milan, 1950), one of which, 'La Jussona' – 'La Cortese' in the keyboard version – borrows only the opening bars from a chanson. Such titles became fashionable at this period. Both ensemble and keyboard versions of 'La Zambeccara' are given in parallel in E. T. Ferand, *Die Improvisation (Das Musikwerk)*, (Cologne, 1956), p. 89.
[85] Complete edition by Sandro dalla Libera (Milan, 1958–9).

The earliest surviving book of *canzoni da sonare* was published by Merulo's pupil Florentio Maschera (Brescia, probably 1582); Banchieri, Gioseffo Guami, and others followed suit; and in 1608 the Venetian printer Alessandro Raverii brought out a notable collection[86] of 36 four-, five- and eight-part canzoni with a generally unnecessary 'Basso generale per l'organo', by Giovanni Gabrieli, Guami, Maschera, Luzzaschi, and others, including the young Girolamo Frescobaldi (1583–1643) and the not long dead Merulo, who ends the volume with a five-part piece of fine thematic workmanship and an interpolated triple-time section. Other pieces showing the variety which could now be accommodated under the title 'canzon' are a 'capricio' in a number of short, sharply differentiated sections by Giovanni Battista Grillo and a composition for sixteen trombones by Tiburtio Massaino. The canzoni by Giovanni Gabrieli in this collection are early and relatively unimportant works; already in the *Symphoniae Sacrae* of 1597 he had published canzoni in which the form was revolutionized by transference from the intimacy of private performance and enjoyment to music for ecclesiastical or state occasions. As many as 12 to 19 instruments are employed, divided into antiphonal bodies in the Venetian choral style; specific instruments are prescribed – cornetti, violini, tromboni – and in one version of a *Canzon in echo* for ten instruments[87] duet sections with organ accompaniment alternate with tutti sections:

Ex. 84

[86] Ed. L. E. Bartholomew (Hays, Kansas, 1965). Four canzoni by the younger Gabrieli ed. Einstein (Mainz, 1933).
[87] *Istituzioni e Monumenti*, ii, p. 181; the other version, p. 180.

There is still a certain amount of imitation, particularly in the openings, but the texture is less polyphonic than in the earlier canzoni, and fast triple-time refrains recur. Two graver pieces without such refrains are entitled 'sonata'[88] and one of them, the *Sonata pian' e forte*,[89] in which cornetto and three trombones alternate and combine with *violino* and three trombones, has become famous not only for its grave beauty but as one of the earliest printed instrumental compositions with dynamic markings. In the posthumously published *Canzoni et sonate* (1615) the instruments are almost always specified. Even in his very early and surprisingly few organ ricercari[90] – notably the one *del 8. tono* on three closely worked subjects, and the one *del 10. tono* (of which the one *del 9. tono* is essentially a shortened version) where a canzon theme alternates with a motive worked in almost too facile descending sequences – Giovanni enters a different world from his uncle's ricercari; the last traces of the 'instrumental motet' have been erased.

DANCE MUSIC IN GERMANY

The Venetians almost ignored dance-music; contemporary German composers of ensemble music, following their keyboard and lute traditions, composed little else. The instrumental publications of the first decade of the seventeenth century, by Christoph Demantius, Melchior Franck, Valentin

[88] The earliest surviving composition so called appears to be a dance-pair, *pass'e mezo* and *padoana*, in the first *Intabolatura di liuto* (Venice, 1561) of Giacomo Gorzanis (*c.* 1525–after 1575).
[89] *Istituzioni*, i, p. 64, and *HAM*, i, No. 173.
[90] Ed. G. S. Bedbrook, *Giovanni Gabrieli: The Keyboard Works* (Kassel, Basel, and London, 1957), and dalla Libera, *Giovanni Gabrieli: Composizioni per organo*, i (Milan, 1957).

Haussmann consist almost exclusively of pavanes, galliards, *Intraden* (pavane-like processional pieces), and Polish dances. Paul Peurl (*c.* 1575–after 1625) further extended the dance-pair in his *Newe Padovan, Intrada, Däntz unnd Galliarda* for four-part strings (Nuremberg, 1611),[91] ten 'variation suites' – padovan, intrada (in triple time), 'dance' and galliarda all being developed from metamorphoses of the same melodic opening. Peurl also wrote four canzoni and these, with a few examples by Hassler and Aichinger, Schein and Scheidt, are practically all that Germany has to show in this genre.

ENGLISH MUSIC FOR CONSORT AND VIRGINALS

England ignored the canzona even more completely. At most one can find traces of the style only in one or two string fantasias by such Italianate Englishmen as Thomas Lupo (d. 1628) and John 'Coprario' (Cooper) (*c.* 1575–1626),[92] hardly even in the instrumental pieces of Morley's *Canzonets to Two Voyces* or the textless 'Air for three voices' (springing from his canzonet 'Lo where with flowery head') in his *Introduction*.[93] But the late Elizabethans and Jacobeans cultivated with the utmost fertility both a free form of ricercar, the fantasia or 'fancy',[94] and the peculiarly English 'In nomine' (see p. 240), as well as dance music and song-arrangements, both for consort (usually for viols, though also 'broken', i.e. for mixed instruments) and for keyboard (usually the small table-harpsichord known as virginals, or organ). Only a very small proportion was published: Antony Holborne's *Pavans, Galliards, Almains*[95] and Morley's *First Booke of Consort Lessons* (both 1599), Dowland's *Lachrimae or Seaven Teares figured in seaven passionate Pavans* ... (1605), Rosseter's *Lessons for Consort* (1609), two fantasias which Byrd included in *Psalmes, Songs, and Sonnets* (1611) and John Adson's *Courtly Masquing Ayres* (also 1611).[96] Individually two Englishmen on the continent fared better; both William Brade (1560–1630) from 1609 onward, and Thomas Simpson (1582–after 1625) from 1610 onward, published in Germany a number of sets of instrumental dances, nearly all their own. As for keyboard music, 'the first musicke that ever was printed for the Virginalls', the famous *Parthenia* containing 21 short preludes and dances by Byrd, Bull, and Gibbons, appeared only in late 1612 or early 1613.[97]

---

[91] Ed. Karl Geiringer, *DTÖ*, xxxvi(2) (vol. 70). Suite No. 3 in Schering, op. cit., No. 157.
[92] See the fantasias by them in *Jacobean Consort Music* (ed. Thurston Dart and William Coates), *MB*, ix (1955), Nos. 10 and 34.
[93] p. 98 of Harman's edition.
[94] A considerable number of these fantasias are really madrigals deprived of their texts. See Richard Charteris, 'John Coprario's Five- and Six-Part Pieces: Instrumental or Vocal', *M&L*, lvii (1976), p. 370.
[95] Four examples in *MB*, ix, Nos. 66–9.
[96] Ibid., No. 54.
[97] Modern editions of Morley's *Lessons* by Sydney Beck (New York, 1959), of Dowland by Peter Warlock (London, 1927); of Brade's collections of 1609, 1614, and 1621, by Helmut Mönkemeyer (New York and London, 1968); separate examples by Brade and Simpson in *MB*, ix; of *Parthenia* by Dart (London, 1960), facsimile ed. O. E. Deutsch (Cambridge, 1943).

While the soft-voiced viol consort was peculiarly suitable for domestic music, there was a standard mixed consort for public occasions, of which we hear in an account (1591) of an entertainment for Elizabeth I at Elvetham in Hampshire: an 'exquisite consort, wherein was the lute, bandora, base-viol, citterne, treble-violl, and flute'.[98] A quantity of dance-music for it is preserved, imperfectly, in the so-called 'Walsingham Consort Books' of approximately the same date,[99] and the combination is depicted accompanying the wedding masque in the Henry Unton memorial painting of a few years later.[100] It is the consort for which Morley and Rosseter published their *Lessons* and which supports the voices in the first seventeen of Sir William Leighton's *Teares or Lamentacions of a Sorrowfull Soule* (1614).

Pl. 43   The standard Elizabethan mixed consort, shown in the Unton memorial painting of *c*. 1596. The 'funeral' part of the same painting shows another consort, of three viols and two theorbos; they could be playing 'Sir Henry Umpton's Funerall' from Dowland's *Lachrimae*.

One composer – and arranger? – who appears prominently in the Morley, Rosseter, and 'Walsingham' collections is the otherwise dim figure of Richard Allison. The repertory consists mainly of pavanes and galliards, with a few popular songs, such as 'Goe from my Window' on which Allison wrote six subtle and intricate variations, and there are good grounds[101] for the assumption that a large proportion of Morley's *Lessons* originated in theatre music. They also inevitably include such universally popular compositions as Dowland's 'Lachrimae Pavin' which seems to have originated as a lute solo, been turned into a song ('Flow, my tears'), arranged for viol consort with six sequels in the 1605 book, and arranged for virginals by Byrd, Morley, and Farnaby.

[98] See Warwick Edwards, 'The Walsingham Consort Books', *M&L*, lv (1974), p. 209.
[99] Fifteen examples, ed. Edwards, in *MB*, xl.   [100] See pl. 43.
[101] See Dart, *PRMA* (1947–8), particularly pp. 5–7.

Dances also figure largely in the repertory for consorts of five or six viols[102] but fantasies were composed in quantity for viol consorts, and later, as in the case of Gibbons's nine published *Fantasies of Three Parts* (*c.* 1620),[103] for consorts in which the highest or two upper instruments were violins. The English took little note of the fantasy before about 1585; the favourite form was still the 'In nomine'. The 130 pieces in a 'Booke of In nomines and other solfainge songs of v:vi:vii:and viii: parts for voyces or Instrumentes'[104] dating from *c.* 1578, some years later than the Mulliner Book, consist of vocal pieces without text and 'In nomines' or other cantus firmus compositions, but includes only a single 'phancy' for five parts by an Edward Blancks who is nearly as obscure as the 'Newman' of the Mulliner Book. Yet this has one interesting feature, an interpolation of seven bars in triple time; similarly one of Byrd's five-part 'In nomines' in the same manuscript[105] ends with a dance-like section in triple time. Such triple-time endings or interpolations are highly characteristic of the English fantasia and Byrd's finest examples, two of those in six parts,[106] are both marked by them. He was the earliest major exponent of the fantasy, for his three-part examples,[107] the five-part,[108] and the keyboard 'fancies' and 'voluntaries' in 'My Ladye Nevells Booke'[109] must date from *c.* 1585–1590. They are comparable with the Italian ricercari of the period, with regular fugal entries at the fifth and well morticed cadential joins. Later Byrd evolved more decidedly instrumental types of theme and differentiated more sharply between the sections. These tendencies were carried much further by the younger men, Gibbons, Coprario, the younger Ferrabosco, Thomas Lupo, and a number of others, who would base a short section on a popular morris-dance tune (as Gibbons does in a four-part viol fantasy) and use motives more clear-cut in rhythmic profile sequentially as Giovanni Gabrieli does.

The only fantasia in *Parthenia* is Gibbons's 'of foure parts',[110] which is appropriate for it is one of the finest of all the keyboard fantasias. The English keyboard repertory, preserved almost entirely in manuscripts and much smaller in quantity than that for solo lute, is no less impressive. It is even more original and varied in type than the consort music, including not only fantasias, 'In nomines', stylized dance-music, arrangements of music from masques and of popular songs, but also miniature genre-pieces, essays in programme music and pure impressionism such as Byrd's 'The Battle' and 'The Bells',[111] variations on ground basses, and sets of variations on popular tunes as distinct from simple arrangements of them. The largest of

---

[102] See *MB*, ix, Nos. 54–75 and 87–94.
[103] The case for this late dating and instrumentation was convincingly argued by Dart, 'The Printed Fantasies of Orlando Gibbons', *M&L*, xxxvii (1956), p. 342.
[104] Brit. Mus. Add. 31390. See the description and list of contents by Jeremy Noble, 'Le Répertoire instrumental anglais: 1550–1585', in *La Musique instrumentale de la Renaissance* (ed. Jean Jacquot) (Paris, 1955), p. 91.
[105] Ed. E. H. Fellowes, *The Collected Works of William Byrd*, xvii, p. 49.
[106] Ibid., pp. 71 and 81.   [107] Ibid., pp. 2, 4, and 6.   [108] Ibid., p. 20.
[109] *William Byrd: Keyboard Music*, ed. Alan Brown, *MB*, xxvii–xxviii, Nos. 25, 27, 46, 61, 64. No. 26 is a version of the five-part string fantasia.
[110] *Orlando Gibbons: Keyboard Music*, ed. Gerald Hendrie, *MB*, xx, No. 12.
[111] *MB*, xxvii–xxviii, Nos. 94 and 38.

all the manuscript collections, the nearly 300 pieces of the so-called 'Fitzwilliam Virginal Book'[112] compiled by a Catholic recusant, Francis Tregian, probably between 1609 and 1619, gives a very fair cross-section. Next to Byrd, the composers most fully represented are two who, although by no means exclusively keyboard composers, are remembered for little else: John Bull (*c.* 1563–1628), a pupil of Blitheman (see p. 240–1), and Giles Farnaby (*c.* 1566–1640). Farnaby is at his best as a miniaturist; his fantasias are of little account but such tiny gems as 'Giles Farnaby's Dream', 'His Rest', 'Farnaby's Conceit' and 'His Humour' are unique, and he was also a master of the art of variation-writing.

It is above all in the sets of variations that the English virginal repertory differs from the consort repertory; Allison's 'Goe from my Window' variations in Morley's *Consort Lessons* are quite exceptional. The principles of variation – ornamentation, thematic reshaping, and so on – had long been in common use. Composition on the conventional melodies-and-basses of the 'Romanesca' type was another form of variation, though a keyboard set such as Andrea Gabrieli's 'Capriccio sopra Il Pass' e mezo Antico'[113] was probably a novelty; Byrd and Farnaby composed sets on 'grounds'. But the extended sets of variations usually on popular songs, but sometimes on dance-tunes or the notes of the hexachord, generally increasing in complication and technical difficulty toward the end, which are arguably the chief glory of virginal music, have been plausibly derived from the *diferencias* of Cabezón (see pp. 236–7). Cabezón was certainly in England with his master, Philip of Spain, for more than a year during 1554–5 when it is improbable that he was not known to Blitheman who was in the service of Mary I. Perhaps also a copy of his belatedly published *Obras de musica* (1578) found its way to England, offering models of song variation. Whatever the prototypes, such variations as Byrd's on 'The Carman's Whistle', 'Sellenger's Round', 'The Woods so wild', Farnaby's on 'Woody-cock' and 'Up tails all', to mention only a few of those in the Fitzwilliam Book, are masterpieces. Byrd's 22 variations on 'Walsingham' present special difficulties including cross-rhythm, but Bull seems to have deliberately trumped them with his even more brilliant and difficult 30 variations on the same tune, which Tregian placed at the head of his anthology: a veritable thesaurus of keyboard devices.

Bull was always, first and foremost, a virtuoso both of technical invention and obviously of performance, even in compositions probably or certainly intended for the organ[114] where he appears as the direct heir of Preston and Blitheman. Only when he essays Farnaby's type of miniature – 'My Self', 'My Grief' (styled 'A Gigge' by Tregian), 'My Choice' – does he curb his virtuosity. When in 1613 he 'went beyond the seas without licence' and settled first at Brussels, then at Antwerp, he was in personal contact with

[112] Ed. J. A. Fuller Maitland and W. Barclay Squire (Leipzig, 1898–9); numerous reprints. But the best texts of the major composers besides Byrd and Gibbons are *Thomas Tomkins* (ed. Stephen D. Tuttle), *MB*, v, *John Bull* (ed. John Steele, Francis Cameron, and Thurston Dart), *MB*, xiv and xix, and *Giles & Richard Farnaby* (ed. Richard Marlow), *MB*, xxiv.
[113] Pidoux's edition, i, p. 36.   [114] See *MB*, xiv.

another expatriate, Peter Philips, and with the Amsterdam organist Sweelinck, both of whom figure in the Fitzwilliam Book.

THE KEYBOARD MUSIC OF SWEELINCK AND PRAETORIUS

The question of priorities with Sweelinck is not easily solved for, whereas his vocal works began to appear in print in 1594, none of his compositions for organ or harpsichord – by far the most important part of his output – were published while he was alive, and all but one of the five manuscript sources dating from his lifetime are English; in fact the Fitzwilliam Book is the earliest. In his fantasias and toccatas[115] it is not difficult to trace Venetian influences, particularly in the six fantasias 'in the manner of an echo' where he takes advantage of the two manuals of the organ to 'echo' motives duly marked f and p. In some of the others there is a clear affinity with Philips's two 'Fitzwilliam' fantasias. (He wrote variations on the early pavane by Philips, dated 1580, in Fitzwilliam.[116]) And there can be little doubt that his song variations were suggested by the English ones;[117] two of the tunes appear also in 'Fitzwilliam' under different names: 'Est-ce Mars' ('The New Sa-Hoo') and 'Von der Fortuna' ('Fortune'). But Sweelinck was no mere imitator, as one sees from his masterly variations on 'Mein junges Leben hat ein Endt'. His application of the variation principle to plainsong, Lutheran hymns, and Huguenot psalms goes far beyond the 'organ hymns' and versets of earlier generations, and differs from his secular variations in that the basic melody is generally preserved intact as cantus firmus in one part or another throughout. The only comparable works are the four monumental organ pieces on 'Ein feste Burg', 'Christ unser Herr zum Jordan kam', 'Wir glauben all', and 'Nun lob mein Seel', the last of which actually consists of two variations, that Michael Praetorius inserted in Part VII of his *Musae Sioniae* (1609).[118] Between them Sweelinck and Praetorius laid the foundations of seventeenth- and eighteenth-century German organ music.

By the second decade of the new century instrumental music in general had developed special properties rendering obsolescent the concept of composition 'da cantare et sonare per ogni instrumento' or 'apt both for viols and voices', while at the same time concerted secular music for voices was beginning to be overtaken in popularity by the vocal solo or duet.

---

[115] *Jan Pieterszn. Sweelinck: Werken voor orgel en clavecimbel*, ed. Max Seiffert (Amsterdam, third, enlarged edition, 1957), with supplement, ed. Alfons Annegarn (1958).
[116] Fitzwilliam, No. 85, and *Werken*, p. 251.
[117] On English influences in Sweelinck, see Alan Curtis, *Sweelinck's Keyboard Music* (London, 2nd edition, 1972).
[118] *Gesamtausgabe der musikalischen Werke von Michael Praetorius*, ed. Friedrich Blume (Wolfenbüttel, 1928–1960), vii.

14

Secular Song (c. 1610–60)

THE TRANSFORMATION OF THE MADRIGAL

The waning popularity of polyphonic song, whether for voices only or for voices doubled by instruments, during the first half of the seventeenth century, is remarkable all over Europe. There was of course no sudden switch to solos and duets with continuo or other independent instrumental accompaniment, yet by the mid-century the old forms of madrigal, polyphonic chanson, and *Lied* were obsolescent. As the Roman polymath Pietro della Valle observed in 1640[1] madrigals were now not often sung, 'nor is there occasion to sing them, since people prefer to hear singing freely by heart with instruments in the hand rather than to watch four or five companions singing with book in hand at a table like schoolboys (*che ha troppo del scolaresco e dello studio*)'. However as late as 1668 another Roman, Mario Savioni (*c.* 1608–1685) brought out a book of five-part *Madrigali morali e spirituali*, explaining that they were to be sung each at the end of one of his previously published *Concerti morali* and adding that he had 'taken care to unite together the aria and the madrigal so as to conform with the character of the concertos'.

The movement of the tide is well illustrated by the successive books of Monteverdi's madrigals. The first four are normal, though the Fourth Book contains pieces, e.g. 'Sfogava con le stelle', with a lot of chordal recitation. The *Quinto Libro* (1605) has an optional continuo part that becomes obligatory in the last six pieces (of which 'Questi vaghi' has 9-part instrumental *sinfonie* into the bargain). The Sixth Book (1614)[2] is similarly divided, even in the pieces without obligatory continuo, and not only in the five-part arrangement of the 'Lamento d'Arianna'.[3] In the extremely emotional 'Sestina: Lagrime d'Amante al Sepolcro dell'Amata' Monteverdi pours out his personal grief for the young singer Caterina Martinelli in passages of declamatory solo or duet which the other voices *accompany*. As for the Seventh and Eighth Books (1619 and 1638), to say nothing of the Ninth, compiled eight years after the composer's death, they contain quasi-operatic ballets and experiments (*Il ballo dell' Ingrate, Tirsi e Clori, Il combattimento di Tancredi e Clorinda*),[4] declamatory or melodic solos or duets

---

[1] *Della musica dell'età nostra*, printed in Solerti, *Le origini del melodramma* (Turin, 1903), p. 148.
[2] The numbering of volumes in Malipiero, *Tutte le opere*, corresponds to the numbers of the Books.
[3] See p. 275.
[4] On the *Combattimento* see p. 317.

over repeated or varied basses, with or without string ritornelli, elaborate vocal and instrumental concerti, and the simplest solo canzonette. 'Con che soavità' in Book VII is for a solo singer and nine instruments disposed in three *cori* – the Gabrieli style in miniature – while 'Ohimè dov' è il mio ben' is a *romanesca* (see p. 237) with two voices singing in close imitation above the bass. Another enchanting piece in the same book, 'Chiome d'oro', is described as a 'Canzonetta a due voci Concertata da duoi Violini Chitarone o Spinetta'; the voices duet (mostly in parallel thirds) over an ostinato bass, each of their five strophes being introduced by one of three ritornelli for the two violini over the same ostinato. The Eighth Book, *Madrigali Guerrieri, Et Amorosi*, opens with an apostrophe to the Emperor Ferdinand III to whom the book is dedicated: 'Altri canti d'Amor'. This is, in effect, what had already been known for a considerable time as a 'cantata' for six voices, four viole, two violini, and string and keyboard continuo, in four strongly contrasted sections (solo and tutti) preceded by a *sinfonia*. It is followed by a setting of Petrarch's 'Hor ch'el Ciel e la Terra el vento tace' which begins with a breathtaking suggestion of total silence by means of more than twenty repetitions of a single triad. It would hardly be an exaggeration to say that there is more variety of treatment, as well as a greater display of creative power, in Monteverdi's 'madrigals' than in the similar compositions of all his contemporaries put together.

Yet they included gifted men, not only the Florentine pioneers of opera who for a time were still active as monodists – Peri's *Le varie musiche* (Florence, 1609), Caccini's posthumously published *Nuove Musiche e nuova maniera di scriverle* (Florence, 1614), Gagliano's *Musiche* (Venice, 1615) – but younger composers: Sigismondo d'India (*c.* 1580–1629), Claudio Saracini (1586–after 1649), and Domenico Belli (*fl. c.* 1616) in the Florentine-Mantuan orbit. It is noteworthy that the Roman Girolamo Frescobaldi (1583–1643) published his two books of *Arie* in Florence in 1630 during his fairly brief service there. In Rome there were Stefano Landi (*c.* 1590–*c.* 1655), Luigi Rossi (1598–1653), and Giacomo Carissimi (1605–74), in Venice Marc' Antonio Negri (*fl. c.* 1612), Alessandro Grandi (d. 1630), Biagio Marini (1597–1665), and Giovanni Berti (d. 1638), who all served under Monteverdi at St. Mark's, and three other composers who did not, Guglielmo Miniscalchi (*fl. c.* 1625), Carlo Milanuzzi (d. after 1647), and the blind Martino Pesenti (*c.* 1600–*c.* 1647). Some continued to write polyphonic madrigals as well as monodic ones; d'India, for instance, published eight books of five-part madrigals during 1606–24 as against five of *musiche* (for Caccini's term was commonly adopted) between 1609 and 1623.[5] In the *musiche* he continued the solo madrigal tradition of Luzzaschi and Caccini, though with a heightened emotional expressiveness reflecting that of such contemporary poets as Giambattista Marino. But in this, which

---

[5] Federico Mompellio has ed. the First Book of madrigals, *I classici musicali italiani*, x (Milan, 1942), and some of the monodies in *Sigismondo d'India e il suo primo libro di 'Musiche de cantar solo'* (*Collectanea Historiae Musicae*, i) (Florence, 1953). 'Forse vien fuor l'aurora', from the First Book of *Musiche*, in Frits Noske, *Das ausserdeutsche Sololied (Das Musikwerk)* (Cologne, 1958), p. 31.

he achieved by bold leaps and chromaticisms of melody and harmony, he was far surpassed by Saracini and Belli (neither of whom composed polyphonic madrigals) whose shock effects are comparable with Gesualdo's of the same period (see p. 267), as in this passage from Belli's 'Ardo ma non ardi' from his *Libro dell' arie a 1 e 2 v. per sonarsi con il chitarrone* (Florence, 1616):

Ex. 85

or the opening of Saracini's 'Tu parti' from his sixth book of *Musiche* (Venice, 1624).[6] Nor did Belli hesitate to give his chitarrone-player jagged leaps and, as he confessed, 'lots of quavers' (*molto serrati di crome*).

CANTADE AND ARIE

By about the time when Belli published his *Arie*, this strophic form which Caccini had clearly distinguished from the solo madrigals in his *Nuove musiche* was overtaking the madrigal in popularity and quickly surpassed it. *Arie* could be simple, tuneful *canzonette*, 'little short songs', as Morley defined them, 'wherein little art can be showed, being made in strains . . . and every strain repeated except the middle;'[7] Caccini's aria VIII, 'Odi, Euterpe' is a canzonetta with only the first 'strain' repeated. Or they could be extended strophic pieces developed from the old principle of the 'conventional' basses, the romanesca and the rest, as some of d'India's are. But the repeated bass was now freely composed, as already in Caccini's aria III, 'Arde il mio petto'. It often marches steadily in even crotchets as in Monteverdi's already mentioned 'Chiome d'oro' (which he styles 'canzonetta' presumably because of its light-handed tunefulness). Indeed Monteverdi produced a classic early example of the strophic-variation solo aria over a marching ostinato – he had come near it years before in 'Qual honor' in *Orfeo* (see p. 274) – in 'Ohimè ch'io cado'.[8] In Grandi's *Cantade et Arie a voce sola* (Venice, 1620) such songs are styled 'cantatas' (*cantade*), probably the earliest use of the term, and the openings of the two strophes of his 'Amor altri' are typical:[9]

---

[6] Quoted in *NOHM*, iv, p. 162.
[7] *Plaine and Easie Introduction*, p. 295 of Harman's edition.
[8] Published in the appendix to Milanuzzi's fourth book of *Ariose vaghezze* (Venice, 1624), though it appeared in Monteverdi's own publications only at the end of his posthumous Ninth Book.
[9] Riemann gives the voice-parts of seven strophes of Grandi's 'Vanne, vatenne Amor' in his *Handbuch der Musikgeschichte*, ii (2) (Leipzig, 1912), pp. 39–45, and the openings of the five strophes of Berti's 'Oh con quanta vaghezza' from his first book of *Cantade et arie* (1624) are shown in parallel in *NOHM*, iv, p. 173.

Ex. 86

The vocal lines of these early cantatas consist mostly of that kind of declamatory melody or nearly melodious recitative that was to be later known as *arioso*. But they also begin to admit a clear differentiation between recitative, arioso, and song within a single piece. D'India does so in 'Torna il sereno Zefiro' from his fifth book of *Musiche* (1623); and Berti distinguishes between recitative and arioso in 'Occhi miei tristi' from his *Cantade et Arie* (1624),[10] and between recitative and aria in 'Da grave incendio' in his second set (1627).[11] In 1623 an elderly Roman organist, Paolo Quagliati (*c.* 1555–1628) included in his *Sfera armoniosa* a *duetto da camera* for two sopranos and *violino obligato* in three sections distinguished by different characters, different metres, and (obviously) different tempi:

Ex. 87

---

[10] Sectional incipits in Nigel Fortune, 'Italian Secular Monody from 1600 to 1635', *MQ*, xxxix (1953), p. 191, and Eugen Schmitz, *Geschichte der weltlichen Solokantate* (Leipzig, 1914), pp. 54–5.
[11] Printed in *NOHM*, iv, pp. 179–80.

(ii)

(iii)

Ex. 87(ii) is a triple-time aria of exactly the same type as those by Berti and d'India just mentioned. Such works as these were the forerunners of the Roman cantatas of the 1630s, the leading composers of which were Landi, Luigi Rossi, and Carissimi.

THE CANTATA IN ROME

In 1619 Landi brought out an opera (see p. 311) and a book of five-part madrigals, and the following year a book of *Arie a una voce*; four more followed during the period 1627–37. He favoured the strophic variation over a slow-moving bass, as in the bass solo 'Superbi colli' in the 1620 book.[12] Much more important as a cantata composer was Rossi, a childhood pupil of

[12] Riemann quotes the first strophe and part of the second, with tremendous coloratura flourishes descending from d' to D, op. cit., p. 46.

de Macque. He was enormously prolific; Alberto Ghislanzoni's thematic catalogue[13] enumerates 263 solo cantatas, canzoni, and arias, and more than a hundred more for two or three voices. Their variety of style and organization is equally remarkable, and it is regrettable that – owing to the fact that merely eight of them were published in his lifetime in miscellaneous collections of *Arie spirituali* (1640) and *Ariette* (1646) – we have few means of determining which are early works, which late. 'Ravvolse il volo' can be dated between 1630 and 1636 by a textual reference, and the famous 'Ferito un cavaliero', a lament for Gustavus Adolphus of Sweden, is almost certainly a late work composed in 1655 in anticipation of the visit to Rome of Gustavus's daughter, Christina, a recent Catholic convert; one cannot imagine a Roman composer celebrating the Protestant hero at any earlier date. Yet both the early *Lamento d'Amore* and the late *Lamento della Regina di Svetia* are in the same form, four recitative sections each ending with a brief arioso refrain – the Queen's cry of 'Datemi per pietade un che m'uccida' – except that the later piece also has an introductory recitative describing the arrival of the 'wounded horseman' from the battlefield. Another cantata which can be dated 1649 by its reference to the execution of Charles I, *La Fortuna* ('Alla ruota, alla benda'), is much more varied and more typical in form:

> Recitative
> Aria I, 4/4
> Recitative
> Aria II, 6/8 (five strophes with continuo interludes)
> Recitative
> Aria I
> Recitative
> Aria III, 6/8
> Recitative
> Aria IV, 4/4
> Recitative
> Aria II

Equally complicated are the *Lamento di Zelemi, turca* ('Con occhi belli e fieri') in 13 sections, four of which consist of an aria repeated as a ritornello, and 'Hor che notte guerriera' for two sopranos and tenor (representing Fortuna, Amore, and Amante), and two violins; the latter includes three recitatives, two arias, a duet, and two terzetti as well as three instrumental *sinfonie*. One of the finest of all, 'Gelosia', published in 1646, opens with a great passionate outburst:

---

[13] *Luigi Rossi: biografia e analisi delle opere* (Milan, 1954), pp. 220 ff.
[14] Recitative in Riemann, op. cit., p. 380 (but with errors); second aria in Dent, 'Italian Chamber Cantatas', *The Musical Antiquary*, ii (1910–11), p. 187.
[15] *HAM*, ii, No. 203, and Riemann, op. cit., p. 381, respectively.

Ex. 88

which is followed by a nine-bar aria in triple time and a fast arioso; the whole scheme is then twice repeated, very freely. Then again there are quite short cantatas, such as 'Pensoso, afflitto', a short recitative followed by two arias,[14] and 'Se dolente', aria-recitative-aria. Some of Rossi's canzoni, e.g. 'Io lo vedo' and 'Difenditi, o core',[15] are simple da capo arias; 'Due labbra di rose' is a strophic duet canzone showing Rossi's purely melodic charm at its best.[16]

The printed collections of 1640 and 1646 in which Rossi's cantatas and canzoni appear also contain works by the Mazzocchi brothers[17] and Marco Marazzoli, all three of whom belonged, like Rossi himself, to the circle who enjoyed the patronage of the Barberini family (see p. 313). The 1646 volume furthermore includes two pieces by another Roman, Carissimi, whose cantatas generally – and they number 130 or more – present the same problem of chronology as Rossi's.[18] Carissimi employed the same variety of forms and styles, and covered an emotional range from the deep tragedy of *Il lamento di Maria di Scozia* to the rich comedy of *Il ciarlatano*. The latter[19] is a good example of his more extended type of cantata with fewer but longer sections than Rossi's:

> Arioso
> Recitative
> Terzetto
> Recitative
> Duet
> Recitative/Arioso
> Terzetto

The opening of the duet will also illustrate one of Carissimi's most striking characteristics, his genuine sense of key:

[16] Luigi Torchi, *L'arte musicale in Italia* (Milan, n.d.), v. p. 190.
[17] Domenico Mazzocchi (1592–1665) had recently (1638) also published five-part madrigals, some with but more without continuo: see the excerpts in Alfred Einstein, *The Italian Madrigal*, ii, pp. 869–71.
[18] The first volume of the cantatas, ed. Lino Bianchi, in Carissimi's *Opere complete* (Rome, 1951–   ), appeared in 1960. Gloria Rose has ed. six of the solo cantatas (London and New York, 1969).
[19] Torchi, op. cit., p. 238. Torchi's continuo realizations must always be ignored.

Ex. 89

O quan - ti so - no a - man - ti e non lo cre - do-

O quan - ti so - no a - man - ti e non lo cre - do - no,

-no!

The slow, uncertain supersession of mode by key had not yet generally revealed the possibilities of tonality for variety and dynamic structure; composers still treated a key very much as a mode, a tonal area within which they could move and from which they wandered uncertainly, and which helped to give unity to a composition. A clear-cut modulation like this from F to B flat, and a little later through C to G before returning to the tonic was still unusual in the mid-seventeenth century. All the movements of *Il ciarlatano*, except two recitatives, begin and end in F major; indeed Carissimi's cantatas are nearly all firmly unified by key. But two solo cantatas, 'Havea la notte oscura' in F major[20] and 'Sospiri ch'uscite' in G minor, venture into wider fields; in the former, for instance, one section begins in B flat and ends in C minor.

By the middle of the century chamber cantatas were being written all over Italy; the composers were as numerous as the madrigalists of the previous century. But the Italian cantata never struck roots abroad even in the modest way the madrigal had done. At least two notable cantata composers, the Roman Giovanni Felice Sances (*c.* 1600–1679) and Pietro (Antonio) Cesti (1623–69), far more famous for his operas,[21] ended their careers in the

---

[20] Ed. Prunières, *Maîtres du chant*, vi (Paris, 1927).
[21] See the following chapter, p. 321. Seven of Cesti's cantatas have been ed. by David L. Burrows (Wellesley Edition, No. 5), (Wellesley, Mass., 1964). A fine example is given in Guido Adler, *Handbuch der Musikgeschichte* (second edition, Berlin, 1930), i, p. 439; it shows *inter alia* how Cesti, like Carissimi at times, allowed the basso continuo to participate thematically:

è nau - fra - gio ba - stan - te il mio do - lo - [re]

B.C.

Imperial Chapel at Vienna, but they failed to transplant the chamber cantata there. Even the term 'cantata' appears not to have been used by a German composer before 1638.

ITALIAN INFLUENCE ON GERMAN SONG

German secular music during the second decade of the century felt Italian influence, but it was the influence of Giovanni Gabrieli, not of the monodists. The composers of the post-Hassler generation (see p. 283) went on publishing polyphonic *deutsche Lieder* of every kind in the old style. Melchior Franck brought out a series of collections under fancy titles – *Recreationes musicae* (1614), *Delitiae amoris* (1615), *Lilia musicalia* (1616) – and at last introduced fa-la refrains in 1621 in his *Newes Teutsches Musicalisches Fröliches Convivium* (Coburg, 1621).[22] The following year Widmann also introduced fa-las in his *Musicalischer Studentenmuth* (Nuremberg, 1622).[23] More progressive than these were the three collections of *Musica boscareccia* (Leipzig, 1621, 1626, and 1628) and *Diletti pastorali* (1624) of the Leipzig *Thomaskantor*, Johann Hermann Schein (1586–1630).[24] Schein had already employed the continuo in a sacred collection, the *Opella Nova* of 1618; in these two secular works it is optional. *Musica boscareccia* is for three voices, two sopranos and bass, soli or 'in ein corpus'. But the bass is figured and Schein obligingly points out alternative methods of performance: two tenors or soprano and tenor instead of the sopranos; bass to be played by trombone, bassoon, or violone; soprano II to be replaced by violin or flute; or simply soprano solo with continuo – by which expedient the German solo song with continuo was born almost by accident. Four sets which Thomas Selle (1599–1663), possibly Schein's pupil, published at Hamburg (1624–35)[25] are modelled on *Musica boscareccia*. Schein's *Diletti pastorali* are more frankly madrigalian and they suggest that he was acquainted with Monteverdi's Seventh Book of 1619.

So also was the greatest German musician of the century, Heinrich Schütz (1585–1672), who actually made a German translation, 'Güldne Haare', of Monteverdi's 'Chiome d'oro'. Later he borrowed from the *Scherzi musicali* of 1632 the ostinato bass and other details of 'Zefiro torna', and the *concitato* effects of 'Armato il cor', in his own *Symphoniae sacrae II* (1647).[26] But he employed the new Italian style in the sacred works which occupied him almost exclusively, so that his secular compositions are few

---

[22] Example in Johannes Wolf, *Music of Earlier Times* (New York, n.d.), No. 63, and a *quodlibet* from the same collection, No. 62.

[23] The *Studentenmuth* has been ed., with other Widmann collections, by G. Reichert, *EDM (Sonderreihe III)* (Mainz, 1959). A typical student song from it is easily accessible in Schering, *Geschichte der Musik in Beispielen*, No. 186.

[24] *J. H. Schein: Neue Ausgabe Sämtlicher Werke*, viii, ed. Adam Adrio. Examples from *Musica boscareccia* in Schering, op. cit., No. 187(a) and H. J. Moser, *Das deutsche Sololied (Das Musikwerk)* (Cologne, 1957), No. 1.

[25] Example in Moser, op. cit., No. 3.

[26] 'Es steh' Gott auf', in *Heinrich Schütz: Neue Ausgabe sämtlicher Werke*, xvi (ed. Werner Bittinger), p. 27.

and for the most part negligible. The real pioneer of the Italian monodic style in Germany was one of his pupils, Johann Nauwach (*c.* 1595–*c.* 1630), who like him had spent some years in Italy. After studying the lute there, Nauwach came home and published a book of *Arie passeggiate*, solo madrigals for 'Chitarrone et altri simili Instr.' (Dresden, 1623). One of these is none other than Caccini's celebrated 'Amarilli', in which Nauwach inserted 'passages' more suggestive of fingers on an instrument than vocal ornamentation, with the necessary additional bits of continuo bass. His setting of Guarini's 'Cruda Amarilli' is modelled, much more freely, on d'India's in his first book of *Musiche*.[27] He also included four strophic *Arien*[28] and continued in this simpler vein in his *Teutsche Villanellen* for one to three voices (1627).[29] Nine of the poems were by Opitz, and Schütz contributed a little strophic duet at the end of the volume.

Seemingly the first German to use the term 'cantata' was another pupil of Schütz, Kaspar Kittel, who had lived in Venice during 1624–9. Kittel published his *Arien und Cantaten* for one to four voices at Dresden in 1638. But what he understood by 'cantata' was the early form, strophic variations over a repeated bass,[30] in two cases the 'Ruggiero', in one the romanesca. Any suggestion of Italianism is stamped out by the steady march of the voices:

Ex. 91

Incidentally, one of Kittell's *Arien*[31] is a setting of the last three strophes of Opitz's 'Nachtklag', the first six of which had been set by Schütz as a madrigal, 'Itzt blicken durch des Himmels Saal' for five voices, two violins, and continuo.[32]

THE NORTH GERMAN AND SAXON COMPOSERS

In the same year as Kittel's *Arien und Cantaten*, yet another of Schütz's pupils, his cousin Heinrich Albert (1604–51) published the first of eight 'parts' of *Arien . . . In ein Positiv, Klavizimbel, Theorbe oder anders vollst.*

---

[27] Parallel excerpts showing both in Einstein, 'Ein unbekannter Druck aus der Frühzeit der deutschen Monodie', *SIMG*, xiii (1911–12), pp. 294 and 290 respectively.
[28] One example, ibid., p. 296.
[29] Example in Moser, op. cit., No. 2; others in Robert Haas, *Musik des Barocks* (Potsdam, 1932), pp. 99–100.
[30] Example in Haas, op. cit., pp. 101–2.
[31] For another example, see Moser, op. cit., No. 5.
[32] *Neue Ausgabe*, xxxvii (ed. Werner Bittinger), p. 98.

Instrument zu singen gesetzt (Königsberg, 1638–50)[33] which enjoyed
enormous popularity; by 1652 the first five *Teile* had reached their third or
fourth editions and a number of separate songs had been republished in
other people's miscellanies. Albert, like most Lutheran composers, mixed
the sacred with the secular and by no means all his songs are solos. Some are
reduced from earlier polyphonic forms, others were expanded into them
(just as Selle promised to do in the preface to his *Mono-Phonetica*, published
at Hamburg in 1636, his earliest really monodic publication).[34] Albert
employs a great variety of styles from recitative to the genuinely strophic,
sometimes introducing violin interludes. He had the advantage of being a
poet himself and a member of a circle of respectable poets, of whom the best
was Simon Dach, at Königsberg; he had wide musical knowledge, not only
of the Italian masters of monody, as he reveals in one of his greatest songs,
'O der rauhen Grausamkeit':[35]

Ex. 92

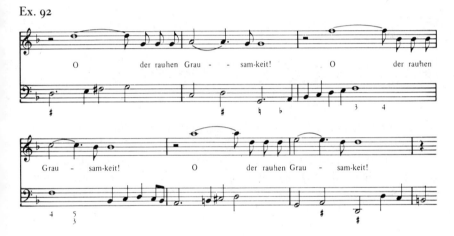

but of other foreign song, French and even Polish, from which he borrowed
with due acknowledgement. But Teutonic *gravitas* marks his most typical
work and he is strikingly responsive to German verse. He is justly regarded
as the earliest master of the German solo song with keyboard – *Positiv* or
Klavizimbel – accompaniment.

At the same time the clergyman-poet Johann Rist (1607–67) provided a
focus for song-composition, comparable with Simon Dach, at Hamburg, a
city which, like Königsberg, was untouched by the Thirty Years' War. Rist
deliberately cultivated a simple, popular style in secular (particularly
moralizing) and religious verse; he was a modest composer himself and in
his earlier collections, from 1641 onward, he also enlisted the help of local
musicians – including Selle in 1651 and 1655. But Rist's influence spread

[33] Ed. Eduard Bernoulli, *DDT*, xii and xiii. There are numerous selections and separate examples, e.g.
HAM, ii, No. 205, Schering, op. cit., No. 193 (three examples), Moser, op. cit., No. 6.
[34] Example in Haas, op. cit., p. 100.
[35] *DDT*, xii, p. 62.

well beyond the so-called Hamburg school and touched such Saxons as Andreas Hammerschmidt (1611–75) in his three collections of *Oden* with instrumental obbligati (1642, 1643, and 1649)[36] and Constantin Christian Dedekind (1628–1715) in his *Aelbianische Musen-Lust* (1657).[37]

Both Hammerschmidt and Dedekind, and indeed Heinrich Albert, were far surpassed in variety and creative power by a young pupil of Samuel Scheidt, Adam Krieger (1634–66) who published in his lifetime little more than a collection of fifty *Arien* for one to three voices with string ritornelli (Leipzig, 1657), though posthumous *Neue Arien* appeared in 1667 (augmented in 1676).[38] At the heart of most of Krieger's work lies the four-square, Lutheran-hymn-like strophic melody as in his earliest known song (which was to appear in a revised form, 'Nun sich der Tag geendet hat', in the *Neue Arien*):

Ex. 93

But Krieger was open to other influences, including Italian operatic song (e.g. 'O schöne Schäferin') and cantata (e.g. 'Fleug, Psyche, fleug'); he varied symmetry and burst the strophic form (e.g. 'Adonis Tod' and 'Ich bin verwundt') with great skill and emotional power, and also commanded a lighter vein (e.g. 'Rheinwein' and 'Es kann nichts angenehmer sein').[39]

THE FRENCH *AIR DE COUR*

French composers of the period, with one exception, were firmly closed to outside influences. They had found their own solution to the humanist problem of mating music with words in *musique mesurée*, the influence of which lingered on although it was no longer practised with doctrinaire thoroughness,[40] and the *air de cour* with lute accompaniment flourished to the near exclusion of polyphonic song, though some of the published lute airs were obviously based on polyphonic originals. The heterogeneity of French solo song at the beginning of the century is shown by the six books of *Airs de différents autheurs* published by the lutenist Gabriel Bataille

[36] Examples from the 1642 volume in Moser, op. cit., No. 7, and Schering, op. cit., No. 194.
[37] Example in Moser, No. 10.
[38] The 1676 edition has been ed. by Alfred Heuss, *DDT*, xix (Leipzig, 1905); there are numerous modern editions of separate songs, e.g. *HAM*, ii, No. 228; Schering, No. 209 (two examples); Moser, No. 12.
[39] *DDT*, pp. 39, 95, 16, 80, 148, and 138.
[40] See D. P. Walker, 'The influence of *musique mesurée à l'antique*, particularly on the *airs de cour* of the early seventeenth century', *Musica Disciplina*, ii (1948), p. 141.

(1575–1630) during 1609–15;[41] each book consists partly of his own compositions, partly of *airs de cour* and psalm-settings by Pierre Guédron (d. 1621), Le Jeune's successor as Compositeur de la chambre du Roi, Guédron's son-in-law Antoine Boësset (1586–1643), the elderly Mauduit, and others. Boësset continued this series of lute *Airs* down to 1632 as well as reviving the four- or five-part *airs de cour* in nine books from 1617 to 1642. They range in style from genuine *musique mesurée* (Guédron's 'Lors que Léandre'), through songs influenced in greater or lesser degree by it (e.g. the same composer's 'Heureux qui se peut plaindre'),[42] to light melodious chansons, ballet airs, and dramatic *récits* like those composed for the court ballets. These *récits* are the most interesting of Guédron's works; it was he who was responsible for introducing them in place of spoken dialogue, thereby taking the *ballet de cour* a significant step nearer to opera, particularly in the *Ballet de la Délivrance de Renaud* (1617) (see also p. 322, n. 44) and *Ballet du Roy sur L'Adventure de Tancrède en la forest enchantée* (1619). There is no stylistic difference between a lute song like 'Quel espoir de guarir':

Ex. 94

and one of his ballet *récits*; indeed some of the latter turn up in the lute books, as Clorinda's despairing 'Toy de qui la rigueur' in *Tancrède* did with a lute accompaniment arranged by Boësset the following year.[43] But there is a considerable difference between this and the monody of Caccini or Monteverdi. Guédron's most popular air, 'Est-ce Mars le grand Dieu des alarmes', in the *Ballet de Madame* (1613), inspired both Sweelinck and Scheidt to write keyboard variations on it and it appears in the Fitzwilliam Virginal Book in an arrangement by Farnaby as 'The New Sa-hoo'.

Whereas Guédron had considerable sense of drama, Boësset had more talent for lyricism and the love-song, and it was his path rather than that of his father-in-law which was followed by the younger composers, of whom François Richard the elder (d. 1650) and Étienne Moulinié (c. 1600–after 1669) were the most gifted. Nor was his popularity limited to France. His songs were mangled and set to German and English verse, for instance in Heinrich Albert's *Arien* where the four-part version of 'Du plus doux de ses

[41] Selection of twenty-four ed. Peter Warlock, *French Ayres* (London, 1926); larger selection of 90 ed. André Verchaly, *Airs de cour pour voix et luth (1603–1643)*, (Paris, 1961).
[42] Warlock, p. 13; opening quoted in *NOHM*, iv, p. 193.
[43] Facsimile in *MGG*, v, cols. 1020–1.

traits' appeared with continuo in 1643 as 'Unser Heil ist kommen'[45] and in Edward Filmer's *French Court-Aires with their Ditties* (London, 1629).[46]

ENGLISH SONG

Unlike the French, the English song-composers were still wide open to Italian influence – and to the new monodic style before the Germans seem to have been aware of it. As already mentioned (see p. 280), Robert Dowland's *Musicall Banquet* of 1610 included Caccini's 'Amarilli' and 'Dovrò, dunque, morire' and a solo madrigal, 'Se di farmi morire', by an early but unimportant monodist, Domenico Maria Melli, and his father succumbed to the new style in at least three of his last songs. (In the *Banquet* the continuo parts were 'realized' in fully written lute parts.) The composer generally credited with the introduction of the *stylo recitativo* into England was Nicholas Lanier (1588–1666), composer, singer, lutenist, Master of the King's Music, and deviser of masques at the court of Charles I, but there is some doubt[47] whether what Ben Jonson said in 1640 – that Lanier 'spake in song' in two of his masques in 1617 – was genuine recitative or only declamatory song. None of this music for *Lovers Made Men* and *The Vision of Delight* has survived, but the earliest piece of Lanier's that we have, 'Bring away this sacred tree' for the Earl of Somerset's Wedding Masque (1613),[48] is close in style to Guédron's *récits* (cf. Ex. 94), and his setting of Walter Raleigh's 'Like hermit poor'[49] is not so very much more declamatory than Ferrabosco's in his *Ayres* of 1609:[50]

Ex. 95

(i) FERRABOSCO

Like her-mit poor in place ob-scure, I mean to spend my days of end-less doubt.

(ii) LANIER

Like her-mit poor in pen - sive place ob - scure, I mean to spend my days of end-less doubt,

while his ending is incomparably more feeble. However during 1625–8 Lanier was in Italy, buying pictures for his royal master, and after his return

[45] *DDT*, xii, p. 119. Similarly Albert's 'So ist es denn des Himmels Will', ibid., p. 93, is based on Moulinié's lute-air 'Est-ce l'ordonance des Cieux' (1635).

[46] Noske, op. cit., No. 7, gives Boësset's 'Je vouldrois bien, ô Cloris' together with Filmer's version of words and melody. This is one of the very many instances in Boësset where the version with lute (1615) was obviously based on the five-part version published two years later.

[47] See McD. Emslie, 'Nicholas Lanier's Innovations in English Song', *M & L*, xli (1960), p. 13.

[48] With later words, 'Weep no more my wearied eyes', in *English Songs (1625–1660)* (*MB*, xxxiii), ed. Ian Spink (London, 1971), p. 1.

[49] Which Playford placed first in his *Select Musical Ayres* of 1652 (see below), the earliest publication of any work of Lanier. See *MB*, xxxiii, p. 187.

[50] *English Lute-Songs* (second series), xvi (ed. Fellowes and Dart).

composed an indisputable recitative on the subject of Hero and Leander, 'Nor com'st thou yet, my slothful love' and a varied-strophe aria, 'No more shall meads'.[51] Lanier seems to have reckoned on lute accompaniment and the credit for the earliest English publication with figured bass must go to Martin Peerson (*c.* 1572–1650)[52] in his *Mottects or Grave Chamber Musicke* (1630). But Peerson must be placed with other essentially conservative musicians such as John Hilton 'the younger' (1599–1657) who were nevertheless conscious of the new trend, as Hilton shows in his *Ayres, or fa la's for three voyces* (1627)[53] and solo songs,[54] and still more in his dramatic dialogues 'Job' and 'King Soloman and the two Harlotts'. The most notable English progressive was Walter Porter (*c.* 1588–1659), who claimed Monteverdi as his 'good Friend and Maestro' and certainly seems to have been acquainted with the master's Seventh Book; indeed one madrigal, 'Wake Sorrow, Wake', can be dated to 1615, earlier than the Seventh Book. His *Madrigales and Ayres of two, three, foure, and five Voyces, with the continued Base, with Toccatos, Sinfonias, and Ritornellos to them. After the manner of Consort Musique* (1632)[55] are fairly described by their title and there is nothing else quite like them in English music.

Like Lanier, Porter was in the royal service, as were the other leading composers of the Caroline period: Robert Johnson (*c.* 1580–*c.* 1634), John Wilson (1595–1674), and the Lawes brothers, Henry (1596–1662) and William (1602–45). Much of their music was originally intended for plays or Court masques; a great deal of it consists of undistinguished melodic declamation,[56] and even the simpler tuneful airs in which they are happiest seldom if ever match the poems of Donne and Herrick, Suckling and Carew, which they set. The best of them was Henry Lawes; even he was far from deserving Milton's great sonnet but he could manage both tragic and colloquial declamation with equal skill in dramatic monologue and strophic air:

Ex. 96

(i) Ariadne Deserted *(Ayres I, 1653)*

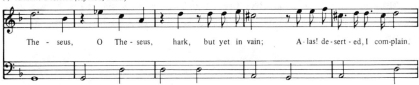

The - seus, O The - seus, hark, but yet in vain; A - las! de - sert - ed, I com-plain.

---

[51] Ibid., pp. 12 and 4.
[52] He had been preceded by the then expatriate Richard Dering whose works were published at Antwerp (see p. 356).
[53] Ed. A. Goodchild (London, 1955). One example in Wolf, *Music of Earlier Times*, No. 66.
[54] *MB*, xxxiii, Nos. 61–7.
[55] Generous extended excerpts in Ian Spink, 'Walter Porter and the Last Book of English Madrigals', *Acta Musicologica*, xxvi (1954), p. 18; see also idem, 'An Early English Strophic Cantata' (Porter's 'Farewell'), *Acta Musicologica* xxvii (1955), p. 138.
[56] For two better examples by Henry Lawes and Wilson, see Noske, op. cit., Nos. 10 and 11. See also Ex. 106.

14. Secular Song (c. 1610–60)

(ii) A Lady to a young Courtier *(Ayres III, 1658)*

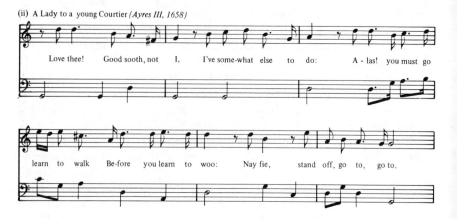

Love thee! Good sooth, not I, I've some-what else to do: A - las! you must go learn to walk Be-fore you learn to woo: Nay fie, stand off, go to, go to.

It is ironical that the Court composers should have had to wait for the establishment of the Commonwealth before their songs were published. John Playford issued his first musical publications, *The English Dancing Master* and *A Musicall Banquet* in 1651. The first[57] is an invaluable collection of popular tunes with instructions for dancing to them, which reached its eighteenth edition around 1728; the second contains pieces for viols and vocal rounds and catches, a peculiarly English form of musical amusement which had flourished briefly in James I's time (Thomas Ravenscroft's collections *Pammelia*, *Deuteromelia*, and *Melismata*, 1609–11), languished for forty years, and now took a very much longer lease of life. In 1652 John Hilton edited for Playford a 'choice collection', *Catch that Catch can*, including many pieces from Ravenscroft as well as some delightful new catches by himself, William Lawes, and others, and in the same year Playford issued *Select Musical Ayres and Dialogues* by Lanier, John Wilson, Henry and William Lawes, and other former Court musicians. In 1653 came the first of three books of *Ayres and Dialogues* by Henry Lawes; the others followed in 1655 and 1658, and beside them Playford's *Breefe Introduction to the Skill of Musick for Song and Viol* (1654) and instrumental music. Thus, after the Civil War, the music of the Court and aristocracy was brought within reach of the ordinary citizens of the Commonwealth.

---

[57] Facsimile edition with introduction and notes by Margaret Dean-Smith (London, 1957).

15

The Early Growth of Opera (c. 1610–60)

THE ENTERTAINMENT OF PRINCES

So far as one of its most important components was concerned, early opera developed *pari passu* with solo song, but its evolution was controlled by other factors. The musico-dramatic form known at first as *tragedia rappresentata in musica, favola recitata in musica, favola rappresentata in musica recitativa*, and similar designations (but not till around 1640 as *opera scenica* or *opera musicale*) had quickly escaped from the antiquarian dilettanti. But for another thirty years it remained solely an entertainment for princes and wealthy aristocrats, mostly at Mantua, Florence, Bologna, Parma, and Rome. During the period 1617–30 Monteverdi composed at least eight operas or quasi-operatic works, nearly all for his old masters, the Gonzaga dukes of Mantua, and all destroyed when the Imperialist army sacked Mantua in 1630. Caccini was dead but Peri was still composing in 1628, when he contributed the music for the part of Clori to Marco da Gagliano's *La Flora* and produced a work of his own, *Jole ed Ercole*, both for a ducal wedding in Florence.[1] Orpheus was still a favourite subject: witness the *Orfeo dolente* (Florence in 1616) of Domenico Belli[2] and *La morte d'Orfeo*, apparently the first opera produced in Rome, before the Papal court (1619), by Stefano Landi. Landi wrote his own libretto and innovated by introducing comic relief in the unlikely person of Charon, who sings what is probably the earliest of all *buffo* arias.[3]

A more important new tendency appeared in another Roman opera (1626), *La catena d'Adone* by Domenico Mazzocchi (1592–1665), who remarks in a note to the published score that he has inserted a number of 'mezz'Arie' which 'break the tedium of the recitative' (*che rompono il tedio del recitativo*). No one has given a completely convincing explanation of what Mazzocchi may have meant by 'mezz'Arie'. But he does, for instance, insert a brief aria-like refrain four times in a recitative scene in Act III for Arsete, the counsellor of the enchantress Falsirena:

---

[1] Five excerpts from *La Flora*, including the fourth variation of one of Peri's songs for Clori, in Hugo Goldschmidt, *Studien zur Geschichte der italienischen Oper im 17. Jahrhundert*, i (Leipzig, 1901), pp. 180 ff; a longish recitative in the earlier Florentine vein, from *Jole ed Ercole*, in Angelo Solerti, *Gli albori del melodramma*, i (Milan, 1904), between pp. 32 and 33.
[2] Rather dubious reconstruction by Antonio Tirabassi (Brussels, 1929).
[3] Seven excerpts from *La morte d'Orfeo* in Goldschmidt, op. cit., pp. 188 ff; his transcriptions are useful though sometimes inaccurate.

Ex. 97

ARSETE

La ra-gion per-de do - ve il sen - - - - - - - -

B.C.

- - - - - so ab - on - da

The important point is that Mazzocchi feared the tedium of recitative, and the theory has been advanced[4] that his score originally contained less of this element, the male alto hero's part being 'full of *canzonette*' which at the singer's request were replaced with recitatives by another composer, the monodist and late madrigalist Sigismondo d'India. As it is, the recitative is broken by melodious solo or ensemble 'arias', actually so called.

At the same time princely festive opera began to make its way abroad, only to be checked by war. In 1627 Schütz composed Martin Opitz's German adaptation of Rinuccini's old *Dafne* libretto (see p. 271) for the wedding of a Saxon princess at Hartenfels, near Torgau, but the Thirty Years War was no time for the birth of German opera and Schütz's score is lost. Two years before, an opera-ballet, *La Liberazione di Ruggiero*[5] after Ariosto, by Caccini's daughter Francesca (1587–c. 1640), had been given in Florence for the benefit of the future Władysław IV of Poland. The prince was so impressed that he had a Polish translation made, brought a scenic engineer from Mantua for a 'fisher idyll' *Galatea* produced at the Warsaw court, and on his accession to the throne in 1632 built a theatre in his palace where a whole series of Italian operas specially composed by members of the Royal Chapel was given. The first of these was by a Pole, Piotr Elert (d. 1653), but most were the work of Marco Scacchi (d. c. 1685). This first important flowering of opera outside Italy, however, was cut short by domestic rebellion and foreign invasion before it could strike roots and even the scores, like Schütz's, have disappeared without trace.

---

[4] By Stuart Reiner in a study ' "Vi sono molt'altre mezz'Arie . . ." ', in *Studies in Music History* (ed. Harold Powers) (Princeton, 1968), p. 241. Goldschmidt gives twelve excerpts from *La catena*, op. cit., pp. 155 ff, and there are more in Reiner's essay and in Anna Amalie Abert, *Claudio Monteverdi und das musikalische Drama* (Lippstadt, 1954), pp. 173–5.
[5] Ed. Doris Silbert, *Smith College Music Archives*, vii (Northampton, Mass., 1945); Goldschmidt gives six excerpts, op. cit., pp. 174 ff.

OPERA IN ROME

Opera in Rome was given a fresh impetus in the 1630s under the music-loving Barberini Pope, Urban VIII, and two Barberini cardinals, his nephews. Even before their magnificent palace was completed by Bernini, they opened the theatre in it, the Teatro delle Quattro Fontane holding three thousand spectators, on 23 February 1632, with a fresh opera by Landi, *Il Sant' Alessio*.[6] For this the libretto was provided by another churchman, Giulio Rospigliosi, later cardinal and finally Pope as Clement IX. Indeed Rospigliosi supplied libretti for a whole series of operas: including *Erminia sul Giordano* (1633)[7] by Michelangelo Rossi (d. after 1670), *Che soffre, speri* (1639)[8] by Domenico Mazzocchi's brother Virgilio (1597–1646) and Marco Marazzoli (1619–62), *Il palazzo incantato* (1642)[9] by Luigi Rossi (1598–1653), *Dal Male il Bene* (1653)[10] by Marazzoli and Antonio Maria Abbatini (*c.* 1595–1677). All these were produced in the Barberini theatre. Marazzoli also composed the last of the Barberini operas, *La vita humana* (1656), to a libretto by Rospigliosi's nephew, Jacopo.

The outstanding feature of these Roman operas was the splendour of the scenery and ingenuity of the scenic effects, which were devised by Bernini himself for *Erminia* and for *Sant' Alessio* when it was revived in 1634 for the entertainment of Władysław IV's brother. Demons and angels flew through the air; there were wonderful scene-changes; there was a great storm in *Erminia* and at the end of *Sant' Alessio* a great cloud descended and then opened to reveal the glory of Paradise. Landi's recitative is sometimes perfunctory, with over-many repeated notes, but sometimes reaches fine expressiveness, particularly in the part of his (castrato) hero. His score is also notable for its choruses, particularly double choruses, which are accompanied – in contrast to the merely continuo supported solos – by the orchestra (three violins and continuo for harpsichords, which are usually joined by *arpe, liuti, tiorbe e violoni*), not merely doubling the voices but sometimes playing independently:

---

[6] Excerpts in Goldschmidt, op. cit., pp. 202 ff.
[7] Ibid., pp. 258 ff.; introductory *sinfonia* in Hugo Botstiber, *Geschichte der Ouvertüre* (Leipzig, 1913), p. 234.
[8] Ibid., pp. 312 ff., and Abert, pp. 222 ff.
[9] Prologue, ibid., p. 385; excerpts in Abert, op. cit., pp. 188 ff; facsimile autograph score, *Italian Opera 1640–1770*, ii, intro. by Howard M. Brown.
[10] Excerpts, Goldschmidt, pp. 325 ff.

Ex. 98

This orchestra is also employed in three unusually extended *sinfonie* to the Prologue and Second and Third Acts, that to the prologue[11] consisting of 11 (slow) bars in quadruple time, a *canzone* of 32 bars with echo-effects of forte and piano emphasized by the scoring:

Ex. 99

7 bars in triple time, and 21 in quadruple.

Just as Landi provided comic relief in *La morte d'Orfeo*, so he did again in *Alessio* with a duet for two frivolous pages who mock the saint.[12] But in *Che*

[11] Ibid., p. 202. The even longer *sinfonia* to Act II is in Goldschmidt, p. 252, and *HAM*, ii, No. 208.
[12] Ibid., p. 210, and *HAM*, ii, No. 209.

soffre, speri his librettist took a bolder step for which he needed other composers, the younger Mazzocchi and Marazzoli. In *Alessio* Rospigliosi had already turned away from the heavily exploited areas of classical mythology and Christian epic to open up the unpromising vein of hagiology; he now struck an infinitely more successful one. *Che soffre, speri* is the earliest *commedia musicale*. It was performed on 27 February 1639, before an audience which included Milton and Cardinal Mazarin. The subject was taken from contemporary life and the chief musical interest lies in the treatment not of the amorous gentry but of the hero's four comic servants and their sons, and the peasants at a fair, who sing partly in dialect:

Ex. 100

and in a quick recitative with many repeated notes which must have been performed quasi-parlando. Here is Egisto conversing with his servants in the second scene:

Ex. 101

There is some realism in the handling of the fair-scene: the impatient cries of the chorus, 'Alla fiera, alla fiera', and the soloists selling combs and mirrors, cups and vases, straw hats.[13] The gentry sing their *arie* and duets, sometimes over ostinato basses, but the expansion of the purely musical and scenic elements at the expense of the dramatic, the recitative, which had hitherto characterized Roman opera, was not merely halted but reversed.

It was not till fourteen years later that Rospigliosi produced his second comic opera, *Dal Male il Bene*, of which Marazzoli composed only the

[13] Quoted in *NOHM*, v, p. 6.

Second Act. He had just spent seven years in Spain as papal nuncio and made the acquaintance of Calderón; the setting is Spanish and the romantic element is stronger. One of the two heroines, Donna Elvira, also anticipates a later operatic character in the words of an aria of genuine pathos, 'Che farò?'[14] But there is also a notable comic character, Tabacco, servant of one of the heroes, with a female counterpart in the pert maid Marina; and the da capo form trio-finale of the First Act, sung by Tabacco, his master, and Elvira, already sounds the characteristic note of the comic-opera finale of the future:

Ex. 102

THE FIRST PUBLIC OPERA-HOUSES

In the meantime an extremely important development had occurred in Venice. England and Spain had had playhouses open to a paying public since the 1570s, France from the beginning of the seventeenth century, but the first such public theatre in Italy was opened only in 1637. This was the San Cassiano in Venice, founded by the patrician family of Tron; it was specifically an opera-house and the first production, on 6 May that year, was an *Andromeda* by Francesco Manelli (*c.* 1595–1667).[15] The success was so great or the rivalry of the wealthy families so keen that during the next four years three more opera-houses were opened: the Teatro dei Santi Giovanni e Paolo, the San Moisè, and the Teatro Novissimo. The Giovanni e Paolo and Novissimo were both inaugurated with operas by Francesco Sacrati (d. 1650), whose works, like Manelli's and those of Benedetto Ferrari (1597–1681),[16] have all disappeared. But the noble impresarios naturally did not forget their great maestro at St. Mark's. Monteverdi had composed no

---

[14] Goldschmidt, op. cit., p. 340.
[15] For a description of the spectacle see Simon Towneley Worsthorne, *Venetian Opera in the Seventeenth Century* (Oxford, 1954), p. 25.
[16] Ferrari had also been the librettist of Manelli's *Andromeda*.

operas since 1630; now the Grimani commissioned from him an *Adone* (lost) for Giovanni e Paolo (1639) and the Vendramini inaugurated their San Moisè the same year with a revival of *Arianna*. In 1641 he produced two new works, *Le nozze d'Enea con Lavinia* (also lost) and *Il ritorno d'Ulisse in patria*,[17] and the following year his final masterpiece *L'incoronazione di Poppea*.[18]

MONTEVERDI'S LOST OPERAS

Owing to the terrible destruction of scores, the only dramatic work of Monteverdi's that we know between those of 1607–8 and the last two Venetian operas is a peculiar experiment 'in genere rappresentativo', *Il combattimento di Tancredi e Clorinda*,[19] performed in the Palazzo Mocenigo in Venice[20] in 1624. A tenor relates the narrative in stanzas 52–68 of *Gerusalemme liberata*, Canto XII, with a great deal of repeated-note quasi-parlando, while actors representing Tancred and Clorinda sing their direct speech. A small ensemble of four viole da braccio plus continuo suggests the trot, canter, and gallop of Tancred's horse, the fall of night, the clash of swords, the fury of the combatants (by rapidly repeated chords, an instrumental effect which disconcerted the players although Biagio Marini had employed it seven years before),[21] and their infighting with sword-pommels, helmets, and shields (by another novel effect: pizzicato chords). When he published the *Combattimento* in 1638, in his book of *Madrigali guerrieri ed amorosi*, Monteverdi claimed in his preface[22] that with it he had created a new genus of music, the *stile concitato* (excited), whereas earlier composers had been content to express the *molle* (soft) and *temperato*. Nowhere else does Monteverdi attempt such vivid realism; the *sinfonia da guerra* in Act II of *Ulisse* is feeble by comparison with the *Combattimento*. But *Ulisse*, despite the great, deeply expressive monologues of Penelope and Ulysses in Act I, the melodic charm of the old herdsman's song, 'Come lieto', which ends the Act, and many fine things in the remainder of the opera, is uneven enough to justify the suspicion that another hand, perhaps Manelli's, had a share in it.

There is also doubt concerning *L'incoronazione*.[23] The earliest opera on an historic subject, it is compact with characters more substantial than those of Ariosto, Tasso, or classical mythology and fully realized in their music: Poppea and Nero and their unfortunate spouses, Seneca, even subordinate characters like Poppea's nurse (who has the most purely beautiful song in the whole opera when she sings her mistress to sleep in Act II, sc.12), and the maid and page who flirt so deliciously in Act II, sc.5 ('Sento un certo,

[17] Ed. Robert Haas, *DTÖ*, xxix (vol. 57), and Malipiero, *Tutte le opere*, xii.
[18] *Tutte le opere*, xiii, and various other editions.
[19] *Tutte le opere*, viii (1); there is also an edition by Denis Stevens (London, 1962).
[20] Now part of Danieli's Hotel. See Domenico de' Paoli, *Claudio Monteverdi* (Milan, 1945), p. 246, n. 1.
[21] See p. 329.
[22] Translation in Oliver Strunk, *Source Readings in Music History* (London, 1952), p. 413.
[23] Alessandro Chiarelli 'L'Incoronazione de Poppea o Il Nerone: problemi di filologia testuale', *Rivista italiana di musicologia*, ix (1974), p. 150.

non so che') and provide the comic relief like Iro in *Ulisse*. Most of the characterization is effected by the recitative, which varies from the driest quick quasi-parlando – Monteverdi sometimes writes only a single sustained note to carry eight or nine syllables – to actual melody, with every nuance between and naturally plenty of scope for his *stile concitato*. In Act I, sc.9, for instance, in contrast with Nero's growing anger, Seneca's dignified recitative flowers into a grandiose melodic phrase at the words

> Per aggrandir l'Impero
> Si assolve de se stesso;

and then drops back into recitative with his contemptuous 'Ma che una feminella . . .'. Conversely the arias – organized strophically, sometimes on da capo lines (e.g. Amore's, Act II, sc.13), or over ground basses – make full use of the expressive vocabulary developed by the madrigalists. Monteverdi's two-part vocal writing tends often to run in thirds, only briefly in the possibly unauthentic final love-duet, more characteristically in the coloratura of Nero's duet with Lucano (Act II, sc.6) as they rejoice over Seneca's death. But there is no distraction from the interplay of characters by the scenic extravagances and choral interruptions of Roman opera.

Three years later, during the carnival of 1645, John Evelyn saw *Ercole in Lidia* by Monteverdi's pupil and successor at St. Mark's, Giovanni Rovetta (*c.* 1596–1668), at the Teatro Novissimo, with 'variety of sceanes painted and contrived with no lesse art of perspective, and machines for flying in the aire, and other wonderfull motions . . . one of the most magnificent and expensive diversions the wit of man can invent'; and the San Cassiano had a chorus for a few years. But the choruses in *L'incoronazione* (of Seneca's household, Act II, sc.3, of 'Consuli e Tribuni' in the penultimate scene) are almost nugatory and could have been sung by a handful of soloists, while the instrumental ensemble in the best source, the manuscript in the Biblioteca Marciana, Venice, consists mainly of only two parts – perhaps taken by only one player each – over the basso continuo. (*Ulisse* is written for four such parts.) The merchant-princes of Venice were not reigning princes or immensely wealthy cardinals; they economized where they could and, although astonishing spectacle was indispensable to the success of opera, the Venetians were adept at producing striking effects with relatively simple means.[24] It is possible that the young Evelyn, who had never seen a Court masque, was easily impressed. All the same the Venetian opera-houses prospered, for two more were opened in 1649 and 1651, making six in all. And this new form of entertainment was available not only to the ordinary citizens of the Republic but to the innumerable foreigners who came for commerce or pleasure. The price of a seat was only two lire.

[24] See Worsthorne, op. cit., p. 24.

FRANCESCO CAVALLI

By far the most important of the Venetian composers, after Monteverdi, was his pupil Francesco Cavalli (1602–76) whose early operas and most of his later ones were produced at San Cassiano, beginning with *Le nozze di Teti di Peleo* (1639). Here, as in his other earlier works, he tends to follow Roman models with plenty of ensembles and short instrumental pieces, e.g. Act I opens with a *sinfonia infernale* and includes two *chiamate*, one marked *alla caccia*, which could be for horns. Similarly a chorus of cavaliers, referring to 'corni e tamburi, e trombe', has instrumental parts which could be for actual trumpets and drums but are more probably for strings imitating them, since in Act II when Chiron is supposed to play his lyre the music consists of a *sinfonia di viole*,[25] and the *passata dell'armata* which ends the First Act of *Didone* (1641) and another *chiamata alla caccia* in the Third are equally ambiguous. In *Didone*, Cavalli's third opera,[26] he had the advantage of a libretto by Giovanni Francesco Busenello who next year provided Monteverdi with the poem of *L'incoronazione*; here already Cavalli showed his dramatic power, particularly in the expressive recitative. But *Didone* has a peculiarity which was to mark later Italian opera, including *L'incoronazione*: the part of Jarba, Dido's rejected lover, who in the end saves her from suicide, is a castrato singing in a higher register than Dido herself; Nerone and Ottone are in the same predicament. And both Jarba's aria in Act III and the final duet are accompanied by all the strings instead of continuo only.[27]

Cavalli was extremely prolific; no fewer than 42 operas are attributed to him and 27 of his scores are preserved in the Contarini collection of the Biblioteca di San Marco. In those of the 1640s he follows, though with less psychological insight and power of characterization, the way pointed by Monteverdi away from the ceremonial princely opera toward what one might call dramatic solo opera for the larger public: drama expressed mostly in expressive recitative monologue and lively recitative dialogue, with the brief 'arias' usually left to the minor characters. But Cavalli did not work to a formula. *L'Egisto* (1643) has an unusual number of duets, 'arias' for two persons, like those with which the shepherd and shepherdess lovers greet the dawn in the first two scenes; in 'Musici della selva',[28] for instance, each melodious strophe (freely imitated in the two violin parts) climaxes in seven bars of recitative. In Act II, sc.6, of the same opera Cavalli introduced the classic example of a type not new even in his own work and employed in so many later operas: the extended *lamento* over a ground bass,[29] usually chromatic.[30] *La Doriclea* (1645)[31] is notable for its number of choral scenes, which were clearly sung by genuine choruses – unlike the *cori* which were

---

[25] The *sinfonia (concilio infernale)* and *sinfonia di viole* are printed by Egon Wellesz, 'Cavalli und der Stil der venezianischen Oper von 1640–1660', *Studien zur Musikwissenschaft*, i (1913), pp. 58 and 59, the *coro di cavalieri* and *chiamata alla caccia* by Goldschmidt, op. cit., i, pp. 391 and 402.
[26] Facsimile score, intro. by Howard M. Brown, *Italian Opera 1640–1770*, i (New York, 1977).
[27] Jarba's aria in Wellesz, op. cit., p. 63, the duet in Abert, op. cit., p. 260.
[28] Facsimile of the autograph, Worsthorne, op. cit., 110–13.

commonly no more than ensembles of soloists. However Cavalli's most popular work was on a libretto by Giacinto Cicognini packed with effective situations. This was *Il Giasone* (1649)[32] which shows him at the height of his powers in the melodious aria with violin imitations (e.g. Jason's 'Delizie contente', Act I, sc.2), in drama (e.g. Medea's conjuration, Act I, sc.15), and in the comic (e.g. the stuttering braggart Demo's 'S'il ballo, s'io canto', Act I, sc.7).[33]

Cavalli's comic vein was worked much more fully in *La Calisto* (1651). But directly after *Giasone* he began a change of direction which was followed by most of his later operas and indeed by later seventeenth-century opera generally. For *L'Orimonte* (1650)[34] he turned to a new librettist, Nicolo Minato, whose texts differentiated more clearly between passages for dramatic/recitative and those for lyrical/aria treatment, as in very early opera. This differentiation became more and more marked in the music of his later Minato operas: *Xerse* (1654),[35] *L'Artemisia* (1656), and the rest. Arias became more important, more numerous, and were given more often to important personages; conversely, recitative became more perfunctory, the *secco* element more pronounced.

CESTI IN VENICE AND VIENNA

It is not impossible that the change was influenced by rivalry. A fortnight after the production of *Giasone*, another opera with a libretto by Cicognini had been given at the opening of yet another Venetian opera-house, Santi

[29] The actual ground bass is anticipated – longer but with fewer repetitions – in Hecuba's lament in Act I, sc. 7, of *Didone*:

Ex. 103

[30] Complete in Abert, op. cit., pp. 270 ff; the opening has often been quoted, e.g. in Donald J. Grout, *A Short History of Opera* (second edition, New York and London, 1965), p. 88.
[31] The introductory *sinfonia* of *Doriclea* is exceptionally in two short movements like a dance-pair – a movement in common time, followed by a presumably faster triple-time variation – closely modelled on the *sinfonia* of *L'incoronazione* even to the extent of borrowing Monteverdi's bass throughout; it is, however, in five parts as compared with Monteverdi's three. The later development of the opera *sinfonia* is discussed on pp. 420 ff.
[32] Act I, ed. Robert Eitner, *Publikationen der Gesellschaft für Musikforschung*, Jg. 11 (Leipzig, 1883); excerpts from Act II in Wellesz, op. cit., pp. 70–77.
[33] Eitner, op. cit., pp. 19, 79, and 44.
[34] Two arias, the second in the A B B' form not uncommon at the time, in Michael Robinson, *Opera before Mozart* (London, 1966), pp. 63 and 64.
[35] Minato's *Xerse* libretto was the basis for Handel's *Serse* of eighty years later. The opening of Cavalli's setting of 'Ombra mai fù' is quoted by Wolfgang Osthoff, 'Handels "Largo" als Musik des Goldenen Zeitalters', *Archiv für Musikwissenschaft*, xxx (1973), p. 179.

Apostoli. This was the *Orontea*[36] of Pietro (Antonio) Cesti (1623–69), a newcomer to Venice who on the strength of this work alone was described by Salvator Rosa shortly afterwards as 'now the glory and splendour of the secular stage'.[37] (It was from a manuscript music-book belonging to Rosa that Burney copied 'Intorno all' idol mio' from *Orontea* for his *General History of Music*.) Cesti's great gift was for melody: sensuous and eminently singable. Two examples, one from Silandra's 'Vieni, vieni' in *Orontea*, the other from Arsete's 'Non scherzi con Amor' in Act I of his Florentine court opera, *La Dori* (1663):[39]

Ex. 104

show (i) his construction of a long descending phrase pivoting on a descending scale and given cohesion by a motivic sequence (the latter already a well-known Venetian device),[40] (ii) his ability to write a sheer catchy tune.

---

[36] Ed. William Holmes (Wellesley, Mass., 1973).
[37] See Frank Walker, 'Salvator Rosa and Music', *Monthly Musical Record*, lxxx (1950), p. 15.
[39] Eitner's partial reprint, *Publikationen*, Jg. 11, p. 116.
[40] Cf. Ex. 108, below, on the same motive as Ex. 104 (ii).

Both *Giasone* and *Orontea* were extremely popular. They were not only revived from time to time in Venice during the next twenty years but performed in a number of other Italian cities. And in 1656 *Orontea* was given at the archducal court of Innsbruck, where Cesti was already established and had produced his *L'Argia* (1655)[41] for the visit of Christina of Sweden. Indeed Cesti spent the rest of his life composing festival court-operas for Innsbruck or Vienna, the most famous of which, *Il Pomo d'Oro* (1667, for the wedding of Leopold I), with its large orchestra including cornetti, trombones, and bassoon, its enormously costly production, its sumptuously printed libretto,[42] is as far from popular Venetian opera as can be imagined. But even before this, as a court entertainment Italian opera had reached not only Poland but France.

ITALIAN OPERA IN PARIS

It will be remembered that Mazarin, himself an Italian, had been present at a performance of *Che soffre, speri*. When his friends the Barberini were obliged for political reasons to leave Rome in 1644 and settled in Paris he lost little time in entertaining them and the French Court with Italian operas. These included a Venetian work of 1641, *La finta pazza* by Francesco Sacrati, which was partly shorn of its music but brightened with fresh ballets by a French composer and striking stage-effects by a celebrated technician Giacomo Torelli, on 14 December 1645, and *Egisto* in February 1646. Then later in that year a composer already associated with the Barberini, the great monodist Luigi Rossi, was invited to Paris; the best Italian singers were engaged, Torelli prepared expensive spectacles, and Rossi's *L'Orfeo* was given before a small and highly select audience on 2 March 1647. Hitherto musico-dramatic entertainments at the French Court had been similar to the Italian intermedii, though with an ever increasing proportion of dancing, as in the famous *Balet comique de la Royne* (1581) devised, but not written or composed, by an Italian known in France as Balthasar de Beaujoyeulx,[43] and the more dramatic *ballets de cour* composed by Guédron.[44] Probably Rossi was suggested by the Barberini brothers on account of the preponderantly spectacular nature of his earlier *Palazzo incantato*,[45] but in *Orfeo* he revealed genuine expressive power, above all in Euridice's arias in the second scene of Act II, the exquisite trio of dryads 'Dormite, begli occhi' (a reworking of a movement from the serenata, 'Hor che in notturna pace'), the chorus of nymphs 'Ah! piangete' following her death,

[41] Facsimile, intro. Brown, *Italian Opera*, iii.
[42] Guido Adler edited what survives of the score, prologue and Acts I, II, and IV, in *DTÖ*, Jg. iii (2) and iv (2) (vols. 6 and 9). His edition also reproduces Ludovico Burnacini's stage-designs.
[43] Facsimile of the original edition (Paris, 1582), ed. Giacomo Caula (Turin, 1965); transcribed Carol MacClintock, *Musicological Studies and Documents, 25* (American Institute of Musicology).
[44] One of Guédron's masterpieces, the *Ballet de la Délivrance de Renaud* (1617), was directed by Mauduit, who with Bataille and Boesset contributed to the score. The music has been printed by Prunières, *Le Ballet de cour en France* (Paris, 1914), pp. 251 ff; one of Armida's dramatic solos is quoted in *NOHM*, v, p. 172.
[45] *Italian Opera*, ii.

and Orfeo's great lament in Act II[46] before the Bacchantes tear him to pieces.

Orfeo had a mixed reception, with predictable hostility on the part of Mazarin's enemies. The wars of the Fronde broke out and the Barberini went back to Rome where their theatre reopened with the significantly named *Dal Male il Bene*. But as soon as the Fronde was over, the Court

Pl. 44   One of Giacomo Torelli's stage-sets for Luigi Rossi's *Orfeo*, performed in the Palais-Royal, Paris, during the carnival of 1647.

resumed its performances, notably in a *Ballet royal de la Nuit* (23 February 1653) with musical *récits* by Michel Lambert (*c.* 1610–1696) and other French composers, in which five roles were danced by a young Florentine dancer and violinist who had already gallicized his name as Jean-Baptiste Lully (1632–87). The following year Mazarin commissioned Francesco Buti, the librettist of Rossi's *Orfeo*, to recruit Italian singers and write another work, *Le nozze di Peleo e di Theti*, for which a Roman composer Carlo Caproli supplied the music and in which the dancers included not only Lully but the 15-year-old Louis XIV who was full of admiration for him. Most of the music is lost but it is clear from the libretto[47] that it was a hybrid of Italian opera and French *ballet de cour*; as Prunières put it,[48] 'Instead of being self-sufficient, the ballet is justified by the comedy and the comedy draws the ballet into the dramatic action'. The marriage was not always so happy. When Mazarin invited Cavalli to Paris in 1660 to provide an opera with text by Buti for the young king's marriage, the master

[46] Romain Rolland published this last as an appendix to his *Musiciens d'autrefois* (Paris, 1908); the other pieces are in Goldschmidt, op. cit., i, pp. 299, 301, 303, and 305.
[47] Which was at once translated into English by that tireless man of letters, James Howell: *The Nuptials of Peleus and Thetis* (London, 1654).
[48] *L'Opéra italien en France avant Lulli* (Paris, 1913).

encountered all sorts of difficulties and had to substitute a performance of his *Xerse* in the Louvre, with an overture and ballet music by Lully. And when at last in February 1662 the real festival opera, *Ercole amante*, one of his finest scores,[49] was produced to inaugurate the new theatre in the Tuileries, he had – despite his deliberate attempt to satisfy French taste with pomp and dancing rhythms – again to accept the insertion of ballet music by Lully, the success of which completely distracted attention from his unusually fine recitatives. But by then Mazarin had died and Lully's royal patron had assumed absolute power. Cavalli returned in disgust to Venice where he resumed his partnership with Minato in *Scipione Africano* (1664)[50] and other operas on historical subjects. Italian opera disappeared from France for many years.

FRENCH *PASTORALES* AND *COMÉDIES-BALLETS*

The music of two short *pastorales* which have some claim to be considered the earliest true operas in French has been lost. They are *Le Triomphe de l'Amour* (1654), a string of airs and instrumental pieces by Michel de La Guerre (*c.* 1605–1679) and *La Pastorale* (called 'd'Issy' because it was tried out there before being presented before the king) (1659) by Robert Cambert (*c.* 1628–1677). Mazarin encouraged Cambert to compose a more ambitious five-act *comédie en musique, comme on faisait en Italie, Ariane et Bacchus* (1659), with a large orchestra; it was rehearsed but, partly owing to the Cardinal's death, not performed and the score of this also is lost. The future lay with Lully who, besides composing and dancing in ordinary ballets, collaborated with Molière in a series of *comédies-ballets*[51] which began in 1664 with the *Le Mariage forcé* and culminated with *Le Bourgeois gentilhomme* (1670), in which Jourdain was played by the author and the Mufti by the composer. Lully had already essayed recitative in French in a ballet, *Les Saisons* (1661):[52]

Ex. 105

and the *comédies-ballets* gave him plenty of opportunities to experiment further. When he turned later to real opera, *tragédie en musique* (see pp. 373 ff.), he was by no means a novice in dealing with French declamation.

OPERA IN GERMANY AND SPAIN

The earliest non-Italian composers to attempt opera in their own language were German. But we do not know what Schütz's German *Dafne* of 1627 was like, nor the *Cleomedes* (Königsberg, 1635) of his pupil Heinrich Albert, since they are lost, and the *Seelewig* (1644) of Sigmund Theophil Staden (1607–55) is merely a curiosity. The prolific Nuremberg poetaster Georg Philipp Harsdörffer published some three hundred didactic *Frauenzimmer-Gespräch-Spiele* for the virtuous, yet at the same time entertaining, education of young women; for nine of these little plays Staden wrote music, mostly strophic songs, but in the one case of *Seelewig* the text was *Gesangsweis auf Italienische Art gesetzt*.[53] German musicians preferred to compose operas in Italian – or were required to do so. For instance, when the Munich Residenztheater was opened in 1657, the new *Hofkapellmeister*, Johann Kaspar Kerll (1627–93) was commissioned to compose an Italian *Oronte* for the occasion; unfortunately his music, like that of his later operas, is lost. (Italian opera had already appeared in Munich in 1653, very soon after the end of the Thirty Years War; indeed it was taken up by several German courts during the 1650s.)

The evolution of opera in Spain from court entertainments, play-music and so on, followed much the same course as in France – with Calderón, who allowed ample scope for music in his plays, taking the role of Molière. It was Calderón who provided the text of the earliest Spanish opera, *Celos aun del aire matan* (Jealousy even of air kills) (1660), set by Juan Hidalgo (d. 1685).[54]

THE ENGLISH MASQUE

In England, likewise, the masque was the immediate predecessor of opera. Masques were usually court entertainments, but Milton's untypical *Comus* (1634) with music by Henry Lawes was performed at Ludlow Castle. James Shirley's *Triumph of Peace* (also 1634), with music by William Lawes and Simon Ives (1600–22), and William Davenant's *Triumphs of the Prince d'Amour* (1635), with music by both Lawes brothers, were the most

[49] Wellesz, op. cit., pp. 94 ff, gives the impressive overture, with trumpets, and the charming page's song, 'Zeffri chi gite', in Act IV.
[50] *Italian Opera*, v.
[51] *Oeuvres complètes de J.-B. Lully*, ed. Prunières (Paris, 1930–), *Les Comédies-ballets*, i, ii, and iii.
[52] Quoted from La Laurencie, *Les Créateurs de l'opéra français* (Paris, new edition, 1930), p. 194.
[53] Schering gives an extensive excerpt in *Geschichte der Musik in Beispielen* (Leipzig, 1931), No. 195.
[54] Act I, all that survives of the music, ed. José Subirá (Barcelona, 1933). Rafaël Mitjana published a recitative dialogue and short air from what he held to be an earlier work of Hidalgo's, *Los celos hacen estrellas* (Jealousy makes stars, where love makes miracles), in Lavignac and La Laurencie, *Encyclopédie de la musique*, Ie. partie, iv (Paris, 1920), p. 2066.

celebrated of the Caroline court masques.[55] Together with the customary songs, choruses, and 'symphonies', they introduce somewhat primitive recitative, e.g. Irene's opening words in *The Triumph of Peace*:

Ex. 106

Incidentally Irene was sung by a tenor: Nicholas Lanier.[56]

The Commonwealth did not put an end to the masque. In 1653 Shirley's *Cupid and Death*,[57] with music by Christopher Gibbons (1616–76), Orlando's son, and Matthew Locke (*c*. 1630–1677), was presented before the Portuguese Ambassador and revived in 1659 with additional long recitatives by Locke. Between those two performances the staunch Royalist Davenant ventured on the production of musical 'entertainments' in a private house (Rutland House, Aldersgate Street) before a small paying audience: *The First Dayes Entertainment . . . by Declamations and Musick* (21 May 1656), with costumes but no real action, the music by Henry Lawes, Charles Coleman (d. *c*. 1664), Henry Cooke (*c*. 1616–1672), and the violinist George Hudson, and in August of the same year *The Siege of Rhodes*, with music by the same composers together with Locke.

THE SPREAD OF PUBLIC OPERA

Davenant himself called *The Siege* 'a Representation by the art of Prospective in Scenes, And the Story sung in Recitative Musick', a variety he describes as 'unpractis'd here; though of great reputation amongst other Nations'.[58] *The Siege* is commonly claimed to be the first English opera, though with what justice it is difficult to say since we have only the libretto and stage-designs.

Historically the most important aspect of Davenant's productions is that they removed English masque/opera from the Court to the field of public

[55] Both ed. Murray Lefkowitz in *Trois Masques à la Cour de Charles Ier d'Angleterre* (Paris, 1970). Songs from *Comus* and *The Triumphs of the Prince d'Amour* are ed. A. J. Sabol in *Songs and Dances for the Stuart Masque* (Providence, R.I., 1959); one song from *Comus* in *HAM*, ii, No. 204.
[56] See p. 308.
[57] Ed. Dent, *MB*, ii.
[58] On both *The First Dayes Entertainment* and *The Siege*, see Dent, *Foundations*, pp. 52 ff.

entertainment. The following year, 1657, Florence – the actual birthplace of opera – also acquired its first public theatre, the Teatro della Pergola, on the initiative of the Accademia degli Immobili. (It was inaugurated with *Il Podestà di Colognole ossia La Tancia*[59] by Jacopo Melani (1626–76), a comic opera with some broadly comic, as well as much beautiful music, e.g. Ciapino's aria in Act II where he imitates in turn the frog, cricket, lamb, owl, and cock.) And before very long, by quite different means, Paris too was to enjoy a public opera.

---

[59] Twelve excerpts in Goldschmidt, op. cit., pp. 349 ff.

16

Instrumental Music (c. 1610–60)

THE BASIC PROBLEM OF INSTRUMENTAL COMPOSITION

Just as the imitative motet had suggested the ricercar and fantasy, and the polyphonic chanson the canzone alla francese, so the new developments in vocal music were also soon reflected in instrumental music. Giovanni Gabrieli's posthumously published *Canzoni et sonate* of 1615[1] show him grappling in different ways with the always basic problem of instrumental composition on any but the smallest scale: the achievement of diversity within unity. In most cases he is content with his earlier method of sharply differentiated sections, one of which recurs as a ritornello. But in a 'Sonata con tre violini'[2] he abandons his massive 'concerto' style for one in which the three instrumental voices 'sing' above the continuo, the sectional seams are less obvious, and the last section is repeated *in toto* before the tiny coda.

Gabrieli's sonata was by no means an isolated example. At Milan in 1610 Gian Paolo Cima (b.*c.* 1570) published *sei sonate*, including one for violin and violone and one for violin, cornetto, and violone. And the Third Book of *Varie Sonate, Sinfonie, Gagliarde, Brandi* [branles] *e Corrente per sonar 2 Viole de braccia ed un Chitarone* (1613) of Salamone Rossi (*c.* 1570–*c.* 1630) – 'il Ebreo', the Jew, as he proudly proclaimed – contains both canzone-like sonatas and variation-sonatas on the romanesca and 'Ruggiero'; the opening of his fourth sonata:

Ex. 107

Ruggiero

---

[1] Ed. Michel Sanvoisin, *Le Pupitre*, No. 27 (Paris, 1971).
[2] Separate edition by Werner Danckert (*Hortus Musicus*, No. 70) (Kassel, 1950).

may be compared with Kaspar Kittel's 'cantata' (Ex. 91). It is worth noting that whereas Rossi here specifies *viole de braccia* (modern violas), his Fourth Book (1622) is for two *violini*, by this time presumably true violins, the instruments which approximate more nearly than any others to the human voice.

INSTRUMENTAL MONODY

Rossi was probably a violinist himself; Biagio Marini (1597–1665) certainly was – at St. Mark's Venice, from 1615 to 1620. Marini's Op. 1 – for opus-numbers were just coming into use – *Affetti musicali . . . a 1, 2, 3* (1617), like Rossi's and almost all instrumental collections of the time end with miscellaneous dances; they include two *sinfonie* 'La Orlandina' and 'La Gardana' for violin or cornetto solo with continuo.[3] These are possibly the earliest true instrumental monodies, unless Marini was anticipated by a composer thought to have been his teacher, Giovanni Battista Fontana (d. 1631). But Fontana's surviving *Sonate* were published long after his death, in 1641; they are remarkable both for virtuosic violin-writing and for a type of singing melody that anticipates Cesti's[4] and are almost certainly late works.

Marini's first essays are formally inchoate: strings of short sections contrasted in material, pace, metre, and – so far as key is established – in key; key was still a means of diversity, not yet of organization. Nor could they be particularly violinistic so long as the cornetto was thought of as an alternative. But Marini temporarily solved the problem of form by following Salamone Rossi in the use of conventional basses.[5] In his Op. 8, *Sonate, Symphonie, Canzoni, Pass'e mezzi, Baletti, Corente, Gagliarde . . . a 1, 2, 3, 4, 5, & 6* (1629) he made a startling innovation, double- and triple-stopping, which he employed in a 'Sonata per il violino per sonar con due corde',[6] a 'Capriccio che due violini sonano quattro parti', and a 'Capriccio per sonare il violino solo contre corde a modo di Lira'. Marini experimented in other directions as well; he had already in 'La Foscarina', Op. 1, No. 13, introduced the repeated-note tremolo – not only for the two violins but for 'trombone o fagotto' and keyboard continuo;[8] he now made another innovation, *scordatura*, tuning the E string down to C in a solo sonata. In Op. 8 he also introduced, in the seventh section of a 'Pass'e mezo concertato a 3', the boldest chromatic progressions – which he sensibly marked slower (*Largo di battuta*).[9]

---

[3] 'La Orlandina' is printed, with an anachronistic key-signature, in Riemann, *Handbuch der Musikgeschichte*, II.2, p. 96; 'La Gardana' in Schering, *Geschichte der Musik in Beispielen*, No. 182.
[4] Cf. the excerpts in Riemann, op. cit., pp. 111–14; his tenth sonata in Franz Giegling, *Die Solosonate (Das Musikwerk)* (Cologne, 1959), No. 3.
[5] e.g. the 'Aria di Romanesca' from his *Arie, Madrigali et Correnti a 1, 2, 3*, Op. 3 (1620), reprinted in *HAM*, ii, No. 199.
[6] Schering, op. cit., No. 183. There is a very short passage of double-stopping in Marini's earlier *Madrigali et Symfonie* (1618).
[8] The passage is quoted in William S. Newman, *The Sonata in the Baroque Era* (Chapel Hill, N.C., revised ed., 1966), p. 103.
[9] Riemann, op. cit., p. 104.

16. Instrumental Music (c. 1610–60)

By the time Marini brought out his Op. 22 in 1655,[10] there had been a great outpouring of sonatas, canzoni, sinfonie, and dances by his contemporaries and by younger men; the Italian instrumental composers of the seventeenth century are as numerous as the madrigalists of the sixteenth. Three of the most significant were Tarquinio Merula (c. 1595–1665), a native of Cremona who spent much of his life there and at Bergamo; Giovanni Battista Buonamente (fl. 1620–37), who served in Mantua, at the Imperial Court, and at Assisi; and Massimiliano Neri (c. 1600–1666), first organist at St. Mark's from 1644 until his death. Buonamente's surviving publications date from 1626–37; Merula made his debut with a book of conventional mosaic-like four-part canzoni in 1615[11] but most of his instrumental music appeared between 1637 and 1651; Neri's two sets of sonatas were published in 1644 and 1651. Some of Buonamente's 'sonatas' are variation-works on popular melodies or conventional basses, but he is outstanding in his construction of more extended sections of non-variation works, thanks to his application of contrapuntal device both to long-breathed phrases and to motivic fragments, sometimes seeming to anticipate the techniques of a much later period:

Ex. 108

from Sonata a tre *(Sonate et Canzoni, 1636)*, Op.6, no.9

And the sections, contrasted as they are, are held together by the recurrence of motives or longer passages. His favourite sonata combinations were *a due* (usually two violins and continuo) and *a tre* (two violins, cello or bassoon, and continuo) – or *a sei* including three or four trombones.

Buonamente was a pioneer in yet another respect. The already quoted titles of Salamone Rossi's Third Book and Marini's Op. 8 are typical of the

[10] The *grave* first movement of Op. 55, No. 2 (printed in Alfred Heuss, 'Die venetianischen Opern-Sinfonien', *SIMG*, iv (1903), p. 475) shows he was now alive to the structural potential of key: a 7-bar phrase modulating from C to G is almost exactly repeated a fifth higher; the return is effected by three statements of a 2-bar phrase in D, G, and C, and clinched by 4 bars in C.
[11] *Tarquinio Merula: Opere complete* (ed. Adam Sutkowski), i (New York, 1974).

period in that they mention, after 'sonatas', *sinfonie* and – as the most popular dances – *corente* and *gagliarde*. These early seventeenth-century 'symphonies' commonly consist of two short sections, each repeated, the second beginning in a related key but ending in the original one; their function seems to have been preludial as in the early operas. The galliard lived on but, instead of the pavane, new triple-time dances appeared: the swift corrento with its 'running' music, and the balletto. (The last two variations of Marini's 'Romanesca' (see p. 329, n. 5) are a 'gagliarde' and a 'corente'.) And Buonamente opened his *Libro quinto* in 1629 with two miniature suites, each consisting of sinfonia, gagliarda, and 'La sua Corrente' thereby giving birth to a new kind of sonata, a series of dances preceded by a non-dance movement. Tarquinio Merula in his *Canzoni overo Sonate concertate per chiesa et camera* of 1637 – the term *canzone* lingered on, though it was now practically synonymous with sonata – Neri in his *Sonate e canzone a 4 da sonarsi . . . in chiesa, & in camera* (1644), and Biagio Marini in his last publication, *Diversi generi di Sonate da chiesa e da camera*, Op. 22 (1655) do not distinguish between sonatas 'for the church' or 'for the chamber', but the distinction between sonatas consisting mainly of dance-movements and those containing none was to be made very soon. Precise terminology is the last thing one must expect of composers of this period, or precision of any kind. Neri's Op. 1 of 1644[12] is for 'diversi stromenti' and the correnti he includes, though really *a quattro*, 'can be played *a tre*, or even *a due*, by leaving out the middle parts'. His *Sonate*, Op. 2 (1651), for three to twelve instruments, manifest traits anticipating the concerto style: virtuoso passages for the violins (as indeed one finds in his Op. 1) and – true mark of a Venetian organist – contrasting of instrumental groups: six wind (cornetti, trombones, and bassoon) against six strings (violins, violas, and tiorba or *viola di basso*). The fugal first section of the second sonata *a tre* in Op. 2[13] shows his ability to construct a 47-bar piece on a single triad-based theme by motivic fragmentation akin to Buonamente's, by sequence, and by modulation to C, F, and so on:

Ex. 109

---

[12] The first sonata is printed in Riemann, *Musikgeschichte in Beispielen* (Leipzig, 1921), No. 98.
[13] Complete in Riemann, *Handbuch*, ii (2), p. 152.

An idiom was beginning to emerge. But it was only fitfully apparent in the early publications of a younger composer whose main work belongs to a later period: Giovanni Legrenzi (1626–90). 'La Cornara'[14] in his first book of sonatas, Op. 2 (1655), might have been written a quarter of a century earlier. But in his Op. 4 the following year, *Suonate da chiesa, e da camera*, he at least marked six pieces specifically 'Sonata da camera'; they are single movements in two sections, each of which is repeated, and only the fifth, 'La Forni', has a tempo marking, 'Adaggio'.[15] They were perhaps intended to be followed by a selection from the dances printed after them.

ENGLISH MUSIC FOR VIOLS

The rest of Europe produced nothing comparable with this outpouring of instrumental solo and ensemble music in Italy. In England the favourite solo instrument was not the violin but, strangely, the bass viol – particularly in its smaller forms, the 'division viol' and 'lyra viol'. Like the treble viol, it was played solo with ornamental variations ('divisions')[16] or with the harpsichord as in the anonymous collection, *Parthenia In-Violata* (1614?),[17] and there were plenty of ayres, fantasias, and so on for two such instruments. The fantasia continued to be the favourite ensemble form, though the extreme paucity of printed sources indicates that it appealed only to a limited public. Coprario (d. 1626) sometimes follows a contrasted-section fantasia with a pair of thematically unrelated dances, alman/ayre or alman/galliard,[18] anticipating the *sonata da camera*, and his idiom tends to be more instrumental particularly when he specifies the use of violins. This tendency is still more marked in the late *Fantasies of Three Parts* (c. 1620) of Orlando Gibbons (see p. 291), in the work of Coprario's pupil William Lawes (1602–45) and in that of John Jenkins (1592–1678), while the *Little Consort of Three Parts* (London, 1656) of Matthew Locke (1622–77) consists of ten suites of dances only (in each case, pavane / ayre / courante / saraband) unified by key – though he includes fantasias in his manuscript suites and was composing duos for bass viols as late as 1652.[19] Apart from their dance-music the English composers were stylistically conservative; they still tended to think polyphonically even when they employed the fashionable Italian layout of two upper parts and bass, and were slow to adopt either the

---

[14] Ed. Søren Sørensen (Copenhagen, c. 1944). Other sonatas in this set in Riemann, *Musikgeschichte in Beispielen*, No. 102, *Old Chamber Music*, iv, p. 152, and *Handbuch*, ii (2), p. 156 (two movements only).
[15] Information kindly supplied by Albert Seay.
[16] A facsimile of the second edition of Christopher Simpson's classic treatise, *The Division Violist*, originally published in 1659, has been brought out by Nathalie Dolmetsch (London, 1956).
[17] Two examples in *Jacobean Consort Music*, ed. Thurston Dart and William Coates (*MB*, ix) (London, 1955), Nos. 96 and 97.
[18] Ibid., Nos. 98, 99, 102, and 103. Thematic catalogue by Richard Charteris (New York, 1977).
[19] A selection from William Lawes's consort music has been edited by Murray Lefkowitz in *MB*, xxi (revised edition, 1971). A selection from Jenkins's fancies and ayres has been edited by Helen J. Sleeper (Wellesley, Mass., 1950), his four-part consort music by Andrew Ashbee in *MB*, xxvi (1969), his five-part music by Richard Nicholson (London, 1970), and his six-part by Donald Peart, *MB*, xxxix (1977). Locke's *Little Consort* has been ed. Michael Tilmouth in *Locke. Chamber Music: I* (*MB*, xxxi, 1971), pp. 57 ff.

term 'sonata' or its style. Jenkins seems to have been the earliest to do so –
with the exception of the expatriate William Young (d. 1672) who published
sonatas with continuo at Innsbruck in 1653 – but unhappily his *Sonatas for 2
Violins and a Base with a Thorough Base for the Organ and Theorbo* (London
1660; Amsterdam 1664) are lost; indeed their very existence has been
questioned.[20] Whether or not he wrote Italianate trio sonatas, Jenkins
commanded a considerable variety of styles not to be accounted for solely by
his longevity: fantasias as dense in polyphony as those of William Lawes,
others as transparent as Martin Peerson's (*c.* 1572–1650)[21] or Simon Ives'
(1600–62),[22] the inevitable duos for bass viols, and a great quantity of dance
music.

FRENCH ENSEMBLE MUSIC

France could show nothing to match this body of consort music, to which a
number of other composers contributed, either in quantity or in quality.
Both André Maugars (*c.* 1580–*c.* 1645), violist for a time in Charles I's
service, later in Richelieu's, and the great theorist Marin Mersenne
(1588–1648) in his *Harmonie universelle* (1636–7)[23] admitted the high level
of English viol playing and composition. Still less was there any question of
Italianate canzonas or sonatas. Whereas Charles I loved intimate consort
music, the French kings preferred the types of instrumental music which
went with balls and ballets and Court entertainments generally; we hear, for
instance, of a concert given before Louis XIII in 1627 by the '24 violons du
Roy' and the '12 hautbois' who took turns in playing ballet airs.[24] Wind
music was much cultivated and Mersenne printed in his *Harmonie* a
Phantasie à 5 pour les cornets[25] by Jehan Henry (1560–1635) – called 'Henry
le jeune' to distinguish him from his father – an expert wind-player and also
a 'Violon ordinaire du roi'. It is a brief trifle of little interest. Mersenne also
printed a much more extended *Fantaisie à 5 pour les violons avec diminutions*
by the same composer[26] but here the interest lies exclusively in the
'diminutions' for the first violin:

Ex. 110

16. Instrumental Music (c. 1610–60)

French ensemble music of this period, other than that for the *ballets de cour*, consists of little more than three fantasies for four viols by Etienne Moulinié (*c.* 1600–after 1669), appended to his fifth book of *Airs de cour* (1639),[27] Nicolas Métru's set of 42 two-part viol fantasies (1642), the *Préludes et allemandes pour orgue et pour les violes* included in the *Meslanges* (Paris, 1657) of the Liègois, Henry Du Mont (1610–84), and a few manuscript *fantaisies* and three *simphonies*, for treble and tenor viols with continuo, by Louis Couperin (*c.* 1626–1661), the first notable figure in a great dynasty of French musicians.

GERMAN DANCES AND *SYMPHONIEN*

In Germany, too, instrumental ensemble music was mostly dance-music. Beside such older composers as Franck and Peurl and the expatriate Englishmen Brade and Simpson (see above, p. 290), who continued to publish collections of dances right up to the eve of the Thirty Years War and exercised wide influence as performers as well as composers,[28] new men appeared: the southern Austrian Isaac Posch (d. *c.* 1622), the Rothenburg cantor Erasmus Widmann (1572–1634), the Leipzig organist Georg Engelmann (*c.* 1575–1632), and two much greater musicians, Hermann Schein (1586–1630), cantor of the Thomaskirche at Leipzig, and his friend the Halle organist, Samuel Scheidt (1587–1654), pupil of Sweelinck and colleague of Michael Praetorius. Schein's *Banchetto musicale* (Leipzig, 1617)[29] is a collection of twenty variation-suites, each consisting of paduane, gagliarde, courante, allemande, and tripla, which far surpass Peurl's in technique and invention. But canzoni are relatively few and fantasies and sonatas almost non-existent. Schein included two sectional canzoni in his *Venus-Kräntzlein* of 1609[30] and one in his *Cymbalum Sionium* of 1615, which, like those by Scheidt in his *Paduana, Galliarda ... Canzonetto* (Hamburg, 1621)[31] and later collections (1622, 1625, 1627) show the unmistakable influence of Giovanni Gabrieli, most of all in Scheidt's canzon for four cornetti.[32] Scheidt employs basso continuo, Schein does not. But in

---

[20] E.g. by John Wilson, *Roger North on Music* (London, 1959), p. 298, n. 32.

[21] One example in *MB*, ix, p. 165.

[22] Opening of a fantasia by Ives in *NOHM*, iv, p. 589.

[23] Facsimile and English translation by Roger Chapman (The Hague, 1957). The 'anonymous' English fantasy which he quotes is by Ferrabosco.

[24] Henri Quittard prints a six-part 'Charivary pour les Hautbois' played on this occasion, in Lavignac and La Laurencie, *Encyclopédie de la musique*, Ire. partie, iii, p. 1249. By 'hautbois' we must understand oboes and bassoons.

[25] Reprinted in Heinz Becker, *Geschichte der Instrumentation* (*Das Musikwerk*) (Cologne, 1964), No. 8.

[26] The entire first section in Quittard, op. cit., p. 1254.

[27] Each is in two sections, the first in imitative counterpoint, the second melodic: see the incipits quoted by Denise Launay, 'La fantaisie en France jusqu'au milieu du XVIIe siècle', *La Musique instrumentale de la Renaissance*, ed. Jean Jacquot (Paris, 1955), p. 337.

[28] See E. H. Meyer, *Die mehrstimmige Spielmusik des 17. Jahrhunderts in Nord- und Mitteleuropa* (Kassel, 1934), pp. 56–7.

[29] Ed. Dieter Krickeberg, *Schein: Neue Ausgabe sämtlicher Werke*, ix (Kassel, 1967).

[30] Ed. Adam Adrio, *Neue Ausgabe*, vi, pp. 39 and 46.

[31] *Scheidt: Werke* ii/iii (ed. Gottlieb Harms) (Hamburg, 1928).

[32] Ibid, ii/iii, p. 21.

one respect Scheidt reverts to the practice of the elder Gabrieli by deriving his canzoni from actual song-tunes, on some of which, e.g. Guédron's 'Est-ce-Mars', he also wrote keyboard variations. Widmann, too, in his *Gantz Neue Cantzon, Intraden, Balletten und Courranten* (Nuremberg, 1618) for 'all kinds of instruments, particularly viols', based a canzona 'auff den Schäfferstantz'.[33] Publication slackened with the outbreak of war and, as the ravages of war became ever more terrible from the late 1620s onward, it nearly stopped altogether. (Engelmann and Widmann died of the plague which was one of the consequences of the war.) Church musicians struggled, as we shall see (below, p. 351), to produce music with reduced forces but there was no demand for dance-music or pleasant chamber-music.

In 1644, when the peace negotiations at Münster had at least begun (though they were not concluded for several years), Scheidt published at Breslau a work of peculiar interest, *LXX Symphonien auff Concerten manir*.[34] These consist of ten pieces for two cantus instruments, bass, and continuo in each of the seven *claves*, which are treated not so much as modes but as keys which have not yet shed all traces of modes: C major, D minor, E (minor and major), F major, G major, G minor, A minor. Like the *sinfonie* of Salamone Rossi and Biagio Marini, they were intended to be played 'before concertos, motets, or spiritual madrigals with instruments as a prelude'. The techniques employed are extremely varied. The opening of 'Die V. Symphonia aus dem G♭ moll' is fairly typical:

Ex. 111

In some of the *Symphonien* the bassus shares in the thematic polyphony with the other parts, in which cases the continuo is merely a skeleton of the bassus.

At the same time new names were beginning to appear. Among those who composed instrumental ensemble music were Andreas Hammerschmidt (1611–75), Erasmus Kindermann (1616–55), Johann Rosenmüller (c. 1619–1684), and the Schütz pupil Matthias Weckmann (1621–74). (Schütz composed no independent instrumental music, though, as we shall see in the next chapter, it played an important part in some of his religious works.) Hammerschmidt published at Freiberg in Saxony in 1636 and 1639 two collections of dances[35] for viols, mostly in five parts with continuo,

[33] *Ausgewählte Werke*, ed. G. Reichert, *EDM. Sonderreihe III* (Mainz, 1959), p. 68.
[34] *Werke*, xiii (ed. Christhard Mahrenholz) (Hamburg, 1962).
[35] Modern edition of the 1636 collection, *Erster Fleiss*, by H. Mönkemeyer (Hanover, 1939).

which were several times reprinted; they include 'Mascharaden', 'Francois-chen Arien', and sarabandes. The sarabande was then still a lively dance which had not quite forgotten its bawdy origin. It had come from Mexico by way of Spain and was now spreading all over Europe; it appears also in the collections of Kindermann and Rosenmüller.

Kindermann's ensemble music is varied: four sets of *Deliciae studiosorum* preferably for wind (Nuremberg, 1640–3), the lost *Neue-verstimmte Violen Lust* for three viols and continuo (Frankfurt a.M., 1652) which seems to have been the earliest German experiment in *scordatura* (unorthodox tuning of the strings), and *Canzoni, Sonatae* (1653) (sectional canzoni which also employ scordatura). Rosenmüller published his first collection of dances in 1645 and nine years later his more important *Studenten-Music* for viols 'or other instruments' with continuo, consisting mainly of ten suites basically built up of paduan / alemanda / courant / ballo / sarabanda but sometimes shorter, sometimes with more than one courant or alemanda. Like Scheidt's *Symphonien* they are definitely tonal and, as the end of the paduan of the C minor suite will show, are sometimes cast in the new Italian string idiom:

Ex. 112

Rosenmüller was to give further examples in a later work (see below, p. 426). Weckmann, on the other hand, in his manuscript sonatas for three or four mixed instruments (cornettino, violino, trombone, bassoon, and continuo), probably written for the Hamburg Collegium Musicum about 1660,[36] shows himself to be a rather eccentric conservative. Indeed both his severe contrapuntal mastery and his bold eccentricity are also revealed in his keyboard works, the former in his chorale variations, the latter in his toccatas – particularly that in A minor.[37]

ORGAN TREATMENT OF LUTHERAN *CHORÄLE*

Some of these – Scheidt above all, Kindermann, Weckmann, to whom we may add the names of Johann Ulrich Steigleder (1593–1635), Heinrich Scheidemann (*c.* 1596–1663), Delphin Strungk (1601–94), and Franz Tunder (1614–67) – were notable organ-composers, particularly of variations and fantasies on *Choräle*.[38] The *Choral*-variations are versets in purpose and derive immediately from those of Sweelinck (see p. 294), whose pupil Scheidt was, while the parentage of the *Choralfantasien* can be traced from the organ hymns in Michael Praetorius's *Musae Sioniae* (see ibid.) and the Latin ones, with the plainsong quite unornamented, in his *Hymnodia Sioniae* (1611). They were played at the end of the service. The classic collection is Scheidt's *Tabulatura Nova* (Hamburg, 1624),[39] 'tabulature' in the sense that the parts are 'tabulated' above each other on separate staves; the contents range from a (Lutheran) organ-Mass and an alternatim Magnificat, to include dances and variations on secular songs, canons, fugues, and an 'echo' in emulation of Sweelinck; the variety of technical device employed in the variations is remarkable. A real tour de force of variation-writing is the *Tabulatur Buch* (1627) of the Stuttgart organist J. U. Steigleder,[40] which consists of forty variations on the 'Vater unser'. Kindermann published *Harmonia Organica*, including two praeambula in each mode and 25 fugues with obbligato pedal parts, at Nuremberg in 1645; but his harpsichord suites (allemande / courante / sarabande) remained in manuscript. Nor were the organ compositions of Scheidemann, Weckmann, Strungk, and Tunder published in their lifetimes. They were preserved in manuscript collections, particularly the great collection of keyboard tablatures in the Ratsbibliothek at Lüneburg[41] which contain North German works for organ and harpsichord of the whole period covered by this chapter, from Sweelinck and Scheidt to Tunder and Weckmann. Based almost entirely on Lutheran hymn music, though

---

[36] *Gesammelte Werke*, ed. Gerhard Ilgner, *EDM* (*Landschaftsdenkmale* 4) (Leipzig, 1942), pp. 1 ff. Weckmann's only instrumental works published in his lifetime, the *Canzonen* of 1650/51, are lost.

[37] Ed. Seiffert, *Organum*, Reihe 4, Heft 3.

[38] That is, on German hymn-melodies and the Latin chants (Kyrie, Magnificat, and so on) used by the Lutheran Church. The German word *Choral* covers plainsong as well as hymn-tune; the anglicized 'chorale', meaning the latter only, is unfortunate.

[39] Ed. Mahrenholz, *Scheidt : Werke*, vi and vii. On pp. 25 ff. of his editorial appendix to vii, Mahrenholz gives the specification of the organ of the Moritzkirche at Halle, built during 1624–5 under Scheidt's direction by Johann Heinrich Compenius, grandson of the founder of the great family of organ-builders. Mahrenholz has printed Part III of the *Tabulatura* in the correct liturgical order, which was not followed in the original edition; see also *MF*, i (1948), p. 32.

[40] Ed. Willi Apel, together with Steigleder's *Ricercar Tabulatura* for young people (1624), *CEKM*, 13.

[41] Ed. Margarete Reimann, *EDM*, xxxvi and xl.

including also some toccatas and preludes (showy concert pieces with fugal episodes),[42] and transcriptions, they constitute a corpus of sober, square-cut keyboard composition which exercised immeasurable influence on the tradition of German music.

There is almost nothing Italianate in it. Only here and there in later works, e.g. a canzon by Scheidemann[43] dated 10 September 1657, can one detect southern influence. In the keyboard music of a younger man, Johann Jakob Froberger (1616–1667), it is much stronger; but then Froberger was a cosmopolitan who spent most of his life in the service of the Habsburgs at Vienna (where the Court Chapel was largely Italian) and Brussels, who actually studied in Rome with Frescobaldi during 1637–41, and made the acquaintance of the French *clavecinistes* and lutenists in Paris in 1652. It is impossible to discuss Froberger, however cursorily, without first considering the work of his chief master.

THE KEYBOARD MUSIC OF FRESCOBALDI

As an outstanding keyboard composer, Girolamo Frescobaldi (1583–1643) appears a somewhat isolated figure in seventeenth-century Italy where, as in England,[44] keyboard and lute music went into a decline while ensemble music flourished. He was set apart even in his musical ancestry for he had little in common with the Venetians. Born in Ferrara, he studied with Luzzaschi but it has been plausibly suggested[45] that he also came under the influence of two Neapolitan associates of de Macque who published several collections of keyboard music during 1603–15: Giovanni Maria Trabaci (c. 1575–1647) and Ascanio Maione (d. 1627),[46] who in turn derived from the Spanish musicians of the Cabezón school at the Viceregal Court of Naples. Frescobaldi's earliest publications consist of a book of madrigals, canzoni contributed to Raverii's collection (see p. 288), and four-part fantasias in score but evidently intended for the organ (1608), a book of *Toccate e partite* (Rome, 1614) and one of *Recercari et Canzoni Franzese* (1615).[47] Neither these toccatas nor the ricercari differ in type from those of Merulo or the Gabrielis, but the canzoni already show Frescobaldi's skill not only in theme-transformation and variation – the partitas are variations on conventional or familiar basses or melodies – but in creating authentic

[42] E.g. the four preludes by Tunder, ed. Max Seiffert, *Organum (4te Reihe, Nr. 6)* (Lippstadt, n.d.); they are perhaps typical of the 'evening performances' (*Abendspielen*) he was giving in the Marienkirche at Lübeck from 1646 onwards, or for the entertainment of the merchants who gathered in the church in the morning before meeting on Change in the Rathaus. The edition of Tunder's *Sämtliche Orgelwerke* by Klaus Beckmann (Wiesbaden, 1974) has been severely criticized.
[43] Lüneberg, Ratsbibl. KN 209.
[44] One aged survivor from the Elizabethan age, Thomas Tomkins, began to compose keyboard music again in his last years – mostly 1647–54 – but did so in the style of his youth.
[45] By Willi Apel, 'Neapolitan Links between Cabezón and Frescobaldi', *MQ*, xxiv (1938), p. 419. See also Roland Jackson, 'On Frescobaldi's Chromaticism and its Background', ibid., lvii (1971), p. 255.
[46] Ricercate by Trabaci have been ed. Oscar Mischiati (Brescia, 1964). See *Neapolitan Keyboard Composers*, ed. Roland Jackson, *CEKM*, xxiv. There is a *canzona francese* by Trabaci in *HAM*, ii, No. 191.
[47] Ed. Pierre Pidoux, *Frescobaldi: Orgel- und Klavierwerke* (Kassel, 1949), iii and ii, but from the editions of 1637 and 1626 respectively.

keyboard texture from tiny motives. It is the spirit rather than the form that distinguishes him from the Venetians, a mystical sweetness that reminds one rather of Palestrina. This excerpt from the ninth toccata shows both the sweetness, typically enhanced by the parallel tenths, and the nature of the motivic work:

Ex. 113

Frescobaldi's harmonic language is predominantly modal, but the pupil of Luzzaschi reveals himself in unexpected chromaticisms, as in the twelfth toccata, which introduce madrigalian idioms into instrumental music. It is tempting to suggest that, while his 'mystical sweetness' calls to mind Guido Reni, his chromaticisms anticipate Bernini's St. Teresa. Chromaticism and mysticism both reappear in the *Secondo Libro di Toccate, Canzone, Versi d'Hinni, Magnificat, Gagliarde, Correnti* of 1627 and still more markedly in the *Fiori musicali* of 1635.[48] This provides music for three specific Masses: versets for Kyrie and Christe, canzoni after the Epistle, ricercari after the Credo, toccatas for the Elevation, all quite short. In two instances, ricercari are prefaced by brief toccatas, a pairing anticipating prelude-and-fugue.

Both the toccatas and the canzoni of the Second Book show a diametrical opposition of formal tendencies: strict monothematicism as the basis of most pieces, complete looseness in others. How far Frescobaldi was from the concept of over-all unity may be seen by comparing 'La Bianchina' in the ensemble canzoni of 1628[49] with the version in the *Canzoni da sonare* of six years later;[50] only the first and fourth main sections and the very short fifth remain, the second and third (and coda) being replaced by entirely fresh music. Indeed in his very practical instructions to performers of his toccatas, Frescobaldi not only suggests great freedom of tempo but permits the player to break off at any marked cadence point.

---

[48] Ibid., iv and v.
[49] Ed. Riemann, *Old Chamber Music*, i, p. 31.
[50] Ed. Hans David, *Canzoni a due canti (Antiqua)* (Mainz, 1933).

After Frescobaldi's death Italian keyboard music more or less petered out for more than half a century, a fact which may be explained by the supersession of the organ by the instrumental ensemble in church music and by Italian lack of enthusiasm for an instrument so incapable of cantabile as the harpsichord. The only notable figure was the opera-composer, Michelangelo Rossi (see p. 313) whose *Toccate e Corenti* for 'organ and harpsichord' were reprinted at Rome in 1657.[51] His correnti are harmless enough but some of the toccatas contain passages of hair-raising chromaticism, for instance the beginning of No. 6 and the end of No. 7. They are interesting curiosities, not to be compared in musical value with Frescobaldi's.

ORGAN MUSIC IN IBERIA AND FRANCE

If Frescobaldi's earlier organ works are conservative by Venetian standards, they are much less so than the organ music that was being published in other Latin countries during the 1620s: the *Flores de Musica* (Lisbon, 1620)[52] of Manuel Rodrigues Coelho (*c.* 1555–*c.* 1635), the *Hymnes de l'Eglise . . . avec les fugues et recherches sur leur plain-chant* (Paris, 1623) and versets for the *Magnificat* (1626)[53] of Jean Titelouze (1563–1633), and the *Facultád Organica* (Alcalá, 1626)[54] of Francisco Correa de Arauxo (*c.* 1575–1663). These were older men; but their humble if often skilful versets and ricercari show that the organ was regarded simply as a utilitarian church instrument, and the younger French organists, even Louis Couperin who was born about the time of Titelouze's second publication, left their compositions in manuscript. It was not till 1660 that the next collection of French organ music appeared: the *Fugues et Caprices*[55] of François Roberday (1624–80), which were printed in score to show the part-writing more clearly and included pieces by 'l'illustre Frescobaldy' and 'Monsieur Froberger'.

FRENCH LUTENISTS AND *CLAVECINISTES*

Non-publication must not, however, always be taken as an indication of non-appreciation – though it probably was so far as organ music was concerned. The lute enjoyed a tremendous vogue everywhere in France, from the Court downward, during the first half of the century as a solo instrument as well as accompaniment to the *airs de cour*; yet the greatest French lutenist-composer, Denis Gaultier (*c.* 1600–1672), and the greatest *claveciniste*, Jacques Champion de Chambonnières (after 1601–*c.* 1671), both members of notable musical families, waited until 1670 to see their work printed – in order to ensure the accuracy of texts. (Chambonnières in his preface actually speaks of the *disadvantage* of publishing one's works.)

---

[51] *Collected Keyboard Works*, ed. John R. White, *CEKM*, 15.
[52] Ed. Santiago Kastner, *Portugaliae Musica*, i and iii (Lisbon, 1959 and 1961); five selected *tentos*, ed. ibid. (Mainz, 1936).
[53] *Titelouze: Oeuvres complètes*, ed. Alexandre Guilmant (Paris, 1898).
[54] Ed. Kastner, *Monumentos de la música espanola*, vi and xii (Barcelona, 1948 and 1952).
[55] Ed. Guilmant and Pirro (Mainz, n.d.).

The harpsichord music of Chambonnières' most famous pupil, Louis Couperin, like his organ music, was never published during his lifetime. Actually the most important source of Gaultier's compositions is not one of the two late printed books but a superb manuscript entitled *La Rhétorique des Dieux*, probably compiled during the 1650s;[56] this contains 62 pieces arranged by modes, each mode being preceded by an allegorical illustration of the mode by Abraham Bosse or his pupil Robert Nanteuil.

Gaultier's modes bear a confusing nomenclature peculiar to seventeenth-century France[57] according to which e.g. *dorien* approximates to D major and *sousdorien* to A major. A number of the pieces bear titles which are explained or commented on in the manuscript; none bears the name of a dance. Yet dance-types are clearly recognizable and constitute suites, not so called, within the mode. Thus the *mode myxolydien* (F major) begins with an allemande 'Apollon Orateur' ('Appolon revestu de l'humanité de Gaultier desploye icy tous les tresors de son bien-dire, et par la force de ses charmes fait que ses auditeurs deviennent tout oreilles'), which is followed by two unnamed courantes,[58] and a sarabande entitled 'Diane au bois'. The next mode, *sousmixolydien* (likewise F major) consists of an unnamed allemande, a courante 'La Caressante' ('Les caresses et les mignardises de cette Beauté, on tant d'attraits que les plus insensibles demeurent d'accord qu'elle merite d'estre aimée.'), and a sarabande. At the end (*mode sousionien*: A minor) comes the most curious suite of all: 'Tombeau de Monsr. de Lenclos', called simply 'allemande' in the printed *Pièces de luth*, 'La consolation aux amis du Sr. Lenclos', and 'La resolution des amis du Sr. Lenclos sur sa mort'. Lenclos, gentleman lutenist, friend of the Gaultiers, and father of the celebrated Ninon, died in 1649 so this was not the earliest of the genre *tombeau*, for Ennemond Gaultier had composed one ten years or so earlier for his teacher René Mezangeau, but it was one of the most famous.[59]

Both the forms and the style of the French lutenists were taken over by their harpsichordist contemporaries – Chambonnières, Louis Couperin, the minor Frenchmen, and the great cosmopolitan Froberger. They easily converted the pseudo-polyphony of the lute-tablature into the real polyphony or, rather, the *style brisé* of the harpsichord notation – the actual sound may not have been so very different, for the big eleven-course theorbo-lute used by Gaultier was very sonorous – and they imitated lute-ornamentation. Sometimes Chambonnières writes suites[60] just like Gaultier's, e.g. one in A minor beginning with 'Allemande la Rare' and followed by courante and sarabande. Sometimes, again like Gaultier, he loosely groups together a considerable number of pieces in the same key, including rondeaux in the simple ABACA ... A form and so-called

---

[56] Facsimile and transcription by André Tessier, *Publications de la société française de musicologie*, I, vi and vii (Paris, 1932–3). This publication also includes the contents of the two printed books, the latter of which has some pieces by Denis's cousin Ennemond Gaultier ('Gaultier le vieux') (*c.* 1580–1651).
[57] Cf. Mersenne, *Harmonie universelle*, III, p. 172.
[58] The French courante was much more staid than the Italian corrento.
[59] Schering printed it, with the 'Consolation', op. cit., No. 215 (a) and (b).
[60] *Oeuvres complètes de Chambonnières*, ed. Brunold and Tessier (Paris, 1925).

'chaconnes' which are not variations on a ground bass but slow rondeaux in triple time.[61] The two sections into which his dances commonly fall differ from Gaultier's in being repeated (apart from the elaborated repeat of the whole piece, called *double*) and in the tendency for the first section to end in or on the dominant. His titles are sometimes dedications in the Italian manner or mark historic events, such as the 'Day of Barricades' in Paris in August 1648, but he never attempts descriptive music as Louis Couperin did in his *Tombeau* for the lutenist Blancrocher,[62] which suggests his friend's fatal fall downstairs and the tolling of funeral bells. Another curious feature of Couperin's work is the number of skeletal *préludes* notated in unbarred semibreves.[63] And there are a number of signs that he was acquainted with Italian music.

FROBERGER'S INTERNATIONAL SUMMATION

All the same it was Froberger who produced the most masterly summation of the organ and harpsichord forms and styles of the period:[64] severe and conservative North German fantasias and ricercari, canzoni and capriccios in the style of Frescobaldi, organ toccatas which look back through Frescobaldi to Merulo and yet forward beyond them,[65] *tombeaux* and suites in the French manner. He was little indebted to the older German ensemble dance-suites which, unlike the French harpsichord suites, were meant to be danced to. Only in one respect does he preserve an older feature ignored by the French, the thematic link between allemande and courante. Of the twelve suites in the best source, the Vienna manuscripts, four consist of allemande / courante / sarabande, and five of allemande / gigue / courante / sarabande (the allemande of No. 12 being a *lamento* for Ferdinand IV, King of Bohemia and Hungary).[66] In one the gigue is placed last and the remaining suite is a set of variations on a popular tune, 'Auff die Mayerin', the seventh, eighth, and ninth *partite* being respectively a courante, a *double* on the courante, and a sarabande. It is noteworthy that, whereas the *lamento* for Ferdinand IV (1654) is an allemande, the *tombeau* 'sur la mort de Monsieur Blancheroche' is marked to be played 'fort lentement à la discretion sans observer aucune mesure' and the *lamentation* for the Emperor Ferdinand III (1657) likewise 'se joue lentement avec discretion'. Froberger's suites employ the keys C, D, G, and A both major and minor, plus F major and E minor; the tonal ambit was expanding.

French culture dominated the German courts after the great war, though music was less deeply affected than, say, architecture; Frenchness was not

[61] E.g. ibid., p. 92. Also in *HAM*, ii, No. 212.

[62] *Oeuvres complètes de Louis Couperin*, ed. Brunold (Paris, 1936), p. 79. Both Denis Gaultier and Froberger also mourned Blancrocher in *tombeaux*.

[63] On their interpretation, see Davitt Moroney, 'The performance of unmeasured harpsichord preludes', *Early Music*, iv (1976), p. 143.

[64] The edition of his works, ed. Guido Adler, in *DTÖ*, Jg. iv (1), vi (2), and x (2) (vols. 8, 13, and 21), needs revision. Adler deliberately garbled the order of the suite-movements.

[65] See the typical example in ibid., iv (1) (vol. 8), p. 5, reprinted in *HAM*, ii, No. 217.

[66] Ibid., vi (2) (vol. 13), p. 32, and *HAM*, ii, No. 216.

absorbed into the essence of German music as Italianism was. It was a fashion which lasted for some seventy years, and Froberger's suites and *tombeaux* were its earliest notable manifestation.

17

Religious Music (c. 1610–60)

When Josquin died in 1521, Western Christendom employed a universal religious music – with national dialects and usages, it is true, particularly in the more popular forms of religious song – but all the same an immediately recognizable organic unity. Within a hundred years that unity was shattered. Not only had the Reformation opened the way for vernacular liturgies and a variety of new practices, Lutheran, Calvinist, Anglican, but Catholicism itself began to employ two divergent styles, corresponding to Monteverdi's *prima* and *seconda prattica*: the Palestrina-Lassus tradition and the new, primarily Venetian concertato style.

Monteverdi found no difficulty in exercising both, side by side. In 1641 he published a second collection of religious music, *Selva Morale e Spirituale*,[1] which includes a Mass in the old *a cappella* style – yet another was published posthumously in 1651 – but, most curiously, also three passages in the *seconda prattica* which Monteverdi says may be substituted in the Credo: a chromatic 'Crucifixus' for four soloists, 'Et resurrexit' for two sopranos, two violins, and continuo, and 'Et iterum' for two altos, bass, and four trombones (or violas). Despite his technical skill in the old style of church music, it is clear that he preferred the *stile concertato* for he employs it in all his other religious music, from the sacred monodies and duets to big, showy compositions such as the seven-part Gloria, with orchestra, in the *Selva*.

The *a cappella* style was most deeply entrenched in Rome itself among the Palestrina epigones and in the geographical extremes of Europe, Poland and the temporarily dual monarchy of Spain and Portugal, both under bigoted Counter-Reforming kings. Yet few even of the more conservative composers were quite immune to the new tendencies, if only the grandiose effects of opposing choirs doubled by instruments. Such was the case with the Roman Asprilio Pacelli (1570–1623), briefly maestro di cappella at St. Peter's but quickly snatched away by the King of Poland to direct his chapel; his *Sacrae Cantiones* (Venice, 1608) include pieces for 12, 16, and 20 voices. Pacelli was succeeded at Warsaw by Giovanni Francesco Anerio (c. 1567–1630), a Palestrina pupil who long followed faithfully in his master's footsteps, though his later madrigals and motets, and his *Teatro*

---

[1] *Tutte le opere*, xv.

armonico spirituale (1619) (see below) reveal him as a progressive. Anerio's pupil and successor at the Polish court, until 1648, Marco Scacchi (d. *c.* 1685) employed both *prattiche* and expounded them on purely Monteverdian lines in a pamphlet published in Warsaw in 1649, and a native member of the Chapel at the same time, Marcin Mielczewski (d. 1651),[2] wrote church music with violins and trombones entirely in the Venetian style. Scacchi's immediate successor as *maestro*, Bartłomiej Pękiel (d. *c.* 1670) composed both 4-part *a cappella* Masses in sixteenth-century style and a *Missa a 14* for three 'choirs': two of voices, the third of instruments. On the whole the Iberian composers – the Spaniards Juan Pablo Pujol (d. 1626)[3] and Juan Bautista Comes (1568–1643),[4] the Portuguese Duarte Lôbo (*c.* 1563–1646),[5] Manuel Cardoso (*c.* 1571–1650),[6] and Felipe de Magalhães (d. 1652) – were more conservative, though Comes's religious villancicos and his vocal dances for Corpus Christi at Valencia are fascinating examples of peculiarly Spanish popular religious music.

In Rome itself the Palestrina tradition was carried on for a time by his pupils like the Anerio brothers and by pupils of pupils, such as Gregorio Allegri (1582–1652), remembered mainly and unfairly for a mediocre Miserere which haunts the pages of musical and non-musical travel-books, but who deserves to be remembered for some fine *a cappella* Masses on the one hand and concertato motets on the other. Another notable composer whose fame depends on a single work – in this case wrongly attributed to him – is Orazio Benevoli (1605–72). The Mass, allegedly for the consecration of Salzburg Cathedral,[7] is for two 8-part choirs, each supported by a large instrumental ensemble with organ, and two additional wind-groups (cornetti and trombones; trumpets and drums), the whole held together by the continuo and requiring a score of 54 staves, though the number of 'real' parts seldom exceeds eight. Other Romans who composed essentially conservative church music on a monumental scale, though less monumental than this, included Benevoli's pupil Ercole Bernabei (*c.* 1621–1687), Paolo Agostini (*c.* 1583–1629), and the opera-composers Abbatini and Virgilio Mazzocchi. Some of the Masses of Giacomo Carissimi (1605–74), e.g. his 12-part 'L'homme armé' are conservative, too, but on the whole he declined in his church music into a concertato, frankly dramatic style. Leichtentritt[8] quotes a passage from a motet of 1647, 'Quis est hic vir' with the comment that it is 'common property of the Roman operas of that time'. It is significant that, while his liturgical music has narrowly escaped oblivion, he is universally recognized as the first great master of oratorio.

[2] *Opera Omnia* (*Monumenta Musicae in Polonia*, series A), ii–iv, ed. Z. M. Szweykowski (Cracow, 1976–   ).
[3] *Opera Omnia*, ed. H. Anglès (Barcelona, 1926–   ).
[4] *Obras musicales*, ed. J. B. Guzmán (Madrid, 1888).
[5] *Composições polifónicas*, ed. Manuel Joaquim (Lisbon, 1945–   ).
[6] Masses, motets, and Magnificat, ed. J. A. Alegria, *Portugaliae Musica*, v, vi, xiii, xx, xxii, lxxvi (Lisbon, 1963–74).
[7] Ed. Guido Adler, *DTÖ*, x(I) vol. 20, and facsimile, ed. Laurence Feininger, *Benevoli: Opera Omnia*, vii (Salzburg, 1969). The ascription to Benevoli was first challenged by Ernst Hintermaier, 'The *Missa Salisburgensis*', *Musical Times*, cxvi (1975), p. 965.   [8] *Geschichte der Motette* (Leipzig, 1908), p. 274.

DRAMATIC DIALOGUE AND ORATORIO

The roots of oratorio lay in the narrative and dramatic dialogues of the Oratorian laudi (see p. 246) and madrigali spirituali. These elements invaded the always fairly simple and popular laudi only in the last decade of the sixteenth century, and in the texts before they affected the music. For instance, the last of a series of five collections of laudi published during 1583–98, primarily for the use of the congregation of the Oratorio della Vallicella, contains a *Dialogo di Christo et della Samaritana*[9] in which the text represents the direct speech of Christ and the woman, but the strophes are all set to the same three-part music. But when the younger Anerio came to treat the same subject twenty years later in his *Teatro armonico spirituale* he did so very differently; the narrative and commenting portions of the text are sung by a chorus, usually in six parts, the direct speech of Christ and the woman by a bass and a soprano soloist with organ continuo:[10]

Ex. 114

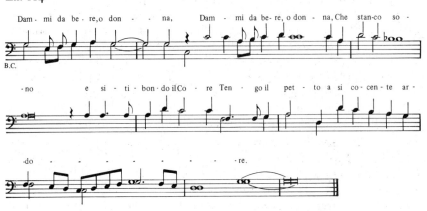

In *La conversione di S. Paulo* Anerio gives part of the narrative to a tenor soloist and introduces an instrumental 'Combattimento: Simphonia a 5' to depict the tumult before Saul's conversion. He has arrived at proto-oratorio though he still talks of 'madrigali' and 'dialoghi'; the term 'oratorio' seems to have appeared only about 1640.

The opera-composers took a hand at about this time. The dozen or so oratorios of Marazzoli are believed to date from 1638–40. They are still unpublished[11] and the oratorios of the Mazzocchi brothers have fared no better, though the sacred monodies in Domenico's *Musiche sacre e morali* (Rome, 1640) probably give a good idea of the style. Luigi Rossi's *Gioseppe, Oratorio per la Settimana Santa*, and *Santa Caterina alla rota* were 'certainly

---

[9] In Domenico Alaleona, *Storia dell'oratorio musicale in Italia* (Milan, 1945), pp. 225–6.
[10] Ibid., complete, pp. 260 ff. Alaleona also prints the *dialoghi*, 'Rispondi Abramo' (p. 251) and the Prodigal Son (p. 270). The Abraham dialogue is also in Günther Massenkeil, *The Oratorio (Anthology of Music)*, (Cologne, 1970), No. 5.
[11] Massenkeil prints a recitative and aria from Marazzoli's *S. Tommaso*, op. cit., No. 6.

performed between 1641 and 1645'.[12] An oratorio at this point was hardly
more than a cantata on a larger scale and Rossi was a master of the cantata
(see pp. 299 ff). In both *Gioseppe* and *Santa Caterina* he employed a
contralto narrator, whom he called *testo* (text) as Monteverdi had called his
narrator in the *Combattimento*; evidently he assumed that the events of Holy
Week did not need one. Here he writes for three soloists, the Virgin, Pilate,
and the Devil – it is not 'Passion music' in the true sense – with choruses of
Jews, pious women, and demons. The orchestra, as in the other two works,
consists of two violins and continuo; it sets the scene with a few preludial
bars:

Ex. 115

and interjects in the ensuing chorus of 'Bàraba!' which, with Pilate's replies,
could well be an excerpt from an opera. The same might be said of
Carissimi's *Jephte*, perhaps his earliest oratorio (before 1650). Carissimi
wrote no operas but as we have seen (pp. 301–2) he was a copious and masterly
composer of cantatas. *Jephte* is full of drama: the battle, with the shattering
bass solo 'Fuggite, cedite'; the joyous coloratura of the narrator (called
historicus, but sung by different soloists) as he describes the daughter
coming out to meet her father, and then of the daughter herself; the tragic
recitative scene of father and daughter; above all her heart-rending lament,
'Plorate, plorate colles', its cadences repeated by a two-part choral echo.
Carissimi introduced a similar echo effect, but for violins, at the end of each
section of Jonah's powerful lament in *Jonas*.[13] He set Latin texts based partly
on the Vulgate, not freely invented Italian ones; he was writing not for the
Vallicella but for the more sophisticated congregation of the Oratorio del
Crocefisso which had always preferred to listen passively to Latin motets
rather than participate in the singing of vernacular laudi.

CONCERTATO CHURCH MUSIC IN VENICE

The Oratorian movement had spread quickly in its early days, naturally
taking with it its characteristic music, but none of the non-Roman
composers was of anything like the stature of Luigi Rossi or Carissimi.
Venice resisted the movement strongly, admitting it only in the 1650s, and
although the performance of vernacular oratorios was not limited to the

---

[12] Alberto Ghislanzoni, *Luigi Rossi* (Rome, 1954), p. 116. Ghislanzoni gives full descriptions with musical incipits.
[13] Carissimi's oratorios have been published in a number of modern editions, notably Janet Beat's *Jephte* (London, 1974). A long excerpt from *Jephte*, ending with the daughter's lament, is printed in Schering, *Geschichte der Musik in Beispielen*, No. 198, Jonah's lament in *HAM*, ii, No. 207.

Oratorians there appear to have been no Venetian oratorios. With four public opera-houses to supply with works, from 1641 onward the ambitious Venetian musician no longer gave priority to religious music of any kind. By

Pl. 45   The Oratorio del Santissimo Crocifisso, Rome, for which Carissimi composed his oratorios.

then Monteverdi had only a couple of years to live and his Vice-Maestro at St. Mark's from 1620 to 1627, Alessandro Grandi, had died at Bergamo in 1630 of the plague so vividly described in Manzoni's *Promessi sposi*. Grandi, even more than Monteverdi, was the protagonist of Venetian church music after Giovanni Gabrieli's death. His earliest essays, five books of *concertato* motets for two or more voices (published 1610–19)[14] are more 'modern' than Viadana's (see p. 252) mainly in their sheer melodiousness, specially marked in the triple-time sections. Then, under the obvious influence of Monteverdi, came three books of motets for one or two voices (1621, 1625,

[14] One example from the First Book in *PRMA*, xc (1967), p. 44; three from the Fourth, *ChW*, xl; one from the Fifth, *PRMA*, p. 47.

348

and 1629) *con Sinfonie d'Istromenti*; they are mostly true monodies,[15] many of them in the strophic-variation form of his secular *Cantade et Arie* (see pp. 297–8). Two excerpts from 'Quam pulchra es' (from Leonardo Simonetti's collection, *Ghirlanda Sacra*, 1625) show the characteristic triple-time aria-like refrain and the melodious character of Grandi's arioso:

Ex. 116

This refrain appears twice more unchanged and the piece ends with a longer triple-time passage swooning from the very 'sickness of love'.

Unfortunately Grandi's successor as Vice-Maestro in 1627, and Monteverdi's as Maestro in 1644, Giovanni Rovetta (*c.* 1596–1668), was not of the same stature although he worthily maintained the Venetian tradition, e.g. in his *Messa e Salmi concertati* of 1639. The same might be said of other contemporaries, while Cavalli, who was ultimately to succeed Rovetta in turn, was typical of the Venetians who preferred opera to church music. Nevertheless Cavalli's *Musiche sacre* of 1656 is the last great native monument of the St. Mark's tradition; it includes *salmi concertati*, hymns and antiphons, a Magnificat, and an impressive ceremonial *Messa concertata* for double choir, two violins, and *violoncino*, with *ripieni e altri instrumenti* ad lib.[16] The Venetian attitude is candidly revealed by another North Italian, Ignazio Donati (d. 1638), in a note to a *Messa concertata* included in his

---

[15] One example from the 1621 book in *MF*, xxv (1972), p. 462.
[16] 'Realized' by Raymond Leppard (London, 1966).

Salmi boscarecci concertati (Venice, 1623); he says he has made the Sanctus and Agnus Dei 'simple and short *alla Venetiana* in order to get them over quickly (*per sbrigarsi presto*) and make room for a *Concerto per l'Elevatione*; *et a qualche Sinfonia alla Communione*'. Indeed by about 1640 we find instrumentally accompanied Masses by Grandi, Rovetta, and Maurizio Cazzati (*c.* 1620–1677) from which Sanctus and Agnus are omitted altogether. It was this last composer, Cazzati, who after moving around to Mantua, Ferrara, and Bergamo, settled at Bologna in 1657 and did more than anyone else to make that city a centre of instrumental church-music; admittedly the seeds had already been sown there by Girolamo Giacobbi (d. 1629), Ercole Porta (d. 1630), and Adriano Banchieri (d. 1634).

VENETIAN INFLUENCE IN GERMANY

In Protestant Germany that crossing of Lutheran hymnody with Venetian techniques initiated by Michael Praetorius in his *Polyhymnia* of 1619 (see p. 260), produced extraordinary results, above all in the work of Heinrich Schütz. The most important form was the *geistliches Konzert*, the sacred concerto; the Mass, usually abbreviated to Kyrie and Gloria only, had never rivalled in musical importance the Catholic Mass. (Church music in the Catholic lands of the Empire remained Italianate in general and Venetian in particular.) The pioneer of the *geistliches Konzert* was Schein in his *Opella nova* (1618 and 1626).[17] Typical is his setting of 'Gelobet seist du, Jesu Christ'[18] which adapts an old German technique for the treatment of hymns: two voices duet freely on fragments of the first line, followed by an unadorned statement of the line by the tenor, the same repeated for each line, and the whole supported by basso continuo. In the monodic pieces Schein dispenses with the unadorned statement.

For a while neither Scheidt nor Schütz attempted the new style in liturgical music, though Schütz did so in his *Aufferstehungshistorie* of 1623 (see below). Scheidt's and Schütz's *Cantiones sacrae* (1620 and 1625 respectively) are motets: Scheidt's, largely German hymn-settings in Michael Praetorius's style, without continuo, Schütz's, Latin and Italianate – indeed not very different from the avowedly 'Italian-madrigalische Manier' of the biblical settings in Schein's *Israelsbrünnlein* (1623). However in his *Pars prima Concertus sacrorum* (1622), Scheidt markedly changed course, making free and independent use of instruments as in 'Sicut locutus est':[19]

---

[17] First collection in *Neue Ausgabe sämtlicher Werke*, iv) ed. Adam Adrio and Siegmund Helms. The other two only in Arthur Prüfer's edition (Leipzig, 1901–23), v–vii.
[18] Ibid., iv, p. 7, and Schering, *Geschichte*, No. 188.
[19] *Gesamtausgabe*, xiv/xv.

Ex. 117

Schütz made the same change in his *Symphoniae sacrae I* (1629)[20] significantly after his second visit to Venice in 1628–9. Their first sacred concertos actually so called appeared only in the 1630s, Scheidt's four collections during 1631–40,[21] Schütz's in 1636 and 1639.[22] To the latter we may add his *Symphoniae sacrae II* (1647)[23] which Schütz expressly described as 'German concertos'. Their example was quickly followed by some of the younger organists mentioned in the last chapter: Hammerschmidt with his *Musicalische Andachten* (beginning in 1639) and *Dialogi oder Gespräche zwischen Gott und einer gläubigen Seelen* (1645), Kindermann with his *Concentus Salomonis* (1642), Tunder and Weckmann in various compositions unpublished during their lives. Kindermann also wrote a notable dialogue *Mosis Plag* (1642).[24] The war had dispersed choirs and reduced musical resources generally, and the earliest concertos were accordingly written – or arranged – for one to four solo voices with continuo but only occasional use of other instruments; publishing his second set in 1634, Scheidt informed purchasers that performing material for up to twelve voices and instrumental symphonies existed and could be supplied to any publisher who cared to print them.[25]

[20] *Neue Ausgabe sämtlicher Werke*, xiii and xiv; all also published separately by the Neue Schütz Gesellschaft.
[21] *Gesamtausgabe*, viii–xii.   [22] *Neue Ausgabe*, x–xii.
[23] Ibid., xv–xvii.
[24] Part I of Hammerschmidt's *Dialogi*, ed. A. W. Schmidt, in *DTÖ*, viii (vol. 16); Tunder's church music in *DDT*, iii, Weckmann's ibid., vi, both ed. Max Seiffert. Weckmann's Annunciation dialogue 'Gegrüsset seist du, Holdselige', nearly all recitative and arioso, with very florid violin writing, verges on the operatic. Examples by Hammerschmidt and Tunder in *HAM*, ii, Nos. 213 and 214, by Tunder and Weckmann in Schering, op. cit., Nos. 211 and 212.
[25] The offer was not taken up. But the original forms of 'Wie schön leuchtet' and 'Nun lob mein Seel' in the first set have been published in the *Gesamtausgabe*, xiv.

351

Both Scheidt and Schütz commanded considerable diversity of styles but Scheidt continued to remain closer to Lutheran hymnody, Schütz to adapt and develop Italian methods; both approach nearer than before to tonal rather than modal feeling. Developing the technique of hymn-variation he had already employed in the *Tabulatura Nova* (see p. 337), Scheidt arrived in his second and third sets of concertos at a species of variation-cantata; thus the eight verses of 'Nun komm der Heiden Heiland'[26] are grouped in three sections, each consisting of two or three variations:

> Verse 1: miniature motet
> 2: duet with tutti coda
>
> 3: variation, with melody in soprano
> 4: variation, with melody in tenor
> 5: canon, with melody in bass
>
> 6: in motet style
> 7: echo chorus
> 8: note-against-note harmonization

But he could also handle the dramatic – and dramatically chromatic – as in the 'Dialogus', 'Kommt her, ihr Gesegneten',[27] between Christ (bass) and the Righteous (soprano and first tenor) and Damned (alto and second tenor) on the Day of Judgement, where the Damned sing (Matthew, xxv, 44):

Ex. 118

---

[26] *Gesamtausgabe*, x, p. 8.   [27] Ibid., ix, p. 20.

Drama and chromaticism came more naturally to Schütz and in particular his monodic concertos – there are none in Scheidt – include masterpieces worthy of Monteverdi; the very first, 'Eile, mich, Gott, zu erretten', marked 'In Stylo Oratorio', is famous and 'Was hast du verwirket', No. 2 in the second set, deserves to be. As a rule, the more voices he introduces, the more conservative the style, so that he seems to fuse the two Monteverdian 'practices'. Yet he also sharply separates them. The *Symphoniae Sacrae II* of 1647, with the tribute to Monteverdi in the preface, the 'tremulus' violin markings in 'Von Gott will ich nicht lassen' and 'Freut euch', the *stile concitato* of piece after piece, the basing of 'Es steh Gott auf' on the Italian master's 'Armato il cor' and 'Zefiro torna', were followed in 1648 by the purely a cappella *Geistliche Chormusik*[28] – though, admittedly, 'Dass ist je gewisslich wahr' dates back to the death of Schein in 1630 and perhaps the transcription of Andrea Gabrieli's 'Angelus ad pastores' ('Der Engel sprach') was made in Venice. This dichotomy persisted; in the *Symphoniae Sacrae III* (1650)[29] the *concitato* is actually heightened in such pieces as 'Saul, Saul' and again there is a free modelling on an Italian piece – 'O Jesu süss' on 'Lilia convallium' in Grandi's 1625 *Motetti*.[30] On the other hand the 'Deutsche Messe' consisting of the first four of the *Zwölf geistliche Gesänge* of 1657[31] is a masterpiece of pure polyphony.

LUTHERAN BIBLE *HISTORIAE*

Two more extended works by Schütz related to the spiritual concertos are *Die Sieben Wortte unsers lieben Erlösers und Seeligmachers Jesu Christi* (probably dating from 1645) and *Historia, Der Freuden- und Gnadenreichen Geburth Gottes und Marien Sohnes, Jesu Christi* (performed in 1660).[32] This is only partly true of his much earlier *Historia der frölichen und Siegreichen Aufferstehung unsers einigen Erlösers und Seligmachers Jesu Christi* (Dresden, 1623), for in this, instead of monody in the seventeenth-century sense, the composer instructs the Evangelist to intone his narrative without '*tact*' and not prolonging any syllable 'more than one is accustomed to do in ordinary slow and comprehensible speech'. Nor has the *Historia* any connection with Italian oratorio. Its ancestor was the *Aufferstehungshistorie* (*c.* 1570) of Antonio Scandello (see p. 258), which had already been imitated by Nicolaus Rosthius (*c.* 1542–1622) and other Saxon composers and had just appeared in two new editions in 1621;[33] these works were in fact triumphant sequels to, and so the musical counterparts of, 'dramatic' Passion music. Schütz largely borrows Scandello's text and his *tonus lectionus* for the Evangelist; but he modernizes, introducing continuo

---

[28] *Neue Ausgabe*, v.   [29] Ibid., xviii–xxi.
[30] Parallel quotations in Hans Joachim Moser, *Heinrich Schütz* (2nd ed., Kassel and Basel, 1954), pp. 520–1.
[31] *Neue Ausgabe*, vii.
[32] Ibid., ii, i, and iii, respectively; various other editions.
[33] Both the Rosthius and Scandello *Historien* have been published in the *Handbuch der deutschen evangelischen Kirchenmusik*, I/3 and 4 (Göttingen, 1937).

throughout, accompanying the Evangelist with a quartet of viole da gamba, and giving his part rhythmical definition at cadential points. He follows Scandello also in giving the part of Maria Magdalena to two sopranos, and the part of Jesus is similarly depersonalized through being sung by alto and tenor; it is only here, in the parts of the 'soliloquents', that the new Italian style is employed. The *Sieben Worte* of twenty years later is another matter; now it is the Evangelist who is depersonalized, sung by various soloists and combinations of soloists, while Jesus is always sung by a tenor and accompanied by two obbligato viols. And the late Christmas *Historia* approximates to 'oratorio'; the declamatory narrative of the tenor Evangelist, accompanied only by continuo, is interrupted by eight *intermedia* for solo angel, three alto shepherds, three tenor Wise Men, and so on, with appropriate instrumental groups – strings, flutes and bassoon, trombones, trumpets – depicting the various scenes of the Nativity in music of great power and beauty.

GERMAN PASSION MUSIC

Schütz also occupies a peculiar place in the history of German 'Passion music' proper. The last German motet-Passion was published by Demantius (see p. 259) in 1631,[34] but the true liturgical or dramatic Passion was to develop new and important characteristics. The Hamburg cantor Selle (see p. 303) in his John Passion of 1643[35] led the way by making two innovations. Dividing his work into three parts, he ends each with a double-choral *intermedium*: on Isaiah, liii, 4–5, on Psalm 22, verses 2–22, and an impressive setting of the hymn 'O Lamm Gottes unschuldig'. One says 'double-choral' but in fact there is a third choir: of instruments. Selle uses instruments throughout: strings and two bassoons, organ for one choir, regal for the other, as well as cornetti and a trombone to accompany Pilate. Jesus (bass) is accompanied by two violins, the Evangelist (tenor) by two bassoons. Traditionally no instruments were allowed in church during Holy Week, so either the Passion was sung in a secular building – as was done at Hamburg at a later date – or Hamburg was a law unto itself, rather as Venice was. In Saxony no such liberties were tolerated. In Schütz's three Passions, a Luke (after 1653), a John (first version 1665), and a Matthew (1666),[36] the soliloquents – Jesus always a high bass, the Evangelist a tenor – intone unaccompanied, without written note-values yet with subtlety of inflection and characterization. Schütz achieves great dramatic power and musical beauty in the choruses, especially in the Matthew Passion, with the simplest means. His only addition to the liturgical text is a final chorus on the words of a hymn, though only in the John Passion does he borrow a hymn-melody, 'Christus der uns selig macht'.

---

[34] Ed. Friedrich Blume, *ChW*, 27.
[35] Ed. Rudolf Gerber, ibid., 26.
[36] *Neue Ausgabe*, ii; various other editions.

CONSERVATISM IN FRANCE AND ENGLAND

Neither France nor England during these years produced religious music comparable in quality or quantity with that of Italy or Germany. It was not only that neither had a composer of the stature of Monteverdi or Grandi or Schütz; in both countries religion itself had problems, which were reflected in church music. Puritan and Huguenot rejected all but vernacular psalms. The Gallican Catholic church had ignored the precepts of the Council of Trent right down to 1615. Then they were accepted by the Romanist faction and applied to music with quasi-puritanical austerity; plainsong was mistakenly and confusedly 'reformed' and polyphony discouraged. Before long the Anglican Church was disestablished, its choirs dispersed and its music suppressed during the Civil War and Commonwealth. It was only with the Restoration in England and the assumption of personal rule by Louis XIV that church music revived in either country.

In France there was a slow transition from polyphony to a more harmonic style and half-hearted adoption of Italian practices. Du Caurroy had left some examples of double-choral writing in his *Preces ecclesiasticae* (1609) but they appear to have been so little noticed that his pupil and successor as director of the Chapelle Royale, Nicolas Formé (1567–1638), could claim his double-choral Mass (Paris, 1638)[37] to be an innovatory work. Formé pitted a small choir, perhaps of soloists, against a larger one, and in the same spirit Guillaume Bouzignac in a number of motets pits a solo voice against the choir, e.g. in 'Dum silentium' where the superius impersonates Gabriel:

Ex. 119

More genuinely progressive was Henry Du Mont (1610–84) who came to Paris in 1640 from Liège, where he seems to have been a pupil of Léonard Hodemont (*c.* 1580–1636). Hodemont's *Sacri concentus* (Liège, 1630) includes some solo motets, *cum basso ad organum* and some with other instruments, and Du Mont's first volume of *Cantica sacra* (Paris, 1652) mixes pieces on these lines with purely polyphonic motets. He was to emerge as a much more significant composer but the bulk of his work belongs to a later chapter (see p. 412).

The greatest English composer of church music throughout these years was Thomas Tomkins (1572–1656). His church compositions were published, as *Musica Deo Sacra*,[38] twelve years after his death, but they belong to a long past age; having spent nearly all his professional life at Worcester Cathedral with only an interlude from 1621 to 1628 at Court, he had no inducement to modify his natural conservatism. Even at Court the wind blew from France rather than Italy and, as we have just seen, France was hardly less conservative than England. The two younger men who would have at least maintained the old style at its best long predeceased him, Weelkes in 1623, Orlando Gibbons in 1625, so we are left with the work of such minor figures as Adrian Batten (1591–1637), a vicar choral at St. Paul's, Robert Ramsey of Cambridge,[39] and the odd anthems of composers more distinguished in other fields: the Lawes brothers, the madrigalist Michael East, the lute-ayre composer Thomas Ford. For Continental influence in English church music we have to turn first to a Catholic, Richard Dering (*c.* 1580–1630). He published two volumes of Latin motets with basso continuo, *Cantiones Sacrae* and *Cantica Sacra*,[40] at Antwerp in 1617 and 1618, before becoming organist to Queen Henrietta Maria in 1625. He also composed *Cantica Sacra* for two or three voices with continuo which Cromwell is known to have delighted in having privately performed for him, but which had to wait till the Restoration before Playford published them in 1662. Much more Italianate is the anthem, 'O praise the Lord', of the English Monteverdian Walter Porter,[41] who opened his book of *Madrigales and Ayres* with it in 1632. Porter was master of the choristers at Westminster Abbey from 1639 to 1644, and during the Commonwealth published some unremarkable settings of metrical psalms: *Mottets of Two Voyces . . . with the Continued Bass or Score* (1657).

VERNACULAR PSALMS

Vernacular psalm-settings flourished more than ever in both England and Scotland. (Indeed also in France, where in rivalry with the old Calvinist translations, new Catholic ones – notably those of Philippe Desportes – were

[37] Sanctus and Agnus, ed. Amédée Gastoué (Paris, 1939).
[38] See above, p. 263, n. 71.
[39] Ed. Edward Thompson, *EECM*, vii.
[40] The latter ed. Peter Platt, ibid., xv.
[41] See p. 309. 'O praise the Lord' is ed. Peter le Huray, *Treasury of English Church Music, 1540–1650* (London, 1965), p. 232.

set by Du Caurroy, the lutenist Gabriel Bataille, and others.) The classic English Psalter of the period was Ravenscroft's *Whole Booke of Psalmes* (1621), the classic Scottish one, *The Psalmes of David in Prose and Meeter* (Edinburgh, 1635).[42] Naturally both borrow heavily from earlier collections, but Ravenscroft not only made some fifty fresh settings of his own but included new ones by Dowland and Tomkins among others. Two years later Gibbons contributed fourteen two-part psalm-settings to George Wither's fresh translation, *Hymnes and Songs of the Church*, and in 1638 yet another translation of the complete Psalter was made by George Sandys, for which Henry Lawes provided twenty-four new tunes 'and a thorough bass, for voice and instrument'. Fifteen of Sandys's versions were set again by Porter in his *Mottets*. But the Wither and Sandys versions were Anglican and we may be confident that the metrical psalms which constituted the only English and Scottish church music from 1644 to 1660 were from earlier collections. The Puritans of New England produced their own translation of *The Whole Book of Psalmes* (Cambridge, Mass., 1640), the so-called 'Bay Psalm Book', the first book to be printed in British North America, but it contained no tunes; the compilers pointed out that the majority 'may be sung in very neere fourty common tunes; as they are collected, out of our chief musicians, by *Tho. Ravenscroft*'.

---

[42] Ed. Richard R. Terry, *The Scottish Psalter of 1635* (London, 1935).

18

The Diffusion of Opera (c.1660–c.1725)

During the first sixty years of its existence opera had been almost exclusively Italian. During the next sixty Italian opera spread all over a Europe not untroubled by war but untroubled by bitter and all-devastating war, and vernacular opera by native composers sprang up beside it. The courts naturally continued to lead but public theatres were opened not only in Italy but in Germany. The Teatro della Pergola at Florence[1] was inaugurated in 1656 with *La Tancia* by Jacopo Melani[2] (1623–76) and two or three months later, in 1657, Munich acquired one, closed by fire in 1674, though like that at Dresden (1667), this was really a court theatre open to the public, not a free commercial undertaking. In that, the example was set by Hamburg, the prosperous Hansa town, northern counterpart of Venice, in 1678. And since opera was becoming the most fashionable and most important form of music, Italian musical hegemony became overwhelming – though not unchallenged.

POPULARIZATION IN VENETIAN OPERA

At Venice during the 1660s the veteran Cavalli continued to produce operas to Minato's libretti (see pp. 320 and 324) but younger men were coming to the fore: Pietro Andrea Ziani (*c.* 1620–1684) and Antonio Sartorio (*c.* 1620–1681). And three or four years after Cavalli's death Giovanni Legrenzi (1626–90) and Carlo Pallavicino (*c.* 1630–1688) made their débuts with *Eteocle e Polinice* (1675) and *Galieno* (1676) respectively. Ziani and Pallavicino excelled in the comic or satirical treatment of pseudo-historical subjects, for instance, the former's *Semiramide* (1671) and the latter's *Messalina* (1680).[3] There had been comic episodes in serious opera ever since Landi, and there continued to be – together with absurd disguises and complicated confusions. But in Ziani and Pallavicino the comedy can be

---

[1] Pictures of the auditorium and stage, from the printed libretto of Cavalli's *Ipermestra* (1658), are reproduced respectively in Robert Haas, *Musik des Barocks* (Potsdam, 1932), p. 151, and *MGG*, iv, col. 385–6.
[2] Excerpts in Goldschmidt, *Studien zur Geschichte der italienischen Oper im 17. Jahrhundert*, i (Leipzig, 1901). pp. 349–73.
[3] Extracts from *Semiramide* in the appendix to Hellmuth Christian Wolff, *Die venezianische Oper in der zweiten Hälfte des 17. Jahrhunderts* (Berlin, 1937), appendix, Nos. 57–61, from *Messalina*, ibid., Nos. 67–76 and, less extended, in Julian Smith, 'Carlo Pallavicino', *PRMA*, xcvi (1969–70), p. 68. Shorter excerpts from both and from other operas of the period in Wolff's chapter in *NOHM*, v, pp. 30 ff.

fundamental. It does not, of course, exclude serious music, e.g. 'Che ti feci' in Ziani's *Candaule* (1679)[4] or 'Misera Erginda' in *Messalina*. The latter is an arioso, a hybrid type which was fast going out of fashion. The sharper distinction of recitative and aria which had begun with Cavalli's later operas (see p. 320) resulted in the emergence of aria-dominated opera – with a growing preponderance of the da capo over the strophic form. Cesti's *La Dori* (1661) had had 32 arias, Pallavicino's *Galieno* (1676) had 71, more than half of them da capo.

A feature dating back to Cesti[6] but first used wholesale by Legrenzi in *Eteocle* is the 'motto' opening: a separate statement of the opening vocal phrase, with an instrumental interjection before the singer repeats it and continues – perhaps a device to catch the attention of the non-connoisseur listener whose tastes had already encouraged the development of 'aria-dominated' opera. For the commercial opera-houses and probably the less cultured courts had already undermined the aesthetic bases of early opera through the popular demand for more melody – even types of melody, 'slumber arias', 'farewell arias' – and more comic relief, and from that day onward genuine success in the opera-house has been impossible without memorable melody. Another ingredient which would appeal to the non-connoisseur but also stimulated a new kind of connoisseurship was vocal agility. Extensive coloratura was a very old feature of Italian song but it was now more and more blatantly exploited to stimulate applause. Emotive words such as 'vittoria' or 'gloria' would not only spark off a display of skill (*bravura*) but call for the addition of a trumpet or pair of trumpets to an orchestra which normally consisted only of strings and continuo harpsichord: e.g. in Sartorio's *Adelaide* (Act I, sc. 1) (1672)[7] and *Antonino e Pompejano* (1677),[8] and Pallavicino's *Amazzoni nelle isole fortunate* (II, 9) (1680).[9] The focus of interest had shifted from drama to song and was soon to shift from song to singer.

COURT OPERA AT NAPLES AND VIENNA

The difference in the operas of the Neapolitan Francesco Provenzale (1627–1704) is very noticeable. Writing for the Spanish Viceregal Court, he needed to make no concessions to popular taste other than the normal interpolation of comic scenes. His coloratura is expressive, not showy,[10] and he remains nearer to Cavalli, of whose *Xerse, Artemisia*, and *Eritrea* he made new versions for Naples, than to his own Venetian contemporaries. Menelippa's often quoted[11] 'Lasciatemi morir' from his *Schiavo di sua*

---

[4] Wolff, op. cit., No. 65.
[6] e.g. 'Dormi ben mio' in his *Orontea* (see p. 321).
[7] Quoted in Schering, *Geschichte der Musik in Beispielen* (Leizpig, 1931), No. 223. Fac. score. intro. H. M. Brown, *Italian Opera 1640–1770*, viii.
[8] Quoted in *NOHM*,v, p. 33.   [9] Quoted in Goldschmidt, op. cit., p. 403.
[10] Goldschmidt prints two examples from *La Stellidaura vendicante* (1674) in 'Francesco Provenzale als Dramatiker', *SIMG*, vii (1905–6), pp. 625–6.
[11] e.g. in *HAM*, ii, No. 222. The transposable ground bass, inherited from Cavalli, remained a favourite device for twenty years after his death. Fac. score of *Lo schiavo*, intro. Brown, op. cit., vii.

moglie (1671) (I, 8) belongs to the older types of arioso melody, as does Ippolita's equally tragic 'Addio Marte' (I, 10):[12]

Ex. 120

remarkable for the importance of the violin parts. (The normal practice was for them to alternate with the voice, accompany unobtrusively, or leave the accompaniment to the continuo.) Another composer working for a court was Antonio Draghi (*c.* 1635–1700) at Vienna, where Cavalli's former librettist Minato was appointed Court poet in 1669; the pair were responsible during the next three decades for nearly 40 full-length operas, to say nothing of *serenate* and other smaller stage-works and oratorios. Many were to celebrate imperial birthdays or weddings and sometimes included an aria or two by Leopold I himself or in later years by Draghi's son, Carlo. The ballet music was also usually by another hand, Johann Heinrich Schmelzer (*c.* 1623–1680), and the stage-designs by Ludovico Burnacini who had already shown his mastery in mounting Cesti's *Pomo d'oro*. It was Cesti rather than Cavalli whom Draghi followed, taking full advantage of his librettist's liking for arias (see p. 320). Before his partnership with Minato – for instance, in *Achille in Sciro* (1663)[13] – they are generally strophic and fairly short, but in his later works the da capo form predominates and is padded out to considerable length by text-repetition and extended coloratura. In *Achille* he had given Ulisse five bars on 'ar-(mi)'[14] as one would expect, but Psiche's last aria in the serenata *Psiche cercando Amore* (1688)[15] is pure bravura. Draghi's recitative is dry and perfunctory;[16] he

[12] Goldschmidt, 'Francesco Provenzale', p. 614.
[13] Five complete excerpts in Max Neuhaus, 'Antonio Draghi', *StMW*, i (1913).
[14] Ibid., p. 185.   [15] Riemann, *Musikgeschichte in Beispielen* (Leipzig, 1921), No. 116.
[16] See the extended scene from *La pazienza di Socrate* (1680) in Schering, op. cit., No. 226.

was keeping abreast of contemporary fashion. Occasionally he takes advantage of the large orchestra of the Court *Kapelle* (which included a number of obsolescent instruments: a quartet of viols, cornetti, theorbo) and once he indulges in a little tone-painting, prefacing *L'albero del ramo d'oro* (1681) with a *sinfonia come di strepito di vento in un bosco* (like the sound of wind in a wood).

'ARIA OPERA'

Alessandro Stradella (1644–82), an aristocratic Roman libertine (but skilled contrapuntist) and the Venetian Carlo Francesco Pollarolo (*c.* 1653–1722) also showed some enterprise in their scoring. Both – for instance, Stradella in his serenata *Lo schiavo liberato* (1674) and a number of later works, Pollarolo in *Onoria in Roma* (1692) – divided their strings into thee-part *concertino* and full *concerto grosso* (see p. 423). Otherwise they are conventional enough.[17] Stradella's *Floridoro* (probably before 1677) has 37 arias (mostly strophic) with continuo accompaniment and 16 with two obbligato violins, no more. In his last opera, *La forza d'amor paterno* (1678)[18] he has a direction that at the end of Arbante's aria in Act I the instruments are to drop out *a poco a poco*. From about the same period dates a work which has often been claimed as 'the first *opera buffa*': Stradella's *Trespolo tutore* (probably 1677). *Che soffre, speri, Dal Male il Bene*, and *La Tancia* (see pp. 313–6 and 327) had been 'comedies in music' but in *Trespolo* the farcical element is paramount. Trespolo himself, the ridiculous guardian (a bass part), and the maid Despina are prototypes in character and music[19] of true *opera buffa*.

In 1679 the future classic master of the 'aria opera', the young Alessandro Scarlatti (1660–1725), made his début in Rome – at first with modest works of the usual semi-seria type showing the influences of Stradella, Provenzale, and Legrenzi. His first *opera seria, Pompeo*, was given in 1683. Even after his move to Naples the next year he was at first content with the conventional chain of da capo arias. (He was stuck with the conventional absurdly complicated plots all his life.) But in 1690 he produced two works which revealed mature power: the intimate *Rosaura* and the brilliant and dramatic *Statira*. In *Statira* more use is made of such devices as orchestrally accompanied recitative and the use of short but sufficiently effective motives in the arias. Elmiro's 'Ah, crudel' in Act II of *Rosaura* is already typical of Scarlatti's vein of heart-easing melody:[20]

[17] Pollarolo had the advantage in later operas – *Gl' inganni felici* (1695), *Griselda* (1701), and others – of libretti by Apostolo Zeno (1668–1750), who did a great deal to condense and simplify the rambling action of contemporary opera and supply composers with better verse. Fac. of *Gl'inganni felici*, intro. Brown, op. cit., xvi.
[18] Vocal score by Alberto Gentili (Milan, 1930).
[19] Complete excerpts in Heinz Heuss, *Die Opern Alessandro Stradellas* (Leipzig, 1906), pp. 85–93.
[20] *Rosaura* (Acts I and II only), is ed. Robert Eitner, *Publikationen älterer . . . Musikwerke*, Jg. xiv, p. 215.

Ex. 121

and Statira's 'Gran tonante' with the lightning (*lampo*) of the violins shows his power of pictorial suggestion:[21]

Ex. 122

[21] From Alfred Lorenz, *Alessandro Scarlattis Jugendoper* (Augsburg, 1927), ii, No. 217. Lorenz's second volume consists entirely of musical examples, including 135 complete pieces.

s'il re-gio splen-do - re por - ta un lam-po di tua ma - e - stà

Pirro e Demetrio (1694)[22] – which reached London, sung partly in English, in 1708 – and *Eraclea* (1700)[23] are perhaps the highwater marks of Scarlatti's 'first Neapolitan period' (1684–1702). Towards the end of it (1697–8) he, a Sicilian by birth, began to introduce a great number of lilting tunes in 12/8 time (in *La caduta dei Decemviri, Il prigioniero fortunato, La donna è ancora fedele*) of the type known as *siciliana*; the example in *La donna*[24] is specifically marked 'Aria detta La Siciliana'. He seems to have been aiming at popular audiences, for the last movement of the overture to *Il prigionero*[25] has a tune played by first and second trumpets in unison to catch the ears of the Neapolitan groundlings:

Ex. 123

In strongest contrast is the masterpiece of Scarlatti's years of wandering (1702–7) in Florence, Rome, and Venice: *Mitridate Eupatore* (Venice, 1707).[26] He never surpassed the tragic grandeur of the opening of Act IV – the solemn march with its antiphony of muted trumpets and timpani on land and on the ship, Laodice's great recitative, 'O Mitridate mio!' and her aria 'Cara tomba', her duet with her brother Eupatore – and there are other fine things in the score, e.g. Eupatore's aria 'Patri Numi'[27] (II, 1). The end of 'Mitridate mio' is a locus classicus of the chromatic harmony of Scarlatti's continuo figuration (e.g. diminished chords with alternative resolutions). With the firm establishment of key and key-relationships (see chap. 21) composers were beginning to move more freely and confidently within the tonal ambit.

[22] Excerpts, ibid., Nos. 246–69.
[23] Ed. Donald J. Grout (Cambridge, Mass, 1974) as the first volume of a projected complete edition.
[24] Lorenz, No. 285. It is distinguished melodically by the flattened supertonic of Sicilian folk music, which Scarlatti harmonizes with the so-called 'Neapolitan sixth' chord.
[25] On Scarlatti's overtures, see below, chap. 20.
[26] The vocal score ed. Giuseppe Piccioli (Milan, 1953), is unreliable.
[27] Complete in Donald J. Grout, *A Short History of Opera* (second edition, New York and London, 1965), p. 175.

Scarlatti's later operas, composed for Naples or Rome, are marked by a number of new developments. Arias are extended, given more inner contrast of key and material (AB/C/AB), the coloratura is more expressive, the accompaniments are more for strings – even without harpsichord. And from *Telemaco* (1718) onward he introduces more quartets or, as he calls them, *arie a quattro*, the melody being passed from voice to voice without differentiation of characters. In *Telemaco*[27a] we find him supporting recitatives with full string chords marked *arpeggio*[28] and *Marco Attilio Regolo* (1719)[29] also has a good deal of accompanied recitative. In *Telemaco* again, as he had already done in *Tigrane* (1715), he accompanies an aria with a *concerto di oubuoè* (two oboes and bassoons) and two horns as well as strings. In *Tigrane* the almost inevitable *buffo* scenes are particularly amusing, being sung in Bolognese dialect with some comic German and Italian. *Il trionfo dell'onore* (1718)[30] is a completely comic opera, Scarlatti's only one. But it is *comica*, not *buffa*, although it has two conventional *buffo* parts, the servants Rosina and Rodimarte, counterparts of the usual buffo couples in the earlier operas. They have a comic scene at the end of Act I,[31] one of the customary places for *buffo* scenes, and join an absurd elderly couple in a 'quarrel' quartet[32] in another conventional *buffo* spot, the penultimate scene of Act III. There is plenty of sparkle also in the other parts, e.g. the rakish hero's 'E ben far, far come l'ape'.

There are no comic scenes in Scarlatti's penultimate opera, *Griselda* (1721),[33] based – but with a number of changes – on Zeno's libretto which Pollarolo had set twenty years before. One significant change was the addition of a quartet, with oboes and trumpets, to end the opera. The Second Act shows Scarlatti's dramatic power at its height: the vigorous coloratura and cutting unison string passages of Corrado's 'Agitata da fiera procella' (sc. 3), the dialogue of Griselda and her cruel husband in the following scene[34] leading to her great declamatory aria, 'Figlio! Tiranno! oh Dio!'.[35]

Scarlatti's younger contemporaries Antonio Lotti (1667–1740) and Francesco Gasparini (1668–1727) produced numerous operas in Venice during the years 1703–16,[36] but his only rival in Naples was a relatively insignificant pupil of Provenzale, Francesco Mancini (1679–1739). Mancini's *Idaspe fedele*[37] was produced in 1710 in London where it probably owed its success as much to the castrato Nicolini's fight with a lion[38] as to the quality of the

[27a] Fac. score intro. Brown, op. cit., xxiii.
[28] See the autograph facsimile in Haas, op. cit., p. 211.
[29] Ed. Joscelyn Godwin (Cambridge, Mass., 1975).
[30] Vocal score ed. Virgilio Mortari (Milan, 1941).
[31] Part of the final duet is quoted in Edward J. Dent, *Alessandro Scarlatti* (second edition, London, 1960), p. 129.
[32] Complete in full score in Dent, 'Ensembles and Finales in 18th century Italian Opera', *SIMG*, xi (1909–10), p. 557.
[33] Ed. Grout (Cambridge, Mass., 1975).   [34] Complete in Schering, op. cit., No. 259.
[35] Opening in Dent, *Alessandro Scarlatti*, p. 165.
[36] Aria from *Alessandro Severo* (1716) by Lotti in Schering, op. cit., No. 270; facsimile of complete opera, Brown. op. cit., xx.
[37] A much revised version of his *Amanti generosi* (Naples, 1704); fac. ibid., xviii.

music. A younger generation of Neapolitans made their débuts with the *Agrippina* (1708) of Nicola Porpora (1686–1768) and the *Pisistrato* (1714) of Leonardo Leo (1694–1744), and the Venetian instrumental composer Antonio Vivaldi (1678–1741) turned to opera with *Ottone in Villa* (Vicenza, 1713) and continued with his usual prolificacy, producing nearly fifty during the next twenty-five years.[38a]

ITALIAN OPERA IN GERMANY

Scarlatti's most significant Italian contemporaries, other than Lotti, were those active in Germany, as Giovanni Andrea Bontempi (*c.* 1624–1705) had been in Dresden (where Lotti went in 1717) and Draghi and others in Vienna. Vienna had always been strongly Italian in culture, and Schütz and his circle, which included Pallavicino as well as Bontempi, had familiarized Dresden with Italianate music well before the latter brought out his *Paride* there in 1662.[39] (Pallavicino's *Gerusalemme liberata* (1687),[40] with its numerous da capo motto-arias, dates from his brief return to Dresden just before his death.) In collaboration with another Italian, Marco Giuseppe Peranda (*c.* 1625–1675), Bontempi also tried his hand in 1671 at a German opera, *Dafne*.[41] At Munich the success of Italian opera was due less to Kerll (see p. 325) than to his pupil Agostino Steffani (1654–1728) though Steffani's earliest opera, *Marco Aurelio*, appeared only in 1681. He had recently visited Paris and become acquainted with Lully's operas, which exercised some effect on him, while his German upbringing from the age of 13 had made him a good contrapuntist, influences which did not pollute his natural stream of Italian melody. And he contentedly conformed to the conventions: drama more or less confined to the recitatives, da capo arias with motto openings, bravura arias in which the singer competed with a solo trumpet,[42] and so on. His ascendancy in Germany was unchallenged. After his last Munich operas, *Alarico il Baltha* (1687)[43] and *Niobe* (1688),[44] he went to Hanover where the new Court opera house was inaugurated with his *Henrico Leone* (1689).[45] Here he produced a number of operas until 1696. Then (always distracted by political and diplomatic activities) he remained silent until during 1707–9 he wrote three for the Elector Palatine at Düsseldorf: *Arminio*, *Amor vien dal destino*, and *Tassilone*. The choice of

[38] Mocked by Addison in *The Spectator*, Nos. 13 and 14 (15 and 16 March 1711) after the production of Handel's *Rinaldo* (see p. 370).
[38a] A good example, *La fida ninfa* (1732) is available in a full score, ed. Raffaello Monterosso (Cremona, 1964).
[39] Ermillo's aria 'Gia trafitto', on a Cavallian chromatic ostinao bass, is printed in Lavignac and La Laurencie, *Encyclopédie de la musique*, Ire. partie, ii, p. 914.
     Full score, ed. Hermann Abert, *DDT*, lv, revised edition by H. J. Moser.
[41] Apollo's aria 'So ist denn nuhn' in Riemann, *Musikgeschichte in Beispielen*, No. 105.
[42] See the example from his *Tassilone* (1709) in Heinz Becker, *Geschichte der Instrumentation (Das Musikwerk)* (Cologne, 1964), No. 3; *Tassilone* has been ed. Gerhard Croll, *Denkmäler rheinischer Musik*, vii (Kassel, 1958).
[43] Ed. Riemann, *DTB*, xi (2); also excerpts from *Niobe, Henrico Leone, La superbia d'Alessandro, Orlando generoso, Tassilone, Amor vien dal destino*, and other operas, ibid., xii (2).
[44] Aria from *Niobe* in idem, *Musikgeschichte in Beispielen*, No. 117.
[45] Aria from Act I in *HAM*, ii, No. 244.

Germanic subjects – Alaric, Henry the Lion, Arminius – is noteworthy. More important: a number of his operas were translated and performed in German, e.g. *La superbia d'Alessandro* (1690) as *Der hochmüthige Alexander* (1695), *Henrico Leone* as *Herzog Heinrich der Löwe* (1696) and *Orlando generoso* as *Der grossmüthige Roland* (1696), all translated by Gottlieb Fiedler for Hamburg.

THE HAMBURG OPERA

The famous Theater am Gänsemarkt at Hamburg had been opened in 1678 with the *Adam und Eva* of Johann Theile (1646–1724). An *Orontes* and other works have been doubtfully attributed to Theile but actually the provision of operas for the first twelve years was in the hands of three other men: Nicolaus Adam Strungk (1640–1700), son of Delphin Strungk (see p. 337), Johann Wolfgang Franck (1644–c. 1710), and Johann Philipp Förtsch (1652–1732).[46] These were very minor masters. The best of them – to judge by what survives of their work – was Franck, whose recitative sometimes flowers into arioso or expressive coloratura and who composed da capo arias (six of those in *Cecrops* having motto openings), while his colleagues preferred strophic and dance songs. The Hamburg composers seem to have known the work of Cavalli and Cesti, and Franck imitates Cesti's broad 3/2 melodies, though without Cesti's quality, as in Mercury's 'O angenehme Nacht'[47] in *Cecrops*, Act V, Sc. 6, the best scene in the opera. Förtsch also translated and adapted Italian works, and during 1689–94 four fairly recent French or Italian operas were performed in the original language: Lully's *Acis et Galatée*, *Achille et Polixène* by Lully and Colasse, *La schiava fortunata* by Cesti and Marc' Antonio Ziani (nephew of Pietro), and Pallavicino's *Gerusalemme*. The last of these was repeated in 1695 in German except for one aria, with the title *Armida*. At the same time the repertory was strengthened by the already mentioned German versions of Steffani and by the appearance of more gifted native composers. First was Johann Sigismund Kusser (1660–1727), an avowed disciple of Lully and teacher of French performing methods, who – after his début as an opera-composer at Brunswick – came to Hamburg for a short time in 1694 and produced his *Erindo*[48] and other operas there. Much more important both as composer and as enduring influence was Reinhard Keiser (1674–1739), who followed Kusser from Brunswick; he poured out a stream of operas from the late 1690s for a quarter of a century, and was responsible for the actual direction of the Hamburg opera from 1703 to 1707. Keiser was a real eclectic

---

[46] Arias by these composers in H. C. Wolff, *Die Barockoper in Hamburg (1678 bis 1738)* (Wolfenbüttel, 1957). Franck's *Die Drey Töchter des Cecrops* (1679), one of three German operas composed for the Court theatre at Ansbach before he went to Hamburg, has been ed. Gustav Friedrich Schmidt, *DTB*, xxxviii (*EDM: Landschaftsdenkmale Bayern*, ii).

[47] Facsimile in *MGG*, iv, col. 659.

[48] Arias, duets, and choruses, ed. Helmuth Osthoff, *EDM: Landschaftsdenkmale Schleswig-Holstein und Hansestädte*, iii. Cloris's 'Ich klage mein Leiden' (p. 40) shows Kusser's expressive power in a typical da capo aria, while Eurilla's 'Schöne Wiesen' (p. 18; also in Schering op. cit., No. 250) reveals the 'disciple of Lully'.

who learned from Lully on the one hand, Steffani on the other, and did not hesitate to introduce arias with Italian texts, as in *Claudius* (1703) and later works, or *plattdeutsch* songs, e.g. Trintje's in Act III of *Der Carneval von Venedig* (1707),[49] beside coloratura da capo arias like Leander's 'Hertz und Fuss eilt mit Verlangen'.[50] His emotional gamut is equally wide: from the despair of the deserted Nero in Act III of *Octavia* (1705)[51] or the tragic resignation of the hero of *Croesus* (1710; revised version 1730; a translation of a Minato libretto)[52] – e.g. his arias 'Niemand kann aus diesen Ketten' (II, 14) and 'Götter, übt Barmherzigkeit' (III, 12) – to the buffo songs of the late and not really characteristic comic opera *Der lächerliche Printz Jodelet* (1726).[53] Keiser is particularly happy with country scenes: in Octavia's 'Wallet nicht so laut' (*Octavia*, II, 6) the sound of the brook is deliciously painted by the incessant triplets of pairs of solo violins and recorders – and in the peasant duet 'Kleine Vöglein' (*Croesus*, II, 1)[54] the bird-song is suggested by a *zuffolo* (probably a flageolet and also used in *Jodelet*) while pairs of oboes and bassoons represent bagpipes. Indeed examples of his enterprising and effective use of woodwind are numerous.

Keiser also collected around him some notable younger men, including the native Hamburger Johann Mattheson (1681–1764), composer, singer, actor, and copious author,[55] who began with *Die Plejades* in 1699, though his best operas were *Die unglückselige Cleopatra* (1704),[56] *Boris Goudenow* (1710), on his own libretto, and *Henrico IV* (1711).[57] Christoph Graupner (1683–1760) produced *Dido* (1707)[58] and *Antiochus und Stratonica* (1708)[59] and then went off to Darmstadt where his later operas appeared. Infinitely more important was Mattheson's friend Georg Friedrich Händel (1685–1759), who came to Hamburg in 1703 and played second violin in Keiser's *Claudius*, soon became harpsichordist, and had his earliest operas, *Almira* and *Nero*, staged early in 1705.[60]

Almira is a typical Hamburg opera, a linguistic hotchpotch (fifteen arias set to the original Italian libretto which Friedrich Christian Feustking had translated), with arias with showy instrumental obbligati (e.g. Almira's 'Chi più mi piace' with solo oboe in I, 3), thoroughly Germanic recitative like the

---

[49] Wolff, *Die Barockoper*, Nos. 114–15. Wolff also gives parallel examples from Keiser's opera and Campra's ballet, *Le Carnaval de Venise* (1699) (see p. 376, n. 85), ibid., Nos. 101–10.
[50] Ed. Wolff, *Deutsche Barockarien aus Opern Hamburger Meister* (Kassel, 1943), ii, p. 4.
[51] Ed. Max Seiffert, *Händel-Gesamtausgabe: Supplement*, Nr. 6 (Leipzig, 1902).
[52] Ed. Max Schneider, *DDT*, xxxvii–xxxviii (Leipzig, 1912; revised edition, H. J. Moser, 1958). Opening of 'Niemand kann' quoted in *NOHM*, v, p. 310.
[53] Ed. Friedrich Zelle, *Publikationen älterer . . . Musikwerke*, Jg. xviii (Berlin, 1892).
[54] Also printed in Schering, op. cit., No. 269.
[55] Beginning with *Das neu-eröffnete Orchestre* (1713), an introduction to music for the *Galant Homme*, the up-to-date man of taste, he went on to publish a great number of prose works, the best known of which are *Der vollkommene Capellmeister* (1739; facsimile, Kassel, 1954) and *Grundlage einer Ehren-Pforte* (1740; ed. M. Schneider, Berlin, 1910).
[56] Ed. George J. Buelow, *EDM*, lxix.
[57] Complete arias from *Boris* and *Henrico IV* in Wolff, *Barockoper*, Nos. 132–5 and 136–8 respectively, and *Deutsche Barockarien*, Nos. 21 and 20 respectively.
[58] Idem, *Barockoper*, Nos. 139–40.
[59] Ibid, Nos. 141–2; *Deutsche Barockarien*, No. 19.
[60] *Almira* was ed. Friedrich Chrysander, *G. F. Händels Werke*, lv, but *Nero* is lost.

one preceding this aria (i) and also curiously instrumental melodic invention (ii), sometimes even more obviously keyboard inspired than in this example:

Ex. 124

and a sarabande, 'Tanz von Asiatern', in the masque of Act III, sc. 3 which was before long to become one of the most famous Handelian airs.

HANDEL IN ITALY

At the end of the following year Handel slipped off to Italy where he stayed till 1710 and produced the opera which first earned him wider fame, *Agrippina* (Venice, 1709).[61] Although Keiser's influence is still perceptible in Ottone's idyllic 'Vaghe fonti' (II, 7) and in the bold exploitation of the orchestra, the work is markedly Scarlattian; Handel had quickly mastered Italian recitative and absorbed Italian melody. His sense of character and situation and his melodic invention (even when he transmuted his own earlier ideas or those of other men, as he did all his life), produced a chain of arias in which Claudio's adagio arietta 'Vieni a cara' (I, 21), brief though it is, is one of the finest links. At the other end is Poppea's often quoted 'Bel piacere' (III, 10), a tune so catchy that it needs no accompaniment – only violins in unison, not even continuo bass – and at the same time vividly suggests by its mixture of 3/8 and 2/4 time her mischievous capriciousness.

[61] *Werke*, lvii.

OPERA IN RESTORATION ENGLAND

In 1710 Handel paid his first visit to London, where Italian opera was still a comparative novelty. Opera in England had got off on the wrong foot with *The Siege of Rhodes* (see p. 326). A poetic play with a superabundance of music provided by any number of composers passed for an opera. Thus in 1674 Shakespeare's *Tempest* – or rather, Dryden and Davenant's perversion of it – was 'made into an Opera' by Thomas Shadwell by the addition of songs and a masque of Neptune and Amphitrite; the songs were composed by John Banister (1630–79), Pelham Humfrey (1647–74), and Pietro Reggio (d. 1685), the instrumental dances and so on by Matthew Locke and Giovanni Battista Draghi (probably Antonio's brother). The same year a French opera *Ariane*, by Louis Grabu, the French 'Master of his Majesties Musick', was performed at the Theatre Royal in Covent Garden, and in 1675 Locke and Draghi again collaborated in music for Shadwell's *Psyche*.[62] Locke published his music as *The English Opera*, although none of the principal characters sings. On the other hand the *Venus and Adonis* (early 1680s)[63] of John Blow (1649–1708), although styled a 'Masque for the Entertainment of the King' (who liked all things French), is a true if miniature opera.[64] It has no spoken dialogue but within its narrow limits Blow managed to enclose, without jarring contrasts, things as disparate as the delicious 'Cupids' spelling lesson' in Act II, and in Act III the lament of Venus who is a fully realized and ultimately tragic character. His treatment of the English language, if not flawless, is immeasurably superior to Grabu's in the latter's second opera, *Albion and Albanius* (1685), to a libretto by Dryden.[65]

PURCELL'S MUSIC FOR THE STAGE

Yet *Albion* as well as *Venus and Adonis*, to say nothing of Cambert – who was in London from 1673 till his murder in 1677 – and Lully's *Cadmus et Hermione* which was performed there by a French company in 1686, all contributed to the dramatic idiom of Henry Purcell (1659–95). The miniature-opera form of *Venus and Adonis* assuredly suggested that of Purcell's only opera, *Dido and Aeneas*,[66] 'Perform'd at Mr. Josias Priest's Boarding School at Chelsey. By Young Gentlewomen' probably in 1689. But Purcell's power of invention was vastly superior to Blow's and not inferior to Lully's, as many numbers of *Dido* bear witness. In the rhythm of

---

[62] Excerpts from the music in *Oxford History of Music*, iii (Oxford, 1902), pp. 291–4, Edward J. Dent, *Foundations of English Opera* (Cambridge, 1928), pp. 117–19, and *NOHM*, v, p. 276.
[63] Ed. Anthony Lewis (Monaco, revised edition 1949).
[64] It has been suggested that Locke's music for Elkanah Settle's *Empress of Morocco* (1671) served as a small-scale model for it; see Lewis, 'Matthew Locke', *PRMA* (1947–48), p. 57.
[65] The excerpts in Dent, op. cit., pp. 166–70, show Grabu's disastrous accentuation. Dent also summarizes and quotes from Dryden's very interesting preface on the problems of opera in English (complete text in *Dramatic Works*, ed. Montague Summers, v (London, 1932)), in which he admits that *Albion* is not really an opera 'because the Story of it is not sung'.
[66] Purcell Society's edition, iii.

the duet and chorus 'Fear no danger' and in the 'Triumphing Dance' he challenges Lully on his own ground, and it is not easy to find in Lully many things finer than Dido's first song, 'Ah! Belinda, I am prest', or as fine as her last, 'When I am laid in earth', with its choral epilogue, 'With drooping wings'. It is tragic that during the five or six remaining years of his life England's greatest dramatic composer wrote no more operas but had to lavish often magnificent work on the plays-with-music which then passed for operas: *The Prophetess, or the History of Dioclesian*, adapted from Beaumont and Fletcher (1690), *King Arthur*, Dryden's sequel to *Albion and Albanius* (1691), and mangled versions of Shakespeare, *The Fairy Queen* (*A Midsummer Night's Dream*) (1692) and the Dryden-Davenant-Shadwell *Tempest* (1695).[67] The last of these illustrates Purcell's abandonment of the French for the Italian style, da capo arias and all, of which 'Arise, ye subterranean winds' happens to be the best known.

ITALIAN OPERA IN LONDON

Ten years passed before Italian opera actually arrived in England and then only half-heartedly and in two obscure works. *Arsinoe, Queen of Cyprus*, described as 'An opera, after the Italian manner: All sung', was produced at Drury Lane on 16 January 1705; the libretto was a translation of a 30-year-old Italian one, the music composed or compiled from Italian songs by Thomas Clayton (*c.* 1670–*c.* 1730). And on 20 April the same year the new Queen's Theatre in the Haymarket was inaugurated with *The Loves of Ergasto* by an obscure German, Jakob Greber, but sung in Italian by Italian singers. More reputable composers, G. B. Draghi and Giovanni Battista Bononcini (1670–1747), were represented in the following year but their works were sung wholly or partly in English. In 1707 Clayton failed catastrophically with his *Rosamond*, despite a libretto by Addison, and a member of the Drury Lane orchestra, Johann Pepusch (1667–1752), concocted a *pasticcio*, *Thomyris*, on airs by half a dozen eminent Italians but partly sung in English. In 1708 a garbled version of Scarlatti's *Pirro* (*Pyrrhus and Demetrius*) (see p. 363) was given at the Haymarket. Soon came an anonymous *Almahide* sung in Italian save for English intermezzi, and Mancini's above-mentioned *Idaspe* entirely in Italian.

Such was the state of opera in England when Handel, recently appointed Electoral *Kapellmeister* at Hanover, visited London. Produced at the Haymarket on 24 February 1711, three months after his arrival, his *Rinaldo*[68] was a milestone in the acceptance of Italian opera in England – though Addison had his fun in *The Spectator*[69] and its success did not immediately eclipse *Idaspe*'s. *Rinaldo* had all the ingredients of success, scenic and musical combined. The famous garden scene (I, 6) had not only

---

[67] Ibid., ix, xxvi, xii, and xix respectively.
[68] *Werke*, lviii.
[69] No. 5, 6 March 1711 and later issues. However in No. 29, 3 April, he or another contributor had some very sensible things to say about *recitativo* in Italian, English, and French.

live birds but idyllic music surpassing Keiser's, the last act not only fights but a famous march, with four trumpets, followed by a superb aria, Rinaldo's 'Or la tromba' (III, 9). Handel had already begun his lifelong practice of borrowing from his own, and other musicians', works: Argante's 'Sibillar gli angui d'Aletto' (I, 3), the duet 'Scherzano sul tuo volto' in the garden scene, 'Fermati!' (II, 6), and the sirens' siciliana 'Il vostro maggio' (II, 3) are all taken from his Italian cantatas; two of Almirena's arias come from *Almira*: 'Combatti da forte' in Act I (sc. 1) and her great 'Lascia ch'io piango' (II, 4) – rivalled in beauty only by Rinaldo's 'Cara sposa' (I, 7) – is simply an expanded yet otherwise unchanged version of the little 'Tanz von Asiatern',[70] while her final 'Bel piacere' (III, 7) is nothing but Agrippina's transposed from G to A. The opening *grave* of the splendid overture[71] likewise came from an Italian cantata. Whether borrowed or newly composed, the thirty arias of *Rinaldo* generally combine melodic beauty with a great deal of genuine characterization, while the element of *recitativo* which, according to *The Spectator*, had so 'startled our English audience', is minimal.

Handel's next few operas, all written for the Haymarket, were markedly less successful and he wrote no more for five years when, permanently settled in England,[72] he opened his series of great mature operas with *Radamisto* in 1720. The King's Theatre was now in the hands of a noble and aristocratic body of directors, known as the Royal Academy of Music, with Handel as 'master of the orchestra'. Serious opera in English had died with the *Calypso and Telemachus* (1712) and *Pan and Syrinx* (1717) of Johann Ernst Galliard (*c.* 1680–1749); the operas chosen to precede and follow *Radamisto* were the *Numitore* of Giovanni Porta (*c.* 1690–1755), an undistinguished Venetian who immediately returned to Italy, and the *Narciso* (Rome, 1714) of Scarlatti's son Domenico (1685–1757) who had already abandoned his short career as an opera composer. Later in the same year the Academy sponsored the *Astarto* of Giovanni Battista Bononcini, a more considerable rival.[73] Bononcini had first attracted attention by his *Serse* (Rome, 1694), based on a revised version of the Minato libretto set by Cavalli (see p. 320).[74] He earned a great international reputation with a series of operas from the enormously successful *Trionfo di Camilla* (Naples, 1697)[75] onward, before the invitation to London. In 1722 his *Crispo* and *Griselda*[76] had some success but he had to compete with a series of

---

[70] It had in the mean time appeared as Piacere's aria 'Lascia la spina' in the quasi-dramatic serenata *Il Trionfo del Tempo* (Rome, 1707).
[71] Also in Schering, op. cit., No. 278.
[72] He had already adopted the familiar English form of his name.
[73] Anthony Ford has ed. a volume of arias from Bononcini's Vienna operas (1699–1710), (London, 1971). See also Ford, 'Music and Drama in the Operas of Giovanni Bononcini', *PRMA*, ci (1974–5), p. 107.
[74] Harold S. Powers, 'Il Serse trasformato', *MQ*, xlvii (1961), p. 481, and xlviii (1962), p. 73, quotes a number of passages in parallel with Handel's setting of 1738, showing that Handel not only appropriated the duet, 'L'amerete? L'amerò' (II, 4) in toto from Bononcini, but borrowed piecemeal elsewhere – even in 'Ombra mai fù' – and also in *Giustino* (1737) and *Faramondo* (1738), magically transforming everything he touched.
[75] Fac. in Brown, op. cit., xvii.

Handelian masterpieces which included *Ottone* (1723), *Giulio Cesare* and *Tamerlano* (1724),[77] *Rodelinda* (1725), *Scipione* (1726), and *Admeto* (1727), and after his *Astianatte* (1727)[78] he gave up the struggle. Indeed after Handel's *Tolomeo* (1728) the Royal Academy itself got into financial difficulty and ceased operations. Handel had deployed for them a wealth of melodic invention in works that were broadly conventional yet often dramatically shattered convention, e.g. Caesar's recitative interruption of Cleopatra's lovely aria 'V'adoro, pupille' in *Giulio Cesare* (II, 1), Scarlattian in style yet often surpassing Scarlatti.

THE GENERAL TRIUMPH OF ITALY

Italian opera had triumphed in London as it had done almost all over Europe. The Imperial Court composer Johann Josef Fux (1660–1741) wrote Italian operas, from *Angelica* (1716) to *Costanza e Fortezza* (1723),[79] with specially heavy scoring for outdoor festivities, and had as *Vize-Kapellmeister* a prolific Venetian, Antonio Caldara (*c.* 1670–1736). The repertory of the Dresden Court, enriched by Johann David Heinichen (1683–1729) and for a year or two by Lotti, was Italian. Even in Hamburg more and more Italian works were given and Georg Philipp Telemann (1681–1767), who took over the direction of the theatre in 1721, wrote Italianate *buffo* intermezzi, *Pimpinone* (1725),[80] with partly Italian words, though his other operas – such as *Der geduldige Socrates* (1721), *Sieg der Schönheit* (1722), and *Emma und Eginhard* (1728)[81] – kept the German tradition alive. The other leading German composers, Keiser and Graupner, had practically abandoned opera, while the most brilliant of the younger men, Johann Adolf Hasse (1699–1783), after a year or two as a tenor at Hamburg, began – with *Antioco* (Brunswick, 1721) – a career as totally dedicated to Italian opera as Handel's. Italian opera was still propagated in its earliest home by such native Venetians as Vivaldi and Tomaso Albinoni (1671–1750). It invaded Spain under the Italophile Philip V and the Teatro de los Caños was built for the Italian company in 1708, though Italian composers were encouraged to set Spanish libretti. Before long it was to carry European musical culture to Russia. France alone held out against it.

THE BEGINNINGS OF FRENCH OPERA

As we have seen (chap. 15) Italian opera had been introduced in France by a

[76] Not to be confused with the opera of the same name by his brother Antonio (1677–1726), who in turn has often been credited with Giovanni's *Camilla* (see *NOHM*, v, pp. 70 and 81). Excerpts from Giovanni's *Griselda* are given ibid., pp. 78–80, and from Antonio's on pp. 82–3. Fac. of Antonio's *Griselda*, Brown, op. cit., xxi.

[77] Fac. in Brown, op. cit., xxvii.

[78] One aria in *HAM*, ii, No. 262.

[79] Ed. Egon Wellesz, *DTO* xvii (2) (vol. 34/35).

[80] Possibly for insertion in Handel's *Rodelinda*. Ed. Theodor Werner, *EDM: Reichsdenkmale*, vi (1936), rev. ed. W. Bergmann (1955).

[81] Excerpts in Wolff, *Barockoper*, Nos. 143–50, 151–2, 153–61 respectively.

gallicized Italian, Cardinal Mazarin, but – as in the case of Cavalli's *Ercole amante* (see p. 324) – it had to be stuffed with ballet to make it palatable to French taste. The real precursors of French serious opera, *tragédie en musique*, were Lully's *comédies-ballets*. Cambert had essayed *comédie en musique* in his lost *Ariane et Bacchus* and when in 1669 his librettist Pierre Perrin was granted the privilege of performing 'Académies d'Opéra, ou représentations de musique en langue françoise', the Académie d'Opéra was inaugurated on 3 March 1671 with Cambert's *Pomone*. This work, like its successor, *Les Peines et les Plaisirs de l'Amour* (1672),[82] was musically an 'opera', a succession of connected airs, ariosi, and recitatives, but dramatically hardly more than a masque or *pastorale*. But a few weeks earlier than *Pomone*, the royal favourite Lully had provided music in some respects more truly operatic in nature for a work of a different kind. Commanded to write at short notice a play which should employ the *décor* and stage-machinery of the *scène des enfers* of Cavalli's *Ercole amante*, Molière set to work on a *tragédie-ballet*, *Psyché*, but was obliged to call on Corneille to finish it and Philippe Quinault to provide the text for *intermèdes* to be composed by Lully. (Lully himself wrote the words for the 'plaintes en italien' of the first *intermède*.) The musical portions are of such power as to constitute, as more than one modern writer has observed, 'almost a *tragédie en musique*', and in 1678 Lully made it into one, preserving all the original music and composing to a substitute text by Corneille's brother, Thomas, the necessary new music. The original *Psyché* was enormously successful; there were no more *comédies-ballets*, and Lully lost little time in intriguing to get the opera monopoly transferred to himself. The permission for an Académie Royale de musique was granted in March 1672. It began operations with a pastiche *pastorale*, *Les Festes de l'Amour et de Bacchus* in November, and the first *tragédie en musique*, *Cadmus et Hermione*[83] to a text by Quinault, the librettist of all Lully's greatest works, was performed in April 1673.

QUINAULT, LULLY, AND *TRAGÉDIE EN MUSIQUE*

The pattern of French serious opera was thus established partly by the taste of the ballet-loving Louis XIV, who took the closest personal interest in each work and always had to be poetically glorified in an act-long prologue, partly by the qualities of his composer who was extremely intelligent but not a great natural melodist. Though a Florentine by birth, Lully was totally gallicized. (In any case French anti-Italian sentiment would not have tolerated Italian texts.) It was not for nothing that he called his works tragedies *en musique* or *lyrique* for they are modelled on Corneille and Racine, alexandrines and all, and his declamation was avowedly based on the 'déclamation enflée et chantante' of the actress Champmeslé, Racine's mistress. Thus at the time when Sartorio and Pallavicino and Draghi were

[82] Prologue and Act I of each of these published in unsatisfactory vocal score by J. B. Weckerlin in the series *Chefs-d'oeuvre de l'opéra français* (Paris, 1881).
[83] Ed. M. Vermeulen, *Oeuvres complètes de J. B. Lully, I. Les Opéras*, i (Paris, 1930).

turning opera into a succession of arias separated by more and more perfunctory recitative, Lully restored recitative to the dominant place it had occupied in the beginnings of opera. Despite the almost slavish following of Quinault's prosody not only in recitatives and airs but in homophonic choruses, mirroring his rhymes and observing his caesuras, Lully again and again rises to such fine passages as Cadmus's farewell to Hermione (II, 4):

Ex. 125

His *airs* are generally short, simple, and mainly syllabic, sometimes melodically charming like Aglante's 'On a beau fuir l'amour' and Charite's 'La peine d'aimer est charmante' in the same opera (I, 3), and the dance-songs which occur throughout his work. Some of his airs, for instance Arcabonne's song in *Amadis* (II, 1):

Ex. 126

became widely popular but the typical Lully air is half-declamatory like Médée's 'Doux repos' in *Thésée* (1675) (II, 1):

Ex. 127

In Lully one tends to remember great scenes rather than beautiful melodies, and there are plenty to remember: the hero's dreams in *Atys* (1676) (III, 4); Amisodar's transformation scene in *Bellérophon* (1679) (II); Méduse in the gorgons' cave of *Persée* (1682) (III, 1); the scene of Protée's questioning and transformations in *Phaéton* (1683) (I, 7); in the final masterpiece, *Armide* (1686), Renaud falling asleep by the river to the murmur of muted violins (II, 3) and Armide finding him (II, 5), Renaud in her toils (V, 1), his escape from them (V, 4), and her rage (V, 5).

Pl. 46   Renaud escapes from Armide's toils in the Fifth Act of Lully's opera (after the engraving by Jean Bérain)

LULLY'S HEIRS AND THE *OPÉRA-BALLET*

Lully's influence on Kusser and Keiser, Steffani and Purcell has already been mentioned. (Purcell borrowed a tune from *Cadmus* in *The Tempest* and imitated the shivering trio of *Isis* (1677) (IV, 1) in *King Arthur*.) The general diffusion of the 'French overture' (see chap. 21) was probably the result of his example. But French opera never seriously competed with the Italian outside France. At home Lully's chief disciples were Pascal Colasse (1649–1709), who completed his hardly begun *Achille et Polixène* (1687), the gamba player Marin Marais (1656–1728), and Henri Desmarets (1662–1741). The best operas of Colasse and Marais, respectively *Thétis et Pélée* (1689) and *Alcyone* (1705), were long famous for their *symphonies de tempête*; the climax of the one in *Thétis* (II, 9) is certainly remarkable:

Ex. 128

But Colasse's fame is based mainly on a work, *Les Saisons* (1695),[84] which borrows liberally from Lully's music, develops a genre cultivated by Lully in his younger days, the quasi-operatic ballet, and is even based on a subject treated by Lully thirty years earlier (see p. 324). This was the precursor of a number of *opéras-ballets* by André Campra (1660–1744) – *L'Europe galante* (1697), *Les Muses* (1703), *Les Festes vénitiennes* (1710)[85] – and his pupil André Cardinal Destouches (1672–1749) – the *pastorale héroïque Issé* (1697), *Les Eléments* (1721),[86] *Les Stratagèmes de l'Amour* (1726). The *opéra-ballet* was a real hybrid, more ballet than opera, for the four *entrées* of *L'Europe galante* are devoted to France, Spain, Italy, and Turkey with no other connection (and only the faintest traces of local colour in the music), and those of *Festes vénitiennes* are similarly disconnected Venetian scenes which underwent various additions and subtractions in later productions. These scores are hybrids in another sense, for Campra qualifies Lullyan air and recitative with a great deal of more 'vocal', Italianate melody and it is not surprising that they were extremely popular.[87]

At the same time neither Campra nor Destouches neglected the *tragédie lyrique*. In *Hésione* (1700), *Tancrède* (1702), *Idoménée* (1712), Campra

---

[84] Vocal scores of *Thétis, Les Saisons*, and most of the operas mentioned further in this chapter, in *Chefs-d'oeuvre de l'opéra français*.

[85] Not to be confused with his ballet *Le Carnaval de Vénise* (1699). Modern edition of the *Festes* by Max Lütolf (Paris, 1972).

[86] To which Lalande contributed the overture and nine other numbers: see *MGG*, iii, col. 239.

appears as a not unworthy successor of Lully, employing a wider range of keys and bolder harmony, and in two respects his superior: in polyphony and in imaginative orchestration. In *Tancrède*, for instance, where the hero in the enchanted forest (III, 3) hears groans and lamentations coming from the trees, Campra lets his audience hear them too:

Ex. 129

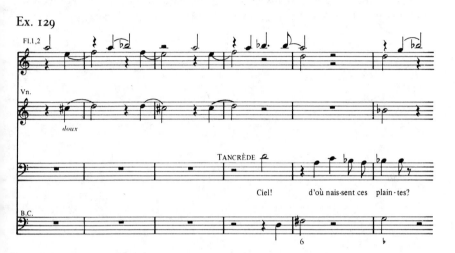

And the overture to *Tancrède* is contrapuntally stronger than any of Lully's (see chap. 20). There are plenty of instrumental *airs* and dances, and the influence of Italianate cantilena is apparent as in the opera-ballets; for instance Clorinde's 'L'impitoyable Amour' (IV, 5).

Such Italianism plays no part in the *tragédies lyriques* of Destouches: *Amadis de Grèce* (1699), *Omphale* (1701), *Callirhoé* (1712), and one or two others. He is essentially Lullyan, particularly in his recitative, but more enterprising even than Campra in his orchestration.[88] His occasionally very unorthodox, probably empirical, but always effective harmony – e.g. in the oracle scene of *Callirhoé* (III, 4) and Leucosie's 'La mer était tranquille' in *Les Eléments* (II, 1) – brought him in his lifetime exaggerated accusations of 'ignorance' and, more recently, exaggerated praise as a 'precursor'.

Lully's *Festes de l'Amour et de Bacchus* and more particularly Campra's *Festes vénitiennes* were the prototypes of *Les Festes de Thalie* (1714) by Jean-Joseph Mouret (1682–1738), who later produced one or two *tragédies*, of *Les Festes de l'été* (1716) of Michel Pinolet de Montéclair (1667–1737) and of *Les Festes Grecques et Romaines* (1723), based on an historical subject instead of

[87] No French composer at this period can have ignored, even if he was uninfluenced by, the literary controversy begun by the Italiophile François Raguenet's *Parallèle des Italiens et des Français en ce qui regarde la musique et les opéras* (1702; English translation, 1709, reprinted in Oliver Strunk, *Source Readings in Music History*, 1952, p. 473) where French opera is at almost every point compared unfavourably with Italian. Le Cerf de la Viéville made a spirited reply, buttressed by references to the work of Lully, in his *Comparaison de la musique italienne et de la musique française* (1704; second part, 1705, incompletely translated in Strunk, ibid., p. 489).
[88] Examples from *Issé* in Becker, op. cit., Nos. 13 and 14.

mythology, by François Colin de Blamont (1690–1760). Colin de Blamont never attempted *tragédie lyrique*; indeed serious opera languished for a time in the hands of minor figures, of whom the inseparable collaborators François Francoeur (1698–1787) and François Rebel (1701–75) were the most noteworthy. They began their career with *Pyrame et Thisbé* (1726) and *Tarsis et Zélie* (1728). But while they held the stage of the Opéra an older and much greater man was waiting in the wings.

19

Secular Vocal Music (c. 1660 – c. 1725)

THE ITALIAN CHAMBER CANTATA

The most popular form of secular vocal music in Italy during the last half of the seventeenth century and for some time afterward continued to be the solo cantata with continuo, with or without other instruments. Beside it flourished the simpler aria, canzone, and canzonetta, the cantata with two or more singers, the chamber duet, and the serenata. About the turn of the century there was even a brief and unsuccessful attempt to revive the unaccompanied madrigal: a few were composed by Lotti, Agostino Steffani, Alessandro Scarlatti, the opera-composer Francesco Gasparini (1668–1727) and Benedetto Marcello (1686–1739). But the solo cantata was the favourite form. Since its musical components, recitative and aria, were also those of opera, it was cultivated particularly by opera composers but also by musicians who wrote no operas, such as Carissimi (see p. 301) and Maurizio Cazzati (c. 1620–1677) who published several sets of arias, canzonette, and cantatas.[1] Giovanni Battista Bassani (c. 1657–1716) left very few operas but published thirteen collections of cantatas under fanciful titles between 1680 and 1703. Benedetto Marcello published only one book of *Canzoni madrigalesche ed arie per camera a 2, 3, 4 voci* (Bologna, 1717), but the proportion of his published to unpublished work was infinitesimal; he left more than two hundred cantatas and duets in manuscript. And this was normal. Pallavicino published solo *Canzonette per camera* (Bologna, 1670) and Legrenzi *Cantate e Canzonette* (Bologna, 1676) and a second book, entitled *Echi di riverenza*, two years later; but both left much more in manuscript. The numerous cantatas of Provenzale and Bernardo Pasquini (1637–1710), the hundreds by Stradella, the perhaps 700 by Alessandro Scarlatti[2] were not published at all in their lifetimes (nor were the hundred-odd duets of Steffani) – and these were the greatest masters of the chamber cantata.

Comparison with the wide publication of madrigals in their heyday suggests that the descendants of those who bought and presumably sang madrigals in the sixteenth century were listeners rather than performers; they probably preferred to sing the canzonette which figure more prominently than cantatas in the published collections. But the comparison does

---

[1] Two examples from his *Cantate morali e spirituali a voce sola*, Op. 20 (Bologna, 1659; reprinted 1679) in Jan Racek, *Stilprobleme der italienischen Monodie* (Prague, 1965), pp. 257 and 260.
[2] See the list in *MGG*, xi, cols. 1488 ff.

define the 'popularity' of the cantata. It was written primarily for performance by professional singers or cultivated amateurs for the delectation of other cultivated amateurs, such persons as those who founded the Roman Accademia dell'Arcadia in 1692, to which Scarlatti and Pasquini were admitted as members in 1706. Manuscript collections of cantatas, as of airs from operas, were made for them and for the Grand Tourists. Some pieces are indeed 'popular' in nature, like the strophic aria 'Lungi, lungi' in Stradella's 'Fermatevi o bei lumi':[3]

Ex. 130

Lun - gi, lun - gi dal mio se - no tuo ve - le - no o nu - do ar - cie - ro.

with its modest coloratura later, or the soprano aria 'Io pur seguirò' in his *serenata a 3 con stromenti* 'Qual prodigio'[4] from which Handel was to borrow liberally in *Israel in Egypt*. Much more typical are (i) the little aria 'Claudio rida' which recurs four times in the cantata *L'incendio di Roma* or (ii) the opening arioso 'In sì lontano lido':[5]

Ex. 131

mi - se - ro,   af - flit - to   e   so - - lo?

This latter, and its continuation, is more finely wrought than most operatic writing of the time; the intimacy of the cantata encouraged such finesse, as is apparent also in the cantatas of Alessandro Scarlatti, the supreme master of the form.

SCARLATTI'S CANTATA MODEL

It was Scarlatti who was mainly responsible for the reduction of the varied aria-forms and straggling overall forms of the cantata to the conventional formula: recitative / da capo aria / recitative / da capo aria. The cantatas of Provenzale had been much more varied, in the tradition of Luigi Rossi and Carissimi. He strings together popular songs ('Squarciato appena avea'), rings the changes of strophic repetition and variation on three not altogether unrelated musical ideas ('La mia speme'), or pours out a long expressive line of continuous melody ('A che mirarmi o stelle'):[6]

Ex. 132

A che,   a che mi - rar - mi o stel - le,   stel - le d'un va - - go

ciel   cru - de stel - le   ma bel - le

Scarlatti's own early cantatas, from 1688 onward, still sprawl freely with a great deal of arioso, strophic arias, and refrain-like movements. Thus

[3] Modena, Bibl. Estense, MSS. Mus. G.209. Quoted in Gino Roncaglia, *La rivoluzione musicale italiana (secolo XVII)* (Milan, 1928), p. 245.
[4] Ed. Chrysander, *Händel-Gesamtausgabe: Supplement Nr. 3* (Leipzig, 1888).
[5] Both quoted in Edward J. Dent, 'Italian Chamber Cantatas', *The Musical Antiquary*, ii (1910–11), pp. 186 and 187.
[6] Quoted in Andrea della Corte and Guido Pannain, *Storia della musica* (Turin, 1944), p. 591. These cantatas are in Naples, Bibl. S. Pietro a Maiella.

381

'Augellin sospendi i vanni' consists of ten movements, of which the first is repeated half-way through, and again at the end; three of the four recitatives run into ariosi;[7] and the two main arias are strophic and built wholly or partly on ground-bass. 'Io morirei contento' consists largely of arioso. In the rather later 'Sarei troppo felice'[8] Scarlatti uses the 'refrain' device with more subtlety to hold together another extended work.

It was in the very numerous cantatas written in Rome during 1703–8 that Scarlatti settled usually for the concise form of two secco (but not perfunctory) recitatives alternating with two da capo arias. His Roman patron, Cardinal Pietro Ottoboni, was perhaps insatiable in his demands for new cantatas and the concise form would have enabled Scarlatti to produce them in quantity without sacrifice of quality; indeed many of them show him at the height of his powers. 'Mitilde, mio tesor'[9] is typical in its boldly modulating recitatives, in the expressive use of a diminished seventh chord (a favourite Scarlattian harmony) at 'aspri tor*men*ti' in the first one, and in the quasi-thematic treatment of the continuo which at the beginning of the first aria anticipates the opening of the voice part and continues in a striking figure which recurs in its own line. The difficulty and importance of Scarlatti's continuo parts are generally attributed to his admiration for an outstanding Roman cellist named Francischiello; that of 'Lascia, deh lascia al fine di tormentarmi più' (1709)[10] was quoted by Johann David Heinichen (1683–1729), in his *Der General-Bass in der Composition* (Dresden, 1728) as particularly difficult for the keyboard-player. Heinichen objected to Scarlatti's *extravagant und irregulair* harmony, though the extravagances of 'Lascia, deh lascia' are mild by comparison with those in the two settings of 'Andate o miei sospiri' *in idea humana* and *in idea inhumana, ma in regolato Cromatico*,[11] the latter written to tease Francesco Gasparini. Nor was Scarlatti's *extravagant und irregulair* harmony, though the extravagances (1717) and 'Là dove a Mergellina' (1725) have passages of winding coloratura more suited to the right hand of a keyboard player than to the voice, while the aria 'Mio cor' in another late work, 'Nel centro oscuro', is marked by jagged leaps.

HANDEL'S ITALIAN CANTATAS AND DUETS

Some of the same characteristics mark the cantatas which Handel wrote in Italy,[12] mostly in Rome during 1707–9 and many certainly for the Marquis Ruspoli and Cardinal Ottoboni who gave weekly concerts in their palaces: continuo parts which really duet with the voice or indulge in tone-painting as in the aria 'Son come navicella' in No. 25, 'Lungi dal mio bel nume';

---

[7] Such ariosi following recitatives came to be known as *cavate*.
[8] Which Dent examines at length in *Alessandro Scarlatti* (London, 1905; revised edition, 1960), pp. 75 ff., quoting the first and last ariosi and first aria complete.
[9] In *HAM*, ii, No. 258.
[10] In Schering, *Geschichte der Musik in Beispielen*, No. 260.
[11] Extended quotations from both in Dent, *Alessandro Scarlatti*, pp. 140 ff.
[12] 72 for voice and continuo in *Werke*, l and li, 28 for various voices and instruments, ibid., lii.

quasi-instrumental vocal writing, e.g. 'Quando non son presente' in No. 9, 'Da sete ardente afflitto'; harmonic daring as in the first recitative of 'E partirai mia vita?', No. 18. It is obvious that he had specific singers in mind, for instance the bass with an enormous compass – probably Giuseppe Boschi – who could manage the terrifying leaps of 'Nel Africane selve', No. 36, the part of Lucifer in the oratorio *La Resurrezione*, and that of Polifemo in *Aci, Galatea e Polifemo* (both 1708),[13] a large-scale cantata or serenata for three voices and an orchestra including oboes and trumpets. The most dramatic of the solo cantatas, and the finest, is *Lucrezia* ('O Numi eterni!') (1709), an eight-movement work remarkable for its range of emotions, its recitative power, its picturesque and expressive coloratura, and its harmonic boldness. Hardly less fine is *Agrippina condotta a morire* (No. 14). At the other end of the scale are such delicious small works as 'Zeffiretto arresta il volo', No. 71, and 'Mi palpita il cor' with flute obbligato, No. 33.

These Italian cantatas, to which he added in later years, served Handel all his life as a quarry for ideas (cf. p. 371). So did the Italian duets[14] composed probably for the most part in 1711–12 for the Electoral Court of Hanover. These duets were evidently written in emulation of those Agostino Steffani had put into final shape for the same Court ten years earlier.[15] Some of Steffani's duets are really lyrical duet-cantatas in several movements, and Handel follows him, sometimes as in 'Tacete, ohimé'[16] actually surpassing the blandness of his melodious style.

MARCELLO'S REACTION AGAINST *BEL CANTO*

The strongest reaction against pure *bel canto* was in the large-scale cantatas[17] and the vernacular psalms of Benedetto Marcello, author of a famous satire on opera, *Il teatro alla moda* (*c.* 1720).[18] Burney, hearing his *Cassandra: un monodramma* fifty years later,[19] accused him of having 'entirely sacrificed the music to the poetry'. Marcello's music always proceeds from the words, as in the final aria of *Demodoco*:[20]

---

[13] *Werke*, xxxix and liii.
[14] Ibid., xxxii.
[15] Sixteen examples, with complete thematic catalogue, ed. Alfred Einstein, *DTB*, Jg. vi(2). One in Schering, op. cit., No. 242. Steffani's only known solo cantata, dating from *c.* 1673, has also been published by Einstein, *ZfMW*, i (1918–19), pp. 457 ff.
[16] *Werke*, xxxii, No. 10.
[17] One of these, *Didone*, with three shorter ones, has been ed. Malipiero, *I classici della musica italiana*, xvii (Milan, 1919).
[18] Translated by Reinhard Pauly, *MQ*, xxxiv (1948), p. 371, and xxxv (1949), p. 85; partial translation by Oliver Strunk, *Source Readings in Music History* (London, 1952), pp. 518 ff. On the *Salmi*, see below, p. 418, n. 103.
[19] 10 August 1770: see his *Present State of Music in France and Italy* (London, 1771, and various modern editions).
[20] Quoted from Andrea d'Angeli, *Benedetto Marcello* (Milan, 1946), p. 94.

Ex. 133

And he is always ready to make picturesque points in the accompaniment, as in the same cantata where he uses strings – exceptionally – to suggest Ulysses' vessel 'ploughing the Ionian waves', or simultaneous tremoli in voice and continuo to illustrate the shaking of the spheres in *Timoteo*, a setting of a free paraphrase of Dryden's *Alexander's Feast*. He indulges in *stravaganze*, sometimes vocal (e.g. in *Medea al sepolcro di Giasone*), sometimes merely whimsical, writing the voice part of 'Senza gran pena non si giunge al fine' in sharps and the continuo in flats or vice versa.[21] Yet comparison of his setting of *Lucrezia* ('O Numi eterni!'), possibly his own poem, with Handel's[22] shows the latter to be not only more 'musical' but, from the opening recitative, more 'extravagant'. Towards the end of his life Marcello composed two larger works for soloists, chorus, and strings, more noteworthy than his oratorios, *Il pianto e il riso delle quattro stagioni dell'anno* (1731) and *Il trionfo della Poesia e della Musica* (1733), which, like Handel's *Il trionfo del Tempo e del Disinganno* (1707), show how the cantata or serenata was becoming expanded. The process is made visible in the difference between Handel's serenata *Aci, Galatea e Polifemo* of 1708 and his quite different English masque, the delightful *Acis and Galatea* of ten years later; he conflated the two as a 'serenata' in 1732.

[21] Second recitative and aria in Carl Parrish, *A Treasury of Early Music* (London, 1959), No. 49.
[22] H. C. Wolff gives a number of parallel quotations in 'Die Lucrezia-Kantaten von Benedetto Marcello und Georg Friedrich Händel', *Händel-Jahrbuch 1957*, p. 74.

THE GERMAN SECULAR *ARIE*

The heyday of the Italian chamber cantata was nearly, though not quite, over by the time of Scarlatti's death; even the much more numerously published canzonette had to compete with printed collections of opera arias. Something similar happened in Germany where the secular chamber cantata never struck very strong roots. The secular German *Arie* of Heinrich Albert and Adam Krieger (see pp. 304–6) was cultivated during the latter part of the century by Johann Theile (1646–1724), the enormously prolific brothers Johann Philipp and Johann Krieger (1649–1725, 1652–1735), and others. The youthful *Weltliche Arien und Canzonetten* (Leipzig, 1667) of Theile are not unfairly represented by the example printed by Schering,[23] held together only by the identity of the last vocal section with the last section of the string ritornello. Nor were the Krieger brothers as gifted as their namesake. Johann's *Neue Musicalische Ergetzlichkeit* (Frankfurt and Leipzig, 1684) consisting of three parts – devotional, secular,[24] and songs from plays – is really successful only when the songs are humorous. His more talented brother published two collections of *Auserlesene Arien* from his operas (Nuremberg, 1690 and 1692)[25] – he directed the Court opera at Weissenfels from 1678 to 1715 – but despite his two years of study in Venice and Rome these are German *Lieder*, not remotely like Italian arias, and although he was familiar with the quasi-operatic type of cantata he practised it not in secular works but in his innumerable church cantatas (see p. 406). Indeed he is credited with having influenced the Weissenfels poets, of whom the most important was Erdmann Neumeister, to provide him with texts that could be introduced beside excerpts from the Bible or from hymns.

ITALIAN INFLUENCE ON THE GERMAN CANTATA

The two collections of *Harmonische Freude musicalischer Freunde* (Nuremberg, 1697 and 1710)[26] by Philipp Heinrich Erlebach (1657–1714) are another matter. Here the full impact of the Italian cantata or opera aria is obvious. Hardly any are simple *Lieder*; the majority are da capo arias with plentiful coloratura and introductions and ritornelli for two violins; one, 'Vertraue doch, mein Herz', No. 3 in the 1710 collection, is a genuine solo cantata with two recitatives and an arioso refrain. One aria in the 1697 set, 'Meine Seufzer, meine Klagen',[27] is a real masterpiece. Keiser followed Erlebach's lead the following year with his *Gemüths-Ergötzung, bestehend in einigen Sing-Gedichten*, seven solo cantatas with violins, remarking in his preface that cantatas had 'quite driven out the former *Teutsche Lieder*'.

---

[23] Op. cit., No. 210.
[24] Example ibid., No. 235.
[25] Two examples ibid., Nos. 236 (*a*) and (*b*).
[26] Ed. Otto Kinkeldey, *DDT*, xlvi–xlvii. Various modern editions of separate numbers, including Schering, op. cit., No. 262, and *HAM*, ii, No. 254.
[27] Kinkeldey, op. cit., p. 43.

Later he published two more sets of cantatas with continuo only, *Divertimenti serenissimi* (1713), six of which have Italian texts, and *Musikalische Land-Lust* (1714). And, as other Hamburg opera composers – Wolfgang Franck and Kusser – had done before him he took care to get collections of airs from his operas into print.

Despite the example of Erlebach and Keiser, the German secular cantata failed to flourish. Mattheson asserted in 1713 in *Das neu-eröffnete Orchestre*, and repeated in *Der vollkommene Capellmeister* a quarter of a century later, that the true nature of the cantata was a vocal solo with continuo only; 'if one added more voices and instruments the work became a serenata' though perhaps this was more allowable in Germany where voices were 'nicht so delicat als in Welschland'. He himself seems to have composed few secular cantatas of any kind, though from 1712 onward he did produce a number of serenatas for weddings in notable Hamburg families. Even more significant is the fact that Scarlatti's critic Heinichen, who had written a considerable number of Italian cantatas in Venice for the singer Angioletta Bianchi, went to Dresden in 1717 as Court *Kapellmeister* and devoted himself to the composition of undistinguished Court serenatas. The more intimate type of solo cantata could be supplied at Dresden for a time by Lotti and later by Giovanni Alberto Ristori (1692–1753).

THE *DRAMME PER MUSICA* OF TELEMANN AND BACH

Two much greater Germans also provided court serenatas, mostly at a rather later period: Georg Philipp Telemann (1681–1767) and Johann Sebastian Bach (1685–1750). However Telemann's *dramma per musica* 'Willkommen, auserwählter Fürst' dates from 1715 and Bach's 'Was mir behagt' (BWV 208),[28] with the lovely aria 'Schafe können sicher weiden', from 1716. It is a serenata in all but name, consisting of 15 numbers (including two choruses), and the orchestra includes flutes, oboes, bassoons, and horns. Telemann, prolific in every genre, went on to pour out solo cantatas with or without obbligato instruments.[29] Bach left only two, unless we accept a couple of dubious and conventional Italian cantatas (BWV 203 and 209). The two authentic works, 'Weichet nur, betrübte Schatten' and 'Ich bin in mir vergnügt' (BWV 202 and 204), both for soprano with obbligato instruments, are more extended alternations of recitative and aria. In a totally different category are *Der zufriedengestellte Aeolus* (1725) and *Vereinigte Zwietracht* (1726) (BWV 205 and 207), consisting respectively of 15 and 11 numbers for four soloists, four-part chorus, and large orchestra including woodwind, trumpets, and drums. Both were *pièces d'occasion* drawn on for later works and both, like Bach's

---

[28] BWV numbers refer to Wolfgang Schmieder, *Thematisch-Systematisches Verzeichnis der Werke J. S. Bachs* (Leipzig, 1950).
[29] See Werner Menke, *Das Vokalwerk George Philipp Telemann's* (Kassel, 1942), pp. 121 ff. A typical example with violin obbligato, with *plattdeutsch* text, is 'Ha, ha! wo will wi hüt noch danzen', ed. Wolf Hobohm (Leipzig, 1971).

other works of the same kind, are styled *dramma per musica*; they belong to a new genre, the enlarged cantata of later times. But before he wrote *Aeolus* Bach had composed at least two annual cycles of church cantatas, more than 200 works (see below, pp. 407–8); it was the Protestant cantata which was the finest consequence of the cantata cult in Germany.

THE FRENCH *AIR*

The cantata was almost unknown in France until the new century, but the tradition of the lyrical *air* of Boësset and Moulinié (see p. 307) was slightly modified through the endeavours of a courtier, Pierre de Nyert, who had returned from Rome obsessed with the idea 'd'ajuster la méthode italienne à la française' by improving the declamation of French song and the diction of French singers, and by teaching them to ornament the second *couplet* of a song. Boësset's last *Livre d'airs* (1643) had already reflected de Nyert's views to some extent. Their best propagandists however were the distinguished singer, lutenist, and composer Michel Lambert (*c.* 1610–1696) and the poetaster, teacher, and composer Bénigne de Bacilly (d. 1690), the latter of whom published in 1668 *Remarques curieuses sur l'art de bien chanter, and particulièrement pour ce qui regarde le chant françois.* Lambert and Bacilly were responsible for an anonymous *Nouveau livre d'airs* (Paris, 1661),[30] in which the words and tunes were by Bacilly, the ornamented versions of the second *couplets* (styled *doubles*) and the continuo probably by Lambert. Bacilly went on to publish several collections of *chansons pour danser et pour boire* and two of *Airs spirituels*. But Lambert was much the better composer and his *Airs à une, II, III et IV parties* (1689) with their little ensembles and their parts for two violins[31] are more ambitious than anything Bacilly attempted. Carissimi's pupil, Marc-Antoine Charpentier, actually composed a cantata *Orphée descendant aux enfers* (*c.* 1683) – not to be confused with his chamber opera *La Descente d'Orphée aux enfers* – for three voices, recorder, flute, bass viol, and harpsichord, but was otherwise content to write *airs sérieux et à boire* like Jean-Baptiste de Bousset (1662–1725)[32] and other younger contemporaries.

THE *CANTATE FRANÇAISE*

In 1703, the year after Raguenet's *Parallèle* (see p. 377, n. 87), two publications marked the advent of two new kinds of song which were to enjoy remarkable popularity in France: a collection of *Brunetes ou petits Airs tendres, avec les doubles et la basse-continue . . . recueillies et mis en ordre par*

---

[30] Two examples in Amalie Arnheim, 'Ein Beitrag zur Geschichte des einstimmigen weltlichen Kunstliedes in Frankreich im 17. Jahrhundert', *SIMG*, x (1908–9), pp. 416–7. Her remarks on the authorship have long been superseded, e.g. by Henry Prunières, 'Bénigne de Bacilly', *Revue de musicologie* (1922–3), p. 156. An example of Lambert's own work, from a posthumous manuscript collection, is given in Noske, *Das ausserdeutsche Sololied (Das Musikwerk)* (Cologne, 1958), No. 13.
[31] Cf. the facsimile of the opening of the dialogue, 'Doutez-vous de mon feu', *MGG*, viii, col. 126.
[32] *Air sérieux* by Bousset in Schering, op. cit., No. 256, *air à boire* in Noske, op. cit., No. 16.

Christophe Ballard,[33] and an anonymous book of *Cantates françoises* put out by Foucault, a dubious business rival of the long established firm of Ballard. The anonymous composer was probably either Jean-Baptiste Morin (1677–1754) or Nicolas Bernier (1664–1734), a pupil of Caldara. In 1706 Ballard published Morin's 'first book' of *Cantates françaises à une et deux voix, mêlées de symphonies*, with a preface explaining that he has for some years had the idea of trying whether 'notre langue ne seroit point susceptible des Compositions de Musique appelées communement en Italie *Cantates*, ou sujets différents de Poësies mêlées d'Airs et de Récitatifs'. He hopes the novelty of such works will please the public, most of whom do not understand Italian words, and he has done his best to preserve 'la douceur de nôtre chant françois, sur des accompagnements plus diversifiez'. And he adds that the cantatas *sans symphonie* can be accompanied by clavecin only, but for the *symphonies* (ritornelli) – and only one piece in the book has them – the bass should be strengthened with a *basse de violle*. Also in 1706 Ballard issued solo cantatas *avec symphonies* in which the cosmopolitan Jean-Baptiste Stuck (*c.* 1680–1755), also known as Battistin, claimed to have joined 'le goût de la musique italienne avec des paroles françaises'.

The popularity of the simple brunette, which was a new name rather than a new genre, was to be expected but the triumph of the 'French cantata' must have astonished Morin and his publisher. His first book was reprinted and he brought out two more in 1707 and 1712; Stuck's reached its fifth edition in 1723, his third book (1711) its third in 1722; Bernier published eight books altogether, of which the fifth (1715), was especially popular. The contrast between the number of editions and the paucity of published Italian cantatas is remarkable; they were, of course, aimed at a totally different public, largely of amateur performers. Naturally the French opera composers hastened to compete and did so with great success. Campra not only brought out a book of cantatas in 1708, in which he too tried to mix 'la délicatesse de la musique françoise' with 'la vivacité de la musique italienne', but also introduced two *cantates* in his *Festes vénitiennes* (see p. 376). One, it is true, is merely a strophic air with flutes but the other – Léandre's 'Suivez-moy' in the fifth *entrée* – consists of a recitative and an air concluding in arioso. His 1708 book was several times reprinted and he published two more in 1724 and 1728.

Montéclair[34] entered the field in 1709, Destouches in 1716, and Jean-Philippe Rameau (1683–1764) composed cantatas (though he did not publish them at the time) as early as 1721, twelve years before he attempted opera. The earliest French woman composer of note, Élisabeth Jacquet de La Guerre (*c.* 1664–1729) published two books in 1708 and 1711. But the finest of all the composers of *cantates* was Louis-Nicolas Clérambault (1676–1749). His first book (1710) contains two dramatic masterpieces,

---

[33] Example in Noske, op. cit., No. 15; a number of others in Paul-Marie Masson, 'Les "Brunettes"', *SIMG*, xii (1910–11), p. 347.
[34] A collection of Montéclair's cantatas has been ed. James Anthony, Barbara Jackson, and Erich Schwandt (Madison, Wis., 1975).

Orphée and *Médée*, both for soprano solo, which show what he might have achieved if he had tried his hand at opera, and the Watteauesque *L'Amour piqué par une abeille*. The form of *Orphée*[35] is typical: the narrative recitative is interrupted by airs *tendre* or *gai*, with a central *air fort lent et fort tendre*, 'Monarque redouté', in which the cry 'Rendés moy ma chère Euridice' is given added poignancy by the violin interjections and entry of a solo flute. *L'Amour piqué*, another soprano piece, is accompanied by continuo only. Typical of the 'Watteauesque' vein common to so many *cantates françoises* is this passage from *L'Isle de Délos* in Clérambault's third book (1716):[36]

Ex. 134

Like the cantata in other countries, the French variety tended to expand – as in Clérambault's *cantate allégorique* for the King's recovery, *Le Soleil vainqueur des nuages* (1721), with its enlarged orchestra – so that it became musically indistinguishable from the older *divertissement*. Or it degenerated into the miniature form known as *cantatille*.

[35] Ed. David Tunley (London, 1972). Tunley's *The Eighteenth Century French Cantata* (London, 1974) is an excellent general survey.
[36] The appoggiaturas – *coulés* in French, hence used punningly here – would take two-thirds of the value of the main note if dotted. The sign + here indicates a mordent.

PUBLIC CONCERTS IN LONDON

In England the accession of a Francophile king in 1660 affected music at Court rather than in the country generally. Playford went on reprinting his collections of the Commonwealth years, sometimes under new titles so that Hilton's *Catch that Catch can* (see p. 310), for instance, reappeared in 1667 with additions – including some Italian songs – and in 1673 was re-titled *The Musical Companion*. Playford's preface to the *Companion* is addressed to his friends of 'the late Musick-Society and meeting, in the Old-Jury, London'. This club may have given John Banister, formerly leader of the King's band, the idea for the combined alehouse and concert-room he opened in Whitefriars in 1672, which led in turn to the professional public concerts at York Buildings, Villiers Street, and the weekly concerts promoted by Thomas Britton over his shop in Aylesbury Street, Clerkenwell, from 1678 onward. We may be confident that most of the new songs Playford published were listened to and sung by those who attended these earliest of all public concerts. There was enough interest in Italian music to justify his bringing out a *Scelta di canzonette italiane de più autori* (Luigi Rossi, Carissimi, Stradella, and others) in 1679, but naturally the repertoire was mostly English and homely – like the four three-part songs contributed to *The Musical Companion* by Thomas Cooke (*c.* 1615–1672), Master of the Children of the Chapel Royal.

THE ENGLISH ODE

Cooke was not only a first-rate singer 'after the Italian manner' and the real founder of the Restoration Chapel Royal; with a much better composer, Matthew Locke, he was one of the initiators of the principal English form of large-scale cantata – though not so called – during the rest of the century: the ode for New Year or the king's birthday and its short-lived sub-species the 'welcome song' of the 1680s. His little New Year ode, 'Good morrow to this year' (1666)[37] and Locke's *New Year's Song* ('All things their certayne Periods have')[38] were followed by the three Court odes (1672–3) of Cooke's pupil and son-in-law Pelham Humfrey (1647–74) and the much more numerous ones of another pupil, John Blow (1649–1708). But the supreme master of the English ode was Purcell, who had in turn been the pupil of Blow. Purcell's early *Welcome Song for His Royal Highness* (the Duke of York) *at His return from Scotland in the year 1682*[39] is typical: a 'French' overture followed by a series of short, well contrasted solos, duets, and choruses. The following year came a delightful work 'Welcome to all the pleasures',[40] an ode for the first of the annual celebrations of St. Cecilia's

[37] Music Library of the Barber Institute, Birmingham, MS 5001. See Rosamond McGuinness, 'The Origins and Disappearance of the English Court Ode', *PRMA*, lxxxvii (1960–1), p. 69.
[38] Oxford, Christ Church, MS. 14.
[39] Purcell Society's edition, xv, p. 52.
[40] Ibid., x, p. 1.

Day at Stationers' Hall. In 1684 the St. Cecilia ode was provided by Blow,[41] in 1685 by another of Cooke's former Children, William Turner (1651–1740). Purcell was to write three other Cecilia odes, the finest of all, 'Hail, bright Cecilia' (1692),[42] and in the years after his death the odes were supplied by Blow (1695), the Italian violinist Nicola Matteis (1696), and Jeremiah Clarke (*c.* 1673–1707) with his setting of Dryden's *Alexander's Feast* (1697) – a falling line. 'Hail, bright Cecilia' is notable for its brilliant festive writing for chorus and orchestra, surpassed only in some of the Birthday Odes for Mary II, particularly those with trumpets: 'Arise my Muse' (1690), 'Celebrate this festival' (1693), which borrows its overture from 'Hail, bright Cecilia', and above all 'Come ye sons of art away', (1694).[43] The Queen drew out the best in Purcell, for during the months between her death and his he composed two deeply expressive Latin elegies on her: 'O dive Custos Auriacae domus' and 'Incassum, Lesbia, rogas',[44] duet and solo cantatas with continuo.

PURCELL'S CHAMBER CANTATAS

In his chamber cantatas – a term he never uses – he seldom introduces violins or 'flutes' (i.e. recorders), and then only in works for two or more voices. Recitative is often the most important element, recitative sometimes breaking into verbally inspired coloratura as in the elegy on the Queen, where the central section 'En nymphas! en pastores!', arioso rather than air, powerfully unified by all-pervading falling fifths, is preceded and followed by such recitatives. The early *Elegy on the Death of Matthew Locke*[45] is a long, less ornate recitative followed by a short two-part chorus. The *Pastoral Elegy* on the publisher Playford, 'Gentle Shepherds' (1687),[46] is much more elaborately organized in six sections on the model of Luigi Rossi or Carissimi, whose work he might have known from Playford's *Scelta*: the first three in A minor, an aria in C major over a descending-scale ostinato, another recitative in A minor, and a final two-part chorus in A major. *Bess of Bedlam*[47] is an appropriately crazy patchwork. Of the more simply organized cantatas, recitative and aria only, 'The fatal hour' is unquestionably the greatest, and not far short of it 'Love arms himself',[48] its bravura recitative introduced by two bars in the bass curiously like those which introduce 'Va superbetto' in Scarlatti's cantata 'Chi mi insegna' (which Purcell could not possibly have known). Another splendid bravura piece, also in C major, opens *Anacreon's Defeat*[49] which is otherwise in C

[41] 'Begin the Song', ed. H. Watkins Shaw (London, 1950).
[42] Purcell Society, viii.
[43] Ibid., xi, p. 36, and xxiv, pp. 36 and 87.
[44] Ibid., xxii, p. 112, and xxv, p. 97.
[45] Ibid., xxv, p. 198.
[46] Ibid., p. 401.
[47] Ibid., p. 45.
[48] Ibid., pp. 36 and 108.
[49] Ibid., p. 174. See Pl. 47.

Pl. 47   The opening of Purcell's solo cantata 'Bess of Bedlam', published in the first volume
of *Orpheus Britannicus* (second edition, 1706), with 'through-bass . . . figur'd for the
Organ, Harpsichord, or *Theorbo-Lute*'.

minor: slow arioso, brisk aria, and brief arioso to conclude. In 'Love arms
himself' and *Anacreon*, as in some of the sacred cantatas, e.g. 'Lord, what is
man?',[50] Purcell adopts the more shapely patterns of Italian coloratura but

[50] Ibid., xxx, p. 62.

his most typical coloratura, like his half-declamatory, half-melodic vocal lines generally, is in the free, expressive tradition of the earlier Stuart composers.

ENGLISH THEATRE SONGS AND CANTATAS

As for Purcell's solo songs, many of them written for plays, they range from the profound arioso setting of George Herbert's 'With sick and famish'd eyes'[51] to such delightful tuneful trifles as 'Ah! how pleasant 'tis to love'.[52] Nor did he despise the popular three-part catch, of which he wrote more than fifty – including such bawdy specimens as 'I gave her cakes'.[53] Playford had published many of the songs and duets in his various collections of *Ayres and Dialogues* from 1675 onward and his son compiled two posthumous volumes devoted solely to Purcell under the title *Orpheus Britannicus* (1698 and 1702).[54] Having paid tribute to his dead friend in an *Ode on the Death of Mr. Henry Purcell*, a duet cantata on Dryden's 'Mark how the lark and linnet sing' (illustrated by two flutes), Blow seemingly essayed to rival him by publishing a big collection of his own songs as *Amphion Anglicus* in 1700.[55] But despite the melodic charm of such songs as 'Tell me no more you love' and *The Self-banish'd*, Blow was not in the same class as Purcell. In his bass songs – for instance, 'Rise, mighty monarch' and 'Arms, arms, arms'[56] – he was obviously writing for the Rev. John Gostling, the English Giuseppe Boschi, whose powers Purcell also tested or exploited again and again; Blow gave him low Es on the word 'down' in both these songs and Purcell took him even lower to D and C, with enormous leaps. Perhaps the best of Blow's twenty or so big odes is 'Awake, awake my lyre', an 'act song' for Oxford University.[57]

   English song of the simpler kind, often introduced in plays, continued to flourish in the hands of such composers as Purcell's brother Daniel (*c.* 1663–1717), John Eccles (1668–1735), Richard Leveridge (*c.* 1670–1758), and Henry Carey (*c.* 1687–1743), all men connected with the theatre. Blow's pupil Jeremiah Clarke, though primarily a church musician, also composed for the theatre and wrote many songs, some of which have survived as 'traditional'. Daniel Purcell, Eccles, and Clarke contributed St. Cecilia Odes. Even the German immigrants around the turn of the century – Wolfgang Franck and Kusser, Pepusch and Galliard – composed a considerable quantity of English songs. Franck, for instance, published a collection of twenty-five, *Remedium Melancholiae*, in 1690,[58] and Galliard was one

---

[51] Ibid., xxx, p. 94.
[52] Ibid., xxv, p. 4.
[53] Ibid., xxii, p. 6: with bowdlerized words.
[54] Facsimile edition, Ridgewood (New Jersey), 1965.
[55] Facsimile edition of six songs from it, ed. G. E. P. Arkwright, *Old English Edition*, xxiii; others ed. Anthony Lewis (Paris, 1938).
[56] Noske, op. cit., No. 12.
[57] Ed. H. Watkins Shaw (London, 1949).
[58] A cantata (recitative and air), 'Still must I grieve', by Franck, in *The Gentleman's Journal* for 1693, was reprinted by W. Barclay Squire in *The Musical Antiquary* (July, 1912), p. 187.

of the first to bring out *English Cantatas after the Italian manner* (n.d.), specifically so called. Pepusch also published two books of *English Cantatas* (*c.* 1710–12) and Daniel Purcell *Six Cantatas for a Voice, with a Thorough Bass, two of which are accompanied with a Violin* (1713), so belatedly did the actual term reach England.

THE RUSSIAN *KANT*

In the European fringe only one type of secular song arrests one's attention at this period, and that for its extreme primitiveness rather than any other quality: the three-part homorhythmic Russian *kant*. Its upper parts nearly always in thirds, it served for more than half a century for every kind of vocal music: vernacular psalms, songs in plays, festive and love songs, and panegyrics on Peter I for his victories over the Swedes. Thus the battle of Poltava (1709), a turning-point in European history, was celebrated in crude tonic-and-dominant harmony:[59]

Ex. 135

Mï zhe dnes' vo · pi · em, ra · dost · no si · tse rtsem:

Vi · vat Petr, vi · vat tsar', vi · vat tsar' Ros · siy · skiy!

---

[59] From S. L. Ginzburg, *Istoriya russkoy muzïki v notnïkh obraztsakh*, i (revised and extended edition, Moscow, 1968), No. 2; this is the second section of the *kant*, preceded by one in A minor mocking the flight of the Swedes. Ginzburg gives ten *kantï*, some later and less primitive; other collections of *kantï* in Nikolay Findeisen, *Ocherki po istorii muzïki v Rossii*, i (Moscow, 1928), musical supplement, and Tamara Livanova, *Sbornik kantov XVIII veka* (Moscow, 1952).

20

Religious Music (c. 1660–1725)

OPERATIC INFLUENCE ON ORATORIO

The influence of operatic forms and styles was not only reflected in secular music; it began to penetrate religious music, the more easily as the religious wars were followed by a complex of reactions: increasing secularization of the climate of thought, tolerance, and downright laxity. As early as Carissimi oratorio had taken on the attributes of non-scenic drama, and before long operatic elements were to infiltrate Passion music and even the Lutheran church cantata and the liturgical music of the Roman church. So far as oratorio was concerned, an important step approximating to opera was the abolition of the *testo*, the narrator. This was mainly due to the most prolific of Roman oratorio-librettists, Archangelo Spagna (*c*. 1632–after 1720), who pointed the way in his *Debora* (1656) which was composed by his friend 'il Sig. Gio. Francesco Rubini' and whose reforms are comparable with those of Zeno in the field of opera.[1] In 1663 he broke away from biblical subjects with his *Pellegrino nella Patria*, on the life of St. Alexis, with which he later claimed he had established oratorio as 'un perfetto Melodramma spirituale'. Choruses were reduced to a minimum, there was plenty of scope for arias, and oratorio gradually took over the dramatic as well as the musical attributes of opera.

ITALIAN *ORATORIO VOLGARE*

All these characteristics are very marked in the oratorios of Stradella, although he never set any of Spagna's libretti. After a Latin oratorio, the title of which is unknown (Rome, 1667), Stradella devoted himself entirely to *oratorio volgare* and his masterpiece, *San Giovanni Battista*, was produced in Rome in 1675. It includes fourteen arias, ranging from Erode's tremendous 'Tuonerà tra mille turbini'[2] to his daughter's pert 'Su, coronatemi'. Both father and daughter are characterized with a dramatic power unsurpassed in Stradella's operas: for instance the scene in which she exasperates her father into giving way and the five notes, spanning nearly

---

[1] In 1706 Spagna published two volumes of his *Oratorii overo Melodrammi sacri*, prefaced by a *discorso dogmatico* which has been reprinted by Arnold Schering, 'Neue Beiträge zur Geschichte des italienischen Oratoriums im 17. Jahrhundert', *SIMG*, viii (1906–7), p. 43, and Domenico Alaleona, *Storia dell' oratorio musicale in Italia* (Milan, 1945), p. 313. Schering also lists the oratorios in the two volumes and those in Spagna's *Fasti sacri* (1720).
[2] In Günther Massenkeil, *The Oratorio (Anthology of Music)* (Cologne, 1970), No. 11.

two octaves, in which he does so ('Battista pera!'), or the final duet contrasting the satisfaction of the one with the heavy heart of the other:

Ex. 136

a joy and depression that neither understands, so that both are left asking themselves, 'Tell me, why?' The chorus is hardly introduced at all but the orchestra is notable for the concertino/concerto grosso division[3] Stradella had already employed in his *Schiavo liberato* (see p. 361). Stradella's next oratorio, *Susanna*, was written in 1681 for Modena where oratorio had made its debut with the *Sansone* of Benedetto Ferrari (1597–1681), a more conventional and obviously considerably earlier work. Ferrari preserves the *testo* and conventional chorus, and beside Dalida (*sic*) and Sansone he introduces abstractions: Ragione (reason) and Senso (sensuality); all the same he makes the most of the love-scenes,[4] which are purely operatic and not at all what a devout congregation would expect to hear. Nor would they have expected to hear the comic duet of the Elders in Stradella's *Susanna*:[5]

[3] See the opening of the daughter's 'Queste lagrime e sospiri', quoted by Carolyn Gianturco, 'The Oratorios of Alessandro Stradella', *PRMA*, ci (1974–5), p. 49.
[4] Schering prints the recitative exchange of the first one, Dalida's seduction and Sansone's hesitant yielding, in the musical appendix of his *Geschichte des Oratoriums* (Leipzig, 1911), p. XXVII.
[5] I am indebted to Carolyn Gianturco for a copy of this duet.

Ex. 137

which might have come from *Il Trespolo tutore*. Susanna's 'distress' aria, on a typical Stradella ostinato bass,[6] is touching but one cannot help noticing Stradella's predilection for young damsels beset by importunate men; the heroine of *Ester, liberatrice del popolo ebreo* has to contend with three. Against this we must set things like Eudosia's great B minor aria in his *Santa Pelagia* (Modena, 1688). But the erotic element, frank or veiled, continued to enliven oratorio in other hands than Stradella's; it was as prevalent in Latin as in Italian works.

Scarlatti, who had produced in Rome some lost Latin oratorios (1679–82), a liturgical *Passio secundum Joannem*,[7] and two Italian oratorios, *Agar et Ismaele esiliati*[8] and *Il trionfo della gratia ovvero La conversione di Maddalena*[9] in 1683 and 1685, also appeared in Modena with one work, as did another of the Roman oratorio-composers, Bernardo Pasquini (1637–1710), better known for his keyboard music (see p. 438). One of the ducal musicians, G. B. Vitali, marked a contemporary event with *L'Ambitione debellata* (1686), the 'conquered ambition' being that of the unfortunate Duke of Monmouth whose fate is moralized over by Faith, Reason, Ambition, and Betrayal. (James II was his master's brother-in-law.) In his *Giona* (1689) God is introduced as a bass soloist in the character of a pitiless operatic despot and the angelic choir observes and narrates. But oratorio never flourished at Modena as it did at Bologna, which was in fact for a number of years the chief centre outside Rome.

The history of non-liturgical Bolognese oratorio begins in 1661 with two

[6] Schering, *Geschichte der Musik in Beispielen*, No. 230.
[7] Ed. Edwin Hanley (New Haven, Conn., 1955). It is dramatically conceived in recitative and arioso, with orchestral tone-painting and a striking scale-descent through a tenth on Christ's last words.
[8] *Tutti gli oratorii di Alessandro Scarlatti*, ed. Lino Bianchi, ii (Rome, 1965). There is a trio from it in Massenkeil, op. cit., No. 12.
[9] Excerpts in *NOHM*, v, pp. 335–6. The first scene is described at length by David Poultney, 'Alessandro Scarlatti and the Transformation of Oratorio', *MQ*, lix (1973), pp. 591–4.

(lost) works by Giulio Cesare Arresti (1617–92). But in this field as in every other, Arresti was completely overshadowed by his enemy Cazzati, although Cazzati's production, begun in 1664 with *Il diluvio* and *Caino condannato*,[10] lasted only about five years. His successor at San Petronio, Giovanni Paolo Colonna (1637–95), a native Bolognese and pupil of Carissimi, also followed him as an oratorio composer with *L'alloro trionfato* in 1672 and a dozen or so later works, and Colonna handed on the torch to *his* pupil G. B. Bononcini who began oratorio composition in the late 1680s.[11] Indeed a number of opera composers contributed Bolognese oratorios in that decade, not only Vitali but Giovanni Battista Bassani (*c.* 1657–1716), Domenico Gabrielli, and Giacomo Antonio Perti, who was at San Petronio from 1696 until his death sixty years later. Perti appears not only to have initiated the composition of Passion-oratorios at Bologna with his *Passione di Cristo* (1694) but to have achieved one of the few performances of oratorio in Venice during the seventeenth century when his *Abramo vincitor de' propri affetti* was given in 1683 at the same time as his opera *Marzio Coriolano*.[12]

At Florence, as at Bologna, oratorio composition was almost entirely in the hands of the opera-composers – notably Antonio Veracini in the latter part of the seventeenth century and his son, Francesco Maria (1690–1768) in the first quarter of the eighteenth. But the Venetian opera-composers faced no demand for oratorio in their own city. Legrenzi's were given at Ferrara, Bologna, even Vienna,[13] but not Venice. The Venetian ice was broken only when Vivaldi, as *maestro de' concerti* at the foundling hospital of the Pietà, gave his Latin *Moyses* (1714) and *Juditha triumphans* (1716)[14] there.

ORATORIO IN VIENNA

Vienna was another matter. Viennese oratorio was initiated in 1660 with a *Sagrifizio d'Abramo* by the Emperor, Leopold I (1640–1705), himself.[15] Leopold composed another half-dozen Italian oratorios as well as two German ones and *sepolcri*, a genre of semi-scenic sepulchre-dramas for Good Friday which were particularly popular in Austria during the latter part of the century. Leopold's *Kapellmeister* Draghi (see p. 360) composed more than forty oratorios and *sepolcri*, and opera-librettists such as Minato, and later Zeno, provided the texts. But Viennese oratorio was less operatic than the native Italian, from which it differed essentially in being Court, not popular, art. In the hands of Fux Viennese oratorio and opera certainly drew nearer to each other, but that was because his operatic masterpiece *Costanza*

---

[10] Unless his (lost) *Espressione in versi d'alcuni fatti di S. Giuseppe* (1659) was a true oratorio.
[11] A deeply impressive prayer from his *Giosuè* (1688) is printed in Schering, *Geschichte des Oratoriums*, appendix, p. XXXI.
[12] A *siciliana* aria from his much later *San Petronio* (1720) is given in Massenkeil, op. cit., No. 16.
[13] A short excerpt from his *Morte del cor penitente* (Vienna, 1705) is quoted in Robert Haas, *Musik des Barocks* (Potsdam, 1932), p. 156.
[14] Autograph facsimile (Siena, 1948); full score, ed. Alberto Zedda (Milan, 1971).
[15] Excerpts ed. Guido Adler in *Musikalische Werke der Kaiser*, ii (Vienna, 1893). The aria from Leopold's *Erlösung des menschlichen Geschlechts* (1679), printed by Schering, *Geschichte der Musik in Beispielen*, No. 225, comes from the same source.

e Fortezza (see p. 372) was, as Quantz remarked, 'mehr kirchenmässig als theatralisch eingerichtet'.[16] However, a more normal approximation of oratorio to opera was general in Vienna, as elsewhere, in the early eighteenth century with Marc' Antonio Ziani (*c.* 1653–1715) and Fux's principal rivals Francesco Conti (1682–1732) and Antonio Caldara (*c.* 1670–1736)[17]; nothing could be more superbly operatic than Conti's *David* (1724).[18]

THE ROMAN ORATORIOS OF SCARLATTI

Yet when all is said and done, the outstanding master of oratorio – as of opera and cantata – in the early eighteenth century was Scarlatti, now at the height of his powers. His early works have already been referred to; the earliest mature one, *La Giuditta vittoriosa*,[19] was given in both Naples and Vienna in 1695. But most of them were composed during his mainly Roman period of 1703–8, some for the oratories but others for the house concerts of such aristocrats as the Marchese Ruspoli and therefore tending – as in the operas and cantatas (cf. pp. 361 and 381) – to make the most of the da capo aria; such were *L'Assunzione della Beata Vergine* (1703), *San Filippo Neri* (1705), *Il Sedecia, re di Gierusalemme* (1706), and the *Oratorio per la Santissima Annunziata* (1708), to name only four out of a score. The lost *Oratorio per la Passione di Nostro Signor Gesù Cristo*, performed in 1708 four days before Handel's *Resurrezione*, was – on the evidence of both title and libretto – an ordinary oratorio on the Passion subject, not a true Passion setting like the early one, *secundum Joannem*. Scarlatti's crowning masterpiece in this form is the nameless *Oratorio a quattro voci* (1717), generally known as *La Vergine addolorata*.[20] It consists almost entirely of recitatives and arias, nearly all for the Virgin and St. John; Nicodemo has a small part, Onia, a Jewish priest, a microscopic one. There are one or two duets and a trio; there is no chorus. But the level of musical invention and the power of profound emotional expression, the 'extravagant harmony', frequently challenge comparison with Bach. This is particularly true of the Virgin's first and last arias, 'Il mio figlio, ov' è?' and 'Figlio, a morte tu ten vai',[21] in the latter of which the 'motto' opening of the voice part is peculiarly poignant:

---

[16] J. J. Quantz, 'Lebenslauf', in Friedrich Wilhelm Marpurg, *Historisch-kritische Beyträge zur Aufnahme der Musik*, i (Berlin, 1755), p. 216. Fux's most notable oratorio, *La fede sacrilega nella morte del Precursor S. Giovanni Battista* (1714), has been ed. H. Zelzer, *J. J. Fux: Gesammelte Werke*, iv (1) (Graz and Kassel, 1959).

[17] On Caldara's oratorios, see Ursula Kirkendale, *Antonio Caldara: sein Leben und seine venezianisch-römischen Oratorien* (Vienna, 1966).

[18] See, for instance, the scene of Saul's madness in Schering, *Geschichte des Oratoriums*, appendix, p. XXXVI.

[19] Ed. Bianchi, *Tutti gli oratorii di Alessandro Scarlatti*, i (Rome, 1964). A later and quite different *Giuditta* is published in iii (1966).

[20] A number of extensive excerpts in Della Corte and Pannain, *Storia della musica*, ii (Turin, 1944), pp. 909–16 and (overture) 934–9.

[21] The middle section of this da capo aria is given in full by David Poultney, op. cit., p. 600.

Ex. 138

THE GERMAN ORATORIO PASSION

La Vergine addolorata is, of course, a Passion oratorio; Bach's *Johannespassion* of five or six years later is something totally different, an oratorio Passion, a German genre which had come into existence quite independently. Its origin was the liturgical Lutheran Passion music, the first form of which had culminated in Schütz's masterpieces (see p. 354). It retained the *testo* which oratorio had abandoned, in the form of the Evangelist's narrative; it employed an increasingly operatic style of recitative but while it was also invaded by the aria the interpolated arias presented only the emotions of a bystander, not of an actor in the drama. Even in Schütz's lifetime North German organists, Thomas Strutius (*c.* 1621–1678) at Danzig and Christian Flor (1626–97) at Lüneburg, a friend of the Hamburg poet Rist (see p. 305), wrote Matthew Passions with interpolated arias and string accompaniments, *symphoniae*, etc. Thus in Flor's Passion the recitative 'Aber Jesus schrie laut, und verschied' (xxvii, 50) is followed by a five-part setting of 'Ecce quomodo', a *symphonia* (with flutes), the second section of the chorus, 'In pace factus est', another *symphonia*, and the first verse of a 12-strophe 'aria' to words by Johann Rist:[22]

Ex. 139

before the Evangelist takes up his tale, 'Und siehe da . . .' (xxvii, 51). Other 'arias' are based on the words and tunes (with interpolations) of well-known hymns: 'O Lamm Gottes unschuldig' and 'Christe, du Lamm Gottes'. At Königsberg it had for some time been customary for the congregation to sing hymns at certain points in Johann Walter's Matthew Passion of 1530, and in 1672 in the same city Johann Sebastiani (1622–83) published his *Leyden und Sterben . . . Jesu Christi nach dem heiligen Matthaeo*[23] with hymn-tunes for a soloist accompanied by viols and continuo. However, a booklet was issued in 1686, with the Passion text, so that the congregation could 'mit lesen und singen' and in the very year of Sebastiani's death a Lüneberg cantor, Friedrich Funcke (1642–99), published a Luke Passion (lost) which is said to have included hymns for congregational participation.

---

[22] From Peter Epstein, 'Ein unbekanntes Passionsoratorium von Christian Flor (1667)', *Bach-Jahrbuch 1930*, p. 78. Epstein gives sixteen pages of musical excerpts, pp. 65–80.
[23] Ed. Friedrich Zelle, *DDT*, xvii (Leipzig, 1904).

PASSION-ORATORIO AT HAMBURG

Hamburg had been the first city to tolerate instrumentally accompanied Passion music (see p. 354). It had opened its opera-house with a work on a Biblical subject (see p. 366); and it was the first place in Germany to accept Passion-oratorio with rhymed texts by the opera librettists, Christian Postel and C. F. Hunold – though without congregational hymns. In 1704 Hunold provided Keiser with libretti for both his opera *Nebucadnezar* and an oratorio, *Der blutige und sterbende Jesus*, which was too gruesome and too sentimental even for the liberal-minded Hamburgers, and in the same year Postel compiled a John Passion partly from the Gospel, partly of his own verses, which was composed by the young Handel.[24] In this early work Handel introduced some extremely dramatic writing for the solo bass who is sometimes the commentator, sometimes Jesus, as in the arioso/aria, 'Es ist vollbracht!/O grosses Werk'; Bach's knowledge of this masterly piece is demonstrated in both text and music of 'Es ist vollbracht!' in his own *John Passion* (1723).[25] A more famous Hamburg Passion libretto – definitely an oratorio – was also drawn on by Bach in the same work: *Der für die Sünden der Welt ermarterte und sterbende Jesus* by Barthold Heinrich Brockes. This provided partly rhymed paraphrase of scriptural text, with soliloquizing arias for the Daughter of Zion and four Believers, and five hymns for the congregation (representing the Christian Church). Brockes' libretto was first composed in 1712, by Keiser who set it sometimes to beautiful but inappropriate Italianate melody:[26]

Ex. 140

TOCHTER ZION

Brich, mein Herz, zer-fliess in Trä-nen, Je-sus

Vn.1,2

Va.

B.C.

---

[24] *Werke*, ix. The attribution to Handel has been disputed (see *NOHM*, v, p. 643, n. 1).
[25] See Friedrich Smend, *Bach in Köthen* (Berlin, 1952), pp. 127ff.
[26] For examples of Keiser's recitative see *NOHM*, v, pp. 659–60, and *MGG*, vii, col. 789.

sometimes (e.g. the Daughter's aria 'Der Gott, dem alle Himmelskreise') to tunes as wretched as the verse. In 1716 it was composed by both Handel[27] and Telemann,[28] in 1718 by Mattheson, and down to 1750 by a number of lesser men. And Bach adapted eight numbers from it for his *John Passion*.[29]

BACH'S PASSIONS

Thus, while Bach reverted in principle to the older type of oratorio-Passion, using the Biblical text for the Evangelist's narrative, the persons of the drama, and the crowd, and familiar hymn words and tunes for congregational participation, he turned to the Hamburg librettists for the lyrical interpolations: the arias and reflective choruses. In the *Passio Domini nostri J.C. secundum Evangelistam Matthaeum*, as he called it (see p. 535), he greatly increased the number of non-Biblical interpolations, twenty-seven instead of twelve, though the texts were all provided by a single poet – and a much better one than Brockes or Postel: Christian Friedrich Henrici ('Picander'). But the ingredients of Bach's *John Passion* were the same as those of Keiser's *Mark* (*c.* 1717)[30] and Telemann's *Luke* (1728);[31] the immense difference lies in the quality of the ingredients. The fact that Bach's two great works – we may disregard his almost completely lost *Mark* and the more than dubious *Luke* – are among the supreme masterpieces of music, while Keiser's and Telemann's numerous Passion compositions of various kinds (discussed in Chapter 25)[32] are not, should not blind us to their close historical relationship.

SACRED DIALOGUES AND *KIRCHENSTÜCKE*

The ancestry of German oratorio before the Passion oratorios must be

[27] *Werke*, xv; *Hallische Händel-Ausgabe*, I/vii.
[28] Ed. Helmut Winschermann and Friedrich Bruck (Hamburg, 1964); the work exists in several revised and extended forms.
[29] For instance, the aria 'Zerfliesse, mein Herze' on a text adapted from that of Ex. 140.
[30] Ed. Hans Grischkat (Stuttgart, n.d.).
[31] Ed. Hans Hörner and Martin Ruhnke, *G.P. Telemanns Musikalische Werke*, xv (Kassel, 1964).
[32] See Hörner, *G.Ph. Telemanns Passionsmusiken* (Leipzig, 1933) and Werner Menke, *Das Vokalwerk Georg Philipp Telemann's* (Kassel, 1942), pp. 78ff. for corrections and additions.

traced not from Catholic oratorio but from such works as Schütz's *Auferstehungs-Historie*, the sacred dialogues of Hammerschmidt and Kindermann (see p. 351), and the *Actus musicus de divite et Lazaro* (1649)[33] of the Stettin cantor Andreas Fromm (1621–83). The text of this last work is drawn from Luke, xvi, 19–25. The first three verses are declaimed by a *prologus*; Lazarus sings two hymns ('Herzlich tut mich verlangen' and 'Mit Fried und Freud') with gamba accompaniment, and a soprano Angel and chorus sing another ('Wie schön leuchtet'); while instrumental sinfonie depict the boozing of Dives and his companions, and see him off to Hell. The *dialogi* and similar works were cultivated in or out of church in the principal Hansa towns, especially at Hamburg by Weckmann with his *Collegium Musicum* from 1660 onward, and at Lübeck at the *Abendmusiken* which came under the direction of Dietrich Buxtehude (1637?–1707) in 1668. Typical of Weckmann's few surviving dialogues is that between Tobias, the Angel, and Raguel, 'Wo wollen wir einkehren',[34] an affair of melodious declamation innocent of any suggestion of the theatrical. Nor is there anything very dramatic in the numerous sacred cantatas[35] – he wrote only two dialogues[36] – of the far more gifted and prolific Buxtehude. He did compose oratorios, though only one survives: *Das allerschröcklichste und allerfreulichste, nämlich Ende der Zeit und Anfang der Ewigkeit, Gesprächsweise in 5 Vorstellungen auf der Operen Art mit vielen Arien und Ritornellen.*[37] This could well be regarded as a 'dialogue' for 'divine voice' (bass), three sopranos who sometimes impersonate sins, sometimes good and evil souls, and chorus, expanded to five acts. But despite being 'after the manner of opera' and although there is a lot of recitative – the 'Göttliche Stimme' has little else – the music is never more dramatic than this:

Ex. 141

[33] Ed. Hans Engel, *EDM: Denkmäler der Musik in Pommern*, v (Kassel, 1936).
[34] Published by Max Seiffert as the work of Johann Rosenmüller, *Organum*, I, No. 21.
[35] Cantatas were not yet so called; such compositions were until many years later known variously as *motetti*, *concerti*, *actus*, and so on, but most often as *Kirchenstücke*.
[36] *Gesamtausgabe*, ed. Wilibald Gurlitt *et al.* (Klecken, later Hamburg, 1925–), iii, p. 93, and *DDT*, xiv, p. 85.

In fact Buxtehude's recitative consists largely of this kind of repeated-note declamation also in his 'cantatas', e.g. 'Der Herr lässet sein Heil verkündigen' in the solo cantata 'Singet dem Herrn'.[38]

THE LUTHERAN CHURCH CANTATA

The 'cantata' – the term, though anachronistic, is convenient – superseded the motet and sacred concerto as by far the most important form of Lutheran church music from *c.* 1660 onward. Its normal place in the service was immediately before the congregational singing of 'Wir glauben all an einen Gott' which in turn was followed by the sermon; in the case of long cantatas in two parts, the second part would follow the sermon or be sung at some later point. The texts were compiled from Biblical passages (often psalms), hymns, devotional verse, alone or variously mingled, and the music is equally heterogeneous: short instrumental *sonate* or *sinfonie* and *ritornelli*, arias, choruses, recitatives. Hymn texts naturally called up hymn tunes, as they had in earlier Lutheran music, and we have already seen (pp. 350 ff.) that instrumental passages and recitative had both appeared long before; the new element intruding into Passion music at the same time was the free religious poem, commenting or contemplative, set usually as 'aria' – a term which could be fairly loosely applied. Thus in Buxtehude's 'Ich habe Lust abzuscheiden'[39] the four stanzas of Michael Walther's poem, 'Spann aus, ach frommer Gott', are sung by first and second soprano (to the same music), bass, and all three soloists. This 'aria' is preceded and followed by a short sonata for two violins and bass, and a 'chorus' for the soloists (from Philippians, i, 23): 'I have a desire to depart, and to be with Christ'.[40] Again: Buxtehude may treat a hymn as Scheidt had done (see p. 352) as a set of variations, some very free, as in 'Jesu, meine Freude'[41] for the same forces as 'Ich habe Lust'. Buxtehude, the classic master of the early 'church cantata', was faithfully followed by his favourite pupil Nicholas Bruhns (1665–97),[42] while the Kantor of the Thomas Church at Leipzig, Johann Schelle (1648–1701), followed his predecessor Sebastian Knüpfer (1633–76) in writing for a true 'chorus' and orchestra with cornetti, trumpets, trombones, and timpani. Probably under pressure from the 'orthodox' Lutheran pastor to emphasize the traditional hymns, Schelle deployed these resources with special effectiveness in hymn-cantatas.[43]

Buxtehude wrote more church cantatas than Bach but his output was far surpassed by the Weissenfels court *Kapellmeister* and opera director,

---

[37] Published in a 'practical' edition by Willy Maxton as *Das Jüngste Gericht* (Kassel, 1939).
[38] *Gesamtausgabe*, i, p. 108.
[39] Surviving in two versions, *Gesamtausgabe*, v, pp. 56 and 62.
[40] Exactly the same form is employed in 'Eins bitte ich vom Herrn' (Psalm xxvii, 4), ed. Seiffert in *DDT*, xiv, p. 15. Part of the seven-stanza 'aria' from this is printed in *HAM*, ii, No. 235.
[41] *Gesamtausgabe*, v, p. 87.
[42] The twelve surviving examples by Bruhns have been ed. Fritz Stein, *EDM: Landschaftsdenkmale Schleswig-Holstein und Hansastädte*, i and ii (Brunswick, 1937 and 1939).
[43] See the examples ed. Schering, *DDT*, lviii/lix. Schering gives four examples by Knüpfer in the same volume.

Johann Philipp Krieger (1649–1725), who produced some two thousand – of which only eighty or so have survived. At Weissenfels Krieger was at least as early as 1696 in contact with the poet and pastor Erdmann Neumeister (1671–1756) who provided composers with texts of a new kind, frankly modelled on those of Italian cantata and opera. He called his first publication (Weissenfels, 1700) *Geistliche Cantaten*, stating in the foreword of 1704 that 'to express myself briefly, a *Cantata* seems nothing other than a piece from an opera, put together from *Stylo Recitativo* and arias' and 'if in an *Aria* the so-called *Capo*, or beginning of the same, can be repeated in a complete *Sensu* at the end it suits the *Music* very neatly (*lässt es in der Music gar nette*)'. This first set of *Cantaten* consists entirely of Bible-paraphrases conceived as texts for recitatives and arias in the Italian sense, although composers sometimes ignored the last-line cue for the da capo. In his later collections, from 1711 onward, Neumeister admitted Biblical texts and hymns but he had given the church cantata a new impulse which even Schelle's very conservative successor as *Thomaskantor*, Johann Kuhnau (1660–1722), was not entirely able to ignore.[44] The later cantatas of Friedrich Wilhelm Zachow (1663–1712) at Halle contain both secco recitatives and da capo arias,[45] while the innumerable cantatas of Kuhnau's pupil Christoph Graupner (1683–1760), from 1709 onward,[46] and Graupner's friend Telemann, from 1711 onward – both opera composers – are naturally full of them. Graupner's 'Ach Gott und Herr' (1711) includes an aria by no means unworthy of Bach:

Ex. 142

[44] See Schering, 'Über die Kirchenkantaten vorbachischer Thomaskantoren' *Bach-Jahrbuch 1912*, pp. 104–5. Four of Kuhnau's cantatas, dating from 1705–18, have been ed. by him, *DDT*, lviii–lix, pp. 224ff.
[45] e.g. 'Die weise Welt'/'A und O bleibt ganz zurükke' in 'Das ist das ewige Leben', ed. Seiffert, *DDT*, xxi/xxii, p. 3.
[46] Seventeen cantatas, ed. Friedrich Noack, *DDT*, li/lii. Excerpts in *NOHM*, v, pp. 766–9.

mat - - ten Au - gen,   ihr   mat - - ten Au - gen,   Herz

RECITATIVE, ARIA, AND HYMN IN BACH'S CANTATAS

Neumeister appears to have been the first poet and Telemann the first composer who deliberately provided complete cycles of cantatas for the church year. Telemann certainly wrote a complete *Jahrgang* at Eisenach in 1711 and many more later, though he often transferred older cantatas – frequently revised – to new cycles. The 1711 cycle and several later ones are entire settings of Neumeister. Bach did not begin to compile *Jahrgänge* until he succeeded Kuhnau at Leipzig in 1723 (Telemann having withdrawn his candidature and Graupner having failed to get release from Darmstadt), nor did he set many of Neumeister's texts, but the score or so of cantatas composed at Weimar during 1714–16 show his awareness of Neumeister's thinking. The elements of recitative and – often da capo – aria are introduced very prominently. A typical example is the tenor 'Komm, Jesu, komm' in 'Nun komm, der Heiden Heiland' (BWV 61), one of the few Neumeister compositions,[47] though the preceding secco recitative soon develops *cavata* (see p. 382, n. 7). Comparing another Neumeister cantata, 'Gleich wie der Regen' (BWV 18), with Telemann's setting, Spitta pointed out how the 'melodic stream in Bach's recitatives' (as here in 'Mein Gott, hier wird mein Herze sein') can lift the music above the words while Telemann's is simply dramatic secco.[48] Yet Bach's other recitatives here – the bass 'Nun wehre, treue Vater' and the tenor 'Ach! Viel' verleugnen' – are positively operatic. There may be a sinfonia or an introductory chorus, or both as in 'Weinen, Klagen' (BWV 12), and there is nearly always a final hymn, but the predominant element is recitative and aria (or duet). On the other hand, true solo cantatas (i.e. for a single soloist) are rare; one is for soprano, 'Mein Herze schwimmt' (BWV 199), another for bass, 'Der Friede sei mit dir' (BWV 158), though here a soprano sings a hymn-verse as counterpoint to an aria.

---

[47] Bach uses Neumeister for the first recitative and the two arias, the second recitative is scriptural, and both choruses are on hymn verses.
[48] *Johann Sebastian Bach*, i (Leipzig, 1873), pp. 489–90. Of the other cantatas described by Spitta in this chapter, one (BWV 160, pp. 495ff.) is by Telemann, another (BWV 142, pp. 481ff.) probably by Kuhnau. BWV 141, 218 and 219 are also by Telemann.

20. Religious Music (c. 1660–c. 1725)

Lutheran hymnody is an important component of Bach's cantatas though he hardly ever composed hymn-variation cantatas like Buxtehude's. One of the rare exceptions is 'Christ lag in Todesbanden' (BWV 4) which could possibly be one of those composed at Weimar. An opening or medial chorus may be based on a hymn-tune, as in 'Nun komm' (BWV 61) and 'Himmelskönig, sei willkommen' (BWV 182), but perhaps most characteristic are the often exquisite quotations of such tunes as counterpoints, e.g. in 'Der Friede sei', usually on solo instruments: trumpet in the tenor aria of 'Weinen, Klagen', violin and viola in unison in the duet of 'Nur jedem das Seine' (BWV 163), organ sesquialtera in the opening aria of 'Komm, du süsse Todesstunde' (BWV 161). One could easily multiply examples from these early Weimar cantatas alone. And it need hardly be said that each quotation makes an extra-musical point; as the alto welcomes the 'sweet hour of death', the solo organ-stop paraphrases – 'Herzlich tut mich verlangen' ('My heart is filled with longing/To pass away in peace' in the familiar English version).

Thus by 1716 the essential elements of Bach's cantatas were already present. The later ones, mostly attributed to the four cycles he composed or compiled from earlier works revised or transcribed at Leipzig for 1723–4, 1724–5, 1725–6, and 1726–7,[49] may differ in maturity of inspiration and technique, in even greater use of hymn-material and (latterly) of adaptation of secular works, but only in those respects.

TELEMANN'S CANTATA CYCLES

Similar developments can be traced in Telemann's cycles. The cantatas of his earliest preserved cycle, for 1716–17, generally consist of an instrumentally introduced chorus, two airs and recitatives, and a hymn.[50] That for 1718–19, which employs the same Neumeister texts and some of the same music as an 'Eisenstadt cycle' of 1711, often gives a new turn to the introductory chorus by opening it in four-part harmony, with the second verse sung in unison against a fugal instrumental background.[51] In the 1721–2 cycle[52] recitatives are sometimes inserted in hymn-settings. In the different conditions at Hamburg, where cantatas had to be provided both before and after the sermon, Telemann began to stamp his cycles with a certain overall unity: thus every post-sermon cantata for 1722–3 includes a

---

[49] On the post-1727 cantatas, see pp. 534–5. The dating of the cantatas by Alfred Dürr, *Studien über die frühen Kantaten J. S. Bachs* (Leipzig, 1951), pp. 49ff., and 'Zur Chronologie der Leipziger Vokalwerke J. S. Bachs', *Bach-Jahrbuch 1957*, p. 5, and by Georg von Dadelsen, *Beiträge zur Chronologie der Werke Johann Sebastian Bachs* (Trossingen, 1958), is usefully summarized in Vernon Gotwals, 'Bach's Church Cantatas Dated: an interim report', *Notes* (Journal of Music Library Association), (Summer, 1964), p. 340.
[50] Menke, op. cit., pp. 35ff.
[51] There is some affinity here with Bach's 1714 cantata 'Nun komm, der Heiden Heiland', which begins with a French-style *ouverture*: unison singing of the first phrase of the hymn-tune, successively by sopranos, altos, tenors, and basses, surrounded by imitative string-writing, and then a *gai* fugal treatment of the third phrase of the tune in triple time for chorus and orchestra.
[52] Probably performed at Frankfurt, although Telemann moved to Hamburg in 1721 (see Menke, op. cit., p. 40).

passage in *siciliana* rhythm, reflecting the operatic vogue for it. And he published as *Der Harmonische Gottes-Dienst* the complete post-sermon cycle for 1725–6; this has been reprinted in modern times[53] and its 72 solo cantatas – mostly aria-recitative-aria – provide the main basis for our judgement of Telemann as a cantata composer. Perhaps unfortunately. For they may, like later publications of excerpts from his cantatas, represent the works in reduced form for private devotion: some, e.g. No. 2, 'Folternde Rache', No. 17, 'Du bist verflucht', No. 33, 'Schwarzer Geist', are very dramatic, not to say operatic. But the fact that a great deal of Telemann's cantata work was published in his lifetime, as against nothing of Bach's (except a couple of very early works), is significant of the aesthetic climate of the period. Telemann's style, smooth, transparent, uncluttered, chimed with the prevailing taste of connoisseurs as well as general public,[54] Bach's did not.

CANTATA ELEMENTS IN OTHER CHURCH MUSIC

The Lutheran *a cappella* motet, often based on hymn-themes – as in the second section of the magnificent double-choral 'Ich lasse dich nicht' by Bach's uncle Johann Christoph Bach (1642–1703) or the middle section of Johann Sebastian's own even finer 'Singet dem Herrn' – generally continues the older tradition. Sometimes however it assumes a cantata-like form with solo movements as in Buxtehude's 'Cantate Domino'[55] or trios and a quartet as in Bach's hymn-motet 'Jesu meine Freude'. As for Bach's church music with orchestra, the Magnificat – and the various sections of the B minor Mass (see below p. 535) – are from a purely musical point of view cantatas without recitative.

Catholic liturgical music of the period in both Germany and Italy shows the same tendency toward structural disintegration – and is sometimes much more theatrical into the bargain. The introduction of operatic forms and idioms in liturgical music in the early eighteenth century is usually, and probably correctly, attributed to the Neapolitans.[56] The 'Stabat Mater' (probably Naples, *c.* 1707) of the prolific cantata composer Emanuele d'Astorga (1680–*c.* 1756) includes solo, duet, and trio 'numbers', but the breaking down of the liturgical text of the sections of the Mass into arias and so on was a more striking innovation. All the same, the supposedly conservative Fux did this in his 'Missa Corporis Christi' (1713),[57] where in the Gloria the 'Laudamus te' is a bass solo with two violins and the 'Gratias agimus' a trio with two clarini. At the other extreme are Fux's *a cappella* Masses, 'Missa S. Caroli' (justly known as 'Missa canonica') and 'Missa Quadragesimalis'[58] in the *stylus antiquus* which he taught in his treatise on

[53] Ed. Gustav Fock, *Telemanns Musikalische Werke*, ii–v (Kassel, 1953–7).
[54] See Martin Ruhnke, 'Telemann im Schatten von Bach?', *Hans Albrecht in Memoriam* (Kassel, 1962), particularly pp. 151–2.   [55] *Gesamtausgabe*, v, p. 29.
[56] Yet the 'Messe Sti. Henrici' of the Salzburger Heinrich Biber, *DTÖ*, xxv (1) (vol. 49) dates from 1701.
[57] Ed. Hellmut Federhofer, *J. J. Fux: Sämtliche Werke*, i, 1 (Graz and Kassel, 1959).
[58] Both ed. J. E. Habert and G. A. Glossner in *DTÖ*, i (1) (vol. 1).

composition, the *Gradus ad Parnassum* (Vienna, 1725),[59] a conscious attempt to revive 'the Palestrina style'. (Actually most of his Masses are in a 'mixed style', the idiom less archaic and the voices instrumentally supported.)

SURVIVAL OF THE 'PALESTRINA STYLE'

The 'Palestrina style', as distinct from the Palestrina spirit, was hardly in need of revival for it had never died. Scarlatti had written *a cappella* Masses, and canonic ones at that, in Rome during the first two decades of the century, as well as the masterly 'St. Cecilia' Mass of 1720 in the newest style.[60] Ever since Monteverdi and Schütz, church musicians – Catholic and Protestant alike – had adopted the stylistic innovations and techniques of contemporary secular music with the right hand and continued, sometimes with less enthusiasm than at others, to employ the austere *prima prattica* with the left. One of the leading Roman composers, Giuseppe Ottavio Pitoni (1657–1743), carried on the 'colossal' style (see p. 345) in a great number of *a cappella* Masses for two, three, or four choirs. But he succumbed for a time, during his sixties, to the attractions of the *stile concertato* with its contrasts of soli with chorus, voices with instruments, which was the norm – if one can speak of a norm in such a variegated scene – for religious music of this period. A greater Roman, Carissimi, composed polychoral Masses with continuo, Masses in the *stylus antiquus* (including one for twelve voices on 'L'homme armé'), a concertato Mass, and a *missa parodia* on one of his own secular cantatas. At Bologna the bi-choral and concerted church style encouraged by Giovanni Paolo Colonna (1637–95), a pupil of both Carissimi and Benevoli, was carried on but considerably modified by his successor Perti. Like his Venetian contemporary Antonio Lotti (1667–1740), he was yet another Janus figure: a cultivator of the quasi-Palestrina style and also a disintegrator of the Mass structure, preferring – as did Vivaldi also – to compose separate Kyries and Glorias, themselves sub-divided, rather than complete Masses.

In the hands of these composers, as in Fux's, the *stylus antiquus* was hardly more than a mere technical idiom. With its aid composers sometimes achieved living masterpieces like Caldara's 'Crucifixus' for four *a cappella* four-part choirs,[61] but it had long ceased to embody anything like Palestrina's spirit. The last relics of modal feeling had been superseded by key, the free flow of parts rhythmically constrained – a process to which the keyboard continuo's chords no doubt contributed.

MOTETS FOR SOLO VOICES

While the *a cappella* Mass thus survived, the *a cappella* motet became nearly

[59] English translation by Alfred Mann (New York, 1943).
[60] Ed. John Steele (London, 1968).
[61] Ed. Mandyczewski, *DTÖ*, xiii (1) (vol. 26).

extinct in the Roman church, lacking as it did the nourishment of the Lutheran hymn-tune whose sturdy march matched the new *a cappella* style. The term 'motet' survived; it was, however, applied not only to concertato motets but to solos and duets with continuo, such as Cazzati's eight books of *Mottetti a voce sola* (1647–78) and Colonna's of 1681 or Carissimi's setting of 'Alma redemptoris mater' for two sopranos and bass (plus continuo), direct descendants (through Donati and others) of Viadana's *Concerti ecclesiastici* (see p. 252). The sacred monody, duet, and trio naturally tended to follow their secular parallels even in the incorporation of operatic forms.[62] So one is not in the least surprised to find that Scarlatti's *Concerti sacri, motetti a 1, 2, 3 e 4 voci con violini* (Amsterdam, *c*. 1705) consist mostly of recitatives and da capo arias with sometimes exaggerated coloratura. While liturgical texts generally obliged composers to prefer the two-part aria form to the da capo, and recitative was hardly employed at all, such settings of sacred texts helped to prepare the way for the cantata-like treatment of Mass-movements.

SPANISH CONSERVATISM

Catholic composers in the western and eastern extremities of Europe were more conservative, especially in Spain. There the leading masters of the turn of the century, José de Torres (1665–1738), organist and then master of the Capilla Real, and Francisco Valls (1665–1747) at Barcelona, were content to demonstrate their mastery of the old contrapuntal devices in *a cappella* works, sometimes harmonically bold and expressive, with no more than continuo support. Indeed it was Torres who wrote and published the first Spanish treatise on continuo playing, *Reglas generales de Accompañar en organo* . . . (Madrid, 1702), and Valls' 11-part Mass 'Scala Aretina' (i.e. on the hexachord) of the same year gave rise to a controversy which rumbled on for a long time.[64] A couple of decades later, however – the work is undated – the musical director of the Pilar at Zaragoza, Joaquin Martínez de la Roca, who dabbled in opera composition, had the temerity to publish a defence of 'el uso de Arietas, Recitados, Cantilenas, Violinos y Clarinetes en el Canto Eclesiástico'.

CHURCH MUSIC OF THE WESTERN SLAVS

The Western Slavs had no such inhibitions to overcome. One of the most splendid of concertato Masses is the 'Missa Sancti Wenceslai' (1661)[65] of Adam Václav Michna (*c*. 1600–76) and at the other end of the period Josef Plánický (1691–1732) published an *Opella ecclesiastica* (Augsburg, 1723)

---

[62] The Bolognese composer Giacomo Perti (1661–1756) composed *sinfonie avanti la messa* and *avanti il Chirie* that would have served just as suitably *avanti l'opera*.

[64] Reminiscent of the Monteverdi-Artusi affair of a century earlier, it hinged on an unprepared dissonant entry of the second soprano in the 'Miserere nobis'. The passage is quoted in Lavignac and La Laurencie, *Encyclopédie de la musique*, 1re. partie, iv, p. 2115.

[65] Ed. Jiří Sehnal, *Musica Antiqua Bohemica*, ser. II, i (Prague, 1966).

consisting of twelve recitatives and da capo arias in the most up-to-date style;[66] but little of equal interest appeared between them. In Poland Jacek Różycki (c. 1630–c. 1707), master of the royal chapel until its absorption into the Dresden court chapel in 1697, wrote either *a cappella* or unadventurous though florid concertato music,[67] and the best composer of the next generation, Grzegorz Gorczycki (c. 1667–1734), master of the Cracow cathedral choir, generally preferred the *stylus antiquus* and when he uses instruments nearly always does so in a very conservative spirit;[68] the late 'Laetatus sum' (1730) is exceptional.[69]

ROYAL TASTE IN FRENCH CHURCH MUSIC

In church music, as in opera, France was a special case. The music of the church, in its most developed forms, was submitted to the taste of the monarch, like that of the theatre. Louis XIV preferred the *messe basse* to the *grand' messe*; consequently Mass composition languished[70] and the *grand* and *petit motet*, often not even on liturgical texts, became the favourite musical forms. The models were established by the composers of the Chapelle Royale, Du Mont (see p. 356), and a little later Pierre Robert (c. 1618–99). Whereas Du Mont's earlier motets had been either polyphonic or solos with organ continuo, he now offered the king *grands motets*, usually on psalm texts, for *petit choeur* of five soloists, *grand choeur* also in five parts, and orchestra which provided not only obbligato accompaniment or doubling of the voices but also a short overture; they fall into several sections,[71] including solo *récits*. The *petit motet*, on the other hand, was sung by one or more members of the *petit choeur* with organ continuo and perhaps an obbligato violin. Some of Du Mont's *petits motets* for two voices are quasi-dramatic dialogues like the earlier German ones (see pp. 351–2) and in a three-sectional *Dialogus de anima* (Paris, 1668) he employs all the resources of the *grand motet*.

Lully's most important religious works are a 'Miserere' (1664) and a massive 'Te Deum' (1677),[72] notable for its great harmonic blocks – a characteristic which tends to overweight his other *grands motets*. At the other extreme of simplicity and restraint are some of his *élévations*[73] and the

[66] No. 2 is printed by Jaroslav Pohanka, *Dějiny české hudby v příkladech* (Prague, 1958), No. 112.

[67] Examples in the series *Wydawnictwo dawnej muzyki polskiej* (various dates and editors, the later editions being always more reliable), Nos. iii, xvi, xliv, lx.

[68] Examples ibid., vii, xiv, xxxvii (the 'Laetatus'), lxiii, lxv.

[69] About 1680 the musicians of the Russian Orthodox Church were introduced to Western polyphony and its (imperfectly understood) principles by a Polonized Ukrainian, Nikolay Diletsky, who had studied with Mielczewski. For two or three decades his pupils poured out a great quantity of liturgical music, including 'sacred concertos' for as many as six four-part choirs (which could not be allowed even continuo support: see pp. 6 and 66); they appear to have had no imitators and their work seems to have had no effect on the further development of Russian music.

[70] In 1669 Du Mont published *Cinq Messes en plain-chant*, plainsong simplified and put in a rhythmic straitjacket by Nivers (see below), which remained popular for more than two centuries (modern edition by Amédée Gastoué, Paris, 1939), and Charpentier left a dozen Masses of varied kinds.

[71] A typical example, 'Quemadmodum desirat cervus', is printed in the musical appendix to Henri Quittard; *Un Musicien en France au XVIIe siècle: Henry Du Mont* (Paris, 1906). Two of Robert's *grands motets* have been ed. Hélène Charnassé in the series *Le Pupitre* (Paris, 1969).

[72] Published in the *Oeuvres complètes*, ed. Prunières: *Les Motets*, i, and ii, p. 41, respectively.

Motets à voix seule, with continuo only (1689), of his coeval Guillaume-Gabriel Nivers (1632–1714). Nivers was the musician who had been entrusted with that drastic simplification of the chants of the Graduale and Antiphonarium (Paris, 1658) which supplied Du Mont with the material for his *Cinq Messes* (see n. 70). Far more important than either was Marc-Antoine Charpentier (1634–1704).

ITALIANATE ELEMENTS IN FRENCH ORATORIO AND MOTET

Charpentier had studied for three years at Rome with Carissimi and now tried, unsuccessfully, to transplant his master's type of oratorio into France. Of his fourteen *historiae*,[74] possibly written for the Jesuit church of St. Louis in Paris, the best known are the *Judicium Salomonis* (1702) and *Le Reniement de St.-Pierre* (which despite its title has a Latin text). On a smaller scale are the *cantica* and the *dialogi* for soloists and continuo, e.g. the *Dialogus inter Magdalenam et Jesum*,[75] recitatives followed by a melodious Italianate duet. The *historiae* show great dramatic power and also complete mastery of the concertato techniques of the *grand motet*. Conversely his *grand motets* include passages of unorthodoxly expressive, not to say dramatic, harmony.

The dramatic and Italianate elements apparent in Charpentier's church music[76] are still more noticeable in that of the next generation: Campra, Michel-Richard de Lalande (1657–1726), Henri Desmarets (1661–1741), as well as Jacques-François Lochon (b. *c*. 1662) and the secular cantata composer Morin (see p. 388) – two mediocre musicians notable mainly for the Italianate nature of their *petits motets* – and a very great one, François Couperin (1668–1733). By 1703 both Campra ('Quis ego Domine') and Lalande ('Nisi quia Dominus') were deliberately combining French and Italian styles in their motets,[77] though Lalande was happiest in the massive

[73] *Les Motets*, iii.
[74] For a detailed discussion, with musical examples, see H. Wiley Hitchcock, 'The Latin Oratorios of Marc-Antoine Charpentier', *MQ*, xli (1955), p. 41. Hitchcock has also ed. the *Judicium Salomonis* (New Haven, 1964) and a Nativity *canticum* (St. Louis, *c*. 1959). There is an edition of *Le Reniement de St. Pierre* by Quittard (Paris, n.d.), from which the scene of Peter's baiting by the maids is given in Carl Parrish, *A Treasury of Early Music* (New York, 1958), p. 244.
[75] Printed in *HAM*, ii, No. 226, where it is oddly said to be from *Le Reniement*. Clérambault also composed an *Histoire de la femme adultère* which has been ed. Donald H. Foster (Macomb, Ill., 1974).
[76] The appearance of Italian influence in French church music is partly attributable to the popularity of the motets of Paolo Lorenzani (1640–1713), a pupil of Benevoli, who came to France in 1678.
[77] See the quotations in *NOHM*, v, pp. 479 and 467 or this passage from Campra's 'Tota pulchra es' (ed. C. Pineau, Paris, 1958):

Ex. 143

choral style where he alternates self-contained chorus numbers and solo ones in the newer 'cantata' manner instead of closely contrasting them in the concertato tradition; he never verges on the operatic as Campra sometimes does. Even before his and Morin's secular cantatas, Campra had adopted the cantata form in his *Motets à I–II et III voix avec la basse continue*.[78]

Couperin also consciously sought to reconcile the French and Italian *goûts* and employed the cantata pattern. But his religious music stands apart, both by its peculiar sense of intimacy and spirituality and by his choice of forms. His only Masses are two early and uncharacteristic *alternatim* organ Masses (1690);[79] he completely neglected the *grand motet*, indeed he hardly ever employs the chorus: only the three-part 'Jubilemus' refrain in the 'Motet de Ste. Suzanne' and two verses of the three psalm-motets composed in 1703–5 *de l'ordre du Roy* where he directs two-part passages to be sung by 'tous les Dessus' or 'Toutes les Tailles' and 'Toutes les Basses-Tailles'.[80] His sole dialogue,[81] fine though it is, is quite undramatic. Couperin achieved his most perfect fusion of styles, indeed his most perfect church music, in three *Leçons de ténèbres à une et à deux voix* (Paris, 1714)[82] composed in the first place for the nuns at Longchamps. He set the initial letters to vocalises, mostly extended and of great beauty, e.g. that on *Beth*:

Ex. 144

Nothing could be farther from Couperin in style or spirit than the rather square-cut, almost secular *grands motets* of Jean-Philippe Rameau (1683–1764), the best of which (*c.* 1718–20) are 'In convertendo' and 'Quam

---

[78] An easily accessible example is 'Cantate Domino' in *HAM*, ii, No. 257.
[79] *Oeuvres complètes de François Couperin*, ed. Maurice Cauchie *et al.* (Paris, 1933), vi. The edition is not quite 'complete'; nine more motets have been ed. Philippe Oboussier in the series *Le Pupitre* (Paris, 1972).
[80] The passages occur ibid., xi, pp. 195, 104, and 122.
[81] Ibid., xii, p. 174.
[82] Ibid., xii, p. 193.

dilecta'.[83] Like the earlier 'Deus noster refugium', these are cantata-like in build, most impressive in the opening operatic tenor *récit* of 'In convertendo' and in the final chorus of the same piece. The probably rather later 'Laboravi clamans'[84] is a dry contrapuntal exercise for five-part chorus with organ continuo.

COMPOSERS OF THE ENGLISH CHAPEL ROYAL

The music of the restored Church of England after 1660 was as susceptible to Charles II's taste as the French church was to Louis's. One of the King's first acts was to appoint Matthew Locke as his 'composer in the private musicke' and Locke, though not at his best as a church musician, supplied in 'Lord, let me know mine end',[85] with its alternation of solos or solo ensembles with choruses (with organ accompaniment), one of the prototypes of what one might almost call the 'Chapel Royal anthems': the work of the youngsters whom 'Captain' Cooke had recruited as 'Children of the Chapel Royal' at the Restoration, Pelham Humfrey, John Blow, William Turner, Michael Wise (*c*. 1648–87), and Thomas Tudway (*c*. 1650–1726). Their precocity is demonstrated by the so-called 'Club Anthem', 'I will always give thanks',[86] of which the first section was written by Humfrey, the little bass solo 'I sought the Lord' by Turner, and the final section by Blow; the work dates from 1664, when Humfrey was 17, Blow 15, and Turner 13. Humfrey's section is preceded and followed by a 'symphony' for four-part modern strings – not viols – which during the first decade of the reign would have been played by three violinists or violists to a part, later by one only to each part, and later still (*c*. 1688) by the organ. We know from the diarists Pepys and Evelyn, and from Tudway, writing many years later,[87] that such violin 'Symphonys and Ritornelles' – 'better suiting a Tavern or a Playhouse than a Church', as Evelyn considered – were demanded by the King, who sent Humfrey to France and Italy during 1665–7 to acquire the latest musical fashions. Yet Humfrey's music is not noticeably French, still less Italianate, except in so far as his grave introductory symphonies – e.g. to 'Almighty God', 'By the waters of Babylon' (his masterpiece), 'Like as the hart'[88] – might be considered Lullyan. His declamation is often a model for free, natural treatment of English.

[83] *J. P. Rameau: Oeuvres complètes*, ed. Camille Saint-Saëns (Paris, 1895–1924), iv, pp. 1 and 112. Copious lengthy extracts in Cuthbert Girdlestone, *Jean-Philippe Rameau* (London, 1957), pp. 78–105. The cut, transposed and simplified vocal scores are to be avoided.
[84] Ibid., v, p. 1.
[85] Ed. Peter le Huray, *Matthew Locke: Anthems and Motets*, MB, xxxviii, p. 89.
[86] Ed. Peter Dennison, *Pelham Humfrey: Complete Church Music: i*, MB, xxxiv, p. 90.
[87] Quoted in E. H. Fellowes, *English Cathedral Music* (revised by J. A. Westrup), (London, 1969), p. 133.
[88] *MB*, xxxiv, pp. 1, 6, 107. See also Pl. 48.

THE ANTHEMS OF BLOW AND PURCELL

The same might be said of Blow, who was even more precocious than Humfrey, for three of his anthems – now lost – were published when he was only 14, and his much longer life allowed him a maturity denied to Humfrey. Blow was a master of both the old *a cappella* style – as in 'O Lord God of my Salvation' and one of his settings of 'God is our hope', both in eight parts (before 1682) – and the vigorous melodic-harmonic style with obbligato instruments of 'And I heard a great voice' and the magnificent Coronation anthem for James II, 'God spake sometime in visions'.[89] As for his contemporaries, if Wise had written nothing more than 'The ways of Zion do mourn'[90] or Turner than his almost Purcellian St. Cecilia's Day anthem for 1697, 'The king shall rejoice', they would deserve to be remembered. But they are hopelessly overshadowed, as even Blow is, by Blow's pupil Henry Purcell.

Like them, Purcell put all the best of his church music – except a grandiose 'Te Deum and Jubilate'[91] for St. Cecilia's Day (1694) – into his anthems. Just as the Catholic and Lutheran cantata and motet were now far more important musically than the Mass, so the Anglican anthem completely pushed into the background the 'service' which was the last remnant of the Mass. Purcell's earlier anthems include a number of *a cappella* works which, with Blow's, constitute the last dying echoes of the Elizabethan style; among the finest, dating from *c.* 1680–2, are the six-part 'O God, thou hast cast us out' and the eight-part 'Hear my prayer, O Lord'.[92] With these may be classed one of his few Latin works, the great psalm-motet 'Jehova, quam multi sunt'.[93] But they are greatly outnumbered by the verse anthems with or without strings, much more homophonic – and very uneven in quality. (The popular 'Rejoice in the Lord alway'[94] is by no means one of the best.) Most of them are marked by the melodic diminished intervals beloved also of Humfrey and Blow, by rhythmic vigour and harmonic boldness,[95] some of them (e.g. 'Why do the heathen so furiously rage' and 'Plung'd in the confines of despair')[96] by the power of the born dramatist. The two latter exploit the powers of the famous bass, Gostling (see p. 393), who in other anthems is given opportunities to display his phenomenal low Ds and Cs. Purcell reached the culmination of what one might call his purely English style in his great Coronation anthem for James II, 'My heart is inditing'.[97] Thereafter the stylistic influence of Italy becomes obvious in such anthems as 'O sing unto the Lord' and 'My song shall be alway'[98] with its bass coloratura.

---

[89] The two last named in *John Blow: Anthems* (ed. Anthony Lewis and Harold Watkins Shaw), *MB*, vii, pp. 62 and 1.
[90] Dearnley, *The Treasury of English Church Music, 1650–1760* (London, 1965), p. 49.
[91] Purcell Society's edition, xxiii, p. 90.
[92] Ibid., xxix, p. 120, and xxviii, p. 135.
[93] Ibid., xxxii, p. 147.   [94] Ibid., xiv, p. 155.
[95] To take one example out of many, the consecutive sevenths at 'in our land' in 'My beloved spake', ibid., xiii, p. 37.
[96] Ibid., xvii, p. 1, and xxx, p. 180.   [97] Ibid., xvii, p. 69.   [98] Ibid., p. 119 and xxix, p. 51.

Pl. 48   Pelham Humfrey's 'Like as the Hart' in the hand of the 18-year-old Purcell (Fitzwilliam Museum MS 88, fo. 7).

HANDEL'S EARLY ANGLICAN MUSIC

Of the younger generation of Anglican church composers the most distinguished was another of Blow's pupils, William Croft (1678–1727), worth remembering for such anthems as 'O Lord, rebuke me not'[99] and 'Hear my prayer, O Lord', and for two fine hymn-tunes, 'St. Anne' and 'Hanover'. Blow's own later anthems, except perhaps 'Praise the Lord, O my soul', an old-fashioned full anthem celebrating the Peace of Ryswick in 1697, added nothing to his stature; but a very much greater man, albeit a foreigner, was to celebrate the Peace of Utrecht in 1713 with a notable 'Te Deum and Jubilate'. Like the 'Dixit Dominus' of 1707, Handel's finest piece of Latin church music, his Utrecht Te Deum[100] is at once Germanic and Italianate – and, as Chrysander pointed out,[101] unmistakeably modelled on Purcell's of nineteen years before. When, about 1717, he began to supply anthems for the private chapel of his patron, the Earl of Carnarvon (later

[99] Dearnley, op. cit., p. 124.
[100] *Werke*, xxxi.
[101] *G. F. Händel*, i (Leipzig, 1858), pp. 388–9.

Duke of Chandos), he used the Utrecht Jubilate – with reduced choral and instrumental forces – for the first of them, 'O be joyful in the Lord'. These so-called 'Chandos anthems',[102] full of borrowings from earlier works and sources for later ones, are very much better than anything the native composers of the day could show, but they are ecclesiastical chamber music,[103] more German cantatas in form than English anthems. Handel's splendid Anglican anthems for royal occasions were to come ten or twenty years later.

---

[102] *Werke*, xxxiv–xxxvi.

[103] Nearly contemporary is another set of works which might be described as religious chamber music, the *Estro Poetico-Armonico* (eight volumes, Venice, 1724–6) of Benedetto Marcello (see pp. 383–4). This is a curious rather than valuable collection of cantata-like settings of Italian paraphrases of the first fifty Psalms for one to four voices with continuo. Its curiosities include a setting of Psalm 16 (AV 17) which begins with two tenors singing in unison the 'canto greco . . . sopra un inno di Dionisio al Sole' which Vincenzo Galilei took for second century A.D. Greek (see p. 268). None of the modern editions of Marcello's Psalms is satisfactory; there is a useful study of them in Andrea d'Angeli, *Benedetto Marcello* (Milan, 1946), pp. 183–270.

21

Instrumental Music (c. 1660–c. 1725)

TONAL ORGANIZATION OF INSTRUMENTAL FORMS

During the last decades of the seventeenth century the final supersession of mode by key was completed. It was a process much more important to instrumental than to vocal music, for as instrumental composers became accustomed to the idea of key-relationship they gradually – and perhaps only half consciously – realized its possibilities for the creation of more extended forms. These could now be diversified by something more than ornamental variation or contrasts of pace and idea, dynamics and opposition of instrumental choirs, yet held together by definite gravitation towards a main key-centre stronger than the subsidiary ones, with no need to rely on thematic relationships or repeated conventional basses. All the instrumental forms drew new strength from the tonal system, but to none was it so vital as to the sonata as it shed the last traces of its origin in the sectional canzone. At the same time the feasibility of large-scale quasi-symmetrical musical structures, without the support of text, was bound to set up a tension – never resolved historically, yet ultimately beneficial – between the 'closed forms' and the free flow of musical ideas.

The sonata conception of the later seventeenth century appears dimly in the work of the musicians of San Petronio at Bologna, Maurizio Cazzati (c. 1620–77) and his pupil Giovanni Battista Vitali (1632–92). And it is perhaps significant of the Bologna cult of the sonata that Legrenzi's third book, Op. 8 (Venice, 1663), was reprinted there in 1671.[1] Before going to Bologna in 1657 Cazzati had already published several sets of pieces which show some evolution from canzone (Op. 2, 1642) to 'trio sonata' for two violins and continuo (Op. 18, 1656),[2] though even in his Op. 55 (1670) his short-winded sections, all in the same key with only passing modulations to the dominant or another neighbouring key,[3] are not so very far from the canzone. He even allows the substitution of cornetto for violin. (In his Op. 35 of 1665 he had included three sonatas for trumpet and strings.) Vitali also writes rather short sections, except in his *Sonate da chiesa*, Op. 9 (Amsterdam, 1684), and relies a good deal on the technique of theme-

---

[1] One, 'La Buscha', for two groups of three instruments plus continuo, *HAM*, ii, No. 220.
[2] No. 9, 'La Martinenga', ed. Werner Danckert in the series *Hortus Musicus*, No. 34. Alfred Heuss printed the second movement of No. 12, 'La Strozzi', in *SIMG*, iv (1903), p. 476, a curious, disjointed piece including a tremolo passage suggestive of some extra-musical meaning.
[3] See, for instance, No. 1, 'La Pellicana', in *HAM*, ii, No. 219.

transformation often employed in canzoni, even in a late work like the last of the two sonatas in his *Artificii musicali* (1689).[4] But in the much earlier Op. 2 (1667) he had shown how to exploit dominant tension, as in this passage from the first movement of the first sonata:

Ex. 145

In the same set, e.g. No. 3, he had hit on the slow / fast / slow / fast arrangement of movements which was later to become more popular than any other.[5] Another composer who worked for a time at Bologna and published there two editions of his trio sonatas, Op. 6[6] (orig. Venice, 1672) was Giovanni Maria Bononcini (1642–78), father of Antonio and Giovanni Battista (see pp. 370 and 394).

THE OPERA *SINFONIA*

At the same time changes were taking place in another variety of instrumental music, the opera sinfonia. Until the 1640s the sinfonie, whether to the opera or to separate acts, had been – if the composers troubled to supply them – usually only short single movements like that to Cavalli's *Ormindo*;[7] Carissimi's oratorio sinfonie are hardly more developed; Landi's sinfonie to *Sant' Alessio* (see p. 314) were quite exceptional. However in *Doriclea* (1645) Cavalli adopted from Monteverdi's *Incoronazione* the plan of two short movements, one slow in common time, the other faster in triple (see p. 320, n. 31), which he sometimes employed again later, e.g. in *Giasone* (1649) and *Calisto* (1651),[8] writing the triple-time

---

[4] A complete edition of the *Artificii* has been ed. by Louise Rood and Gertrude Smith, *Smith College Music Archives*, xiv (Northampton, Mass., 1959).
[5] Both Cazzati and Vitali also published collections of ensemble dances, some specifically *alla francese*, and Cazzati a set of *Correnti e Balletti per spinetta* (1662).
[6] No. 9 is ed. Erich Schenk, *Die italienische Triosonate (Das Musikwerk)*, (Cologne, n.d.), No. 3.
[7] In Heuss, op. cit., p. 469.
[8] Published respectively in Robert Eitner, *Publikationen der Gesellschaft für Musikforschung*, Jg. 11, p. 3, and Egon Wellesz, 'Cavalli und der Stil der venetianischen Oper', *StMW*, i. p. 77.

section of the latter in a species of canon so primitive, note-against-note and in even note-values, that it would not be worth mentioning if it had not been so often imitated later. Cesti's *Argia* (1655) is on the same plan but adds a quick 4/4 passage. These were far surpassed in more ways than one by the overture the gallicized Italian Lully provided in 1658 for his *Ballets d'Alcidiane*.[9] Whereas Cavalli, writing for the commercial Italian theatre, could reckon on only a small body of players – perhaps sometimes only one to each of his five string parts, plus continuo players – Lully commanded the resources of a great court, no less (according to a contemporary chronicler)[10] than 'octante instrumens', of which the simple five-part score gives no hint: the flutes simply doubled the violins. These were exceptional circumstances but they give a warning that larger instrumental forces would soon be in more general use and that it would be effective to contrast such a tutti with a trio, perhaps for two flutes or oboes and bassoon, like *grand motet* and *petit motet*, as Lully proceeded to demonstrate in the overtures to his ballets *Les Saisons* (1661) and *Le Triomphe de Bacchus* (1666).

The movements of the *Alcidiane* overture are longer than Cavalli's: the slow first in dotted rhythm, the second also in common time but a more respectable fugato than that of *Calisto*. When in 1660 he provided an overture as well as ballet music for the Paris production of Cavalli's *Xerse*, Lully did even better and reverted to what was to become the normal triple time for the fugal movement, pulling it back at the end with a duple *grave*. Cavalli's own sinfonia to *Ercole amante* (Paris, 1662)[11] only demonstrates his incapacity as an instrumental composer, while Cambert in the *première ouverture* of *Pomone* (1671) follows a respectable dotted *mouvement grave* with a fortunately brief note-against-note fugato and a movement in common time unredeemed by its *à trois* contrasts. But the pattern of the 'French overture' with its two movements, amorphous in themselves, was now well established; Lully employed it in all his operas, sometimes expanding the final *grave* (as in *Xerse*), sometimes omitting it altogether. (The chaconnes which are the other large-scale instrumental pieces in his operas of course presented no structural problems; the splendid one in *Roland* (1685) only happens to be longer.) His sense of key was the limited one of his contemporaries, but like Vitali (cf. Ex. 145) he soon discovered how to establish cadential tension, as at the end of the *grave* of the *Cadmus* overture (1673):

---

[9] Ed. A. Dieudonné, *Oeuvres complètes de J.-B. Lully, Les Ballets*, ii.
[10] Quoted by Henry Prunières, 'Notes sur les origines de l'ouverture française', *SIMG*, xii (1910–11), p. 426, n. 30).
[11] Wellesz, op. cit., p. 94.

Ex. 146

in a way that was soon to become commonplace.

When Marc' Antonio Ziani (1653–1715), a nephew of Pietro Ziani, produced a revision of Cesti's *Schiava fortunata* in Venice in 1674, he supplied a model 'French overture',[12] but the other Venetians showed no disposition to follow him.[13] Cesti's overture to *La Dori* (1663)[14] and Pallavicino's to his first opera, *Demetrio* (1666), had consisted of four short sections. In Cesti's overture to *Le disgrazie d'Amore* (1667)[15] 18 bars marked 'Stanze dell'Allegria' are followed by a saraband in two (repeated) sections: 12 bars proceeding from tonic to dominant and 15 in reverse – an extremely popular pattern for dance-movements. His *Pomo d'oro* (see p. 322) was in every respect a special case. And whereas Cesti had been generally content with five-part strings, now in the 1670s the Venetians were more interested in exploiting the solo trumpet concertante than in formal organization. Sartorio's use of a pair of trumpets in the short *sinfonia* to his *Adelaide* (1672)[16] was admittedly motivated by the following aria: the heroine hears 'trombe guerriere'. Pallavicino pits it against the strings in the three-movement *sinfonia* of *Diocletiano* (1675),[17] where it prefaces a scene of triumph, as does the elder Ziani in his parallel piece for *Candaule* (1679). Pallavicino's *Le Amazoni nell' isole fortunate* (also 1679) is introduced by *largo*, *sarabande*, and *grave* for two violins and continuo only.

Of Stradella's operas, which date from the late 1670s, *Corispero* has no sinfonia, that to *Floridoro* consists of a *grave* and a fugal *allegro*; *Trespole tutore* has an *allegro*, the theme of which grows out of a brief intrada, and is rounded off by a 3/2 passage. Much more extended is the sinfonia with solo trumpet to the *Inventione per un Barcheggio* (in other words, 'water music') of 1681:[18] a *spiritosa e staccata* (26 bars), a 3/2 movement (68 bars), a 40-bar canzone, and a 3/8 gigue-like finale of 122 bars.

---

[12] Complete in Heuss, op. cit., p. 470.
[13] The French *ouverture* was before long adopted in other countries: e.g. by Blow for *Venus and Adonis* (early 1680s), Purcell for *Dido and Aeneas* (late 1680s), the cosmopolitan Steffani for *Orlando generoso* (Hanover, 1691), and Fux from his *Concentus musico-instrumentalis* (Nuremberg, 1701) onward. (See also p. 426, n. 30).   [14] Eitner, op. cit., p. 86.   [15] Ibid., p. 178.
[16] Schering, *Geschichte der Musik in Beispielen*, No. 223.   [17] Ibid., No. 224.
[18] The *sinfonia* has been ed. Owen Jander (North Easton, Mass., 1963); incipits in Heinz Heuss, *Die Opern Alessandro Stradellas* (Leipzig, 1906), pp. 71–2.

THE CONCERTO GROSSO

The most interesting feature of Stradella's instrumental writing is not the forms but his frequent employment of the antiphony between three solo strings (concertino / little consort) and the full body of strings (concerto grosso / grand consort) already noted in the accompaniments to arias in his serenatas and oratorios (see pp. 361 and 396). This, with other kinds of antiphony, is employed in his manuscript collections of *sinfonie a più istrumenti* which must be among the earliest independent genuinely orchestral pieces that have come down to us. Some of his sinfonie are for solo instruments only;[19] one for two violins and bass and two cornetti and bass, and one for solo trumpet, two *chori* each of four-part strings, and continuo, are doubtful cases. But when string concertino is pitted against string concerto grosso there can be no doubt. Georg Muffat (1653–1704), who had sat at Lully's feet in Paris as a boy, tells us that he heard Arcangelo Corelli (1653–1713) perform such concertos 'with a great number of players' (*mit grosser Anzahl Instrumentisten*) at Rome in 1682. He promptly went back to Salzburg and published his *Armonico tributo*,[20] which he prefaced with a fourfold explanation in German, Italian, Latin, and French of the way this novel type of music was performed. The interplay of concertino with concerto grosso in Stradella may be illustrated by this passage from a sinfonia in D (Modena, Bibl.Est.Mus.F. 1129, no. 2), a work consisting of a 4/4 *allegro* (24 bars preceded by four slow bars), 75 bars in 3/4, another 4/4 *allegro* (22 bars, introduced by eight slow bars), and a 6/8 finale of 41 bars:

Ex. 147

[19] Notably the long, straggling specimen for violin, cello, and continuo printed by Schering, op. cit., No. 229.
[20] Ed. Schenk, *DTÖ*, 89.

In textures of this kind, as in Lully's 'fugal' allegros, counterpoint had lost all its inner dynamism and is reduced to a bustling enlivenment of a harmonic basis controlled by the steady march of the basso continuo. Even thematic ideas tend to be conceived in harmonic rather than melodic terms.

THE TRIO SONATA

If Stradella was really the first to employ the concerto grosso – for the designation was later (*c.* 1700) applied to the musical form itself – Corelli was its classic master as he was also of the trio sonata with its much longer ancestry. Corelli's *Concerti grossi*, Op. 6, were published only posthumously (Amsterdam, 1714) though most of them must have been composed at the same period as his trio sonatas, Opp. 1–4 (Rome, 1681, 1685, 1689, 1694, and a number of nearly simultaneous editions elsewhere) or his Op. 5 for solo violin and continuo (1700), which would obviously have been better commercial propositions.[21] In these sonatas, and on the title-pages of three sets, he proclaimed himself 'Bolognese' which he was by education. Opp. 2, 4, and the second part of 5 are *da camera* with at most (e.g. Op. 3, Nos. 2 and 6) a slow movement in the relative minor; each consists of slow *preludio* followed by (usually) three or four dances unified by key: mostly allemandes and correntes and ending with giga or gavotte. They are delightfully melodious and violinistic, and make only modest demands on technique, but they cannot compare in interest with Opp. 1, 3, and the first part of Op. 5, *da chiesa*, in which Corelli shows himself the direct heir of G. B. Vitali and G. M. Bononcini. Almost all the trio sonatas *da chiesa* are in four movements, most of them laid out as slow / fast / slow / fast, the first quick movement generally fugal, the finale often in 6/8 or 12/8 time. In the solo sonatas, Op. 5, he allows himself an extra quick movement. The last four concertos of Op. 6 are planned like the *sonate da camera* and it is difficult to

---

[21] The *concerti grossi* are often performable without the ripieno parts, as simple trio sonatas.

understand why Nos, 1–8 were *not* planned like the *sonate da chiesa*; Nos. 3 and 6 have one additional movement each like the solo sonatas, the others even more. Incidentally, the finale of No. 6 is more carefully organized tonally than is usual with Corelli.

THE INFLUENCE OF CORELLI'S STYLE

What puts Corelli above his contemporaries in this field is not mastery of form or even quality of invention but the seemingly effortless creation of a style. It could be imitated – and was very successfully imitated by his mysterious English pupil, 'Giovanni' Ravenscroft (d. *c.* 1708) who published a set of twelve trio sonatas at Rome in 1695.[22] One has only to look at the *sonate de chiesa* of Antonio Caldara (*c.* 1670–1736) and Vitali's son Tomaso (1663–1745) who each published an Op. 1 in 1693, or the Op. 1 (1694) of Tomaso Albinoni (1671–1750) – from which the young J. S. Bach is thought to have borrowed material for two keyboard fugues (BWV 950 and 951) – to see how the Corelli style influenced his younger Italian contemporaries; or to study their later works to find how little they added to it during his lifetime.

The style reached England very soon. The vogue of Italian violin music had been started, according to Roger North, by the violinist Nicolà Matteis who came to England about 1672. After a time 'came over Corelly's first consort that cleared the ground of all other sorts of musick whatsoever';[23] there is evidence that quantities of Italian music, printed and in manuscript, were imported *c.* 1680–1; and in 1683 Purcell, who two or three years before had been writing viol fantasies modelled on those in Locke's suites of the 1650s, published his *Sonnata's of III Parts* in which, as he claimed in his preface, he had 'faithfully endeavour'd a just imitation of the most fam'd Italian Masters' – though North notes that they were 'clog'd with somewhat of an English vein'.[24] (A second set of trio sonatas was published posthumously in 1697.) The 'fam'd Italian Masters' certainly included Cazzati, G. B. Vitali, and the lesser-known Roman, Lelio Colista (1629–80),[25] whom he selected – in his 1694 revision of Playford's *Introduction to the Skill of Musicke* – as an exemplar for instrumental fugal writing, which certainly plays an exceptionally important part in his own sonatas.

The impact of the Italian sonata in France was manifest a little later with Couperin's *sonades*, composed *c.* 1692 when, as he said later, he was first 'charmés de celles du signor Corelli', though the trio sonatas of Jean-Ferry Rebel (1666–1747), said to date from the 1690s, are not in the least Corellian. It was not until 1724 that Couperin published his splendid

---

[22] See William S. Newman, 'Ravenscroft and Corelli', *M&L*, xxxviii (1957), p. 369. Ravenscroft's second sonata, at one time attributed to Caldara, is given in Einstein, *A Short History of Music* (fifth edition, London, 1948), p. 276.
[23] *Roger North on Music*, transcribed and ed. by John Wilson (London, 1959), p. 310.
[24] Ibid, p. 310, n. 65.
[25] See Michael Tilmouth, 'The Technique and Forms of Purcell's Sonatas', *M&L*, (1959), particularly pp. 113–20. The sonatas are published in vols. v and vii of the Purcell Society's edition, but should be referred to in the revised editions.

programmatic *grande sonade en trio, Le Parnasse ou l'Apothéose de Corelli*, in 1725 that he published the companion apotheosis of Lully[26] in which Corelli and 'the Italian muses' welcome him to Parnassus and 'Apollon persuade Lulli et Corelli que la réunion des Goûts François et Italien doit faire la perfection de la Musique', and in 1726 that he very belatedly brought out three of his early *sonades* with fresh titles,[27] and each followed by a suite of six to eight dances, in the collection *Les Nations*. But despite this deliberate attempt at a 'réunion des Goûts', Couperin's music is always more French than Italian, always bursts the Corellian forms, and is always more keyboard than violin music – as he nearly admits in the *avis* to the Lully *Apothéose* where he says he has been accustomed to perform his trio at home 'à deux Clavecins, ainsi que sur tous autres instruments'. Corellian influence had by then already appeared in the solo violin sonatas (1707) of Élisabeth Jacquet de La Guerre (*c.* 1664–1729), of Jean-Baptiste Senallié (*c.* 1687–1730) from 1710 onward, and Louis Francoeur (1692–1745) in 1715 and 1726 – the trio sonata never won much favour in France – but even before Couperin raised Corelli to Parnassus, the first sonata collections of Francoeur's better known brother François (1698–1787) and Jean-Marie Leclair (1697–1764), published in 1720 and 1723 respectively, show that Corelli's style was being superseded by Vivaldi's (see p. 428).

GERMAN EXPERIMENTALISM

In Germany the influence of Italian instrumental music was sporadic. Johann Rosenmüller (1619–84) did a good deal to propagate it by his example; his last work, the *Sonate à 2.3.4. è 5 Stromenti da Arco & Altri* (Nuremberg, 1682),[28] stands up well to comparison with his Italian contemporaries. While the already mentioned Georg Muffat was a complete cosmopolitan who attempted a 'réunion des Goûts' long before Couperin and followed up the Italianate sonatas and concertos of the *Armonico tributo* with two *Florilegia* (1695 and 1698)[29] in which suites of dances are introduced by Lullian overtures,[30] another Salzburg musician, Heinrich Biber (1644–1704), the greatest German violinist of the age, looked inward and occupied himself with glorifying the Mysteries of the Rosary and with experiments against the very nature of the instrument: profuse multiple stopping and *scordatura* (unorthodox tuning) in order to facilitate it.[31] Biber also took the violin into much higher positions than Corelli. Some northern musicians – e.g. the eclectic Johann Philip Krieger (1649–1725) in his Op. 2

[26] *Oeuvres complètes de François Couperin*, x, ed. Amédée Gastoué (Paris, 1933), pp. 7 and 53.
[27] 'La Pucelle' was re-named 'La Françoise', ibid., ix, p. 9, 'La Visionnaire' became 'L'Espagnole', p. 65, and 'L'Astree' 'La Piemontoise', p. 225.
[28] Modern edition by E. Pätzold (Berlin, 1954–6) and various separate editions.
[29] Ed. Heinrich Rietsch, *DTÖ*, Jg.i (2) and ii (2) (vols. 2 and 4).
[30] A form popular not only in France but also in Germany, where the precursor was probably Lully's follower Kusser (see p. 366) with his *Composition de Musique* (Strasbourg, 1682).
[31] Biber's *Sonatae Violino solo* have been ed. Guido Adler, ibid., (Jg. v (2)) (vol. 11), the sonatas 'zur Verherrlichung von 15 Mysterien aus dem Leben Mariae' by Erwin Luntz, ibid.(Jg. 12(2) vol. 25). No. 6 in Schering, op. cit., No. 238.

(1693) and Buxtehude in his Opp. 1 and 2 – substituted the viola da gamba for the second violin in their trio sonatas. The six *parties* (suites of dances preceded by French overtures) of Krieger's *Lustige Feld-Music* (1704) are for four-part wind. Everywhere there was experiment and the exploration of byways, but the main road lay through Italy.

TORELLI'S RITORNELLO FORM

That road was marked out mainly by two men only five or six years younger than Corelli: Giuseppe Torelli (1658–1709) and Alessandro Scarlatti. At the time when Corelli had just published his trio *sonate da chiesa*, both employed the same over-all pattern, Scarlatti in his *Rosaura* overture (1690), Torelli – who spent two periods of his life at Bologna, where nearly all his published works appeared – in three of his *Sinfonie a tre e Concerti a quattro* (1692). The second concerto of this opus is in the quick / slow / quick mould, which from 1696 became the norm for Scarlatti's overtures[32] and hence for Italian overtures in general. It is difficult to determine the chronology of Torelli's sonatas, *sinfonie*, and concertos, many with the trumpets so often favoured by Bolognese composers. But in 1709 his brother published the posthumous Op. 8 which is a real milestone in the history of instrumental music. Op. 8 is made up of six concertos in which the concertino consists of two violins only, and six in which it is reduced to a single solo violin. But Torelli's 'discovery' of the solo concerto, which had been foreshadowed in passages of his *Concerti musicali a quattro* (Augsburg, 1698) and of Albinoni's *Concerti a cinque*, Op. 2 (Venice, 1700), was of less moment than his method of constructing extended single movements that were at the same time diversified and satisfactorily unified. In earlier works he had demonstrated his skill in inventing strongly profiled themes and counter-subjects which could be modified and fragmented, and in sophisticating the simple return of dominant to tonic, e.g. by inserting a four-bar parenthesis: E major (D, C, B, E) – A minor.[33] In Op. 8 he emphasizes the key-structure by introducing each tutti with the same striking theme which recurs as a species of ritornello, its appearances being accentuated by the much more florid, often non-thematic nature of the solo passages. Thus in the first movement of No. 7[34] we have a 12-bar ritornello in D minor beginning:

Ex. 148

[32] E.g. *La caduta dei Decemviri* (1697), printed in Carl Parrish, *A Treasury of Early Music* (London, 1959), p. 264; *Eraclea*, with its pair of trumpets, (1700), in Robert Haas, *Musik des Barocks* (Potsdam, 1932), p. 207; the solo cantata, 'Sulla sponda del mare', and the oratorio *Sedecia* with its concertino/concerto grosso effects (1706), in Hugo Botstiber, *Geschichte der Ouvertüre* (Leipzig, 1913), pp. 247 and 252.

followed by two bars of solo; two bars only of ritornello in F major, followed by another tiny solo and a 12-bar passage in which tutti and solo alternate, cadencing in B flat, C, D minor; ritornello in A minor, 13 bars, followed by 12 of solo passage work; ritornello in D minor as at the beginning. In the first movement of No. 8 in C minor[35] the 'head' of the ritornello, here preceded by two solo bars, consists of four tutti chords of which the fourth is the dominant (Ex. 149i), and the key scheme of the movement as stamped out by the ritornelli is:

> C minor
> G minor
>   C minor but melodically changed to lead into E flat (Ex. 149ii)
> C minor as at first
> G minor but ending on the dominant chord and so introducing the
>   brief solo slow movement.

Ex. 149

The schemes are different but both rest securely on the tonal pillars of the ritornelli: tonic, relative major, minor dominant.[36]

VIVALDI AND HIS FOLLOWERS

Three years after Torelli's death a remarkable collection of concertos entitled *L'Estro Armonico* was published at Amsterdam where Estienne Roger with an edition of Corelli's Op. 1 (*c.* 1700) had initiated a flourishing music business in which Italian instrumental works bulked heavily. *L'Estro Armonico* consisted of eight concerti grossi and four solo violin concertos by the Venetian violinist Antonio Vivaldi (1678–1741), who had already published two sets of Corellian *sonate da camera* for trio (Op. 1, Venice, 1705) and for solo violin (Op. 2, Amsterdam, 1709). His position at the Ospedale della Pietà (see p. 398) put him in charge of a considerable number of well-trained girl musicians, not only orphans but also fee-paying

---

[33] In the second movement of a *sonata a quattro*, No. 46 in the thematic catalogue appended to Franz Giegling, *Giuseppe Torelli* (Kassel, 1949).
[34] Schering, op. cit., No. 257.
[35] Miniature score, ed. Ernst Praetorius (London, 1939).
[36] Both these concertos – the first movement of No. 7, and No. 8 transposed to A minor – were transcribed for organ by Johann Gottfried Walther (1684–1748), and published in his *Gesammelte Werke für Orgel*, ed. Seiffert, *DDT*, xxvi–xxvii, pp. 343 and 350. Walther also transcribed two concertos from Albinoni's Op. 2, ibid., pp. 285 and 289.

pupils, not only string-players but oboists and harpsichordists, and his concertos were naturally composed for himself and them. Two of the concerti grossi, Nos. 2 and 11,[37] preserve the Corellian trio concertino. No. 2 is even cast in the four-movement *chiesa* mould – as are two of those for 4-violin concertino – and neither makes effective use of the ritornello structure. On the other hand No. 8, which dispenses with the cello, is in the opera-overture form and the three tutti chords characteristic of overture openings provide the 'head' of the ritornello. It is a typical Vivaldi work with well defined themes, sequentially worked motives, sharp differentiation between tutti and soloists (who are given a lovely duet in the slow movement), and some enterprising violin writing in the finale. Of the four solo concertos, all in the three-movement form, Nos. 9 and 12 are outstanding – the slow movement of No. 9 spun with almost hypnotic effect from a mere four-note motive, that of No. 12 expanding a short initial theme with ever-longer breath in a golden melody worthy of Corelli or Scarlatti. In the same year (1712) that *L'Estro Armonico* appeared, as his Op. 3, Vivaldi composed a solo concerto for 'la Solemnità della S. Lingua di S. Antonio in Padua'[38] – in which the tutti is augmented by a pair of oboes – with a written-out cadenza for the soloist. Displays of virtuosity for violinists had already appeared in opera scores – for instance, the introduction to the aria 'Ti rendo ancor la palma' in Scarlatti's *Laodicea e Berenice* (1701)[39] – and improvised ornamentation was an ancient custom, but Vivaldi's practices of either indicating the place for a cadenza by writing 'Qui si ferma a piacimento' when the orchestra is to stop until the final tutti (as he does in the first movement of the 'S. Antonio' concerto) or writing out a cadenza of nearly 40 bars incorporating material from the first movement as well as the finale (as at the end of the same work), seem to have been new. New also is the cadenza's venture into the extremely high register, demanding the twelfth position, considerably more than Torelli had asked for – and Corelli had been content with the third.[40] The element of technical showmanship for its own sake was before long to become a *sine qua non* in solo concertos by performer-composers.

Vivaldi continued to publish sets of concertos up to about 1730, perhaps the most important being Opp. 6 and 7 (*c.* 1716–17), 8 (*Il Cimento dell' Armonia e dell' Inventione*) (*c.* 1725), and 9 (*La Cetra*) (1728). The first concerto of Op. 6 is outstanding in its power and passion; the first four of Op. 8 (Nos. 76–9 of the complete edition) are named after the seasons, 'Autumn' having a 'hunt' finale and 'Winter' 'shivering' trills, while the fifth is headed 'La tempesta di mare'; another storm at sea (No. 150) opens Op. 10, a set with solo flute – which figures delightfully in the third concerto

---

[37] Most of the works mentioned here are easily available in miniature scores. Vivaldi's vast output of instrumental music was ed. G. F. Malipiero (Milan, 1947–71). The thematic catalogues by Mario Rinaldi (Rome, 1945) and Marc Pincherle (Paris, 1948) have been superseded by Peter Ryom's (Copenhagen, 1973).   [38] No. 312 in the complete edition.
[39] Pincherle quotes a violin cadenza from the Third Act of *Mitridate Eupatore* in his *Antonio Vivaldi et la musique instrumentale* (Paris, 1948), i, p. 68.
[40] Other concertos with notable cadenzas are Nos. 55, 112, and 136. In the last the solo instrument is *scordato* and the tutti consists of two four-part groups.

(No. 42), 'Il gardelino' (The goldfinch). But Vivaldi's published concertos are far outnumbered by the hundreds he left in manuscript: solo concertos for cello, the various wind instruments (including horn and trumpet), even mandoline, and the most varied groupings of concertino and ripieno instruments in the *concerti grossi*, with infinite variety in the treatment of the material.

Vivaldi's *Estro Armonico* appears to have been less quickly appreciated in Italy than in Germany, particularly in Saxony. The *Concerti grossi*, Op. 1 (Amsterdam, 1721), of Pietro Locatelli (1695–1764), a pupil of Corelli, are still heavily under his master's influence and Albinoni reveals that of Vivaldi for the first time in his *Concerti a cinque*, Opp. 7 and 9 (Amsterdam, 1719 and 1722), though admittedly we do not know the dates of composition. But Johann Joachim Quantz (1697–1773) narrates in his autobiographical sketch[41] how at Pirna, near Dresden, in 1714 he saw for the first time Vivaldi's violin concertos: 'As an entirely new kind of musical pieces they made no little impression on me. I did not fail to collect quite a store of them. Vivaldi's splendid *Ritornelle* served me in later times as a good example'.[42] At exactly the same time the young Duke Johann Ernst of Saxe-Weimar (1696–1715), pupil of that connoisseur of Italian concertos J. G. Walther, was composing a set of *Six Concerts à un Violon concertant*, Op. 1. And there can be little doubt that it was in these years (1715–17) that the Weimar Court organist and *Hofmusicus* Sebastian Bach made keyboard arrangements[43] of four of the Duke's concertos (two of them from Op. 1), an oboe concerto by Alessandro Marcello (1684–1750), Benedetto's elder brother, published at Amsterdam in 1716, and no fewer than nine by Vivaldi (five from *L'Estro Armonico*,[44] the others from Opp. 4 and 7). The Saxon cult of Vivaldi was given stronger impetus in 1717 by the return of the Dresden Court violinist Georg Pisendel (1687–1755), who had been studying with Vivaldi and brought back a large collection of his master's works – including both sonatas and concertos dedicated to himself[45] – and the appointment as *Kapellmeister* of Johann David Heinichen (1683–1729) who had composed a very Vivaldian concerto grosso in Venice two years before.

BACH AT CÖTHEN

In December of that year (1717) Bach moved to the small Calvinist Court of Cöthen. No church music was required of him and he was free to concentrate on instrumental music, mostly for violin or harpsichord or both,

[41] Facsimile reprint in Willi Kahl, *Selbstbiographien deutscher Musiker des* XVIII. Jahrhunderts (Cologne, 1948), p. 104.

[42] However Quantz was disenchanted by Vivaldi's later concertos: see his *Versuch einer Answeisung, die Flöte traversiere zu spielen* (1752), modern edition ed. Schering (second ed., Leipzig, 1926). p. 241.

[43] BWV 592–7 for organ, 972–87 for harpsichord; the differentiation of tutti and solo would be easy on any instrument with two manuals.

[44] But in at least one case (see Pincherle, op. cit. i, p. 237) using a manuscript copy, not the edition. Bach's arrangement for four harpsichords (BWV 1065) of Vivaldi's Op. 3, no. 10, an undertaking no less – or more – questionable than the operations of Busoni and others performed on Bach himself in the twentieth century, is customarily dated much later.

[45] For instance, Nos. 322, 323, and 325 of the collected edition.

but also including some memorable concertos: the solo violin concertos in A minor and E, the concerto in D minor for two violins, and the *Six Concerts avec plusieurs Instruments* of which a fair copy was dedicated in 1721 to the Markgraf of Brandenburg although they had clearly been written in the first place for Prince Leopold of Cöthen, his *Kapellmeister*, and their little group of players.[46] Closest to the Vivaldi pattern are the A minor solo concerto and the one for two violins. The first movement of the E major covers a wider tonal span; instead of a simple tonic ritornello, it begins with a self-contained 52-bar tonic / dominant / tonic section. Bach could thus confidently sweep through C sharp minor, B minor, A major, B minor again, F sharp minor, and even touch on G sharp minor, setting up all sorts of prolonged dissonant tensions (particularly on diminished sevenths), before a note-for-note repetition of his opening 52 bars. By exactly the same process he could construct a 427-bar first movement for the fourth 'Brandenburg'. All the 'Brandenburgs' explore the varied possibilities of the concerto grosso: in No. 3 the nine string players constitute the *concertino* and simply coalesce into three 'real' parts as the *ripieno*, No. 6 is really a 'double concerto' for the viole da braccio, and No. 5 a triple concerto for flute, violin, and harpsichord (which alternately acts as continuo and solo instrument). Here the slow movement is a pure trio-sonata piece for the soloists, while the virtuoso writing and long, unaccompanied cadenza for the harpsichord in the first movement foreshadow the solo harpsichord concerto of the near future. In No. 1 Bach turns the concerto into a kind of suite by the addition of a minuet and *polacca*, each with its trio (literally) for wind. In two other suite-like works from this period, the *ouvertures* in C (oboes, bassoon, and strings) and B minor (flute and strings), Bach was of course following not an Italian pattern but a favourite Franco-German one adopted by Kusser and Georg Muffat (see p. 426), J. C. F. Fischer in his *Journal de Printems* (Augsburg, 1695),[47] Fux in his *Concertus musico-instrumentalis* (Nuremberg, 1701),[48] and wholesale by Telemann.

In the Cöthen years Bach was eager to experiment: with sonatas and partitas (including fugues and the celebrated chaconne) for violin alone and suites for cello alone; with a 'trio sonata' (BWV 1015) (on the *chiesa* pattern, like its companions in the set) for violin and harpsichord in which the keyboard player's right hand replaces what would normally be the second violin; with 'concerto' movements, no doubt suggested by his earlier transcriptions, as preludes to the so-called 'English suites' for harpsichord (Nos. 2 and 3, and less obviously Nos. 4 and 5); with a demonstration in the 24 preludes and fugues which constitute the first part of *Das wohl temperirte Clavier* that the tonal spectrum explored in the E major violin concerto[49]

---

[46] Friedrich Smend, *Bach in Köthen* (Berlin, 1951), pp. 24–5; the only extra players needed were two horns for No. 1. Bach's later concertos, including transcriptions of some of the Cöthen ones, date from the period from 1729 onward when Bach took over the direction of the Leipzig Collegium musicum founded by Telemann.

[47] Ed. Ernst von Werra, *DDT*, x.   [48] Ed. Heinrich Rietsch, *DTÖ*, Jg. xxiii (2) (vol. 47).

[49] Indeed earlier by Pachelbel in his suites and J. C. F. Fischer in his *Ariadne Musica* (1702) (see below, p. 441), which Bach certainly knew.

could, by a minuscule adjustment of the tuning of keyboard instruments,[50] be completed and music composed in any major or minor key. But, except in the last area, his experiments did not lead into the future; he was not a 'progressive' composer like Telemann or Graupner, or Johann Friedrich Fasch (1688–1758) who studied at different times with both of these. Moving to Leipzig in 1723 and henceforth more deeply involved than ever in Lutheran church music, he became more and more introverted and Germanic.

TELEMANN'S ECLECTICISM

Bach's German contemporaries worked in opera centres where Italianism was paramount or at courts dominated by French fashions. For a composer such as Telemann, French models were at least as important as Italian ones. As he related in both his *Lebens-Lauff* of 1718 and his autobiography of 1740,[51] it was at the little court of Sorau in Brandenburg during 1704–6 that he widened his knowledge of the '*Ouvertüren* with their additional pieces' of 'Lulli, Campra and other good masters' and devoted two years to the composition of some two hundred such overtures. When at Eisenach (1706–11) he was obliged to produce 'a fair quantity' of concertos, he confessed that his heart was not in the work 'though at least it is true that they mostly smell of France'. The opening of a concerto grosso for flutes, oboe, and violin probably dating from his early Frankfurt days (1711 onward), when he was in close touch with Graupner at Darmstadt, perhaps indicates what he meant:

Ex. 150

---

[50] Not strictly 'equal temperament' as is commonly asserted. For an authoritative yet not excessively technical discussion of Bach's 'good temperament' see J. Murray Barbour, 'Bach and *The Art of Temperament*', *MQ*, xxxiii (1947), p. 64.
[51] Facsimile reprints in Kahl, op. cit., particularly pp. 221–2 and 205.

The dotted rhythm is that of the *ouverture*. But in later years Telemann preferred to introduce the concerto element in his suites,[52] which he did copiously,[53] rather than compose concertos as such. The 'French smell' of Telemann's suites was considerably heightened by his free introduction of quasi-programmatic elements and non-dance pieces with fancy-titles (*galanteries*, as they were called). Georg Muffat had given titles – 'Blanditia', 'Impatientia', 'Nobilis Juventus', 'Splendidae Nuptiae', and the like – to the 'fascicules' (suites) of his *Florilegia* (see p. 426) and separate titles to numbers in 'Constantia', 'Entrees des Fraudes' and 'des Insultes', which suggest that they were excerpts from actual ballets, as were the earlier French suites. Indeed Muffat actually tells us this was so in the case of the second suite of the *Florilegium secundum*, 'Laeta Poesia'. The 'Gigue pour des Anglois' of 'Nobilis Juventus'[54]

Ex. 151

433

catches the English flavour so perfectly that it is hard to believe it is not a genuine English tune. Telemann was much addicted to French types of dance and French fancy-titles for individual pieces (e.g. 'Les Scaramouches', 'Rossignol', 'Harlequinade') all his life. Owing to the impossibility of establishing a chronology of his vast output, it is impossible to say *when* he embarked on the composition of programme suites but his Hamburg 'Wasserouverture' for strings and woodwind, 'qui représente l'eau avec ses divinités) ('Sarabande: Die schlaffende Thetis', 'Bourrée: Die erwachende Thetis', and so on) is dated 1725.[55] Still more programmatic is the *Ouverture Burlesque de Quichote* for strings only, in seven movements including Quixote's attack on the windmills and his 'amorous sighs' for Dulcinea, Sancho tossed in the blanket, and the gallops of Rosinante and Sancho's ass.

All this was a rather superficial manifestation of French fashion. Much deeper and more permament in its effects was the vogue for short-breathed symmetrical melodic phrases less closely related to song, for thinner textures less cluttered with polyphony, for Gallic types of ornament, and for more static basses, which smoothed the way for fundamental changes of style spread over the next half-century. Bach's essays in the French style are not very French.

THE GERMAN KEYBOARD SUITE

Except for transcriptions, dances were the only common ground of instrumental ensemble music and keyboard music; the other keyboard forms developed in very different ways, apart from acute national differences. The general plan of the Froberger keyboard suite (see p. 342), but with the gigue now always placed last – allemande / courante: sarabande / gigue – was adopted with various additions and variations by Pachelbel and Buxtehude,[56] and by most German composers down to Bach and Handel. Additional movements were most often French dances (minuet, gavotte, bourrée, and various others) or *doubles* (see p. 342), and Kuhnau seems to have been one of the earliest to add non-dance preludes to the *Partien* of his *Neue Clavier Übung* (two sets, 1689 and 1692). This innovation – anticipated in the lute suites (*Delitiæ Testudinis*, 1667)[57] of Esaias Reusner (1636–79) – was quickly adopted. It appears in J. C. F. Fischer's *Musicalisches Blumen-Büschlein* of 1696 – and in the suites of Purcell's posthumous *Choice Collection of Lessons for the Harpsichord or Spinnet* published in the same year, in the *Sechs Musicalische Partien* (1697) of Johann Krieger

[52] As did Handel in his two loose suites of *Water Music* (1715 and 1717).
[53] See the lists in Horst Büttner, *Das Konzert in den Orchestersuiten G. Ph. Telemanns* (Wolfenbüttel, 1935), pp. 77–84. [54] *DTÖ*, Jg 2 (2) (vol. 4).
[55] Incipits, not altogether accurate, in Karl Nef, *Geschichte der Symphonie und Suite* (Leipzig, 1921), pp. 94–5.
[56] Their suites were not published in their lifetime. Pachelbel's have been ed. Seiffert, *DTB* ii (1), and numerous separate editions (e.g. *HAM*, ii, No. 150). Buxtehude's *Klaveraverker* are ed. Emilius Bangert (Copenhagen, second ed., 1944). [57] Example in *HAM*, ii, No. 233.

(1652–1735), younger brother of Johann Philipp (see p. 426), in the so-called *Sonate d'intavolatura* (Rome?, 1716) of Domenico Zipoli (1688–1726), the best Italian keyboard composer of the period, in Handel's *Partien* of *c*. 1706[58] and the first collection of his *Suites de pièces pour le Clavecin* (London, 1720), and in Bach's 'English' suites. (The 'French' ones[59] all begin with the allemande.) It was apparently the Lüneburg organist Georg Böhm (1661–1733) who first composed a full-length French *ouverture*-suite for harpsichord;[60] the type never became widely popular though in later years Bach (BWV 828 and 831), Handel (Suite No. 7), and Telemann produced fine examples.[61]

FRENCH MUSIC FOR CLAVECIN

Böhm, who – like Fischer and Muffat – reveals French influence in his profuse ornamentation, may well have derived the idea of a keyboard *ouverture* from the *Pièces de clavecin* (1689)[62] of Jean-Henry d'Anglebert (1628–91), which include arrangements of 'Diverses Chaconnes, Ouvertures, et autres Airs de Monsieur de Lully': *inter alia*, the overtures to *Proserpine* and *Cadmus* (with the unfortunate G of Ex. 146 tactfully removed), and such favourite excerpts as the chaconne in *Phaéton* and the dream scene of *Atys*. These arrangements are interwoven with d'Anglebert's own dances in three sets, each in one key and introduced by a *prélude* with minimal rhythmic definition. He ends with a *tombeau* for Chambonnières, whose pupil he had been, and five fugues for organ. Another Chambonnières pupil, Nicolas Lebègue (1630–1702), had already published two books in 1677 and 1687[63] containing eleven similar sets of dances, with preludes followed by allemande, courante, and sarabande before the varied dances; like d'Anglebert, he eschewed fancy names. Incidentally, Lebègue kept well abreast of Lully (cf. Ex. 146) in his bold treatment of cadence, indeed going well beyond him in the boldness of his chromatic harmony. The two suites (1702 and 1703) of Louis Marchand (1669–1732) and those of Clérambault (Paris, 1704) reflect to some extent the fashionable 'goût de la musique italienne'; so also do those of Gaspard Le Roux (1705) and Élizabeth Jacquet de La Guerre (1707); even Rameau's *Premier Livre* (1706)[64] includes a 'Vénitienne'. Yet they are all still recognizably in the Chambonnières–Louis Couperin tradition. Le Roux clings to the old unmeasured type of *prélude*, as rather surprisingly does Rameau in the first

[58] Kuhnau, ed. Päsler, *DDT*, iv; Fischer, ed. Werra, in Fischer's *Sämtliche Werke für Klavier und Orgel* (Leipzig, 1901); Purcell, *Purcell Society*, vi; Krieger, ed. Seiffert, *DTB*, xviii; Marchand, first suite (D minor), in Gino Tagliapietra, *Antologia di musica antica e moderna*, x (Milan, n.d.); Zipoli, *Sonate*, ed. L. F. Tagliavini (Heidelberg, 1959).
[59] Perhaps so called because one autograph bears a non-autograph inscription: 'Sex Sviten pur le Clavessin'.
[60] Ed. J. Wolgast, *Sämtliche Werke*, i (Leipzig, 1927).
[61] An understandably very immature earlier *ouverture*-suite by Bach (BWV 822) dates from *c*. 1702 when he was in close proximity to Böhm at Lüneburg and is known to have heard the French orchestra maintained at the court of Celle nearby.
[62] Ed. Marguerite Roesgen-Champion, *Publications de la Société française de musicologie*, I, viii (Paris, 1934). Three pieces from the G minor set in *HAM*, ii, No. 232.
[63] Ed. Norbert Dufourcq (Monaco, 1956).   [64] *Oeuvres complètes*, i, and numerous other editions.

part of his prelude before breaking into an Italianate flow of 12/8 quavers in the second part. Marchand's *préludes* are partly measured.

Rameau's *Premier Livre* is not, however, really characteristic; by the time he published his next collection in 1724, the greatest of all the French *clavecinistes*, François Couperin, had produced the first three of his four *Livres* (1713, 1716–17, 1722, 1730),[65] in the second of which – indeed already in the fourth *ordre* of *Livre 1* – all pretence of being dance suites is abandoned.[66] Couperin's *ordres* are not suites but collections of exquisite genre-pieces like 'La Fleurie ou la tendre Nanette' in the first *ordre* of all, with usually enigmatic titles.[67] Some are dedicatory (e.g. 'La Superbe ou La Forqueray' in the 17th), some delicately imitative (the bird-pieces of the 14th), some frankly programmatic (the battle sequence of the 10th), some miniature ballets ('Les Fastes de la grande et ancienne Mxnxstrxndxsx'[68] in five tiny *actes*, No. 11, and 'Les Folies françoises, ou les Dominos'), and all are profusely ornamented in the essentially French lute-derived manner. Rameau in his 1724 *Pièces* was obviously challenging Couperin (particularly in 'Le Rappel des Oiseaux' and 'Les Soupirs')[69] but his robust talent was more at home in the dance forms. And in the same year Jean-Francois Dandrieu (1682–1738) included a 'Concert des Oiseaux' in his *Premier Livre de Pièces de Clavecin contenant plusieurs divertissements dont les principaux sont les caractères de la Guerre, ceux de la Chasse et de la Fête du Village.*

FRENCH ORGAN MUSIC

French organ music of this period was closely related to *clavecin* music in its light weight, melodiousness, and profusion of ornament – and this despite the strict limitations on church music of the *Ceremoniale parisiense* of 1662. (Or perhaps *because* the *Ceremoniale* attempted to ban all instruments except the organ.) The new style was inaugurated by none other than Nivers, the simplifier of plainsong (see p. 413), who was a pupil of Chambonnières; he published *Livres d'orgue* in 1665 ('cent pièces de tous les tons de l'Eglise'), 1667, and 1675, in which he makes great play with dialogues between solo stops or very simple groupings. This excerpt from a 'Dialogue de Voix humaine et de Cornet' is typical:

---

[65] *Oeuvres complètes*, ii–v, and many other editions.
[66] On the other hand his *Concerts royaux* (*Oeuvres*, vii), published at the same time as *Livre III* but composed at the time of *Livre I*, are simple dance-suites with preludes. The suites of Marin Marais (1656–1728), nominally for viols da gamba but, like Couperin's *Concerts*, mostly playable 'sur toutes sortes d'instrumens' (*Livres*, 1686, 1701, 1711, 1717, 1725), are collections rather like Couperin's ordres and hardly less lavishly ornamented.
[67] See Wilfrid Mellers' 'Notes on the Titles' in his *François Couperin and the French Classical Tradition* (London, 1950), p. 356.
[68] I.e. the *Ménestrandise*, or musicians' guild, which Couperin disliked.
[69] Cuthbert Girdlestone also has an appendix on titles in his *Jean-Philippe Rameau* (London, 1957), p. 591.
[70] A *noël* by Lèbegue is given in *HAM*, ii, No. 231. The works of all these composers have been published in the series *Archives des maîtres de l'orgue* (ed. Alexandre Guilmant and André Pirro) (Paris, 1898–1914) and in various later editions.
[71] *Archives*, v. p. 70. The melody is the third-mode one for Vespers at Corpus Christi (*Liber Usualis*, p. 957).

Ex. 152

In the same vein are the *Livres d'orgue* of Lebègue (1676, 1678–9, 1685), Nicolas Gigault (*c.* 1624–1707) (*Livre de Musique*, 1685), André Raison (d. 1710) (*Livres*, 1688 and 1714), and Jacques Boyvin (*c.* 1653–1706) whose two *Livres* (1689 and 1700) were written expressly to exploit the resources of his big new organ at Rouen. The repertory consists of organ Masses, hymn versets, and settings of *noëls*.[70] Almost everything is highly ornamented; Lebègue's pupil, Nicolas de Grigny (1672–1703), the best of the school, whose sole *Livre* (1699) consists of an organ Mass and 'les hymnes des principales festes de l'année', smothers the melody of 'Pange lingua'[71] (in the left hand) with ornaments:

Ex. 153

Couperin's two Masses (1690)[72] are more restrained, while Clérambault's *Livre* of 1710 is the most cheerfully worldly – and Italianate – of all.

ITALIAN KEYBOARD MUSIC

Italian keyboard music of this time was conservative. Besides Zipoli whose 'sonatas' (see above, p. 435) consist half of organ versets and Mass movements, half of harpsichord suites, the one outstanding master was Zipoli's teacher, Bernardo Pasquini (1637–1710), the most celebrated Roman organist and harpsichordist after Frescobaldi. Pasquini also numbered among his pupils Johann Philipp Krieger and Georg Muffat (who learned from him 'die welsche Manier auf dem Clavier'). Like his Spanish contemporary, Juan Cabanilles (1644–1712), he was essentially conservative: still employing (*c.* 1691–*c.* 1705) Frescobaldi's forms – toccata, ricercar, and *canzone francese* – though with more up-to-date methods of articulation and types of material as in this passage from a toccata:[73]

Ex. 154

It is ironical that, on the strength of a dozen curious manuscript 'sonatas' for two harpsichords (written as two figured-bass parts only and dated 1704), Pasquini has been regarded as a pioneer of the keyboard sonata – an expression which the imprecision of seventeenth-century terminology makes almost meaningless.

---

[72] *Oeuvres complètes*, vi.   [73] Collected works, ed. M. B. Haynes. *CEKM* 5.

KUHNAU AND THE HARPSICHORD SONATA

As we have seen, 'sonatas' of various kinds had been written throughout the century, some of them for solo keyboard instruments. But the earliest harpsichord sonatas roughly comparable with the Corellian *sonata da chiesa* appear to have been the one in B flat which Kuhnau appended to the suites of the second set of his *Neue Clavier Übung* (Leipzig, 1692) and the seven which constitute his *Frische Clavier Früchte* (1696).[74] If Kuhnau was not actually a pioneer, he seems to have considered himself to be one, for he remarks in the preface to the *Clavier Übung* 'warumb sollte man auff dem Claviere nicht eben, wie auff andern Instrumenten, dergleichen Sachen tractiren können? da doch kein einziges Instrument dem Claviere die Praecedenz an Vollkommenheit jemahls disputirlich gemacht hat' ('Why should not one be able to manage such things [as sonatas] on the *Clavier* just as on other instruments? for no single instrument has ever challenged the *Clavier*'s superiority in completeness'), going on to explain that all the same, in contrast with an instrumental ensemble, sacrifices or compromises have to be made in 'the continuity of voices' on a keyboard instrument. Kuhnau's B flat sonata opens with a movement apparently moderate in pace – he seldom marks tempi – followed by a fugue, also in B flat, in fast-flowing semiquavers; a 3/4 Adagio in E flat and C minor, and a short 3/4 Allegro (G minor and B flat major), after which the first movement is to be repeated: evidence, underlined by extended reference to the first movement also in the fugue, of Kuhnau's striving for over-all unity. The first two *Früchte* sonatas resemble each other in general plan:

Suonata prima	*Suonata seconda*
Moderate, 4/4 (G minor)	Moderate, 4/4 (D major)
Short *Adagio*, 4/4 (B flat)	Short slow, 4/4 (B minor to D)
Allegro, 4/4 (B flat)	Quick, 6/8 (D major)
Slow, 3/4 (E flat to G minor)	Short slow, 4/4 (G to E major)
Fast, 3/4 (G minor)	Fast, 3/4 (A minor to D major)

In each case the first movement is based on two mutually complementary components, neither particularly striking in profile, presented at once and worked together into neighbouring keys as in this vigorous excursion in C minor in No. 1, which well illustrates Kuhnau's normal texture:

Ex. 155

---

[74] Complete keyboard works, ed. Päsler, *DDT*, iv, and various separate editions.

Both central movements are showy, *clavier*istic affairs; the finale of No. 1 is mildly fugal; that of No. 2 makes almost incessant use of a descending six-note scale figure. This general plan is modified in the other sonatas. In No. 3, for instance, the central movement is a fugue, flanked by two melodious slow movements, and the finale is a gigue although not marked as one. No. 6 begins with a *ciaconna*. Unfortunately the *Früchte* have been overshadowed by Kuhnau's next keyboard publication, the *Musicalische Vorstellung einiger Biblischer Historien in 6.Sonaten* (1700),[75] each of which illustrates an Old Testament story in three to eight movements, some naïvely illustrative (e.g. the combat of David and Goliath in No. 1) and needing the composer's glosses to make them intelligible, some very fine (Saul's melancholy in No. 2, though even this suffers from the outbreaks of Saul's madness). But there was nothing novel in illustrative keyboard music; Kuhnau may well have known, for instance, the suite *La Ribellione di Ungheria* (1671)[76] of the Viennese Italian Alessandro Poglietti (d. 1683) – though this has nothing of his own crude realism – or Kerll's *Battaglia* (1686).

SURVIVAL OF OLDER KEYBOARD FORMS

Kuhnau's *Clavier Früchte* went into five further editions during 1700–24, yet harpsichord composers were in no hurry to follow his lead. They – or the public they wrote for – still preferred the suite or the favourite old keyboard forms of ornamental variations or variations on a ground bass (sometimes in the up-to-date form of the Lullian chaconne). Kuhnau's contemporary Pachelbel practised both forms of variation with consummate mastery in works suitable for either harpsichord or organ: the six sets of variations on 'arias' in his *Hexachordum Apollinis* (1699) and six manuscript *ciacone*. Two airs, each with five ornamental variations, are included in Handel's first collection of suites; indeed his conception of the suite is very liberal; No. 2 has no dance movement at all and might as well have been called a sonata:

> *Adagio*, 4/4 (F major, closing on the dominant of D minor)
> *Allegro*, 4/4 (F major)
> *Adagio*, 3/4 (D minor)
> Fugue (allegro), 4/4 (F major).

[75] No. 4, illustrating Isaiah, xxxviii, is printed in *HAM*, ii, No. 261.
[76] Ed. Hugo Botstiber, *DTÖ*, Jg. xiii (2) (vol. 27), p. 32.

As with Kuhnau the Allegro is showy and the second Adagio is similarly equivalent to that of Kuhnau's *suonata prima*.

The only other large-scale keyboard form – if one can so describe anything so formless – was the toccata, which had changed little in its essence since Merulo (see p. 287): a quasi-improvisatory display-piece with fugal interludes. In the hands of Kerll – probably, like Froberger, a pupil of Frescobaldi, the last great master of the toccata, though a much younger one – and *his* pupil Franz Xaver Anton Murschhauser (1663–1738) the polyphonic element was reduced but the improvisatory element given more motivic coherence. And this was the general tendency in the various keyboard species, whether entitled toccata, capriccio, fantasia, canzone, or whatever, while the imitative polyphonic element became separated and developed its own existence usually under the name of fugue. In the Magnificat versets of Kerll's *Modulatio Organico* (Munich, 1686)[77] these elements are sharply distinguished. And whereas Georg Muffat reveals his usual eclecticism in a compound of German, French, and Italian styles and forms in his *Apparatus musico-organistico* (Salzburg, 1690),[78] the *Ariadne Musica*[79] (cf. p. 431, n. 49) of that other eclectic J. C. F. Fischer, its twenty keys foreshadowing Bach, the short toccata-style preludes and the appended fugues are sharply distinguished.

THE LUTHERAN ORGAN COMPOSERS

All these composers were South Germans and Catholics; consequently the Lutheran hymn, such an important component of most German organ music, plays no part in theirs. It plays an enormous part in that of Buxtehude, who towers above all the other Lutheran organ composers of the latter part of the century: Vincent Lübeck (1654–1740), Georg Böhm[79a] Zachow, Bruhns. They all continued the traditions of Tunder and Weckmann, Buxtehude with a copiousness and exuberance that often suggest improvisation. In his treatment of hymns, say 'Ein feste Burg' or 'Von Gott will ich nicht lassen', he will smother the melody in as much ornamentation, though a totally different kind of ornamentation, as Nicolas de Grigny, and the interludes between the phrases are freely non-thematic or disguisedly thematic. In large-scale fantasies – on 'Wie schön leuchtet' or the huge "Gelobet seist du' – he will follow through the successive stanzas of the hymn in variations on the grandest scale, held together by the basic melody. His toccatas, which he usually styles 'Praeludium cum fuga',[80] were probably intended not to follow a service, possibly for the Lübeck *Abendmusiken* but more likely for the morning entertainment of the

[77] Ed. R. Walter (Altötting, 1956).
[78] Ed. ibid, (Altötting, 1957). A fine passacaglia from it in *HAM*, ii, No. 240.
[79] Ed. Werra, op. cit.; example in *HAM*, ii, No. 247.
[79a] On Böhm's hymn treatments, see F. J. Müller-Buscher, *Georg Böhms Choralbearbeitungen für Tasteninstrumente* (Laaber, 1978).
[80] The stress is really on 'praeludium'; Bach headed his great Prelude and Fugue in B minor (BWV 544) simply 'Praeludium pro Organo pleno cum pedale obligato'.

merchants (see p. 338, n. 42). They are large-scale works.[81] Whereas Tunder was content with one fugue, Buxtehude generally prefers two – of which the second may be in a different measure and may be connected with the first by the briefest transition (sometimes suggesting recitative) or by a whole 'movement' of a couple of dozen bars. The work always begins and almost always ends with a display of virtuosity and the various sections are unified only by key, not thematically despite occasional and probably accidental motivic connections. Buxtehude's pupil Bruhns introduced even greater variety of sections, whereas Böhm and in at least one case Vincent Lübeck[82] employed thematic variation to relate them.

Pachelbel's keyboard music contrasts strongly with that of the North Germans. Instead of juxtaposition of unrestrained virtuosity with fugal sobriety, his 'toccata' writing is itself sober and motivically integrated while the fugue is no longer an episode but an independent piece at the end like Fischer's in his *Ariadne Musica*. His contrapuntal mastery is demonstrated at its finest in a collection of nearly a hundred 'Magnificat fugues', preludes or versets (though very few are based on the actual Magnificat tones).[83] Again in contrast with Buxtehude, the melodies in Pachelbel's *Choräle zum praeambulieren* (1693) are unornamented and each phrase is prefaced by a miniature fugal exposition of it in diminished note-values, a procedure which dates back a century and a half to Heinrich Finck (see pp. 180–1). On the other hand, Pachelbel's hymns for home performance on the harpsichord in his *Musicalische Sterbens-Gedancken* (1683) are *partite*, sets of ornamental variations, just as Buxtehude had written a variation dance-suite, with sarabande, courante, and gigue, for harpsichord on 'Auf meinen lieben Gott', and as the very young Bach was to do in BWV 766–8.

Among the organ composers who show considerable affinity with Pachelbel was Bach's uncle Johann Christoph (1642–1703),[84] while his elder brother of the same name (1671–1721) was actually a pupil of Pachelbel's. Yet another direct link between Pachelbel and the greatest of the Bachs was J. G. Walther, born and brought up in Erfurt under Pachelbel's shadow, Sebastian's relative (through their mothers) and colleague for nine years at Weimar, and an outstanding master of composition on Lutheran hymns. (Like Pachelbel he composed both ornamental variations more suitable for harpsichord than organ[85] and stylistically quite different versets, which are also a form of variation,[86] for church use.) In his Lüneburg years (1700–3) Bach must have heard Böhm play, and possibly studied with him; in 1705, from Weimar, he went on a prolonged visit to Lübeck to hear Buxtehude. No one was better placed than

---

[81] There are numerous editions; easily accessible examples in Schering, op. cit., No. 249, and *HAM*, ii, No. 234 (an unusually extended piece).
[82] Toccata in G minor.
[83] Ed. Botstiber and Seiffert, *DTÖ*, Jg. viii (2) (vol. 17); one example in *HAM*, ii, No. 251. Other organ works ed. Seiffert, *DTB*, Jg. iv (1), and numerous later editions.
[84] Prelude and fugue in *HAM*, ii, No. 237.
[85] For example, 'Herr Jesu Christ, dich zu uns wend' and 'Jesu, meine Freude', *DDT*, xxvi–xxvii, pp. 92 and 129.   [86] E.g. 'Gottes Sohn ist kommen' ibid., p. 77.

he to aggregate – and given his creative genius, to crown – the whole art and technique of German organ music of the previous century.

BACH'S EARLIER KEYBOARD WORKS

The hand of Buxtehude lies heavy on Bach's earliest organ music. The C minor fugue of BWV 549 collapses into the toccata style well before the end; the so-called *Praeludium und Fuge* in A minor (BWV 551) is really a Buxtehudean toccata with two fugues, the first supplying the greater part of the prelude; while the toccata in E (BWV 566) differs from the prototypes only in the decisiveness with which the sections are marked off. This virtuosic exuberance effervesces with more technical assurance in the preludes and fugues and toccatas ascribable to the years 1708–10 at Weimar and explodes in the barely coherent rhetoric of the D minor toccata (BWV 565) commonly known as 'toccata and fugue'. And the same may be said of the harpsichord toccatas of the same time (BWV 912–16), though the E minor (914) is more restrained and the later ones in F sharp minor and C minor (910 and 911) are mature masterpieces. These last were probably written at Cöthen (*c.* 1720) by which time Bach had already taken leave of the toccata form in his organ works, settling for separate preludes (however named) and fugues which remain strictly thematic to the end (534, 536, 537, 540, 542). In these works of the later Weimar years (*c.* 1716–17) he invents themes that are strong in profile and develops large-scale forms from them, not by the introduction of contrasts but by extended key-range. The crowning masterpiece is the G minor (BWV 542), the astounding harmonic language of the preludial fantasia resolved into an unforgettable fugue-theme which manages to suggest in its first two bars in turn tonic, dominant, and relative major. From the same period dates the Chromatic Fantasia and Fugue for harpsichord; Bach was indeed ready to embark on the fugues of *Das wohl temperirte Clavier*.

At about the same time as the completion of what we know as the first book of the *Wohl temperirtes Clavier* at Cöthen in 1722[87] 'for the profit and use of musical youth desirous of instruction', Bach also compiled an *Orgel-Büchlein* 'wherein an inexperienced organist (*ein anfahender Organist*) is given guidance in all sorts of ways of treating a hymn (*einen Choral durch-zuführen*), as well as becoming competent in use of the pedal. . . .' The didactic purpose of both collections relates them to other music, including the *Auffrichtige Anleitung* (commonly known as the 'two – and three-part inventions') and the 'French suites', written for the instruction of his eldest son, Wilhelm Friedemann (1710–84) and his second wife, Anna Magdalena, and the elaborate autograph titles suggest that they were intended for publication. Although he was to write later, larger, and arguably greater keyboard fugues and *Orgelchoräle*, both collections are remarkable not only for their technical mastery but for their wealth and variety of invention.

---

[87] The second book was compiled more than twenty years later.

21. Instrumental Music (c. 1660–c. 1725)

There is relatively little in Bach's early compositions for harpsichord or clavichord – and many of these *Clavier* pieces are definitely for one or the other, some for either – that foreshadows these preludes and fugues. But one can trace the way – though with uncertain chronology – to the *Orgel-Büchlein* from such early efforts as 'Gelobet seist du, Jesu Christ' (BWV 722), 'In dulci jubilo' (BWV 729), and 'Lobt Gott ihr Christen' (BWV 732) perhaps dating from *c.* 1705, where he was content to play the phrases of the hymn in full chords and separate them by inept skirmishes, to the masterly treatments of the same tunes (BWV 604, 608, and 609) in the *Büchlein*. On the way we find a good deal of Buxtehudean elaboration (e.g. in 'Herr Jesu Christ' (709), and 'Ein' feste Burg' (720) which is known to date from 1709) and also adaptation of Pachelbel's favourite method ('Allein Gott in der Höh') (717) and two settings of 'Valet will ich dir geben' (735 and 736), and we notice many lovely things like 'Herzlich tut mich verlangen' (727) and a number of essays in canon and fugue. The *Orgel-Büchlein* itself is a thesaurus of devices for treating the tunes – as well as an anthology of musical poems on Lutheran hymnody.

Not much organ music was printed in Germany at that time but, as we have seen, harpsichord music in plenty. It is perhaps an indication how far Bach was out of touch with contemporary taste that neither the *Wohl temperirtes Clavier* nor the *Auffrichtige Anleitung* found a publisher in his lifetime. His earliest printed keyboard work was the first of the six partitas (BWV 825–830), which he published at his own expense in 1726; the rest appeared in the following years, the complete set in 1731 as *Clavir-Übung bestehend in Praeludien, Allemanden, Couranten, Sarabanden, Menuetten, und anderen Galanterien*. He rightly assumed that the public preferred dances to fugues.

Changes in Opera (c. 1725–90)

THE CHALLENGE TO *OPERA SERIA*

When Alessandro Scarlatti died in 1725, *opera seria* had reached its apogee although its best librettist, Pietro Metastasio (1698–1782), had only just appeared on the scene. There was no immediate decline, for Vivaldi, Caldara, Porpora, and Leo were in full production and a brilliant Venetian who had first attracted attention by his dialect comedies, Leonardo Vinci (*c.* 1695?–1730), had entered the *seria* field with his *Publio Cornelio Scipione* (1722). Handel in London was at the height of his powers and in 1721 another Italianized German, Johann Adolf Hasse (1699–1783), himself a singer – later a pupil of Porpora and, briefly, of Scarlatti, later still the husband of one of the most famous singers of the age, Faustina Bordoni – made his debut as a composer with his *Antioco* (Brunswick, 1721). But it inevitably happens that when a musical style has fully ripened, it can only over-ripen and decay. *Opera seria* might set its bounds wider still and wider, establishing itself more strongly at the Court of Madrid after the acquisition of Naples by the Spanish Bourbons in 1735 and carried to that of St Petersburg the following year by the *Forza dell' amore e dell'odio* of Francesco Araja (1709–*c.* 1770). But in its chief strongholds it was being challenged – as *tragédie-lyrique* was being challenged in France – by new and more popular forms of musical play.

The challenge, which speeded the natural process of decay, came from two sides. Opera, as we have seen (pp. 316 and 358–9) had been popularized since its inception, notably in Venice and Hamburg. But the rapidly expanding population of Europe must have lowered the standard of what was 'popular' and in any case *opera seria* was – particularly outside Italy – art for connoisseurs or those who wished to be considered as such. There were audiences eager for less sophisticated forms of musical theatre. On the other hand, as we see from Marcello's *Il teatro alla moda* (*c.* 1720) (cf. p. 383), the connoisseurs themselves were becoming dissatisfied with the conventions of 'aria opera' with its ridiculously complicated plots.

METASTASIAN OPERA

Metastasio, a genuine poet and dramatist, and a man of wide learning, did not destroy the existing conventions but he injected new life and psychological truth into them. He had an acute sense of what kinds of drama and verse were suited to music and a very clear idea of what kind of music should be married to his verse (to which he always imagined a musical setting). He restored the chorus, giving it dramatic roles when appropriate, but entrusted the *commenting* role of the chorus to solo arias which inevitably hold up the action. His first full-length libretto, *Didone abbandonata*, was set by Domenico Sarri (1679–1744) (Naples, 1724), Albinoni (Venice, 1725), and Vinci (Rome, 1726).[1] And this stampede to compose Metastasio was not unique. In 1730 his *Artaserse* was composed for Rome by Vinci, whose last opera it was, and for Venice by Hasse, who made later versions of it in 1740 and 1760;[2] it was set by dozens of later composers including Thomas Arne (1710–78) who made his own English translation in 1762.[3] Such favourite libretti were not only sometimes translated but often adapted to satisfy the whims of a singer or suit local conditions: *Alessandro nell' Indie* was written for Vinci (Rome, 1729); two years later altered versions were produced in London by Handel (*Poro, re dell' Indie*) and Dresden by Hasse (*Cleofide*);[4] it was still being composed half a century later. Equally popular were *Demetrio* (1731), *L'Olimpiade*,[5] and *Demofoonte* (both 1733), all three written for Caldara who became Metastasio's favourite composer after Vinci's death.

But Caldara died too in 1736 and Metastasio's closest and happiest association for many years – it lasted till *Ruggiero* (1771)[6] – was with Hasse. It was to Hasse that he addressed a very long letter (20 October 1749) concerning *Attilio Regolo*, in which after describing his conception of the 'physiognomy' of the various characters he goes on to express at great length and in considerable detail how he wishes his poem to be set. To begin with the recitatives, 'it seems to me that they can be animated by the instruments':

Thus in Act I I find two places where instruments can be useful to me. The first is the whole of Attilio's harangue to Manlio in scene II at the line:

A che vengo! Ah fino a quando!

After the words 'A che vengo!' the instruments should begin to make themselves heard, now resting, now accompanying or reinforcing, to give warmth to an oration already excited in itself, and I should be glad if they do not abandon Attilio until after the line

La barbara or qual è Cartago o Roma?

I believe moreover, particularly in this case, that it is necessary to guard against the

---

[1] Fac. of Vinci's setting in Brown, *Italian Opera 1640–1770*, xxix.

[2] See the comparative tables of arias in O. G. Sonneck, 'Die drei Fassungen des Hasse'schen *Artaserse*', *SIMG*, xiv (1913), p. 235. Excerpts from Vinci's setting are given in *NOHM*, v, p. 116–18, and in Donald J. Grout, *A Short History of Opera* (2nd ed., London, 1965), pp. 203–4, an aria which Hasse shamelessly plagiarized in 1760.

[3] Excerpts from Arne's *Artaxerxes* in Michael F. Robinson, *Opera before Mozart* (London, 1966), pp. 125–7, and *NOHM*, vii, p. 259.

[4] Excerpts from Vinci's *Alessandro* and Hasse's *Cleofide* are given in *NOHM*, v, pp. 119 and 143–4 respectively, in both cases with Handel's parallel settings in *Poro*. In *Original Vocal Improvisations (Das Musikwerk)* (Cologne, 1972), p. 143, Hellmuth Christian Wolff gives a complete aria from *Cleofide* in its original form and with the embellishments sung by the composer's wife.

[5] Fac. of Caldara's *Olimpiade*, Brown, op. cit., xxxii. Vivaldi's setting, the year after Caldara's, is considered to be one of the best of his fifty or so operas. His composition of Metastasio's *Siroe* (Reggio, 1727) is lost.

[6] Ed. Klaus Hortschansky (Cologne, 1973).

446

unsuitability of making the song wait more than the bass alone requires (*di far aspettare il canto più di quello che il basso esigerebbe*), for all the warmth of the oration will become tepid, and the instruments will enervate the recitative instead of animating it . . .

Again, at the end of Act II, 6, the hero has finished his 'Tu palpiti' standing and he must be given time to sit down:

For that reason, so that he may get to his seat slowly, stopping from time to time and showing himself deep in thought, and repeating if you like a few words from the beginning of the scene, the instruments must anticipate him, help him and support him . . .

This Hasse faithfully did.[7]

That *opera seria* remained very much 'aria opera' was largely due to the cult of the virtuoso soprano soloist – female like Bordoni-Hasse and Cuzzoni or castrato like Caffarelli and Farinelli. Each had to be given a certain number of arias of contrasted types – *patetica, bravura, parlante, brillante* – to display variety of accomplishment. Metastasian opera actually had fewer arias but they were much longer; Vinci in his *Artaserse* found no difficulty in expanding a simple four-line strophe into a full da capo aria ('Perche tarda e mai la morte'). But the relative paucity of arias in Metastasio's libretti made them unacceptable in England, as the Modenese diplomat Giuseppe Riva explained:[8] 'few verses of recitative and many arias is what they want over here'. Operas from Italy had to be 'revised or rather deformed' for London – which is precisely what Niccolò Haym did with Metastasio's *Siroe* for Handel's setting in 1728.

When Handel embarked on opera management on his own account in 1729, he used two more of Metastasio's libretti – the already mentioned *Poro* (1731) and *Ezio* 'deformed' by Paolo Rolli (1732)[9] – but nothing else during his remaining nine years of operatic composition; except Vivaldi, no composer of *opera seria*, not even Porpora, was so little drawn to Metastasio. He towers above his contemporaries by the quality of his purely musical invention, particularly in this latter series in *Orlando* (1733), *Ariodante* and *Alcina* (1735), *Serse* (1738), and last of all *Deidamia* (1741). In the operas of the last three or four years he introduces a number of delightful short airs, perhaps intended to attract a wider public, but by comparison with the continental Metastasians he had become a conservative figure writing for audiences who, even if aristocratic, were connoisseurs of singing and song rather than of musical drama.

The Metastasian composers did not, of course, set only Metastasio and they were by no means consistently faithful to his dramatic ideals, but he was so overwhelmingly more popular than any other librettist that it is

---

[7] See the long excerpt in Guido Adler, *Handbuch der Musikgeschichte* (Berlin, second edition, 1930), p. 724.
[8] Letters to Muratori (1725–6), translated in Otto Erich Deutsch, *Handel: A Documentary Biography* (London, 1955), pp. 185–6 and 197.
[9] Rolli's compression of Metastasio's recitative is nicely illustrated by Ex. 82 of *NOHM*, v, where 20 bars of the original, set by Hasse the year before, are shown beside the 9 bars to which Rolli reduced them.

justifiable to speak of the mid eighteenth century as 'the Metastasian period' of *opera seria*. The most gifted of the younger composers was Giovanni Battista Pergolesi (1710–36) whose best serious opera was *L'Olimpiade* (Rome, 1735)[10] in which he shows his command of genuine pathos:

Ex. 156

He had already shown his command of mock pathos in Tracollo's 'A una povera Polacca' in *Livietta et Tracollo*,[11] intermezzi in another Metastasio opera, *Adriano in Siria* (Naples, 1734). And this was not his first incursion into a field which was to bring him far more fame than any of his serious operas and was in fact to produce a genre ultimately fatal to *opera seria* itself.

DIALECT COMEDY AND COMIC INTERMEZZI

Comedy had long played a part in Italian opera. *Buffo* scenes for servants and suchlike, often in dialect, had been common enough in Scarlatti and his contemporaries (see p. 364). And at Naples there was a special cult of the dialect *cummedeja in museca* from 1709 onward, in which Vinci had participated with his *Lo cecato fauzo* (1719), *Le zite 'n galera* (1722),[12] Leo with *La 'mpeca scoperta* (1723), and other works by both. Side by side with these there had grown up the practice of removing the *buffo* scenes from serious opera and compensating for their loss by intercalating two *buffo* acts, with entirely independent characters and action, between the acts of an *opera seria*. Domenico Sarri, for instance, inserted intermezzi (*Dorina e Nibbio*) in his pioneer setting of Metastasio's *Didone* (1724). And Pergolesi, having first attracted attention with a Neapolitan dialect comedy, *Lo frate 'nnamorato* (1732),[13] asked its librettist – Gennaro Federico – to supply the

[10] Fac. ed. Brown, op. cit., xxxiv; vocal score in the not very satisfactory *Opera Omnia*, ed. Filippo Caffarelli (Rome, 1939–43), xxiv. Parallel quotations with Leo's *L'Olimpiade* (1737) in *NOHM*, v, pp. 125–6.
[11] *Opera Omnia*, xi. A mock tragic recitative and aria, also for Tracollo, are given in Carl Parrish, *A Treasury of Early Music* (London, 1959), p. 317.
[12] Fac. Brown, op. cit., xxv; excerpts in Nicolo d'Arienzo, 'Le origini dell'opera comica', *Rivista musicale italiana*, vi (1899), p. 473.
[13] *Opera Omnia*, ii. A thematic catalogue of Pergolesi's complete works has been compiled by Marvin Paymer (New York, 1977).

text for intermezzi to his serious opera, *Il prigioniero superbo* (Naples, 1733);[14] the result, which like most successful intermezzi assumed an independent existence, was *La serva padrona*.[15] This is one of those works which, though by no means prototypes, have come to be regarded as prototypes – largely in this case because of the furore aroused by its second production in Paris in 1752 (see below, p. 456). Its two singing characters – there is also a mute part – rich old man and scheming maid, are just as much stock figures as Metastasio's virtuous heroes and heroines and magnanimous monarchs, and the comic idiom of rapid and exaggerated repetition of words and musical motives was well established: for instance in Vinci's intermezzi *Serpilla e Bacocco* (also known as *Il giocatore*) (Venice, 1718).[16] But Pergolesi's transparent, totally uncontrapuntal score is very delightful and he manipulates his puppets with uncommon skill, giving them a semblance of flesh and blood, and introducing, for instance, a melodic tic common at the time, symptomatic of the approach of 'sensibility':

Ex. 157

[14] Ibid., xx.
[15] Ibid., xi; miniature full score, ed. Karl Geiringer (Vienna, 1925); duet concluding the first intermezzo in *HAM*, ii, No. 287.
[16] See the excerpt in *NOHM*, v, p. 121.

22. Changes in Opera (c. 1725–90)

ENGLISH BALLAD OPERA

Opera seria had already been challenged in England by a rival less elegant than *opera buffa*. In 1728 John Gay produced a low-life satire partly on contemporary politics and politicians, partly on Handelian opera and its *prime donne*, entitled *The Beggar's Opera*. The music consisted of popular tunes of the day, including some by Purcell, Handel, and other known composers; these were harmonized by Pepusch who had been one of the pioneers of *pasticcio* opera (see p. 370) and who contributed a 'French' overture with a fugue subject partly based on Lucy's 'I'm like a skiff on the Ocean tost' in Act III. The music contributes little or nothing to the drama but includes more haunting simple tunes than any Italian opera. It was enormously successful and other 'ballad operas' quickly followed. The most notable of these was *The Devil to Pay* (1731) (text by Charles Coffey; music arranged by the German musical director of Drury Lane, 'Seedo' or Sidow). This was translated into German and performed in Berlin, probably with the original tunes, in 1743 and again as *Der Teufel ist los* in a new translation and with fresh music by J. C. Standfuss (d. *c.* 1759) (Leipzig, 1752).[17] It thus became the forerunner of a new type of *Singspiel*: comic opera with spoken dialogue – unlike *opera buffa* which always retained recitative.

THE PRECURSORS OF *OPÉRA COMIQUE*

It is tempting to claim *The Beggar's Opera* and *Der Teufel ist los*, like *La serva padrona*, as 'prototypes'; in fact they only crystallized hitherto inchoate types of musical theatre. To some extent this is true also of French *opéra comique* but the crystallization was long delayed. The term *opéra comique* was first applied to some of the performances of the *comédiens italiens du Roy* before their expulsion on grounds of indecency in 1697. They mixed music with words, and the music consisted of *vaudevilles* (popular street tunes), airs like those mentioned in Chapter 19, and quite often *airs* from Lully's operas – all provided with new texts, of course. This sort of entertainment was carried on at a lower level at the two annual Paris fairs, the Foire Saint-Germain and the Foire Saint-Laurent, and the term *opéra comique* was used once more by the two companies performing at Saint-Germain in 1715 when they were given official recognition by the Opera proper (the Académie royale de musique). The new set-up was inaugurated with a parody by Le Sage, *Télémaque*, but as yet pieces with a plot and continuous action were exceptional and the nature of the music may be judged from this vaudeville in *Télémaque*:

---

[17] One song in Schering, *Geschichte der Musik in Beispielen*, No. 309a.

Ex. 158

Le grand dieu Nep - tune est en co - lè - re; Ho, ho! Tou - re - lou - ri -

-bo! Rien ne peut le sa - tis - fai - re: Ho, ho! Tou - re - lou - ri - bo!

Le Sage wrote for the Foire off and on until 1738, and from 1723 onward Rameau contributed original numbers to pieces by Alexis Piron. One of these – for a display by two Louisiana Indians – he published as 'Les Sauvages' in his *Nouvelles Suites de Pièces de Clavecin* (*c.* 1728); he used it again in the final *entrée* of his *ballet héroïque*, *Les Indes galantes* (1735), the libretto of which – an early example of an American subject – was by Louis Fuzelier, one of the Foire writers. Mouret also composed for the Foire.

But while the number and quality of original contributions rose, the music still consisted of hotch-potches even after the advent of Charles-Simon Favart, a brilliant librettist who is justly regarded as the literary founder of true *opéra comique*. Favart's first great success, *La Chercheuse d'esprit* (1741), was musically a mixture of parodied Lully, vaudevilles, and a very little original composition. (Rameau had already joined Lully as a victim; Favart's *Les Amours de Gogo* (1739), based on his *Fêtes d'Hébé*, was forbidden by the police, but *Arlequin Dardanus* was given at the Théâtre-Italien two months after the opera itself.) The ingredients of *opéra comique* all existed; it was *La serva padrona* that induced the catalysis – but not until 1752.

ITALIAN OPERAS OF THE MID-CENTURY

By 1752, however, *opera buffa* had not developed much either. The composers of Pergolesi's generation, who survived him by many years, were almost exclusively interested in *seria* and Metastasio was still the favourite poet. The one rather older man in whose hands comic opera – *commedia musicale* rather than intermezzi – was maturing was Leonardo Leo. But he died in 1744 aged only 50, after demonstrating in *Amor vuol sofferenze* (also known as *La finta Frascatana* and *Il cioè*) (Naples 1739) that a ridiculous, pompous character need not be a puppet:[18]

---

[18] Antiphonal orchestras were an old, if unusual, operatic device employed by Scarlatti, e.g. in *La caduta dei Decemviri*, and more recently by Pergolesi in *Adriano in Siria* (1734).

Ex. 159

that light music need not be flimsy, and that he possessed a fund of enchanting melody. Act I ends with an embryonic form of later comic finale: an ensemble in which, after the climax, one character is left alone on the stage. But Leo was a rather isolated figure; nearest to him stands Nicola Logroscino (1698–1765), whose importance seems to have been overrated.[19] Although Hasse, working away at the virtually complete composition of Metastasio, did not disdain occasional intermezzi,[20] his younger compatriot, Carl Heinrich Graun (1704?–1759) apparently did. Enticed away from Brunswick, where he had been writing German operas, by the future Frederick the Great, Graun settled down at the newly built Berlin Hofoper to produce *opere serie*. These included the customary grapplings with *Artaserse* (1743),[21] *Demofoonte* (1746), and other Metastasian libretti but also – in accordance with his royal master's French tastes – Italian translations of Corneille, Racine, and Quinault.

The younger Italians – Baldassare Galuppi (1706–85), Egidio-Romoaldo Duni (1709–75), Davide Perez (1711–78), Domingo Terradellas (1713–51) (really an Italianized Catalan), Niccolò Jommelli (1714–74) – poured out almost nothing but *opere serie*, the vast majority Metastasian, during the 1730s and 1740s and indeed in some cases afterwards. The same is true of

---

[19] Fac. of his *Governadore* (Naples, 1747), Brown, op. cit., xlii; the Act I finale is printed as a supplement to Kretzschmar, *Gesammelte Aufsätze über Musik*, ii (Leipzig, 1911).
[20] *La contadina astuta* printed in Pergolesi's *Opera Omnia*, xi, is his.
[21] Fac. in Brown, op. cit., xl.

Jommelli's exact contemporary, Christoph Willibald Gluck (1714–87), who began his career with settings of *Artaserse* (1741) and *Demofoonte* (1742) and, except for participation in a few *pasticci*, continued with Metastasio or Metastasio's literary disciples until the middle 1750s. Actually Jommelli had begun with two comic operas for Naples, *L'errore amoroso* (1737) and *Odoardo* (1738), and the librettist of the first one, Antonio Palomba, who also wrote the libretto of Terradellas's only *commedia*, tempted him again into the comic field with *L'amore in maschera* in 1749. In the same year he also produced *Don Trastullo*, the first of his few intermezzi – and the inevitable *Artaserse*; indeed he continued composing Metastasio till the end of his life. The one notable exception was a rather dim figure, Rinaldo di Capua (*c.* 1710–after 1770), who composed only a few *serie* (including a *Didone* given at Lisbon in 1741) but obviously preferred the comic vein. This he began to work in 1738 with *La commedia in commedia* for Rome; his intermezzi *La donna superba* and *La Zingara* were given in 1752 and 1753 respectively in Paris where they rivalled the *Serva padrona*.

Galuppi, after composing a series of Metastasio operas, was diverted by a dramatist as different as possible from Metastasio, yet no less distinguished: Carlo Goldoni. The poet of exalted antiquity was supplanted (though not finally till 1760) by the poet of everyday Venetian contemporaneity. Goldoni had given Galuppi a serious libretto, *Gustavo primo, Re di Svezia* as early as 1740. But it was only in 1749 – the year also of his *Artaserse* and *Demofoonte* – that Galuppi composed *L'Arcadia in Brenta* (Venice, 1749), and then *Il mondo della luna* and *Il mondo alla roversa* (1750), his masterpiece *Il filosofo di campagna* (1754),[22] and a series of others until he was invited to St Petersburg by Catherine II in 1756. These were three-act works in which, beside plentiful opportunities for satire, light-handed rhythmic wit and sparkle, and delicious tunes, Goldoni offered the composer real characters (e.g. Nardo, the 'peasant philosopher') and real feelings to express, as in Lena's song in Act I of the same opera:

Ex. 160

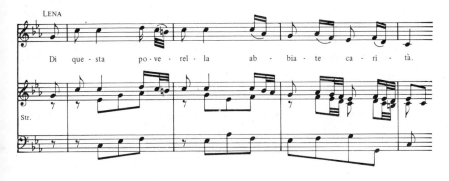

---

[22] Vocal score, ed. Virgilio Mortari (Milan, 1938). One aria in *HAM*, ii, No. 285.

Galuppi was no longer tied to the da capo aria but would cast a solo in two contrasted sections. He also seems to have been the pioneer of the so-called 'chain finale', ending an act with a series of short sections in which the music was entirely controlled by the stage action.

Duni changed course even more drastically. He produced the last of his Metastasio operas, *Olimpiade*, in 1754 at the court of the Francophile Duke of Parma, where the French company was performing Lully and Rameau, and was persuaded to set two French libretti – Favart's three-act *Ninette à la cour, ou Le caprice amoureux* (partly a pasticcio) (1755) and his old *Chercheuse d'esprit* (1756) – as well as an Italian *melodramma giocosa*, Goldoni's *La buona figliuola* (based on Richardson's novel *Pamela*) (also 1756). He hankered after a Paris production of a third French work, *Le Peintre amoureux de son modèle* (1757), and its immediate success at the Foire Saint-Laurent decided him to settle there and spend the rest of his life composing *opéras comiques*.

RAMEAU AS THE HEIR OF LULLY

In France the old French-versus-Italian polemic (see p. 377, n. 87) had long been revived. Couperin's 'réunion des Goûts' was a dream-armistice which ended when Rameau at the age of fifty, after tentative dabblings in theatre music, brought out his first *tragédie lyrique*, *Hippolyte et Aricie*, in 1733. *Hippolyte* was followed by *Castor et Pollux* (1737), *Dardanus* (1739), and the *opéra-ballets Les Indes galantes* (1735) and *Les Fêtes d'Hébé* (1739).[23] They were, from overture to final or near-final chaconne, 'Lullyan operas transposed from the key of Louis XIV to the key of Louis XV', as someone has said. Rameau himself wrote in the preface to *Les Indes galantes*:

Toujours occupé de la belle déclamation et du beau tour de Chant qui règnent dans le récitatif du grand Lully, je tâche de l'imiter, non en copiste servile, mais en prenant comme lui la belle et simple nature pour modèle.

Yet each, from *Hippolyte* onward, provoked a storm of controversy in which the name and works of Lully were constantly invoked by the hostile critics who found Rameau's scores unintelligible, lacking in melody, dissonant, too 'learned', and over-orchestrated. It was perhaps against the Italianate works of Campra and Mouret that they were measured, for it was the want of Italian qualities that the self-called *lullistes* complained of. And the fact that Rameau had published a *Traité de l'Harmonie réduite à ses principes naturels*

---

[23] The only important full score not included in the *Oeuvres complètes* is *Zoroastre*, which has been ed. Françoise Gervais (Paris, 1964).

[24] A typical product of the Age of Reason which did much to encourage a 'vertical' (harmonic) rather than 'horizontal' (contrapuntal) approach in the teaching of composition by putting forward a scientifically based, logical harmonic system instead of the empirical addition of chords to the basso continuo. One of Rameau's conceptions was that of a *basse fondamentale* ('root') which was not necessarily the actual bass: e.g. the 6/3 chord on E and the 6/4 on G had the same root as the triad on C, of which they were *renversements*. Chords of the seventh and so on were built up in thirds from the *basse fondamentale*. In all this, as in his other theories of chord-formation and dissonance treatment, Rameau laid the foundations of harmony teaching for nearly two hundred years. Important excerpts from the *Traité* are translated in Oliver Strunk, *Source Readings in Music History* (London, 1952), p. 564.

(1722)[24] and a number of other theoretical writings prejudiced amateurs against a 'learned' musician.

Rameau's harmonic vocabulary is certainly more varied than Lully's and his orchestral palette is richer; his orchestra includes pairs of flutes, oboes, and bassoons (plus, of course, horns in a hunting scene), used independently of the strings, and it is employed with bravura, e.g. the 'thunder' in *Hippolyte* (I.4) and the boiling waves (III.9) suggested by demisemiquaver string scales in contrary motion. Most astonishing of all is the passage, 'Où cours-tu, malheureux?' in the trio of the Parcae (II.5), with its division of functions: sustained woodwind chords and two separate string patterns (violins divisi).[25] (We hear the beginning of modern orchestration.) In marked contrast, in the older style he gets delightful effects with solo flute and strings only: Aricie's 'Temple sacré' (I.1), Phèdre's 'Cruelle mère' (III.1), Aricie asleep (V.3) – where he successfully challenges comparison with Lully's sleeping Renaud in *Armide*, as he was to challenge the dream scene in *Atys* with the one in *Dardanus* (IV.1) – and the shepherdess's 'Rossignols amoureux' in the last scene of all. Or he will be content with the purely Lullyan trio of two oboes and bassoon for delightful little dances.

Rameau's basic conception of opera is purely Lullyan and owes nothing to Italian *opera seria*. Whereas the contrast of recitative and aria is more marked than ever in Metastasian opera, it is nearly indistinct in Rameau. He will descend with the greatest skill from the emotional height of a great monologue like Thésée's 'Puissant maître des flots' (*Hippolyte*, III.9) to a lower one, using fragments of orchestral accompaniment to cover the transition. He can write beautiful melodies but gives them as often to instruments as to the voice; if a singer has a coloratura passage (e.g. L'Amour's 'flammes' in the final scene of the Prologue) it is picturesque, not virtuosic display; when one of her followers has one on 'enchaînez' a little earlier, the singer is only repeating note for note what the orchestra has already played half-a-dozen times. The two great *opéra-ballets* naturally aim more at entertainment and admit, for instance, an increase – always textually justified – of vocal coloratura; they became really popular, particularly *Les Indes galantes*.

Perhaps discouraged by so much adverse criticism Rameau withdrew from the scene for several years, reappearing with a drastic rewriting of *Dardanus* in 1744. The next year he contributed, on royal command, two works to the wedding celebrations of the Dauphin at Versailles: a *comédie-ballet* on Voltaire's *Princesse de Navarre*, and a *comédie lyrique*, *Platée*. In both of these occasional Italianate traits appear: the finale of the three-movement, non-Lullyan overture to the *Princesse*, the bravura da capo *ariettes* for La Folie in *Platée* (II.5 and III.4). But his powers were failing. Except for the one-act ballet *Pygmalion* (1748) and the *tragédie lyrique Zoroastre* (1749), he wrote little more of significance. But the overture to *Zoroastre* is again symptomatic of change; for one thing, it is programmatic

---

[25] *Oeuvres complètes*, vi, p. 183. The passage is quoted in full score in Girdlestone, *Jean-Philippe Rameau* (London, 1957), p. 154.

– the dotted-rhythm first section depicts the tyranny of Abramane, the brief second a rebirth of hope, the third the triumph of Zoroastre; for another, this third movement is based on two themes suggesting the style of Johann Stamitz whose symphonies were just becoming known in Paris (see below, p. 488). Ex. 161 (ii) is ultimately brought back in the tonic key.

Ex. 161

THE *QUERELLE DES BOUFFONS*

Now in his old age Rameau was to be drawn into the bitterest of all the campaigns of the Franco-Italian war, sparked off by a revival of Destouches' *Omphale* in January 1752. This provoked the Baron von Grimm, an aggressive young German who had settled in Paris, to publish a *Lettre sur Omphale* attacking French opera and praising Italian, which he had known in Dresden, though paying tribute to the 'sublime' *Platée* and 'divine' *Pygmalion*. In April Grimm's friend, Jean-Jacques Rousseau (1712–78), joined anonymously in the ensuing skirmish of pamphlets with a *Lettre à M. Grimm* in which Rameau was damned with very faint praise indeed. And then on 1 August a little Italian company opened a series of performances at the Opera with *La serva padrona* (prefaced with an overture by Telemann), which had been given in Paris in 1746 and fallen completely flat. Now it created a sensation. The Italians followed it with a *Giocatore* (probably a pasticcio version), *Il maestro di musica*[26] by Pietro Auletta (c. 1698–1771) and others, and Rinaldo di Capua's *La donna superba*. Next year they gave

[26] Ed. Caffarelli in Pergolesi, *Opera Omnia*, xxv.

Pergolesi's *Livietta e Tracollo*, Rinaldo di Capua's *La Zingara*, and Jommelli's *Il paratajo*, among other works. The success was enormous and provoked the pamphlet war known as the *querelle des bouffons* between the pro-Italian faction and the patriots – the *bouffons* were of course the Italian company. Rousseau fired off a *Lettre sur la musique française* and Grimm his *Le petit prophète de Boehmisch-Broda* (both in 1753).[27] Grimm's is a heavy-handed skit, Rousseau's a reasoned if not always a reasonable attack on the aesthetic of French opera, particularly on the Lully-Rameau type of recitative, to which Rameau himself replied in *Observations sur notre instinct pour la musique* (1754).

THE RETURN TO NATURE

Rousseau had already given a practical demonstration of his ideas in the words and music of a one-act *intermède*, *Le Devin du village*.[28] It was performed before the King at Fontainebleau on 18 October 1752 with overture and recitatives by other hands but repeated at the Académie royale on 1 March next year with the composer's own recitatives and probably his own overture. It is an attempt at an Italian intermezzo in French and, despite its terribly jejune music, it had numerous performances not only in France. It is historically important solely on account of its subject which embodies a great deal of the essence of Rousseauism: simple sentiment, return to nature, justice for the common people. Colette's opening ariette, which quickly became immensely popular, is a fair example of Rousseau's melodic invention:

Ex. 162

It is twice interrupted by her secco recitative, in which every couple of bars or so have such indications as 'ferme', 'ironie et dépit', 'animé', 'douleur', 'menace', 'douleur tendre'.

[27] Excerpts from both in Strunk, op. cit., pp. 636 and 619 respectively.
[28] The best modern vocal score is ed. C. Chaix (Geneva, 1924); full score ed. Roger Cotte. The final *vaudeville* – strophic song for the soloists, with choral refrain – is given in *HAM*, ii, No. 291.

Six months later Favart put on a parody, *Les Amours de Bastien et Bastienne*.[29] This also made theatrical history, for Mme Favart, who played Bastienne, insisted on dressing like a real peasant girl in a simple linen dress with simple hair-style and wooden sabots, a sensational innovation. The text was also closer to nature than Rousseau's for it imitated peasant speech; the tunes were mostly popular ones – for instance, instead of Colette's opening *ariette*, Bastienne sang 'J'ai perdu mon ami' to the tune of 'J'ai perdu mon âne'. But they also included one from *Titon et l'Aurore*, a new work by Jean-Joseph Mondonville (1711–72), who was succeeding Rameau as the champion of French serious opera, as well as one from the *Devin* itself.

Pl. 49 Justine Favart as Bastienne in *Les Amours de Bastien et Bastienne* (1753), after a portrait by Charles-André Vanloo. She made theatrical history by dressing as a real peasant girl.

[29] A German version of the text was composed by the 12-year-old Mozart in 1768.

458

In this same year (1753) Antoine Dauvergne (1713–97) brought out *Les Troqueurs*, a one-act *intermède* much more Italianate than *Le Devin*; it was in fact originally passed off as the work of an Italian composer and deceived the *bouffonistes*. Favart poured out comic works of every kind: parodies, as of Mondonville's *Titon* (*Raton et Rosette*), translations of the *Serva padrona* and then of the other things performed by the *bouffons*. Duni came to Paris (cf. above, p. 454), and in 1756 François-André Philidor (1726–95), hitherto better known as a chess-player and writer on chess (though he came of a dynasty of musicians), put together a pasticcio setting of a translation of *The Devil to Pay* (see p. 450) for the Foire Saint-Laurent. He went on to give the Foire a one-act piece of his own, *Blaise le savetier* (1759), and followed it with a number of other, mostly one-act, operas of which the most popular was *Le Maréchal ferrant* (1761). At the same time Pierre-Alexandre Monsigny (1729–1816) appeared on the scene with *Les Aveux indiscrets* (1759) and *Le Cadi dupé* (1761). (By an odd chance Gluck also set the same libretto, by Pierre Lemonnier, the same year; it was the sixth of the *opéras comiques* he had written since 1758 for the Viennese court where, under a Francophile Intendant of the Imperial Theatres, Count Durazzo, French comedy was in vogue.) With these three – Duni, Philidor, and Monsigny – *opéra comique*, always with spoken dialogue, reached its mature form, officially acknowledged by the amalgamation of the Foire company with the Comédie italienne in 1762.

THE REJUVENATION OF ITALIAN OPERA

1762 was also a notable date in the history of *opera seria*, for on 5 October Gluck's *Orfeo ed Euridice* was produced at the Burgtheater, Vienna (see below, p. 464). Italian opera had recently been rejuvenated by a number of composers younger than Galuppi and Jommelli, all Neapolitans by birth or education: Tommaso Traetta (1727–79), Pasquale Anfossi (1727–97), Niccolò Piccinni (1728–1800), Pietro Guglielmi (1728–1804), Antonio Sacchini (1730–86), and Gian Francesco di Majo (1732–70). Their view of opera was shared by Bach's youngest son, Johann Christian (1735–82), who had gone to Italy to study in 1756, and they were soon joined by Giovanni Paisiello (1740–1816). To all of them except di Majo, opera was an affair of music rather than of drama. Metastasio was still their favourite librettist – Traetta's first notable successes were *Didone* (1757), *Olimpiade* and *Demofoonte* (both 1758), di Majo set nine Metastasio libretti,[30] J. C. Bach started his career with *Artaserse* and *Catone* (both 1761) and *Alessandro nell' Indie* in 1762 – but they translated him into a very different musical idiom, as

---

[30] Fac. of his *Adriano in Siria* in Brown, op. cit., xlix. Poro's 'Se mai più saro geloso' in Act I of di Majo's *Alessandro nell' Indie* (1766) is given complete in Bücken, *Musik des Rokokos und der Klassik* (Potsdam, 1929).

we may see by comparing Bach's setting of the First Act duet in *Alessandro*[31] with Handel's of thirty years earlier.[32] Handel's melody is a reminder of a solemn oath, Bach's a charming piece of 'sensibility'. The difference between Handel's passionate setting of Cleofide's 'Digli ch'è il mio tesoro' in Act II and Bach's elegant one is still more striking:

Ex. 163

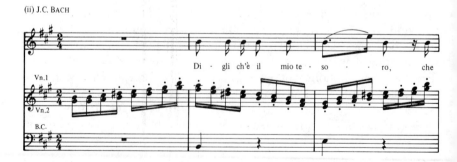

[31] Quoted in *NOHM*, vii, p. 46.
[32] *Werke*, xxvii, p. 34.

m'a - mi, ch'io l'a - do - ro,

Incidentally Bach's anticipation of Mozart's *Don Giovanni* minuet was paralleled also in 1762 by di Majo's even closer anticipation of 'Vedrai, carino' in Semira's 'Bramar di perdere' in *Artaserse*.

The role of the orchestra was becoming more significant, particularly with Jommelli, who was serving a Rameau-loving duke at Stuttgart, and with Traetta who during 1758–65 was at Parma, where Duni had changed his heart after hearing Lully and Rameau. Their orchestra was important not only in the accompaniment of arias but particularly in the *recitativi accompagnati* where its interjections are quasi-thematic, as in Traetta's *Sofonisba* (1762) and *Ifigenia in Tauride* (1763), a real masterpiece,[33] and in Jommelli's *Fetonte* (1768).[34] The Neapolitans frequently introduced and accompanied their arias, which were less and less often full da capo ones, with elegant orchestral passages of melting sweetness like the introductions to 'Bell' alma se ancora' in Piccinni's *Ciroe* (1759) and Jove's aria in the First Act of di Majo's *Astrea placata* (1760),[35] and the Son's aria in Act III of Traetta's *Sofonisba*.[36]

Ex. 164

(i) PICCINNI
Ob. solo

[33] Both are notable for their vocal ensembles and whole 'composed-through' scenes – such as that of the Furies in *Ifigenia* (II.4). Fac. of them both in Brown, op. cit., xlvii.
[34] See the excerpts from these operas in *NOHM*, vii, pp. 36–41. *Fetonte* has been ed. complete by Hermann Abert, *DDT*, xxxii–xxxiii; excerpts from the Traetta works by Hugo Goldschmidt in *DTB*, xiv (1) and xvii.
[35] Quoted by Hermann Abert, *W. A. Mozart* (Leipzig, 1919), i, pp. 251 and 236. For an example of di Majo's dramatic power, see Orestes' prayer in his *Ifigenia in Tauride* (1764), quoted in Martin Cooper, *Gluck* (London, 1935), p. 32.
[36] Ed. Goldschmidt, *DTB*, xvii, p. 157.

(ii) DI MAJO

(iii) TRAETTA

Piccinni often employs the techniques and idioms of comic opera in his serious works; conversely in his comic *Cecchina ossia la buona figliuola* (1760),[37] on the Goldoni libretto already set by Duni, his Cecchina is truly Richardson's Pamela, a creature of charm and pathos:

Ex. 165

SENTIMENT IN *OPÉRA COMIQUE*

Something very similar developed in *opéra comique*. Just as the buffoonery of the intermezzi and dialect *commedie musicali* were refined and emotionally filled out as in the *Figliuola*, so the vaudevilles of the Foire had no sooner

---

[37] Ed. Giacomo Benvenuti, *I classici musicali italiani*, vii.

developed into a form marked by such accomplished works as Monsigny's *Rose et Colas* (1764) and Philidor's *Tom Jones* (1765)[38] than *opéra comique* began – with Duni's *École de la jeunesse* (1765) and the *Lucile* (1769)[39] of André-Ernest-Modeste Grétry (1741–1813), an admirer of the *Figliuola* – to sound the *larmoyant* note[40] introduced in the non-musical theatre some years earlier. In Monsigny's *Le Déserteur* (1769) it went further, broke into accompanied recitative at two points, and nearly touched the tragic. Monsigny and Philidor were actually emboldened to compose *tragédies lyriques*: *Aline* (1766) and *Ernelinde* (1767).[41] Philidor's is stylistically not so very different from *Tom Jones* but with recitative – lively Italianate recitative, both *secco* and accompanied – instead of spoken dialogue.

GLUCK IN VIENNA

It is against a background of French influence and 'bourgeois sensibility' invading every kind of opera and undermining the pompous classicism of both *tragédie lyrique* and *opera seria* that we see Gluck's *Orfeo* (1762) and *Alceste* (Vienna, 1767)[42] in true perspective, not simply as essays in the 'reform' of Metastasian *opera seria*.

After his *Artaserse* of 1741 he had during the next twenty years composed more than a dozen other Metastasio libretti. Then under the Durazzo regime in Vienna he was composing a series of *opéras comiques* and in 1761 what is perhaps the earliest of independent, genuinely dramatic ballets,[43] *Don Juan*, to a scenario based on Molière's *Festin de pierre*, and inspired by the *Lettres sur la danse, et sur les ballets* (Lyons, 1760),[44] of the Stuttgart ducal ballet-master Noverre. Gluck's next work was *Orfeo ed Euridice*, an *azione teatrale per musica* to mark the nameday of the Emperor. The libretto was not by Metastasio, though he was still the Court poet; instead, Durazzo commissioned it from his friend Ranieri Calzabigi, who totally rejected the complicated Metastasian type of plot but retained a good deal of Metastasian diction (including cliché phrases), and produced a poem that is less, not more, dramatic than the typical Metastasio effort: the simple myth-with-a-happy-ending and the fewest possible trimmings. This libretto was revolutionary; the music with which Gluck clothed it was not. He writes *recitativi accompagnati* on the lines Jommelli and Traetta were following at the same time and although he innovates by supporting *secco* recitative with

[38] The First Act duet from *Tom Jones* is quoted in *NOHM*, vii, p. 213, the Second Act duet in Michael Robinson, *Opera before Mozart* (London, 1966), p. 155.
[39] Ed. François Fétis, François Gevaert, *et al.*, *Collection complète des oeuvres de Grétry* (Leipzig and Brussels, 1883–1936), ii. The quartet 'Où peut-on être mieux qu'au sein de sa famille' in *Lucile* enjoyed enormous popularity in France for more than half a century.
[40] There was no doubt a direct influence from Richardson whose works had, according to Horace Walpole (letter of 31 August 1765), 'stupefied the whole French nation'.
[41] Vocal score of Philidor's *Ernelinde* by César Franck (Paris, 1883).
[42] *Sämtliche Werke*, ed. Rudolf Gerber *et al.* (Kassel, 1951–   ), Series 1, i and vii.
[43] Rameau's *Pygmalion* still embodies vocal remnants of opera.
[44] English edition, *Letters on Dancing and Ballets*, by Cyril Beaumont (London, 1930). Noverre advocated the replacement of 'artificial' formal ballet by a combination of pantomime with dancing, the *ballet d'action*.

string chords instead of keyboard continuo the nature of the recitative itself is unchanged. The organization of e.g. the opening of Act I as a complex of chorus and recitative followed by strophic song alternating with recitative, and the entire scene in Hades, derives from Rameau. So does the extensive employment of ballet and chorus. What stamps *Orfeo* as a work of genius is the skill with which Gluck welds together elements of *opera seria* and *tragédie lyrique* so that no one notices their disparity, the dramatic power of the first two acts, and such imaginings as the exquisite 'Che puro ciel' in which the finesse of the orchestration[45] surpasses anything of its kind that had preceded it.

How little Gluck regarded himself as a reformer of opera may be seen from his next works: a setting – with bravura coloratura arias – of Metastasio's *Trionfo di Clelia* (1763) which Hasse had composed the year before, *La rencontre imprévue* (1764),[46] his best *opéra comique* (later performed in German translation as a *Singspiel, Die Pilgrimme von Mecca*), the one-act *Parnaso confuso* (1765)[47] specially written for him by Metastasio, and *Telemacco* (also 1765)[48] on a cut-down version of an *opera seria* libretto which Scarlatti had composed in 1718. In 1769, after *Alceste*, he was willing to insert a long and empty bravura aria at the end of Act I of *Orfeo* for the castrato Giuseppe Millico – and to keep it as the *ariette (sic)* 'L'espoir renaît' in the Paris version of the opera.

GLUCK'S REGENERATION OF ITALIAN OPERA

It was not until the *tragedia in musica Alceste* (1767) and his, or Calzabigi's, dedicatory manifesto when the score was published two years later, that he frankly stepped forward as a reformer.[49] He and his poet, he claims, had avoided 'florid descriptions and sententious morality'; ritornelli holding up the action, the da capo, 'superfluity of ornaments'; 'sharp contrast between aria and recitative' which could be softened by the treatment of 'the concerted instruments'. 'The overture ought to apprise the spectators of the nature of the action.' Above all he had striven for 'a beautiful simplicity'. This was open revolt against Metastasian *opera seria*, though similar criticisms had been made before, notably by the polymath Francesco Algarotti in his *Saggio sopra l'opera in musica* (1755).[50] And Diderot in the third *entretien* to his play *Le Fils naturel* (1757) had made positive suggestions foreshadowing Gluck's aesthetic.

[45] Quoted in score in Alfred Einstein, *Gluck* (London, 1936), p. 75, and Guido Adler, *Handbuch der Musikgeschichte* (second ed., Berlin, 1930), ii, p. 731. The magic lies entirely in the orchestration. Gluck had already used the musical substance – the oboe solo, the horn sounds, the violin sestuplet semiquaver figure – in the introductions to arias in *Ezio* (1750) (to paint the murmuring of a brook) and *Antigono* (1756) (Demetrio's farewell to life, taking its cue from the words 'l'onda fatal', the 'fatal wave'). Both passages are quoted in score by Ernst Kurth, 'Die Jugendopern Glucks', *Studien zur Musikwissenschaft*, i (Vienna, 1913), pp. 239–44.
[46] *Werke*, Series 4, vii.
[47] *Werke*, Series 3, xxv.
[48] Ibid., Series 1, ii.
[49] Complete English translation of the dedication in Einstein, op. cit., p. 98, and Strunk, op. cit., p. 673.
[50] Long excerpt in Strunk, ibid., p. 657.

Rameau's *tragédie lyrique* did not suffer from these defects of *opera seria* and, as we have seen (p. 455–6), he had composed a programmatic opera overture twenty years before. So for that matter had Gluck himself; the overture to his *Contesa de' numi* (1749) certainly suggests the 'contest of the divinities'[51] and he prefaced his *opéra comique L'isle de Merlin* (1758)[52] with an *ouverture descriptive* (storm and shipwreck – calm and rescue) which he had little difficulty in adapting as the introduction to *Iphigénie en Tauride* (1779). The overture to *Alceste*, in D minor and scored for a large orchestra with horns and three trombones, does indeed 'apprise the spectators' of an action on tragic heights. And the action itself, though not as skeletal as that of *Orfeo*, is stripped of inessentials and marches inevitably to the happy ending, matched by music of great dramatic power (e.g. the Oracle's brass-accompanied 'Il rè morrà s'altri per lui non muore') and made memorable by Alceste's great free-form arias, 'Ombre! larve! compagne di morte' (better known with the later text, 'Divinités du Styx'), 'Ah, per questo', 'Non vi turbate'. But soloists and chorus interchange freely and naturally, as the action demands.

GLUCK'S FRENCH OPERAS

Gluck's third and last collaboration with Calzabigi, *Paride ed Elena* (Vienna, 1770),[53] was a failure despite the – for Gluck – unusually sensuous beauty of much of the music. His essays in the regeneration of Italian opera with elements of *tragédie lyrique* were over, but after a fallow period he opened an epoch in *tragédie lyrique* itself with the production in Paris in 1774 of the *tragédie-opéra Iphigénie en Aulide*.[54] This was on a libretto adapted from Racine by a French diplomat, François du Roullet, and was followed four months later by a drastically revised version of *Orfeo: Orphée et Eurydice*.[55] (In 1776 came a still more drastic revision, with du Roullet's collaboration, of *Alceste*; these revisions in accordance with French taste, involving additional ballet and the transformation of Orpheus from male alto to tenor, were by no means all for the better.) *Iphigénie* also made use of a great deal of borrowed material – including the opening phrase of the overture (and Agamemnon) which comes from *Telemacco* – and is a remarkable amalgam of French and Italian styles and methods. The French text is set most scrupulously as Italianate recitative; there are half a dozen da capo arias (one actually so marked), Achilles' 'Cours et dis-lui' (Act II) that Rameau might have written, Iphigenia's 'Adieu, conservez' (Act III) which could be by Traetta, and the final shattering D minor unison for chorus and orchestra (with bass drum) after the conventional D major chaconne, which only Gluck could have thought of. But above all there are extended scenes like that between Achilles and Agamemnon, and Agamemnon's monologue, at

---

[51] See the excerpts in Kurth, op. cit., p. 225.
[52] *Werke*, Series 4, i.
[53] Ibid., Series 1, iv.
[54] Ibid., Series 1, v.
[55] Ibid., Series 1, vi.

the end of Act II, or Clytemnestra's swoon in Act III, to say nothing of innumerable subtle details elsewhere, which surpass in dramatic power anything in opera that had gone before.

Iphigénie en Aulide was a sensational success. But the pro-Italian party in Paris withheld their applause, although Rousseau was won over by the opera's 'truth to nature', and when it was known that Gluck – greatly daring – was composing an *Armide* on the Quinault libretto Lully had used ninety years earlier, the pro-Italians had the idea of bringing Piccinni to Paris[56] and offering him another Quinault libretto (drastically compressed by Marmontel). This was *Roland*. *Armide* was produced in September 1777, *Roland* four months later, and Paris was torn by the faction warfare of *gluckistes* and *piccinnistes*. *Roland*,[57] though styled *tragédie lyrique*, is in many respects Italian opera with French text; where Lully had set 'O supplice horrible!' in the hero's mad scene (III.6) thus:

Ex. 166

Piccinni deals with the words in typical *accompagnato* manner, like many such passages in Gluck:

---

[56] He had just demonstrated his tragic powers in new versions (Naples, 1774) of his Metastasian operas *Alessandro nell' Indie* (1758) and *Olimpiade* (1761).
[57] Vocal score, ed. Gustave Lefèvre, *Chefs d'oeuvre de l'opéra français* (Paris, 1882).

Ex. 167

and follows this with a beautiful instrumental *andantino amoureux* very much in the vein of Ex. 164 (i). Roland's fine monologue which constitutes the whole of III.2 is quite Gluckian in conception. Gluck's *drame héroique Armide* is Franco-Italian in a different sense, as *Iphigénie en Tauride* is; the score contains even more borrowings from earlier works but is exceptional in Gluck's output for its sensuous beauty. This is accentuated in the handling of the orchestra; it is the orchestral background to Renaud's 'Plus j'observe' in Act II[58] that puts it on a par with Lully's setting, not the vocal line.

In *Iphigénie en Tauride* (1779),[59] based on a good libretto by Nicolas-François Guillard, Gluck achieved a final, perfect integration of the disparate elements. Despite the usual borrowings from the past, it is a nearly flawless masterpiece. The principal characters are strongly and subtly delineated in powerful or beautiful music; dramatic complexes of recitative, arioso, and chorus are composed through; the only interruption of the first scene of Act I is Iphigenia's short and exceptionally lovely 'O toi, qui prolongeas mes jours', dramatically justified even in its da capo, and the rest of the Act – even the wild Scythian ballet – is all continuous drama.

[58] In Schering, op. cit., No. 313.
[59] *Werke*, Series 1, ix, and miniature score, ed. Hermann Abert (Leipzig, n.d.).
[60] Ed. Daniel Heartz in *Mozart: Neue Ausgabe sämtlicher Werke* (Kassel, 1956), Series 21.

MOZART'S *OPERE SERIE*

This highest point of Italianized *tragédie lyrique* was followed two years later by the highest peak of later *opera seria*, the *Idomeneo* (Munich, 1781)[60] of Wolfgang Amadeus Mozart (1756–91). Up to then Mozart had made only two boyish essays in serious opera. *Idomeneo*, based on Giambattista Varesco's adaptation of a French libretto set by Campra in 1712, however firmly rooted in the Italian style, would have been very different if Mozart had not known Gluck – particularly *Alceste*. Ilia's 'Se il padre perdei' in Act II and her 'Zeffiretti lusinghieri' might have been written by J. C. Bach – Mozart's favourite 'Italian' – or di Majo, but Electra has many Gluckian traits and the High Priest in Act III borrows an *accompagnato* figure from the High Priest in *Alceste*; the ensuing priestly march is Gluckian, as of course is the vast ballet. Most important of all is the amount of 'continuous drama' involving the chorus. Mozart returned to *opera seria* only once, at the very end of his life, with a mangled version of Metastasio's *Clemenza di Tito* (1791) for which the *secco* recitatives were probably supplied by his pupil Franz Xaver Süssmayr; he had found other and more congenial media for seriousness.

OPERA IN PARIS BEFORE THE REVOLUTION

The sun of *opera seria* had indeed set. Few of any note appeared after *Idomeneo* – Pietro Guglielmi's *Enea e Lavinia* (Naples, 1785) and a few by a younger man, Domenico Cimarosa (1749–1801), generally remembered by one comic masterpiece, *Il matrimonio segreto* (1792); but the hybrid, Italianized *tragédie lyrique* flourished in Paris through the 1780s.

At first there was a vogue for setting Quinault, consequent on Gluck's *Armide* and Piccinni's *Roland*. In 1779, the year of the second *Iphigénie*, J. C. Bach came to Paris with *Amadis des Gaules*; the following year Piccinni brought out an *Atys* and Philidor a *Persée*, his first 'serious' work since *Ernelinde*. In 1780 also, another *comique* composer, Grétry, entered the tragic field with an *Andromaque*[61] based on Racine. In 1781 Piccinni boldly challenged comparison by composing a far from contemptible *Iphigénie en Tauride* (to a different libretto)[62] and Marmontel provided him with good libretti for *Didon*[63] in 1783 and *Pénélope* in 1785, where – without rising to the tragic height of Dido – he shows what he had learned from Gluck (particularly the dramatic involvement of the chorus) without forgetting his own nationality (as in Dido's 'Ah! que je fus bien inspirée' (II.3)). He certainly did not forget it in his *opéra comique Le faux Lord* (1783).[64]

At the same time other Italians were coming to Paris to challenge him. Sacchini arrived from England in 1783 with French adaptations of earlier

---

[61] Fétis and Gevaert, op. cit., xxxvii–xxxviii.
[62] See Julian Rushton, '*Iphigénie en Tauride*: the operas of Gluck and Piccinni', *M & L*, liii, (1972), p. 411, for musical examples from Piccinni.
[63] Ed. Lefèvre, *Chefs d'oeuvre de l'opéra français* (Paris, 1881).
[64] One air in *HAM*, ii, No. 300.

works: *Renaud* (from *Armida*: Milan, 1772) and *Chimène* (from *Il Gran Cidde*: Rome, 1764); in 1784 a *Dardanus* set to an adaptation of the libretto sanctified by Rameau; in 1786 an *Oedipe à Colone* to one by Guillard,[65] the librettist of Gluck's second *Iphigénie*. These were all performed at Versailles. But four months after Sacchini's death *Oedipe* was given at the Paris Opera with the massive choral resources it demanded and quickly established itself as one of the finest and most successful works in Gluck's immediate wake. And younger men arrived: Gluck's pupil, Antonio Salieri (1750–1825) and Luigi Cherubini (1760–1842). Salieri, who had already written a number of *opere serie* and *buffe* including a Metastasio *Semiramide* (Munich, 1782), came to Paris the same year. He produced three *tragédies* – the 'horror opera' *Les Danaïdes* (1784), *Les Horaces* (1786), and *Tarare* (1787)[66] to a libretto by Beaumarchais which reflects the current fermentation of liberal ideas, and then went back to Vienna where *Tarare* was converted into *Axur, rè d'Ormus* with a libretto by Lorenzo da Ponte. Cherubini, who also had a dozen or so *opere serie* to his credit, made his Parisian début in 1788 with *Démophoon*, the libretto being Marmontel's version of Metastasio's *Demofoonte*;[67] but his first notable success was *Lodoïska* (1791) and his work as a whole, entirely French, belongs to a later chapter.

Lodoïska was described as a *comédie heroïque* and produced at the Théâtre Feydeau, but it was not all comic; Salieri's *tragédie Tarare* became the *opera tragicomica Axur* and he described later Viennese operas as *eroicomico*[68] and even *filosoficocomico*. The old clear-cut division between serious and comic opera had broken down and new terms were needed. Since Monsigny and Philidor had shown that opera could reflect near-tragic crises in the lives of ordinary people as well as historical or mythological characters, Grétry in particular had not only enriched his scores by his admiration for Gluck and by essays in naïve ingenuity[69] but expanded the range of subjects with the fairy-tale *Zémire et Azor* (Beauty and the Beast) (1771) which became popular all over Europe during the 1770s, the Spanish *L'Amant jaloux* (1778), the medieval *Aucassin et Nicolette* (1779), and the oriental *Caravane du Caire* (1783). After this he produced the best of all his *paysanneries, L'Épreuve villageoise* (1784), and then broke new ground with *Richard Coeur-de-Lion* (also 1784).[70] This was one of the earliest of the 'rescue operas' which were to be so popular during the next twenty years, and notable also for the employment throughout the opera in various forms of

[65] Which Grétry had attempted in 1785 but wisely abandoned after the first act.
[66] Vocal scores of *Danaïdes* and *Tarare*, ed. Lefèvre, op. cit. (Paris, 1881 and 1882).
[67] Another French version of *Demofoonte* was the *Démophon* (1789) of a brilliant young German, Johann Christoph Vogel (1758–88), an impassioned Gluckist who did not live to see its success.
[68] A description Haydn had already applied to his *Orlando Paladino* (Esterháza, 1782) and Paisiello to his *Rè Teodoro in Venezia* (Vienna, 1784).
[69] The overture to *Le Magnifique* (1773) was played with the curtain up, showing two girls in a room talking while in the street outside a procession passes with trumpets, a military band, chanting of priests, all treated naturalistically and finally dying away. That to *Aucassin and Nicolette* is twice interrupted by Aucassin's father calling from behind the scenes. In *Andromaque* the heroine's recitatives are always accompanied by three flutes.
[70] Fétis and Gevaert, op. cit., xiii, xxi, xxxii, xxii, vi, and i respectively.

Blondel's *romance* 'Une fièvre brûlante', which is thus (as Grétry himself put it) 'le pivot sur lequel tournait toute la pièce' and one of the earliest of all deliberate and unmistakable operatic 'reminiscence themes'. *Richard* is styled *comédie avec ariettes* but Blondel's 'Ô Richard! mon roi!' in Act I (which the band played at the fatal royal banquet at Versailles on 1 October 1789) and Richard's 'Si l'univers entier m'oublie' in Act II are worthy of any 'heroic' opera, and the spectacular final assault on the castle was a foretaste of what was to become known as 'grand opera'.

Another composer whose intelligence, like Grétry's, tended to outrun his musical ability was Alexandre (Nicolas) Dezède (*c.* 1742–92). However the 'tearful' tradition was kept up by him and by Grétry's disciple Nicolas-Marie Dalayrac (1753–1809) in his *Nina, ou La Folle par amour* (1786) and *Les deux petits Savoyards* (1789).

SERIOUS ELEMENTS IN *OPERA BUFFA*

There was also, after Piccinni's *Figliuola*, a 'tearful' element in *opera buffa*, but it never got the upper hand as it did in *opéra comique* and there are few Italian Rousseausque innocents. But more serious characters were introduced and, since the *buffa* composers were often the leading *seria* composers – Piccinni, Guglielmi, Traetta – the methods and idioms of *seria* were employed more and more in *buffa*. Their mockery of serious opera, as in Piccinni's *La bella verità* (1762) and Jommelli's *La critica* (1766), is deliciously pungent; Traetta did not shrink from parodying Gluck's *Orfeo* and making fun of 'Che farò' in the Second Act of his *Cavaliere errante* (1778). Yet in the First Act of the same opera he can sound the note of genuine pathos:[71]

Ex. 168

It was Piccinni and his pupil Anfossi who were foremost in cultivating the sentimental strain, but when one compares the latter's setting of Calzabigi's *Finta giardiniera* (Rome, 1774) with Mozart's (Munich, 1775)[72] – his earliest mature *opera buffa* – it is not the Italian who is the more sentimental:

[71] Example from Abert, *W. A. Mozart*, i, p. 421.
[72] *Werke* (Leipzig, 1879–86), Series 5, ix.

Ex. 169

ANFOSSI

Un ma - ri - to oh Dio! vor - re - i   a - mo - ro - so e pien d'af - fet - to

MOZART

grazioso

Un ma - ri - to oh Dio! vor - re - i   a - mo - ro - so e pien d'af - fet - to

And in the second section, 'Ah, mi fugge', of Serpetta's later aria, 'Una voce sento', the not yet 19-year-old Mozart goes beyond the 'tearful' incongruously to the tragic.

Piccinni could create comic figures musically in the round, as well as oppressed heroines; in the *Buona figliuola* the roistering German soldier Tagliaferro beside Cecchina.[73] Both have memorable arias, but Piccinni is at his most characteristic in simpler, small-scale songs. (*Opera buffa* songs were much more varied in form than those in *seria*.) Or he will carry along a scene with tiny, sparkling orchestral motives which may build up to a musical-dramatic climax in the finale of an act. His finales sometimes take the form of a free rondo, like that to Act I of the *Figliuola* where the little duet for Sandrina and Paoluccia returns again and again, varied or unaltered. Galuppi's type of 'chain finale' (see p. 454) was now extended both dramatically and musically, with crises and sudden reversals of fortune embodied in a succession of musical episodes usually held together by nothing more than key. One of Piccinni's finest is that to Act II of *Enea nel Cuma* (1775), a burlesque treatment of Book VI of the *Aeneid*. All in all, he was the leading *buffo* composer of the generation which includes not only his compatriots Traetta, Guglielmi, and the late developer Giuseppe Sarti (1729–1802) whose earliest success was *Le gelosie villane* (1776), but two Austrians: Florian Leopold Gassmann (1729–74) and Franz Joseph Haydn (1732–1809),[74] though it must be admitted that the latter's operas, composed for the private theatre of Prince Nikolaus Eszterházy, are of slight importance by comparison with his work in other fields.

The most noteworthy of the younger Italians was the Neapolitan Paisiello. He seems to have been one of the earliest to introduce in an overture tunes from the opera itself (the one-act *Duello* of 1774) and anticipated Traetta in making fun of Gluck in *Il credulo deluso* (also 1774) and *Socrate immaginario* (1775):[75]

[73] Tagliaferro's 'Star trompeti, star tampuri' is ed. H. C. Wolff, *Die Oper I* (*Das Musikwerk*, 38) (Cologne, 1971), No. 20.
[74] Gassmann's best known work, *La Contessina*, has been ed. Robert Haas, *DTÖ*, Jg. xxi (1) (vol. 42–4); copious excerpts from his other operas, *Studien zur Musikwissenschaft*, ii (1914), pp. 137–211. Haydn's are in Series 24 and 25 of the Haydn-Institut edition of the *Werke*.
[75] Vocal score of *Socrate*, ed. G. Barini (Florence, 1939).

Ex. 170

Much more important: he enriched the orchestral palette of *opera buffa* by more frequent use of the woodwind in general and the clarinet in particular. His earlier operas, like those of his younger contemporaries Giuseppe Gazzaniga (1743–1818),[76] Cimarosa, the Spaniard Vicente Martín y Soler (1754–1806), maintain the true *buffa* tradition, but sentiment appeared with the character of Rosina in *Il barbiere di Siviglia* (St Petersburg, 1782). There is more of it in *Il Ré Teodoro* (1784), perhaps his masterpiece – with its superb septet finale to Act I, beginning as 'a murmur, a whisper' ('Che sussurro, che bisbiglio') and proceeding crescendo – and it overflows in *L'amor contrasto* (better known by its later title, *La molinara*) (1788) and *Nina o sia La pazza per amore* (on a version of the French libretto set by Dalayrac three years before) (1789).[77] Yet there are beautiful things in *Teodoro* and *Nina*; *La molinara* has a delightful Second Act finale and Rachelina's 'Nel cor più non mi sento', with its waspish violin figure, should not be judged by Beethoven's miserable piano version in the variations he wrote on it in 1796.

The young Austrian who was to eclipse them all for posterity, though not for their contemporaries, originated nothing; the genre, warmly humanized *opera buffa*, with all its vocal and orchestral idioms and resources, was fully mature. What Mozart brought to it was overwhelming creative genius. But not first in *opera buffa* itself; before doing that he applied its resources to *Singspiel*.

THE DEVELOPMENT OF *SINGSPIEL*

That modest form had not developed far from its humble beginnings (see p. 450) until it was taken up by Johann Adam Hiller (1728–1804) in the 1760s. Beginning with *Lisuart und Dariolette* (Leipzig, 1766), on a libretto translated from that of Duni's *La fée Urgéle* (1765), Hiller's *Singspiele – Lottchen am Hofe* (1767) (*Ninette à la cour*, cf. p. 454), *Der Dorfbalbier* (1771) (*Blaise le savetier*, cf. p. 459)[78] and the rest – were nearly all modelled on *opéras comiques* with the substitution of simple German *Lieder* for the *airs*. Most of them were first produced at Leipzig. The production of *Die Jagd* at Weimar in 1770, however, seems to have inspired Goethe to write a number of – not very successful – *Singspiel* libretti.

[76] Gazzaniga's *Don Giovanni* has been ed. Stefan Kunze (Kassel, 1974).
[77] Vocal scores of *Nina* and *La molinara* by C. Gatti (Milan, 1940) and A. Rocchi (Florence, 1962) respectively.
[78] Song from *Lisuart* in *HAM*, ii, No. 301; excerpts from *Lottchen am Hofe* in *NOHM*, vii, pp. 82–3; song from *Der Aerndtekranz* (1771) in Schering, op. cit., No. 309b.

473

In February 1775 a more sophisticated musician took up the *Singspiel*; this was the Bohemian-born Georg Benda (1722–95) who had a fortnight earlier attracted attention with a one-act 'duodrama' (spoken word and mime with orchestral accompaniment), *Ariadne auf Naxos*.[79] His *Dorfjahrmarkt*[80] and its successor the *comische Operette Der Holzhauer* (1778) (= Philidor's *Le Bûcheron* (1763)) not only employ an orchestra larger than Hiller's but introduce recitative, arias, and other elements of *opera buffa* and even occasionally *seria*. These appear also in the *Bergknappen* (1778)[81] of the Viennese Ignaz Umlauff (1746–96), the *Adelheit von Veltheim* (Frankfurt, 1780) of Christian Gottlob Neefe (1748–98), and the *Belmont und Constanze* (Berlin, 1781) of Johann André (1741–99),[82] and the two latter, both on 'Turkish' subjects, introduce *opera buffa* type finales. But poor André's *Singspiel* was to be totally overshadowed fourteen months later by Mozart's *Entführung aus dem Serail* (Vienna, 1782), based on a shameless adaptation of the same libretto.

Except for the patches of spoken dialogue, *Die Entführung* is really *opera buffa* – and *opera buffa* of the highest order. Blonde's second aria in Act II, 'Welche Wonne', belongs to the world of *Singspiel*; her first at the beginning of the Act emphatically does not; and one has only to compare Pedrillo's subtle and enchanting *romanze* 'In Mohrenland' with André's square-cut Germanic setting:

Ex. 171

Im Moh - ren-land ge - fan - gen war ein Mä - del hübsch und fein

to see that we have to do not only with very different composers but with very different genres. The finales are unremarkable as *opera buffa* types. That to Act I, like André's, is a terzet, that to Act II a quartet in seven contrasted sections which do not advance the action, while the third finale is a 'vaudeville' beginning with solo strophes sung by the characters in turn, with tutti refrain – Osmin recalls the words and music of his 'Erst geköpft, dann gehangen' from Act I – and the piece ends with a quartet and chorus. Where Mozart really steps out of the *opera buffa* world it is to enter that of *seria* – splendidly in Constanze's Act I aria, 'Ach, ich liebte' (except that, as he admitted to his father, its coloratura element was 'a sacrifice . . . to the flexible throat of Mlle. Cavalieri' (letter of 26 September 1781)) and her 'Traurigkeit' (II.10), disastrously from the dramatic point of view in her

---

[79] Ed. Alfred Einstein (Leipzig, 1920); excerpts in *NOHM*, vii, pp. 77–9. *Ariadne* was probably suggested by reports of J. J. Rousseau's *scène lyrique Pygmalion* (Lyons, 1770), which reached Paris in 1775 and Germany in 1779.
[80] Ed. Theodor Werner, *DDT*, lxiv; excerpts in *NOHM*, vii, pp. 86–8.
[81] Ed. Haas, *DTÖ*, Jg, xviii (1) (Vol. 36). Excerpts in *NOHM*, vii, pp. 92–4.
[82] André had already composed two of Goethe's libretti, *Erwin und Almire* (1775) and *Claudine von Villa Bella* (1778). He was later to be better known as a music-publisher.

musically superb 'Martern aller Arten' with its 60 bars of concertante instrumental introduction.

MOZART'S OPERATIC MASTERPIECES

Mozart made no such 'sacrifices' or misjudgements when he turned to true *opera buffa* – totally humanized *opera buffa* – in *Le nozze di Figaro* (Vienna, 1786). Beaumarchais's play, skilfully adapted by da Ponte, offered him at least half-a-dozen characters more substantial and more subtle than those of *Die Entführung* and his musical embodiment of them begins even in the recitatives. The characterization is developed and the action advanced mainly in the duets and trios and larger ensembles. Susanna, for instance, who has the *prima* female part, not the *seconda*, participates in all six duets of the opera, both trios, the sextet, and all the finales; her first aria, in Act II, is an action aria, her second, 'Deh vieni', is the last in the opera and adds the final exquisite stroke to her character. When just before this, Figaro, who is far indeed from the old conventional *buffo* man-servant, sings to the men in the audience 'Aprite un po' quegl' occhi', its 'comedy' is rendered ironic by the anguished *accompagnato* that has immediately preceded it. The musico-dramatic action of the very long Second Act finale, roughly two-thirds of the entire Act, has never been surpassed; the 'chain' type here reaches its highest development, crisis succeeding crisis in an organic key-structure beginning in E flat, moving to the dominant on Susanna's surprising appearance, changing suddenly to G when Figaro enters, and then winding back through a chain of fifths (C major, F, B flat) to the original tonic. And it is noteworthy that *Figaro*, like all Mozart's operas from *Idomeneo* onward, ends in the key of the overture.

In *Don Giovanni* (Prague, 1787) the D minor opening of the overture is a foretaste of an element of *seria* lacking, except in passing, in *Figaro*. Leporello's 'Notte e giorno faticar', the conventional *opera buffa* opening with the soliloquy of a comic servant, is cut short by the appearance of Giovanni and Donna Anna and the murder of her father. Elvira is anything but a comic character and her music practically never slips into the *buffa* idiom; her 'Bisogna aver coraggio' in the finale of Act I is exceptional. And the Act II finale from the change to the minor key and the knocking on the door is exceedingly powerful *opera seria* – with the thread of Leporello's buffoonery running through it. There is the same masterly characterization as in *Figaro* – Leporello is by no means a mere buffoon. And there are even more remarkable devices, such as three little stage-bands playing three different dances, in 3/4, 2/4, and 3/8, simultaneously,[83] or the evasion of characterization when confronted with a colourless personality like Ottavio, by giving him the loveliest melodies in the opera, 'Dalla sua pace' and 'Il mio tesoro'. This last device served Mozart well in *Così fan tutte* (Vienna, 1790)

---

[83] A minuet alone as background music had been introduced by Galuppi in *La partenza ed il ritorno dei marinari* (1764) and Piccinni in *I viaggiatori* (1775).

which is a return to pure *opera buffa*. This time da Ponte provided him with familiar stereotype figures whose activities he covered with the most sensuously beautiful music. When the element of *seria* appears, as in Fiordiligi's 'Come scoglio', it is richly ironic, for whatever the lady's soul is like 'in faith and love', it is not 'like a rock unmoved by winds and tempest'.

After *Così* Mozart turned again, in 1791, to *Singspiel* – but a *Singspiel* the like of which had never been composed before nor has been since. To appreciate to the full the extraordinariness of *Die Zauberflöte*, one should compare it with other Viennese *Singspiele* of the same period, with the justly popular *Doktor und Apotheker* (1786)[84] and *Das rothe Käppchen* (1788) of Karl Ditters von Dittersdorf (1739–99), the *romantisches Singspiel Oberon, König der Elfen* (1789) of Mozart's Czech friend and brother-Freemason Paul Wranitzky (Vranický) (1756–1808), or *Kaspar, der glückliche Vogelkrämer* (1790) and *Kaspar der Fagottist oder Die Zauberzither* (1791, less than four months before *Die Zauberflöte*) by Wenzel Müller (1767–1835). Yet that is hardly necessary; the heterogeneity of the *Zauberflöte* has no operatic parallel. The subject is compounded of romantic fairy-tale, buffoonery, and symbols of the Freemasonry which probably meant more to Mozart than the Catholic faith itself. The musical idioms include those of *opera seria* (the opening scene, the Queen of the Night); the romantic side of *opera buffa* (the young lovers) and its comic side (Monostatos's 'Alles fühlt'); *Singspiel* (Papageno and Papagena); Gluck at his most ethereal and his most solemn (the three boys, Sarastro and the priests); even Lutheran hymn-prelude (the men in armour). Yet all these disparate styles are subsumed into a very real unity comparable with that which marks each of Mozart's great instrumental works of the same period. This is particularly remarkable in the two 'finales' which contain nearly half the music of the entire work, above all the second with its various scene changes and its extremes of solemnity and buffoonery, moving tonally from E flat and C minor, through F and C (the romantic pair), G, C, and G (the comic pair), back to the solemnity of C minor and E flat.

Such a work could have no successor, least of all in the genre of *Singspiel* from which it burst, but it did influence the evolution of German romantic opera, just as, on a very different musical level, the final scene of Grétry's *Richard* and the choral effects of Sacchini's *Oedipe* were to point the way to Parisian *grand opéra*. It is significant that in the end really successful vernacular German opera developed not from imitation of Italian opera but from the humbler native *Singspiel*. The Hamburg enterprise had declined and fallen after Telemann's *Flavius Bertaridus* (1729); and isolated works such as the Wieland settings *Alceste* (Weimar, 1773)[85] and *Rosemunde* (Mannheim, 1780) of Anton Schweitzer (1735–87), and the *Günther von Schwarzburg* (Mannheim, 1777)[86] of the Metastasian Ignaz Holzbauer (1711–83), were only flashes in the pan.

---

[84] Vocal score by Richard Kleinmichel (Leipzig, 1890); excerpt in *HAM*, ii, No. 305.
[85] Excerpts in *NOHM*, vii, pp. 67–70.
[86] Ed. Kretzschmar, *DDT*, viii–ix; excerpts in *NOHM*, vii, pp. 72–5.

OPERA IN SPAIN

A similar pattern is traceable in all the peripheral countries from Spain and England to Poland and Russia. From 1730 onward opera in Spain was completely dominated by Neapolitan or Parmesan Metastasians – Francesco Coradini, Giovanni Battista Mele (b. 1701), and Francesco Corselli (d. 1778) – and the most influential person at the Spanish Court from 1737 to 1759 was the famous castrato Farinelli. The composers sometimes set Spanish texts, as when they collaborated in a Spanish version of *La clemenza di Tito* in 1747, but the repertory was mainly Italian, composed either by immigrants or by the greater Italian masters.

About 1760 the tide began to turn when the Spanish libretti, original or translations, of Ramón de la Cruz became popular. Cruz began his collaboration with the composer Rodriguez de Hita (1704–87) in an Italianate serious opera, *La Briseida* (Madrid, 1768), but they at once found their real *métier* in the *zarzuela burlesca* dealing with scenes of popular life, *Las segadoras de Vallecas* (also 1768) and *Las labradoras de Murcia* (1769). On similar lines is *Los jardineros de Aranjuez* (1768) by Pablo Esteve (d. 1794), who had made a very successful Spanish version, with additional music by himself, of Piccinni's *Buona figliuola* (Madrid, 1765). But even this form of *zarzuela* with its miniature counterpart, the *tonadilla escénica*, was hard pressed by the competition of *opera buffa*.

THE ENGLISH *PASTICCI*

Except for Arne's *Artaxerxes* (see p. 446), the few English attempts at vernacular *opera seria* – Arne's *Rosamond* and other still-born works by Johann Friedrich Lampe (1703–51) and John Christopher Smith 'the younger' (1712–95) in a London season of 1732–3; Smith's two Shakespearean efforts, *The Fairies* (after *A Midsummer Night's Dream*) (1755) and *The Tempest* (1756); and the *Dido, Queen of Carthage* (adapted from Metastasio) (1792) of Stephen Storace (1763–96), brother of the original Susanna in *Figaro* – were even less successful than the German ones. On the other hand the so-called ballad operas (see p. 450) and *pasticci* – compiled from popular melodies, borrowings from foreign operas, and a greater or lesser amount of original music by the compiler – flourished and spread to Scotland, Ireland, and the American colonies. (*The Beggar's Opera* reached Kingston, Jamaica, in 1733 and New York in 1750.) Among the more successful were Arne's *Love in a Village* (1762), *The Maid of the Mill* (1765) by Samuel Arnold (1740–1802), *Lionel and Clarissa* (1768) by Charles Dibdin (1745–1814), and *The Duenna* (1775) on Sheridan's libretto, with music by his father- and brother-in-law, the two Thomas Linleys (1733–95 and 1756–78), Sacchini, and others. *The Duenna* also introduced Scottish tunes, and *The Poor Soldier* (1783) by William Shield (1748–1829) Irish ones, reflecting a fashion noticeable in other fields (see pp. 603 and 631).

Storace's best work of this kind was his very successful *No Song, no Supper* (1790),[87] which includes borrowings from Grétry's *L'Amitié à l'épreuve* and *L'Épreuve villageoise*.

OPERA IN POLAND

Poland knew of nothing but Italian opera under both the Vasa dynasty and the Saxon kings. Indeed when Augustus III was driven from Dresden by the Seven Years War and settled in his Polish capital he naturally took his favourite Hasse with him[88] and Warsaw enjoyed a brilliant series of Hasse productions, including at least two new Metastasio settings, *Il sogno di Scipione* (1758) and *Zenobia* (1761). Then came an invasion of *opéras comiques* and other foreign works, and the earliest Polish libretto, *Nedza uszczeześliwiona* (Misery made happy) (1778),[89] is on the simplest *opéra comique* or *Singspiel* lines. It was set by Maciej Kamieński (1734–1821), a composer of Slovak origin, and one of his later works, *Balik gospodarski* (1780), is on a translation of Favart's *Le bal bourgeois*. Kamieński's Polishness never goes far beyond the occasional use of mazurka or polonaise rhythms, but there is a good deal more of it in *Zółta szlafmyca* (The yellow nightcap) (1788), which seems to have been a collective work in which he may have had a hand. The national note was sounded more loudly still in *Krakowiacy i Gorále* (Cracovians and mountaineers) (1794) by the Czech-born Jan Stefani (*c.* 1747–1829), on an up-to-date libretto with political undertones; Poland was seething in the aftermath of the Second Partition and the *deus* who intervenes is a young student not *ex* but *cum machina*, a portable but powerful 'electrical machine'.

THE BIRTH OF RUSSIAN OPERA

In Russia the Italians had an almost complete monopoly of the Imperial opera for nearly half a century after Araja's advent (see p. 445). When he left in 1762 he was followed in turn by Galuppi, Traetta, Paisiello, Sarti, Cimarosa, and Martin y Soler, though none stayed as long as he. In 1755 Araja actually set a Russian libretto, *Tsefal i Prokris*, though his knowledge of the language seems doubtful, and other foreigners were encouraged to follow him. Conversely, Catherine II sent two of her subjects, Maksim Sozontovich Berezovsky (1745–77) and Dmitry Stepanovich Bortnyansky (1751–1825), to study in Italy and their *opere serie* were produced there: Berezovsky's Metastasian *Demofoonte* at Leghorn, which was then being used as a base by the Russian fleet, in 1773, and Bortnyansky's *Creonte* (Venice, 1776) and two later works. After his return to Russia, Bortnyansky composed two little *opéras comiques*, *Le faucon* (1786)[90] and *Le fils rival*

---

[87] Ed. Roger Fiske, *MB*, xvi.
[88] Hasse lost his house and library through the Prussian bombardment of Dresden in 1760, which also destroyed a number of Schütz manuscripts.
[89] Full score ed. Alina Nowak-Romanowicz and Piotr Poźniak, *Opery Polskie*, ii (Cracow, 1978).
[90] Ed. A. S. Rozanov, *Pamyatniki russkovo muzikalnovo iskusstva*, v.

(1787), for the Court – which had already heard works by Duni, Philidor, and Monsigny.

These were all false starts. The roots of Russian vernacular opera were the equivalents of early English ballad-opera: plays incorporating numerous songs to popular melodies specified in the libretti. The one-act *Anyuta* (Tsarskoe Selo, 1772) is known only in libretto form, but a fragment survives from *Lyubovnik-koldun* (The lover-magician) which dates from the same year:

Ex. 172

The arranger/compiler was probably the Moscow theatre conductor Iosif Kerzelli, who solved the problem of harmonizing a mainly pentatonic tune, with A as its final, by treating it as if it were in G major; the same problem and similar drastic solutions haunted Russian musicians for more than fifty years. By far the most successful of these folk-tune plays was *Melnik – koldun, obmanshchik i svat* (Miller – magician, deceiver and match-maker) (Moscow, 1779), on a subject resembling Rousseau's *Devin*[91] in that star-crossed village lovers are brought together by a good-natured charlatan. The music was compiled by a theatre violinist named Mikhail Matveyevich Sokolovsky.[92]

At the same time operas with original music, though often borrowing popular melodies, began to be staged in Moscow and St Petersburg: Kerzelli's *Rozana i Lyubim* (Moscow, 1778), and the St Petersburg operas

---

[91] A Russian adaptation of which, *Derevenskoy vorozheya* (The village fortune-teller), with original music by Kerzelli, had been given in Moscow and published the year before.

[92] His score is lost and the earliest surviving one dates from 1805; the vocal score published in 1884, wrongly attributed to Fomin, has no more connection with the original than the modern versions of *The Beggar's Opera* with Pepusch. Excerpts from the 1805 score – and most of the other works mentioned here – are published in S. L. Ginzburg, *Istoriya russkoy muziki v notnïkh obraztsakh*, i (second edition only, Moscow, 1968).

of Vasily Alekseyevich Pashkevich (1742–97): *Neschastie ot kareti* (Misery caused by a carriage) (1779), *Sanktpeterburgskoy gostinïy dvor* (St Petersburg bazaar) (1782) and *Skupoy* (The Miser) (1782),[93] suggested by Molière's *L'Avare*. For Pashkevich's serious opera *Fevey* (1786) the libretto was written by Catherine II herself. Indeed the Empress provided several other libretti: the opera-ballet *Novgorodsky bogatïr Boeslaevich* (1786), composed by Evstigney Ipatevich Fomin (1761–1800); *Gore-bogatïr Kosometovich* (The woeful knight Kosometovich) (1789), a satire on her enemy Gustav III of Sweden, composed by Martin y Soler who constructed an overture on three Russian tunes; and *Nachalnoe upravlenie Olega* (The early reign of Oleg) (1790), really a play with incidental music, in which Sarti and Pashkevich collaborated. Of the Russian composers, by far the most talented was the Italian-trained Fomin who was equally successful in the racy, thoroughly Russian *Yamshchiki na podstave* (Coachmen at the relay-station) (1787);[94] an Italianate *opera buffa* on the *conquistadores* in South America, *Amerikantsï* (composed 1788; produced 1800); and a duodrama on Benda's lines, with final ballet, *Orfey i Evridika* (1792). The clarinet solo representing Orpheus's song shows his assimilation of Italian cantilena:

Ex. 173

while this song from *Yamshchiki* illustrates his adaptation of folk-melody:[95]

Ex. 174

(i) FOLK-SONG

Da - ra - ga - ya tï mo - - - - - ya

ma - tu - - - - shka, _____

[93] Ed. F. M. Levashev, *Pamyatniki*, iv.
[94] Ed. I. M. Vetlitsina, ibid., vi.
[95] As printed (a tone higher) in Vasily Trutovsky's 'collection of Russian simple songs with notes', the earliest publication of Russian popular tunes. The first part came out in 1776, the second, in which this song appears, in 1778. Modern edition of all four parts ed. Viktor Belyaev (Moscow, 1953).

(ii) FOMIN

Re - ti - vo serd - - tse mo - - - - - - - lo -
- dets - - - ko - e,

This dualism was to persist in Russian music for many years.

23

Orchestral and Chamber Music (c. 1725–90)

During the second quarter of the eighteenth century the most popular types of orchestral music were still the concerto above all, with or without solo instruments, and the 'French' overture – now less favoured except in Germany – with its retinue of dances and *galanteries*. Bach abandoned the composition of original concertos but busied himself with the arrangement for harpsichord and orchestra of earlier works for other solo instruments. He did however, compose, probably *c.* 1730, two splendid overtures (suites) in D (BWV 1068 and 1069). Telemann included both overtures and concertos in his *Musique de Table* (Hamburg, 1733),[1] a collection of three 'productions' as he calls them which appeared at three-monthly intervals, each 'production' consisting of '1 Ouverture avec la Suite, à 7 instrumens; 1 Quatuor; 1 Concert, à 7; 1 Trio; 1 Solo: 1 Conclusion, à 7'. It is clear from the *soli* and *tutti* markings that the overtures and *galanteries*, the four-movement concertos, and the *conclusions* are genuine orchestral music for a body of strings. The other pieces – each in four movements – are for soloists (chamber music in the modern sense); the demarcation was by no means always as clear even thirty years or more later. The next few years saw the publication of Handel's sets of concertos:[2] *Concerti grossi*, Op. 3 (1734), *Concertos for the Harpsichord or Organ*, Op. 4 (1738), *Twelve Grand Concertos*, Op. 6 (1740), and a 'second set' of keyboard concertos five of which are simply, and the sixth partly, transcriptions from Op. 6 (1740). A third set 'for the harpsicord or organ', Op. 7, was published posthumously in 1761; the autographs bear various dates from 1740 to 1751. The Op. 3 set are specifically for a concertino of two violins and cello, and concerto grosso of 'two other violins', viola, and bass, but parts for pairs of flutes, oboes, and bassoons were published as well. As so often with eighteenth-century concertos, the date of publication may be far from the date of composition. The fugal third movement of No. 2 is taken direct from the overture to the Brockes Passion of 1716, No. 4 appeared the same year, as a new sinfonia for *Amadigi*, and the rest also include earlier work. The Op. 6 set are for strings only, though four have autograph oboe parts. Handel is here at the height of his powers as an instrumental composer; only one concerto, No. 5, has

---

[1] Ed. Seiffert, *DDT*, lxi, and Johann Philipp Hinnenthal, *Telemann-Ausgabe*, xii–xiv. Miniature score of third 'production', ed. Walter Bergmann (London, n.d.).
[2] *Werke*, xxi, xxviii, xxx, and xlviii. Op. 3, 6, and 7 are published complete in miniature score.

movements borrowed from earlier works (in this case the *Ode for St. Cecilia's Day* of the previous year). He often seems to scorn mere technical finesse and formal conventions, his superb and exuberant inventiveness sometimes spilling over into six or even seven movements. If the concerti grossi are uneven in quality, the keyboard concertos are still more so. It is noteworthy that, whereas Bach's are practically all transcriptions, Handel's – despite the high proportion of transcription and adaptation – do include a certain amount of original composition.

In Italy Vivaldi, the classic master of the form, appears to have gone on composing concertos at least until 1739. Of his younger contemporaries, Francesco Geminiani (*c.* 1680–1762) published several sets of concerti grossi in London between 1732 and 1746,[3] Pietro Locatelli (1695–1764) several sets, nearly all at Amsterdam, from 1721 to 1762.[4] Even Giuseppe Tartini (1692–1770), who composed a vast number of violin concertos, published two sets of concerti grossi at Amsterdam in 1728 and 1734. The concerto grosso, then, was by no means extinct yet, though it was going out of fashion. The various kinds of solo concerto found ever more favour with composers and public, and on the other side (as it were) the concerto grosso – as well as the overture-suite – was superseded more insidiously by an outgrowth of opera: the concert sinfonia.

THE CONCERT 'SINFONIA'

The haphazard terminology of the seventeenth century made no distinction between sinfonia and concerto. The term 'sinfonia' had long been applied occasionally to various kinds of concerted instrumental music; as we have seen (p. 423), the earliest concerti grossi were styled *sinfonie*. Torelli in his Op. 5 (1692) (see p. 427) distinguished between the *sinfonie a 3* and the *concerti a 4:* the concertos have an additional – viola – part and he says all the instruments should be 'multiplied', whereas he seems to have envisaged solo performance of the sinfonie[5] which were essentially *sonate da chiesa*. The one three-movement work foreshadowing the quick-slow-quick plan of the Italian opera sinfonia is a concerto. So with Albinoni's *Sinfonie e concerti*, Op. 2 (1700): the four-movement sinfonie are individually described as *sonate*, which is what they are, and the mostly three-movement concerti are orchestral in nature.

The earliest genuinely orchestral three-movement sinfonie played at concerts were unattributed opera symphonies. Such are at least two of the symphonies by Vivaldi preserved in the Dresden Landesbibliothek;[6] according to a manuscript of 1740, he performed them at the Ospedale della

[3] The Op. 3 set are all available in miniature score.
[4] Op. 7, No. 12, available in miniature score. Locatelli's *Introduttioni teatrali*, Op. 4, Nos. 1–6 (Amsterdam, 1735), are concerti grossi with four-part concertino, in the three-movement opera symphony form and with slow movements sometimes nourished by the up-to-date idioms of *opera buffa*; they have been ed. Arend Koole, *Monumenta Musica Neerlandica*, iv (Amsterdam, 1961).
[5] Franz Giegling, *Giuseppe Torelli* (Kassel and Basel, 1949), p. 38.
[6] Three of them ed. Ludwig Landshoff (Leipzig, 1935).

Pietà at Venice, but one has been identified as the overture to his *Arsilda regina di Ponto* (1716) and another[7] as that to *L'incoronazione di Dario* (1717). Unfortunately we do not know how soon Vivaldi began using his opera symphonies as concert works or when he began the composition of concert symphonies.[8] A claim has been made for Johann Joachim Agrell (1701–65), a Swede in the service of the Court at Kassel, as the pioneer of the concert symphony *c.* 1725, but his earliest published set did not appear until 1746. Be that as it may, the earliest important Italian composer of 'chamber' symphonies, the Milanese Giovanni Battista Sammartini (*c.* 1700–75), much more prolific in this field than Vivaldi, began by adding slow movements and brief finales to the one-movement sinfonie[9] to Acts II and III of his opera *Memet* (1732).

THE NEW INSTRUMENTAL IDIOM

The real distinction between symphony and concerto was brought about by the general change of musical idiom which took place almost imperceptibly mainly during the second quarter of the century and affected the symphony, with its close relationship to opera, much earlier than the concerto. Symptomatic of the new style were the tendency to replace long melodic lines and polyphonic or quasi-polyphonic texture by short antithetic or repeated melodic motives and simple harmonies which often dissolved into bustling passage-work; the close juxtaposition of contrasted ideas; and the infusion of elegant and sentimental ornamentation (reflecting the general cultural climate). These raised few problems in the usually short slow movements and allegro or minuet finales; but in the first movements the motor-rhythmic drive of the concerto allegro, its tonal and thematic unity and variety dependent on the pillars of the ritornello and its reliance on soli-tutti antitheses for contrast, was inadequate for the sinfonia allegro when this became more extended. And the empty sound of repeated or broken chords which served well enough as preface to an opera performance would hardly have charmed the Venetian audiences who went to listen to the girls' orchestra at the Pietà.

The new 'juxtaposition of contrasted ideas' may be illustrated by comparing the opening of Vivaldi's *Incoronazione* symphony (1717) with that of a symphony by Graupner, with the same initial theme, of perhaps twenty years later:

Ex. 175

(i) VIVALDI

f [repeated ***p****]*

---

[7] Ibid., No. 1.
[8] Ibid., No. 3 is probably one.
[9] Ed. Bathia Churgin, *The Symphonies of G. B. Sammartini*, i (*Harvard Publications in Music*, 2) (Cambridge, Mass., 1968), Nos. 17a and 12.

(ii) GRAUPNER

Vivaldi's theme is played in bare octaves; Graupner's is harmonized. The first real contrast in Vivaldi's movement occurs at bar 20, an idea used once later – in both cases to effect modulation; indeed all that happens is repetition of the initial theme in various keys. Graupner's movement, like many others of the period, is essentially a mosaic of thematic particles, easily arranged and rearranged in different orders: such is the Allegro of Sammartini's Op. 2, No. 11[10] (Paris, 1742), which is articulated by vestiges of the concerto-ritornello principle. Key is used only haphazardly as an organizing factor; most often – as in the Graupner movement – no more than a devious progression from tonic to dominant in the first section (which may be repeated) and from dominant, supertonic minor, or other key back to the tonic in the second. Sammartini's F major Allegro ends with a dominant chord 'resolved' in the ensuing *affettuoso* which is also in F. This is a relic of a *sonata da chiesa* practice, found also in Vivaldi's early *Incoronazione* where the dominant of C major closes into an andante in C minor.

EMBRYONIC SONATA-FORM

One of the earliest composers to emphasize key-contrast by strongly contrasted themes seems to have been the Czech František Václav Miča (Mitscha) (1694–1744) in the overtures to an opera and cantatas composed for his master Count Questenberg at Jaroměřice around 1730. In the sinfonia to his serenade *Operosa Terni Colossi Moles* (1735)[11] the first subject (i) cadences very vigorously in the dominant which is then confirmed by a markedly contrasting, though related, 'second subject' (ii), and after a modulating middle section, the movement ends with a recapitulation of the 'first subject' (but no more) and brief coda:

Ex. 176

(i)

---

[10] Complete in the appendix to Karl Nef, *Geschichte der Sinfonie und Suite* (Leipzig, 1921), p. 318.
[11] Complete in condensed score by Vladimir Helfert, *AfMW*, vii (1925), p. 128. The Symphony in D published in 1946 and attributed to F. V. Miča is by his nephew, František Adam Miča (1746–1811).

(ii)

Sammartini in such an early symphony as No. 4 in Churgin's edition[12] was content to construct his dominant passage from a continuation of the first subject, and the over-all form is essentially the familiar tonic-dominant (repeated), dominant (or relative minor)-tonic pattern. But in a later symphony, in G major,[13] although the second subject is by no means as discrete as Miča's, he breaks out of that pattern by a tiny innovation – the insertion of a *tonic* appearance of the first subject in the second section – thus:

First section	First subject (5 bars): tonic
(repeated)	Second subject (12 bars): dominant
Second Section	First subject (4 bars dominant, plus 12 bars modulating)
(repeated)	*First subject (6 bars): tonic*
	Second subject (12 bars): tonic

By making that tiny insert and so recapitulating both subjects in the tonic key, he had arrived at a rudimentary form of what was to become known much later as 'sonata-form' or 'first-movement form'. In later terminology the first section was described as 'exposition', the second as 'development and recapitulation' – and its total repeat was to survive at least until the finale of Beethoven's last quartet, Op. 135.

Sammartini was not alone; indeed there is no evidence that he was the originator. The Viennese Mathias Georg Monn (1717–50) employed this embryonic 'sonata-form' in the finale of a symphony in D (1740) and the first movement of a later one in B flat,[14] and the Italian Giovanni Benedetto Platti (*c.* 1700–63) did so, with slightly more sophisticated transition passages, in some of the allegros of his *VI Sonates pour le Clavessin sur le Goût Italien*, Op. 1 (Nuremberg, 1742).[15] In the same city and year Carl Philipp Emanuel Bach (1714–88), second surviving son of Sebastian and least Italianate of mid-century composers, published *Sei Sonate per cembalo*,[16] dedicated to the King of Prussia, the first of which opens with a poco allegro in this form. It was evidently well known by that time, though so far it was only one of a great number of experimental forms in which

---

[12] Printed in a largely bogus form in *HAM*, ii, No. 283.
[13] Miniature score, ed. Newell Jenkins (London, 1956).
[14] Ed. Karl Horwitz and Karl Riedel, *DTÖ* Jg. xv (2) (vol. 31), pp. 37 and 51; finale of the D major in *HAM*, ii, No. 295.
[15] Ed. Lothar Hoffmann-Erbrecht, *Mitteldeutsches Musikarchiv* (I, iii) (Leipzig, 1954); one such movement in *HAM*, ii, No. 284.
[16] Ed. Rudolf Steglich, *Nagels Musik-Archiv*, vi and xv (Hanover, 1927).

composers sought to give both cohesion and variety to extended in-strumental movements. Another Viennese, Georg Christoph Wagenseil (1715–77), in a D major symphony of 1746[17] brings back the first subject in the tonic after the dominant but his movement has no second subject. Monn himself in the opening movements of his 1740 symphony and one in G major nine years later was content with the old simpler binary form. Incidentally, while Sammartini occasionally substitutes a minuet for the fast triple-time finale, both Monn and Wagenseil sometimes introduce it as a fourth movement after or, less often, before the slow one.

THE CONCERTO IN MID-CENTURY

The mixture of forms and styles is even more confused in the concertos of this period. Despite the infusion of modern idioms, even such 'progressive' musicians as Tartini, Hasse,[18] Monn, and C. P. E. Bach continued to rely heavily on the ritornello principle[19] with its varied-key landmarks, rather than on clearly defined tonic and dominant areas with a sense of gravitation toward the tonic; the final tonic tutti of the concerto movement was not a tonal goal reached after tension, and Tartini's frequent marked repeats of the first tutti-and-solo do not make them 'expositions'. The only general-izations one can make about the mid-century concerto are that the harpsichord was becoming more and more popular as the solo instrument, while the concerto grosso soon followed the overture-suite into oblivion after about 1750, except in England. There Sammartini's brother Giuseppe (*c.* 1693–1751) published several sets from 1738 till his death[20] and a Dutch immigrant, Pieter Hellendaal (1721?–1799), published *Six Grand Concertos* in 1758, and Geminiani's pupil Charles Avison (1709–70) no fewer than six sets during 1740–69, while the older works of Handel, Geminiani, and the rest were reprinted for a quarter of a century.

Instead of the 'concertino' of the old concerto, *concertante* instruments (particularly wind) began to play a part in the symphony, though the *sinfonia concertante* proper was a later development (see below, p. 496).

THE SYMPHONY AT PARIS

The popularity of the new type of orchestral music was closely connected with the spread of the public concert of the type provided by Vivaldi in Venice. Handel had accustomed London to subscription concerts in

[17] Ed. Horwitz and Riedel, op. cit., p. 16.
[18] See Pippa Drummond, 'The Concertos of Johann Adolf Hasse', *PRMA*, xcix (1972–3), p. 91. Modern editions of Hasse flute concertos – his favourite form – ed. Schering, *DDT*, xxix–xxx, p. 33, and ed. Richard Engländer (Wolfenbüttel, 1935, and London, 1953).
[19] See, for instance, the two examples by Monn in *DTÖ*, Jg. xix (2) (vol. 39), pp. 52 and 92, and the very typical A minor Concerto by C. P. E. Bach, dated 1750 (miniature score, ed. Wilhelm Altmann, Leipzig, 1938). The latter and Monn's G minor Concerto both exist in two forms, the solo harpsichord parts being transcribed from the originals for cello.
[20] On the confusion of the brothers' compositions in the contemporary editions see Henry G. Mishkin's study in *MQ*, xlv (1959), p. 361.

theatres, centred mainly on his own music, and since 1725 Paris had had the Concert spirituel, founded by Anne-Danican Philidor, the much older half-brother of the opera composer, in a hall of the Tuileries. But most public concerts in London were still given in taverns, just as in Leipzig Sebastian Bach's famous Collegium Musicum performed in coffee-houses; it was only in 1744 that the rival Grosses Concert moved to a larger hall which could accommodate an orchestra of two dozen and an audience of two or three hundred. However the symphony in particular became really fashionable after a contact between two private, aristocratic centres: the Court Chapel of the Elector Palatine at Mannheim and the private theatre of the Parisian Maecenas Alexandre de La Pouplinière, where regular concerts were directed by Rameau.

In 1741 the Elector acquired a violin virtuoso of Bohemian origin, Johann Stamitz (1717–57), who became *Konzertmeister* and built up an orchestra of outstanding quality partly from his fellow-countrymen. One of these, Franz Xaver Richter (1709–89), had already had *Six grandes Simphonies* (for strings) published in Paris in 1744 before going to Mannheim. In 1751 Stamitz himself visited Paris, where his symphonies were already known and where La Pouplinière had recently added two clarinets (which were then rarities) and two horns to his orchestra; in 1754 he returned and was entrusted with the direction of La Pouplinière's concerts for nearly a year. There he made the acquaintance of François-Joseph Gossec (1734–1829), a young native of Hainault who had just published a set of trio sonatas and was soon, probably under Stamitz's influence, to produce a set of *Six Symphonies à 4 parties* (now lost) and four more sets during 1759–62.

Like the earlier symphonies of Sammartini, the *VI Simphonies dans le goût italien, en trio* (Paris, 1740) of Louis-Gabriel Guillemain (1705–70) and other French symphonies of the period, Richter's *Grandes Simphonies*, and Stamitz's own Op. 1, *Six Sonates à trois ou avec tout l'orchestre* (Paris, *c.* 1755), these could be played either by soloists or by several players to a part according to the size of the auditorium. The keyboard continuo was common to both methods and even when symphonies were described as *a più instrumenti*, the additional instruments – usually a pair of woodwind (flutes or oboes often unspecified) and a pair of horns – were frequently dispensable though they gradually took over more obligatory parts. Indeed this was how they were printed when the vogue for them swept Paris in the 1750s: not in score but in sets of usually eight parts: two for violins, one for viola, one for bass (used by cello, double bass, bassoons, and keyboard), two each for woodwind and horns. And publication, especially when pairs of trumpets, timpani, and (exceptionally) clarinets – as in Nos. 1 and 2 of Gossec's Op. 5 – were added, led to standardization in the constitution of the orchestra. From about 1757 onward Huberty, La Chevardière, and other Parisian publishers flooded the market with symphonies by Stamitz, Richter, Sammartini, Gossec, the Viennese Wagenseil, Stamitz's Austrian colleague at Mannheim, Ignaz Holzbauer (1711–83), another Czech, the cellist Anton Filtz (*c.* 1730–60) and others. They were issued usually in sets of six, sometimes by *divers auteurs*, sometimes separately at monthly intervals as *symphonies périodiques* or in London, when the vogue reached there a few years later, as 'periodical overtures'. In 1762 Breitkopf of Leipzig brought out the first of a series of thematic *Cataloghi delle Sinfonie* which he was prepared to supply in carefully hand-copied parts, not printed ones. As for Italy, the birthplace of music-printing, and Vienna, hand-copying was now the normal practice.

STAMITZ AND THE YOUNGER SYMPHONISTS

Stamitz worked on a comparatively large scale. He not only adopted the four-movement form, with the minuet extended by a trio section; as a rule in his first movements the tonic and dominant areas of what we may call the exposition both include several strongly contrasted ideas; there is no double-bar and repeat; and the second section is some form of return from dominant to tonic. But he was no slave to routine; in the *Sinfonia pastorale*, Op. 4, No. 2 the main themes of both 'subjects' (which are played by the wind) are recapitulated in the tonic as are those in No. 5 of the set 'by various authors' published as *La Melodia Germanica*;[21] in No. 3 of the same set[22] there is only a brief reference to first-subject material in the tonic at the end of the movement, and in Op. 5, No. 2[23] the first-subject themes are recapitulated partly in the dominant, partly in the tonic. By the fire of his imagination, his skill in exploiting subtle relationships, and his control of broad, slow-moving harmonic bases, he contrives to weld into satisfying wholes the sharp thematic contrasts which must have excited contemporary audiences by their novelty. For instance the first of the *Melodia Germanica*[24] symphonies opens with a sharp call to attention and one of those crescendi for which the Mannheim orchestra and composers were famous (i) and in the dominant area provides both relationship (ii) and strong contrast (iii):

---

[21] First movement and finale in Lothar Hoffmann-Erbrecht, *Die Symphonie (Das Musikwerk)* (Cologne, 1967), p. 59.
[22] Ed. Riemann, *DTB*, vii (2), p. 1. Stamitz's three contributions to *La Melodia Germanica* were posthumously published as his Op. 11.
[23] Riemann, op. cit., p. 55; first movement in *HAM*, ii, No. 294.
[24] Riemann, op. cit., iii (1), p. 14.

Ex. 177

Stamitz's idiom, with its 'sighing' appoggiaturas and syncopated themes, is closely related to that of contemporary Italian opera. His love of crescendo effects was shared with – possibly derived from – Jommelli, and the Italianate nature of his slow movements may be illustrated by comparison of that of the third *Melodia Germanica* symphony:

Ex. 178

with the song from Galuppi's exactly contemporary *Filosofo di campagna* quoted on p. 453 (Ex. 160).

Stamitz died in 1757 – two years before Handel – but was succeeded by a whole generation of younger Mannheimers: Christian Cannabich (1731–98), a pupil of Jommelli and his successor as *Konzertmeister*; his son Carl (1745–1801) who studied with Cannabich, Richter, and Holzbauer; Carl Joseph Toeschi (d. 1788); and Ernst Eichner (1740–77). At the same time new talents appeared in Vienna: Florian Leopold Gassmann (1729–74); Carlos d'Ordoñez (1734–86), Spanish only by parentage; Leopold Hofmann (1738–93); Johann Wanhall (Jan Vaňhal) (1739–1813), a Czech; Carl Ditters von Dittersdorf (1739–99); and the genius who was ultimately to tower high above them all, Franz Joseph Haydn (1732–1809) – to say nothing of his far from negligible brother Michael (1737–1806), who (like Mozart's father) spent the greater part of his life in the archiepiscopal service at Salzburg. The youngest of the Bachs, Johann Christian, also made a belated debut as a composer of concert symphonies after his move to London in 1762, where he went into partnership with Karl Friedrich Abel (1723–87) in the giving of public concerts (1764–81).[25] These were of the same generation as Traetta and Piccinni, Sacchini and di Majo. The age of 'sensibility' had dawned, and the musical idiom generated by the concept of stylized representation of codified emotions was obsolete.

DIVERSITY OF INSTRUMENTAL FORMS

Concerted instrumental music became increasingly diversified. The concert symphony, carried on the wave of fashion, became ever more important – and also more different from the opera sinfonia, of which the one-movement

---

[25] Abel, the son of Sebastian Bach's gamba-player and himself a former gambist in the Dresden orchestra under Hasse, also composed six sets of symphonies, one of which – his Op. 7, No. 6 (1764) – was later reprinted as a work of the child Mozart (K. 18). A complete edition of Abel's works has been edited and published by Walter Knape (Cuxhaven, 1966–   ).

form, as in Gluck's *Orfeo*, was increasingly favoured. And lighter forms resembling the symphony but usually with more movements and diverse instrumentation became popular and flourished under a variety of names which defy clear definition and are often interchangeable: serenade, divertimento, *cassazione*, *notturno*, and others. They were intended for social and festive occasions and, when wind instruments predominated, for outdoor performance. Some might be played orchestrally but performance by solo instruments was evidently more common. Haydn's early *divertimenti a quattro*,[26] written during the 1750s, are the works we know as his string quartets Opp. 1 and 2, yet we cannot be sure that these were intended for solo performers. According to his early biographer, Griesinger,[27] Op. 1, No. 1 was written for four specified players, but No. 3 exists with horn parts and No. 5 as a 'sinfonia' with both oboes and horns. When La Chevardière published Nos. 1, 2, 3, and 4 in 1764 with two quartets by Toeschi he described them as *Six Simphonies ou Quatuors Dialogués*. Certainly the harmony of some of the early quartets shows that Haydn expected a bass to double the cello an octave lower. Yet, so far as terminology was concerned, as late as 1772 the Op. 20 set which are solo quartets beyond shadow of doubt are described on the autograph as *divertimenti a quattro*.

HAYDN'S EARLY SYMPHONIES

Haydn composed a considerable number of divertimenti for strings, strings and wind, or wind only, in three to six or eight parts and as many as five or six movements, before his earliest true symphonies which date from about 1758.[28] The one which he told Griesinger was his first, and which is accordingly numbered 1 in modern editions, is pure Stamitz in its opening[29] but shows nothing of Stamitz's command of form; Haydn was for some time content with variants of the older binary type of first movement. But his variants are innumerable. His early symphonies are remarkable above all else for diversity of every kind: form, style (with curious throw-backs to the outmoded), instrumentation. The first three written at Eisenstadt after his appointment as *Vice-Capellmeister* to the Princes Eszterházy in 1761 are entitled 'Le Matin', 'Le Midi', and 'Le Soir' (with a finale headed 'La Tempesta'); the descriptive element is minimal but the second movement of 'Le Midi' is an accompanied *recitativo* for solo violin[30] and the third a virtuoso coloratura duet for the violin and a solo cello – all three symphonies include movements with concertante parts for violin and cello. The one flute

[26] The master edition of Haydn's music is *Joseph Haydn Werke*, produced by the Haydn Institut, Cologne (Munich and Duisburg, 1958–   ).
[27] Georg August Griesinger, *Biographische Notizen über Joseph Haydn* (Leipzig, 1810); modern edition, ed. Franz Grasberger (Vienna, 1954), p. 13.
[28] The standard work on Haydn's symphonies is H. C. Robbins Landon, *The Symphonies of Joseph Haydn* (London, 1955; supplement, London 1961). Landon has also edited the complete symphonies in miniature score (Vienna, 12 vols., 1963–8).
[29] Quoted in Hoffmann-Erbrecht, *Die Symphonie*, p. 15.
[30] An effect repeated ten years later in the Adagio of the quartet, Op. 17, No. 5.

(two are employed only in the third movement of 'Le Midi') is independent of the oboes and, like the single bassoon – and in one brief passage the horns – has a few genuine solos. The first movement of 'Le Soir' is cast in the sonata-form key-pattern but with unmemorable themes. The symphonies of the next three or four years also have peculiar features: concertante movements (in Nos. 13, 24, and the misnumbered 36), adagio first movements (e.g. Nos. 11, 18, 21, 22, 34). In the Adagio of No. 22 a pair of cors anglais alternate with a pair of horns, all playing *ff*, in a broad hymnlike melody against the incessant quaver accompaniment of muted strings. Sometimes, as in No. 19, Haydn adopts a device of which he was fond all his life, the so-called *fausse reprise*, bringing back the first subject in the tonic at bar 5 after the double-bar but only in passing; the real reprise begins more than 30 bars later.

Haydn soon became internationally known, for in 1768[31] La Chevardière followed up the already mentioned *Simphonies* (really quartets) with another set (similarly titled) which did include four genuine but pre-1761 symphonies (Nos. 15, 25, 32, and 33) as well as two divertimenti. But so far he must have given an impression of gifted eccentricity, for instance by ending the Presto assai of No. 23 dying away pianissimo to a single pizzicato chord, or by writing a pair of symphonies, Nos. 72 (wildly misnumbered) and 31 (both 1765) with concertante parts for four horns, violin, and cello. The first ten bars of the allegro development of No. 12 (1763) are a tonal wilderness. No. 49 in F minor (1768), another symphony with an adagio first movement, has an allegro second in sonata-form opening with great leaps on the violins: $c''–c'/d\flat''–e\natural'/b\flat''–g$. However when Charles Burney visited Austria in 1772 it was not Haydn who 'like another Shakespeare . . . pushed art further than any one had done before him', whose 'genius was truly original, bold, and nervous'; it was Johann Stamitz. Haydn is mentioned only with other notable composers and as the author of 'some exquisite quartets', perhaps those of Op. 9, in which the first violin is very much the predominant partner, or the new Op. 17.

The removal of the Eszterházy court to the new great palace at Eszterháza in 1766 practically isolated Haydn, now *Capellmeister*, and his musicians for the greater part of each year. But, as he told Griesinger, he could experiment as he liked with his orchestra:[32] 'I was cut off from the world . . . and so I had to be original.' So, as he matured, eccentricity became marked individuality. This was disliked by North German critics[33] who pilloried him with Dittersdorf and Filtz for mixing the serious with the comic, 'particularly as there is more of the latter than the former in their works; and

---

[31] It was not until ten years later that music-publication was begun in Vienna by the firm of Artaria.
[32] It was modest in size: not more than four first violins, four seconds, two violas, and two basses, pairs of oboes, bassoons and horns. Flautists and clarinettists were extras and, except during 1780–1, there were neither trumpets nor timpani (see Dénes Bartha and László Somfai, *Haydn als Opernkapellmeister*, Budapest, 1960, pp. 47–8).
[33] See Burney, *A General History of Music from the Earliest Ages to the Present Period*, four vols. (London, 1776–89). Modern edition in two vols. ed. Frank Mercer (London, 1935), ii, p. 959.

as for rules, they know but little of them'. The Austrians were naturally more open to wider influences from Italy.

THE PIANO CONCERTOS AND SYMPHONIES OF J. C. BACH

At Vienna Dittersdorf and Leopold Hofmann, like the younger Mann-heimers (particularly Cannabich), extensively cultivated the keyboard concerto, a genre which Haydn rather neglected. That neglect in itself shows his aloofness from the fashionable, for the solo concerto – above all, the keyboard concerto – had begun to run the symphony close in popularity. In fact by the time C. P. E. Bach moved from Berlin to Hamburg in 1767 he had written forty keyboard concertos (a few of them originally for flute, oboe, or cello) but only nine symphonies. Bach's much younger brother and pupil Johann Christian, after becoming completely Italianized (cf. p. 459), sounded a new note in his instrumental music, the so-called 'singing allegro',[34] exemplified by the opening of the first concerto of his Op. 1 set (London, 1763) – by no means his earliest concertos. The solo instrument is specified as the *clavecin* but when it takes up that opening theme:

Ex. 179

it is clear that it demands an instrument with more cantabile potential than the harpsichord. London did not hear the pianoforte until 1767 – Paris two years later – and Bach seems to have been the first to play a solo on it publicly (2 June 1768) but he must have known it from his Berlin days and his Op. 1 was probably composed with it in mind. They are intimate, modest works with only 'deux Violons et une Violoncelle' – thus really quartets – and Nos. 1–3 and 5 are in only two movements, the second usually a minuet; No. 4 has slow movement and presto finale, No. 6 a slow movement and some rather puerile variations on 'God save the King' (Queen Charlotte being the dedicatee). Far from being virtuoso display pieces, they are well within the reach of cultivated amateurs.[35] Formally they demonstrate the infiltration of the sonata-form idea into the *galant* concerto; the ghost of the ritornello still haunts his concertos but their rationale is thematic contrast and key contrast-and-reconciliation.

Two years after his first concertos, Bach published his first set of six symphonies in London, where a Scottish pupil of Stamitz, the Earl of Kellie

---

[34] Anticipated by his brother in a B flat concerto of 1751, ed. in its probably original form for cello by W. Schulz (Leipzig, 1938). Its roots were, of course, in Italian opera.
[35] In 1772 his brother Emanuel published at Hamburg at his own expense six 'easy' harpsichord concertos 'at the request of numerous amateurs'. The 'accompaniment' was for two violins, violetta, bass, and pairs of flutes and horns *per rinforza*. There is a modern edition of No. 2, ed. Ludwig Landshoff (Wilhelmshaven, 1967).

(1732–81), also published a set of six at about the same time. (The symphonies of Boyce and Arne are for the most part overtures to odes or theatre pieces, in an older idiom.) Bach had already composed opera sinfonie, some of which were published as concert pieces among the collections of *symphonies périodiques*, and the Op. 3 set are not markedly different: elegant, beautifully fashioned, with occasional evidence of Mannheim influence. The Op. 6 set (*c*. 1770), in the first two of which Bach adopts sonata-form proper, are another matter. No. 6 in G minor[36] is a masterpiece bursting with the passion Mozart was to associate with that key, yet dying away *pp* at the end like Haydn's No. 23. In the C minor Andante più tosto adagio, for strings only, instead of honeyed melody we get a stern opening unison, 'yearning' chromaticism (i), and dissonant anguish (ii):

Ex. 180

HAYDN AND STRING-QUARTET STYLE

Similar passionate emotion permeates much of Haydn's work of the same period: notably the E minor Symphony, No. 44, the Quartets (*divertimenti a quattro*), Op. 20, Nos. 3 and 5, the Piano Sonata in C minor. Yet in these same works he imposes stricter discipline on himself; the minuet of the E minor Symphony proceeds in close canon at the octave between violins and basses throughout; in No. 47 both minuet and trio are totally reversible; and the tragic F minor Quartet, No. 5, has a final fugue with two subjects, the first sometimes inverted simultaneously with the original form. No. 6 of the same set ends with a three-subject fugue, No. 2 with a four-subject one. But these are strange fugues, all three marked to be played *sotto voce* throughout,

[36] Miniature score, ed. Richard Platt (London, 1974).

exercises not in the manner of J. S. Bach but of J. J. Fux or F. X. Richter.[37] It was one solution to the problem of giving the instruments equally interesting parts.

Already in Opp. 9 and 17 Haydn had made the final distinction between quartet and string symphony; the virtuoso passages for first violin are solo music and the cello parts are unthinkable as orchestral basses. Richter too had made it, less spectacularly, in his *Six Quartettos*, Op. 5 (London, 1768).[38] It was above all in the texture of such movements as the first Allegro of Op. 20, No. 1, where he found a more fertile solution than fugue to the problem of instrumental parity, that Haydn differentiates his quartet style. There is nothing of this motivic 'goldsmiths' style' in the symphonies written at about the same time: the already mentioned No. 44 (not even in the exquisite Adagio), Nos. 45 (the 'Farewell'), 46 (with its extraordinary recall of the minuet near the end of the finale), and 48 ('Maria Theresia'), which salutes the visiting Empress with trumpets and drums. One does, however, notice that oboes and horns are more often freed from their roles of merely doubling or supplying a 'binding' stratum of sustained sound.

THE *SYMPHONIE CONCERTANTE*

This freedom is something quite different from the concertante element, as in the horn-writing of the earlier No. 31. But the concertante element was flourishing elsewhere in the symphony at this very time. A set of six symphonies by C. P. E. Bach (Hamburg, 1773), though for strings only, demand a string concertino, and his younger brother had just produced a number of *simphonies concertantes*, specifically so called, which were published in Paris or Amsterdam.[39] This was a hybrid form which flourished, particularly in Paris from *c.* 1770 for a couple of decades and in Germany from *c.* 1780: not so much symphony as concerto but with more than one solo instrument. The *symphonie concertante* was usually in two movements, hardly ever more than three, and ended with a rondo, minuet-and-trio, or variations – essentially a light-weight, 'popular' form of orchestral music. It was probably brought to Paris by Carl Stamitz, who wrote more than twenty, and Cannabich, and taken up there by the Italian violinist-composer Giovanni Giuseppe Cambini (1746–1825) who is said to have composed about eighty. Jean-Baptiste Davaux (1742–1822) wrote a number of *symphonies concertantes*, as did Joseph de Saint-Georges (1739–99);[40] but the best Parisian symphonists – Gossec, Henri-Joseph Rigel (1741–99), Simon Le Duc (*c.* 1745–77) – appear to have contributed

[37] There is a *sinfonia da camera* for four-part strings by Richter (ed. Walter Upmeyer, Hanover, 1931), which ends with a similar, though less learned, fugue; it is in two sections – tonic-dominant/dominant-tonic – each repeated. And in 1773 Gassmann published six quartets, *Chacun avec deux fugues.*
[38] Ed. Riemann, *DTB*, xv.
[39] There are several modern editions of separate symphonies from the elder brother's set; two of Johann Christian's have been published in miniature score by Fritz Stein (Leipzig, 1935) and Alfred Einstein (London, 1947).
[40] See p. 506.

only a handful between them. Significantly, it was in Paris, during April 1778, that Mozart wrote his first *sinfonia concertante* (K. Anhang 9)[40a] for the Concert spirituel, where its performance was prevented by an intrigue of Cambini's. Next year, back in Salzburg, he essayed two more, K. 364 and the unfinished K. Anh. 104, as well as the fine concerto for two harpsichords, K. 365.

MOZART'S DEVELOPMENT AS INSTRUMENTAL COMPOSER

The young Mozart had begun to show his mettle as an instrumental composer four or five years earlier. Under the influence of the symphonies of Sammartini and J. C. Bach which he heard at the Salzburg Académies during 1772, he produced a series of symphonies four of which – K. 130, 132, 133, and 134 – cannot be dismissed as remarkable juvenilia; they are vigorous four-movement works which bear comparison with the work of most of his mature contemporaries. In the summer of 1773 he composed six string quartets, K. 168–73, very different from earlier efforts in the vein of Sammartini; indeed he had already in the first movement of K. 157 (bars 25ff.) demonstrated in passing that he had not much more to learn about instrumental parity in quartet style:

Ex. 181

The lessons are not always applied; the slow movement of K. 170 is simply an accompanied violin solo; K. 168 and K. 173 follow the fashion for fugal finales. And the originally Italianate quintet, K. 174, written under the influence of Michael Haydn's C major quintet and recast under that of his G major,[41] looks both ways. But this quintet was immediately followed by a more exciting 'first', the harpsichord concerto K. 175, which Mozart continued to play nine or ten years later – though with a new finale, the rondo, K. 382, a lighter-weight piece than the contrapuntal, sonata-form original ending. Indeed, with all its indebtedness to J. C. Bach, K. 175 is more firmly knit by thematic entries than Bach's most mature concertos and scored for a much larger orchestra, with oboes, horns, trumpets, and drums. Also from the winter of 1773–4 date the earliest of Mozart's really memorable symphonies, the fiery and passionate G minor, K. 183, and the A

[40a] Doubtfully authentic in its surviving form.
[41] Both ed. Hans Albrecht (Lippstadt, 1952).

major, K. 201, which, according to Wyzewa and Saint-Foix,[42] is closely
modelled on a symphony in the same key by Michael Haydn.

In 1775 Mozart broke more new ground with five delightful violin
concertos. He was never nearer to J. C. Bach than in the first of them, K.
207, and K. 218 is very closely modelled on one in the same key (D major)
formerly attributed to Luigi Boccherini (1743–1805).[43] Another Italian who
may have influenced Mozart to some extent was Pietro Nardini (1722–93)
who had published his Op. 1 violin concertos a few years before. (Those of
Mozart's close contemporary Giovanni Battista Viotti (1755–1824) did not
appear till 1782.) But the ultimate products, particularly K. 218 and 219,
with their amusingly variegated rondo-finales,[44] are completely Mozartean.
During the next year or so he composed a great deal of divertimento-type
music at Salzburg, including such delightful things as the *Serenata notturna*
for two orchestras, the *Notturno* for four, and the 'Haffner' Serenade (K.
250), but no symphonies or string quartets and only two harpsichord
concertos, K. 238 and 271.

Then in 1777 he made an extended expedition, discovering at last at
Augsburg a type of pianoforte (made by Johann Andreas Stein) which really
satisfied him by its expressive possibilities and the efficient damping which
remedied the weakest point of the earlier piano; it is significant that the two
keyboard sonatas written at Mannheim next month (K. 309 and 311) were
published in Paris as 'pour le Clavecin ou le Forte Piano'.[45] He spent the
winter months at Mannheim where he probably got to know J. C. Bach's
quintets, Op. 11,[46] dedicated to the Elector Karl Theodor; at any rate the
second theme of the first Allegro of No. 6:

Ex. 182

stuck in his mind – to be thrown up years later in the finale of his piano
quartet, K. 478, and piano rondo, K. 485. Mozart also heard the very last of
the famous Mannheim orchestra, for while he was there Karl Theodor
succeeded to the Bavarian Electorate and moved his court to Munich, taking
with him Cannabich and a number of the players – who were now allowed to
give public performances. After writing some quartets and concertos with
flute for a wealthy amateur flautist, Mozart himself moved on to Paris where

[42] *Wolfgang Amédée Mozart*, ii (Paris, 1936), p. 126. The model has been ed. C. A. Sherman (Vienna, 1968).
[43] Elsa von Zschinsky-Troxler, 'Mozarts D dur-Violinkonzert und Boccherini', *ZfMW*, x (1927–28), p. 415. On Mozart's genuine indebtedness to Boccherini, see Hans Keller, 'Mozart and Boccherini', *The Music Review*, viii (1947), p. 241.
[44] The rondo – either of the simple 'French' type or the more sophisticated 'sonata-rondo' in which the first return of the main subject is followed by a species of development – became particularly popular as a finale form during the last quarter of the century.
[45] On the whole question of Mozart's keyboard instruments, see Nathan Broder, 'Mozart and the "Clavier" ', *MQ*, xxvii (1941), p. 422.
[46] Ed. Rudolf Steglich, *EDM*, iii.

he suffered the already mentioned fiasco of the *sinfonia concertante*, K. Anh. 9, but scored a popular success with a rather uncharacteristic three-movement symphony in D, K. 297. This was his first for four years – and the first in which he added clarinets and timpani to his forces.[47] (He continued to use timpani, but clarinets only as afterthoughts in K. 385 and 550; K. 543 is the only symphony with clarinets in the original score.) Another uncharacteristic Paris work was the concerto for flute and harp commissioned for the Duc de Guines and his daughter.

After his return to Salzburg Mozart's instrumental ensemble music again mainly took the divertimento form. During the years 1779–81 he wrote only two three-movement symphonies, K. 319 and 338, to which he added minuets in 1782. (In 1780 he had written 12 bars in full score of a minuet for K. 338, a wonderful little work all air and fire, but then inexplicably broke off.) A *sinfonia concertante* for violin and viola (K. 364), a *Concerto a due cembali* (K. 365), and a quartet for oboe and strings (K. 370) complete the tale.

THE BACH BROTHERS AND HAYDN

These were the years in which C. P. E. Bach published his last and finest symphonies (in 1780, but they had been composed four years earlier), the *Orchester Sinfonien mit zwölf obligaten Stimmen*,[48] of which No. 3 opens with one of the most memorable Promethean gestures of late eighteenth-century music (i), a gesture to which Haydn was to respond in rather different mood in the opening of his Symphony No. 78 of 1782 (ii):

Ex. 183

---

[47] In 1773 the orchestra of the Concert spirituel had consisted of 13 first violins, 11 seconds, 4 violas, 10 cellos, 4 basses, 2 flutes, 3 oboes, 2 clarinets, 4 bassoons, and pairs of horns, trumpets, and timpani (see Adam Carse, *The Orchestra in the XVIIIth Century*, Cambridge, 1940, p. 25). The Mannheim orchestra of the same period was rather weaker in strings.

[48] They are three-movement works. Neither of the Bach brothers ever adopted the four-movement structure which was becoming normal for the symphony – whereas the concerto remained a three-movement form.

They were also the years in which Johann Christian published *his* last set, the six of Op. 18 (*c.* 1781), of which Nos. 1, 3, and 5 are for double orchestra –an old Italian opera device (cf. 451, n. 18) resulting in a sub-species of *sinfonia concertante* – No. 2 is the overture to his *Lucio Silla* (written for Mannheim in 1776) and No. 4 borrows its Haydnish Andante from the overture to *Temistocle* (Mannheim, 1772).[49] Haydn also was resurrecting opera movements in his symphonies: the overture to *Il mondo della luna* (1777) reorchestrated as the first movement of No. 63,[50] the 'hunt' prelude to Act III of *La fedeltà premiata* (1780) as the finale of No. 73 (1781).

HAYDN, MOZART, AND STRING QUARTET TEXTURE

From 1775 to 1781 Haydn, like Mozart, rather neglected the major instrumental ensemble forms. He was preoccupied with opera at Eszterháza, not so much his own works – and he produced nothing remotely comparable with *Idomeneo* (1781) – but the conducting of other people's.[51] He wrote only a dozen or so symphonies, mostly *c.* 1779, of which the most remarkable is No. 70, a D major symphony with a D minor slow movement (*specie d'un canone in contrapunto doppio*) and a D minor finale consisting mostly of a three-subject fugue also in invertible counterpoint but with the most whimsical D major coda. In Nos. 53 and 63 (*c.* 1777) he began the practice, later a favourite one, of casting slow movements in the form of variations on alternate themes, major and minor. He wrote no quartets at all for nine years, until in 1781 he announced the forthcoming publication of a set of six (Op. 33) written 'auf eine ganz neue besondere Art'. By this 'quite new peculiar manner' he clearly meant not only instrumental parity but the weaving of texture from the motivic fragmentation and remoulding of themes. It was not quite as new as he claimed but it had never before been practised with such consistency and mastery as in the first movement of No. 2, where the motive *x* of the opening theme:

Ex. 184

is soon being handed from first violin, to cello, to viola, to cello-cum-second violin, and so on, and the first three notes of Ex. 184 introduce the short second-key area. Hardly a bar is not derived from it, and the end of the movement:

[49] Miniature scores of No. 2, ed. Gwilym Beechey (London, 1971), and No. 4, ed. Alfred Einstein (Leipzig, n.d.).
[50] Cf. the passage from both quoted in Landon, op. cit., pp. 361–2.
[51] In 1778, for instance, four first performances (operas by Guglielmi, Piccinni, Anfossi, and Gazzaniga) and five revivals (by Piccinni, Paisiello, and three by Dittersdorf). See Bartha and Somfai, op. cit., pp. 74ff.

Ex. 185

is reached by a quasi-logical evolution in which there is no false link. By no means everything is as tightly woven, but the principle underlies even the slow movements of Nos. 4 and 6 and such lighthearted movements as the final rondo of No. 3 and the scherzando of No. 1. In Op. 33 Haydn calls his fast minuets *scherzi* or *scherzandi*; he had already marked the 'menuetto' of Op. 20, No. 4 *alla zingarese* and it would have been absurd to style the Austrian *Ländler* of Op. 33, No. 2, or the Czech *sousedska* of No. 5, a minuet. (Throughout his life he had a quick ear for the characteristic rhythms and melodic idioms of all the various races of the Habsburg dominions.) But these innovations were not carried into the symphonies. Haydn never called his symphonic minuets *scherzi*, though some are obviously quite fast. 'Thematic open-work' is employed only occasionally, as in the development section of the C minor symphony, No. 78.

Thematic open-work is, however, employed with superb craftsmanship in a quartet (K. 387) that Mozart completed on the last day of 1782 and in two others, K. 421 and 428, of next summer. They were the first three of the set which were appropriately dedicated 'al Signor Giuseppe Haydn . . . Dal Suo Amico W. A. Mozart'.[52] (The fugal writing of the finale of K. 387 was a natural consequence of his preoccupation with fugal studies during 1782.) The influence of the 'new peculiar manner' was not limited to composers but ultimately induced a new way of listening to chamber music and later to instrumental music in general: as (to quote Goethe's famous phrase) to 'the conversation of four intelligent people'.[53] The connoisseur might admire the 'science' of fugal writing but appreciation of quasi-conversational texture – and quasi-logical form – was well within the capacity of those who,

[52] With a most affectionate personal letter (1 September 1785); they had got to know each other much better during the previous winter.
[53] Letter to Carl Friedrich Zelter (9 November 1829).

like Diderot, wanted to understand music without having to learn it ('je voudrais bien la savoir et ne la point apprendre'). Mozart did not, however, adopt Haydn's tight weave, his striving toward thematic relationship; he preferred marked thematic contrasts and now began to provide another type of music for connoisseurs in which thematic contrast within the movement was exploited to the full.

MOZART AND THE PIANO CONCERTO

So far he had written few piano concertos, and none for five years. Now, between the winter of 1782–3 in Vienna and early December 1786, he produced no fewer than fifteen. During the same period he composed only one symphony, the so-called 'Linz' (K. 425), though it is true he immediately followed the C major Concerto (K. 503) with a three-movement symphony in D for performance at Prague. It is on these fifteen concertos from K. 413 to K. 503, not on his symphonies despite the three final masterpieces in E flat, G minor, and C major of 1788, that Mozart's fame as an orchestral composer is most firmly based. Strangely, he returned to the piano concerto only twice later: K. 537 in 1788 and K. 595 in the last year of his life.

The three earliest of this outpouring of concertos, K. 413–5, are stylistically not so very different from the later concertos – Op. 13 (*sic*) (1777) and Op. 7 (*c.* 1780) – of J. C. Bach, or those of Bach's protégé Johann Samuel Schröter (1752–88) who published two sets of piano concertos in London, Op. 3 (1776) and 5 (*c.* 1780), which Mozart admired.[54] Like Bach's concertos, K. 413–5 can – as Mozart pointed out to the French publisher Sieber (letter of 26 April 1783) – also be played *a quattro*, i.e. as chamber music with the wind parts omitted. (He had confided to his father (28 December 1782) that there were passages aimed at '*connoisseurs alone . . .* yet so that the non-connoisseurs will be content without knowing why'.) Whether the pianist played with the strings, continuo-wise, in performances *a quattro*, is doubtful; J. C. Bach's Op. 11 quintets were initially published (*c.* 1776) with the bass figured, though the continuo was redundant; but the case was very different with larger ensembles where, however unnecessary for harmonic filling, the continuo player directed the performance. The piano always played continuo during the tuttis in normal performances of Mozart's concertos;[55] conversely, accompaniments to the pianist's solos were played by strings soli. The earlier mature concertos, including K. 449, are for modest orchestras with hardly more than pairs of oboes and horns; the trumpet and timpani parts of K. 415 appear first in an edition of 1802. The rondo finales of the violin concertos, K. 218 and 219, are recalled in the

---

[54] He wrote cadenzas for Schröter's Op. 3, Nos. 1, 4, and 6, and – as Konrad Wolff has shown (*MQ*, xliv (1958), p. 350), the finale of the E flat Concerto, K. 482 (1785), is an exact reminiscence of the opening of Schröter's Op. 5, No. 6. There is a modern edition of his Op. 3, No. 3, ed. K. Schultz-Hauser (Mainz, 1964).

[55] See, for instance, the miniature score of K. 415, ed. Hans F. Redlich (London, 1954). All editions published during the nineteenth century and the first half of the twentieth were tampered with.

final Tempo di minuetto of K. 413 and the C minor episodes in the finale of K. 415. Even K. 449 a year later is potentially a miniature work, with *ad libitum* oboe and horn parts, and the idiom is still that of ideally instrumentalized Italian opera. But the magical chromatic thirds or tenths of the first movement of K. 450 and Andante of K. 451 belong, like the other concertos of 1784, to a more symphonic type.

There is a curious family likeness about the marchlike repeated notes, anticipated in K. 415, of the opening themes of K. 451, 453, 456, and 459, which seem to announce a more orchestral style; the opening tuttis are completely symphonic and the wind-group often plays a totally independent role; and by this time Mozart had evolved a quasi-symphonic first-movement plan. (The slow movements may be in sonata-form-without-development, a rondo, or variations; the finales are generally rondos.) The orchestra propounds as many as half-a-dozen ideas, all in the tonic except for a passing modulation or two; the soloist then freely repeats the first two of these, slips into the dominant – often doing so with an entirely new theme – and may or may not repeat all the rest in a 'second exposition'. Next comes a short tutti in the dominant on one or two of the original ideas and usually including the last of them if omitted by the soloist. In a middle section, either 'development' or on new material, and in a recapitulation of most or all of the themes in the tonic, soloist and orchestra have ample scope for interplay. A final tutti, interrupted by the soloist's cadenza, refers back to the end of the first tutti. Such a scheme offered not only infinite opportunity for the composer to display his skill in manipulating the most disparate musical ideas but a frame of reference for the listening connoisseur who could enjoy both the performance as such and the surprises in the play of musical ideas.

All the more striking must have been the impact of some of the concertos of the next group: K. 466, 467, 482, 488, 491, and 503 (1785–6). Not merely are they more symphonic, the wind treated much more freely, and the themes less disparate; the frame of reference itself is shattered. The agitated syncopated minor chords and threatening bass figure of the first tutti of the D minor, K. 466, are not taken up later by the piano; instead it utters a cry, a plea, and the movement becomes a dramatic dialogue between soloist and orchestra. Here again is that passionate note of personal emotion we have already noticed in C. P. E. Bach and Haydn (cf. Ex. 183); indeed the opening of Haydn's C minor Symphony seems to be echoed in the opening of Mozart's concerto in the same key, K. 491. The age of elegance was coming to an end; the age of romanticism – deeper and more personal than 'sensibility' – was dawning.[56] Both first movements, the D minor and the C minor, end pianissimo – the piano adding simple arpeggios to the C minor by way of prelude to the *sancta simplicitas* of the Larghetto. Not all the concertos of this group are impassioned; the first solo of the C major, K.

[56] Compare also the G minor piano quartet, K. 478, which likewise dates from 1785. In that same year a 15-year-old Rhinelander, Ludwig van Beethoven (1770–1827) also composed three piano quartets; the first includes an E flat minor Allegro con spirito in which passion is at least well simulated.

467, begins with a little surprise that must have delighted the cognoscenti, but the work as a whole is as serenely classical as most of Mozart's compositions in that key; K. 482 has only similar, minor surprises; and the A major K. 488 belongs structurally to the 1784 group though it over-shadows the best of them by its surpassing loveliness. (In both 482 and 488 oboes are replaced by clarinets.) Then after an interval, partly filled by *Figaro*, another piano quartet (K. 493)[57] and the isolated string quartet in D (K. 499), came the greatest of the C major concertos, K. 503, as Olympian as the so-called 'Jupiter' Symphony itself. It was completed two days before the 'Prague' Symphony – in which Mozart exploited that independence of the wind-group which he had recently developed in the concertos.

MOZART'S LAST INSTRUMENTAL WORKS

Of the two later piano concertos, K. 537 (1788) – known as the 'Coronation' because Mozart played it, with K. 459, at Frankfurt two years later on the occasion of the coronation of the Emperor Leopold II – is disappointing and the tired beauty of K. 595 (1791) does not bear comparison with Mozart's last concerto of all, K. 622, for another instrument: the clarinet.[58] He had already written his last symphonies in 1788; the solemn, euphonious E flat; the passionate, 'romantic' G minor with its revolutionary division of a melodic phrase between strings/wind/strings, its 'chords' of simultaneous chromatic appoggiaturas; and the C major which includes such extremes as *opera buffa* – a snatch, which dominates the beginning of the development of the first movement, from an insert arietta (K. 541)[59] written for the Vienna production of Anfossi's *Gelosie fortunate* three months earlier ⁴/₄ and the fugal finales of Michael Haydn as exemplified in his symphonies in the same key of 1784 and that same year 1788.[60] Mozart had already half-remembered the opening of the younger Haydn's E flat symphony of 1783[61] in the first Allegro of his own, and he now planned the finale of his great C major on the same broad lines as Haydn's of 1784: an introduction, a 20-bar fugal exposition followed by a great deal of imitative writing introducing new themes and moving to the dominant; a development also with much imitation and widening the tonal area; a tonic recapitulation (omitting the 'fugal exposition') but otherwise normal; and a brilliant coda. Mozart was able to generate divine fire by rubbing together his dry contrapuntal sticks; Michael Haydn was not – but Mozart picked up a bit of one of his sticks:

---

[57] Mozart's chamber music with piano is discussed in the next chapter.
[58] Originally for an instrument recently constructed by the virtuoso Anton Stadler and his brother in which the mechanism of the normal clarinet was adapted to the basset-horn's slightly lower register.
[59] Which Haydn cut when preparing the Eszterháza production (Bartha and Somfai, op. cit., p. 55).
[60] Ed. respectively by Otto Schmid (Leipzig, 1895) and Lothar Herbert Perger, *DTÖ*, Jg. xiv (2) (vol. 29), p. 1.
[61] Ed. Perger, op. cit., p. 34.

Ex. 186

During the last five years of his life, as his interest in orchestral composition faded – except for the three great symphonies and a great quantity of dance music (36 minuets and nearly sixty *Deutsche* and *Ländler*) which, as Imperial *Kammerkompositeur*, he had to provide for court balls – Mozart turned more and more to chamber music. After closing the set of quartets dedicated to Haydn with the A major, K. 464, and the C major, K. 465, the one with its extraordinary end, the other with its extraordinary beginning, he wrote the D major, K. 499, dedicated to his publisher, Hoffmeister, in 1786 – and then during the last five years of his life only the three, K. 575, 589, 590, for the cello-playing King of Prussia; during the same period Joseph Haydn wrote nearly two dozen – including one set, Op. 50, for the same monarch. But Mozart's finest chamber music of this period was for the trio of piano, violin, and cello,[62] a medium of totally different origin in which Haydn began to be seriously interested at about the same time, and for string quintet – which Haydn altogether neglected though his younger brother did not. As we have seen (p. 497), Mozart's youthful B flat quintet, K. 174, was modelled on two by Michael Haydn. But that was fourteen years behind him. In the meantime Boccherini had popularized the medium – though writing for two cellos instead of two violas – by the publication of at least forty string quintets, and was to go on pouring them out for the rest of his life, charming and technically polished. But K. 515 and 516 (1787) and K. 593 and 614 of the last year of Mozart's life have nothing to do with Boccherini or Michael Haydn; they show him at the height of his powers, K. 516 in G minor being – except for the final rondo – perhaps the most tragic thing he ever wrote. And the quintet for clarinet and strings that came between the pairs of string quintets has a strong claim to be considered among the loveliest.

THE SYMPHONY DURING THE 1780S

During 1785–6 Haydn, who had begun to show traces of his younger

[62] See below, p. 527.

friend's influence in the few and rather experimental symphonies of the early 'eighties, composed six very fine ones, Nos. 82–7, for the recently founded Concert de la Loge Olympique of Paris. This orchestra, directed by Joseph de Saint-Georges, himself a composer of symphonies and concertos,[63] was even larger than that of the Concert spirituel, with forty violins and nearly a dozen string basses, and in two of the Paris symphonies, 82 and 86, Haydn took the fullest advantage of its resources – except that he never used the clarinets. (The rest of the woodwind are as emancipated, notably in the slow movements, as in Mozart's work of the same time.) The slow movement of No. 86 is an astonishing 'capriccio', while in those of 82 and 84 he draws near the French *romance* and in No. 85, which became such a favourite of Marie Antoinette that it was nicknamed 'La Reine', borrows an actual one, 'La gentille et jeune Lisette'. The subject of the rondo finale of No. 85 is a contredanse.[64] Three of the six have slow introductions – by no means an innovation, of course, but specially characteristic of his latest and finest work; four of the five dating from 1788–9 have them, and all but one of the last twelve. The introduction to No. 92 in G major (1789), nicknamed 'the Oxford' because Haydn played it there in 1791 when he was given an honorary doctorate, ends with a typical mystification: instead of the normal dominant harmony, an ambiguous augmented sixth which an innocent ear might take for the dominant seventh of A flat. Haydn's mastery of form and texture which he handles with the utmost plasticity and inexhaustible novelty were now at their height, as he proceeded to demonstrate also in the eighteen quartets Op. 50 (1787), 54 and 55 (1788), and 64 (1790), above all in the last set. Here – for instance in outlines softened by chromaticisms of unmistakable origin, such as

Ex. 187

Allegro spiritoso

(bar 21)

in the first movement of Op. 50, No. 4 – Haydn begins to draw from Mozart the interest on his earlier loans.

1790 was a climacteric year. The death of Prince Nikolaus Eszterházy at the end of September, and the immediate disbandment of the musical and theatrical establishment at Eszterháza by his successor set Haydn free to

---

[63] His *symphonie concertante*, Op. 13, has been published by Barry S. Brook, *La Symphonie française dans la seconde moitié du XVIIIe siècle* (Paris, 1962).
[64] The opening of the finale of Mozart's E flat Symphony is strikingly like a contredanse (K. 565, No. 1) which he composed four months later.

travel abroad for the first time and to enjoy in person his European celebrity. His greatest works were still to come; they belong to later chapters (see pp. 596, 617, and 656). And the following year death removed his only serious rival. Of his nearest contemporaries Dittersdorf had just closed his career as a symphonist with twelve mildly programmatic *Simphonies exprimant [les] métamorphoses d' Ovide* (first performed in 1786) and turned to chamber music with two sets of string quintets (1782 and 1789) and one of quartets (1788).[65] They are amiable light-weight works, sometimes eccentric in structure and reflecting the styles of both Haydn and Mozart without their genius, as in the Mozartean opening of No. 6:

Ex. 188

The ever prolific Boccherini is also open to the charge of euphonious weakness, but with less justice; at his best, as in some of his later symphonies and in the finale of this quartet, Op. 8, No. 6[66] (1769):

Ex. 189

[65] Nos. 1, 2, and 5 are available in miniature score.   [66] Ed. Enrico Polo (Milan, *c.* 1936).

he is neither weak nor over-euphonious. As for the younger Italians, Salieri's few symphonies and concertos are forgotten – perhaps unjustly; Muzio Clementi (1752–1832) had only just emerged as a symphonic composer with two works, Op. 18 (1786); and Cherubini's meagre instrumental music, other than his overtures, was still to come. Despite the violin concertos of Giovanni Battista Viotti (1755–1824), the best of which also lay in the future (see p. 598) and – like most of the music of Salieri, Cherubini, and Clementi – were composed in foreign lands, the long ascendancy of Italy in orchestral and chamber music was already over and it was being threatened, or was about to be threatened, in other fields.

24

Music for or with Keyboard (c. 1725–90)

We have seen how the *Clavier*, the 'keyboard' – harpsichord or organ – maintained its place, though with diminishing importance, as a continuo instrument in ensemble music, how the harpsichord came to rival and eventually actually to surpass even the violin as the favourite solo instrument with orchestra, and how during the last decade or so of the period the new pianoforte threatened the supremacy of the harpsichord. At the same time solo music for keyboard became increasingly popular, especially with the advent of the new instrument with its greater powers of expression and command of nuance – qualities which particularly appealed to the Age of Sensibility and actually led to the development of new types of solo song and of chamber music.

THE LATER CLAVIER MUSIC OF BACH, HANDEL, AND THEIR GERMAN CONTEMPORARIES

Surprisingly, the great period of organ music was over by the time of Bach's death in 1750. Even Bach's output of organ music during the last quarter-century of his life was not great in bulk, however superb in quality: the three great preludes and fugues in B minor, C major, and E minor (BWV 544, 547, 548), the preludes of 545 and 546, and the third part of the *Clavier Übung*,[1] published in 1739, which consists of 21 *Choral* preludes prefaced and concluded by the E flat Prelude and Fugue (BWV 552). (The second part of the *Clavier Übung* (1735) consists of imitations of orchestral styles for two-manual harpsichord – the 'Concerto after the Italian taste' and the B minor 'Overture in the French style' – and the fourth, probably 1742, of the so-called 'Goldberg variations' also for two-manual harpsichord.) Of the *Sechs Chorale von verschiedener Art* published by Georg Schübler of Leipzig in the late 1740s, five are transcriptions from cantata movements. The eighteen which Bach was preparing for publication just before his death are largely new versions of old compositions. Another work prepared for the printer at the same time was *Die Kunst der Fuge*, a crowning demonstration of contrapuntal mastery surpassing even the *Musikalisches Opfer* of 1747. While the latter includes two trio movements, with flute and violin, the *Art*

---

[1] See p. 444.

of Fugue is for a keyboard instrument alone – and the fact that it was written in score, like the fourth of the canonic variations on 'Vom Himmel hoch' (BWV 769) and the six-part ricercare of the *Opfer*, suggests that the instrument Bach had in mind was the organ. If so, the *Art of Fugue* is the last great monument not only of Bach's art and classical 'harmonic polyphony' but of classical organ music. The inflexibility of the organ was as unsuited to the music of 'sensibility' as harmonic polyphony was to its melodious and dynamically subtle style.

Handel had already written the best of his keyboard music, except perhaps for two or three of the *Six Fugues or Voluntarys for the Organ or Harpsichord* published in 1735, above all the noble sixth. In the same year his old Hamburg friend Mattheson, who had praised his fugues in *Der vollkommene Capellmeister*, dedicated to him *Die wol-klingende Finger-Sprache in zwölff Fugen.*[2] If Handel's keyboard fugues are less tightly woven than Bach's, the fugal theorist's are looser still; in a combination of three themes, as at the end of his No. 10, Mattheson produces a harmonic rather than a polyphonic effect; the music coagulates – and dissolves in an empty semiquaver flurry of broken 6/3 chords or sixths:

Ex. 190

(The small notes are non-thematic)

Telemann's *Fugues légères et petits jeux a clavessin seul* (1738–9)[3] are even more liquescent; they differ little in texture from the frankly melodious sets of 'petits jeux' which follow each one. Telemann was happier in the small forms of his *Fantaisies pour le clavessin: 3 Douzaines* (1733)[4] which he multiplies into large ones: the first *fantaisie* of the first *douzaine* consisting of allegro-adagio-allegro repeated, and the second of presto-adagio-presto repeated, after which the whole of No. 1 is to be played again, thus conjuring nine movements out of four – a process repeated with each pair of

[2] Modern edition by Lothar Hoffmann-Erbrecht, *Mitteldeutsches Musikarchiv* (I.1) (Leipzig, 1954).
[3] Modern edition by Martin Lange (Kassel, 1929).
[4] Modern edition by Max Seiffert (Kassel, 1935).

fantaisies. But Telemann's best harpsichord works are keyboard overtures, *VI Ouvertüren nebst zween Folgesätzen bei jedweder* (*c.* 1745),[5] like Bach's B minor, but with 'two following movements . . . trifling with French, Polish or what-not, and Italian', in the shape of slow movement and quick finale instead of a suite of dances. The last outstanding master of the German keyboard suite was the Viennese Court organist, Gottlieb Muffat (1690–1770), Georg's son, who left six fine *Partien*, as he calls them, in his *Componimenti musicali* (Augsburg, *c.* 1736).[6] Nos. 1 and 5 begin with French overtures and, like so many German composers of the period. Muffat was fond of French genre-titles. At his best, as in the dances of the third *Partie*, he is not so very inferior to Bach himself, and despite the clear-cut, balanced melodic phrases of his upper parts and occasional passages of quasi-recitative (e.g. the final adagio of the fantaisie No. 4), he is less 'progressive' than Telemann. His manuscript compositions include a great quantity of toccatas, ricercari, canzoni, and other studies in out-dated forms.

Nor was Telemann in his fifties and sixties more than an open-minded man sensitive to a changing climate. The real German progressives were Bach's two eldest sons: Wilhelm Friedemann and Carl Philipp Emanuel. While their father was bringing out the last part of his *Clavier Übung* and compiling the second book of the *Wohl temperirtes Clavier*, Emanuel was publishing his first two sets of *Sonate per cembalo*, the six dedicated to Frederick II of Prussia and the six dedicated to the Duke of Würtemberg (Nuremberg, 1742 and 1744),[7] and Friedemann published his D major sonata in 1745 and his E flat in 1748.[8] Both brothers adopted the Italian concerto/*sinfonia* three-movement form: fast-slow-fast. And, more impor-tant, as we have seen (p. 486), Emanuel sometimes employs embryonic sonata-form; so too does Friedemann in his E flat sonata. Equally 'progressive' are the nature of the themes, the phasing out of polyphony (most marked in all three movements of the fifth 'Prussian' sonata), and the high proportion of personally expressive passages – carried to an extreme in the recitatives of the slow movement of the first 'Prussian' sonata.

DOMENICO SCARLATTI AND THE HARPSICHORD SONATA

We have also seen that an Italian composer, Platti, working at Würzburg, likewise published a set of harpsichord sonatas revealing traces of embryonic sonata-form in 1742. (A second set followed *c.* 1746.) But their artistic value and historical importance have been much exaggerated. What is curious about them is that they appeared such a short time after the first keyboard sonatas of two almost exact Italian contemporaries of *Sebastian*

---

[5] Modern edition by F. Oberdörffer (Berlin, 1940).
[6] Ed. Guido Adler, *DTÖ*, Jg. iii (3) (vol. 7). A seventh *Partie* is a ciacona with 38 variations.
[7] Modern editions by Rudolf Steglich, *Nagels Musik-Archiv*, Nos. 6, 15, 21, and 22.
[8] Modern edition by Friedrich Blume, ibid., 78. Friedemann's other sonatas are ed. Blume, ibid., 63 and 156.

Bach, both Neapolitans. The delightful *Sonate ... divise in studii e divertimenti* (Naples, c. 1730),[9] six pairs of more or less fugal 'studies' coupled with tonally and sometimes motivically linked divertimenti, of Francesco Durante (1684–1755) are the by-product of a notable church-composer and teacher of composers (see p. 548). The case of the thirty *Essercizi* of Domenico Scarlatti (1685–1757), published in London in 1738, is very different. The son of Alessandro Scarlatti, Domenico had between 1703 and 1718 composed fourteen mediocre operas; like his numerous serenatas and cantatas they are completely under the shadow of his father. In 1720 he entered the Portuguese royal service and became the music-master of the king's daughter, who in 1729 married the Prince of the Asturias (later Philip V of Spain, Farinelli's patron) and took Domenico with her to Spain. There he spent the rest of his life and began a new career as a composer almost exclusively for the harpsichord; of his more than 550 'sonatas',[10] the vast majority are preserved in fifteen manuscript volumes originally belonging to his royal mistress. Thus Sebastian Bach's contemporary in years was the contemporary of his sons as a keyboard composer and the *Essercizi* of 1738 by which he first became known to the public, and later selections during his lifetime, represent only a tiny proportion of his output. Formally the basic pattern, however varied in detail, is the old conventional progress from tonic to dominant (marked by a new idea) and from dominant or other key back to the tonic. The majority, particularly those of his last eight years, were intended to be played as pairs, like Durante's, e.g. K. 115–6, 119–20, 132–3, 208–9, 215–16, and many others, the second piece being usually quicker and in 3/8 time like the finale of a Neapolitan opera sinfonia. They constitute a thesaurus of harpsichordal invention and device, born out of the very spirit of the instrument. Their technical demands are formidable – leaps, crossing of hands, note-repetition – and the harmony is daringly unorthodox,[11] pure keyboard harmony with scant regard for orthodox part-writing – but not crazy, as his method of notating *acciaccature* might lead one to suppose (cf. the opening of the second section of K. 215).

'THE SCARLATTI SECT IN LONDON'

Owing to his seclusion as a royal pet, Scarlatti's influence on his contemporaries was negligible. Even his young Portuguese colleague Carlos Seixas (1704–42) and his Spanish pupil Antonio Soler (1729–83), both composers of great ability, show very much less of it than one would expect.[12] One recognizes that they worked with much the same forms and

---

[9] Modern edition by Bernhard Paumgartner (Kassel, n.d.).
[10] See the catalogue in Ralph Kirkpatrick, *Domenico Scarlatti* (Princeton, 1953), p. 442. Complete edition, ed. Kenneth Gilbert (Paris, 1973–   ). Kirkpatrick has edited an excellent selection of *Sixty Sonatas* in two vols. (New York, 1953). 'K.' numbers refer to Kirkpatrick's catalogue.
[11] A family complaint: cf. p. 382.
[12] Seixas's harpsichord sonatas are ed. Santiago Kastner, *Portugaliae Musica*, x (Lisbon, 1965); selected sonatas ed. idem, *Cravistas portuguezes*, i and ii (Mainz, 1935 and 1950). Complete edition of Soler's sonatas, ed. Samuel Rubio (Madrid, 1957); various modern editions of selected works.

textures, but both were of too marked individuality to adopt the older man's idiosyncrasies. It was only in England, oddly enough, that these made any impression – as a result of the championship of Thomas Roseingrave (1690–1766), who had been on intimate terms for some years with Scarlatti in Italy and supervised the London production of his opera *Narciso* (originally *Amor d'un ombra*) in 1720. Roseingrave published an enlarged and revised collection of the sonatas in 1739; he had already brought out fifteen *Voluntaries and fugues made on purpose for the organ or harpsichord* (*c.* 1728)[13] of his own in which he displays unorthodox harmony and bold modulations akin to his idol's. Later, Burney in his *General History* (iv (1789), p. 665) names as 'the head of the Scarlatti sect in London' Joseph Kelway (*c.* 1702–82), who published six highly eccentric sonatas in 1764. The more sober Englishmen of the time – Maurice Greene (*c.* 1695–1755), Thomas Arne (1710–78) and James Nares (1715–83), Greene's successor as organist of the Chapel Royal – published Italianate, but not Scarlattian collections of 'lessons' for harpsichord. Greene's (1750)[13a] are unconnected single pieces, but seven of Arne's eight (1756) are genuine sonatas in several movements, some of which (e.g. the second of No. 1, the first Allegro of No. 3, the first movement of No. 4) employ the key-structure of the true sonata-form though without markedly profiled second subjects. The same may be said of the third 'lesson' (cf. the second movement) of Nares's second collection (1759).[14] (His first collection had appeared in 1747.) Just how Italianate Arne's keyboard writing is may be seen by comparing the first movement of his second sonata with the Allegro of the first of G. B. ('Padre') Martini's *Sonate per l'organo e il cembalo* (Bologna, 1747)):[15]

Ex. 191

(i) MARTINI

(ii) ARNE

---

[13] Modern edition by Vernon Butcher (London, n.d.).

[13a] Facsimile of original edition, intro. Davitt Moroney (London, 1977).

[14] Nares's 'lesson' was reprinted complete by J. A. Fuller Maitland, *Oxford History of Music*, iv (Oxford, 1902), p. 329, and has been ed. Henry G. Ley (London, 1926). Facsimile edition of Arne's sonatas intro. Gwilym Beechey and Thurston Dart (London, 1969).

[15] Modern edition by Hoffmann-Erbrecht, *Mitteldeutsches Musikarchiv*, I. v (Leipzig, 1954).

24. Music for or with Keyboard (c. 1725–90)

The same kind of wreathing, triplet-sown melodic line, the same three-part lay-out with the inner part starting off the beat (and in this case employing even the same little rhythmic motive), open Galuppi's Op. 1, No. 4 (London, 1756).[16] Galuppi's very large number of harpsichord sonatas, only a tiny proportion of which was published in his lifetime, belong to the world of elegance and 'sensibility' – and also of *opera buffa*. Sometimes he is content to write arietta melody with a left-hand part of the type traditionally associated with the name of Domenico Alberti (*c.* 1710–*c.* 1740), a minor composer who certainly exploited it:[17]

Ex. 192

Sometimes, however, Galuppi miraculously distils the essence of Italian song into a pure keyboard idiom:

Ex. 193

Galuppi was no formal innovator but the variety of his work and the quality of the best of it were unrivalled by any of his contemporaries in Italy. They were fairly numerous but two stand out: Domenico Paradisi (or Paradies) (*c.* 1710–91) and Giovanni Rutini (1723–97). Paradisi's fame rests almost entirely on the twelve *Sonate di gravicembalo* published in London in 1754 which became enormously popular and were often reprinted.[17a] They are well-made works with 'close juxtaposition of contrasted ideas' (cf. p. 484), as in the opening of No. 10, and sometimes approximate to sonata-form, as in the same movement. The keyboard writing is extremely effective but as a melodist, even at his best (in the 'aria' second movement of No. 3), he is not

[16] No. 35 in Fausto Torrefranca's 'Catalogo tematico delle sonate per cembalo di B. Galuppi', *Rivista musicale italiana*, xvi (1909), pp. 872ff., which is the nucleus of later lists. The best edition is Hedda Illey's (Rome, 1969–); her first volume has a thematic catalogue which accepts and continues Torrefranca's.
[17] Ex. 192 is from Torrefranca's No. 27, Ex. 193 from No. 26.
[17a] Ed. H. Ruf and H. Bemmann (Mainz, 1971).

to be compared with Galuppi. Whereas Paradisi spent his life entirely in Italy and England, Rutini – like Galuppi – was one of the cosmopolitans who travelled even as far as St Petersburg. And his style is more cosmopolitan. The heavy chords and thematic fragments of the initial Largo e staccato of the first sonata of his Op. 1 (Prague, 1748), and the Recitativo middle movement of the second, already announce the advent of a personality and that personality is fully developed in the three sets, Opp. III, V, and VI, which he published *c.* 1757–60. His masterpiece is Op. V, No. 5 in F minor; the plangency of its first movement:

Ex. 194

and the dramatic urgency of the second:
have few parallels in the Italian keyboard music of the period.[18] Rutini's later publications show a marked lowering of standards; he was evidently

Ex. 195

---

[18] The modern Italian editions of Paradisi and Rutini are grossly over-edited, and the gigue finale of Rutini's Op. VI, No. 6, in *HAM*, ii, No. 302, does not show him at his best.

aiming at a wider public. They are easy pieces for less gifted amateurs or students and, with Op. X (1776), he began to add violin parts in accordance with the recent fashion (see below, p. 518). Like Galuppi and Paradisi, he preferred the two-movement type of sonata though both he and Galuppi wrote a great number in three movements – and the pair often consists of two fast movements.

THE DECLINE OF ORGAN MUSIC IN GERMANY

With their German contemporaries, the three-movement type was the rule: as we have already seen, Emanuel Bach adopted it in all his 'Prussian' and 'Würtemberg' sonatas. Like most German keyboard music, these pay much less attention to virtuosic effectiveness than the Italian but much more to the expression of personal emotion. Indeed in the last of the six sonatas (*achtzehn Probe-Stücke*) which Emanuel appended to his famous treatise 'on the correct way to play the clavier' (*Versuch über die wahre Art das Clavier zu spielen*: Berlin, 1753),[19] the Adagio dissolves into an unbarred slow cadenza, and the eighteenth *Probestück* is a written-out 'free fantasia', direct expression of naked 'sensibility'. There was no scope for 'sensibility' on the organ and Emanuel soon gave up playing it; his only organ works are seven sonatas composed (1755–8) for the chamber-organ of the Princess Amalie, his royal master's sister, and only one of these employs the pedals.[20] Even his father's most faithful pupil, Johann Ludwig Krebs (1713–80), who wrote genuine and valuable organ music (fugues and hymn preludes) had published two sets of *Klavierübung* (1743 and 1749) on hymn-themes 'which can be played not only on the organ but on the harpsichord (*Klavier*)'. Another of Sebastian's pupils, Johann Philipp Kirnberger (1721–83), a learned theorist, composed little or no genuine organ music but did publish late in life a set of fugues 'pour le Clavecin ou l'orgue'. Outside the immediate Bach circle the Salzburg organist Johann Ernst Eberlin (1702–62) published *IX Toccate e fughe* for the organ (1747), of which a fugue in E minor had the honour of passing for Sebastian's work far into the nineteenth century. With those and with a handful of pieces by the great might-have-been, Wilhelm Friedemann, the tradition of Bach organ music hardly survived its greatest master. His best 'modernist' pupils, other than Emanuel – Christoph Nichelmann (1717–62) and Johann Gottfried Müthel (1728–88) – ignored the organ altogether except for three or four organ pieces by the latter, which include a wildly exuberant pedal-study.[21] Müthel

---

[19] There are several modern editions, including a facsimile (Leipzig, 1957) and an English translation by William J. Mitchell (London, 1949). The treatise – probably suggested by the much less comprehensive *Kunst das Clavier zu spielen* (Berlin, 1750) of Friedrich Wilhelm Marpurg (1718–95) – is still invaluable for its teaching on ornamentation and was enormously influential in revolutionizing the method of fingering.

[20] From 1759 dates a concerto 'per l'Organo overo il Cembalo concertato' with an outstandingly beautiful Adagio in A flat, the strings playing *con sordini*.

[21] See the quotation in Reinhold Sietz, 'Die Orgelkompositionen des Schülerkreises um Johann Sebastian Bach', *Bach-Jahrbuch 1935*, p. 65.

was a hothead of proto-romanticism, whose sonatas 'pour le Clavessin' (Nuremberg, 1756),[22] are obviously modelled on Emanuel's *Probestücke*.

GERMAN KEYBOARD MUSIC FOR AMATEURS

Emanuel himself began to turn his eyes in another direction, to a less skilled and less demanding public. Around 1740–3 Krebs had published 'easy preludes in the present taste' and, reflecting his great master, an 'easy concerto . . . after the Italian *Gusto*' and an overture 'after the French *Goût*' to which he appended sixteen 'Galanterien vor Frauenzimmer anzusehen' (to be regarded as for females). Before long Nichelmann followed with a set of six *Breve Sonate . . . massime all'uso delle Dame* (chiefly for the use of ladies) and a second set a few years later. And Marpurg published at Leipzig in 1756 and 1757 two *Raccolte* of new keyboard pieces of very moderate difficulty by himself, C. P. E. Bach, Nichelmann, and others. During 1761–3 the Berlin publisher Birnstiel produced nine similar miscellanies under the title *Musikalisches Allerley*, while his rival Winter retorted with four of a *Musikalisches Mancherley*, and a *Musikalisches Vielerley* appeared at Hamburg in 1770. C. P. E. Bach not only contributed to all of these but published separately *Sonaten mit veränderten Reprisen* (1760) for 'beginners and those amateurs who . . . have neither time nor patience to devote themselves to exercise of any difficulty' and are given 'varied repeats' since they would be unable to invent their own ornamentation. Two 'continuations' followed, then six easy sonatas (1766) and six more 'à l'usage des Dames' (1770). A number of other sonatas were included in the various miscellanies but Bach is also represented in them by a great number of minuets, polaccas – the polonaise fashion was already widespread – and (like Nichelmann, Marpurg, and Kirnberger) short pieces with fancy names, 'Les langueurs tendres', 'La Complaisante', 'La Capricieuse', which are French in little but their titles.

KEYBOARD MUSIC WITH OPTIONAL ACCOMPANIMENT

In France itself the art of the *clavecinistes*, after reaching its apogee in Couperin's Fourth Book (1730) and Rameau's *Nouvelles Suites* of about the same date, petered out through the work of the light-weight composers François D'Agincour (1684–1758) and Louis-Claude Daquin (1694–1772), who published their books in 1733 and 1735 respectively – the latter's *Nouveau Livre de Noëls pour l'Orgue et le Clavecin* (c. 1745) continues the French tradition of *clavecin*-like organ music (see p. 436) – to the three books (1751 onward) of Pierre-Claude Foucquet (1694–1772) and the 1759 book of Claude Balbastre (1727–99), who were composers of no weight at all. But another publication of Rameau's indicates the way the wind of fashion

---

[22] Ed. Hoffmann-Erbrecht, op. cit., I. 6. Müthel's music, like C. P. E. Bach's, often seems more suited to the big German clavichords of the mid-century than to the harpsichord.

was beginning to blow. This was the *Pièces de clavecin en concerts, avec un violon ou une flûte, et une viole ou un deuxième violon* (1741).[23]

Works for obbligato harpsichord not merely accompanying but duetting with one or two 'melody instruments' were not new but they were uncommon. J. S. Bach had written some at Cöthen *c.* 1720 but they had not been published. And in France Jean-Joseph Cassanéa de Mondonville (1711–72) brought out three *opera* which in themselves document changing fashion: violin sonatas with continuo (1733), sonatas for two violins or flutes with continuo (1734), *Pièces de Clavecin en Sonates, avec accompagnement de Violon* (*c.* 1734).[24] In Op. 3 the title is more noteworthy than the reality; the violin 'accompanies' but it is not dispensable. But in the similarly titled Op. 25 (after 1741) of Michel Corrette (1709–95), an immensely prolific composer of every kind of instrumental music, and the Op. 13 (1745)[25] of Louis-Gabriel Guillemain (1705–70) it can be dispensed with. Guillemain, himself an outstanding violin virtuoso, actually admits in his preface that he had originally conceived the pieces for *clavecin* alone, but 'in order to conform to the present taste' he had added a violin part which must be played with 'grande douceur' so as to allow the keyboard instrument to be easily heard: 'On pourra . . . exécuter ces sonates avec ou sans accompagnement; elles ne perdent rien de leur chant puisqu'il est tout entier dans la partie de clavecin.'[26] (Conversely, Guillemain's *Amusement* (1762) is one of the earliest French examples of unaccompanied violin music.)

The new combination was adopted with enthusiasm by the German keyboard composers who invaded Paris when the Seven Years War ended in 1763, and gave the *coup de grâce* to the *clavecinistes*. Only one of them seems to have neglected it, Johann Gottfried Eckard (1735–1809) whose first publication (1763) is notable for his claim that he had tried to make it 'd'une utilité commune au Clavecin, au clavichorde, et au Forté et piano'. Leontzi Honauer (*c.* 1735–*c.* 1790) composed both solo and violin-accompanied sonatas. Johann Schobert (*c.* 1740–1767) added optional accompaniments not only for violin but for bass and a pair of *cors de chasse*, thus arriving at prototypical 'piano trios' and 'piano quartets' (with two violins instead of the later violin and viola)[27] and, with his Op. 11, at a type of concerto a little more fully scored than the contemporary ones of Christian Bach (cf. p. 494).[28] Bach himself, on coming to London, published sonatas with violin (or flute) and cello (Op. 2, 1764) before solo sonatas (Op. 5, 1768). And the very first printed works of the child Mozart (K. 6–15) were sonatas with accompaniments for violin (Opp. I and II, Paris, 1764) or violin/flute and cello (London, 1765); as the autographs show,[29] some at least were

---

[23] Ed. Saint-Saëns, *Oeuvres complètes*, ii.
[24] Ed. Marc Pincherle (Paris, 1935).
[25] Op. 13, No. 2, is printed in the appendix to Eduard Reeser, *De klaviersonate met vioolbegeleiding* (Rotterdam, 1939).
[26] Quoted in Lionel de La Laurencie, *L'École française de violon de Lully à Viotti* (Paris, 1922–4), ii, p. 8.
[27] See below, p. 527.
[28] Modern editions of Schobert's work ed. Riemann, *DDT*, xxxix, and elsewhere.
[29] See the facsimiles in Robert Haas, *Wolfgang Amadeus Mozart* (Potsdam, 1933), pp. 45 and 46.

originally written for keyboard only, and it is not impossible that the violin parts were added by the boy's father.

Schobert was very much a man of his age, thinking like the Mannheimers, writing for the keyboard like the Italians; as with all the other early composers of violin-accompanied sonatas his violin parts rarely add anything of much interest. They may lend emphasis or rhythmic variety or fullness to the harmony, underline keyboard melody at the third or sixth, play a snatch of counter-melody, but they seldom make any independent thematic contribution. If there is a cello part it seldom does anything but double the bass. His Op. 16, No. 4, is exceptional; after the double bar in the first movement violin and cello momentarily take over from the keyboard:

Ex. 196

and in the minuetto they do so throughout, the clavecin merely accompanying. Similar exceptions occur in J. C. Bach and Boccherini: in Bach's Op. 2, No. 1, and Boccherini's Op. 5 (Paris, 1768). Here the violin imitates the piano – the keyboard instrument Boccherini clearly had in mind – or vice versa, and in the third sonata it is absolutely obligatory. This is a prototype of the true duet sonata. The keyboard sonata 'with accompaniment' was at first little more than simple ensemble music for modestly gifted amateurs. To the same category belong the four-hand sonatas for piano only which began to appear at about the same time, with the child Mozart's K. 19d,

which he played with his sister in London in July 1765, and three by J. C.
Bach possibly composed *c.* 1770, though published much later.

THE SOLO SONATAS OF J. C. BACH AND THE YOUNG HAYDN

Both piano-duet and violin-piano duet were to outgrow beyond recognition
these modest beginnings but neither was to have such a glorious future as
the sonata for piano solo. As we have noticed, J. C. Bach did not publish his
earliest solo sonatas till 1768 and his partner Abel wrote none at all; Abel's
sonatas are either 'accompanied' or with roles reversed in the old way – for
one or two melody instruments with continuo. Bach's Op. 5 sonatas[30] are
with one exception either in the Italian keyboard style with tonic-dominant /
dominant-tonic first movements (Nos. 1, 3, and 5) or Mannheim-
symphonic with sonata-form first movements (Nos. 2 and 4); the exception
is No. 6, obviously written much earlier, which is a prelude and fugue with
incongruous rondo finale. His eldest brother, Friedemann, had temporarily
abandoned the sonata for the fashionable form of the polonaise (*c.* 1765),
though some of his polonaises, particularly the adagio ones in E flat minor
and F minor, Nos. 6 and 10, are quite remarkably unfashionable examples of
agonized proto-romanticism:[31]

Ex. 197

During the 1760s Haydn composed a score or more of keyboard sonatas,
most of which he called 'Parthia' or 'divertimento'; indeed they are
generally on the same plan as the harpsichord divertimenti that Wagenseil
had been publishing in sets during 1740–63,[32] most often fast-slow-minuet

[30] Facsimile editions of Op. 5 and Op. 17, with introduction by Christopher Hogwood (London, 1976).
[31] The detailed dynamic markings are the composer's own. No. 2, in C minor, is printed in *HAM*, ii, No.
288. There are several modern editions of all twelve.
[32] Four divertimenti ed. Blume, *Nagels Musik-Archiv*, 36.

or fast-minuet-fast, but with more substance – and more finesse when the substance is slight:[33]

Ex. 198

(i) WAGENSEIL: No. 3 of *Tre Divertimenti* (1761)

(ii) HAYDN: Finale of *Sonata, No. 12* (1767)

Haydn soon began to show his true quality, first in his slow movements – the Andante of No. 19 and the extraordinarily 'romantic' D flat Adagio of No. 46 (if it is really as early as Larsen says)[34] – then throughout the C minor, No. 20 (1771), which has already been mentioned as the peer of the Symphony No. 44 and some of the Op. 20 quartets (cf. p. 495). And there is the same preoccupation with contrapuntal devices; the minuet finale of No. 25 is a canon and in No. 26, as in Symphony No. 47, minuet and trio are totally reversible. Nos. 19 and 20 suggest the influence of C. P. E. Bach, whose 'Prussian' sonatas had delighted him twenty years earlier,[35] and it is perceptible here and there in Haydn's first published set of sonatas, Nos. 21–26 (Vienna, 1774), not only in technical details but in the dynamic urgency, the abrupt contrasts of capricious humour, the tendency of even the slow-movement themes to 'speak' rather than 'sing'. Haydn was not a keyboard virtuoso like the Bachs or Mozart but he was a master of keyboard styles. When he translates it is from instrumental ensemble, never as Christian Bach and Mozart do from opera.

MOZART AND THE PIANOFORTE

It so happened that in that same year, 1774, Mozart turned to piano composition for the first time since his childhood. First came a four-hand

---

[33] The Haydn sonata is numbered according to Anthony van Hoboken, *Joseph Haydn: Thematisch-bibliographisches Werkverzeichnis (Instrumentalwerke, i)* (Mainz, 1957), XVI: 12.
[34] Jens Peter Larsen, *Die Haydn-Überlieferung* (Copenhagen, 1939), p. 217.
[35] Georg August Griesinger, *Biographische Notizen über Joseph Haydn*, modern edition by Franz Grasberger (Vienna, 1954).

sonata (K. 358) with a beautiful singing slow movement,[36] then half-a-dozen solo sonatas (K. 279–284). The first five show little orginality – K. 279 and K. 283 are completely Italianate – except for the wonderful consoling adagio first movement of K. 282, which dissolves into angelic frivolity in its eleventh bar. K. 284 is a different matter; the idiom is more Franco-German than Italian and original genius is manifest in the first movement and some of the final variations. Mozart played it at Augsburg in 1777 on the new Stein piano (see p. 498) on which he said it 'came out incomparably'. The next month, at Mannheim, with that instrument in mind, he wrote two sonatas, K. 309 and 311, one of them for Christian Cannabich's daughter; they take advantage of forte / piano contrasts; the sound of the superb Mannheim orchestra was in his ears. And probably some of the more recent sonatas of J. C. Bach were under his hands, for, among general similarities, both allude to the same little motive in the latter's not yet published Op. 17, No. 6.[37] Before leaving Mannheim he also wrote his first violin sonatas, or as he called them to his father (letter of 14 February 1778) 'Clavier duetti mit violin', K. 296, 301–3, 305. They naturally belong to the same musical world as the piano sonatas but are not, as the original Paris edition describes them, piano sonatas 'Avec Accompagnement D'un Violon'; they were written to surpass the 'not bad' *Divertimenti da camera* for harpsichord and violin of Joseph Schuster (1748–1812).[38] Two more violin sonatas, K. 304 and 306, perhaps also K. 378, followed in Paris in the summer, and five piano sonatas, K. 310, 330–3. One of the latter, the A major (K. 331), seems with its variation first-movement – several independent sets of variations on French songs date from the same time – its pretty minuet, and its *alla turca* finale to be deliberately aimed at Parisian taste.[38a] On the other hand the A minor (K. 310) surpasses even the E minor violin sonata (K. 304) in passionate intensity and its companions remind one of J. C. Bach only to remind one also how far Mozart at 22 had already surpassed the older man. And then for six years he wrote no more solo piano sonatas.

CLEMENTI AND SOME CONTEMPORARIES

Before he returned to this field in 1784 with his powerful C minor (K. 457), after exploring other keyboard forms – fantasies, fugues, even a suite (overture and three dances) more or less in Handel's style – some outstanding sonatas by older composers had appeared, to say nothing of many run-of-the-mill sonatas by such German mediocrities as Johann

---

[36] The first four bars are identical, except that they are in 3/4 time instead of 4/4, with the first four bars of the opening Allegro of a string quartet in the same key (K. 160) of the year before – a 'singing allegro' indeed.

[37] Bach, andante, bars 12–13; K. 309, andante, bars 33–4; K. 311, rondo, bars 19–20. Bach had been in Mannheim, most recently in 1776, and may well have given Rose Cannabich copies. Cf. also p. 498.

[38] One of Schuster's divertimenti is printed in the appendix to Richard Engländer, *Die Dresdner Instrumental-Musik in der Zeit der Wiener Klassik* (Uppsala and Wiesbaden, 1956).

[38a] Nevertheless Wolfgang Plath believes that K. 330–3 were composed later. See *Mozart-Jahrbuch 1976–7*, p. 171.

Wilhelm Hässler (1747–1822), Daniel Gottlieb Türk (1750–1813), and Johann Franz Xaver Sterkel (1750–1817), published from the mid-seventies onward. A young Italian of the same generation, Muzio Clementi (1752–1832), brought to England as a boy of fourteen, was already remarkable as a pianist, not yet as a composer. His early sonatas – solo, four-hand, or violin / flute-accompanied – are either directly in the Italian tradition or derived from Italy through J. C. Bach. The opening themes of Op. 1, No. 5 (London, *c*. 1770) and Op. 2, No. 3 (*c*. 1773):

Ex. 199

(i) Op.1, no.5

Larghetto

(ii) Op.2, no.3

Moderato

Fl. or Vn.

are cast from the same moulds as the openings of Bach's Op. 5, No. 3, and Op. 17, No. 5. (It must again be emphasized that the late publication (*c*. 1779) of Bach's second collection of solo sonatas does not preclude earlier circulation of copies.) It was another ten years or so before Clementi began to emerge as a notable composer – even then not an outstanding one – the founder of true pianoforte technique and later still an innovator in piano structure. But during the years of Mozart's neglect of the piano sonata, the old master of the form, C. P. E. Bach, returned to the field with the first four collections of his crowning masterpieces, the *Clavier-Sonaten für Kenner und Liebhaber*[39] (1779, 1780, 1781, and 1783; two more collections followed in 1785 and 1787), which also included rondos (from the second collection onward) and *freye Fantasien* (from the fourth). Haydn, too, published two sets of six sonatas – Nos. 27–32 (Berlin and Amsterdam, 1778) and 35–9, with 20 belatedly (Vienna, 1780) – and two sets of three: 33, 34, and 43 (London, 1783) and 40–2 (Speyer, 1784). The enterprising new publisher Bossler, of Speyer, had already (October 1783) printed another set of three sonatas – by a not yet 13-year-old, Ludwig van Beethoven. It is noteworthy that these last show little or nothing of the influence of the boy's principal teacher at Bonn, Christian Gottlob Neefe (1748–98), or Neefe's idol C. P. E. Bach;[40] much more that of J. C. Bach, 'Mannheim', and, according to Schiedermair,[41] of Sterkel; and the opening of the Allegro assai of the second sonata is a portent:

---

[39] The best modern edition is that by Carl Krebs and Hoffmann-Erbrecht (Leipzig, 1953).
[40] Neefe's twelve sonatas of 1773 (modern edition by Walter Thoene, *Denkmäler rheinischer Musik*, x–xi, Düsseldorf, 1961 and 1964) were dedicated to Emanuel Bach.
[41] Ludwig Schiedermair, *Der junge Beethoven*, (Leipzig, 1925), pp. 270ff.

Ex. 200

C. P. E. BACH'S INFLUENCE ON HAYDN

Haydn's 1780 set was described as 'per il Clavicembalo o Forte Piano', that of 1784 as 'pour le Pianoforte'; Bach's first collection 'for connoisseurs and amateurs' were indeterminate *Clavier-Sonaten*, the five later ones specifically 'fürs Fortepiano'. The new instrument was establishing its paramountcy. But Bach clung to the end of his life, for his most intimate utterances, to his real favourite, the clavichord. The second sonata of the first collection employs the *Bebung* (throbbing) effect possible only on the clavichord, and he also wrote for it two separate pieces: a rondo, 'Farewell to the Silbermann Clavier' (1781) and an extraordinary fantasia headed 'Very sorrowful and entirely slow. C. P. E. Bach's feelings' (*Sehr traurig u. ganz langsam. C. P. E. Bachs Empfindungen*) (1787).[42] In the sonatas he exploits not so much the 'singing' potential of the piano, like his young brother, but what one might call its 'recitative' potential: its flexibility of expression, its suitability for sudden dramatic contrasts (as in a passage near the end of I, No. 6), for declamation, for the powerful development of lapidary or emotional ideas. The 'fantastical and far-fetched' nature of his music, of which critics had already complained,[43] is carried to the extreme in these collections; they are bursting with intellectual vigour, emotional (largely harmonic) tension,

---

[42] Ed., with the 'Farewell', Alfred Kreutz (Mainz and London, 1950). Bach later added a violin accompaniment; the first page of the autograph, at one time owned by Haydn, is reproduced in Ernst Fritz Schmid, *Carl Philipp Emanuel Bach und seine Kammermusik* (Kassel, 1931), facing p. 148.
[43] Burney's defence in his *Present State of Music in Germany* (1773) is still valid: see Percy Scholes, *Dr. Burney's Musical Tours in Europe*, (London, 1959), ii, p. 218.

violent contrasts not only of dynamics but of key. The rondos which open III and IV are wholly delightful but the innocent themes of the second rondos of II and III become – very typically – involved in strange adventures; the simple 6/3 chords of the D major rondo in II are distorted into harmonies comparable with Friedemann's (cf. Ex. 197) and the rondo structure itself dissolves into an unbarred passage as from a fantasia. The gay third rondo in IV completely dissolves into fantasia and is followed by two characteristically rhapsodic fantasias. Similarly in the first sonata of V the somewhat perfunctory and unorthodox first movement dissolves into a brief Adagio which is a mere transition to the delightful andantino finale. Although one of the pioneers of embryonic sonata-form (see pp. 486 and 511), Bach seldom employs fully developed sonata-form. To take the first movements of three of the finest *Kenner und Liebhaber* sonatas, in III, No. 3 (F minor), the insignificant second subject is totally overshadowed by the powerful, often quoted opening theme, and in V, No. 2, the second 'subject' is no more than a key area embodied in scales and broken chords; only the D minor, III, No. 2, has something like a definite second subject. Instead of beautifully wrought structures to be listened to as 'pure' music, Bach provides shaped and stylized improvisations, sequences of musical-intellectual events communicating emotional experiences.

Haydn's indebtedness to, and affinity with, Emanuel Bach have always been generally recognized; his admiration for the older man was lifelong – and warmly reciprocated. But by 1780 his creative personality was strongly developed and, while one can detect relationships in some of the sonatas of his 1778 set (e.g. No. 29, the Adagio of 30, 31, and the very fine B minor, No. 32), it was the depth of perversity for an English writer[44] to declare that Haydn was deliberately caricaturing the eccentricities of Bach's style. Haydn's piano sonatas of this period are sometimes bold but never 'fantastical and far-fetched'. On the contrary, some of them (e.g. Nos. 35 and 40, and the later 47) are rather tame and more obviously intended for amateurs than anything in Bach's sets, except perhaps the sixth collection. And there is more than a suspicion of Italian texture or material in the first movements of Nos. 27, 30, and 37. But there is nothing tame in the sonatas 29–32; even the innocent-seeming sonata-form finale of 32 generates surprising energy in development and coda. No. 36 is another outstanding minor-mode sonata, with a first movement notable for the cohesive effect of the motive in ♪♫ | ♩ rhythm and for the harmonic tension of the latter part of the development. One looks in vain for *durchbrochene Arbeit* comparable with that of the nearly contemporary Op. 33 quartets, though it is sketchily implied in the two movements of No. 42 and there is more of it in the E flat, No. 49 (dated 1 June 1790), a worthy forerunner of that other E flat, 52, which belongs with the greatest quartets and symphonies to the last phase of Haydn's instrumental music.

[44] *The European Magazine*, 6 October 1784.

THE ACCOMPANIED KEYBOARD SONATAS OF HAYDN AND MOZART

Up to 1784 Haydn, like C. P. E. Bach, had bothered very little with the accompanied keyboard sonata in any form. He had composed old-fashioned trio sonatas for two violins and continuo in his youth[45] and more than 120 trios for Nikolaus Eszterházy's favourite instrument, the baryton (a relative of the viola da gamba), viola, and bass (cello). A number of these 'baryton trios' were published in arrangements sometimes by Haydn himself for other trio combinations – including keyboard, violin, and cello. (Hoboken, XV, 2, is one example.) But his attention was first seriously drawn to the trio for piano 'accompanied by violin and cello' when he began supplying the London publisher William Forster with easily saleable compositions; in 1784–5 he sent Forster two sets (Hob. 4–10) which continue, as it were, the line of solo sonatas from No. 42 onward. It is true that the violin part is indispensable but it could be restored to the pianist's right hand without much harm and the cello hardly ever does more than double the piano's bass; only in the A major (Hob. 9) – an Adagio and Presto, one in condensed, the other in extended sonata-form – is the cello given any independence, allying itself often in parallel tenths with the violin. In the first of the half-dozen published by Artaria during 1789–90 (Hob. 11), the cello has no independence; in 13 and 14 it has a little and is even briefly necessary. Only in 15 do violin (or flute) and piano genuinely duet on nearly equal terms. There are beautiful things in these works but half of Haydn's total output of piano trios was still to come.

Mozart found his way to the piano trio, which he had so far essayed (with K. 251) only among his Salzburg divertimenti (see p. 499), at about the same time as Haydn and after several false starts. Having settled in Vienna in 1781 and begun work on *Die Entführung*, he published as Op. II a set of six violin sonatas of which four, K. 376, 377, 379, and 380, had been recently composed; they are genuine duet sonatas, though the piano tends to lead the dialogue. The G major (K. 379) was his finest violin sonata so far, perhaps without even that qualification.[46] But planning a second set the next year, to be dedicated to his young bride, he ran into trouble. K. 402 was to be in the same form as K. 379 and the initial slow movement, if not the peer of its counterpart, is not unworthy to stand beside it, but the ensuing Allegro – a fugue – was abandoned half-way through and was posthumously completed by Maximilian Stadler. Two movements of the weak 403 were finished but Stadler again had to complete the finale; only two fragments survive of a C major sonata (K. 404), and of the C minor only the piano part of yet another initial Adagio (the 28-bar exposition),[47] with five bars of the violin part. A

---

[45] The first movement of one of them is given in Schering, *Geschichte der Musik in Beispielen*, No. 311. It is from a set published as 'Op. 5' in Paris, 'Op. 8' at Amsterdam.
[46] Even the form of K. 379, the slow movement placed before the sonata Allegro, is striking. And this beautiful Adagio is itself half a sonata-form movement, the development interrupted to modulate without a break into the Allegro.
[47] Ingeniously completed by Stadler as a full sonata-form movement, described as a 'Fantasie' (K. 396) for piano.

little later three separate attempts at movements for piano trio, collectively numbered 442 by Köchel, shared the same fate.

In the years 1784–6, specially rich in piano concertos (see pp. 502ff), Mozart also introduced the piano in a number of chamber compositions as well as giving it two remarkable works on its own: the C minor sonata (K. 457) to which he later prefixed the Fantaisie (K. 575), publishing them together. One might challenge any suggestion of influence from C. P. E. Bach on the sonata, with its passionate upward-leaping opening theme, were it not also manifest in the nature of the fantasia and the plan of the slightly later rondo K. 485, with its theme borrowed from Bach's brother (see p. 498). But Bach is surpassed in the sonata and sublimated in the fantasia; where Bach is Dionysian, as Nietzsche would have put it, Mozart is – as always – Apollonian. There is nothing comparable in the sonatas, either solo or duet, of these and the last years. What one finds instead is a juxtaposition of the confident and virtuosic, spilling over from the piano concertos, with the engimatic – a juxtaposition typified by the great A major violin sonata, K. 526, and in the contrast between the melancholy A minor rondo (K. 511) and the almost symphonic four-hand sonatas (K. 497 and 521), all dating from 1786–7.

MOZART'S PIANO QUARTETS AND TRIOS

It was late in 1785 that Mozart first turned his attention to the piano quartet. The combination was so unfamiliar that three years later a writer in the Vienna *Journal des Luxus und der Moden* could describe the popularity of K. 478 and 493 as 'a bizarre phenomenon . . . an ephemeral *manie du jour*'. There had indeed been few earlier examples. Schobert had published *3 Sonates en Quattuor pour le Clavecin avec accompagnement de deux Violons et Basse ad libitum*, Op. 7 (Paris, 1767) and posthumously Op. 14, No. 1, in 1770.[48] Georg Joseph Vogler ('Abt Vogler') (1749–1814) wrote a two-movement *Notturno en Quattuor* (Paris, 1778; later editions in Vienna, London, and elsewhere) for the classic combination, with viola instead of second violin. Mozart himself, despite the stimulus he never failed to draw from the key of G minor, seems not always particularly happy with the medium as such in K. 478; in the E flat, K. 493, he handles the combinations and antitheses of string group and piano more plastically; yet he never wrote for piano quartet again. Instead he turned at last to the piano trio – not at first, in the G major, K. 496 (1786), with complete success, for the cello is still the inferior partner. In the B flat, K. 502, its emancipation is considerably advanced and in K. 542, the very fine E major, and 548 (both 1788) the process is complete. K. 564, which followed them in three months, is another matter; it is an original piano sonata with string parts extracted or added. It was his last work for piano and strings.

---

[48] Op. 7, No. 1, and Op. 14, No. 1, ed. Riemann, *DDT*, xxxix, pp. 94 and 83.

Mozart continued to write for piano alone. The last sonatas (K. 533/494, 570 and 576) combine the keyboard style developed in the concertos with the intensified dissonance which so often crops up at this period. It also marks a movement greater than any in the sonatas, the tragic and sublime Adagio in B minor (K. 540), and two delightful trifles, the gigue (K. 574) and the minuet which Köchel wildly misnumbered 355. But it is not heard in the last piano composition of all, the fine set of variations (K. 613) on a song from a *Singspiel, Der dumme Gärtner*, with words by the *Zauberflöte* librettist Schikaneder – who also sang the song.

THE 'KEYBOARD SONG'

In May and June 1787 Mozart composed half-a-dozen songs with piano accompaniment, two of which are masterpieces demonstrating what the advent of the instrument could do for solo song: 'Als Luise die Briefe ihres ungetreuen Liebhabers verbrannte' and 'Abendempfindung'. He had of course written such songs, nearly all settings of German words, before – to say nothing of a great number of Italian concert arias and 'insert' arias with orchestra – but it is significant that he showed little interest in the genre before he made the acquaintance of the improved piano. The eighteenth-century German 'keyboard song' had sprung from two main sources, themselves by no means unrelated: theatre song (cf. p. 385) and popular song, both often with words fitted to a pre-existing melody. In England the two sources had actually mingled in *The Beggar's Opera* and continued to do so in the later ballad-operas and other forms of dramatic entertainment. These, like the songs at the London pleasure-gardens – Vauxhall, Marylebone, Ranelagh – were orchestrally accompanied and, when published, were supplied with nothing more than a simple bass. They were of course printed in considerable quantity, but few original keyboard songs appeared in England during this period before Storace's *Eight Canzonetts with an accompaniment for a Piano Forte or a Harp* (c. 1782) (which includes a noteworthy setting of part of Gray's 'Elegy'). French song was in the same state; the *cantate* had died out and popular *airs* and *romances* from the theatre were published without accompaniment or with continuo only. The break-through was made by the German-born Aegidius Martini (1741–1816) with his *Airs du Droit de Seigneur et Trois Romances Nouvelles avec Accompagnement de Harpe*[49] *ou Forte Piano* (1784); he explained that he had felt obliged to write out the accompaniments to the *airs* from his *opéra comique, Le Droit de seigneur*, himself because the versions in circulation 'did not conform at all to the score'; as for the three *romances* – one of which was the charming 'Plaisir d'amour' – he announced that he had prepared alternative string parts 'so that they could be accompanied with the orchestra'.

[49] Recent improvements in the pedal-harp, made by Jean Henry Naderman and the Cousineaus (father and son), helped to popularize it for a time but as a domestic instrument it was in the end unable to compete with the piano.

GERMAN DOMESTIC SONG

Whereas the Mediterranean lands never had a tradition of what might be called 'domestic' song – for neither the solo madrigal nor the now moribund solo cantata was exactly domestic – the *bürgerlich* German had long been accustomed to modest music-making in the home and during the eighteenth century a new impulse was given to German song by the efflorescence of German poetry. Telemann's publications of songs and selected arias from his operas, side by side with keyboard pieces, in *Der getreue Music-Meister* (Hamburg, 1728)[50] and *Singe-, Spiel- und Generalbass-Übungen* (1733 and 1734)[51] represent the better side of the German continuo-*Lied* (sometimes with violin obbligato) before that efflorescence. The immensely popular compilations, *Sperontes Singende Muse an der Pleisse*, which began to appear at Leipzig in 1736 and continued with new editions and three *Fortsetzungen* until 1751, represent the worse. 'Sperontes', the pseudonym of Johann Sigismund Scholze (1705–50), simply fitted or failed to fit verses to existing tunes from a wide variety of sources.[52] As a counterblast a cultured amateur, Johann Friedrich Gräfe (1711–87) published at Halle in 1737 the first part of his *Sammlung verschiedener und auserlesener Oden* 'to which some melodies have been prepared by the most celebrated masters of music' (including C. P. E. Bach and C. H. Graun).[53] And from Hamburg came two collections – Telemann's *24 Oden* (1741) and the first part of the *Sammlung neuer Oden und Lieder* (1742) of Johann Valentin Görner (1702–62)[54] – which not only drew on the verse of such new poets as Friedrich von Hagedorn, but gave more thought to its setting.

NORTH GERMAN ODE SETTINGS

The initiative next passed to the Berlin poets and composers represented in the three volumes of *Berlinische Oden und Lieder* (Leipzig, 1756, 1759, and 1763) edited and partly composed by Marpurg. But they were overshadowed by C. P. E. Bach's first song publications: *Gellerts Geistliche Oden und Lieder* (Berlin, 1758) and the secular *Oden mit Melodien* (1762). The Gellert odes are a real landmark, not only as a collection of 55 settings of one distinguished poet, but for their frequent subordination of melody to text, as in the 'Busslied' (i), or their text-heightening, as in 'Trost eines schwermüthigen Christen' (ii):

---

[50] Selection ed. Dietz Degen (Kassel, 1941).
[51] Ed. Max Seiffert (Berlin, 1914); one example in Schering, *Geschichte der Musik in Beispielen*, No. 299.
[52] Ed. Buhle and Moser, *DDT*, xxv–xxxvi; two examples in Schering, ibid., No. 289.
[53] Leopold Mozart paid Gräfe the compliment of borrowing twenty of his songs, though with fresh, pious texts, for the *Notenbuch* he presented to his seven-year-old son in 1762 (ed. Hermann Abert, Leipzig, n.d.).
[54] Ed. together by W. Krabbe, *DDT*, lvii. Separate examples by Görner in Schering, op. cit., No. 300, and Moser, *Das deutsche Sololied* (*Das Musikwerk*) (Cologne, 1957), No. 18.

Ex. 201

They are also notable for the free treatment of strophic form (with not always successful struggles to adapt the first-stanza melody to the later ones), and not least the writing out of the accompaniment which, as Bach says in his preface, he did not wish 'left to the caprice of a wooden (*steif*) continuo-player'. It is true the upper part of the accompaniment always doubles the voice[55] but inner parts are sketched in, and there are little preludes, interludes, and postludes. Older composers, e.g. Kirnberger in his *Oden mit Melodien* (Danzig, 1773), continued to supply only a figured bass, but the *Singspiel* composer and educator, J. A. Hiller, wrote out the keyboard parts for his *Lieder für Kinder* (1769). Gluck in his settings of Klopstock's odes, first published in the *Göttinger Musenalmanach* for 1774–5,[56] sometimes provided a more genuinely pianistic texture though the highest part never fails to double the declamatory rather than lyrical vocal line.[57] This is indeed music of the Age of Enlightenment.

[55] The sharing of ornaments must have raised problems.
[56] Collected by Artaria (Vienna, 1785); ed. Gustav Beckmann, *Veröffentlichungen der Gluckgesellschaft*, iii (Leipzig, 1917). One example in Moser, op. cit., No. 25.
[57] Opening of 'Sommernacht' quoted in *NOHM*, vii, p. 350.

LYRICAL SONG AND NARRATIVE BALLAD

A truer reflection of the new lyrical poetry of Gleim, Claudius, and Hölty is to be found in the songs of Joseph Anton Steffan (Štěpán) (1726–97), the earliest Viennese composer of German *Klavierlieder*, Johann André (1741–99), who founded a new genre, the 'through-composed' narrative ballad, with his first setting of Bürger's 'Lenore' (1775),[58] and two Kirnberger pupils, Johann Abraham Peter Schulz (1747–1800) and Johann Friedrich Reichardt (1752–1814). Schulz, who was among those who contributed to a temporary revival of the German solo cantata, published *Gesänge am Klavier* in 1779 and three collections of *Lieder im Volkston bey dem Klavier zu singen* (Berlin, 1782, 1784, and 1790); some of these are tiny yet delightful trifles but Schulz defined the deliberate limitations of his art all too clearly in the preface to the 1785 reprint of his first collection *im Volkston*: 'In all these songs I have endeavoured to sing in popular vein rather than for art's sake (*mehr volksmässig als kunstmässig*), so that even unpractised amateurs, provided they are not totally lacking in voice, may easily pick up the song and bear it in memory'. His extremely simple setting of Claudius's 'Der Mond ist aufgegangen' did indeed become very popular, a *Volkslied* in the German sense of the word, but it can hardly compare with Reichardt's more *kunstmässig* one, to say nothing of Schubert's (which is no masterpiece). Reichardt – critic as well as composer, and a man of all-round culture – was more gifted creatively, more skilful technically, and much more prolific. His seven hundred songs show a fascinating development from 'songs for the fair sex' (*Gesänge fürs schöne Geschlecht*, Berlin, 1775) and three collections of *Oden und Lieder* (1779–81), which include the Claudius 'Der Mond', to the Goethe songs of his last years. Nearly all his best work belongs to a later chapter (see p. 644).

The vogue of the *Klavierlied* in Vienna, which began in 1778 with the publication of the first of Steffan's three *Sammlungen deutscher Lieder für das Clavier*, coincided exactly with the production of Umlauff's *Bergknappen* (see p. 474) in the new Burgtheater. It was this which gave *Singspiel* the stamp of Imperial approval, and the influence of *Singspiel* is often apparent in domestic song. The fourth song of Steffan's first *Sammlung*, a setting of Claudius's 'Phidile', is a case in point. But his very first song, Gleim's address to the February violet ('Das Veilchen im Hornung'),[59] has a melodic charm that places it in a different class from the rather pedestrian, homespun work of the Berlin composers:

---

[58] André made three later versions, two of which are published in *EDM*, xlv, pp. 18 and 46; the latter is a vocal score of one for four soloists, chorus, and orchestra (1788).

[59] Both these Steffan songs are printed in the appendix to Irene Pollak-Schlaffenberg, 'Die Wiener Liedmusik von 1778 bis 1789', *Studien zur Musikwissenschaft*, v (1918), p. 140. The same author edited a selection of Viennese songs of the period by Steffan, Kozeluch, and others in *DTÖ* Jg. xxvii (2), vol. 54, where the two Steffan songs are on pp. 1 and 3.

Ex. 202

However neither Steffan nor Haydn, who published two volumes each of twelve songs in 1782 and 1784, nor Leopold Kozeluch (Koželuh) (1747–1818) who brought out two sets in 1785, thought it necessary to print a separate voice-part. Both Haydn and Kozeluch introduce the *Singspiel* element, Kozeluch frankly in 'Was nennest du mich spröde', Haydn with more subtlety in his treatment of Lessing's 'Lob der Faulheit'.[60] But all three – naturally Haydn above all – could sound deeper notes: Steffan in 'Seid mir gegrüsst, ihr Täler' and the Herder ballad 'Edward', Kozeluch in his Italianate 'Liebeserklärung eines Mädchens',[61] Haydn in 'Die Verlassene' and 'Gebet zu Gott'. Haydn's greatest piano-accompanied song, however, was to come later: the Italian solo cantata *Arianna a Naxos*, consisting of two recitatives and two arias, the second recitative preceded by a remarkable passage of chromatic melody and harmony for the piano suggesting the unhappy heroine clambering up the rock as Theseus's ship disappears.

MOZART'S *DEUTSCHE ARIEN*

Artaria published *Arianna* in 1790 as 'accomp. del clavicembalo o fortepiano'. The piano had been specifically mentioned as the accompanying instrument, solely or as alternative to the *Clavier*, for several years. When Artaria published two pairs of *Deutsche Arien* (*sic*) by Mozart in 1789, he still described them as 'zum Singen beym Clavier' though the accompaniments are obviously pianistic. In the earliest of them, the setting of Goethe's 'Veilchen' (1785), as also to some extent in its companion 'Das Lied der

[60] Moser, op. cit., No. 31.
[61] Pollak-Schlaffenberg, op. cit., p. 141.

Trennung', Mozart composed a strophic poem non-strophically and with a vocal line so independent of the accompaniment that it had to be written on a third stave. 'An Chloe' in the other pair is not in the same class but the already mentioned fourth song, 'Abendempfindung', is astonishing – not only by its beauty. Within 12 bars we are aware not of 'sensibility' but of profoundly German romanticism, an impression deepened at the words 'Werdet ihr an meinem Grabe weinen, trauernd meine Asche seh'n'. In another of the 1787 songs, 'Als Luise', not published in the composer's lifetime, Mozart creates in the direct speech of a girl burning her faithless lover's letters perhaps his most tragically passionate *recitativo accompagnato*. Nothing in the songs of his immediate successors anticipates so surely the advent of the declamatory or lyrical nineteenth-century *Klavierlied* as this song and 'Abendempfindung'.

25

Religious Music (c. 1725–90)

Although the second quarter of the eighteenth century was illuminated by a number of supreme masterpieces of religous music, these were a sunset glory. The reasons for a general decline of church music were varied; it was not wholly attributable to the indifferentism or deism of Enlightenment. There was a good deal of religious fermentation but it was mostly unorthodox; the *Herrnhuter* (successors of the post-Hussite Bohemian Brethren), the Methodists, the Swedenborgians, were equally opposed to rationalist Enlightenment and to the official church-establishments, Catholic and Protestant alike. The *Herrnhuter* and the Methodists evolved their own hymnodies but had no influence on major religious music, which naturally remained under the control of ecclesiastical authority. The Catholic courts, royal and episcopal, liked their church music to be as colourful and theatrical as their rococo churches – only tempered here and there by the 'strict style', often to be equated with dullness, which most markedly differentiated religious from secular. As for the Protestants, the Calvinists had always rejected a musical rite and the Lutherans had for some time concentrated on the sermon, preceded and sometimes followed by a cantata often with strong dramatic elements (cf. p. 406) as well as hymnic ones; now they began to demand that church music should no longer be regarded as a function of worship but rather as an instrument of congregational edification. It was not a climate in which genuinely religious music could be expected to flourish.

BACH'S LAST CANTATAS AND *MATTHEW PASSION*

In Lutheran music the giant figure of J. S. Bach practically blots out everything else, though his production of church music – not only of organ music (cf. p. 509) – fell off markedly after the mid-1730s when his life was embittered by a quarrel with the Rector of the Thomasschule at Leipzig (1736–8) and the deterioration of his sight particularly from about 1740. Having completed the fourth cycle of cantatas (cf. p. 408), he needed to provide only a dozen new cantatas during 1728–9 and another dozen or so during the period 1730–5 – even if we count the six cantata-like 'parts' which constitute the *Weihnachts-Oratorium* for Christmastide 1734. (Twelve numbers of the *Christmas Oratorio* are based on festive secular

534

compositions for the royal-electoral family.) It is possible that 'Wär' Gott nicht mit uns' (BWV 14) was Bach's last cantata. The opening chorus is one of his most strenuous contrapuntal feats though the cantata as a whole is not to be compared with such other late ones as 'Ich steh' mit einem Fuss im Grabe' (156); the crowning masterpiece among the *Choral* cantatas, 'Wachet auf' (140); the festive solo cantata 'Jauchzet Gott' (51); or 'Sehet, wir geh'n hinauf' (159) which might be a preface to the *Matthew Passion* (probably 1727).[1] Not only is the cantata text, for the Sunday before Lent, by Henrici ('Picander'), the librettist of the *Passion*; it is a looking forward to Good Friday and in the second number, 'Ich folge dir nach', the soprano soloist sings in counterpoint the sixth verse of 'O Haupt voll Blut und Wunden'.

One may well speak of the 'librettist' of the *Matthew Passion*, for the non-scriptural, non-hymnic text is not a patchwork like that of the *John Passion* but the sole work of Picander. And it bulks so much larger than in the earlier, more dramatic work that the liturgical origin is almost lost sight of; the *Matthew Passion* is nearly an oratorio. Framed by its great opening double chorus, 'Kommt, ihr Töchter', and its great closing double-choral 'Ruhe sanfte, sanfte ruh' ', it stands as one of the transcendant monuments of Christian musical art.

One problem of the *Matthew Passion* is the relationship of the work as we know it to the version performed at Leipzig on the Good Fridays of 1727 and 1729. No doubt it was substantially the same but the earliest surviving manuscript of the full score is a copy made by Bach's pupil, and later son-in-law, Johann Christoph Altnikol (1719–59) at some time after 1744,[2] and Bach's autograph fair copy, which differs in details, is obviously later still.

THE 'B MINOR MASS'

Problems of another kind surround the so-called – not by Bach himself – 'B minor Mass'. That it is another great monument of Christian music is incontestable; its precise nature remains debatable. The two sections which Bach himself styled 'Missa' and sent to the king-elector on 27 July 1733, with a petition for the title of court composer, were the Kyrie and Gloria: a complete Lutheran Mass-composition (cf. p. 207). Even the Latin text is that of the Lutheran liturgy used in Saxony (e.g. in the Gloria, 'Domine Fili unigenite Jesu Christe *altissime*'). In the autograph score (not later than 1739) this 'Missa' ('No. 1') is followed by three other cantata-like compositions, each with a separate title-page and list of sources: 'No. 2 Symbolum Nicenum' (the Credo), 'No. 3 Sanctus' (first chorus only),[3] 'No.

---

[1] The fact that between November 1728 and March 1729 nine numbers were adapted as funeral music for Bach's old master, Leopold of Anhalt-Cöthen, has led to the mis-dating of the Passion. See Joshua Rifkin, 'The Chronology of Bach's Saint Matthew Passion', *MQ*, lxi (1975), p. 360, and Robert L. Marshall, 'Bach the Progressive', ibid., lxii (1976), p. 313.
[2] Complete facsimile in *Neue Bach-Ausgabe*, Serie II, 5a. The best edition of the definitive full score is that by Alfred Dürr, ibid., II, 5.
[3] For which a separate score and parts dating back to 1724 exist: see Dürr, 'Zur Chronologie der Leipziger Vokalwerke J. S. Bachs', *Bach-Jahrbuch 1957*, p. 77.

4 Osanna / Benedictus / Agnus Dei et Dona nobis pacem'. The Missa already included two numbers, 'Gratias agimus' and 'Qui tollis', adapted from cantatas (BWV 29 and 46); there are three more such borrowings in the Credo, and another – the 'Osanna' – in the Sanctus. The whole series can hardly be regarded as a unified musical conception and 'Nos.' 2, 3, and 4 may have been intended not to complete an actual Catholic Mass but as a series of quasi-cantatas on the lines of a Mass – possibly a gesture of gratitude to the Catholic king-elector when the Lutheran composer was belatedly given the court appointment in 1736.[4] A work so compiled was bound to be uneven but after the stupendous Kyrie the Christe and second Kyrie, after the overwhelming Sanctus the Osanna, are a necessary relief; and the Credo, often a stumbling-block for composers, is a series of triumphs.

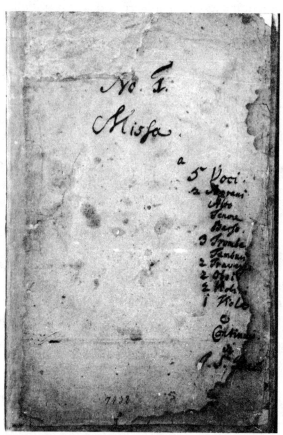

Pl. 50   First of the four title-pages of Bach's so-called 'B minor Mass'. 'No. 1 Missa' applies only to Kyrie and Gloria; it is followed by 'No. 2 Symbolum Nicenum' (the Creed), 'No. 3 Sanctus', and 'No. 4. Osanna, Benedictus, Agnus Dei et Dona nobis pacem'.

[4] Friedrich Smend's notes to his edition, *Neue Bach-Ausgabe*, II, 1, have been seriously criticized by Georg von Dadelsen, *MF*, xii (1959), p. 315.

Bach's four later Masses, BWV 233–6, Kyrie-Gloria pairs seemingly commissioned by a Bohemian count *c.* 1737–8, were probably his last church compositions other than organ-hymns. They were also among the last of a dying genre. Not many even of his own generation contributed much to it; there are a few by Telemann, by Gottfried Heinrich Stölzel (1690–1749), whose *Missa canonica* was modelled on Fux's, and by the Graun brothers.[5] The opening of an E flat Mass by Johann Gottlieb Graun (1703?–1771), roughly contemporary with Bach's last Masses, is typical of the solid square-cut style of Lutheran church music of the mid-century:

Ex. 203

THE CHURCH CANTATA IN DECLINE

Carl Heinrich Graun's most successful church work was his 'Te Deum' of 1757 celebrating Frederick the Great's victory at Prague. But the favourite form was the cantata, to which all these composers contributed though none so copiously as Telemann and Graupner, each of whom left more than 1400. Bach's brief successor as *Thomaskantor*, Johann Gottlob Harrer (1703–55), duly produced a cycle of 48, and was followed by Johann Friedrich Doles (1715–97), a pupil of Bach who translated the musical idiom of his master's cantatas into that of the mid-century while preserving their forms; they illustrate the contention in his preface to one of them, on Gellert's song 'Ich komme vor dein Angesicht' (Leipzig, 1790), that 'church music should have the easy comprehensibility and consequence of the rhythms, the simple and powerful harmony and the heart-melting melody, which one often finds particularly in the new operas'. Even Friedemann Bach in the cantatas he composed at Halle during 1746–64 often lapses into routine, though at his best – as in the Ascension Day cantatas 'Gott fähret auf' (1748) and 'Wo geht die Lebensreise hin' (perhaps ten years later) – he is no unworthy son of his father. 'Wo geht' has a fine opening chorus, the second part of which is a fugue 'Und der Herr, mit heller Posaune', and Friedemann is often at his best in such choruses: e.g. 'Alle Lande sind seiner Ehren' in 'Heilig', and 'Alle Tale' in 'Es ist eine Stimme eines Predigers in der Wüste'. This last work is typical of his unevenness; a brilliant trumpet opening, with some Italianate vocal coloratura, is followed by the superb, almost Handelian double fugue 'Alle Tale sollen erhöhet werden' and some platitudinous solos. The choral suggestion of the 'wilderness' is Friedemann at his most imaginative, but it is the bass solo before the final hymn that is more typical of the Lutheran cantata around 1760:

Ex. 204

The church cantata was not yet dead; Doles left some 160 and another of Sebastian Bach's pupils, the Dresden organist Gottfried August Homilius

[5] Excerpts from the *Missa canonica* and another Mass of Stölzel's, and from one by C. H. Graun are printed in *NOHM*, v, pp. 573–8.

(1714–85) composed more than a hundred, including a complete cycle a few years before his death; but, like the Lutheran Mass, it was moribund.

PASSION AND ORATORIO IN THE AGE OF SENSIBILITY

The forms which survived most successfully in the changing religious climate were the Passion composition and the oratorio, which indeed had long beeen drawing closer to each other. The scriptural Passion, however interlarded with non-scriptural elements as in Bach,[6] lived on most healthily in Hamburg in the works of Telemann and, after him, C. P. E. Bach. Bach borrowed overmuch from his predecessor and from his own father but Telemann produced a new, or mainly new, Passion every year from 1722 to 1767, steadily rotating through Matthew, Mark, Luke and John. Two of the best earlier ones are the *Luke* for 1728,[7] the five sections of which are prefaced by *Vorbereitungen* in the form of Old Testament parallels, and the *Matthew* of 1730.[8] With the passage of time Telemann increased the non-scriptural element more and more, as in the *Mark* of 1759,[9] at the same time simplifying the hymn-settings in accordance with the new trend. Nor did he neglect the Passion oratorio. He had been among the earliest to set the Brockes libretto (see pp. 402–3) and in 1729 he composed both text and music of *Seliges Erwägen* which was immensely popular for many years. (It was drastically revised in 1740.) This was followed by *Die gekreuzigte Liebe* (1731) to a text by the opera-librettist Johann Ulrich von König.[11] At about the same time C. H. Graun entered the field with a work known under various titles (e.g. *Das Versöhnungsleiden Jesu*) (Brunswick, 1730).

The vogue of the tears-and-blood Passion oratorio reached its height during the 1750s. It even extended to Catholic Salzburg with *Der blutschwitzende Jesus* (1750)[12] by the court and cathedral organist Eberlin. Eberlin converted this, perhaps unintentionally, into part of a Passion trilogy by adding *Der verurteilte Jesus* (1754)[13] and a lost *Der gekreuzigte Jesus*. Yet a fourth Passion oratorio, *Das Leiden unseres Heilands* (1755) is on a German version of Metastasio's somewhat operatic *Passione* in which the characters are Mary Magdalene, Peter, John and Joseph of Arimathaea, first set in its original form by Caldara (Vienna, 1730) – and by Salieri in 1776. Eberlin's was not the first German version of the Metastasio, for one by Gottlob Harrer had been heard in 1751 in – of all places – the Thomaskirche in Leipzig, where Bach's old congregation were edified by the Magdalen sobbing:

---

[6] In the very conservative Matthew Passion (1736) of Johann Theodor Römhild (1684–1756), ed. Karl Paulke (Lepizig, 1921) there are no non-scriptural elements other than congregational hymns.
[7] *Telemanns Musikalische Werke*, xv.
[8] Ed. Kurt Redel (Liechtenstein, 1963).
[9] Ibid.
[11] Not to be confused with Telemann's friend, the Frankfurt cantata-composer and hymn-book compiler, Johann Balthasar König (1691–1758).
[12] Ed. Robert Haas, *DTÖ* Jg. xxviii (1) (vol. 55).
[13] Examples of recitative and *turbae* in *Studien zur Musikiwissenschaft*, viii (1921), pp. 35–7.

Ex. 205

The typical oratorio of the Age of Sensibility, however, was C. H. Graun's *Der Tod Jesu* (Berlin, 1756).[14] This was a setting – less bad than is often asserted, less good than more than a century of popularity in Prussia suggests – of a poem by the Berlin poet K. W. Ramler, ' the poetic drill-sergeant of his age'. The best music is in the sturdy, if square-cut, choruses ('Sein Oden ist schwach', 'Hier liegen wir'), the worst in the flaccid solo-writing:

Ex. 206

and the dull harmonization of the hymns, a foretaste of the Lutheran hymn-style of the later Enlightenment.

---

[14] One example in Schering, *Geschichte der Musik in Beispielen*, No. 308; another in Günther Massenkeil, *The Oratorio (Anthology of Music)* (Cologne, 1970), No. 18.

Ramler's libretto was also set by Telemann (1757) and another Bach son, Johann Christoph Friedrich (1732–95), in 1769. (The 'Bückeburg Bach' was more successful with a better poet, Herder, who supplied the texts for his *Die Kindheit Jesu* and *Die Auferweckung Lazarus* (both 1773).)[15] Judging from some surviving fragments, Friedrich also composed Ramler's *Auferstehung und Himmelfahrt Jesu*, a sequel to *Der Tod Jesu*. Telemann laid hands on it in 1760, and Emanuel Bach in 1777–8, though his score was published only ten years later. This last is a masterpiece indeed, 'the first major work on the Continent written under the impression of Handel's *Messiah*'.[16] It towers above all the German oratorios of the previous quarter-century, including such fine non-Passion works as Telemann's *Tag des Gerichts* (1761)[17] and Bach's own *Israeliten in der Wüste* (1769).[18] The first German performance of *Messiah* had been given in Hamburg, under Thomas Arne, in 1772, and Bach himself performed it three years later.[19] There is little or no Handelian influence in the style of the *Auferstehung und Himmelfahrt*; what impressed Bach was evidently Handel's vivid dramatic sense, the monumentality, and the thunderbolt effects. The recitative 'Judaea zittert', after the first chorus, is striking in itself, the persistent drum-roll accompaniment still more so, and after the triumphant bass solo with trumpets. 'Der König zieht in sein Reich', the work is crowned by an extended chorus 'Gott fähret auf mit Jauchzen' in which the sudden fortissimo D flat after C minor, first for unison chorus unaccompanied,[20] then in tutti orchestral chords, is only one of the hammer-blows. Hardly less impressive are the male-voice entry after a silent bar:

Ex. 207

and the concluding fugue, 'Alles, was Odem hat, lobe den Herrn'.

HANDEL'S ENGLISH ORATORIOS

Handel had closed his career as an oratorio-composer in 1757 with the final version of the secular *Triumph of Time and Truth*, a pastiche. As we have seen (pp. 399 and 402), he had opened it as a composer of German Passion-oratorio and Italian fashionable oratorio and then abandoned it. He resumed it accidentally in 1732 when his masque *Haman and Mordecai (c.* 1720) was performed privately without scenery and then publicly without stage-costumes or action, the Bishop of London having objected to the theatrical enactment of a Biblical story. The original *Haman* was half pastiche from earlier works, the new form – *Esther* – was more than half.[21] So was its successor, *Deborah* (1733),[22] a subject no doubt suggested by Maurice Greene's *Song of Deborah and Barak* (1732);[23] *Athalia* (also 1733), modelled on Racine's tragedy, has a very much greater proportion of new music. But he was still preoccupied with Italian opera and, while he composed Dryden's *Alexander's Feast* in 1736 – one of those English odes (cf. pp. 390–1) which are nearly short secular oratorios, and furbished up his 1707 *Trionfo del Tempo* in 1737, he turned to true oratorio with *Saul* and *Israel in Egypt* only in 1739 when his operatic venture was nearly on its last legs. These two masterpieces, both marked by those borrowings from other composers which have raised so much controversy, are profoundly different: *Saul* as dramatic as any opera, *Israel* a great choral fresco with minimal solo relief, most of the text taken direct from the Bible. Neither owes anything to German or Italian oratorio; *Israel in Egypt* is a work *sui generis*, *Saul* develops the formula adumbrated in *Esther* and developed in *Deborah* and *Athalia*, an Old Testament story chosen for its dramatic possibilities. If there is any debt, it is perhaps to the English ode and to Purcell (notably 'Birth and fortune I despise' and the Witch's 'Infernal spirits').[24] The characterization, particularly of Saul himself, is what one

[15] Both ed. Georg Schünemann, *DDT*, lvi; excerpt from *Lazarus* in Massenkeil, op. cit., No. 19.
[16] Schering, *Geschichte des Oratoriums* (Leipzig, 1911), p. 373.
[17] Ed. Max Schneider, *DDT*, xxviii; one chorus *HAM*, ii, No. 272.
[18] Ed. Herbert Drux, *EDM*; miniature score, ed Gábor Darvas (London, 1971).
[19] Presumably Hamburg had a trumpeter able to cope with the first trumpet part. But playing in the high (*clarino*) register was a dying art. It was not yet dead, for Piccinni wrote for it in his *Iphigénie en Tauride* (Paris, 1781) and the *Messiah* part was played by 'Mr. Sarjant' in the Handel Commemoration in Westminster Abbey in 1784; but Johann Ernst Altenburg in his *Versuch einer Anleitung zur heroisch-musikalischen Trompeter- und Pauken-Kunst* (Halle, 1795; translated Edward H. Tarr, Nashville, Tenn., 1974) admitted that nowadays 'the right embouchure' was 'uncommonly difficult'. When Mozart reorchestrated *Messiah* for Vienna in 1789 he rewrote the trumpet parts in the medium register with its limited choice of notes, which had been the symphonic norm since the middle of the century (cf. p. 488).
[20] Quoted in *NOHM*, vii, p. 331.
[21] See Winton Dean, *Handel's Dramatic Oratorios and Masques* (London, 1959), pp. 199 and 207.
[22] Ibid., p. 230.
[23] Vocal score ed. Frank Dawes (London, 1950). Greene's powers are better displayed in his somewhat Handelian *Forty Select Anthems* (1743; numerous modern editions).
[24] Dean, op. cit., p. 291, detects in the latter a specific affinity with Purcell's scena 'In guilty night' (*Purcell Society*, xxxii, p. 128) on the same subject.

would expect from a great opera composer; there is drama *en gros et en détail*, in the scene at Endor and in the sudden modulation and javelin cast at the end of Saul's 'A serpent in my bosom warm'd'; and there are great choral set-pieces – 'Hallelujah', 'Envy! eldest born of Hell!', 'Mourn, Israel' 'Gird on thy sword'. The religious element is less than secondary but the Biblical subject and occasional references to Jehovah made a strong appeal to the secular religiosity of superior middle-class England.

Messiah (1741) is a totally different matter. Handel had produced his last two operas and they had both failed. Now Charles Jennens, the librettist of *Saul*, selected and adapted for him an inspired patchwork of passages from the Bible and Prayer-Book adverting to the promise of a Messiah's coming and the Nativity ('Part the first'), Christ's Passion and ascension, and the going forth of the apostles (Part II), Christ as Redeemer (Part III). The vast preponderance of Old Testament texts is astonishing; in Part I Luke, ii, is drawn upon for the shepherds' vision (three recitatives and 'Glory to God'), Matthew for three sentences, and the rest is mostly Isaiah; in Part II, still more surprisingly, the Passion and Ascension are not narrated but shown in the prophetic mirror, as it were, of the Old Testament; only in the short Part III is the New Testament, mostly I. Corinthians, xv, practically the sole source. Yet such is the splendour of the music with which Handel clothed all this that the strange basis is forgotten, if noticed at all. He never surpassed the beauty or power of the solos, though he sometimes equalled them, and the choral thunderbolts – 'Wonderful! Counsellor' in 'For unto us', 'He is the King of Glory' in 'Lift up your heads', 'for the Lord God' in 'Hallelujah' (and the fugal entry 'And he shall reign' is no less shattering in a different way) – are the most Jovian that even he ever hurled.

Handel returned again and again to *Messiah* to alter it, mostly on account of the available soloists, but he never returned to the same kind of oratorio. Immediately after the composition of *Messiah* and before its performance (1742) he went back in *Samson* to the *Saul* formula – dramatic treatment of an Old Testament story – and repeated it with infinite variety of resource and invention in *Joseph and his Brethren* (1744), *Belshazzar* (1745), *Joshua* (1748), *Solomon* (1749), and *Jephtha* (1752). Three times, in *Judas Maccabaeus* (1747), *Alexander Balus* (1748), and *Susanna* (1749), he turned to the Apocrypha and once – *Theodora* (1750) – to Christian hagiography, his only Christian oratorio besides *Messiah*. Comparable with these but frankly secular were *L'Allegro, il Penseroso ed il Moderato* (two thirds based on Milton, one third Jennens) (1741), a superb setting of Congreve's *Semele* 'after the Manner of an Oratorio' (1744), and a hardly inferior 'Musical Drama' *Hercules* (1745). Much later came the short *Choice of Hercules* (1751) and the final version of *The Triumph of Time and Truth* (1757), neither of which contains much new music. Yet there was no real decline in Handel's powers in his last years; he never wrote a more delightful melody than 'Sweet rose and lily' in *Theodora*; he himself held 'He saw the lovely youth' to be 'far beyond' the *Messiah* 'Hallelujah'; and if the final, profoundly tragic chorus 'Oh love divine' is a transformation of Dejanira's 'Cease, ruler of the day' in *Hercules*, it is a transformation like the miracle at Cana. More interesting than these self-borrowings and borrowings from other composers are the cases where Handel reveals the continuity of a vein of invention; Didmus's 'With courage fire me' is not a borrowing of Ruggiero's 'La bocca vaga' in *Alcina*, fifteen years earlier, but it is cast from the same mould:

Ex. 208

(i) ALCINA

La boc - ca va - ga, quell' oc - chio ne - ro, lo sò, t'im - pia - ga

(ii) THEODORA

With cou - rage fire me, or art in - spire me,

ENGLISH COMPOSERS OF ORATORIO

Handel's example was naturally the model for a certain amount of English oratorio composition. Greene's *Jephtha* (1737), Boyce's *Solomon* (1743) and Arne's *Death of Abel* (on a translation of Metastasio's *Morte d'Abele*) (1744) and *Judith* (1761) are perhaps the least feeble. A revival of *Judith* in 1773 is at least memorable for the circumstance that for the first time the boys and counter-tenors of the chorus were replaced by women's voices. Pasticcio oratorio sprang up beside pasticcio opera (see p. 477); in 1763 John Brown prefaced his once celebrated *Dissertation on the union and power . . . of poetry and music* with an oratorio libretto, *The Cure of Saul*, which was performed with a score concocted from Handel, Purcell, Corelli and Benedetto Marcello but composed single-handed by Samuel Arnold (1740–1802) in 1767. Other pasticci were prepared exclusively from Handel's music, the most successful being a *Redemption* (1786) put together by Arnold. Arnold's own *Prodigal Son* (1773) was held to be his best work. However he is remembered not by these efforts but by the collected edition of Handel's works on which he embarked in 1787; with all its faults and despite its incompleteness, it was the first attempt at a complete edition of any one composer's music.[25] In refreshing contrast to all this mediocre imitation of Handel by native composers is the *Joas* of Johann Christian Bach (London, 1770), a setting of Metastasio's libretto (untranslated) and quite free from Handelian influence.

---

[25] While English music – oratorio and church music, opera and instrumental music alike – touched a very low level, the period witnessed the real birth of English musical scholarship. Boyce published his great collection of three volumes of *Cathedral Music* (1760–77), which Arnold continued when he died. Charles Burney published the first volume of his *General History of Music, from the Earliest Ages to the Present Time* and Sir John Hawkins all five of his *General History of the Science and Practice of Music*, both in 1776. Burney's fourth and last volume did not appear until 1789.

LITURGICAL MUSIC AND ORATORIO IN FRANCE

In France oratorio practically died out with Marc-Antoine Charpentier. But in the field of church music *grand motets* and *petit motets* – types as peculiarly French as the anthem was peculiarly Anglican – continued to be composed by such men as Mouret and Blamont, and later with more up-to-date orchestral writing by Boismortier (solo motets, 1728), Esprit Blanchard (1696–1770) (motets from 1736 onward),[26] and Mondonville. Beginning in 1739 with his 'Lauda Jerusalem' Mondonville composed a series of *grands motets* for the Concert spirituel (see p. 488) and during his directorship of the Concert (1755–62) he produced there two *motets françois*, *Les Israëlites à la montagne d'Horeb* (1758) and *Les fureurs de Saül* (1759), and a secular one, *Les Titans* (1761). The music is lost but the libretti show that they were actually very short oratorios; in any case they were only flashes in the pan. The real revival of French oratorio occurred only after 1773 when the direction of the Concert was taken over by Gossec and Le Duc. In 1774 they gave a *Samson*[27] by Nicolas-Jean Méreaux (1745–97), *Le Sacrifice d'Isaac* by Mozart's future enemy Cambini,[28] Rigel's *La Sortie d'Egypte*,[29] and a *Nativité* by Gossec himself[30] believed to have been written for Mondonville in 1759. These works were repeated a number of times but the composers' later oratorios never achieved quite the same success. Gossec's greatest triumph in religious music remained the very early *Messe des morts* first given in 1760 in the Dominican church in the Rue St-Jacques, where he produced a 'terrible' effect by announcing the Last Judgement in the 'Tuba Mirum' by a band of four clarinets, eight bassoons, four trumpets, four horns, and three trombones concealed high up in the church while the orchestral strings made a pianissimo *frémissement*. Unfortunately the *orchestre éloigné* plays nothing more terrible than a fanfare in bare octaves on the common chord of E flat, the same harmony as the *frémissement*.

The Concert spirituel also introduced oratorios by non-French composers: *Esther* by the Alsatian Johann Friedrich Edelmann (1749–94), best known as a composer of 'accompanied' *clavecin* sonatas; another *Esther* (1786),[31] perhaps a French version of an earlier work, by Sacchini; Salieri's *Le Jugement dernier* (1788);[32] and part of Haydn's *Sieben Worte* (see p. 552) in 1789. Owing to its length, only excerpts from Philidor's enormously successful *Carmen seculare* (originally performed in London, 1779),[33] could be given at the Concert spirituel. But the Concert sponsored the first performances of works – motets and an ode on a text by Jean-Baptiste Rousseau (1785) – by a more remarkable composer than Philidor: Jean-François Le Sueur (1760–1837). After two years at Saints-Innocents, where a Mass and 'Stabat Mater' were given, Le Sueur was appointed *maître de chapelle* at Notre Dame in 1786. Finding that choral music was

---

[26] Excerpt from his Fontenoy *Te Deum* (1745) in *NOHM*, v, p. 491.
[27] Excerpt in Donald H. Foster, 'The Oratorio in Paris in the 18th Century', *Acta Musicologica*, xlvii (1975), p. 86.   [28] Ibid., p. 88.   [29] Ibid., p. 90.
[30] Ed. Douglas Townsend (New York, 1966); excerpt in Massenkeil, op. cit. No. 20.
[31] Excerpt in Foster, op. cit., p. 103.   [32] Ibid., pp. 106 and 108.   [33] Ibid., pp. 98–100.

accompanied there only by cello, bassoons, basses and organ, he at once enlisted Court influence for permission to engage a full orchestra for the four main festivals of the year, and celebrated the first of the festivals, the Assumption of the Virgin, with a dramatic Te Deum. He went on to compose an *Oratorio de Noël* and similar oratorios for Easter, Pentecost, and the Assumption of 1787, each a conflation with the complete Ordinary of the Mass. The music of only one, the Christmas Oratorio, survives and this only in the drastically altered version published forty years later.[34] Le Sueur printed *Exposés* of each work, explaining that church music should 'imitate nature' and is 'therefore dramatic', and his essays show exactly how he interwove the Mass movements with the oratorio elements, familiar chants and, in the first work, *noëls*, 'melodies heard first in one situation and reappearing in another, analogous to it'. So much innovation was too much for the Chapter; they soon found a pretext for dismissing their young *maître*, but he was to reappear as an opera-composer and celebrator of the Revolution.

ORATORIO IN ITALY

In Italy oratorio continued to flourish particularly at Bologna. At Naples Leonardo Leo, who had first made his mark with *Il trionfo della castità di San Alessio* in 1713, continued the Scarlattian tradition in his *Oratorio per la Ss. Vergine del Rosario* (1730) and two later masterpieces on Metastasio's libretti: *Sta. Elena al Calvario* (1734) and *La morte d'Abele* (1738).[35] But these two works were produced at Bologna and it was at Bologna that two oratorios by Leo's chief rival as a Neapolitan church composer, Francesco Durante (1684–1755), were performed in 1740 and 1755. It seems that the last notable Neapolitan oratorios were two rather doubtfully attributed to Vinci, *Gionata* (1729) and *Il sacrificio di Jephte* (1731), and Pergolesi's *dramma sacra*, *La Conversione di San Guglielmo Duca d'Aquitania* (1731)[36] and his *Morte di San Giuseppe* (probably also 1731).[37] The best of Porpora's oratorios seems to have been *David e Bersabea* (1734), written – like several of his operas – in London in deliberate rivalry with Handel. Porpora, Leo, Vinci, and Pergolesi were opera composers – Durante, remarkably, was not – and their oratorio music is close in style to their opera music. Pergolesi's *San Guglielmo* actually includes two *buffo* parts, the Capitano Cuesemo and the Dèmone. The Captain, a Neapolitan dialect part, is the hero's comic attendant, who mocks the Devil's threats:

Ex. 209

(Orch. *colla voce*) Se n'e - ra ve - nu - to lo tri - sto for - fan - te co "Va, te de - spe - ra!"

---

[34] The two forms of Kyrie and Gloria are compared ibid, pp. 120–1, musical excerpts, pp. 122 and 124–6. [35] Excerpts from the latter in *NOHM*, v, pp. 344–6.
[36] The version in *Opera Omnia*, iv, is a later one, not by the composer. [37] *Opera Omnia*, i.

LITURGICAL MUSIC IN ITALY

Their liturgical music is also frequently operatic: in form (the 'cantata Mass' with solo arias), in treatment of the orchestra (often augmented with brass), and in dramatic expressiveness and vocal display. The last point is well illustrated by the aria 'Judicabit' from a 'Dixit Dominus' by Durante quoted in the *New Oxford History of Music*,[38] which also shows characteristic near-doubling of the voice by violins. This is shown again in the opening of a Mass by Durante, typical also in its close-canonic beginning and its speedy collapse into a more 'modern' type of cadence:

Ex. 210

[38] v. p. 394.

which appears to have served as a model for the opening of the famous 'Stabat Mater' for soprano, alto, and strings (1736) of his pupil Pergolesi.[39]

Durante also wrote much more genuine polyphony than this – and more solid and striking harmony, as in his two settings of 'Misericordias Domini' for two four-part choirs. He composed a *Missa alla Palestrina*. But in the end it is the 'polyphonic-concertante' style of Ex. 210 that seems most characteristic. Sharp stylistic contrasts were, of course, common at this time; Pergolesi's 'Stabat Mater' is a *locus classicus*. And Durante handed on his techniques to more than one generation of pupils: to Traetta, Piccinni, and Sacchini, even to the young Paisiello. One thinks of them only as opera composers but they all wrote oratorios – Piccinni, *Gioas* (Naples, 1752) and *Morte di Abele* (Naples, 1758); Sacchini, *San Filippo Neri* (Bologna, 1766); Traetta, *Rex Salomone* (Venice, 1766); Paisiello a *Passione* (Warsaw, 1784) – as well as their quota of Masses and other church music.

While Durante was immensely influential, his Neapolitan contemporary Leo is generally considered the greater of the two. His Masses, 'short' (Kyrie/Gloria) cantata-Masses like Pergolesi's, date from the 1730s; they are supplemented by independently composed Credos and so on. But his best known works date from his last years: a 'Miserere' for two four-part choirs and continuo (1739)[40] and the finest of several settings of 'Dixit Dominus', also for two choirs with orchestra (1742).[41] The 'Dixit' shows the usual contrast of styles – very difficult and florid soprano solos but 'Tu es sacerdos' set as a triple fugue – while the 'Miserere' is an impressive essay in the up-dated 'Palestrina style' to which Durante also leaned occasionally but which was still being practised more successfully and wholeheartedly by the now elderly Venetian Antonio Lotti (see p. 410).[42] But even Lotti did not totally eschew the modern style,[43] and, ironically, his pupil Galuppi distinguished himself by the light weight, even downright frivolity, of the numerous oratorios he wrote for the Venetian conservatories from 1740 onward.[44] The oratorios of the Neapolitan Jommelli, a disciple of Leo, particularly his Metastasio settings, *La Betulia liberata* (Venice, 1743), *La Passione* (Rome, 1749), and *Isacco* (Rome, 1750), are much more considerable though naturally very operatic. His large output of church music, much of it written for the Ducal Chapel at Stuttgart (1753–70) shows the usual mixture of styles: masterly fugues beside smooth concertante effects. His Requiem of 1756[45] is perhaps his finest church composition.

[39] Miniature score, ed. Alfred Einstein (London, 1949). The work as a whole is modelled on Scarlatti's setting.
[40] Excerpt in *NOHM*, v. p. 392. It profoundly impressed Wagner at Naples in 1880: see C. F. Glasenapp, *Das Leben Richard Wagners*, vi (Leipzig, 1911), p. 323.
[41] Ed. Charles V. Stanford (London, 1879).
[42] His *a cappella* Masses have been ed. Hermann Müller in *DDT*, lx, presumably on the strength of the two years he spent at Dresden (1717–19).
[43] See, for instance, the solo 'Laudamus' in a Kyrie/Gloria (Brit. Lib., Add. MS. 24297).
[44] A Mass by him has been ed. H. Bäuerle, *Altklassische Messen*, vii (Leipzig, 1927).
[45] Vocal score, ed. Julius Stern (Leipzig, 1866).

HASSE AT DRESDEN

Hasse at Dresden, a near-contemporary of Leo and absolutely Italian in spirit, accepted the modern style completely except for the occasional conventional gesture: e.g. the square-cut fugal 'Christe' in his Requiem for Augustus III of Saxony (1763), but the Lacrymosa from the same work[46] is more typical. He composed his adored Metastasio's oratorio *Giuseppe riconosciuto* (1741) and made two settings of his *Sant' Elena al Calvario* (1746 and 1772). Both in these and in two other notable oratorios, *I pellegrini al sepolcro di Nostro Redentore* (1742)[47] and *La conversione di Sant' Agostino* (1750),[48] he pays more attention to the chorus than he does in his operas, and his accompanied recitatives are particularly fine. The solo writing, as also in his liturgical music,[49] is unmistakably operatic. In the Age of Enlightenment it was not to be expected that church music would be saturated with mystic awe or ardent devotion; emotion was rationalized or sentimentalized, or even drained away so that nothing was left but 'pure' music. However pleasant the opening of Hasse's *Litanie della Beatissima Virgine* (performed by members of the Imperial family at Vienna in 1761), it is a very complacent prayer for divine mercy:[50]

Ex. 211

---

[46] In Schering, *Geschichte der Musik in Beispielen*, No. 310.
[47] Excerpts in *NOHM*, v, pp. 347–8.
[48] Ed. Schering, *DDT*, xx; example of accompanied recitative in *HAM*, ii, Ni. 281.
[49] See the examples in *NOHM*, vii, p. 292.
[50] Facsimile in *MGG*, v, col. 1774.

RELIGIOUS MUSIC AT VIENNA

Caldara and Fux had kept contrapuntal church music alive in Vienna, and by Viennese influence in Prague and Salzburg, and Fux's disciple Wagenseil continued the tradition for a while. But after their deaths in 1736 and 1741, and Wagenseil's defection first to opera (in 1745) and then to instrumental composition, the most influential musician in the *Hofkapelle* was Georg Reutter 'the younger' (1708–72).[51] In his oratorios, which include settings of Metastasio's *Betulia liberata* (1734) and *Gioas, re di Giuda* (1735) – and actually very much more in his 80 Masses and other liturgical music – Reutter followed the 'Neapolitan' tradition, with solos more operatic than those in his own operas. He did, however, strengthen a trend toward the 'orchestral' Mass by his use of brass and drums – surprising since Maria Theresa, no lover of music like her father, the Emperor Charles VI, and engaged in one desperate war after another, drastically reduced her musical establishment. In 1772 Reutter was succeeded by Gassmann, who at once marked his advent with a performance of *his* setting of *La Betulia liberata* at a public concert – the first in Vienna – of the *Musikalische Sozietät der Witwen und Waisen* which he had just founded. He also set about a reformation of the Imperial Chapel, and in the same year Johann Georg Albrechtsberger (1736–1809) was appointed second organist. Both were admirably qualified to fuse the polyphonic tradition with modern conceptions of melody and instrumentation. Albrechtsberger was an outstanding contrapuntist, Gassmann had been a pupil of the greatest Italian exponent of the old style, 'Padre' Martini at Bologna,[52] and although Gassmann soon died his successor, Giuseppe Bonno (1711–88), practised an eclecticism in his church music which by no means excluded the *stile antico*.[53] The only liturgical compositions by Albrechtsberger in print are two instrumental movements[54] for the accompaniment of the Gradual in accordance with eighteenth-century Viennese practice. Gassmann's church music, much admired by both Haydn and Mozart, dates mostly from 1772–3; it turns its back on Neapolitan worldliness; while it admits solo passages in cantata-Masses, it does not admit coloratura. His fugal writing is decidedly harmonic, as indeed is his choral writing in general in accordance with ecclesiastical policy.[55] His masterpiece was a Requiem[56] cut short by

---

[51] Reutter had to wait till 1747 for his official appointment as *second Kapellmeister*, and till 1769 to become first although he had long exercised all the functions. A selection of his *Kirchenwerke*, ed. Norbert Hofer, has been published in *DTÖ*, vol. 88.

[52] A rather later pupil of Martini's was the Russian Berezovsky, who learned to compose 'spiritual concertos' on entirely different lines from those mentioned on p. 412, n. 69. They are mostly four-part compositions in several contrasted movements; the best known (printed in S. L. Ginzburg, *Istoriya russkoy muziki v notnikh obraztsakh*, second edition, Moscow, 1968, p. 33) is a setting of Psalm 71, vv. 9–13, the final section of which, 'Let them be confounded', has been claimed as the first Russian fugue.

[53] See Alfred Schienerl, 'Giuseppe Bonnos Kirchenkompositionen', *Studien zur Musikwissenschaft*, xv, p. 62.

[54] Ed. Oskar Kapp, *DTÖ*, Jg. xvi (2) (vol. 33), pp. 46 and 54. On his church music generally, see Andreas Weissenbäck's study in *Studien zur Musikwissenschaft*, xiv, p. 143.

[55] See pp. 553–4.

[56] Ed. Franz Kosch, *DTÖ*, Jg. xlv (vol. 83), p. 55. See also Kosch, 'Florian Leopold Gassmann als Kirchenkomponist', *Studien zur Musikwissenschaft*, xiv, p. 213.

his death after the 'Dies irae', like a more famous Requiem nearly eighteen years later, which it curiously foreshadows in its opening:

Ex. 212

HAYDN AT ESZTERHÁZA

Greater composers were working outside Vienna, though within its sphere, but the greatest was not yet particularly drawn to church music. Haydn celebrated the transfer from Eisenstadt to Eszterháza in 1766 with a big Neapolitan cantata-Mass in E flat, his first important liturgical work; it is scored for a large orchestra and *concertante* organ (whence it is known as the 'great organ Mass') and the solo parts have brilliant coloratura.[57] The *Missa Sancta Caeciliae* (*c.* 1770) is on similar lines, the *Missae Sancti Nicolai* (1772) and *Sancti Joannis de Deo* of the same period are more modest. In the latter Haydn adopts the deplorable practice of telescoping the texts in a short Mass, so that in the Gloria, for instance, the sopranos sing 'Gratias agimus', the altos 'Domine fili', tenors 'Domine Deus', and basses 'Et in terra' all

[57] Haydn's Masses are published in five volumes of the *Werke*, Series XXIII (various editors).

simultaneously. The *Sancti Nicolai* opens with a pleasant 6/8 Kyrie marked by parallel thirds like Ex. 211, and no less complacent, but there are a beautiful Benedictus and a solemn purely chordal Agnus Dei in G minor – the key Haydn adopted for his 'Stabat Mater' of about the same time. Even the finer *Missa Cellensis* (1782), commissioned as a votive offering for the pilgrimage-church at Mariazell, suffers from the same heterogeneity, with a coloratura soprano singing the Gratias and simultaneous texts in the Resurrexit. Equally Neapolitan in conception is Haydn's sole oratorio of the Eszterháza period, *Il ritorno di Tobia* (Vienna, 1775), raised to a higher level by its fine choruses. His *Sieben Worte des Erlösers am Kreuze* originated in a series of orchestral pieces commissioned for the Oratory of La Cueva at Cadiz in 1785; the adaptations for chorus and orchestra (which Haydn himself styled an 'oratorio') and for string quartet were made later.[58]

CHURCH MUSIC AT SALZBURG

Much more prolific as a church composer was his brother Michael at Salzburg, as was natural in the service of a Prince-Archbishop. Until 1762 the leading figure had been Eberlin (see pp. 516 and 539), who numbered among his pupils Leopold Mozart (1719–87) and Anton Cajetan Adlgasser (1729–77), both composers of (among other things) church music and oratorios.[59] When Michael Haydn joined them as *Orchesterdirektor*, after Eberlin's death, he had already composed a quantity of church music in which he quickly turned his back on his great brother's improprieties. He was just the man for the Archbishop who succeeded in 1772, Hieronymus von Colloredo-Waldersee, who set about a reformation of church music in the spirit of Enlightenment. The Mass for his master's saint's day (1777) is not festive but profoundly serious and the orchestra is limited to oboes, bassoons, and trombones.

Leopold Mozart's precocious son ultimately found it harder to be so accommodating. He was indeed precocious if the C minor Mass, K. 139, was really written in 1768, when he was not quite 12, as experts now believe. He went on to compose another full-size Mass, four *missae breves*, Kyries, Offertories, Litanies, hymns, before the advent of the new Archbishop. On a visit to Italy in January 1773 he wrote the brilliantly operatic solo cantata-motet 'Exsultate, jubilate' for the castrato Rauzzini, but resolved on his return to Salzburg to master the local tradition. To that end he scored no fewer than nineteen church compositions, 16 by Eberlin, three by Michael Haydn, from the parts.[60] The first fruits of his studies were an incomplete

[58] The orchestral and vocal versions are ed. Hubert Unverricht, ibid., Series IV and XXVIII.
[59] Lengthy examples in full score from a 'Veni Sancte Spiritus' and the Crucifixus of a *Messa solenne* (1764) by Leopold Mozart, the Benedictus of a *Missa brevissima* by Eberlin, and a 'Te Deum' (1760) by Michael Haydn on which the young Mozart modelled his K. 141, are given in Wilhelm Kurthen, 'Studien zu W. A. Mozarts kirchenmusikalischen Jugendwerken', *ZfMW*, iii (1920–1), pp. 366ff. Eberlin's Offertory 'Benedixisti Domine' is given complete in Hermann Abert, *W. A. Mozart*, ii (*Notenbeilage* III).

Missa brevis without orchestra (K. 115) and a solid *Missa in honorem SSmae Trinitatis* without soloists (K. 167) – but with an orchestra which, like that of K. 139, includes four trumpets and drums. His other Salzburg church music down to 1777, including eight Masses (mostly *breves*), generally follows the same tradition of chordal choral writing, leavened by a certain amount of imitative counterpoint and festooned with lively violin parts. The outstanding exceptions are his second *Litaniae Lauretanae* (K. 195) and second *Litaniae de venerabili altaris sacramento* (K. 243); following the examples of his father and Michael Haydn, he writes 'cantata-litanies' in strongly contrasted movements; the solos are quite operatic and sometimes (e.g. the Agnus Dei of K. 195) very lovely – the expression of a Catholicism as joyous and innocent and exuberant as the pilgrimage churches of Balthasar Neumann and Dominikus Zimmermann. After the interlude of his tour in the West, Mozart composed in 1779 and 1780 the two finest of his Salzburg Masses, both in C and both for the same large forces: K. 317, known as the 'Coronation Mass' from the probability that it was written for the annual coronation of the image of the Virgin at Maria am Plain near Salzburg, and K. 337, not improbably for the next year's ceremony. In both cases it is possible to identify with some confidence the relevant instrumental pieces, K. 329 and 336, which replaced the Gradual in the Mass in accordance with custom; these two are the last of Mozart's fifteen so-called 'Epistle sonatas'.

In 1781 Mozart, increasingly unhappy in the conditions at Salzburg, broke away. In Munich, just before the actual break, he wrote a deeply tragic isolated Kyrie in D minor (K. 341) and after it in Vienna he began in 1782 a great 'cantata-Mass' in C minor (K. 427), stylistically no longer a mixture of disparate elements but a compound, which was apparently never finished. The torso was performed – how we do not know – in the Peterskirche at Salzburg in 1783 and two years later Mozart himself pillaged the Kyrie and Gloria for an Italian oratorio *Davidde penitente* (his only oratorio other than a juvenile setting of *Betulia liberata*). Even as a torso it is his supreme masterpiece of church music – and almost his last.

THE REFORM OF CHURCH MUSIC BY JOSEPH II

It was no mere coincidence that Haydn also wrote no more Masses for fourteen years after his *Missa Cellensis* and that his brother appears to have written no important ones between 1782 and 1793. A more powerful champion of Enlightenment than the Prince-Archbishop had appeared in 1780 when the death of Maria Theresa released her son, Joseph II, from her leading-strings. Already in 1749 an 'enlightened' Pope, Benedict XIV, had issued an encyclical laying down the law on a number of church-musical subjects. Plainsong was his ideal but polyphonic music with 'organ or other

---

[60] London, Brit. Lib. Add. MS. 41633. The incipits are given in Köchel's *Verzeichnis* (third edition, ed. Einstein, Ann Arbor, 1947), Anh. 109. One of the Eberlin works is the 'Benedixisti' mentioned in n. 59 above.

instruments' would be tolerated, provided no worldly and theatrical elements were introduced, and provided they only supported the sung text without interfering with its comprehensibility. (Hence the essays in choral homophony, allowing clear declamation of the words, and the separate, decorative role of the orchestra.) A Viennese Court decree of 1754 went further and forbade the use of trumpets and drums in the service. All this was honoured at least as much in the breach as in the observance, but Joseph II and his Prince-Archbishop were much more severe. In the interests of simplicity, wider comprehensibility and 'edification', parish churches were in 1782 ordered to replace instrumental music by German 'spiritual songs' and to celebrate the Mass in German. The following year Colloredo took the Office music in hand, vetoed the Epistle sonatas, and instructed Michael Haydn to make simple settings of the Graduals and Offertories. He complied and in the course of the next decade composed no fewer than 117 Graduals[61] and 45 Offertories, as well as eight German Masses, which were soon accepted as models and used all over Austria, The Archbishop presented a specially fine copy to St. Stephen's at Vienna.

MOZART'S LAST RELIGIOUS COMPOSITIONS

The accession in 1790 of Leopold II, who reversed nearly everything his brother had done, prepared the way for an easing of the church situation. But Leopold was no lover of music and no admirer of Mozart; the commission to compose *La clemenza di Tito* for his coronation as King of Bohemia was given by the Bohemian Estates, not by him. In any case time was running out for Mozart. In June 1791 he wrote the exquisitely simple 'Ave verum corpus' for voices, strings, and organ, probably for the church choir at Baden bei Wien. And the following month he received an anonymous commission to compose a Requiem Mass. Work on it was hindered by the composition of *Clemenza* and the Clarinet Concerto, the production of *Zauberflöte*, and physical exhaustion. He still struggled with it on his death-bed but only the first number, Introit and Kyrie, was completed in full score; seven of the eight numbers of the 'Dies Irae' were left complete in voice-parts and continuo, with indications of the scoring; he wrote only eight bars of the 'Lacrymosa'. The Requiem was finished by his pupil and copyist Franz Xaver Süssmayr (1766–1803), the 'Domine Jesu' and 'Hostias et preces' possibly by another close friend, Josef Eybler (1765–1846). But the unevenness of the result is not attributable solely to the 'other hands'. The Introit is profoundly tragic, the Handelian Kyrie/Christe double fugue no more than a technical triumph, the 'Tuba mirum' unequal, the 'Recordare' touchingly beautiful. . . . Yet the Requiem and the 'Ave verum' are – unless we include, as we might well do, his Masonic compositions, e.g. the *Maurerische Trauermusik* (1785) and *Kleine Freimaurer Kantate* (1791) – the only religious music Mozart wrote during

[61] Nine examples ed. Anton M. Klafsky, *DTÖ*, Jg. xxxii (1) (vol. 62).

the last eight years of his life, when his creative powers were most fully developed. Both – like the late songs and *Zauberflöte* – show how the last great Italianate German composer was at the age of thirty-five turning more and more into a German musician. Ethereal as it sounds, the little motet might almost be a Protestant hymn and much of the Requiem is an afterglow of Bach and Handel. Even *La clemenza* was, to the Neapolitan ears of Leopold II's wife, a 'dirty German mess' (*porcheria tedesca*); she would have been astonished if anyone had suggested that the world's greatest music during the next hundred years might be largely written by Germans.

Interlude

26

The Music of India[1]

THE BEGINNINGS OF INDIAN MUSIC

Despite numerous European contacts with India from the sixteenth century onward, neither Portuguese nor Dutch, French nor English, preoccupied by commerce, military rivalry, and conquest, took any interest in her music until the end of the eighteenth. Seemingly the earliest European to do so was Francis Fowkes who published a paper 'On the Vina of the Hindus' in 1788.[2] He was followed by the great orientalist Sir William Jones in an essay 'On the musical modes of the Hindus'[3] and for very many years Indian music remained the affair of orientalists, not European musicians. There was no relationship with Western music comparable with that which subsisted at times between Arabic and Western music, and the orientalists were interested in history and theory to the almost complete exclusion of the living practice. Confusion arises when the same technical terms or names of instruments are applied in describing both. For instance, the modern *vīṇá*, a stringed instrument with frets fastened to a bamboo tube with two gourd resonators, is not even descended from the *vīṇá* mentioned in the oldest theoretical treatise, the *Nāṭyasāstra* (early first millennium A.D. but probably incorporating earlier material). *Vīṇá* is really a generic term for stringed instruments; in early periods it was applied to a species of short lute and the instrument of Bharata's treatise was probably an arched harp played with a *kona* (plectrum). On the other hand, tube- or stick-zithers – the real progenitors of the modern *vīṇá* – first appear in iconography of the 6th–7th century, after which little more is seen of the lute and harp types. Frets are mentioned in Śārṅgadeva's *Saṃgītaratnākara* (*c.* 1200–50), which mentions *vīṇás* with only one string or as many as 22.

Long before the *Nāṭyasāstra*, the Vedic period (*c.* 1500–800 B.C.) provides suggestions of Indian music in the same way that the Old Testament suggests the nature of that of the Jews. How the hymns of the great Sanskrit collection, the *Rigveda*, were intoned we simply do not know, though precise accuracy of transmission was so essential, owing to the frightful consequences of even slight error, that it is possible modern intonation of Rigvedic texts[4] has not been much modified in the course of

---

[1] The whole sub-continent, not the modern Republic.
[2] *Asiatic Researches*, i (1788), p. 295.
[3] Ibid., iii (1792), p. 55.
[4] E.g. the fragment quoted in *NOHM*, i, p. 200.

three millennia. Considerably wider in compass, six or even seven notes, are the formulae of the *Sāmaveda*, based on hymns from the *Rigveda* and actually sung, not merely intoned, in the course of offerings and sacrifices. These formulae, *sāmans*, seem to have been originally independent melodies, later texted melodies.

To the Hindu, music was not a thing-in-itself any more than it was to the Greeks. He believed in the power of music – or rather *sāmgīta*, the combination of vocal music, instrumental music, and dance – to influence the whole workings of the universe; he believed in its power to help the self break from the endless cycle of birth, death, and rebirth and become absorbed into the spirit of the universe, *Nirvāṇa*, as is duly set forth in the *Samgītaratnākara*, the basis of our knowledge of what we may call the classical system of Indian music.

THE MUSICAL SYSTEM

Like the music of the West, that of India is based on the octave. It could exist in three registers: *mandra* (soft), *madhya* (middle), and *tāra* (sharp), thought to be produced by breast, throat, and head respectively. The octave was divided into 22 theoretically equal *śrutis*, not in succession – there was no such thing as a scale of *śrutis* – but to define the intervals between the notes of the scales: 2 *śrutis* = a semitone, 3 = an intermediate note, 4 = a whole tone. The principal scale was the *ṣadjagrāma* (commonly abbreviated to *sa-grāma*) and from it was derived another, the *madhyamagrāma* (abbreviated to *ma-grāma*), so called because it began on the note *madhyama*, the 'middle note'. Each note had a name and the first syllable of each name provided a solmization syllable for the note and the interval below it, thus the *ṣadjagrāma* consisted of:

> sa ri ga ma pa dha ni
> 4 3 2 4 4 3   2   *śrutis* to the interval

Two of these intervals – but only two – could be altered: *ni* taking two *śrutis* from *sa* in the register above, rising a semitone and called *kākalī-ni* (soft *ni*), and *ga* borrowing from *ma* and becoming *antara-ga* (medium *ga*).

Modern Indian practice has abandoned *śrutis* and defines scales in terms of tones and semitones, though these are not precisely fixed. In certain *rāgas* (see below) a particular note may be slightly more or less sharp or flat than usual, and undefined microtones occur in profusion in the expressive improvised ornamentation so important in Indian music. Unlike Western music, which has almost completely abandoned intervals smaller than the semitone in its theory and gradually developed a complicated system of harmony, Indian music has ignored harmony other than the age-old universal drone and developed an extremely complex monodic system.

From the two basic scales were derived seven classes of mode called *jāti*, starting from *sa*, *dha*, *ni*, and *ri* of the *sa-grāma* and *ma*, *ga*, and *pa* of the *ma-grāma*. Melodies classed in the same *jāti* might be pentatonic, hexatonic, or heptatonic. And from the *jātis* were derived the melodic formulae known as *rāgas* (colours), a term which appeared as early as the eighth century A.D., and have supplied the essential matter of Indian music through the centuries. Śārṅgadeva in his *Saṃgītaratnākara* calls them the 'children' of the *jātis*, and reckons and duly classifies 264 of them. Very important were the first note of the *rāga* (*graha*), the note most dwelt on (*aṃśa*), and the final (*nyāsa*), which might or might not be identical, though in modern practice all *rāgas* have effectively the same final (*sa*) and the first note is usually not specified though in practice it is generally the same as the final. All these characteristics of the *rāga* are emphasized in the prelude (*ālāpa*) to a performance based on it, and already placed in relation to the *sa* of the mode (sounded by the drone). Like the Muslim *maqām* (see p. 197), each *rāga* has its own extra-musical association of emotion or time of day and so on, and the performance of one *rāga* must be completed before the performer is free, if he wishes, to take up another. Only in certain specific forms is it permissible to 'modulate' from one *rāga* to another – and then only to a closely related one.

Whereas the *ālāpa* – which may last as long as an hour – is an improvisation in free rhythm, the main part of the performance is based on a composed melody conforming to the *rāga* on which the singer or player improvises variations within the limits of the time-measure known as *tāla*. These rhythmic patterns are continually repeated; the basic one may be marked by hand-claps or left unmarked, the drum may emphasize it with a simple pattern of strokes or especially in the South, provide a continuous and often extremely complex rhythmic counterpoint to the melody. The *tālas* may consist of anything from five to sixteen, or even more, beats grouped asymmetrically, e.g. 10 as $2+5+3$, 12 as $4+4+2+2$, 16 as $4+8+4$, and the cross-rhythms set against the basic pulse by both soloist and percussion player build up great tension which is ultimately resolved on the first beat of a *tāla*-cycle. This main part of the performance, after the *ālāpa*, consists of a number of parts usually different in register; the first – called *sthāyī* in the North, *pallavī* in the South – is repeated as refrain after the other parts, thus:

North India: 1. *sthāyī:* middle octave, emphasizing the 'tonic' (*sa*)
Refrain
2. *antarā*: higher register, emphasizing the octave of the 'tonic'

Refrain
3. *sañcārī*: varied repeat of 1.
4. *ābhog*: varied repeat of 2.
Refrain

South India: 1. *pallavī = sthāyī*
　　　　　　　Refrain
　　　　　　　2. *anupallavi = antarā*
　　　　　　　Refrain
　　　　　　　3. *caraṇam = sañcārī* and *ābhog*
　　　　　　　Refrain

Parts 3 and 4 in the Northern tradition are now normally omitted.

At the end the soloist usually returns to *sa*, which is heard continuing in the drone after the melody has ceased.

Pl. 50(i)　The *sārangī* has three strings played with a bow and forty to fifty sympathetic strings.

　　　(ii)　North Indian ensemble with (left to right) *sitar*, *sārod*, *tambura*, and *tāblā* (Jodhpur, Rajasthan).

DIFFERENCES OF NORTH AND SOUTH

There are other differences between North and South Indian music. For instance, the same name may be applied to different *rāgas*, North or South, or identical *rāgas* may have different names and are differentiated by subtle details. Comparing the Southern *rāga Ābherī* with the Northern *rāga Bhimpalālsī*, which have identical notes in both rising and falling forms, the South Indian musician Subrahmanya Ayyar[5] remarks:

The difference is largely due to the small variations in the microtonal changes of the *svaras* [notes] in the ascent and descent. . . . The Northern Indian musician may be aware of the 22 *śrutis* in the octave but he has not attempted to use them in his *rāgas* to a very large extent . . . This feature is seemingly responsible for the feeling of monotony that the South Indian feels in listening to Hindustani *rāgas*.[6]

Ayyar suggests that the vocal music of the North has been influenced by the technique of the bowed *sāraṅgī* with its glissandi of nail on string and its

---

[5] *The Grammar of South Indian (Karnatic) Music* (Madras, second, enlarged edition, 1951), p. 123.
[6] The Hindustani ornamental style is slow and sensuous, that of the South light and rapid.

'sympathetic' strings, that of the South by the more intimate and expressive plucked *vīṇá*; conversely, of course, it is arguable that the instrumental style in each case has been influenced by the vocal.

These differences flowed from the Islamic conquest of Northern India – 'Hindustan' proper, a word with a Persian suffix – during the eleventh and twelfth centuries. Persian became the official and literary language, and unconverted Hindus used the Persianized form of their own language known as Urdu or Hindustani, whereas the South was conquered later and more briefly; even the Mogul emperors failed to establish a long ascendancy there. The Hindus preserved and the Muslims accepted to some extent their belief in the magical power of music, even its Buddhist overtones, but Persian and Urdu types of song came into existence and Persian instruments such as the double-reed pipe *shahnāi*, the Persian *surnā*, were adopted. The *shahnāi* reached the South but characteristically under a Hindu name: *nāgasvaram*. The popular *sitar*, with movable frets and sympathetic strings, is of Persian origin and significantly, is said to have appeared first in Delhi in the twelfth century. The Persian *tanbūr* (see p. 191) became the *tambūrā* which sounds *sa*, *pa*, and upper *sa* as a multiple drone, and the pairs of drums, *tablā*, are obviously named from the Islamic *ṭabl*. (Another kind of drum, the horizontal *mṛdaṅgam*, is – like the *tablā* – tuned to *sa* as a percussive 'drone'; this too has a Hindustani name, *pakhavāj*.) Other direct borrowings in the North are the *rabāb* (the Persian *rubāb*: see p. 195), now called *sārod*, and the short straight trumpet *nafari* (the Persian *nafar*), an instrument not used in classical music.

Arthur Fox Strangways summed up his general impression of the difference between Muslim and Hindu singing thus:

The Mohammedan prefers the more cheerful *Rāgs* – *Khamāj*, *Kāfi*, and the *Kaliāns*; and the simpler rhythms. . . . With these he takes a considerable amount of liberty, concealing the rhythm, especially, by interspersed rests, and broken phrases that run counter to it, so that it would be unintelligible sometimes without the drummer. He has the performer's instinct; he rivets the attention of the audience as a whole, and the less able singer is apt to tear a passion to pieces rather than not challenge their admiration. . . . The Hindu . . . is at his best in the quieter *Rāgs* like *Bhairavī*, or the more characteristic such as *Vasant or Bibhās* or *Toḍī*, and in the more irregular rhythms. . . . His singing is less broken up with rests, and he luxuriates in cross-rhythm. His song gives much more the impression of coming from the heart, and of reaching out for sympathy rather than for applause.[7]

The impact of the Muslim invasion was the most important event in the history of Indian music until the arrival of the Christian missionaries. They introduced, *c.* 1900, the portable harmonium which by general consent has done immeasurable harm. Other imported instruments, such as the

[7] *The Music of Hindostan* (Oxford, 1914). pp. 89–90.
[8] A. M. Chinnaswami Mudaliyar gives sixty of Tyāgarāja's songs in his *Oriental Music in European Notation* (Madras, 1892) but European notation of Indian music – of which there is plenty – bears the same relation to the music as a cheap Victorian lithograph of a master painting does to the original. Indian music must be listened to, not read, and there are fortunately plenty of authentic recordings.

Hawaiian guitar, to say nothing of electronic amplification, have also played havoc, while modern education has largely substituted class-training in music for the individual instruction of a pupil by a master. Indian music, vocal and instrumental, is essentially a solo art.

One might almost go so far as to say that Indian music has no history. More accurately, its history is of slow, deep changes. Treatise succeeds treatise, each refining or expanding the theory of the system, often confusing it with modern practice; names of great musicians such as Tyāgarāja of Tanjore (1767–1847) appear but their work is preserved mainly through oral tradition.[8] Composer and interpreter are one and the same. It is as if Paganini or Liszt had published nothing for want of an adequate notation. It may seem incredible that an extremely complex and exquisitely sensitive monodic system should have flourished for two thousand years without essential changes – and without devising an adequate notation beyond the letter pitch-notation of *sa–ri–ga* and their modifications. The explanation lies in the very ethos of Indian music, so different from that of the West, the endless, quasi-mesmeric flow of melody, with associative emotional overtones that few Westerners can hope to catch, a sound image of cosmic infinity or of *cetana*, the movement of life. It is perhaps not too fanciful to find parallels in the masterpieces of Indian art, the wall-paintings of the Ajaṇṭā caves or the 'descent of the Ganges' sculpture at Māmallapuram.

27

The Music of Eastern Asia

EARLY CHINESE MUSIC

Of the high-culture musics of Eastern Asia the one with the longest documented history is that of China with its near relatives in Japan, Korea, and Vietnam. Some of the others are more distantly related, some – those of Cambodia, Thailand, and Indonesia – hardly at all. None, not even Burmese, has any but tenuous or occasional connection with Indian. Although the Chinese have a double-reed wind instrument called *so-na*, they are more likely to have acquired it directly from the Persian *surnā* along the Central Asian trade-route followed by Marco Polo than from the Hindustani *shannāi*. Only belief in the transcendental nature and power of music was shared by the Chinese with the Indians (and Greeks). As early as *c.* 250 B.C. a treatise systematized the relationship of musical sounds to the cosmic order – a relationship almost certainly recognized by the ancient Babylonians (see p. 21), and possibly Egyptians, and later by the Persians and Arabs – and at nearly the same time another treatise showed that the notes of the scale could be arithmetically derived from bamboo pitch-pipes.[1] Long before this we have texts referring to instruments and even surviving instruments: egg-shaped ceramic flutes, a zither-like instrument, various kinds of drum, and L-shaped 'sounding stones' (*ching*) suspended from a frame and struck with a stick. Melodic percussion and instruments of the zither type are characteristic of Eastern Asian music generally.

According to the encyclopedic *Ch'un-ch'iu* (Spring and Autumn) (239 B.C.) of Lü Pu-wei, the note given by the first pitch-pipe became the basis of the entire Chinese musical system. It was called *huang-chung* (literally 'yellow bell') and the Jesuit missionary Joseph Amiot, the earliest European to write extensively about Chinese music,[2] reckoned that it sounded F below middle C, probably a slight miscalculation. From the 'yellow bell' two series of notes were computed in ratios of 2:3 and 4:3, rising in perfect fifths and descending in perfect fourths – F C G D A E etc. The six notes (*lu*) of the lower series, F. G. A B C♯ D♯, were female (*yin*), the six (lu) of the upper series, C D E F♯ G♯ A♯, male (*yang*). But this was theory or, rather, the

[1] *NOHM*, i, p. 94.
[2] 'Mémoire sur la Musique des Chinois tant anciens que modernes', *Mémoires*, vi (Paris, 1780). An earlier Jesuit, Jean-Baptiste du Halde, had printed five Chinese melodies in his general description of China published in 1735; they are reproduced, a third too low, in *SIMG*, ii (1900–1), pp. 526–8. No. 1 was printed, at the correct pitch but with an error in bar 3, by Rousseau in his *Dictionnaire de musique* whence Weber borrowed it in his incidental music for Schiller's *Turandot* in 1809.

basis of theory; the oldest practical scale was pentatonic. There are very early references to 'five notes' and the names – *kung* (F), *shang* (G), *chiao* (A), *chih* (C), *yü* (D) – appear before the *Lü-shih Ch'un-ch'iu*, as also did two auxiliary notes, probably *pien-chih* (B) and *pien-kung* (E). It is characteristic of the Chinese scholar's conception of the relation of music to social as well as cosmic order that even the 'five notes' were symbolic, *kung* of the Emperor, *shang* of his chief minister, *chiao* of his subjects, *chih* of state affairs, and *yü* of material things; they also corresponded to the 'five virtues', 'five colours', 'five elements', 'five planets', and 'five directions' (the main points of the compass, plus centre). They could be played in the ritual music on the strings of the oldest form of *ch'in*, a long, narrow species of zither, together with a larger zither, *sê*, two panpipe-like instruments, the *p'ai hsiao* or true panpipes and the *shêng* with free-reed pipes and a small wind-chest, and tuned stones and bells.

We owe practically all this information to Lü Pu-wei, whose treatise escaped the holocaust of books on Chinese culture ordered by the last of the Ch'in emperors in 212 B.C. Under the Han dynasty (206 B.C.–A.D. 220) various theorists tried to close the gap between the twelfth fifth, and the octave of the fundamental by continuing the cycle of perfect fifths, arriving by working back and forth within the octave at infinitesimal intervals, 60 to the octave. The pentatonic scale could begin on any one of the five notes, giving five different 'modes' named after the initial/final of a melody in the mode in accordance with the seasons. The Han theorist Ching Fang (*c.* 40 B.C.) talks about a twelve-note scale related to the twelve months, hours, and signs of the zodiac. Each note has a different name: *huang-chung* (F), *ta-lü* (F♯) *r'ai-ts' ou* (G), *chia-chung* (G♯), *ku-hsien* (A), *chung-lü* (A♯), *jui-pin* (B), *lin-chung* (C), *i-tsê* (C♯), *nan-lü* (D), *wu-i* (D♯), *ying-chung* (E). He says, 'For the musical degrees, at the winter solstice one takes *huang-chung* as prime, *t'ai-ts'ou* as major second, *ku-hsien* as major third, *lin-chung* as fifth, *nan-lü* as major sixth, *ying-chung* as diminished octave, *jui-pin* as diminished fifth,' and goes on to explain that the initial of the mode is transposed according to the day and 'the second and fifth follow in conformity with their nature'. However this practice of ritual transposition according to month and hour[3] was not a constant feature of Chinese ritual music but fell into disuse again and again only to be revived. Under the Han emperors an Imperial Bureau of Music (*Yüeh-fu*) was established to supervise all these matters and maintain an archive of national ritual melodies – indicating the existence of a system of notation (probably the names of the notes as listed).

FOREIGN INFLUENCES ON CHINESE MUSIC

During the first six centuries of the Christian era Chinese court music was affected by various foreign influences. First, along the Central Asian trade-

---

[3] The ninth-century Arab theorist Ishāq al-Kindī (see pp. 193–4) describes a similar use of particular modes proper to the hours of day, week, and month.

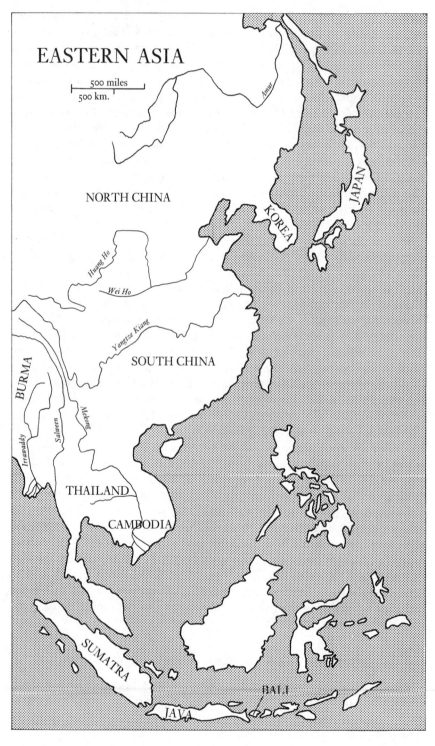

route came Buddhist missionaries with their own ritual chants. Buddhism became enormously influential for several centuries (though it never replaced Confucianism as the state religion) and coloured all the Chinese arts with second-hand Central Asian tints. And new instruments came from Western Asia: the Persian lute *barbat* = the Chinese *p'i-p'a*, the long Persian lute *setar* ('three strings') which also gave its name to the Indian *sitar* = the Chinese *san hsien* ('three strings'), the Persian harp *jank* = the Chinese *k'ung hou*. The imperial court had for centuries employed orchestras of hundreds of musicians, perhaps playing in unison or octaves, plus fifths and fourths broken up in rhythmic figuration, in marked contrast with the solo music of India. Now foreign orchestras from newly conquered areas of Central Asia delighted the court and there was a recognized and popular category of 'foreign music'. Small orchestras of *ch'in*, *sè*, *chêng* (yet another zither), *p'i-p'a*, and *hsiao* (a vertical flute) accompanied the puppet plays that appeared at this time.

MUSIC UNDER THE T'ANG, SUNG, AND YÜAN EMPERORS

Music flourished under the T'ang emperors (618–907). One of the earliest, T'ai-tsung, approved a new formulation of theory: twelve-note scales including all the semitones, founded on each of the seven basic modes. A later one, Hsüan-tsung the Ming-Huang Emperor, personally instructed a band of three hundred young musicians in an academy known as the Pear Garden (with a girls' section, the Garden of Everlasting Spring) and is said to have been able to detect a single player's wrong note; he is also believed to have composed.[4] The choral ballets, developing away from purely ritual forms to secular ones, have even been claimed – rather doubtfully – as one of the cradles of Chinese drama beside the early puppet plays.

From the T'ang period also date purely instrumental pieces in a number of connected movements, as many as seven or eight, something like the Islamic *nauba* (cf. p. 199). A large body of secular music of this period has survived as the T'ang music (*Togaku*) of the Japanese Court, borrowed by the Japanese before 850 (see below, p. 569). A piece for voice and *ch'in* survives from the Sung Dynasty (960–1126). The tablature indicates finger-positions, not pitch, of short phrases.[5] The vocal stanzas alternate with equally brief instrumental interludes.

The Sung were driven to South-East China, where they reigned for another half-century, by Tatar invasion. The first Tatar (Yüan dynasty) emperor, Kubilai ('Kubla Khan'), introduced a 'Mongol scale' identical with the Western F major scale but a compromise was established, retaining the Chinese B natural but adding the Mongol B flat. The Yüan emperors preserved the ritual transpositions and also developed the classical theatre.

---

[4] A tune ascribed to him, though from a much later source, is printed in *NOHM*, i, p. 107.
[5] See the examples in ibid., pp. 102–3, 105, 109–10.

THE MING PERIOD

Under the Sung the puppet theatre had evolved through children dressed as puppets to adult musical theatre. Performances in the north were accompanied by the flute, and flute notation consequently remained the notation of theatre music, though in the south the *p'i-p'a* was used. During the long supremacy of the purely Chinese Ming emperors (1368–1644) the southern 'opera' developed greater importance and a variety of styles, of which the most important was that known as *k'un-ch'ü* – with numerous acts comprising both song and declamation, melodies recurring in association with particular feelings or situations,[6] and a varied orchestra including *ti-tzŭ* (transverse flute), *shêng, so-na, san hsien, p'i-p'a*, and percussion. Latterly actresses were excluded and all roles were played by males.

An outstanding monument of the Ming period was the great musical encyclopedia, *Yüeh-lü ch'üan shu*, published in 1606 by Prince Tsai-yü. This includes a history of Chinese music and not only preserves numerous old ritual melodies but attempts reconstructions of the original orchestral accompaniments.[7] The prince was also a remarkable theorist who hit on the concept of equal temperament before any European, and calculated the length of equal-tempered pitch-pipes using the twelfth root of 2.

THE MANCHUS AND 'PEKING OPERA'

At the same time Jesuit missionaries were not only introducing European music in their churches but writing about it in Chinese. However, its influence long remained infinitesimal even under the Manchu emperors (Ch'ing dynasty) who ruled from 1644 until the Revolution of 1912. During the last years of the Manchus a tide of Westernization had already begun to flow in other areas besides music and, particularly since the Second World War, many Chinese musicians have now become highly proficient on Western instruments and some have composed for them.

One notable feature of the late Manchu period was the rise of a new type of musical theatre known as 'Peking opera' or *ching-hsi*, which surpassed the classical southern style (*k'un-ch'ü*) in popularity without entirely supplanting it:

Superficially the most obvious difference between *k'un-ch'ü* and *ching-hsi* lies in the rejection of the *tz'ŭ* form of lyric in favour of the less strict *ch'ü*. While *k'un-ch'ü* makes use of only two rhythms: a 2/4 with the first beat strongly accented, and a 4/4 with the first beat strongly accented and the third beat divided into two quavers, *ching-hsi* makes use of a considerable number of rhythms, both regular and irregular.[8]

---

[6] Three examples, ibid., pp. 116–17.
[7] Brief excerpt in score, ibid., p. 103. Tsai-yü's account of his reasoning is given at length in Maurice Courant, 'Chine et Corée', *Encyclopédie de la Musique et Dictionnaire du Conservatoire*, Ire partie, i, pp. 121ff.
[8] Laurence Picken, *NOHM*, i, p. 128.

CHINESE INFLUENCE ON JAPAN

The basic pentatonicism of Chinese music is shared with Japan, Korea, and Annam (the modern Vietnam). In the two latter lands Chinese musical culture has come to overlay a substratum of indigenous music. The instruments were similar, sometimes even in name, with all sorts of variants; for instance, in the sixth century A.D. a Korean minister is said to have invented a zither-like instrument, *komūngo*, suggested by the Chinese *ch'in* but played differently. T'ang court music came flooding into Japan during the eighth and early ninth century, while during the Sung the Confucian ritual music and instruments were imported into Korea, where the Chinese ritual style, called *a-ak*, came to predominate in religious ceremonies, while the indigenous music predominated in secular court ceremonies and in popular music. It was through the visit of a Korean orchestra of eighty players that Chinese-style music, *sankangaku*, first reached Japan in A.D. 435.

A hundred years later the Emperor Kimmei asked for Korean music-masters to be sent to Japan, and the introduction of Buddhism under his aegis led to the performance of temple dances, *gigaku* (*gaku* = music). In the eighth century the staffing of the imperial court-music still included masters of the Korean styles but also twelve masters and sixty students of *Tōgaku* (Chinese T'ang music). Annamese music, *Rinyûgaku*, was soon added to the mixture but the instruments were mostly of Chinese origin: various kinds of flute, the double-reed *hichiriki* (the Chinese *pi-li*), the *shō* (= *shêng*), the *sō* or *koto* (= *chêng*), the *biwa* (= *p'i-p'a*), the zither *wagon* (one of the few indigenous Japanese instruments), the long lute *samisen* (= *san hsien*), and various kinds of gong and drum. Not only the Chinese instrumentarium but Chinese theory was taken over. The Japanese note-names for the twelve-note scale, however, are those of *modes* beginning on these degrees. In some instances these are Sino-Japanese forms of the Chinese modal names: E *hyōjō* (Japanese) = Chinese *p'ing-tiao*, G *sōjō* = *shuang-tiao*, B *banshiki* = *pán-shê*, A *ōjiki* = *huang-chung*; in other cases the names are purely Japanese: F♯ *shimomu*, C♯ *ramimu*, etc. The principal tunings of stringed instruments are arrived at by measuring a perfect fifth and fourth from the fundamental and then, like the Chinese, by rising fifths or falling fourths, though for practical purposes only from the first note to the fifth in the sequence. A mode such as *hirajōshi* can be modified by flattenings or sharpenings – apart from the microtonal embellishments which are important in Japanese music. Modes are classified as male (*ryo*) (with major third) or female (*ritsu*) (with minor third). Two other popular modes, *kumoi* and *iwato*, admit semitones respectively between the second and third (or first-second and fourth-fifth) degrees of the scale and first-second and third-fourth degrees.

The T'ang Court repertory (*Tōgaku*) and the Korean repertory (components of the Court music) include both purely instrumental pieces and orchestrally accompanied dances (*bugaku*) foreign in origin but assimilated as Japanese by the ninth and tenth centuries. The names of eminent musicians have been preserved, notably Hakuga-no-Sammi (918–80) from whom a collection of fifty pieces of the T'ang repertory has survived in flute-tablature. A great deal of the *gagaku*[9] tradition has been preserved in manuscript part-books since the early ninth century. It is of several kinds: *saibara* are songs, believed to be modelled on folk-songs, taken into the court repertoire, *Tōgaku*, the T'ang Court repertory, and *Komagaku*, the Korean repertory, all played today by an orchestra of *shō*, *ryūteki*, and *hichiriki* which carry the melody, and *koto* and *biwa* which play conventional accompaniment patterns, gong, and drums.[10]

During the thirteenth and fourteenth centuries the popular song and dance entertainments known as *dengaku* and *sarugaku* gradually developed into a serious dramatic form, *saragaku-no-nō*, later called simply *nō*, with two actors who employed recitative, a chorus, a transverse flute, and percussion instruments. It was an unrealistic drama which adumbrated the spirit of Zen Buddhism, and the *shōguns* who now ruled Japan instead of the nominal emperors – particularly Yoshimasa (1435–90) – personally intervened in the organization of the *nō* actors.

JAPANESE MUSIC UNDER THE *SHŌGUNS*

Music flourished under the Tokugawa *shōguns* who ruled from the beginning of the seventeenth century to the middle of the nineteenth. They expelled the Jesuit missionaries and all but a handful of the foreign traders who had lately appeared in Japan, established Confucianism as the official religion, and effectively sealed off the country from all outside contacts. A new form of lute, the *samisen* (Chinese *san hsien*, see p. 567), had recently found its way to Japan from Okinawa and quickly became popular thanks to the superb playing of the master Ishimura. About 1600 another master of the instrument, Sawazumi, used it to accompany his recitation of scenes from popular novels, later bringing in puppets to represent the action. In the course of a century and a quarter this type of entertainment absorbed and was finally overwhelmed by elements from the popular theatre, *kabuki*, which was not formalized like the *nō* plays. Another outstanding musician of the early Tokugawa period was the blind *koto*-player Yamazumi (1614–85) who took the name of Yatsuhashi and settled in Edo (the modern Tokyo). Yatsuhashi invented an important new instrumental form for his instrument, the *danmono*, a suite of pieces in numbered sections. (*Dan* is a Sino-Japanese word for 'step' or 'rung', but here it has its original Chinese meaning (from *tuan*): a musical section.) Each *dan* is of a specific length and is divided into two parts, the second considerably longer than the first; each *dan* is played a little faster than its predecessor, but the tempo is gradually

[9] *Gagaku* is court music generally, *Tōgaku* specifically T'ang.
[10] There are a number of editions of *gagaku* in Western notation, the most recent being the *Complete Gagaku Music in Western Notation*, ed. Shukehiro Shiba (Tokyo, i– , 1968–). But, as with other Asian musics, Western notation cannot convey the finesses of pitch and interpretation, least of all the ornamentation (which is customarily improvised). However, Eta Harich-Schneider in the examples in her *History of Japanese Music* (London, 1973) has attempted to do this.

slowed in the second part of the last *dan*. Yatsuhashi had an outstanding successor in Ikuta (1655–1715) who developed a virtuoso style of composition though he neglected another of Yatsuhashi's inventions, the *kumi-uta*, which is rather like the *danmono* but with a subordinate voice-part.

Pl. 52 Players of hand-drum and *biwa*. At the feet of the blind *biwa* player lie a pitchpipe and a small recorder. Illustration by Tosa Mitsunobu from the *Shokunin Zukushi Uta-awase* (1744).

THE IMPACT OF THE WEST

The hermetic Japanese world was cracked in the 1850s by armed foreign intrusion and shattered in the 1860s by the Meiji restoration. Earlier than the Chinese and much more thoroughly, the Japanese hastened to adopt not only Western dress and Western armaments but Western music. Their own was not abandoned; indeed *gagaku* ceased to be a Court preserve and began to be performed in public. But the army adopted European bands and from 1874 onward the Court musicians had to learn European instruments side by side with the traditional ones. In the 1880s Western music began to be taught in the schools, where the piano or harmonium became an obligatory instrument. A new kind of Japanese ensemble-music for *kotos* or *samisens* came into existence, while on the other hand the first symphonic orchestra was established in 1897. With their astonishing capacity for assimilation in every field, it not surprising that Japanese performers of Western music are now commonplace. Composers have been slower in adopting Western techniques, ranging from German romantic to post-war *avant-garde*. Outstanding among the older Westernized composers was Kōsaku Yamada (1886–1965), namesake of a celebrated nineteenth-century *koto* player. Yamada, a pupil of Max Bruch and decidedly Germanic, contributed to most genres, including opera; his *Ochitaryu tennyo* (The fallen angel) was composed in 1912 but not performed till 1930. His almost exact contemporary Kiyoshi Nobutoki (1887–1965) composed mostly solo songs and choral music. From the much younger men one might single out Akira

571

Miyoshi (b. 1933) composer of orchestral and chamber works which include an interesting hybrid, an Octet for *shakuhachi* (similar to the Chinese *hsiao*), three *kotos*, and strings. Yet so far no Japanese composer has won anything more than *succès d'estime* in Europe or America.

THE MUSIC OF INDONESIA

The musics of the Malayan archipelago – Javanese, Balinese, Sumatran, and the rest – differ from both the Chinese and the Indian genera in their freedom from religious or cosmic associations and in not being constructed from the cycle of fifths. It is true that one of the two Javanese modes, *slendro*, which takes its name from an Indian dynasty of the ninth and tenth centuries, is pentatonic like the Chinese – though the octave tends to be wrongly divided into five equal steps – and that the predominance of melodic percussion instruments (except in northern Sumatra) recalls the early Chinese 'sounding stones'. But that is all. The orchestra (*gamelan*) consists of the bowed *rebab* (the Persian-Arabic *rabāb*: see p. 195), *gambang* (a xylophone-like instrument with wooden or metal bars), *gendèr* (freely vibrating metal plates with bamboo resonators, suspended in a frame), *saron* and *demoeng* (resembling the *gendèr* but without resonators), *bonang* (tuned gongs in a frame), *réjong* (a pair of tuned gongs), *angkloeng* (a tuned bamboo rattle), *soeling* (vertical flute), *tjengtjengs* (cymbals), and other percussion of indefinite pitch. (The single-reed *selompret* is seldom included in the *gamelan*.) These play together in free heterophony, each instrument ornamenting the melody according to its nature[11] and producing sounds that delighted Western ears, including Debussy's at the Paris Exposition Universelle in 1889, and later inspired Messiaen (see p. 847).

Besides the pentatonic mode *slendro*, Indonesian music employs another called *pelog*, in which the octave is divided into seven. This mode, or five- or four-note selections from it, is particularly favoured in Bali also. Indeed the main difference between the musics of Java and Bali consists not in the systems or instruments but in the manner of performance:

Javanese gamelans have an incredibly soft, legato, velvet sound; the hammers and mallets that are used to strike the metallophones and gongs are padded so thickly as to eliminate all shock. Tempos are slow and stately, and there is little change in dynamics; the prevailing mood is one of untroubled calm and mystic serenity. Balinese music, on the other hand, is vigorous, rhythmic, explosive in quality; the gamelans sound bright and percussive; hard hammers of wood or horn are used for many instruments, and the thin clash of cymbals underlies every tone; only the great gongs are gently struck. While the classic calm of Javanese music and dance is never disturbed, music and dance in Bali is turbulent and dramatic, filled with contrast and bold effects.[12]

---

[11] See the page of score in *NOHM*, i, p. 169; the complete composition is given in Daniel de Lange and Joh. F. Snelleman, 'Les Indes orientales néerlandaises', *Encyclopédie de la Musique*, Ire partie, v, pp. 3160–4. And cf. the Thai score in *HAM*, i, No. 3.
[12] Colin McPhee, 'The Five-tone Gamelan Music of Bali', *MQ*, xxxv (1949), p. 251.

Part IV
The Ascendancy of Germany

Introduction

The musical ascendancy of Germany – ethnic not political Germany – was neither as long nor as complete as that of Italy had been. It cannot be dated from Handel and J. S. Bach for the one was Italianate, the other little known beyond Protestant Germany. The Mannheim composers were the earliest portent, significantly in the field of orchestral music, with Bach's son, Carl Philipp Emanuel, who was to influence Haydn. It was the excitement of romanticism that powered the heartbeat of German music during its greatest age and romanticism itself was essentially German despite its origin in Rousseauesque sensibility. Early landmarks of romanticism include Goethe's *Götz von Berlichingen* (1772), Klinger's *Sturm und Drang* which provided a label for the whole early period (1775), and Schiller's *Die Räuber* (1781) in literature, Haydn's minor-key symphonies of the early 1770s, the third of Emanuel Bach's *Orchester-Sinfonien* (1776), his *Fantasien* and *Abschied von meinem Silbermannischen Clavier* (1781), Mozart's *Deutsche Arien* (1787) and B minor Adagio, K. 540 (1788) in music. It was German writers – Schiller, the Schlegels, Tieck, Novalis, E. T. A. Hoffmann – who tried to define the nature of romanticism, and mainly German writers – Scott and Byron (and later Hugo) were the principal exceptions – who supplied composers with subjects and verses.

The belated flowering of German lyric poetry gave a tremendous stimulus to song composition and the *Klavierlied* of Zumsteeg and his contemporaries came to full bloom in the hands of Schubert and Loewe, and continued to blossom profusely with Schumann and Franz and Cornelius, Brahms and Hugo Wolf. But one of the most striking features of the period was the supremacy of instrumental music, the vast enlargement of its area of competence. (Even in pure virtuosity the instrumental performers – Paganini, Liszt, and the rest – now overshadowed the vocalists). After Beethoven, neither symphony, piano sonata, nor string quartet could ever be the same; none but a tame conservative could ignore his challenges. Even if the classical genres remained 'simply' music, their forms and textures had been opened up and, in the case of the piano, mechanical improvements made possible quasi-orchestral conceptions on the one hand and the quasi-cantabile and introvert broodings of true romantic piano music on the other. The symphony with chorus, the symphony with programme, the concert overture which in mid-century became the symphonic poem, were all

574

attempts to give music new dimensions. While piano music often challenged the orchestra, the art of orchestration tended from Liszt and Wagner onward to make orchestral texture quasi-pianistic in finesse. All the vital music of the century is of the nature we generally recognize as 'romantic': 'music as a record of the most subtle and intimate personal emotions and impressions, music as a rhetorical language addressed to large audiences . . . music fertilized more richly than ever before by literature and painting, with the vast expansion of tonality, the complication of chromatic harmony and texture in general, and the richness and rarefaction of orchestration that were developed by the striving for wider and more refined expressive power.'[1] And while Berlioz refined the orchestral palette and Liszt and Rimsky-Korsakov gave it additional brilliance, while Chopin spread the magic of chromaticism and fine texture over piano music and Chaykovsky showed Mahler how private emotion could be expressed in public rhetoric, it was mainly German composers – particularly Wagner and his train – who embodied these tendencies.

The German ascendancy was not a matter of all-pervading influence as the Italian had been; it was due to the pre-eminence of a number of individual composers, from Beethoven, Weber, Spohr, Schubert belatedly, Mendelssohn, and Schumann to Brahms, Bruckner, Hugo Wolf, Richard Strauss, Reger, Mahler, and most of all of course Wagner. The most improbable non-Germans fell under Wagner's spell – Chabrier and Debussy, Puccini, Rimsky-Korsakov, Sibelius – albeit their music may show few traces of their infatuation. Other factors limited the extent of German influence. Italy had her own operatic masters and Paris remained cosmopolitan in taste. Moreover one consequence of the French Revolution and the defeats, and later the victories, of the Napoleonic wars was the awakening of acute national consciousness among various European peoples, none more than the Germans themselves. It stimulated the development of German romantic opera, throwing into the shade the old popular *Singspiel* or glorifying it as in *Freischütz*. But while providing fertile ground for the works of Spohr, Weber, and Marschner, and limiting the hegemony of Italian opera, at the same time nationalism hindered Germany from acquiring a similar universal ascendancy.

Italy's musical, as distinct from her political, nationalism was unconscious; it was as natural for an Italian to write Italian music as to speak Italian. In countries with less deeply rooted musical traditions it was deliberate. Glinka in Italy, his 'second fatherland', and saturated in *Italicismo*, was 'gradually led by homesickness to the idea of writing in Russian style' and around the middle of the century a whole group of younger talents were to follow him. Smetana at Weimar in 1857, angered by the tactless remark of a Viennese in Liszt's circle, 'swore then and there' that he would 'beget a native Czech music' and although brought up to speak and write German, and with imperfect knowledge of Czech, he went on to fulfil

[1] *NOHM*, x, p. 1.

his vow. A few years later the Belgian Peter Benoit, caught up in the *Vlaamse Beweging*, turned decisively from the composition of French texts to the composition of Flemish ones. Norwegian composers who went to Leipzig to study returned home to write Norwegian music; like the Russians they found a cathartic agent in their native folk-music. The French composers who succumbed to Wagner fought desperately to assert their own Gallicism; the disaster of the Franco-German War only spurred them to challenge the Germans in their most successful field and military defeat actually promoted a rebirth of French instrumental music. Britain and America alone remained totally under the German spell.

All the same, the national composers generally failed for a long time to win the international recognition granted to their German – and Italian operatic – contemporaries. Admittedly few of them were of equal stature but their unique qualities were often devalued by the application of Germanic standards of judgement; the successful non-Germans, such as Dvořák and Grieg, were those who could be regarded almost as honorary Germans. Not until the first decade of the twentieth century were the new voices of Debussy and Musorgsky attentively listened to by the musical world in general.

During that first decade romantic music had reached the degree of refinement which in the history of art frequently conceals immanent decadence. Melodic sensitivity (particularly to poetry), chromatic harmony developed to a degree that made tonality nearly meaningless on paper and quite meaningless to ear and mind, extreme density and subtlety of motivic relationship and texture, over-enrichment of orchestral sound had been carried to the uttermost. Germanic techniques – for all this was essentially Germanic – were exhausted. Reaction had already set in, indeed several reactions: the quasi-*art nouveau* style of Debussy and his *pointilliste* technique, the cool, compressed symphonic writing of Sibelius, the bold and novel rhythms and colours of Russian music revealed to Western Europe by Dyagilev's seasons of ballet and opera, the naïve, down-to-earth diatonic or modal music of the English folk-song school. But none was German; they were as much anti-German as anti-romantic. The early non-tonal works of Schoenberg up to *Pierrot lunaire* must be regarded as the death-cramp of romanticism.

Schoenberg himself brooded in silence for some years during the First World War and after it before setting in motion a Germanic reaction, but by then Germany had lost her almost unchallenged lead in the European consort.

28

Opera (1790–1830)

By the 1790s the greatest period of Italian ascendancy was over, even in its special field of opera. Of the older masters, Salieri in Vienna wrote three or four more works, including a *Falstaff* (1799) remembered only because Beethoven composed piano variations on the duet 'La stessa, la stessissima'; Paisiello and Martín y Soler produced little of any significance; only Cimarosa worthily continued the tradition for, as we shall see, the younger generation were of little account until a brilliant star emerged half way through this period. The greatest Italian composer of the time was Cherubini. But Cherubini was living in France and composing French operas. He could have found no better milieu, for Revolutionary Paris was the most exciting operatic centre of Europe. Not directly because of the Revolution, though a by-product of the Revolution became a focus: the 'École gratuite de musique de la Garde Nationale parisienne' was first re-named 'Institut national de musique' and then, in 1795, incorporated with Gossec's 'École royale de chant' as the 'Conservatoire de musique'. Five *inspecteurs des études* were appointed: Gossec, Grétry, Le Sueur, Cherubini, and Étienne-Nicolas Méhul (1763–1817). Gossec (and, later, Méhul) was professor of composition, Henri Berton (1767–1844) was professor of harmony, Charles-Simon Catel (1773–1830) of theory. All composed operas[1] in the Gluck tradition but, as Berton claimed in later years,[2] fertilized it with Haydn's plastic method of treating symphonic themes. Similarly, they varied the fashionable heroic-classicism with occasional essays in horror (e.g. Le Sueur's *Caverne* (1793) and Cherubini's *Médée* (1797)), just as the painter David did in his 'Murdered Marat'. Their later foreshadowings of romanticism in subjects from Ossian, Le Sueur's *Ossian ou Les Bardes* (1804) and Méhul's *Uthal* (1806), were not uninfluenced by the knowledge that Ossian was Napoleon's favourite poet.

Cherubini was by far the most gifted of the group, as Méhul was of the native 'Conservatoire composers'; Gossec and Grétry had seen their best days. Neither 'horror operas' nor 'rescue operas' were new to the Paris stage (see pp. 470–1) but Cherubini, by power of invention and mastery of technique, raised both to a higher plane. His first Paris success, *Lodoïska*

---

[1] As did the violin professor Rodolphe Kreutzer (1766–1831), whose *Astianax* (1801) and *Aristippe* (1808) were successful in their day. He is now better known as the dedicatee of a sonata.
[2] *De la musique mécanique et de la musique philosophique* (1826).

(1791), was with a rescue-opera and the political events of the next few years made the genre painfully apposite. *Eliza ou le Mont Saint-Bernard* (1794) showed his gift for musical scene-painting[3] and *Médée* is a tragic masterpiece, yet neither succeeded like *Les deux journées* (1800), a classic rescue-opera of

Pl. 53   Title-page of Le Sueur's *La Caverne* showing the underground cave in which the heroine is held captive by brigands.

the years when such rescues belonged to the past. No earlier *opéra comique* can have opened with such solemnity and mystery as the andante of the *Journées* overture or with such assured mastery as the allegro that follows;[4] Cherubini had not admired Haydn's symphonies for nothing and Haydn's gift of the autograph of the 'Drum-roll' (see p. 597) when Cherubini visited Vienna to produce another 'rescue' work, *Faniska*, in 1805, was no empty gesture. The opening of the melodrama 'Il fait un chaleur', just before the last finale of the *Journées*, breathes for eight bars the air of one

[3] One effect in Act II, sc. 4 – a clarinet call in the mountains, answered by a distant clarinet and followed by thunder – anticipates Berlioz's 'Scène aux champs' (see p. 668).
[4] Easily available in miniature score, as are the overtures to *Médée* and *Anacréon*.

greater even than Haydn, one who when asked in 1817 whom, excluding
himself, he considered the greatest living composer, answered 'Cherubini'.[5]
Not all of *Les deux journées* is on anything like this level; the First Act duet,
'Me séparer de mon époux?' is very fine, but the first two numbers,
Antonio's 'Un pauvre petit Savoyard' and his father's 'Guide mes pas' are
closer to Grétry or Dalayrac than to Beethoven. And these two numbers are
employed as reminiscence-themes like Grétry's 'Fièvre brûlante'; 'Un
pauvre petit Savoyard', for instance, is recalled by the orchestra when
Antonio is calming his sister in the finale of Act I, and when his father cries
'Il est sauvé, l'homme au manteau' in the finale of Act II. The reminiscence-
theme was by no means the peculiar property of the Conservatoire
composers but they were particularly fond of it; Cherubini had already
employed it in *Médée*, as had Méhul in *Ariodant* (1799); Le Sueur was to do
so in *Ossian* and Catel in *Sémiramis* and *Les Bayadères*. Nor were they
content with straightforward reminiscence. Méhul employs in *Ariodant*
(1799) a theme marked 'cri de fureur' and specially associated with the
revengeful Othon (i) which undergoes a number of transformations:
insinuated when Ariodant's beloved but threatened Ina appears during his
air, 'Oui, mon bonheur est assuré' (ii), accompanying the hero's anguish (iii),

Ex. 213

and thundered out *fff* at the end of Act II after Ina's words 'Donnez-moi la
mort'. Catel followed suit in his *Sémiramis* (1802) and, more subtly, in
Les Bayadères (1810), Berton belatedly in *Virginie ou les Décemvirs* (1823).

The post-Gluckian style was overlaid with noisy triumphs and heroic
triadic themes; except Cherubini and Méhul the Conservatoire composers

[5] Alexander Wheelock Thayer, *Life of Beethoven*, rev. and ed. Elliot Forbes (Princeton, 1964), ii, p. 683.

were not notable melodists. But they were all daring experimenters with the orchestra: timbres, textures, sharp contrasts of colour and dynamics. In *Eliza* Cherubini writes passages for solo horn or oboe, in *Médée* for flute and bassoon, that one would expect to find in a concerto but not in an opera score. He accompanies the heroine's prayer in Act I of *Faniska* – and Méhul opens the *Ariodant* overture – with three solo cellos plus bass. The end of the *Anacréon* overture (1803) is marked by the most brilliant antitheses of timbre: a phrase is tossed to and fro between horns/bassoons and woodwind/divided violas, or three ideas are combined – (i) melodic phrase on first violins and first bassoon in octaves, (ii) another on first flute and first oboe in octaves, (iii) thematic figure on second violins. Le Sueur had an exaggerated belief in the ability of the orchestra alone to express specific emotions and suggest stage gestures and movement; his *Caverne* overture shows extreme dynamic contrasts:

Ex. 214

presumably reflecting the horror of the gloomy cave in which the heroine is held captive by brigands, with her maid and Gil Blas, as it repeatedly strikes her. The contrasts are not pictorial but psychological. For his *Ossian* eleven years later, an early example of truly *grand opéra*, he demanded, and was given, eight harps. Méhul in his much more modest *Uthal*, in one act with spoken dialogue, went to the other extreme and renounced violins – for the sake of the viola timbre. But Méhul was peculiarly sensitive to timbre; in his early *Mélidore et Phrosine* (1794)[6] there is an extraordinary passage for four

---

[6] The production of which was delayed by the censor of the *Comité de salut public* on the ground that the spirit of the opera was 'not republican': 'le mot "liberté" n'y est pas prononcé une seule fois'. This premature socialist realist was guillotined the following year.

horns playing stopped notes in the First Act finale when Aimar is dying;[7] and his last notable work, and his most Gluckian, *Joseph* (1807), in which he almost dispensed with the female voice, is saved from dullness not so much by its dramatic scenes (e.g. Siméon's remorse in Act I) as by the masterly choral and orchestral scoring.

THE *LÉONORES* OF GAVEAUX AND BEETHOVEN

The part of Reuben in *Joseph* was sung by the tenor Pierre Gaveaux (1761–1825), himself the composer of several operas, the best known of which is *Léonore ou L'Amour conjugal* (1798). The librettist was Jean Nicolas Bouilly, who provided two of Méhul's *livrets* and was soon to give Cherubini *Les deux journées*, which Beethoven considered one of the two best libretti known to him.[8] (The other was Étienne de Jouy's for *La Vestale* (see below).) He also thought well enough of *Léonore* to accept a close translation of it by his friend Joseph Sonnleithner when he was commissioned to compose an opera for the Theater auf der Wieden, and his own *Leonore* was produced on 20 November 1805, appropriately before an audience largely of French officers from the army occupying Vienna in the aftermath of Austerlitz. This version, in three acts, with the overture known as '*Leonore*, No. 2', was revised four months later (the text by Stephan von Breuning) in two acts with '*Leonore*, No. 3'.[9]

The definitive version, with much more drastic changes in text (by Friedrich Treitschke) and music, was produced – as *Fidelio*, the title actually used for the 1805 production but immediately dropped – in 1814. The changes were innumerable and include such major ones as the insertion of the chorus of prisoners returning to their cells and the almost entirely new final scene in the courtyard, as compared with the end of *Leonore* in the torch-lit dungeon; they effectively disguise the nature of Beethoven's original essay in French rescue-opera. There is little in the First Act of *Leonore* – equivalent to the first five numbers of *Fidelio*, plus a feeble trio for Marcelline, Jaquino, and Rocco – to distinguish it stylistically; the first two bars of 'O wär' ich schon' were saved by the substitution of two bars originally conceived instrumentally;[10] the first phrase of Rocco's aria actually echoes Gaveaux, whose score Beethoven possessed:

---

[7] Quoted by Berlioz in his *Traité de l'instrumentation et d'orchestration modernes* (Ex. no. 42). Earlier, in the Second Act finale of *Euphrosine ou le tyran corrigé*, he had used the horns 'with upturned bells': a shattering effect to crown a climax which Berlioz considered 'le plus terrible exemple de ce que peut l'art musical *uni* à l'action dramatique, pour exprimer la passion'.

[8] According to Bouilly, *Mes Récapitulations* (Paris, 1836–7), ii, pp. 81 and 179, both *Léonore* and the *Journées* were based on incidents under the Terror in which he was personally concerned.

[9] 'No. 1' was composed in 1807 for a projected performance at Prague. A vocal score of the 1805 and 1806 versions was ed. Erich Prieger (Leipzig, second edition 1907).

[10] See the sketch in Gustav Nottebohm, *Ein Skizzenbuch von Beethoven aus dem Jahre 1803* (Leipzig, 1880), p. 67.

Ex. 215

(i) Maestoso

Sans un peu d'or, un peu d'ai - san - ce, Re - te - nez bien cet - te le - çon,

(ii) Allegretto non molto

Hat man nicht auch Gold bei - ne - ben, kann man nicht ganz glück - lich sein,

and the march, which originally opened Act II, might easily be the work of a Conservatoire composer. The most famous dramatic stroke in the entire work – the off-stage trumpet-call announcing the arrival of the *deus ex machina*, and its previous interruption of the overture – was taken directly from a 'Conservatoire' work, also on a libretto by Bouilly: Méhul's *Héléna* (1803), which had just been given in Vienna.[11] It is only with the appearance of Pizarro that *Leonore* becomes really Beethovenian, though even 'Ha! welch' ein Augenblick!' is not beyond the scope of the composer of Créon's aria in Act I of *Médée*. Few of the things that stamp *Fidelio* as a masterpiece *sui generis* appear in *Leonore*; the end of Act II (from Pizarro's reappearance), the wonderful end of 'Gott! welch' Dunkel hier!', the still more wonderful continuation of 'In des Lebens Frühlingstagen' with Florestan's hallucination, all belong only to the final version. The 'fifth' leap, E flat-B flat, of 'Tödt' erst sein Weib!', was originally a third, G-B natural, and was covered by the orchestra.

SPONTINI AND 'EMPIRE CLASSICISM'

In France Cherubini's successes in the field of rescue-opera were trumped by a younger Italian who arrived in Paris in 1804: Gasparo Spontini (1774–1851). Spontini had already produced a dozen or more Italian operas in the vein of Piccinni and Paisiello; his first essays in France were unsuccessful; but he then received a revelation – not from the French Gluckists but from the *Alceste* and two *Iphigénies* of Gluck himself, which he now heard for the first time. The result was *La Vestale* (1807), a model of 'Empire classicism'. The old *tragédie lyrique* had been spectacular and Spontini now transposed it from the key of Louis XIV to the key of Napoleon I. He provided military triumphs and religious ceremonies for one of his Imperial patrons and a drama of human passions for the other, the Empress Josephine, and the two elements are skilfully fused. *La Vestale* is a masterpiece. It is almost completely through-composed, the joins between the numbers carefully contrived, almost concealed, so that one gets long

---

[11] The entire passage from Méhul's overture is given in full score in Hugo Botstiber, *Geschichte der Ouvertüre* (Leipzig, 1913), pp. 155–62.

continuous stretches like the scene between Julia and the High Priestess, and then Julia alone, in the First Act, linked by orchestral reminiscence (of the Gluckian morning hymn) with the previous number and by key (dominant-tonic) with the following march. Again in Act II there is an unbroken sequence of song and accompanied recitative beginning with Julia's 'Toi que j'implore' and continuing through her duet with Licinius. Thematic reminiscence and quasi-symphonic working of orchestral figures contribute to the sense of continuity. The melodic language, Italianate or Gluckian rather than French, sometimes foreshadows the clichés of the next half-century, e.g. in Cinna's 'Dans le sein d'un ami fidèle' (i), in Licinius's part in the Act II duet (ii) and (iii), in Julia's prayer in the finale of Act II (iv):

Ex. 216

PARISIAN *GRAND OPÉRA*

The subject of Spontini's next opera, *Fernand Cortez* (1809), was suggested by Napoleon himself. Spontini and his librettist, Étienne de Jouy, repeated the formula of spectacle-and-love-story but with much more emphasis on spectacle – marching armies, even horses on the stage – and orchestral noise. But Spontini was not merely a noisy orchestrator; there are many fine effects in *La Vestale*, and in *Cortez* he followed the experimental path of Méhul by introducing a distant stage band in Act III with oboes and clarinets muted 'en refermant le bas de l'instrument dans une bourse de peau'.

Thus, with Catel's *Bayadères* – another Jouy libretto – the following year, Parisian *grand opéra* was now fully developed. Cherubini made an unsuccessful essay in it with *Les Abencérages* (1813) – Jouy yet again – and Spontini's *Olimpie* (1819) also failed, though it has his finest overture and, after the most drastic revision, with a German libretto by E. T. A. Hoffmann, was successful when it was given at Berlin in 1821. Nor was

583

Berton's *Virginie* (1823) a masterpiece. The golden age of *grand opéra* dawned with *La Muette de Portici* (1828) by Daniel Auber (1782–1871) and *Guillaume Tell* (1829) by Gioacchino Rossini (1792–1868).[12] Both were new-comers to this style of opera, though Rossini had long won universal fame in other fields (see below) and Auber had begun to make a reputation in the field of *opéra comique*, particularly after his *Leicester* (1823), based on Scott's *Kenilworth*, and *Le Maçon* (1825). Both, as well as *La Muette*, were on libretti partly by Eugène Scribe (1791–1861) who was to become by far the most important French librettist of the next thirty or forty years.

ROMANTIC *OPÉRA COMIQUE*

There had been no outstanding *opéras comiques* since *Les deux journées*, for although *Joseph* had spoken dialogue and was produced at the Théâtre de l'Opéra-Comique, it was more reasonably described as a 'drame . . . mêlé de chant'. Méhul was not without musical wit, as he demonstrated in the ensembles of his best comic works, the one-act *L'Irato* (1801) and *Les deux aveugles de Tolède* (1806); but his real inclination was toward romantic *opéra comique*, e.g. *Héléna* (1803), *Gabrielle d'Estrées* (1806), like his colleague Berton (*Aline, Reine de Golconde* (1803)) and the older Dalayrac (*Gulistan* (1805)). A young protégé of Méhul's, with a natural gift for the comic, Adrien Boieldieu (1775–1834) after some early successes took himself off to Russia from 1804 to 1811, and found on his return that the most popular composer of *opéra comique* was an old friend (but later bitter enemy), Nicolò Isouard (1775–1818). Isouard, better known at the time by his Christian name only, was a Maltese by birth, Neapolitan by training, but purely French in origin, and in a series of unpretentious works during the first decade of the century with the help of excellent librettists he restored the true *bouffon* quality to the French musical theatre. In 1810 he produced his masterpiece *Cendrillon*; then, challenged by the success of Boieldieu's *Jean de Paris* (1812) and *Nouveau seigneur de village* (1813), he sounded a more romantic note in his *Joconde* (1814). But Boieldieu was not only a fine orchestrator in the new French manner; he was also a better composer than Isouard, as he proceeded to demonstrate in *Le petit Chaperon Rouge* (1818), a direct challenge to *Cendrillon*. (Both were styled *opéra-féerie*.) In the same way he totally eclipsed Auber's *Leicester* with a Scott romantic *opéra comique*, *La Dame blanche* (1825), on a libretto conflated by Scribe from *Guy Mannering* and *The Monastery*. Not only was Isouard dead; his temporary revival of French comic opera was stifled by a new fashion. Rossini's *dramma giocoso*, *L'Italiana in Algeri* (Venice, 1813), was given in Paris in 1817, just a week after *La Cenerentola*, based on a translation of the libretto of *Cendrillon*, had been produced in Rome.

---

[12] See chapter 35.

SIMON MAYR AND FERDINANDO PAER

Rossini certainly fertilized French opera; neither Boieldieu nor Auber, still less Méhul's pupil Louis-Joseph-Ferdinand Hérold (properly Herold) (1791–1833), escaped his influence. What was more important, he electrified Italian opera, which at the beginning of the century had been in the hands of the veteran Nicola Antonio Zingarelli (1752–1837), last of the eighteenth-century Neapolitans, and such men as Guglielmi's son Pietro Carlo (*c.* 1763–1817), the Bavarian-born Simon Mayr (1763–1845), the *buffo* composer Valentino Fioravanti (1770–1837), and Ferdinando Paer (1771–1839), by birth Parmesan but a real eclectic who worked in Vienna (1798–1804) before settling in Paris in 1808. Paer, who first attracted wide attention with *Camilla* (Vienna, 1799), knew his Mozart and Gluck – and the French Gluckists. The following tune from the Achilles-Patroclus duet in the Second Act of his *melodramma eroico Achille* (Vienna, 1801) (i) might have been written by Méhul or Boieldieu, while the heroine's cavatina in his *dramma semiserio Leonora* (Dresden, 1804) is purely Italian (ii):

Ex. 217
(i)

Paer's opera is on an Italian version of Bouilly's libretto, with the characterization considerably modified and recitative instead of spoken dialogue. While Beethoven could not have heard it, Paer may well have shown him the score; his Leonore in the equivalent scene of his original version (her Act II monologue) out-does Paer's in coloratura, and has interpolated demisemiquaver passages for solo horn and bassoon like Paer's.

Another Italian opera on the same subject was Mayr's *L'amor coniugale* (Padua, 1805) in which the names of the characters are changed and the whole compressed into a single act. Much more important were Mayr's *Ginevra di Scozia* (Trieste, 1801) and numerous other works in which, coming under precisely the same influences as Paer, he was able – since his entire creative life was spent in Italy – to transmit these influences to his adopted country. He induced the conservative Italian public to accept the important choral scenes and larger ensembles in general, and the far richer orchestration, which had long been normal in Paris and Vienna. In the best of his later operas, *La Rosa bianca e la Rosa rossa* (Genoa, 1813) and *Medea in*

Corinto (Naples, 1813) he had the advantage of texts by Felice Romani, the most skilful and prolific Italian librettist of the nineteenth century.

ROSSINI'S CONQUEST OF EUROPE

Mayr was not a great creative personality and he and his contemporaries were completely eclipsed by the generation born in the 1790s, among whom Rossini was only *primus inter pares*. One of them, Gaetano Donizetti (1797–1848), was actually a pupil of Mayr's and Saverio Mercadante (1795–1870), a pupil of Zingarelli's came heavily under Mayr's influence. A greater than Mercadante – Vincenzo Bellini (1801–35) – was also a Zingarelli pupil. But Rossini was the eldest and the first in the field. After half a dozen one-act *buffo* works, he produced at Venice in 1813 two operas which by the end of the decade had conquered all Europe, the *melodramma eroico Tancredi* (based on Voltaire's *Tancrède*) and the *dramma giocoso L'Italiana in Algeri*. And in 1816, still only twenty-four, he brought out his greatest *commedia* and his greatest tragedy: *Almaviva o sia L'inutile precauzione* (soon renamed *Il barbiere di Siviglia*) at Rome and *Otello* at Naples. Then – to name only the most famous – came *Cenerentola* and *La gazza ladra* (both 1817), *Mosè in Egitto* (1818), his Scott essay *La Donna del lago* (1819), *Maometto II* (1820, but better known in its French version, *Le Siège de Corinthe*, 1826), and *Semiramide* (1823). In 1824 he settled in France where he remodelled not only *Maometto* but *Mosè*, composed the delightful comedy *Le Comte Ory* (1828) and opened, and prematurely closed, a new chapter in his creative life with *Tell*.

It is hardly possible to speak of a maturing in Rossini's Italian operas; he reached his best very quickly and the exuberant and infectious high spirits, the real secret of his success, are present in his very earliest works. *Tancredi* already bears the hall-marks of his style: the long-drawn *crescendi* of the overture (purely dynamic climaxes), the use of tiny, incessantly repeated motives in the orchestra, the melodies patched together from disparate fragments, as in the hero's famous 'Di tanti palpiti' in the First Act:

Ex. 218

Rossini's melodic invention was short-breathed and often surprisingly instrumental in nature (cf. the cabaletta, 'Io sono docile', of 'Una voce' in *Il*

barbiere); he conceals the thinness by coloratura – fully written out in order to curb the customary ornamentation by the singers. (The title part of *Tancredi* was sung by a castrato; Rossini regretted the dying out of what one can hardly call the breed.) Some of these elements were inherited from his eighteenth-century predecessors but his increasing introduction of vocal ensembles and his orchestral writing in *Tancredi* derive from Simon Mayr – the orchestra of the *Barbiere* is very large for a *commedia*. And whereas his late eighteenth-century compatriots had introduced *seria* elements in comedy, Rossini reverses the process; in *Tancredi* (e.g. the Second Act duet for Tancredi and Argirio) *buffa* music is employed in a serious situation. The skilful blend of pathos with comedy in *Cenerentola* and *La gazza ladra* of course had antecedents reaching back to Piccinni and Anfossi (see p. 471). But unfair comparison with Mozart defined Rossini's limitation; the *Barbiere* is superb *opera buffa*, *Figaro* transcends *opera buffa*. In the pure *buffa* field Figaro's 'Largo al factotum' and Basilio's 'Calunnia', the finale of Act I and the quintet of Act II – both typical of Rossini's almost Mozartean skill in welding a number of contrasted musical sections into continuous action – have few equals. Nor has the Third Act of *Otello*, an opera in which he dispensed with keyboard-accompanied recitative, many equals in Italian serious opera. The off-stage song of the gondolier, 'Nessun maggior dolore', is not only an exceptionally beautiful long-breathed melody; it establishes a doom-laden atmosphere, and when Desdemona echoes its opening and continues it in her willow song,[13] Rossini touches a rare height of tragic power. Nor is the dramatic conclusion of the opera so much inferior, for Rossini in the face of all precedents insisted on retaining the tragic ending. He had failed in a half-hearted attempt to do that in *Tancredi*, succeeded in his second Voltaire opera, *Maometto II*, but ruined the end of his third, *Semiramide*, by the final chorus.

Rossini conducted the first Italian performance of Spontini's *Cortez* at Naples in February 1820, and *Maometto* (still more the revised Paris version) and *Semiramide* show how his eyes had thus been opened to *grand opéra*. Both, for instance, introduce stage-bands. And in *Semiramide* there are embryonic reminiscence themes; it can hardly be chance that the heroine begins her cavatina 'Bel raggio lusinghier', her 'L'alto Eroe' in the finale of Act I, and the duet at the beginning of Act II, with the same motive – which is also subtly recalled in her prayer near the end of the opera – or that the quartet 'Giuro ai numi, a tè Regina', more familiar as the horn quartet in the overture, is more than hinted at when she sings 'La madre rea punisci' in her duet with Arsace in Act II.

THE ROMANTIC MELANCHOLY OF BELLINI

Of Rossini's contemporaries, Mercadante, the most intelligent but not the most gifted, scored his first success with *Elisa e Claudio* (Milan, 1821), the

---

[13] The melody of the gondolier's song and a substantial excerpt from 'Assisa a'piè d'un salice' in full score are given in the Handbook to *The History of Music in Sound*, viii (London, 1958), pp. 35ff.

facile and prolific Donizetti his with *Zoraide di Granata* (Rome, 1822). *Zoraide* was *opera seria*; Donizetti's earliest notable *buffa* works were *Il borgomastro di Saardam* (Naples, 1827) and *La regina di Golconda* (Genoa, 1828). Their full development came in the years when Rossini had retired from the field. Bellini's case was different. He wrote no *opere buffe*, although his first stage work, *Adelson e Salvini* (Naples, 1825), included a comic bass singing in Neapolitan dialect and, in accordance with a passing Neapolitan fashion, the dialogue was spoken.[14] But *Adelson* also had an aria for the heroine, 'Dopo l'oscuro nembo', in which the very essence of Bellini's sensuous melancholy is already distilled. After beginning his partnership with Romani, the librettist of all but one of his later operas, with the *melodramme Il pirata* and *La straniera* (Milan, 1826 and 1827), he wrote *I Capuleti e i Montecchi* (Venice, 1830), an unequal work the best parts of which left permanent marks on the vocabulary of musical romanticism. Nelly's song from *Adelson* was introduced to crown Giulietta's scena in Act I:

Ex. 219

and provided with its 'piangendo' a cliché which appears everywhere from Donizetti and Mercadante to Chopin.

Nor is Bellini's melody limited to sensuous melancholy, as he shows in the finale of Act II with the glorious phrase for the lovers, 'Se ogni speme è a noi rapita'. He was to go on to *La Sonnambula*, a variation on the *Gazza ladra* theme, and *Norma*, a variation on the *Vestale* theme, with a tragic end (both Milan, 1831), and finally to *I Puritani* (Paris, 1835) in which he ventured on slightly more sophisticated harmony (e.g. at Elvira's 'quì il giurava' in 'Quì la voce' in Act II, and her 'quanto tempo! lo rammenti?' in the Third Act duet). But through all these works runs the constant thread of melody, a descendant of the golden melody of that other Sicilian, Alessandro Scarlatti, only more vibrant, more pathetic (in the original sense), more *romantic*.

GERMAN OPERA AFTER MOZART

Italian composers were seldom romantics, for romanticism was originally a

---

[14] The score printed by Ricordi reflects a later revision, never performed.

literary movement and their literary interests did not spread very far beyond libretti. Even in France Grétry, Le Sueur, and Berton were exceptional. The real home of romanticism, literary and later musical, was Germany, and it was in the cultural climate of romanticism that German opera at last began to flourish when the wars with France were over.[15] Until then – during the last decade of the old century and the first of the new one – there was little but Viennese *Singspiel*. (The *Singspiele* of the non-Viennese, such as Reichardt and Zumsteeg, are quite insignificant.) After *Die Zauberflöte* there was of course nothing remotely comparable, not even Beethoven's *Leonore*, only such pleasant works as *Die Schwestern von Prag* (1794) by Wenzel Müller (1767–1835), the one-act *Dorfbarbier* (1796) of Johann Schenk (1753–1836),[16] the 'romantic-comic' *Donauweibchen* (1798) of Ferdinand Kauer (1751–1831) with its various continuations and imitations by himself and others,[17] *Der Spiegel der Arkadien* (1794) and *Soliman der Zweite* (1799) by Mozart's faithful Süssmayr, the *Waisenhaus* (1808) and *Schweizerfamilie* (1809) of Joseph Weigl (1766–1846).

The only German who attempted a higher flight in the 1790s was Peter von Winter (1754–1825), a pupil of 'Abt' Vogler and Salieri. Winter was a complete eclectic who composed Italian, German, and French operas. His German operas include *Das unterbrochene Opferfest* (Vienna, 1796), a rescue opera set in Peru, *Das Labirint* (Vienna, 1798), a foolhardy setting of Schikaneder's sequel to *Die Zauberflöte, Marie von Montalban* (Munich, 1800), and an Ossian opera, *Colmal* (Munich, 1809), which has some claim to be considered 'romantic'. The general naïvety of Winter's melodic writing is typified by the quartet 'Kind! Willst du ruhig schlafen' in Act II of the *Opferfest*, on which Beethoven wrote some piano variations; the extended finale of Act I is much better though it fails to redeem the promise of its opening:

Ex. 220

Add *Agnes Sorel* (Vienna, 1806) and a few other pieces by Haydn's Czech disciple Adalbert Gyrowetz (Jírovec) (1763–1850), and the tale of German opera before the dawn is complete. It is all the darker by comparison with German instrumental music of the same period.

[15] It must be remembered that Italian opera was Court-supported at Berlin till 1806 and at Dresden and Munich for another quarter of a century.
[16] Full score ed. Robert Haas, *DTÖ*, Jg. xxxiv (vol. 66).
[17] Including a Russian version, *Lesta, dneprovskaya rusalka* (St. Petersburg, 1804), for which – and three sequels – additional music was supplied by a Venetian, Catterino Cavos (1776–1840), and Stepan Ivanovich Davïdov (1777–1825).

28. Opera (1790–1830)

THE DAWN OF GERMAN ROMANTIC OPERA

The dawn was a little slow in breaking. The earliest gleam was *Silvana* (Frankfurt, 1810) by another Vogler pupil, Carl Maria von Weber (1786–1826).[18] *Silvana*, which has the novelty of a dumb heroine who mimes and dances, was actually described as a *romantische Oper* and the hero's aria 'Ich liebe dich!' in Act II bears within half-a-dozen bars two of the international hall-marks of romantic operatic melody; we have already met one of them in *La Vestale* (Ex. 216, iii):

Ex. 221

Darf ich dich fra - gen: Schlägt zärt - lich auch dein Herz für mich? O
lass mir die - se Au - gen sa - gen

There is also some 'romantic' orchestration, but the *Singspiel* element survives in the songs of the hero's squire, who was modelled on a character in Kauer's *Donauweibchen*. Weber's one-act *Abu Hassan* (Munich, 1811) is an excellent specimen of pseudo-oriental *Singspiel* but he wrote no more for the stage for ten years. Before he did so, he had heard and published a warmly appreciative criticism[19] of an opera, *Undine* (Berlin, 1816), by a composer much better known as a man of letters: Ernst Theodor Amadeus Hoffmann (1776–1822). Hoffmann was not only the most stimulating of thinkers about music in his day and the creator of such fictitious figures as the Kapellmeister Kreisler who in turn were to inspire real musicians; he was also a gifted and quite competent composer. For *Undine*, based on the recently published story by La Motte Fouqué, one of the classics of German literary romanticism, he produced a score with few *Singspiel* elements other than spoken dialogue and, despite some conventional dross, shot through with characterizing or picturesque orchestral and harmonic effects, particularly for Undine herself and her uncle, the daemonic water-spirit Kühleborn. Typical is the theme, always in the same key, heard first in the introduction to Act II, before and after her disappearance at the end of the Act:

---

[18] A fellow student with Weber was Jakob Meyer Beer (1791–1864) who after some essays in *Singspiel* composed Italian operas, from *Romilda e Costanza* (Padua, 1817) to *Il Crociato in Egitto* (Venice, 1824), as 'Giacomo Meyerbeer'. After the success of *Il Crociato* in Paris (1825) he found his true *métier* in French *grand opéra* (see pp. 705–7).

[19] *Allgemeine musikalische Zeitung*, 19 March 1817; reprinted in Weber's *Ausgewählte Schriften*, ed. Rudolf Kleinecke (Leipzig, 1892), p. 117; trs. Oliver Strunk, *Source Readings in Music History* (London, 1952), p. 802.

Ex. 222

and symphonically developed in the final scene when she has her human
lover 'zum reinen Liebestod erkoren'.

SPOHR AND WEBER

There is more of the pure spirit of romanticism in *Undine* than in the *Faust*
which Louis Spohr (1784–1859) produced at Prague a month later,[20] but
less human passion. Spohr's Faust has little in common with Goethe's; he is
torn between two women and his big scena in Act II demonstrates the
composer's symphonic treatment of 'reminiscence' or 'association' themes.
The overture had, according to the 'programme' printed in the libretto,
been dominated by a semiquaver motive suggesting 'Faust's sensual life and
the intoxication of debauchery' and this pervades the scena, now worked
imitatively in melody and bass, now generating passage-work; near the
beginning it is temporarily quelled by a quotation from the duet he has sung
with the innocent Röschen in the First Act:

Ex. 223

[20] In two acts, with spoken dialogue which was replaced by recitative in a later three-act version.

The witches also have two themes, always in B minor. Yet how half-heartedly Spohr was committed to German romanticism may be seen from *Zemire und Azor* (Frankfurt, 1819) on a libretto translated from the one Grétry had set and, as he admitted in his autobiography, musically influenced by Rossini's *Tancredi*. But in 1821 Weber's *Freischütz* surpassed in popularity and influence anything Spohr had done and in Berlin itself completely eclipsed the German version of Spontini's *Olimpie*[21] produced a month earlier. Two years later Spohr brought out *Jessonda* at Kassel and Weber *Euryanthe* at Vienna; in 1825 came Spohr's *Berggeist* also at Kassel, in 1826 Weber's *Oberon* in London.

The immediate success of *Freischütz* all over non-Mediterranean Europe was due to the combination of effective plot, sharply defined national quality at a time when the overthrow of 'international' French rule had made Europe acutely conscious of national individuality, and above all the charm and *élan* of Weber's melody, the high lights and deep shades of his orchestra, which left Spohr a second best even in Germany. It was not quite free from Italianisms – even Rossini's *Otello* (cf. p. 587, n. 13) is echoed in Ännchen's 'Einst träumte meiner sel'gen Base' in Act III – and it remains much closer than *Faust* to traditional *Singspiel* and hence to German popular music. Associative themes are practically limited to two or three connected with Caspar, one – first heard in bars 26–29 of the overture – purely harmonic/orchestral and always heard at the same pitch and nearly identical scoring. But such arias as Caspar's 'Hölle Netz' and Agathe's great scena 'Wie nahte mir der Schlummer'[22] and the concerted pieces, above all the finales, show Weber's full power as a dramatist.

CONTINUOUS TEXTURE AND REMINISCENCE THEMES

There is nothing of *Singspiel* in *Euryanthe*; even the inevitable huntsmen's chorus has 'schmetterndc Hörncr' which were echoed in German symphonic music fifty years later. This was a *grosse heroisch-romantische Oper* and Weber's finest achievement as an operatic craftsman; the musical texture is continuous, the joins between the numbers being often bridged by interrupted cadences, and there are a number of instances of thematic reminiscence. The theme associated with Eglantine, perfectly suggesting her viperine nature, is no ordinary reminiscence theme; it is more expressive and more plastically treated than such themes in Méhul and Catel. Appearing first at the beginning of Act I, sc. 3, where it provides interludes to the recitative dialogue, it is woven into the accompaniment of the following aria, and triumphs when Eglantine successfully deceives the heroine; fragments of it recur through her great revenge scena; in the finale of Act II it reminds us of her when her partner in crime is lying successfully;

---

[21] See p. 583. Spontini went on to compose original German operas for Berlin, in the last of which, *Agnes von Hohenstaufen* (1829), he deliberately and successfully assimilated elements from Spohr and Weber.
[22] Weber was justifiably accused of taking the first four bars of its final section note for note from a piano concerto (1813) by Ludwig Böhner (1787–1860).

and it turns up again in Act III when Euryanthe tells how 'Eglantine's pleading caresses' wheedled her secret out of her.

Jessonda is another continuous-texture opera with reminiscence themes. But Spohr's themes are ineffective. Nadori's recitative 'Still lag auf meiner Seele', for instance, is punctuated by two ideas heard later in the opera; but neither characterizes him or is striking enough to be memorable. There are fine things in *Jessonda* – many in Act I, above all in the finale,[23] and Tristan d'Acunha's monologue, 'Durch Fluthen, Flammen' in Act III. Spohr demonstrates his command of the romantic idiom, the melodic hall-marks of 'question motives', rising chromatic appogiaturas, frequently chromatic harmony, plastic figuration, and orchestral finesse, but too little of *Jessonda* is on the level of its best. In *Der Berggeist* the level is still lower; even the figure associated with the Earth Spirit himself is commonplace. The work has a place in history only because it is totally through-composed in scenes, themselves connected, instead of 'numbers' – although there are naturally residual traces of numbers. Whereas Spohr and Weber were closest in *Jessonda* and *Euryanthe*, they were never farther apart than in *Der Berggeist* and *Oberon*. Far from being through-composed, *Oberon* was formally a reversion to chivalrous/oriental *Singspiel*, yet the fire and beauty of the separate numbers are unsurpassed in romantic opera. Not only the overture and the big arias but the choruses and such solos as Oberon's 'Fatal vow!' and Huon's little prayer in Act II, show Weber at the height of his achievement – including his achievement as a brilliant and delicately subtle orchestrator.

Of the same generation as Spohr and Weber but far less significant was Konradin Kreutzer (1780–1849) who first attracted attention with a romantic opera *Libussa* (Vienna, 1822) and never rose higher than *Das Nachtlager von Granada* (Vienna, 1834). The young native Viennese who was a far greater composer than any of them, Franz Schubert (1797–1828), is a classic example of the musical genius with no gift for the theatre; his stage-works are full of lovely music but only three were performed in his lifetime, two in 1820: the one-act 'farce with song' *Die Zwillingsbrüder* and a 'magic play (*Zauberspiel*) with music', *Die Zauberharfe*, the overture to which was published *c*. 1827 as 'Ouvertüre zum Drama *Rosamunde*'. (The actual *Rosamunde* music (1823) was, like Weber's *Preciosa* of two years earlier, incidental to a play.)

MARSCHNER AND 'HORROR OPERA'

Oberon was Weber's last work and his place was hardly filled by Heinrich Marschner (1795–1861), though his *grossen romantischen Opern Der Vampyr* (Leipzig, 1828) and *Der Templer und die Jüdin* (Leipzig, 1829) successfully exploited respectively the vein of supernatural horror worked in *Der Freischütz* and *Der Berggeist*, and the vogue of Walter Scott. In such

---

[23] Excerpts in score in *Handbook*, op. cit., pp. 22–6.

passages as the vampire Ruthven's scena 'Strauchle auf der Bahn des Rechten' and Bois Guilbert's 'Mich zu verschmähen!' he displays genuine dramatic power: neither of his villains is wholly evil and he commands the harmonic vocabulary and orchestral technique to make them convincing. Nor is Rebecca's prayer in Act III of the *Templer* a simple aria. On the other hand, despite extended through-composed sections there is a considerable *Singspiel* element – folkish choruses and so on – in both operas and Marschner admits spoken dialogue with or without *melodrama* accompaniment.

NATIONAL OPERA IN PERIPHERAL EUROPEAN COUNTRIES

Consciously national opera was by no means confined to Germany. Russian opera had already found its own voice, as we have seen, and in the aftermath of the Napoleonic war the most completely Russianized of the Italian immigrants, Cavos (see p. 589, n. 17), based an extremely successful work with a strongly national flavour on an episode in Russian history: *Ivan Susanin* (St. Petersburg, 1815). Polish opera took an upward turn with *Jadwiga, królówa Polski* (Jadwiga, Queen of Poland) (Warsaw, 1814) and *Nowe Krakowiaki* (New Cracovians) (1816) by Karol Kurpiński (1785–1857) and the *Król Lokietek* (King Dwarf) (1818), also historical and intensely patriotic, of Joseph Elsner (1769–1854). History again supplied the subject of one of the earliest Hungarian operas, *Béla futása* (The flight of Béla IV) (Kolozsvár (Cluj), 1822)[24] by József Ruzitska (dates unknown), in which recognizably Hungarian elements modify the common European idiom as Russian and Polish elements do in the other operas. The *Dráteník* (Tinker) (Prague, 1826) of František Škroup (1801–62) is less obviously Czech; it is a *Singspiel* comedy of bourgeois manners. But nine years later Škroup did produce a historical patriotic opera, *Libušin sňatek* (The marriage of Libušc).

Sweden and Denmark had had vernacular operas on subjects from national history, sometimes even incorporating traditional melodies, ever since *Gustaf Vasa* (Stockholm, 1786) by the German-born Johann Gottlieb Naumann (1741–1801), and another German – Christoph Ernst Friedrich Weyse (1774–1842) – gave the Danes a delightful *syngespil* in his *Sovedrikken* (The sleeping draught) (Copenhagen, 1809). But the earliest genuinely romantic-historic *syngespil* was *Elverhøj* (The fairies' hill) (1828) by yet a third German, Friedrich Kuhlau (1786–1832); foreigner though he was, Kuhlau skilfully adapted folk-melodies.[25]

Spain and Portugal were untouched by either historic patriotism or romanticism. The latter had a distinguished native composer, the appropriately named Marcos Portugal (1762–1830), but his style was completely Italian and he wrote Italian as well as Portuguese works, while Spain could

---

[24] See the bass song in Bence Szabolcsi, *A Concise History of Hungarian Music* (Budapest, 1964), musical appendix No. XIII (i).
[25] See the example in John Horton, *Scandinavian Music: a Short History* (London, 1963), p. 81.

show nothing more characteristic than the one-act *tonadillas* of Manuel García (1775–1832), famous tenor and founder of a dynasty of famous singers. The old Italian influence became more overpowering than ever after the Napoleonic war, when Rossini swept all before him. The one native composer of talent, Ramón Carnicer (1789–1855), was completely swamped by it and wrote only Italian operas despite his cherished hope of one day founding a 'truly national lyric theatre'. Marcos Portugal spent the last twenty years of his life in Brazil but appears to have done little there.

OPERA IN NEW YORK AND LONDON

In New York the extremely humble foundations of American opera were laid by two immigrant Englishmen, James Hewitt (1770–1827) with *Tammany, or The Indian Chief* (1794) and Benjamin Carr (1768–1831) with *The Archers* (1796), but Hewitt's music is entirely lost[26] and only two pieces from Carr's have survived. In England Storace had died in 1796, leaving no worthy successor, and when Henry Bishop (1786–1855) appeared with *The Maniac, or The Swiss Banditti* (1810) it was only to demonstrate his incapacity to lift English opera out of the rut of ballad opera and pasticcio. A cobbler of English perversions of foreign masterpieces, Bishop's own operas are romantic in subject but never in feeling. Except for some showy songs, e.g. 'Lo, here the gentle lark' from his pasticcio *The Comedy of Errors* (1819), and the sentimental 'Home, sweet home' which he inserted in *Clari, or The Maid of Milan* (1823), he left little memorable music, and his one opera without spoken dialogue, *Aladdin* (1826), was a total failure.

[26] Unless the song 'Alkmoonok', printed by Oscar Sonneck, *Miscellaneous Studies in the History of Music* (New York, 1921), p. 63, is part of it. Sonneck also printed a song from *The Archers*, ibid., facing p. 74, and a rondo from the overture, arranged for piano, in *SIMG*, vi (1904–5), p. 490, as well as 'Alkmoonok', p. 464.

29

Orchestral Music (1790–1830)

In 1792 the greatest living composer was Joseph Haydn. His visit to London, begun the previous year, was the result of his European fame and the twelve symphonies he wrote for it and for his second visit of 1794–5 seemed to crown his eminence. Yet his greatest chamber music, his greatest piano music, his greatest Masses, and the two masterpieces of oratorio were not yet written. Only in the field of opera did he remain insignificant, although the opera he composed for London but failed to produce there, *Orfeo ed Euridice (L'anima del filosofo)*, demonstrates his power to write for the stage not only beautiful but strongly dramatic music (e.g. the chorus of Furies, 'Urli orrendi'). And even in opera the influence of his symphonic writing was acknowledged in France (see p. 577). To the wider public he was first and foremost a composer of symphonies. And the last twelve, Nos. 93–104, eclipsed almost all that had gone before.

There are Mozartean elements – the singing Allegros of Nos. 93 and 104, the Andante of No. 95, the extraordinary chromatic passage for flute and oboes (tonally pointed by the string interjections) in the first movement of No. 97, the heart-melting chromatic counterpoints near the end of the slow movement of No. 104, and perhaps the brilliant fugal elements in the finales of Nos. 95 and 101. And there are suggestions from the folk-music of the various peoples of the Habsburg dominions: *Ländler* and *Deutsche* in the trios of the *minuetti* (which are usually allegrettos, though that in No. 94 is marked 'allegro molto'), Croat tunes in the Andante of No. 103, and one common to both Czechs and Croats in the finale of No. 104. But all these are distilled into music that could have been written by no one but Haydn. There are one or two weak movements – the Andante of No. 94, the 'Surprise', and the Allegretto of No. 100, the 'Military'[1] – but otherwise Haydn's power of invention and technical skill function at their highest level. All but one have slow introductions, all very different in treatment and sometimes in function. The one exception is No. 95 which could not have had an introduction; nothing could have preceded the bare octave statement of the powerful theme, a theme of the dramatic type now commonly

---

[1] The 'military' section, bars 152 to the end, was tacked on to a 'Romance' from a lyra concerto of 1786, at the time when Britain was engaged in the opening campaigns of the war with Revolutionary France – perhaps in October 1793 when Marie Antoinette was executed, since the main theme is related to a favourite work of hers (cf. p. 506).

associated with the key of C minor, which ties into strongly knotted imitation and expands with such energy that the end of the development is fused with the recapitulation without perceptible join. Bars 2 and 3, repeated as the last two bars, of the introduction of No. 97 provide the codetta of the Vivace and introduce the coda of this festive, triumphant movement. (The Presto assai finale is equally exuberant, reminding the listener at one point of the first movement's abrupt turn from C to E flat, and positively wanton in its humour and high spirits.) The Adagio introduction of No. 98 sounds in the minor the theme which opens the Allegro in the major; that of No. 103, the 'Drum-roll', undergoes much more extraordinary changes into a dancing violin figure (bar 74ff.), into a bass (bar 112ff.), and reappears in its original grave form before its last lightning transformation. The finale of the 'Drum-roll' is remarkable in a different way: for its domination by the repeated-note figure ♪ ♩♩♩ | ♩ which appears in almost every bar. The delightful Andante of No. 101, the 'Clock', has done much to earn that symphony its deserved popularity but neither this nor the corresponding movement of No. 96, with its exquisite chamber-music finesse, is one of the very greatest slow movements. For those one must turn to the adagios: the sublime opening of the one in No. 98 – which must have been conceived as a variation on 'God save the King' and was converted into another prayer, the 'Agnus Dei' of the *Harmoniemesse* (see below, p. 657) ten years later; the deeply felt one of No. 99 with its wonderful woodwind writing; that of No. 102 (an orchestral version of the slow movement of the F sharp minor Trio (see p. 617) with a solo cello playing the left-hand piano part); and, if only because of the last page, No. 104. There are new things in these scores: in all but one of the last six Haydn introduced clarinets for the first time. And there are old: Haydn 'presided' at the harpsichord or piano, a relic of the continuo practice, and opened the coda of the finale of No. 98 with a passage of semiquaver figuration which he wrote into the performing score.[2]

REFUGEE COMPOSERS IN LONDON

Among other composers who produced their own works in these two memorable series of concerts promoted by the violinist composer Johann Peter Salomon (1745–1815) or in their own benefit concerts was Gyrowetz, who confessedly took Haydn's symphonies as his models and had the temerity to challenge Haydn's *Symphonie concertante* for oboe, bassoon, violin, and cello (March, 1792) with one of his own for the same soloists, plus flute, three months later. Another disciple, Ignaz Pleyel (1757–1831) brought out a new symphony in that same spring. The piano composer Johann Wenceslaus Dussek (1760–1812) produced several 'new concertos' during 1791–4, and the violinist Viotti, who had conducted Haydn's 'Paris' symphonies in the French capital, where their impact wrought considerable changes in his hitherto rather jejune concerto writing, made his London

---

[2] Reproduced in H. C. Robbins Landon, *The Symphonies of Joseph Haydn* (London, 1955), p. 767.

début early in 1793. Austrians, Czech, Italian, they had all fled from the storm in Paris and made their home for a time at least in London. They were followed in 1796 by Daniel Steibelt (1765–1823).[3]

POPULARITY OF THE CONCERTO

The quantity of concertos produced by Viotti and Dussek followed naturally from their eminence as performers, but the general preference for the concerto rather than the symphony as the major orchestral form, all through the 1790s, already shown by Mozart during the last ten years of his life, was very marked. From under Haydn's great shadow crept such minor symphonists as Pleyel, Johann Franz Sterkel (1750–1817), and Friedrich Witte (1770–1837) who *c.* 1796 produced a C major symphony, heavily influenced by late Haydn, which was for a time accepted as an early work by Beethoven.[4] Yet Haydn's influence was at first more fruitful in the field of the concerto, which he had cultivated very little himself. But Viotti had learned from him and also enjoyed a fascinating mutual relationship with Mozart,[5] and before he left Paris he had fathered a group of violinists and concerto-composers – Rodolphe Kreutzer (see p. 577, n. 1), Pierre Baillot (1771–1842), Pierre Rode (1774–1830) – whose influence both as technicians and as composers was widespread. The Adagio of his Concerto No. 22 (*c.* 1803):[6]

Ex. 224

surpasses anything in the contemporary symphonic literature outside Beethoven and the Adagio of Kreutzer's No. 13 is not so far inferior. In his No. 23 Viotti writes a quasi-military first movement of a type enthusiastically adopted by his French disciples, e.g. in Kreutzer's Nos. 14(i) and 18 (ii) and Rode's No. 6 (iii):

---

[3] Clementi's pupil, Johann Baptist Cramer (1771–1858), had, like Clementi himself, lived in England since childhood.
[4] Miniature score, ed. Fritz Stein, as Beethoven's 'Jenaer Symphonie' (Leipzig, 1911).
[5] See Boris Schwarz, 'Beethoven and the French Violin School', *MQ*, xliv (1958), pp. 433–4.
[6] Miniature score, ed. Alfred Einstein (Zürich, 1929).

Ex. 225

Nor was Viotti's influence limited to the violin concerto; a number of his works were transcribed more or less freely by Dussek and others, and the fioriture in the Larghetto of Dussek's piano concerto, Op. 29,[7] for instance:

Ex. 226

are closer to Viotti's than to earlier piano writing. The more widely spaced left-hand arpeggios are equally symptomatic of the piano-style of the near future. Dussek also followed the French 'military' concertos in a 'Concerto militaire', Op. 40 (1802) for piano, one of the earliest works in which use of the sustaining pedal is indicated.

---

[7] Quoted from Hans Engel, *Die Entwicklung des deutschen Klavierkonzerts von Mozart bis Liszt* (Leipzig, 1927), musical appendix, No. 114.

BEETHOVEN'S YEARS OF SYMPHONIC COMPOSITION

Since there were more piano virtuosi than virtuosi of the violin, except in France, piano concertos flourished particularly. The young Beethoven showed the same preference; a fragment of a violin concerto movement in C (*c.* 1791)[8] got considerably further than an earlier sketch for a symphony, but he had completed a piano concerto in E flat[9] as early as 1784. He performed a second, Op. 19, in 1795, and a third ('No. 1') in C, Op. 15, with a martial first movement in the French violin-concerto style, in 1798. Before he composed the C minor Concerto (*c.* 1800) he must have finished his First Symphony which was performed on 2 April 1800. The Second Symphony followed in 1802 and was performed together with its predecessor and, for the first time, the C minor Concerto on 5 April 1803. None of these works is mature Beethoven, though in all three he displays his power of large-scale thinking even in the slow introduction to the Second Symphony; the First is a virile specimen of Haydn epigonism, with a hint of Mozart – whose spirit haunts the concerto – in the second subject of the finale; the Second is more powerful and more imaginative (e.g. the wonderful beginning of the coda to the finale); both concerto and Second Symphony have lovely lyrical slow movements and the concerto is marked by many unmistakably Beethovenian strokes like the thematic entry of *pp* drums after the first-movement cadenza. The piano is no longer treated as a continuo instrument in the tutti, as it had been as late as Op. 15.

All but the in every way exceptional last of Beethoven's symphonies were written during the years 1799–1812, and from the same period date a triple concerto for piano, violin, and cello (1804), the G major and E flat (so-called 'Emperor') piano concertos (1806 and 1809), the Violin Concerto (1806), and the overtures to *Leonore* (see p. 581), to Heinrich von Collin's *Coriolan* (1807) and Goethe's *Egmont* (1810). The epoch-marking work was the Third Symphony, completed early in 1804 and originally entitled 'Bonaparte' but given without a title when first performed in February 1805, and later, when Napoleon was again at war with Austria, described as 'Sinfonia eroica, composta per festeggiare il sovvenire di un grand' Uomo'.[10] The triadic opening theme and the rhythms of the *marcia funebre* do indeed relate it to the music of the Revolution (cf. p. 579 and below, p. 654), but it was a symphonic revolution in itself. It stands out by its vast scale, much longer than any earlier symphony, the urgent rhythmic drive sustained throughout the first and third movements, the close thematic argument of the first, the variation-form of the finale and its gradual build-up, a drastic break with traditional types of finale. As for the greatest of all funeral marches, its

---

[8] Full score in Ludwig Schiedermair, *Der junge Beethoven* (Leipzig, 1925), p. 427.
[9] Miniature score, ed. Willy Hess (London, 1961).
[10] The universally believed legend of Beethoven tearing up the title-page on hearing of Napoleon's coronation as emperor (based on stories by Schindler, based on Moritz Lichnowsky, and Ries) is false. Three months after the coronation Beethoven told Breitkopf and Härtel that 'the symphony is really entitled "Ponaparte" ' (*sic*) and in 1810, when Napoleon had married an Austrian Archduchess, he considered dedicating the C major Mass to him (see *MGG*, i, col. 1530).

stature may best be measured by comparison with the slow movement of a symphony, also in E flat and composed in 1804, by Mozart's pupil Anton Eberl (1765–1807):

Ex. 227

This was played at the concert in which the *Eroica* was given its first hearing, when a critic who claimed to be one of Beethoven's 'most sincere admirers', found in the *Eroica* 'too much of the shrill and bizarre' to be grasped as a whole. He had nothing but praise for the First Symphony, also in the programme, and for Eberl's.

Beethoven's habit of working on several major works simultaneously and over extended periods forbids one to say that such-and-such was 'composed' in a certain year, but the G major Piano Concerto, the Fourth Symphony, and the Violin Concerto were all completed in 1806. All three are outstandingly genial in both the English and the German senses of the word: the warmth and mellowness of serene invention set off by Olympian high spirits. But while the concertos open up fresh perspectives the symphony, despite its total permeation with the qualities of the mature Beethoven, is formally a step backward from the *Eroica* to the conventional symphony, except that the trio of the third movement is repeated to produce an ABABA structure. In one of the loveliest of his slow movements he begins by recalling the first movement of the C minor Concerto and goes on in a long-breathed melody that is a happier younger sister to 'In des Lebens Frühlingstagen'. The piano concerto begins not with a tutti but with five solo bars, after which the orchestra continues pianissimo; its violin companion also begins quietly with a thematic drum-figure and calm woodwind; neither could be further from the conventional opening tutti. And both proceed unconventionally. Increasing deafness since 1802 inhibited Beethoven's appearances as a virtuoso and, although the concertos demand virtuosity, they are not so much display-pieces as symphonic dialogues for soloist and orchestra – in the Andante con moto of the G major Concerto an extremely dramatic dialogue of totally opposed ideas, in the Larghetto of the violin work for the most part a meditation for the orchestra on which the soloist comments. Both the first two movements of the Violin Concerto are marked by even-crotchet four-note motives of a type found in Viotti (No. 20) and Rode (No. 8) but sublimated here by their context. Like Viotti, he took care to publish a piano version of the solo part.

If the Fourth Symphony was superficially orthodox, the pair completed in 1807–8, No. 5 in C minor and the *Symphonie pastorale*, No. 6, were as novel in form as in content; only the slow movement of the Fifth picks up and idealizes Haydn's form of 'double variation' (see p. 500). This

Andante con moto is the only passage of relative repose between the shattering motivic concision of the first movement and the great unbroken stretch of music that follows: scherzo unlike any earlier scherzo,[11] culminating in a long crescendo into the finale which it later interrupts, and finale unlike any earlier finale, with orchestra suddenly augmented by piccolo, trombones, and double bassoon, seeming to celebrate some great military triumph. In the Sixth Symphony there are again interruptions and connections, but the 'meaning' is not implicit, the composer's secret. On the contrary he made it as explicit as possible in a whole series of verbal explanations, of which we may accept as the definitive form that printed in the programme-book for 22 December 1808, when the Fifth and Sixth symphonies were first played:

Pastoral Symphony, more expression of feeling than painting. 1st piece: pleasant feelings which awaken in men on arriving in the countryside. 2nd piece: scene by the brook. 3rd piece: merry gathering of country people, interrupted by 4th piece: thunder and storm, into which breaks 5th piece: salutary (*wohltätige*) feelings combined with thanks to the Deity.[12]

Between the symphonies the G major Concerto, with Beethoven as soloist, was also given its first performance,[13] believed to have been the last during his lifetime. He at once began the sketches for another, in E flat, which was completed in 1809 and proved a failure when his protégé Karl Czerny (1791–1857) introduced it to Vienna in February 1812. The reason is not difficult to understand, for the 'Emperor' is even less a display concerto than the G major; the opening massive tutti chords and the answering sweeping arpeggios of the soloist announce the setting up of two equal powers and the military nature of the first movement gives one licence to think of an army dominated by a hero. Beethoven forbids the soloist to 'make a cadenza' and instead provides him with a brief threatening flourish which dies into a background for distant marching. When the piano enters in the Adagio its fioriture are *pp espressivo* without the faintest suggestion of display, and when the main theme comes back it soon turns itself into an exquisite harplike orchestral instrument. For a time the display concerto, however poeticized, was to hold the field but just as Beethoven's innovations in the symphony gradually inspired imitators so, more belatedly, his conception of the concerto was to transform that also.

The E flat Concerto was followed by another 'heroic' work, the *Egmont* overture. (It is tempting to regard the C minor *Coriolan* as a parergon to the

---

[11] But obviously referring deliberately to Mozart's G minor Symphony: see Gustav Nottebohm, *Zweite Beethoveniana* (Leipzig, 1887), p. 531.

[12] A much more verbose programme in French was prefixed by one of Vogler's pupils, Justin Heinrich Knecht (1752–1817), to his *Portrait musical de la Nature, ou Grande Simphonie* (Speyer, *c.* 1784). It is printed in full in George Grove, *Beethoven and his Nine Symphonies* (London, 1896), p. 192.

[13] The programme of this unique concert also included the much earlier concert aria, 'Ah, perfido', Op. 65, the Gloria and Sanctus from the C major Mass, a solo improvisation (of which we may have a recollection in the Fantasie, Op. 77), and another improvisation 'in which the orchestra gradually entered, and finally the chorus' which sang a poem partly by the poetaster Christoph Kuffner – that is, the so-called Choral Fantasia, Op. 80, for which Beethoven later provided a written-out improvisation for publication.

Fifth Symphony written at the same time, in the same temper as its first movement, and thematically quite as taut and even more subtle.) Next came another pair of symphonies, 7 and 8, both completed in 1812. The first is on a very large scale from the poco sostenuto introduction onward and, as always with Beethoven, his inventive vitality sustains the largest structures without flagging; instead of a normal slow movement he provides a strangely hypnotic Allegretto, processional in character (he wished it not to be taken too fast); then, presto, comes a most brilliant scherzo, and the symphony is crowned by a Dionysian finale. The other, in F like the Pastoral, was once described by Beethoven himself as a 'little symphony' and is superficially a reversion to a type of twenty years earlier; the first movement is concise, the third actually a 'tempo di minuetto'; between them comes a short Allegretto scherzando as different as possible from the Allegretto of No. 7, humorous and delightful. It is in the fiery finale that the 'little' symphony becomes both big and great, for after a more or less normal sonata-form movement Beethoven enters upon a 'coda', or second development-and-recapitulation (significantly altered), nearly as long as what has gone before, with a sense of opening up vast new vistas.

PIANO CONCERTOS BY BEETHOVEN'S CONTEMPORARIES

The activities of Beethoven's contemporaries during these years now seem pitiful if not contemptible; they did not seem so at the time. The symphonies and piano concertos of Eberl and, from 1803 onward, of Joseph Wölfl (1773–1812), a pupil of Leopold Mozart and Michael Haydn, were more agreeable, because less shocking, than Beethoven's even to cultivated ears in Vienna and London. Wölfl paid tribute to the fashion for 'military' first movements; one work, with which he probably toured Germany as a virtuoso during 1799–1801, was actually styled *Grand Concert militaire*. His Op. 36 (1806), known as 'The Calm' from its middle movement, was enormously successful in London; indeed a composer who could score as imaginatively as he does in his Op. 26 (before 1803) (see Ex. 228, p. 604)[14] was at the least a not inconsiderable talent. So, too, was Eberl who is rather unfairly represented by Ex. 227; his concertos in C and E flat (1803 and 1804) and his Concerto for two pianos (1805) show influences from Beethoven's earlier concertos but also very respectable craftsmanship. Even the showman Steibelt wrote one by no means contemptible concerto in E minor (*c.* 1797) before turning to 'L'Orage' (1798) with slow movement on an *air écossais* and pastoral finale interrupted by the storm, and a fifth (1807 or earlier) also with a Scottish slow movement and a *chasse* finale. Cramer's concertos from the D minor of 1802 onward are of no great significance, but younger men were coming along to cultivate this fertile field: Mozart's pupil, Johann Nepomuk Hummel (1778–1837), Beethoven's, Ferdinand

---

14 Engel, op. cit., No. 132.

Ex. 228

Ries (1784–1838), and Weber. Ries was the first to enter it, with a C major Concerto in 1806, but showed himself at his best only after coming under the influence of Clementi's pupil John Field (1872–1837) (see pp. 613–4) in St. Petersburg where he wrote his C sharp minor Concerto in 1812. Two excerpts from Ries's first movement (i) and finale (ii) show how the keyboard style of Dussek (cf. Ex. 226), Italian *morbidezza*, and 'yearning' appoggiaturas were now being fused. The implied inner parts for the left hand, doubling the melody at the octave and tenth are also common in Field:

Ex. 229

Hummel's most noteworthy early concerto was his brilliant, heavily orchestrated C major of 1811; his best appeared nearly ten years later. Weber's two (1810 and 1812) show that, although a brilliant pianist himself, he was unaware of, or unsympathetic to, the new keyboard style. He entered into the spirit of the solo instrument much more in the concertino and two concertos (1811-13) for the famous clarinettist Heinrich Bärmann and the Bassoon Concerto for another member of the Munich Court Orchestra.[15] It is only in the orchestration of the slow movements of the piano concertos that Weber shows superiority; in the first the orchestra is cut down to two horns, violas, two solo cellos, and bass, in No. 2 the first half is played solely by muted violins *divisi a 4* and a solo viola, a truly romantic sound.

INNOVATIONS IN OVERTURE AND SYMPHONY

Weber had already produced that characteristic sound in the slow movement of his youthful first symphony (1807): a passage for two horns and two bassoons, rich in diminished triads. Otherwise the symphony and

---

[15] All the Weber concertos are published in miniature score, ed. Max Alberti (London, 1954-9).

an immediate successor are insignificant, as is another work of the same year, a *Grande Ouverture pour les Fêtes musicales d'Allemagne* (*scil.*, the Napoleonic Confederation of the Rhine), really a revised version of the overture to a lost opera, *Peter Schmoll*. But in 1811 he rewrote the overture to another lost opera much more drastically; this was entitled *Ouvertüre zum Beherrscher der Geister* – a non-existent work, the opera was called *Rübezahl*. It carries much further Cherubini's separation of orchestral timbres: all strings or all woodwind in octaves opposed to other bodies, a passage played by a choir of woodwind and horns with only the quietest independent string accompaniment, the same passage played by an unaccompanied brass choir. By such means he achieves effects of great brilliance, perhaps unprecedented.

The concept of a one-movement 'concert overture' had a precedent of a sort in the three-movement concert *sinfonia* of the previous century (see pp. 483–4), but Weber's old master, Vogler, had already in 1806 made a real symphonic innovation when he marked the new status of Bavaria as a kingdom independent of the Empire by remodelling his C major Symphony of 1799 into a *Baierische National-Sinfonie* with a chorus singing in one movement 'Ich bin ein Baier, ein Baier bin ich'. Six years later, when Bavaria had changed sides in time to be on the winning side in 1814, Munich heard another symphony with chorus, the *Schlachtsymphonie* of Peter von Winter, while in Vienna Beethoven composed a concert overture, Op. 115, perhaps with an eye on the Congress festivities, based on themes conceived for a choral setting of parts of Schiller's 'Lied an die Freude'.[16]

The symphony enjoyed a brief revival in France during 1809–11 after the Bohemian immigrant Anton Reicha (1770–1836) had finally settled in Paris and written two more symphonies there. Probably spurred on by two performances of Beethoven's First Symphony by the student orchestra of the Conservatoire under Baillot's pupil François-Antoine Habeneck (1781–1849), Méhul composed four, of which the G minor (1809) was the most noteworthy;[17] and the veteran Gossec, who had not written a symphony for thirty years, produced one in F, *à 17 parties*, at the same time.

The piano concerto had never enjoyed much popularity among French composers but the violin concerto continued to flourish, particularly in the hands of Baillot. To the French school of violin-concerto composers we must also reckon two Germans, Andreas Romberg (1767–1821) – not to be confused with his cousin Bernhard Romberg (1767–1841), a notable producer of cello concertos – and Spohr, who was well known as a violinist before he emerged as a composer. Spohr frankly modelled his playing and at first his concertos on Rode's, but already the A major of 1804 has an introductory adagio more like that of a Haydn symphony than the 10-bar

---

[16] Beethoven envisaged the possibility of a performance on the evening of Francis I's name-day, whence the popular title *Ouvertüre zur Namensfeier*. The opening bars of the allegro were to have followed, and bars 55–9 to have accompanied, a curious staccato, syllabic setting of Schiller's first two lines: cf. Nottebohm, *Beethoveniana* (Leipzig, 1872), pp. 41–2.
[17] Numerous excerpts in Alexander Ringer, 'A French Symphonist at the Time of Beethoven', *MQ*, xxxvii (1951), p. 543.

opening of Rode's No. 5 (1800), and with his third (C major, 1806) he began
to develop a more symphonic style. In No. 6 (G minor, 1809) he went
further, with antitheses between soloist and orchestra particularly in the
slow movement where the orchestra is answered by violin recitative. In
three of these early concertos Spohr adopts Rode's occasional practice of
strengthening the bass in loud passages with a trombone.[18] Weber had done
the same in his *Peter Schmoll* and the habit of using the trombone as a sort of
heavy bassoon persisted for some thirty years. However when in 1811 Spohr
was commissioned to compose a symphony, his first, for a musical festival at
Frankenhausen[19] he wrote – like Weber in his *Geister* overture of the same
year – for three trombones, not merely for their power and weight as
Beethoven had done in the finales of the C minor and the Pastoral, but as an
enrichment of the orchestral palette. Spohr's First Symphony was
acclaimed, like those of Eberl and Wölfl, for its freedom from *Bizarrerie und
Affektation*. It is, like so much of his music, euphonious and amiable but
lacking in energy and profile; only in the slow movement are these qualities
transfigured by imaginative orchestration:

Ex. 230

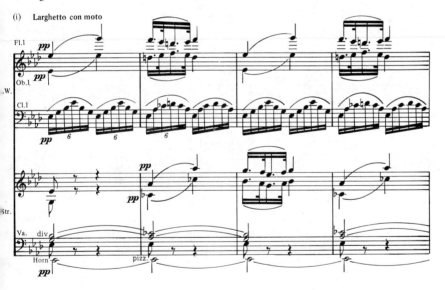

[18] Often described as *trombone di basso* but almost certainly a tenor, since the true bass trombone was
almost unknown in France.
[19] Where the year before his conducting, 'with a roll of paper', clearly and effectively without fuss and
grimaces, had been favourably commented on. The Frankenhausen festivals were the first German
Musikfeste and Spohr was one of the pioneers of 'conducting' in the modern sense.

The old-fashioned nature of the scherzo compares badly with the fire of that in the veteran Cherubini's only symphony, composed for the London Philharmonic Society in 1815:

Ex. 231

(i) SPOHR

Similar dry fire informs the D major Symphony by Clementi[20] performed by them in 1819. Spohr's Second Symphony was written for the same Society in 1820 and is even less notable than the First. Ferdinand Ries also wrote a number of symphonies for the Philharmonic (e.g. No. 2 in C minor, 1814, and No. 3 in A flat, 1816) but failed lamentably to follow the way pointed by his great master. These were not vintage years for the symphony. Yet all the time an unknown youth in Vienna was composing works no weaker than those of his seniors and sometimes lit up by flashes of an inspiration denied to them – but not one was given a public hearing during his life. Nor were his two later masterpieces which surpass all contemporary symphonies except Beethoven's.

SCHUBERT'S EARLY ORCHESTRAL MUSIC

Even the very first of Schubert's symphonies, written in 1813 when he was sixteen, is not to be dismissed as mere student work. (For that, one must look at the unrevised form of his concert overture in D of the previous year (D. 26).)[21] The Andante would have done no discredit to Spohr and the Minuetto, especially the trio, no discredit to anyone but Beethoven. The theme of the Andante of the Second Symphony (1815) is near enough to the corresponding movement of Ries's Second, of the previous year, to emphasize their common parent, Haydn, but the chromatic-romantic shadow which falls across the end of the variations is purely Schubertian. The models in these early symphonies, including No. 4 in C minor (1816) on which Schubert later wrote the title *Tragische*, are – as with so many symphonies of the time – mostly Haydn, sometimes Mozart, the first two of Beethoven, or – in the finales of Nos. 2 and 3 – *opera buffa*. But the Schubertian note is always sounded and it dominates No. 5 in B flat (also 1816). The winter of 1816–17 brought a new influence to Vienna: Rossini's. It is apparent in three overtures written at this time: the B flat (D. 470) which begins with what must be a deliberate quotation of 'Una voce poco fa',[21a] the D major (D. 556), and the C major (D. 591), later described

---

[20] Alfredo Casella (Milan, 1938).
[21] D numbers refer to Otto Erich Deutsch, *Schubert: Thematic catalogue of all his works* (London, 1951). For the unrevised form see the *Revisionsbericht* to the *Gesamtausgabe* (Leipzig, 1897), p. 28; Schubert already writes for three trombones. [21a] In *Il barbiere*.

by Schubert's brother as 'im italienischen Stile'.[22] And it left traces on the second and fourth movements of the Sixth Symphony (C major, 1818), where an early-Beethovenian type of scherzo is sandwiched between them.

THE SYMPHONY IN THE 1820S

Schubert went on to write three fully mature symphonies: one in E (D. 729) (1821) which he left incomplete, the immortal B minor (1822) popularly known as 'Unfinished' though there are reasons for supposing that it was not, and the 'great' C major (probably 1825).[23] The E major would clearly have been a totally Schubertian symphony surpassing the earlier six. The B minor is nothing of the sort; it is like no previous symphony by Schubert or anyone else and it remains inimitable. The opening theme of the Allegro moderato is unlike that of any known earlier symphony both in its nature and in its statement; all the material is melodious and *ipso facto* unsuitable for symphonic treatment, yet when fragmented it yields motives which Schubert weaves into a superb orchestral argument full of power and passion. The Andante is so exquisite that listeners are unwilling to be awakened from its dream, but the opening of the third movement[24] is a deliberate, even brutal shattering of the dream and, if it be accepted that the finale was the great tragic march which has come down to us as the first entr'acte of the *Rosamunde* music, Schubert intended the symphony to end not with triumph but with heroic acceptance of fate. The Andante con moto of the C major is another tragic march, a companion piece to the Allegretto of Beethoven's Seventh. Whereas the power of the B minor symphony is essentially melodic, that of the C major is essentially rhythmic. The scale is much larger than that of any 'normal' symphony of the period yet the great structures never sag, for they are not only impelled by tremendous rhythmic impetus but sustained by wide-ranging key-schemes.

These two masterpieces belong only to the secret history of the 1820s; the C major emerged – and then only in a shortened version – in 1839, the B minor a quarter of a century later still. (The total ignoring of Schubert's symphonies during his lifetime – No. 6 was publicly performed three or four weeks after his death – can be explained by the fact that he was neither a virtuoso performer nor the holder of an official post and was therefore unable to publicize himself by concertos or to exert influence.) Consequently the musical world remained ignorant of the new dimension he had given his orchestra by the free use not only of horn tone like Weber and others but of trombone harmony much more poetic than Spohr's and, in the C major Symphony, of pianissimo trombone melody – in fact treating them like horns capable of a full chromatic scale – which gives these scores

---

[22] He gave the same description, much less aptly, to the D major overture (D. 590), from which Schubert later adapted the introductory adagio for his *Zauberharfe* ('*Rosamunde*'). One of the so-called 'Italian' overtures was his first work to get a public performance (1 March 1818).
[23] See John Reed, *Schubert: the final years* (London, 1972), pp. 71ff.
[24] The composition sketch is complete, but for the trio; the first twenty bars are complete in full score.

unprecedented warmth and colour. The new dimension had to be discovered afresh and added by other means.

Between these two great works, chronologically, lies an even greater – Beethoven's Ninth. Long in gestation, it was completed in 1823 and performed on 7 May 1824. A symphony with chorus was not a novel idea; as we have noticed, Vogler and Winter had had it and as recently as 1820 Steibelt had introduced a chorus in the final 'Bacchanalian Rondo' of his E flat Piano Concerto, No. 8.[25] Beethoven himself had made a preparatory experiment in his Fantasie, Op. 80. But these great choral/orchestral variations on stanzas from Schiller's ode to liberty, equality, and fraternity[26] were epoch-making. And they come as the finale to three purely orchestral movements at least equally great: a first movement of monumental musical thinking in terms of a new kind of orchestral polyphony, chamber music for giants; the most brilliant of all Beethoven's moto perpetuo scherzi, in full sonata-form; and a sublime transformation of Haydn's scheme of 'double variation', the second theme different in pace (andante instead of adagio molto), time (3/4 instead of 4/4), and key (D and G instead of B flat).

Naturally there was nothing remotely comparable among the other symphonies of the 1820s, not even the 'Great National Symphony' No. 3 in G by Clementi (1823),[27] in which 'God save the King' was subjected to all sorts of contrapuntal ingenuity, and certainly not Spohr's Third, in C minor (1828), though it is one of his best. The most promising younger men had not yet developed. A more than promising symphony was composed by a young Basque musically educated in Paris, Juan Arriaga (1806–26), and the Czech Jan Václav (Hugo) Voříšek (Worzischek) (1791–1825), though older than Schubert, produced another single symphony (1823)[28] – notable for the national feeling of its scherzo. His fellow-countryman Johann Wenzel Kalliwoda (1801–66) never quite fulfilled the promise of his First Symphony (1825) though the falling off in Nos. 2 and 3 (1829 and 1830) is less marked than in the three later ones. The composer of the Largo of No. 1:

Ex. 232

[25] When it was given at a Philharmonic concert in London two years later the chorus sang:
    The terrors fierce of war
    Now yield their hoarse alarm.
[26] Written in 1785 and rumoured to have been intended to *Freiheit* (liberty), not *Freude*. A note in Beethoven's sketch-books (Nottebohm, *Beethoveniana*, p. 41) 'Fürsten sind Bettler' refers to a line in the original poem, 'Bettler werden Fürstenbrüder' (Beggars become princes' brothers) which was prudently altered to 'Alle Menschen werden Brüder'.
[27] Torso completed by Pietro Spada (Milan, 1977).

does not deserve total oblivion. At the same time stronger talents were beginning to emerge in Germany and France: the astonishingly precocious Felix Mendelssohn-Bartholdy (1809–47) and Hector Berlioz (1803–69). Mendelssohn's 'First' Symphony in C minor – it was actually his thirteenth – dates from 1824 and is technically even more assured than Schubert's, written at nearly the same age; the first movement suggests an attempt to emulate Beethoven, the second is a very sister of Kalliwoda's, just quoted, but enfeebled by chromatic harmonies in the Spohr manner, the 6/4 allegro molto 'minuetto' full of genuine vigour – though in 1829 it was replaced by a shortened orchestral version of the scherzo from a string octet (see p. 625). But the real Mendelssohn showed himself in 1826 in the concert overture to *A Midsummer Night's Dream*, a flawless masterpiece of orchestral invention from the magical opening wind chords and fairy shimmer of violins to the equally magical end. This was something quite new in music, a miracle which the mature Mendelssohn was never able to repeat.

NEW TRENDS

The man who later acquired that power was about to show his quality in two works of quite a different nature. On 26 May 1828 – two or three months after the inauguration of the Société des Concerts du Conservatoire at which Habeneck introduced Beethoven's mature symphonies to the Parisian public – Berlioz gave a concert of his own compositions including the concert overture *Waverley*, written the year before, and the overture to a never completed opera *Les Francs Juges*. *Waverley* already shows the hand of a brilliant and daring orchestrator familiar with the scores of Cherubini, Spontini, and Rossini. *Les Francs Juges* is another matter; it was the prelude to a 'horror opera' and the tremendous brass unisons do indeed induce a sense of terror. The manner is Berlioz's but the musical language is not yet quite his own; the second subject of the allegro assai might have come from Cherubini or any of the 'Conservatoire composers', the intense dynamic contrasts and oppositions in particular from his teacher Le Sueur.

No such ultra-romantic nightmares haunt the concertos of the period, not even the two (*c*. 1818 and 1826) by the demonic virtuoso of the violin, Niccolò Paganini (1782–1840).[29] There had been formal experiments,

---

[28] Ed. Jan Racek and František Bartoš, *Musica Antiqua Bohemica*, xxxiv.
[29] Paganini's rival and – for many years – friend, the Polish virtuoso Karol Lipiński (1790–1861), left four concertos, of which the second, *Concerto militaire* in D, Op. 21, adapts Ukrainian folk-melodies in the second and third movements.

however. In 1816 Spohr cast his Violin Concerto No. 8 *in modo di scena cantante* without a break:

> Accompanied recitative (allegro: A minor)
> Cavatina (adagio: F major—A flat—F)
> Recitative (andante: modulating)
> Aria (allegro moderato: A minor, etc. ending in A major –
>   essentially sonata-like but with a lyrical episode in E flat
>   and B instead of a development)

It is one of his best works. And in 1821 Weber composed a somewhat similar *Concert-Stück* 'for piano with accompaniment of the orchestra' illustrating a literary programme. Five years before he had contemplated a piano concerto in F minor, in three movements depicting farewell, absence, and return; now he devised a more elaborate programme[30] about a Crusader's wife sitting alone (larghetto affettuoso: F minor), visualizing his death in battle (allegro passionato: F minor), hearing an approaching procession (tempo di marcia: C major), and reunited with her husband (presto assai: F major). The programme is naïve; the joining of the sections is naïve, though the piano's headlong rush 'con molto agitazione' after the march, during which it has been silent, shows the musical dramatist really visualizing action. All the same, Weber more effectively than Spohr created a condensed-concerto form which was to be taken up in the future.

The normal piano concerto of the period was very different; the models were not Beethoven – or Weber – but Dussek and Field. Instead of being given a more important role, the orchestra was reduced to a subservient one, sometimes totally dispensable. In the late 1790s Pleyel had contrived his *Deuxième Simphonie Concertante* for piano and violin so that it could be played *sans Orchestre*, and Field published his concertos as continuous piano music with tutti and solo indications and occasional cues where the soloist had to be silent for a moment. However he printed the orchestral parts of the tuttis, and an autograph solo part of No. 1 (1799) shows no vestige of a continuo role. Hummel's A minor Concerto (*c.* 1820), one of the best and long one of the most influential concertos, was scored like his C major of 1811, for a symphonic orchestra with pairs of horns, trumpets, and drums – but this time only the strings are obligatory.

THE PIANO CONCERTO IN THE 1820S

Field was a young Irishman originally employed by his teacher Clementi, who had joined a London piano-manufacturing firm at the turn of the century, to demonstrate his instruments. His earliest concertos[31] seem to have been designed to show off the beauties of the high register; the ornamentation of the slow movement of No. 1, variations on 'Within a mile

---

[30] Printed complete in John Warrack, *Carl Maria von Weber* (London, 1968), p. 237.
[31] Full scores of Nos. 1–3 ed. Frank Merrick, *MB*, xvii.

of Edinburgh town', again and again touches c'''' and the delightfully frivolous rondo theme begins on and constantly returns to b♭'''; in the first movement of No. 2 occurs an episode in B major in which Field demonstrates that his instrument can also 'sing' con espressione in that octave. It was this singing potential and the exquisite fioriture, though so far not much more plastic than Dussek's, that early impressed listeners, and in the 'military' Allegro moderato of No. 3 he went on to write groups of 13, 17, and 19 demisemiquavers. His first four concertos were published at St. Petersburg in 1814, but it was only after their reissue by Breitkopf in 1815–16 that they made their full impact; No. 5 followed in 1817, No. 6 in 1823, and No. 7 in 1835. Field was no master of large-scale structure – or of orchestration; his first movements sound like orderly compilations from improvisation – that of No. 7 is so episodic that one passage, transposed but practically unchanged, was published separately as a solo nocturne; only in Nos. 5 and 7 does he avoid the 'march' type; he makes concessions to popular taste, as in No. 5, 'L'incendie par l'orage', where for the 'storm' episode in the first movement he asks for a second piano 'parce qu'un seul Pianoforte serait trop faible pour exprimer l'orage'; his orchestral material is generally commonplace; even his piano-writing, ornaments and all, is often – side by side with his innovations – plain and old-fashioned. But it is the innovations that founded his influence and have justly preserved his reputation: the romantic poetry of his ornamentation, the chromatic veils concealing conventional harmony, the vast variety of new piano textures. This passage near the end of the first movement of No. 5 is typical of the more virile virtuoso element in Field:

Ex. 233

Field's spirit and technique make themselves felt in Cramer's E major (Op. 56, 1817) and the Larghetto of Weber's *Conzert-Stück*, and much more strongly in Hummel's two concertos, Op 85 in A minor, which was to become a model for younger composers, and Op. 89 in B minor (*c.* 1827). Hummel had now outgrown the influence of his teacher Mozart but his training shows in his superior mastery of form and orchestration. (In the B minor he reduces the orchestra to four horns and bass, a richly romantic sound.) Its immediate successors were of the essentially 'brilliant' type. He was, however, still writing for the Viennese piano whose nature he describes in his *Klavierschule* (Vienna, 1828), an instrument which

allows the player to give his performance every possible nuance, speaks clearly and promptly, has a round flute-like tone ... which distinguishes it well from the accompanying orchestra and does not demand exertion that would make fluency difficult ... These instruments are therefore to be treated in accordance with their character; they allow neither violent attack and pounding of the keys with the whole weight of the arm, nor a ponderous touch; the power of the sound must be produced by the elasticity (*Schnellkraft*) of the fingers only.

Hardly less popular in the coming years than Hummel's A minor, and dating from the same year, was the third, in G minor, of Ignaz Moscheles (1794–1870), which introduces the finale with a piano recitative:

Ex. 234

a device Moscheles also employed in the middle movement of his Op. 56 (1825). Beside these the first, D minor, concerto (*c.* 1823) of the Gallicized Friedrich Kalkbrenner (1785–1849) deserves a place; influenced by Hummel's A minor work and also by Field and perhaps Weber, its promise was not fulfilled in its successors, brilliant and elegant as they are.

Field, Hummel, Kalkbrenner, and also Spohr, contributed to the idiom and technique of the concertos of the young Pole who was to eclipse them all. Fryderyk Chopin (1810–49) composed his first showpiece for piano and orchestra in 1827; it was not a concerto but five variations, with introduction and *alla polacca* finale, on 'Là ci darem' from *Don Giovanni*. They were publicly acclaimed by a young German of his own age as the work of 'genius' and if the whole work were on the level of the G flat section of the fifth variation Schumann would hardly have been exaggerating; as it is, freed from the needs to construct large-scale form and to write extensively for the orchestra, Chopin gives a remarkable revelation of exuberant virtuosity, virtuosity of musical imagination no less than of technique. In his next works for piano and orchestra, the *Fantaisie sur des airs nationaux polonais* and the concert rondeau *Krakowiak* (both 1828) he never approached this level, and in his two concertos – F minor (1829) and E minor (1830) – with all their beauties he was hampered by his limited structural ability and orchestral sense (though he does not score as badly as is sometimes asserted).[32] The opening of the F minor in one detail (chromatically descending thirds) reflects the opening of Kalkbrenner's D minor, and the opening of the E minor was clearly written with that of Hummel's A minor in mind. The recitative middle section of the Larghetto of the F minor is modelled on the equivalent passage in Moscheles' E flat concerto, Op. 56, but accompanied by tremolo strings as in his G minor (Ex. 234). Except for a 'Polonaise brillante' he never wrote for orchestra again. yet despite their weaknesses and their incomplete revelation of the young Chopin's genius, they are the only examples of the 'brilliant' concerto which have survived in the modern repertory. Indeed the heyday of the 'brilliant' concerto was nearly over. As Beethoven's mature works became more familiar, the concerto, like the symphony, was soon to develop on quite different lines.

---

[32] See Abraham, 'Chopin and the Orchestra' in *Slavonic and Romantic Music* (London, 1968).

30
Chamber Music (1790–1830)

The overall picture of instrumental music for smaller ensembles during this period naturally has much in common with that of orchestral music: the supreme eminence of Haydn during the first decade, the emergence of Beethoven and his production of chamber masterpieces during a relatively short period (1806–12) followed by almost complete silence until 1824, while the stage was occupied mainly by Spohr and Hummel and Weber, and Schubert remained in the wings, though two or three works were publicly performed in Vienna during 1824–8. Again Beethoven re-emerged with staggering new music and the young Mendelssohn appeared with fresh and delightful works.

HAYDN'S LAST CHAMBER WORKS

The six quartets which make up Haydn's Op. 71 and 74 were composed in 1793 between his two visits to London and in some ways reflect his preoccupation with symphonic composition. He sometimes seems to forget he is not writing for a body of strings and in the first movement of Op. 71, No. 3, near the beginning of the development, he does actually forget that he has no bass doubling the cello an octave lower. Op. 71, No. 2, is unique among his quartets in having an adagio introduction, albeit a very short one. Finest of the six is Op. 74, No. 3, with its wonderful E major slow movement. Very striking, too, is the effect of the D flat trio to the F major Minuetto of Op. 74, No. 2; the 'warm' deep flat keys were to become more and more popular during the next thirty years. Half a dozen piano trios (Hob. 18–23) were probably composed during the same year as these quartets and he wrote eight more (Hob. 24–31) before returning to the quartet; they are the apogee of his work in this medium. Haydn never achieved a true trio style; the piano is always the dominant partner, the cello almost a sleeping one; but these trios are compact of superb music. The first movement of the C major (Hob. 27) is as powerful as the first movement of a symphony; Hob. 26, in F sharp minor, actually gave its slow movement to a symphony (cf. p. 597). It is ironical that the other universally known movement of these fine works is the rondo all'ongarese finale of Hob. 25. In 1797 Haydn returned to the string quartet with the six familiar masterpieces that make up Op. 76: the 'Kaiser', No. 3, the 'Largo', No. 5, and their companions, and in 1799 the two of Op. 77, the second of which, the F major, was described by Tovey as 'perhaps Haydn's greatest instrumental composition'. But the old man had not finished yet. In 1803, two years after Beethoven had published his Op. 18, he composed the two middle movements of a quartet in B flat, beneath which he wrote two lines in which, like Prospero, after his 'heavenly music' he broke his staff and owned his strength 'most faint'.

BEETHOVEN'S EARLY CHAMBER MUSIC

Beethoven turned to the string quartet almost as belatedly as to the symphony. As we have seen (p. 503, n. 56) his earliest chamber works were piano quartets and while still at Bonn he made some jejune essays in piano trio writing (e.g. the Variations, Op. 44) as well as a string trio, Op. 3, which he later tried to turn into a piano trio.[1] But his most important chamber work at Bonn was the eight-part wind *Parthia*, Op. 103, for the Elector's *Tafelmusik*, which he drastically rewrote in 1797 as a string quintet, Op. 4. His three piano trios, Op. 1, were performed in Vienna in 1793 or very early 1794 in the presence of Haydn who was himself engaged in trio composition, as we have just seen; Op. 1 was therefore in all probability composed or revised during Beethoven's brief period of study with him. There is much that is Haydnish in Op. 1: the very long codas of the first movements of Nos. 1 and 2, the adagio introduction of No. 2 (foreshadowing the allegro theme as in some of Haydn's last symphonies: cf. p. 597), the scherzos. But the string writing is more emancipated, particularly for the cello, and above all in the C minor, No. 3, which is already marked by Beethoven's individual stamp. Haydn approved of Nos. 1 and 2 but not of No. 3, whence his pupil's revolt. After, or perhaps at the same time as, some serenade-like compositions for strings and/or wind, Beethoven produced (1796–7) a group of works in which his personality emerges more clearly: the cello sonatas, Op. 5, the string trios, Op. 9, and the violin sonatas, Op. 12. Least clearly in the two cello sonatas for the cello-playing Frederick William II of Prussia, for whom Mozart had written his last quartets, but they are historically notable as probably the earliest genuine duet sonatas for cello and piano. The violin sonatas, dedicated to another teacher (Salieri), are also genuine duets but surpassed in value and idiosyncrasy by the Op. 9 trios. Op. 9, No. 1, has a Haydnish adagio introduction with an unobtrusive figure (bar 3) later employed to lead back into the recapitulation of the allegro, and in all three one finds similar subtleties, but the most striking feature is the complete command of both form and texture. As in Op. 1, the C minor work (No. 3) is the most characteristic.

The six quartets, Op. 18, followed immediately after Op. 9, if indeed the composition of the two sets did not slightly overlap. It seems that No. 3 in D

[1] This version, which breaks off in the slow movement, was published by Wilhelm Altmann, *ZfMW*, iii (1920–1), p. 135.

was the earliest, No. 1 in F the next, though Beethoven revised it vigorously before publication.[2] One sketch for the end of the Adagio of No. 1 is marked 'les derniers soupirs',[3] and the adagio which introduces and interrupts the *Deutsche* finale of No. 6 is entitled 'La Malincolia', another indication of an emotional 'programme'. An innovation was the interruption of the Adagio cantabile of No. 2, with its suggestion of an operatic duet for first violin and cello, by an allegro growing out of its cadential motive. It is possible to detect the influence of Haydn in No. 4, of Mozart in Nos. 3 and 5, and – more surprisingly – of a humbler Viennese, older than Mozart, Emanuel Alois Förster (1748–1823), one of Beethoven's earliest friends in Vienna, who had published sets of quartets in 1793 (Op. 7) and 1798 (Op. 16). (He went on to publish a third set, Op. 21, in 1802, three sets of string quintets (1801–3), and a good deal of other chamber music.)[4] Beethoven later called him his 'alter Meister' and regarded him as a master of quartet composition. The Adagio of his Op. 7, No. 5, has been suggested as the – far surpassed – prototype of that in Beethoven's Op. 18, No. 1, and since Beethoven probably discussed Förster's work on his Op. 16 while it was in progress he may well have been impressed by his older friend's ideas. Certainly Förster's quartets, however inferior to Haydn's, are more Beethovenian than, for instance, Wölfl's Opp. 4 and 10 (1798 and 1799).

Very close in spirit to Op. 18 is the String Quintet, Op. 29, of which the 'interrupted' finale echoes that of Op. 18, No. 6, the fiery Presto being twice held up by a short 'andante con moto e scherzoso' (1801). Thematically close to the quartets but much more relaxed is the six-movement serenade-like Septet for strings, clarinet, horn, and bassoon (1800), one of Beethoven's most popular early works; three years later he published his own arrangement of it for piano, clarinet (or violin), and cello, Op. 38, in which the piano takes the string parts, the clarinet retains its original part, and the cello acts as general deputy. An even more masterly transcription is his string quartet version, in F, of the E major Piano Sonata, Op. 14, No. 1 (1802). From the same years (1801–3) date all but one of Beethoven's violin sonatas: Op. 23, Op. 24, the three of Op. 30, and Op. 47, dedicated to Rodolphe Kreutzer who never played it. The opening theme of the F major, Op. 24, with its wide, plastic curves, is the very prototype of German romantic melody from Weber onward, and the whole sonata sustains and varies the mood. The Op. 30 sonatas are more powerful, indeed the second, in C minor, is positively symphonic in feeling. Like Op. 24, it is in four movements – an innovation – and the harmonic warmth of its A flat Adagio is another anticipation of the romantic idiom. Op. 47 is very different: a brilliant showpiece which Beethoven himself described as a *Sonata scritta in un stilo molto concertante quasi come d'un Concerto.*[5]

---

[2] The original version has been published by Hans Josef Wedig (Bonn, 1922).
[3] Nottebohm, *Zweite Beethoveniana*, p. 485.
[4] Karl Weigl published the quartets, Op. 16, Nos. 4 and 5, and the Quintets, Opp. 19, 20, and 26, in *DTO*, Jg. xxxv(i) (vol. 67).
[5] Nottebohm, *Ein Skizzenbuch von Beethoven aus dem Jahre 1803* (reprinted Leipzig, 1924), p. 74.

DUSSEK AND LOUIS FERDINAND

Kreutzer himself composed string quartets and string trios but no chamber music with piano; his violin sonatas are solo sonatas *avec basse*. Indeed little French chamber music dates from this period and even in the German lands composers were only just beginning to explore the possibilities of a combination of non-subordinated piano with strings, though Beethoven had led the way to the duet sonata and was soon to do so to the trio. The experiment of piano with three strings which Mozart and the 15-'year-old Beethoven had tried twenty years earlier had led nowhere; perhaps it was felt that the light-weight piano of the time was no match for a trio of strings;[6] now it was to be tried again by Dussek and his friend and pupil Prince Louis Ferdinand of Prussia (1772–1806) who composed not only piano quartets but piano quintets. Indeed Louis Ferdinand's quintet, Op. 1, in C minor, for piano 'with accompaniment' of string quartet (Paris, 1803)[7] seems to have been the precursor; Dussek's Op. 41 is really a piano quartet with optional double-bass. The prince was no mere dilettante either as pianist (as Beethoven admitted) or composer; one of his finest works is the F minor Piano Quartet, Op. 6,[8] in which he shows his command of genuine proto-romantic melody (i) while in the Larghetto of his *Nocturno*, Op. 8, for piano, flute, strings, and two optional horns he aligns himself with Dussek and anticipates Field (ii):

Ex. 235

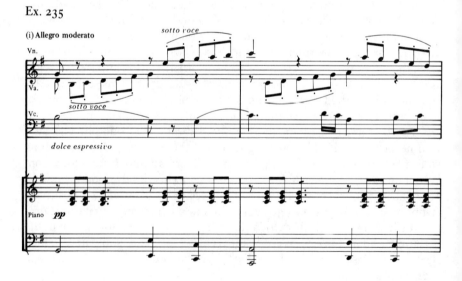

[6] In the quintets for piano and wind, a much more tricky combination, by Mozart (1784) and Beethoven (1797) the greatest care is taken not to 'cover' the piano as a partner.
[7] Ed. Kretzschmar, *Prinz Louis Ferdinand: Musikalische Werke* (Leipzig, 1910), p. 1.
[8] Ibid., p. 267.

Eberl, who had also composed piano quartets in 1803–4, went on in 1806 to add a clarinet in Op. 41 and an oboe in Op. 48 to this combination. Dussek, Eberl, and the Prince all cultivated the piano trio and Hummel entered the field with his Op. 12 in 1804.

BEETHOVEN'S MIDDLE-PERIOD CHAMBER MUSIC

Such was the background to the three quartets, Op. 59, composed by Beethoven in 1806 to the commission of Andrey Razumovsky, the Russian ambassador in Vienna, which occasioned the introduction of Russian folktunes in Nos. 1 and 2. The Op. 18 quartets had continued the tradition of Haydn and Mozart; the 'Razumovskys' opened a new chapter in the history of quartet writing. They are symphonic in their organization and dimensions. In No. 1 all four movements are in full sonata-form; in the first movement of No. 2 Beethoven demands a repeat of development and recapitulation, casts the Molto adagio again in full sonata-form, repeats the trio of the Allegretto (and the main Allegretto itself a third time), and ends with a huge sonata-rondo. In the fugal finale of No. 3 he presses to the very limit of chamber-music style, bordering on the orchestral. He seldom wrote more beautiful slow movements than those of the first and second 'Razumovskys', and that of the third has only one counterpart, the Allegretto of the Seventh Symphony, but sometimes these great quartets are marked by a brusque power – for instance the opening of No. 1, the finale of No. 3 – which roughens the polish of the classical chamber-music style and again suggests the symphonic.

The A major Cello Sonata, Op. 69 (1808), is another spacious work allied in feeling to the Violin Concerto and marked by the same type of 'even-note crotchet' motives (cf. p. 601) in the first and last movements. They appear again in the finale of the first of the two trios, Op. 70, of the same year, memorable for its symphonic/dramatic slow movement on a theme which seems to be associated with a witches' chorus in a projected opera on *Macbeth*.[9] Op. 70, No. 2, opens with an even-crotchet motive but the quasi-symphonic urge had expended itself; the E flat trio is an exquisite study in chamber-music writing from beginning to end, with a third movement that is pure Schubert-before-Schubert. The same intimacy and fine workman-ship characterize the E flat Quartet, Op. 74 (1809); only the scherzo is at all symphonic. In the *Quartetto serioso*, Op. 95 (1810), there is an abrupt change of style; the moods are wilful and enigmatic, the themes scrappy; the musical thought is condensed and elliptical, the modulations sudden and unexpected. Yet the disparate elements in the texture are tightly woven by a master-hand. Op. 95 remained for fourteen years an isolated work; it was immediately followed in 1811 by Beethoven's greatest trio, Op. 97, and in 1812 by his greatest violin sonata, Op. 96, both dedicated to the Archduke Rudolph, a pair of Olympian works, untroubled, with profoundly beautiful slow movements but slightly disappointing finales. Beethoven sometimes reached such heights that he found it difficult to descend from them. And except for two more cello sonatas, Op. 102 (1815) – the first an experiment in form, the second notable for his only extended slow movement for cello and piano, and a flight in the face of nature in the form of a fugal finale – and a few odds and ends like the quintet arrangement of the trio, Op. 1, No. 3 (1817), he abandoned chamber music for twelve years.

VARIED CONCEPTS OF CHAMBER MUSIC

Beethoven's lifelong striving for equality of partnership in his chamber music was not shared by most of his contemporaries. Spohr, who began his career as a quartet composer in 1807, frankly regarded himself as the soloist and his colleagues as suppliers of accompaniment; he often describes his compositions as *quatuors brillants*. Weber, being a pianist, gave himself the most showy role in his piano quartet (1809) and when he wrote a clarinet quintet he provided his friend Bärmann (cf. p. 605) with a real virtuoso part. Baillot, who was in Russia during 1805–8, published a number of *airs*

---

[9] See Nottebohm, *Zweite Beethoveniana*, p. 226.

russes (and *français*) *variés* for violin with string quartet accompaniment and about the same time Ivan Ivanovich Vorobyev (1776–1838) composed a 'Russian Quartet, No. 2' on two folk-tunes which is likewise for solo violin with accompaniment. Again, the earliest concerted works published by Field were two *divertissements* (Moscow, 1810) for piano with very subordinate string quartet accompaniment, movements from which reappeared as solo 'nocturnes'. However Hummel's Septet for piano, flute, oboe, viola, cello, double bass, and horn (1816) is different; here is real partnership, indeed it is one of his finest works, but all the same the pianist composer is decidedly the senior partner.

In Spohr's Nonet (1813) and Octet (1814),[10] both for strings and wind, the usual predominance of his first violin had to be modified – as a matter of fact, it is also in his G major String Quintet, Op. 33, No. 2, written at the same time – but some of the partners were more senior than others and he admitted in his autobiography[11] that in the Octet 'besides myself' it was mainly the clarinettist and the two horn-players 'who found opportunity to distinguish themselves'.

Another notable octet for strings and wind is the Op. 96 (1817) of that cosmopolitan Czech Reicha, though regrettably another such work of his, consisting of a string quartet in G and a wind quartet in E minor (1811) which could also be played simultaneously, seems to be lost. Reicha, a prolific composer of every kind of chamber music who delighted in the most diverse technical challenges, was particularly skilful in writing for wind and his 24 wind quintets, Opp. 88, 91, 99, and 100, are masterpieces of their kind;[12] he treats the horn much more freely than Spohr as in this passage from the Andante poco adagio of Op. 100, No. 6:

Ex. 236

---

[10] Both available in miniature score (London, n.d.)
[11] Kassel and Göttingen (two vols. 1860 and 1861), i, p. 203.
[12] Op. 88, No. 3, and Op. 91, Nos. 3 and 5, have been ed. Racek, Hertl, and Smetáček, *Musica Antiqua Bohemica*, xxxiii.

Though his melodic-harmonic idiom is here much more conservative than Spohr's, he was capable of the most hair-raising experiments, including even polyrhythm and polytonality. His pupil George Onslow (1783–1852), a Frenchman of English parentage, a prolific composer of chamber music who also produced a string-wind nonet, alternates the rather stiff diatonic style of his master at his most sober with the chromatic sideslipping of Spohr and Weber exemplified in the String Quintet, Op. 19:

Ex. 237

All these string/wind octets and nonets have of course been thrown into the shade by the delightful Octet which Schubert composed in 1824; but this had to wait till 1827 for a public performance and another twenty-six years for (incomplete) publication, whereas Spohr, Reicha, and even Onslow (a wealthy amateur) were published at once.

CHAMBER COMPOSITIONS OF SCHUBERT'S YOUTH

Schubert had already essayed an octet in F for wind only (D. 72), of which only a fragment of the first movement, the minuet, and the finale survive, but the string quartet was his favourite chamber medium. He had already made at least eight essays in it and was working on two more (D. 68 and 74) at nearly the same time as this octet; two or three months later he produced the E flat, Op. 125, No. 1 (published in 1830). This is a beautifully written work, with a prestissimo Beethovenian scherzo, but neither this nor its close successors – the D major and B flat, Op. 168 (both 1814), the G minor (1815), and the E major, Op. 125, No. 2 (1816)[13] – is mature Schubert though Op. 168 is very near. Nor are the four sonatas for violin and piano (1816–17) or even the light-hearted, loquacious five-movement Piano Quintet which derives its nickname from its fourth movement, variations on the song 'Die Forelle'; the 'Trout' Quintet is, like the Octet of 1824, indoor serenade music. These are full of delightful things that only Schubert could have written but the 'great' Schubert shows himself first in the C minor String Quartet of 1820 – and that, alas, is a torso: a wonderful Allegro assai, commonly known as the *Quartettsatz*, and part of an Andante which Schubert probably abandoned on noticing that he had inadvertently plagiarized Beethoven's 'In des Lebens Frühlingstagen', which was to haunt him again a few months later in his setting of Goethe's 'Geheimes'.

CHAMBER MUSIC DURING THE 1820s

The continuity of Schubert's instrumental composition depends on melodic expansiveness. Viennese in a sense that Beethoven never was, brought up in a partly Italianate ambience which affected even popular music, his basic ideas are either extended melodies or melodic snatches which change and proliferate spaciously, rarely germinal motives. It is sometimes dramatic but not as Beethoven's is dramatic; it is lyrical drama. The chamber works of Schubert's master period – the A minor Quartet (1824), the D minor (with the variations on 'Der Tod und das Mädchen') (begun in 1824), the G major (1826), the B flat Trio (1827 – its E flat companion is markedly inferior), and the great C major String Quintet (1828) – are marked not only by even more wonderful melodic invention but by heightening of this 'lyrical drama' and by superb organization and control of the thematic and tonal expansiveness.

Of these, only the A minor Quartet and E flat Trio were publicly performed and published in Schubert's lifetime,[14] while such eminences as Spohr and Hummel had no difficulty in either respect. They were at the height of their powers: Hummel with his *Grand Trio concertant*, Op. 83 (1820), his very fine *Grand Quintetto* with piano, Op. 87 (1821), and his piano trios, Opp. 93 and 96 (1822), and Spohr, in mid-career as a quartet composer, embarking on the experiment of 'double quartets' in D minor (1823) – opening with one of those jagged themes the late eighteenth century had associated with C minor – and E flat (1827). It was an interesting idea, which he pursued later in his long life, but he found no followers. The young Mendelssohn preferred to write a straightforward string octet and in 1825, at the age of sixteen, produced a work which in its allegro leggierissimo scherzo anticipates his *Midsummer Night's Dream* vein[15] and, as a whole, stands beside Spohr at his best. He had already composed three quartets 'for

---

[13] This last has a passage in the first movement, bars 49–52, where Schubert has written one harmonic progression in the violin parts and another for the two lower instruments: a curious mental lapse.
[14] The first movement only of the G major Quartet was performed by the Schuppanzigh Quartet at the same concert as the E flat Trio.

piano with accompaniment . . .' (1822–5), of which at least the third, in B minor, shows much more than promise, and a string quartet (1823); he was to go on to write another in A minor, Op. 13 (1827) and a third in E flat, Op. 12 (1829). Op. 12 has some interesting points – the modelling of the opening on that of Beethoven's Op. 74, the bringing back of the first theme of the Allegro to end the finale very poetically – but the quartet is always remembered above all for its second movement, the Canzonetta which replaces the scherzo with more midsummer-night dreaming as in the Octet. The same element had also appeared in the intermezzo of Op. 13, which likewise ends with the adagio that had begun it. But we know from Mendelssohn's song 'Frage' that bars 13–15 ask a question, 'Ist es wahr?' ('Is it true?') and the coda gives the reassurance that 'thou' art always there and ever true. And there are other striking features: the bold, unusual textures (e.g. the poco più animato of the slow movement), the recitatives, accompanied and unaccompanied, of the finale and its references to earlier movements.

There is nothing in non-German chamber music of the period to compare with this. Donizetti had written eighteen string quartets during 1817–21, trifles light as air; the four that Rossini published at Milan in 1826 are merely quartet arrangements of six *Sonate a quattro* (with double bass) written in 1804. They are certainly no better than Arriaga's (Paris, 1824). The earliest surviving Russian string quartet, the E flat of Aleksandr Aleksandrovich Alyabyev (1787–1851),[16] dates from 1815; it is a dry work, as is Glinka's first completed quartet (1830), but Alyabyev was more successful with his third, in G (1825), which has a slow movement based on his song 'Solovey' (My nightingale):

Ex. 238

BEETHOVEN'S LAST QUARTETS

Such was the chamber music of the 1820s, the background against which Beethoven's contemporaries judged the five quartets he composed during

[15] A vein which, as John Horton has pointed out (*Mendelssohn Chamber Music*, London, 1972, p. 10), Cherubini had already exploited in his E flat Quartet composed in 1814 (not 1809) though unperformed and unpublished for nearly twenty years.
[16] Ed. B. V. Dobrokhotov (Moscow, 1952).

1824–6 after the performance of the Ninth Symphony. Written in deafness and spiritual isolation, they included much that was not easily comprehensible even to later generations. His inner ear could accept a degree of dissonance painful to physical ears of the time; the essence of the music often lies less in themes or melodies than in the web of sound woven from the particles of highly developed *durchbrochene Arbeit* and fragments of harmonic polyphony; not only are there structural innovations but the outlines and cadences of orthodox forms are veiled by the texture and the frequently unclear tonality; tempi change at unexpected points within a movement. All this is least apparent in the E flat, Op. 127, the first to be composed, though even here some of the variations of the beautiful Adagio must have worried contemporary players and listeners. It is much more apparent in the next two, Op. 132 in A minor and Op. 130 in B flat. That they were thought of as a pair is demonstrated by the opening of Op. 132 that provided the theme of the original finale of Op. 130, the 'Grosse Fuge' which Beethoven withdrew on the advice of his friends and published separately as Op. 133. (He substituted a harmless Allegro, a rather incongruous sequel to the profoundly beautiful cavatina fifth movement.) The Allegro ma non tanto of Op. 132 is motivically related to the Scherzando vivace of Op. 127, and its middle section consists mainly of a mysterious extended quotation (bar 22ff.) of the first part of an A major allemande for piano dating from 1800.[17] Another 'allemande' (Alla danza tedesca) provides the fourth movement of Op. 130. These two quartets are above all memorable for their three slow movements: the Andante con moto – a *locus classicus* of motivic *durchbrochene Arbeit* – and Cavatina of Op. 130, and the sublime variations entitled 'A convalescent's devout song of thanksgiving to the Deity' in Op. 132. These variations are an exact counterpart of those in the Ninth Symphony: 'double variations' with the second theme, again in triple time and D major, headed 'Feeling new strength'. And the quartet continues on the same lines as the symphony; a lively alla marcia is begun but soon broken off – the first violin rejects it in a recitative which says as clearly as words 'O friends, not these sounds'; and the quartet ends with a passionate Allegro on material that Beethoven had at one time contemplated employing in an instrumental finale to the Ninth Symphony.

The C sharp minor Quartet, Op. 131, hints at a relationship with Op. 132 and Op. 130 in bars 16–17 of its second movement and the third variation of its fourth movement. For decades after Beethoven's death even such musicians as Wagner found this quartet difficult to understand, and the ostinato in the middle section of the Vivace of Op. 135 in F, a much less problematic work, must have seemed to his contemporaries to be quite crazy. Variation slow movements provide the heart of both these quartets, very long (the fourth movement) in Op. 131, very short – the whole work is

---

[17] Ed. Arnold Schmitz, *Beethoven: Unbekannte Skizzen und Entwürfe* (Bonn, 1924), p. 3 of transcriptions. Bars 9–16 of the allemande melody are first divided between viola and first violin and then the viola takes up the first eight bars.

much shorter – in Op. 135. The numbering of the seven movements of Op. 131 is deceptive; the extraordinary fugal Adagio is certainly very much more than the old 'slow introduction' but the third and sixth movements are only transitions. Let no one be deceived by the brevity and apparent simplicity of Op. 135; the first movement teases the listener with a Haydnish 'false reprise' and when the real reprise comes it is the subtlest in all Beethoven. He teases again in the finale with the curious musical mottos, 'Must it be? It must be!' It is just possible that they, and the recitative of Op. 132, suggested points in the finale of Mendelssohn's Op. 13[18]; if so, this would be the only evidence of the impact of the late quartets on any music for many years to come.

---

[18] Opp. 132 and 135 were published in Berlin a few weeks before Mendelssohn completed his Op. 13.

31

Piano Music (1790–1830)

While organ music passed through the darkest period in its history, constant improvement of the mechanism of the pianoforte and its ever-growing popularity led not only to the changes in writing for the instrument mentioned in Chapter 29 but to changes in the nature of its repertory. The sonata remained the pre-eminent form but the set of variations, the rondo, the fantasia, the miniature, which had so far been mainly the province of the amateur performer became increasingly important and increasingly difficult. They were now composed for the professional and the really accomplished amateur as well as for humbler pianists. And long familiar types of keyboard music – the artistic exercise in a specific technical difficulty and the dance intended only to be listened to – were idealized and poeticized and turned into show-pieces for virtuosi; the exercise became an *étude*, perhaps an *étude de concert*, and dances were styled *brillante*. The miniature more and more often became a romantic poem.

Even Haydn's last piano works, the great E flat Sonata of 1794 and still more the even finer *Andante con variazioni* of the previous year, foreshadow some of these developments. A worthy successor stepped into his shoes when in March 1796 Beethoven dedicated to him the three sonatas, Op. 2. These were not Beethoven's first published sonatas; three respectable juvenilia had appeared in 1783 and Op. 2 also looks backward, for the slow movement of No. 1 and passages in the first movement of No. 3 are based on material from one of the piano quartets written in 1785.[1] But the fire and drive of the quick movements of Op. 2, the emotional depth of the Largo appassionato of No. 2, the by no means superficial brilliance of No. 3, already show the hand of the young master. And during the next nine years Beethoven produced a series of works which, even if he had written no later ones, would have established him as the greatest of all composers of piano sonatas: the *Grande Sonate*, Op. 7, with another profound slow movement (1797),[2] the three of Op. 10, where in the first movement of No. 3 he comes very close to a passage in the finale of the quartet Op. 18, No. 5 (1798), the *Grande Sonate pathétique*, Op. 13 (1799), the pair of Op. 14, of which he

---

[1] See p. 503, n. 56.
[2] The duet sonata, Op. 6, is vastly inferior, like practically all piano duet music up to this time. The heyday of the nineteenth-century duet really dawned with the publication of Weber's *Huit Pièces*, Op. 60, in 1819 and Schubert's Variations, Op. 10, in 1822.

transcribed No. 1 for quartet[3] (also 1799), the B flat, Op. 22, retrograde yet with a markedly 'pre-romantic' slow movement, published in 1802 at the same time as Opp. 26, 27, and 28: Op. 26, with its variation first movement and its funeral march 'on the death of a hero' (possibly the Russian Field-Marshal Suvorov), the pair Op. 27, each 'quasi una fantasia', the second of which unluckily suggested to the poet Ludwig Rellstab many years later a vision of a boat on Lake Lucerne in the moonlight, and Op. 28, soon described as 'Pastorale' in a pirated English edition. The three of Op. 31 (comp. 1801–2) include another retrograde-but-with-pre-romantic-slow-movement example (No. 1) and a powerful work with extraordinary recitatives in the first movement (No. 2). From the same period date the publication of Beethoven's first set of Bagatelles, Op. 33, and his first serious sets of variations – other than the mostly trivial ones for amateurs – Op. 34 on an original theme, and Op. 35 on a bass and melody from his ballet *Die Geschöpfe des Prometheus* (1801), the identical material on which he was to write the variations of the *Eroica* finale. And then during 1804–5 came three separate sonatas, of which the delightful two-movement Op. 54 in F seems crushed between its two great neighbours, the brilliant and powerful C major, Op. 53, dedicated to the composer's benefactor Count Ferdinand von Waldstein,[4] and the F minor, Op. 57, universally known as the 'Appassionata', a work so overwhelming that Beethoven seems to have felt disinclined to write more piano sonatas until 1809. He did, however, in 1806 compose another fine set of variations, the 32 in C minor.

The only piano composer comparable with the young Beethoven was Clementi, his senior by eighteen years. Clementi had already produced some seventy sonatas by 1790, largely to exhibit his virtuosity – above all, his passage-playing in thirds, sixths, and octaves – but also revealing poetic sensitivity and great technical skill as a composer. Then in 1795 he published in Vienna two sonatas, Op. 34, which are very much more substantial; indeed the first, in C, originated as a concerto, the second, in G minor, as a symphony. The latter, in particular – with its slow introduction transformed into the first theme of the Allegro con fuoco and reappearing in its original form in the middle of the development, its beautiful Poco adagio and its fiery finale – yields nothing to early Beethoven. Without denying the Italian tradition to which he belonged, he surpassed his predecessors in both emotional power and command of large-scale structure, and it is not surprising that Beethoven, even in later years, 'had the greatest admiration for [Clementi's] sonatas, considering them the most beautiful, the most pianistic of works, both for their lovely, pleasing, original melodies and for the consistent, easily followed form of each movement'.[5] The passionate energy of the first Allegro of the B minor, Op. 40, No. 2, matches

---

[3] Miniature score, ed. Wilhelm Altmann (Leipzig, 1910).
[4] Waldstein (1762–1823) was himself a respectable composer. A symphony in D by him has been ed. Ludwig Schiedermair, *Denkmäler rheinischer Musik*, i (Düsseldorf, 1951).
[5] Anton Schindler, *Biographie von Ludwig van Beethoven* (Münster, 1860); English ed. by Donald MacArdle, trans. Constance Jolly (London, 1966), p. 379.

Beethoven's, while the second movement – an austere, declamatory Largo mesto e patetico interlocked with a Scarlattian 6/8 allegro – is purest Clementi; the lovely E major slow movement of its companion, Op. 40, No. 1, and the 'perpetual canons' of its third movement seem to have been written in deliberate, and not unsuccessful, rivalry with Haydn. Unfortunately, after Op. 40 (1801–2) Clementi wrote no more sonatas for eighteen years.[5a] (The pair, Op. 41, were earlier works.) Like Cramer and Pleyel, he devoted himself instead to business activities, music-publishing – he was one of Beethoven's publishers – and the manufacture and sale of pianos.

NEW PIANO TEXTURES

Clementi's direct pupils included Cramer, Field and Kalkbrenner, and his influence was widespread. Of Mozart's, Eberl is remembered not for his piano sonatas (1792–1806) but for his variations, some of which (e.g. the set on a song from Dittersdorf's *Der Gutsherr*) were long attributed to his master – as indeed was his C minor sonata. The younger pupil Hummel was to emerge as a more significant sonata composer, though not yet; his Op. 2 in C, written at 15, is purely Mozartean in style. But in Op. 13 (1803) he pays tribute to Haydn, to whom it is dedicated, by basing the opening subject on a plainsong Alleluia in long notes over a staccato quaver bass in the manner of Haydn's Symphony No. 22 in the same key; there is keen awareness of the newer piano textures (the Adagio is particularly good) and of harmonic colour (the side-slipped diminished sevenths 22 bars before the end of the finale); Op. 20 in F minor and the 'Sonata di bravura', Op. 38 (1807 and 1808), are finely wrought but not consistently inspired. And then, as with Clementi, piano-sonata composition was laid aside – in Hummel's case for eleven years.

Notable among the other near-contemporaries of Beethoven who skilfully employed the sonorous quasi-contrapuntal broken-chord figuration and the contrasts of scoring one finds in his Opp. 22–27 were Dussek, Steibelt, and Cramer. It has even been claimed that the finale of Cramer's Op. 23, No. 1 in A flat (1799) gave Beethoven hints for the finale of his Op. 26; Steibelt in his G major, Op. 64 (1802) accompanies fioritura-embellished cantabile with wide-spread left-hand broken chords in the same style as Dussek's Concerto Op. 29 (cf. Ex. 226); like Dussek in his Op. 40 of the same year, he provides pedal markings. Both Cramer and Steibelt were over-prolific sonata composers, their work notable for skilful texture rather than structure – or inspiration. Dussek was another matter. Even in such an early work as his G minor, Op. 10, No. 2 (*c.* 1789), which has an optional violin part, he shows his skill and virility. Like Steibelt he could stoop to rubbishy battle-pieces, as in his 'characteristic sonata' on the Battle of Camperdown; like Cramer he exploited the English drawing-room market by introducing in his Op. 25 (another 'accompanied' work) popular

[5a] See, however, n. 11a on p. 637.

Scottish and English tunes. At the other extreme, the sonatas of his last years, the F sharp minor, Op. 61 (*Élégie harmonique sur la mort du Prince Louis Ferdinand de Prusse, en forme de Sonate*) (1807), the A flat, Op. 70 (*Le Retour à Paris*) (also 1807), above all the F minor, Op. 77 (*L'Invocation*) (1812), surpass all except Beethoven's of the same period (Opp. 78, 79 and 81a,[6] 1809, and Op. 90, 1814). The *Élégie harmonique* is an extraordinary work in two movements: the first, a Tempo agitato full of subtle changes of mood, preceded by a long declamatory introduction which reminds one that as a young man in the 1780s Dussek had studied in Hamburg with C. P. E. Bach, the second a Tempo vivace over-long for its insufficiently varied material but redeemed by an exquisite episode in G flat major. The finale is again the weakest of the four movements of Op. 70; the other three are masterly. And Op. 77 is a masterpiece without qualification: the power and passion of the first movement, the canonic minuet with its delightful trio, the warmth and depth of the Adagio, the enigmatic, far from superficial rondo finale, make it one of the greatest piano sonatas of the early nineteenth century. Dussek's variety of keyboard textures and of harmonic colour were enormously influential.

THE POETIC MINIATURE

When Dussek visited Prague in 1804 he enchanted his young fellow-countryman Václav Tomášek (1774–1850) by his playing, and seemingly inspired him to compose four sonatas – as well as two concertos and a couple of symphonies – during the following year. But Tomášek was no sonata-composer, as may be seen by the curiously old-fashioned first movement of the C major sonata, Op. 21 (1805),[7] and in 1808 he tells us he determined to 'take refuge in the poetic and see whether it were not possible to transplant the various types of poem into the realm of music, thus broadening the hitherto narrow boundaries of musical poetry. My first attempt consisted of six piano eclogues . . . pastorals but quite different in melody, harmony, and rhythm from the old type of *pastorale*'.[8] attempts to express the feelings of a simple shepherd. The first set of *Six Eglogues*, Op. 35, was published in 1810; in the same year he completed two volumes of designedly Homeric *Rhapsodies pour le Pianoforte*, Opp. 40 and 41; and in 1818, side by side with his fifth set of *Eglogues*, he composed *Tre Dithyrambi*, Op. 65 (Prague, 1823). The loosely constructed rhapsodies and dithyrambs make more exacting technical demands, though the piano style is old-fashioned, but the simpler eclogues are more appealing, especially when snatches of folk-melody cross the simple shepherd's mind:

---

[6] Op. 81a is the *Lebewohl, Abwesenheit und Wiedersehn (sic)* (Farewell, Absence and Return); Beethoven disliked the French title given it by Clementi.
[7] Ed. Franz Giegling, *Die Solosonate (Das Musikwerk)* (Cologne, 1959), No. 15.
[8] *Vlastní životopis* (Prague, 1941).

Ex. 239

Except in their 'poetic' intention, Tomášek's *Eglogues* are not so very different from some of the *Bagatelles*, e.g. No. 3, that Beethoven had published in 1803.

The first outstanding master of the poetic miniature for piano was Field. He was no more a genuine sonata-composer than Tomášek; his first three, Op. 1 published in 1801, are insignificant two-movement works notable only for the delightful scherzando finale of No. 1, and surpassed by the E flat minor Sonata, Op. 3, No. 1 (1803)[9] of his friend George Frederick Pinto (1785–1806). Field's fourth sonata, in B major (published in 1813) is full of delightful, completely Fieldian music, but the moderato cantabile first movement – again there are only two – suffers from that discontinuity of invention, that lack of sustained impulse, which are the weakness of so many first movements of the period; the second subject could pass for a nocturne. In the interval since Op. 1 Field had published variations on English and Russian songs, including an *Air Russe favori varié pour le piano* (Moscow, 1809) which is a *tour de force*; the short-breathed 'Russian air' is the famous 'Kamarinskaya' which is treated with great variety of device, including underlining by chromatic scales:

Ex. 240

In 1812 he published at St. Petersburg his *Premier Nocturne*, the first of the compositions on which his fame mainly rests. Not all the pieces now so called were so originally (cf. pp. 614 and 623) but the nocturne style easily embraced them; in radical contrast with Tomášek's homely eclogues with their square-cut ternary form and outworn pianistic idiom, it was elegant, exploiting a wide range of limpid sonorities, and by no means

[9] Modern edition by Nicholas Temperley (London, 1963).

confined to Italianate fioritura-decorated melody for the right hand and widespread arpeggios for the left. The typical Field nocturne is idyllic, seldom rising to passion, music for an aristocratic drawing-room. Less well-known are Field's essays in idealized dance music (e.g. the four-hand *Grande Valse* published in 1815) and poeticized *exercices* such as this example for the left hand:

Ex. 241

which he might well have called an *étude* since Cramer had used this term first for a collection of *exercices* (*Étude pour le pianoforte en 42 exercices*, Leipzig, 1804) and applied it to single pieces from 1818 onward.

DANCE MUSIC FOR PIANO

The scandalously erotic waltz, an updated form of the *Ländler*, had just achieved general European popularity; Byron's poem on it was published in 1813. It naturally had to be made available for pianists. Hummel's *Tänze für den Apollosaal*, Op. 27 (1808) seem to have been the earliest piano waltzes and in 1812 Weber published anonymously *Sechs Favorit-Walzer* (of the Empress Marie Louise) for piano and also orchestrated them. Seven years later he composed the first concert waltz for piano, the *Aufforderung zum Tanze*, which like the *Concert-Stück* for piano and orchestra (see p. 613) had a secret programme.[10]

It was also Weber who exploited the concert polonaise in his *Grande Polonaise*, Op. 21 (1808) and *Polacca brillante*, Op. 72 (1819). The polonaise had long existed as a keyboard dance for the performer's or listener's pleasure; Friedemann Bach's (see p. 520) were certainly not meant to be

[10] Printed in Warrack, op. cit., p. 191.

danced to and the much more authentic piano polonaises of Prince Michał
Kleofas Ogiński (1765–1835), published all over Europe from *c.* 1792
onward, were likewise poetic miniatures. The same may be said of most of
the polonaises of Joseph Xaver Elsner (1769–1854), a Silesian who
polonized himself very thoroughly. Elsner published piano polonaises from
1803 onward, at first modelling them on Ogiński's, and his last, in F minor
(1821):

Ex. 242

in turn provided the model for the opening of one in G sharp minor, which
far surpassed it, by his most famous pupil – Chopin.

THE PIANO SONATA: 1816–26

The element of virtuosic exuberance and empty rhetoric in Weber's concert
polonaises, indeed in so much of his piano music, is a source of weakness in
his piano sonatas. It suggests that their emotion is no more than well
simulated and emphasizes, instead of concealing, the lack of genuine unity
and continuity in the first movements; it brings about the collapse of the
splendid opening of the A flat Sonata, Op. 39 (1816) in twenty bars. Yet
there are fine things in the sonatas; the 'grief' in the Moderato (*con duolo*) of
the E minor, Op. 70 (1822) rings true, and the finale of the A flat is,
exceptionally, not a presto but a moderato e molto grazioso sonata-rondo
with a second subject laid out in a way that the composers of the coming
generation were to delight in:

Ex. 243

1816 was the year not only of Weber's Op. 39 and of his Op. 49 in D minor but of Schubert's first completed sonata (D. 459), a heterogeneous work long known as 'Fünf Klavierstücke', and of Moscheles's *Grosse Sonate* in E, Op. 41, notable for the appearance in the finale of a Hungarian gypsy tune familiar through the fifth of Brahms's Hungarian dances (see p. 775). (Moscheles had already published (Vienna, 1814) a *Sonate mélancolique*[11] remarkable in that it is not only in one large movement but almost monothematic, the second subject being rhythmically related to the first.) 1816 was moreover the year in which Beethoven returned to the piano sonata in the grand manner he had abandoned after the *Appassionata*.

Beethoven described his A major Sonata, Op. 101, as 'für das Hammerclavier' – as he also did Op. 106 and Op. 110 – but tradition has unanimously decided to reserve the distinction for Op. 106. The first movement of Op. 101 suggests anything but 'the grand manner'; it opens unassumingly with a far from striking theme; there is no really contrasting 'second subject' – it flows naturally, imperceptibly, from the first; it is one of the shortest of all Beethoven's first movements. Its greatness lies in the 'most intimate feeling' (*innigste Empfindung*), its intense compression, the elision of joins. The mood is shattered by a brusque, powerful march in a 'wrong' key (F major) with a sketchy trio mostly in two-part canon. A 'longing' (*sehnsuchtsvoll*) *una corda* Adagio of only twenty bars, in A minor, dissolves in a cadenza and a brief recall of the first movement, and this leads without a break into a big sonata-form finale with much contrapuntal writing – in fact the whole long development is a fugue. With Op. 106 in B flat (1818) the grand manner reaches a peak; this is the longest as well as arguably the greatest of all Beethoven's sonatas: a titanic first movement (he was using the powerful piano sent him by Broadwood), the most capricious of scherzos, an immensely long and profoundly beautiful Adagio in F sharp minor, and a page of modulating Emanuel Bachian fantasy leading to a gigantic fugue of the type adumbrated in the finale of the third 'Razumovsky' quartet but far surpassing it. Op. 109 in E (1820) is less breathtaking but even more unconventional: an eight-bar vivace first subject is immediately cut short by a rhapsodic adagio second subject – a total reversal of the method of Op. 101 except in the absence of transitions. (It might be said that the first movement of Op. 101 is all transition.) Then after a scurrying prestissimo also in sonata-form, with a mysterious una corda end to the development, comes a most beautiful set of variations as long as all the rest of the sonata. In the A flat, Op. 110 (1821), a spacious cantabile first movement is again cancelled, as it were, by a brusque Molto allegro; what follows – and again it is the major part of the sonata – is beyond all precedents. It begins, it is true, with things that C. P. E. Bach would have understood, a brooding soliloquy from which emerges a heart-rending arioso dolente, but the fugue which follows, is interrupted by the arioso, and then returns inverted and rises to a completely non-fugal hymn of triumph,

[11] Modern edition by William S. Newman, *Thirteen Keyboard Sonatas of the 18th and 19th Centuries* (Chapel Hill, North Carolina, 1947).

is *sui generis*. So also is Op. 111 (1822), in two movements only; a monumental Maestoso and Allegro con brio charged with all the power and passion one expects of Beethoven in C minor and transcending all his other C minor movements with the possible exception of the Allegro of the Fifth Symphony, and variations on an 'arietta' in C major that become transcendental in another sense, passing into an other-worldliness comparable in spirit, though not at all comparable in substance, with the last molto adagio of the 'Heiliger Dankgesang' of the A minor Quartet. This was not Beethoven's last piano composition, for the following year he produced the *33 Veränderungen über einen Walzer von Diabelli*, Op. 120, which are a classic demonstration of the art of making much out of nothing, and completed two collections of *Bagatellen*, Opp. 119 and 126, some of which – e.g. Op. 119, No. 11, Op. 126, Nos. 1 and 3 – are tiny masterpieces.

That Beethoven had now moved into a different orbit from any of his contemporaries is most vividly demonstrated by comparison with the sonatas of the re-emergent Clementi and the last two of Hummel's. Clementi had reappeared as a composer in 1817 with the simultaneous publication in London, Paris, and Leipzig of the first volume (Nos. 1–27) of his *Gradus ad Parnassum, or the art of playing on the Pianoforte exemplified in a series of exercises in the strict and in the free styles*; the second volume (Nos. 28–50) appeared in 1819, the third (Nos. 51–100) in 1826. Many, indeed most, of the pieces in this extraordinary collection are not mere utilitarian exercises but living music of the most diverse types. Contrapuntal devices figure prominently – nothing could be more delightful and natural than the 'Canone per moto contrario e per intervalli giusti', No. 73 – and in the 'free style' he offers a great 'Scena patetiica', No. 39, of sustained power, a nine-page adagio longer than most sonata slow movements. Not only did a whole generation of pianists cut their teeth on the *Gradus*, the composers among them found it a thesaurus of pianistic devices and textures. Between the second and third books of the *Gradus* he published a feeble sonata in B flat, Op. 46, two remarkable Capriccios, Op. 47 – No. 2 begins with an Adagio in 5/4 time – and three sonatas, Op. 50, dedicated to Cherubini. The third and weakest of the sonatas has attracted special attention on account of its title, 'Didone abbandonata (Scena tragica)', and the markings of the three movements: (i) diliberando, e meditando (ii) dolente (iii) agitato, e con disperazione. The other two sonatas are masterly: technically superb and revealing Clementi's great powers of energy and expression. But – he had only gone on from where he had left off. One can compare Op. 50, Nos. 1 and 2, with Beethoven, but the Beethoven of twenty years earlier.[11a]

Hummel, on the other hand, had matured remarkably since his Opp. 20 and 38. In Op. 81 (F sharp minor, 1819), if not in Op. 106 (D major, 1821), he is no longer a Mozart epigone but a proto-romantic; colourful and exciting, it influenced the coming generation almost as much as his A minor

[11a] Leon Plantinga believes the Op. 50 sonatas were actually composed much earlier. See his *Clementi: His Life and Music* (London, 1977), p. 216.

Concerto (see p. 615). In the first movement the sharply contrasted ideas (with sudden changes of tempo and dynamics) are related by motivic subtleties and swept along by sheer power of oratory; the exposition is very long, the development hardly more than an excursion to a remote key, leading back to a masterly return of the opening theme, itself expanded from a three-note motive, (Ex. 244 (i)) in the bass. The slow movement is Field-like, a *dolente* melody dissolved into a wealth of silvery fioritura, and the brittle finale draws its second subject from a suggestion in the second subject of the first movement. The difference between the romantic approach and the classical may be illustrated by comparing the opening of this Hummel sonata with that of a sonata by his pupil Voříšek published the following year.[12] Like Hummel's it opens with bare octaves (ii), but Voříšek's are the beginning of a long-breathed paragraph which needs no motivic connections to sustain it; everything is clear and concise and when the second subject (iii) appears – already at bar 26 – it has the noble simplicity of the young Beethoven (as indeed has the trio of the scherzo).

Ex. 244

[12] Voříšek had already rivalled his earlier teacher Tomášek in a collection of rhapsodies, Op. 1 (1818). There is a modern edition of his Op. 20 sonata by Ludvík Kundera, *Musica Antiqua Bohemica*, iv.

Voříšek died in 1825, leaving beside the Sonata a piano Fantasia, Op. 12, and a set of *Impromptus*, Op. 7[13] (Vienna, 1822), which seem to have been the progenitors of Schubert's five years later. Both Schubert and Voříšek contributed 'German dances' to an album published for the carnival of 1823 and, with Czerny, Hummel, Kalkbrenner, Tomášek, Moscheles, the boy Liszt and many others, single variations on the Diabelli waltz which provoked Beethoven to compose his own great set. Schubert's contributions were not quite the first of his works to appear in print. In 1821 he had published a number of songs (including 'Der Wanderer', Op. 4, No. 1) and a collection of *Originaltänze* (waltzes and *Deutsche*), Op. 9; the next piano compositions to appear were some undistinguished piano duet variations, Op. 10, and in 1823 a Fantasia in C, Op. 15, and more dances, Op. 18. Before the Fantasia he had written more than half a dozen piano sonatas, the best of which – dating from 1817–19 – were published posthumously as Opp. 120, 122, 164, and 147, but although they contain a great deal of delightful, unmistakably Schubertian music none, not even the A major, Op. 120, of 1819 can compare with the Fantasia. Nor can the A minor, Op. 143, that he wrote a few months after it. Stylistically they are old-fashioned in the sense that Schubert, anything but a concert pianist, ignored the latest pianistic idioms; the Andante of his Op. 122 is near enough in content to that of Weber's Op. 39, written the year before, to reveal his limitations.

The C major Fantasia is not only more adventurous pianistically; it is in another sense epoch-marking – probably the earliest instance of a four-movement work of sonata plan in which all the movements are not only connected but based on the same motto-theme, which the Adagio reveals as a quotation from the song 'Der Wanderer':

> Die Sonne dünkt mich hier so kalt,
> die Blüthe welk, das Leben alt,
> und was sie reden, leeren Schall,
> ich bin ein Fremdling überall.

(The sunshine seems so cold to me, the flowers faded, life grows old, and what they say is empty sound, I am a stranger everywhere.)

The Fantasia was composed immediately after the B minor Symphony and is equally unique. The Allegro con fuoco is not in sonata-form but evolved organically from the opening motto-theme which before long (E major, *pp*) throws out a little three-note pendant, first as a variant of its third bar, which gradually takes on a life of its own – particularly when it re-enters (E flat, *dolce*, *pp*) after a big climax. The C sharp minor Adagio consists of five variations, with interludes, on the song-theme itself, Schubert's most virtuosic piece of piano-writing, and is followed by a presto scherzo in A flat in which the motto is metrically modified (bars 3–4 and 7). Presently the dancing rhythm is embodied in an enchanting tune in C flat major – the Wanderer's melancholy long forgotten – and there is a middle section in D

---

[13] Modern editions in *Musica Antiqua Bohemica*, xx(2), p. 63, and i.

flat, derived from the E flat dolce of the first movement. The presto ends on the dominant of C major which returns with the motto in its original form (but with a long fresh pendant) in the stormy final Allegro.

Schubert published only four more piano sonatas in his lifetime: an early duet sonata in B flat, Op. 30, not to be compared with the fine C major of 1824 which had to wait till 1838 before it saw the light (as a 'Grand Duo'), and three solo works, Opp. 42, 53 and 78, composed 1825–6 and quickly published. Fine as these three are, they do not challenge the supremacy of the 'Wanderer' Fantasia; the work that might have done if Schubert had completed it is their C major companion (D. 840). Yet Op. 78, from beginning to end a sublimation of Viennese song and dance and march, has a unique niche in the gallery of Schubert's sonatas. Another 'unique' work is the F minor duet Fantasia of 1828, more loosely organized than the 'Wanderer' but compact of beautiful music, not least beautiful the Italian-operatic love-duet in the second movement. Also to the last year of Schubert's life belong the three great – but stylistically conservative – sonatas in C minor, A and B flat which Schubert intended to dedicate to Hummel. (When he belatedly issued them in 1838 the composer-publisher Diabelli dedicated them to Schumann.)

In considering Schubert's piano music one must, more than with any of his contemporaries or predecessors, take into account the small-scale pieces as well as the large: the *divertissements*, variations, marches, polonaises and other dances and so on, for four hands, the two sets of *Impromptus* (1827), the *Moments musicaux* (collected and published in 1828), above all the innumerable little waltzes, *Ländler*, *deutsche*, and *écossaises*[14] for two. Schubert's piano dances were no doubt originally intended to be danced to in intimate surroundings but it is difficult to think of such gems as the seventeen 'Deutsche Tänze' (D. 366) – e.g. Nos. 2, 9, 12 – as anything but tiny love-poems.

THE NEW GENERATION

Among the rising generation the small-scale pieces were liable to be more important, certainly more characteristic, than their sonatas. The G minor Sonata which the precocious Mendelssohn wrote in 1821, like the less precocious B flat of 1827, was sensibly laid aside; both appeared posthumously as Opp. 105 and 106. But he did publish the E major, Op. 6 (1826), a work interesting mainly for its evidence of formal – not stylistic – influence from Beethoven's later sonatas: the recitative fantasies and andante interludes linking the Tempo di minuetto with the finale, and the return of music from the beginning and end of the first movement at the end of the finale. But he had already written (*c.* 1824) a *Rondo capriccioso*, prefaced by a Weberian andante, which is the purest *Midsummer-Night's-Dream* Mendelssohn, and some at least of the *Sieben charakteristische*

---

[14] Probably not Scottish even in remote origin. The early nineteenth-century *écossaise* was the precursor of the polka.

Stücke, Op. 7 (pub. 1827) which demonstrate his skill in various styles, including – for short laps – that of J. S. Bach. In the third of *Trois Fantaisies ou Caprices*, Op. 16, he hit on the type of polished, melodious piece he was to make famous as 'songs without words' and indeed followed it immediately with the first book of *Lieder ohne Worte* (originally entitled *Melodies for the Pianoforte*), Op. 19 (1830). But he wrote no more true sonatas for the piano although the F sharp minor *Phantasie* (pub. 1833, but probably composed several years earlier) is described on the autograph as *Sonate écossaise*.

Chopin, a year younger, composed his first sonata, in C minor, in 1828, but failed to get it published; it is a dull and almost completely uncharacteristic work and eleven years passed before he embarked on another. Yet he had already written the 'Là ci darem' Variations (see p. 616) and a number of polonaises (including the already mentioned G sharp minor, the D minor, Op. 71, No. 1, and the B flat minor with its trio based on 'Vieni fra questa braccia' from Rossini's *Gazza ladra*), mazurkas (Op. 68, No. 2, and the original version of Op. 7, No. 4), and a nocturne (Op. 72, No. 1), all far more Chopinesque than the sonata. His earliest published works, other than a childish polonaise of 1817, were the C minor Rondo, Op. 1 (Warsaw, 1825) and the *Rondo à la Mazur*, Op. 5 (1826; pub. 1828). He had not yet outgrown the influence of Hummel and Field, Weber and the Kalkbrenner who could write the F minor Sonata, Op. 56 (*c.* 1824), and perhaps of his fellow-countrywoman Maria Szymanowska (1789–1831). But his own personality was emerging – and his nationality. The *Rondo à la Mazur* and the Op. 68, No. 2, mazurka are already marked with the sharpened fourth so characteristic of Polish folk-melody but rarely found, and then only decoratively, in Szymanowska's *Vingt-quatre Masurkas ou Danses Nationales de Pologne. Arrangées pour le pianoforte* (Leipzig, *c.* 1826).[15] In the years to come, Chopin was to stand almost alone in the flood of German or German-influenced piano music.

[15] Modern edition, Moscow, 1956.

32
Solo Song (1790–1830)

During his second visit to Britain Haydn enriched English music with twelve songs to English words, mostly by Anne Hunter, widow of the famous Scottish surgeon John Hunter: two sets of *Six Original Canzonets* (1794 and 1795). The first set includes the well known 'My mother bids me bind my hair' and one of his best songs, 'Fidelity', the second set, the curiously English-sounding 'Piercing eyes' ('Why asks my fair one?'). Finer than any of the *Canzonets* are two rather later English songs, 'O tuneful voice' and 'The Spirit's Song'. In all these, contrary to his practice in his earlier *Lieder*, he writes a separate voice-part distinct from the accompaniment. He had already added accompaniments for violin and figured bass to *A Selection of Original Scots Songs in Three Parts. The Harmony by Haydn* (London, 1792) for the publisher William Napier, who brought out another set three years later. At the same time a more important publisher, George Thomson of Edinburgh, was embarking on the publication of Scottish – and at a later date Welsh and Irish – songs with 'Accompanyments for the Violin & Piano Forte' provided in the first place by Pleyel (1793), later by Kozeluch (1798). Dissatisfied with some of their efforts, he persuaded Haydn to replace a number of them with fresh accompaniments – 'a delicate Accompaniment in *Notes* for both hands' and ad libitum parts for violin and cello – and then to undertake two further sets (1802 and 1805) alone.[1] Unhappily neither Haydn's folk-song arrangements nor his original settings of English verse inspired imitation by native composers; British solo song of the period consisted for the most part of popular skimmings from theatre music. The settings for voice and piano of verses from Scott's *Lady of the Lake* – 'He is gone on the mountain', 'Ave Maria! Maiden mild!' – (1811) by Mozart's pupil Thomas Attwood (1765–1838) are quite exceptional.

THE *ROMANCE* IN FRANCE

Nor was French song in much better state. During the first excitements of the Revolution composers turned from the *romance* to more virile types of song, performed less often as solos than as unison choruses, revo-

---

[1] In 1814 Thomson recruited Beethoven, in the first place to set Irish airs, and in 1826 Weber and Hummel.

lutionary or even counter-revolutionary. One of these, the 'Réveil du Peuple' (1795) of Gaveaux, the composer of *Léonore* (see p. 581), became a sort of royalist hymn after the 'Thermidorian reaction' and was banned under the Directory. All the same the *romance* began to revive in the calmer climate of the Directory[2] and Noske[3] distinguishes two main types, 'the German-influenced expressive song with relatively significant piano-part' cultivated by Méhul, Jadin, and others, and the 'more or less abstract but graceful melody with subordinate accompaniment' preferred by Boieldieu and Charles-Henri Plantade (1764–1839), until the general commercialization of the *romance* about 1830. He also detects a parallelism between the set of nine *Odes d'Anacréon* published by Cherubini and Méhul[4] in 1798 and the classical paintings of David and Ingres.

THE *LIED* IN THE 1790s

The main stream of solo song flowed in Germany where, besides Beethoven, two minor but not negligible talents had appeared: Carl Friedrich Zelter (1758–1832) and Johann Rudolf Zumsteeg (1760–1802). Schiller's friend Zumsteeg began to publish unpretentious songs, some without independent voice-part, from 1784; they were republished posthumously in the last three volumes (1803–5) of his *Kleine Balladen und Lieder*; but he first attracted attention in 1792 with his setting of Bürger's narrative ballad 'Des Pfarrers Tochter von Taubenhayn'. Then came other ballads, including the relatively short 'Ritter Toggenburg' (Schiller) (1797), one of his best, and a setting of Bürger's 'Lenore' (1798) which totally eclipsed André's (see p. 531) by its dramatic power. Nor was he mainly a ballad composer; he was really more successful with ordinary *Lieder* where he could capture a mood, as in his setting of Kosegarten's 'Nachtgesang', and sound emotional depth with simple means and in tiny space (e.g. the two eight-bar strophes in which he enshrines Gaudenz von Salis's 'Das Grab').

Beethoven's earliest songs, apart from a couple of boyish efforts without independent voice-part, are a collection composed in the early 1790s, surprisingly published in 1805 as Op. 52. Some of these too hardly need a separate stave for the voice; the best of them, the Goethe 'Mailied', is not markedly better than, say, Zumsteeg's 'Wahre Minne'. Much more Beethovenian are the songs of 1795: 'Adelaide', a beautiful cavatina-and-cabaletta aria which, as Matthisson gladly admitted, completely over-shadowed his poem, '"Seufzer eines Ungeliebten" und "Gegenliebe"', a miniature cantata, and the simple hymnic 'Opferlied'. Next year came the big dramatic scena with orchestra, 'Ah! perfido' (also published in 1805 with a late opus-number). But the mature Beethoven emerged as a song-writer only in the six *Lieder von Gellert* (1803), especially in the lapidary 'Vom

---

[2] Witness the *Premier recueil de six romances* (1796) from which 'La Mort de Werther' by Louis Emmanuel Jadin (1768–1853) is reprinted by Frits Noske, *Das ausserdeutsche Sololied* (*Das Musikwerk*) (Cologne, 1958), No. 21.
[3] Ibid., p. 9.
[4] Example in ibid., No. 22.

Tode' and 'Gottes Macht und Vorsehung'. Even 'In questa tomba oscura' (1807), powerful as it is, is less impressive than 'Vom Tode'.

THE INSPIRATION OF GOETHE

In the *Egmont* year, 1810, he published several other Goethe settings – the four unsuccessful attempts at 'Nur wer die Sehnsucht kennt' which he had made in 1808, an equally unfortunate 'Kennst du das Land?', Op. 75, No. 1, a 'Song of the Flea', Op. 75, No. 3, which as some wit said suggests the flea but not Mephistopheles – and three more, as Op. 83, in 1811. Only the year before a vastly inferior composer had set 'Kennst du das Land?' to a tune which does indeed catch Mignon's 'childish innocence of expression'.[5]

Ex. 245

Reichardt (see p. 531) published his four books of *Goethes Lieder, Oden, Balladen und Romanzen mit Musik*[6] in 1809 and *Schillers lyrische Gedichte in Musik gesetzt* two years later. The 128 Goethe setttings include striking part-declamatory songs such as 'Prometheus' and the *Harzreise* 'Rhapsodie', and a remarkable strophic setting of 'Erlkönig', but Reichardt is happiest with purely lyrical poems: 'Schäfers Klage' (see Ex. 246 (i)), 'Trost in Tränen', 'Die schöne Nacht'. It hardly needs to be said that much of his work – often without independent voice-parts – falls to lower levels. But Beethoven and Reichardt were far from having a monopoly of Goethe. The poet's own favourite composer, his friend Zelter had been setting his songs since 1796; now in 1811–12 he brought out four volumes of *Sämmtliche Lieder, Balladen und Romanzen*. He composed altogether 75 by Goethe, which pleased the poet particularly because, as he told August Wilhelm von Schlegel, 'so far as I can judge, they never originate in inspiration (*ein Einfall*) but are a fundamental reproduction of poetic intentions', a quality exemplified in *his* 'Schäfers Klagelied' (Ex. 246 (ii)) which musically hardly bears comparison with Reichhardt's. Then in 1815 Tomášek followed the fashion with nine volumes of *Gedichte von Goethe für den Gesang*, Opp. 53–61, 41 songs in all, including an 'Erlkönig' (Op. 59, No. 1) and a 'Kennst

---

[5] In *Wilhelm Meisters Lehrjahre* (Book III, Chap. 1) Goethe describes in detail how she sang it.
[6] Ed. Walter Salmen, EDM 58 and 59.

du das Land' (Op. 54, No. 1) for which Goethe declared his special liking. He too set the 'Schäfers Klagelied' (Op. 56, No. 1).

The young Schubert made his first Goethe settings in the last months of 1814. (Hitherto he had kept almost exclusively to Schiller and Matthisson.) They included 'Gretchen am Spinnrade', first of his master songs, 'Trost in Thränen', and 'Schäfers Klagelied' (Ex. 246 (iii)), which (transposed to E minor and with four bars of piano introduction) was his first song to be performed in public (28 February 1819):

Ex. 246

(i) REICHARDT

(ii) ZELTER

(iii) SCHUBERT

It is clear that he took Zelter's setting as a model – on which he improved considerably. It was a common practice of Schubert's in his youth to work from such models, but the models were usually Zumsteeg, in whose songs he could 'wallow for days together' and for whom he retained a life-long admiration. 'Hagars Klage' (1811), 'Die Erwartung' and the Kosegarten 'Nachtgesang' (both 1815), 'Ritter Toggenburg' (1816), and the first two versions of 'Das Grab' (1815–16) – even the third (1817) in one detail – were all modelled on Zumsteeg's settings.

CYCLES AND COLLECTIONS OF *LIEDER*

Schubert's songs were his earliest compositions to be published; even so, they were not revealed to the world at large until 1821 and in the meantime Beethoven had made his last important contribution to the literature of song with his cycle *An die ferne Geliebte* (1816), settings of six poems by a young medical student, Alois Jeitteles. The songs run on without a break and are clinched by the fact that the music of the first song reaches its real climax only when it returns at the end of the cycle. A true 'song cycle' like this, a collection united by poetic theme as well as by poet, was then fairly novel, although Beethoven himself had foreshadowed it in his *Gellert-Lieder* and Weber in the first book (1814) of *Leyer und Schwerdt*,[7] settings of Körner's patriotic poems of the War for Freedom. In the year after the *Ferne Geliebte* Weber published a true cycle, *Die Temperamente beim Verluste der Geliebten*, the second of which, 'Der Schwermüthige', is one of his most beautiful songs. He was a very uneven song-composer, though consistent in his choice of bad poets, but at his best – in 'Was zieht zu deinem Zauberkreise' (comp. 1809), 'Unbefangenheit' and 'Sind es Schmerzen' (both 1813), and 'Das Mädchen an das erste Schneeglöckchen' (1819) – he is very good indeed. The composer of *Freischütz* showed his hand in two sets of pseudo-*Volkslieder*, Op. 54 (1818) and Op. 64 (1822). Spohr too was a fairly prolific song-composer, more 'operatic' than Weber; he made a rather fine setting of 'Gretchen am Spinnrade' in his first volume of *Deutsche Lieder*, Op. 25 (pub. 1810):

Ex. 247

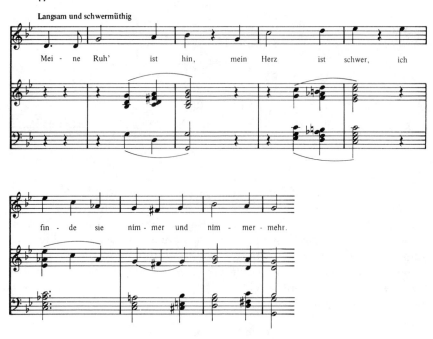

and a fussy, point-underlining one of 'Kennst du das Land' in his second one, Op. 37 (1816). And in the wings beside Schubert was standing a young man only a few months older than himself who had composed music to 'Erlkönig' and Herder's translation of 'Edward' in 1818: Carl Loewe (1796–1869).

[7] The second book consists of male-voice quartets: see p. 665.

THE GRADUAL REVEALING OF SCHUBERT

Loewe had to wait till 1824 before his 'Erlkönig' was published (as his Op. 1, No. 3). Schubert was more fortunate; he had composed his setting in 1815 and it was sung at an evening concert of the Gesellschaft der Musikfreunde on 25 January 1821; in April Cappi & Diabelli published it as Op. 1 and 'Gretchen am Spinnrade' as Op. 2. In the course of the same year appeared Opp. 3–7, eighteen songs including 'Heidenröslein', 'Schäfers Klagelied', 'Memnon', 'Meeres Stille', 'Der Tod und das Mädchen', and 'Der Wanderer', some early, some recent. These songs opened Schubert's path to fame as a song-writer though many years were to pass before he was generally recognized as a master of anything else. The publications of 1822–3 included the *Gesänge des Harfners* from *Wilhelm Meister* and other Goethe songs, Schiller's 'Gruppe aus dem Tartarus' and Rückert's 'Sei mir gegrüsst', those of 1824 the *Schöne Müllerin* cycle. In 1825 appeared 'Die junge Nonne' and more Goethe songs including the three of Op. 19, 'An Schwager Kronos', 'An Mignon' and 'Ganymed', 'reverentially dedicated to the poet' who never even acknowledged their receipt. 'Ave Maria' and six other songs from a translation of *The Lady of the Lake*, another set from *Wilhelm Meister* (including a duet version of 'Sehnsucht' as demanded by the story, as well as a fourth solo version), 'Auf dem Wasser zu singen', 'Du bist die Ruh' ', the third version of 'Der Jüngling am Bache', and two masterpieces composed nine or ten years before – 'Lied eines Schiffers' and 'An die Musik' – were published during 1826–7, and in 1828 came the *Winterreise* cycle and at least three outstanding Goethe songs, 'Der Musensohn', 'Auf dem See', and 'Über allen Gipfeln'. In that last year Schubert discovered two new poets, Heine and Rellstab, and planned to publish a Rellstab set and six separate Heine songs; in the end these were all issued, together with his last song, J. G. Seidl's 'Die Taubenpost', under the collective title *Schwanengesang* in May 1829. The total of posthumously published songs runs to nearly four hundred; they do not include many masterpieces though 'Grenzen der Menschheit' is nothing less, and they do include some beautiful things published immediately after the composer's death: 'Am Tage aller Seelen' ('Litanei'), the Claudius 'An die Nachtigall' ('Es liegt und schläft'), the 'Wiegenlied' wrongly attributed to the same poet, and A. W. von Schlegel's translation of 'Hark, hark, the lark'. ('Was ist Sylvia' had already appeared in 1828.)

A study of Schubert's outpouring of songs *per se* would most naturally be chronological; historically it is more important to comprehend its gradual public revelation, an approach which has the further advantage of showing what he himself considered most valuable. For instance he was caught up in the Ossian vogue and made eight settings from Eduard Harold's translation in 1815–16, but thought none of them worth publishing. He took the same view of his Körner settings (1815). But he had already composed 'Gretchen' in 1814 and 'Erlkönig' and thirty other Goethe songs in 1815 – 'Meeres Stille', 'Der du von dem Himmel bist', 'Erster Verlust', 'Heidenröslein',

'Rastlose Liebe', the first and best 'Nur wer die Sehnsucht' (which he did not publish), to name only a handful of the best known. (Goethe usually struck the best out of him; he by no means needed great poetry to produce great music but verse such as Goethe's, and at the end of his life Heine's, obviously excited his creative invention to a high pitch.) It is difficult to speak of the 'development' of a composer who could produce such songs as these at 18 and the All Souls' 'Litanei', 'An Schwager Kronos', 'An die Nachtigall', 'Lied eines Schiffers', and 'An die Musik' a year or two later. One notices changes. He grew out of his fondness for the *scena* type of his youth but still employed it, more or less compressed, in 'Gruppe aus dem Tartarus' and 'Ganymed' (both 1817), 'Prometheus' (1819), and later still in 'Kriegers Ahnung' (1828). Richard Capell[8] detected 'a new phase of Schubert's lyric art' characterized by 'compactness, delicacy, and psychological refinement' in the 1821 settings from Goethe's *West-östlicher Divan* ('Geheimes', 'Verloren', the two 'Suleika' songs) and those of 1822–3 from Rückert's *Östliche Rosen* ('Sei mir grüsst', 'Dass sie hier gewesen', 'Du bist die Ruh', 'Lachen und Weinen'). Certainly the exquisite, perfumed harmonies of 'Dass sie hier gewesen' were new, but Schubert was reacting to the pseudo-orientalism of the verses as he always reacted to his poets. He did so again to Wilhelm Müller in his two song-cycles, *Die schöne Müllerin* and *Winterreise*. Or rather he reacts to the two groups of poems: the idyll-with-a-tragic-end is reflected in homely vignettes, often near to folk-music, the sound of the mill-stream again and again pervading the piano part; the almost unrelieved misery of the winter journey inspired more tragic and ironic music. The fortuitous collection of the so-called *Schwanengesang* naturally has no such unity. On the contrary it shows the diversity of mood and method customary in Schubert's groups. The Rellstab vary in style from the purely melodious 'Ständchen' to the more than half declamatory 'Aufenthalt', near *Winterreise* in mood, near 'Erlkönig' in method. Of the Heine songs only 'Das Fischermädchen' is purely melodious, and as such far inferior to 'Ständchen', 'Ihr Bild' a wonderful and faithful arioso translation of Heine into music. But in 'Der Atlas', 'Die Stadt', 'Am Meer', and above all 'Der Doppelgänger' Schubert – not by any means for the first time – adds a completely new dimension to an already fine poem.

By his inexhaustible fund of melodic invention and infinite variety of stylistic approach, to say nothing of his injection of heightened harmonic colour and his bolder contrasts of tonality, Schubert effected a revolution in *Klavierlied* which often demanded as ideal interpreters musicians more sophisticated and better equipped technically than the domestic performers who were happy with Zumsteeg and Reichardt and could cope with a great deal of Beethoven and Weber, and also more sensitive and intelligent than most opera-orientated professional singers. His music nurtured such interpreters and after his death stimulated a great flowering of German

---

[8] *Schubert's Songs* (London, 1928), pp. 155–6 and 201.

song-composition. But it hardly affected the work of two almost exact contemporaries who began to publish songs at about the same time as himself, did most of their best work in that decade, but lived on into the third quarter of the century – Marschner and Loewe.

THE GERMAN NARRATIVE BALLAD

Marschner was an enormously prolific composer of *Klavierlieder*; he left more than 400. Beginning with Schiller and Matthisson settings, he first made his mark with his Op. 12 (1822), three songs from a story, 'Märthchen', by Friedrich Kind, the librettist of *Freischütz*, the third of which, 'Der Schiffmann', is in the supernatural-horrific vein he was to exploit so successfully in his operas. In the same year he set three stanzas of 'Lenore', Op. 27, No. 7 – not Bürger's but the original poem Arnim and Brentano had published in the second volume of *Des Knaben Wunderhorn* (Heidelberg, 1808) – which Kind had introduced in his play *Schön Ella*. In later years he expanded Gertrud's song 'Des Nachts wohl auf der Haide' in Act II of *Hans Heiling* (see p. 711) into a ballad 'Das Flämmchen auf der Haide', Op. 80, No. 12, and later still produced a very fine ballad, 'Die Monduhr', Op. 102, No. 2. Marschner's lyrical songs are not of much account.

Nor were Loewe's. Another admirer of Zumsteeg – he was particularly fond of singing his 'Ritter Toggenburg' and 'Lenore' – Loewe made his debut, as already mentioned, with an 'Erlkönig' and an 'Edward' which he never surpassed in all his great output. Wagner is said to have considered Loewe's 'Erlkönig' 'noch viel besser' than Schubert's and his 'Edward' is certainly superior to Schubert's ('Eine altschottische Ballade'). The third ballad of Loewe's Op. 1, Uhland's 'Der Wirtin Töchterlein', is much less remarkable; the subject lacks drama – and drama, action that he could visualize and suggest in picturesque accompaniment motives, was the life-source of Loewe's inspiration. In 'Walpurgisnacht', Op. 2, No. 3, which with 'Edward' and the Herder 'Elvershöh', Op. 3, No. 2, was one of those Wagner used to sing 'with inimitable expression',[9] Körner's 'Treu-Röschen', Op. 2, No. 1, and 'Herr Oluf', Op. 2, No. 2,[10] Loewe was back with the supernatural shudder.

After his three sets of ballads, Loewe published in 1826 four sets of *Hebräische Gesänge, Gedichte und Balladen* (translations of Byron's *Hebrew Melodies*), Opp. 4, 5, 13, and 14, the first of which, 'Herodes Klage um Mariamne' shows him at his best outside the ballad field. Lyrical song was his weak area. In 1828 he published *Gesammelte Gesänge, Romanzen und Balladen*, Op. 9, in ten books, 53 songs in all, divided into 'Night Songs', 'Songs of Longing', 'Cheerful Songs', and so on. The 'Nachtgesänge'

[9] Hans von Wolzogen, *Erinnerungen an Richard Wagner. (Neue, um das Doppelte vergrösserte Ausgabe)*, (Leipzig, n.d.), p. 32.
[10] Herder's translation from the Danish, in which 'Erlkönigs Tochter' waylays the hero, suggested to Goethe his own companion piece. But 'Erlkönig' is a nonce-word; the Danish 'Ellerkonge' means elf-king.

include Heine's 'Lotosblume' and Goethe's two famous 'Nachtlieder'; 'Die Lotosblume' is set with impeccable workmanship, over-dramatized and with only a passing touch of lyrical feeling, 'Über allen Gipfeln' and 'Der du von dem Himmel bist' are quite uninspired. Uhland's 'Graf Eberhards Weissdorn' figures, a little oddly, among the 'Gesänge der Sehnsucht'; Loewe's setting is no masterpiece but he has no emotion to cope with, except the old knight's nostalgia in the last stanza, only a simple story to tell – and he does it very pleasantly. 'Mädchen sind wie der Wind', one of the 'Heitere Gesänge', a humorous trifle, is better still:

Ex. 248

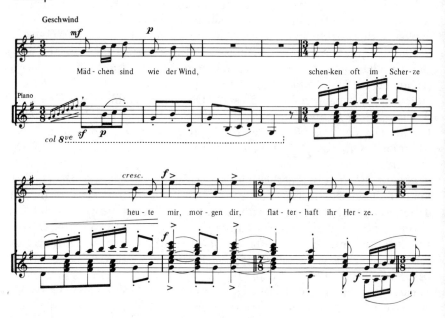

Humour was one of Loewe's strong suits and in humorous narratives like the *Drei Balladen*, Op. 20 – Goethe's 'Hochzeitlied', 'Der Zauberlehrling', and 'Die wandelnde Glocke' – he has few equals; the actual tale of the sorcerer's apprentice is told in C major, a breathless *vivacissimo* near-patter, the spell abruptly each time in D flat – and back to C without modulation. The similar description of the elves' wedding (C major) is likewise placed between the narrative opening (E major and minor) and close (E major). Loewe's later work is marked by impoverished invention and self-repetition, though now and again the old power breaks through as in 'Archibald Douglas' at

> Nur lass mich atmen wieder auf's neu
> Die Luft im Vaterland

and in 'Der Nöck'.

THE ART-SONGS OF THE WESTERN SLAVS

Against this overwhelming background of German song must be set the modest appearance of Slavonic art-song. After a lifetime devoted almost exclusively, so far as song-writing was concerned, to German texts Tomášek turned after 1820 to Czech poets. He had indeed already in 1813–14 published two books of settings mostly of his friend Václav Hanka, Opp. 48 and 50, prefacing the first with a 'Word to Patriots' in which he propounded the suitability of Czech – a language despised and neglected under the Habsburgs – for singing. Now he composed another Hanka set, Op. 71 (1823), and in 1825 six *Starožitné písné* (Ancient Songs) from Hanka's forgery, the so-called Králové Dvůr manuscript, then believed to be a genuine specimen of old Czech literature. Like Ossian, it stirred imaginations and Tomášek rightly felt that his settings were sounding a new, national note.

The emergence of the Polish 'art-song' dates from the same period. Polish had always flourished as a literary language and the political and military disasters of the 1790s had called forth a quantity of vocal mazurkas and polonaises. Elsner (see p. 594) had been publishing Polish songs rather in the vein of Zumsteeg's lyrical songs since 1803, and in 1818 he issued a treatise on the musical treatment of Polish verse-metres and rhythms. But the real flowering was inspired by the poetry of Mickiewicz which acted as a catalyst, as Goethe's above all had done in German song. In 1825 the opera-composer Kurpiński set Mickiewicz's sonnet 'Do Niemna' ('To the Niemen') and soon after another setting was made by the violin virtuoso and composer Lipiński:

Ex. 249

nie - gdyś czer - pa - łem — w nie-mo - wlę - ce dło - - nie,

('Niemen! where are the waters I used to scoop with childish hands?')

The pianist Szymanowska[11] had already published three Niemcewicz songs in 1816 and now in 1828 she also turned to Mickiewicz, first composing his ballad 'Switezianka' and then three songs from his *Konrad Wallenrod*, the first of which, 'Piesn do Wilii' ('Song to Vilia'), has two voice-parts composed above her so-called 'nocturne' (really a study in incessant semiquaver sextolets for the right hand), 'Le Murmure' (Paris, 1824). It was one of Mickiewicz's accomplishments to improvise verses to his own piano-playing and Szymanowska had recently heard him improvise to 'Le Murmure'.

BIRTH OF THE RUSSIAN ART-SONG

Russian solo song with piano first took the form either of French-style *romances* or of imitations of folk-song, so called 'Russian songs': forms which often merged. They were nearly all anonymous but evidently the work of ill-equipped dilettanti. The best of these was Nikolay Alekseyevich Titov (1800–75), one of a family of such composers, who published his first *russkie romansï* in 1820; one song of his, 'Kovarny drug' (Insidious friend, but dear to my heart), was immensely popular for many years. Much more accomplished was Alyabyev whose song 'My nightingale' has already been mentioned in connection with his Third Quartet (see p. 626) where the string parts are a great improvement on the original piano accompaniment. His best songs, in which his wider range of harmony, his imaginative accompaniments, his varied and extended forms, his wide choice of subjects, place him far above his predecessors, began with his exile to Siberia in 1828: 'Irtïsh', a strophic song, each strophe beginning with quietly melancholy narrative but bursting into powerful direct-speech protest (1828), 'Grob', a through-composed setting of a translation of Salis's 'Das Grab' (1829):

---

[11] On these composers see above, pp. 594, 613, n. 29, and 641 respectively.

Ex. 250

('Dark and awful is the quiet grave!')

'Vecherny zvon', Kozlov's gloomy translation of Moore's 'Those evening bells'[12] composed with a striking 'tolling' piano-part (1830). Then came some memorable Pushkin settings: 'Dva vorona' (The two crows), 'Zimnaya doroga' (The winter road), and others. Also during the 1820s the future opera-composer Aleksey Nikolayevich Verstovsky (1799–1862) developed the narrative ballad – or 'dramatic cantata' as he called it – a genre which did not particularly interest Alyabyev, with 'Tre pesni skalda', Zhukovsky's version of Uhland's 'Die drei Lieder' (1823), and Pushkin's 'Chernaya shal' ('The black shawl'). Both of these were originally with orchestra but the dramatic and picturesque elements in the ballad encouraged Russian song-composers to enrich their piano accompaniments, both harmonically and in figuration. And the advent of Pushkin provided a catalyst more effective than Mickiewicz, hardly less so than Goethe. A real efflorescence was on the way.

---

[12] Moore's poem, published in his *Selection of Popular National Airs*, is said to be written to the tune 'The Bells of St. Petersburg'.

653

33

Choral Music (1790–1830)

The general decline in church music all too evident through the greater part of the eighteenth century continued during the early years of the nineteenth. The Lutheran church could show nothing better than the collection of dull church cantatas that Zumsteeg composed in 1795 and published during 1803–5, the Anglican the Services and anthems of Attwood, John Clarke [-Whitfeld] (1770–1836) and William Crotch (1775–1847). The one Englishman who could have far surpassed them, the Bach missionary Samuel Wesley (1766–1837), turned Catholic and wrote his finest works, the great double-motet 'In exitu Israel' and the hardly inferior five-part 'Exultate Deo', as well as several Masses, for the Roman church. Russia had found in Bortnyansky, whose psalm-*kontserti* and *kheruvimski* (cherubic hymns) date from 1796 onward, the classic master of Orthodox church music, and Catholic Austria, having a composer of genius, stood out. But in once-Catholic France church music passed into total eclipse with the Revolution.

THE OPEN-AIR FESTIVALS OF THE FRENCH REVOLUTION

Not immediately. The fall of the Bastille was saluted with a 'Te Deum' in Notre Dame. It was pointed out that God the Father of mankind could hardly be an aristocrat and Jesus was hailed in a sermon as 'la divinité concitoyenne du genre humain'. And Gossec's 'Te Deum' of 1779 was sung at the *Fête de la Fédération* in the Champ de Mars on the first anniversary of the fall of the Bastille, the first of the great open-air festivals of the Revolution. It was rescored for male voices with wind-band, *bande de tambours*[1] and *pièce d'artillerie*, music of a type essential if revolutionary music was to rise above the level of 'Ça ira' sung to an old *contredanse* tune. Gossec obliged with a similarly orchestrated 'Ronde nationale', a 'Hymne à la Liberté', and other works (1792) as well as a purely instrumental 'Marche lugubre' which made an enormous impression and was played at Mirabeau's funeral (1791). After his victory at Valmy in 1792 Kellermann wished a 'Te Deum' to be sung on the battlefield but was ordered by the Minister of War to substitute the then very new 'Hymne des Marseillais' of the amateur Claude Joseph Rouget de Lisle (1760–1836). This was soon adopted officially as the 'hymne de la République' and in 1793 it was arranged by

---

[1] In the 'Judex crederis' the bass drum was struck, *pp*, with timpani sticks.

Gossec for soloists, chorus, and band for the celebration (10 August) of the anniversary of the storming of the Tuileries. On the same day Pleyel's *Révolution du 10 Août, ou le Tocsin allégorique* for chorus, orchestra, additional trumpets, fifes and drums, seven church bells, and cannon, was performed at Strasbourg. God was soon supplanted by Reason, honoured at once in hymns and other works by Gossec, Méhul, Catel, and Boieldieu, and in 1794 by a Supreme Being whose *Fête* (8 June) Gossec celebrated in a hymn for soloist, chorus, and wind-band which became one of his most popular compositions. A few weeks later Méhul commemorated the victory at Fleurus in a similarly scored 'Chant du départ' which became a 'second "Marseillaise" '. The refrains not unfairly represent the normal revolutionary musical idiom and level of inspiration:

Ex. 251

(i) GOSSEC: *Hymne à l'Être suprême*

(ii) MÉHUL : *Chant du départ*

For five years the festivals, anniversaries, victories of the Republic, and the funerals of its heroes were observed with *hymnes* and *chants* by Gossec, Méhul, Catel, Le Sueur, Berton, and even Cherubini whose *Hymne du Panthéon* (1794) for Marat's interment and *Ode sur le 18 fructidor* (1798) were among the few compositions of any distinction. The *coup d'état* of 18–19 brumaire, 1799, brought a dramatic change. Napoleon was no Christian but he ended the rites of the Supreme Being, re-opened the churches, and released the imprisoned priests; as First Consul he concluded the Concordat with the Pope and sealed it with a 'Te Deum' – probably

Berton's – in Notre Dame. Paisiello was appointed director of his private chapel, for which he composed a *Messa pastorale* (1802).

The last notable music of the Republic was two colossal *scènes lyriques* by Méhul and Le Sueur which were performed in the 'Temple de Mars' (Dôme des Invalides) in 1800. Méhul composed a *Chant national* for the Bastille anniversary for tenor and bass soloists, three choirs – one female, with two harps and a horn, placed in the dome, the other two male – and three orchestras. Two months later it was trumped by Le Sueur with a *Chant du 1er vendémiaire en faveur du rétablissement de la Paix* for four choirs and four orchestras. When Paisiello wished to return to Italy, and Méhul declined the succession, the post was offered to Le Sueur on Paisiello's recommendation. Méhul's *Messe solennelle* composed for Napoleon's coronation in 1804 was set aside and replaced by one by Paisiello, who also wrote a 'Te Deum' with double orchestra for the occasion. Le Sueur provided a coronation march adapted from his *Chant des Triomphes de la République* of 1794 and transposed the opening chorus of the *Chant du 1er vendémiaire*, 'Jour glorieux, jour de mémoire', from C minor to A minor for an 'Ora pro nobis' in his *Oratorio pour le couronnement*. The same useful quarry yielded material for other church music; for instance the chorus 'Et l'avare Albion' was easily recast as the motet 'Veni sponsa'.

HAYDN'S SYMPHONIC MASSES

At the other extreme from pagan France, Catholic Austria – unlucky in war – saw her greatest composer of those years producing church music which was long to outlive the fruits of French victories in the field. Haydn, who had composed no church music for fourteen years and written his last symphony the year before, was moved to compose in 1796 the first of a series of Masses for the Kalvarienbergkirche at Eisenstadt, *Missa in tempore belli* – Napoleon was driving the Austrians out of Italy – also known as the *Paukenmesse* from the drum-rolls and trumpetings of the long Agnus Dei. The Kyrie is almost symphonic in organization, the 'Et incarnatus' particularly lovely. A little later came the *Missa Sti. Bernardi de Offida*, a saint very recently canonized, also known as the *Heiligmesse* from the quotation of the hymn, 'Heilig, heilig, heilig' in the Sanctus; Haydn displays his contrapuntal mastery in the fugal Kyrie and canonic 'Et incarnatus', though this is immediately eclipsed by the profundity of the purely chordal 'Crucifixus'. The *Missa in Angustiis* is another 'Mass in time of war', completed on 31 August 1798 just a month after Nelson's victory at the Nile which – at least temporarily – relieved the 'straits' of the allies; whether or not it 'inspired' the latter part of the Mass the work acquired the nickname of *Nelsonmesse* and was performed when he was entertained at Eisenstadt in 1800. It is a composition of extraordinary virility, scored for three trumpets, drums, strings, and organ only: the Kyrie in D minor again symphonically organized, a splendid D major fugue ('in gloria Dei Patris') to end the 'Quoniam', an 'Incarnatus' which stands beside Haydn's great symphonic slow movements, and a *coup de théâtre* for trumpets and drums at the end of the Benedictus before the major 'Hosanna in excelsis'. The *Theresienmesse* of 1799, dubiously associated with the wife of Francis II, is a much more modest work scored for pairs of clarinets, trumpets, and drums, upper strings only, and the organ reduced to a continuo instrument; in the Credo both 'Incarnatus' and 'Crucifixus' luxuriate in flat keys, B flat minor and D flat major. The main key is B flat major, as with the *Heiligmesse* and the two final masterpieces: the so-called *Schöpfungsmesse* (1801) and *Harmoniemesse* (1802). The nicknames derive from a quotation from *Die Schöpfung* (see below, p. 660) in the 'Quis tollis' in the one case and the prominence of the wind section in the other. As a matter of fact both are scored for full symphonic orchestra with woodwind in pairs, and organ – which has a cheerful solo in the *Schöpfungsmesse*. Peculiarly touching is Haydn's return in the Agnus of the *Harmoniemesse* to the F major Adagio of Symphony No. 98 (see p. 597).

THE MASS IN PROVINCIAL AUSTRIA

During the 1790s Haydn's brother had composed simple Masses in the style favoured at Salzburg (cf. p. 554), little more than four-part harmonizations of plainsong with figured bass for organ;[2] only in the *Missa in honorem S. Ursulae* (1793) does he introduce a modest instrumental accompaniment. In December 1800 the war was literally brought home to Michael Haydn when Salzburg was temporarily occupied by the French who looted his house. As a gesture of compensation, the music-loving Empress Maria Theresa commanded him to compose a Mass, the *Missa solemnis sub titulo Stae. Teresiae* (1801) which naturally had to be given a full orchestral accompaniment though, as always, he was more observant of strict ecclesiastical propriety than his brother. A second commission from the Empress[3] produced a *Missa St. Francisci*[4] with Te Deum (1803) for the Emperor's name-day; in this, his most festive work, he still holds fast to a familiar intonation:

Ex. 252

Cre - do   in u - num De - - um,   Pa - trem o - mni - po - ten - - tem,

Joseph Haydn's successor as *Kapellmeister* at Eisenstadt was Hummel who published two Masses in B flat and E flat in 1805, the first with the parts of the service through-composed, except that the 'Dona nobis' is separate, the second a 'cantata-Mass'. (The 'Et incarnatus', for instance, has a ten-bar

---

[2] Two of these, dating from 1794, have been ed. Anton Klafsky, *DTÖ*, Jg. xxii (vol. 45), pp. 110 and 126.
[3] Another work which owed its inception to the Empress was Eybler's Requiem (1802).
[4] Klafsky, ibid, p. 1.

orchestral introduction with an effective oboe solo probably suggested by the clarinet which Haydn had used at the same point in his *Harmoniemesse*.) One of the best movements is the Benedictus:

Ex. 253

But Hummel at his most inspired was to be eclipsed – though Prince Eszterházy did not think so – by another Mass for Eisenstadt in 1807: Beethoven's in C. (It is odd that practically all the most important compositions of the most impressive Christian ritual from 1796 to 1807 should have been written for one small church in the Austrian provinces, albeit a princely one.) Beethoven's C major Mass is not one of his outstanding masterpieces but no important work of his full maturity could be devoid of great passages; we find them here in the tremendous opening of the Gloria, the awed opening of the Sanctus. Perhaps the finest single movement is, surprisingly, the Credo – particularly from the mystery of the incarnation and the drama of crucifixion and resurrection onward. Again, in the Benedictus he surpasses Hummel not by melody but by a lovely fabric of motivic open-work for the solo voices in a harmonic framework beautifully orchestrated.

CHERUBINI'S FIRST MASSES

The following year Cherubini, who had shown little interest in church music since his youth in Italy, composed a *missa brevis* – Kyrie and Gloria only – also for a village church under princely auspices, at Chimay near Charleroi. In 1809 he extended this to a full-length, indeed very long, Mass in F which achieved a sensational success when performed in Paris. Two years later he composed the first of his real masterpieces in this field, the *Messe solennelle* in D minor. Here the rival Beethoven most admired, a master of drama, counterpoint, and orchestration, extended himself in a cantata-Mass far too long for liturgical use except for some great occasion – but it is worthy of a great occasion. (The 'Amen' of the Credo extends to more than two hundred bars.) The choral entry with the Kyrie:

Ex. 254

after twenty bars of orchestral introduction, establishes the level of what is to follow and the protracted pianissimo end of the movement is no less impressive. Outstanding in the Gloria are the 'Gratias agimus', which might be the slow movement of a late Haydn symphony, and in which one fine stroke succeeds another – the bass phrase 'Propter magnam gloriam tuam', the woodwind writing at 'Domine Fili' – the B minor 'Qui tollis' with its great climax on 'suscipe deprecationem', the Amens of 'Cum Sancto Spiritu'. In the Credo one is struck by the crystalline sweetness of the three alternating choirs – woodwind only, unaccompanied trio of soprano and alto soloists, trio of tenor and bass soloists with pizzicato accompaniment; the 'Crucifixus' is not dramatized but represented as a deeper mystery than the Incarnation; the shattering brass of the Resurrection soon die away and the soloists in turn take up 'Et in Spiritum Sanctum' in another movement recalling Haydn. After that there is a slight falling-off, though the first enunciation of the 'Benedictus' is exquisite. Toward the end romantic chromaticism slightly dyes a work otherwise classic in the truest sense. As

659

we shall see, the church music of the post-war years was even more imbued with the spirit of romanticism.

HAYDN'S ORATORIOS

With a little sophistry it might be argued that that spirit had already touched non-liturgical religious music in Haydn's oratorio *Die Schöpfung*, but the symptoms – the prefatory 'Representation of Chaos', the flight of 'hell's spirits black' in Uriel's first aria, the various pictorial touches, the scoring of the introduction to Part III – are merely accidental. Haydn had been deeply impressed by the monster performances of Handel's oratorios in London in May 1791 and when he left in 1795 after his second visit he took with him a *Creation* libretto said to have been compiled for Handel from Genesis and the seventh and eighth books of *Paradise Lost*. He did not set it at once. On his way to London he had heard or seen at Passau an adaptation of his orchestral *Sieben Worte des Erlösers* (see p. 552) with voice-parts adapted by the local *Kapellmeister*, Joseph Friebert, and his first care on returning to Vienna was to improve this version. He invited Mozart's patron Van Swieten to revise the text, an operation in which he drew on Ramler's *Der Tod Jesu* (see p. 540); nor did Haydn entirely discard Friebert's voice-parts.[5] He revised his own orchestral score, adding clarinets and trombones, and composed a new orchestral piece as an introduction to the second part of the work.

Swieten also made a German translation – and, it is said, the deplorable English re-translation – of the *Creation* libretto on which Haydn began work after the *Missa in tempore belli*. The oratorio was not finished until April 1798 but was performed at once in the Schwarzenberg Palace at Vienna and then again and again semi-publicly and publicly within a few months; in 1800 it was given twice in London in the spring, at Worcester later, and in Paris under Steibelt in December. It was Haydn's most successful work in his lifetime; he himself regarded it as his crowning masterpiece and all the evidence, including that of the voluminous sketches, shows that it cost him enormous effort. After the remarkable 'Chaos' and Raphael's first recitative – the narrator or *historicus* of early oratorio is replaced by three archangels – the overwhelming C major chord on 'Let there be *light*' is a truly Handelian thunderbolt; indeed it far overtops Handel's comparable 'And light was over all' in the *Samson* chorus 'O first-created beam'. Of such grand conceptions – 'Awake the harp', 'The heavens are telling', 'Achieved is the glorious work' – and such lovely passages as the description of the 'limpid brook' in Raphael's 'Rolling in foaming billows' Haydn might well be proud; he was probably much less proud of the touches of topical realism in that same aria, in Gabriel's 'On mighty pens', and Raphael's accompanied recitative 'Straight opening her fertile womb' – or even of the old-fashioned

---

[5] See the examples in score quoted by Adolf Sandberger, *Ausgewählte Aufsätze zur Musikgeschichte* (Munich, 1921), pp. 273–7.

coloratura of 'With verdure clad'. And after the already mentioned introduction and the duet with chorus 'By thee with bliss' there is a marked falling off in almost the whole of Part III.

Pl. 54   Haydn (seated in the foreground) being honoured with a fanfare of trumpets and drums before the performance of *Die Schöpfung* in the Aula of the Old University, Vienna, on 27 March 1808. This was his last public appearance. Salieri conducted and Konradin Kreutzer can be seen sitting at the piano. The painting was commissioned by Princess Herminegild Eszterházy for the lid of a casket which she presented to the 76-year-old master.

The *Creation* was immediately followed (1801) by another work of the oratorio type, though secular in nature: *Die Jahreszeiten*. The libretto was concocted from James Thomson's *The Seasons* by Van Swieten, who again made a re-translation. Haydn was not attracted by it and composed it only under heavy pressure from the librettist; among other things he is said to have disliked the pictorial element and he certainly described the imitation of the croaking frog in the last number of 'Summer' as 'dieser französischer Quark' (this French trash), so it is possible that similar things in *The Creation* were inserted against his better judgement. There is not much 'great' music in *The Seasons*, though the final fugue is nothing less, but a great deal of delightful music, some of which – like Hanne's spinning song in 'Winter', for which Van Swieten borrowed a poem by Bürger – belongs to the world of *Singspiel*. But the three characters who replace the archangels of *The Creation* – the farmer Simon, his daughter Hanne, and the peasant Lucas – are not so much *dramatis personae* as 'narrators' in fancy dress; their view of country life is, like Thomson's early eighteenth-century view, conventionally idealized, not subjectively romanticized. The score is

661

enlivened with genre-pictures, as of the hunt in 'Autumn', and with some of Haydn's most colourful orchestration; there is a thunderstroke, French Revolutionary rather than Handelian, near the end of 'Spring': the *ff* tutti, in B flat after D major, at 'Ewiger, mächtiger, gütiger Gott!' (One must quote the original German since the various English texts are in confusion.) But the quintessence of *The Seasons* is to be found in such things as Hanne's aria 'Welche Labung', in 'Summer', which are not new Haydn but familiar Haydn at nearly his best.

ORATORIO AFTER HAYDN

No one could describe *Christus am Ölberge* (1803) as first-period Beethoven at nearly his best. Christ's agony on the Mount of Olives roused him to merely conventional operatic music, and the advent of the coloratura soprano Seraph is calculated to induce agony in the listener; she becomes tolerable, and Christus human, only in their duet 'So ruhe dann mit ganzer Schwere'. On the other hand, the final chorus with its fugal entries, 'Preiset ihn, ihr Engelschöre', is really impressive. Indeed after Haydn oratorio reached its nadir, marked by such forgotten efforts as Paer's *Trionfo della Chiesa* and *Passione di Gesù Cristo*, written for Parma in 1804 and 1810, Eybler's *Die vier letzten Dinge* (1811), Spohr's *Das jüngste Gericht*[6] and Crotch's *Palestine* (both 1812), and Morlacchi's *Isacco* (1817).

The work that might have marked the beginning of a rebirth was Schubert's Easter cantata, *Lazarus* (1820), planned in three acts, of which the third – the actual raising from the tomb – was never composed and even the second is incomplete. Yet the torso is remarkable in that each act is through-composed, the arias and choruses embedded in richly devised and orchestrated accompanied recitative; for instance the violin phrase that punctuates Nathanael's 'Sieh', unsrer Freunde sind schon Viele versammelt' near the end of Act II is exquisite. And when Jemina, who was Jairus's daughter, comes to relate her own death and ascension in a truly Schubertian scena, 'So schlummert auf Rosen', her account of her reception into Heaven is accompanied by high woodwind chords perhaps suggested by the introduction to Part III of *The Creation*. Above all, the entire score is permeated by what one can only call romanticism.

CATHOLIC MUSIC IN THE POST-WAR PERIOD

The Catholic Europe which emerged after the war was very different from that of the eighteenth century. In France the Revolution had produced the usual results of persecution – renewal and intensification of faith – and after the politic official Christianity of the Empire the restored Bourbon monarchy revelled in ecclesiastical ceremony. Cherubini and Le Sueur were appointed joint superintendents of the Chapel Royal and Cherubini was

[6] Properly 'The Last Judgement'. But that title is misleadingly given in England to his *Die letzten Dinge* (1826), from which the quartet and chorus 'Selig sind die Toten' is still occasionally performed.

kept busy with official compositions. The first, the C minor Requiem (1816) for the anniversary of the execution of Louis XVI, is a masterpiece which Beethoven preferred to Mozart's, saying that if he ever wrote a Requiem he would take Cherubini's as his model.[7] There followed a more modest Mass in C (1816), a number of Kyries followed by motets, and Masses (1819 and 1825) for the coronations of Louis XVIII (which never took place) and Charles X. The last, the Coronation Mass in D, is perhaps the last great and living example of 'pure' musical classicism.

On the other hand in Catholic South Germany religious music, in common with literature and painting, was infected with that variety of romanticism which Goethe dismissed as the 'neukatholische Sentimentalität' of Wilhelm Wackenroder's *Herzensergiessungen eines kunstliebenden Klosterbruders* (1797). (Yet it was not Wackenroder[8] but his disciple A. W. von Schlegel who claimed that Protestantism was unsuited to the production of religious art.) Wackenroder's book strongly influenced the group of painters nicknamed the Nazarenes, headed by the Viennese Overbeck, who turned Catholic and settled in Rome. There Schubert's friend Leopold Kupelwieser joined them in 1823. And Schubert's *Lazarus* could well be described as 'Nazarene music' – 'Nazarene' being not necessarily a depreciatory adjective.

There is nothing even faintly Nazarene in Weber's Masses in E flat and G. Both were composed for the Dresden Hofkirche, the first for the name-day of King Frederick Augustus in 1818, the second for his golden wedding in 1819; the singers were Italians, including a castrato soprano whom Weber provided with preposterous coloratura in the Gloria of the G major Mass. For the E flat he borrowed in the Kyrie from a Mass in the same key written about 1801, and in Gloria, Credo, and Sanctus from three still earlier fughettas.

The case of Schubert is quite different. His first four Masses (1814–16) and other church music of this period, including four settings of 'Salve regina', were written when he was still under the tutelage of Salieri. They were composed for and performed at the church in the Liechtental district where he was born; indeed No. 1 in F was a festival Mass with an orchestra of strings, woodwind, and horns for the church's centenary. All four, and his two later Masses, are peculiar in that they fail to assert belief 'in one holy, catholic and apostolic church', an omission for which various explanations have been offered – carelessness, defiance of orthodoxy, conformity with some local practice – all possible but none completely convincing. Musically they might be described as a reconciliation of Mozart with Salieri: lovely innocence, as in the Agnus of the G major Mass (No. 2), and more than competent fugal writing. Schubert's most impressive early fugue, however, is the 'Alleluia' which constitutes the greater part of a Gradual, 'Benedictus es', for chorus, orchestra, and organ dating from 1815. Much more Schubertian and more significant is a religious but non-liturgical work

---

[7] Thayer-Deiters, *Ludwig van Beethovens Leben* (second edition, Leipzig, 1923), v, p. 329.
[8] Wackenroder, a Berliner, had studied music with Reichardt and Zelter.

composed in 1816, a setting for soprano, tenor, and bass soloists, chorus, and orchestra of Klopstock's paraphrase of 'Stabat Mater' in which Goethe might well have detected traces of 'Catholic sentimentality': e.g. the chorus 'Liebend neiget er sein Antlitz', the bass solo 'Sohn des Vaters'. And when after several years barren of notable religious music Schubert set Moses Mendelssohn's translation of Psalm 23, 'Gott ist mein Hirt', for women's voices and piano, the music is of very 'Nazarene' sweetness. Again in the A flat Mass which occupied him off and on from 1819 to 1822, Kyrie, Benedictus, Dona nobis are very bland.

In the great E flat Mass of his last year this element appears only in the Credo, where in the 'Incarnatus' it is transfigured by the sheer beauty of sound. But as a whole the Mass is no mere incitement to romantic devotion but a great ritual composition from the solemn orchestral chords and ostinato bass rhythm that open the Kyrie to the ineffable peace of the 'Dona nobis'. One of the most impressive passages occurs in the Gloria where at 'Domine Deus . . . qui tollis peccata mundi' the trombones in octaves *ff* (and other wind later), against a shuddering string background, intone references to the opening of 'Dies irae'.

'MISSA SOLEMNIS'

The E flat Mass stands as far above the Mass in D, a far from contemptible work which Hummel published in the same year (1828) as, it must be admitted, it does below the D major which Beethoven had published the year before. (The composition had been spread over the years 1819–23.) No special significance is implied by the epithet 'solemnis' always attached to Beethoven's work; it was a common enough description for a full-scale Mass; Cherubini's D minor and his Coronation Mass for Charles X were both styled *messes solennelles* and Rossini had collaborated in a *messa solenne* for Naples in 1820. Nevertheless Beethoven's D major deserves some special epithet, not because it was originally intended for a great ceremonial occasion – the enthronement of his pupil, the Archduke Rudolph, to whom he had dedicated a number of other masterpieces, as Archbishop of Olmütz – but because it is as unique in its way as Bach's B minor. Like that, it is liturgically impracticable – though not so long as Cherubini's D minor – and should be regarded as a grand musical poem inspired by the liturgical text. From a purely musical point of view, the outstanding peaks in a work of exceptional altitude are the fugues on 'in gloria Dei Patris' in the Gloria and 'Et vitam venturi saeculi' in the Credo – indeed the mysticism, tragedy, and triumph of what precedes it, from 'Et incarnatus' onward; the mysticism again of the awed Sanctus; the violin solo that floats down like the dove of the medieval Holy Ghost and hovers over the Benedictus; the 'petition for inner and outward peace' (*Bitte um innern und äussern Frieden*) as Beethoven marked the 'Dona nobis'; and the trumpets and drums and agonized recitatives which make this the most powerfully dramatic movement he ever wrote.

SECULAR MUSIC

The new century brought forth no secular choral works remotely comparable with Haydn's *Seasons*. (The finale of the Choral Symphony is, after all,
not a separate work.)[9] Beethoven's cantata *Der glorreiche Augenblick* for the
first peace celebration (1814) and Weber's, *Kampf und Sieg*, for the second
(1815), are mere *pièces d'occasion* unworthy of the composers and the events.
In 1815 Beethoven also set Goethe's *Meeresstille und Glückliche Fahrt* 'for
four voices' with orchestra, the seven pages of calm sea very beautifully, the
resumed voyage redeemed from commonplace only by some picturesque
touches. The four voice-parts are marked *coro* but the line between quartet
and chorus is not always firmly drawn in vocal music of this period.

Social male-voice music flourished particularly in England and Germany, in England particularly after the foundation of The Glee Club by
Samuel Arnold and others in 1787, in Germany after the *Liedertafel*
founded by Zelter in Berlin in 1809. Strictly the glee, a peculiarly English
form, was an unaccompanied piece – tuneful and mainly chordal but with
some polyphonic interest – for three or more solo male voices. But in fact
choral performance, accompaniment, and even female voices, sometimes
crept in; 'Glorious Apollo' (1790) by Samuel Webbe (1740–1816), one of
the founders of the Club, was sung at every meeting – first with three voices
to a part, then in full chorus. Webbe was one of the best of the glee-
composers; his 'Discord, dire sister' and 'When winds breathe soft' deserve
not to be forgotten. Among the best of the other glee-composers were
Richard Stevens (1757–1837), who made a number of attractive Shakespeare settings, and John Callcott (1766–1821). None of these distinguished
himself in other fields. The original Berlin *Liedertafel* was consciously
patriotic – Prussia was then at her lowest ebb – but it was quickly copied
elsewhere, for instance, in Zürich in 1810. The general run of *Liedertafel*
music was inferior to the better English glee but the level was raised from
time to time by the participation of more distinguished composers. Weber,
for instance, composed 'Das Turnierbankett' in 1812 for Zelter's Berlin
club, though his best-known male-voice pieces are those of the second book
of *Leyer und Schwerdt* (1814) (see p. 646), including the famous 'Lützow's
wilde Jagd' – which Schubert set the following year 'for two voices or two
horns' but never published. Spohr signalized his return to Germany and to
composition after his travels in Italy with a set of male-voice songs, Op. 44
(1817), one of which, the setting of Goethe's 'Dem Schnee, dem Regen'
'later became a favourite with the *Liedertafeln*'.[10] Marschner's membership
of a literary-artistic club in Leipzig, 'Der Tunnel an der Pleisse', in 1828
sparked off a considerable production of such quartets/choruses which he
published as *Tunnellieder*. But the outstanding master was of course
Schubert.

[9] One work composed in Vienna about 1807, Reicha's setting of Kosegarten's *Die Harmonie der Sphären*
for double chorus and orchestra, is remarkable at least for its employment of eight timpani tuned to G, A
flat, A, B flat, C, D flat, D, E flat, which play three- or four-part chords.
[10] *Selbstbiographie*, ii, p. 55.

33. Choral Music (1790–1830)

Schubert's biggest secular vocal work was the setting of *Mirjam's Siegesgesang*, which Grillparzer wrote specially for him, for soprano solo, mixed choir, and piano (1828). But mixed voices and female voices alone appealed to him, as to all his contemporaries, less than male voices. He wrote for them with or without piano accompaniment, once ('Nachtgesang im Walde') with accompaniment for four horns, once ('Hymnus an den Heiligen Geist') with full wind ensemble. Most of his male-voice pieces might be described not unfairly as very good *Liedertafel* stuff and a number of them – Opp. 11, 16, 17, 28, 64, 81, and the 'Boat Song' in the *Lady of the Lake* set – were published during his lifetime. But two pieces stand out: his fifth setting of Goethe's 'Gesang der Geister über den Wassern', Op. posth. 167 (1821), for four tenors and four basses, two violas, two cellos, and bass, and 'Mondenschein' (1826) for two tenors, three basses, and dispensable piano. Very different, both are masterpieces.

34

Orchestral Music (1830–93)

For many years orchestral music had drawn many of its idioms, even some of its forms, from opera. That era ended with ripe Haydn and Beethoven, and the general ascendancy of German music involved the ascendancy of instrumental music since German opera was long overshadowed by German instrumental music. As we shall see in the next chapter, the orchestral element became ever more important in opera until its predominance actually rejuvenated opera and made it once again for a time the most influential area of Western music. Yet the great orchestral forms faced more than one crisis. Beethoven's influence was fatal, in every sense of the word, for the symphony. It was inescapable for two generations, whether composers submitted to it or tried to ignore it; sometimes it was paralysing. As late as *c*. 1871 Brahms could tell the conductor Hermann Levi, 'I shall *never* compose a symphony! You have no idea what a man such as I am feels like when he hears a giant like that marching behind him.'[1] He had already begun and abandoned symphonies, though he was to finish one of them a few years later.

THE SYMPHONIES OF BERLIOZ

There was, however, one notable exception. During the early part of 1830 Berlioz wrote or compiled, and on 5 December performed, a *Symphonie fantastique* which owed nothing to Beethoven and a great deal to opera. He had first heard Beethoven's Third, Fifth, and Seventh Symphonies in 1828 and been completely bowled over by them; the following year he published a 'Notice biographique de Beethoven', quoting Fétis's translation of a German description of the Ninth, and parenthetically claiming to have 'read' the score. (It was not performed in Paris till 1831 when he was in Italy.) The Berlioz of the *Fantastique* was indebted to one of his teachers, Le Sueur, for the idea of an *exposé* (cf. p. 546), in this case a programme which should be 'considéré comme le texte parlé d'un opéra, servant à amener des morceaux de musique, dont il motive le caractère et détermine l'expression', which was distributed to the audience; to Cherubini's *Médée* overture for the plan of the first Allegro (sonata form with the subjects reversed in the

---

[1] Max Kalbeck, *Johannes Brahms*, i (1) (Berlin, 1908) p. 165.

recapitulation) and some short-breathed string figures; and to the operas of the 'Conservatoire composers' generally for the idea of a reminiscence-theme associated with the heroine of the symphony, recurring in modified forms in each movement. And this 'motto theme', borrowed from his cantata *Herminie* (1828), is the slender tie which holds together such disparate elements as the melody of the introduction – *Rêveries. Passions* (originally a song, 'Je vais donc quitter pour jamais', written in boyhood), the second and fifth movements – *Un bal* and *Songe d'une nuit du Sabbat* (one probably, the other almost certainly composed for a *Faust* ballet in 1828), the third – *Scène aux champs* (adapted from Act II of *Les Francs Juges* see p. 612), and the fourth – *Marche au supplice* (taken, all but the last 14 bars, from the *marche lugubre* in the last act of the same opera). However novel as a symphony and as a conception, the *Fantastique* is distillation – a highly individual distillation – of French 'Conservatoire opera'; Berlioz himself spoke of it as a *drame instrumental*. Its romanticism is 'horror romanticism', not – despite its autobiographical origin – the romanticism of subjective expression.

Berlioz followed the *Symphonie fantastique* with a *Grande Ouverture du 'Roi Lear'* (1831) and a second symphony, *Harold en Italie* (1834), which borrows its hero, but nothing else, from Byron's *Childe Harold*. This is a programmatic *sinfonie concertante*, the solo instrument being a viola which 'impersonates' the hero. But the hero is only an observer of scenes[2] – in the mountains ('Scènes de mélancolie, de bonheur et de joie'), passing pilgrims singing their evening prayer, an Abruzzi mountaineer serenading his mistress, brigands carousing – and his personal theme, recurring in all four movements, which had previously impersonated Diana Vernon and Mary, Queen of Scots,[3] is not transformed like the *idée fixe* of the *Fantastique*. The influence of Beethoven is apparent in *Harold*: of the first movement of the Seventh Symphony in the first allegro, of its Allegretto in the pilgrims' procession, and the opening of the finale of the Ninth in the 'souvenirs de scènes précédentes' which interrupt the beginning of the brigand scene. While the four movements of *Harold* correspond freely with those of a normal symphony, *Roméo et Juliette* (1839) – 'symphonie dramatique, avec choeurs, solos de chant et prologue en récitatif choral' – completely shattered the old symphonic framework and opened the way to a new, hardly definable conception of 'symphony'. It is true that the traditional four movements are embedded in it:

No. 2: Romeo alone and the Capulets' ball (Andante malincolico, leading to Allegro)
No. 3: Love scene (Adagio) – after the allegretto chorus of the young Capulets

---

[2] Like Byron's Harold, Berlioz's could say:
    I live not in myself, but I become
    Portion of that around me.
[3] In two abandoned works, a *Rob Roy* overture and a *fantaisie dramatique, Les derniers Instans de Marie Stuart*.

No. 4: Queen Mab (Scherzo: Prestissimo)
No. 6: Scene at the tomb (Allegro agitato), with distorted reminiscences of No. 3

These are purely orchestral and the first three include some of the most exquisite music Berlioz ever wrote, full of what one can only call 'orchestral imagination' of the highest order. But the tomb scene, based like other details of the symphony on Garrick's acting version of the play, illustrates the action point by point and could be used for a mimed performance on a stage – or in the mind of an imaginative listener. Yet this symphonic core, which is not unified by key, is surrounded by other elements: No. 1, which consists of (*a*) an orchestral introduction (the riot in the streets and the Prince's intervention), (*b*) the *prologue en récitatif choral*, culminating in the love-theme of No. 3, (*c*) two *strophes* for contralto commenting on this, (*d*) a 'Queen Mab' scherzetto for tenor and chorus; No. 5, Juliet's funeral procession, a scene inserted by Garrick, for chorus and orchestra; and No. 7, a *grand opéra* finale with renewed quarrel, recitative and *air* for Friar Laurence, and double-choral oath of reconciliation.

In 1840 Berlioz wrote a fourth symphony, again on a different pattern: a *Symphonie funèbre et triomphale* – originally *Symphonie militaire* – for the official commemoration of the tenth anniversary of the July Revolution. Intended for outdoor performance and scored for a huge wind-band (to which Berlioz later added optional string parts and, near the end of the final 'Apothéose', a chorus), it is in the direct tradition of the monumental compositions of Gossec and his colleagues in the 1790s. The first movement is a funeral march fit for heroes, and the central 'Oraison funèbre' is none the worse for the fact that its trombone solo originated as a tenor recitative and cavatina in the last Act of *Les Francs Juges*. Berlioz went on to write two more concert overtures, both extremely brilliant, in 1844 – *Le Carnaval romain*, based on music from *Benvenuto Cellini* (see p. 707), and *Le Corsaire*, dubiously after Byron since it was first performed as *La Tour de Nice* and then re-named *Le Corsaire rouge* from Fenimore Cooper's *The Red Rover* – and in 1848 the masterly *March funèbre pour la dernière scène d'Hamlet*. But no more symphonies.

SPOHR AND THE PROGRAMME-SYMPHONY

Berlioz's symphonies are, in the biological sense, sports. They had little or no immediate influence on the symphony as a form though it is possible that they encouraged Spohr, who long before had provided his *Faust* overture with a printed programme (see p. 591), to break out in such experiments as the 'characteristic tone-painting in form of a symphony', *Die Weihe der Töne* (1832). Like the *Fantastique*, this has a programme – a poem by Karl Pfeiffer which Spohr had originally intended to set as a cantata and which he told Wilhelm Speyer (letter of 9 October 1832) 'must be printed and distributed in the hall or read aloud before the performance' – and it has a meaningless

and barely perceptible motto-motive which appears at the very beginning
(i), in the ensuing allegro (ii), and later, e.g. in the 'march to battle' (iii):

Ex. 255

The programme is a 'Creation' poem beginning with the 'numbed silence of
Nature before the creation of Sound' (26 bars of largo introduction) and
proceeding to the (allegro) awakening of life, the normal second subject
being replaced by a burst of bird-song and the development by conventional
storm music depicting the 'tumult of the elements'. The second movement
has three components, lullaby (3/8), dance (2/8), and serenade (3/16), which
are rather unnaturally combined later, and the third movement consists of
march to battle/feelings of those left behind/return of the victors, and coda
'Te Deum'. The most interesting innovation is the slow finale, perhaps the
first of its kind: 'Funeral music' (the hymn 'Begrabt den Leib') and
'Consolation in Tears'. After a conventional Fifth Symphony (1837) Spohr
made a more novel experiment, an *Historische Symphonie* (1839) 'in the style
and taste of four different periods. I. Bach-Handel period, 1720; II. Adagio,
Haydn-Mozart period, 1780; III. Scherzo, Beethoven period, 1810; IV.
Finale, latest period of all'. Bach and Handel are characterized by a fugue
interrupted by a pastoral *siciliana*, Haydn and Mozart by a typical Spohr
larghetto; the 'Beethoven' scherzo opens promisingly with a theme on three
timpani tuned to G, D, E flat but fails to fulfil the promise, and
contemporaneity is satirized by the noisy over-orchestration of exceedingly
trivial ideas. The *Historische* was followed by *Irdisches und Göttliches im
Menschenleben* (1841) for two orchestras, a large one representing the
'earthly' element, and one of eleven solo instruments the 'divine', and the
three movements are entitled 'World of childhood', 'Victory of the
passions', and 'Final victory of the divine', where both orchestras join in an
adagio coda. Last of all, between normal Eighth and Tenth symphonies
(1847 and 1857), came a fairly conventional two-movement *Die Jahreszeiten*
(1850), 'Winter-Spring' and 'Summer-Autumn'. Despite his unsuccessful
satire of the 'latest period of all', and despite the limitations of his talent,

Spohr's programme symphonies at least demonstrate an openness to innovatory ideas that was not shared by his younger German contemporaries.

MENDELSSOHN'S ORCHESTRAL FORMS

First among these was Mendelssohn who had already produced a very respectable symphony at the age of 15 (see p. 612). None of its successors, their composition spread over several years – the *Reformationssinfonie*, No. '5' (1829–30), the 'Italian', No. '4' (1833), the *Lobgesang*, No. '2' (1840), the 'Scottish', No. '3' (1831–42) – was quite conventional, but their unconventionality was calculated not to shock the most genteel listener. 'Classical' techniques were applied to non-classical musical ideas. The *Reformation* Symphony, celebrating the tercentenary of the Augsburg Confession, introduces the 'Amen' of the Dresden liturgy in the first movement and 'Ein' feste Burg' in the finale, but except for the Allegro vivace second movement it is a lifeless work. Mendelssohn himself later took the view that it should be burned but it was unfortunately published twenty years after his death. The *Lobgesang*, a disastrous attempt to follow Beethoven in a symphony with choral finale, is equally regrettable.

The 'Italian' Symphony, conceived in Italy at the same time as Berlioz's *Harold* when the two young men were rather uneasy comrades, is a different matter; the opening is brilliant, full of youthful *élan*, and while genuine inspiration quickly fades, Mendelssohn's skilled craftsmanship sustains the sheer momentum of the movement. The Andante con moto has been nicknamed 'pilgrims' march' though the tramping bass seems to march on organ-pedals quite as much as on a dusty road; like Berlioz's, it reflects the Allegretto of Beethoven's Seventh. There is a touch of genuine romanticism in the middle section of the third movement, and the saltarello finale in A minor (the tonic minor of the symphony) recaptures the zest of the first movement. There is little zest in the 'Scottish', bar the delightful Vivace second movement, but there is evocative melancholy in the slow introduction, a travel impression of Holyrood Palace, which is recalled at the end of the first allegro. Indeed the whole symphony is marked to be played without a break: one of Mendelssohn's little innovations. But this ponderous work, with its grandiose final Allegro maestoso assai, is far inferior to another travel impression from Scotland, the piece originally entitled *Ouvertüre zur einsamen Insel*, later *Die Hebriden* (1830), later still *Isles of Fingal* (1832), and finally published in 1835 as *Fingals Höhle*. This is a masterpiece comparable with the *Midsummer Night's Dream* overture (see p. 612). The opening bars, jotted down at Tobermory (before Mendelssohn had seen Fingal's Cave), by themselves at once conjure up a vision of grey sea and lowering cloud and, in contrast with so many of his later works, the continuation while less inspired than the opening does not depreciate it. How fine, for instance, is the *pp* ending!

Mendelssohn's three mature concertos, G minor (1831) and D minor

(1837) for piano and E minor (1844) for violin, all break gently with convention. But they break. The old concerto idea is dead; they are simply sonata-like show-pieces for soloist and orchestra. The orchestra begins with no more than a few introductory bars – not even those in the Violin Concerto. All three are played without a break, the same linking music being used at the end of the first movement of the very Weberian G minor concerto and the beginning of the finale. The finale also briefly recalls the second subject of the first movement, though not its *echt romantisch* major/minor repeat and its continuation in D flat. Equally romantic is the E major slow movement, which Mendelssohn was to half remember when he came to write the nocturne in his incidental music for *A Midsummer Night's Dream* in 1842. The ever-popular Violin Concerto is quintessential Mendelssohn: light-handed, a pleasant, strikingly effective first movement, skilful transition passages, a sentimental slow movement, and a finale in which the old fairy magic of the early *Dream* overture alternates with commonplace.

CONCERT OVERTURES OF THE 1830S

In none of his other overtures did Mendelssohn reach the level of the *Dream* or *Fingal's Cave*. The one on Goethe's *Meeresstille und Glückliche Fahrt* (1828–32) is commonplace and obvious. That to Grillparzer's *Märchen von der schönen Melusine* (1833) is pervaded by a charming theme suggesting flowing water, but the rest of the material is as flaccid as much of Spohr. As for *Ruy Blas* (1839), since Mendelssohn thought Victor Hugo's play 'quite detestable' and mocked at his own overture, it is reasonable to surmise that with its histrionism and heavy trombone scoring it is a deliberate parody of Berlioz. Beside these we may place the overtures of his disciples, the Englishmen George Macfarren (1813–87) and William Sterndale Bennett (1816–75), the Dane Niels Gade (1817–90). Their youthful works, Sterndale Bennett's *Parisina* (1835), *Naiads* (1836), and *Wood-nymphs* (1838), Macfarren's *Chevy Chace* (1836), Gade's *Efterklang af Ossian* (1839), were their best; they went on to write symphonies – Bennett had already composed three or four, and three piano concertos, before *Parisina*, Macfarren six before *Chevy Chace*, but they were still-born; Gade's Fourth in B flat (1850) is appropriately dedicated to Spohr. But Ossian is genuinely evoked in the first theme of his overture:

Ex. 256

which is later on played *ff* by woodwind, horns, and trombones in octaves, accompanied by great full arpeggiated chords on violins, violas, and harp. And if Sterndale Bennett is to Berlioz what Samuel Palmer was to Delacroix, there is genuine watercolour poetry in *The Naiads*:

Ex. 257

Macfarren's *Chevy Chace* is a brilliant 'hunting' overture with a beautiful andante first statement of the old ballad tune to 'God prosper long our noble king' by violins divisi in four parts, and when one has deciphered the untidy autograph score[4] – it was never published – one understands why it was admired by both Mendelssohn and Richard Wagner.

Wagner himself[5] was at the same time learning to orchestrate, mainly by writing overtures. Some of them – the D minor of 1831 and the C major with final fugue of 1832, like the C major Symphony also of 1832 – are hardly more than exercises in classical scoring. The overture to Raupach's *König Enzio* in the same year shows that he had been studying Cherubini's *Anacreon*, while the Andante of the Symphony finds him conflating within three bars (18–20) echoes of Beethoven's Ninth, Seventh, and Fifth. Yet in another overture begun at the same time, though not finished till 1836, *Polonia*, afterglow of the Polish Rising and partly based on Polish melodies, he looks forward forty years to the funeral march not of an heroic nation but of a single hero:

[4] Cambridge, Fitzwilliam Museum.
[5] 1813–83.

Ex. 258

The overture (1834) to his opera *Die Feen* (see p. 705), Weberian as it is, reveals more of his future self than the first movement of an E major Symphony which he sketched seven months later.

In all these essays his sole conception of structure was conventional sonata form. Next year he temporarily and unsuccessfully broke with convention in an overture to his friend Theodor Apel's play *Christoph Columbus*, of which he later gave an amusing description in *Mein Leben*.[6] After 32 bars of *pp* 'sea' music, chords and murmuring diminished sevenths in E flat, allegro molto agitato, the key suddenly changes to D and *pp* trumpets sound a fanfare representing a '*fata morgana*, the surmised land which the hero again and again thinks he sees'. After more 'sea', always in E flat but growing to *ff*, interrupted by more trumpet calls (D and B flat, later C, D, and E flat), comes a longer, more connected stretch of 'sea' music, now with 'a powerful, yearning and striving theme' (Columbus himself?) which was 'the only comprehensible thing in the rolling sea of its surroundings'.

[6] Munich (1911), p. 120.

The end is all too obviously copied from that of Mendelssohn's *Glückliche Fahrt* which Wagner had just conducted, but with six trumpets instead of Mendelssohn's three.

CHANGES IN THE ORCHESTRAL BRASS

The trumpets of *Columbus* are the old 'natural' instruments. Mendelssohn never took advantage of the new valve mechanism for brass. Berlioz had clung to natural horns, though he sometimes introduced *trompettes à pistons* – but from the first, like most French composers, he preferred *cornets à pistons*. Wagner had, as we have seen in Ex. 258, written for valve-trumpets as well as a pair of natural ones in *Polonia*. In his next three overtures – *Ouvertüre zu Goethes Faust. Ier Theil* (January 1840; revised in 1855 and called *Eine Faust-Ouvertüre*), to *Rienzi* (October 1840) and *Der fliegende Holländer* (November 1841) (see pp. 713–4) – he scored for pairs of valve and natural horns and valve and natural trumpets, though he had yet to evolve that free use of valve-horns which was to revolutionize the sound of the nineteenth-century orchestra. All three show the influence of Beethoven's Ninth Symphony: *Faust* and the *Dutchman* in choice of key and actual material, while in the original version of the *Rienzi* introduction the melody of Rienzi's prayer was played by cellos and basses like the 'Freude' melody in the symphony[7] before being taken up in full, harmonized scoring.[8]

SCHUMANN AND THE SYMPHONY

While Wagner was composing these overtures, another German master entered the field of orchestral composition: Robert Schumann (1810–56). He had already made several uncompleted essays, notably a symphony in G minor (1833)[9] and two or three piano concertos. But his real beginning was in 1841 with two symphonies, in B flat and D minor (the latter completely revised and numbered '4' in 1851), an 'Overture, Scherzo and Finale', Op. 52 – in other words a symphony with no slow movement – and a *Fantasie* in A minor for piano and orchestra which was converted into a concerto by the addition of two more movements in 1845. Both symphonies, and Op. 52 to an even greater extent, suffer from the fact that Schumann was essentially a lyrical piano miniaturist; his themes are not particularly orchestral and do not lend themselves readily to large-scale expansion – the allegro theme of the D minor is more like passage-work than a genuine theme – so he does

---

[7] See John Deathridge, *Wagner's 'Rienzi': a reappraisal based on a study of the sketches and drafts* (Oxford, 1977), pp. 131–2.
[8] Both *Faust* and the *Dutchman* underwent considerable changes, the latter particularly in 1846, 1852, and 1860, removing a great deal of heavy brass, adding more poetic endings, and so on. (See Paul Machlin, 'Wagner, Durand and *The Flying Dutchman*: the 1852 revisions of the overture', *M & L*, lv (1974), p. 410.) The 1860 version of the *Dutchman* substitutes 21 bars in pure *Tristan* style for the original music and there was a similar, though less awkward, insertion (pp. 21–2 of the Eulenburg miniature score) in *Faust*.
[9] Miniature score, ed. Marc Andreae (Frankfurt, 1972).

what he can with modulation and sequence. Like Mendelssohn's best symphonies, they are 'absolute' music with a light extra-musical connotation in the case of the B flat and the later E flat (1850).

The B flat is known to be a 'Spring' symphony and the opening horn and trumpet call was verbally inspired by the last line of a poem by Adolf Böttger: 'Im Thale blüht der Frühling auf' (In the valley Spring begins to bloom); in diminution it provides the first allegro molto theme and a reminiscence of it is played by the trombones, marcatissimo, in the finale ('Spring's farewell'). Near the end of the slow movement the same instruments, *pp*, sound a new idea which is immediately taken up as the theme of the scherzo, which follows without a break. (It has two trios, the first in 2/4 time.) By such devices Schumann tries to mute the 'suite'-like feeling of the work as a whole. He originally intended to call Op. 52 'Suite'. In the D minor Symphony this striving for organic unity is carried further; the 'passage-work' first subject is put into the major to provide the second subject, in the development it punctuates on the strings a new idea played by the wind, and then on the violas, poco marcato, it accompanies a fresh *dolce* melody of the first violins:

Ex. 259

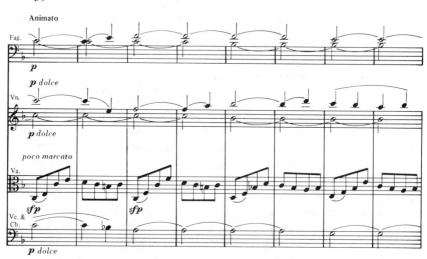

It also plays an important part in the Largo which connects scherzo with finale without a break. The quaver-moving theme of the slow introduction to the symphony also provides much of the *romanza* slow movement, with a triplet arabesque version on a solo violin, and – inverted – in the scherzo while the trio is based on the triplet-arabesque variant. When he drastically revised the symphony in 1851, reorchestrating with a heavy hand, he tightened the quasi-organic unity still further; it is true he took out the 'passage-work' theme from the equivalent of Ex. 259 but he inserted it elsewhere, in the slow introduction and on violas, cellos, and basses in the first four bars of the finale. Further, he directed that the whole work, which he first thought of calling a 'Symphonistische Phantasie', be played without a break. In this form, a determined attempt at a compressed, unified type of symphony, the work is an historic milestone as important as Berlioz's strivings in the opposite direction.

In his C major Symphony, No. '2' (1846), he actually borrows his unifying device from Berlioz and Spohr: a motto-theme heard at the beginning and near the end of the first movement, at the end of the 2/4 scherzo (second movement), and near the end of the finale.[10] But whereas Berlioz's motto-themes are at least symbols, Schumann's is no more than a rubber-stamp, though more effective than Spohr's (Ex. 255), and later symphonists were content to use the device in the same way. He does not introduce it at all in by far the finest movement, the Adagio, (quoted in the finale, bars 215ff.). In his E flat Symphony, No. '3', the so-called 'Rhenish' (1850), Schumann turns his back on unifying devices and composes his most suite-like work. It even has five movements: an exuberant *lebhaft* (he now abandoned Italian tempo markings) in which he at last achieves long paragraphs of organic, 'logical' symphonic thought; a leisurely so-called scherzo originally entitled 'Morning on the Rhine'; a tender romantic *nicht schnell*; a profound and impressive *feierlich* Adagio inspired by a great ceremony in Cologne Cathedral (a movement which lifts the work above, say, Mendelssohn's 'Italian' which it resembles in genre); and a rather square-cut open-airy finale with references to the Cathedral movement.

THE ROMANTIC CONCERTO

Schumann's Piano Concerto is as innovatory as his D minor Symphony. He had told his bride Clara 'I can't write a concerto for virtuosi; I must think of something a little different'. The result was certainly not a bravura piece; even less than Mendelssohn's is it a concerto in the classical sense. The material of the first movement is very Mendelssohnian and he follows Mendelssohn in dispensing with an opening tutti, but instead of a brilliant cadenza he provides a rather dreamy written-out quasi-improvisation; the slow movement is essentially an intimate, almost chamber-music conversation for piano and orchestra; and even the finale has fire – and charm – without fireworks. In his last years of sanity he produced other works for solo instruments and orchestra but generally preferred to call them *Concertstück, Fantasie, Concert Allegro*. The only concertos were for cello (1850) and for violin (1853); neither shows him at his best and the Violin

---

[10] The new theme on the oboe at bar 280 and the violin reply (bars 288–91) refer to the first song of Beethoven's cycle *An die ferne Geliebte* (see p. 645) ('nach den fernen Triften sehend, wo ich dich Geliebte fand') and at bar 418 Schumann quotes, not for the first time in his music (see p. 763), from the last song, 'Nimm sie hin denn, diese Lieder', followed by the motto-theme *pp*. It is tempting to guess at a hidden programme for the whole symphony: the struggle against obstacles to marriage in the first movement, yearning and devotion in the third, and love triumphant in the finale.

Concerto is conventional even in beginning with more than fifty bars of tutti. Nor are the independent overtures Schumann composed in 1851, to Schiller's *Braut von Messina*, Shakespeare's *Julius Caesar*, and Goethe's *Hermann und Dorothea*, memorably inspired. His best overtures are those to his opera *Genoveva* (1848) (see p. 713), to Byron's *Manfred* (1848), and to Goethe's *Faust* (1853). The *Manfred* is a masterly character study, as indeed is the *Faust*; both are marked by the rather angular themes that originated in Schumann's study of Bach's fugues. Even the rather thick scoring is not ineffective in *Manfred*, and in the following incidental music, for instance Manfred's adjuration to the Witch of the Alps, Schumann scores more light-handedly and imaginatively than anywhere else except perhaps in the sunrise (composed 1849) in the *Szenen aus Goethes 'Faust'*.

Mendelssohn, Schumann, and Berlioz had no serious rivals or successors during the 1830s and 1840s. None of the five violin concertos of Ferdinand David (1810–73),[11] a pupil of Spohr, challenge comparison with Mendelssohn, although he contributed much advice to his friend's work and was the first to perform it; his own first (published in 1837) is likewise in E minor and likewise with connected movements. The later piano concertos of Moscheles[12] and the F minor Concerto of Adolph Henselt (1814–89) are much finer. Moscheles was now following in the wake not of Hummel but of Weber and Mendelssohn's G minor; his No. 6 (*Concerto fantastique*) (1833) is in four movements, of which the last three are connected and the second and third look back thematically to the first. His masterpiece was No. 7 in C minor (*Concerto pathétique*) (1836) in which the virtuoso element is played down and the form is novel: an allegro maestoso followed by an allegro agitato alternating with andante espressivo, the theme of the agitato (i) being completely transformed in the second andante (ii), and again in the third movement, allegro con brio (iii):

Ex. 260

---

[11] The *odes-symphonies* of Ferdinand's French namesake and exact contemporary, Félicien David (1810–76) – *Le Désert* (1844) and *Christophe Colomb* (1847) – are feeble successors to *Roméo et Juliette*, despite some imaginative orchestration and the introduction in *Le Désert* of genuine melodies from the Middle East, where David had travelled. There are three movements: introduction for speaker and chorus, and 'marche de la caravane' interrupted by a *simoom*; invocation to Night (tenor solo), 'fantaisie arabe' and 'danse des almées' (orchestra only), chorus 'La liberté au désert', and 'rêverie du soir' (tenor); Sunrise, with 'chant du muezzim' and 'départ de la caravane' (chorus). The four movements of *Christophe Colomb* are similarly organized.
[12] See p. 615 on features of his earlier ones.

Moscheles' last concerto, *Pastorale* (1838), is interesting only in that it has a hidden programme which he revealed in a letter to Mendelssohn. The novelty of Henselt's Concerto (1844) lies less in the architecture than in the piano style. It is a full-blooded romantic virtuoso concerto, complete with dramatic introductory tutti (allegro patetico). Instead of a development, muted strings introduce a new hymnlike idea which is then taken up by the piano in great chords and sweeping arpeggios needing three staves for their notation. The slow movement is a very beautiful Chopinesque nocturne in D flat, with typically widespread left-hand part and a middle section in C sharp minor which demands four staves to show its then novel layout:

Ex. 261

'TONE-PICTURES', 'OVERTURES', AND 'TONE-POEMS'

The Henselt concerto is in the mainstream of romantic orchestral music; the symphonies – *Sérieuse* and *Capricieuse* (both 1842), *Singulière* and E flat (both 1845) – of the Swede Franz Berwald (1796–1868) stand right outside it. To begin with, they are not, like so much romantic music, essentially piano music orchestrated but conceived directly for orchestra. The most characteristic ideas are mainly diatonic, classical in their simplicity; the forms are clear and concise, the textures spare and transparent with long-held pedal-notes and motives much repeated. There is no romantic emotion or rhetoric; the symphonies are 'absolute music', though Berwald did also write what he called *Tongemälde* (tone-pictures), of which the best is *Erinnerung an die norwegischen Alpen* (1842). Yet 'pure' as his music may be, it can communicate an indefinable *frisson* as in the second subject of the Adagio (in the middle of which occurs the scherzo) of the *Symphonie singulière*:[13]

Ex. 262

---

[13] Miniature score (Copenhagen, 1947).

In the very year of Berwald's *Symphonie singulière* a Russian musician visiting Spain composed a *Capriccio brillante* on the Aragonese *jota*, later styled 'Spanish Overture, No. 1', which was orchestrated in a manner remarkable for its bright, pure, transparent colouring. Mikhail Ivanovich Glinka (1804–57) had already displayed an outstanding orchestral sense in his overture and incidental music to Nestor Kukolnik's tragedy *Knyaz Kholmsky* (1840), which still reveals his respect for the beloved *Médée* overture of Cherubini, even more in the overture and dances in his second opera, *Ruslan i Lyudmila* (1842) (see p. 719). In 1848 he produced a companion piece to the *Capriccio* – *Recuerdos de Castilla* (later rewritten as 'Night in Madrid: Spanish Overture No. 2') – and a 'Wedding song and Dance song' on two Russian folk-tunes, later named *Kamarinskaya* after the dance-tune. Glinka had earlier tried unsuccessfully to base a symphony on Russian themes; he had tried unsuccessfully to write a three-hand piano piece on the 'Kamarinskaya' tune; now in 1848 he produced something much smaller than a symphony but infinitely more important to the development of Russian music than the First Symphony of Anton Rubinstein (1829–94) two years later. *Kamarinskaya* proved to be a model for extended orchestral treatment of folk-themes without destroying their essence, setting them in relief against ever-changing backgrounds as Field had done with this very tune forty years earlier (see Ex. 240).

Glinka's adoption of the term 'overture' for his Spanish pieces is significant of its general use in the mid-century for almost any one-movement orchestral piece with a more or less descriptive title. But it was soon to be rivalled by another vogue-term of which we get a hint in the long 'explanation' which the Anglo-Alsatian Henry Litolff (1818–91) wished to be printed 'on the back of the programme' when his overture *Maximilien Robespierre* (1850) was performed: 'The tone-poem (*Tondichtung*) forms not merely the musical introduction to Robert Griepenkerl's tragedy of the same name but also gives . . . a quite independent life- and character-picture of the national hero. . . .' And he goes on to give a much more detailed 'programme' than Berlioz ever provided. More important than *Robespierre* were the concert-overtures of the same period which the Hungarian pianist-composer Franz Liszt (1811–86) roughed out and first, since he did not trust his knowledge of orchestration, handed for scoring to a young friend, August Conradi (1821–73), composer of symphonies (and later of operettas). From the beginning of 1850 Conradi's versions were superseded by those of

Liszt's factotum Joachim Raff (1822–82), always under Liszt's supervision,[14] and in this way Liszt himself gradually mastered an individual
orchestral style indebted less to Berlioz – Liszt's music was basically too
pianistic to profit much from him – than to Meyerbeer.[15] Indeed one
has only to examine the score of Meyerbeer's overture to his brother's
tragedy *Struensee* (1846), a work one could easily supply with a programme
as precise as Litolff's to *Maximilien Robespierre*, in order to recognize Liszt's
indebtedness not only to Meyerbeer's scoring in pure instrumental groupings – note the dynamic markings – such as the opening:

Ex. 263

and the repetition of this theme by brass choir (horns, valve trumpets,
trombones, and ophicleide) but also to his instrumental recitative or arioso
(the cello theme in C sharp minor which immediately follows).

Liszt's earliest *Concert-Ouvertüren* were *Ce qu'on entend sur la montagne*
and *Die vier Elemente* which Raff 'partly scored and clean copied' in January
1850. The former, also described as *Bergsymphonie* and *Méditation
Symphonie*, had been suggested by an ode in Victor Hugo's *Feuilles
d'automne*; the other originated as an overture to four projected male
choruses with words by Joseph Autran – 'La Terre', 'Les Aquilons', 'Les
Flots', 'Les Astres' – with the collective title *Les quatre Élémens*. In 1849
came an overture for Goethe's drama *Tasso*, in 1850 an overture to Liszt's

---

[14] Autograph facsimiles of the opening of *Tasso* in Liszt's original sketch, Conradi's score, Raff's score,
and various emendations by Liszt, are given at the end of Peter Raabe, *Franz Liszt* (Stuttgart and Berlin,
1931), ii.
[15] See p. 590, n. 18, and below, pp. 705–7.

choruses from Herder's *Der entfesselte Prometheus*, in 1851 an orchestral version of the fourth of his *Études d'exécution transcendante* (see p. 762) which he had named *Mazeppa*, and in 1854 an orchestral prelude (and postlude on the same themes) to a performance of Gluck's *Orpheus* at Weimar, a prelude, *Festklänge*, to Schiller's 'Huldigung der Künste', an orchestral piece *Hungaria*, interesting for its national flavour, and possibly the definitive form of *Heroïde funèbre*, the first movement of a long projected 'Revolutionssymphonie'. When these works were published in 1856–7 they were styled *symphonische Dichtungen* (symphonic poems) and provided, possibly by Liszt himself, possibly by his mistress the Princess Carolyne von Sayn-Wittgenstein, with prefaces and in one or two cases with *ex post facto* 'programmes'. Thus *Die vier Elemente* was rechristened *Les Préludes* and prefaced by a completely spurious quotation allegedly 'd'après Lamartine', while a middle section, 'allegretto mosso con grazia', was inserted in *Tasso* and the piece was now said to suggest three cities associated with different stages of the poet's life: Venice, Ferrara, and Rome.

INNOVATIONS IN CONCERTO AND SYMPHONY

Liszt claimed later that throughout his first period at Weimar (1848–61) he had been inspired by 'une grande idée: celle du renouvellement de la Musique par son alliance plus intime avec la Poésie; un développement plus libre, et pour ainsi dire, plus *adéquat* à l'esprit de ce temps'.[16] But this fertilization of music did not imply the subordination of musical forms to literary ideas. He introduces tone-painting of a type long familiar, but his titles and programmes are only general clues to the extra-musical meanings, like Beethoven's and Berlioz's and Spohr's. It was only later that he occasionally, as in the *Zwei Episoden aus Lenaus 'Faust'* (1860) – particularly the first, the 'Procession at night' – attempted musical depiction of a succession of events. The peculiarity of his large-scale forms, their lack of organic continuity, was conditioned not by literary programmes but by the fact that they are essentially enlargements and elaborations of the symmetrically disposed sectional forms typical of romantic piano music[17] (see Chapter 37); and his cohesive, unifying device – sometimes only partially successful, sometimes brilliantly so – is the centuries-old one of theme-transformation, most recently practised by Schubert in the 'Wanderer' Fantasia (which Liszt arranged for piano and orchestra) and by Berlioz, Moscheles, and others. He was almost justified in his claim[18] that *Les Préludes* was 'construirt' from:

---

[16] Letter of 16 November 1860, *Franz Liszts Briefe*, iii (Leipzig, 1894), p. 135.
[17] Basically pianistic, too, was his requirement of almost unprecedented flexibility of performance in his orchestral music: e.g. 'a poco a poco più di moto' spread over 48 bars in *Les Préludes*, and the R . . . . . and A. . . . signs in *Orpheus* indicating 'slight Ritardandi and Accelerandi'.
[18] Letter of 24 May 1856, ibid., viii, p. 127.

683

Ex. 264

But it was 'constructed', it did not grow.

Liszt had already constructed two piano concertos, conceived in the 1830s and completed in 1849 though subsequently revised two or three times, on similar lines. The first of them, in E flat, was dedicated to Litolff – very appropriately, for Litolff, a pupil of Moscheles, had in his B minor *Concerto symphonique* (1844) introduced the scherzo in the concerto, an innovation which Liszt adopted. Indeed Litolff and Liszt have much in common; in all his *concertos symphoniques*, particularly the D minor (1854), Litolff makes the orchestra the equal, if not the superior, partner of the piano as Liszt does both in his concertos and in the exactly contemporary *Totentanz* on the 'Dies irae', though Litolff does not connect the movements as Liszt does; his scherzos, too, have a 'demonic' quality akin to the finale of Liszt's *Faust* Symphony and the second of the *Episoden aus 'Faust'*, the 'Dance in the Village Inn (Mephisto Waltz)'. But Litolff's invention is far less memorable than Liszt's.

Eine Faust-Symphonie in drei Charakterbildern (1854) might be regarded as a triptych of three of his finest symphonic poems. The character-portraits are of Faust, Gretchen, and Mephistopheles, the scherzo-finale being based on mocking distortions of Faust's themes, and in 1857 Liszt had the not altogether happy idea of adding an epilogue in which a solo tenor and male chorus (plus organ) sing Goethe's closing words, the chief Gretchen theme being adapted for 'the Eternal Feminine'. *Eine Symphonie zu Dantes Divina Commedia* (1856) was also originally conceived as a triptych but ultimately a choral setting of the Magnificat, for women's voices, was substituted for a representation of Paradise. Instrumental recitative and themes derived from it always play an important part in Liszt's music and at the beginning of the *Dante* Symphony he actually prints the words – the famous inscription on the portal of Hell – under the notes, as he does later in the movement when the cor anglais sings 'Nessùn maggior dolore. . . .'

THE 'NEW GERMAN SCHOOL'

Elements of Liszt's music – notably its frequent incoherence as pure music, the bold unorthodoxy of its harmony, the element of empty showiness which was an unlucky legacy of his career as a virtuoso pianist – aroused intense hostility among many German musicians, a hostility which he compounded by his championship as conductor of the 'progressive' works of Berlioz, Wagner, and younger men. But enmity was counterbalanced by the enthusiastic devotion of his disciples, some of whom talked of a 'new German school' of composition. Prominent among them were Peter Cornelius

684

(1824–74), nephew of the 'Nazarene' painter, the Czech Bedřich Smetana (1824–84), and the pianist-conductor Hans von Bülow (1830–94), who was soon to become Liszt's son-in-law. And there were admirers among the less conservative composers beyond the close circle; for instance the Russian pianist Anton Rubinstein (1829–94) dedicated his non-programmatic second symphony, the *Ocean*, in its original four-movement form (1852)[19] to Liszt. Strangely, the members of the close circle were in no hurry to adopt the designation 'symphonic poem' and Bülow was not even able to decide what his first orchestral essay was supposed to illustrate. Composed *c.* 1853 as an overture to an unsuccessful tragedy, *Ein Leben im Tode* by Karl Ritter, it existed for several years as an untitled *Fantaisie*; in 1859 it was performed as 'a Symphonic Prologue to Byron's *Cain*' and two years later Liszt suggested Schiller's *Räuber* as possible alternative to *Cain*; in 1866 it was published as *Nirwana. Symphonisches Stimmungsbild*, in 1881 as *Nirwana. Orchesterphantasie in Ouvertürenform*. On the other hand, his orchestral *Ballade nach Uhlands Dichtung 'Des Sängers Fluch'* (1863) clearly reflects the sequence of events in the poem. Smetana seems not even to have heard the term 'symphonic poem' in 1858, for he described his *Richard III* in a letter as 'a sort of musical illustration, composed in one movement yet neither overture nor symphony, in short something that awaits a name'.[20] Both *Richard III* and its successor, described on the autograph score as '*Wallenstein's Camp*/by Fr. Schiller/orchestral composition' (1859), were performed in Prague in 1860 as 'fantasias'; in his diary of this period Smetana refers to them and to *Hakon Jarl* (1861), inspired by Adam Öhlenschläger's tragedy, as 'symphonies'; it was only later that he began to refer to them in correspondence as 'symphonic poems'.[21]

DEFECTIONS FROM THE LISZT CAMP

There were defections from the 'new German' group. As early as 1853 Raff was beginning to tire of his role, to feel oppressed by Liszt's overpowering personality, and to challenge his views, though he stayed at Weimar until 1856. The young leader of the Grand Ducal orchestra at Weimar, Joseph Joachim (1831–1907), whose overtures to *Hamlet* and Hermann Grimm's *Demetrius* (*c.* 1854) were much admired by Liszt, had already left in 1853 in the most friendly circumstances. But Joachim was almost immediately drawn into the Schumann circle, where the influence of Schumann's widow and her young friend Johannes Brahms (1833–97) was hostile to the 'new German' outlook. Joachim was attracted particularly closely to Brahms whose first big orchestral work, the D minor Piano Concerto (1858), underwent revisions at his hands.

---

[19] In 1864 Rubinstein added two more movements, in 1882 a seventh.
[20] Also in 1858 his pupil Jan Ludevít Prochazka (1837–88) began a symphony inspired by Vítězslav Hálek's poem *Alfred*, the first movement of which seems to have been the earliest Czech work to be styled 'symphonic poem'.
[21] Information kindly supplied by the late Alfons Waissar, formerly Director of the Smetana Museum at Prague.

Brahms was not at this time considered – so far as he was considered at all, for he was not yet well known – a conservative but rather, like Schumann and his circle generally, a neo-romantic. When the first of his two orchestral serenades, Opp. 11 and 16 (1858 and 1860), was performed at Hanover a local critic thought he was concerned 'above all to find a central point of unification between Beethoven and the newer romantic schools (including Berlioz), in order to gain a firm basis for further researches'.[22] But in that very same month, March 1860, a belligerent Brahms and unwilling Joachim were drawing up a public declaration 'deploring and condemning . . . the productions and new unheard-of theories of the leaders and followers of the so-called "New German" school . . . as contrary to the innermost nature of music'. Brahms was privately anxious to mention Liszt by name 'lest we should be accused of obduracy against Wagner, etc.',[23] but this was never made clear. Among others who signed or promised to sign were Carl Reinecke (1824–1910), Clara Schumann's half-brother Woldemar Bargiel (1828–97), and Max Bruch (1838–1920), but owing to premature publication in the Berlin *Echo* in May only four signatures appeared and the 'declaration' proved a very damp squib although it did draw an unfortunate line of demarcation. In 1862 Brahms left North Germany for Vienna where his music did become a 'central point' but not one of unification, and it was long before it included another purely orchestral work.

The most important music for orchestra being written at this time was indeed of the 'New German School' but it was not by Liszt and it was not for the most part composed for the concert-hall. The master who re-volutionized orchestral writing in the middle of the century was Wagner in his operas (see below, pp. 723–6). All the same, much of his music was performed in concert-halls, often before the complete works were staged; for instance, the three concerts he gave in Paris in January and February 1860 included not only the overtures to the *Holländer* and *Tannhäuser*, and the prelude to *Lohengrin*, but the prelude to *Tristan* (with the exquisite ending[24] which he wrote specially for these concerts). And the overture to *Die Meistersinger* was performed in Leipzig in October 1862, nearly six years before the first production. But these latter masterpieces, one a superb example of the most subtle scoring of advanced chromaticism, the other of diatonic orchestral polyphony, had no immediate influence on the music of the concert-hall.

SYMPHONIC MUSIC IN THE 1860S

The veteran Gade trudged on in the old Mendelssohn-Schumann line, reaching his Eighth Symphony in 1871 but never recapturing the in-spiration of his earliest days. His contemporary Robert Volkmann

---

[22] Max Kalbeck, *Johannes Brahms*, i (Berlin, 1908), p. 402.
[23] *Johannes Brahms im Briefwechsel mit Joseph Joachim* (Berlin, 1908), i, p. 274.
[24] It was published at once by Breitkopf in this form, so infinitely preferable to the musically senseless botching on of the 'Liebestod'.

(1815–83) surprisingly produced a first symphony, in D minor, in 1863 with a powerful opening promising more than it was quite able to fulfil:

Ex. 265

And the following year the forty-year-old Anton Bruckner (1824–96) also began a D minor Symphony (known as No. 'o') completed only in 1869 after the earliest ('Linz') version of his No. 1 in C minor (1866). Of the generation born *c.* 1840 Max Bruch is remembered not by the two symphonies he published in 1870 but by the first (G minor, 1868) of his three violin concertos, Hermann Goetz (1840–76) by his Symphony in F (1873). The man who was to emerge as one of the leading orchestral composers of the latter part of the century, the Czech Antonín Dvořák (1841–1904), had written three symphonies by 1873 while he was still a viola player in the Prague National Theatre orchestra but none had yet been performed. The finest 'new' symphony of the 1860s was Schubert's 'Unfinished', performed at last on 17 December 1865 and published the following year. But the typical symphonist of the period was Raff, a latter-day Spohr, a middle-of-the-road composer prepared to break with tradition but not to follow the lead of Liszt and Wagner. Beginning with *An das Vaterland* (1863), all but two of his eleven symphonies are tepidly programmatic. No. 3, *Im Walde* (1869), is in three parts (*Abtheilungen*): I – 'In the day: Impressions and emotions', II – 'Dreaming' (adagio) and 'Dryads' Dance' (scherzo), III –

687

'Night. Quiet stirring of night in the forest. Passing of the "wild hunt" with Holda (*Frau Holle*) and Wotan. Daybreak'. Night in the forest is suggested fugally; the 'wild hunt' is the only really pictorial element in the symphony. Raff's Fifth Symphony, *Lenore*, is likewise in three sections: I – 'Love's happiness' (two movements, allegro and andante quasi larghetto), II – 'Separation', III – 'Reunion in death. Introduction and Ballade (after Bürger's "Lenore")'. Again it is only the last section with its allusions to 'separation' and 'love's happiness' and the Berliozian gallop of the ghostly lover's horse that is programmatic. But the genuine note of the demonic was quite beyond Raff's powers. Still weaker are the *Alpensinfonie* (1877) and the four symphonies uninspired by the seasons from which they derive their titles (1878–82) with which he closed his symphonic output.

Even such a conservative musician as Joseph Rheinberger (1839–1901) was tempted to write a *Wallenstein* symphony – or *sinfonische Tongemälde*, as he called it (1867) – consisting of 'Prelude' (allegro con fuoco), 'Thekla' (adagio), 'Wallenstein's Camp' (scherzo), and 'Wallenstein's Death'. And Sterndale Bennett in 1862 so far moved with the times as to cast his fantasie-overture *Paradise and the Peri* not in sonata form but as an Introduction ('a Peri at the gate of Eden') and three Scenes – the young Indian warrior, the Egyptian lovers, the repentant Syrian sinner – each prefaced by a quotation from Moore's poem and the last returning to the material and key of the Introduction. There are a few programmatic suggestions but there is nothing 'New German' in the musical substance. One Englishman domiciled in Germany, Henry Hugo Pierson (properly Hugh Pearson) (1815–73), actually outdid the New Germans in one work, his 'Symphonic poem to the tragedy *Macbeth*' (pub. 1874), where the programmatic principle is reduced to absurdity, the music being incoherent in itself and comprehensible to the score-reader thanks only to the liberal scattering of poetic quotations.

Actually the younger New Germans were more interested in opera or piano music or songs than orchestral music for the concert-hall. Liszt himself wrote no more important orchestral works after 1860. One of his brightest hopes, Felix Draeseke (1835–1913), completed an enormous symphonic movement, *Julius Caesar*, based on a single motive, in 1860 but he then came under Wagner's spell and later turned completely away from programme-music. In fact Wagner generally supplanted Liszt as the standard-bearer of modernism and the name of the cause was now 'music of the future', not 'New Germanism'. Wagner himself adopted the word *Zukunftsmusik* (originally applied in mockery) in September 1860, four months after the appearance of the Brahms-Joachim attack on the New German School.

LISZT'S INTERNATIONAL PROTÉGÉS

Liszt, however, continued his benevolent look-out for rising talents in all countries. He did not particularly influence the music of the Norwegian

Edvard Grieg (1843–1907), for instance – beyond persuading him to give the second subject of his Piano Concerto (original version, 1868) to the trumpet instead of the cellos – but he encouraged him and furthered the performance of his music. (Grieg and his compatriot Johan Svendsen (1840–1911) found their own way from the Schumann-Gade idiom to a national style flavoured by folk-music; as early as 1866 Grieg had introduced a *hardingfele* – hardanger-fiddle – tune in the coda of his concert overture *In Autumn*.) Liszt had encouraged Smetana from 1856 onward; later he became a leading champion of the new generation of Russian composers.

The influence of Liszt and Berlioz during the 1860s was nowhere stronger than in Russia where Mily Alekseyevich Balakirev (1837–1910), a disciple of Glinka in his last years, was its focus. Balakirev's early orchestral works include an *Overture on Russian Themes* (1858), an overture and incidental music to *King Lear* (1859), and a *Second Overture on Russian Themes* (1864). This last, like so many orchestral works of the mid-century, underwent a number of revisions; when it was first published in 1869 it was described as a 'musical picture',[25] *1000 Years*, in allusion to the founding of a Russian State by Rurik in 862. In its final form of 1889 Balakirev's overture, reorchestrated but unchanged in substance, became a 'symphonic poem' *Rus* and the three folk-tunes were now alleged to 'characterize three elements of our history: paganism, the Muscovite way of life, and the semi-feudal, semi-republican element later revived among the Cossacks.' In the hands of Balakirev and two brilliant amateur disciples – Aleksandr Borodin (1833–87) and Nikolay Rimsky-Korsakov (1844–1908) – and Rubinstein's professional pupil Pyotr Ilyich Chaykovsky[26] (1840–93) a remarkable flowering of orchestral music began, much of it inspired by Russian literature or folk-music: Chaykovsky's overture *Groza* (The Storm), to Ostrovsky's play (1864), his First Symphony (1866), the 'symphonic fantasia' *Fatum* (1868), the first version of the overture-fantasia *Romeo and Juliet* (1869), Rimsky-Korsakov's First Symphony (original form, 1865), his 'musical picture' *Sadko* (1867) and the first version of his 'second symphony' *Antar* (1868) – a programmatic work with motto-theme suggested by *Harold in Italy* so far as plan is concerned but, like *Sadko*, deriving its musical language partly from Liszt and Balakirev – and Borodin's Symphony No. 1 in E flat (1867). Of the four symphonies Borodin's is decidedly the best. Rimsky-Korsakov's First is juvenile and jejune, and *Antar* – attractive and very brilliant in its later forms – is, as the composer came to recognize, a 'symphonic suite' rather than a symphony. Chaykovsky's G minor is a compilation: two sensitive and poetic movements corresponding to the work's title, 'Winter Daydreams', the scherzo an orchestral version of one written for a piano sonata, and a noisy extrovert

---

[25] Rubinstein had described his *Faust* (1864), all that remains of a projected *Faust* symphony, as a 'musically characteristic picture' and he applied the same term to his *Ivan IV* and *Don Quixote* (1869 and 1870).
[26] The element of mechanical manipulation in Chaykovsky's music, when inspiration fails, is usually pure Rubinstein.

finale; like *Antar*, it is a rather suite-like symphony. Borodin's too, with its Berliozian scherzo, its quasi-oriental andante, and its Schumannesque finale, is open to the same criticism, but the first movement is strikingly original in invention and construction. The thought-processes are by no means those of normal sonata-form: the theme (I*ab*) propounded in the adagio introduction is at once dissected in the allegro and rearranged in dizzying patterns to which the two scraps of 'second subject' (II*a* and *b*) are presently added, and it is only in the andantino coda that the cello line reveals the one-ness of *all* the thematic material:

Ex. 266

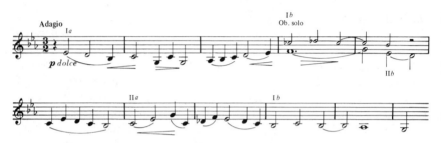

Whereas Rimsky-Korsakov's Third Symphony (C major, first version 1873) is a dry and colourless essay in pseudo-classicism, Chaykovsky's Second (C minor, first version 1872)[27] is the most national of all his symphonies, with material borrowed from Russian and Ukrainian folk-music. But the unrelated second movement, originally a wedding march from a destroyed opera, *Undine*, again suggests a suite and that suggestion is yet stronger in his Third Symphony (D major, 1875) with its alla tedesca second movement and polonaise finale. A much better work is the all-too-famous B flat minor Piano Concerto[28] of the same year, which derives its sense of unity from the wealth of sensuous, basically Italianate yet completely Russianized melody – often in D flat – of which Chaykovsky had produced an earlier example in the love-theme of *Romeo and Juliet*. A similar melody, this time in G flat, serves as love-music in his 'fantasia' *Burya* (Shakespeare's *Tempest*) (1873), a Lisztian patchwork of episodes: calm sea – Ariel raising the storm – Prospero chords – storm – the lovers – Ariel and Caliban – the lovers – Prospero chords – calm sea.

The masterpiece of Russian orchestral music of this period was Borodin's Second Symphony, in B minor (1876). The opening may have been suggested by Volkmann's (see Ex. 265) which had been played at St. Petersburg in 1865, but Borodin's theme (Ex. 267, i) is more compressed and more powerful, and he gives the movements extraordinary unity

---

[27] The first movement was completely rewritten in 1880, as was that of the First Symphony in 1874, in neither case for the better.

[28] Its powerful chordal effects and other features of the piano-writing seem to have been suggested by Rubinstein's D minor Concerto, No. 4, Op. 70 (1864). Rubinstein's E minor Concerto, Op. 25 (1850), is also marked by melodic and harmonic characteristics commonly regarded as Chaykovskian.

through a white heat of inspiration by which this idea is fused (iii) with the utterly different second subject (ii):

Ex. 267

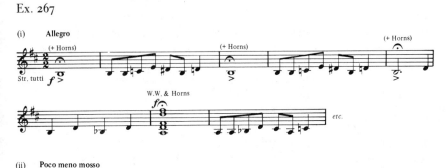

This Allegro is followed by a brilliantly original scherzo, a sensuous D flat Andante, and a 'heroic' and gorgeously coloured finale, the whole being unified by the fact that much of the material was drawn from a temporarily abandoned opera, *Prince Igor* (see p. 732).

RENAISSANCE IN FRANCE AFTER 1871

In France also there was, particularly after the war of 1870–1, a reawakening of interest in instrumental music. With Berlioz diverted to opera and choral works, French orchestral music had languished under the Second Empire. The hybrid of *ode-symphonie* initiated by Félicien David had been continued in the *symphonie orientale Le Sélam* (with text by Théophile Gautier) (1850) of Ernest Reyer (1823–1909) and the *Vasco de Gama* (1860) of Georges Bizet (1838–75). Pure symphonies had tended to be pleasant lightweight works in the styles of half a century earlier; such were the two by Charles Gounod (1818–93) and Bizet's C major, all three dating from 1854–5, and the E flat Symphony (1853) of Camille Saint-Saëns (1835–1921). Bizet also completed another C major symphony, a quasi-programmatic one entitled *Roma*, in 1868 and produced a post-war overture *Patrie* in 1873, but he was essentially a man of the theatre and his best purely orchestral work is his incidental music for Daudet's *L'Arlésienne* (1872). The renaissance of French orchestral music began with the foundation in 1871, even before the war was over, of the Société nationale de musique in which the prime mover was Saint-Saëns, a devoted Lisztian. With him were associated a number of prominent musicians, including the Liègois César Franck (1822–90) and his pupil Henri Duparc (1848–93), and Édouard Lalo (1823–92), whose five-movement *Symphonie espagnole* for violin and orchestra (1875) exemplifies a number of general tendencies of the time: approximation of symphony and concerto, suite-like expansion, exploitation of extra-national idioms.

For the concerts of the Société Saint-Saëns wrote his first *poème symphonique*, *Le Rouet d'Omphale* (1872). The form was still so unfamiliar in France that he described it as 'un nouveau moule qui fera époque dans l'histoire de l'art'.[29] But his work is less Lisztian than he claimed; based on an earlier rondo for piano, it stems from the French tradition of elegant pictorialism. As he says in his preface to the score, 'the subject . . . is feminine seductiveness . . . The spinning-wheel [an anachronism] is only a pretext chosen solely from the point of view of rhythm and the general style of the piece. Those interested in the search for details will detect at letter J Hercules groaning in the bonds he is unable to break and at letter L Omphale mocking his vain efforts.' These faint 'details' provide the middle section of a ternary form. The plan of *Phaéton* (1875) is similar; in *Danse macabre* (also 1875) variations on an earlier song of the same name enclose a valse parody of 'Dies Irae' and are framed by a few touches of realism (Death's fiddle and dawn cockcrow); only in *La Jeunesse d'Hercule* (1877) does Saint-Saëns suggest a sequence of events – and show what he had learned from Liszt's treatment of the orchestra.

Still more clearly narrative is Duparc's *Lenore* (1874), not only German in subject but influenced by Wagner's, rather than Liszt's, orchestration, harmony, and *Leitmotiv* technique (see p. 723). At least equally Germanic are the early orchestral works of a younger pupil of Franck's, Vincent d'Indy (1851–1931), the *Piccolomini* overture (1874) – renamed *Max et Thécla* as the central movement of a trilogy on Schiller's *Wallenstein* in 1880 – and the *ballade-symphonie La Forêt enchantée* (after Uhland's 'Harald') (1878). Franck himself had in 1872 composed a *poème-symphonie* in three movements for soprano, chorus, and orchestra, entitled *Rédemption*, (see p. 757) of which the central *morceau symphonique* was for orchestra only; the work was a total failure but two years later Franck produced an almost completely new orchestral movement with the same title.[30] However he went on to write a genuine symphonic poem, *Les Éolides* (1876), suggested by Leconte de Lisle's poem and influenced by Wagner (also a little by Berlioz), and later (1882) actually succumbed to the vogue of German orchestral ballads in the heavy-handed *Chasseur maudit* after Bürger's 'Der wilde Jäger'. Neither Franck nor his band of disciples was as yet particularly interested in 'pure' orchestral music, but Saint-Saëns, by the time he published his Second Symphony, in A minor, in 1878, could point to four elegant, Lisztian, but by no means unoriginal piano concertos in D major (1857), G minor (1863),

---

[29] See *Revue de musicologie*, i (1922–3), p. 170.
[30] All that remains of the original is the very end, pp. 47ff., of the miniature score, ed. André Coeuroy (Leipzig, 1936).

E flat (1869), and C minor (1875). No. 4 is an interesting experiment in a form he used in later works: two parts, the first consisting of allegro moderato and andante, the second of scherzo, a transitional and much altered recall of the andante, and finale. The best of his concertos, No. 3 for violin, in B minor, came later (1881).

THE ADVENT OF BRAHMS

In central Europe the Lisztian symphonic poem was being cultivated by Smetana and his young compatriot Zdeněk Fibich (1850–1900). Smetana began his cycle of six, *Má vlast* (My Country), written in ever-increasing deafness, with *Vyšehrad* and *Vltava* in 1874, completing it in 1879 with *Blaník*. Fibich composed *Othello* (1873), *Záboj, Slavoj a Luděk* (also 1873), from which Smetana borrowed the 'Vyšehrad' theme in his cycle, and *Toman a lesní panna* (Toman and the wood-nymph) (1874), while a third Czech, Dvořák, so far eschewing programme-music, was writing his Third, Fourth, and Fifth symphonies (1873–5) and an unsuccessful Piano Concerto on traditional lines (1876). Of the symphonies, No. 5 in F (long known as 'No. 3') is the earliest of those which have earned Dvořák his place among the greatest masters of the late-nineteenth-century symphony as the most nearly Schubertian symphonist after Schubert. During the same years (1873–6) Anton Bruckner (1824–96) was also completing the original versions of *his* Third, Fourth, and Fifth Symphonies, the earliest thoroughly mature ones, though – like Dvořak's – they were slow to make their way in the world. On the other hand Raff at Wiesbaden, whom Liszt thought superior in imagination to Brahms, was still producing symphony after symphony[31] and was one of the most performed composers of the day; in Vienna Karl Goldmark (1830–1915) followed in his train with a suite-like 'rustic wedding' symphony, *Ländliche Hochzeit* (1876), in five pictorial movements of which the fourth, 'Im Garten', shows how Wagner's influence was now liable to appear in unlikely places:

Ex. 268

Such was the scene on which Brahms belatedly appeared, at first tentatively, as it were, with his Variations on a theme he supposed to be

[31] Raff also cultivated the orchestral suite – in Hungarian, Italian, and Thuringian suites – a form revived by the aged Franz Lachner (1803–90) during the 1860s long after he had abandoned symphonic composition. A comparable form, the serenade, was successfully cultivated from 1874 onward by Brahms's disciple, Robert Fuchs (1847–1927).

Haydn's (1873), then with three master-works, the Symphonies in C minor and D major (1876 and 1877) and the Violin Concerto (1879). The first movement of the C minor Symphony, minus the slow introduction, had been completed as early as 1862; even before then he had worked on a symphony, originally a sonata for two pianos, the first movement of which he converted into the first movement of the D minor Piano Concerto of 1858; but as we have seen (p. 667) he was long paralysed by the ghost of Beethoven. His instrumental music in the intervening period had been almost entirely for chamber ensembles and his mature orchestral style is essentially an extension of his chamber style. He had a habit of completing works first for two pianos; the two-piano version of the Op. 56 Variations was actually published side by side with the orchestral one and is not markedly inferior except for the loss of horn sound. Brahms wrote for natural horns in different crooks – in fact his scoring is always intensely conservative, deriving from Beethoven and Schumann – but drew exquisite sounds from them, above all at the end of the seventh variation.

His skill in variation writing was also the salvation of his symphonies, for his ideas tended to come, like Schumann's, in balanced melodic phrases, not as the pregnant motives he needed in order to work on the Beethovenian lines he was aiming at; but the master of variation disguises the four-squareness of cadence-points and often draws his 'symphonic' continuation from the variation or even the bass rather than the melody. The opening of the Second Symphony is a classic case, that of the *Tragische Ouvertüre* (1880) a more compressed one. Brahms could not match the rhythmic drive and thematic argument of Beethoven's first movements, but he did offer rich thematically woven textures and deeply satisfying thinking-in-sound which made a profound appeal to musicians who were repelled by the contemporary trends of literary influence on orchestral music and effective scoring for its own sake. Nor does he reach the depths of Beethoven's slow movements, though he nearly does in the Fourth Symphony (1885), or write a true scherzo at all. The conductor Hermann Levi confided to Clara Schumann[32] that he 'had doubts about the two middle movements' of the First Symphony; 'beautiful as they are, they seem to me more suitable for a serenade or suite than an otherwise so grandly planned symphony'. Beethoven himself had provided an alternative to the scherzo in the Allegrettos of his Seventh and Eighth, and three times out of four Brahms accepts it; the wistful Poco allegretto of his Third Symphony (1883) is charming – but it is very nearly a song-without-words. As for the boisterous 2/4 Allegro giocoso of the Fourth Symphony, its heavy Teutonic humour comes from the same world as the *Akademische Fest-Ouvertüre* of 1880. The finale of Brahms's First deliberately challenges comparison with Beethoven's Ninth by its chief allegro theme and brings off a *coup de théâtre* in the coda when the più allegro is suddenly interrupted, *ff*, by the solemn

---

[32] Letter of 22 November 1876, Berthold Litzmann, *Clara Schumann: Ein Künstlerleben*, iii (Leipzig, 1908), p. 343.

chords already heard on trombones and bassoons, *piano*, in the slow introduction to the finale. The merely noisy ending of the Second is far inferior; the quiet one of No. 3 very beautiful and with few precedents outside Haydn. But there are probably no precedents at all for the chaconne finale of No. 4.

Brahms's concertos belong very much to the world of his symphonies. The D minor Piano Concerto partly originated in a symphony; the first movement of the Violin Concerto is the younger sister of that of the D major Symphony; the B flat Piano Concerto (1881) is in four movements, of which the second is a true scherzo – the whole is really a symphony for piano and orchestra. The solo parts are always very difficult, but the element of virtuosic display, though indispensable, is minimized and nearly disappears altogether in the *Doppel-Konzert* for violin and cello (1887).

THE SYMPHONIES OF BRUCKNER

If Brahms and Liszt wrote for orchestra like pianists, in accordance with their diametrically contrasted types of pianism, Bruckner orchestrated like the organist he was: in great blocks of sound, changing his instrumental groups like so many stop-combinations, even with the pauses an organist needed to manipulate them in the days before such devices as 'combination pistons' were introduced. He was quite as conscious of Beethoven 'marching behind him' as Brahms was but the ghost did not worry him. He accepted its presence. He began his Third Symphony in D minor (1873)[33] with a trumpet theme which practically quotes, but in the tonic, the opening of Beethoven's Ninth. And he nearly did it again with a solo horn, and a tiny but magic transformation, at the beginning of No. 4 in E flat (first version 1874). Another feature borrowed in No. 4 from the same Beethoven passage, the *pp* string tremolo, was also to open Bruckner's Seventh (1883), Eighth (1887), and Ninth (unfinished in 1894). Such openings promise vast spaciousness and the promise is fulfilled, but the great spaces are filled not with Beethovenian dynamism (or closely woven Brahmsian texture) but with thematically often undistinguished, harmonically slow-moving blocks of cyclopean masonry in primary orchestral colours, frequently with a massive brass choir predominating. Prolonged ostinato figures and pedal-points support these monumental blocks. The slow movements are real adagios, not songs-without-words, the scherzos true scherzos, and the finale provides the dynamic and thematic crown. These features are foreshadowed in Bruckner's earlier symphonies, even in No. o, but they are all first fully established in No. 3. The second subject of the first movement of No. 3 is a characteristic 'double theme' (one on second violins, the other on violas and then solo horn), and the third is presented with one strand on all woodwind

---

[33] It was recast in 1878, eliminating deliberate quotations from Wagner, and again in 1888–9. For the various versions of Bruckner's symphonies, particularly Nos. 'o', 1, 2, 3, 4, and 8, in some of which his disciples had a hand, see, for instance, Erwin Doernberg, *The Life and Symphonies of Anton Bruckner* (London, 1960), pp. 222–5.

and brass in octaves, the other on tutti strings in octaves; it is succeeded by a *Choral* (so marked by the composer in the trumpet parts) for brass choir. It was the Adagio of this work which earned Bruckner his nickname, *der Adagio-Komponist*. Scherzo and trio are equally characteristic and the finale again has a 'double' second subject (total antithesis of brass and strings) and the tremendously brassy crown is provided by the opening theme of the symphony now at last in a major setting. This procedure of bringing back material from the beginning of a symphony for a noisy triumphant finish was repeated in Nos. 5, 6, and 7; in No. 8 Bruckner went further, without increasing the impressiveness, by combining the chief themes of all four movements in 12 ear-splitting bars of C major triad.

Bruckner styled No. 4 *Romantische Symphonie*; it is the only one with faint programmatic suggestions such as the delightful 'double' second subject of the *ruhig bewegt* first movement where the viola theme confessedly expresses the mood in which the composer listened to the song of the great tit (first violins), and the hunting scene which replaced the scherzo of the original version. Even the usual Adagio is replaced by an Andante said to have sprung from the idea of an unlucky lover and his 'vain serenade'.[34] The most striking new features of the Fifth Symphony, in B flat, which Bruckner considered his 'contrapuntal masterpiece', are the note-for-note reappearance of the very slow triplet crotchets of the Adagio as the molto vivace crotchets of the scherzo (with the diguised reappearance of the Adagio oboe theme on the woodwind in octaves in the scherzo), and the review of themes from the previous movements – the ghost of Beethoven's Ninth again – at the beginning of the finale. No. 6 in A is remarkable for an unusually fascinating, enigmatic scherzo, No. 7 in E for traces of Wagner's influence – up to this point rarer than one would expect considering Bruckner's almost canine devotion to the older man – in the 'instrumental arioso' nature of the opening theme, the second allegro theme and its later inversion, and the noble Adagio with its four tubas, written under the dread of Wagner's imminent death. Wagner shows again in the first subject of the Allegro moderato of the Eighth and the *Tristan*esque syncopated *pp* string chords in its slow movement, but practically disappears from the three completed movements of the Ninth.

DVOŘÁK: HEIR OF SCHUBERT

Whereas Bruckner is a freak (in the biological sense), a composer *sui generis*, Dvořák – so akin to him in his peasant origin, his personal naïvety – stands clearly in the Viennese classical tradition, the heir of Schubert in his seemingly spontaneous melodic invention and treatment of the orchestra. While Bruckner parades his contrapuntal achievements, Dvořák seems to think naturally in contrapuntal terms. He also ended a symphony – No. 5 in

---

[34] See Max Auer, *Anton Bruckner: Sein Leben und Werk* (third, completely revised edition, Leipzig, 1941), p. 284.

F (1875), his earliest mature one – with a recall of its opening, but almost unobtrusively on a single trombone covered by a trumpet fanfare. (Such trumpet 'signals' became his favourite method of intensifying a tutti *ff*.) Dvořák writes for the orchestra 'from within' as it were, as neither Brahms nor Bruckner did; he was one of the few great composers who have actually been orchestral players – he was a violist – and, although his two sets of *Slovanské tance* (1878 and 1887) and his set of ten *Legendy* (1881) were originally written for piano duet, his orchestral sense was basic and ensured the natural effectiveness of his scores. His thinking tends to be discursive. His slow movements are not 'profound' though he nearly achieves profundity in the Seventh Symphony (1885) written under the direct stimulus of Brahms's Third. (The second subject of the first movement pays more open tribute to his friend, its first two bars being identical even in key with the opening of the slow movement of Brahms's B flat Piano Concerto.) But they are full of enchanting effects such as the descending scales in sixths in the Adagio of No. 8 (1889) or the cor anglais solo in the Largo of No. 9 (*Z nového světa* – From the New World) (1893). The scherzos are dancelike; in two instances, those of No. 6 (1880) and No. 7, typical Czech *furiants*, with crossing of triple with duple rhythms – a dance introduced also in the *Slavonic Dances*, Op. 46, Nos. 1 and 8, and as the finales of the *Česká suita* and Violin Concerto (both 1879), and various non-orchestral works. After his greatest achievement as a symphonic thinker, the D minor, No. 7, Dvořák relaxed in his last two symphonies, the G major and the *New World*, the latter curiously inspired by Negro spirituals and in the two middle movements by the Amerindian *Song of Hiawatha* yet totally Czech – its pentatonic patterns are common to both Negro and Czech folk-music – and then asserted his full powers for the last time in the great B minor Cello Concerto of 1895.

Dvořák's music is profoundly Czech in a way that Smetana's, for all his patriotism, seldom is. He was a natural Czech speaker whereas Smetana learned Czech only in maturity, and the speech-patterns of the language influenced his melodic patterns and in some cases – Nos. 1 and 4 of the *Legends* and four of the late symphonic poems, *Vodník* (The Water Goblin), *Polednice* (The Noonday Witch), *Zlatý kolovrat* (The Golden Spinning-Wheel), and *Holoubek* (The Wood-Dove) (1896) – his themes were based on actual lines of Czech verse.[35] He seldom quotes national melodies; those in the overtures *Josef Kajetán Tyl* (often known as 'My Country') (1882) and *Husitská* (1883) were exceptions for which there were special reasons. But their spirit subtly permeates not only avowedly 'Slavonic' works like the *Dances* and the three *Rhapsodies* of 1878, which are really more 'Smetanové' than 'Slovanské', but the symphonies and concertos, the *Symfonické variace* (1877), where the oboe interjects a sly hint of furiant in the twenty-first variation, and the *Scherzo-capriccioso* (1883) where the same dance more than hints at its presence.

[35] See Gerald Abraham, *The Tradition of Western Music* (London and Berkeley, 1974), pp. 73–4.

Until nearly the end of his life when he composed the cycle of overtures, *Příroda, Život a Láska* (Nature, Life, and Love = *Nature, Carnival, Othello*) (1891–2), and then the circumstantially programmatic symphonic poems, Dvořák was no more interested in programme-music than Brahms or Bruckner. It was otherwise with Chaykovsky. Despite his repeated expressions of distaste for it, he had, as we have seen, written programmatic music in his younger days and he went on doing so in the fantasia *Francesca da Rimini* (1876), the Berliozian *Manfred* 'symphony in four pictures, after Byron' (1885), the overture-fantasia *Hamlet* (1888), and the 'symphonic ballad' on Adam Mickiewicz's poem 'Wojewoda' (1891). And of course his symphonies also have subjective programmes: that of the Fourth in F minor (1876), confided in a letter to his benefactress Nadezhda von Meck, is extremely well known, the Fifth in E minor (1888) is dominated by the motto-theme – presumably of 'fate' – which opens it, shatters the love-yearnings of the Andante cantabile, casts its shadow over the valse, and is triumphantly accepted in the finale. As for the Sixth in B minor, the *Pathétique* (1893), its programme remains an enigma, as he wished it to be, though it is not without clues (e.g. the reference to 'resting with the saints' from the Requiem, on the four-part brass choir at bar 201 of the first movement). Indeed, except for the three Suites (1879, 1883, and 1884), the Violin Concerto (1878), and the piano concertos (No. 2 in G, 1880, the Concert Fantasia, 1884, and the one-movement No. 3, 1893), Chaykovsky composed very little absolute music for orchestra. Even the three later symphonies are suite-like as wholes, nor are the separate movements organic; the first movements are essentially symmetrically disposed episodes connected, as the composer ruefully admitted, by all too obvious 'seams' and their unity emerges, particularly in the Sixth, from their emotional content. Such naked expression of personal emotion, such storms of passion and protest, embodied in powerful, very highly coloured yet subtle orchestral writing, completely distracts attention from structural shortcomings.

One particularly incongruous ingredient in Chaykovsky's symphonies is the element of French ballet-music, his love of which dates from a performance of the *Giselle* (1841) of Adolphe Adam (1803–56), which he saw as a boy. It was greatly stimulated by the *Sylvia* (1876) of Léo Delibes (1836–91) which he heard only after he had completed his own first full-length ballet, *Lebedinoe ozero* (Swan Lake) (1876). French influence is naturally strong in his other great ballets, *Spyashchaya krasavitsa* (Sleeping Beauty) (1889) and *Shchelkunchik* (Nutcracker) (1892), and is responsible for many delightful numbers in the suites, operas, and other works. The incongruity results when it appears in the first movement of the Fourth Symphony, the third of No. 5, and the middle movements of the *Pathétique*.

At the same time as Chaykovsky's last three symphonies, exceptional orchestral virtuosity was being developed by another Russian composer for very different ends. Besides relatively modest compositions on Russian folk-melodies – a one-movement Piano Concerto (1883), a *Simfonietta* (1884), a Fantasia for violin and orchestra – Rimsky-Korsakov made his first revision of *Antar* (1875), wrote a brilliantly fantastic *Skazka* (Legend) (1880), and reached a climax of pyrotechnic orchestration in a style derived from Glinka and Liszt in an *Ispanskoe kapriccio* (1887), where, as he insisted, orchestration is the 'very essence of the composition', a *Voskresnaya* (Easter) Overture on liturgical themes (1888), and a symphonic suite *Shekherazada* (1888). This fantastic evocation of the *1001 Nights* in which various themes were associated with various characters – the solo violin theme with Sheherazade herself – has four movements which were at one stage given titles although there is no musical reflection of any story. The suite is, in fact, like Islamic art: an affair of coldly beautiful patterns without human emotion.

From the beginning of the 1880s date several other notable Russian orchestral pieces: Borodin's 'musical picture' *V Sredney Azii* (In Central Asia) and Rubinstein's Fifth Symphony in G minor, specifically titled *Russkaya* (both 1880), and Balakirev's symphonic poem *Tamara* after Lermontov's poem (1882). *Tamara* is a masterpiece of rich orchestral, quasi-oriental colour and in Borodin's charming little 'picture' of a caravan with its military escort approaching and passing, an oriental tune is contrasted and combined with a Russian folk-tune. Rubinstein also employs an oriental – at least Crimean Tatar – pentatonic pipe-tune for the scherzo of his *Russian Symphony*, though the middle section is intensely Russian in its cantilena; indeed both first movement and finale are thoroughly national in feeling – only blemished at times by Germanic text-book harmony. And younger talents began to appear. Antony Stepanovich Arensky (1861–1906) produced a Chopinesque Piano Concerto in 1882, two symphonies in 1883 and 1889 (of which the second, in A, is in one movement with slow-movement and scherzo episodes), and a very attractive Suite in G minor including two numbers in 5/4 time, an 'Air de danse' and 'Basso ostinato'. Potentially stronger was Aleksandr Konstantinovich Glazunov (1865–1936) whose First Symphony was composed in 1884. His early works, including the symphonic poem *Stenka Razin* (1885) and the 'symphonic picture' *Kreml* (1890), suggested the advent of a considerable master but in his Fourth Symphony (E flat, 1893) he struck a vein of fluent, suave melody, harmony, and orchestration which he found it all too easy to work in later works until within ten years he tired of repeating himself.

ORCHESTRAL COMPOSITION IN THE WEST

In the West there was a kind of false dawn of orchestral composition in countries where it had long ceased to flourish or had never flourished at all. In Italy Giovanni Sgambati (1841–1914) produced a piano concerto (1880) and a Symphony in D minor (1881). In Poland, where the most distinguished recent orchestral music had been the two violin concertos (1853 and

1862) of Henryk Wieniawski (1835–80), Zygmunt Noskowski (1846–1909) composed two symphonies – A major (1875) and C minor (*Elegijna*, with a finale headed 'Per aspera ad astra') (1879) – and a concert overture, *Morskie Oko* ('Sea Eye', the name of a lake in the High Tatras) (1875). (A Third Symphony, *Od wiosny do wiosny*, 'From Spring to Spring', a 'seasons' symphony, followed much later in 1903.) There was also a stirring in the English-speaking lands. Hubert Parry (1841–1924) composed four symphonies between 1882 and 1889, Alexander Mackenzie (1847–1935), a violin concerto in 1885, and Charles Villiers Stanford (1852–1924) four symphonies (1882–94) of which No. 2, the 'Irish', introducing national melodies, is perhaps the best. With his *Land of the Mountain and the Flood* overture (1887) the young Hamish MacCunn (1868–1916) showed a promise he failed to fulfill. Another concert overture, *Froissart* (1890), by Edward Elgar (1857–1934) was a foretaste of greater things. The American George Chadwick (1854–1931) made his debut in 1879 with a *Rip van Winkle* overture, following it with symphonies in C (1882) and B flat (1888) and a number of symphonic poems, and Horatio Parker (1863–1919) composed a Symphony in C minor in 1885. But the most gifted American of this generation was Edward MacDowell (1861–1908). A pupil of Raff, MacDowell early produced two symphonic poems, *Hamlet and Ophelia* (1885) and *Lancelot and Elaine* (1888), an equally romantic Suite (1891) and two piano concertos (1885 and 1890).

Almost all these 'Anglo-Saxons' studied in Germany and their work is technically conservative and unoriginal. But by the mid-1880s the French were recovering from their awe of German music (which in any case meant 'Wagnerian', not in the least 'Brahmsian'), though the influence of Lisztian techniques was still powerful. It marks a whole series of French symphonies: Saint-Saëns' No. 3 in C minor ('à la mémoire de Franz Liszt') (1886), Lalo's G minor Symphony and d'Indy's *Symphonie pour orchestre et piano sur un Chant montagnard français* (both 1887), Franck's D minor (1888), and the B flat Symphony (1890) of his pupil Ernest Chausson (1855–99), who had first attracted notice with a symphonic poem *Viviane* in 1882. The Saint-Saëns is in two parts, an inflated repetition of the form of his piano concerto in the same key (cf. p. 693): I. Adagio introduction to allegro moderato – poco adagio; II. Allegro moderato (=scherzo and trio) – maestoso transition to allegro finale. There are a number of theme-transformations – some fairly obvious, as when the first allegro theme reappears on the woodwind at bar 17 of the scherzo, and as the fugue-subject of the finale, others (such as the trombones' hint, toward the end of the scherzo, that they have not forgotten the melody of the adagio) more subtle. The orchestration is not only skilful, as one expects of Saint-Saëns, but unusual: the organ is introduced in the D flat Adagio where it duets with the orchestra (half the divided first violins, violas, and cellos in three octaves, molto espressivo, while the rest of the strings accompany pizzicato):

Ex. 269

A piano is used for washes of scale and arpeggio in the scherzo and has a quasi-Berliozian passage, *à 4 mains*, in the Maestoso.

D'Indy's three-movement Symphony, consisting almost entirely of transformations of the haunting Cévenol theme proposed by the cor anglais, not only has a virtuoso piano part throughout but makes free use of the harp – a 'Lisztian' orchestral instrument which neither Brahms nor Bruckner, Dvořák or Chaykovsky (except in *Manfred*) would have used in a symphony. But Franck did and Chausson wrote for two harps. Both Franck and Chausson adopt the three-movement scheme which originated in Liszt's *Faust* – Franck's opening, the 'motto' theme, is borrowed from that of *Les Préludes* – but despite this superficial similarity and the thematic recall in both finales, the two works are very different. Franck presents his all-too-memorable material in 'organistic' orchestration in the two outside movements – the middle Allegretto with its ingenious combination of scherzo with slow movement is much more attractively scored, as are the *Variations symphoniques* (really 'Introduction, variations, and finale') for piano and orchestra of 1885 and *Psyché*, 'poème symphonique pour orchestre et choeur' (1888) – whereas Chausson treats less striking themes more subtly and with many passages of delightful orchestration. The two 'inside' movements of Lalo's Symphony, and also the slow introduction to the first movement, are drawn from an early, unproduced opera *Fiesque*; the saltarello finale is marked by the piquant, light-handed scoring characteristic of so much French music of the period.

Even some of the French Wagnerians could forget much of what they had learned at Bayreuth, as Emmanuel Chabrier (1841–94) did in his exuberant rhapsody *España* (1883) and *Marche française* (re-named *Joyeuse marche*) (1888). Chabrier here shows himself a direct heir of Berlioz. Another strong orchestral influence was Jules Massenet (1842–1912) who had been composing sets of *Scènes napolitaines, pittoresques, alsaciennes* and so on from *c.* 1865 onward, suites which were surpassed by the *Impressions d'Italie* (originally subtitled 'Symphonie sentimentale et pittoresque') (1891) of his pupil Gustave Charpentier (1860–1956).

THE YOUNG STRAUSS AND HIS CONTEMPORARIES

The same Italian scenes – specifically two of them, Sorrento[36] and Naples – had been painted with a very different orchestral palette five years before. Richard Strauss (1864–1949) had composed two symphonies, in D minor and F minor (1880 and 1884), the second of which – modelled on Beethoven, Mendelssohn, and Schumann, with the fashionable thematic recall of the three previous movements in the coda of the finale – won Brahms's approval. Then a close friendship with Alexander Ritter (1833–96), an unsuccessful composer of Lisztian symphonic poems,[37] led to a sharp change of direction. Returning from a holiday in Italy, Strauss composed in 1886 a *sinfonische Fantasie, Aus Italien*, which announced the arrival of a masterful new personality. *Aus Italien* employs a musical language that owes more to Liszt and Wagner than to Schumann and his followers; it is very Teutonic by comparison with Charpentier's Italy yet subtly permeated with an Italian *morbidezza*, remote from the vulgar cheerfulness of 'Funiculi, funicula' in the finale. The scoring is already of virtuoso quality, heard at its most astonishing near the beginning of 'Am Strande von Sorrent' in the *ppp* chromatic sestolets of violins in the highest register, piccolo, and flutes, embroidering a sustained C major chord. Both the brilliance and the Italianism are still more marked in *Don Juan* (after Lenau's dramatic frag-

---

[36] Charpentier's fourth movement, 'Sur les cimes', looks down on Sorrento from the hills, Strauss's third stays on the beach, but the mood of calm is common to both.
[37] His best orchestral work, the 'symphonic waltz', *Olafs Hochzeitsreigen*, a grim piece of programme-music, was not composed until 1891.

ment) (1888); the first of the memorable horn themes comes straight out of the First Act of Rossini's *Tell* (Arnold's 'Il faut donc vaincre ma *flamme?*'). Next came the tragic *Macbeth* (also 1888; revised 1890) and *Tod und Verklärung* (1889), for which Ritter supplied two versions of a poetic programme *ex post facto*. In these *Tondichtungen* – Strauss never used the term '*symphonic* poem' – continuous webs of orchestral polyphony, rather like sustained passages from Wagnerian music-drama deprived of voice-parts, leave only vestigial remains of the traditional forms. (They are most apparent in *Macbeth*.) Narrative has supplanted architecture and only creative imagination of a high order could sustain such narrative at length.

At that time Strauss stood alone among his compatriots. Of the potential rivals of his own age, one – Hugo Wolf (1860–1903) – had tried orchestral composition and failed, the other – Gustav Mahler (1860–1911) – was only just beginning. Wolf's symphonic poem *Penthesilea* (1883), a triptych based on Kleist's tragedy in which the heroine kills Achilles instead of being killed by him, and then dies in insane frenzy, reaches its highest point in the middle movement, Penthesilea's dream of the rose-festival in which the Amazons ravish their captives. But the outer movements suggest music orchestrated rather than music thought directly in terms of the orchestra as Strauss's always does. Mahler completed his First Symphony in 1888, a work which Raff, had he lived to hear it, might have greeted as a continuation of his own life-work by a more daring and gifted younger spirit. It is suite-like, originally in five movements divided into two parts, with a strange programme suggested by Jean Paul Richter's novel *Titan*:

Part I: From the days of youth. 1. Spring and no end; 2. Flower chapter (andante); 3. Full Sail (scherzo).
Part II: Commedia umana. 4. Shipwrecked. A funeral march in Callot's manner (The Hunter's Funeral); 5. Dall'inferno al Paradiso (allegro furioso), the sudden expression of a heart wounded to its depths.

The 'flower chapter' (see pl. 54, p. 704) was soon removed but the suite-like impression remains; nothing could be further in conception and execution from Strauss's tone-poems – or the compression of the contemporary French symphonies. But a new way was opened for the symphony in the coming century.

Pl. 55   Opening of the 'Bluminen-Kapitel' (flower chapter), after Jean Paul's *Siebenkäs*, which was originally the second movement of Mahler's First Symphony but later discarded. (Autograph score in the University Library at Yale.)

35

Opera (1830–93)

In contrast with the pre-eminence of German instrumental music, German opera melted little ice during the 1830s and 1840s outside the German and Habsburg lands and their closest neighbours; its international future really depended on a young man who certainly composed a very promising romantic opera, *Die Feen* (based on Gozzi's *La donna serpente*), in 1834 though it was never produced in his lifetime. In Italy – and outside Italy – the vogue for Bellini and Donizetti, and of course the now silent Rossini, was at its height and some notable lesser talents began to make their presence felt: Mercadante (cf. pp. 586–8) and the Ricci brothers, Luigi (1805–59) and Federico (1809–77). Giuseppe Verdi (1813–1901), who was to eclipse them all, made his début with *Oberto* in 1839. But the prestige of Paris as an international opera-centre was undiminished, indeed higher than ever under the Orleans monarchy. Auber's *Muette de Portici* (1828) and Rossini's *Guillaume Tell* (1829) were followed by Meyerbeer's *Robert le Diable* (1831), Auber's *Gustave III* (1833), the *Juive* of Fromental Halévy (1799–1862) in 1835, and Meyerbeer's *Les Huguenots* in 1836 at the Opéra, while Auber's *Fra Diavolo* (1830), *Cheval de bronze* (1835) and *Domino noir* (1837), Hérold's *Zampa* (1831) and *Pré aux clercs* (1832), and Adolphe Adam's *Postillon de Longjumeau* (1836) appeared at the Opéra-Comique. It is instructive to compare the later fate of these justly famous and successful operas with that of the orchestral music of the same period. Their fame and success were not due solely to their musical qualities and not only is it always more difficult to perform – and so keep alive – an opera as compared with a work for the concert-hall, but *grands opéras* of the Parisian type depended heavily on elaborate and impressive staging, to say nothing of large orchestra and chorus. They were operatic dinosaurs, foredoomed to extinction by their own nature.

Most of them were created by Scribe who provided Auber's *comiques* as well as *grands* libretti, Halévy's for *La Juive*, and above all Meyerbeer's. It was Meyerbeer, a totally international figure, a German Jew who Italianized his name and composed his best operas to French words, who was Spontini's true heir in the sphere of spectacular *grand opéra*. Musically he was the inferior of Rossini, the Rossini who exerted his full powers in *Guillaume Tell*. *Tell* was founded, rather unstably, on Schiller's play but Rossini lavished on it not only Italian cantilena (Arnold's 'Ah! Mathilde, idole de mon âme', mentioned on p. 703) and Italian *slancio*, as in the headlong 'Que du ravage' at the end of Act I, but orchestral invention of a high order (e.g. the superb introduction to Mathilde's 'Sombre forêt', itself a beautiful air, in Act II). He commands every kind of dramatic situation from the big choral scene of the Rütli oath (finale of Act II) to the quiet tension of the passage where the hero tells his son 'Sois immobile, et vers la terre incline un genou suppliant', a passage greatly admired both by Berlioz, who quotes it in his *Traité d'instrumentation*, and by Wagner. And the whole work is given a peculiar unity by the saturation of many pages of the score, beginning with the andante of the overture and the introduction to Act I, with Swiss – or acceptably pseudo-Swiss – idioms.

Neither Auber's *Muette* nor Halévy's *Juive* reaches the level of *Tell*. Auber was really much better at comedy than tragedy; *Fra Diavolo* sparkles from the patter-duet in Act I to the last act finale and the rascally hero has a part ranging from the light romantic (his barcarolle 'Agnes la jouvencelle') to the comic variety of 'Je vois marcher' in Act III; the Chinese fantasy of *Le Cheval de bronze* is delightful. There is little scope for comedy in *La Muette* but the hero, the Neapolitan fisherman Masaniello, like Tell a hero of revolt, has a barcarolle, 'Amis, la matinée est belle', which is effectively quoted when he is out of his mind in the last scene, and a rather broken-backed cavatina when he comforts his dumb sister; but Auber can do nothing better for the heroic side of his character than the patriotic duet with his friend Pietro in Act II, which belongs to the world of the 1790s. However the heroine has three extended orchestral dances with catchy tunes before she finally leaps into the lava from Vesuvius.

These are typical ingredients of a Scribe libretto: a *truc* (the heroine who can only mime or dance), an element of horror, and startling spectacle (a volcanic eruption). But he must be given credit for daring to end operas tragically. In *La Juive* he surpasses himself in horror when the heroine is thrown into a cauldron of boiling oil at the very moment when her Jewish supposed father reveals her identity to her true father, the Cardinal, who has vainly tried to save them. But despite the melodrama, and the coloratura of Rachel's princess rival, *La Juive* is dramatically and musically one of the finest of the *grands opéras*. It was not for nothing that Halévy, himself a Jew, had been a pupil and friend of Cherubini. In workmanship as well as invention – not only here but in the later *Reine de Chypre* (1841) – he is far superior in this field to nearly all his French contemporaries. The characterization is particularly fine in the duets and other ensemble pieces and his more sensuous melodies are not so much directly Italian as Chopinesque Italian: e.g. Rachel's 'Pour lui, pour moi, mon père' in the final trio of Act II, or Éléazar's appeal to her at the end of Act IV:

Ex. 270

which is even more striking when played by a pair of cors anglais in thirds than when sung. There is an Italian element in Meyerbeer's *Robert le Diable* – appropriately in Isabelle's music for she is a Sicilian princess – and a good deal more in *Les Huguenots*: Raoul's *romance* 'Plus blanche que la blanche hermine' in Act I, Marguerite's 'O beau pays de la Touraine', the E flat melody of Valentine's 'Parmi les pleurs', above all the love-duet in Act IV, the most beautiful Meyerbeer ever wrote. But in neither, nor in his later operas, is there one character – not even Valentine – as live and musically realized as Halévy's Rachel and Éléazar. But *Robert* with its supernatural ingredient is 'romantic', as they are not; indeed some of the music was originally conceived for a *Faust* opera. The mastery of his orchestration has already been mentioned (see p. 682) and he demonstrates it again and again, as in the scene of the opening of the tombs and the appearance of the wanton nuns in Act III of *Robert*, the chorus of bathing girls in Act II of *Huguenots*, the Act IV duet – and the tocsin that shatters it.[1] But he usually thinks more of effect than of characterization and delights in such onomatopoeic nonsense as Marcel's 'Piff, paff' song in Act I and the 'Rataplan' *couplets* in Act III. It was such things as these, and the exciting ensembles – above all the *bénédiction des poignards* in Act IV – that appealed to the public as much as the spectacular stage effects. These, and Scribe's horrors and *trucs*. *Les Huguenots*, like *La Juive*, ends with a father inadvertently ordering his daughter's killing, the considerably later *Prophète* (1849) with the hero blowing up a palace and burning both his mother and himself. The *truc* in *Robert* is the introduction of resurrected but lascivious nuns, in *Huguenots* of bathing beauties, in *Le Prophète* of a roller-skating ballet supposedly on a frozen pond. Though it is true that Meyerbeer was the direct heir of Spontini, he reflects the bourgeois taste of the Orleanist monarchy whereas Spontini reflected the military taste of the Empire.

Berlioz's *Benvenuto Cellini* (1838) came in refreshing contrast. Conceived as an *opéra semi-seria* with spoken dialogue, it was converted into *grand opéra* and subsequently underwent a number of changes. Musically it is delightful and some of the best passages were embodied in the two overtures, the actual one and the later *Carnaval romain* (cf. p. 669). There is some justifiable Italianism – Térésa's cavatina and cabaletta in the first

---

[1] Berlioz quotes all four passages in his *Traité*.

scene, Ascanio's barcarolle and a genuine Italian melody for the workmen ('Bienheureux les matelots') in the third. But the libretto – not Scribe's – is poor and the audience no doubt felt that the final casting of the statue of Perseus[2] was a tame substitute for boiling oil or a volcanic eruption. *Benvenuto Cellini* failed at once as a drama and has never been very successful.

Pl. 56   Coronation scene in Act IV of Meyerbeer's *Le Prophète*: the first London performance at Covent Garden (24 July 1849) with Mario as John of Leyden and Pauline Viardot as Fidès.

Very much more so was Donizetti's *La Favorite* (1840) which appealed by its more theatrical, much less subtle music despite its relative lack of sensational elements and its quiet, tragic ending. Already that year Donizetti had conquered Paris with an *opéra comique*, *La Fille du régiment*, and he repeated his triumph with *Don Pasquale* (1843), while throwing off a *semi-seria*, *Linda di Chamounix*, for Vienna in 1842. (His last serious operas for Paris and Vienna were not nearly as successful as *La Favorite*.) Except for Auber – *Les Diamantes de la Couronne* (1841), *Le Duc d'Olonne* (1842), *La Part du diable* (1843), *La Sirène* (1844) – he had little competition in the *comique* field, and the work that might have trumped *La Favorite* had to wait

---

[2] The actual statue was cast not for a Pope but for Cosimo dei Medici and stands in the Loggia della Signoria at Florence.

a quarter of a century for its performance in Paris while its author and composer was keeping the wolf from his door by making vocal scores and other arrangements of – supreme irony – *La Reine de Chypre* and *La Favorite*. Wagner's *Rienzi*, which has all the ingredients of a successful *grand opéra*, an insurrectionary hero in the line of Tell and Masaniello, memorable tunes, impressive choruses, noisy and effective orchestration, lavish stage-effects, and a final conflagration with Rienzi, his sister and her lover buried in the ruins of the Capitol, was instead produced at Dresden in 1842. It quickly opened Wagner's way to greater things.

ITALIAN ROMANTIC OPERA

Most of Donizetti's work was, of course, Italian and there for some years his supremacy was undisputed, with Rossini silent and Bellini dead after *Beatrice di Tenda* (1833) and *Puritani* (see p. 588) (1835). Outstanding in his great and very uneven output were *Anna Bolena* (1830), *L'elisir d'amore* (1832), *Lucrezia Borgia* (1833), *Gemma di Vergy* (1834), *Lucia di Lammermoor* (1835) – and *Don Pasquale* (1843), a variation of themes as old as Harlequin, Columbine, and Pantaloon for which Donizetti himself wrote much if not all of the libretto. He was more virile than Bellini and commanded a more extended range of expression; like him he draws heavily on the common stock of contemporary Italian melodic clichés and conventional forms, yet he breaks out of the forms and welds together the 'numbers' – again like Bellini (cf. the Second and Third Acts of *Puritani*) and, for that matter, Meyerbeer – in long continuous stretches. A fine example of Donizetti's through-composition, largely arioso, occurs as early as the final scene of *Anna Bolena*, a 'mad scene' more subtle than the famous show-piece in *Lucia*; another is the opening scene of Act III of *La Favorite*, punctuated by significant orchestral reminiscences of Fernand's *cavatina* in Act I, 'Un ange, une femme inconnue'. If his melody seldom achieves the vibrant, *morbido* quality of Bellini's, it can be as varied and memorable, witness Fernand's 'Ange si pur', Ernesto's serenade 'Com'è gentil la notte' in *Pasquale*, and 'Una furtiva lagrima' in *L'elisir d'amore*, a comedy whose plot emerges from the telling of the tale of that other love-potion which united Tristan and Isolde. The wedding sextet in *Lucia* is justly celebrated but it is no more than typical of Donizetti's skill in ensemble. A simpler example is the delightful contrast between Norina's cantabile 'or bisogna del progetto' and her victim's patter 'altro a fare non mi resta' in the Third Act duet of *Pasquale*.

Donizetti had nothing to fear from the competition of such operas as Mercadante's *Giuramento* (1837) and *Vestale* (1840) and Federico Ricci's *Prigione d' Edimburg* (1838) or the *Saffo* (1840) of Giovanni Pacini (1796–1867); but at just this time Verdi's *Oberto* appeared at Milan (1839) and began to make the rounds of Italy while his *Nabucodonosor* ('*Nabucco*') (1842) quickly carried his name to Vienna, Berlin, Paris, and London, indeed to all Europe and across the Atlantic. The young (and not so young) Verdi was heavily indebted to Bellini – the great hit of *Nabucco*, the chorus 'Va, pensiero, sull' ali dorate':

Ex. 271

is completely Bellinian – and later to Donizetti. But Verdi's melody, even in these early works, was more passionate, more coarsely energetic than his exemplars'. His popularity in his homeland was enormously helped by his subjects: Italian audiences saw in the Hebrew captivity of *Nabucco* an analogy with their own political plight and in *I Lombardi alla Prima Crociata* (1843) they identified with the Lombard crusaders, while the shattering unison chorus in the conspiracy scene (Act III) of *Ernani* (1844):

Ex. 272

generates much more genuine martial fire than Meyerbeer's *bénédiction des poignards* which was obviously its model. Altogether there is a great deal of fire in *Ernani*, notably in the final terzetto, and a great deal of vulgar energy; indeed these were to be Verdi's strongest suits in the operas of the next few years. For subjects he turned from Victor Hugo to Byron (*I due Foscari*, 1844), Schiller (*Giovanna d'Arco*, 1845), and after two total failures to Shakespeare (*Macbeth*) and Schiller's *Räuber* (*I masnadieri*) (both 1847, though *Macbeth* was thoroughly revised in 1865). He had effectively introduced a reminiscence theme, Silva's horn, in *Ernani*[3] and developed the device further in *Foscari* – and this was commented on; so slowly did foreign ideas get accepted in Italian opera. In all these works until *Macbeth* sympathetic audiences could easily recognize political allusions. But *Macbeth*, even in its original form, was a real step forward. Here for the first time Verdi, with Lady Macbeth, created a living character musically in the round and the sleep-walking scene is the finest thing he had done so far, superbly underlined by the orchestral writing.[4] Verdi significantly wrote to Salvatore Cammarono, who was supervising the Naples production, 'Note that the principal pieces of the opera are the duet for the Lady and her

---

[3] He had employed a simple reminiscence as early as *Oberto*. See Joseph Kerman, 'Verdi's Use of Recurring Themes', in *Studies in Music History*, ed. Harold Powers (Princeton, 1968), p. 495.
[4] Another fine piece of orchestral expression, supporting the chorus of Scottish exiles in the last Act, is mature Verdi of the 1865 version.

husband, and the sleepwalking: if these don't come off, the opera is done for; and they must on no account be sung – they must be acted and declaimed with the voice very dark and veiled (*con una voce ben cupa e velata*).' Beautiful singing was no longer the be-all and end-all. After another failure, *Il Corsaro* (1848), based on Byron, and the frankly political *Battaglia di Legnano*, produced in Rome on 27 January 1849, twelve days before the proclamation of the Roman Republic, came another change. The subject of *Luisa Miller* (also 1849), based on Schiller's *Kabale und Liebe*, a sort of tragic counterpart of *Sonnambula*, obliged Verdi to abandon the heroic for a more intimate style. Incidentally, the *Battaglia* and *Luisa Miller* are among the minority of operas of this period which have full-length overtures.

GERMAN ROMANTIC OPERA

The outstanding German opera-composer of the 1830s was Marschner, for Spohr was long silent after the failure of his *Alchymist* (1830) (on Washington Irving's 'Student of Salamanca' in *Bracebridge Hall*). Encouraged by the success of the scenes with country-folk, drinking songs, and so forth in *Der Vampyr* and *Templer und Jüdin*, Marschner composed a comic opera entirely in this vein, *Des Falkners Braut* (The Falconer's Bride) (1832), which was published with alternative Italian text in the hope of performances it never had; even in Germany, despite a few good tunes (which tend to peter out) and a patriotic finale (discomfiture of French troops by armed German peasants), it never became popular. But the following year Marschner retrieved this defeat with *Hans Heiling*, a masterpiece of the 'romantic shudder'. Heiling, the earth-spirit, arouses pity as well as terror. The key point of the work is his aria in Act I, 'An jenem Tag', which yields the material for reminiscence-themes; characteristically it runs out in an orchestral postlude against which Anna, the mortal he loves, *speaks*. Marschner was fond of *Melodram* and introduces it very effectively; one example, 'Des Nachts wohl auf der Haide', spoken by Anna's mother as she anxiously waits for the girl's return, is the most chilling passage in the entire score; another, at the beginning of Act III when Heiling recognizes his defeat, is opened by a horn-call heard first in the overture – which comes *after* the long, through-composed scenic *Vorspiel*. That call was to be remembered by both Brahms and Dvořák, and another theme that was to cast its shadow forward is the one to which Heiling's mother threatens Anna in Act II, altogether a very powerful scene:

Ex. 273

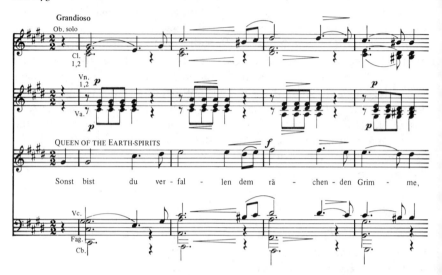

Curiously Marschner himself inadvertently remembered the opening, also in C sharp minor but in 6/8 time, for Dilafrose's love-song, 'Es sang so süss die Nachtigall' in his oriental comic opera *Der Bäbu* (1838). Neither *Der Bäbu* nor his serious *Schloss am Ätna* (1836), which has a demonic Sicilian *marchese*, won much success.

The master of German opera who made his début at this juncture was Albert Lortzing (1801–51). The son of an actor and actress and himself both actor and singer, and often librettist, his stage sense more than compensated for the modesty of his creative talent and his technical limitations. The second of the two operas he brought out at Leipzig in 1837, *Die beiden Schützen* (The two riflemen) and *Czaar und Zimmermann* (Tsar and Carpenter), proved one of the most successful of all German operas. (In the first performance he himself sang the part of the carpenter who changes clothes with Peter the Great, and his mother had a small role.) He had already produced a number of little *Singspiele* and pasticci; in 1830 he refurbished and re-scored J. A. Hiller's *Die Jagd* (see p. 473) and sang in it. A vein of *Singspiel* runs through most of his work, particularly in *Der Wildschütz* (The Poacher) (1842) and *Der Waffenschmied* (The Armourer) (1846) which became nearly as popular as the *Czaar*, and it does not disappear entirely in his most ambitious work, the 'romantic magic-opera' *Undine* (1845). In *Undine* he enlivens La Motte Fouqué's story with two less romantic characters, the hero's page Veit and a butler Hans, and the water-spirit Kühleborn even has to sing a duet with Veit; altogether his conception is much more conventionally operatic than Hoffmann's (see p. 590) and rivals his musical magic only at the very end with the chorus of water-spirits softly singing 'Schwanensang, Schwanenklang'. But reminiscence themes occur in *Undine* as freely as in any of the other German operas produced in that same year – and they include not only Spohr's swan song after long silence, *Die Kreuzfahrer*, and Marschner's last significant work, *Kaiser Adolph von Nassau*, but Wagner's *Tannhäuser*.

All four of these works are variations on chivalrous themes, as are Schumann's only opera, *Genoveva*, another which makes free use of reminiscence themes (too subtle to be effective), and Wagner's *Lohengrin* (both 1850). These mark the end of the great wave of German romantic opera that had begun with Spohr and Weber. As for German comic opera, it died with Lortzing, for the *Alessandro Stradella* (1844) and *Martha* (1847) of Friedrich von Flotow (1812–83), are more French than German in feeling and the delightful *Lustigen Weiber von Windsor* (1849) of Otto Nicolai (1810–49) is half-Italian – though it has a German-romantic final scene, Windsor Forest by moonlight, familiar from the slow introduction to the overture. Flotow and Nicolai had worked in France and Italy respectively and written French and Italian operas before their German ones. Nor did the rebirth begin with the Liszt disciple Cornelius's *Der Barbier von Bagdad*, as it should have done, for after a single performance at Weimar in 1858 it disappeared for many years. What came instead, after an interval, were the Viennese operettas of Franz von Suppé (1819–95) and Johann Strauss (1825–99).

THE NOVEL ELEMENTS IN WAGNER

Contemplating the many lively Franco-Italian passages of Wagner's *Measure for Measure* opera *Das Liebesverbot* (The Love Ban) (1836), it is tempting to speculate what he might have done with true comic opera. His protean genius was capable of adapting to anything, as he soon demonstrated by his exercise in Spontinian-Meyerbeerian *grand opéra*, *Rienzi*, and while he did not find what proved to be his true direction until *Der fliegende Holländer* (1843)[5] the earlier turnings and twistings were not wasted experience. He had begun to sketch the *Dutchman* before *Rienzi* was finished but the difference was drastic. From the five long acts, the cumbersome plot, the stage spectacle of *Rienzi*, Wagner turned to a three-act work which he originally intended to be played without breaks between the acts, with action almost entirely emotional or symbolic, chorus used sparingly and to dramatic purpose, scenery limited to two bits of coast and two ships, and a domestic interior. And the music is unified by the derivation of much of it from Senta's ballad in Act II, though Wagner exaggerated when he claimed later[6] that

---

[5] Produced at Dresden on 2 January; the following day the first performance of *Don Pasquale* was given in Paris.
[6] *Eine Mitteilung an meine Freunde* (Leipzig, 1852; *Richard Wagners Gesammelte Schriften*, ed. Julius Kapp (Leipzig, 1914), i; the passage quoted is on p. 152. The earliest sketch, wordless and on the same sheet as sketches for the *Rienzi* overture, is in the Burrell Collection in the Curtis Institute, Philadelphia; it is equivalent to bars 97–111 of the overture and the material is of course used in the ballad. Probably the earliest sketch with text is reproduced in facsimile in Kapp, *Richard Wagner: eine Biographie* (Berlin, 1910), pictorial appendix, p. 23.

in this piece I unconsciously set down the thematic germ of the whole music of the opera . . . In the final working-out of the composition this thematic image (*Bild*) spread itself quite involuntarily as a complete web over the whole drama; all I had to do was to develop the various thematic germs contained in the ballad each in its own direction in order to have all the principal moods of the poem before me in definite thematic shapes.

This was the point when the long familiar *Erinnerungsmotiv*, the thematic reminiscence, began to become what was much later known as *Leitmotiv*, the thematic clue. The characters, the action, the 'principal moods' of the *Dutchman* are so few, so simple and so inter-related that thematic reminiscences connected with any of them were almost bound to spread themselves 'as a web over the whole drama' – a web made possible only by the extreme concentration of the plot. This was the only new element. The symphonic handling of the orchestra, the blending and interweaving of recitative and arioso, the organization of more and more extended musico-dramatic sections had long been commonplace, though in Wagner's hands they do not seem commonplace. And the *Dutchman* is still a number-opera, despite the skill with which the numbers are dovetailed in; the melodic language still lapses into French or Italian idioms, as in the Daland-Dutchman duet in Act I, the ensemble for Mary and the girls after the ballad, Daland's aria 'Mögst du, mein Kind', and Erik's cavatina. The curse-theme itself is a recollection not only of the opening of the Ninth Symphony but of the scene of Ruthven's demonic possession in *Der Vampyr*.

If the *Dutchman* is the nearly pure essence of German romantic opera, *Tannhäuser* (1845) must be regarded as a hybridization with grand opera and *Lohengrin* (1850) as a sublimation of the compound. The whole Tournament of Song in *Tannhäuser*, from the march onward, and the end of the opera, with soloists and chorus, plus trombones, singing in unison 'Der Gnade Heil' against the persistent figure in the upper strings as in the overture are very Meyerbeerian. But the musical idiom, compounded though it still is of elements from Beethoven and Spontini, Spohr, Weber and Marschner, Bellini and Meyerbeer, is gradually fusing into an amalgam recognizable as Wagnerian. The fusion of recitative with arioso and song already noticeable in the *Dutchman* is carried further, as in Tannhäuser's narration of his pilgrimage, and Wagner wished even apparent recitative to be sung with precise observance of note-values, not declaimed.[7] There are still 'numbers' and still plenty of innocent diatonic melody and harmony, as in Elisabeth's 'Der Sänger klugen Weisen' (Act II, sc. 2), though the proportion of chromatic harmony and, consequently, melody has grown. There is still a certain amount of conventional orchestral figuration and interjection.But transitions are made more subtly: the Es on flute, oboe, and harp at the end of I.1 unobtrusively prepare the 'Glocken frohes Geläute' at

---

[7] See the very long letter of 8 September 1850 to Liszt, who had just produced *Lohengrin* at Weimar, *Breifwechsel zwischen Wagner und Liszt* (Leipzig, third edition, 1912), particularly pp. 73 and 79.

bars 18ff. of I.2; the so-called 'pulse of life' figure is also prepared, though differently, in III. 3, at Wolfram's last desperate 'Heinrich!' and faded out on second violins and violas at his 'Noch soll das *Heil dir Sünder* werden!'

Bolder transitions are effected by means of interrupted cadences: the dominant chord will be followed by another dominant seventh, by a diminished seventh, or an unexpected concord, sometimes marking a peripeteia – as when Elisabeth sees Tannhäuser at the beginning of II.2 or his entrance at the beginning of III.3 – but not always. The harmony is sometimes very bold, nowhere more so than in bars 17ff of the overture: a harmonic sequence stepping abruptly in thirds, and each two-bar limb of the sequence dissolved into a stream of mainly semitonally moving parts. Harmonically most fascinating of all are the distant calls of the sirens in the Venusberg scene, as the most fascinating orchestral effect is that of the violins *divisi à 8*, and half-muted, in the same scene – even in the original version. In the version he made for the Paris production of 1861 Wagner actually brought off the feat of gilding refined gold.[8]

In *Lohengrin* it is the refinement of the scoring that strikes one more than anything else. The grand-operatic element in the work is reponsible for great stretches where refinement is out of the question, but even the vulgar introduction to Act III opens with six bars of positively Berliozian brilliance. *Lohengrin* was the first work in which Wagner wrote for four valve-horns and for woodwind in threes instead of the traditional pairs, and though he does not treat this more complete wind band very differently from that of earlier operas, he employs it independently still more than in *Tannhäuser*: Elsa's first appearance, Lohengrin's greeting to the King (I.3), the chromatic chords accompanying Telramund's 'Du wilde Seherin' (II.1), a long passage at the beginning of II.2 and a number of other places. The whole body of violins is also divided into three equal parts in II.2 (Elsa's 'Der morgen nun mein Gatte heisst . . .'), but the effect has nothing of the exquisite subtlety of the prelude with its four solo violins and the remainder also *divisi à 4*. However, the euphony of a great deal of the *Lohengrin* score is due not only to the relatively high proportion of primary orchestral colour and diatonic harmony but also to the increased fluidity of the inner harmonic texture in which the horns often participate – most noticeably in bars 36ff of the prelude, more characteristically in this passage in II.2:

---

[8] Cf. pp. 147ff. and 859ff. of the miniature score.

Ex. 274

Characteristic, also, is the instrumental nuancing of phrases as here in III.2 where Lohengrin's melody is underlined first by oboe, then by violins, but heard complete on neither:

Ex. 275

The numerous reminiscence themes are treated more plastically, too, especially the group associated with Ortrud which are distorted by alteration of the intervals and dissolved into passage-work; near the end of II.1, when Telramund seats himself beside Ortrud, her chief theme is blared out by three trombones and tuba in the manner of the brass recitatives of *Rienzi*; near the end of the altercation of II.5 Ortrud's 'Er ist besiegt' is underlined by solo trumpet and trombone sounding softly through the whole vocal and instrumental texture. *Lohengrin* is full of such contrasts; the 'numbers' are not yet completely dissolved into the musico-dramatic stream; the chorus when Lohengrin is first sighted ('Seht! Seht!') is naturalistic but when he actually appears the chorus (and its orchestration) would pass unnoticed in *Rienzi*, while the final chorus of Act I derives, as Wagner himself once remarked, 'more from Spontini than from Weber'[9] and that of the procession to the minster perhaps from the bridal chorus in Auber's *Muette*.

NATIONAL OPERA IN EASTERN EUROPE

While French, Italian, and German opera dominated European and

[9] Wolzogen, *Erinnerungen an Richard Wagner*, p. 26.

American stages, vernacular opera was putting out shoots in other countries during the 1830s and 1840s. In Russia the precursor was Aleksey Nikolayevich Verstovsky (1799–1862), whose 'romantic-legendary' *Pan Twardowski* (1828), *Vadim* (1832), and *Askoldova mogila* (Askold's Grave) (1835), all with spoken dialogue, were written under the shadow of Méhul, Cherubini, and Weber but with a fair amount of Russian flavour. The aria of the hero, Krasicki, in Act I of *Twardowski* – Pan Twardowski was a legendary Polish Faust – though not particularly Russian, is nevertheless the prototype of melodies in later Russian opera:

Ex. 276

O, dni scha-stli-vïkh na-slazh-de - - niy Bes-pech-noy yu-no-sti mo-ey,

(O happy days of my endless youth)

The music of *Askold's Grave* is much more distinctively national particularly in the choruses, many passages from which, such as this from the First Act:

Ex. 277

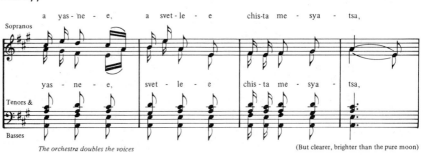

The orchestra doubles the voices

(But clearer, brighter than the pure moon)

have the genuine ring; it is not surprising that Verstovsky's opera remained popular for sixty years despite its partial eclipse by a more famous work. This was Glinka's *Zhizn za Tsarya* (Life for the Tsar: originally – and again since the Revolution – named after its hero, Ivan Susanin) (1836).

Glinka was a very much stronger talent than Verstovsky and the very first numbers of his opera – the beautiful peasant chorus, Antonida's almost unaccompanied cavatina (in which the coloratura is not so Italianate as to destroy the Russianness), the unison chorus accompanied by pizzicato strings suggesting balalaikas – perfectly create the ambience for the drama that is to follow. And it is a real drama, which reaches its climax near the end of Act IV where Susanin waits for the dawn and the certain death he will suffer for refusal to betray the whereabouts of the young Tsar, and no fewer than six reminiscence themes recall those who are dearest to him. Glinka's second opera, *Ruslan i Lyudmila* (1842), based on a fantastic-humorous poem by Pushkin, is hopelessly undramatic but full of delightful and harmonically bold music, much more original than that of its predecessor, and therefore – apart from lack of a patriotic theme – less likely to appeal to the Imperial court circle. Both operas were immensely influential musically but each had its special band of admirers; Chaykovsky preferred the first one, Balakirev, Borodin, and Rimsky-Korsakov the second. The bard's song in the opening scene of Act I and the 5/4 chorus in honour of the Slavonic love-god, Lel, also in Act I, were the main sources of the so-called 'Russian heroic style' as well being melodically influential. The oriental or quasi-oriental element in Russian music, stimulated by military penetration of the Caucasian lands, owes most of its conventions to *Ruslan* (Persian chorus, Ratmir's aria, and the Lezgian dance in Act III, Ratmir's *romans* in Act V). Even more important are the harmonic innovations, different from any in Western European music, which are employed for fantastic effects: the descending whole-tone scale which is the theme of the evil magician Chernomor, for instance, is combined when he abducts Lyudmila with a treble descending in major thirds and followed by alternation of unrelated chords pivoting about a single note.[10] Chernomor's march in Act IV, which Liszt transcribed for piano in 1843, and the barbaric *lezginka*[11] are two other astonishing pieces.

Neither the Czechs nor the Poles had as yet produced any opera composer comparable with Glinka. After his *Libušin sňatek* (1835) (see p. 594), Škroup did not attempt any more Czech operas; nor did anyone else until 1847 when Jiří Macourek (1815–after 1863) brought out his *Žižkův dub* (Ziska's oak). The Hungarians were more fortunate in Ferenc Erkel (1810–93) whose *Hunyadi László* (Ladislas Hunyadi) (1844) and *Bánk bán* (The Palatine Bánk) (comp. 1852 but unperformed for political reasons until 1861), were founded on subjects from Hungarian history in the fifteenth and early thirteenth centuries; despite their Italianate musical basis they are thoroughly stamped with Hungarian traits.[12] The fine overture to *Hunyadi László* makes much use of the familiar triplet motive from the so-called 'Rákóczi march' which is treated as the reminiscence-theme of the Hunyadi family throughout the opera; equally Hungarian is another theme in the overture, taken from a chorus in Act III, scene 1:

Ex. 278

35. Opera (1830–93)

The contemporary vernacular operas of the other peripheral European lands, from Scandinavia to Iberia, were much less noteworthy. Yet an Irishman, Michael Balfe (1808–70), was winning international recognition. Balfe began his career as a singer and as composer of three Italian operas; he conquered London with *The Siege of Rochelle* (1835), *The Maid of Artois* (1836), and, most successful of all, *The Bohemian Girl* (1843) which reached New York the following year, Madrid in 1845, Vienna in 1846, and afterwards was played all over Europe – its tunes were irresistible. His *Le Puits d'amour* (1843) and *Les quatre fils Aymon* (1844) were *opéras comiques* and *L'Étoile de Séville* a *grand opéra* composed for Paris. Nor was Balfe the only successful composer of English opera. John Barnett[13] (1802–90) had led the way with *The Mountain Sylph* (1834), the first true opera in English since the mid-eighteenth century. *The Night Dancers* (1846) by Edward Loder (1813–65) also had considerable success. But the only work which came within measurable distance of challenging *The Bohemian Girl* was *Maritana* (1845) by another Irishman, William Vincent Wallace (1812–65). And in the same year as *Maritana*, 'the first publicly performed opera with continuous music by a native American composer . . . modelled on the styles of Donizetti and Meyerbeer'[14] was given in Philadelphia; it was *Leonora* by William Henry Fry (1813–64).

OPERA DURING THE 1850s

In Paris during the 1850s the veterans Auber and Halévy continued to compose without repeating their earlier triumphs, Meyerbeer signally failed with *L'Étoile du Nord* (1854), partly a re-hash of his Berlin *Singspiel, Ein Feldlager in Schlesien*, of ten years earlier, and Adam made a notable comeback after a decade of near silence with three successful *opéras comiques*: *Giralda* (1850), and *La Poupée de Nuremberg* and *Si j'étais roi* (both 1852). Of the younger talents Ambroise Thomas (1811–96) first attracted general attention with *Le Caïd* (1849), Louis Maillart (1817–71) with *Les Dragons de Villars* (1856), and Gounod (see p. 691) – pupil of Paer, Halévy, and Le Sueur with *Sapho* (1851). By far the most gifted of these was Gounod, who was soon to set French serious opera on a fresh path. For after a delicious *opéra comique, Le Médecin malgré lui* (1858), he composed an opera which was technically *comique* but actually tragic and very quickly provided with

---

[10] See the extended example in David Brown, *Mikhail Glinka: A Biographical Study* (London, 1974), pp. 213–4.

[11] Ibid., pp. 227 and 229.

[12] See, for instance, the long excerpt from Act III of *Bánk bán* in Bence Szabolcsi, *A Concise History of Hungarian Music* (Budapest, 1964), musical appendix, XIII (ii); translation of the heroine's farewell to her son, before she drowns herself and the child, p. 234.

[13] His father's name was originally Beer and he was a cousin of Meyerbeer; cf. p. 590, n. 18.

[14] Donald Jay Grout, *A Short History of Opera* (New York and London, second edition, 1965), p. 492. The first outstanding opera to come from the New World was the completely Italianate *Il Guarany* (1869) of the Brazilian Carlos Gomes (1836–96).

recitative instead of speech.[15] The utter inadequacy of *Faust* (1859) if measured by Goethean standards, and its immense popularity for many years, have obscured the fact that it is a masterpiece of its kind – a new kind of French opera that accepted most of the musical conventions of Halévy and Meyerbeer but applied them to less spectacular and sensational subjects with more scope for lyrical melody than for dramatic effects. Even the church scene and the final *apothéose* are sincerely religious in intent, not merely effective, for Gounod was above all *dévot*. It is a masterpiece badly flawed by vulgarities and commonplace, but at its best as in the garden scene – above all, Marguerite's appearance at her window – it is very fine. If there are Italianate clichés in Faust's first arioso, the first of them is the very same that Wagner had recently borrowed as a *Leitmotiv* in *Die Walküre*. Much of the *kermesse* scene might have come from an Auber *opéra comique* but it is magically interrupted by the vision of Marguerite at her spinning-wheel with music to which Faust will later sing 'Ô nuit d'amour! Ciel radieux!'. And there are subtle touches: Siebel's pretty 'flower song', pure Gounod, is surpassed when the orchestra takes over the tune in the next scene and reaches its true climax with the words 'Un baiser lui dira le reste!'.

The renaissance of French opera was thus only just begun and in the meantime, during the 1850s the two outstanding opera-composers of Italy and Germany were very differently occupied. Verdi was producing the familiar works of his mature second period: *Rigoletto* (1851), *Il trovatore* and *La traviata* (*La Dame aux camélias*) (both 1853), *Les Vêpres siciliennes*, his first *grand opéra* (1855), *Simon Boccanegra* (1857), *Un ballo in maschera* (1859), *La forza del destino*, written for St. Petersburg (1862). All except *Traviata*, a first-night fiasco, were immediate successes and *Rigoletto* and *Trovatore* enjoyed a world popularity challenged only by *Faust*. Wagner on the other hand was living in political exile, mostly in Zürich, writing a quantity of prose-works – of which the most important was *Oper und Drama* (1851) – the poems of a vast tetralogy, *Der Ring des Nibelungen* (1853), the music of the first two parts of the tetralogy, *Das Rheingold* (1854) and *Die Walküre* (1856), the 'composition sketch' of Acts I and II of the third part, *Siegfried* (1857), and another complete opera, *Tristan und Isolde* (1859). None of these new works was yet performed; as for performance of earlier ones, *Rienzi* and the *Holländer* now lay dormant, *Tannhäuser* was making its way all over Germany but little further, and *Lohengrin* was not to cross the German border – except to Riga which was culturally German – until 1862. Wagner's European fame really began with the Paris production of *Tannhäuser*, in French and with stylistically incongruous 'improvements' and additions, on 13 March 1861. From then on, the word 'Wagnerian' quickly became synonymous with everything 'advanced' or unconventional in opera or music generally, and when *Faust* was performed at Darmstadt the same year Gounod was said to have 'adopted Wagner's principles'.

Both Verdi and Wagner were refining their art, Wagner much more

---

[15] For Strasbourg in 1860 but given in this form, and with ballet, at the Paris Opéra only in 1869.

rapidly and thoroughly so that the difference between *Lohengrin* and *Tristan* is very much greater than that between *Rigoletto* and *Ballo in maschera*.[16] But Verdi also developed. The quartet in *Rigoletto*, justly famous for its musical quality and the differentiation of the characters, is surpassed both musically and dramatically by that in Act I of *Un ballo* and the individual characters, when stripped of their preposterous Bostonian disguises, have a truth to life very different from that of the earlier stagy figures. Verdi was capable of staggering from the melodramatic puppets of *Trovatore*, who exist mainly to sing unforgettable tunes, to the living personae of *Traviata* practically at the same time, but he developed as slowly and surely as the tide comes in though successive waves may suggest the opposite. The very opening duet of *Rigoletto* is an advance on his previous treatment of text; in the final duet he rises to his greatest tragic ending so far. In *Trovatore*, one of the last 'romantic horror' operas, there is more than a little of the old vulgarized Bellini and also, perhaps because of an approach from the Paris Opéra, for the first time some influence from Meyerbeer. But *Traviata* marks a further advance in technical skill and emotional subtlety with the Violetta-Germont duet and the card-playing scene in Act II, and there are few more moving passages in nineteenth-century opera than that when in the Third Act, Alfredo's 'di quell' amor, quell' amor ch'è palpito dell' universo' from the First, is brought back on two solo violins *pp*, as Violetta reads his father's letter.

Les Vêpres siciliennes, on a Scribe libretto, is pure *grand opéra*, a failure in itself but source of a cross-fertilization which was to produce remarkable later works, of which *Simon Boccanegra* was the first but not – at any rate in its original form, for it was vigorously revised in 1881 – the finest. *La forza del destino* is another of these with a further new strain, this time from *opera buffa* in the person of Fra Melitone. Between them came the *Ballo in maschera*, where the Parisian influence derives from Auber rather than Meyerbeer: dramatically much more clear-cut than *Boccanegra* or *La forza*, where ever more accomplished music is lavished on stagy characters and confused plots. In the *Ballo* the predominant underlying pulse of Verdi's music is still that of the march, but the melodic patterns of the march now evolve more plastically (e.g. 'E posso alcun sospetto' in the finale of Act I) and the single motives are whipped up in what were later to be known as the 'workings up' (*Steigerungen*) of *Tristan* – as at 'nulla, più nulla' and so on in Ulrica's first scene.

WAGNERIAN MUSIC-DRAMA

One of the fundamental differences between Verdi and Wagner was that the practical Italian always thought and worked in terms of the existing operatic conventions within which he achieved a mastery surpassing all his

---

[16] Based respectively on Hugo's *Le roi s'amuse* and Scribe's libretto *Gustave III*, set by Auber in 1833, censorship – Austrian in Venice, papal in Rome – enforced their transposition from the Paris of Francis I to the Mantua of a nameless duke and from Stockholm to Boston, Mass.

contemporaries. With all his care for the finest nuances as well as the broad effects of dramatic expression, his scores are essentially musical projections of stage-plays with characters – at any rate in intention – from real life. Wagner, brooding in exile from his homeland and the practical world of the opera-house, beheld in dreams a new kind of musical drama which would by-pass the stage-play with its complicated plot and realistic characters. As early as 1844 he had written that an opera subject should be suitable for musical treatment only: 'I would never take a subject that might be used just as well . . . for spoken drama'.[17] Now in conceiving the *Ring* tetralogy which had sprung from a projected opera, *Siegfrieds Tod*, he saw it as a subject totally suitable for music and as different from a stage-play or opera libretto with all its convolutions of prosaic plot as could possibly be imagined. (It is noteworthy that when, twenty years later, he transformed *Siegfrieds Tod* into *Götterdämmerung* as the fourth part of the tetralogy and had to deal with human beings instead of gods and demi-gods, giants and dwarfs, and something like normal drama, he unavoidably approached more nearly to romantic grand opera than in the previous, but later conceived, parts.) There were to be no more 'numbers' but a continuous chain of 'musical-poetic periods . . . determined musically by a principal key'.[18] The emotional content is to be expressed, melodically and harmonically, by the orchestra; the voice-part will be neither recitative nor quasi-instrumental melody as in conventional opera but, floating on the surface of the orchestral stream, supply a 'connecting and elucidating link between verbal speech and musical speech' and thus give that precision of expression which pure instrumental music cannot achieve.[19] The old, familiar reminiscence theme would now have a more important role: 'melodic motives (*Momente*) of premonition or reminiscence' would 'act as signposts of feeling through all the complex structure of the drama' and 'by their related recurrence produce a unified artistic form . . . extending over the entire drama'.[20] The mere reminiscence theme was to become what was much later[21] dubbed 'clue theme' (*Leitmotiv*).

Thus dreaming in an ideal world, free from practical limitations, he laid out the score of *Das Rheingold* for an orchestra including quadruple woodwind, eight horns (four of the players doubling on a type of tenor tuba which did not yet exist, *Waldhorntuben*), four trumpets, five trombones, and six harps, with string parts sometimes more suited to virtuoso soloists than to ordinary orchestral musicians. In *Rheingold* he often employs it for vast fresco effects – for instance brass and harps only, near the beginning of sc. 2 – but from *Walküre* onward he drew on the wide palette much more selectively, sometimes writing for strings alone almost in quartet style, and reserving his great tutti for things like the ride of the Valkyries at the beginning of Act III and the fire-magic at the end. The 'love-duet' at the

---

[17] Letter of 30 January 1844, *Sämtliche Briefe*, ii.
[18] *Oper und Drama*, in *Gesammelte Schriften*, ed. cit., xi, p. 262.
[19] Ibid., pp. 278 and 281.
[20] Ibid., pp. 308 and 310.
[21] In 1871 by an obscure Wagnerian, Gottlieb Federlein.

end of Act I is very different from those of conventional opera. Wagner's harmony also became more bold, particularly in the music associated with the evil Mime in *Siegfried*. Dissonant procedures long accepted as quasi-colour effects in the piano music of Chopin and Liszt (see below p. 762) often sounded much harsher when transferred to the orchestra – though the orchestra could also soften asperities – and incessant modulation concealed key-schemes in themselves too vast to be easily perceptible. And this harmonic language, with its lack of resting points – the expected resolutions of dissonance being always deferred – and the 'yearning' of accented rising chromatic appogiaturas, reached its apogee in the opera which in 1857 interrupted the composition of *Siegfried*: *Tristan and Isolde*. Directly in the second bar of the prelude to *Tristan* the G sharp appoggiatura is prolonged and played by both oboes, the resolution on A is merely a quaver played by the first only. The progression ends on a dominant seventh in A minor – which is never resolved; the process is repeated to end on the dominants of the relative major, C, and its own dominant, E. Thus to ellipsis is added polarization of key; the tonic chord of A minor is never heard throughout the prelude. The basic thematic material of *Tristan* consists to an astonishing extent of the clichés of earlier Italian and German opera transformed by their harmonic background, plastically moulded and remoulded, and coloured by an orchestral palette no larger than that of *Lohengrin* but handled with the finesse of chamber music. And not only do the themes and harmonies and colours shade and melt into each other; the very forms do so. The moulding of the 'Ring' theme into that of 'Valhalla' at the end of the first scene of *Rheingold* is a comparatively crude instance of the kind of transition Wagner effects in *Tristan* and later scores. He justly claimed in 1859 that his 'finest and deepest art' was now 'the art of transition, for my whole texture consists of such transitions'.

The performance of *Tristan* under Bülow at Munich in 1865 marked the beginning of a new dialect of the musical language of the Western world. It was followed in 1868 by the performance of a work which hardly spoke that dialect at all, *Die Meistersinger von Nürnberg*. For the first time Wagner was able to show power to create in music living characters instead of incarnate passions, embodiments of ideas or myths, and figures from operatic stock. After the tense claustrophobic tragedy of *Tristan* came a relaxed open-airy romantic comedy with the crowds and church-scene – but not the other conventions – of grand opera; instead of chromatic harmony, predominantly diatonic polyphony. And this polyphony is wonderfully enriched by the participation of the horns, which are seldom silent. Wagner had employed the horns with great freedom and sensitivity in the early parts of the *Ring* and in *Tristan*; in *Meistersinger* he uses them as constantly and flexibly as the woodwind, so that the basic sonority is not of strings but of strings-plus-horns. And the clue-themes are not only combined as *tours de force* as in the overture but intertwine freely and naturally as in this quite insignificant passage in Act III shortly before Beckmesser essays the prize-song:

Ex. 279

This is totally thematic, for (*a*) is the 'St. John's Day' motive, (*b*) part of the 'Meistersinger', and (*c*) and (*d*) 'guild assembly' themes, and the transition from (*a*), which has just been predominant, to (*b*), which is about to predominate, is subtly bridged by suffixing the last two notes of (*a*) also to (*b*). When Wagner returned at last to the *Ring*, completing *Siegfried* in 1871 and *Götterdämmerung* in 1874, he had thus made considerable advances in technique and power of characterization; in *Parsifal* (1882) he exploited the contrast between his diatonic style and *Tristan*esque harmony, carried to an extreme in the introduction to Act III, in order to characterize the opposition of good and evil powers. However *Parsifal* reveals a slight weakening of creative vigour. It was the performance of the complete *Ring* in the specially built 'festival playhouse' at Bayreuth, 13–17 August 1876, before a brilliant international audience, which established Wagner as the dominating cultural figure he long remained.

Pl. 57   Wotan and Fricka, followed by Froh, Freia, and Donner, cross the rainbow-bridge to Valhalla while Loge calls to the lamenting Rhine-maidens in the valley below: last scene of the first production of *Das Rheingold*, staged separately at Munich on 22 September 1869.

THE LAST PHASE OF *GRAND OPÉRA*

Meanwhile true *grand opéra* in its final phase in the last years of the Second Empire was represented by Gounod's *Reine de Saba* (1862), the second part of Berlioz's *Les Troyens*, as *Les Troyens à Carthage* (1863),[22] Meyerbeer's posthumous *L'Africaine* (1865), and Verdi's second French opera *Don Carlos* (1867), and might be said to sputter out with Ambroise Thomas's *Hamlet* (1868). Both *Les Troyens* and *L'Africaine* end with the suicide of unhappy queens as their faithless lovers sail away, and Sélika's 'La haine m'abandonne, mon coeur est désarmé' is by no means an unworthy counterpart of Dido's 'Je vais mourir'; indeed Meyerbeer's opera, particularly the Fifth Act, includes some of his finest music. But the work as a whole is very unequal, while the truly Virgilian beauty of *Les Troyens*, least sensational, even least dramatic, of grand operas, gives it an extraordinary unity; it is characteristic that in the intensity of their passion – in the 'Nuit d'ivresse' duet – the lovers are subdued by the enchantment of the night. *Don Carlos* is another unequal work. As in *Les Vêpres siciliennes* Verdi seems to have felt obliged to challenge Meyerbeer on his own ground – unsuccessfully. But Schiller's tragedy provided him with characters less simple than most of those he had had to deal with in earlier operas; his power of dramatization had continued to develop, and musically his more symphonic writing for the orchestra led Bizet to declare that 'Verdi n'est plus italien; il veut faire du Wagner'.[23] Yet superb as much of it is, particularly in the four-act version of 1884, with Italian text, it is flawed by weaknesses and banalities carried on from earlier days.

Aida (1871) is also Meyerbeerian grand opera, particularly *à L'Africaine*, though it was composed to an Italian libretto for Cairo. Even musical details inevitably remind one of Meyerbeer, e.g. 'O terra addio' in the last duet recalls the duet in the same key (G flat) in *Les Huguenots*. But Aida's 'Vedi? di morte l'angelo', the exquisite voice-part matched by the exquisite orchestral sound (which surpasses even the subtlety of the Berliozian introduction to Act III, the moonlit Nile and starry sky) is as far beyond Meyerbeer's reach as the full-blooded melodic inspiration of most of *Aida*. Despite such banalities as the 'Su! del Nilo' chorus in Act II, it was Verdi's greatest work so far.

The man who was, as librettist, to help him surpass *Aida* – Arrigo Boito (1842–1918) – was at that time the leading champion of Wagner in Italy; a month or so before the first performance of *Aida* he had had a hand in the first Italian performance of a Wagner opera (*Lohengrin*).[24] He had himself composed an opera, *Mefistofele* (1868), but his wide culture and literary skill were not matched by his musical invention or technique. He took Goethe seriously and his conception embraces episodes from both parts of *Faust*, a great fresco of evil and good forces, the 'wager between God and the Devil'

[22] The first part, *La Prise de Troie*, was not performed until 1890.
[23] Hugues Imbert, *Portraits et études* (Paris, 1894), p. 160.
[24] He was the 'Italian friend' to whom Wagner addressed an open letter on this occasion. See Wagner's *Gesammelte Schriften*, ed. cit., xiii, p. 104.

as he calls it in his preface to the score. He threw over most of the conventions of Italian opera, though he gave Margherita coloratura to suggest her soul '*flying* away like a sparrow from the forest' and frequently relied on its idioms (Mefistofele's 'Popoli! e scettro e clamide' in the Brocken scene, the last duet of Faust and Margherita – and quite beautifully in the arioso 'Odi la voce' that precedes it – the Faust-Elena duet in the 'classical Walpurgis Night'). He proudly pointed out that he had made Elena's attendants sing in classical metres, that, as in Goethe, she asks Faust the secret of rhyme and thus 'classic and romantic art are married, Grecian beauty with Teutonic'. But, more importantly, his music fails miserably to rise to crucial passages, as when Faust promises to surrender his soul at the moment he is able to say, 'Arrestati, sei bello!'

RUSSIAN OPERA

Wagner had already acquired a champion in Russia in the person of Aleksandr Nikolayevich Serov (1820–71), whose conversion was effected by a performance of *Tannhäuser* at Dresden in 1858. Like Boito he was a man of wide general culture, an admirer of German literature and music, and a composer of technically weak but not unsuccessful operas; he appeared on the scene at a time when Russian opera, indeed Slavonic opera generally, was on the eve of efflorescence. Glinka's immediate successor had been Aleksandr Sergeyevich Dargomïzhsky (1813–69), whose *Esmeralda* was originally set to Hugo's own libretto on *Notre-Dame de Paris*[25] of which he belatedly made a Russian translation. *Esmeralda* is true *grand opéra*, considerably influenced by *La Juive* which had been heard in St. Petersburg in 1837 and of course completely un-Russian. His second opera, *Rusalka* (1856), was not *grand* but romantic and the shadow of Halévy was replaced by Glinka's and something of Weber's. It is based on a dramatic poem by Pushkin, a variation of the 'Undine' story with hints from *Lesta, dneprov-skaya rusalka*,[26] the most striking character being a miller greedy for money who encourages his daughter's love for a prince but goes mad when she is deserted, drowns herself, and becomes a *rusalka* (a seductive water nymph). Musically – in melodic power, orchestration, technical skill – Dargomïzhsky was decidedly Glinka's inferior; he comes nearest to him in his occasional introduction of folk-tunes and his numerous folkish intonations. Dramatically the *sapog*, one might say, is on the other foot. Whereas Glinka's duets and ensembles are essentially musical compositions with little or no differentiation of characters or emotions, *Rusalka* develops further the dramatic sense and power of characterization already shown in *Esmeralda*. And Dargomïzhsky exhibits this not only in the Miller's crudely effective crazy laughter when he too has gone mad with remorse (finale of Act III) but much more subtly, as for instance in the hypocritical smoothness of the Prince's reply to Natasha's furious challenge, 'You're going to marry?':

[25] Made for Louise Bertin (1805–77), of the family who owned the *Journal des Débats*. Her opera was produced in 1836.   [26] See p. 589, n. 17.

Ex. 280

Chtozh de - lat? sud'-be dolzhnï mï po-ko-ryat'· sya; su - di sa - ma, su - di sa -

-ma ved' mï ne vol' - nï zhen se - be po serd - tsu brat

(What can we do? We must submit to fate: judge for your*self*, judge for yourself, we're not free to take wives according to our hearts' desire . . .)

The year after the production of *Rusalka* Dargomïzhsky stated his aim to make 'the sound the direct expression of the word. I want truth.' And in a third opera (see below, p. 730), still not quite finished at his death, he carried that effort to an extreme.

In 1857 Verstovsky reappeared after a long silence with *Gromoboy*, based on the first part of Zhukovsky's poem, 'The Twelve Sleeping Maidens' the second part of which had provided the subject of his *Vadim* a quarter of a century earlier. Other Russian operas of the period are of little account and Rubinstein preferred to compose German ones, e.g. *Feramors* on Moore's *Lalla Rookh* (Dresden, 1863). Then came Serov's *Yudif* (Judith) (also 1863) which he started with an Italian text, setting the final scene of Judith triumphing with the severed head before switching to Russian. There is nothing Wagnerian about it, as might have been expected; except for the simplicity of the plot, it is pure *grand opéra* in the vein of Spontini, to whom Serov had devoted one of his first critical articles (he was a fiery polemicist), and Meyerbeer (who had been an earlier idol); the quasi-orientalism of the 'Assyrian' music is derived from Glinka's *Ruslan*. A young ex-Guards officer, Modest Petrovich Musorgsky (1839–81), wrote to Balakirev who was guiding his steps in composition that '*Judith* is the first opera on the Russian stage since *Rusalka* that has to be taken seriously' and a few months later began an opera, *Salammbô*, with a number of dramatic parallels and some striking musical affinities.[27] This came to nothing though some of the music was used in a later masterpiece. Serov himself next turned to a Russian quasi-historical subject, *Rogneda* (1865), with melodramatic plot and spectacular scenes such as the hunt in Act III in which dogs from the Imperial Kennels appeared; however most of the music is authentically Russian in flavour and much of it – including the opening scene with the witch, the dance of *skomorokhi*[28] in Act II, the 7/4 hunting chorus, and the chorus of pilgrims at the end of Act III – favourably impressed Rimsky-Korsakov. And Serov must be given credit for his naturalistic treatment of

---

[27] See the musical illustrations in Abraham, 'The operas of Serov', *Essays presented to Egon Wellesz*, ed. Jack Westrup (Oxford, 1966), particularly pp. 177–8. Musorgsky's unfinished *Salammbô* was ed. Pavel Lamm (Moscow and Leningrad, 1939).   [28] See above, p. 95.

the chorus: the crowd jeering at the Pecheneg prisoners in the finale of Act I, the picking out of 'one tenor', 'one bass', 'another bass', 'some altos', and so on in the finale of Act V. In his early Spontini article he had written that 'in *musical* drama what matters first and foremost is drama' and he had hailed *Rusalka* with enthusiasm.

In 1866 Dargomïzhsky himself embarked on a much bolder experiment in drama-with-music, 'sound as the direct expression of the word'. (Russian intellectuals had been obsessed with the conception that beauty exists only in 'that which speaks to us of life' ever since Chernïshevsky had enunciated it in his *Aesthetic Relationships of Art to Reality* in 1855.) This was nothing less than a setting of one of Pushkin's 'little tragedies', *Kamenny gost* (The Stone Guest) on the Don Juan story, just as it stands, without adaptation. The voice-parts are almost entirely recitative or arioso:

Ex. 281

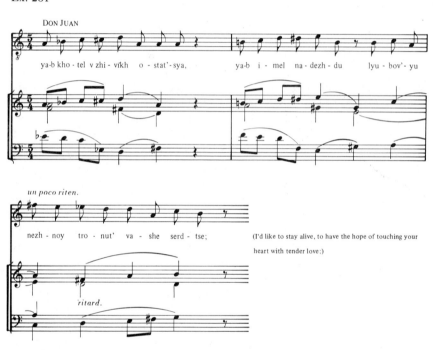

The orchestra generally accompanies but has reminiscence-themes, notably music in the whole-tone mode (including whole-tone tetrads) symbolizing the statue; the score is completely without key-signatures. Although Dargomïzhsky was certainly not unacquainted with Wagner, there are only the faintest – probably accidental – traces of Wagnerian influence. *The Stone Guest* fascinated the Balakirev circle, who took part in domestic performances of it and finished it after the composer's death. Musorgsky, who used to sing Leporello and Don Carlos, was tempted to trump

Dargomïzhsky by setting Gogol's prose comedy, *Zhenitba* (The Wedding), on similar lines but fortunately abandoned it after the First Act in favour of another project, an opera based much more freely on Pushkin's chronicle play *Boris Godunov*. This in its original form of seven scenes only was completed in 1869 but rejected by the opera committee of the Imperial Theatres; the definitive version in four acts, of which the Third was entirely new while other sweeping changes were made, was complete by 1872 and produced in 1874.[29]

In *Boris* Musorgsky turned to account a quantity of material from the abandoned *Salammbô* of 1863 and there are relics of *grand opéra* in *Boris* itself. But he had learned from Serov's naturalistic handling of the chorus in *Rogneda* and from his own 'truthful' setting of prose texts, with empirical but strikingly suggestive harmony, in songs and the *Marriage* experiment, with the result that *Boris* was – apart from the fact that it has no 'plot' in the normal sense – something entirely new, and non-Wagnerian. The character-drawing is superb; even the Verdi of *Don Carlos* could not have created in music a more subtly complicated figure than the protagonist, and the minor characters, above all the simpleton left alone on the stage at the end, are wonderful vignettes; only those of the inserted, Polish, Third Act are failures and the music is correspondingly weak though the Gounod-like love-duet is pretty. The disconnected scenes of *Boris* presuppose some knowledge of Russian history but non-Russian audiences willingly accept them for the sheer power and beauty of the musical invention. Musorgsky went on to compose scenes of hardly inferior beauty in another historical opera, *Khovanshchina* (The Khovansky plot), but this, with a comic opera on Gogol's Ukrainian story, 'Sorochinskaya yarmarka' (Sorochintsy Fair), was left incomplete and can be staged only in forms by other hands which doubtfully represent his intentions.

In the mean time another of the Balakirev circle, the half-French, half-Lithuanian César Cui (1835–1918) had set a fairly faithful translation of Heine's tragedy *William Ratcliff* (1869), with some highly effective scenes and a very beautiful love-duet in Act III. But Cui's music is, not surprisingly, often French in nature, now like Gounod, now like Auber. A fortnight before *Ratcliff*, Chaykovsky produced an intensely Russian work, *Voevoda* (on a play by Ostrovsky), rich in folk-tunes.[30] Indeed three other operas of the early 1870s, besides *Boris*, are saturated in the folk-idiom and actual folk-melody: Serov's *Vrazhya sila* (Hostile power) (1871), also based on an Ostrovsky play, Rimsky-Korsakov's *Pskovityanka* (The Maid of Pskov) (1873), and Chaykovsky's *Oprichnik* (1874). Even Rubinstein, who usually preferred to compose German operas for the German public, wrote

---

[29] A vocal score showing both initial and definitive versions was ed. Pavel Lamm (Moscow and London, 1928; rev. ed., London, 1968), the full score, ed. David Lloyd-Jones (London, 1975). Unhappily *Boris* has become better known in the well-intentioned but misguided versions made by Rimsky-Korsakov with wholesale rewriting of melody and harmony and totally new orchestration.

[30] Dissatisfied with it, the composer transferred some of the music to other works and destroyed the score. It was reconstructed from the surviving material by Lamm and published in 1953 (full score and vocal score) as supplementary volumes of the *Polnoe sobranie sochineniy* of Chaykovsky's works.

731

a Russian *Demon* on Lermontov's poem (1875). *Hostile Power*, Serov's third and best opera, is a 'naturalistic' affair of peasant life, which he ended with a murder that is not in Ostrovsky. *Pskovityanka* and *Oprichnik* are both set in the time of Ivan the Terrible, who actually appears in Rimsky-Korsakov's opera where his divided character, akin to that of Boris Godunov, is musically depicted with a skill that usually deserted the composer when he had to deal with realistic characters.[31] *Oprichnik*, which contains a good deal of the music discarded from *Voevoda*, is downright melodrama and the pesudo-oriental music of Rubinstein's Caucasian opera might not unfairly be described as second-hand *Ruslan and Lyudmila*. He was more successful with another Lermontov subject, *Kupets Kalashnikov* (The merchant Kalashnikov) (1880). This was composed just before his G minor Symphony (see above, p. 699) and, as in that, he took great and not unsuccessful pains to assimilate his style to that of the avowed nationalists; even the crowd is often treated like that in *Boris*. It is a powerful and moving work but its end, the unjust execution of the hero on the orders of the 'terrible' Tsar, made it unacceptable to the authorities.

Kalashnikov and Chaykovsky's *Orleanskaya Deva* (using Zhukovsky's wonderful translation of Schiller's *Jungfrau von Orleans*)[32] (1881) are really the last Russian *grands opéras*, and even in the *Maid* Agnes's arioso in Act II, which might belong to Gounod's *Faust*, betrays his admiration for the new more lyrical type of French opera. Already before this Chaykovsky was involved in a vogue for comic-fantastic opera based on Gogol's short stories. Serov, just before his death, had begun a *Noch pered Rozhdestvom* (Christmas Eve); Musorgsky's *Sorochintsy Fair* has already been mentioned; Chaykovsky based his *Kuznets Vakula* (Vakula the smith) (1876), one of his most fresh and delightful works, on 'Christmas Eve';[33] and Rimsky-Korsakov chose *Mayskaya noch* (May night) (1880), finding in this lyrical and fantastic piece a much more congenial vein than the drama of *Pskovityanka*, a vein which he worked at greater length and with more skill in his treatment of Ostrovsky's 'Spring tale' *Snegurochka* (Snow Maiden) (1882). Overflowing with fresh, very Russian melody and bright, transparent harmonic-orchestral colour, diversified by piquant mosaics of tiny motive particles in the music associated with Tsar Berendey, this was in its way as unprecedented as *Boris*. So also was the opera, *Knyaz Igor*, on which Borodin began to work again in 1874 but which was still unfinished at his death in 1887 and had to be completed by Rimsky-Korsakov and Glazunov (perf. 1890). So again was Chaykovsky's operatic masterpiece, *Evgeny Onegin* (1879). Yet these four very disparate works have something in common: not one is covered by Joseph Kerman's definition of opera as 'a

---

[31] The original *Pskovityanka* was ed. A. N. Dmitriev in the *Polnoe sobranie sochineniy* of Rimsky-Korsakov's works (Moscow, 1966), in full and vocal scores. On the great differences between this and the 1895 version, the one generally known, see Abraham, '*Pskovityanka*: the original version of Rimsky-Korsakov's first opera', *MQ*, liv (1968), p. 58.

[32] In which the Anglophobe composer replaced the romantic fantasy of Schiller's ending with the horror of Joan's burning.

[33] In 1885 he revised it, replacing arioso by recitative in order to speed up the action, and in this form it was performed two years later as *Cherevichki* (The little shoes).

musical form of drama'. *Boris* is a selection of scenes from a play that is itself not a drama but a chronicle in dramatic form. *Igor* stages with gorgeous and virile music scenes suggested by a medieval monkish chronicle and, to a less extent, a medieval prose-poem. *Snegurochka* is a fairy-tale in music, with pantheistic overtones. Pushkin called his *Onegin* a 'novel in verse' and Chaykovsky made of it a novel in music. Each has dramatic scenes, some of which – not many in *Igor* – are held together by a narrative thread. Collectively and involuntarily they delivered a blow to operatic convention comparable with that which Chekhov was shortly to give to the spoken play. Chaykovsky was acutely conscious of the unsuitability of his 'lyrical scenes' for performance by operatic veterans on large stages, and dreamed of performance by young students; but *Onegin* succeeded because it had characters with whom he could for once identify – as Musorgsky could identify with the most varied characters – and Tatyana's letter-scene from which his entire conception flowered is his finest piece of stage-music. *The Maid of Orleans* also sprang from one scene, Joan's narrative in Act II, but the identification and inspiration then ran out and the work never broke out of the Meyerbeerian mould. Nor does *Mazepa* (1884) or *Charodeyka* (The Sorceress) (1887). He succeeded better in *Pikovaya dama* (The Queen of Spades) (1890), a Pushkin story padded out with a great deal of eighteenth-century pastiche, because he could identify with the wretched 'hero'. Both here and in the very Frenchified one-act *liricheskaya opera, Iolanta* (1892), the voice-parts often declaim over essentially orchestral music in a way that shows he had not completely escaped the influence of Wagner.

POLISH AND CZECH OPERA

Opera in the Western Slav languages was slower in maturing than Russian opera, mainly perhaps because of the political situations in Poland and Bohemia. Neither had opera-houses comparable in resources with the Imperial Theatres in St. Petersburg and Moscow; Prague had no Czech-language opera-house at all until November 1862 when the Provisional Theatre was opened. It was Stanisław Moniuszko (1819–72) with his *Halka* (first version, 1854) who did for Polish opera what Glinka had done for Russian, giving it its first work of lasting value; but Moniuszko was no Glinka and *Halka* is much more conventional than *Life for the Tsar*. Its heroine is twin-sister, except in her purely mortal nature, to that of Dargomïzhsky's, *Rusalka*: a village girl betrayed by an aristocratic lover when he wants to marry a woman of his own class, who goes out of her mind and jumps into a river. But Moniuszko, who had up to then composed only operettas, clothed this melodrama in dramatic and colourful music, basically Italianate but with Polish inflections (to say nothing of plentiful mazurka and polonaise rhythms) and with all the customary apparatus of thematic reminiscence, church choruses behind the scenes, and so on. Halka herself is a real person, characterized in naïve and passionate and mournful songs of which the most moving of all is the lullaby she sings to her dying baby in the last scene,[34] 'Who will rock you in your eternal sleep?':

Ex. 282

The final curtain is a master-stroke of irony: the steward runs from the church and orders the crowd to strike up a merry song as the gentry are just coming out.

Moniuszko followed *Halka* with two delightful one-act comic operas, *Flis* (The Raftsman) (1858) and *Verbum nobile* (A nobleman's word) (1861), and the more ambitious *Straszny dwór* (The haunted château) (1865), a four-act comedy of two misogynic young aristocrats and the two girls who captivate them. But neither Moniuszko himself in his later works nor his successors – his pupil Henryk Jarecki (1846–1918), Ludwik Grossmann (1835–1915), Władysław Żeleński (1837–1921) – attracted extra-national attention. The Czechs were more successful, yet they too had to wait till 1892 before their great hit, Smetana's *Prodaná nevěsta* (The sold bride) (produced in 1866) with its brilliant comedy overture, gained international success.

The *Bride* began its career modestly, its two acts expanded from what the librettist originally wrote as one, with spoken dialogue; the two acts were later inflated to three and dances were inserted, and in 1870 the spoken dialogue was replaced by recitative for a prospective performance at St. Petersburg. Smetana introduced few actual folk-melodies – the *furiant* in Act II is one of them – but the now gay, now sentimental music has a not easily definable Czech flavour and successfully covers the thinness of the plot. But the *Bride* was not the first of Smetana's operas, nor typical of them. A few months before, he had produced *Braniboři v Čechách* (The Brandenburgers in Bohemia), a serious opera on a patriotic historical subject. The first original Czech opera to be given in the new Provisional Theatre at Prague, *Vladimír, bohův zvolenec* (Vladimir, chosen of God) (1863) by František Skuherský (1830–92), was such another though the subject was Bulgarian and, ironically, Skuherský set a German libretto, *Der Apostat*, which had to be translated. (Smetana himself had been brought up

---

[34] An exact parallel to that of Erkel's Melinda in *Bánk bán* (see p. 720, n. 12).

German-speaking, had great difficulty in setting Czech in his early operas, and was never quite confident in the language.) The *Brandenburgers* was also preceded by *Templáři na Moravě* (The Templars in Moravia) (1865) by Karel Sěbor (1843–1903), though Smetana could not have known it or Skuherský's opera while he was working on the *Brandenburgers*.

Both *Vladimír* and *The Brandenburgers* were regarded as 'Wagnerian', though Smetana in a newspaper criticism accused his rival of introducing Wagnerisms half-heartedly, and too much mixed up with old-fashioned recitative.[35] His own score is really more Lisztian than early-Wagnerian in idiom, but reminiscence themes are introduced generously; the choruses of the folk-scenes are very solid and diatonic, and as always he avoids quotation or imitation of folk-melody which he regarded as a very superficial manifestation of national feeling. He was no more able than anyone else at that time to avoid set numbers though he dovetails them in quite skilfully. He employed the same musico-dramatic formula for his next two operas, *Dalibor* (1868) and *Libuše* (completed in 1872, but held back for the opening of the National Theatre in 1881). *Dalibor* might be described dramatically as a Czech variation on the theme of *Fidelio*; musically it is notable for the Lisztian metamorphoses of the 'Dalibor' theme, first heard when the curtain rises in Act I. *Libuše*, originally intended to mark the coronation of Franz Josef as King of Bohemia – which never happened – is as Smetana himself said, 'not an *opera* on the old lines but a festival tableau, musico-dramatic nourishment'[36] and it ends with Libuše's prophecy of the glorious future of the Czech people, shown in six tableaux. Yet the libretto, like that of *Dalibor*, was originally written in German. Of Smetana's later operas, *Dvě vdovy* (Two widows) (1874), *Hubička* (The Kiss) (1876), *Tajemství* (The Secret) (1878) and *Čertova stěna* (The Devil's wall) (1882), the last was styled 'comic-romantic', the others as simply 'comic' – though *The Secret* is no less romantic. *The Kiss* approaches most nearly the peasant simplicity of *The Bride* but the texture is continuous and more sophisticated, and the heroine, Vendulka, is characterized by music much more beautiful than anything in the early work; the love-duet in Act I of *The Bride* is prettily sentimental, but has nothing of the tender poetry of that in Act I, sc. 4 of *The Kiss*. Many pages of *The Two Widows*, literally a 'drawing-room comedy', a number-opera originally with spoken dialogue, have a peculiar sweetness as if some air from St. John's Night in *Die Meistersinger* had blown in – as perhaps it had.

Of the younger Czech opera-composers – Vilém Blodek (1834–74), Karel Bendl (1838–97), Zdeněk Fibich (1850–1900), Karel Kovařovic (1862–1920) – none was the equal of Dvořák, despite his weak dramatic sense. They tended to be eclectic, as much German in feeling as Czech. Completely under the spell of Wagner, Dvořák also began by composing a German libretto, *Alfred*, but suppressed the result, and the original version of his first Czech opera, *Král a uhlíř*. (The King and the Charcoal-burner), is

---

[35] *Národní Listy*, 3 January 1865.
[36] František Bartoš, *Smetana ve vzpomínkách a dopisech* (Prague, 1940), p. 221.

so heavy-handed that he withdrew it after rehearsal, scrapped all the music and made a totally new setting (1874) which, as Otakar Šourek remarked, is 'much nearer to Lortzing than to Wagner'.[37] He followed it with two more comic operas, the one-act *Tvrdé palice* (The pig-headed ones) (comp. 1874, perf. 1881) and two-act *Šelma sedlák* (The rascal peasant (1878), a *tragická opera*, *Vanda* (1876), and a *historická opera*, *Dimitrij* (1882), the action of which is the historical sequel to the events in *Boris Godunov*.[38] In the comic works he drew nearer to Smetana but *Vanda* and *Dimitrij* are survivals of grand opera in the old sense. They are all surpassed by *Jakobin* (1889). Here his style had reached full maturity and he lavished his warm flow of melody, the rich colours of his orchestral palette, and the technical skill which is so easy that one is hardly aware of it (as in the combination of children's chorus with orchestral dance in the schoolmaster-musician's *serenáda* near the beginning of Act II) on a subject dear to his heart: life in a village where this schoolmaster-musician, significantly named Benda, becomes a secondary hero. *Jakobin* is very musical, not very dramatic; the climax of dramatic tension – and it is very great – comes when Julie behind the scenes in III.5 begins the simple lullaby which is to soften her father-in-law's heart. There is much play with motives, and Dvořák, like Smetana, will often dream over a repeated motive as if unable to tear himself from it, but he will also treat one with Lisztian plasticity, so that that of the hero, Bohuš, is for instance unobtrusively incorporated in Julie's lullaby (i), played by the oboe when she tells the old man she learned her song from his son (ii), accompanies his cry of grief for the lost son (iii), and leads the orchestral passage when Julie tells him 'He is still alive!' (iv):

Ex. 283

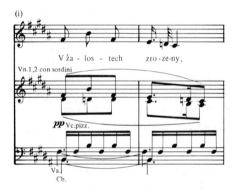

[37] *Dvořákovy skladby orchestrální*, ii (Prague, 1946), p. 33.
[38] A great deal of *Dimitrij* was re-composed in a revision of 1894, though not all of it as in the case of *Král a uhlíř*.

After *Jacobin* Dvořák wrote no more operas for ten years.[39] His younger compatriot Fibich was more intellectual, less musically gifted. His first effort, *Bukovin* (1874), is curiously Weberian; he then discovered Wagner and his second, *Blaník* (1881), already shows some of the consequences. *Nevěsta Messinská* (on Schiller's *Braut von Messina*) (1884) shows all of them. Despite lingering traces of Smetana's influence, it is the most Wagnerian opera anyone had composed so far; Fibich had great dramatic ability and assured command of Wagner's harmonic-polyphonic-orchestral technique; his *Leitmotive* are true clue-themes woven into the texture; indeed there are many pages of *The Bride of Messina* one would take to be Wagner's if only they were marked by his creative genius. But Fibich's is not to be despised; his funeral march for Don Manuel is not equal to Wagner's for Siegfried but it is quite impressive, and when the brothers meet in temporary reconciliation (I.5) he shows he can not only clinch a climax but relax without a sense of anticlimax:

---

[39] His later ones, and Fibich's, are referred to below, p. 799.

Ex. 284

Unhappily, after this Fibich abandoned opera for eleven years and elected instead to outdo his eighteenth-century compatriot, Georg Benda (see p. 474), in the field of melodrama. But the music of his *Hippodamia* trilogy – *Námluvy Pelopovy (Pelops's wooing) (1890)*, *Smír Tantalův* (The atonement of Tantalus) (1891) and *Smrt' Hippodamie* (The death of Hippodamia) (also 1891), each in four acts – is vastly inferior to that of *The Bride*.

DIVERSITY OF NON-WAGNERIAN OPERA

The long hesitation of the Germans to follow Wagner's lead is curious. Even the best of the Lisztians, Cornelius, failed to advance beyond the Wagner of *Lohengrin* in *Der Cid* (1865), though it has some fine scenes such as the duet for Chimene and the title-hero in Act II, and his unfinished *Gunlöd* is still less Wagnerian even in its harmony. And by the time Draeseke came to write his *Gudrun* (1884) he had left the progressive camp. Most of the other German composers – Bruch with his *Loreley* (1863), Rubinstein in his German operas, *Feramors* (1863) and *Maccabäer* (1875), Goldmark with *Die Königin von Saba* (1875) – had never belonged to it. Comic opera was naturally even further removed. The outstanding work in this area was Goetz's *Der widerspenstigen Zähmung* (The Taming of the Shrew) (1874), Wagnerian only in its occasional hints of *Meistersinger*. Despite its humour and such melodic beauties as Katharina's outburst near the end of Act III:

Ex. 285

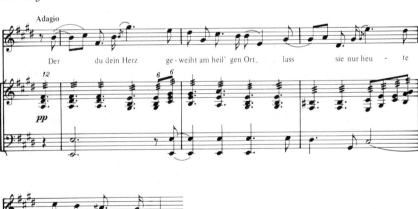

it was eclipsed in the same year by a mere operetta, *Die Fledermaus* (The Bat) by Johann Strauss, who went on to produce one gay masterpiece after another in this genre. When at last a genuinely Wagnerian opera employing the techniques of *Meistersinger* appeared in 1893, the *Hänsel und Gretel* of Engelbert Humperdinck (1854–1921), it owed its immediate success – like *Die Fledermaus* – to its wealth of delightful melody.

Similarly in France the best operettas of Jacques Offenbach (1819–80), from *Orphée aux enfers* (1858) and *La belle Hélène* (1864) down to the less frivolous, posthumously produced *Contes d'Hoffmann* (1881), have shown more staying power than most of the genuine *opéras comiques* of their day.[40] Berlioz's *Béatrice et Bénédict* (1862) is as much in a class by itself as *Les Troyens*; he employed two of its best numbers, Béatrice's 'Il m'en souvient' and the final *scherzo-duettino*, in the overture – and it is the overture which has survived best. 'Serious' *opéra comique* – like Félicien David's *Lalla-Roukh* (1862), Bizet's Gounodesque *Pêcheurs de perles* (1863) and Italianate *Jolie Fille de Perth* (1867), Thomas's *Mignon* (1866), and Gounod's *Roméo et Juliette* (1867) – is another matter. But among the genuinely comic, Gounod's *Philémon et Baucis* (1860) stands almost alone. After the war with Germany and the Commune an inferior operetta composer, Alexandre Charles Lecocq (1832–1918), scored successes – first in Brussels – with *La Fille de Madame Angot* (1872) and *Giroflé-Girofla* (1874), and 1872 also saw two delightful one-act *opéras comiques* on the Paris stage: Bizet's *Djamileh* and Saint-Saëns' *La Princess jaune*, both on oriental subjects. Saint-Saëns was to go on for many years putting new vintages into obsolescent bottles – spectacular *grand opéra* with *Samson et Dalila* (1877) and *Henry VIII* (1883), genuine *opéra comique* with *Phryné* (1893), to name only his chief successes – but Bizet lived to produce only his final masterpiece, *Carmen* (1875). *Carmen* is, of course, the most tragic of *opéras comiques*, though the grossness of the error of his friend Ernest Guiraud in replacing the spoken dialogue with accompanied recitative is now generally recognized. Like the works of Gounod and Thomas, it follows in the Auber-Halévy tradition, but it transcends them and not only modernized and re-vitalized the tradition but brought it closer to real life. And this 'realism', quite different from Russian word-and-note realism, was to influence opera as different as Chaykovsky's and that of the Italians of the coming generation. The musical realization of Carmen herself, of Don José and Escamillo, the teeming and vital melodic invention, the Spanish local colour – not the less effective for being mostly spurious[41] – combined to make it one of the world's most popular operas.

Bizet's near contemporary Léo Delibes (1836–91) had been composing operettas and full-length dramatic ballets, the second of which, *Coppélia*, was produced two or three months before the outbreak of war and became

---

[40] As with Offenbach and Strauss, the British Arthur Sullivan (1842–1900), whose partnership with the librettist William Schwenck Gilbert began modestly with *Trial by Jury* in 1875, turned out a series of comic masterpieces culminating in *The Yeomen of the Guard* (1888) and *The Gondoliers* (1889) which completely overshadowed not only his own *Ivanhoe* (1891) but the serious operas of Stanford and Goring Thomas (1850–92).

outstandingly successful. After the war he composed a sparkling comic opera, *Le Roi l'a dit* (1873), and an even more delightful ballet, *Sylvia* (1876), but his essay in serious *opéra comique* on an historical subject, *Jean de Nivelle* (1880), was less successful and the tragic *Lakmé* (1883), despite its melodic charm and oriental flavour, seems very pale beside *Carmen*. Two older composers appeared on the scene, Reyer after a long silence with *Sigurd* (1884), Lalo making his début at 65 with *Le Roi d'Ys* (1888). The latter is a striking and individual work, which introduces Breton folk-melodies, but it is not at all Wagnerian except perhaps at times in the orchestration. Nor is *Sigurd*, despite its quasi-Wagnerian subject and Reyer's enthusiasm for the Wagner of *Tannhäuser* and *Lohengrin* – and for *Meistersinger* after hearing it in London.

WAGNER'S INFLUENCE IN FRENCH OPERA

The first really Wagnerian French opera was Chabrier's *Gwendoline* (1886). (A literary landmark in the French cult of Wagner – for his ideas as much as his music – was the foundation the year before of the *Revue wagnérienne* whose contributors included Verlaine, Mallarmé, and Swinburne.) *Gwendoline* is by no means wholly Wagnerian; its Wagnerism, like its 'Nordic' plot with its Danes and perfidious Saxons which could easily have been laid in medieval France or Italy, is only skin-deep. But it has a dozen or so genuine *Leitmotive* which are modified, transformed, combined, and woven into a more or less continuous orchestral texture. Incidentally, one of them is a 'Walhalla' theme first heard in D flat in the overture and when Harald sings it ('Peut-être l'heure était venue') in Act I, sc. 4. Some of the modifications of the 'Gwendoline' motive, which occurs far more often than any other, are almost too subtle to be noticed – as is the bitterly ironic quotation by the orchestra, near the end, of her father's hypocritical blessing in the 'Épithalame'. There is a great deal of Wagnerian appoggiatura harmony and rising Wagnerian sequences. But there is also a great deal that is purely French. It goes without saying that the declamatory vocal line is, but the cantabile and its harmonization are also apt to be very French, not only in the set-numbers of which a few survive: e.g. Gwendoline's *légende* and spinning-song, and Harald's 'Je vis dans la bourrasque amère'. Harald's already mentioned version of the 'Walhalla' theme is pure Gounod. Yet sometimes the fusion of Frenchness and Wagnerism as in the prelude to Act II is perfect and produced exquisite results:

---

[41] The renaissance of indigenous Spanish opera began with the *zarzuelas grandes* of Francisco Barbieri (1823–94), *Pan y toros* (Bread and bulls) (1864) and *El barberillo de Lavapiés* (The little barber of Lavapiés) (1874), continued with those of Ruperto Chapí (1851–1909) – particularly *La tempestad* (1882) – and took a further step forward with *Los amantes de Teruel* (1889) and later works by Tomás Bréton (1850–1923). Bréton also contributed with outstanding success to the *género chico*, the 'little [one-act] kind' of zarzuela, with *La Verbena de la Paloma* (The Vigil of Our Lady of the Dove) (1893)

Ex. 286

Chabrier was more true to himself and the French tradition in the gay and brilliant *Le Roi malgré lui* (1887), where his bold harmony – for instance, the unresolved major ninth chords in the prelude – is by no means always Wagnerian. Even before his death the cause of French Wagnerian opera had passed into the less gifted hands of Alfred Bruneau (1857–1934). Perhaps influenced by the success of *Cavalleria rusticana* (see below), Bruneau opted for realistic subjects and, from *Le Rêve* (1891) and *L'Attaque du moulin* (1893) onward, found them in the novels and short stories of Zola. He also was a bold harmonist; he introduced passages in the whole-tone mode in *Le Rêve*; but in melodic invention and technical finesse he was far inferior to Chabrier and his employment of the Wagnerian apparatus of *Leitmotive* and so on is crude and sits oddly on the many old-fashioned *opéra comique* textures.

Bruneau had been a pupil of Massenet, and it was Massenet who was the central figure of French opera for many years. He was the direct heir of Gounod and the failure of the older man's *Polyeucte* in 1878, with Saint-Saëns's inability to repeat the achievement of *Samson*, left him in hardly challenged pre-eminence. He had already scored a considerable success with *Le Roi de Lahore* in 1877; with *Hérodiade* (1881), *Manon* (1884) *Le Cid* (1885), *Esclarmonde* (1889) he went from triumph to triumph in a career that was really crowned by his masterpiece *Werther* in 1892 though he went on composing operas for another twenty years. He adopted and adapted what he wanted from Wagner – the melody in the orchestra, the continuous (if rather attenuated) texture, the characterizing themes – but, except perhaps in *Esclarmonde*, there is nothing Teutonic in his music. Its essence is all to be found in the opening scene of Act II of *Manon*: the warm sensuous cello theme of Des Grieux, the *p et léger* semiquaver figure that characterizes one aspect of Manon herself, the tender, facile but haunting theme of Des Grieux's love (which returns with devastatingly emotional effect when Manon is dying). And as he matured Massenet refined and subtilized his technique, particularly his orchestration which can be exquisitely sensitive as in the Third Act of *Esclarmonde* when the heroine's voice is first heard off-stage, and in many passages of *Werther*.

LATE VERDI AND *VERISMO*

If Wagner made only a superficial impression on French opera-composers, he made none at all on the Italians after Boito. The *Gioconda* (1876) of Amilcare Ponchielli (1834–86), with a libretto by Boito based on Victor Hugo's *Angelo*, is a crude and violent work owing something to Meyerbeer, something to Verdi, but its crudity and violence were to make an impression on two of Ponchielli's pupils, Giacomo Puccini (1858–1924) and Pietro Mascagni (1863–1945). The best of the younger men so far was Alfredo Catalani (1854–93) whose *Elda* (1880) failed until it was largely rewritten as *Loreley* (1890), whose *Dejanice* (1883) was doomed to long neglect, and whose masterpiece *La Wally* was still to come in 1892; he too was to influence Puccini and Mascagni to some extent.

The great master of them all remained silent after *Aida*. And then in 1887 he broke his silence with one of the greatest masterpieces of all opera, an *Otello* for which Boito adapted, often actually translated, Shakespeare with extraordinary felicity, and Verdi translated Shakespeare's poetry and characters into music of supreme genius. The Verdi of *Otello* was not a 'new' Verdi but the old one almost transfigured; the old power without the old vulgarity – so that a patch of full-throated melody like Desdemona's 'E un dì sul mio sorriso', in the finale of Act III, causes a passing shock. There is nothing Wagnerian, though there are hardly any set-numbers – and they, the *brindisi* in Act I, the choral serenade to Desdemona in Act II, her 'willow' song, are always dramatically justified. There are no *Leitmotive* yet the reminiscence, at the very end, of 'Un bacio . . . ancora un bacio' from the wonderful love-duet in Act I is the most poignant stroke in all Verdi. The balance between voice and orchestra is superbly handled, the orchestra always alive and producing the profoundest effects with the utmost economy; the unaccompanied cor anglais anticipating the willow song before the curtain goes up on Act IV prepares a mood of intense melancholy, and the open fifths of the two clarinets in their lowest register fall like a stone on the heart.

Otello exercised no influence on the work of the young generation whose conception and depiction of jealousy and murder were far from Shakespearian. Paradoxically, in the name of *verismo* they turned their backs on this model of musico-dramatic truth and wrote crude melodramas: Puccini's *Edgar* (1889), Mascagni's one-act *Cavalleria rusticana* (Rustic chivalry) (1890), and the *Pagliacci* (The clowns) (1892) of Ruggiero Leoncavallo (1858–1919). In fact 'verism' was equated by Mascagni and Leoncavallo not with truth but with 'realism', with scenes of common life as in *Carmen* and Bruneau. The immediate and lasting success of *Cavalleria* was certainly due to its wealth of powerful vulgar melody, comparable with that of early Verdi, though in fairness to Mascagni it must be admitted that Lola's *stornello* is charming and that, as he quickly went on to demonstrate in the pleasant idyll of *L'amico Fritz* (1891), he was capable of much better things. Puccini took a still greater step forward from *Edgar* to *Manon Lescaut* (1893). Consciousness of Massenet shows in the efforts to avoid the scenes from Prévost's novel he had selected – an effort which had unfortunate effects on the dramatic scheme – rather than in the music. Puccini's tender, feminine vein of melody has a good deal in common with Massenet's, but more in later works than in *Manon Lescaut* where, on the other hand, it is impossible not to notice the unexpected influence of *Tristan* in Manon's 'Cedi, son tua!' and the rest of the love-scene in Act II, and in the beginning and end of the intermezzo between II and III. But *Manon Lescaut* as a whole is very Puccinian, a worthy opening to a new chapter in the history of Italian opera.

Eight days after the first performance of *Manon Lescaut* in Turin another chapter was closed in Milan with *Falstaff*, a *commedia musicale* for which Boito had presented Verdi with another near-perfect libretto. It was a new venture for Verdi who had never attempted comic opera since his failure with *Un giorno di regno* (The reign of a day) half a century before. But his last comedy is as great as his last tragedy, technically even finer, the union of words and music even more perfect, generally in a unique style of quasi-parlando, interplaying with a feather-light, almost impressionistic orchestra. Fenton's 'Dal labbro il canto estasïato vola' at the beginning Act III, part 2, is an exquisite example and as characteristic of the young man as his love-making in the Act I duet with Nannetta. As for Falstaff himself, he is Verdi's most complete characterization. And the master found the perfect ending to it all, a scherzo-fugue in which all the characters join: 'Everything's a jest. Man's born a joker . . . Every man mocks his fellow, but he who laughs last laughs well and heartily!'

36
Choral Music (1830–93)

The choral music of this period is so vast in bulk, so unequal in quality, above all so heterogeneous – from the monumental composition for soloists, chorus, and orchestra to the totally unsophisticated part-song or anthem – that it is almost impossible to achieve a conspectus. Even the boundaries of 'choral music' were blurred by hybridization with the symphony as in Mendelssohn's *Lobgesang*, Félicien David's *odes-symphonies*, and Berlioz's *Roméo et Juliette*, or opera as in Berlioz's *Damnation de Faust* and Schumann's *Szenen aus Goethes 'Faust'*. The outstanding fact that faces one is the low level of church music, Catholic and Protestant alike; it was produced in great quantities by mediocre and worse than mediocre composers while the real masters tended to neglect it almost completely or seize the opportunities of the Catholic rite for dazzling *pièces d'occasion*. The tide began to turn only when a plainsong revival injected new blood.

ORATORIO IN GERMANY

The only kind of religious music that really flourished was extra-ecclesiastical and sometimes doubtfully religious: oratorio. The veteran Spohr composed *Des Heilands letzte Stunden* (1835) and *Der Fall Babylons* (1840), and a hymn, *Gott du bist gross* (1836), a sort of miniature oratorio of the type that flourished in England as 'sacred cantata'. Religiosity incited Spohr to his most mawkish chromaticism while, as so often happened in oratorio, the heathen inspired vigorous and dramatic music like the chorus in which the besieging Persians threaten vengeance to sleeping Babylon, and the operatic master shows in Belshazzar's colourfully accompanied recitative when he sees the writing on the wall.

Even more operatic is *Die Zerstörung Jerusalems* (The Destruction of Jerusalem) (1832) by the master of the narrative ballad, Loewe, with its debts to Spontini and Rossini. Loewe followed this with a curiosity, *Die eherne Schlange* (The bronze serpent) (1834) for male voices only, in which the Israelites, among other oddities, sing 'Das Vorbild ist geschwunden, das Urbild ist enthüllt' (The symbol has passed away, the ideal is revealed') to the melody of 'O Haupt voll Blut und Wunden'. Elements of opera and ballad are very obvious in Loewe's later oratorios, *Die sieben Schläfer* (The Seven Sleepers of Ephesus) (1835) and those in which the religious strand is even less obtrusive: *Gutenberg* (also 1835) and *Johann Hus* (1843). *Palestrina* (1841) naturally hinges on the Council of Trent with the performance of a fragment of the 'Missa Papae Marcelli' opening Part III, the composer's wife listening at the cathedral door and presently joining in; Palestrina himself sings music that is infinitely more Leonine than Praenestine.[1] But Loewe's works and the other German oratorios of the period – the *Christus* trilogy after Klopstock (1837/1841/1842) of Sigismund Neukomm (1778–1858), Ferdinand Hiller's *Zerstörung von Jerusalem* (1840), the *Mose* (1841) of Adolf Bernhard Marx (1795–1866), all highly thought of in their day – were eclipsed by Mendelssohn's *Paulus* (1836) and *Elias* (1846).

Mendelssohn had directed the first public performance of Bach's *Matthew Passion* for a hundred years in 1829 and the conception of *St. Paul* was obviously influenced by it: witness the narrator and the interpolated hymns, one of which, 'Wachet auf' opens the overture. There is something Bachian in the opening chorus with its cries of 'Herr! Herr!' But the sense of drama that informs the Bach Passions was weak in Mendelssohn; he could manage nothing more dramatic than the 'Steiniget ihn' chorus.[2] The finest things in the work are the idyllic 'Siehe, wir preisen selig' and the would-be Bachian 'Aber unser Gott ist im Himmel' built like a chorale prelude around 'Wir glauben All' an einen Gott'. Mendelssohn's lack of dramatic power is a more serious weakness in *Elijah* which, like several of Loewe's oratorios, is a counterpart of romantic opera: it has definite characters – not only Elijah, but Obadiah, Ahab, the widow, the priests of Baal – and dramatic scenes of several numbers which in the case of the confrontation with the heathen priests are connected without a break. As in *Hans Heiling* the overture comes second, presumably suggesting the drought Elijah has just prophesied. But only in the Baal scene does Mendelssohn develop any dramatic strength, particularly in the priests' choruses and Elijah's 'Ist nicht des Herrn Wort wie ein Feuer?'. Jehovah is effectively acclaimed in the chorus 'Der Herr ging vorüber', pictorial rather than dramatic, but far too much of the work is saturated with that sanctimonious complacency which at the time passed for religious emotion. The once marvellous inspiration of the composer of the early instrumental works is stifled in it, though it shines out once in the chorus 'Siehe, der Hüter Israels'.

Three years before *Elias*, a genuinely dramatic composer had shown what could be done in the way of dramatic religiosity. In his 'biblische Szene' *Das Liebesmahl der Apostel* (Love Feast of the Apostles), performed in the Frauenkirche at Dresden in 1843, Wagner employed a male chorus of 1200 and a correspondingly huge orchestra. At first the chorus, divided in three choirs with twelve bass soloists, often in unison, representing the Apostles, sings unaccompanied; then a semi-chorus of 'voices from on high' in the cupola of the church sings 'Seid getrost! Ich bin euch nah', 'a sound as of a

---

[1] See, for instance, his cavatina in Part I quoted by Schering, *Geschichte des Oratoriums* (Leipzig, 1911), p. 417.
[2] It is as difficult for an Anglo-Saxon audience – or chorus – to realize that Mendelssohn set German words as for a German one to grasp that the original text of *Messiah* is English.

'rushing mighty wind' sweeps up through the orchestra (beginning with a *pp* drum-roll and a tremolo chord on cellos *divisi a 4*), and a work which till then has been deeply impressive begins to deteriorate into what might be the final overpowering chorus of a *grand opéra*.

THE 'SACRED CONCERT' IN FRANCE

There can be little doubt that Wagner's grandiose conception was suggested by Berlioz's *Grande Messe des Morts* (1837), itself suggested by the monumental works of the first Revolution (see pp. 654–6). Conceived for performance in the Invalides, this needed a chorus of at least two hundred and an orchestra including quadruple woodwind, twelve horns, sixteen timpani, and four brass groups placed at the angles of the choral-orchestral mass which enter at the 'Tuba mirum' of the 'Dies irae' and in the course of the 'Lacrymosa',[3] while their trombones also participate in the 'Agnus Dei'. But beside these sensational passages Berlioz placed others of restrained and quiet beauty, above all the 'Sanctus' with its subtle scoring when it returns after the wonderful long-breathed melody of the fugal 'Hosanna'. There is a certain piquancy in the fact that three months after the performance of Berlioz's Requiem, the second (D minor) Requiem of his old enemy Cherubini was also given its first performance (1838). Composed for much more modest forces – three-part male choir and normal orchestra – this too is a masterpiece, a wonderful end to a long career, but a masterpiece of a different kind. It is a genuine liturgical Mass whereas Berlioz's like his equally monumental 'Te Deum' (comp. 1849 but not perf. till 1855), is really what he himself in his *Mémoires* called a 'vast sacred concert': the third, very large, unison choir in the 'Te Deum' 'represents the mass of the people participating from time to time in a vast sacred concert', which tempts one to conjecture that he was influenced by the thinking of the Liberal Catholic publicist Lamennais. Liszt certainly was. In 1834, the year of Lamennais's *Paroles d'un croyant*, he wrote an article on the future of church music, a fragment of which was later published in the *Gazette musicale*[4] in which he deplored the broken link between the Church and 'the people' and called for the creation of

a new music which for want of a better term we may call 'philanthropic' (*humanitaire*) which shall be devotional, strong and effective, which shall unite on a colossal scale theatre and church, which shall be at the same time dramatic and sacred, splendid and simple, ceremonial and sincere, fiery and free, stormy and calm, clear and profound. The Marseillaise . . . and the beautiful hymns to Liberty are the formidably splendid forerunners of this music.

---

[3] Such forces could, of course, be gathered only with government assistance and a pretext for the commissioning was after some difficulty found in the burial of General Damrémont, killed in the assault on Constantine in the Algerian war.
[4] German translation, 'Über zukünftige Kirchenmusik', *Gesammelte Schriften*, ii (1881).

INFLUENCE OF THE PLAINSONG REVIVAL

The young Gounod likewise declared that 'the path of religious art had been lost in France for so long' and needed 'courageous and capable restorers',[5] but his prescription for restoration was quite different. He was then in Vienna, on his way back from Rome where during his laureateship he had been profoundly impressed by plainsong and Palestrina, and he had just had performed in the Karlskirche a Requiem (1842), from which the 'Dies Irae' theme was to reappear in the church-scene of *Faust*, and an *a cappella Messe de Saint-Charles* (1843), 'à peu près dans le style de la chapelle Sixtine'. And more powerful forces were working toward a revival of plainsong in France. The Benedictine Dom Prosper Guéranger, abbot of Solesmes, was a militant advocate of the restoration of the Roman liturgy and with this end in view recognized the value, indeed the necessity, of restoring the original chant, a matter that was being ventilated at the same time by Jean-Louis-Félix Danjou (1812–66), organist of Notre-Dame. In the course of his researches Danjou unearthed among other treasures the Montpellier manuscript known as H.159 which with its double neumatic/Boethian notation provided such a valuable key (see above, p. 82), but the best palaeographic work was done at Solesmes.[6]

The influence of plainsong on Gounod was, after all, slight – even slighter than that of Palestrina. His *Messe solennelle* (*Sainte-Cécile*) (1855) begins with a Gregorian intonation, D E G, but nothing comes of it and little came of his 'courageous restoration' of church music; by that time he had written three operas. Liszt had already used the same intonation in his *Missa quattuor vocum ad aequales concinente organo* (1848) and was to continue to do so as a 'sound symbol of the Cross' in later works. But his church music at this period was intensely personal and romantic, as in the settings of Psalms XIII and CXXXVII (1855 and 1859), while in the splendid *Missa solennis* for the consecration of the restored cathedral at Gran (Esztergom) (1856) he came near to realising his old ideal of a *musique humanitaire*. On the other hand Berlioz, turning from the monumental to the intimate in his delightfully naïve *trilogie sacrée L'Enfance du Christ* (1854), introduced the second part, 'La Fuite en Égypte', with 'une petite ouverture fuguée', in F sharp minor with flattened leading-note, which he had written in 1850, enshrining the spirit though not the letter of plainsong. Liszt followed suit in the Kyrie of his *Missa choralis* (1865):

---

[5] Letter quoted in J.-G. Prod'homme and A. Dandelot, *Gounod (1818–1893): sa vie et ses oeuvres* (Paris, 1911), i, p. 89.
[6] The history of the plainsong revival is long and troubled. Diffusion of the Solesmes versions was hindered by a reprint of the 'Medici' version (see p. 247) which enjoyed Papal protection from 1873 to 1903. Dom Joseph Pothier's *Mélodies grégoriennes* did not appear till 1880, his Gradual in 1883, the Solesmes Antiphoner in 1891, and the compendium, *Liber usualis*, in 1896. Dubious rhythmic theories deprive the 'Solesmes tradition' of historical authority but the great series of source-facsimiles, *Paléographie musicale*, begun by Dom André Mocquereau in 1889, is of inestimable value.

Ex. 287

SECULAR ORATORIOS

French oratorios were rarities at this period and neither Félicien David's *Moïse au Sinaï* nor César Franck's jejune *églogue biblique*, *Ruth* (both 1846) can compare with *L'Enfance*. But in the same year as these two works Berlioz himself produced a remarkable specimen of what might be called 'secular oratorio' – though he himself called it *légende dramatique* – with *La Damnation de Faust*. Expanded and slightly altered from *Huit scènes de Faust* (in Gérard de Nerval's translation) published in 1829, the *Damnation* is typically Berliozian in having a ramshackle over-all structure while including some of his finest and most original music. The eight scenes were the Easter hymn, the peasant chorus, the delicious 'Concert des Sylphes', the songs of the rat and the flea, Marguerite's wonderful, haunting 'Roi de Thulé' and her *romance*, 'D'amour l'ardente flamme'. This was *Faust* without Faust. But in the *Damnation* he is handsomely restored – watching the sunrise in Hungary (because he has to hear Berlioz's hair-raising arrangement of the 'Rákóczi march'), brooding in his study, making love to Marguerite, invoking 'Nature immense' – and the characters of Mephistopheles and Marguerite are filled out.

Schumann's *Scenen aus Goethes 'Faust'*, on which he worked spasmodically from 1844 to 1850, adding the overture in 1853, ignores Berlioz's picturesque inessentials and concentrates almost entirely on the dramatic scenes and character-drawing: the garden scene, Gretchen praying to the statue of the Virgin and tormented in the cathedral, Faust's blinding and death. Much of the music is more dramatic than one expects of Schumann and the idiom is sometimes close to Wagner's of the same period; as for the picturesque, the sunrise scene, despite its unusually poetic scoring, cannot compete with Berlioz's equivalent 'scene on the banks of the Elbe'. In Part III Schumann breaks away from drama and measures himself wonderfully against the sublimity of Goethe's final scene, beginning 'Alles Vergängliche', but failing, as every composer has failed, to find the right music for 'Das Ewig-Weibliche'. Schumann had come late to choral music. His first essay consisted of three Heine settings with orchestra (1841) which he converted with no more success into solos and a duet with piano, Op. 64, No. 3. Then came what he described as 'an oratorio . . . not for an oratory', *Das Paradies und die Peri* (1843), its text selected from a German translation of that favourite subject of the period, Moore's *Lalla Rookh*. (The oriental subject and the nature of the work were probably suggested by Marschner's *Klänge aus Osten*, an 'overture, songs and choruses', which he had heard, admired – and compared with Berlioz's *Roméo et Juliette* – in 1840.) The local colour is pale and the romantic fire of the early Schumann of the piano works has sunk rather low. There are delightful pages such as the chorus of the spirits of the Nile, 'Hervor aus den Wässern', and striking effects like the alternation of string and wind chords when the tenor sings 'Doch eine Stille, fürchterlich, liegt über diesen Himmelsfluren', but *Das Paradies* as a whole sinks under the weight of so much square-cut, block-chordal choral writing. This was a feature of most German choral composition at the time; even Mendelssohn's only important secular choral work, *Die erste Walpurgisnacht* (1832, revised 1843), also suffers from it; presumably the quality of the largely amateur choirs imposed a style that might be described as inflated *Liedertafel*.

Both Mendelssohn and Schumann composed a considerable quantity of part-songs of no great interest, but Schumann persisted in turning out compositions for soloists, chorus, and orchestra, of which the short *Requiem für Mignon* (1849), intimate and tender until nearly the end, is by far the best. *Der Rose Pilgerfahrt* (The Pilgrimage of the Rose) (1851), a homely, rather mawkish counterpart to *Paradies und die Peri*, has one beautiful solo number, the tenor's 'Und wie ein Jahr verronnen ist' where the affinity with Wagner shows again. During 1851–3 Schumann experimented with a new type, the ballad-cantata for soloists, chorus and orchestra – *Der Königssohn, Des Sängers Fluch, Vom Pagen und der Königstochter*, and *Das Glück von Edenhall* – lit up only spasmodically by flashes of harmonic or orchestral inspiration. But nothing lights up his only two liturgical works, the C minor Mass and Requiem composed for the Catholics of Düsseldorf (both 1852).

RELIGIOUS MUSIC IN ENGLAND

Nor was Mendelssohn very happy in his church music, of which the most ambitious piece was the festival cantata *Lauda Sion* (1846), which comes to real life only in the treble solo 'Caro cibus'. And it is a treble solo, 'O for the wings of a dove', which has kept alive his most popular church composition 'Höre meine Bitten' (Hear my prayer). Some of his church music was composed to English words – two Magnificats and Nunc dimittis, a Te Deum and Jubilate, half-a-dozen Anglican anthems – mostly during his last years, and it is easy to see why they impressed the English public. The only native church musician of real distinction was Samuel Sebastian Wesley (1810–76), son of Samuel Wesley (see p. 654), whose Service in E (1845) stands out in Anglican liturgical music, as among Victorian anthems do his 'The Wilderness' (one of a volume of twelve anthems published in 1853) and the later 'Thou wilt keep him in perfect peace' and 'O Lord, thou art my God'. Pierson, whose *Jerusalem* (1852) is one of the few mid-Victorian oratorios of any distinction, neglected church music altogether. *Jerusalem* brought a draught of generally unwelcome fresh air and another draught came from a different quarter. Just as the anti-Gallican tendency in the Roman church in France had sparked off a revival of plainsong there, the Oxford Movement in England turned men's minds to the possibility of adapting plainsong to Anglican ends – a process which Sebastian Wesley denounced as a return to barbarism. *Laudes Diurnae*, containing 'the Psalms and Canticles adapted to Gregorian Tones' for the use of All Saints', Margaret Street, London, was published in 1843, and Thomas Helmore (1811–90), Master of the Children of the Chapel Royal, published *The Psalter and Canticles noted* (1850) and *A Hymnal Noted* (1858) which were adopted in High Church circles. A similar revival of plainchant with German words was soon mooted in Prussia, and in both countries demands for standard hymnals including hymns of all periods in trustworthy forms led to the publication of the *Deutsches Evangelisches Kirchen-Gesangbuch* (1854) and *Hymns Ancient and Modern* (1861).

LITURGICAL MUSIC IN BAVARIA AND AUSTRIA

Catholic Bavaria and Austria had nothing comparable with Gallican aberrance to combat, no cause like the Roman tendency of the Oxford Movement to advance. But dissatisfaction with the general low level of church music led there also to renewed study of the Palestrina style, stimulated by such books as Justus Thibaut's *Über Reinheit der Tonkunst* (Heidelberg, 1824) and R. G. Kiesewetter's on Palestrina (Leipzig, 1834)[7] and the compositions and missionary work of Caspar Ett (1788–1847) in Munich (where the Nazarene painters (cf. p. 663) first won recognition in their homeland); it culminated in the launching of a complete edition of Palestrina's works[8] comparable with that of Bach's[9] begun in 1851. Restoration of 'the good old style' of plainsong was also prescribed in

---

[7] This was really a condensation of Giuseppe Baini's *Memorie storiocritiche della vita e delle opere di G.P. · da Palestrina* (Rome, 1828).
[8] *Giovanni Pierluigi da Palestrinas Werke* (Leipzig, 1862–1907).
[9] *Johann Sebastian Bach's Werke* (Leipzig, 1851–99).

Ludwig I's church-music rescript of 1830, but the best intentions led in the end to the unfortunate republication at Regensburg (Ratisbon) in 1871 of the 'Medici' version.

Conservative Austria preserved a link with the old tradition stemming from Fux in the 35 Masses and other church music of another notable contrapuntist, Simon Sechter (1788–1867), and the work of his greatest pupil, Bruckner. Bruckner's only important works before his study with Sechter (1855–61) were a Requiem in D minor (1849), modelled on Mozart's, and *Missa solemnis* in B flat minor (1854), where in the Credo he again leans heavily on the Mozart Requiem (opening of the 'Recordare'). Even in the much more mature D minor Mass (1864) he gives evidence of close study of Haydn's *Missa in angustiis*, not only echoing themes in the Kyrie but following the old master's symphonic organization of the movement. But in the D minor Bruckner moved into the middle of the nineteenth century: the more plastic themes (e.g. the cello melody in the middle of the Benedictus), the bolder, more chromatic harmony, the more extensive orchestral writing, even thematic cross-quotation and allusion from movement to movement, reveal an unexpected if only superficial affinity with the Liszt of the Esztergom *Missa solennis*. He had already introduced drama (the orchestral crescendo before 'Et surrexit') in the B flat minor; he now injects a more personal emotion.

In the following year he heard the first performance of Liszt's oratorio *Die Legende von der heiligen Elisabeth* at Pest, was deeply impressed by it, and met the composer. From then onward he was drawn more and more into the Liszt-Wagner orbit and turned from mainly liturgical to mainly symphonic composition, but not before he had composed two more fine Masses – in E minor for eight-part choir and wind (1866) and F minor for soloists, chorus, orchestra, and organ (1868) – to say nothing of a massive 'Te Deum' (1881)[10] for the same forces as the F minor Mass. In the Kyrie and Sanctus of the E minor Bruckner seems to be challenging comparison, not unsuccessfully, with Palestrina, though Palestrina's ghost did not inhibit his introduction of hair-raising dissonances in the 'Miserere' of the second Agnus. In the 'Incarnatus' of the F minor he comes nearer than anywhere else to Liszt. Bruckner's F minor Mass was to some extent autobiographical, connected with a nervous collapse and his recovery from it; a quotation from the second Kyrie is introduced in the finale of his Second Symphony and the 'Benedictus' is quoted near the end of the slow movement. A similar quotation of the opening string figure of the 'Te Deum' in the sketches for the uncompleted finale of the Ninth Symphony gave rise to an improbable theory that Bruckner had contemplated using the 'Te Deum' to conclude the symphony.

---

[10] The dates given are for the completion of the original versions; as with his symphonies, Bruckner revised again and again.

LISZT'S MASSES AND ORATORIOS

The most surprising contemporary Mass was the *Petite Messe solenelle* (1863) of the septuagenarian Rossini, originally accompanied only by two pianos and harmonium and performed privately in the presence of Meyerbeer, Auber and Ambroise Thomas, later orchestrated, and performed publicly in 1869. The Gloria is very fine and the mass as a whole is less operatic than the much better known *Stabat Mater*.[11] Liszt's *Missa choralis* for four voices and organ of 1865[12] has already been mentioned; it is a bold essay in an up-to-date church style which should reconcile the traditional modes with modern harmony. His next Mass, for the coronation of the Emperor Franz Josef as King of Hungary in 1867, was necessarily very different; it had to be not only festive but Hungarian, and various Hungarian themes are worked into it: for instance from the 'Rákóczi march' at 'Laudamus te' in the Gloria, while another from the same source is floated by a solo violin over the Benedictus, *adagio molto*:

Ex. 288

Curiously, for the Credo Liszt simply borrowed one from Du Mont's *Cinq Messes en plain-chant* (see p. 412 n. 70). In his Requiem (1868) for male voices, organ, trumpets, trombones, and timpani Liszt returned to the severity of the *Missa choralis*.

Liszt's two completed oratorios, the *Legend of St. Elisabeth* (1864) and *Christus* (1867), are conceived on totally different lines, one so operatic that stage-performances were given as early as 1881, the other partly liturgical, but both making full use of a large orchestra which is given a high proportion of purely instrumental music. Determined to honour the Hungarian princess with 'authentic' music, Liszt based her personal theme on an old antiphon, 'Quasi stella matutina' *In festo sanctae Elisabeth*, not realizing that it was intended for St. Elizabeth, queen of Portugal; he was luckier with the theme in Part II, heard first in the orchestra, associated with his heroine's deeds of charity, which he found in the *Lyra Coelestis* (1695) of the Esztergom canon György Náray with the words 'Szent Örzsébet asszony életérül' (St. Elizabeth, lady preserver of life). A third theme, suspiciously

---

[11] The first six numbers of which, redeemed only by a few passages such as the exquisite horn-writing at the beginning of the 'Quis est homo' duet, date from 1832; the last four, including the anguished harmonies of 'Quando corpus' and the vigorous double fugue 'In sempiterna secula', were added in 1841.
[12] Not to be confused with another *Missa quattuor vocum* (male voices only) originally dating from 1848 but completely revised in 1869.

dancelike in its original form, is connected with Hungary itself. From these, and original ideas, treated as in his symphonic works Liszt created a quasi-operatic fresco of some dramatic power (e.g. the characterization of the wicked Landgravine Sophie) and great beauty, as in the miracle of the roses.

Pl. 58   Liszt conducting the first performance of his *Legende von der heiligen Elisabeth* in the Redoute at Pest on 15 August 1865 to commemorate the 25th anniversary of the Pest Conservatoire (after a drawing by Bertalan Székely).

Borrowed themes are used plentifully also in *Christus* but they are all plainsong, though naturally cast in modern rhythmic moulds: e.g. the Advent introit 'Rorate caeli' which both opens and closes the work, the unaccompanied soprano solo 'Angelus ad pastores', the 'Stabat Mater dolorosa' in Part III.[13] Part I is a miniature 'Christmas oratorio' in which after a 'Stabat Mater speciosa', the song of the shepherds and the arrival of the Three Kings are represented by two extended orchestral movements. Part II consists of the Beatitudes, the Lord's Prayer, the founding of the Church (Matthew, xvi. 18), the miracle of the tempest (Matthew, viii. 24–26), with a very realistic orchestral storm, and the entry into Jerusalem, Part III of the agony in the garden, 'Stabat Mater dolorosa', and the Resurrection with 'O filii et filiae' set to the traditional tune. Despite Liszt's usual tendency to rely overmuch on dynamics to achieve climax, *Christus* is a masterpiece unmatched by any other oratorio of the mid-century.

[13] *Liber Usualis* (1949 edition), pp. 353, 397, 1874 respectively.

ORATORIO IN DECLINE

A Fleming, Peter Benoit (1834–1901), entered this field with his *Lucifer* (1866) and followed it with *De Schelde* (1869), *De Oorlog* (The War) (1872) and other oratorios which have never made any impression outside his native land. The same must be said of the works provided by British composers for great choral festivals in London and the provinces where oratorio was considered the highest form of musical art. Sterndale Bennett's *Woman of Samaria* (1867), Sullivan's *Prodigal Son* (1869), *Light of the World* (1873), and *Martyr of Antioch* (1880), and the productions of lesser musicians appealed to an appetite not satisfied by the works of Handel, Mendelssohn, and Spohr. Sullivan's most ambitious failure was his big secular cantata, *The Golden Legend* (1887), where the feebleness of his invention hardly needs to be demonstrated by comparing his Prologue with Liszt's setting of the same words, *Die Glocken des Strassburger Münsters* (1873). Foreign composers also wrote for the English market, Gounod his *Rédemption* (1882) and *Mors et Vita* (1884) for Birmingham, Dvořák *Svatá Ludmila* (1886) for Leeds. A younger Englishman, Hubert Parry, raised hopes with *Judith* in 1888 and *Job* in 1892, as did Horatio Parker with *Hora novissima* (1893) in America, which were never fulfilled. Oratorio was a dying form and the galvanic treatment it was given at the turn of the century (see below, p. 798) only prolonged its demise without averting it.

THE 'ORATORIO OF SENTIMENT'

In France, it is true, it enjoyed an unexpected popularity – not in the first place because of Gounod (who returned to Mass composition in 1870 after a fifteen-year break and wrote more than a dozen of various kinds during his last years) but on account of Massenet's sensuous and sentimental 'drame sacré' *Marie-Magdeleine* (1873), with its love duet for Jesus and the Magdalen, and his 'mystère' *Ève* (1875). But his more ambitious 'légende sacrée' *La Vierge* (1880) was a total failure, though it may be said to have repaid Massenet's debt to Gounod by contributing to *La Rédemption*. There is no Massenet in *Mors et Vita* but too much pure Gounod for the realization of such a grandiose conception: a triptych like Liszt's *Christus*, of which Part I consists of a *prologus* followed by a complete Requiem Mass, Part II of the Last Judgement, and Part III of the Vision of St. John. The Requiem naturally challenges comparison not only with Berlioz's but with a more recent one, also overpoweringly dramatic and more nearly a concert oratorio than a liturgical composition: Verdi's *Messa da Requiem* of 1874. One has only to compare, say, Gounod's descending arpeggio on 'Rex tremendae' with Verdi's – and the two are sufficiently alike to make comparison inevitable – to recognize his debility. Or his flaccid 'Lacrymosa' with Verdi's piteous cry. Verdi's pure melody can be operatic but superb (the soprano's 'signifer sanctus Michael' in the Offertorium): Gounod's never rises above that of the orchestral 'Judex' (which incorporates one of his handful of recurrent themes, the one he associated with 'the happiness of the blessed'), an epitome of the sentimental piety of the period. (A very similar theme in Saint-Saëns' 'poème biblique' *Le Déluge* (1876), first played by a solo violin in the Prelude, symbolizes 'the innocent happiness of man' in the days of the patriarchs.) And there is plenty of sentimental piety in Franck's 'poème-symphonie' *La Rédemption* (1872), already referred to on p. 692, *Les Béatitudes* on which he worked spasmodically from 1869 to 1879, and the 'scène biblique' *Rébecca* (1881).

By far the best of these is *Les Béatitudes* and even that is startlingly unequal. Each beatitude is presented by antithetic choirs – one celestial, the other voicing the money-grubbers in the first beatitude, the pessimists in the second, Pharisees, tyrants, and so on – while the baritone Voice of Christ always intervenes near the end singing, or accompanied by, a characteristic theme variously modified. It may be quoted as it appears in the second movement, in order to show how Franck can sometimes express ineffable sweetness by purely diatonic discords instead of his all too common saccharine chromaticism:

Ex. 289

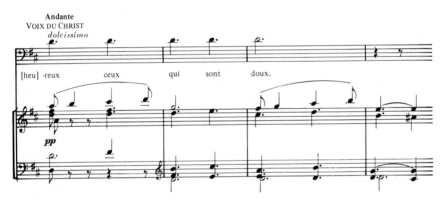

The fourth and eighth beatitudes are consistently fine. But Franck could express evil, chorally or in the person of Satan who is heard in the last two numbers, only in terms of bad opera. Yet each movement is redeemed by exquisite passages for the celestial choir and its accompanying orchestra: 'Heureux ceux qui pleurent' in No. 3, 'À jamais heureux les miséricord-dieux!' in No. 5, 'De l'enfant la sainte ignorance' in No. 6, the first section of the quintet of peacemakers in No. 7. The quiet pulsation of alternating chords accompanying Christ at the end of No. 4 is no less memorable, and the end of No. 8, when the 'Christ' theme mounts in waves of orchestral sound bearing the choral 'Hosannas!', is overwhelming. The paradisal bliss of some passages of the *Béatitudes* is paralleled in French religious music only by Gabriel Fauré (1845–1924) in the Sanctus and final antiphon 'In paradisum' of his Requiem (1887).

LITURGICAL MUSIC IN GERMANY AND RUSSIA

Franck never competed with the very prolific Gounod in the field of liturgical music. He had written one or two Masses and some motets in earlier days, a group of *offertoires* in 1871, but they are of little significance. Saint-Saëns' church music consists mostly of motets. But liturgical music was not flourishing anywhere at this period. In the German lands the only noteworthy successor to Bruckner was Rheinberger who on being appointed director of the Bavarian Court Chapel in 1877 embarked on the composition of Masses both *a cappella* and with organ. The finest is probably the one in E flat, Op. 109, for two four-part *a cappella* choirs, which might be described as Palestrina weakened by diminished sevenths. But similar appointments to the Russian Imperial Chapel drew only a small response, and that neither very important nor very interesting, from Balakirev and Rimsky-Korsakov during the 1880s. On the other hand when Chaykovsky in 1878 set the Liturgy of St. John Chrysostom (see p. 65), which he admired very much as literature, his publisher had to fight a lawsuit with the Imperial Chapel which claimed a monopoly in the printing of religious music. He went on in 1881 to make what he called an 'essay in the harmonization of liturgical chants' of the *Vsenoshchnoe Bdenie* (the 'Vesper Service'). All these were extremely simple harmonizations with no contrapuntal interest, but in three *kheruvimskiya* (cherubic hymns) and a few other pieces (1884–5) he was a little more venturesome, only to be reproved by Balakirev for introducing 'anti-ecclesiastical dance-rhythms' in the tenor and bass parts of his setting of an old Kiev chant:

Ex. 290

Yet this third *kheruvimskaya* was later declared to be 'as important in Russian sacred music as *Life for the Tsar* in Russian secular music'.[14] It marked the beginning of a renaissance.

THE CHORAL WORKS OF BRAHMS

The one outstanding piece of Protestant religious music during these decades was neither liturgical nor an oratorio. Brahms's *Ein deutsches Requiem* (completed in 1868 after years of spasmodic work) was the composition of a man who, like Chaykovsky and many other non-believers of the time, accepted the Christian ethic and admired the Bible as literature. Nevertheless it may be called 'Protestant' since a composer's inheritance may be as important as his beliefs and Brahms's North German background was Lutheran, as he was to demonstrate repeatedly: in *a cappella* motets spread over thirty years, in the eight-part *Fest-und Gedenksprüche* of 1889, and in the organ preludes of 1896. The *German Requiem* begins and ends with beatitudes. 'Blessed are they that mourn' and 'Blessed are the dead which die in the Lord'; the latter, of course, comes from Revelation (xiv, 13) not the sermon on the Mount, but 'Selig sind, die da Leid tragen' is the equivalent of Franck's 'Heureux ceux qui pleurent' and comparison beautifully illustrates the differences of Lutheranism and Catholicism: Franck's theatrical lead-up, the rather bland assurance of the 'voix du Christ', the bliss and ecstasy of the *choeur céleste*, contrasted with the noble human consolation of Brahms's music, illuminated here and there by harp-sounds but darkened as a whole by the absence of violins. For the second

---

[14] N. Kompaneysky in *Russkaya muzïkalnaya gazeta*, 31 October 1904.

movement of his *Requiem*, 'Denn alles Fleisch es ist wie Gras', Brahms borrowed a sarabande-like movement from the abandoned symphony mentioned on p. 694. There is comfort – the chorus 'Wie lieblich' and the soprano solo 'Ihr habt nun Traurigkeit' – but it is really only the trombone chords heralding the Last Judgement which bring release in the almost Bachian fugal 'Herr, du bist würdig'. Brahms's later compositions involving chorus and orchestra are shorter and with one exception, the *Triumphlied* (1871) for the victory of German arms, secular. Two are Goethe settings for soloist and male chorus – the almost operatic *Rinaldo* (1868) and the *Rhapsodie* (1869) suggested by Brahms's discovery of J. F. Reichardt's setting of the same verses from the *Harzreise im Winter* – and four pieces for chorus and orchestra only: the Hölderlin *Schicksalslied* (Song of Destiny) (1871), the *Triumphlied* (from Revelation, xix),[15] the Schiller *Nänie* (1881) and the *Gesang der Parzen* (1882) from Goethe's *Iphigenie auf Tauris*. The last fifteen bars of the 'Song of the Fates' are one of the most 'modernistic' passages in the whole of Brahms's work.

THE NARRATIVE BALLAD

A favourite secular form was the narrative ballad on more or less Schumannesque lines. Such were Gade's *Elverskud* (Elf-king's daughter) (1853) and *Den Bjergtagne* (The Mountain Thrall) (1873), Max Bruch's *Odysseus* (1872), ten scenes from the *Odyssey*, Grieg's *Landkjaenning* (Landfall) (also 1872 but drastically rewritten in 1881), Mahler's *Das klagende Lied* (original version, 1880), Dvořák's *Svatební košile* (The Wedding Dress, generally known as *The Spectre's Bride*) (1884), Horatio Parker's *The Ballad of a Knight and his Daughter* (1884), Stanford's *The Revenge* (1886) and *The Voyage of Maeldune* (1889). This was a genre Parry wisely never attempted but his Milton setting *Blest Pair of Sirens* (1887) was a notable indication that English choral writing was beginning to feel blood circulating in its veins once more.

---

[15] Brahms omitted the words of the second part of xix: 2, 'for he hath judged the great whore', but provided the music for them in three bars of orchestral unison the meaning of which would have been perfectly clear to the conquerors of Paris.

37

The Dominance of the Piano (1830—93)

During the greater part of the century the piano – vastly improved in sensitivity by Sébastien Érard's double-escapement action (1823) and in resonance by the one-piece cast-iron frame produced by the American firm of Chickering (1862),[1] to mention only the most important innovations – played a completely dominant role in all the more intimate musical forms. Its solo music changed *pari passu* with that of the orchestra: while the conventional symphony was cultivated less and less, the sonata for piano alone became less vital than other forms, by no means all 'miniature'. But just as it assumed heroic roles in the concerto, so it became the favourite and dominant partner in chamber ensembles while the string quartet lost its classic pre-eminence. In solo song too, the voice was less often accompanied than partnered by the piano and sometimes found itself the less important partner. Even orchestral music was sometimes conceived in pianistic terms; Brahms would write the original version for two pianos. For good or ill, the hand on the keyboard – particularly the German hand – ruled the musical world.

THE PARISIAN PIANIST-COMPOSERS

For a time the pianistic centre of Europe was Paris; the most famous virtuoso-composer of the old generation, Kalkbrenner, was living there and so were the two outstanding younger men, Chopin from 1831, Liszt from 1828 to 1834, to say nothing of such lesser lights as Ferdinand Hiller (till 1835), Johann Peter Pixis (1788–1874), and Henri Herz (1806–88). All these were foreigners, but Paris also had a native virtuoso-composer in Charles-Valentin Alkan (1813–88). Virtuosity was still during the 1830s the most obvious characteristic of major piano music. The climax of sheer virtuosity in Chopin's work was touched in the concertos and other compositions for piano and orchestra (see p. 616) and the *Douze grandes Études* Op. 10 (pub. 1833) and the *Douze Études*, Op. 25 (pub. 1837). Compared with Liszt's *Grandes Études* (pub. 1839) and *Bravourstudien nach Paganini's Capricen* (pub. 1840)[2] it is not high; indeed Liszt's studies are so extremely difficult

---

[1] The dates are those of the Paris *Expositions* at which they were launched.
[2] No. 1 borrows its prelude from Paganini's No. 5, the rest being a transcription of Paganini's No. 6. No. 3 is based not on a caprice but on the 'Campanella' ('Rondeau à la clochette') from Paganini's Concerto No. 2 in B minor (see p. 612).

that he was constrained to make them less so in the *Études d'exécution transcendante* (1852), where they were now given such titles as 'Mazeppa' and 'Feux follets', and *Grandes Études de Paganini* (1851) respectively. Liszt also displayed his transcendent technique not only in his *fantaisies* and *réminiscences* of operas, of which that on *Don Juan* (*c.* 1843) is outstanding, but in the transcriptions he made as propaganda for Schubert's songs (1835 onward), Berlioz's *Symphonie fantastique* (1834), and other works he admired. (It was perhaps Liszt's versions of Berlioz and Beethoven symphonies that suggested to Alkan the idea of an original *Symphonie* for piano: Nos. 4–7 of his *Douze Études dans les tons mineurs*, Op. 39 (*c.* 1850).)

What strikes one most in Chopin's studies is not their technical brilliance but their iridescent harmony, common in all his mature music but most noticeable in the *études*. Here the harmony, projected on a screen of plastic motive-patterns, is the very essence of the music: showers of diminished sevenths, broken-up or side-slipped, 'suspensions' unobtrusively repeated but long unresolved, intercalated 'foreign' chords (interdominant in function) or whole passages, so that 12 bars before the end of Op. 10, No. 7, C major is apparently dissolved for four bars yet never really left. The passages at the end of Op. 25, No. 7, and 13 bars before the end of the second of the *Trois nouvelles études* (1840) are *loci classici* of Chopin's harmony in which key is richly extended without any sense of modulation.

Whatever Chopin touched turned to poetry, even an exercise for the right hand playing solely on the black keys. (When Alkan writes a white-key study, the *allegro barbaro* No. 5 of his *Douze Études dans les tons majeurs*, Op. 35 (1847), it is merely vigorous octave-playing mainly in F with B natural instead of B flat.) His nocturnes are more romantically poetic than Field's. His valses, mazurkas, and polonaises are ideal, not real dances, and these 'miniature' forms were sometimes considerably extended from 1841 onward: the C sharp minor Mazurka, Op. 50, No. 3, the Polonaises, Op. 44 and 53, the *Polonaise-fantaisie* of 1846, and the *Barcarolle* of the same year which is a vast nocturne. It is characteristic of the period that he wrote only two mature piano sonatas and the Cello Sonata of 1847, and characteristic of Chopin that his mastery of large-scale structure is much less apparent in these than in the forms he developed for himself. Some of these – notably the scherzos – are very obviously sectional; but in the *Polonaise-fantaisie*, the F minor Fantaisie (1841), and the ballades, particularly No. 3 in A flat (1841) and No. 4 in F minor (1842), he achieves great sweep and power of continuous thought; phrase-structure and transitions are subtilized, and the forms truly organic. They are, moreover, purely musical – or, if they have extra-musical significance, Chopin carefully suppressed it. Whether or not the ballades were inspired by Mickiewicz's ballads (and it may be true that the F major Ballade, No. 2, with its final catastrophe was suggested by the poet's 'Switez'), they are not programme music – despite their palpable but undemonstrable narrative flavour – and Chopin never used a descriptive title.

When Liszt turned to the intimate piano piece from 1835 onward it was with quite different intent. The *Apparitions* (1835) and the pieces in the *Album d'un voyageur* (1842), later recast in the first 'year' of *Années de pèlerinage*, are reactions to persons, to political events (the workers' rising at Lyons), to specific places in Switzerland, or expressions of religious moods and thoughts (*Harmonies poétiques et religieuses*). They are often rhapsodic and smothered in indications of the poetic content – 'Extrêment lent avec un profond sentiment d'ennui', 'lento disperato', 'avec coquetterie'. Pseudo-recitative, a device seldom used by Chopin but all the more effective when he does use it, is all over the place. Liszt allowed his first Ballade (1849) to be published in France as a crusader's song (*Chant du Croisé*) and the crusaders who march in it anticipate the stiff jerky puppets who march in *St. Elisabeth*. And then in 1839 he began to compose songs – much more copiously than Chopin ever did – and at once turned the earliest group, settings of three Petrarch sonnets, into piano pieces and inserted them in the second 'year' of the *Années de pèlerinage*. Similarly the three *Liebestraüme* of 1850 are transcriptions of song-settings of Uhland and Freiligrath.

SCHUMANN'S PIANO MUSIC

Schumann also paid his tributes to Paganini: *Studien nach Capricen von Paganini*, Op. 3 (1832) and *Études de concert d'après des Caprices de Paganini* (1833). He also turned three early songs into piano music and wrote little for the piano that had no extra-musical meaning. But Schumann would never have become a virtuoso, even if he had never damaged a hand; he was as profoundly introvert as Liszt was flamboyantly extrovert. Both drew heavily on literary sources, as Chopin almost never did, but Liszt frankly exploited his whereas Schumann would often conceal or only hint at them, so that Liszt appears exuberantly many-sided while Schumann is always himself behind varied masks. The title of *Papillons* (1832), based largely on polonaises and waltzes written in frank imitation of Schubert's, is a double play on words, for butterflies are metamorphoses of larvae and in German *Larve* means not only a grub but a character in a mask. Both Liszt and Schumann were preoccupied with titles, frequently changing them, to a degree that would have seemed strange to an earlier generation. Thus *Carnaval: scènes mignonnes sur quatre notes* (1835, pub. 1837) was originally called *Fasching: Schwänke auf vier Noten für Pianoforte von Florestan*. The four notes were A, E flat, C, B natural which in German spelled four letters of peculiar significance to him, ASCH or SCH . . A . ., and Florestan was one of two characters invented as persons in a contemplated novel, which he discovered later to be projections of himself and put forward as composers of a number of his other works. And the title *Faschingsschwank* was transferred to Op. 26 (comp. 1839). In the three-movement C major *Fantasie* (comp. 1836, pub. 1839), originally *Obolen auf Beethovens Monument: Ruinen-Trophaen-Palmen*, he contrives by quotations from a Beethoven song (see p. 677, n. 10) to pay tribute to a greater master and at the same time send a message, hinted at in the Friedrich Schlegel epigraph, to his 'distant beloved'. He quotes the 'beloved's' own 'Notturno', Op. 6, No. 1, in his *Novelletten* (1838), Nos. 1 and 8 ('*Stimme aus der Ferne*'), and greets Sterndale Bennett with a quotation from *Der Templer und die Jüdin* ('Du stolzes England, freue dich') in the *Études symphoniques* (1834, pub. 1837).

These intimate miniatures enshrine the essential Schumann. Of the large-scale piano works only the great C major *Fantasie* is wholly successful. Of the sonatas – F sharp minor (comp. 1835), 'No. 3' in F minor ('Concert sans orchestre') (1836), and 'No. 1' in G minor (1838)[3] – the F sharp minor was partly assembled from earlier compositions and the G minor built round the slow movement, one of the early songs, just as Chopin built his B flat minor Sonata (1839) round a *marche funèbre* written two years before.

ROMANTIC PIANO MUSIC: 1830–50

A more curious 'assembled' sonata was Loewe's *Grande Sonate élégique* (*sic*), Op. 32, the three movements of which were composed in 1819, 1825, and 1834. Like Loewe's other sonatas – the E major, Op. 16 (1830) with *ad lib.* parts for tenor and soprano in the slow movement, and the *Zigeunersonate*, Op. 107 (1847) in five movements each with a title and in one case with stage-directions – its only virtue is oddity. Equally odd – by reason of its numerous indications of spiritual autobiography scattered throughout the score – but of much more musical value is Alkan's Op. 33 (*c.* 1847). The piano sonatas of the Mendelssohn epigones – Wilhelm Taubert (1811–91) (Opp. 20, 21, and 35, 1835–41), Sterndale Bennett (F minor, 1837) and Gade (E minor, 1839) – are not odd but rather dull.

Except for the *Variations sérieuses* of 1841 Mendelssohn himself never attempted large-scale piano solo composition after the Op. 28 *Phantasie* but devoted himself almost exclusively to *Lieder ohne Worte*, of which seven more books were composed between 1833 and 1845. Their domestic poetry is too seldom lit up by fancy comparable with Schumann's – Op. 30, No. 1, Op. 62, No. 1, and Op. 67, No. 3 are among the exceptions. And the same must be said of the miniatures of Sterndale Bennett, who never recovered the youthful freshness of his *Three Musical Sketches* (1835), of Taubert's various sets of *Minnelieder*, Gade's *Akvareller* (1850), and the innumerable piano pieces of the amiable but spineless Hungarian Stephen Heller (1814–88). Félicien David's *Mélodies orientales* (1836), later incorporated in his *Brises d'Orient*, have at least the interest of being – unlike Schumann's *Bilder aus Osten* (1848) – genuine travel impressions of the East. Smetana had begun to compose *Bagatelles et Impromptus* (1844), *Albumblätter* (1845 and 1849), *Hochzeitsszenen* (1849), and less Germanic polkas. But the outstanding second-rank piano composer of the period was Henselt, whose *Douze Études caractéristiques de concert*, Op. 2 (1837), each headed by a

---

[3] The definitive finale was written in that year, replacing a Presto passionato of 1835. On Schumann's drastic changes in the first movement (1833), see the extended examples in Linda Roesner 'Schumann's Revisions in the First Movement of the Piano Sonata in G minor, Op. 22', *19th Century Music*, i (1977–8), p. 97.

poetic motto in French, are inferior only to Liszt's and Chopin's while his *Ballade*, Op. 31 (1846), is worthy of the composer of the F minor Concerto (see p. 679).

In 1835 Henselt settled permanently in Russia where native piano music was mostly of the light salon type published all over Europe, mostly by amateurs and often in *Albums musicaux* and their kind. Even Glinka's piano pieces are mostly only superior examples of the type, but his four-hand *Capriccio sur des thêmes russes* (1834) is an early and striking demonstration of his skill in treating folk-material and his *Souvenir d'une mazurka* (1847) though Chopinesque is individual. More important as a piano composer was his friend Ivan Laskovsky (1799–1855), an officer in the War Ministry and pupil of Field, who published ephemeral valses and so on in the albums but whose more significant pieces appeared posthumously.[4] These include an extended *Ballade* in F sharp minor and some ingenious variations on two Russian themes, one of them 'Kamarinskaya'. The best of his shorter pieces is one of his *Pensées fugitives* (a favourite tag of the day, used also by Henselt and Smetana):

Ex. 291

PIANO-DOMINATED CHAMBER MUSIC

The two great German masters of these years seem to have marked their disillusionment with the solo piano sonata by turning to chamber music in which the piano was either a prominent partner or makes itself felt in theme and texture. In 1837–8 Mendelssohn, who had almost completely neglected this medium for ten years, produced a group of three string quartets, Op. 44, and a Cello Sonata (B flat), and followed them in 1839 with a Piano Trio in D minor. Schumann, who had never tried it after his failure with a youthful

---

[4] *Oeuvres complètes pour piano de Jean Laskowsky* (St Petersburg, 1858).

piano quartet, composed in 1842 a Piano Quintet (an unpopular com-bination), a Piano Quartet (almost equally unpopular), and a group of three string quartets, Op. 41. (String quartets were seldom published in groups after the classical age; Rubinstein's Op. 17 and 47, published in 1855 and 1857, were almost the last.) Mendelssohn completed his total of chamber music with another cello sonata (D major) and a quartet 'Capriccio' in 1843, another Piano Trio (C minor) and a String Quintet in B flat in 1845, and the F minor Quartet and two separate movements in 1847, Schumann his with two Piano Trios (D minor and F) in 1842, a third Trio and the first two of three violin sonatas[5] in 1851, and – true to his predilection for separate pieces – various *Fantasiestücke, Romanzen* and their kind, all with piano, during 1849–53.

This corpus of work includes many delightful movements – and moments: the scherzi of Mendelssohn's E flat Quartet, Op. 44, No. 3, and C minor Trio, the Andante espressivo of his D major Quartet, the finale of Schumann's Quintet and the third movement of his D minor Violin Sonata. Some are deeper than delightful: the Adagio of Mendelssohn's F minor Quartet, the march movement of the Schumann Quintet and the Andante cantabile of the Piano Quartet. But the parts do not, except in the case of the Piano Quintet, add up to wholes and none is wholly true to the medium. In both Quintet and Quartet Schumann too often simply uses the strings to double the piano or as an antithetic block. Mendelssohn again and again – the opening movements of the D major and F minor Quartet and the B flat String Quintet – writes orchestrally with a great deal of 'scrub' tremolo, or like Schumann he shows, for instance in the Adagio and finale of the E flat Quartet, Op. 44, No. 3, the hand of the keyboard composer or, as in the D minor Trio, allows the actual piano to dominate everything.

Piano-writing and piano-'feeling' also dominate the *Trois trios concertans* which the young César Franck published as his Op. 1 in 1841. A fourth in one movement, originally intended as the finale of No. 3, came out the next year with a dedication to Liszt. No. 2 was properly described as a *trio de salon* but Nos. 1 (F sharp minor) and 4 are interesting as presaging both in the nature of the thematic material and in its transformation and cross-quotation the Franck of many years later. He wrote no more chamber music at the time. Indeed French chamber music was then almost non-existent except for the string quintets with double bass, of Félicien David – four sets of six, *Les quatre saisons* (1845–6) – and his friend the expatriate Englishman Onslow (see p. 624) whose flow of production was unstoppable. At the same time another English amateur who stayed at home, John Lodge Ellerton (1801–73), was turning out string quartets with equal industry, equal competence and equal lack of divine fire; like Sterndale Bennett, he could just avoid platitude, as in the opening of No. 39 in F:

---

[5] No. 3 in A minor has been ed. Oliver Neighbour (London, 1956).

Ex. 292

and he wrote in an outdated style but he was, if we except the Bennett of the A major Trio (1839), the best British chamber-music composer of the day.

THE FRENCH *MÉLODIE*

The piano-dominated solo song was essentially German, firmly established by Schumann in 1840; the greatest French song-composer of the 1830s, Berlioz, could not even play the piano. But he sang and most of the non-German song-composers sang. Berlioz's mature *mélodies* – a fairly new name for the solo song – stand in roughly the same relation to the *romances* of the previous quarter-century as Schubert's mature songs to the older German *Klavierlied*. Except for the Victor Hugo 'Captive' (1832, rewritten and orch. 1848) and 'La mort d'Ophélie' (1848) the best are in four sets: *Neuf mélodies imitées de l'anglais* (Thomas Moore, trans. Thomas Gounet) (1830), *Nuits d'été* by Théophile Gautier (1834, pub. 1841 and 1856), *Fleurs des landes* and *Feuillets d'album* (collections pub. 1850). The best of the 'Irish melodies' is 'Le Coucher du soleil' ('How dear to me the hour'), the accompaniment of which is improved in the orchestral version; the impassioned 'Élégie' ('When he who adores thee') is ruined by a disastrous accompaniment. 'La Captive' was not only orchestrated but rewritten in a freer form, but the piano accompaniment is harmless and the voice-part is one of those subtle, indefinably fascinating melodies, like the 'Roi de Thule' in *Faust*, that only Berlioz could write. The Gautier set opens with a sparkling and effective 'Villanelle' and follows it with the masterly 'Spectre de la rose'; 'Absence' is also very fine but suggests in voice and accompaniment the influence of the *Lied*. In sharpest contrast, the piano-part of 'Au cimetière' is amateurish beyond belief yet interesting for the B flat which intrudes inexplicably on the D major chord six bars before the end and disappears unresolved in the first version of the song – Berlioz later repented of his temerity – an effect of pure colour perhaps hinting at the 'chant plaintif' of the dove perched on the yew-tree. 'La Mort d'Ophélie', on Ernest Legouvé's paraphrase of 'There is a willow grows aslant a brook', is only half effective in its original form, overwhelmingly tragic with orchestra as the second of the *Tristia*, Op. 18.

Berlioz was almost alone among French composers of *mélodies*. Naturally David did not fail to exploit his oriental vein in *Les Perles d'Orient* (1845), *Sous les palmiers* (1845),.and other collections, and while the 'Tristesse de l'odalisque'[6] from the *Perles*, a Gautier setting, does not equal 'La Captive' it is a beautiful song. Slighter in workmanship are the songs of Henri Reber (1807–80). But many French songs of the period were the work of foreigners. Meyerbeer published *Six elégies et romances* in 1839. In the handful that Wagner composed in Paris *c.* 1840 the best is the urgent, if *Lied*like setting of Hugo's 'Attente'; his Ronsard 'Mignonne, allons voir si la rose' is rather solidly Teutonic and his setting of a translation of 'Die beiden Grenadiere' anticipated by a few months Schumann's idea of introducing the 'Marseillaise' at the last stanza. But the finest of the foreign songs are Liszt's Hugo settings of 1844, two of which – the exquisitely light-handed 'Comment, disaient-ils' and the warmly romantic 'Oh! quand je dors' – are masterpieces. The piano parts are generally important and Wagner's 'Dors, mon enfant' could with little adjustment be played as a piano solo.

SOLO SONG IN THE SLAV LANDS

That cannot be said of the songs of Alyabyev (see p. 652–3), whose productivity continued unabated; however imaginative his accompaniments, they are still backgrounds; like practically all Russian composers of the time, he was himself a singer. As for Aleksandr Varlamov (1801–48), composer of the well-known 'Krasny sarafan' (1833), and Aleksandr Gurilev (1802–56), their numerous songs get nothing more than support from the piano; the vocal lines, however, influenced by folk-music, contributed to the crystallization of a national idiom. Even Glinka's earlier songs are often Italianate, indeed sometimes settings of Italian texts. The earliest of his maturity was the declamatory *fantaziya* 'Nochnoy smotr' (Night review) (1837).[7] In the same year came the Pushkin 'Gde nashe roza' (Where is our rose?),[8] a 17-bar gem mostly in 5/4 time. But both of these are exceptions among Glinka's songs. His norm is the lyrical *romans* and he produced some beautiful specimens: 'Ya pomnyu chudnoe mgnoven'e' (I remember the marvellous moment) (1840), another Pushkin setting, the Russian flavoured 'Zhavoronok' (The lark) and the Italian flavoured 'K Molli' ('To Molly'). The two latter are included in *Proshchaniya s Peterburgom* (Farewell to Petersburg) (1840), a collection in which Glinka seems to have deliberately set out to demonstrate his versatility: the near-operatic, the ballad, bolero, cavatina, barcarolle, drinking song. Very soon (*c.* 1847–8) Dargomïzhsky, yet another singing composer, grew out of his rather amateurish beginnings as a *romans* composer and was composing such songs as the Lermontov settings 'I skuchno, i grustno' (It's boring and

---

[6] *Das ausserdeutsche Sololied (Das Musikwerk)* (Cologne, 1958), ed. Frits Noske, No. 26.
[7] Zhukovsky's translation of Zedlitz's 'Die nächtliche Heerschau', which Loewe had set in 1830 – a finer song.
[8] Complete in David Brown, *Mikhail Glinka* (London, 1974), p. 149.

sad) and 'Mne grustno' (I'm sad because I love you), in which pure lyricism is tempered by acute sensitiveness to the text. But his special place in the history of Russian song was earned by later work (see below pp. 784–5).

It is impossible to deny Chopin a place in the history of Polish song but it is only a small one. Most of his seventeen posthumously published songs are early pieces, most of them are mazurkas, and the piano-writing is incredibly unChopinesque. His two best vocal mazurkas are on Mickiewicz's 'Moja pieszczotka' (My sweetheart) (1837) and Stefan Witwicki's 'Pierścień' (The ring) (1841), and a snatch of mazurka begins and ends his finest song, the tragic, complex 'Śpiew grobowy' (Song from the grave) (1836). Two years later Moniuszko published in Berlin, and originally in German, three Mickiewicz settings including one of 'Moja pieszczotka'. In 1843 he went on to publish the first of his twelve *Śpiewniki domowe* (Songbooks for the home), a corpus of more than three hundred songs: narrative ballads, lyrical songs, light songs revealing the operetta composer, and dance-songs (mazurkas, krakowiaks, and so on). In 1835 Loewe had published five settings of translations of Mickiewicz's ballads, Opp. 49 and 50, and these clearly incited Moniuszko to try his hand. His first essay was 'Trzech Budrysów' (The three Budrys, Loewe's Op. 49, No. 3) (1840) and two more, 'Świtezianka' and 'Panicz i dziewczyna' (Loewe's 'Switesmädchen' and 'Der junge Herr und das Mädchen'), were published in his first *Śpiewnik*. Moniuszko's playful setting of 'Moja pieszczotka' catches the spirit of the poem more accurately than Chopin's well-known melody (Op. 74, No. 12). The opening of 'Dąbrowa' (The oak-wood) (comp. *c.* 1851) is a good example of his lyrical vein:

Ex. 293

(Oak-wood, little oak-wood, you have a good master)

Czech solo song in those days rarely rose above the level of sentimental popular song; all but one of Smetana's early songs are German and even the few songs of his much later maturity do not show him at his best.

THE SPATE OF ROMANTIC *LIEDER*

In Germany the narrative ballad continued to flourish in the hands of Marschner and Loewe. Marschner's 'Die Monduhr', Op. 102, No. 2,[9] his version of Uhland's 'Die Rache', Op. 160, No. 2, and Loewe's 'Archibald Douglas' (as late as 1858) are among the most powerful they ever wrote. Of the younger masters of German song, Mendelssohn, Schumann, Liszt, and Robert Franz (1815–92), neither Mendelssohn nor Franz was attracted to the ballad form. One of Liszt's earliest German songs was a quite impressive setting of Uhland's 'Die Vätergruft' (1844) and in later years he achieved a real masterpiece with 'Die drei Zigeuner', but with his tendency to overdramatize, he also treated as dramatic ballads poems that are really lyrics, not only 'Die Loreley' and the 'König in Thule' but 'Kennst du das Land?'. Schumann, on the other hand, had little dramatic gift, yet the earliest in the great outpouring of songs released in February 1840 was a setting of Heine's 'Belsatzar', later published as Op. 57. Other ballads followed – Chamisso's 'Die Löwenbraut', 'Die rote Hanne' (Béranger, trs. Chamisso), Heine's 'Beiden Grenadiere', all in the same wonderful year, and Schiller's 'Der Handschuh' (1850) – but they are far from the best or most characteristic of Schumann's songs. For that, one must turn to the lyrical ones – which paradoxically often admit a narrative element (e.g. the Eichendorff *Liederkreis*, Op. 39, Nos. 4, 7, 10, 11).

What is characteristic is that he began by setting Heine. Nearly forty Heine songs, including the Op. 24 *Liederkreis* and the *Dichterliebe* cycle, date from 1840; no other poet excited him to the same degree. He drew on Eichendorff for the Op. 39 *Liederkreis* and Chamisso for *Frauenliebe und -leben* (more 1840 songs), and Rückert for the *Liebesfrühling* cycle (1841) and naturally numerous other poets, but not even Goethe meant so much to him as Heine. And the same may be said of his contemporaries. Heine was the German embodiment of the spirit of that age and the musicians' treatment of him is, so to speak, a touchstone for their natures. Goethe took second place with them, Lenau and other obvious choices, including translations of Byron, Scott and Moore, came after, and some composers had peculiar favourites, e.g. Mendelssohn and Franz in their friends Karl Klingemann and Wilhelm Osterwald.

Mendelssohn was not one of the greatest song-writers, though he began with a fine gloomy setting of the folk-poem 'Es ist ein Schnitter', Op. 8, No. 4 (1830) and ended with another great acceptance of death in Eichendorff's 'Nachtlied', Op. 71, No. 6 (1847). Between them lies a great deal of merely amiable, facile music – among which must be included his best-known Heine songs: 'Gruss', Op. 19, No. 5, and 'Auf Flügeln des Gesanges', Op. 34, No. 2. His unimaginative Volkslied-like 'Allnächtlich im Traume', Op. 86, No. 4 – 'und's Wort háb ich vergessen' set to the same music as 'zu deinen süssen Füssen' – is not to be compared with Franz's Op. 9, No. 4, still less with Schumann's in the *Dichterliebe*. And those two latter also demonstrate

---

[9] In *Romantik in der Tonkunst (Das Musikwerk)*, ed. Kurt Stephenson (Cologne, 1961), No. 6.

the difference between very fine and *hors de concours*, for Franz's setting is masterly – the throbbing *pp* left-hand chords and ghostly spread right-hand intervals at 'Du siehst mich an . . . wehmüthiglich', the climax, the pause, and the end are more imaginative than Schumann's – and yet they are swept out of mind by Schumann's all-through spontaneous impetus. So many of Franz's songs are like this, deeply felt, with admirable word-setting, beautifully fashioned partnership of voice and accompaniment, but lacking the final touch of genius. Only now and again, as in the extremely simple little Lenau song, 'Bitte', Op. 9, No. 3, does a Franz setting sound inevitable. But Schumann's, particularly with Heine, often make any other composition of the poem unthinkable. He has been accused of not understanding Heine and the same charge lies against Franz and Liszt; they took Heine's poems at their face-value and were inspired by it; keener insight might well have resulted in poorer music – or no music at all. For that generation the value of a song still lay not in the poem but in what the musician made of it. Like Schubert, Schumann could make little master-pieces – for instance, 'Der Nussbaum', Op. 25, No. 3, and some of the *Frauenliebe* songs – out of mediocre poems.

The role of the piano in Schumann's songs and to a slightly lesser extent in Franz's is more important than in earlier lyrical songs. It not only duets with the voice, as in 'Der Nussbaum'; its harmony, not merely supporting, conveys what the voice alone cannot say, as in 'Stille Tränen', Op. 35, No. 10, and in that song as in so many others the piano continues for some time in wordless commentary after the voice is silent. And when the voice is not silent it is often merely the surface of a self-sufficient piano-part. (The already mentioned 'Bitte' is one of a number of similar cases in Franz.) Since so many of Schumann's instrumental melodies are 'rhyming' and stanzaic in pattern, and some are known to have been verbally inspired, it is tempting to regard a song like the Eichendorff 'Wehmuth', Op. 39, No. 9, – and there are many like it – as a piano piece from which the composer has neglected to discard the verbal inspiration.

In Liszt's German songs, most of which are later – or later versions of early ones – than Schumann's, the piano parts are important but in a different way. There is little doubling of the voice and the piano-writing is surprisingly simple in texture though not in harmony. Instead of coalescing, the roles of voice and piano are well differentiated. A poem is often dissected and the half-declaimed sentences punctuated by the piano. The second version of 'Morgens steh ich auf und frage' (1859) is typical, and comparison with Franz's setting, Op. 25, No. 4, neatly characterizes both composers – for Franz subsumes the whole poem in four phrases, four melodic arcs, twenty bars as compared with Liszt's 46. (Schumann's naïve Op. 24, No. 1 is one of his failures.) Liszt tends to dramatize detail even in an undramatic poem, e.g. 'Anfangs wollt ich fast verzagen'; Franz – intent on lyricism – tends to play down dramatic or ironic elements even in Heine. He is never more dramatic than in 'Verfehlte Liebe' though this is a perfect example of the Schumannesque piano-piece-with-voice-doubling. But when Liszt is obliged to concentrate, as in the scathing 'Vergiftet sind meine Lieder' (1844),[10] he achieves a masterpiece, one of the most terrible hate-songs ever written. The *morendo* end of the piano-part is typical of the unconventionality of Liszt's songs, an unconventionality which became even more marked in those of his old age (see below, p. 789).

ORGAN MUSIC IN MID-CENTURY

The 1850s at Weimar were Liszt's most prolific period. He sought new fields, composing not only for orchestra but for organ: a fantasia and fugue on the chant of the three anabaptists in the First Act of Meyerbeer's *Prophète*, 'Ad nos, ad salutarem undam' (1850), and the first version of a prelude and fugue on BACH (1855). He was not the first major nineteenth-century composer to write for the organ. Mendelssohn's handful of preludes and fugues (*c.* 1839) are of no great account and his six so-called sonatas, Op. 65, (1839–45) are really a collection of voluntaries written for the English market. Schumann's six fugues on BACH (1845), impressive as a demonstration of the skill he had now achieved in the devices of academic counterpoint, are a more significant symptom of a tendency that was to become very important half a century later: an anti-romantic reaction. (In that it leaned on Bach, it was also a symptom of historicism parallel with the leaning on plainsong.) It was followed up by Schumann's disciple Brahms – yet another pianist writing organ music – in a little group of organ fugues dating from 1856–7, likewise Bachian pastiche.[11] Liszt's organ music is not Bachian and his fugues are not fugal when the exposition is over. In the earliest the *fuga* is no more than one variation near the end of a series of rhapsodic variations, or rather theme-transformations, in which the second phrase of Meyerbeer's theme, 'iterum venite, miseri', is sometimes worked separately. Equally the BACH work is essentially a brilliant romantic improvisation on the theme, not a 'Präludium und Fuge'.

PROBLEMS OF LARGE-SCALE INSTRUMENTAL FORM

Liszt's tendency to improvisation was more successfully, though by no means completely, tamed in his solution of that problem of piano-sonata structure which had defeated Mendelssohn and Schumann. Completed in February 1853, when he had already embarked on one-movement symphonic poems, his B minor Sonata combines the elements of the several-movement sonata within the framework of a distended first-movement form, the slow movement serving also – by an afterthought – as second subject, and is given specious unity by theme-transformation. Classical argument is superseded by romantic rhetoric. Liszt's model was adopted by

[10] All these songs are compositions of Heine.
[11] Those interested in such matters should note that in the subject of the A flat minor Fugue Brahms hit on a 10-note row: eleven notes, of which only A flat is repeated.

few, of whom the best and most immediate was Julius Reubke (1834–58) in his B flat minor Piano Sonata, a real if unoriginal masterpiece, and more freely and on a smaller scale in his *Sonate für Orgel (Der 94ste Psalm)* (both 1857). The Organ Sonata, which is also related to Liszt's 'Ad nos' and is prefaced by the verses 1–2, 3, 6–7, 17, 19, and 22–3 of the psalm by way of programme, was not published till 1871. Two years earlier Rheinberger had published the first of his twenty organ sonatas, Op. 27 in C minor, very conservatively romantic while Reubke's is almost orchestral in style. With these – and with the best of Franck's again very different *Six pièces* (1862) – began a revival of interest in organ music, impossible so long as its exponents were such men as Louis Lefébure-Wély (1817–70) and Gustav Merkel (1827–85). Franck himself was to approach most nearly to Bach in the second of his *Trois chorals* (1890), a free passacaglia in B minor.

It is significant that even Liszt did not return to the piano sonata. Nor did Brahms after his early essays, Opp. 1, 2, and 5 (1852–3). Rubinstein waited more than twenty years before adding a fourth to his first three, Opp. 12, 20, and 41 (1854–5). Chaykovsky's C sharp minor (1865) is a student work which had only one successor, the clumsily written G major thirteen years later, and Grieg's E minor of the same year, modelled on Gade's, is not much better. The best piano sonata of the 1860s was the C sharp minor *Sonata quasi fantasia*, Op. 6, of Liszt's disciple, Felix Draeseke (1835–1913). Draeseke's is a curious work, Lisztian in the material of its first movement (Introduzione e Marcia funebre) but not in plan; the second movement is a Chopinesque presto Intermezzo (Valse-Scherzo) in D flat, and the E major finale often suggests Schumann despite its harkings back to the first movement. What all except Brahms lacked was the sustained and spreading inventive power of a Haydn or Beethoven.

Brahms was not afraid to model the opening of his Op. 1 on the opening of Op. 106 or to wake echoes of the Adagio molto of the first 'Razumovsky' quartet near the end of the slow movement of his Op. 5. There is much Schumann too – the verbally inspired themes of the slow movements of Opp. 1 and 2, and the 6/8 A minor theme ('Mein Herz ist im Hochland') in the finale of Op. 1, the pianistic workmanship – even a hint of Liszt in Op. 2. But instead of a splendid row of successors, Brahms turned – after the Schumannesque *Balladen*, Op. 10, of which at least No. 1 was verbally inspired – to variation writing: variations on the Hungarian song 'Ez a kis lány, hamis kis lány' (This little girl, naughty little girl) (1853), variations on Schumann's 'Albumblatt', Op. 99, No. 4 (1854), variations on an original theme (1856), variations and fugue on Handel's aria in the B flat Suite in his Second Collection (1861), four-hand variations on a theme Schumann imagined had been dictated by the spirits of Schubert and Mendelssohn (1861), two sets of variations on Paganini's Caprice, No. 24, to say nothing of the variations from his B flat Sextet (1860) which he arranged for piano. Some of these, notably the early Schumann set, Op. 9, are as romantically autobiographical – with concealed quotations, and unpublished inscriptions on the autograph – as anything by Schumann himself, but they were above all the school of composition in which he learned that art of transmuting symmetrical melodies into themes (see above, p. 694) which is the basis of his instrumental style. He had already in the F sharp minor Sonata, Op. 2, brought off a supra-Lisztian transformation of andante into scherzo and he repeated the trick later, but his own peculiar art of transmutation was different. It may be illustrated by comparing bars 7–10 of the Grave of the String Quintet, Op. 88 (1882), with the corresponding passage in the piano saraband of 1855 on which it is based:

Ex. 294

(i)

(ii) transposed

The alternative Allegretto vivace and Presto in the same movement are founded on a piano gavotte of the same early period[12] and it is not insignificant that, just as Brahms's orchestral music was apt to be completed first in two-piano forms, even a piano-less chamber work like Op. 88 should look back to pianistic origins. And of his twenty-four full-length chamber works only eight – the sextets, Opp. 18 and 36 (1860 and 1865), the three string quartets (Opp. 51 and 67) (1873–5), the string quintets, Opp. 88 and 111 (1882 and 1890), and (supreme masterpiece) the Clarinet Quintet, Op. 115 (1891) – are without piano. If Brahms early abandoned the sonata for piano solo, he continued until 1894 – the two clarinet sonatas, Op. 120 – to write very fine sonatas for piano with other instruments, music notable for the same kinds of rich texture, the same solid thinking-in-sound, that mark

[12] See Robert Pascall, 'Unknown Gavottes by Brahms', *M & L*, lvii (1976), p. 404.

his orchestral music. And in the 1880s he was still an important influence on the brilliant young men who were soon to reject his aesthetic *in toto :* Hugo Wolf and Richard Strauss. Wolf's D minor String Quartet seems to have been written mostly in 1879–80 and, while much of it is a wild striving to out-do late Beethoven, the more sober passages are unmistakably Brahmsian, as is Strauss's C minor Piano Quartet (1884). But Strauss's Violin Sonata (1884) is much more Straussian and the ancestry of Wolf's one-movement *Italian Serenade* (1887) for string quartet, but orchestrated later, is to be traced in Berlioz (*Carnaval romain*) and Liszt (first *Mephisto Waltz*).

THE PIANO MINIATURE

Until quite late in life Brahms took relatively little part in the proliferation of small-scale piano music. He composed Hungarian dances and Schubertian waltzes for piano duet either alone (Op. 39, 1865) or with *ad libitum* voices (*Liebeslieder* and *Neue Liebeslieder*, 1869 and 1874), in 1878 a set of eight *Clavierstücke* (capriccios and intermezzos), Op. 76, and in 1879 two powerful, more extended *Rhapsodien*, Op. 79, which might perhaps have been more accurately styled 'ballades'. But his most finely polished miniatures, the twenty beautiful poems – partly verbally inspired – of Opp. 116–19, came only in 1891–3.

The freshest flowers in the proliferation of piano poetry were Grieg's, the strangest those of the septuagenarian Liszt. Grieg's early pieces from the *Vier Stücke*, Op. 1 (1861) to the first book of *Lyriske Stykker*, Op. 12 (Copenhagen, 1867) were written under the sign of Leipzig and Gade, though contact with the songs and piano-pieces of Halfdan Kjerulf (1815–68) and Rikard Nordraak (1842–66) attracted him to specifically Norwegian music, and the decisive catalyst was his discovery in 1869 of the collection of Norwegian folk-music, *Ældre og nyere Fjeldmelodier* (Old and new mountain melodies), published in piano arrangements by the organist Ludvig Mathias Lindeman in 1853 and 1867. Lindeman's collection had already been drawn on to some extent by Kjerulf in his *XXV Udvalgte norske Folkedandse* (1861) and *Norske Folkeviser* (1867) for piano; Grieg now followed suit with *25 Norske Folkeviser og Dandser* (Norwegian folk-songs and dances) in 1870. From then on he evolved a personal idiom based partly on such folk-characteristics as the sharpened fourth in both major and minor scales, drone basses, and so on, partly on the most advanced harmony of Liszt and (to a less extent) Wagner. His short piano pieces, mostly collected in successive books of *Lyrical Pieces* vary in quality from domestic salon-pieces to such miniature poems as the 'Gjætergut' (Shepherd Boy) and 'Klokkeklang' (Bell sounds) (Op. 54, Nos. 1 and 6) in the fifth book (1891). He seldom ventured on more extended forms, evading their problems by writing variations as in the *Ballade i form av variasjoner over en norsk folketone*, Op. 24 (1875) or stringing miniature forms together as in the *Firhaendige Danse* (usually known as 'Norwegian dances'), Op. 35 (1881), or unsuccessfully meeting the problem head on – as in his three violin sonatas (F major, 1865; G major, 1867; C minor, 1887) and his G minor String Quartet (1878). Not even a motto-theme, a quotation from his song 'Spillemænde' (Minstrels), Op. 25, No. 1, can hold the quartet together; it is, moreover, open to the charge of being *klaviermässig* (pianistic), despite Grieg's rejection of it.[13]

Grieg was in later years to widen his harmonic vocabulary still further, particularly in his arrangements of folk-melodies, the very fine *Norske Folkeviser*, Op. 66, of 1896 and the *Slåtter*, Op. 72 (1902), but the naked clashing of opposed open fifths in the earlier 'Klokkeklang' belongs to the world of dissonant, skeletal textures of the death-haunted pieces Liszt had recently been writing: 'Nuages gris' (1881), 'Csárdás macabre' (1882), and the later 'Unstern / Sinistre / Disastro'. These were so far unpublished but Grieg might have known the 'Trauervorspiel und Trauermarsch' of 1885 (Leipzig, 1887) in which an angular ostinato, *Wie Glocken-Geläute* ('like bell sounds'), produces extraordinary clashes with the *risoluto* right-hand part:

Ex. 295

In such music as this the pianistic language of romanticism was already dead.

Elsewhere it continued to flourish exceedingly, not only under the hands of Grieg but in those of the Schumann epigones, of whom perhaps the best was the immensely prolific Theodor Kirchner (1823–1903). Between 1872 (*Lieder ohne Worte*, Op. 13, and *Neue Davidsbündlertänze*, Op. 17) and 1889 (*Acht Notturnos*, Op. 87) Kirchner published nearly sixty collections of well-made pieces. In the non-Teutonic countries the language was employed all too often by eminent composers in the production of marketable sub-standard work. Most of Chaykovsky's and Dvořák's piano music is of this type, though in fairness to Dvořák it must be said that, like Schubert, he had the knack of throwing off enchanting, seemingly effortless trifles like the Waltzes, Op. 54 (1880). Aiming higher, he scored only what a marksman calls a 'magpie' with his *Tema con variazioni*, Op. 36 (1876). But piano works of such dimensions were rare.

Among the few, two Russian and some French are outstanding. The Russian pieces, Balakirev's 'oriental fantasia' *Islamey* (1869) and the *Kartinki s vïstavki* (Pictures from an exhibition) (1874) of his former disciple Musorgsky, could hardly be more different in character. *Islamey* is a

[13] Letter to Max Abraham, his Leipzig publisher, 28 October 1878.

Pl. 59 V. A. Hartmann's project of 1869 for a city-gate and bell-tower at Kiev, surmounted by suggestions of a traditional woman's head-dress and an old Slavonic helmet. It was shown in the posthumous exhibition of his sketches, water-colours, and designs at the Petersburg Academy of Arts in March 1874 and inspired the last of Musorgsky's *Pictures from an exhibition*.

dazzling exhibition of pianistic virtuosity in the Liszt manner and equally dazzling inventive virtuosity in its exploitation of three unpromising scraps of Tatar and Kabardinian tunes; the *Pictures* – musical reactions to a collection of designs and sketches by the architect Viktor Hartmann, connected by the composer's 'promenades' as he strolls round the exhibition – are so little conventionally pianistic that at least three vandals have been tempted to deface Musorgsky's bold black-and-white crayon strokes with orchestral colour.

In the same year as Musorgsky's *Pictures* Saint-Saëns produced his *Variations sur un thème de Beethoven* (the trio of the minuetto of Op. 31, no. 3) for two pianos, Op. 35, which tower above his earlier piano pieces and the *Variations chromatiques de concert* (1868) of Bizet. (Bizet's best piano music is found in the delightful four-hand *Jeux d'enfants* (1871)). Saint-Saëns's

Variations and, in the miniature field, *Jeux d'enfants* marked the beginning of a revival of French piano music although Bizet soon died and Saint-Saëns was more interested in other media. The actual revival was due mainly to three men: Franck, Chabrier, and Fauré. Fauré was essentially a miniaturist, a sensitive, poetic craftsman, though some of the numerous impromptus, nocturnes, and barcarolles composed from 1883 onward are fairly extended pieces, e.g. the G and G flat Barcarolles, Opp. 41 and 42, of 1885. But his first notable piano composition, the Ballade, Op. 19 (1881), later rewritten for piano and orchestra, is a really big work. Chabrier's *Pièces pittoresques* were also first performed publicly in 1881; like his later piano pieces, they are unpianistic – some were orchestrated later – but delightful and historically important for their anti-romanticism.

It was the intensely romantic Franck who was to invent a new kind of piano sonata, though not actually so called, with his *Prélude, Choral et Fugue* (1884) and *Prélude, Aria et Final* (1887), forms already adumbrated in the 'Prélude, fugue et variation' of the *Six pièces pour grand orgue* (see above, p. 773). In both these triptychs the three movements are organically related by thematic transformation and cross-references; near the end of the 'fugue' – which is no more fugal than Liszt's – the 'prélude' pattern and 'choral' theme in the right hand are combined with the 'fugue' subject in the left; in the parallel position of the later work the principal theme of the 'prélude', *dolcissimo*, is combined with the opening theme of the 'aria', *meno dolcissimo*. Both compositions suffer from unidiomatic piano-writing.

FRENCH CHAMBER MUSIC

This is less noticeable in Franck's two chamber works with piano, the Quintet of 1879 and the Violin Sonata of 1886, though the pianistic idioms are merely conventional. Few composers have been able to write piano quintets in which the piano has not to fight for its life against the strings – Dvořák in his lovely A major (1887) is one of the exceptions – and in his passionate F minor Franck acquits himself very well. As for the Sonata which came between the piano triptychs, it is one of Franck's most limpid, delightfully lyrical compositions. Then contrarily, having dispensed with the piano, he proceeded to write a String Quartet (1889) as stodgy in texture – except in the scherzo – as the triptychs. The chamber music and solo piano music of Franck's disciples cannot be compared with his own; perhaps the best example is Chausson's curious *Concert* (1891) for violin, piano, and string quartet. Nothing could be much less Franckian than the G major Violin Sonata (1892) of the youngest disciple of all, Guillaume Lekeu (1870–94), crude and vulgar in its piano-writing, but bringing blasts of fresh air with its vigorous, long-breathed diatonic themes and, in the slow movement, 'le sentiment d'un chant populaire'. A more Gallic strain of chamber music stemmed from Saint-Saëns who published in 1867 a Piano Trio in F, clear, fluent, and classical. And in 1876 his pupil Fauré composed a Violin Sonata in A, Op. 13, to which one can apply precisely the same adjectives, following it three years later with a Piano Quartet in C minor, Op. 15, even more delightful, with one of the most whimsical and original of scherzi.[14] Fauré's second Quartet, G minor, Op. 45 (1886), is a more powerful conception but lacks the charm of the earlier light open-textured works; after it he wrote no more chamber music for twenty years.

Something of Fauré's indefinable poetic spirit is perceptible in the String Quartet of a musician, Claude Debussy (1862–1918), who had so far published only songs and a few pleasant piano pieces such as the *Deux Arabesques* written in 1888. Debussy's Quartet was composed in 1893 the year of *Falstaff* and the *Pathétique* Symphony and Brahms's last piano pieces, and is in essence farther from all of them than they are from each other. They are monuments of an age drawing to a close and this was a symptom of the future, for although it is modelled to a surprising extent on Grieg's G minor Quartet and borrows Franck's techniques of theme-transformation and cross-reference between movements the appearance of organic structure is purely superficial. Debussy's music begins to be an art of fluid arabesques, of sonorities for their own sakes, of sensations rather than emotions; it was affected by his passion for *art nouveau*, impressionist painting, and symbolist poetry, and its savouring of musical sounds purely as such hinted at a new kind of absolute music.

CHAMBER MUSIC IN RUSSIA

It was not only in France that chamber music entered on a particularly flourishing period. Both Russians and Czechs gave the world works it has gladly accepted, together with some it has not. First came Chaykovsky's three string quartets (1871, 1874, and 1876) and Rimsky-Korsakov's F major Quartet (1875) and String Sextet (1876). Chaykovsky scored an immediate success with his No. 1 in D, thanks to the beautiful folk-melody of the first 16 bars of the Andante cantabile and the pizzicato ostinato of the cello in the middle of the movement; the rest of the quartet is unremarkable, as are the F major and E flat minor – except for the beautiful Andante funebre of the latter. As for the Rimsky-Korsakov works, they are little better than exercises in German classical styles. Neither Chaykovsky nor Rimsky-Korsakov was really at home in this medium. Borodin's case was very different; he was a cellist who had taken part in chamber music all his life and had already half-a-dozen chamber works behind him when he composed his two published quartets: A major (1879), 'stimulated by a theme of Beethoven' (in the finale of Op. 130), often alluded to but never quoted, and D major (1885). The effectiveness and variety of Borodin's quartet-writing are astonishing, particularly in the First Quartet, and the voluptuous euphony of the Notturno of the Second is unmatched in Russian chamber music.

---

[14] Fauré's scherzo seems to have suggested the trio in the equivalent movement of Lalo's Trio in A minor (1880). Lalo orchestrated his scherzo in 1884.

Chaykovsky later composed a Piano Trio (1882) and a String Sextet (1890). Neither was very successful. The Trio, dedicated 'to the memory of a great artist' (Rubinstein's brother Nikolay), consists of a Pezzo elegiaco and a long set of variations on a theme associated with a happy day in the country in May 1873; but, as Chaykovsky admitted, it is really 'symphonic music adapted for trio'.[15] A month or so after Chaykovsky's Trio, Rimsky-Korsakov's 17-year-old pupil Glazunov completed his First Quartet (D major) and a Second, in F, followed in 1884; he sounds 'inspired depth' (as Cui said) in the slow movement of No. 2 but the finale betrays its origin as an orchestral conception. Glazunov's other early quartet compositions – the set of *Novelletti* (1886), the Third (*Slavyansky*) Quartet, in G (1888), the Suite in C (1891), and several separate movements – show him reverting to an older Russian conception of chamber music: music to be enjoyed by players not quite of the first rank rather than listened to by intellectuals with their heads in their hands. The sterner note in Russian chamber music was sounded by Chaykovsky's disciple Sergey Taneyev (1856–1915), whose First Quartet (B flat minor, Op. 4) was composed in 1890, and in the later quartets of Glazunov himself.

THE CHAMBER MUSIC OF DVOŘÁK

Czech chamber music during these years was almost completely dominated by Dvořák, but the two string quartets of Smetana – whose only other chamber work was the G minor Piano Trio of 1855 – are peculiarly interesting in that they are avowedly autobiographical and programmatic. The first (E minor, 1876) is actually entitled 'Z mého života' (From my life) and its first three movements recall the composer's youth – his love of art and his romantic yearnings, his merry life and love of dancing and dance-music, his first love – while the fourth indicates his joy in composing *national* music, annihilated by the high E of the first violin symbolizing the persistent sound which announced the onset of ultimately total deafness. The second (D minor, 1883) 'continues where the first ended, after the catastrophe. Imagine the whirlpool of music in a man who has lost his hearing'.[16] In that same year Dvořák also composed a work with a strong autobiographical content, the F minor Trio, Op. 65; overshadowed by the death of his mother, it also reflects a crisis of temptation to forswear his Czechishness for the sake of the advantages to be gained in Czechophobe Vienna, and there is no doubt a cryptic significance in the allusion in the first movement to his song 'Zezhulice' (The Cuckoo) from Op. 7 (1872). Such veiled autobiography is as rare in Dvořák as in Brahms who did admit more than once[17] that his C minor Piano Quartet, Op. 60 (final version, 1874) was 'a sort of illustration' (*etwa eine Illustration*) to the last chapter of Goethe's *Werther*. For the rest, their chamber music is as 'purely musical' as

---

[15] Letter to Nadezhda von Meck, 13/25 January 1882.
[16] Conversation with Václav Zelený, 9 March 1883.
[17] *Billroth und Brahms im Briefwechsel*, ed. Otto Gottlieb-Billroth (Berlin and Vienna, 1935), p. 211.

Beethoven's or Schubert's – which does not of course exclude the rarefaction of emotion. When he wrote the F minor Trio, Dvořák had already produced a quantity of chamber music some immature, but also including four string quartets, rich in invention and beautifully written – in E (1876), D minor (1877), E flat (1879), and C (1881) – and a String Sextet (1878), all bearing opus-numbers arbitrarily added by the publisher Simrock with total disregard of chronology. Nowhere does Dvořák reveal his affinity with Schubert more obviously than in these quartets, an affinity that extends to a decline of inspiration in final movements yet never occludes his own delightful musical personality. The delicious *alla polka* of the D minor Quartet, the *dumka* (alternating slow and fast sections) of the E flat, the *dumka* and *furiant* of the Sextet, and the *furiant-cum-waltz* of the F minor Trio are of course outside Schubert's range. (In 1891 he was to write a trio consisting entirely of six *dumky*.) Dvořák's next important chamber work after the F minor Trio was the A major Piano Quintet (1887), an outstanding masterpiece which has not unjustly overshadowed the E flat Piano Quartet of two years later. In 1892 he went to America where the following year he composed not only the *New World* Symphony but three comparably attractive and technically over-relaxed chamber works: the F major String Quartet, the E flat String Quintet, and a Sonatina in G for piano and violin which has eclipsed his somewhat Brahmsian Sonata in F of 1880. The greatest masterpieces of his string quartet output, the G major and A flat, particularly the former, were written after his return to Europe in 1895.

CZECH SONG

One of the curiosities of Dvořák's chamber music is a set of twelve short pieces for string quartet, entitled *Cypřiše* (Cypresses)[18] which he arranged in 1887 from songs in a cycle composed in 1865. The original cycle of sixteen, inspired by love for a girl who was later his sister-in-law, were his earliest attempts at songwriting; they are rather crude, with faulty declamation, but he was haunted by them and in 1882 rewrote four of them which were published with additional German texts as *Vier Lieder*, Op. 2; finally in 1888, after the quartet versions, he restored eight of the twelve in song form as *Liebeslieder*, Op. 83. Quotation of a single bar will show what different forms (ii) and (iii), Dvořák conjured from the original (i), and how much more imaginative is his quartet than his piano texture:

---

[18] Miniature score (Prague, 1957).

Ex. 296

He was not a born song-writer, nor was Smetana or Fibich. In 1871 Fibich had set three poems from the 'Králové Dvůr manuscript' (see p. 651) – 'Skřivánek' (The lark), 'Róže' (The rose), and 'Opuščená' (The deserted girl) – and the following year Dvořák composed the same three with three others, including the already mentioned 'Zezhulice', as Op. 17. Fibich set more German than Czech texts – his Heine ballads 'Loreley' and 'Tragödie', Op. 7, Nos. 3 and 4 (1872–3), foreshadow the future opera-composer – but like Dvořák he was attracted by Vítězslav Hálek's *Večerní písně*, five of which he composed as Op. 5 (1871). Dvořák's eleven settings date from 1876 and were published as Op. 3, Op. 9, Nos. 3 and 4, and Op. 31, and in 1880 Smetana chose five of the poems for his only mature songs, almost the only ones to Czech texts. (Nos. 1 and 2 perfectly exemplify the pianistic song to which words have been fitted.) The pressure to compose German texts was very strong and Dvořák's earliest mature songs, the *Zigeunermelodien* (1880) – including the extremely popular 'Als die alte Mutter' – were set not to Adolf Heyduk's original poems but to German versions; the lovely little lullaby 'Schlaf' mein Kind' (1885) is another of a number of similar cases. The terribly unequal *Biblícke písně* (Biblical songs) (1894) were originally composed to seventeenth-century Czech texts from the 'Kralice Bible' and the voice-parts then completely rewritten and spoiled in the process to fit German translations.

The Králové Dvůr poems also attracted the Polish composer Żeleński who set five of them as his Op. 10 (probably *c.* 1863) when he was studying in Prague. Żeleński, with Zygmunt Noskowski (1846–1909) who first made his mark as a song-writer with 'Sen' (The dream), a setting of a translation of Heine's 'Ich hab' im Traum geweinet' (1872), was mainly responsible for the continuation of the Moniuszko tradition in Polish song.

SOLO SONG IN RUSSIA

The output of neither Poles nor Czechs is remotely comparable in quantity or quality with the great outpouring of Russian song at this period, the result perhaps of the musical nature of the language and the volume of Russian lyric poetry. Even such composers as Rubinstein, Chaykovsky, and Rimsky-Korsakov who, like Dvořák, were not born song-writers, turned out very many respectable and sometimes inspired songs. Rubinstein generally preferred German words, which he set in the manner of Mendelssohn or Schumann; good examples are the Hoffmann von Fallersleben 'Siehe, der Frühling währet', Op. 33, No. 5 (1856), and 'Bedeckt mich mit Blumen', Op. 76, No. 5 (1867), from the Geibel and Heyse *Spanisches Liederbuch*. Best of all are the *Wilhelm Meister* settings (not all solos), Op. 91 (1872), but his essays in German orientalism – the *Zwolf Lieder des Mirza Schaffy*, Op. 34 (1854) and Heine's 'Der Asra', Op. 32, No. 6 (1856) – are much better known. Rubinstein's Russian romantic songs are inferior but he did quite early score a surprising success with *Shest basen I. Krïlova* (1851), delightfully humorous treatments of six of Krïlov's fables.

Chaykovsky's songs are mostly of the arioso-*romance* type, with inflated and rather clumsy piano parts; his favourite approach – to model a melodic idea on a key-phrase in the text and allow it to dominate the whole song – appears in some of his earliest, e.g. 'Net, tolko tot, kto znal' (Mey's translation of 'Nur wer die Sehnsucht kennt'), Op. 6, No. 6 (1869) and the Apukhtin 'Zabït' tak skoro' (To forget so soon) (1870), and recurs until his very last, 'Snova kak prezhde' (Again, as before, alone), No. 6 of the set of Daniel Rathaus songs, Op. 73 (1893). Chaykovsky is at his characteristic best when the poem opens up his vein of lyrical passion as in Aleksey Tolstoy's 'O, esli b ti mogla' (If thou couldst for one moment'), Op. 38, No. 4 (1878), yet two of his finest songs are in the strongest possible contrast, the dramatic ballad 'Korolki' (The corals), Op. 28, No. 2 (1875), Mey's translation of a Polish poem by Władysław Syrokomla, already composed by Moniuszko, and the exquisite 'Legenda', No. 5 of *16 Pesen dlya detey* (Songs for children), Op. 54 (1883), translated by Aleksandr Pleshcheyev from an English original.

The truly characteristic Russian songs of the period flowed from other sources: two quite different ones, Liszt and Dargomïzhsky. Balakirev and his circle, though professed disciples of Glinka, were also admirers of Liszt and Schumann, exponents of the pianistic song, and Balakirev was like them a pianist, not a singer. His earliest songs (1858) include a Glinka-ish

'Barkarolla', Russified Schumann – 'Kolïbelnaya pesnya' (Cradle song), 'Vzoshel na nebo mesyats yasny' (The bright moon rose in the sky), 'Pridi ko mne' (Come to me) – and a Russified Lisztian setting of Lermontov's 'Pesnya Selima' (Selim's song). The styles are not only Russified but personalized in beautiful melodies and harmonically subtle piano parts, and the songs of the next few years are Lisztian in parentage – particularly the Lermontov pieces, 'Evreyskaya melodiya' (Hebrew melody, after Byron's 'My soul is dark'), 'Otchego' (Why), 'Pesnya zolotoy rïbki' (Song of the golden fish), and 'Slïshu li golos tvoy' (When I hear thy voice) – yet 'The Golden Fish' and the intoxicating Pushkin 'Gruzinskaya pesnya' (Georgian song) (1863), in both of which the piano is at least as important as the voice, are the purest Balakirev. After 1865 he abandoned song-writing for thirty years but in that very same year his youngest disciple, Rimsky-Korsakov, began to compose songs consciously modelled on his, 'the melodies . . . conceived instrumentally so to speak, i.e. not in close connection with the text but only harmonizing with its general content, or evoked by the harmonic basis which sometimes preceded the melody'.[19] In 'Plenivshis rozoy, solovey' (Enslaved by the rose, the nightingale), Op. 2, No. 2 (1866), for instance, the voice sings (partly unaccompanied) for only 20 of the song's 48 bars, in 'V temnoy roshche zamolk solovey' (In the dark grove the nightingale is silent), Op. 4, No. 3 (also 1866) for 19 bars out of 43. On the other hand Rimsky-Korsakov was capable of beautiful, simple and simply accompanied melody, e.g. the cradle song from Mey's *Pskovityanka*, Op. 2, No. 3, which he later incorporated in his opera (see p. 731), though the melody, like those of Balakirev – and Dvořák for that matter – is as much instrumental as vocal. Except for a small group, much more conventional in melody and accompaniment (1882–3), he also abandoned solo song from 1870 to 1897.

The more important stream of Russian song, proceeding from vocal lines born from the words and suggesting the character uttering them, flowed from Dargomïzhsky. (His setting of 'The Golden Fish', less striking than Balakirev's, is more faithful to Lermontov.) In the early 1860s he developed a type of short dramatic or comic scene for voice and piano, notably two based on Russian translations of Béranger, 'Stary kapral' ('Le vieux caporal') and 'Chervyak' ('Le Sénateur', literally 'The Worm') which he performed himself, half-acting as he sang. 'Chervyak' has such performance directions as 'very humbly', 'screwing up the eyes', but the music of the 'worm's' self-portrait is itself comic and dramatically true. In 'Mne vse ravno', again with a vocal line supported by the simplest piano chords, he creates a very different self-portrait – of a pseudo-Byronic hero 'all passion spent':

---

[19] Rimsky-Korsakov, *Letopis moey muzïkalnoy zhizni* (fifth edition, Moscow, 1935), p. 290.

Ex. 297

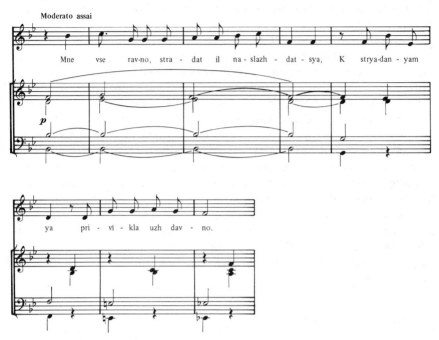

Dargomïzhsky was no more than an original talent but his example fired a genius. Musorgsky showed considerable creative power already in his early, more or less lyrical songs – like Dargomïzhsky he was himself a singer. They are illuminated by imaginative empirical harmony, and with the Nekrasov 'Kalistratushka' (a peasant remembering the lullaby his mother sang) he indicated the line he was to take with greatest success: the self-portrait drawn in flexible, unsymmetrical cantilena that is now more, now less lyrical as the subject demands. A whole series followed during 1866–8, nearly all to his own words: 'Svetik Savishna' (Darling Savishna – the village beauty wooed by the village idiot), 'Seminarist' (whose thoughts keep wandering to a pretty girl as he tries to memorize the Latin nouns of the third declension), 'Ozornik' (the ragamuffin – who jeers at an old woman), 'Sirotka' (the begging orphan), and others. Side by side came lyrical songs and also lampoons – 'Klassik' (The classicist) and 'Raëk' (The peepshow) – amusing ephemera. Musorgsky's final realistic masterpieces are to be found in the cycle *Detskaya* (The nursery) (1872), in which a child's speech is rendered in a sort of musical prose with extraordinary accuracy, completely free from adult sentiment, and supported by vividly suggestive, totally unorthodox harmony. After *The Nursery* Musorgsky turned away from naked realism and composed two cycles to words by his friend Arseny Golenishchev-Kutuzov: *Bez solntsa* (Sunless) (1874), filled with subjective pessimism, and *Pesni i plyaski smerti* (Songs and dances of death) (1875–7) in which Death serenades a sick girl, dances with a drunken peasant lost in a snowstorm,

785

rides over a battlefield. After these wonderful incitements for a great musical dramatist, his later lyrical settings of Aleksey Tolstoy (1877) are very disappointing.

Two other members of Balakirev's circle composed songs. Cui, half-French, half-Lithuanian, and a pupil of Moniuszko, was immensely prolific and quite eclectic, setting poems in Russian, Polish, French, and German with equal facility and sometimes, as with Pushkin's 'Sozhzhennoe pismo' (The burned love-letter), Op. 33, No. 4 (1886), considerable success.[19a] Borodin wrote a bare dozen mature songs but half of them, to his own words or his own translations of Heine, are masterpieces or near-masterpieces: 'Spyashchaya knyazhna' (The sleeping princess), with its mesmeric unresolved syncopated seconds and shattering whole-tone passages in the accompaniment (1867),[20] 'Morskaya tsarevna' (The Sea-king's daughter), 'Pesnya temnavo lesa' (Song of the dark forest), an epic fragment comparable with Musorgsky at his best, 'Falshivaya nota' (The false note) and 'Otravoy polnï moi pesni' (Heine's 'Vergiftet sind meine Lieder') (all four 1868), and 'More' (The sea), a fine descriptive ballad (1870). 'Iz slëz moikh' (Heine's 'Aus meinen Tränen') (1873) and the later songs are weaker.

THE MÉLODIE: 1855–93

French song-composers were slow to recognize the possibilities of an imaginative, finely wrought piano part. Gounod is not of course to be judged as a song-writer by his infamous 'Ier Prélude de Bach ... Arrangé pour chant' with a text by Lamartine ('Le livre de la vie est le livre suprême') (1852) (not 'Ave Maria' originally) or the dreadful songs to English words that he poured out from 1870 onward. His two hundred songs include some charming things besides the Hugo 'Sérénade' of 1857 but their accompaniments tend to be thin – often quite justifiably – or based on conventional figuration. To compare his *Six mélodies* of 1855[21] with Lalo's *Six* of the same year is to realize at once how much more enterprising the slightly younger man was in the treatment of the piano: for instance in No. 5, Hugo's 'Oh! quand je dors'. Neither Delibes nor Bizet was a prolific song-writer but both produced some attractive things, among them the former's 'Les Filles de Cadix' (1863) and the latter's 'Adieux de l'hôtesse arabe' (1866), another Hugo song. But Massenet was very prolific, putting the best of his work into a series of song-cycles on the lines of Schumann's which he called *Poèmes – d'avril* (1866), *du souvenir* (1868), *pastoral* (1872), *d'octobre* (1876), *d'amour* (1879), *d'hiver* (1882) and so on – framed by the piano and in which the piano plays an ever more important part.

[19a] Even better, a perfect miniature, is his later Pushkin setting, 'Tsarskosel'skoe statuya', Op. 57, No. 17. The statue at Tsarskoe Selo depicts La Fontaine's 'La laitière et le pot au lait'.

Noske, op. cit., No. 25.

One of these, 'O ma belle rebelle', in Noske, op. cit., No. 27.

In the late 1860s stronger talents appeared: Saint-Saëns' young friend Fauré and Franck's pupil Henri Duparc. (Saint-Saëns' own *mélodies* are numerous, dextrous, and undistinguished.) Both composed mainly the poems of Gautier, Baudelaire, and the *Parnassiens*,[22] Leconte de Lisle, Sully Prudhomme, and Verlaine (who was a *Parnassien* in his younger days), but their careers were strikingly different. Fauré published his first song, the feeble Hugo 'Le Papillon et la fleur' in 1869 and nearly a score more, all composed earlier, during the next ten years; they include the popular 'Après un rêve' and the more characteristic 'Sylvie'. About 1880 he resumed song composition with the delightful Leconte de Lisle 'Nell', went on to produce such diverse masterpieces as the Sully Prudhomme 'Les Berceaux', the Armand Sylvestre 'Le Secret', another Leconte de Lisle song 'Les Roses d'Ispahan', the Villiers de l'Isle-Adam 'Les Présents'. With 'Les Présents' he paired as Op. 46 his first Verlaine setting 'Clair de lune' (*c.* 1887) and, having discovered Verlaine, proceeded to compose 'Spleen' (*c.* 1889), the *Cinq mélodies* (1890), and the cycle *La Bonne Chanson* (1892) which established him as arguably the greatest of all French song-composers.

The case of Duparc is strange. Like Borodin he composed a mere handful of songs, between *c.* 1868 and *c.* 1884, and then (mentally distressed by the gradual advance of glaucoma) no more for the rest of his long life. But the handful includes such classics of French song as the two Baudelaire settings, 'L'invitation au voyage' and 'La Vie antérieure' (*c.* 1870 and 1884), the Gautier 'Au pays où se fait la guerre' and 'Lamento' (*c.* 1869 and 1883), 'Le manoir de Rosemonde' (*c.* 1879) with its dramatic declamation and nervous energy and intensity, and – finest of all – the Leconte de Lisle 'Phidylé' (*c.* 1882). The last two and 'L'invitation au voyage' were later orchestrated; Duparc's piano parts, while always extremely important, are seldom purely pianistic in nature like Fauré's. And his vocal lines are rather more controlled by the words than those of Fauré's pre-Verlaine songs. It was only with the Op. 58 *Cinq mélodies* and above all *La Bonne Chanson* that Fauré achieved quite perfect fusion of poem with music, though the tender lyrical expansiveness of the earlier ones never lapses into the sentimental or commonplace; they are always stamped by that 'sobriety and purity' which he himself considered essentially French. Duparc never completely renounced his inheritance from Liszt and Wagner and Franck; when Fauré blurs the sense of key it is more likely to be through the influence of plainsong modes than of romantic chromaticism.

Related to both Franck and Fauré is Chausson, even less productive of songs than Duparc; his bare dozen were all written during 1879–87. The delicious Gautier trifle 'Les Papillons' and his Leconte de Lisle settings, 'Nanny', 'Le Colibri', and 'La Cigale', are Fauréan, the Villiers de l'Isle-Adam 'L'Aveu' and the Gautier 'Caravane' Franckish. And he treated Verlaine's 'La lune blanche' with more than Fauréan restraint in 1885 before Fauré had composed any Verlaine at all, six years before he set the

---

[22] So called from the review *Le Parnasse contemporain* (1866–76).

poem in *La Bonne Chanson*. Chausson has also been claimed as a link between Fauré and Debussy and it is true that Debussy's early songs reveal affinities with Fauré (the Verlaine 'Green' of 1888, afterwards published among the *Ariettes oubliées*) while there is a recollection of the unresolved seconds of Borodin's 'Spyashchaya krasavitsa' in the Baudelaire 'Jet d'eau' (1889). The amalgam that was Debussy's personal style had not yet formed even in the first set of Verlaine *Fêtes galantes* (1892) and the *Proses lyriques* to his own words (1893).

THE LATE NINETEENTH-CENTURY *LIED*

Neither French *mélodie* nor Russian *romans* challenged the prestige of German *Lied*, represented during the second half of the century above all by Brahms whose work is essentially a prolongation of the line of Schubert and Schumann. That other notable traditionalist, Robert Franz, went on until 1884 composing and refashioning earlier songs hitherto held back but, as he himself admitted, it is impossible to trace any artistic development: 'I hold my Op. 1 to be no better and no worse than my Op. 52'.[23] The younger men, Cornelius and later Adolf Jensen (1837–79), were drawn into the Liszt orbit though Schumannians at heart. Jensen spices his songs – e.g. 'Als einst von deiner Schöne' (from the *Lieder des Hafis*, Op. 11, of 1863), 'An deinem Finger' (from the *Liebeslieder*, Op. 13), 'Wie so bleich ich geworden bin?' (from the Chamisso cycle *Dolorosa*, Op. 30)[24] – with Lisztian, even Wagnerian harmony:

Ex. 298

The great majority of Cornelius's earlier songs – among them the miniatures of Op. 1 (1853), the *Brautlieder* (Nuptial songs) (1856), the *Weihnachtslieder* (Christmas songs) (also 1856) – are settings of his own poems. (The dates given are for the earliest versions; Cornelius often revised and often drastically rewrote; the original version of 'Die Könige' in the *Weihnachts-*

[23] Rudolph Procházka, *Robert Franz* (Leipzig, 1894), p. 37.
[24] Stephenson, op. cit., No. 11.

lieder bears no relation to the well-known later one in which the voice relates while the piano plays in solemn chords 'Wie schön leuchtet der Morgenstern' – Liszt's idea.) More Lisztian are the settings of three Bürger sonnets (1859) and the Hebbel songs of 1861–3. Cornelius commanded a wide range of technique and expression from the delicate Hölty 'Auftrag', Op. 5, No. 6, to the powerful 'Zum Ossa sprach der Pelion', Op. 5, No. 5 (both 1862); another song of the same year, 'Warum sind denn die Rosen so blass?', is (significantly) one of his only two Heine songs. Liszt himself went on writing songs when Cornelius was dead. None is of great significance though two tiny pieces, his third setting of 'Was Liebe sei' and the 14-bar 'Einst' (both 1879) are noteworthy for their endings on unresolved diminished sevenths; the devaluation of dissonance had been going on for a long time but the convention of the final 'concord' was to be unconscionably long-lived. In 'Was Liebe sei' the separation of piano part from un-accompanied declamation is total.

Before Liszt's death in 1886 Hugo Wolf had composed the Mörike 'Mausfallen-Sprüchlein' (Mousetrap motto) (1882), Strauss his Op. 10 which includes 'Zueignung' (Dedication) and 'Allerseelen' (All Souls') (1882–3), and Mahler the *Lieder eines fahrenden Gesellen* (Songs of a wayfarer) (1884). And Brahms was in full spate with some 170 songs behind him and a score more to come. Brahms's earliest songs, Opp. 3, 6, and 7 (pub. 1853–4) already point along what were to be the main lines of his *Lieder* work. Apt to be inspired to melody even in an instrumental piece, vocal melodies came easily to him; he did not need the subtler poets, the words of traditional songs would serve equally well, as they did in Nos. 4 and 5 of Op. 7. It is obviously unfair to compare his 'In dem Schatten meiner Locken', Op. 6, No. 1, written when he was not yet 19 with Wolf's in the *Spanisches Liederbuch* nearly forty years later; it is in fact an attractive song; but it is a straightforward, unsubtle melodic mirror of the words. It is said that Brahms would judge a song brought to him for comment by first covering up the right-hand piano part; the essentials were vocal melody and the bass. His peculiar art lay in his skill in disguising the original melodic idea by rhythmic extension and phrase-overlapping and the accompaniment by endlessly inventive variation. (The first of his occasional strayings from the norm was the Mörike 'An eine Äolsharfe', Op. 19, No. 5 (1858) which Wolf was, as it were, to translate into Wagnerian terms in 1888; but the parallels with Brahms are striking.) If the poem gave Brahms a beautiful melody which did not fit the words, as in 'Wie bist du, meine Königin', Op. 32, No. 9 (1864), so much the worse for the words. He may be said to have reached maturity in the fifteen *Romanzen aus Tiecks 'Magelone'*, Op. 33 (Nos. 1–6, 1861–2, the rest in 1869); no one but he could have composed No. 4, 'Liebe kam aus fernen Landen' (Love came from distant lands) or No. 9, 'Ruhe, Süssliebchen' (Sweetheart, rest). After that one can only pick familiar masterpieces at random. 'Von ewiger Liebe' and 'Die Mainacht', Op. 43, Nos. 1 and 2, the almost too familiar 'Wiegenlied', Op. 49, No. 4, the eight Daumer songs, Op. 57, 'Meine Liebe ist grün' and 'O wüsst' ich doch', Op.

63, Nos. 5 and 8, 'Vergebliches Ständchen', Op. 84, No. 4, and 'Feldeinsamkeit', Op. 86, No. 2, all came in the decade 1868–78. Then six years' silence was broken by the two songs for contralto with viola obbligato, Op. 91, followed by another five years of song writing, less prolific but marked by even finer craftsmanship in such things as the 'Sapphische Ode', Op. 94, No. 4, 'Wir wandelten', Op. 96, No. 2, 'Wie Melodien zieht es mir', 'Immer leiser wird mein Schlummer' and 'Auf dem Kirchhofe', Op. 105, Nos. 1, 2, and 4, and two enchantingly gay songs, the 'Ständchen', Op. 106, No. 1, and 'Das Mädchen spricht', Op. 107, No. 3. Quite different from all that had gone before but returning to the mood of *Ein deutsches Requiem* are the great meditations on death from the Bible and Apocrypha, the *Vier ernste Gesänge* of 1896.

If Wolf's dislike of Brahms and his music was to some extent pathological, there were also aesthetic grounds for it. Not only was he a Wagnerian, a young 'progressive', but his basic approach to song composition was different. One might put it crudely that Brahms was primarily inspired by the sound of a poem, Wolf by its sense. And he would bury himself for a time in the work of one poet, as Brahms seldom did, producing a near-symbiosis. A song melody existing in its own right, the rule in Brahms, is the exception in Wolf. (The popular 'Verborgenheit' – 'Concealment' – is one such exception.) 'Verborgenheit' is one of the 43 Mörike songs he composed in a typical state of continuous excitement in three months of 1888. He had already set one or two Mörike poems, including the 'Mausfallen-Sprüchlein' already mentioned and in 1886 'Der König bei der Krönung', but it was only now that Mörike became a real catalyst. Ten more Mörike songs were composed in October and November, after a short spell of Eichendorff, but then no more. The next catalyst was Goethe who drew from him 50 songs between the end of October and the end of January 1889. Next were the *Spanisches Liederbuch* of Geibel and Heyse (November 1889–April 1890) and then Heyse's *Italienisches Liederbuch* from which inspiration came in spurts, a few songs in late 1890, fifteen in December 1891, 24 in one month in the spring of 1896. Finally, in rough parallel with Brahms's *Ernste Gesänge*, Wolf composed translations of three poems by Michelangelo in March 1897 just before his mental collapse. Concentrating almost exclusively on songs, he had produced more in ten years than Brahms in forty. Wolf reacted not only to the poem but to the poet. There is enormous variety in the Mörike songs – 'Fussreise', 'Auf einer Wanderung', 'In der Frühe', 'Denk es, O Seele', 'Schlafendes Jesuskind', 'Gesang Weylas' to mention only a few of the best known – yet they all reflect the spirit of the gentle Swabian poet. He turns to Goethe and matches not only the classical epitaph on 'Anakreons Grab' but rises to the greatest Goethe in 'Prometheus' and 'Grenzen der Menschheit'; he tries a fall with the *Wilhelm Meister* songs and, like his predecessors, gives Mignon beautiful music that is somehow not quite right. The Spanish songs, 10 sacred, 34 secular, naturally explore a very different world – not superficially Hispanic yet reflecting deeper, particularly darker, strains in the Spanish nature and again with wide variety from 'Herr, was trägt der Boden hier' to 'Mögen alle bösen Zungen'. And the *Italian Book*, which begins with the exquisite 'Auch kleine Dinge' and finally boils over with the exuberant pertness of 'Ich hab in Penna', explores another. One hardly needs to be told that Wolf composed at the piano; his piano parts are at least as important as, often more important than, the voice – the equivalents of Wagner's orchestra. They can be Wagnerian in texture, witness the long passage in the Mörike 'Auf einer Wanderung' beginning 'Ach hier, wie liegt die Welt so licht!' and leading to the final climax, and late Wagnerian in harmony as in the first two bars of 'Schon streckt ich aus' in the *Italian Book*.

There is – astonishingly – nothing Wagnerian (or Brahmsian) in the early songs of Wolf's exact contemporary Mahler. Nor was there any artistic sympathy between them after their student friendship. Mahler was not inspired by great verse; most of his earliest songs are settings from the Arnim and Brentano collection of folk-poems, *Des Knaben Wunderhorn*, and for the *Lieder eines fahrenden Gesellen* he wrote his own words, slightly sophisticated imitations of Austrian folk-poetry accurately reflected in the music. From the first Mahler seems to have envisaged orchestral accompaniment for his songs and the *Wayfarer* ones were actually orchestrated in the 1890s. Wolf also orchestrated some of his songs, with not very happy results; all the same, the *Orchesterlied* was soon something to be reckoned with.

SOLO SONG IN SCANDINAVIA

The influence of the German *Klavierlied* was felt not only in France and Bohemia but perhaps even more strongly in Scandinavia. Grieg's Opp. 2 and 4 (1861 and 1864) are all to German texts, all but one by Heine and Chamisso; he returned to German poets in Op. 48 (1889) and the circumstance that his later songs were published in Germany with German words long gave the impression that he went on setting them. In fact the German versions are often unfortunate, sometimes disastrous. Gade and his pupil Kjerulf had already composed a great many Schumannesque songs to Danish or Norwegian as well as German words and some of Kjerulf's Bjørnson songs – 'Synnøves Sang', Op. 6, No. 3 (1859), which with its hummed conclusion[25] gave Grieg a hint for Solveig's song in his music to *Peer Gynt*, and 'Prinsessen' in his Op. 14 (1865) – are thoroughly Norwegian in flavour. Grieg's betrothal (and later marriage) to a singer in 1864 gave him a lifelong inducement to write songs. Living in Denmark during 1863–6, he turned first to Hans Andersen in his set of *Hjertets Melodier* (Melodies of the heart), Op. 5 (1864); they included two immediate successes, 'To brune Øine' (Two brown eyes) and 'Jeg elsker dig!' (I love you) – the latter being one of the dozen of which he later made monstrously overloaded piano transcriptions as Liszt had done – and the powerful 'Min Tanke er et

---

[25] Quoted by Dag Schjelderup-Ebbe in 'Modality in Halfdan Kjerulf's Music', *M & L*, xxxviii (1957), p. 241.

mægtigt Fjeld' (My thought is a mighty mountain). Andersen also inspired the delightful long-breathed melody of 'Hytten' (The Hut), Op. 18, No. 7 (1869). But the best of Grieg's songs are those which match the Norwegian poems of Bjørnson (first in 'Prinsessen', 1871) and Ibsen (first in 1876). Besides 'The Princess', Bjørnson gave him 'Det første Møte' ('The first meeting', one of those later chosen for string-orchestral transcription), the virile 'Tak for dit råd' (Thanks for thy counsel), Op. 21, Nos. 1 and 4 (1872–3), and the masterly 'Fra Monte Pincio', Op. 39, No. 1, Ibsen his most perfect song, 'En svane' (A swan), Op. 25, No. 2 (1876). Grieg orchestrated the accompaniments of the last two in 1894, and of course both Solveig's songs in *Peer Gynt* – her lullaby at the end of the play outdoes the familiar one in Act IV – are orchestral songs. Bjørnson and Ibsen naturally wrote in *riksmål*, literary Norwegian; in 1877 Grieg was excited by the poems of Aasmund Vinje in the dialect-based *landsmål*, now known as 'New Norwegian' to produce a whole set of songs, Op. 33, three of which – 'Våren' (Spring), 'Den Sårede' (The wounded heart), and 'Fyremål' (The goal) – he later transcribed for string orchestra (Op. 33, Nos. 2 and 1, and Op. 53, No. 1). Twenty years later he set eight more *landsmål* poems, the *Haugtussa* cycle, Op. 67, and it is in these two collections, Opp. 33 and 67, that he is least open to the charge of writing songs in the German tradition – though such *riksmål* songs as the Bjørnson 'Dulgt kjaerlighed' (Hidden love), Op. 39, No. 2 (1873) are also totally Norwegian.

ENGLISH SONG

English solo song also entered a new and more promising phase under German auspices. Henry Hugo Pierson was the first Englishman to try his hand at the more sophisticated *Klavierlied*; unequal composer though he was, he broke away from English conventions of song-writing even in his early Burns settings, Op. 7 (*c.* 1841). His considerable output of songs,[26] ranging from the tender lyric to the big dramatic ballad, includes numerous German ones and he spent the latter part of his life in Germany, but he was happier with English than with German poets. He was one of the earliest to tackle Shelley (*c.* 1839)[27] and he is at his best with Tennyson, as in 'Claribel' and the *humoreske* composition of 'The white owl in the belfry sits'. The young Parry thought it worth his while to spend a long vacation studying with Pierson at Stuttgart, and Parry was before long (*c.* 1873–82) to make his courageous attempts to compose Shakespeare sonnets. Then came the first two sets of his *English Lyrics* (pub. 1886), models of English prosody though weighed down by pedestrian piano parts. They were not a dawn but they heralded a dawn. Much the same may be said of the songs of Edward MacDowell on the other side of the Atlantic (from 1883 onward) though

[26] Six are included in *English Songs (1800–1860)* (*MB*, xliii), ed. Nicholas Temperley and Geoffrey Bush.
[27] While still an undergraduate at Cambridge. See Alice and Burton Pollin, 'In Pursuit of Pearson's Shelley Songs', *M & L*, xlvi (1965), p. 322.

MacDowell, instead of going to fine poets as Parry did, was paralysed by the idea of translating great poetry into music and generally preferred to write his own regrettable verse.

38

The Decline and Fall of Romanticism
(1893–1918)

During the twelve or fifteen years after 1893 musical romanticism enjoyed its final efflorescence and began to show symptoms of decadence. Fundamentally German, its decline was closely associated with the decline of German musical supremacy which was given its final blow by the war of 1914–18. But there were no signs of decline around the turn of the century.

The most brilliant of the younger generation of European composers was Richard Strauss, and Strauss was following up his early 'tone-poems' with a series of programmatic works. *Till Eulenspiegels lustige Streiche* (1895), *Also sprach Zarathustra* (1896), *Don Quixote* (1897), *Ein Heldenleben* (1898), *Symphonia domestica* (1903) are marked by ever-increasing realism on the one hand (the bleating sheep in *Don Quixote*, the acid sneers of the hero's critics in *A Hero's Life*, the squealing baby in the *Domestica*) and on the other by ever-increasing exuberance of invention and the employment of large orchestras – *Heldenleben* and the *Domestica* need quadruple woodwind and eight horns – in thematic polyphony which carries Wagner's style to its *ne plus ultra*. At the same time he had entered the field of opera with *Guntram* (1894), first of the ruck of more or less Wagnerian German operas which succeeded *Hänsel und Gretel* – Wolf's *Corregidor* (1896), the *Evangelimann* (1895) of Wilhelm Kienzl (1857–1941), and *Der arme Heinrich* (1895) and *Die Rose vom Liebesgarten* (1901) by Hans Pfitzner (1869–1949). Strauss followed *Guntram* with the much more accomplished one-act *Feuersnot* (1901) which owed its success partly to the folk-elements common to the Humperdinck, Pfitzner, and Kienzl works and much more to the scandal of the erotic subject and the explicitly erotic music accompanying the heroine's defloration. In *Salome* (1905), a longer one-act work to Oscar Wilde's play, the healthy eroticism of *Feuersnot* was perverted and the scandal and success were much greater but the psychological characterization of the music is masterly. Strauss was encouraged to become primarily an operatic composer; he must have realized that there were limits to purely instrumental explicitness. At first, in *Salome* and *Elektra* (1909) his opera scores suggest tone-poems realized in terms of dialogue and stage-action. But from *Rosenkavalier* (1911) onward he ensured popularity with the great opera-going public by a stronger infusion of the diatonic lyricism which had always been present in his music.

Strauss thus gradually ceded the role of leading Central European symphonist to Mahler who had followed his suite-like First Symphony with a Second (1894) in the first movement of which 'the hero of my D major Symphony is borne to the grave'.[1] The whole Symphony has a subjective programme; the third movement is based on one of his *Wunderhorn* songs ('Des Antonius von Padua Fischpredigt') another *Wunderhorn* poem, 'Urlicht', is sung by a contralto soloist as the fourth, while the choral finale is a setting of Klopstock's ode 'Auferstehen, ja auferstehen' which Mahler had just heard sung at Hans von Bülow's funeral. The whole symphony plays for nearly two hours and the giant orchestra gave Strauss the precedent for that of *Heldenleben* and the *Domestica*. The Third Symphony (1896) was conceived as 'a musical poem embracing all the stages of evolution step by step. It begins with inanimate nature and rises to the love of God'.[2] It is cast in two 'sections' (*Abteilungen*), the first consisting of a gigantic purely instrumental movement in inflated sonata-form, the second of five shorter ones: a Tempo di minuetto ('the flowers in the field'), a Scherzando ('the animals in the wood') still instrumental but based on the early *Wunderhorn* song 'Ablösung im Sommer', a very slow movement in which an alto soloist sings Nietzsche's midnight song from *Zarathustra* ('the voice of Man'), a lively one in which the alto and choirs of boys and women sing the 'Poor beggar-children's song' from *Des Knaben Wunderhorn* ('the voices of angels'), and an instrumental slow movement in which the instruments seem to be struggling for precise utterance as in a subjective symphonic poem. Mahler himself said in the letter already quoted that the *Motiv* of this movement was

> Vater, sieh an die Wunden mein!
> Kein Wesen lass verloren sein!
> (Father, look upon my wounds! Let no living thing be lost!)

This is 'the voice of God as Love'. Yet another movement on a *Wunderhorn* poem, 'Wir geniessen die himmlische Freuden', was transferred to become the finale of the Fourth Symphony (1900). Some passages in these ramshackle but fascinating structures are as specifically programmatic as anything in Strauss; one manuscript of No. 3 has such marks as 'Das Gesindel' (The mob) at fig. 44 and 'Die Schlacht beginnt' (The battle begins) at 49; many are completely subjective; Mahler kept inventing and changing programmatic titles and hints but always ended by trying to suppress them altogether. But before Strauss extended the symphonic poem into a new kind of music-drama, Mahler had already removed all defining limitations from the 'symphony' although he was to withdraw to purely instrumental conceptions in Nos. 5 (1902), 6 (1905), 7 (1905), 9 (1910), and the unfinished 10, and put his vocal writing into the separate compartment

---

[1] Letter of 26 March 1896 to Max Marschalk, *Gustav Mahler Briefe* (Berlin, Vienna, and Leipzig, 1924), pp. 188–9.
[2] 1 July 1896 to Anna Bahr-Mildenburg, ibid., p. 161. On the complicated history of this work see P. R. Franklin, 'The Gestation of Mahler's Third Symphony', *M & L*, lviii (1975), p. 439.

of *Orchesterlieder*: the *Fünf Lieder nach Rückert* and *Kindertotenlieder* (Elegies for children), also by Rückert. Both sets (composed 1901–4) are intimate songs, the orchestra small, almost of chamber dimensions, and they include such exquisite miniatures as 'Ich atmet' einen linden Duft'. As for the two-movement Eighth Symphony (1907), vast settings of the 'Veni Creator' and the end of *Faust*, for a colossal force of soloists, choruses and orchestra, and the six-movement *Lied von der Erde* (1908) for contralto, tenor, and normal orchestra, neither is a symphony within any normal definition of the word.

THE INFLUENCE OF BACH

Diametrically different though Mahler and Strauss were in personality and musical idiom – Strauss extrovert, self-assured, brilliant depictor of characters not his own, in the stylistic line of Wagner and Liszt, Mahler introvert, constantly changing his mind, always concerned with his own thoughts and emotions, in a line deriving remotely from Schubert and approaching Wagner only occasionally – both were romantics, even extreme romantics, in that music was for them essentially a language, a medium for expression or suggestion. It is indeed difficult to conceive music more vividly descriptive than Strauss's, more subtly emotional than Mahler's. But they had a younger contemporary, Max Reger (1873–1916), who held with the nineteenth-century conservatives that musical ideas and structures could be ends in themselves. Reger's idol was Bach and organ works figured early and constantly in a great outpouring of music of every kind except opera. He was not an anti-romantic; he could admire Wagner and Strauss; but he admired Brahms more and the essential Reger is to be found in the *Phantasien* and fugues on hymn-melodies or original themes. He loved to archaize and his counterpoint, however harmonically based, is more genuinely linear than the free polyphony of Wagner, Strauss or Mahler. Yet his approach to Bach was very much that of his day; like his teutonized Italian friend Ferruccio Busoni (1866–1924) – and like the Bach scholars André Pirro and Albert Schweitzer – he was conscious of a mission to demolish the still lingering conception of Bach as a dry academic composer and he would play Bach fugues with free tempi and long built-up crescendi, an approach naturally reflected in such compositions of his own as the *Variationen und Fuge über ein Thema von J. S. Bach* for piano, Op. 81 (1904). His dense chromatic harmony early showed a tendency to clot his texture. The apparatus of romanticism is not applied to romantic ends; despite such things as the passionate first movement of the C minor Piano Quintet (1898), the tender Andante semplice of the orchestral Serenade in G (1906), and the powerful *Sinfonischer Prolog zu einer Tragödie* (1908), Reger was an absolute musician in the sense that Brahms was.

SCHOENBERG'S CHANGE OF COURSE

Of Reger's almost exact Teutonic contemporaries – Alexander von Zemlinsky (1872–1942), Arnold Schoenberg (1874–1951), Franz Schmidt (1874–1939), Franz Schreker (1878–1934) – by far the most important proved to be Schoenberg, typical of the rising generation in his initial admiration for both Brahms and Wagner. In 1899 he composed a string sextet inspired by Richard Dehmel's poem *Verklärte Nacht*, a Straussian symphonic poem in black-and-white instead of colour; in 1901 – though the orchestration was not finished till 1911 – a Wagnerian–Straussian work for soloists, choruses, and an orchestra of more than Mahlerian dimensions based on a translation of Jens Peter Jacobsen's *Gurresange*. There are some beautifully romantic things in the *Gurre-Lieder* – for instance, Tove's first song 'O, wenn des Mondes Strahlen' – a surprising addiction to strict canon in the choral writing, and the innovation of a speaking part with both 'pitch' and rhythm precisely indicated in musical notation. Next, and in strong contrast to the diatonic idiom of a great deal of the *Gurre-Lieder*, came a true symphonic poem, *Pelleas und Melisande*, after Maeterlinck (1903). Strauss had suggested the subject, some of the music is Straussian and the orchestra is practically identical with that of *Ein Heldenleben* but handled with much less skill. Strauss's thematic polyphony is sometimes over-rich, Schoenberg's is dense; the complicated texture, more suitable for chamber music, is often made opaque instead of more luminous by the orchestration. Both in *Pelleas* (at fig. 16) and in the third of the *Sechs Orchester-Lieder*, Op. 8 (1904) – 'Sehnsucht', a *Wunderhorn* song – there is a hint of Mahler.

After *Pelleas* Schoenberg began a retreat from romanticism and became increasingly preoccupied with the problems of construction. In *Verklärte Nacht* and *Pelleas* he had constructed long single-movement compositions with contrasted sections suggested by the sections of the poem or episodes of the play and organically related by a small number of basic themes corresponding to the human characters, as Strauss did in the *Domestica*. It was therefore not too difficult for Schoenberg to adapt the method in abstract works, the D minor String Quartet (1905) and *Kammersymphonie* for 15 solo instruments (1906), though with the shadowy programmes he also discarded the adipose tissue and revealed the hard bone-structure. The thematic material is also harder in the Chamber Symphony. In *Pelleas* Schoenberg had introduced a couple of chords of superimposed perfect fourths, promptly resolving them; now – with Salome's dance no doubt in mind[3] – he not only opened the Symphony with a quartal theme on the horn but built up a tremendous fourth-chordal fanfare as the climax of the development. The opening horn theme is followed by equally non-diatonic whole-tone music, but other thematic shapes are Wagnerian or Straussian.

Schoenberg's Second Quartet (1908) reverts to the four-movement form but advances even more boldly into new territory. The most obvious novelty, following Mahler's wholesale introduction of voices in the symphony, was the appearance of a soprano soloist singing poems by Stefan George, 'Litanei' and 'Entrückung' – as it were, a prayer and the answer to it – in the third and fourth movements (both slow). The Quartet begins in F sharp minor and ends with an F sharp major chord but Schoenberg had by now all but abandoned even the pretence that key still had any meaning for him, or that the centuries-old methods of large-scale architecture by altered repetition of thematic complexes had much more. With sense of key lost, the tonal tensions on which the methods depended no longer existed – just as the tensions produced by dissonance had become flaccid. The pattern of sonata-form is still discernible in the first movement; the second has a D minor key-signature, a middle section with a D major signature, and is freely repeated after it; the third consists of variations. But Schoenberg had really come to the end of large-scale construction; his thinking was collapsing in upon itself, so to speak, to produce musical substance of small magnitude but extraordinary density. It was exuded by a process that he later called 'developing variation' (*entwickelnde Variation*) which took the place of varied repetition. Thus by 1908 Schoenberg, who had disciples in Anton von Webern (1883–1945) and Alban Berg (1885–1935), had prepared a future crisis in Western music.

BELATED WAGNERISM

During these years when Strauss and Mahler, Reger, Pfitzner, and the rest, occupied the centre of the musical scene German influence dominated a vast amount of non-German music wherever romanticism was not yet extinct. In England, for instance, Edward Elgar (1857–1934), a stronger personality than any British composer since Purcell, belatedly applied Lisztian and Wagnerian harmony and orchestration and the *Leitmotiv* technique first in the moribund forms of cantata (e.g. *King Olaf*, 1896) and oratorio – *The Dream of Gerontius* (1900), *The Apostles* (1903), *The Kingdom* (1906). He went on to reveal his sensitive, emotional self in the orchestral *Variations on an Original Theme (Enigma)* (1899), and a First Symphony (1908). At the same time a younger man who was to write very different music in maturity,

[3] He could not then have known Mahler's Seventh Symphony, with its quartal passage in the slow introduction, nor did he probably know of Erik Satie's quartal chords in the music for Sar Péladan's *Le Fils des étoiles* (1891) any more than he could have foreseen Vladimir Rebikov's in the 'musico-psychological tale' *Bezdna* (The Abyss, on Leonid Andreyev's story) (1907):

Ex. 299
(i) SATIE   (ii) REBIKOV

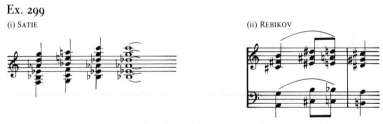

It is characteristic of both Satie (1866–1925) and Rebikov (1866–1920) that neither could do anything better with his invention than simply sideslip it unmodified.

Gustav Holst (1874–1934), heard *Tristan* 'and for the next ten years he was held by the binding tyranny of its spell'.[4] And the Hungarian Béla Bartók (1881–1945) was similarly bowled over by hearing *Zarathustra* and *Heldenleben* in 1902 and modelled his *Kossuth* (1903) quite closely in form, though not so much in texture, on *Heldenleben*. Both Holst and Bartók were emancipated from the German thrall – *c.* 1905–6 in both cases – by the discovery of their native folk-song. As for the Czech composers, Fibich had succumbed to Wagner early in the 1880s (see p. 737) and in his later operas – *Hedy* (Byron's Haidee) (1896), *Bouře* (on Shakespeare's *Tempest*) (1895), *Šarka* (1897), *Pad Arkuna* (The fall of Arkun) (1900) – Wagner contends with Smetana for the upper hand. Much the same might be said of Dvořák's last three, *Čert a Káča* (The Devil and Kate) (1899), *Rusalka* (1901) and *Armida* (1904), which are surprisingly more Wagnerian than their predecessors; but Dvořák always regarded *Tannhäuser* as Wagner's best work and *Rusalka* in particular is stamped over all by his own musical personality. The new note sounded in *Její pastorkyňa* (Her step-daughter) by Leoš Janáček (1854–1928), produced at Brno in 1904, remained unnoticed for twelve years or more when it soon became famous as *Jenůfa* (see below, p. 837).

In Russia the mature Wagnerian music-drama became generally known only with the *Ring* performances in 1889; *Die Meistersinger* and *Tristan* did not follow till 1898. Their effect was most marked on Rimsky-Korsakov who proceeded to enrich his already mature orchestral style and to adapt *Leitmotiv* techniques, in so far as they could be adapted to textures more Lisztian than Wagnerian, in three spectacular operas, *Mlada* (1892), *Noch pered Rozhdestvom* (Christmas Eve, on Gogol's story) (1895) and *Sadko* (1898). Thenceforth he steered an erratic, mostly experimental operatic course in which the best works – *Skazka o Tsare Saltane* (The tale of Tsar Saltan) (1900), *Kitezh* (1907) and *Zolotoy petushok* (The golden cockerel, after Pushkin) (1909) – were the most Russian although the quasi-Wagnerian element never completely drained away. Germanic influences penetrated elsewhere in Russian music, superficially in the songs and instrumental music of Sergey Taneyev (1856–1915), Sergey Rakhmaninov (1873–1943), specially in that of the somewhat Brahmsian Nikolay Metner (1880–1951), but most profoundly in the thought as well as the music of Aleksandr Skryabin (1872–1915).

A typical Russian intellectual of the period of political repression when the optimistic positivism of the 1860s had long been superseded by escapist religious, philosophical or artistic cults, Skryabin began by composing exquisite piano miniatures – notably the sets of preludes, Opp. 11, 13, 15–17 (mostly 1895) – a much less characteristic Piano Sonata in F minor (1893) and Concerto (1897), and two fine specimens of the late-romantic piano sonata, Opp. 19 and 23 (both 1897). Skryabin's orchestral music was always essentially piano-music orchestrated and a great deal of his First Symphony (1900) belongs to the age of Schumann and Liszt. Its most interesting

---

[4] Imogen Holst, *The Music of Gustav Holst* (London, 1951), p. 5.

feature is its plan, a conventional four-movement symphony in E minor framed by two movements in E major based partly on the same material, one purely orchestral, the other with mezzo-soprano, tenor, and chorus singing a poem of his own, more or less equating art with religion. It was now that he really discovered Wagner whom he placed beside Liszt, 'the ideal type of artist', and also Nietzsche's gospel of the Superman and glorification of the artist type; a planned 'Nietzschean opera' came to nothing, but the Second Symphony (1902) and Fourth Sonata (1903) were Wagnerian as well as Lisztian. Combining the roles of Superman – Nietzsche's 'Caesar with the soul of Christ'[5] – and of Messiah in his strange unbalanced mind, he dreamed of 'a fusion of all the arts' uniting art 'with philosophy and religion in an indivisible whole to form a new gospel', and styled his Third Symphony (1904) *Le divin poème* in an attempt to represent the evolution of the human spirit struggling with its past and evolving through Pantheism to an 'intoxicated affirmation of its liberty and unity with the universe (the divine "Ego")'.

He next tried to put his thoughts into words, *Poema Ekstaza (Le Poème de l'Extase)* (Geneva, 1906),[6] the first 224 lines of which loosely provided the programme of an orchestral piece with the same title, while another quotation was printed as an epigraph to the Fifth Sonata (both 1907). The orchestra of the *Divine Poem* is already large and that of *Ecstasy* is of *Heldenleben* dimensions, plus an organ; indeed some of the music itself is Straussian, Strauss modified by Skryabin's feathery piano style. Much of it is still diatonic and *Ecstasy*, like the Second Symphony and the *Divine Poem*, ends on an emphatic C major chord. Skryabin had not yet found the musical language for his ultimate goal, a quasi-liturgical 'mystery' in which music, dance, poetry, colours and scents would combine to induce 'a supreme final ecstasy' – and the end of the world. In the piano *Morceaux*, Opp. 56 and 57 (1908), we can see him with one foot still in the world of *Ecstasy* (Op. 56, No. 2) but leaning forward with his hand almost on the *trouvaille*, at the end of Op. 56, No. 4:

Ex. 300

This is, after all, only a sophistication of something already discovered by Satie and Rebikov (cf. Ex. 299).

[5] Nietzsche, *Aufzeichnungen aus dem Nachlass zur Erklärung von 'Also sprach Zarathustra'*, No. 81.
[6] English translation by Hugh Macdonald, *The Musical Times*, cxiii (1972), p. 26.

THE WAGNERIAN SUNSET IN THE LATIN LANDS

Romanticism and Germanic music had affected that of the Latin peoples variously, the Iberians least of all. However Felipe Pedrell (1841–1922), collector of folk-music and founding father of Spanish musical nationalism, had composed in 1891 an intensely patriotic Catalan opera *Els Pireneus* (The Pyrenees) (perf. 1902) in the idiom of Lisztian oratorio, with much thematic reminiscence, and liberally laced with Catalan and Moorish melodies, troubadour songs – with examples of *tenso*, *lai*, and *sirventès*[7] – and anachronistic borrowings (the action of the three parts passing in 1218, 1245, and 1285) from the works of the Valencian organist Juan Bautista Comes (1568–1643). Pedrell's next opera, *La Celestina* (comp. 1902), was on similar lines. A stronger impulse from Central Europe is perceptible in the orchestral music of Conrado del Campo (1876–1953), first from César Franck, then from Strauss, particularly in the symphonic poem *La divina comedia* (1904). However the real rejuvenation of Spanish music was to come from another quarter (see below, p. 804).

Italy was another matter. The renaissance of Italian instrumental music was mainly due to the Liszt disciples Sgambati (see p. 699) and Busoni, and the more Brahmsian Giuseppe Martucci (1856–1909). Busoni also went on to embrace other German music, from Bach to Brahms, but the romantic vein shows in the *Symphonisches Tongedicht* (1893) and in the planning of the Violin Concerto (1897) and the colossal Piano Concerto with male choral finale on an excerpt from Adam Oehlenschlæger's *Aladdin* (1904).[8] Both Sgambati and Martucci championed Wagner's music without being much influenced by it. On the other hand, as we have seen (p. 744), Puccini was familiar with it when he wrote *Manon Lescaut*. But Puccini's Wagnerism was purely superficial, an affair of continuous texture and quasi-*Leitmotiv*; it was hardly a more important component of his operas than Massenet's type of melody. He soaked up such elements from every quarter like a sponge but the sponge remained unmistakably Puccinian; the warm, luscious, *morbide* melodies, harmonies and orchestration of *La Bohème* (1896), *Tosca* (1900), and *Madama Butterfly* (1904), the vocal lines levelling into quasi-parlando, swelling as imperceptibly into melody, could have been written by no other composer. Leoncavallo's Wagnerism was of the same order; it shows in *I Medici* (1893) and in *his Bohème* (1893), notably at the beginning of Act III.

As we have seen in Chapters 34–7 Wagnerism had struck deeper roots in France. But Vincent d'Indy, looking back in 1930,[9] decided that even in Chabrier's *Gwendoline* it was 'more apparent than real'. Franck, always more Lisztian than Wagnerian, employed quasi-*Leitmotive* in his posthumously produced operatic failures, *Hulda* (comp. 1886) and *Ghiselle* (1899), but Franck's Wagner was essentially the Wagner of *Tannhäuser* and

---

[7] See p. 100.
[8] A play for which the Danish symphonist Carl Nielsen (1865–1931) later provided incidental music.
[9] *Richard Wagner et son influence sur l'art musical français*, p. 69.

Lohengrin. Much more genuinely Wagnerian were the works of his disciples, d'Indy's *Fervaal* (1897) and Chausson's *Le Roi Arthus* (posthumously produced in 1903[10]). Both composers wrote their own libretti, both employed true *Leitmotive*, both – particularly Chausson who sometimes comes dangerously near to quotation from *Tristan* – adopted Wagnerian harmony and textures; both occasionally reveal the Frenchman behind the German mask, e.g. Grympuig's address to the chiefs in *Fervaal*, II.3, and the labourer's song in *Arthus*, II.1. Wagnerism could also be crossed with Massenet and *verismo*, as Charpentier demonstrated with great popular success in *Louise* (1900). Another hybrid that was being composed by a friend of Chausson's, during the early 1890s at the same time as *Fervaal* and *Arthus* marked both an end and a beginning, the end of Wagnerian domination in France and the emergence of a new music.

THE LANDMARK OF *PELLÉAS*

Debussy's *Pelléas et Mélisande* (1902) is the earliest major musical landmark of the twentieth century. In some respects – the emotional restraint, the total suppression of eloquence – it seems the complete antithesis of Wagnerian music-drama. But Debussy himself confessed his difficulty in escaping from the old magician's spell; there is a whiff of *Tristan*, Act II, in *Pelléas* and a stronger one of *Parsifal*; d'Indy was able to enumerate ten *thèmes-conducteurs* in the score[11] and other commentators have found more. All the same, there is even less of Wagner in the musical stuff of *Pelléas* than there is of Rimsky-Korsakov, Balakirev, or Massenet in Debussy's orchestral *Prélude à 'L'après-midi d'un faune'* (1894) suggested by Mallarmé's poem. *L'après-midi* and *Pelléas* are further stages in that deliquescence of texture and structure already noticeable in Debussy's String Quartet (cf. p. 779) and Maeterlinck's play was the perfect alembic. Its dreamlike action was the pretext for, and connecting thread of, these mosaics of motives and non-functional harmonies in which the note-combinations exist for their own sake, and colour and lay-out are more important than context, while contrast is quite as important as connection. The very opening bars of *Pelléas* are suggestive: four not merely diatonic but modal (d'Indy's 'forest' theme) followed by two on whole-tone chords ('indecision' or Golaud). The church modes were much in French composers' minds at the time; Bruneau had introduced whole-tone harmony in *Le Rêve*; the under-stated vocal lines, so different from Wagnerian declamation, had prototypes not only in Musorgsky's songs but in Massenet's and even Gounod's; the finesse of the *Pelléas* orchestra was not so outstanding against the background of contemporary French scoring. But taken together these elements, fused by genius, added up not simply to a masterpiece of the mortal sickness of romanticism but to a denial of the essence of romanticism, music-as-a-

---

[10] Under d'Indy at Brussels where earlier in the same year he had conducted the first performance of his own second opera, *L'Étranger*.
[11] Op. cit., pp. 79–81.

language, and the resuscitation of music-for-sound's-sake alone – albeit very novel sounds. This too was very much in the air at the time; Grieg's 'Klokkeklang' (see p. 776) is a fairly crude example; and Debussy himself was soon to carry it further in his orchestral *Nocturnes* (1897–9), where 'Sirènes' is the most perfect exemplar of his *pointilliste* technique, the three 'esquisses symphoniques' *La Mer* (1903–5), the two sets of *Images* for piano (1905 and 1907), and later works.

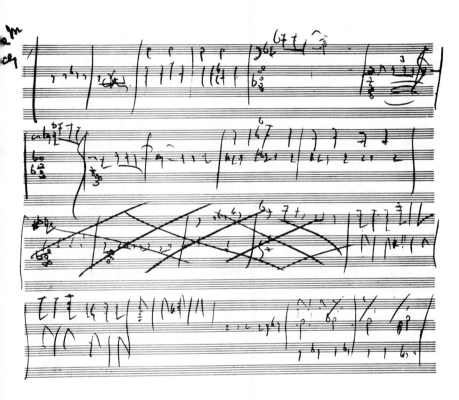

Pl. 60   Composition sketch for the opening of Act V of Debussy's *Pelléas et Mélisande*; the curtain rises on a room in the castle where Mélisande lies dying.

CROSS-CURRENTS IN FRENCH MUSIC

Debussy's influence was widespread, most importantly on his younger compatriot Maurice Ravel (1875–1937), a pupil of Fauré. It is evident in five *Miroirs* for piano (1905) and the three pieces inspired by Louis Bertrand's

Gaspard de la Nuit (1908). But Ravel was generally more inclined to line-drawing than Debussy, producing a variety of neo-classicism. His String Quartet in F (1903) sprang from 'une volonté de construction musicale' and the same was evidently true of his piano *Sonatine* (1905) and *Introduction et Allegro* for harp accompanied by string quartet, flute and clarinet (1906). Indeed Debussy himself had leaned the same way in *Pour le piano* (1894–1902) and the *Trois chansons de France* (1904) and was to do so much more markedly in his later years. At the same time d'Indy was turning to a far more rigorous kind of classicism in his E major Quartet (1897), Symphony No. 2 in B flat (1903), and Piano Sonata (1907), a classicism marked by thematic density, taut construction and sometimes (e.g. near the end of the Symphony) harsh, angular canonic writing. Yet he found it difficult to exorcise the spirit of romanticism completely; the basic themes of the Symphony symbolize good and evil, and his orchestral *Jour d'été à la montagne* (1905), through which blows the fresh air of folk-melody, is frankly romantic, picturesque, even programmatic. As for the younger men in his shadow – Albéric Magnard (1864–1914), Paul Dukas (1865–1935), Albert Roussel (1869–1937), and the rest – they were eclectics of a type common at this period. The symphonies of Magnard and Roussel (e.g. the latter's No. 1, entitled *Le Poème de la forêt* (1904–6)) are basically romantic, influenced to some extent by Debussyan techniques, while Dukas passed from his Franckish-d'Indyish C major Symphony of 1896 by way of the programmatic *L'Apprenti sorcier* on Goethe's ballad (1897) and the splendidly classical *Variations, interlude et final sur un thème de Rameau*[12] for piano (1903) to a Maeterlinck opera, *Ariane et Barbe-Bleue* (1907). *Ariane* could hardly have been written without *Pelléas*, but is more Wagnerian, harsher harmonically, its brilliant orchestration – at such passages as the pouring out of the precious stones in Act I and the moment when Ariane lets in the light to the darkened hall in Act II – learned from Rimsky-Korsakov and Strauss. But Dukas's material, even in the most poetic moments (as when Ariane reveals the beauty of the other wives and when they choose after all to stay with Blue-Beard) is open to the criticism he made of Strauss's: 'Les thèmes . . . éveillent rarement . . . l'impression du sentiment qu'ils prétendent évoquer. Ce sont de purs graphismes symboliques'.[13]

INDIVIDUAL ECLECTICS

Such eclecticism, such cross-currents were typical of the period. Strauss and Debussy seemed to be the opposite poles of contemporary music, yet a Dukas, a Skryabin and a Schreker could learn from both. Usually it was Debussy who opened up new paths. It was his piano music and Ravel's that showed the way for Isaac Albéniz (1860–1909) and Manuel de Falla (1876–1946) to compose respectively the four sets of *Iberia* (1906–9) and the *Quatre pièces espagnoles* (1908) with which Spain re-entered the field of

[12] 'Le Lardon' in Rameau's *Pièces de Clavecin* of 1724.
[13] *Les Écrits de Paul Dukas sur la musique* (Paris, 1948), p. 488.

European music. Debussy, discovered only in 1907, was after folk-song the principal agent of Bartók's liberation from the German tradition; he quickly celebrated his liberation by writing a set of piano *Bagatelles* (1908) which have been described as 'a miniature thesaurus of the new harmonic and tonal devices of the period': bitonality, counterpoint of chord-blocks, fourth chords, the non-functional sideslipping of dissonances. Similarly the Englishman Ralph Vaughan Williams (1872–1958) was liberated by folk-song and study with Ravel in 1908 and composed his very English Housman song-cycle *On Wenlock Edge* in 1909, English even in its conservatism, its rejection of the more exciting novelties of the European *avant-garde* gathered together by Bartók.

The case of Busoni was different, the Italian and German elements in his make-up so amalgamated that he stands alone, unmistakably individual despite his eclecticism. His lifelong friend the Finn Jan Sibelius (1865–1947) was another such, Frederick Delius (1862–1934), English by birth, German by ancestry, Scandinavian by musical sympathy, French by domicile, a third. Sibelius was so sensitive to the charge of eclecticism that he flatly denied not only his ravishment by Wagner, particularly *Parsifal*, still in 1894, but the effect of all other influences – including Finnish folk-music – on his style. In fact, his susceptibility to composers as diversified as Borodin, Grieg, and Bruckner is revealed in his First Symphony (1899) though it bears the overall stamp of his own personality, an unmistakable individuality manifest even more clearly in the orchestral *En Saga* (first version 1892; revised 1901) and the four *Legends* – including *Tuonelan Joutsen* (Swan of Tuonela) – of 1893–5. In such early works as the *Swan* Sibelius was already producing unique 'granite' orchestral sonorities and although he was always liable to turn aside to similar picturesque works he went on to write a remarkable series of 'abstract' symphonies. In the first movement of No. 2 (1902) he adapts to his own ends the structural principle of Borodin's First (see p. 690); in strongest contrast with his contemporaries he uses the 'classical' orchestra with only pairs of woodwind and in the Third Symphony (1907) one notices not only emotional coolness and economy of texture but elision of structural inessentials, a process carried to the extreme in No. 4 (1911) where the first subject of the opening movement, after six bars of introduction, consists of 20 bars, the transition of 5, and the second subject-plus-codetta of 22, a compression paralleled but not excelled in his Seventh and last Symphony (1924). Nothing could be more completely antithetic in every respect to the contemporary Germanic symphony.

Delius's distinctness was of a different nature. His music is frankly romantic; he admired Wagner – and Strauss's *Don Juan*; when he uses impressionistic methods as in the orchestral piece *In a Summer Garden* (1908) he does so to romantic ends. In *A Mass of Life* (1905), with a text drawn from Nietzsche's *Zarathustra*, he employs very large – though not quite Straussian or Mahlerian – forces. His drifting harmony, as empirical and piano-based as Musorgsky's, derived from late Grieg, envelops much of his music in a dreamy haze of nostalgia; whether his subject is star-crossed lovers as in his opera *Romeo und Julia auf dem Dorfe* (1901; perf. 1907), after a story by Gottfried Keller, or an English folk-tune as in the orchestral rhapsody *Brigg Fair* (1907), he sees it through much the same poetic haze.

Such eclectic figures, such cross-currents of musical language had of course been known before but probably never in such quantity especially if we count less individual eclectics like Dvořák's pupil Vítězslav Novák (1870–1949) and the Hungarian Ernö Dohnányi (1877–1960), who changed course several times, and younger men feeling their way such as the Pole Karol Szymanowski (1882–1937) (see p. 839) and the Spaniard Joaquin Turina (1882–1949). The great majority of composers were still content to use the language of late romanticism, with or without chic impressionistic techniques or slight national accents.

HYBRIDIZATION OF FORMS AND MEDIA

Nor was the process of hybridization confined to the language of music. It began to confound forms and media, so that their specific history becomes much less important than the history of musical language and of new concepts, some of them derived from extra-musical artistic movements. Opera was invaded by ballet, not in the long familiar form of divertissement but as an integral part of the work (Rimsky-Korsakov's *Mlada* and *Kashchey bessmertny* (Kashchey the immortal) (1902), Strauss's *Salome*). *The Golden Cockerel* was before long – in 1914 – performed as a ballet with the voice-parts sung off-stage. Solo song was introduced in chamber music with Schoenberg's Second Quartet or accompanied by piano and string quartet (*On Wenlock Edge*), while soloists and chorus took over entire symphonies (Mahler's Eighth and Vaughan Williams's Walt Whitman *Sea Symphony* (1910)). Composers wrote for orchestra with a textural finesse that would formerly have been reserved for chamber music; conversely *Verklärte Nacht* was a 'symphonic' poem for string sextet and Schoenberg's first chamber symphony for 15 solo instruments was followed ten years later by Schreker's for 23.

Schreker had already in 1908 taken the chamber orchestra into the theatre for his music to Oscar Wilde's *The Birthday of the Infanta* and in 1909 Holst completed a chamber opera, *Savitri*, lasting thirty minutes with three characters and an 'orchestra' consisting of two string quartets, double bass, two flutes and cor anglais. Intimate theatre was not, however, always content with modest forces; Schoenberg's *Monodram, Erwartung* (Expectation) (also 1909), demands quite a large orchestra. This was another field in which Rebikov was an insufficiently gifted pioneer. In 1900 he had published a set of *Melomimiki*, a genre which he defined as 'a species of scenic art in which mime and instrumental music' (in this case for piano) 'combine in an indivisible whole; it differs from ballet in that dances play no part in it and from pantomime in that the part of music is no less important than that of mime'. These were followed by short 'vocal scenes' for soloist in costume with scenery and *Melodeklamatsii* (precisely notated rhythmic declamation to piano) (1905). *La Tragédie de Salomé* by Florent Schmitt (1870–1958), an out-and-out French eclectic, was originally conceived in 1907 as a *mimodrame* with small orchestra for Loie Fuller, an American dancer who made much play with effects of colour and lighting. Schoenberg's *Erwartung* and still more his *Die glückliche Hand* ('The hand of fate' as he called it) followed in this line.

THE CRISIS OF 'EXPRESSIONISM'

Erwartung was peculiarly important to Schoenberg, for the concentration of the dramatic action in one character not only chimed with the fashionable concept that dominated so much *avant-garde* art of the time, expressionism – which has been defined as 'the morbidly intense expressive content of concentrated particles of speech or line or sound' – but provided a temporary solution for the problem that faced him after the Second String Quartet. The implosion of his musical thought had deprived him of the means of extended construction. Tonality and repetition, even varied repetition, were discarded and what he described as the 'emancipation of dissonance' made the heightening and relaxation of tension impossible. While shreds of thematicism are still perceptible in the first two of the *Drei Klavierstücke*, Op. 11 (1909), they are only vestigial in No. 3. Music of such density was not only extremely difficult to apprehend; it could not be expanded without destroying its very nature. Very similar to Op. 11, No. 3, is the first of the *Fünf Orchesterstücke*, Op. 16, written at nearly the same time, but the density is somewhat lightened by the orchestral colouring, while No. 3 is actually a 'colour'-composition, static chords almost imperceptibly changing timbre. The settings of poems from Stefan George's *Das buch der hängenden gärten* from the same year are also miniatures but the extended text of *Erwartung* supplied a continuous support for continuous composition with varied emotional expression. Schoenberg's disciples naturally shared his crisis. Webern's *Fünf Sätze* for string quartet, Op. 5 (1909), are very close to Schoenberg's Op. 11, though his six *Stücke für Orchester*, Op. 6 (1910), have more light and air despite the enormous orchestra involved; Berg in his two-movement String Quartet, Op. 3 (1910), however eschews such extreme puritanism and achieves extended instrumental forms in which themes at transposed pitch are atonal substitutes for key-changes. Schoenberg himself drastically clarified his textures in his *Sechs kleine Klavierstücke*, Op. 19 (1911) but they are *klein* indeed, the longest only 17 bars, three of them only 9.[14] In *Pierrot lunaire* (1912), settings of 'thrice-seven poems' translated from Albert Guiraud for a singer (who is generally required to speak at approximate musical pitches) and five instruments, and the expressionist drama *Die glückliche Hand*

---

[14] Webern's *Sechs Bagatellen* for string quartet, Op. 9, and five *Stücke für Orchester*, Op. 10 (1911–13), are smaller still. Op. 10, No. 4, is six bars long and plays for about 20 seconds.

(comp. 1910–13), involving three nameless characters, choral *Sprechstimme*, a very large orchestra, and carefully 'orchestrated' schemes of coloured lighting, he relies more and more on canon and inversion and ostinato for purposes of structure as well as texture. The outbreak of the 1914 war temporarily released him and his followers from the need to find a way out of this cul-de-sac; all three were called up for periods of military service.

Bartók was not one of Schoenberg's 'followers'. He had discovered him (the Op. 11 *Klavierstücke*) only in 1910 and Schoenberg's harmony had affected him only superficially when he composed his opera *A kékszakállú herceg vára* (Duke Bluebeard's castle) (perf. 1918) in 1911. But *Bluebeard's Castle* is an 'expressionistic' drama which the poet Béla Balázs had based on Maeterlinck with drastic modification and compression – only one act and two characters, Bluebeard and Judith (Ariane) – and Bartók's music might be described as half way between *Ariane et Barbe-Bleue* and *Erwartung*.

ARTIFICIAL HARMONIC CONSTRUCTION

In the meantime Skryabin had discovered what he called his 'synthetic harmony' on which he exclusively based his *Prométhée: le Poème du Feu* (comp. 1908–10). The 'poem of fire' is scored for mammoth orchestra and piano, with organ, wordless chorus, and a keyboard (musically notated) intended to control the flooding of the concert-hall with intense light coloured in accordance with his associations of sound and colour. The 'synthetic harmony' consisted of chords made up of fundamental notes with their 9th, 10th, 11th, 13th, and 14th upper partials arranged in fourths (e.g. C, F♯, B♭, E, A, D) which – neglecting the tempered tuning of the piano – he considered should provide 'perfect' combinations of sound.[15] In *Prometheus* and the post-Promethean piano music, including Sonatas 7–10 and a number of preludes (1911–14), the basic harmony is treated freely with plenty of 'foreign' appoggiaturas and passing notes which mollify its impact. Nevertheless Promethean music remains an occult language, packed with precise meaning to the composer himself alone, another dead end of extreme romanticism and at the same time a symptom of anti-romanticism in its artificial constructivism, an antinomy similar to that of *Pierrot lunaire*. At the same time another form of artificial constructivism was being introduced to Western Europe by a more popular and exciting Russian invasion. In 1907 the impresario Sergey Dyagilev had organized in Paris a series of orchestral concerts including excerpts from Rimsky-Korsakov's *Mlada* and *Christmas Eve*, in which he had experimented with an artificial idiom (e.g. a scale of alternate tones and semitones). (Brilliantly coloured by his scoring, this provided an unreal fantastic foil to the real, human elements in his operas.) The following year a concert performance of the introduction and wedding-march from *The Golden Cockerel*, in which this element is developed much further, was outstandingly successful. And

---

[15] Rebikov's chords sideslipped in Ex. 299(ii) and Skryabin's own penultimate chord in Ex. 300 lack only the 9th partial, in the latter case G natural, of the full 'Promethean' chord.

in 1909 Dyagilev revealed the full splendour of the art of ballet developed under the aegis of the Imperial Court: a combination of a new kind of choreography, as much mime as dance, splendid *décor*, and music of almost symphonic quality.

INFLUENCE OF THE DYAGILEV BALLET

The outstanding sensations of the second season (1910) were *Sheherazada*, with music from Rimsky-Korsakov's suite, and *Zhar-ptitsa* (The Fire-Bird) composed by his pupil Igor Stravinsky (1882–1971), a score reflecting not only the master's latest style but here and there Skryabin's and Debussy's. 1911, when the company also visited Rome and London, brought a second Stravinsky ballet, *Petrushka*, and in 1912 French composers entered the field. Ravel's *Daphnis et Chloé* had been commissioned by Dyagilev but he also orchestrated piano works – *Ma mère l'oye* (1908) and *Valses nobles et sentimentales* (1911) – for rival undertakings. (For one of these Dukas composed his *poème dansé La Péri* and Florent Schmitt re-scored his *Tragédie de Salomé* for full symphonic orchestra.) In 1913 Dyagilev brought out Debussy's *Jeux* and a French company Roussel's *Le Festin de l'araignée* (The Spider's banquet) but these were totally eclipsed by the sensation of Stravinsky's third ballet *Vesna svyashchennaya* (The Rite – properly 'the consecration' – of Spring). In these 'scenes from pagan Russia' six-note blocks of piled up fourths and fifths were pounded out by a monumental orchestra of four-fold woodwind, eight horns and so on in powerful yet subtle rhythms, provoking riots in the theatre and at subsequent concert performances.

The *Rite* was bracketed in the bewildered minds of the great majority of the musical public with *Prometheus* and Schoenberg's *Five Orchestral Pieces*; very different from each other, all three works seemed to have passed the limits of comprehensibility.

THE RETREAT FROM ROMANTIC EXCESS

However, Skryabin died in 1915 and Schoenberg and Stravinsky soon changed course. Even Strauss seems to have felt he had ventured far enough into cacophony in *Elektra* (1909) and retreated through the romantic bitter-sweetness of *Rosenkavalier* (1911) and the still more *pastiché Ariadne auf Naxos* (1912) to the bland *Kitsch* of the Dyagilev ballet *Josephslegende* (1914) and the diatonic platitudes of the *Alpensymphonie* in which he deployed a mammoth orchestra in his weakest symphonic composition. It is tempting to see something parallel in Debussy's music for d'Annunzio's *Le Martyre de saint Sébastien* (1911) and *Jeux*. But the simplicity and economy of the *Douze Études* for piano and *En blanc et noir* for two pianos (both 1915), and the three chamber *Sonates* of 1915–17, are not 'concessions'; they are a retreat from impressionism but an advance to a new classicism paralleled in Ravel's Piano Trio (1915) and *Le Tombeau de Couperin* for piano (1917), and the later works of Fauré. The new classicism had many faces; Debussy's *Martyre*, Sibelius's extremely condensed Fourth Symphony, and Busoni's opera *Die Brautwahl* all date from 1911 but are no more alike than *Petrushka* and *Rosenkavalier*, yet all three exist in a cool climate. It was, incidentally, a climate in which the terminal symptom of romantic excess, the mammoth orchestra, did not flourish much longer. Holst's suite *The Planets* (comp. 1914–17), perhaps the earliest English work to absorb a little Stravinsky and something of Schoenberg's Op. 16, No. 3, was among the last really lavish scores, and Stravinsky himself turned from the vast orchestra of the *Rite* to the small group of *Renard* ('histoire burlesque chantée et jouée') (1917) and the smaller one of *L'Histoire du soldat* ('à réciter, jouer et danser') (1918).

Romanticism, if dying, was not yet dead. To the majority of audiences, other than connoisseurs, it offered more normal and agreeable forms of contemporaneity: Rakhmaninov's D minor Concerto (1909) and his piano Preludes and *Études-Tableaux*, Opp. 32 and 33 (1910 and 1911), Mahler's *Lied von der Erde* (1908; perf. 1911) and Ninth Symphony (1910; perf. 1912), Elgar's Violin Concerto (1910), Second Symphony (1911) and *Falstaff* (1913), in the field of Italian opera *L'amore dei tre re* (The love of the three kings) (1913) by Italo Montemezzi (1875–1952) and the *Francesca da Rimini* (1914) of Riccardo Zandonai (1883–1944), and in Central Europe Schreker's erotic-fantasy opera *Der ferne Klang* (1909; perf. 1912), a surprisingly successful synthesis of Debussy and *verismo* with Straussian orchestration. British composers in particular cultivated various forms of nature-poetry, sometimes incorporating folk or folk-inspired melody: Delius's *On hearing the first Cuckoo in Spring* (1912) and *North Country Sketches* (1914), Vaughan Williams's *The Lark Ascending* (1914), and the tone-poems of Arnold Bax (1883–1953), *The Garden of Fand* (1916), *Tintagel* and *November Woods* (both 1917). It was Bax who later defiantly stated the *credo* of the romantic composer in two sentences: 'My music is the expression of emotional states. I have no interest whatever in sound for its own sake'.

Interlude

39

The Music of Black Africa and America

GENERAL CHARACTERISTICS

'Black Africa' is by no means a simple contradistinction from 'white Africa', least of all where music is concerned. Much of Africa belongs culturally to the Arab world; Indonesia has left its mark on Madagascar: and there is an enclave, Ethiopia, preserving – like Armenia – its own dialect of early Christian music. Unlike European, Arabic, Indian, and Chinese music, that of black Africa has no age-old theories, no notation; all we know of it is based on direct observation of practices, observation of little scientific value until little more than half a century ago. Black Africa includes very many peoples whose languages are often quite distinct, yet one authority[1] has detected 'underlying unities' in their musics and attempted to 'give an overview of the characteristics of this musical system' which is 'reasonably cohesive', and another[2] has declared roundly that 'the music of Africa south of the Sahara is one single main system', modified in varying degrees in some areas by Arab influence, e.g. among the Swahili-speaking peoples along the east coast.

Instruments derived from Arab models, such as the *rabāb* (see p. 195) are found in these areas, and the songs of the Tutsi in Ruanda and Hima in Uganda use

a hummed introduction which sets the general modality for the music and text which follow, clearly akin to the Arabic *maqām*. The style of voice production, ornamentation of melodic line, general melodic characteristics, and the use of intervals smaller than half tones all suggest Arabic influence.[3]

The same influence is apparent here and there on the west coast; in Nigeria it is overwhelmingly preponderant with the Hausa, less so with the Yoruba, and non-existent among the Ibo.

Whereas Arabic music, indeed Asian music generally, is remarkable for its concentration on successive pitch-sounds with exquisitely subtle distinctions and ornaments – and European music for its luxuriant exploitation of simultaneous pitch-sounds – the most obvious aspect of pure black African music is the primacy of rhythm. All African music rests on a

[1] Alan P. Merriam, 'African Music' in *Continuity and Change in African Cultures*, ed. William R. Bascom and Melville J. Herskovits (Chicago, 1959), pp. 49 and 80.
[2] A. M. Jones, *Studies in African Music* (London, 1959), i, p. 222.
[3] Merriam, 'African Music Reexamined in the Light of New Materials from the Belgian Congo and Ruanda-Urundi', *Zaïre*, vii (1953), p. 251.

rhythmic basis that includes the rich and complex polyrhythms essential to what is commonly known as 'hot' rhythm. The nickname itself is derived from 'a linguistic concept of West African tribesmen':

A compelling rhythm is termed 'hot'; the more exciting the rhythms, the 'hotter' the music. . . . The essential criteria of Negro musical rhythm may all be understood as overt manifestations of the concept 'hot'. Everywhere, Negro music differs from the music of impinging non-Negro groups in being 'hotter'.[4]

Hence the most important African instruments are percussive; the numerous ones which are not actually percussion instruments are played percussively[5] – and dance, even hand-clapping, is as important as song.

AFRICAN INSTRUMENTS

There are innumerable types of drum, the names and uses of which vary from tribe to tribe, of rattles, gongs, etc. Xylophones with calabash resonators, sometimes so large as to need more than one player, are called *timbila* or *malimba* by the Chopi of Mozambique, who have orchestras of them. Related to the xylophone, though not percussive, is the peculiarly African *sansa*, a sound-board to which are fastened metal or sometimes bamboo tongues capable of quickly altered tuning, freely vibrating and played by the thumbs and first fingers. In southern Africa the *sansa* is known as the *mbira*, which in some versions is mounted inside a gourd resonator. Besides vertical and transverse flutes and panpipes, there are 'musical bows', such as the Ruanda *umunaki* and southern African *chipendari*, which are struck or plucked, the bow being held to the open mouth which acts as resonator – though many types have calabash resonators.

In west Africa metal bells, called *gankogui* by the Ewe of Ghana, are used to establish a fundamental rhythm for an ensemble; they are sometimes accompanied by a calabash rattle (*axatse*). But the most important instruments are the drums, for which the Ewe names are *atsimevu*, the 'master-drum', *sogo*, *kidi*, and *kagan* (see pl. 61). Each is tuned successively higher but there is no precise pitch or precise interval. The lowest, *atsimevu*, is tuned first, the *sogo* rather higher, the *kidi* about a fifth higher than the *atsimevu*, and the *kagan* a sixth or seventh higher. What matters is not so much pitch as rhythm – and the tone-quality of the stroke. The *atsimevu* player uses both stick and hand, and can produce different sounds by striking different parts of the drum-skin. The smaller drums are played with two sticks, either freely or muted. And there are two ways of muting and thereby raising or lowering pitch: by holding down the stick after the stroke or by placing the other stick soundlessly on the drum before the stroke. The possible nuances of tone-quality and pitch are very numerous.

On the drum music are superimposed the rhythms of hand-clapping

---

[4] Richard A. Waterman, ' "Hot" Rhythm in Negro Music', *JAMS*, i (1948), p. 24.
[5] See Merriam, 'African Music Reexamined', pp. 248–9.

which, like the drum rhythms, take their time from the fundamental rhythm of the *gankogui* – as do the seemingly free rhythms of the song.[6] The commonest pattern of hand-clapping all over black Africa is:

or the variant:[7]

The sung melody is essentially, but by no means always, a free stylization of spoken intonation; there is 'a constant conflict and accommodation between

Pl. 61   Ewe ensemble (Ghana) consisting of three drums – *atsimevu* (master-drum), *sogo*, and *kidi* – flanked by players of *axatse* (calabash rattles) and *gankogui* (double bell).

musical tendencies and the curves traced by the speech-tones of the song-text';[8] and the vocal rhythms are freely elaborated from the clapping rhythms. The numerous scales are sometimes close to, but never identical with, Western diatonic scales; for instance the Ghanaian Ewe tend to sing in a 'major' scale which avoids the fourth degree and slightly flattens the seventh. Another African scale flattens the third as well as the seventh. And there are different styles of chorus-singing:

First, there is that four-square, virile, rather slow but very forceful type of chorus sung by the Zulus in South Africa [and also in Kenya, Uganda, and Tanganyika]. A different type of chorus is exemplified by the Bemba in Northern Rhodesia [the present Zambia, as well as by the Yoruba in far distant Nigeria], whose choruses, in parallel thirds, have an even, *legato*, wave-like flow which is intensely musical. Yet again, a third type of chorus-work is employed by the Nsenga on the eastern border of [Zambia, and by the Ganda of Uganda]. This is a rapid style of bright cheery singing.[9]

There is singing not only in unison and parallel thirds but in parallel fifths

[6] Jones, op. cit., ii, gives 'full scores' of chorus, clapping, and instrumental percussion.
[7] See ibid., i, pp. 212–3, for variants in different parts of the continent.
[8] George Herzog, 'Speech Melody and Primitive Music', *MQ,* xx (1934), p. 466.
[9] Jones, op. cit., i, p. 214.

and fourths.[10] Sometimes polyphony is produced by overlapping of chorus-leader and chorus, and canon has been observed in West African xylophone music.[11]

CONTACT WITH WESTERN MUSIC

Contact with modern Western music, as earlier with Islamic music, has adulterated the African tradition, for the black African is adept at assimilation and the process has been made easier by the circumstance that the African and Western musical systems are not totally incompatible. Both at home and dragged away from home to slavery in Latin or Anglo-Saxon America, he has long been exposed to Christian hymns and Western dance-music and popular song, liked them, and adopted or adapted them. European instruments have largely supplanted African ones, though they may be played in a non-European way; for instance, the guitar has taken the place of the *sansa* as the most popular instrument for solo performance or accompanying a song but 'as a rule we shorten the strings by tying a bar of wood, a *capodasta*, across them and so never use the greatest (lowest) notes at all'.[12] But the supreme irony is the adoption of jazz – the Ewe and other West African tribes now *swing* their traditional songs – by which process they are resuming their own property.

When the enslaved Africans, mostly from the west, were taken across the Atlantic, those settled in Latin America – Spanish, Portuguese, or French – were more fortunate than their brethren in North America. Their masters were more easy-going and did not, for instance, regard sexual intercourse with them with the abhorrence felt by the Anglo-Saxons who regarded the African generally as a contemptible inferior. The *mestizo* assimilated to his masters and gradually adopted their music while at the same time contributing to it much of his own; indeed Latin American music has become a fascinating compound of Spanish or Portuguese, Amerindian, and Negro elements varying in proportion according to each country. (Chilian is almost purely Spanish; Paraguayan is rich in Amerindian elements but has no African; Brazilian and Venezuelan include all three; Cuban has no Amerindian.) The Haitians, still nearly pure Negroes, have actually preserved drum-ensemble playing in polyrhythms and there is a remnant of African rhythm in the Cuban figure known as *cinquillo*:

a *gankogui* pattern, the same as the *samba* (which the Ewe call *conga*). Drum ensembles have also survived in Trinidad and, with Yoruba names, in the

---

[10] See *NOHM*, i, pp. 74ff., Exs. 118, 120, 123, 124, 128, 129, 131–3, 138–9.
[11] Herzog, 'Canon in West African Xylophone Melodies', *JAMS*, ii (1949), p. 196.
[12] Hugh Tracey, *Ngoma* (London, 1948), p. 72. A Zambian dance-song of the type called *saba-saba*, with guitar accompaniment, is given in Jones, op. cit., i, p. 263.

cult music of Bahia in Brazil.[13] Indeed, a Brazilian musicologist, F. R. Valle, has said that 'of the three principal lines forming the Brazilian race, the African branch is incontestably the one which has exercised most influence in our music',[14] and quoting him, Richard Waterman goes on to particularize:

African percussion instruments, played in the African manner, are responsible for the distinctive flavour of Brazilian dance rhythms. Brazilian popular music utilizes to a great extent the multiple metres of African polyrhythm, and to an even greater extent the African characteristic of 'off-beat phrasing' of melodic rhythms.[15]

The Mozambique *malimba* has become the Guatemalan *marimba*, and not only instruments but dances preserve African names; the *samba* and *conga* have already been mentioned, and the Cuban *rumba* and Argentine *tango* are African in origin although the tango has become completely hispanicized in the course of centuries.

NEGRO MUSIC IN NORTH AMERICA

Thus much of the substance of African music, however modified, has survived in Latin America. None at all has survived in North America, only the spirit. Crushed and degraded, the North American Negro forgot his traditional music, except perhaps underground and untraceably, and it was not until the mid-eighteenth century that he was offered any other. The Methodists and Baptists seem to have been the first to think of christianizing him; teaching him hymns they quickly found that, as one Presbyterian divine noted in 1755, 'the *Negroes*, above all the Human Species that I ever knew, have an Ear for Musick, and a kind of extatic delight in Psalmody'.[16] At the same period domestic slaves began to be successfully trained as violinists and wind-players. But this was a totally foreign music, eagerly adopted but not offering much scope for African expression. This came belatedly in the nineteenth century in the more lively 'spiritual' songs of the religious revivalist 'camp meetings'. It was through these and through traditional Irish and Scottish tunes sung by their masters that the African ethos began to manifest itself in work-song on the plantation and in banjo-playing,[17] first in the stressing of off-beats and in syncopation. Even before the Civil War and emancipation, Negro versions of 'spirituals' had begun to attract attention – a Negro form of 'Roll, Jordan, roll' was published in Philadelphia in 1862 – and in 1867 William Francis Allen and other white champions of the black published in New York a collection of 136 *Slave Songs of the United States*.

---

[13] Herskovits, 'Drums and Drummers in Afro-Brazilian Cult Life', *MQ*, xxx (1944), p. 477.
[14] *Elementos de folk-lore musical brasiliero* (São Paulo, 1936), p. 61.
[15] Op. cit., p. 27.
[16] Quoted in Robert Stevenson, 'Protestant Music in America', in the English-language edition of Friedrich Blume, *Protestant Church Music* (New York, 1974), p. 680.
[17] See Hans Nathan, 'Early Banjo Tunes and American Syncopation', *MQ*, xlii (1956), p. 455.

CAKEWALK, RAGTIME, AND BLUES

The nineteenth-century history of Negro music in the United States is blurred by its exploitation in the sometimes pseudo-Negroid songs of Stephen Foster (1826–64), the exuberant piano-pieces – 'La Bamboula', 'Le Bananier', 'Le Banjo' – of Louis Gottschalk (1829–69), born in New Orleans (which had been 'Latin' until 1803 and was always a hotbed of negritude), and on the lowest level by the 'nigger minstrels' who were usually whites with blacked faces. Even these minstrel troupes with their banjos took up a genuinely Negroid dance in simple syncopated rhythm, the cakewalk, and popularized it not only throughout America but in Europe during the closing years of the nineteenth century. The cakewalk was the direct precursor of ragtime, a type of (usually) piano music in which the right hand executed lively syncopated rhythms over a square sober 4/4 beat in the left. It is classically exemplified in a set of studies, *The School of Ragtime; six exercises for piano* (1908), by the Texan Negro Scott Joplin (1869–1917). But cold definition and the printed page give no idea of the true, quasi-improvisatory nature of the music in which the essential African-ness shows itself. All accounts of Black dancing speak of its 'intoxication', its 'frenzy', and the rhythms of the music are imbued with the quality known as 'hot'.

Pl. 62   Fate Marable's jazz-band on a Mississippi steamboat (*c.* 1918). The trumpeter (fourth from the left) is Louis Armstrong.

Side by side with ragtime there developed a type of melancholy solo song which probably developed from the singing of spirituals. It commonly employed the scales mentioned on p. 814, with the seventh and often the third degree slightly flattened. This presented a difficulty for the accompanying pianist, who solved it by playing the 'true' note together with the semitone below, while the singer might modify the flattening of the third to different degrees in the same performance.[18] These dubious notes were said to be 'blue', whence the songs themselves were styled 'blues'.

[18] Winthrop Sargeant, *Jazz Hot and Hybrid* (New York, 1946), pp. 148ff.

39. The Music of Black Africa and America

While ragtime was essentially pianistic and the blues were vocal, the style which emerged *c.* 1915 and before long invaded the world of 'serious' music (see pp. 823–4) was essentially for instrumental ensembles, originally quite small, consisting basically of cornet, saxophone, trombone, guitar, piano, double bass, and percussion. This was jazz, a word for which too many origins have been found for any of them to be credible. Born in New Orleans out of ragtime and blues – and 'hotter' than either – and sometimes based in early days on old French quadrille-tunes, its glorification of percussive rhythm may perhaps be regarded as a reincarnation of the African spirit in a strange, originally European body.

Part V
The Fragmentation of Tradition

Introduction

From the beginnings of Western music, if not earlier, until well into the twentieth century it is not difficult to trace a continuous evolutionary web of musical thinking and practice. The first threads of the warp were plainsong, the first woof the polyphonic methods of treating it. Then secular elements were interwoven. The pattern became enriched by instrumental elements; we have the written evidence of keyboard music and see that the same melodies were liable to appear in church music, secular song and as dance-tunes. Modal harmony was gradually moulded by increasing use of *musica ficta* into tonal harmony, which in turn made possible new ways of extending cohesive instrumental composition. Incorporation with drama introduced a fresh complication and national characteristics impinged. Yet through it all the web of tradition was continuous; despite the variants the main pattern was easily recognizable. Great cultural and spiritual and political upheavals – Renaissance Humanism, the Reformation, the Thirty Years War, the French Revolution – modified it only in passing. Even such a drastic innovation as the Florentine *recitativo* was gradually assimilated to the melodic tradition in *arioso* and finally in Wagner's scores. Monteverdi could employ his *prima prattica* and *seconda prattica* side by side; the Western tradition was strong enough to absorb both.

The first signs of a more serious crisis showed early in the twentieth century. A sense that the great tradition was approaching a dead end was reflected in Debussy's non-functional harmony, in Skryabin's experiments with a completely new harmonic system, and in Schoenberg's revolt against tonality. Debussy's innovations were easily absorbed like most of the earlier ones; Skryabin's were after a time rejected as some earlier ones – for instance, sixteenth-century *musique mesurée* – had been rejected. But Schoenberg's refused to be rejected. The first negative form of non-tonality was succeeded by a positive form, a substitute for tonality, 'composition with twelve notes'. This too found little acceptance because it was at first an artificial exercise in pure constructivism; the succession of notes and coincidence of notes, being deliberately dissociated from all traditional melodic lines and harmonics, were completely meaningless. It was only when Schoenberg and his disciple Alban Berg found ways of humanizing twelve-note music that its potential musical meaning began to be perceptible. A musical Esperanto came to be recognized as a musical language.

Such composers as Bartók occasionally infused twelve-note elements into tonal music and there was no longer any reason why dodecaphony should not be ultimately absorbed, as 'serial music', into the Western tradition.

At the same time however, the tradition itself was weakening in the hands of tired veterans and epigones, as well as being undermined by other innovations than Schoenberg's. In Germany itself Hindemith propounded a new, if less radical, tonal system. Jazz began to leak into Western music generally and aesthetic – not linguistic – confusion flowed from various forms of anti-romanticism: neo-classicism, 'utility music', the deliberately nonsensical musical equivalent of 'Dadaism'. Polytonality and microtonal music, like the pre-First War quartal harmony, did affect the basic language but were absorbed with other components into an eclectic *lingua franca* – linear, angular, half-heartedly tonal, and generally shy of extra-musical significance – a cross-bred weakling scion of the great line of Western music. Nevertheless it was recognizably a descendant and it served, with numerous personal modifications, many composers all over the world. Nerveless and flaccid though it is, it continues to serve, but it is the language of rearguard composers. The advance-guard attaches little or no value to tradition in any form or in any field, moral, economic, political, artistic. The language of pure musical tradition is, ironically, still kept alive mainly in the Soviet Union in a political oxygen tent.

While the Western tradition emerged thus cracked and enfeebled after the Second War, the process of fragmentation soon went much deeper and resulted in wide open breaks. *Musique concrète* and electrophonic music opened up exploration of an art of pure sound completely lacking in the associations normal music had imperceptibly acquired during the centuries, and therefore devoid of meaning and incapable of communication. Serialism was no longer limited to melodic note-rows but now applied to all the other elements of music: rhythm, pitch, metre, dynamics. And in escape from these cerebral straitjackets a new freedom, or rather licence, was permitted: aleatory music, the music of chance procedures. Music was composed by programmed computers. Instruments were used against their own nature; pianos were 'prepared' by inserting foreign objects between the strings, and orchestral instruments were subjected to similar distortion while singers were expected to cope with the appallingly unvocal. Scores were replaced by geometrical or fanciful diagrams.

If music continues to evolve in these directions we may be obliged to face the probability that most of the vast treasures accumulated by the Western tradition will have to be enjoyed as splendid museum-pieces in the same way that we enjoy the music of the distant past – and no doubt will long continue to be so enjoyed. But there is another hope. Western music, like Western culture in general, has become pre-eminent among the musics of the world but it is not the only one. Others even older – the most important ones sketchily indicated here in brief 'interludes' – have during the last thirty years aroused much interest not only among eminent and learned musicians but also among Western audiences. So far, most attempts to cross-fertilize them with Western music and vice versa have not been particularly happy. Yet it is not beyond possibility that, given 'world enough and time', mankind may evolve a universal culture that will include a genuine world music.

40

Music between the Wars (1919–45)

The world, and particularly the Europe, which emerged from the war of 1914–18 provided a musical milieu bewilderingly different from that of the past. The Habsburg Empire was fragmented, so that Vienna remained the capital only of a small republic while Prague and Budapest became the chief cities of genuinely independent states. The powerful Hohenzollern Empire was replaced by the shaky Weimar Republic while that of the Romanovs had already gone down in still more drastic revolution. Poland at last regained her independence. And these new states were torn by civil war, foreign invasion, counter-revolution, and economic crises of which the German *Billion* inflation of 1923–4 was only the most immediately spectacular, the world crisis of 1930 the most serious. Social and economic conditions did not encourage European composers to embark on sumptuous operas and monumental orchestral scores even if they had wanted to. The great gainer from all this was America. The United States were wealthier and more powerful than ever; to musicians they offered more financial prosperity and political security than anywhere else in the world. As early as 1915 the Parisian Edgard Varèse (1885–1965) had moved there and the Swiss Ernest Bloch (1880–1959), the first outstanding Jewish nationalist composer, followed in the next year. Rakhmaninov fled there in 1918 from the Russian Revolution, spent six years there and returned in 1939 to make it his final home. Hitler's rise to power and the outbreak of another war lead to further emigrations: Schoenberg, Schreker's pupil Ernst Křenek (1900–   ), Kurt Weill (1900–50), Stravinsky, Bartók, the Czech Bohuslav Martinů (1890–1959), and two brilliant exponents of new kinds of anti-romanticism, the Frenchman Darius Milhaud (1892–1974) and the German Paul Hindemith (1895–1963), though the last two returned to Europe after the war.

This foreign influx naturally stimulated native American composers, who at the same time found obvious sources for a new and American idiom in ragtime and jazz. Satie and Stravinsky had already introduced ragtime movements in the ballet *Parade* (1917)[1] and *L'Histoire du soldat*, and Milhaud composed a whole ballet, *La Création du monde* (1923) in jazz idioms, when the former Busoni pupil Louis Gruenberg (1884–1964)

[1] See below, p. 827.

entered the field with *The Daniel Jazz* (also 1923) for tenor and eight solo instruments and went on to compose a *Jazz Suite* for orchestra (1925) and an opera *The Emperor Jones* (1931; perf. 1933). A composer from a much humbler background but with greater natural gifts, George Gershwin (1898–1937), scored an immense popular success with an essay in 'symphonic jazz', *Rhapsody in Blue* (1924), a success he managed to repeat only once – with a 'folk opera' *Porgy and Bess* (1935). Another variety of pure Americanism, the bizarre unintegrated mixture of daring sophistication and homespun crudity in the music of Charles Ives (1874–1954), remained generally unknown until *c.* 1930 though his *Concord Sonata* for piano had been privately printed in 1919 and *114 Songs* in 1922. On the other hand other Americans of Gershwin's generation began to be heard in European concert-halls, notably Roger Sessions (1896–), Roy Harris (1898–) and Aaron Copland (1900–). (Significantly both Harris and Copland studied in Paris, not as the previous generation had done in Germany.) Such works as Copland's ballets *Billy the Kid* (1938) and *Appalachian Spring* (1944) and Harris's Third Symphony (1939) are very conservative by comparison with the avant-garde *Hyperprism* (1924) and *Ionization* (1931) of Varèse but did much more to establish the international standing of American music.

CONTEMPORARY IDIOMS IN BRITAIN

British composers were equally cautious in their acceptance of fresh concepts. Elgar's Cello Concerto and Delius's for violin, both 1919, were the last real masterpieces of English romanticism though Bax in his seven symphonies (1922–39), chamber and piano music, and some of his contemporaries fought a gallant rearguard action. Yet composers who did know their Stravinsky and at least the Schoenberg of the *Fünf Orchesterstücke*, Holst and Arthur Bliss (1891–1975), absorbed little from them beyond the mildly Stravinskian rhythms of Holst's choral *Hymn of Jesus* (1917) and Bliss's *Conversations* for six solo instruments (1919) or the quartal harmonies of Bliss's *Colour Symphony* (1922) and Holst's *Choral Symphony* on poems by Keats (1924). Nor can it be claimed that the younger generation – Edmund Rubbra (1901–), William Walton (1902–), Lennox Berkeley (1903–), Constant Lambert (1905–51), Alan Rawsthorne (1905–71) and Michael Tippett (1905–) – marched in the vanguard of contemporary music. One or two, nevertheless, did attract international notice. A string quartet by Walton was, with Bliss's Rhapsody for soprano, tenor, and six solo instruments, performed at the first festival of the International Society for Contemporary Music in 1923.[2] Dyagilev commis-

[2] The Society and the League of Composers in America did invaluable work in the period between the wars to propagate new tendencies, and the influence in Britain of the British Broadcasting Company (later Corporation), particularly from 1927 when it began to transmit special concerts of contemporary music, was incalculable. From the middle of this decade broadcasting, together with the introduction of electrical recording for the gramophone in 1925, soon led to an enormous widening of the musical public generally.

sioned a ballet, *Romeo and Juliet*, from Lambert (1926). Walton's *Façade* originally for chamber ensemble accompanying the rhythmic recitation of poems by Edith Sitwell (1923), his overture *Portsmouth Point* (1925) and *Sinfonia concertante* for piano and orchestra (1927), Lambert's setting of Sacheverell Sitwell's *The Rio Grande* for piano, chorus, and orchestra (1928), his Piano Sonata (1929) and Concerto for piano and nine instruments (1913), were written under the shadow of jazz, Stravinsky, and their young French contemporaries (see below, pp. 828–30). But these were overshadowed in turn by a more unexpected influence, that of Sibelius whose last three symphonies had been completed after the war (No. 5, 1919; No. 6, 1923; No. 7, 1924). In a book written in 1933 Lambert hailed Sibelius as 'of all living composers the most interesting and stimulating to the post-war generation' and his Fourth and Seventh Symphonies as 'two of the most astonishing creative efforts of our time'.[3] Not only Walton's Viola Concerto (1929) and First Symphony (1935) adopt Sibelian procedures but the symphonies of older men: Bax's Fifth (1932) which was dedicated to him, Vaughan Williams's Fourth (1934) and Fifth (1943) (also dedicated to him). They are equally apparent in the earlier symphonies of Rubbra (from 1936 onward) and faint echoes are still perceptible in the opening of Tippett's first Piano Sonata (1937) and Concerto for Double String Orchestra (1939) and in Rawsthorne's *Symphonic Studies* (1938). British musicians of the time, like British politicians, could not remain unaffected by Continental developments but seemed equally determined not to get deeply involved in them. Only Elisabeth Lutyens (1906–   ) began to turn to twelve-note technique (see below, pp. 834–5) in her *Fantasy for Five Strings* (1937) and Chamber Concerto, No. 1, for nine instruments (1939). The rising star of English music, Benjamin Britten (1913–76), was content in such works as the *Variations on a Theme by Frank Bridge* for string orchestra (1937) to produce novel and individual effects from a basically diatonic idiom.

THE MAIN STREAM IN PARIS

The main stream of Western music flowed not through London or New York or even Vienna or Berlin but through Paris. Paris was still bemused by the Dyagilev ballet and Stravinsky made France his home throughout the inter-war years while a younger expatriate, Sergey Prokofyev (1891–1953), spent most of his time there from 1923 until he made a definitive return to his homeland in 1936. Both exercised very great influence on radical musicians throughout the Western world but particularly in France; both made extraordinary twists and turns in their creative evolution. After the switch from the *Rite of Spring* to *L'Histoire du soldat* Stravinsky produced in 1920 two very different works, the ballet *Pulcinella* based on pseudo-Pergolesi material[4] and the severely neo-classical *Symphonies d'instruments à*

---

[3] *Music Ho!* (London, 1934), p. 327.
[4] A number of spurious works were long attributed to Pergolesi.

vent from which any suggestion of emotion or the picturesque was rigidly excluded. Then came two more 'Russian' works, his last, the one-act comic opera *Mavra* (1922) and the ballet *Les Noces* (1923, but largely written some years earlier), and further neo-classical ones: a wind *Octuor* (1923), a piano Sonata and Concerto for piano and wind (both 1924), an 'opera-oratorio' *Oedipus Rex* (1927), and two more ballets in 1928, *Apollon Musagète* for strings only and a Chaykovsky pastiche, *Le Baiser de la fée*. In the three last, in particular, he adopted a seemingly ingenuous diatonic and rhythmically simple idiom perhaps derived from his young French colleagues. Prokofyev after leaving Russia had completed an opera *Lyubov k trem apelsinam* (Love for three oranges, after Gozzi) in 1919 and a ballet *Shut* (The Buffoon) for Dyagilev in 1920; both were produced in 1921 and confirmed the widespread impression that he was simply an extravagant *farceur*. (His delightful *Classical Symphony* of 1917 was taken to be a parody.) But before settling in Paris he had also begun a very different work, an opera *Ognenny Angel* (The fiery angel), on a story by the symbolist poet Valery Bryusov; it was never performed in his lifetime and much of the music was transferred wholesale to his Third Symphony (1928). For Dyagilev he wrote two more ballets, *Le Pas d'acier* (1927) and *Le Fils prodigue* (1929) the latter of which was similarly turned to account in the Fourth Symphony (1930). In that same year 1930 Stravinsky composed a very different symphony[5] a *Symphony of Psalms* for chorus and orchestra on Latin texts from the Vulgate,[6] not quite the earliest evidence of his religiosity but one of the most impressive. The setting of 'Laudate Eum in cymbalis' at the end (see Ex. 301) induces an effect of mystical hypnosis comparable with that of the 'Dona nobis' of Josquin's 'Pange lingua' Mass four centuries earlier.[7] Stravinsky had travelled a long way since the days when he was one of the main influences on the young French composers who emerged soon after the war; he was to continue along it in the Violin Concerto (1931), the ballet *Jeux de cartes* (1936), the *Dumbarton Oaks* Concerto for chamber orchestra (1938), and later works.

The older men were still active. Debussy was gone but Fauré produced masterpieces of neo-classical chamber music, including a piano quintet, a piano trio and a string quartet, during 1921–24, d'Indy's third and last opera, the unsuccessful *Légende de saint Christophe*, was given in 1920, and Ravel continued to compose – the delightful *fantaisie lyrique L'Enfant et les sortilèges* (1925), and three very mildly jazzy compositions, a sonata for violin and piano (1927) and two piano concertos, one for left hand only (both 1931) – until a brain tumour silenced him. Roussel after the belated staging of his sumptuous Indian *opéra-ballet Padmâvatî* in 1923, changed course in the classical ballet *Bacchus et Ariane* (1930) and adopted unadulterated neo-classicism in a string quartet (1932) and Fourth Symphony (1934). And an

---

[5] Both Stravinsky's and Prokofyev's, like Roussel's Third and Honegger's First, were commissioned to commemorate the fiftieth anniversary of the Boston Symphony Orchestra in 1931.
[6] Authorized Version: xxxix, 12–13, xl, 1–3, cl complete.
[7] See pp. 176–7.

almost exact contemporary, hitherto prolific but not much noticed, Charles Koechlin (1867–1950), emerged as a neo-classicist and exploiter of new techniques. But it was a third contemporary, that equivocal figure Satie, whom the young French chose as their mascot.

Ex. 301

SATIE AND *LES SIX*

Satie was an amusing *blagueur* of minuscule creative talent discovered by Ravel as a 'precursor' in 1911 and later taken up by Jean Cocteau, the choragus of the French literary *avant-garde* a few years later. When Dyagilev commissioned Cocteau to devise a *ballet-réaliste, Parade*, with costumes and stage-designs by Picasso, he turned to Satie for the music (1917). The result sparked off a typical Parisian theatrical riot. Satie's music is childishly simple but for the introduction of a typewriter, a ship's siren, and other playful eccentricities, yet in his pamphlet *Le Coq et l'Arlequin*[8] Cocteau hailed it as 'an architectural masterpiece' and Satie's as the 'poetical imagination of childhood moulded by a master technician'. Satie's *faux-naïf* music appealed to his admirers by its negative qualities; it was an extreme reaction against the rich and complicated textures of both romanticism and

[8] English translation by Rollo H. Myers (London, 1921).

impressionism, 'un language ferme, net et dépouillé de tout agrément imagé' as Stravinsky described it.[9] Picasso's collaboration in *Parade* induced culture-snobs to talk of Cubism but in fact it has much more in common with the deliberately outrageous anti-art, anti-sense movement known as 'Dada' which originated at about the same time.

Parade aroused the enthusiasm of a young French musician, Francis Poulenc (1899–1963), who a few months later wrote an amusing *Rapsodie nègre* for baritone, piano, clarinet and string quartet, and his friend Georges Auric (1899–19), a former pupil of d'Indy. Three weeks after the first performance of *Parade* the music was repeated in a concert organised by Auric and some other young musicians, together with a trio by Auric himself, six settings of Guillaume Apollinaire by Arthur Honegger (1892–1955) and a piano duet by Louis Durey (1888–1979). Early in 1919 the circle was joined by Milhaud (1892–1974), a Conservatoire-trained composer who had been serving under Paul Claudel in the French Legation in Brazil, and another Conservatoire product, Germaine Tailleferre (1892–19), to form what was later rather stupidly dubbed 'le groupe des *Six*'. In fact their talents and temperaments were very different; Durey and Tailleferre proved to be unimportant; Poulenc and Auric were the most faithful to Satie; Milhaud and Honegger were much more substantial and prolific figures. But for a long time they were all tarred with the same brush and grouped with Stravinsky and Prokofyev as the most advanced exponents of musical radicalism. In the years when Schoenberg was struggling in semi-obscurity with the problems of post-romantic music, they lightheartedly bypassed them.[10]

Satie himself was not always a joker. His *drame symphonique Socrate* (1918), a setting for female voices and chamber orchestra of translated excerpts from three of Plato's Dialogues, almost deserves the praise Cocteau had lavished on *Parade*; the simplicity of the death of Socrates is touching:

Ex. 302

et la but a - vec u - ne tran - quil - li - té   et   u - ne dou - ceur   mer - veilleu - se.

[9] *Chroniques de ma vie* (Paris, 1935), ii, p. 18.
[10] Their non-French admirers included the Englishman Lord Berners (1883–1950) and the American Virgil Thomson (1896–1978). Thomson's opera *Four Saints in Three Acts* (comp. 1928; prod. 1934) and Berners' ballet with chorus *The Wedding Bouquet* (1936) both have texts by Gertrude Stein.

But his two later ballets, *Mercure*, another Picasso collaboration, and *Relâche* (both 1924), were total failures. Milhaud also essayed ballet. The first to be produced, *Le Boeuf sur le toit* (1920), took its title from a Brazilian popular song and exploited Brazilian dance-rhythms as in his piano

Pl. 63 Fernand Léger's maquette for the décor of the original production of Milhaud's ballet *La Création du monde* at the Théâtre des Champs-Élysées, Paris, on 25 October 1923.

Saudades do Brazil (Memories of Brazil) a little later, but Cocteau took over and produced the scenario of a *clownerie* in the line of *Parade*. The impression that Milhaud was just such another joker was not softened by the facts that his *Cinq Symphonies* for chamber ensembles (1917–22) were symphonies only in the early seventeenth-century sense, that he composed descriptions of agricultural machinery found in a catalogue (*Machines agricoles*, 1919) and a *Catalogue de fleurs* (1920), and by the company he kept and his harmonic experiments. Although Milhaud dedicated his Fifth String Quartet to Schoenberg and conducted performances of *Pierrot lunaire*, his harmony was not in the least Schoenbergian. The basis of his music is diatonic melody – popular, jazz, sometimes even neo-Bachian – and although in early works he thickens it into quartal or quintal chords (*Saudades*, Nos. 9 and 11) he prefers to employ it in textures that are not merely polyphonic but polytonal with strands in two or three or even more simultaneous keys, often 'anchored' by a quasi-ostinato bass.

Poulenc, with his early love of street songs and popular dance music, was the most anti-romantic of the *Six*, although in his charming Ravelian *Mouvements perpétuels* for piano (1918) he had revealed his admiration for Chabrier (shared by the whole group). He joined with Milhaud, Honegger, Auric and Tailleferre in a characteristic Cocteau skit, *Les Mariés de la Tour Eiffel* (1921) and then decided on a three-year course of study with Koechlin, at the end of which he gave Dyagilev a delightful, slightly Stravinskian ballet score, *Les Biches* (1924). But Cocteau's influence was waning – Milhaud's *Le Train Bleu* in the same year was the last notable Cocteau ballet – and with his *Concert champêtre* for harpsichord and orchestra[11] (1928) and *Aubade* for piano and chamber orchestra (1929) Poulenc put buffoonery behind him without losing his sense of fun. He wrote some of the best of his songs and piano music during the 1930s and turned to liturgical music with *Litanies à la Vierge Noire* (1936), followed by a number of *a cappella* works (1937–41), including a Mass. (Cocteau himself came under the influence of the Catholic philosopher Jacques Maritain.) Similarly Milhaud after throwing off three *opéra-minutes* in 1927 produced two of his most ambitious and impressive works, the operas *Christophe Colomb* (on a Claudel libretto) (1930) and *Maximilien* (1932), and composed a series of concertos and a vast quantity of incidental music for the theatre during the 1930s. Honegger, a d'Indy pupil and Swiss by parentage, had no frivolous past to live down, other than such jazz wild oats as the Clarinet Sonatina (1922); he disliked Satie's music and had no use for Cocteau's aesthetic though he set six of his poems (1920 and 1923) and based an opera, *Antigone* (1927), on his libretto after Sophocles. His technically accomplished early String Quartet (1917), is romantic, as the superscription of the first movement indicates: 'Appassionato (*Violent et tourmenté*)'. And his earliest noteworthy orchestral piece, *Pastorale d'été* (1920), is based on simple diatonic melodies. His incidental music to René Morax's play *Le Roi David* (1921) was expanded into a *psaume symphonique* and followed by similar biblical operas or 'stage oratorios': *Judith* (1926), *Cris du monde* (1931), *Jeanne d'Arc au bûcher* (text by Claudel) (1935, perf. 1938), *Nicolas de Flue* (1939). The powerful unison opening of his First Symphony (1930):

Ex. 303

[11] For Wanda Landowska. Manuel de Falla had written his Concerto for her in 1926.

proclaimed the lifelong admirer of Beethoven, and the very fine Second, for string orchestra with solo trumpet in the finale (1941), and its successors demonstrated that he could write symphonies as varied as Beethoven's. Even his best known orchestral piece, the notorious *Pacific 231* (1923), is not only a graphic impression of a powerful locomotive but itself a tensely wrought piece of musical 'machinery'.[12]

ONDES MARTENOT AND QUARTER-TONE MUSIC

Of the younger Frenchmen who emerged in the 1930s the most significant were Olivier Messiaen (1908–   ) and Jean Françaix (1912–   ). Françaix first attracted attention with a delightful Concertino for piano and orchestra (1932), wrote a series of ballets including *Le Roi nu* (after Andersen) (1935) and *Le Jugement du fou* (after Rabelais) (1938), and during 1939–42 a formidable oratorio *L'Apocalypse de Saint Jean* for soloists, chorus, and two orchestras – of which the second, including saxophones, cornet, harmonium among other unpleasing instruments, fittingly represents hell. Messiaen has always been much preoccupied with heaven. Organist and Catholic mystic, pupil of Dukas, one of the founders in 1936 of a new but short-lived *groupement* that styled itself 'Jeune France', he was a far more significant figure than Françaix. Very typical of his earlier works are *Les Offrandes oubliées* (1930), a *méditation symphonique* on the mystery of the Eucharist, a set of nine meditations for organ on *La Nativité du Seigneur* (1935), and another organ work, *Les Corps glorieux* (1939). Messiaen was always very willing to supply not only prose-poetic glosses to his works but also explanations of the technical innovations they embody. These were by no means as far-reaching as in those of his maturity (see below, p. 847) but he had already experimented with the *ondes Martenot*, an electrophonic instrument invented by Maurice Martenot,[13] writing a *Fête des belles eaux* for six *ondes* (1937) and *Deux monodies en 1/4 de ton* for a single one (1938). Up to then the only important composers to experiment with quarter-tones (on normal instruments or specially constructed pianos) had been a Czech pupil of Schreker, Alois Hába (1893–1972), and his brother Karel (1898–   ); the incunabula of quarter-tone music were Hába's string quartets Opp. 7 and 12 (1920 and 1922) and his opera *Die Mutter* (prod. Munich, 1931). Hába, who was encouraged by Busoni to compose sixth-tone music as well, was like Messiaen influenced toward microtonal composition by study of non-European musics.

THE CONTEMPORARY SPIRIT IN ITALY

While Spanish music tended to preserve a relationship with French – Falla's most popular work, the ballet *El sombrero de tres picos*, was written for Dyagilev and originally produced in 1919 as *Le Chapeau tricorne* – the

---

[12] His *Rugby* (1928) may have been suggested by Martinů's *Half-Time* (1925).
[13] See his *Méthode pour l'enseignement des ondes musicales* (Paris, 1931).

Italians rejected everything French as emphatically as everything German. Whereas the attempted revival of instrumental music by Sgambati and Martucci had been inspired by German models, Ottorino Respighi (1879–1936) and his contemporaries studied old Italian music. Respighi himself orchestrated lute airs and dances, Ildebrando Pizzetti (1880–1968) edited Francesco Veracini, Gian Francesco Malipiero (1882–1973) Monteverdi, and Alfredo Casella (1883–1947) Vivaldi and Domenico Scarlatti. The first movement, marked *sinfonia*, of Casella's Partita for piano and orchestra (1925) and Pizzetti's *Concerto dell' estate* (Seasons concerto) (1928), with its *gagliarda e finale* third movement, were avowedly suggested by the old concerto grosso. Malipiero's *Prima sinfonia, in quattro tempi come le quattro stagioni* (1933), with its concertante element, stands in the same relationship to the old Italian *sinfonia*, and Respighi's Toccata for piano and orchestra (1928) to the Frescobaldian toccata. They were also fascinated by the church modes, rather belatedly. Hitherto these had played little part in Italian composition except in the short-lived oratorios of Dom Lorenzo Perosi (1872–1956), but they permeate a good deal of Malipero's music and in 1922 Respighi produced a violin *Concerto gregoriano*, in 1930 a *Metamorphoseon modi XII* for orchestra. Neither of the latter ever won anything like the popularity of the brilliant scores in which this one-time pupil of Rimsky-Korsakov displayed his virtuosity: *Fontane di Roma* (1917), *Pini di Roma* (1924), *Vetrate di chiesa* (Church windows) (1926), *Trittico botticelliano* (1927), and the rest. Both liturgical chant and colourful orchestration mark two of Respighi's operas: the one-act *Maria egiziaca* (St. Mary of Egypt) (1932) and *La fiamma* (1934).

Puccini and Busoni both died in 1924, leaving not quite finished operatic masterpieces. Busoni had long ceased to be an Italian composer and he wrote the libretto of *Doktor Faust* in German; *Turandot*, with all its harmonic modernity (including polytonality at the beginning of Acts I and II), and the justified exoticism of its melody and harmony, is intensely Italian – the greatest Italian opera since *Otello* and *Falstaff*. The younger men were determined to break away from the long tradition of which it was the apogee but their achievement fell far short of Puccini's, as Malipiero demonstrated in his triptychs, *L'Orfeide (La morte delle maschere, Sette canzoni,* and *L'Orfeo)* (1925) and *Tre commedie goldoniane* (1926), in which the basic idea – but nothing else – must have been suggested by Puccini's *Trittico (Il tabarro, Suor Angelica,* and *Gianni Schicchi)* (1918). Like Casella in his *La donna serpente* (after Gozzi) (1932), Malipiero wakens echoes of eighteenth-century *opera buffa* but he is better at depicting genre scenes than in creating characters. Pizzetti does just that. Writing his own libretti for *Dèbora e Jaéle* (1922), *Fra Gherardo* (1928), *Orsèolo* (1935), he created strong dramas and well defined characters in words and music which, despite his own theories, is sometimes rather Puccinian – as in this passage from the First Act of *Gherardo*:

Ex. 304

Among the Italian contemporaries of 'Jeune France' two are outstanding: Goffredo Petrassi (1904–   ) and Luigi Dallapiccola (1904–   ). Petrassi, a protégé of Casella, despite the influences of Stravinsky and Hindemith continued the process of revitalizing old Italian forms: dances in his orchestral Partita (1932), Palestrina and the later Romans in a setting of *Psalm IX* for chorus and orchestra (1936). In the fine *madrigale drammatico*, *Coro di morti* (on a text by Leopardi) (1941), the male chorus might almost be singing a latish Monteverdi madrigal while they are accompanied by brass, percussion, and three pianos which sometimes play chords of continuous thirds extending from the bottom to the top of the piano compass. Dallapiccola also produced an orchestral Partita in the same year as Petrassi's and paid tribute to Italy's past by preparing a 'performing version' of Monteverdi's *Ritorno d'Ulisse* in 1942. But his interest in Busoni's ideas had, with other factors, made him receptive to Germanic developments and he became the Italian pioneer of the twelve-note technique, at first tentatively and interwoven with diatonic music in *Tre Laudi* for soprano and 13 instruments (1937), then in a one-act opera *Volo di*

notte (based on Saint-Exupéry's novel *Vol de nuit*) (1940) and *Canti di prigionia* for chorus and string-less orchestra (1941). In the second of three sets of *Liriche greche – Cinque frammenti di Saffo* for soprano and 15 instruments (1943) – he went on to rigorous twelve-note writing with canons by inversion, contrary motion, and so on. It was, as it were, a preparatory exercise for his most important work, the opera *Il prigioniero* (comp. 1944–48, perf. 1950).

THE TWELVE-NOTE ROW

Experiments with new types of opera were naturally not confined to France and Italy. In Germany Strauss did not innovate, except in making *Intermezzo* (1924) autobiographical and introducing a game of *Skat*. *Die Frau ohne Schatten* (1919), *Arabella* (1935), *Die schweigsame Frau* (1935), and the rest are old musical variations on new dramatic themes. Schreker had no new sensations to titillate the public after *Die Gezeichneten* (The branded) (1918) and *Der Schatzgräber* (The treasure digger) (1920). The innovators were Alban Berg, Paul Hindemith, Ernst Křenek, and Kurt Weill. The novelty of Berg's *Wozzeck* (comp. 1917–21, perf. 1925) consisted not in its musical language – freely atonal in Schoenberg's pre-war idiom, with *Sprechstimme* in Act I, sc. 2, Act II, sc. 3 and 4, etc. – but in the psychological penetration of the squalid tragedy and in the imposition of definite musical forms on the dramatic action, so that Act I proceeds as suite, rhapsody, march, and so on, Act II is a five-movement symphony, and III a series of 'inventions' on a theme, a note, a rhythm, etc. It is also noteworthy that the 21 variations of the passacaglia (Act I.4) are based on a theme, shown here as it is played by a solo clarinet 'without expression' before the passacaglia begins:

Ex. 305

including all twelve notes of the chromatic scale.

Schoenberg had in 1914 begun a sketch for the scherzo of a projected symphony with a similar theme or 'note-row':[14]

Ex. 306

[14] See Josef Rufer, *The Works of Arnold Schoenberg* (trans. Dika Newlin) (London, 1962), fac. 22, facing p. 108.

but it was only seven years later that he realised that the exclusive use of such a twelve-note row in a composition would not only safeguard absolute atonality by ensuring that no note would be heard more than another but at the same time solve the old problem of atonal structure (cf. p. 807). A single row – which could be rhythmically varied, reversed, inverted, transposed, used vertically in chords as well as horizontally, treated canonically or as an ostinato – made extended atonal composition perfectly feasible. At first he experimented with it only in short pieces. The piano Prelude, Op. 25, No. 1, dates from July 1921, the other pieces of the Suite did not follow until 1923 when he became more and more fascinated by the idea; and at last in the Wind Quintet, Op. 26 (1923–4) he satisfied himself that it could indeed provide the basis of extended composition. Then came a whole series of twelve-note works including the Third and Fourth Quartets (1927 and 1936), the orchestral Variations, Op. 31 (1928), the unfinished opera *Moses und Aron* (1930–2), and concertos for violin (1936) and piano (1942). Berg adopted the technique first in his *Lyrische Suite* for string quartet (1926), Webern in his String Trio (1927). Webern continued to employ it in the tight forms he always favoured; tightest of all is the String Quartet, Op. 29 (1938). Berg on the other hand by introducing diatonic cells in the basic row of his Violin Concerto (1935) was able to reconcile the twelve-note idiom with such more substantial diatonic elements as Bach's hymn 'Es ist genug' (from BWV 60) and an Austrian folk-tune. His development of his second opera, *Lulu* (a combination of two plays by Wedekind), not quite finished at his death in 1935, from a single basic row is fascinatingly sophisticated;[15] the row again contains diatonic cells. In *Lulu* Berg also reconciled twelve-note technique with jazz: an off-stage jazz band, including saxophones, jazz trumpets, and banjo, is heard in the First Act.

HINDEMITH AND *GEBRAUCHSMUSIK*

Whereas Berg's operas might be regarded as examples of romanticism in putrescence, those of his younger contemporaries are diverse forms of reaction against romanticism. Not immediately: Hindemith's first one-act opera, the expressionist *Mörder, Hoffnung der Frauen* (Murder, hope of women) on a text by the painter Kokoschka (comp. 1919, perf. 1921), and its immediate successors, *Sancta Susanna* and the 'Burmese puppet play' *Das Nusch-Nuschi*, seem not only to parody Wagner but to echo him. Hindemith's antiromanticism passed through several phases marked in his instrumental music: first the influences of jazz and Stravinsky, then experiments with polytonality and quartal harmony in the *Kammermusik nr. 1* for twelve players (1921) and *Suite 1922* for piano, later vigorous linear, non-harmonic counterpoint in the Rilke song-cycle *Das Marienleben* (1923; partly rewritten 1948) and the orchestral concerti grossi entitled *Kammermusik*, Nos. 2–4 (1924–5). His first full-length opera, *Cardillac* (1926;

---

[15] See the analysis in Mosco Carner, *Alban Berg* (London, 1975), pp. 205–12.

new version 1952), is basically couched in this neo-classical, inexpressive instrumental idiom, relieved only in such passages as the Act III quartet, and like Berg in *Wozzeck* (though his texture is much simpler) he imposes definite musical forms – as indeed he had already done in *Das Marienleben*.

The astonishing success of Křenek's *Jonny spielt auf* (Johnny strikes up) (1927), with its Negro jazz-musician hero, sparked off a vogue for contemporary opera-subjects (*Zeitoper*), humorous, satirical, sometimes with cabaret elements as in Weill's *Dreigroschenoper* (Threepenny opera, an updated version of Gay's *Beggar's Opera*) (1928) and *Aufstieg und Fall der Stadt Mahagonny* (Rise and fall of the town of Mahagonny) (1930), both with libretti by Brecht. Even Schoenberg contributed a one-act twelve-note opera, *Von Heute auf Morgen* (From today till tomorrow) (1930), and Hindemith wrote two, the one-act *Sketsch*, *Hin und zurück* (There and back) (1927) and the three-act *Neues vom Tage* (The day's news) (1929; revised 1953).

Another activity to which Hindemith devoted himself in these years was *Gebrauchsmusik* (utilitarian music for amateur singers and players, for films, and so on); in 1930 both he and Weill composed school operas, *Wir bauen eine Stadt* (We're building a town) and *Der Jasager* (The Yea-sayer), for which Brecht again supplied Weill with a libretto, and in the same year appeared the first numbers of the *Schulwerk*, employing new types of melodic percussion instruments, of Carl Orff (1895–19). The composition of *Gebrauchsmusik* no doubt contributed to a mellowing of Hindemith's music, perceptible in the oratorio *Das Unaufhörliche* (The unceasing) (1931), the *Philharmonisches Konzert* (1932), the opera *Mathis der Maler* (1934; perf. 1938) – from which, taking a hint from Prokofyev's practice, he extracted a symphony – and a concerto entitled *Der Schwanendreher* (named after a folk-song) for viola and small orchestra (1935).

The score of *Mathis* completed, Hindemith felt the need to codify his musical language and the profusion of empirical harmony in current use. His text-book, *Unterweisung im Tonsatz*,[16] is in three parts, the first theoretical, the other two giving exercises in two- and three-part writing; it rejects amorphous atonality (and quarter-tone music) and instead of the long-outdated distinction between consonance and theoretical dissonance proposes a method of classifying degrees of harmonic tension based on the natural laws of acoustics. It is logical and ingenious; it was the basis of his own later music and led to his drastic rewriting of *Das Marienleben*, *Cardillac* and *Neues vom Tage*; it naturally influenced his pupils; but it won no general acceptance. The element of euphony inherent in it was particularly marked in the ballet *Nobilissima Visione* (on the life of Francis of Assisi) (1938).

Křenek, had after *Jonny*, also turned to relative euphony in a song-cycle, *Reisebuch aus den österreichischen Alpen* (Travel book from the Austrian

[16] Mainz, 1937 and 1939; English edition, *The Craft of Musical Composition*, London and New York, 1942. There are useful summaries of the theoretical part in Ian Kemp, *Hindemith* (London, 1970), pp. 35–40, and *NOHM*, x, pp. 336–8.

Alps) (1929), and the *grosse Oper Leben des Orest* (1930), but then became a convert to twelve-note technique and composed in it what he called a *Bühnenwerk mit Musik* (stage-work with music), *Karl V* (comp. 1930–3). But there was no place for such works and their composers in Nazi Germany and nervous Austria after 1933; *Lulu* and *Mathis* had to be given in Zürich and *Karl V* was produced in Prague in 1938. Křenek immediately afterwards left for the United States where he set about the composition of *a cappella* choral works and the popularisation of twelve-note music with *12 Short Piano Pieces*, Op. 83.[17] Hindemith followed him to America in 1939 and launched a series of notable compositions: a ballet in the form of variations for piano and strings, *The Four Temperaments*, and a cello concerto (1940), a Symphony in E flat (1941), and *Ludus Tonalis*, a set of twelve three-part piano fugues linked by interludes (1942).

CZECH OPERA

The experiments of Schoenberg and Hindemith and the high jinks of *Zeitoper* had little influence outside the German-speaking lands between the wars, though Schoenberg had one whole-hearted disciple in the Greek, Nikos Skalkottas (1904–49). The strongest creative personality in the 'successor States', Béla Bartók, had exploited 'motor rhythm' – e.g. in the *Allegro barbaro* for piano of 1911 – when Hindemith was still in his teens but, while he was always keenly aware of Schoenberg's music and, like the French-Swiss Frank Martin (1890–1978),[18] occasionally wrote twelve-note themes (see below, p. 840), he never employed twelve-note technique.

In neighbouring Czechoslovakia the equally individual Janáček, encouraged by the belated success of *Jenůfa* (see p. 799 at Prague (1916) and Vienna (1918), embarked on a remarkable series of operas. He had for several years been trying to extract a libretto from Svatopluk Čech's *Výlety pana Broučka* (Mr. Brouček's excursions – Janáček modified the title to *Výlety páně Broučkovy*), a Swiftian satire with a vulgar, cowardly, materialistic Prague petty bourgeois hero who is transported in drunken dreams to the moon and to the Hussite time. He finished the 'Excursion to the Moon' first as an independent work and then rather unfortunately decided to add the 'Excursion to the Fifteenth Century' (1918); the whole opera was produced in 1920. Nothing could be more different from the 'veristic' plot of *Jenůfa* and Janáček changed his ground in each succeeding work: *Kát'a Kabanová* (1922), a realistic drama on Ostrovsky's *Storm*, *Příhody lišky Bystroušky* (Experiences of the little vixen Quick-Ears) (1924), a fantasy of animals and humans, *Věc Makropulos* (The Makropoulos Case) (1926), on Karel Čapek's contemporary play with a three-hundred-year-old heroine, and *Z mrtvého domu* (From the house of the dead) (1930), on Dostoevsky's account

---

[17] He also published a text-book, *Studies in Counterpoint based on the twelve-tone technique* (New York, 1940).
[18] Martin's secular oratorio *Le Vin herbé* (1942) is a classic example of the integration of twelve-note materials in eclectic textures.

of his prison-life in Siberia, an opera without drama or even story but with *characters*. It was characters that mattered supremely to Janáček, characters and 'the reality behind phenomena' as he put it; in the two Russian operas everything is real, in *Makropulos* everything but the heroine herself, and in the two fantastic operas reality provides a frame or a support. (The moon-people and the fifteenth-century Prague citizens of *Brouček* are all double dream-transfigurations of 'real' characters from the inn-scenes, and there are similar parallels between the animal and the human characters of the *Vixen*.) Janáček provided them all with dramatically *under*stated music, often a mosaic of lapidary motives, many of them verbally inspired though devoid of verbal or dramatic significance, and he employed the same laconic, intensely individual language in the *Zápisník zmizelého* (Notebook of one who vanished) for voices and piano (1919), probably suggested by Rebikov's 'musico-psychological tales' which had interested him, in his string quartets (1923 and 1928) and in his great *Glagolská mše* (1926), a Catholic Mass with Church Slavonic text.

The only Czech opera of the 1920s that rivalled Janáček's in success, though very inferior musically, was *Švanda dudák* (Schwanda the bagpiper) (1927) by Jaromír Weinberger (1896–19) who afterwards took refuge in America – as did the more gifted, versatile and immensely prolific Bohuslav Martinů (1890–1959). Weinberger was German-orientated, Martinů French; he lived in Paris – where one of his closest friends was the German–Swiss Conrad Beck (1901–) – from 1923 to 1940 and studied with Roussel. His large output was very uneven but two outstandingly interesting works are the fantasy dream-opera *Julietta* (1938) and the *Polní mše* (Field Mass) (1939), part-Mass, part cantata, intended for open-air performance for the Czech troops in France. Martinů also enjoyed the distinction of having composed, in 1935, what seem to be the earliest operas for radio: *Hlas lesa* (Voice of the forest) and *Veselohra na mostě* (Comedy on a bridge).

EAST EUROPEAN MASTERS

Still more completely Gallicized was the Romanian Georg Enescu (1881–1955) who studied with Massenet and Fauré and whose masterpiece, *Oedipe*, was composed to a French text and produced at the Paris Opéra in 1936. It is a score as subtly wrought and almost as daring as that of *Wozzeck*, of which it sometimes reminds one – as in the awakening of the Sphinx in Act II, sc. 3:

Ex. 307

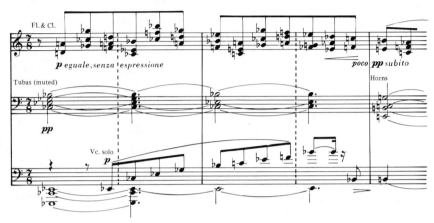

Another somewhat isolated East European figure was Enescu's almost exact contemporary, the Pole Szymanowski. Szymanowski was one of the few composers influenced throughout his life by Skryabin (as well as by Strauss and Reger and, later, by Stravinsky and Ravel). His most characteristic mature works are the opera *Król Roger* (King Roger) (comp. 1924; prod. 1926), Skryabinian in its mixture of mysticism, eroticism, and orgiastic ecstasy, the Fourth Symphony (with piano concertante) (1932), and the nationalistic ballet-pantomime *Harnasie* (1935).

Yet a third isolated East European contemporary of these two – isolated despite his lifelong friendship with Zoltán Kodály (1882–1967), composer of the choral-orchestral *Psalmus Hungaricus* (1923) and the folk-opera *Háry János* (John Hary) (1926), and teacher of a whole generation of Hungarian composers, isolated despite his world fame – was Bartók. Bartók's isolation was rooted in the single-mindedness with which, while keenly aware of everything that was going on around him, he always managed to follow his own line. He studied not only Hungarian folk-music, like Kodály, but that of Bulgaria and Romania, the Arabs and the Turks, and learned from them much more than from his European peers. He wrote no more stage works after *Bluebeard*, the 'dance-play' *A fából faragott királyfi* (The prince carved from wood) (1917), and the 'pantomime' *A csodálatos mandarin* (The wonderful mandarin) (comp. 1919; prod. 1926), no more solo songs after the five settings of poems by Endre Ady, Op. 16 (1916), and only one notable composition for chorus and orchestra, the *Cantata profana* (1930). His way lay almost entirely through instrumental music: concertos for piano (1926, 1931, and 1945) and violin (1938), the *Musik für Saiteninstrumente, Schlagzeug und Celesta* (Music for strings, percussion, and celesta) (1936) and the Concerto for orchestra (1943), but most importantly perhaps in chamber music: the last five string quartets (1917, 1927, 1928, 1934, 1939), the two sonatas for violin and piano (1921 and 1922), and the sonata for solo violin (1944).

The way ran parallel with the most advanced musical thinking of the time but at a little distance from it. As we have seen (pp. 808 and 837), Bartók was familiar with all the resources of contemporary harmony and the Ady songs show that he was prepared to accept to a limited degree Schoenberg's atonal harmony though not his doctrinaire anti-tonality and dense textures. His dissonance emphasizes his characteristic percussiveness and although non-functional is not anti-functional; large-scale structure thus presented him with no difficulties. Bartók's relationship to Stravinsky was similar; the erotic ecstasy of the end of the *Mandarin* is comparable with that of the *Rite of Spring*, but comparison serves only to show how Bartók refined and clarified. The *Mandarin* and the sonatas for violin and piano show signs of a shift toward increased clarity in his own style, a shift carried further in the First Piano Concerto and the Piano Sonata of the same year (1926) which may be described as neo-classical – like *Cardillac*, Stravinsky's Piano Sonata and even Schoenberg's Third Quartet (so far as texture and formal structure are concerned), all of the same period. The Third String Quartet juxtaposes fine thematic work in the *prima parte* and its *ricapitulazione* (centred on, but not 'in', C sharp) with a folkish second movement. The Fourth Quartet, similarly 'on' C, brought a relaxation, a process continued in the Second Piano Concerto and later works down to the Violin Concerto – in which Bartók characteristically, perhaps contemptuously, strings together a succession of *different* twelve-note rows (first movement, bars 73ff.) firmly anchored to a sustained A and finally dissolved in a glissando for the soloist – and the Concerto for orchestra. It should be noted that Bartók also produced *Gebrauchsmusik*, mostly in the form of piano music for children, from 1908 onward.

Bartók had political difficulties under the Hungarian regency (from 1919); *Bluebeard's Castle* and *The Wood-carved Prince* could not be produced because the librettist was an exiled Communist, the *Mandarin* because the subject was considered obscene. The German composers, and soon the Austrians, had difficulties after 1933 not only if they were Jews or composed operas on 'degenerate' subjects but even if they were non-Jews like Hindemith and persisted in writing music in the contemporary idioms which the authorities considered decadent and anarchic, 'cultural Bolshevism'. The only kind of modernism acceptable in the Third Reich was the rhythmically hypnotic, totally diatonic neo-primitivism of Orff's scenic cantatas *Carmina Burana* (1937) and *Catulli Carmina* (1943) and his opera *Die Kluge* (The clever woman) (1943). Ironically, the authorities in the land of Bolshevism itself were at the same time trying to suppress precisely the same kind of music as 'formalistic' and anti-proletarian.

MUSIC IN RUSSIA AFTER THE REVOLUTION

After the Revolution, the Commissar of Education, Lunacharsky, appointed as head of its music section an avant-garde composer, Arthur Lourié (1892–1966), disciple of Debussy, Skryabin and Schoenberg. The direction of the conservatoires was exclusively in the hands of Rimsky-Korsakov pupils: Glazunov, Mikhail Ippolitov-Ivanov (1859–1935), Reinhold Glier (1875–1956), and Maximilian Steinberg (1883–1946). Until the end of the Civil War and Polish War in 1921, composition ran mostly in the channels of choral folk-song arrangement and 'mass-songs' for the Red Army and workers. Then Lourié emigrated to France and the musical education of the masses in both popular and 'classical' music was taken seriously in hand. But there was a setback and then a schism. The Association of Proletarian Musicians (APM), formed in 1923, denounced not only contemporary music but the 'bourgeois' classics and demanded a 'Soviet music' immediately comprehensible to workman and peasant; they were opposed in 1924 by an Association for Contemporary Music (ASM from its Russian initials) who denied that 'music is ideology' and interpreted 'contemporary' in the international sense. ASM were at first the more successful and, full musical contacts with the outside world having been established, such operas as *Der ferne Klang, Love for Three Oranges, Wozzeck, Mavra, Jonny spielt auf* and the *Dreigroschenoper* were performed, though familiar classics were provided with new, politically acceptable libretti as had been done not only in Tsarist Russia but in other autocratic states in the early nineteenth century. Mahler's symphonies enjoyed a vogue in Leningrad during 1925–7. But before long the balance changed; ASM collapsed in 1931 but the triumphant Proletarians were so technically incompetent that teaching standards fell disastrously. Finally the Central Committee of the Communist Party intervened in 1932, suppressed crude proletarian art with one hand and contemporary 'formalism' (art for art's sake) with the other, and gave Soviet musicians (and artists and writers) the motto 'Socialist realism'. In the Soviet Union, as in Nazi Germany, music was to be strong, healthy, optimistic, worthy of its country's past.

The first notable work to emerge after the Revolution was the Sixth Symphony (1924) of Nikolay Myaskovsky (1881–1950), a conservative late-romantic pupil of Glier, and it is noteworthy less for its musical quality than for its 'monumental' dimensions, which made it a model for a number of later Soviet symphonies, and for the nature of the finale suggested by Verhaeren's play *Les Aubes*, glorifying revolution by the treatment of 'La Carmagnole' and 'Ça ira' and mourning its dead heroes with 'Dies irae' and a folk-song with religious text which is taken up by an *ad libitum* chorus. In 1925 the best of Myaskovsky's pupils, Vissarion Shebalin (1902–63), made his debut with a First Symphony which had the bad luck to be totally overshadowed by another 'first', the F minor Symphony of a Steinberg pupil, Dmitry Shostakovich (1906–75). Shostakovich's symphony, his leaving exercise at the Leningrad Conservatoire, is a sprightly attractive work, some of which might have been written by Prokofyev, and quickly made its way abroad: the first Soviet work to do so. 1925 also saw the real beginnings of Soviet opera with *Za krasny Petrograd* (For Red Petrograd) by Arseny Gladkovsky (1894–1945) and *Orliny bunt* (Revolt of the eagles) by Andrey Pashchenko (1885–19). Gladkovsky's 'musico-dramatic chronicle' in-

841

cluded scenes satirizing the Whites with 'grotesque' music by one Prussak, a nonentity; it was fiercely criticized but in 1930 Gladkovsky without collaborator produced a new 'opera-oratorio' version with a new libretto, entitled *Front i tïl* (Front and rear). Pashchenko's folk-songish crowd scenes won more success but his attempt at folk-theatre with popular song and clowning, *Tsar Maksimilian* (1929), definitely did not. The tide of Western modernism flooded in and Aleksandr Mosolov (1900–73) won temporary international notoriety with the first movement, 'Zavod' (Foundry), of his ballet suite *Stal* (Steel) (1926), in which he tried to emulate Honegger's *Pacific 231*. Shostakovich reflected Prokofyev, Stravinsky, and Hindemith in his early piano music but his next two symphonies, inscribed 'To October: symphonic dedication' (1927) and 'First of May' (1929), single-movement works with final chorus, were unsuccessful attempts to reconcile the 'contemporary' with the 'proletarian'. In his first opera, *Nos* (The nose) (1930), after Gogol's story, he came down heavily on the 'contemporary' side with a score the godparents of which were *Mavra* and Prokofyev, Hindemith and Křenek. Shostakovich was one of the few genuine modernists who composed piano music; like chamber music and solo song it was left in the hands of Myaskovsky and his circle. The 'proletarians' were, of course, hostile to such bourgeois art-forms. Ballet, however, was acceptable provided the subject was revolutionary and the music con-servative, and Glier scored the first real ballet success in 1927 with his *Krasny mak* (The red poppy). Earlier in the same year he had begun the official stimulation of native art in the Caucasian republics with his Azerbaydzhanian opera *Shakh-Senem*.

THE CONCEPT OF 'SOCIALIST REALISM'

These heady, happy days did not end suddenly with the Party's edict in 1932 for at first no one was quite sure what 'Socialist realism' meant in terms of instrumental music. It took four years for composers to learn. The symphonic works of 1932–3 show various approaches. The most obvious was to play for safety by bringing in chorus and in some cases brass bands; it was adopted by one of the older composers, Yury Shaporin (1887–1966), a very fine if conservative musician, in his C minor Symphony with a 'past-and-present' programme, by Lev Knipper (1898–19) in his Third (*Dalnevostochnaya*/Far Eastern) glorifying the Far Eastern Red Army, and by Shebalin in his 'dramatic symphony' *Lenin* (on Mayakovsky's poem). All three are monumental, programmatic, and spiced with revolutionary tunes. Others relied on a title or epigraph. Steinberg's Fourth, *Turksib*, celebrated the opening of the Turkestan-Siberia railway; Myaskovsky's Twelfth was dedicated 'To the 15th Anniversary of the Revolution', its three movements reflecting 'The Russian countryside before, during and after the struggle for the new life', and his pupil Dmitry Kabalevsky (1904–) based his First on a programme from Viktor Gusev's poem 'The Year 1917'. Others continued to write abstract music. The returned prodigal Prokofyev's elegiac *Simfonicheskaya pesn* (Symphonic song), his first composition after his not yet final settlement in his fatherland, was criticized crushingly (though his amusing, light-handed music to the film *Poruchik Kizhe* which came next was welcomed) and Shostakovich's Piano Concerto, with solo trumpet and strings, was not saved by its lyrical patches; its vulgarity and its 'modernistic' motor-rhythms were fatal. Shostakovich had already composed an opera freely based on Leskov's story *Ledi Makbet Mtsenskovo uyezda* (The Lady Macbeth of the Mtsensk District) (prod. 1934). The music is a stylistic hotchpotch; whereas the passacaglia entr'acte connecting the two scenes of Act I and practically the whole of Act IV are splendidly tragic, Shostakovich and his librettist introduced a strong element of politically motivated caricature quite foreign to Leskov, farce rendered in very feeble music. All the same the opera was extremely successful. It was greeted as 'a most significant landmark in the development of Soviet musical art', stood as such for exactly two years, and was then dramatically toppled. On 28 January 1936 *Pravda* denounced *The Lady Macbeth* as 'a deliberately discordant, confused stream of sounds' and much more to the same effect; it was 'modernist formalism' of the worst kind – *Kulturbolschewismus*, in fact.

The work authoritatively approved at the same time as the correct model for Soviet opera was *Tikhy Don* (The quiet Don, after Sholokhov's novel) by Ivan Dzerzhinsky (1909–78), which had been produced three months earlier, melodious but technically barely competent. Dzerzhinsky vainly tried to repeat his success by composing the sequel, *Podnyataya tselina* (Virgin soil upturned) (1937), and others wrote in the same vein only much better: Kabalevsky in *Master iz Klamsi* (The master of Clamecy, based on Romain Rolland's *Colas Breugnon*) (1938) and Tikhon Khrennikov (1913–) in *V buryu* (In the storm) (1939). But when a greater than either of these, Prokofyev, produced a Civil War opera, *Semyon Kotko* (1940), it was greeted with a storm of criticism. However the success of his ballet *Romeo and Juliet*, hitherto known only by the orchestral suites from it, was some compensation.

Shostakovich was so shaken by the *Lady Macbeth* affair that he withdrew his already completed Fourth Symphony and wrote a Fifth (1938) which he described as 'a Soviet artist's practical creative reply to just criticism'. The Sixth (1939) suggests that his regeneration was imperfect and at the same time he turned more seriously to chamber music with the first of his remarkable series of string quartets (1938) and a Piano Quintet (1940). The problem of Socialist realism in instrumental music remained unsolved, though the works of a newcomer from Armenia, Aram Khachaturyan (1903–78), a First Symphony (1934), a Piano Concerto No. 1 (1936) and a Violin Concerto (1940), were well received, perhaps on account of their novel colouring of Armenian and Uzbek folk-music. Khachaturyan's ballet *Schastye* (Happiness) (1939) was also popular – and still more so when it was recast with a new scenario as *Gayane* in 1942. Russian composers had no comparable novelties to offer; indeed novelty was not required; on the contrary composers were pressed into stylistic retrogression – witness, for instance, Myaskovsky's Symphonies 17 and 18 (both 1937) in comparison with No. 10 (1927). But the probability of war began to turn attention to patriotic rather than the now rather threadbare revolutionary themes and in 1939 both Prokofyev and Shaporin glorified princely heroes of the Middle Ages, Alexander Nevsky in the cantata which Prokofyev evolved from his music to Eisenstein's film, and Dmitry Donskoy in the 'symphony-cantata' *Na pole Kulikovom* (On the field of Kulikovo) on a cycle of poems by Blok, two outstanding masterpieces of Soviet music.

When war actually came in 1941 Shostakovich celebrated the defence of Leningrad in his Seventh Symphony, with a programmatic first movement part of which suggests the inexorable advance of the Germans. Composers were evacuated wholesale to the Caucasus and, the authorities having other matters on their minds, cultural surveillance was relaxed, with the result that he went on to compose a truly monumental and tragic Eighth (1943) which after the war was condemned, with Prokofyev's Sixth (1947), as 'formalistic' and suppressed for nearly ten years. Residence in the Caucasus naturally interested musicians in local folk-music and in 1941 Prokofyev was moved to compose a string quartet (his No. 2) and Myaskovsky a symphony (his Twenty-third) on Kabardinian themes. Operas on heroic subjects proliferated; both Kabalevsky and Dzerzhinsky found them in contemporary events. But most of them were poor things and all were outclassed by the one which Prokofyev completed in its first version in 1942 (partially prod. 1946): *Voyna i mir* (War and Peace). Tolstoy's novel was an impossible subject, yet by selecting eleven – in the final version thirteen – scenes showing Andrey's love for Natasha and Kuragin's seduction on the one hand and big war set-pieces on the other, a procedure for which he had precedents in *Boris, Khovanshchina* and *Prince Igor*, and setting them to music that is by turns lyrical, dramatic, and epic, Prokofyev was able to create a masterpiece more worthy of his great predecessors than any earlier Soviet opera.

MUSIC DURING THE SECOND WORLD WAR

The war had the effect of suppressing 'cultural Bolshevism' all over the European continent. The main stream of Western music now flowed more strongly than ever across the Atlantic. Paris had lost its lead during the 1930s and the stream there dwindled to a trickle under the Occupation. Honegger wrote little, Poulenc a high-spirited throw-back in the form of the *opéra bouffe Les Mamelles de Tirésias* (1944) but also such lovely things as the *a cappella* cantata *Figure humaine* and perhaps his best song, the Aragon setting 'C' (both 1943), while Messiaen likewise turned his back on worldly things in his *Quatuor pour la fin du temps* (1941) and an immensely long piano work, *Vingt Regards sur l'Enfant-Jésus* (1944). In embattled Britain, in much the same spirit, Vaughan Williams produced a serene diatonic/modal Fifth Symphony. Tippett, however, made a strong political gesture with his oratorio *A Child of our Time* (1941) and later went to prison for refusing military service. The real surprise of British music was the development of Britten from a composer of great technical facility always seeking problems to solve (e.g. the setting of Rimbaud in *Les Illuminations* (1939)), into an exquisitively sensitive poet (the *Serenade* for tenor, horn, and strings (1943)), and a musical dramatist capable of creating in *Peter Grimes* (1945) the first English opera since Balfe's and *The Mikado* to win international success.

America had native composers of comparable ability – Sessions, Harris, Copland, Elliott Carter (1908–), William Schuman (1910–), Samuel Barber (1910–) – but their work was inevitably overshadowed by that of the great immigrants: Stravinsky's Symphonies in C (1940) and 'in three movements' (1945), Hindemith's in E flat (1941), Schoenberg's *Ode to Napoleon Buonaparte* and Piano Concerto (both 1942), Bartók's Concerto for orchestra (1943) and Sonata for solo violin (1944), Rakhmaninov's *Symphonic Dances* (1940). Britain had her immigrants too – Egon Wellesz (1885–1974), Roberto Gerhard (1896–1970), Mátyás Seiber (1905–60), Franz Reizenstein (1911–68) – but they were not in the same class as composers and they wrote little or nothing during the war.

41

Cross-currents after 1945

THE ECLECTIC LANGUAGE

The termination of the Second World War was followed by a short period of cultural stagnation comparable with that after the First, only to be followed by experiments far more revolutionary than those of the 1920s and far more fundamental. At first the reaction against experimentalism that had begun in the mid-1930s continued. Romantic self-expression died with Richard Strauss in 1949 – or, rather, in his exquisite swan-song *Vier letzte Lieder* (Four last songs) in 1948. It was possible at that time to write that all over the Western world composers had acquired something very like a common language:

an eclectic language, embodying many of the results of earlier experiment ... melodically rather angular, predominantly linear in texture, continually crossing the frontier between tonality and atonality, unsentimental but not without restrained or ironically masked emotion and sometimes opening up real depths.[1]

They employed it with innumerable personal variations of harmonic acerbity, melodiousness and tonal reference. But in that very year 1948 occurred two unconnected events which were ultimately to open a wider cleft than ever. In February the Central Committee of the Communist Party in Moscow denounced an opera *Velikaya druzhba* (The great friendship) (1947) by the Georgian-born Vano Muradeli (1908–70) in terms nearly identical with those applied in 1936 to *The Lady Macbeth of Mtsensk* and attacked as 'anti-national formalists' Prokofyev, Shostakovich, Myaskovsky, Shebalin and Khachaturyan. And in March a Frenchman, Pierre Schaeffer (1910–), began to think of a 'symphony of noises' (*Symphonie de bruits*) and began to collect suitable 'objects': bells, an alarm-clock, rattles, two musical merry-go-rounds (*tourniquets à musique*). Experimenting, he recorded 'natural' and musical sounds on discs (later on tapes) and distorted and combined them imaginatively in sound-*collages* which he called *musique concrète*. A *concert de bruits* was broadcast by the Radiodiffusion française in October. A more complete opposition to music easily understandable to the common man than this music totally incomprehensible to the common man was hardly possible.

[1] Gerald Abraham, *A Hundred Years of Music* (London, second edition 1949), p. 295.
[2] *Turangalîla* is a Sanskrit compound. *Turanga* means time flowing, rhythm, movement, *Lîla* love, divine play.

846

MESSIAEN'S GRAND SYNTHESIS

A much more important work, almost equally incomprehensible to the common man, also dates from 1948: Messiaen's ten-movement *Turangalîla-Symphonie*. Messiaen emerged as a sort of nucleus figure in the post-war years and *Turangalîla* summed up his technical evolution so far. His melodic vocabulary was vast, drawn from sources as different as the plainsong modes and the *rāgas* of Indian music, what he called *modes à transpositions limitées* (invented by himself, although they include Rimsky-Korsakov's scale of alternate tones and semitones), the songs of a great many birds (which he notated with extreme care), but not twelve-note rows. His harmony was equally wide-ranging: added-note chords, quartal or quintal chords, Skryabinian aggregations of the harmonic overtones (see p. 808). Most individual of all was his treatment of rhythm, stimulated by study of the isorhythmic techniques of *ars nova* (see pp. 118–9) and the 'proportions' of the early fifteenth century (see p. 146). He borrowed not only Indian 'modes' but Indian rhythms – and the title of his symphony[2] – and something of the ethos of Indian music. Messiaen's rhythms are infinitely subtle – a dotted semiquaver or a demisemiquaver may be tied to a crotchet; the familiar symmetries are disrupted and the evasive patterns may be 'serialized', the time-values being augmented or diminished in arithmetical progression with each repetition, or they may be reversed or employed in canon like melodic patterns (but independently of them). The method may be illustrated by this rhythmic and melodic *canon cancrizans* for flute and oboe, accompanied by solo violin and solo basses, with piano, celesta, vibraphone, and percussion used together in a special ensemble 'resembling that of an East Indian *gamelan*', in the third movement of *Turangalîla*:

Ex. 308

THE DARMSTADT *FERIENKURSE*

At the same time musicians in Germany were beginning to catch up with the
lost years. As early as the autumn of 1945 the eclectic symphonist Karl
Amadeus Hartmann (1905–63) launched a series of concerts under the title
'Musica Viva' which revealed to them a wide range of music unknown under
the Nazis; these were broadcast and spread to other centres under the

848

direction of Wolfgang Fortner (1907–   ), a composer who had hitherto practised neoclassicism in the veins of Hindemith and Stravinsky, but who now turned to a more advanced idiom in his Symphony (1947) and experimented with his own variety of twelve-note technique in his Third String Quartet (1948). Fortner was also involved from the start in the Internationale Ferienkurse für neue Musik (vacation courses for new music) instituted at Darmstadt-Kranichstein in 1946. Hindemith directed the courses in 1947. But the real international importance of Darmstadt as a hotbed for advanced composers dates from the arrival of René Leibowitz (1913–72), a Parisian Pole who had studied with Webern in Vienna, in 1948 and of Messiaen in 1949. Leibowitz was the missionary expounding the twelve-note gospel,[3] Messiaen the creative artist but not yet a convert. But Messiaen in the fourth of his *Quatre études de rhythme* for piano, 'Mode de valeurs et d'intensité' written at Darmstadt in 1949, advanced a new constructional device which he christened *paramètres*. ('Parameter' is a mathematical term denoting the constant quantity in the equation of a curve.) He employs 'modes' of pitch (three twelve-note series), of 'attack' (twelve varieties, e.g. accent, wedge-staccato, dot-staccato, and so on), of dynamics (seven degrees), and of note values (twelve multiples of ♪, twelve of ♪, twelve of ♪). While these limits are constants, Messiaen moved fairly freely within them and even broke right out of them, though in the third of the *Quatre Études, Île de Feu 2*, he experimented with the constant association of pitch with note-value so that e.g. E natural is always a minim, A flat always a crotchet. In 1952 he attempted to employ similar ideas in *musique concrète: Timbres-durées*.

TOTAL SERIALIZATION

Messiaen's line of thought was extended with doctrinaire severity by his two most distinguished pupils, Pierre Boulez (1925–   ) and Karlheinz Stockhausen (1928–   ). Besides Messiaen, Boulez also studied with Leibowitz from whom he imbibed what one might call the ingrown serial microtechnique of Webern; he became more interested in the treatment of small segments of the row than in the orthodox twelve-note row. During 1951–2 he dabbled briefly with *musique concrète* and constructed *Études* I and II for it; but a much more important work of the same years was the *Premier livre* of *Structures* for two pianos in which complete twelve-note rows not only constitute the linear element but control all the others. The first section, though unpropitious as pure sound, is simple enough to demonstrate the technique:

---

[3] He was also a composer, but his compositions attracted much less notice than his books, *Schoenberg et son école* (Paris, 1947; English translation, New York, 1949) and *Introduction à la musique de douze sons* (Paris, 1949).

Ex. 309

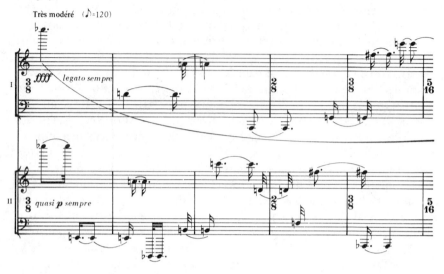

Piano I plays the basic row:

Eb	D	A	Ab	G	F♯	E	C♯	C♮	Bb	F	B
1	2	3	4	5	6	7	8	9	10	11	12

Piano II its inversion: 1 7 3 10 12 9 2 11 6 4 8 5

Boulez constructs two 'permutation tables', number-squares consisting of (*a*) all the transpositions of the original row, (*b*) the transpositions of the inversion. (The second rows of (*a*) and (*b*) yield the second section of the piece and so on.) And these tables are used to determine the note-values, dynamics and varieties of attack. The bottom row of (*a*) is

12 10 11 7 1 2 9 3 4 6 8 5

that of (*b*): 5 4 8 2 1 7 6 3 10 9 11 12

and to obtain the note-values these numbers are treated as multiples of a demisemiquaver: thus $12 = \flat \times 12 = \,\downarrow$.. The values for Piano I are prescribed by the bottom row of (*b*) in reverse, those for Piano II by that of (*a*) in reverse. Dynamics and attack, which are constant for each section, are determined by similar methods; in Ex. 309 the index figures for Piano I are both 12, indicating *ffff* and *legato sempre*, for Piano II 5, i.e. *quasi p* and 'normal'. Having chosen his basic row, the composer decides on tempi and the register in which each note is to be played but everything else is predestined. Pure constructivism for its own sake, without regard for communication with a listener, would seem to have reached its *ne plus ultra*, but in fact it was carried much further by Boulez himself in the *Deuxième livre* of *Structures* (1956 and 1961) and by other exponents of 'total serialization'. And the genuine sensitive musician in Boulez enabled him in *Le Marteau sans maître* (The masterless hammer) (begun 1953, perf. 1955, final version 1957) – his career has been littered with disowned works, rewritten works, and works-in-progress – to illuminate total serialization with fascinating, mostly percussive and transparent sound and also to relieve it by freer passages. *Le Marteau* is a setting of three surrealist poems by René Char (one set twice) for alto with small groupings of flute, guitar, viola, vibraphone, xylorimba, and percussion (including two pairs of bongos, maracas, triangle, gongs, and cymbals) plus a purely instrumental prelude and three *commentaires* on one of the poems. It remains his most accessible mature work.

ELECTRONICALLY PRODUCED SOUND

Total serialization and *musique concrète* were not the only new techniques of the 1950s. Herbert Eimert (1897–1972) demonstrated possibilities of electronically produced sound far more sophisticated and much further removed from normal musical sounds than those of Martenot and his rivals, first in 1951 at Darmstadt where they impressed Messiaen, Boulez – and Stockhausen. For Stockhausen in that year revelation succeeded revelation. Until recently he had been familiar only with Schoenberg and Berg; now he was introduced both to mature Webern and to a recording of Messiaen's 'Mode de valeurs et d'intensité' which so completely fascinated him that he decided to go to Paris and study for a time with Messiaen and Milhaud. There he encountered but rejected *musique concrète* and returned to join Eimert in the Cologne Radio studio for electronic music. His earliest compositions in this phase – *Kreuzspiel* for oboe, clarinet, bass, piano, and percussion (1952), the first four *Klavierstücke* (1953), and *Kontra-Punkte* for ten instruments (1953) – were not, however, electronic but serial. *Kontra-Punkte* is 'totally serial' in the Boulez sense but Stockhausen lacked something of Boulez's fundamental musicality and was the victim of doctrinaire mathematical obsessions. It is doubtful whether the human ear can apprehend the rhythmic/metrical subtleties of, say, the opening of *Klavierstück II*:

Ex. 310

What follows is notated in single bars of 4/8, 6/32 (two), 4/8, 1/8, and so on. Also in 1953 Stockhausen composed his first electronic works, two *Studien* in the manipulation of pure sine-tones[4] and nearly two hundred individual frequencies selected according to serial plans. *Studie II* was the first electronic composition to be published, not in the form of a musical score (which would be impossible) but as a graph-like diagram showing tone-heights (in frequencies), durations (so many centimetres with the tape played at 76·2 centimetres a second), changes of timbre, and dynamics.

INDETERMINACY

Stockhausen made radical experiments in every direction. In *Zeitmasze* (Tempi) for five woodwind (1956) the instruments are often required to play in independent, unsynchronized tempi and in *Gruppen* for three orchestras each with its own conductor (1957) he embarked on what he called 'Instrumentalmusik im Raum' (in space), the orchestras sometimes playing freely in different tempi, sometimes together, sometimes echoing or answering each other. (As he confessed, 'It is difficult to perform this music in existing concert-halls'.) Already in the *Gesang der Jünglinge* (Song of the youths in the fiery furnace, Book of Daniel, 3) (1956) for 'manipulated' human voice and electronically generated sounds he had asked that the five loudspeaker groups be placed all round the audience. On the same principle and more ambitious is *Carré* (Square) (1960) for four orchestras and choirs. The 'indeterminate' principle of *Zeitmasze* and *Gruppen* dominates in a different form the *Klavierstück XI* (1956): nineteen groups of notes are printed on a large sheet of paper and the pianist plays one group at random at whatever speed and dynamics he likes, but at the end are directions for tempo etc. of the next group which again must be picked at random. Compared with these eccentricities, Stockhausen's much later *Mantra* for two pianos and percussion (1970) and the final version of *Momente* (1972) seem almost conservative.

---

[4] Sounds without overtones.

THE AVANT-GARDE IN AMERICA

To some extent these methods had been anticipated by the American John Cage (1912–), a pupil of the bold but rather naïve experimenter Henry Cowell (1897–1965), an early admirer of Ives. Neither Cowell's piano 'tone-clusters' (played with the flat hand, forearm or wood blocks) nor Cage's 'prepared piano' (pitch and timbre altered by objects attached to the strings) had much future, though Cowell's direct attacks on the piano strings (treating it like a harp) offered obvious possibilities. Cage, who had studied with Schoenberg as well as Cowell, followed his first piece for prepared piano, *Bacchanale* (1938), with *Imaginary Landscape No. 1* (1939) which involves two record-players of variable speed with other instruments; in 1951 his *Imaginary Landscape No. 4* demanded twelve radios each controlled by two 'players' and a conductor. But Stockhausen denied any influence from Cage and summed up his work as an 'anarchistic protest against the European tradition . . . in a musical no-man's-land'.[5] He was much more sympathetic to another American, Earle Brown (1926–), a pioneer of 'aleatory' (indeterminate) music comparable with the plastic mobiles of Alexander Calder, whose orchestral *Folio: November 1952* may well have prompted his own essays in indeterminacy. In Brown's *Available Forms II* (1962) two large orchestras and two independent conductors seem extravagant means to dubious ends. A pioneer in another direction, total serialization, was Milton Babbitt (1916–), a mathematician by training, who began feeling his way toward it in his *Compositions* for various instruments around 1947–8. At about the same time a hitherto very conservative modernist, Elliott Carter, began to experiment with 'metrical modulation' (non-symmetrical changes of speed) producing a remarkable First String Quartet (1951) and going on to his own version of 'music in space' in a Second Quartet (1959) and a very fine Double Concerto for piano, harpsichord, and two chamber ensembles (1961). Varèse re-emerged after many years of silence with *Déserts* (1954), alternations of instrumental and electronic music, and a *Poème électronique* (1958), while another immigrant, Křenek, adopted total serialization in his *Quaestio Temporis* (Investigation of time) for chamber orchestra (1960).

INTERNATIONAL DISCIPLES OF STOCKHAUSEN

Nevertheless the focal point of advanced modernism remained in Europe, for Stockhausen, not only by his works but by stimulating writings and personal charisma, had gathered disciples from many countries. One Italian, Luigi Nono (1924–) had appeared at Darmstadt even before himself with orchestral *Variazioni canoniche* on a note-row by Schoenberg (1950) and was very close to him during the 1950s; another, Dallapiccola's pupil Luciano Berio (1923–), came in contact with him in 1954 and founded the Milan electronic institute the next year. His disciples included

[5] 'Arbeitsbericht 1952–3', *Texte* i (Cologne, 1963).

the Belgian Henri Pousseur (1929–   ), the Argentinian Mauricio Kagel (1931–   ), the Hungarian György Ligeti (1923–   ), the Englishman Cornelius Cardew (1936–   ), who actually collaborated with Stockhausen in the preparation of *Carré*, the Japanese Makoto Shinohara (1931–   ), the Swede Bo Nilsson (1937–   ), and the Pole Włodzimierz Kotoński (1925–   ). Kotoński visited Darmstadt during 1957–60, and then worked in the 'experimental studio' of the Polish Radio at Warsaw, and it was he who provided the point of contact between the composers of his own country and the Western avant-garde. His own *Muzyka kameralna* for 21 instruments and percussion (1958), *Musique en relief* for six instrumental groups, and *Etiuda na jedno uderzenie w talerz* (Study on a single cymbal-stroke) (both 1959) are cautious but attractive essays. Similarly the orchestral *Jeux vénitiens* (1961) and open-work String Quartet (1965) of Witold Lutosławski (1913–   ) are easier for most listeners to accept than the severely cerebral or wildly experimental work of their Western colleagues; and Krzysztof Penderecki (1933–   ) scored an immediate success with his extraordinarily effective *Tren: Ofiarom Hiroszimy* (Threnos: for the victims of Hiroshima) for 52 strings (1961) and produced with his *Passio et mors Domini nostri Iesu Christi secundum Lucam* (1965, but incorporating a choral 'Stabat Mater' of 1963) one of the most remarkable monuments of truly contemporary Christian art. At the same time the State publishing-houses of other East European countries brought out avant-garde music: in Hungary the remarkable Op. 1 String Quartet (1961) of György Kurtág (1926–   ) and in Czechoslovakia the very advanced Third Quartet (1963) and *Hudba pro 5* (Music for 5) for oboe, clarinet, bassoon, viola, and piano (1964) of the Stockhausen-influenced Marek Kopelent (1932–   ).

Like the Poles, the Italian avant-garde preserved what one might call a sense of 'immanent song' that is missing from the Central Europeans. In Nono's *Il canto sospeso* (The suspended song) (1956) – settings of excerpts from the last letters of members of the European Resistance condemned to death – for soloists, choir, and large orchestra, although he splits up words syllabically between different voices in the last movement, he likes to give his singers long-sustained notes or declamation on repeated notes in the old Italian manner and even allows them to expand:

Ex. 311

Di - co ad - di·o   a tut - ti   e   pian - go.

(I say goodbye to all, and weep.)

Moreover the basic row is very simple, the notes alternately rising and falling by semitones; he used it again in later works. And Berio in his *Circles* (1960), settings of E. E. Cummings for soprano, harp, and two percussion players obviously suggested by Stockhausen's *Zyklus* (1959) for one percussion-player, breaks into a similar kind of distorted cantabile. In the same way innate Frenchness has always tempered the self-discipline of Messiaen and usually Boulez's. Bird-calls increasingly infest Messiaen's compositions – the third and sixth of the *Sept Haikai* for chamber ensemble (1952), the *Oiseaux exotiques* for piano, wind, and percussion (1956), the *Premier Catalogue d'oiseaux* for piano (1956–8), *Chronochromie* (The colour of time), 'permutations of thirty-two durations' for orchestra (1960), *Couleurs de la Cité Céleste* for piano and orchestra (1963) in which bird songs from New Zealand, Brazil, and Canada are among the elements brought together to illuminate five quotations from the Book of Revelations, the colossal *Transfiguration de Notre Seigneur Jésus Christ* (1969). Yet it is impossible not to perceive that something at least of his techniques, as of Boulez's, derives ultimately from Debussy. However it was a pupil of Messiaen's – and of Milhaud and Honegger, not of Stockhausen – a trained architect who had collaborated with Corbusier, the Greek Iannis Xenakis (1922–   )[6] who programmed a computer to compose two pieces which were performed in Paris in 1962. Another novelty was the laying of impious hands on the masters of the past. In the third movement of his *Sinfonia* for eight voices and orchestra (1968) Berio parodied in succession the third movement of Mahler's Second, Ravel's *La Valse*, *Der Rosenkavalier*, and the scherzo of Beethoven's Ninth, and in 1970 Kagel deformed Beethoven electronically in *Ludwig van*.

MODIFIED SERIALISM

The European avant-garde had pressed so far forward that it was completely out of touch with the main body of the musical public, not a totally novel state of affairs but more serious than in the cases of Schoenberg or Stravinsky or Debussy – or Wagner. Confronted with *musique concrète*, aleatory music, electronic music, many musicians felt it was not unreasonable to deny that this was 'music' at all, particularly when shown a 'score' like that of Stockhausen's *Zyklus* for one percussion-player (1959) (see Plate 64). It was certainly not music that expressed or communicated anything, but rather a massive exploration of the possibilities of organized or random sound on lines only to be expected in an age obsessed with technological exploration, which might conceivably lead to an art of sound quite different from music as we know it, developing its own techniques and gradually establishing its own ethos. Alternatively it might develop as an acceptable adjunct to normal music as the twelve-note idea, which had seemed so outrageously anti-musical a quarter of a century earlier, was now being accepted in various modified forms. Those who wanted symphonic bread were outraged by the offer of electronic stone but they were now prepared to put up with a certain amount of dodecaphonic grit in their bread.

---

[6] Protagonist of 'stochastic' music (from the Greek στόχος, conjecture).

Barber put some in his Piano Sonata (1949) and he was followed by other Americans – Sessions and Copland – and the Englishman Peter Racine Fricker (1920–) during the 1950s. K. A. Hartmann, Fortner, Boris Blacher (1903–75) and his pupil Giselher Klebe (1925–), and Fortner's brilliant pupil Hans Werner Henze (1926–), who also studied with Leibowitz, likewise adopted twelve-note technique in varying degrees so far as it suited them. Henze's Violin Concerto (1947) and his first three symphonies (1947–51) announced the appearance of a major talent who was soon to develop in a different field.

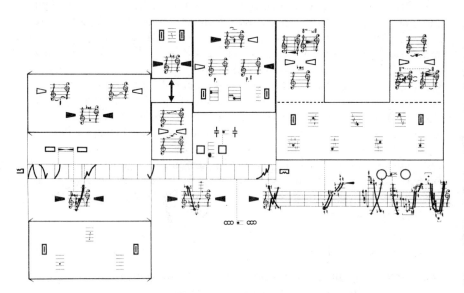

Pl. 64   No. 12 of the cycle of seventeen 'periods' of Stockhausen's *Zyklus für einen Schlagzeuger*. The player may begin with any period but must end with the same one. The rectangles at top and bottom of the left-hand column contain directions for vibraphone and African slit-drum respectively; between them are directions for side-drum, guero, and marimba; other instruments involved are untuned bells, triangle, tam-tam, and 'high-hat'.

THE POST-WAR SYMPHONY

The real *avant-garde* of the day were not interested in the symphony; their techniques were totally unsuited to the large-scale instrumental forms and it remained the domain of middle-of-the-road or frankly conservative musicians mostly British or Russian: the veteran Vaughan Williams with his last four (1947, 1952, 1956, and 1958); Rubbra who pluckily continued to plough his own furrow; Sessions in a comparable series; Walton's Second (1961); three striking works by Fricker (1949, 1951, and 1960); Tippett's three (1945, 1957, 1972), the Second Symphony (1958) of Lennox Berkeley and Rawsthorne's Third (1964); Hindemith's *Harmonie der Welt* (1951) which stands in the same relation to his opera of the same name (1956) as his

Mathis Symphony to the *Mathis* opera. Britten fought shy of the true symphony. His *Spring Symphony* (1949) is vocal throughout, characteristically skilful settings of a dozen poems and symphonic only in that its four 'parts' correspond to the conventional four movements, and his Symphony for cello and orchestra (1963) is a counterpart to Prokofyev's *Sinfonia concertante* for cello and orchestra (1952)[7] and, like it, a tribute to the Russian cellist Mstislav Rostropovich.

In Russia, of course, conservatism was the official policy. Prokofyev's Sixth Symphony, acclaimed in Leningrad in October 1947 was two months later in Moscow caught in the storm that destroyed Muradeli's *The Great Friendship* (see p. 846); his Seventh and last (1952) was, like Shostakovich's Second Piano Concerto (1957), originally intended for juvenile audiences. Shostakovich's Tenth (1953), arguably his finest, was attacked as 'pessimistic' but defended as 'an effort to overcome tragedy'. Nos. 11 (*The Year 1905*) and 12 (*The Year 1917*), composed in 1957 and 1961, are frankly programmatic dedications to the unsuccessful and the successful revolution, in a musical idiom comprehensible to mass audiences. No. 13 (1962) is a cantata-like setting of poems by Yevtushenko for baritone, male chorus, and orchestra, No. 14 (1969), a symphony only in the sense that Mahler's *Lied von der Erde* is a symphony, a cycle of eleven poems on the theme of death by Lorca, Guillaume Apollinaire, Küchelbecker, and Rilke. His Fifteenth and last (1971) is purely instrumental, autobiographical and enigmatic with an unrevealed programme to which the only clues are quotations from Rossini and Wagner.

TWELVE-NOTE MUSIC IN THE USSR

During his last years Shostakovich produced a series of string quartets similarly autobiographical and enigmatic, particularly No. 8 (1960) and Nos. 12, 13, 14, and 15 (1968, 1971, 1973, 1974), brooding more and more agonizingly on thoughts of death and culminating in the six Adagio movements of No. 15. Nos. 12 and 13 are remarkable also in that twelve-note passages are introduced, though only non-thematically as Bartók had done thirty years before (see p. 840). However, genuine serialism had already gained a foothold in the Soviet Union, the pioneer being Andrey Volkonsky (1933–), a pupil of Shaporin, who gave a public performance of his twelve-note *Musica Stricta* for piano in 1957. It was contemptuously dismissed but he persevered and was inspired by Stockhausen's *Kreuzspiel* to compose a *Game in Three* for violin, flute, and harpsichord (1962). He found sympathetic colleagues – Edisson Denisov (1929–), Sergey Slonimsky (1932–), the Estonian Arvo Pärt (1935–), Boris Tishchenko (1939–) – and in December 1965 the Composers' Union held a conference on 'genuine and apparent innovation in contemporary music'. Next year Slonimsky's *Concerto buffo* (1964), serial and with an element of 'controlled

---

[7] A reworking of his Cello Concerto of 1938.

improvisation' like his *Dialogï* for wind quintet (also 1964), was performed and then published. And in 1968 the official organ of the Union published a by no means unsympathetic discussion of Pärt's *Polifonicheskaya simfoniya* (1963), Tishchenko's Third Symphony (1967) and the Second Violin Concerto of Alfred Shnitke (1934–),[8] all twelve-note compositions. *Musique concrète* and electronic music have not attracted the Soviet avant-garde but the Estonian Kuldar Sink (1942–) has employed them in music for films.

Advanced music of any kind was naturally unthinkable in Russian opera or ballet, with their large audiences. Only one or two works in each category stand out from the quantity of 'correct' compositions of the post-war years. Even the best composers failed. Prokofyev's opera *Povest o nastoyashchem cheloveke* (Story of a real man) (1948; prod. 1960), with its 'clear melodies and the simplest possible harmonic language', was unworthy of him; and Shostakovich's *muzïkalnaya komediya, Moskva, Cheremushki* (Cher-yomushki is a Moscow suburb) (1958), is pure rubbish. The outstanding operas of the 1950s were Shaporin's long worked-on *Dekabristï* (The Decembrists) (prod. 1953), essentially a series of fine historical tableaux, and Shebalin's *Ukroshchenie stroptivoy* (The Taming of the Shrew) (1957). Prokofyev was still adding fresh music to his ballet *Kamenny tsvetok* (The stone flower) (prod. 1954) when he died in 1953 on the same day as Stalin. Khachaturyan's ballet *Spartak* (Spartacus) (1956) was an unashamed – and successful – essay in the vein of *Gayane*, and *Konek-Gorbunok* (The little humpbacked horse) (1955) by Shaporin's pupil Rodion Shchedrin (1932–) was another popular ballet.

POST-WAR OPERA

It is not only in the Soviet Union that opera composers have found advanced idioms a bar to success. Schoenberg's never completed *Moses und Aron* (comp. 1930–2) owed its sensational acclaim when it was at last produced in 1957 not to the music, though it is one of his finest scores, but mainly to sensation – the orgy scene. Even *Wozzeck* is not exactly a repertory opera and performances of *Lulu* or Dallapiccola's infinitely less 'difficult' *Prigioniero* are notable events. As for the 'space-opera' *Aniara* (1959) of the Swede Karl-Birger Blomdahl (1916–68), launched with considerable publicity, it was still-born. The only twelve-note opera composer to achieve repeated success is Henze, and he has been exceptionally free-and-easy in his attitude to twelve-note composition, putting sensuous effect before orthodoxy. It was his vein of frank melody that gave him his first operatic success, *Boulevard Solitude* (1952), an updated *Manon Lescaut*, and he continued on similar lines in *König Hirsch* (King Stag) (1956), *Der Prinz von Homburg* based on Kleist's play (1960), the chamber opera *Elegy for Young Lovers* (1961), and *The Bassarids* (1966). The passage from the first scene of *The*

[8] Mikhail Tarakanov, 'Novaya zhizn' staroy formï', *Sovetskaya muzïka* (1968), No. 6, p. 54.

Prince of Homburg quoted as Ex. 312 (see p. 860) is a typical example of nearly diatonic 'serialism' with plenty of note repetition. The 'series' played by the flute after a false start is sung by the heroine and inverted by the Electress.

More conservative still have been the English, headed by Britten who was admired by Henze and Shostakovich alike. Britten's world-wide success was due not only to his power of creating characters in terms of music and evoking mood and atmosphere with a few deft touches but to his vocal set-pieces, like Peter Grimes's 'Now the Great Bear and Pleiades', and his melody, as in Ellen's solos in the same score. Each opera that followed was made memorable by similar strokes: to name only a few in each, Lucia's arietta in Act II.2 and the choral lullaby in his first chamber opera, *The Rape of Lucretia* (1946), one tune after another in its comic companion *Albert Herring* (1947), the shanties and ballads – and the little First Act scene of the flogged Novice – in the all-male *Billy Budd* (1951), Essex's lute-songs in *Gloriana* (1953), the nursery tunes, the Governess's aria in the fourth scene, Miles's haunting little 'Malo, malo' tune in the sixth, of *The Turn of the Screw* (1954), in his masterpiece *A Midsummer Night's Dream* (1960) a profusion in which Oberon's 'I know a bank' is only one little gem. Many more examples could be adduced from his children's operas, *The Little Sweep* (with audience participation) (1949) and *Noye's Fludde* (1958), his 'parables', *Curlew River* (1964) and its successors, and his television opera *Owen Wingrave* (1971).

Musical conservatism comes naturally to the English – Britten's brief flirtation with the twelve-note idea (not serial composition) in *The Turn of the Screw* is characteristic – and Britten was not alone in realizing the vital need to meet opera audiences half way. Walton did so in *Troilus and Cressida* (1954), giving them a positively Italianate aria in Cressida's 'At the haunted end of the day' in Act II, and a much younger man, the twelve-note composer Nicholas Maw (1935–), wisely and drastically modified his style in *The Rising of the Moon* (1970). Three of Maw's contemporaries underline the point with opposite extremes: Malcolm Williamson (1931–) with the frankly popular appeal of *Our Man in Havana* (1963) and *The Violins of Saint-Jacques* (1966), Harrison Birtwistle (1934–) with the uncompromising *Punch and Judy* (1968) and Peter Maxwell Davies (1923–) with his *Taverner* (1972) – though Davies became much more approachable in his chamber opera, *The Martyrdom of St. Magnus* (1977). It is Tippett's refusal to make concessions in *The Midsummer Marriage* (comp. 1952; prod. 1956), *King Priam* (1962), and their successors that has militated against his exercises in philosophical symbolism; he is essentially an instrumental composer, happiest in the 'ritual dances' of *The Midsummer Marriage*.

STRAVINSKY: THE LAST YEARS

Stravinsky, perhaps wisely, neglected opera during the last twenty years of

Ex. 312

his life – after neglecting it for a quarter of a century before that. *The Rake's Progress* (1951) may be claimed as an American opera for the libretto is English and one of the librettists, W. H. Auden, was – like the composer – American by naturalization while the other, Chester Kallman, was American by birth. Whereas the 1922 *Mavra* is an amusing travesty of early nineteenth-century comic opera, the 1951 *Rake's Progress* is a brilliant *travesti* – in the literal sense of a change of clothes – of eighteenth-century, particularly Mozartean, *opera buffa* not merely in being a 'number opera' with airs and duets and recitative both secco and accompagnato, but in its scoring and much of the orchestral figuration and vocal lines. Like the finest eighteenth-century *opere buffe*, Mozart's, it is touched with pathos. Altogether it has everything to make it acceptable to the opera public, even familiar clichés like Tom's song in Act III, sc. 3:

Ex. 313

The Rake's Progress marks one limit of Stravinsky's neo-classical wanderings though he followed it with a work that is neo-classical in a different direction. After his first essay in composing an English text, he felt 'a strong desire to compose another work in which the problems of setting English words to music would reappear, but this time in a purer, non-dramatic form'. Accordingly he chose four poems and set them as a *Cantata* (1952) for soprano, tenor, female chorus and instrumental quintet, a work of severe beauty in which the most remarkable movement is the tenor solo 'Tomorrow shall be my dancing day', a *cantus cancrizans* in which the first eleven notes interlock with their retrograde form, this with their inversion, and this again with their retrograde-inversion:

Ex. 314

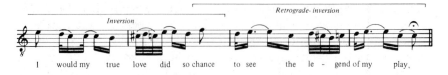

The same devices were further developed in a Septet for piano, wind, and strings (1953) and *In Memoriam Dylan Thomas* (1954) where a tenor solo, Thomas's 'Do not go gentle into that good night', is framed by two 'dirge-canons' for antiphonal quartets of trombones and strings. This remarkable work is entirely based on a theme – or series – of five different notes the inversions and retrogressions of which are duly marked in the published score.[9] Stravinsky had thus arrived at serialism in its simplest form, though not yet twelve-note composition. This was adopted first in three movements of the *Canticum Sacrum ad honorem Sancti Marci nominis* (1955), an outstanding masterpiece of modern music first performed in St. Mark's the following year, for tenor and baritone soloists, chorus, and three orchestral groups obviously suggested by the later music of Giovanni Gabrieli: woodwind only, trumpets and trombones, and harp, organ, violas, and double-basses. After a brief quasi-plainsong 'dedicatio' to the city of Venice, comes a diatonic choral/purely orchestral section, 'Euntes in mundum' which is repeated totally and exactly in retrograde at the end, 'Illi autem profecti'. The second movement, a tenor solo, 'Surge, aquilo', with wisps of counterpoint for woodwind and harp, is strictly on a twelve-note series and the texture suggests the influence of Webern; the third and fourth movements are based with more liberties but great ingenuity on another, closely related series. This juxtaposition of diatonic and twelve-note elements is again apparent in the delightful ballet *Agon*, begun in 1953 before *In Memoriam Dylan Thomas* when Stravinsky was only toying with serial procedures, and completed in 1957 when he had completely accepted them. Again there is a seventeenth-century element, for the dance-types in *Agon* (the Greek word means primarily a gathering to watch contests) – bransle, saraband, gaillarde – were modelled on those described and illustrated in Mersenne's *Harmonie universelle* (see p. 333).

Stravinsky's first composition entirely based on a single twelve-note series was *Threni (Lamentationes Jeremiae Prophetae)* for six soloists, mixed chorus, and fairly large orchestra (1958); and in *Movements* for piano and orchestra (1958), *The Flood* (1961), *Abraham and Isaac* (1964), *Requiem Canticles* (1966), he proceeded to explore in extreme concentration the possibilities of post-Webernian techniques – always with unexpected and highly personal twists. In *Abraham and Isaac*, a 'sacred ballad' for baritone and small orchestra composed on the Hebrew text of Genesis xxii, the voice-part is, in his own words, 'partly *bel canto* – melismatic – and partly an

---

[9] New York, 1954. A similar analysis of the tenor solo, by Hans Keller, has been printed in *Tempo*, No. 35 (Spring, 1955), p. 16.

interval-speech of single syllables'. In the *Requiem Canticles* for contralto and bass soloists, chorus and orchestra, the text a drastically abbreviated version of the Requiem Mass, twelve-note serial writing is contrasted with passages ('Libera me') in which the chorus sings simple repeated block chords.

Stravinsky was a catalytic reconciler of opposites. He ultimately adopted techniques originally intended to annihilate tonal gravitation and employed them to serve a new and neo-classical music by no means out of touch with tonality. Beginning with the absorption of contemporary Russian music (Rimsky-Korsakov, Skryabin), he had gone on to soak up everything truly contemporary that suited his genius, and then to incorporate sympathetic elements from the nineteenth century, the eighteenth, and finally from the seventeenth. He was one of the great foci on which rays of tradition converge and when he died in 1971 – not long after Hindemith and Pizzetti, and soon followed by Milhaud, Shostakovich, and Britten – an era ended.

Bibliography

Suggestions for further reading, by specialist scholars

General Histories

Of the various comprehensive histories of music conceived during the latter half of the eighteenth century only Burney's *General History . . . from the Earliest Ages to the Present Period* (four vols., London, 1776–89; modern edition by F. Mercer, London, 1935, reprinted New York, 1957) retains much interest for the general reader – mainly because of its survey of what was then 'the present period'. But the foundation-stone of scientific history is Forkel's *Allgemeine Geschichte der Musik* (two vols, Leipzig, 1788 and 1801). The two great nineteenth-century histories are the *Geschichte der Musik* (three vols., Breslau, 1862–8) of A. W. Ambros and the *Histoire générale de la musique* (five vols., Paris, 1869–76) of F.-J. Fétis. Neither was completed by its author but Ambros's work was posthumously revised and extended by other hands; thus the fourth volume was almost completely rewritten by Hugo Leichtentritt (Leipzig, 1909) who brought the story down to *c.* 1650, and the fifth (Leipzig, 1882) is a collection of musical examples to the third (compiled and edited by Otto Kade).

Hugo Riemann produced a *Handbuch der Musikgeschichte* in five 'half-volumes' (Leipzig, 1904–13) but the time had now come for collective histories, of which the first was *The Oxford History of Music* in six volumes shared between five authors and edited by W. H. Hadow (Oxford, 1901–5); an 'introductory volume' was added in 1929, the first two volumes were drastically revised, and a seventh volume (1850–1900) was brought out in 1934. However the five volumes which constitute the *1ère Partie – Histoire de la musique* – of the *Encyclopédie de la musique* of Albert Lavignac and Lionel de La Laurencie (Paris, 1913–22) had already shown the advantages of enlisting numerous specialist editors as well as the need to widen the ethnic bounds to include world, not merely European, music. So indeed had the more modest but very valuable *Handbuch der Musikgeschichte* edited by Guido Adler (Frankfurt, 1924; greatly enlarged ed. in two vols, Berlin, 1930). *The New Oxford History of Music* (ten vols, London, 1954–) has a group of editors and many contributors. Less ambitious collective histories are *Man and his Music* (four vols, London, 1957–9) by Alec Harman, Anthony Milner, and Wilfrid Mellers), and *A History of Western Music* (five vols., London, 1973–), ed. F. W. Sternfeld.

There are also general histories of particular categories. In 1905 Hermann Kretzschmar launched a series of *Kleine Handbücher der Musikgeschichte nach Gattungen* (Leipzig) with Arnold Schering's *Geschichte des Instrumentalkonzerts bis auf die Gegenwart*, and contributed to it his own *Geschichte der Oper* (1919). The series also included Leichtentritt's *Geschichte der Motette* (1908), Schering's *Geschichte des Oratoriums* (1911) Hugo Botstiber's *Geschichte der Ouvertüre und der freien Orchesterformen* (1913), Georg Schünemann's *Geschichte des Dirigierens* (1913), and Karl Nef's *Geschichte der Sinfonie und Suite* (1921); only the first parts were published of Kretzschmar's *Geschichte des Neuen deutschen Liedes* (from Albert to Zelter) (1911), Eugen Schmitz's *Geschichte der Kantate und des geistlichen Konzerts* (the secular solo cantata) (1914), and Peter Wagner's *Geschichte der Messe* (to 1600) (1913). Other category histories are Riemann's *Geschichte der Musiktheorie im IX–XIX Jahrhundert* (Berlin, 1898; rev. ed., 1920), Otto Klauwell's *Geschichte der Programmusik von ihren Anfängen bis zur Gegenwart* (Leipzig, 1910), Maurice Emmanuel's *Histoire de la langue musicale* (two vols, Paris, 1911) Joseph Müller-Blattau's *Grundzüge einer Geschichte der Fuge* (Kassel, 1931), Otto Ursprung's *Die Katholische Kirchenmusik* (Potsdam, 1931), Friedrich Blume's *Die Evangelische Kirchenmusik* (Potsdam, 1931; English ed., extended and with a vast amount of material by various hands, covering other fields, as *Protestant Church Music: a History*, New York, 1974), Gotthold Frotscher's *Geschichte des Orgelspiels und der Orgelkomposition* (two vols., Berlin, 1935), Walter Georgii's *Klaviermusik* (Berlin and Zürich, 1941; revised and extended ed., 1950), Donald J. Grout's *A Short History of Opera* (two vols., New York and London, 1947; rev. ed. in one vol., 1965), Bence Szabolcsi's *A melódia története* (Budapest, 1950; English ed., *A History of Melody*, London, 1965), William S. Newman's *A History of the Sonata Idea* (three vols., Chapel Hill, N.C., 1959–69), Denis Stevens (ed.), *A History of Song* (London, 1960), and Howard E. Smither, *A History of the Oratorio* (three vols., Chapel Hill, 1977). The best monograph on the history of orchestration is that by Gabriel Pierné and Henry Woollett in the Lavignac/La Laurencie *Encyclopédie de la musique, 2e Partie*, iv (Paris, 1929), pp. 2215–2286 and 2445–2718.

Substantial comprehensive histories of Western national musics, as distinct from studies of periods, are rare. Hans Joachim Moser's *Geschichte der deutschen Musik* (three vols., Stuttgart, 1920–4) and Yury Keldïsh's *Istoriya russkoy muzïki* (three vols., Moscow and Leningrad, 1947–54) are exceptions. (Gerald Seaman's *History of Russian Music* (Oxford, 1967) never got beyond the first volume.) The collective Polish *Z dziejów polskiej kultury muzycznej* (two vols., Cracow, 1958 and 1966) is in the same class. Even single-volume histories of any value are not very numerous; they include *A History of Music in England* by Ernest Walker (Oxford, 1907; rev. and enlarged ed. by J. A. Westrup, 1952), *A History of British Music* by Percy M. Young (London, 1967), *America's Music: From the Pilgrims to the Present* by Gilbert Chase (New York, 1955; 2nd ed., 1966), *The Music of Spain* by Gilbert Chase (New York, 1941; 2nd ed., 1959), *Historia de la Música Española* by José Subirá (Barcelona, 1953), *A magyar zenetörténet kézikönyve* by Bence Szabolcsi (Budapest, 1947; 2nd. ed., 1955; English ed., *A Concise History of Hungarian Music*, Budapest, 1964), *Česká hudba* by Jan Racek (Prague, 1958), and *Scandinavian Music: A Short History* by John Horton (London, 1964).

GERALD ABRAHAM

Chapter 1. *Mesopotamia and Egypt*

MESOPOTAMIA

Useful general surveys of Mesopotamian music are given by W. Stauder, 'Die Musik der Sumerer, Babylonier und Assyrer' in H. Hickmann and W. Stauder, *Orientalische Musik* (Leiden, 1970), pp. 171–243, with extensive bibliography; Stauder, 'Sumerisch-babylonische Musik' in *MGG*, xii, cols. 1737–1752;

Bibliography

A. Spycket, 'La musique instrumentale mésopotamienne', in *Journal des Savants* (1972), pp. 153–209; and, more briefly in a wider setting, M. Duchesne-Guillemin, 'La musique en Égypte et en Mesopotamie anciennes', in Roland Manuel (ed.), *Histoire de la musique* (Encyclopédie de la Pléiade, 9) (Paris, 1960), pp. 353–62. A detailed study of Sumerian music is offered in H. Hartmann, *Die Musik der sumerischen Kultur* (Frankfurt, 1960). A handy conspectus of ancient near-eastern, including Mesopotamian, instrument types, with a folding chart illustrating them in their chronological settings, is given in M. Wegner, *Die Musikinstrumente des alten Orients* (Munster, 1950); and individual types are discussed in R. D. Biggs, 'The Sumerian Harp' in *The American Harp Journal*, i, 3 (1968), pp. 6–12; M. Duchesne-Guillemin, 'La harpe à plectre Iranienne: son origine et sa diffusion', in *Journal of Near Eastern Studies*, xxviii (1969), pp. 109–15; and S. A. Rashid, 'Zur Datierung der mesopotamischen Trommeln und Becken' in *Zeitschrift für Assyriologie*, lxi (1971), pp. 89–105. For a discussion of the interpretation of cuneiform musical texts see A. D. Kilmer, 'The Discovery of an Ancient Mesopotamian Theory of Music' in *Proceedings of the American Philosophical Society*, cxv (1971), pp. 131–49.

T. C. MITCHELL

EGYPT

The musicologists most concerned with ancient Egypt have been Curt Sachs and Hans Hickmann. A bibliography of the former appears in *MQ*, xxvii (1941), of the latter in *Ethnomusicology*, ix (1965) and xiii (1969). Comprehensive bibliographies will appear in the *New Grove Dictionary of Music and Musicians* (1980) under the articles on these scholars and on 'Egypt: Ancient Music'.

Specialized works on iconography have been Max Wegner, *Die Musikinstrumente des alten Orients* (Münster, 1950), and Hickmann 'Ägypten', vol. 2, Part 1 (Leipzig, 1961) in the series *Musikgeschichte in Bildern*. From Hans Hickmann's other voluminous writings one would initially choose *Musique et vie musicale sous les Pharaons* (Paris, 1956); '45 siècles de musique dans l'Egypte ancienne', *La Revue musicale* (Paris, 1956); 'La chironomie dans l'Egypte pharaonique', *Zeitschrift für ägyptische Sprache und Altertumskunde*, lxxxiii (1958). Other scholars who have treated the subject at length are W. C. Hayes, *The Scepter of Egypt* (New York, 1953; Harvard, 1959); H. G. Farmer, 'The Music of Ancient Egypt', *NOHM*, i, ed. E. Wellesz (1957); and J. Vandier, *Manuel d'archéologie égyptienne*, iv, I (Paris, 1964).

For the study of individual instruments in museum collections there are three main catalogues: for Berlin, C. Sachs, *Die Musikinstrumente des alten Ägyptens: Mitteilungen aus der Ägyptischen Sammlung*, Bd. iii (Berlin, 1921); for Cairo, H. Hickmann, *Catalogue général des antiquités égyptiennes du Musée du Caire: Instruments de musique, nos. 69201–69852* (Cairo, 1949); for London, R. D. Anderson, *Catalogue of Egyptian Antiquities in the British Museum, iii: Musical Instruments* (London, 1976). As well as Hickmann's invaluable series of articles on various instruments (mainly in Egyptological periodicals), Lise Manniche has contributed two useful monographs, *Musical Instruments from the Tomb of Tut'ankhamūn* (Tut'ankhamūn Tomb Series, vi, Griffith Institute, Oxford, 1976) and *Ancient Egyptian Instruments* (Munich, 1975).

W. V. DAVIES

Chapters 2 and 3. Greece and the Hellenistic-Roman World

A useful modern *Bibliography of Sources for the Study of Ancient Greek Music* was compiled by T. J. Mathiesen (New Jersey, 1974), containing nearly 1,000 entries covering about 400 years, and more recently S. Michaelides, *The Music of Ancient Greece* (London, 1978), has conveniently assembled a vast amount of information, historical, technical, and biographical about music and musicians. The detailed study of Greek musical theory, promoted in the nineteenth century by such scholars as Gevaert, Rossbach, and Westphal, has been pursued in the present century by, amongst others, R. P. Winnington-Ingram, *Mode in Ancient Greek Music* (Cambridge, 1936, repr. Amsterdam, 1968), O. J. Gombosi, *Die Tonarten und Stimmungen der antiken Musik* (Copenhagen, 1939), J. Chailley, 'Le mythe des modes grecs', *Acta Musicologica*, xxviii (1956), pp. 137–63. Winnington-Ingram has also contributed (along with J. F. Mountford) an excellent article, *Music*, in *The Oxford Classical Dictionary* (2nd ed. Oxford, 1970), and a synopsis of work from 1932 to 1957 in *Lustrum*, iii (Göttingen, 1959). Remarkable for its elegant compression of basic material remains Th. Reinach's *La Musique grecque* (Paris, 1926), and the general ground is well covered by I. Henderson in her chapter on *Ancient Greek Music* in *NOHM*, i (London, 1957) and by G. Reese in Chapter ii of his *Music in the Middle Ages* (New York, 1940). Of course Reese, like E. J. Wellesz, *A History of Byzantine Music and Hymnography* (2nd ed., Oxford, 1961), and other chapters in *NOHM*, i, pursues the subject beyond the Greek classical and Hellenistic eras.

Details of musical instruments may be found in Sachs, *The History of Musical Instruments* (New York, 1940), and, along with many illustrations, in M. Wegner, *Das Musikleben der Griechen* (Berlin, 1949), and *Griechenland* in the *Musikgeschichte in Bildern* series (Mainz, 1963). On the lyre, Winnington-Ingram's 'The Pentatonic Tuning of the Greek Lyre', *Classical Quarterly* vi (1956), pp. 169–86, and on the *aulos*, A. A. Howard's article in *Harvard Studies in Classical Philology*, iv (1893), pp. 1–60, are important, and, on the *hydraulus*, J. Perrot's *The Organ from its Invention in the Hellenistic Period* (Paris, 1965, Eng. trans. London, 1971).

The most thorough study of music in Roman life and literature is that of G. Wille, *Musica Romana* (Amsterdam, 1967), which may be supplemented by the iconographic evidence in G. Fleischhauer, *Etrurien und Rom*, in the *Musikgeschichte in Bildern* (Mainz, 1964). The Greek ethical views about music, brilliantly assembled and analysed by H. Abert, *Die Lehre vom Ethos in der griechischen Musik* (Leipzig, 1899, repr. 1968) have been discussed again by W. D. Anderson, *Ethos and Education in Greek Music* (Harvard, 1966). The major ancient writers of purely technical musical treatises are not all readily accessible in translation – notable exceptions are Aristoxenus, *Harmonics*, in vol. xiv of the Loeb Library *Moralia* (London, 1967); and, in German, Aristides Quintilianus, trans. R. Schäfke (Berlin, 1937) and Ptolemy and Porphyry, trans. I. Düring (Göteborg, 1934). There is an English translation of the later Byzantine writer, Manuel Bryennius, who reveals the characteristic antiquarian interest of later ages in Greek musical theory, in the edition of G. H. Jonker (Groningen, 1970). The most convenient collection of actual musical documents (all post-classical, and mostly fragmentary) is that of E. Pöhlmann, *Denkmäler altgriechischer Musik* (Nuremberg, 1971).

E. K. BORTHWICK

Chapter 4. Music in the Christian World

The music of the Christian liturgies may be studied partly through facsimiles and partly through modern editions, most of which take the form of 'official' editions for present-day (though because of liturgical reform considerably restricted) use. Both facsimiles and transcriptions are included in the series *Monumenta Musicae Byzantinae* (Copenhagen, 1935–). The most significant collection of facsimiles of Latin chant is the series *Paléographie Musicale*, published by the monks of Solesmes (Solesmes, 1889–). To this should be added *Graduale Sarisburiense* (1894) and *Antiphonale Sarisburiense* (1901–25), both edited by W. H. Frere (reprinted 1966). Modern editions of chant are quite numerous, particularly if one includes the books of the Benedictine, Dominican, and Cistercian orders: even so, they by no means include the whole medieval repertory between them. Some of them are difficult to obtain, and in others the layout has been changed in the most recent editions, making reference difficult. The most generally serviceable is the *Liber Usualis* (English edition, Tournai, 1934 and reprints), which contains chants for the Mass and Offices in a continuous sequence. The *Graduale Sacrosanctae Romanae Ecclesiae* (Tournai, 1938 and later editions) contains many more chants of the Mass. The *Antiphonale Sacrosanctae Romanae Ecclesiae* (Tournai, 1949) and *Antiphonale monasticum pro diurnis horis* (Tournai, 1934), similarly contain additional chants for the hours, though not for Matins. A few chants for Matins are included in the *Liber Usualis*; more are in the *Liber responsorialis . . . juxta ritum monasticum* (Solesmes, 1895), which is now difficult to find. Offertories with their verses were published by C. Ott in his *Offertoriale* (Tournai, 1935). The chants for the Ambrosian rite are published in the *Antiphonale missarum juxta ritum Sanctae Ecclesiae Mediolanensis* (Rome, 1935) and in the very rare *Liber vesperalis* (Rome, 1939); but in any case the complete repertory of the earliest manuscripts is given in square notation in *Paléographie musicale*, vi. Modern scholarly editions include the several volumes of *Monumenta Monodica Medii Aevi*, ed. B. Stäblein (Kassel and Basel, 1956–), and Dom A. Hughes, *Anglo-French Sequelae* (Burnham and London, 1934). There are also numerous extracts in various anthologies, including *Das Musikwerk*, xviii, ed. F. Tack (Cologne, 1960).

The standard work on Byzantine chant is E. Wellesz, *A History of Byzantine Music and Hymnography* (2nd ed., Oxford, 1961), to which may be added his *Eastern Elements in Western Chant* (Oxford, 1947). The literature on Gregorian chant is very extensive, but the following are outstanding: A. Gastoué, *Les origines du chant romain: l'antiphonaire grégorien* (Paris, 1907); P. Wagner, *Einführung in die gregorianischen Melodien*, 3 vols. (final edn., Leipzig, 1911–21, repr. Hildesheim, 1962; English translation of vol. i, *Introduction to the Gregorian Melodies*, London, 1907); P. Ferretti, *Esthétique grégorienne* (Paris, 1938); W. Apel, *Gregorian Chant* (London, 1958). On the liturgy: L. Duchesne, *Christian Worship* (English translation of the 5th ed. of his *Origines du culte chrétien*, London, 1951); J. A. Jungmann, *The Mass of the Roman Rite* (English version of his *Missarum Sollemnia*, 2nd ed., New York, 1954). On the notation of chant, G. Suñol, *Introduction à la paléographie musicale grégorienne* (Paris, 1935) is still probably the most accessible general treatise; volume ii of Wagner's *Einführung* is devoted entirely to the subject, while H. M. Bannister's *Monumenti vaticani di paleografia musicale latina*, 2 vols. (Leipzig, 1913) is an astonishingly full collection of facsimiles illustrative of its development.

Many medieval liturgical texts can be found assembled in the fifty-five volumes of *Analecta hymnica medii aevi*, ed. G. M. Dreves, C. Blume, and H. M. Bannister (Leipzig, 1886–1922), to which a comprehensive index (*Register*, ed. M. Lütolf, Bern and Munich, 1978) has recently been added. For theoretical sources, see the bibliography to the next two chapters, adding the important recent edition of Aurelianus of Réomé, *Musica Disciplina*, by L. Gushee (*Corpus Scriptorum de Musica*, xxi): a translation of this by J. Ponte was published by the Colorado College of Music Press in 1968.

JOHN CALDWELL

Chapters 5 and 6. Early Polyphony and the Proto-Renaissance

THEORY OF NOTATION AND EARLY POLYPHONY

The texts – not always from the best sources – are conveniently assembled in Gerbert, *Scriptores ecclesiastici de musica sacra potissimum* (3 vols., St. Blaise, 1784, repr. Milan, 1931 and Hildesheim, 1963): Hucbald, *Alia Musica, Musica enchiriadis* and *Scholia enchiriadis*, and the *Dialogus* attributed to Odo are in vol. i, the *Micrologus* and other writings by Guido of Arezzo are in vol. ii. There is a translation of *Musica enchiriadis* by L. Rosenstiel (Colorado College Music Press, 1976) and a critical edition of the *Micrologus* by J. Smits van Waesberghe in *Corpus Scriptorum de Musica*, iv; there is also an edition of *Alia musica* by J. Chailley (Paris, 1965), and one of *Musica enchiriadis* by H. Schmid is promised.

The later *organum* treatises include chapter 23 of the *De musica* by John of Afflighem or John Cotton (Gerbert, op. cit., vol. ii and *Corpus scriptorum de musica*, vol. i); *Ad organum faciendum*, edited from four sources by H. Eggebrecht and F. Zaminer, with German translation (Mainz, 1970); and *Der Vatikanische Organum-Traktat Ottob. lat. 3025*, ed. F. Zaminer (Tutzing, 1959).

Facsimiles of practical sources (Winchester troper, St. Martial and Compostela MSS) are included in the books of Apel, Holschneider, and Parrish cited below; there is a complete facsimile and transcription of the Compostela MS ed. W. M. Whitehill and G. Prado (3 vols., Compostela, 1944). Transcriptions are available in a variety of sources: a start may be made with the excellent selections in the *Historical Anthology of Music* and the *Oxford Anthology of Music: Medieval Music*. There is also a complete transcription, into modern plainsong notation, of the Compostela MS by P. Wagner, entitled *Die Gesänge der Jakobusliturgie zu Santiago de Compostela* (Freiburg-im-Schweiz, 1931).

Further reading: W. Apel, *The Notation of Polyphonic Music* (5th ed., Cambridge, Mass., 1953) and C. Parrish, *The Notation of Medieval Music* (London, 1958) provide facsimiles from both theoretical and practical sources, and ample explanations. Apart from the references in the text, the following, in German, are of particular importance: M. Markovits, *Das Tonsystem der abendländischen Musik im frühen Mittelalter* (Bern and Stuttgart, 1977) (on the tonal system as presented by early medieval theorists) and A. Holschneider, *Die organa von Winchester* (Hildesheim, 1968) (on the *organa* of the Winchester troper in Cambridge, with plates and some attempted transcriptions).

Bibliography

TROPE, SEQUENCE, AND LITURGICAL DRAMA

There is an important edition of tropes in P. Evans, *The early trope repertory of St. Martial de Limoges* (Princeton, 1970); a complete edition is initiated with *Introitus-Tropen I*, ed. Günther Weiss (*Monumenta Monodica Medii Aevi*, iii: Kassel etc., 1970). Early sequences (without texts) are represented primarily by Dom A. Hughes, *Anglo-French sequelae* (Burnham and London, 1934, repr. Farnborough, 1966); there are also transcriptions of those of Notker by Crocker (below). There is a transcription with facsimile by G. Tintori of the 'Fleury' play-book, entitled *Sacre rappresentazioni nel manoscritto 201 della Bibliothèque municipale di Orléans* (Cremona, 1958) and several transcriptions of individual plays into modern rhythmic values by W. L. Smoldon: *Officium pastorum, Peregrinus, The Play of Herod, Sponsus,* and *Visitatio sepulchri* (London 1964–72) and *The Play of Daniel* (Plainsong and Medieval Music Society, 1960, rev. D. Wulstan, 1976) – also available in an edition by Noah Greenberg (New York, 1959).

Further reading: on tropes, see especially P. Evans, op. cit.; A. Planchart, *The Repertory of Tropes at Winchester* (2 vols., Princeton, 1977). The series *Corpus troporum*, published by the University of Stockholm, will eventually encompass the complete publication of all the early texts: two volumes have appeared, *Cycle de Noël*, ed. R. Jonsson (1975; includes a musical study by N. Sevestre and many valuable plates) and *Tropes de l'alleluia*, ed. O. Marcusson (1976). R. Crocker, *The Early Medieval Sequence* (Berkeley, Calif., 1977) approaches the sequence from the point of view of the texted versions (especially those of Notker); like P. Dronke, 'The Beginnings of the Sequence', in *Beiträge zur Geschichte der deutschen Sprache und Literatur*, lxxxvii (1965), pp. 43–73, he tends to discount the traditional view of the early close association of the sequence with the liturgical Alleluia. Dronke's views are summarized in his *The Medieval Lyric* (London, 1968, 2nd ed. 1978), pp. 38–9. The standard work on Notker, with the complete texts of his sequences, is W. von den Steinen, *Notker der Dichter und seine geistige Welt* (2 vols., Bern, 1948). Liturgical drama will be covered by W. L. Smoldon, *The Music Drama of the Medieval Church* (London, 1980), which supplements and corrects K. Young, *The Drama of the Medieval Church* (2 vols., Oxford, 1933, repr. 1951, 1962). Another recent important work is D. Dolan, *Le drame liturgique de Pâques en Normandie et en Angleterre au moyen-âge* (Paris, 1975), with its own substantial bibliography.

SECULAR AND OTHER NON-LITURGICAL MONOPHONIC SONG

Several important sources are available in facsimile: those marked * also include complete musical transcriptions. Latin songs: K. Breul, *The Cambridge Songs* (Cambridge, 1915); B. Bischoff, *Carmina Burana* (New York, 1967). See also the facsimiles of W[1], F, and Fa in the next section. Troubadours and trouvères: P. Aubry, *Le chansonnier d'Arsenal* (Paris, 1909, incomplete); J. Beck, *Le chansonnier Cangé* (2 vols., Paris and Philadelphia, 1927)*; J. and L. Beck, *Le manuscrit du roi* (2 vols., London and Philadelphia, 1938)*; F. W. Bourdillon, *C'est decausï & de nicolete* (Oxford, 1896; his non-facsimile edition with music was published Manchester, 1930); A. Jeanroy, *Le chansonnier d'Arras* (Paris, 1925); P. Meyer and G. Raynaud, *Le chansonnier français de Saint-Germain-des-Prés* (Paris, 1892); U. Sesini, *Le melodie trobadoriche nel canzionere provenzale della Biblioteca Ambrosiana R.71 Sup.* (Turin, 1942)*. German song: K. K. Müller, *Die Jenaer Liederhandschrift* (Jena, 1896; note also the 2-volume diplomatic transcription by

G. Holz, F. Saran and E. Bernouilli, Leipzig, 1901, repr. Hildesheim, 1966, and the more recent facsimile by F. Gennrich, Langen-bei-Frankfurt, 1963); H. Rietsch, *Gesänge von Frauenlob, Reinmar von Zweter und Alexander* (*DTÖ*, xx.2 (71), Vienna, 1913)*; W. Schmieder and E. Wiessner, *Lieder von Neidhart* (*DTO*, xxxvii.1 (71), Vienna, 1930); F. Gennrich, *Die Colmarer Liederhandschrift* (Langen-bei-Frankfurt, 1967: cf. P. Runge, *Die Sangweisen der Comarer Hand-schrift und die Liederhandschrift Donaueschingen*, Leipzig, 1896); F. Delbono, *Oswald von Wolkenstein: Handschrift A* (Graz, 1977). Spanish song: H. Anglès, *La musica de las Cantigas de Santa Maria del Rey Alfonso el Sabio* (3 vols., Barcelona, 1942–64)*; P. Vindel, *Las siete canciones de amor* (Madrid, 1915). Italian song: F. Liuzzi, *La Lauda e i primordi della melodia italiana* (2 vols., Rome, 1935)*.

The texts of the Cambridge Songs were edited by K. Strecker, *Die Cambridger Lieder* (Berlin, 1926), and of *Carmina burana* by A. Hilka, O. Schumann, and B. Bischoff (4 vols., Heidelberg, 1930–70). For troubadour texts, R. T. Hill and T. G. Bergin, *Anthology of the Provençal Troubadours* (2nd ed., 2 vols., New Haven, 1973) is invaluable. There are numerous editions of individual troubadour and trouvère poets: to his *Bernart von Ventadorn* (Halle, 1915, including editions of all texts and facsimiles of all songs with music) C. Appel added later his *Die Singweisen Bernarts von Ventadorn* (Halle, 1934). A complete edition of the troubadour melodies has been completed by F. Gennrich, *Der musikalische Nachlass der Troubadours* (3 vols., Darmstadt, 1958–60 and Langen-bei-Frankfurt, 1965); and a similar exercise has been initiated by H. van der Werf, *Trouvères-Melodien I* (*Monumenta Monodica Medii Aevi*, xi, Kassel etc., 1977). This approach, though well-intentioned, does not do justice to the songs as musico-poetic entities. For this purpose F. Gennrich, *Lo gai saber: 50 ausgewählte Troubadourlieder* (Darmstadt, 1959) is admirable. The works of Adam de la Halle were edited by Coussemaker (Paris, 1872, repr. Farnborough, 1966), and more recently by N. Wilkins (*CMM*, 44, 1967); *Le Jeu de Robin et de Marion* was edited by E. Langlois (Paris, 1896), and more recently by F. Gennrich (Langen-bei-Frankfurt, 1962). There are two editions of J. de l'Escurel: F. Gennrich (Langen-bei-Frankfurt, 1964) and N. Wilkins (*CMM*, 30, 1966). Note also A. Jeanroy, L. Brandin and P. Aubry, *Lais et descorts français du XIIIᵉ siècle* (Paris, 1901). German song has been dealt with by R. J. Taylor, *Die Melodien der weltlichen Lieder des Mittelalters* (2 vols., Stuttgart, 1964: also his *The Art of the Minnesinger*, 2 vols., Cardiff, 1968); individual editions include A. D. Hatto and R. J. Taylor, *The Songs of Neidhart von Reuental* (Manchester, 1958), F. Gennrich, *Neidhart-Lieder* (Langen-bei-Frankfurt, 1962), and J. Schatz and O. Koller, *Oswald von Wolkenstein: Geistliche und weltliche Lieder* (*DTÖ*. ix.1 (18), Vienna, 1902). An excellent small selection from the main repertories is F. Gennrich, *Troubadours, Trouvères, Minne- und Meistersinger (Das Musikwerk*, ii: Cologne and London, 1960).

Much of the above contains a substantial amount of commentary. In addition the following bibliographical works are indispensable: A. Jeanroy, *Bibliographie sommaire des chansonniers français du moyen-âge* (Paris, 1918); A. Pillet and H. Carstens, *Bibliographie der troubadours* (Halle, 1933); and H. Spanke, *G. Raynauds Bibliographie des altfranzösischen Liedes* (Leiden, 1955). The earlier standard commentaries by P. Aubry, *Trouvères et troubadours* (Paris, 1909) and J. Beck, *La musique des troubadours* (Paris, 1910) are still very readable; F. Gennrich, *Grundriss einer Formenlehre des mittelalterlichen Liedes* (Halle, 1932) and *Rondeaux, Virelais und Balladen* (2 vols., Dresden 1921 and Göttingen 1927, with music) are standard. For Latin song, F. J. E. Raby, *A History of Christian-*

Bibliography

Latin Poetry (2nd ed., Oxford, 1953) and *A History of Secular Latin Poetry in the Middle Ages* (2nd ed., 2 vols., Oxford, 1957), with P. Dronke, *Medieval Latin and the Rise of European Love-Lyric* (2 vols., 2nd ed., 1968) are essential. A recent valuable work in English is H. van der Werf, *The chansons of the Troubadours and Trouvères* (Utrecht, 1972), while P. Dronke, *The Medieval Lyric* (2nd ed., London, 1978) is a highly attractive introduction to the whole field from a primarily literary point of view. English song is best studied with the aid of the references given in the masterly article of C. Page, 'A catalogue and bibliography of English song from its beginnings to *c.* 1300', *Research Chronicle of the Royal Musical Association*, xiii, pp. 67–83, with facsimiles; and mention must finally be made of J. Stevens, ' "La grande chanson courtoise": the chansons of Adam de la Halle' in *PRMA*, ci (1974–5), pp. 11–30.

POLYPHONY IN THE LATE TWELFTH AND THIRTEENTH CENTURIES

Facsimiles are available as follows (using the recognized *sigla*: a star indicates the inclusion of transcriptions): W^1: J. H. Baxter, *An Old St. Andrews Music Book* (London, 1931, to be used with Dom A. Hughes, *Index to the facsimile edition of MS. Wolfenbüttel 677*, Edinburgh and London, 1939); W^2, F, and Ma: ed. L. Dittmer in his series *Publications of Medieval Musical Manuscripts* (New York: Institute of Medieval Music), ii (1960), x–xi (n.d.), and i (1957) respectively; St. V: E. Thurston, *The Music in the St. Victor Manuscript* (Toronto, 1959); Ba: P. Aubry, *Cent motets du XIIIe siècle* (3 vols., Paris, 1908, repr. New York 1964)*; Mo: Y. Rokseth, *Polyphonies du XIIIe siècle* (4 vols., Paris, 1935–9)*; Hu: H. Anglés, *El Codex musical de Las Huelgas* (3 vols., Barcelona 1931)*; Tu: A. Auda, *Les 'motets wallons' du manuscrit de Turin: Vari 42* (2 vols., Brussels, 1953) and Fa: P. Aubry, *Le Roman de Fauvel* (Paris, 1907).

Editions, apart from those incorporated in the above, include transcriptions of the Leoninus *organa* by Waite (see below); of the three- and four-part organa by H. Husmann, *Die drei- und vierstimmigen Notre-Dame-Organa* (Leipzig, 1940, repr. Hildesheim and Wiesbaden, 1967); J. Knapp, *Thirty-five Conductus for Two and Three Voices* (Yale, 1965); E. Thurston, *The Works of Perotin* (New York, 1970); G. A. Anderson, *The Latin Compositions in Fascicules VII and VIII of . . . Wolfenbüttel Helmstadt 1099 (1206)* (New York, 1968–76); and the same author's *Motets of the Manuscript La Clayette* (*CMM*, 68, 1975) and *Compositions of the Bamberg Manuscript* (*CMM*, 75, 1977). There is an attractive selection in *Das Musikwerk*, ix (Cologne and London, 1962). (For the motets of Fa see bibliography to next two chapters.)

The fundamental work · of reference is F. Ludwig, *Repertorium organorum recentioris et motetorum vetustissimi stili* (Halle, 1910, only vol. i, pt. 1 published; reprinted Hildesheim, 1964, and supplemented from proof-sheets of later parts, and other material, both by L. Dittmer in his series *Musicological Studies*, xvii, and F. Gennrich in *Summa Musica Medii Aevi*, vii–viii). Gennrich has also added his own useful *Bibliographie der ältesten französischen und lateinischen Motetten* (Darmstadt, 1957). For English-speaking readers much of the essential information is conveyed in W. Waite, *The Rhythm of Twelfth-Century Polyphony* (New Haven and London, 1954, with transcription of the two-part organa of W^1). The periodical literature is apt to become dated, but the following are still essential: W. Waite, 'The Abbreviation of the Magnus Liber', *JAMS*, xiv (1961), pp. 147–58; H. Husmann, 'The Enlargement of the Magnus Liber Organi . . .' ibid., xvi (1963), pp. 176–203; and idem, 'The Origin and Destination of the *Magnus Liber Organi*' in *MQ*, xlix (1963), pp. 311–30. There are, alas, no reliable English translations of the major theorists, but there are excellent editions, with German translation, of Anonymus IV by F. Reckow (2 vols., Wiesbaden, 1967) and of Johannes de Garlandia by E. Reimer (2 vols., Wiesbaden, 1972). Other editions superseding those of Coussemaker include those of Hieronymus de Moravia by S. Cserba (Regensburg, 1935) and of Franco by G. Reaney (*Corpus Scriptorum de Musica*, xviii).

JOHN CALDWELL

Chapters 7 and 8. Ars nova and the European Synthesis

THE FOURTEENTH CENTURY IN FRANCE

The *Roman de Fauvel* MS was edited in facsimile by P. Aubry (Paris, 1907); its motets are given complete in *Polyphonic Music of the Fourteenth Century*, i, ed. L. Schrade (Monaco, 1956). This volume also includes the remaining known works of Philippe de Vitry and the so-called Masses of Toulouse, Tournai, and Barcelona. The works of Machaut were edited by F. Ludwig and H. Besseler (4 vols., Leipzig, 1926–43, repr. Wiesbaden, 1954) and by L. Schrade, *Polyphonic Music of the Fourteenth Century*, ii–iii (Monaco, 1956): these are still the best editions of Machaut's works, though of many separate editions of the Mass that by D. Stevens (London, 1973) is clearly presented. More sacred and secular music of the fourteenth and early fifteenth centuries is found in *CMM*, 11, 13, 21, 29, 36, 37, 39 and 53, and in *Polyphonic Music of the Fourteenth Century*, v; there is also W. Apel, *French Secular Music of the Late Fourteenth Century* (Cambridge, Mass., 1950).

A recent introductory study of value is G. Reaney, *Machaut* (London, 1971). The standard biography of Machaut is still A. Machabey, *Guillaume de Machault* (2 vols., Paris, 1955). Reaney gives a good bibliography of Machaut; the sexcentenary of his death in 1977 was commemorated in a number of journals, especially *Early Music*. Other aspects of the period are dealt with in *NOHM*, iii, ch. 1, and its bibliography.

THE FOURTEENTH CENTURY IN ITALY

The standard editions include *CMM*, 8, 36, 37, and 57 (Faenza Codex), and *Polyphonic Music of the Fourteeth Century*, iv (Landini), vi–ix (secular music), xii (sacred music), and the following separate editions: L. Ellinwood, *The Works of Francesco Landini* (Cambridge, Mass., 1939); T. W. Marrocco, *Fourteenth-Century Italian Cacce* (2nd ed., Cambridge, Mass., 1961); and J. Wolf, *Der Squarcialupi Codex* (unreliable) (Lippstadt, 1955).

See *NOHM*, iii, ch. 2, for further bibliography. Of more recent publications note especially *L'Ars nova italiana del trecento* (3 vols., Certaldo, 1962–70), and K. von Fischer, 'The Sacred Polyphony of the Italian Trecento', *PRMA*, c (1973–4). The standard work on Ciconia, with edition of the music, is S. Clercx-Lejeune, *Johannes Ciconia* (2 vols., Brussels, 1960).

Bibliography

ENGLISH MUSIC TO ABOUT 1470

Much of the material is available in facsimile in H. E. Wooldridge, *Early English Harmony*, i (London, 1897) and J. Stainer, *Early Bodleian Music*, i (London, 1901); the second volume in each case contained transcriptions, some of them of dubious value. The St. Andrew's manuscript (W¹) was edited in facsimile by J. H. Baxter, *An Old St. Andrew's Music Book* (London, 1931). The music from Worcester was first edited by Dom A. Hughes, *Worcester Medieval Harmony* (London, 1928), with some good facsimiles, and latterly by L. Dittmer, *The Worcester Fragments* (American Institute of Musicology, 1957). An edition of all late thirteenth- and fourteenth-century music is planned for *Polyphonic Music of the Fourteenth Century* in 3 volumes. The Old Hall Manuscript was edited in 3 volumes by A. Ramsbotham, H. B. Collins, and Dom A. Hughes (London, 1933–8), and more recently by M. Bent and A. Hughes (*CMM*, 46).

Fifteenth-century music is included in *MB*, iv (*Medieval Carols*, ed. J. Stevens) and viii (*The Works of John Dunstable*, ed. M. Bukofzer: 2nd ed., revised by B. Trowell, M. Bent, and I. Bent, 1970); *Early English Church Music*, viii (*Fifteenth-Century Liturgical Music*, I, ed. A. Hughes); and G. McPeek, *The British Museum Manuscript 3307* (London, 1963). There is a large number of single editions available, and a considerable quantity of English music in *Sechs* [later *Sieben*] *Trienter Codices*, ed. G. Adler and others (8 vols. to date: *DTÖ*, vii. 1–2 [14–15], xi. 1 [22], xix. 1 [38], xxvii. 1 [53], xxxi [61], xl [76], 120).

The literature includes especially F. Ll. Harrison, *Music in Medieval Britain* (2nd ed., London, 1963). Many topics of interest are dealt with in M. Bukofzer, *Studies in Medieval and Renaissance Music* (London, 1951). Numerous articles continue to apear in such journals as *Musica Disciplina, Journal of the American Musicological Society, Music and Letters*, and the *Proceedings* and *Research Chronicle* of the Royal Musical Association. The standard work on the carols, with complete edition of the English-language texts, is R. L. Greene, *The Early English Carols* (2nd ed., Oxford, 1977).

FIFTEENTH-CENTURY MUSIC ON THE CONTINENT, *c.* 1420–70

The contents of the Oxford Canonici MS were edited in a series of older editions: J. Stainer, *Dufay and his Contemporaries* (London, 1898: the transcriptions are largely superseded but there is an excellent description of the MS by W. B. Nicholson); J. Marix, *Les musiciens à la cour de Bourgogne au XVᵉ siècle* (Paris, 1937); C. Van den Borren, *Polyphonia sacra* (London, 1932, repr. 1962) and *Pièces polyphoniques profanes de provenance liégeoise* (Brussels, 1950). The complete works of Dufay are edited by G. de Van and H. Besseler as *CMM*, 1; those of Walter Frye as *CMM*, 19, ed. S. Kenney. The 'L'homme armé' Masses of Dufay, Busnois, Caron, Faugues, Regis, Ockeghem, de Orto, Basiron, Tinctoris, and Vacqueras are edited by L. Feininger as *Monumenta polyphoniae liturgicae*, I (Rome, 1947–). A great quantity of music from the period is in the edition of the Trent codices already cited. The chansons of Binchois have been edited by W. Rehm (Mainz, 1957).

For Oswald von Wolkenstein, see bibliography to chapters 5 and 6; for the *Lochamer* and *Glogauer* song-books, and the early German keyboard repertory, see the references in the text.

Standard literature on the period includes C. Van den Borren, *Guillaume Dufay* (Brussels, 1925: in French); C. Hamm, *A Chronology of the Works of Guillaume Dufay* (Princeton, 1962, repr. with corrections 1967); E. Sparks, *Cantus Firmus in*

874

Mass and Motet, 1420–1520 (Berkeley and Los Angeles, 1963); M. F. Bukofzer, *Studies* (cited above); J. Marix, *Histoire de la musique et des musiciens de la cour de Bourgogne sous le règne de Philippe le Bon* (Strasbourg, 1939); H. Moser, *Paul Hofhaimer* (Stuttgart, 1929, repr. Hildesheim, 1965: in German); L. Cuyler, *The Emperor Maximilian I and Music* (London, 1973). There is also a large periodical literature: see the journals already cited, and *Acta musicologica*, which carries material in various languages including English. The 1975 volume of the *Journal of the American Musicological Society* included several important articles on Dufay.

JOHN CALDWELL

Chapter 9. The Impact of the Renaissance

The concept of Renaissance in musical history is discussed in F. Blume, *Renaissance and Baroque Music: a comprehensive survey* (New York, 1967). For more detailed continuous accounts of the period, one has to turn to Gustave Reese's *Music in the Renaissance* (London, 1954), chapters VIII–XII of *NOHM*, iii (London, 1960), and in German H. C. Wolff, *Die Music der alten Niederländer* (Leipzig, 1956). E. H. Sparks, *Cantus firmus in mass and motet 1420–1520* (Berkeley/Los Angeles, 1963) and F.Ll. Harrison, *Music in Medieval Britain* (London 1958) continue their studies with this era. The only ample study of a major composer in English is ed. E. Lowinsky, *Josquin des Prez* (London, 1976), a series of essays which cover many aspects of both his life and works. On a lesser figure is E. B. Warren, *The Life and Works of Robert Fayrfax* (*MSD* xxii, AIM 1969). The most valuable periodical literature on individual composers is mentioned in the footnotes, to which may be added N. Davison, 'The motets of Pierre de la Rue', *MQ*, xlviii (1962), p. 19. On secular music J. Stevens, *Music and Poetry in the Early Tudor Court* (London, 1961). While the frottola has no major study in English, the discussion of its place in the development of the madrigal will be found in J. Haar (ed.), *Chanson and Madrigal 1480–1530* (Cambridge, Mass., 1966) and an ample account in Italian is F. Luisi, *La Musica Vocale nel Rinascimento* (Turin, 1977). The introductions to H. Hewitt's edition of *Harmoniae Musices Odhecaton* and *Canti B* (Cambridge, Mass., 1946 and 1967); L. Cuyler's of *H. Isaac's Choralis Constantinus Bk III* (Ann Arbor, 1950); and E. Lowinsky's of *The Medici Codex of 1518* (*Monuments of Renaissance Music*, 3 vols, Chicago, 1968) all contain valuable historical material and the final essay '*Caput*: a liturgico-musical study' in M. Bukofzer, *Studies in Mediaeval and Renaissance Music* (New York, 1950) gives insight into the development of the cyclic mass.

EDITIONS

A tremendous amount of music of the period is available in collected editions. That of Josquin, *Werke* (Amsterdam 1926–69), suffers in some respects from antiquated editorial procedures which make a new edition desirable; it is nevertheless quite usable. Only the Masses have so far appeared in Ockeghem, *Collected Works* (1947–); Obrecht has fared only a little better in the latest edition, *Opera Omnia*, ed. Smijers and Marcus van Crevel (1953–), but the previous edition, *Werke*, ed. J. Wolf (Leipzig, 1908–21, photo reproduction 1966) although using old clefs, is a truly complete edition. The *CMM* series contains various editions in varying states of completion: Brumel (5), Gafurius (10) Compère (15), Fayrfax (17), Agricola (22),

Bibliography

Ghiselin-Verbonnet (23), Andreas de Silva (49), Genet (58), Hayne van Ghizeghem (74). The works of Isaac are available partly in *DTÖ* x and xxxii; partly in the edition by Cuyler mentioned above; and in *CMM*, 65. The Eton Choirbook is available in *MB*, x–xii (x in rev. 2nd ed.), as is an ample selection of songs and consort pieces in *Music at the Court of Henry VIII* (*MB*, xviii, rev. ed. 1969). For practical editions and individual compositions consult the footnotes. The series *Das Chorwerk* also contains a large number of volumes devoted to music of the period.

DENIS ARNOLD

Chapter 10. Music in the Islamic World

The most important collection of translated source materials is contained in R. D'Erlanger, *La musique arabe*, i–iv (Paris, 1930–59). This includes works by al-Fārābī (d. 950), Ibn Sīnā (Avicenna, d. 1037), Ṣafī al-Dīn (d. 1294), and al-Lādhiqī (late fifteenth century), thereby providing a representative selection of the theoretical literature, aspects of which are surveyed in L. Manik, *Das arabische Tonsystem im Mittelalter* (Leiden, 1969). A tenth-century work containing practical as well as theoretical information is al-Ḥasan b. Aḥmad b. 'Alī al-Kātib, *La perfection des connaissances musicales. Kitab kamāl adab al-ghinā'* (tr. A. Shiloah, Paris, 1972). A representative example from the same period of the cosmological approach to music is to be found in A. Shiloah, 'L'épitre sur la musique des Ikhwan al-Safa', tr. annotée, *Revue des études islamiques*, xxxii (1964) and xxxiv (1966). For further material and references see H. G. Farmer, 'The influence of music: From Arabian sources', *PRMA*, lii (1925–6), p. 89. The debate on the legal admissibility of music and the Sufi defence of music are illustrated in J. Robson, *Tracts on listening to music* (London, 1938), D. B. Macdonald, 'Emotional religion in Islam as affected by music and singing . . .', *Journal of the Royal Asiatic Society*, 1901, 1902. The most comprehensive bibliography of (Arabic) source materials is H. G. Farmer, *The sources of Arabian music* (Bearsden, 1940, rev. ed. Leiden, 1965).

For general history and background, H. G. Farmer, *A History of Arabian music to the XIIIth century* (London, 1929, repr. 1967) is still useful, while among the more informative survey articles are H. G. Farmer, 'An outline history of music and musical theory', in A. U. Pope, *A survey of Persian art* (London, 1938), Farmer, 'The music of Islam', in *NOHM*, i (London, 1957), and the even more substantial H. Hickmann, 'Die Musik des arabisch-islamischen Bereichs', in *Handbuch der Orientalistik. Erste Abteilung. Ergänzungsband IV. Orientalische Musik* (Leiden/Köln, 1970), with an appendix on European instrument names of Arabic origin. Farmer's *Islam* (*Musikgeschichte in Bildern, Band III, Lieferung 2*) (Leipzig, n.d.) may serve as an introduction to instruments, while the controversial question of Arab musical influences is dealt with (in rather polemical fashion) in his *Historical facts for the Arabian musical influence* (London, 1930). For a more recent discussion of this topic see E. B. Perkuhn, *Die Theorien zum arabischen Einfluss auf die europäische Musik des Mittelalters* (Walldorf-Hessen, 1976).

Further useful survey articles which contain material on modern practice include those by Rouanet (North Africa) and Raouf Yekta (Turkey) in A. Lavignac and L. de La Laurencie, *Encyclopédie de la musique*, i (Paris, 1922). Among other general works (varying considerably in size and scope) which deal with present-day practice the following may be noted: M. Barkechli and M. Maroufi, *La musique tradi-*

tionelle de l'Iran (Tehran, 1963), N. Caron and D. Safvate, *Les traditions musicales: Iran* (Paris, 1966), M. D'Erlanger, *La musique arabe*, v and vi (Paris, 1930–59), S. Jargy, *La musique arabe* (Paris, 1971), L. E. R. Picken, *The Folk Musical Instruments of Turkey* (London, 1975), K. and U. Reinhard, *Turquie (les traditions musicales)* (Paris, 1969), H. H. Touma, *Die Musik der Araber* (Wilhelmshaven, 1975), and E. Zonis, *Classical Persian music, an introduction* (Cambridge, Mass., 1973). For an introduction to religious music in Islam consult the relevant articles in Porte J. (ed.), *Encyclopédie des musiques sacrées*, i (Paris, 1968).

OWEN WRIGHT

Chapters 11 and 12. Music of the Reformation and Counter-Reformation

The fullest account of the proposed reforms of the Council of Trent is given in L. Lockwood, *The Counter-Reformation and the Masses of Vincenzo Ruffo* (Vienna/London/Milan, 1970) while a briefer study which contains transcripts of the main documents is K. G. Fellerer's 'Church Music and the Council of Trent', *MQ*, xxxix (1953), p. 576. There are no comprehensive studies of the major Netherlands composers in English. J. Schmidt-Görg, *Nicolas Gombert, Kapellmeister Kaiser Karls V. Leben und Werk* (Bonn, 1938) and K. Ph. Bernet Kempers *Jacobus Clemens non Papa und seine Motetten* (Augsburg, 1929) are two fundamental works, while E. Lowinsky's book *Secret Chromatic Art in the Netherlands Motet* (New York, 1946) and an article 'Matthaeus Greiter's *Fortuna*: An Experiment in Chromaticism and in musical Iconography', *MQ*, xlii (1956), p. 500 and *MQ*, xliii (1957), p. 68 offers insights into the mental approach to music of the humanists; as does the fascinating study by D. P. Walker, 'Musical Humanism in the 16th and Early 17th Centuries', *Music Review*, ii (1941), pp. 1, 111, 220, and 288 and iii (1942), p. 55. On the later composers of church music the major detailed study in English of Palestrina's music is K. Jeppesen *The Style of Palestrina and the Dissonance* (rev. ed. London, 1946) but for chronology and a more general view of the style a German book, K. G. Fellerer's *Palestrina* (rev. ed. Düsseldorf, 1960), is necessary. Lassus has no English biographer, but there is an extremely comprehensive monograph in German, W. Boetticher, *Orlando di Lasso und seine Zeit (1532–1594)* (Kassel and Basel, 1958), and, although ageing, C. van den Borren, *Orlande de Lassus* (Paris 1920; later editions in several languages) is still useful. No up-to-date account of Victoria's music is available, although he and Morales are discussed at some length in R. Stevenson, *Spanish Cathedral Music in the Golden Age* (Berkeley and Los Angeles 1961).

The music of the Venetian school of composers is not yet treated in depth in any single study although three books are available on its principal composer, Giovanni Gabrieli: C. v. Winterfeld, *Johannes Gabrieli und sein Zeitalter* (Berlin, 1834, repr. 1965), E. Kenton, *Life and works of Giovanni Gabrieli* (Rome, 1967) and D. Arnold, *Giovanni Gabrieli and Music of the Venetian High Renaissance* (London, 1979). There are several works on Monteverdi which deal with both madrigals and church music, such as L. Schrade, *Monteverdi, Creator of Modern Music* (New York, 1950) and D. Arnold, *Monteverdi* (London, 1963), while a comprehensive account of the background to his early religious works is to be found in J. G. Kurtzman, 'Some

Bibliography

Historical Perspectives on the Monteverdi Vespers', *Analecta Musicologica* Bd 15 (1975), p. 29. The origins of church music using basso continuo are dealt with in F. T. Arnold, *The Art of Accompaniment from a Thorough Bass as practised in the XVII and XVIII Centuries* (Oxford, 1931), also in F. Mompellio *Lodovico Viadana, Musicista fra due secoli* (Florence, 1967). The standard work on the music of the Lutheran church is F. Blume, *Die Evangelische Kirchenmusik* (Potsdam, 1931, Eng. ed. New York, 1974) and of the Anglican church, P. le Huray, *Music and the Reformation in England 1549–1660* (London, 1967); the later English composers for the Catholic rite are dealt with in F. L. Harrison, *Music in Medieval Britain* (London, 1958) and H. Benham, *Latin Church Music in England* c. *1460–1575* (London, 1977). Monographs in this sphere are few but P. Doe, *Tallis* (2nd ed. London, 1976) is useful, and a large gap on Byrd is partly filled by J. Kerman, 'Byrd's Motets: Chronology and Canon', *JAMS*, xiv (1961), p. 359.

The standard work on the madrigal is A. Einstein *The Italian Madrigal* (three vols., Princeton, 1949). Useful essays on the origins of the madrigal are contained in J. Haar, *Chanson and Madrigal 1480–1530* (Cambridge, Mass, 1964). The most up-to-date account of the development of the chanson is the chapter by C. van den Borren in *NOHM* iv, while on English music, the article by P. Brett, 'The English Consort Song', *PRMA* lxxxviii (1961–2), p. 73 summarizes the progress of non-madrigalian forms, and J. Kerman, *The Elizabethan Madrigal* (New York, 1962) is the fullest account of Italianate music. W. Apel, *The History of Keyboard Music to 1700* (Bloomington, Indiana, 1972) is the most comprehensive English account of this topic, although still worth supplementing by the classic, O. Kinkeldey, *Orgel und Klavier in der Musik des 16 Jahrhunderts* (Leizpig, 1910); on the important English school of composers, J. A. Caldwell, *English Keyboard Music before the 19th Century* (Oxford, 1973) and C. van den Borren, *The Sources of Keyboard Music in England* (London, 1913) are both useful. There is no such account of ensemble music, but a valuable if idiosyncratic study of its English development is contained in E. H. Meyer, *English Chamber Music* (London, 1946), and there are several valuable articles on particular genres: R. T. Dart, 'Morley's Consort Lessons of 1599', *PRMA*, lxxiv (1947–8), p. 1, R. Donington and R. T. Dart, 'The origins of the In nomine', *ML*, xxx (1949), p. 101, and G. Reese, 'The Origins of the English "In nomine" ', *JAMS*, ii (1949), p. 7. Venetian ensemble music is dealt with in S. Kunze, *Die Instrumentalmusik Giovanni Gabrielis* (Tutzing, 1963) and also the works on this composer by Arnold and Kenton mentioned above.

EDITIONS

Editions of music of this period are so many that for those of the works mentioned in the text, the reader must be referred to the footnotes. The most important source of collected editions of composers is the series *Corpus Mensurabilis Musicae* which includes the works of Willaert, Clemens non Papa, Gombert, Giovanni Gabrieli, Rore, Festa, Ludford, Verdelot, Wert, Arcadelt, Mouton, Sandrin, Merulo (sacred music only), Claudin de Sermisy, Crecquillon, and Marenzio (sacred music). Palestrina's music has been the subject of two collected editions, one edited mainly by Germans (Leipzig, 1862–1903) which contains a certain amount of interesting supplementary material not contained in the more recent *Le Opere Complete* (Rome, 1939–   ) which however has the advantage of modern clefs and views on underlay. Lassus's works are collected in two complementary series, the first (Leipzig, 1894–1926) containing the greater part of the motets and the bulk of the secular music (not always taken from the best sources) and the newer set (Kassel, 1956–) important mainly for the Masses. Victoria's music is completely available in the *Opera Omnia* (Leipzig, 1902–13) and that of Morales in the series *Monumentos de la música española*, Vols 11, 13, 15, 17, 20, 21, 24, and 34.

The collected works of Byrd were first published nearly complete (London, 1937–) and a revised and amplified edition is in progress. The *Sämtliche Werke* of J. Walter (Kassel, 1953–70), Senfl (Basel/Wolfenbüttel, 1937–) and Rhau (Kassel, 1955–), Lechner (Kassel, 1954–), and Hassler (Wiesbaden, 1961–) are the most important modern sources for German music. Janequin's *Chansons polyphoniques* (Monaco, 1965–71) and Goudimel's *Oeuvres complètes* (New York, 1967–) are similarly important for French vocal music. The work of the English school of church musicians is largely contained in two series, *Tudor Church Music* (London, 1922–9) and *Early English Church Music* (London, 1963–), especially important for its complete edition of Tallis's Anglican music (Vols. 12 and 13) and the anthems of Tomkins (Vols 5, 9, 14) to which must be added Weelkes, *Collected Anthems* (*MB*, xxiii). The keyboard works of individual composers are referred to comprehensively in the footnotes, although it must be noted that many of the earlier editions of English keyboard collections are less accurate than the volumes of separate composers in *Musica Britannica*: Tomkins (v), Bull (xiv, xix), Gibbons (xx), Farnaby (xxiv), Byrd (xxvii, xxviii). There are two collected editions of Sweelinck, *Werken van Jan Pieterszoon Sweelinck* (Leipzig, 1894–1901) and a newer, not yet complete *Werke* (Amsterdam, 1943–). Similarly, although ensemble music is largely scattered throughout various series, vol 1 of *Monuments of Renaissance Music* must be mentioned as containing the *Musica Nova* of Willaert and others; and the first two volumes of *Istituzioni e Monumenti dell' Arte Musicale Italiana* for not only editions of G. Gabrieli's early instrumental pieces, but also valuable prefatory matter. The most notable anthology of large-scale ensemble music is contained in L. E. Bartholomew, *Alessandro Raverij's Collections of 'Canzoni per Sonare' Venice 1608* (2 vols. Fort Hayes, 1965).

DENIS ARNOLD

Chapters 13 and 14. Secular Music (c. 1560–1660)

The literature on the late madrigal centres on Einstein's above mentioned study (see page 878); on the principal composers of madrigals the following are useful: Boetticher's monograph *Lasso* (see page 877), C. MacClintock, *Giaches de Wert : Life and Works* (American Institute of Musicology, 1966), the biographical studies of Monteverdi (see page 877); H. Engel, *Luca Marenzio* (Florence, 1956) and D. Arnold *Marenzio* (London, 1965); G. Watkins, *Gesualdo, the man and his music* (London, 1973). The forms of English secular music are dealt with in P. Brett, 'The English Consort Song, 1570–1625', *PRMA*, lxxxviii (1961–2) p. 73 and J. Kerman, *The Elizabethan Madrigal* (New York, 1962), while as studies of individual composers, two books by D. Brown, *Thomas Weelkes, A biographical and critical study* (London, 1969) and *Wilbye* (London, 1974), D. Stevens, *Thomas Tomkins 1572–1656*, and D. Poulton *John Dowland* (London, 1972) are all valuable. There is no comparable survey of German madrigalian music, although R. Schwarz, 'Hans Leo Hassler unter dem Einfluss der italiënischen Madrigalisten', *VfMw*, ix (1893), p. 1 is a substantial contribution. An outline survey of the late madrigal is contained

879

in G. Rose, 'Polyphonic Italian Madrigals of the 17th century', *ML*, xlvii (1966), p. 153.

On the origins of monody and opera there is a vast literature. The sixteenth-century academic discussions and experiments are dealt with in N. Pirrotta's book *Li due Orfei da Poliziano a Monteverdi* (Turin, 1975) and article 'Temperaments and Tendencies in the Florentine Camerata', *MQ*, xl (1954), p. 169. C. Palisca covers the ground from a different aspect in 'Girolamo Mei: Mentor to the Florentine Camerata', *MQ*, xl (1954), p. 1 and *Girolamo Mei. Letters on ancient and modern music to Vincenzo Galilei and Giovanni Bardi* (AIM, 1960). The Monteverdi literature mentioned above is relevant, and to it must be added A. A. Abert, *Claudio Monteverdi und das musicalische Drama* (Lippstadt, 1954). N. Fortune, 'Italian Secular Monody from 1600 to 1635; an Introductory Survey', *MQ*, xxxix (1953), p. 171 remains a good overall study of Italian song forms, though amplified by greater detail in his chapter in *NOHM*, iv. Although much cataloguing and editing of seventeenth-century cantatas has taken place in recent years, no detailed stylistic study has been published and the clearest exposition remains E. J. Dent, 'Italian Chamber Cantatas', *The Musical Antiquary*, ii (1910–11), pp. 142 and 185. English song has fared somewhat better with an overall survey, I. Spink, *English Song: Dowland to Purcell* (London, 1974), while there are relevant chapters in M. Lefkowitz, *William Lawes* (London, 1960). The general history of instrumental music is as in the bibliography for Chapters 11 and 12. To this the following specialized works must be added: O. Neighbour, *The consort and keyboard music of William Byrd* (London, 1978), A. Curtis, *Sweelinck's keyboard music* (Leiden/London, 1969), T. Dart, 'Morley's Consort Lessons of 1599', *PRMA*, lxxiv (1947–8), p. 1, and S. Kunze, *Die Instrumentalmusik Giovanni Gabrielis* (Tutzing, 1963).

EDITIONS

Of the madrigal composers, Monteverdi's complete œuvre is available in Vols. 1–10 of *Tutte le opere* (Asolo/Vienna 1926–42, reprinted 1968 with revisions in Vol. 8). Marenzio is less fully served with only the first six books for 5 voices in years 4 and 6 of *Publikationen älterer Musik* (Leipzig, 1929 and 1931 respectively); only one volume of a new series containing *Il Settimo Libro de Madrigali a 5vv* has so far appeared. Gesualdo's madrigals are contained in *Sämtliche Werk*, i–iv (Hamburg, 1957–67), while work of English composers is contained in *The English Madrigal School* (London, 1913–24, gradually being reprinted and revised as *The English Madrigals*) and that of the Danes in *Dania Sonans*, ii and iii (Copenhagen 1966, 1967). The major madrigal comedies by Croce, Banchieri, and Vecchi are available in the series *Capolavori Polifonici del Secolo XVI* (Rome, 1939–); madrigals and the other music of intermezzi are contained in A. C. Minor and B. Mitchell *A Renaissance Entertainment* (Missouri, 1968) and D. P. Walker, *Musique des Intermèdes de La Pellegrina* (Paris, 1963). The quasi-monodies of Luzzaschi are published complete in Luzzasco Luzzaschi, *Madrigali per cantare e sonare a uno, due e tre soprani* (Brescia/Kassel 1965). Caccini's *Le Nuove Musiche* is best studied in the edition by H. Wiley Hitchcock (Madison, 1970), with ample prefatory material. The most valuable collection of monody remains that of K. Jeppesen, *La Flora* (3 vols., Copenhagen, 1949–) while a broader spectrum including other countries is provided by C. MacClintock, *The Solo Song 1580–1730* (New York, 1973). The English song is available in the comprehensive series *The English School of Lutenist*

Song Writers (London 1920–   ) later called *The English lute songs*, and for the later repertoire in the anthology ed. I. Spink, *English Songs 1625–1660*, MB, xxxiii (London, 1971). The cantata repertoire is badly represented in modern editions and the available scattered examples are referred to in the footnotes. The most readily available anthology of German song is H. J. Moser, *The German Solo Song* (Cologne, 1957, English version 1958). Of the earliest operas Monteverdi's *L'Orfeo* is available in many editions, not all very accurate: that in the Collected Edition (Vol. 11) and ed. E. Tarr (Paris, 1974) may be consulted. The latter contains interesting additional material concerning the libretto and ornamented versions of the vocal line.

W. Apel, *The History of Keyboard Music to 1700* (Bloomington, Indiana, 1972) is the most comprehensive account of this topic in English, although still worth supplementing by the classic, O. Kinkeldey, *Orgel und Klavier in der Musik des 16 Jahrhunderts* (Leipzig, 1910); while on the important English school of composers, J. A. Caldwell, *English Keyboard music before the 19th century* (Oxford, 1973) and C. van den Borren, *The Sources of Keyboard Music in England* (London, 1913) are both useful. There have been many recent publications of lute music, often in facsimile, of which may be mentioned *The Collected Lute Music of John Dowland*, ed. D. Poulton and B. Lam (London, 1974), Galilei, *Il Fronimo* (facsimile Bologna, 1969), J-B. Besard, *Thesaurus Harmonicus* (facsimile Geneva, 1975), and *Oeuvres pour luth seul de Jean-Baptiste Besard* (ed. A. Souris, Paris, 1969).

DENIS ARNOLD

Chapter 15. The Early Growth of Opera (c. 1610–60)

The development of opera just after its origin is reasonably well treated, with much recent research published in serious journals. The literature on Monteverdi mentioned above contains studies of his later operas. A. A. Abert's work is especially valuable, and contains extensive analyses also of Roman operas. The Venetian background of these works is dealt with in S. T. Worsthorne, *Venetian Opera in the Seventeenth Century* (Oxford, 1954) and with more detail, H. C. Wolff, *Die Venezianische Oper in der zweiten Hälfte des 17. Jahrhunderts* (Berlin, 1932). Much information is contained in a valuable series of articles by R. Giazotto, 'La Guerra dei Palchi', in *Nuova Rivista Musicale Italiana*, i (1947), pp. 245 and 467, iii, p. 906, and v, p. 1034 and ed. M. T. Muraro, *Venezia e il melodramma nel seicento* (Florence, 1976). On composers of the next generation, useful information may be found in J. Glover *Cavalli* (London, 1978) and H. Prunières, *Cavalli et l'opéra Venetien aux XVIIIe siècle* (Paris, 1931); on Cesti there is W. C. Holmes, 'Comedy-Opera-Comic Opera' in *Analecta Musicologica*, v (1968), p. 92 and on 'Giacinto Andrea Cicognini's and Antonio Cesti's *Orontea* (1649)' in ed. W. W. Austin, *New Looks at Italian Opera* (New York, 1968), also C. V. Crowther 'The Operas of Cesti', *Music Review*, xxxi (1970), p. 93; and, on the Roman scene, W. Witzenmann 'Die Römische Barockoper *La vita humana ovvero il Trionfo della Pietà*', *Analecta Musicologica*, xv (1975), p. 158. Two books are the standard sources for the early history of opera in France, H. Prunières *L'Opéra italien en France avant Lulli* (Paris, 1913) and R. Rolland *Histoire de l'opéra en Europe avant Lully et Scarlatti* (Paris, 1931). A useful summary is also in J. R. Anthony, *French Baroque Music from Beaujoyeulx to Rameau* (London, 1973, rev. 1978). E. J. Dent's *Foundation of*

Bibliography

English Opera (London, 1928) is the standard account of its subject, which may be supplemented by the literature on Purcell (see p. 886).

Modern editions of complete operas of this period are rare, although extended extracts may be found in various studies as mentioned in the footnotes to this chapter. The later dramatic works of Monteverdi are to be found in the Collected Edition; most other editions meant for practical use are substantially altered and cut and should not be trusted. The only two Cavalli operas currently available are in this kind of edition, freely arranged by R. Leppard, *L'Ormindo* (London, 1969) and *La Calisto* (London, 1975). Cesti's *Orontea* is, on the other hand, available in an accurate version (Wellesley College, 1973). Of the pre-operatic entertainments in France and England, the Beaujoyeulx *Ballet comique de la Royne* (1582) is available in two complete editions: ed. J. W. Weckerlin and ed. C. MacClintock (AMI, 1971). For Lully there is an as yet incomplete *Oeuvres complètes* (Paris 1930–   ). The complete music to masques (as far as it survives) is to be found in *Masque in honour of the marriage of Lord Hayes* (1607) (*The Old English Edition*, Vol. 1, London/Oxford, 1889); *Cupid and Death* in *MB*, ii (London, 1951).

Facsimiles of earlier scores, both printed and manuscripts, are not uncommon, although they often provide only the skeleton of the work. The most important are those of Monteverdi's *L'Orfeo* (Augsburg, 1927 and London, 1972) and *L'Incoronazione di Poppea* (Milan, 1938); M. da Gagliano's *La Dafne* (Bologna, 1970); D. Mazzocchi's *La Catena d'Adone* (Bologna, 1969); M. Rossi's *Erminia sul Giordano* (Bologna, n.d.); S. Landi, *Il S. Alessio* (Bologna, 1970). The series *Italian Opera 1630–1770* (introductions by H. M. Brown, New York, 1977) so far includes Rossi *Il Palazzo Incantato overo La Guerriera Amante* and Melani *Ercole in Tebe*.

DENIS ARNOLD

Chapter 16. Instrumental Music (c. 1610–60)

Although there has been a great deal of research in this sphere in recent years, most of it has remained in theses and is thus not generally accessible. The clearest general account of the development of instrumental music with continuo is still that by H. Riemann *Handbuch der Musikgeschichte*, ii, (2nd ed., Leipzig, 1912) and S. Bonta, 'The uses of the sonata da chiesa', *JAMS*, xxii (1969), p. 54, and the set of papers published in J. Jacquot, (ed.) *La Musique instrumentale de la Renaissance* (Paris, 1955) are also useful. W. S. Newman, *The Sonata in the Baroque Era* (Chapel Hill, 1966, rev. London/New York, 1972) contains a systematic examination of the sonata; and E. Selfridge-Field, *Venetian Instrumental Music from Gabrieli to Vivaldi* (Oxford, 1975) examines the music of one of the more important schools of composition. E. Schenk, *The Italian Trio Sonata* (English version, Cologne, 1955) has a long and interesting preface. English viol music has no study more modern and comprehensive than Meyer (see p. 878) but several articles contain important material, notably R. Charteris, 'John Coprario's Five-and Six-part pieces: Instrumental or vocal?' *ML*, lvii (1976), p. 370 and A. Ashbee, 'The four-part consort music of John Jenkins, *PRMA*, xcvi (1969–70), p. 29, while Lefkowitz on *Lawes* (see p. 880) provides an analysis of that composer's oeuvre in this field. On keyboard music, Apel (see p. 878) is indispensable, but there are few stylistic (as opposed to biographical) studies of individual composers, although prefaces to editions are sometimes useful.

EDITIONS

The nearest to an overall anthology of continental ensemble music of the period remains H. Riemann, *Old Chamber Music* (4 vols. London, 1896), heavily overedited but nonetheless full of interesting and characteristic pieces. There are few collected editions of individual composers, a notable exception being that of S. Rossi, *Sinfonie, gagliarde, canzone 1607–08* (3 vols., New York, 1965–71). Otherwise, only individual items as mentioned in the footnotes are generally available, the most ample selection being of Marini's sonatas contained in the musical appendix to D. J. Iselin, *Biagio Marini, sein Leben und seine Instrumentalwerke* (Basel, 1930); while William Young's sonatas were published in the Oxford Orchestra Series (London 1930). English composers are better represented by several volumes in *MB, Jacobean Consort Music* (ix), W. Lawes, *Select Consort Music* (xxi), Locke, *Chamber Music* (xxxi and xxxii), Jenkins *Consort Music of Four Parts* (xxvi) and *Six Parts* (xxxix). Jenkins is further represented in the collected edition published by the Viol da Gamba Society – his consort music for viols in 4 parts (London, 1978), 5 parts (London, 1971), and 6 parts (London, 1976). German composers are generally represented in the collected editions of Scheidt, *Werke* (Hamburg, 1923) and Schein, *Neue Ausgabe sämtlicher Werke* (Kassel/Basel 1963–).

Keyboard music is better provided for, the collected edition of Frescobaldi, *Orgel und Klavierwerke* (ed. Pidoux, Kassel 1949–) being supplemented by music of contemporaries and followers in the series *CEKM*: G. Strozzi (xi), M. Rossi (xv), Neapolitan keyboard composers (xxiv), Frescobaldi's own manuscript legacy (xxx), and an anthology of Vatican manuscripts (xxxii). The works of the Iberian school are as referred to in the footnotes; those of Chambonnières are to be found not only in the edition mentioned in the footnotes but also in the facsimile edition of his first book of keyboard pieces (New York, 1967), useful for showing the original notation; L. Couperin's music is best consulted in his *Pièces de Clavecin* ('Le Pupitre', Paris, 1970). A useful cross-section of the period, with excellent prefatory matter on methods of performance will be found in the series edited by H. Ferguson, *Early Keyboard Music in France* (London, 1966), *Germany* (1970), and *Italy* (1968).

DENIS ARNOLD

Chapter 17. Religious Music (c. 1610–60)

There is no overall account of seventeenth-century church music in English, the nearest being the relevant sections of general histories, notably M. Bukofzer, *Music in the Baroque Era*, (London, 1948) and *NOHM* iv and v. In German, there is an extended section on this period in K. G. Fellerer (ed.), *Geschichte der Katholischen Kirchenmusik* (Kassel, 1976). The Monteverdi literature (see pp. 877–8) treats of his Venetian church music, to which must be added R. Smith Brindle, 'Monteverdi's G minor Mass' *MQ*, liv (1968), p. 352. Little has been written on the Roman school, but there are a number of articles dealing with individual Venetian composers and topics: D. Arnold, 'Alessandro Grandi, a disciple of Monteverdi', *MQ*, xliii (1957), p. 171; J. Roche, 'Giovanni Antonio Rigatti and the development of Venetian Church Music in the 1640s', *ML*, lvii (1976), p. 256; D. Arnold, 'Cavalli at St

Bibliography

Mark's', *Early Music*, iv (1976), p. 266; J. Roche, 'Anthologies and the Dissemination of Early Baroque Italian Sacred Music', *Soundings*, iv (1974), p. 6. The oratorio now has a comprehensive study in English, H. E. Smither, *A History of the Oratorio*, the baroque being dealt with in Vols 1 and 2 (Chapel Hill, 1977); and the same author discusses, in more detail, 'Carissimi's Latin Oratorios: their Terminology, Functions and position in Oratorio History', *Analecta Musicologica* 17 (1976), p. 54. The readily available literature in English on German religious music is largely that on Schütz, notably H. J. Moser, *Heinrich Schütz, his life and work* (English version, St Louis, Miss., 1959); while the French study, A. Pirro's *Schütz* (Paris, 1913), is still worth reading. J. R. Anthony's generalized study (see p. 881) contains a section on church music and Le Huray (see p. 878) performs the same function for England.

EDITIONS

Monteverdi's later church music is printed in Vols 15 and 16 in the *Opera Omnia* (the first edition of these volumes was not read in proof; the reprint of 1967/8 is more accurate); Benevoli's genuine music is contained in an as yet incomplete *Opera omnia* (Rome, 1966–) and Carissimi's similarly in the series of the *Istituto Italiano per la Storia della Musica: Monumenti iii* (1951–). The work of minor composers is scarcely published at all in modern editions, although the series *Das Chorwerk* contains a certain amount of it (especially vols 12, 14, 16, 34, 40, 70, 107, 116, and 117). The excellent *Cantio Sacra* (Cologne, 1954) contains a vast and representative number of solo motets of the period; while the Faber Baroque Series (London 1968–) is devoted to concertato music. The text of Cavalli's *Missa Concertata* (London, 1966) is freely edited in Leppard's 'realization' but is nevertheless usable for study purposes. Of the two collected editions of Schütz's music the *Sämmtliche Werke* (Leipzig, 1885–1927) maintains old clefs and note values; the *Neue Ausgabe sämtlicher Werke* (Kassel/Basel 1955–) is not yet complete, and modernizes these features, sometimes transposing the music, not always to its advantage. A selection of the works of Hammerschmidt is included in *DDT*, xl and *DTÖ*, xvi; of Tunder in *DDT*, iii; of Weckmann in *EDM*, ii and *DDT*, vi. There is very little French church music of this period readily available except in D. Launay, *Anthologie du motet latin polyphonique en France (1609–1661)* (Paris, 1963), but the *EECM* series contains ample sources for Tomkins (v, ix, xiv), Ramsey (vii), and Dering (xv).

DENIS ARNOLD

Chapter 18. The Diffusion of Opera (c. 1660–c. 1725)

Much of the literature concerning the opera of the earlier seventeenth century (see Chapter 15) applies to the later part of the century. For the newer developments two works of H. C. Wolff are important: *Die venezianische Oper in der zweiten Hälfte des 17 Jahrhunderts* (Berlin, 1937) and *Die Barockoper in Hamburg 1678–1738* (2 vols. Wolfenbüttel, 1957). M. Robinson, *Naples and Neapolitan Opera* (Oxford, 1972) is more informative on the later period but contains information also about this era; R. M. Isherwood, *Music in the Service of the King* (Ithaca, 1973) fills in the background of French opera, as does D. J. Grout, 'Some Forerunners of the Lully

884

Opera', *ML*, xxii (1941), p. 1. On England, in addition to the study by Dent (see pp. 881–2) and the various monographs on Purcell (see p. 886), the early chapters in R. Fiske, *English Theatre Music in the Eighteenth Century* (London, 1973) are informative. On individual composers there are few full-length studies, an exception being E. J. Dent's *Alessandro Scarlatti: his life and works* (2nd ed., London 1960). Articles which give general stylistic assessments (as distinct from editorial or bibliographical studies) include J. Smith, 'Carlo Pallavicino', *PRMA*, xcvi (1969–70), p. 57; C. Gianturco, 'Caratteri stilistici delle opere teatrali di Stradella', *Rivista Italiana di musicologia*, vi (1971), p. 211; J. A. Westrup, 'A. Scarlatti's *Il Mitridate Eupatore* (1707)' in W. W. Austin (ed.) *New Looks at Italian Opera* (Ithaca, 1968), p. 133. W. Dean, *Handel and the Opera Seria* (Berkeley, 1969), Dent's chapter 'Handel on the Stage' in G. Abraham (ed.), *Handel: a Symposium* (London, 1954), and, discursively, P. H. Lang, *George Frideric Handel* (New York, 1966) provide a basis for further study of that master's operas.

EDITIONS

There are few full scores of operas of the period in modern editions, and not many more vocal scores. A new collected edition, *The Operas of Alessandro Scarlatti* (Cambridge, Mass 1974–) has so far published four works. The early works of Handel are in the Chrysander editions of the *Werke* (Leipzig 1858–94); the newer *Hallische Händel-Ausgabe* (Kassel, 1958) has not yet published them. There is an incomplete *Oeuvres complètes* of Lully (Paris, 1930–) and the relevant works of Purcell are available in the *Complete Works* (London, 1878–). Keiser's *Die grossmütige Tomyris* is available in the new series *Die Oper* (Munich 1975–), Pallavicino, *La Gerusalemme liberata*, in *DDT*, lv (1916). Two volumes of *DTB* [*DDT* 2 folg], xi [ii] and xii [i], are devoted to Steffani, as is the *Denkmäler rheinischer Musik*, viii (1958). Blow's *Venus and Adonis* is in a modern edition (Monaco, 1949) and Campra, *Les Festes vénitiennes* is in the series *Le Pupitre*, xix (Paris, 1972).

Otherwise, the material is largely limited to extracts (as mentioned in the footnotes) and facsimiles of original sources including the following from the series *Italian Opera 1640–1770* (introductions by H. M. Brown, Chicago): A. Sartorio, *L'Adelaide* (1978); B. Pasquini, *L'Idalma overo Chi la dura la vince* (1977); P. A. Ziani, *L'innocenza risorta, overo Etio* (1978); C. Pallavicino, *L'Amazone corsara, overo L'Alvida regina de Goti* (1978); A. Steffani, *Le Rivali concordi* (1977); C. F. Pollarolo, *Gl'inganni felici* (1977); A. Lotti, *Alessandro Severo* (1977); A. M. Bononcini, *Griselda* (1977); A. Scarlatti, *Telemaco* (1978).

DENIS ARNOLD

Chapter 19. Secular Vocal Music (c. 1660–c. 1725)

There is no comprehensive study of the Italian cantata and few smaller studies in any depth. For an outline, H. Prunières, 'The Italian Cantata of the XVIII Century', *ML*, vii (1926), pp. 38 and 120 analyses some works of the period. E. J. Dent, *Alessandro Scarlatti* (London, rev. 1960), A. Lewis 'The Songs and Chamber Cantatas' in G. Abraham (ed.), *Handel. A Symposium* (London, 1954), O. Jander,

'The Prologues and intermezzos of Alessandro Stradella', *Analecta Musicologica*, vii (1969), p. 87, C. Timms 'Revisions in Steffani's chamber duets', *PRMA*, xcvi (1969–70), p. 119 all contain useful information on small segments of the topic. In contrast, D. Tunley *The Eighteenth-Century French Cantata* (London, 1974) is an ample and well-documented survey. For English composers it is necessary to consult the literature on Purcell which includes monographs by J. A. Westrup (London, rev. 1960), R. Sietz (Leipzig, 1955), and F. B. Zimmermann (London, 1967), as well as a comprehensive catalogue by Zimmermann (London, 1963) and R. E. Moore's *Henry Purcell and the Restoration Theatre* (Cambridge, Mass., 1961). An excellent introduction to the background of the period is provided by John Harley's *Music in Purcell's London* (London, 1968). There is also H. W. Shaw 'The Secular Music of John Blow, *PRMA*, lxiii (1936–7), p. 1, and R. McGuinness, *English Court Odes 1660–1820* (Oxford, 1971).

EDITIONS

Collected editions of Italian cantatas are non-existent, but selections of the major composers exist as follows: Legrenzi *Cantatas and Canzonets for solo voice* (2 vols., Madison, 1972); Carissimi, *Six solo cantatas* (London, 1969); Bassani, *Cantate a voce sola* (Venice, 1963); Steffani, *Ausgewählte Werke, DTB* (or *DDT* Zweite Folge), vi (2) (Leipzig 1905). The cantatas of Scarlatti and Marcello are not available except in isolated numbers as referred to in the footnotes. Handel's cantatas and duets are contained in the old series of his *Werke*, vols 32 (1 and 2), 50, 51 (Leipzig, 1858–94); they are not yet in the *Neue Ausgabe*. Other German composers are represented only in scattered individual editions. Purcell's songs and cantatas are mainly collected in his *Complete Works* (London, 1878–) Vols 25 and 27; also useful for a general coverage of English composers are the facsimiles of Playford's *Harmonia Sacra* (New Jersey, 1966) and Blow's *Amphion Anglicus* (New Jersey, 1965). The individual editions of French cantatas are listed in Tunley, op. cit. p. 239.

DENIS ARNOLD

Chapter 20. Religious Music (c. 1660–c. 1725)

H. E. Smither's *History of the Oratorio* (see p. 884) is especially useful, although A. Schering *Geschichte des Oratoriums* (Leipzig, 1911, repr. Hildesheim, 1966) still offers valuable insights. The introduction to the series of extracts in G. Massenkeil, *The Oratorio* (Cologne, English version 1970) offers a summary of the genre's history. On individual composers, the most complete study is that of U. Kirkendale *Antonio Caldara: Sein Leben und seine venezianisch-römischen Oratorien* (Graz/Cologne, 1966); D. Poultney, 'Alessandro Scarlatti and the Transformation of Oratorio', *MQ*, lix (1973), p. 591 (also the previously noted work of Dent – see p. 885) and C. Gianturco, 'The Oratorios of Alessandro Stradella', *PRMA*, ci (1974–5), p. 45, fill in gaps on Italian composers. A. Schnoebelen, 'Performance practices at San Petronio in the Baroque', *Acta Musicologica*, xli (1969), p. 37 gives valuable information about the important Bologna school.

Although the literature on the Lutheran church cantata is large, most of it centres on the work of J. S. Bach. The best general account of the form in English is in

F. Blume, *Protestant Church Music* (English ed. New York, 1974), p. 251, in which there is also a detailed bibliography for individual composers. A. Pirro's study (in French) *Dietrich Buxtehude* (Paris, 1913) remains useful. The fundamental re-dating of Bach's cantatas contained in A. Dürr, *Die Kantaten von Johann Sebastian Bach* (Kassel/Basel, 1971) is now to be found in an appendix to the 1978 reprint of the most ample study in English, W. G. Whittaker, *The Cantatas of Johann Sebastian Bach* (2 vols. London, orig. 1959), while the interesting discussion of the researches leading to these conclusions is A. Mendel, 'Recent Developments in Bach Chronology', *MQ*, xlvi (1960), p. 283. A brief but useful account of passion music is B. Smallman *The Background of Passion Music. J. S. Bach and his predecessors* (rev. ed. New York, 1970). For a general description of the French School, see J. Anthony op. cit. (p. 881) with additionally H. W. Hitchcock's 'The Latin oratorios of Marc-Antoine Charpentier', *MQ*, xli (1955), p. 41 and the chapter in W. Mellers, *François Couperin and the French Classical Tradition* (London, 1950).

For those wishing to investigate further, the pages of the journal *Recherches sur la Musique française classique* (Paris, 1960–) provide many articles on individual composers and institutions. A summary of developments in England is contained in C. Dearnley, *English Church Music 1650–1750* (London, 1970). On individual composers J. A. Westrup (see p. 880) offers the best account of Purcell; P. Dennison writes on 'The church music of Pelham Humfrey' in *PRMA*, xcviii (1971–2), p. 65; while both Latin and Anglican music are discussed in the chapter by B. Lam, 'The Church Music', in G. Abraham (ed.), *Handel: a symposium* (London, 1954).

EDITIONS

For both the oratorio and church music, collected editions of various composers provide a valuable source, especially Alessandro Scarlatti, *Tutti gli oratorii* (Rome, 1964–); J. J. Fux, *Sämtliche Werke* (Kassel/Basel, 1959–); D. Buxtehude, *Werke* (Klecken/Hamburg, 1925–); Telemann, *Musikalische Werke* (Kassel/Basel, 1950–); Lully's as yet unfinished *Oeuvres complètes* (Paris, 1930–); F. Couperin, *Oeuvres complètes* (Paris, 1932–3); Rameau, *Oeuvres complètes* (Paris, 1895–1913); H. Purcell, *Complete works* (London, 1878–). The complete corpus of Bach's church music is contained in the *Werke*, issued by the Bach-Gesellschaft (Leipzig, 1851–1926); and the *Neue Ausgabe sämtlicher Werke* (Kassel/Basel, 1954–) has made good progress in this sphere, in an edition using modern editorial practices and with ample critical commentaries. The *Werke* of Handel (Leipzig, 1858–94) includes all his church music, as well as some works previously ascribed to him. The *Hallische Händel Ausgabe* (Kassel, 1955–) has made less progress in the church music, though including Passion music (I/2 and I/7) and the early 'Dixit Dominus' (III/1). For lesser composers whose works are included in the national *Denkmäler* series see the references in the footnotes; to which may be added P. Humfrey, *Complete Church Music* in *MB*, xxxiv and xxxv, and M. Locke, *Anthems and Motets*, *MB*, xxxviii. Useful individual editions include A. Scarlatti, *Audi Filia* (London, 1961), *Dixit Dominus* (London, 1975) and the *St John Passion* (Madison, 1974) with an informative introduction by A. Schnoebelen.

DENIS ARNOLD

Chapter 21. Instrumental Music (c. 1660–c. 1725)

The situation recorded in the bibliography to chapter 16 is largely the same for the period, and the general accounts – by Riemann, Newman, Selfridge-Field, Schenk, and Apel – also discuss this later period. To these must be added studies of particular composers and genres. The concerto is dealt with in a discursive but interesting and orderly way in Arthur Hutchings, *The Baroque Concerto* (London, 1961, 3rd rev. ed. 1973) although this does not displace the older work by Arnold Schering, *Geschichte des Instrumentalkonzerts* (Leipzig, 1905, 2nd ed. 1927), while two articles by Michael Talbot on 'The Concert Allegro in the early 18th Century', *Music and Letters* lii (1971), pp. 8–18 and 159–72 are useful. The standard work on Corelli is M. Pincherle, *Corelli et son temps* (Paris, 1954) translated as *Corelli, his life, his work* (New York, 1956) which may be supplemented by two multilingual congress reports, *Studi Corelliani* (1972) and *Nuovi Studi Corelliani* (1978) both published as *Quaderni della Rivista Italiana di Musicologia* (Florence). Vivaldi is still better represented by M. Pincherle, *Vivaldi: Genius of the Baroque* (Paris 1955, English translation New York, 1957), though the work from which this derives, *Antonio Vivaldi et la musique instrumentale* (two vols, Paris, 1948) may also be read with profit; while W. Kolneder's *Antonio Vivaldi, his life and work* (Wiesbaden, 1965, English translation London, 1970) and the more up-to-date and comprehensive M. Talbot, *Vivaldi* (Master Musicians series, London, 1978) are indispensable. The general survey of French music by J. R. Anthony mentioned in the bibliography to chapter 15 gives the clearest outline of the stylistic development of instrumental music in France, and C. L. Cudworth's article ' "Baptist's Vein": French Orchestral Music and its influence from 1650 to 1750', *PRMA* lxxxiii (1965–7), pp. 29–47, offers a more limited but interesting account of this topic.

On keyboard music Mellers's study of Couperin (see chapter 20) deals not only with that composer but with the French background. Handel's keyboard music receives a chapter in G. Abraham's aforementioned symposium. Surprisingly, there is no really satisfactory account of Bach's instrumental music. C. S. Terry's *Bach's Orchestra* (London, 1932) gives valuable background material; C. H. H. Parry's *Johann Sebastian Bach*, (London, 1909) and Schweitzer's *J. S. Bach* (English edition London, 1911) must be used with caution although both were epoch-making in their day.

EDITIONS

The enormous amount of music of the period available is such that for individual items and anthologies the reader must be referred to the footnotes. Collected editions of Purcell, Couperin, Telemann, Bach, and Handel have already been referred to; to these must be added Corelli (that of Joachim and Chrysander – London 1888–91 – is being replaced and supplemented by a new one – the *Historisch-kritische Gesamtausgabe* Cologne, 1976–); *Vivaldi* (edited by various hands, of mixed scholarly tastes, Milan 1947–) and Albinoni (newly begun and as yet consisting of a few numbers only – Zurich, 1974). Of importance for the Bologna school is a series called *Italian 17th and 18th century sinfonias and sonatas for trumpets and strings* (anonymously edited, published by Musica Rara, London). The music of many French keyboard composers is now available, notably in the following publications: d'Anglebert, *Pièces de Clavecin*, ed. K. Gilbert in *Le*

Pupître 54 (Paris, 1975); Böhm, *Sämtliche Werke. Klavier und Orgelwerke . . .* newly edited by G. Wolgast (Wiesbaden, 1952–); Gigault, *Livre de musique pour l'orgue* in *Archives des Maîtres d'Orgue* 4; Kuhnau, *DDT*, Six Biblical Sonatas ed. K. Stone (New York, 1953); Lebègue, *Oeuvres complètes d'Orgue* in *Archives des Maîtres d'Orgue* 9, *Pièces de Clavecin* (1677, 1687) ed. Dufourcq (Monaco, 1956); Marchand, *Pièces d'Orgue* in *Archives des Maîtres d'Orgue* 3 and 5 and *Pièces d'Orgues du grand Marchand* ed. J. Bonfils (Paris, 1974); Pachelbel, *DTB* incomplete; Bernardo Pasquini, collected keyboard works in *Corpus of Early Keyboard Music* v (7 vols, *AIM*, 1964–8); Raison, *Livre d'Orgue* in *Archives des Maîtres d'Orgue* 2; LeRoux, *Pièces for harpsichord* ed. A. Fuller (New York, 1956).

DENIS ARNOLD

Chapter 22. Opera (c. 1725–90)

General accounts of operatic developments during this period can be found in chapters 14–17 of D. J. Grout, *A Short History of Opera* (2nd ed., London, 1965), R. Haas's chapter 'Die Oper im 18. Jahrhundert' in G. Adler (ed.), *Handbuch der Musikgeschichte* (2nd ed., 2 vols., Berlin, 1930), and M. F. Robinson, *Opera before Mozart* (London, 1966). Neapolitan opera is the subject of Robinson's book *Naples and Neapolitan Opera* (Oxford, 1972) and two articles both entitled 'The Neapolitan Tradition in Opera' by H. Hucke and E. Downes in the *Report of the Eighth Congress of the International Musicological Society, New York 1961* (Kassel, 1961). E. J. Dent's article 'Ensembles and Finales in 18th Century Italian Opera', *SIMG*, xi (1909–10), pp. 543–69 and xii (1910–11), pp. 112–38, is still useful, and an important recent contribution is D. Heartz, 'The Creation of the Buffo Finale in Italian Opera', *PRMA*, civ (1977–8), pp. 67–78. On operatic reform see D. Heartz, 'From Garrick to Gluck: the Reform of Theatre and Opera in the mid-Eighteenth Century', *PRMA*, xciv (1967/8), pp. 111–27. Studies of individual composers of Italian opera include E. Warburton, 'J. C. Bach's Operas', *PRMA*, xcii (1965–6), pp. 95–106, W. Bollert, *Die Buffoopern Baldassare Galuppis* (Bottrop, 1935), G. Donath, 'Florian Leopold Gassmann als Opernkomponist', *Studien zur Musikwissenschaft*, ii (1914), pp. 34–211, A. Mayer-Reinach, 'Carl Heinrich Graun als Opernkomponist', *SIMG*, i (1899–1900), pp. 446–529, R. Gerber, *Der Operntypus Johann Adolf Hasses* (Leipzig, 1925), J. Abert, *Niccolo Jommelli als Opernkomponist* (Halle, 1908), H. Abert, 'Paisiello's Buffokunst und ihre Beziehungen zu Mozart', *Archiv für Musikwissenschaft*, i (1918–19), pp. 402–21, and H. Bloch, 'Tommaso Traetta's Reform of Italian Opera', *Collectanea Historiae Musicae*, iii (1963), pp. 5–13.

Major books on Gluck include M. Cooper, *Gluck* (London, 1935), A. Einstein, *Gluck* (revised ed., London, 1964) and P. Howard, *Gluck and the Birth of Modern Opera* (London, 1963), whilst a catalogue is A. Wotquenne, *Thematisches Verzeichnis der Werke von Chr. W. v. Gluck* (Leipzig, 1904). His letters are published in English edited by H. and E. H. Mueller von Asow as *The Collected Correspondence and papers of Christoph Willibald Gluck* (London, 1962). Haydn's operas are discussed in H. Wirth, *Joseph Haydn als Dramatiker* (Wolfenbüttel, 1940), and his general operatic activity in D. Bartha and L. Somfai (edd.), *Haydn als Opernkapellmeister* (Budapest, 1960), and the articles by J. Harich, 'Das Repertoire des Opernkapellmeisters Joseph Haydn in Eszterháza (1780–1790)' and

Bibliography

H. C. Robbins Landon, 'Haydn's Marionette Operas and the Repertoire of the Marionette Theatre at Esterház Castle', both in *Haydn Yearbook*, i (1962).

Of the numerous surveys of Mozart's operas may be singled out E. J. Dent's *Mozart's Operas* (2nd ed., London, 1947), C. Osborne, *The Complete Operas of Mozart* (London, 1978) and G. Abraham's chapter, 'The Operas', in *The Mozart Companion* (London, 1956). H. Abert's *Don Giovanni* (London, 1976) is a translation from his full biography of the composer. Two studies of *Figaro* are S. Levarie, *Mozart's Le Nozze di Figaro: A Critical Analysis* (Chicago, 1952), and F. Noske, 'Social Tensions in *Le Nozze di Figaro*', *ML*, l (1969), pp. 45–62. Important background to *Die Entführung* and *Die Zauberflöte* is found in W. Preibisch, 'Quellenstudien zu Mozarts "Entführung aus dem Serail" ', *SIMG*, x (1908–9), pp. 430–76, and E. M. Batley, *A Preface to The Magic Flute* (London, 1969).

For French *opéra-comique* see G. Cucuel, *Les Créateurs de l'opéra-comique français* (Paris, 1914) and C. E. Koch, 'The Dramatic Finale in the Opéra Comique of the Eighteenth Century', *Acta Musicologica*, xxxix (1967), pp. 72–83. The best work on Grétry is S. Clercx, *Grétry* (Brussels, 1944) and on Monsigny there is P. Druilhe, *Monsigny, sa vie, son oeuvre* (Paris, 1955). The *querelle des bouffons* is the subject of N. Boayer's *La Guerre des Bouffons et la musique française 1752–54* (Paris, 1945), and the eighteenth-century pamphlets themselves have been reprinted as *La Querelle des Bouffons* (Geneva, 1973).

For England R. Fiske, *English Theatre Music in the Eighteenth Century* (London, 1973) is the standard work. Accounts of Russian opera are found in G. Seaman, *History of Russian Music*, vol. 1 (Oxford, 1967) and D. Lehmann, *Russlands Oper und Singspiel in der zweiten Hälfte des 18. Jahrhunderts* (Leipzig, 1958). M. N. Hamilton's *Music in Eighteenth Century Spain* (Urbana, 1937) is a good survey, while J. Subirá's *La tonadilla escénica* (3 vols., Madrid, 1928–30) is the main study of this form of Spanish opera. Accounts of the *Singspiel* include E. Istel, *Die Entstehung des deutschen Melodramas* (Berlin, 1906), V. Helferts, 'Zur Geschichte des Wiener Singspiels', *ZfMW*, v (1922–3), pp. 194–209, and W. H. Rubsamen, 'Mr. Seedo, Ballad Opera, and the *Singspiel*', in *Miscelánea en homenaje a Monseñor Higinio Anglés* (Barcelona, 1958–61), ii, pp. 775–809. On ballad opera itself see E. M. Gagey, *Ballad Opera* (New York, 1937).

PETER WARD JONES

Chapter 23. Orchestral and Chamber Music (c. 1725–90)

Works on French orchestral music include B. S. Brook, *La symphonie française dans la seconde moitié du XVIIIᵉ siècle* (3 vols., Paris, 1962), G. Cucuel, *Études sur un orchestre au XVIIIᵉ siècle* (Paris, 1913), M. Brenet, *Les concerts en France sous l'ancien régime* (Paris, 1900), and C. Pierre, *Histoire du Concert Spirituel 1725–1790* (Paris, 1975). On English symphonies there is C. L. Cudworth, 'The English Symphonists of the Eighteenth Century', *PRMA*, lxxviii (1951–2), pp. 31–51.

H. Hell, *Die neapolitanische Opernsinfonie in der ersten Hälfte des 18. Jahrhunderts* (Tutzing, 1971) is an important introduction to the early Italian symphony, while N. Zaslaw, 'Towards a Revival of the Classical Orchestra', *PRMA*, ciii (1976–7), pp. 158–87, gives a good summary of eighteenth-century orchestral resources. H. Botstiber, *Geschichte der Ouvertüre* (Leipzig, 1913) still has much valuable material. The major study of Haydn's symphonies is H. C. Robbins Landon, *The Symphonies of Joseph Haydn* (London, 1955, supplement, 1961), and a shorter survey is the same author's *Haydn Symphonies* (London, 1966). The best succinct account of Mozart's symphonies is J. P. Larsen's chapter, 'The Symphonies' in *The Mozart Companion* (London, 1956), whilst G. de Saint-Foix, *The Symphonies of Mozart* (London, 1947) is still useful. Studies of other composers' symphonies include E. Suchalla, *Die Orchestersinfonien Carl Philipp Emanuel Bachs* (Augsburg, 1968), F. Tutenberg, *Die Sinfonik Johann Christian Bachs* (Wolfenbüttel, 1928), F. Torrefranca, 'Le origini della sinfonia. Le sinfonie dell'imbrattacarte (G. B. Sanmartini)', *Rivista musicale italiana*, xx–xxii (1913–15), and P. Gradenwitz, 'The Symphonies of Johann Stamitz', *Music Review*, i (1940), pp. 354–63.

The general literature on the concerto of the period includes H. Engel, *Das Instrumentalkonzert*, vol. 1 (Wiesbaden, 1971), A. Schering, *Geschichte des Instrumentalkonzerts* (2nd ed., Leipzig, 1927), H. Daffner, *Die Entwicklung des Klavierkonzerts bis Mozart* (Leipzig, 1906), and H. Uldall, *Das Klavierkonzert der Berliner Schule* (Leipzig, 1928). Three valuable articles are B. S. Brook, 'The Symphonie Concertante: an Interim Report', *MQ*, xlvii (1961), pp. 493–516, E. J. Simon, 'The Double Exposition in the Classic Concerto', *JAMS*, x (1957), pp. 111–18, and J. R. Stevens, 'An 18th-Century Description of Concerto First-Movement Form', *JAMS*, xxiv (1971), pp. 85–95. L. Crickmore, 'C. P. E. Bach's Harpsichord Concertos', *ML*, xxxix (1958), pp. 227–41 provides a concise survey of his output. For Mozart there is C. M. Girdlestone, *Mozart's Piano Concertos* (London, 1948), A. J. B. Hutchings, *A Companion to Mozart's Piano Concertos* (2nd ed., London, 1950), A. H. King, *Mozart Wind and String Concertos* (London, 1978), P. F. Radcliffe, *Mozart Piano Concertos* (London, 1978), and the chapters by F. Blume and H. C. Robbins London in *The Mozart Companion* (London, 1956).

PETER WARD JONES

Chapter 24. Music for or with Keyboard (c. 1725–90)

A comprehensive study of the sonata is found in W. S. Newman, *The Sonata in the Classic Era* (2nd ed., New York, 1972), and a short account of the Italian sonata is K. Heuschneider, *The Piano Sonata of the Eighteenth Century in Italy* (Cape Town, 1967). L. Hoffmann-Erbrecht's *Deutsche und italienische Klaviermusik zur Bachzeit* (Leipzig, 1954) is important, as is the article by R. Kamien, 'Style Change in the Mid-18th-Century Keyboard Sonata', *JAMS*, xix (1966), pp. 37–58. For English keyboard music see J. A. Caldwell, *English Keyboard Music Before the Nineteenth Century* (London, 1973). P. Barford's *The Keyboard Music of C. P. E. Bach* (London, 1965) is the only substantial study in English, though somewhat abstruse and over-philosophical in approach. R. Kirkpatrick's *Domenico Scarlatti* (Princeton, 1953) remains a definitive work. F. Torrefranca's *Giovanni Benedetto Platti e la sonata moderna* (Milan, 1963) is valuable, though extravagant in its claims. Clementi now has a full study in L. Plantinga, *Clementi, His Life and Music* (London, 1977) to complement A. Tyson's *Thematic Catalogue of the Works of Muzio Clementi* (Tutzing, 1967). The development of the string quartet is the subject of L. Finscher's *Studien zur Geschichte des Streichquartetts* (Kassel, 1974–), and the string trio's history is traced in H. Unverricht, *Geschichte des Streichtrios* (Tutzing, 1969). Also useful is J. Webster, 'Towards a History of

Viennese Chamber Music in the Early Classical Period', *JAMS*, xxvii (1974), pp. 212–47. Two studies of French chamber music are G. Cucuel, *La Pouplinière et la musique de chambre au XVIIIᵉ siècle* (Paris, 1913) and L. de La Laurencie, *L'école française de violon de Lully à Viotti* (3 vols., Paris, 1922–4). On individual composers there is E. F. Schmid, *Carl Philipp Emanuel Bach und seine Kammermusik* (Kassel, 1931), R. Hughes, *Haydn String Quartets* (London, 1966), R. Barrett-Ayres, *Joseph Haydn and the String Quartet* (London, 1974), and A. H. King, *Mozart Chamber Music* (London, 1968).

The major study of German eighteenth-century song is still M. Friedlaender, *Das deutsche Lied im 18. Jahrhundert* (2 vols., Stuttgart, 1902), with many complete examples. A detailed work on C. P. E. Bach's songs is G. Busch, *C. P. E. Bach und seine Lieder* (2 vols., Regensburg, 1957). On English song see H. D. Johnstone, 'English Solo Song, *c.* 1710–1760', *PRMA*, xcv (1968–9), pp. 67–80, and M. Boyd, 'English Secular Cantatas in the Eighteenth Century', *Music Review*, xxx (1969), pp. 85–97.

PETER WARD JONES

Chapter 25. Religious Music (c. 1725–90)

For a recent account of Bach's passion music see P. Steinitz, *Bach's Passions* (London, 1979). W. Dean's *Handel's Dramatic Oratorios and Masques* (London, 1959) is a standard work, while there are two full studies of *Messiah*, J. P. Larsen, *Handel's Messiah* (London, 1957) and H. Watkins Shaw, *A Textual and Historical Companion to Handel's Messiah* (London, 1965). F. Blume's *Protestant Church Music* (London, 1975) has good chapters on this period. General accounts in German are A. Schering, *Geschichte des Oratoriums* (Leipzig, 1911), and A. Orel, 'Die katholische Kirchenmusik seit 1750', in G. Adler ed., *Handbuch der Musikgeschichte* (2nd ed., 2 vols., Berlin, 1930). A major article is D. H. Foster, 'The Oratorio in Paris in the 18th Century', *Acta Musicologica*, xlvii (1975), pp. 67–133. The main work on Haydn's masses is C. M. Brand, *Die Messen von Joseph Haydn* (Würzburg, 1941). Mozart's church music is well discussed by K. Geiringer in *The Mozart Companion* (London, 1956), and an important article on the *Requiem* is F. Blume, 'Requiem but no Peace', *MQ*, xlvii (1961), pp. 147–69.

PETER WARD JONES

Chapter 26. The Music of India

For a general account of Indian history and culture, A. L. Basham's *The wonder that was India* (London 1954; published in paperback by Fontana, 1971) is recommended. The same author has also edited *A cultural history of India* (Oxford, 1975), which comprises more specialized articles by various authors. These include one of the best short accounts of Indian music, by N. A. Jairazbhoy; see also the article by Jairazbhoy on 'South Asian music' in *Encyclopaedia Britannica*, 15th ed., vol. 17. Other general accounts include A. H. Fox Strangways' book *The music of Hindostan* (Oxford, 1914), a valuable and sympathetic study if now somewhat outdated in matters of detail; chapter IV of *NOHM*, i (London, 1957), by A. A. Bake; and

Captain C. R. Day's *The music and musical instruments of southern India and the Deccan* (London, 1891), also somewhat outdated. Of Indian books in English the most useful are perhaps those of P. Sambamoorthy (*South Indian music*, Madras, 6 vols.), N. Ghosh (*Fundamentals of rāga and tāla*, Bombay, 1968), and B. C. Deva (*Indian music*, New Delhi: Indian Council for Cultural Relations, 1974). A useful survey of the literature of Indian music in English is H. Powers' review article 'Indian music and the English language', in *Ethnomusicology*, ix (January 1965).

The historical development of Indian music was first explored by J. Grosset, 'Inde: histoire de la musique . . .' in A. Lavignac (ed.), *Encyclopédie de la musique*, i (Paris, 1913), and more recently by E. te Nijenhuis, *Indian music, history and structure* (Leiden, 1974). For a detailed account of the history of Indian musical instruments, see C. Marcel-Dubois' *Les instruments de la musique de l'Inde ancienne* (Paris, 1941); a more general account will be found in C. Sachs, *The history of musical instruments* (London, 1940), chapters 7 and 11.

Few translations of Sanskrit texts are available. The *Nāṭyaśāstra* has been translated, somewhat unsatisfactorily, by Manomohan Ghosh (vol. I, Calcutta, 1951; vol. II, including the chapters on music, Bibliotheka Indica no. 272, Calcutta, 1961). More reliable are the translations of the *Dattilam* (*c.* 5th century AD) by E. te Nijenhuis (Leiden, 1970) and M. Lath (New Delhi, 1978); each of these provides an extensive commentary drawing on the evidence of the *Nāṭyaśāstra* and other early texts. The first chapter of the *Saṃgītaratnākara* of Śārṅgadeva has been translated with commentary by C. Kunhan Raja (Adyar Library Series no. 51, Madras, 1945). In *A history of Indian literature*, ed. J. Gonda, vol. VI fasc. 1, 'Musicological literature' (Wiesbaden, 1977), E. te Nijenhuis summarizes the contents of all published Sanskrit texts on music. N. A. Jairazbhoy has written a valuable article on 'An interpretation of the twenty-two śrutis', in *Perspectives on Asian music: essays in honor of Dr Laurence E. R. Picken*, published as volume VI, nos. 1 and 2 of the American journal *Asian Music* (1975). Studies of Indian musical notation include E. te Nijenhuis, *The rāgas of Somanātha* (2 vols. Leiden, 1976), in which melodies notated (with special signs for ornaments) in the 17th century are transcribed and compared with modern performances of the same rāgas; W. Kaufmann, *Musical notations of the Orient*, vol. I (Bloomington, 1967) includes a chapter on Indian notation-systems; see also D. R. Widdess, 'The Kuḍumiyāmalai Inscription: a seventh-century source of Indian music in notation', in *Musica Asiatica* 2, ed. L. E. R. Picken (London, 1979). Aspects of Vedic music and Vedic notation-systems have been studied by, among others, R. Simon, 'Die Notationen der vedischen Liederbücher', in *Wiener Zeitschrift für die Kunde des Morgenlands*, xxvii (1913), J. F. Staal, *Nambudiri Veda recitation* (The Hague, 1961), and most recently by W. Howard, *Sāmavedic chant* (New Haven, 1977).

Most studies of contemporary Indian music concentrate on the concept of rāga. W. Kaufmann's *The rāgas of North India* (Bloomington, 1968) includes many valuable examples of melodies illustrating the majority of common (and many less common) North Indian rāgas. The same author's *The rāgas of South India: a catalogue of scalar material* (Bloomington, 1976) includes fewer musical examples, most rāgas being illustrated only by the characteristic ascending and descending scale-forms. A. Daniélou's *The rāga-s of northern Indian music* (London, 1968) contains musical examples, but the introductory historical account and the treatment of temperament in this work are open to question (see N. A. Jairazbhoy and A. W. Stone, 'Intonation in present-day North Indian classical music' in

Bibliography

Bulletin of the School of Oriental and African Studies, xxvi, 1963). Deeper analysis of the structure of North and South Indian rāgas is to be found in N. A. Jairazbhoy, *The rāgas of North Indian music* (London, 1971), and J. Kuckertz, *Form und Melodiebildung der Karnatischen Musik Süd-Indiens* (2 vols., Wiesbaden 1970). See also H. Powers, 'Mode and rāga', in *MQ*, xliv (October, 1958), and 'An historical approach to the classification of rāgas' in *Selected reports in ethnomusicology*, vol. 1, no. 3 (1970).

RICHARD WIDDESS

Chapter 27. The Music of Eastern Asia

The most copious bibliography of works in European languages on Chinese music (1483 items) is that assembled by Fredric Lieberman: *Chinese Music, an annotated bibliography* (Society for Asian Music, New York, 1970). Attention may also be drawn to the existence of the Chinese Music Archive of the Music Department of the Chinese University of Hong Kong, Shatin, New Territories, Hong Kong, founded by Dale Craig, whither enquiries may be directed. No single, adequate account of Chinese music, covering the wide range of genres and styles currently practised, defining the Chinese musical language in musical terms, and at the same time affording a summary history in terms of musical documents, is as yet available in any language, not excepting Chinese. Chapter II of *NOHM*, i (1957), and the brief section on Chinese music in William P. Malm's *Music Cultures of the Pacific, the Near East, and Asia* (New Jersey, 1967), may serve as additional background reading for the more curious.

A single Chinese manuscript of the late ninth century, a lute-score in tablature, from Tunhuang, Kansu Province (Bibliothèque nationale, Paris, Pelliot 3808) has so far resisted all attempts to transcribe it. The late Hayashi Kenzō published a complete transcription, but his reading is not convincing as music. A score for five-stringed lute, dated 842, is preserved in the Yōmei Bunko Library in Kyoto and has been transcribed by R. F. Wolpert: 'A ninth-century score for five-stringed lute', in *Musica Asiatica 3* (London, 1980). A manuscript lute-tutor, written in Yangchow in 838, and including modal preludes and tuning-testing pieces for 27 different mode-keys, survives in a manuscript copy written in 920/1 (see R. F. Wolpert: 'A ninth-century Sino-Japanese lute-tutor', in *Musica Asiatica 1*, (London, 1977). pp. 111–65).

Tunes from the repertory of entertainment-music at the T'ang Court, borrowed by the Japanese, are preserved in scores in flute-tablature and have been transcribed by A. J. Marett: 'Tunes notated in flute-tablature from a Japanese source of the tenth century', in *Musica Asiatica 1*, pp. 1–59 (London, 1977). This borrowed repertory includes not only pieces performed at court during the T'ang Dynasty but also pieces at least a century older, known to have been popular in the entertainment music of the preceding dynasty, the Sui.

An outstanding historical study of music, theatre, and dance, in the T'ang period was made by Martin Gimm in his detailed examination and translation of a short monograph on music, completed about the year 900: *Das Yüeh-fu tsa-lu des Tuan An-chieh* (Wiesbaden, 1966).

Virtually the entire body of printed Chinese musical documents from the early thirteenth until the mid-fourteenth century has now been published in transcrip-

894

tion. Twelve melodies for song-texts from the *Book of Songs* (*Shi Jing*) and believed to date from the eighth century were printed (*c.* 1220) in a general exegesis of commentaries on the *Canon of Rites* by Chu Hsi, the renowned Neo-Confucian philosopher of the Sung Dynasty (see 'Twelve ritual melodies of the T'ang dynasty', in *Memoriae Belae Bartók sacra*, Budapest, 1956, 1957, pp. 147–63). Rulan Chao Pian was able to work from a copy of the first posthumous printing of Chu Hsi's work, and she also published transcriptions of these melodies in her major historical study of Chinese music: *Sonq Dynasty musical sources and their interpretation* (Cambridge Mass., 1967), pp. 157–72. Ten hymns to local divinities, both texts and melodies by the Sung Dynasty poet and musician, Chiang K'uei, have been translated and transcribed: 'Chiang K'uei's "Nine songs for Yüeh"', in *MQ*, xliii (1957) pp. 201–19. These same melodies are also transcribed by Rulan Chao Pian, op. cit., pp. 176–86.

Seventeen secular songs by Chiang K'uei, composed during the latter half of the twelfth century, have also been translated and transcribed: 'Secular Chinese songs of the twelfth century', in *Studia Musicologica*, viii (Budapest, 1966) pp. 125–71; transcribed also, but not in mensural versions, by Rulan Chao Pian, op. cit., pp. 101–22. A single song with accompaniment for seven-stringed zither, also by Chiang K'uei, has been translated, transcribed, and a vocal line reconstructed from the zither-part: 'A twelfth-century Chinese secular song with zither-accompaniment', in *Asia Major*, xvi (1971) pp. 102–20. All seven musical items in notation from a popular Chinese encyclopedia, dating from late Sung times, and known from Yüan (fourteenth century) and later copies, were transcribed by Rulan Chao Pian (op. cit., pp. 131–3). Measured versions, respecting duration-signs and percussion marks in the original printings of two song-melodies – a shorter melody-type in 4/4, and a larger in 8/4 – as well as two movements of a *Lion-Dance Suite* (*Prelude* in 8/4 and *Broaching* in 6/4) have been (or are being) published. The former were printed in: 'Musical sources and music of the Sonq Dynasty', in *Journal of the American Oriental Society*, lxxxix, (1969), pp. 600–21 – see p. 611; 'A Lion-Dance of the Song Dynasty' will be published in *Musica Asiatica 4.*

The early documentation of Chinese Buddhist chant surviving in Japan is copious as compared with what survives in China. The special field of Chinese chant (*Fan-pei* = Japanese *Bombai*) was well reviewed in the Buddhist encyclopedia *Hōbōgirin* (fasc. 1 (1929), 2 (1930), pp. 93–113) (includes many musical examples). A summary of the field in English is to be found in Eta Harich-Schneider: *A history of Japanese music* (London, 1973) – see pp. 307–42. A recent study by W. Giesen: *Zur Geschichte des buddhistischen Ritualgesangs in Japan* (Kassel, 1977), brings much new historical material to the account of transmission, notation, differentiation, etc.

Major studies of particular genres of Chinese music include a musical study of Peking opera by Gerd Schönfelder: *Die Musik der Peking-Oper* (Leipzig, 1972), to be read in parallel with *The rise of the Peking opera* by Colin P. MacKerras (Oxford, 1972). A contrasting analysis of a single type of aria, also examined by Schönfelder, is to be found in Rulan Chao Pian's essay: 'Text-setting with the *shipyi* animated aria', in *Words and Music: the scholar's view* (Cambridge Mass., 1972), pp. 237–70. Attention should also be drawn to the continuing publication of *Chinoperl News*, Cornell University, New York (seven annual volumes to date) providing a forum for the discussion of aspects of Chinese oral literature and music. Fredric Lieberman's doctoral dissertation: *The Chinese long zither ch'in: a study based on the 'Mei An ch'in-p'u'*, Parts I and II (Ann Arbor and London, 1977), makes available a wealth of materials on all aspects of the technology of construction, technique, and repertory, of the seven-stringed zither, *ku-ch'in*, and focuses attention on a late, and – very unusually – a measured, edition of part of that repertory.

That the arithmetical cycle-of-fifths procedure applied to pipes by the Chinese may have been inspired by reports of Babylonian tuning-procedures begins to look possible in the light of recent studies of Babylonian and Hurrian cuneiform inscriptions. These show that the generation of a diatonic scale by cycle-of-fifths tuning-procedures on lyres was known in Babylon towards the end of the third millennium B.C. (see M. Duchesne-Guillemin: 'Déchiffrement de la musique babylonienne', in *Accademia nazionale dei Lincei, Problemi attuali di scienza e di cultura*, Quaderno no. 236 (1977) pp. 1–24). Borrowings of astronomical and divinatory procedures by the Chinese from Babylonian sources, made on several separate occasions, show that, long though the path of transmission might appear to be, cultural borrowing nevertheless occurred (see L. E. R. Picken, *Folk Musical Instruments of Turkey*, London, 1975, pp. 588–90, 600–9). At the more recent end of the time-scale, as late as the eighteenth century, and at the other end of Asia, Chinese musical influence – directly exerted by Chinese performers – profoundly affected Thai and (in turn) Burmese, court music, when the entire court of Siam was captured in the sack of Ayuthia (1767) and transferred to Ava, the royal city in Upper Burma (M. C. Williamson, 'A biographical note on Myá-wadi Ủ Sá, Burmese poet and composer', in *Musica Asiatica 2* (London, 1979), pp. 151–4); indeed, as the same authority notes, one of the four harp-tunings of Burmese art-music – Chinese-type pentatonic – seems to date from this time.

For Japanese music, the accounts available to the general reader are more extensive than those for Chinese music. T. F. Piggott's *The music and musical instruments of Japan* (2nd ed. London, 1909) is still useful and remarkably sympathetic in tone for its time. W. P. Malm's *Japanese music* (Tokyo, 1959) and E. Harich-Schneider's *A history of Japanese music* (London, 1973), provide all that the beginner can require.

Detailed and more advanced specialized studies include W. P. Malm's *Nagauta : the heart of Kabuki music* (Tokyo, 1963) with analyses of the type of art-song distinguished as 'long song' (*naga uta*), and W. Adriaansz's *The kumiuta and danmono traditions in Japanese koto music* (Berkeley Calif., 1973). For the Tōgaku musical tradition as seen from the Japanese point of view, reference may be made to '*Music of a Thousand Autumns*', *the Tōgaku style of Japanese court music*, by R. Garfias (Berkeley, Calif., 1975).

General accounts of Korean music are available in *Survey of Korean Arts, Traditional Music* (Seoul, 1973), and in the writings of Lee Hye-ku. More detailed studies include those of J. Condit, 'A fifteenth-century Korean score in mensural notation', in *Musica Asiatica 2* (London, 1979), pp. 1–87, and of R. C. Provine, Jr, 'The treatise on ceremonial music (1430) in the Annals of the Korean King Sejong', in *Ethnomusicology*, xviii, (1974), pp. 1–29.

A full and detailed account of Thai instrumental music is given in *The traditional music of Thailand* by D. Morton (Berkeley Calif., 1976), with excellent illustrations and transcriptions.

In search of further information relating to musics of Indonesia, the reader will find much of interest and value in the publications of Colin McPhee, in *Music in Java* (two vols, The Hague, 1949), by Jaap Kunst, and in Mantle Hood, *The nuclear theme as a determinant of 'patet' in Javanese music* (Groningen, Djakarta, 1954).

LAURENCE PICKEN

Chapter 28. Opera (1790–1830)

General studies of the opera of the period include Ernst Bücken, *Der heroische Stil in der Oper* (Leipzig, 1924), E. J. Dent's *The Rise of Romantic Opera* (Cambridge, 1976), and Karl Wörner, 'Beiträge zur Geschichte des Leitmotiv in der Oper', *ZfMW*, xiv (1931–2), p. 151. Important national studies are S. Goslich, *Beiträge zur Geschichte der deutschen romantischen Oper zwischen Spohrs 'Faust' und Wagners 'Lohengrin'* and Winton Dean, 'Opera under the French Revolution', *PRMA*, xciv (1967–8); some account of Polish opera of the time is given in G. Abraham, 'The Early Development of Opera in Poland' in *Essays on Opera and English Music*, ed. Sternfeld, Fortune, and Olleson (Oxford, 1975).

Beethoven's *Fidelio* is dealt with in much of the vast literature on his work in general and the monographs include W. Hess, *Beethovens Oper Fidelio und ihr drei Fassungen* (Zürich, 1953) and Maurice Kufferath, '*Fidelio*' de L. van Beethoven (Paris, 1913); Winton Dean's chapter in *The Beethoven Companion*, ed. Arnold and Fortune (London, 1971), is outstanding. Schubert's operas, usually given rather short shrift in the general Schubert literature receive more extended examination by A. Hyatt King in *Schubert: a Symposium*, ed. Abraham (London, 1946) and by E. N. McKay, 'Schubert's Music for the Theatre', *PRMA*, xciii (1966–7). Weber's operas are well studied in John Warrack, *Carl Maria von Weber* (2nd ed., Cambridge, 1976) and there is an interesting monograph on *Der Freischütz* by H. W. von Waltershausen (Munich, 1920). On Marschner the most extended work is still H. Gaartz, *Die Opern Heinrich Marschners* (Leipzig, 1912); on Hoffmann, see Gerhard Allroggen, *E. T. A. Hoffmanns Kompositionen* (Regensburg, 1970) – and for a short study, Abraham, 'Hoffmann as Composer' in *Slavonic and Romantic Music* (London, 1968).

For the work of opera composers in France one must turn to small but compact biographies: *Auber* by Arthur Pougin (Paris, 1873) and C. Malherbe (Paris, 1911); *Boieldieu*, by Lucien Augé de Lassus (Paris, 1927); *Herold*, by A. Pougin (Paris, 1906); *Méhul*, by René Brancour (Paris, 1910). There is a larger, two-volume biography of Boieldieu, *Boieldieu, sa vie et son oeuvre*, by Georges Favre (Paris, 1944–5). On Italians working in Paris we have *Cherubini: Memorials illustrative of his life*, by Edward Bellasis (London, 1874) – still readable and useful; *Cherubini*, by Basil Deane (London, 1965); *Spontini*, by Charles Bouvet (Paris, 1930) – short, concise, and well illustrated.

The three greatest Italians are well provided for, with important works in Italian – *Gioacchino Rossini*, by Guido Radiciotti, 3 vols. (Tivoli, 1928–29); *Donizetti: Vita-Musiche-Epistolario*, by Guido Zavadini (Bergamo, 1948) and *Bellini secondo la storia*, by Francesco Pastura (Parma, 1959) – together with compendious volumes in English, all by Herbert Weinstock – *Donizetti* (London, 1964); *Rossini: A Biography* (London and New York, 1968); *Vincenzo Bellini* (London, 1972). Another important Donizetti book is that by William Ashbrook (London, 1965). A handier study of Bellini is Leslie Orrey's (2nd ed. London, 1973); more intensive research on him and his period has been undertaken by Friedrich Lippmann, 'Quellenkundliche Anmerkungen zu einigen Opern Vincenzo Bellini' and 'Vincenzo Bellini und die italienische opera seria seiner Zeit', in *Analecta Musicologica*, iv (Cologne and Graz, 1967) and vi (Cologne and Vienna, 1969) respectively. On Donizetti see also Winton Dean, 'Donizetti's serious Operas', *PRMA*, c (1973–4).

LESLIE ORREY

Chapter 29. Orchestral Music (1790–1830)

The best works on Haydn's last symphonies are Robbins Landon's (see bibl. to chap. 23) and H. J. Therstappen, *Joseph Haydns sinfonisches Vermächtnis* (Wolfenbüttel and Berlin, 1941). All Beethoven's instrumental music is studied in detail in such symposia as the Arnold and Fortune *Beethoven Companion* (see p. 897), the *Neues Beethoven Jahrbuch* ed. Adolf Sandberger from 1924 to 1942, and the *Beethoven-Jahrbuch* published by the Beethovenhaus, Bonn, from 1954 onward. On the orchestral music we have in English George Grove's classic *Beethoven and his Nine Symphonies* (London, 1896) and Donald Tovey's brilliantly idiosyncratic *Essays in Musical Analysis* (London, 1935–39), dealing with the symphonies in i and ii, the concertos in iii, and the overtures in iv, and at the other end of the scale two good BBC Music Guides: Robert Simpson's *Beethoven Symphonies* and Roger Fiske's *Beethoven Concertos and Overtures* (both 1970).

There is also a Music Guide to *Schubert Symphonies* by M. J. E. Brown (1970) and Tovey wrote on three Schubert symphonies in his first volume. *Schubert: a Symposium* (see p. 897) includes an extensive chapter on 'The Orchestral Music' by Mosco Carner, while John Reed, *Schubert: the final years* (London, 1972), should be read for his re-dating of the 'great' C major Symphony. The symphonies of their contemporaries are mostly discussed only in general studies but Clive Bennett has written on 'Clementi as Symphonist', *MT*, cxx (1979), p. 207.

For the concertos of the lesser contemporaries of Beethoven and Schubert one must turn to Arnold Schering, *Geschichte des Instrumental-Konzerts* (Leipzig, 2nd ed. 1927), and Hans Engel, *Das Instrumentalkonzert* (Leipzig, 1932). Engel has also written on *Die Entwicklung des deutschen Klavierkonzerts von Mozart bis Liszt* (Leipzig, 1927). As regards the violin concerto, Arthur Pougin's out-dated *Viotti et l'école moderne de violon* (Paris, 1888) awaits supersession but a modern view of the subject is provided by Boris Schwarz, 'Beethoven and the French Violin School', *MQ*, xliv (1958), p. 431.

LESLIE ORREY

Chapter 30. Chamber Music (1790–1830)

On Haydn's late quartets see R. Hughes, *Haydn String Quartets* (see bibl. to chap. 23). Beethoven's chamber music is given a lengthy study by Vincent d'Indy in *Cobbett's Cyclopedic Survey of Chamber Music* (see ibid.), and two chapters, by N. Fortune and R. Simpson, in *The Beethoven Companion* (see bibl. to chap. 28). The earliest substantial study of the string quartets is Theodor Helm's (Leipzig, 1885), drawn on heavily in J. de Marliave's of 1925 (English edition, London, 1928). More up-to-date are D. G. Mason, *The Quartets of Beethoven* (New York, 1947) and J. Kerman, *The Beethoven Quartets* (London, 1967). Basil Lam's penetrating BBC Music Guides, *Beethoven String Quartets I* and *II* (London, 1975), also discuss the string trios, Opp. 3 and 9, and quintet, Op. 29. On the violin sonatas W. Engelmann, *Beethovens Kompositionspläne* (Augsburg, 1931) is full of interest.

The article on Schubert's chamber music in *Cobbett*, ii, is by Willi Kahl; J. A. Westrup wrote the chapter on it in *Schubert: a Symposium* (see bibl. to chap. 28) and also a BBC Music Guide (1969). H. Truscott's articles on the quartets in D minor and G major, *Music Review*, xix (1958), p. 27, and xx (1959), p. 119, should not be overlooked.

Other chamber combinations have been somewhat neglected, though there is a good monograph on the piano quartet: Joseph Saam, *Zur Geschichte des Klavierquartetts bis in die Romantik* (Strasbourg, 1933).

The general articles in *Cobbett* on Hummel and Spohr are worth consulting and John Horton deals admirably with early Mendelssohn in a Music Guide, *Mendelssohn Chamber Music* (1972).

LESLIE ORREY

Chapter 31. Piano Music (1790–1830)

Unlike William S. Newman's monumental *The Sonata in the Classic Era* (Chapel Hill, N.C., 1963) and *The Sonata since Beethoven* (Chapel Hill, 1969), Kathleen Dale's *Nineteenth-Century Piano Music* (London, 1954) covers the smaller as well as the larger forms. Newman, however, is concerned with every kind of sonata, not merely that for piano. He is particularly good on the composers overshadowed by the giants. Of those, of course, Beethoven has the largest literature, ranging from Tovey's *Companion to Beethoven's Pianoforte Sonatas* (London, 1935) and Willibald Nagel's two-volume *Beethoven und seine Klaviersonaten* (Langensalza, 2nd, much revised, edition, 1923) to the chapters by H. Truscott and P. Barford in *The Beethoven Companion* (see bibl. to chap. 28) and the Music Guide, *Beethoven Piano Sonatas* (1967) by Denis Matthews. J. S. Shedlock, *Beethoven's Pianoforte Sonatas* (London, n.d.) discusses the origin and values of various readings. Another aspect of Beethoven's piano composition is examined in J. V. Cockshoot, *The Fugue in Beethoven's Piano Music* (London, 1959).

By far the most extensive study of Schubert's sonatas is Hans Költzsch, *Franz Schubert in seinen Klaviersonaten* (Leipzig, 1927); for the English reader there is Philip Radcliffe, *Schubert Piano Sonatas* (London, 1967), a BBC Music Guide, and Kathleen Dale discusses the piano music in general in *Schubert: a Symposium* (see bibl. to chap. 28). Piano music also bulks very largely in M. J. E. Brown, *Schubert's Variations* (London, 1954). Clementi has recently been the subject of Riccardo Allorto's *Le Sonate per Pianoforte di Muzio Clementi* (Florence, 1959) and Leon Plantinga's *Clementi: His Life and Music* (London, 1977), while Patrick Piggott's *Life and Music of John Field, 1782–1837, Creator of the Nocturne* (London and Berkeley, 1973) is the most complete study in English of this composer. Dussek is dealt with in Leo Schiffer, *J. L. Dussek: seine Sonaten und seine Konzerte* (Leipzig, 1914) and also in Paul Egert, *Die Klaviersonate im Zeitalter der Romantik* (Berlin, 1934) beside Cherubini, Cramer, Schubert, Weber, Spohr, and others. For the smaller forms see W. Kahl, 'Das Lyrische Klavierstück Schuberts und seiner Vorgänger seit 1810', *AfMW*, iii (1921), pp. 54 and 92.

LESLIE ORREY

Chapter 32. Solo Song (1790–1830)

On the songs of Zelter and Zumsteeg, see G. Wittmann, *Das klavierbegleitete Sololied Karl Friedrich Zelters* (Giessen, 1935), F. Szymichowski, *J. R. Zumsteeg als Komponist von Balladen und Monodien* (Stuttgart, 1932), and E. G. Porter,

'Zumsteeg's Songs', *MMR* lxxxviii (1958), p. 135; also Hermann Kretzschmar, *Geschichte des Neuen deutschen Liedes* (Leipzig, 1911), pp. 305ff and 330ff.

Beethoven's songs are analyzed in depth in Hans Boettcher, *Beethoven als Liederkomponist* (Augsburg, 1928) and discussed by Leslie Orrey in *The Beethoven Companion*. There is an excellent French book by Henri de Curzon, *Les Lieder et airs détachés de Beethoven* (Paris, 1905). But in this field the Beethoven literature is far outweighed by Schubert's. In English the classic study is Richard Capell's *Schubert's Songs* (London, 1928; reprinted 1973); on a smaller scale are Alec Robertson's chapter in *Schubert: a Symposium* and M. J. E. Brown's Music Guide *Schubert Songs* (1967). The German literature is vast but Paul Mies, *Schubert, der Meister des Liedes* (Berlin, 1928) must be singled out for its thoroughness and comprehensiveness. Books on special areas range from Edith Schnapper, *Die Gesänge des jungen Schubert* (Bern and Leipzig, 1937) to Arnold Feil, *Franz Schubert: Die schöne Müllerin – Winterreise* (Stuttgart, 1975). Dietrich Fischer-Dieskau gives a singer's reaction in *Auf den Spuren der Schubert-Lieder* (Wiesbaden, 1971), of which there is an English translation, *Schubert: a Biographical Study of his Songs* (London, 1976). Schubert is paired with Loewe in A. B. Bache's *The Art Ballad: Loewe and Schubert* (Edinburgh and London, 1890) and Loewe is treated on his own in H. Bulthaupt, *Carl Loewe: Deutschlands Balladencomponist* (Berlin, 1898) as well as in a curious little monograph, *Reitmotive: ein Kapitel vorwagnerischer Charakterisierungskunst* (Langensalza, 1911). For French song, see H. Gougelot, *La Romance française sous la Révolution et l'Empire* (Paris, 1938). There are chapters on Czech, Polish, and Russian song, by G. Abraham, in Denis Stevens (ed.), *A History of Song* (London, 1960).

. LESLIE ORREY

Chapter 33. Choral Music (1790–1830)

On the choral music of the French Revolution see Constant Pierre, *Les hymnes et chansons de la Révolution* (Paris, 1904) with his edition of scores by Gossec, Lesueur, Catel, and others – *Musiques des fêtes et cérémonies de la Révolution française* (Paris, 1899) – and Henri Radiguer, 'La musique française de 1789 à 1815' in Lavignac and La Laurencie, *Encyclopédie de la musique, 1re partie,* iii (Paris, 1921), p. 1562. The church music of Cherubini is discussed in Bellasis and Deane (see bibl. to chap. 28).

On Haydn's later church music see C. M. Brand, *Die Messen von Joseph Haydn* (Würzburg, 1941), A. Schnerich, 'Zur Geschichte der späteren Messen Haydns', *ZIMG*, xv (1913–14), p. 328, and 'Zur Chronologie der Messen Haydns, *ZfMW*, xvii (1935), p. 472. On his oratorios we have Tovey's fine studies of *The Creation* and *The Seasons* in *Essays in Musical Analysis*, v (1937) and a number of articles on special aspects: M. Friedländer, 'Van Swieten und das Textbuch zu Haydns "Jahreszeiten"', *Jahrbuch Peters*, xvi (1909), p. 47, H. Schenker, 'Die Chaos-Musik der "Schöpfung"' in *Das Meisterwerk in der Musik*, ii (Munich, 1926), K. Geiringer, 'Haydn's Sketches for "The Creation"', *MQ*, xviii (1932), p. 299. Michael Haydn's church music is discussed at length in A. M. Klafsky, 'Michael Haydn als Kirchenkomponist' *Studien zur Musikwissenschaft*, iii (1915), p. 5.

The literature on Beethoven's *Missa solemnis* must be headed by Tovey's essay (op. cit.). The Mass is set in historical perspective by Warren Kirkendale, 'New Roads to Old Ideas in Beethoven's *Missa solemnis*', *MQ*, lvi (1970), p. 665. The same Beethoven bicentennial number contains an important article by Alan Tyson, 'The 1803 Version of Beethoven's *Christus am Oelberge*' (p. 551) and the choral music in general is dealt with in *The Beethoven Companion* by Denis McCaldin. In the recent German literature J. Schmidt-Görg's *Missa Solemnis* (Bonn, 1948) and *Drei Skizzenbücher zur Missa solemnis* (three vols., Bonn, 1968–70) are particularly valuable.

Schubert's church music and secular choral music are discussed by A. E. F. Dickinson in *Schubert: a Symposium*, and by C. A. Rosenthal and A. Loft in the American edition, *The Music of Schubert* (New York, 1947). On his Masses see O. Wissig, *Franz Schuberts Messen* (Leipzig, 1909), A. Schnerich, *Messe und Requiem seit Haydn und Mozart* (Vienna, 1909), and L. Bonvin, 'Franz Schuberts Es-dur Messe', *Musica Sacra*, lviii (1928). There is an excellent survey of 'Schubert's Settings of the "Salve Regina" ' by M. J. E. Brown, *ML*, xxxvii (1956), p. 234. 'Carl Maria von Webers Messen, Jähns 224 und 251' are studied at length by B. A. Wallner, *ZfMW*, viii (1925–6), p. 530.

On the oratorios of this period see A. Schering, *Geschichte des Oratoriums* (Leipzig, 1911), pp. 382–406.

LESLIE ORREY

Chapter 34. Orchestral Music (1830–93)

The wider implications of musical romanticism are discussed in Friedrich Blume's *Classic and Romantic Music* (London, 1970) and in such studies of the movement as a whole as Jacques Barzun's *Classic, Romantic and Modern* (New York, 1961) and George Steiner's *The Death of Tragedy* (London, 1961).

On the symphony, the first volume of Robert Simpson's compilation *The Symphony*, 'From Haydn to Dvořák' (London, 1966) contains essays on Berwald by Robert Layton, on Berlioz by David Cairns, on Mendelssohn, Schumann, Brahms, and Dvořák by Julius Harrison, on Liszt by Humphrey Searle, on Franck and Borodin by John Manduell, on Bruckner by Deryck Cooke, and on Chaykovsky by Hans Keller. Tovey's fine essays on Brahms's and Mendelssohn's symphonies are found in the first volume of his *Essays in Musical Analysis* (London, 1935). The second volume (1935) is devoted to symphonies by Schumann, Franck, Bruckner, Chaykovsky, Dvořák, and others. The third volume (1936) deals with concertos and the fourth (1936) with 'Illustrative Music', including overtures and symphonic poems.

Composers of this period were prolific in writing of their own lives and works, and such writings can often be recommended as providing the best kind of immediate commentary on their music and the circumstances of its composition. In this category should be listed the following: Berlioz, *Memoirs*, trans. David Cairns (3rd ed. London, 1977); Spohr's *Autobiography* (English trans. London, 1865; annotated German ed. Tutzing 1968); Mendelssohn *Letters*, trans. Gisela Selden-Goth (New York, 1945); Schumann *Music and Musicians* (English trans. London, 1876 and 1880), selected in Henry Pleasants, *The Musical World of Robert Schumann* (New York, 1965); Wagner's *My Life* (English trans. London, 1911); Glinka, *Memoirs*, trans. Richard Mudge (Norman 1963); Rimsky-Korsakov, *My Musical Life* (English trans. New York, 1942).

On individual composers, the following should be consulted: on Berlioz: Jacques Barzun, *Berlioz and the Romantic Century* (3rd ed. New York, 1969), Hugh Macdonald, *Berlioz Orchestral Music* (BBC Music Guide, London 1969), and Brian Primmer, *The Berlioz Style* (London, 1973). On Mendelssohn, English studies include Philip Radcliffe, *Mendelssohn* (Master Musicians, London, 1957) and Eric Werner's *Mendelssohn* (New York, 1963); readers of German will find more specialized essays in *Das Problem Mendelssohn*, ed. Dahlhaus (Regensburg, 1974). On Schumann there are *Schumann: a Symposium* (ed. Gerald Abraham) (London, 1952) and Gerald Abraham's article 'Schumann' in *Grove's Dictionary* (5th ed.); Leon Plantinga's *Schumann as Critic* (New Haven, 1967) takes a specialist viewpoint. On Liszt, Humphrey Searle's essay on the orchestral music in Alan Walker's symposium *Liszt: the Man and his Music* (London, 1970) may be supplemented by his book *The Music of Liszt* (London, 1954). General studies of Brahms include Karl Geiringer's *Brahms: his Life and Work* (rev. ed. London, 1961) and Hans Gál's concise *Brahms* (London, 1963). The symphonies and concertos are treated by John Horton in a BBC Music Guide (London, 1969).

Smetana is the subject of studies by Brian Large (London, 1970) and John Clapham (London, 1972), and the latter's *Dvořák: Musician and Craftsman* (London, 1966) should be consulted. For Berwald see Robert Layton's biography (London, 1959) and for Grieg Gerald Abraham's symposium (London, 1948).

On Russian music collections of essays by Gerald Abraham provide a wide coverage of biographical and critical matters in the period from Glinka to Glazunov: *Studies in Russian Music* (London, 1935), *On Russian Music* (London, 1939). *Masters of Russian Music* (with M. D. Calvocoressi, London, 1936), and *Slavonic and Romantic Music* (London, 1968). On individual Russian composers one should read David Brown's *Glinka* (London, 1974), Edward Garden's *Balakirev* (London, 1967), *Tchaikovsky: a Symposium* (ed. Gerald Abraham) (London, 1946), John Warrack's *Tchaikovsky* (London, 1973) and Edward Garden's *Tchaikovsky* (Master Musicians, London, 1973). V. V. Stasov's *Selected Essays on Music* (English trans. London, 1968) provide useful contemporary testimony to the work of the Handful.

The best survey of late 19th-century French music is Martin Cooper's *French Music from the Death of Berlioz to the Death of Fauré* (London, 1951). Julien Tiersot's *Un demi-siècle de musique française (1870–1919)* (Paris, 1924) provides a useful treatment of the same period in French and Laurence Davies's *César Franck and his Circle* circumscribes a large number of French composers of the period. On Bizet one should read Mina Curtiss's *Bizet and his World* (New York, 1958) for a closely documented biography, and Winton Dean's *Bizet* (3rd ed. London, 1975) for balanced advocacy.

Bruckner's symphonies are analysed by Erwin Doernberg in *The Life and Symphonies of Anton Bruckner* (London, 1960) and by Robert Simpson in *The Essence of Bruckner* (London, 1967), and the confusion concerning editions and versions of the symphonies is elucidated by Deryck Cooke in four articles in the *Musical Times* of January, February, April, and May 1969 (vol. cx): 'The Bruckner Problem Simplified'. Strauss's tone poems receive full and lucid treatment in the first volume of Norman del Mar's *Richard Strauss* (London, 1961).

For American music see H. Wiley Hitchcock, *Music in the United States* (Englewood Cliffs, 1969) and Wilfrid Mellers, *Music in a New Found Land* (London 1965).

HUGH MACDONALD

Chapter 35. Opera (1830–93)

Many opera guides give synopses and some historical background to nineteenth-century operas, and among these should be mentioned Kobbé's *Complete Opera Book* (revised ed. London, 1972) and Gerhard von Westermann's *Opera Guide* (London, 1964). Donald Jay Grout's *A Short History of Opera* (2nd ed. New York, 1965) provides an informative history, and Edward Dent's little general introduction *Opera* (London, 1965) is full of insights. An unusual approach to opera is taken by Patrick Smith in *The Tenth Muse* (New York 1970), a historical study of the libretto as a genre. More tendentious approaches are found in Joseph Kerman's *Opera as Drama* (New York, 1956) and Peter Conrad's *Romantic Opera and Literary Form* (Berkeley, 1977).

On the origins of Romantic opera one should consult Dent's *The Rise of Romantic Opera* (Cambridge, 1976) and Winton Dean's article 'Opera under the French Revolution' in *PRMA*, xciv (1967–8), and for German opera of the early nineteenth century John Warrack's *Weber* (2nd ed. Cambridge, 1976). On Meyerbeer one should read Martin Cooper's essay in *Ideas and Music* (London, 1965) and W. L. Crosten's *French Grand Opera* (New York, 1948). For Italian opera there are books on Rossini by Francis Toye (London, 1934) and Herbert Weinstock (New York, 1968). On Bellini there is Leslie Orrey's book in the *Master Musicians* series (London, 1969) and on Donizetti books by Herbert Weinstock (New York, 1964) and William Ashbrook (London, 1965). Verdi is the subject of a rapidly expanding literature, of which the most useful are likely to be: Julian Budden, *The Operas of Verdi* (London, vol. 1 1973, vol. 2 1978), Charles Osborne, *The Complete Operas of Verdi* (New York, 1970), and Frank Walker's *The Man Verdi* (London, 1962), an incomparable study of Verdi's life and character. Puccini is best studied in Mosco Carner's *Puccini: a Critical Biography* (London, 1958) and William Ashbrook's *The Operas of Puccini* (London 1969).

Wagner's operas are copiously documented. His own writings are found in Ashton Ellis's nearly unreadable translation in eight volumes (London, 1892–9), although a useful selection therefrom was made by Goldman and Sprinchorn in *Wagner on Music and Drama* (New York, 1964). Bryan Magee's *Aspects of Wagner* (London, 1968) is brief and penetrating; Ernest Newman's *Wagner as Man and Artist* (London, 1914) is a no-nonsense analysis of Wagner in theory and in practice; Hans Gál's *Wagner* (London, 1976) is a concise, non-partisan approach. Elliott Zuckerman's *The First Hundred Years of Wagner's Tristan* (New York, 1964) is a fascinating history of the cult of Wagner. The individual Wagner operas are summarized by Ernest Newman in *Wagner Nights* (London, repr. 1968) and his monumental *Life of Richard Wagner* in four volumes (repr. Cambridge, 1977) is indispensable for serious students of Wagner. Lorenz's theories of Wagner analysis are usefully summarized by Gerald Abraham in *A Hundred years of Music* (4th ed. London 1974), a Jungian interpretation sustains Robert Donington's *Wagner's Ring and its Symbols* (2nd ed. London 1969), and Deryck Cooke's *I Saw the World End* (London, 1979) is a study of the origin and character of the text of *The Ring*.

For Russian, Czech, and French composers of opera, see the bibliography to chap. 34, with the addition of M. D. Calvocoressi's *Mussorgsky* in the *Master Musicians* series (1946, rev. 1974) and his separate *Mussorgsky* (London, 1956), Gerald Abraham, 'Tchaïkovsky's Operas' in *Slavonic and Romantic Music* (London, 1967), and N. Van Gilse van der Pals, *N. A. Rimsky-Korssakow:*

Opernschaffen (Paris and Leipzig, 1929). On Berlioz's *Les Troyens* read David Cairns's essay in his *Responses* (London, 1974).

HUGH MACDONALD

Chapter 36. Choral Music (1830–93)

General surveys of choral music include Percy Young's *The Choral Tradition* (London, 1962) and Alec Robertson's more particular *Requiem* (London, 1967). The sacred music of the period is the subject of Arthur Hutchings's *Church Music in the 19th Century* (London, 1969).

The oratorio as a genre is treated in Arnold Schering's classic *Geschichte des Oratoriums* (Leipzig, 1911) (in German), and English choral music of the period may be studied in J. A. Fuller-Maitland's *English Music in the XIXth Century* (London 1902, repr. 1976) and Eric Blom's *Music in England* (London, 1942). Tovey's essays on the Verdi and Brahms Requiems and on two other Brahms choral works will be found in the fifth volume of his *Essays in Musical Analysis* (London, 1937).

For individual composers discussed in this chapter (Mendelssohn, Schumann, Liszt and Brahms) see the bibliography to chap. 34. Cherubini's choral works are considered in Basil Deane's *Cherubini* (London, 1965).

HUGH MACDONALD

Chapter 37. The Dominance of the Piano (1830–93)

Widely divergent approaches to nineteenth-century piano music are illustrated by Kathleen Dale's *19th-Century Piano Music* (London, 1954) – selective and discursive – and William S. Newman's *The Sonata Since Beethoven* (Chapel Hill, 1972) – exhaustive and scientific. Denis Matthews's compilation *Keyboard Music* (Newton Abbot, 1972) takes the middle way. For additional literature on individual composers and national schools, see the bibliography to chap. 34. For Chopin one may consult Gerald Abraham's *Chopin's Musical Style* (London, 1939), Arthur Hedley's *Chopin* (Master Musicians, London, 1947) and Alan Walker's symposium *Frederic Chopin* (London, 1966).

For the repertoire of chamber music see Cobbett's *Cyclopedic Survey of Chamber Music* (2nd ed. London, 1963). The posthumous volume of Tovey's *Essays in Musical Analysis* (London, 1944) is devoted to piano and chamber works by, among others, Chopin, Schumann, and Brahms.

Denis Stevens's symposium *The History of Song* (London, 1960) surveys a wide conspectus of 19th-century song of all nationalities. For French song one should consult Frits Noske's *French Song from Berlioz to Duparc* (English trans. New York, 1970), and for individual composers one may supplement the reading suggested in the bibliography to chap. 34 with the following: Eric Sams, *The Songs of Robert Schumann* (London, 1969); Eric Sams, *The Songs of Hugo Wolf* (London, 1961): Frank Walker, *Hugo Wolf* (London, 1951).

HUGH MACDONALD

Chapter 38. The Decline and Fall of Romanticism (1893–1918)

Among the more useful general books covering the period are: W. W. Austin, *Music in the Twentieth Century*, (New York, 1966); M. Cooper, *French Music from the Death of Berlioz to the Death of Fauré* (London, 1951); M. Cooper, (ed.), *NOHM*, x: *The Modern Age 1890–1960* (London, 1974); P. Griffiths, *A Concise History of Modern Music* (London, 1978); E. Salzman, *Twentieth-Century Music* (Engelwood Cliffs, N.J., 2nd. ed., 1977); J. Samson, *Music in Transition: a Study of Tonal Expansion and Atonality 1900–1920* (London, 1977); N. Slonimsky, *Music since 1900* (4th ed. New York, 1972); H. H. Stuckenschmidt, *Twentieth-Century Music* (London, 1969).
The literature on individual composers includes:

BARTÓK

B. Bartók, *Essays* (ed. B. Suchoff) (London, 1977); T. Crow, (ed.) *Bartók Studies* (Detroit, 1976); E. Lendvai, *Béla Bartók: an Analysis of his Music* (London, 1971); H. Stevens, *The Life and Music of Béla Bartók* (2nd ed., New York, 1964); J. Ujfalussy, *Bartók* (Budapest, Eng. trans., 1971).

BUSONI

F. Busoni, *Entwurf einer neuen Asthetik der Tonkunst*, (Trieste, 1907; Eng. trans., New York, 1911, many subsequent editions); F. Busoni, *Gesammelte Aufsätze* (Berlin, 1922; Eng. trans., London, 1957); E. J. Dent, *Ferruccio Busoni* (London, 1933, reprinted 1974); H. H. Stuckenschmidt, *Busoni* (Zurich, 1967; Eng. trans., London, 1970).

CHAUSSON

P. Barricelli, and L. Weinstein, *Ernest Chausson* (Norman, Oklahoma, 1958).

DEBUSSY

J. Barraqué, *Debussy*, (Paris, 1962); D. Cox, *Debussy Orchestral Music* (BBC Music Guide, London, 1975); F. Dawes, *Debussy Piano Music* (BBC Music Guide, London, 1969); C. Debussy, *Monsieur Croche et autres écrits* (ed. F. Lesure) (Paris, 1971; Eng. trans., London, 1977); E. Lockspeiser, *Debussy: his Life and Mind* (2 vols., London, 1962 and 1965); R. Nichols, *Debussy* (Oxford Studies of Composers, London, 1973); L. Vallas, *Les idées de Claude Debussy* (Paris, 1927; Eng. trans., London, 1929; new edition, New York, 1967); A. B. Wenk, *Claude Debussy and the Poets* (Berkeley, Calif., 1976).

DELIUS

T. Beecham, *Frederick Delius* (London, 1959); E. Fenby, *Delius as I knew him* (London, 1936, reprinted 1966); P. Heseltine, *Frederick Delius* (London, revised edition 1952); A. Hutchings, *Delius* (London, 1948).

ELGAR

E. Elgar, *A Future for English Music and Other Lectures* (ed. P. M. Young) (London, 1968); M. Kennedy, *Portrait of Elgar* (London, 1968); M. Kennedy, *Elgar Orchestral Music* (BBC Music Guide, London, 1970); D. McVeagh, *Edward Elgar: His Life and Music* (London, 1955).

FALLA

R. Arizaga, *Manuel de Falla* (Buenos Aires, 1961); R. Crichton, *Manuel de Falla: Descriptive Catalogue of his Works*, (London, 1976); S. Demarquez, *Manuel de Falla* (Paris, 1963); J. Jaenisch, *Manuel de Falla und die spanische Musik* (Zurich, 1952); J. Pahissa, *Manuel de Falla* (London, 1954); K. Pahlen, *Manuel de Falla und die Musik in Spanien* (Olten, 1953); J. B. Trend, *Manuel de Falla and Spanish Music* (London, 1930).

HOLST

I. Holst, *Gustav Holst: a Biography* (London, 1938, 2nd ed., 1969); I. Holst, *The Music of Gustav Holst* (London, 3rd ed., 1974).

JANÁČEK

M. Brod, *Leoš Janáček* (Vienna, 1956); M. Ewans, *Janáček's Tragic Operas* (London, 1977); H. Hollander, *Leoš Janáček: his Life and Work* (London, 1963); J. Vogel, *Leoš Janáček: his Life and Works* (London, 1963).

MAHLER

P. Barford, *Mahler Symphonies and Songs* (BBC Music Guide, London, 1970); D. Mitchell, *Gustav Mahler* (2 vols., London, 1958 and 1976).

PUCCINI

G. Adami, *Puccini* (Milan, 1935); M. Carner, *Puccini* (London, 2nd ed. 1975).

RAKHMANINOV

G. Norris, *Rakhmaninov* (Master Musicians, London, 1976).

RAVEL

R. Myers, *Ravel: Life and Works* (London, 1960); R. Nichols, *Ravel* (Master Musicians, London, 1977); A. Orenstein, *Ravel: Man and Musician* (New York, 1975).

ROUSSEL

B. Deane, *Albert Roussel* (London, 1961); A. Hoérée, *Albert Roussel* (Paris, 1938); M. Pincherle, *Albert Roussel* (Geneva, 1957).

SCHOENBERG

B. Boretz and E. Cone (ed.), *Perspectives on Schoenberg and Stravinsky* (Princeton, N.J., 1968); R. Leibowitz, *Schoenberg et son école* (Paris, 1947; Eng. trans., 1949, reprinted 1975); G. Perle, *Serial Composition and Atonality: an Introduction to the Music of Schoenberg, Berg and Webern* (Berkeley, Calif., 4th ed. 1978); A. Payne, *Schoenberg* (Oxford Studies of Composers, London, 1968); C. Rosen, *Schoenberg* (London, 1975); J. Rufer, *The Works of Arnold Schoenberg* (New York, 1963); A. Schoenberg, *Style and Idea* (New York, 1950, enlarged edition ed. L. Black, London, 1975); H. H. Stuckenschmidt, *Arnold Schoenberg: Leben, Umwelt, Werk* (Zurich, 1974; Eng. trans., London, 1977).

SIBELIUS

G. Abraham, (ed.), *The Music of Sibelius* (London, 1947); R. Layton, *Sibelius* (Master Musicians, London, 1965); E. Tawaststjerna, *Sibelius* (Eng. trans., London, vol. i, 1975).

SKRYABIN

H. Macdonald, *Skryabin* (Oxford Studies of Composers, London, 1978).

STRAUSS

N. Del Mar, *Richard Strauss: a Critical Commentary on his Life and Works* (3 vols., London, 1963, 1969, 1972); W. Mann, *Richard Strauss: a Critical Study of his Operas*, London, 1964; W. Schuh, *Betrachtungen und Erinnerungen* (Zurich, 1957; Eng. trans., London, 1957); R. Strauss and H. von Hofmannsthal, *A Working Friendship* (London, 1961); F. Trenner, *Richard Strauss: Dokumente seines Lebens und Schaffens* (Munich, 1954).

STRAVINSKY

B. Boretz and E. Cone (ed.), *Perspectives on Schoenberg and Stravinsky* (Princeton, N.J., 1968); I. Stravinsky, *Chroniques de ma vie* (Paris, 1935; Eng. trans., London, 1936, 2nd ed. 1975); I. Stravinsky, *Poétique musicale* (Cambridge, Mass., 1942; Eng. trans., Cambridge, Mass., 1947); R. Vlad, *Stravinsky* (Rome, 1958; Eng. trans., London, 3rd ed. 1979); E. W. White, *Stravinsky: the Composer and his Works* (London, 1966).

VAUGHAN WILLIAMS

F. Howes, *The Music of Ralph Vaughan Williams* (London, 1954); M. Kennedy, *The Works of Ralph Vaughan Williams* (London, 1964).

PAUL GRIFFITHS

Chapter 39. The Music of Black Africa and America

BLACK AFRICA

A lot more has been written about African music or about specific aspects of it than one might think. L. J. P. Gaskin's *Select Bibliography of Music in Africa* (London, International African Institute, 1965) lists no less than 3,370 titles of books or articles. Brief summaries of the earliest publications were given in an earlier work by D. H. Varley: *African Native Music: an Annotated Bibliography* (London, 1936) and this treatment was continued in A. P. Merriam's article, 'An Annotated Bibliography of African and African-derived Music since 1936' (in the journal, *Africa*, xxi, No. 4, 1951). A. P. Merriam has also covered sound-recordings in his book, *African Music on LP: an Annotated Discography* (Evanston, Illinois, 1970). Later writings and recordings have been regularly listed by the American journal, *Ethnomusicology*, in its 'Current Bibliography and Discography' section.

An early pioneer in African music research was the German scholar, E. M. von Hornbostel (1877–1935) who also collaborated with Curt Sachs. Especially notable were Hornbostel's two papers in the journal, *Africa*, entitled 'African Negro music' (in Vol. i 1928, pp. 30–62); and 'The Ethnology of African Sound-instruments' (in Vol. vi, 1933, pp. 129–154, and 277–311). Among books on instruments, P. R. Kirby's *The Musical Instruments of the Native Races of South Africa* (London, 1934) is an outstanding work, as also K. P. Wachsmann's treatment of instruments in M. Trowell and K. P. Wachsmann: *Tribal Crafts of Uganda* (Oxford, 1953); Olga Boone's *Les Xylophones du Congo Belge* (Tervuren, 1936); and J. S. Laurenty's *Les Cordophones du Congo Belge et du Ruanda-Urundi* and *Les Sanza du Congo* (Tervuren, 1960 and 1962).

A. M. Jones' *Studies in African Music* (2 vols., London, 1959) mainly deals with music and drumming of the Ewe people of Ghana, besides expressing the author's general impressions and theories about music found elsewhere in Africa. The same writer's *Africa and Indonesia* (Leyden, 1964) posits an Indonesian origin for African xylophones. *Essays on Music and History in Africa* (ed. K. P. Wachsmann) (Evanston, Ill., 1971), and *Essays for a Humanist: an offering to Klaus Wachsmann* (New York, 1977) provide a variety of papers by leading scholars. The Ghanaian ethnomusicologist J. H. Nketia has written several books. These mostly concern the music of Ghana, but his work, *The Music of Africa* (New York, 1974) provides wider coverage. Other African ethnomusicologists include J. Kyagambiddwa (Uganda), M. Djenda (République Centrafricaine), M. S. Eno Belinga and P. C. Ngumu (Cameroun), Fela Sowande, T. K. Etundayo Phillips, L. E. N. Akwueme, S. Akpabot, Akin Euba, and Mosun Omibiye (Nigeria). Gerhard Kubik of Vienna has done research in many different areas. Some of his papers are reprinted in his *Theory of African Music* (Urbana, Ill., 1979). Gilbert Rouget of the Musée de l'Homme, Paris, has specialized in West Africa (especially Dahomey). His papers have appeared in various periodicals (see Gaskin's *Select Bibliography . . ., et al.*) as have also the works of many others, such as A. V. King and D. K. Rycroft of the School of Oriental and African Studies, London (who have specialized in Hausa and Manding music, and in Zulu and Swazi music, respectively), and J. Blacking of Queen's University, Belfast (Venda music). Theses and dissertations based on musical field research in various parts of Africa have in recent years been presented at many of the major universities in Africa, Europe, Britain and America. *The New Grove Dictionary of Music and Musicians* (London, 1980) will contain a large selection of authoritative articles on African instruments and on the music of different regions.

In the 1960s UNESCO issued a collection of LP recordings of African music, with documented commentaries (published by Bärenreiter-Musicaphon, Kassel). Further material of this kind has been issued by the Musée Royale de l'Afrique Central, Tervuren, Belgium; by the Musée de l'Homme, and OCORA, Paris; and in America by Ethnic Folkways and other companies. The principal sound-archive for indigenous African music is the International Library of African Music, set up by the late Dr Hugh Tracey. Their catalogue, issued in 1973, lists 210 LP records, resulting from their own field recordings in Central, Eastern, and Southern Africa. They also publish the authoritative annual journal, *African Music* (editor: Andrew Tracey), which since its inception in 1954 has presented a wide range of analytical papers by a variety of leading international scholars working in this field. The Library was formerly in Roodepoort, Transvaal, but is now housed at Rhodes University, Grahamstown, 6140, South Africa.

DAVID RYCROFT

AFRO-AMERICAN MUSIC

A methodical basis for the study of Afro-American music is to be found in a symposium edited by Dominique-René de Lerma, *Black Music in our Culture: Curricular Ideas on the Subjects, Materials and Problems* (Indiana, 1970), in which twenty contributors plot the way to specialized studies, with thorough listings of books, films, and recordings. A useful general survey of black American art is to be found in Margaret Just Butcher's *The Negro in American Culture* (New York, 1957, repr. 1969). Specifically musical trends are discussed in vol. 2 of Richard A. Waterman's *African Influence on the Music of America* (Chicago, 1952).

There are various studies of black American music that survey the whole subject beyond the bounds of popular music and jazz. Pioneer works which helped to create an interest in black music were James M. Trotter's *Music and Some Highly Musical People* (Boston, 1879; repr. New York, 1968); Langston Hughes' *Famous Negro Music-Makers* (New York, 1935; repr. 1957); and Maud Cuney-Hare's *Negro Musicians and Their Music* (Washington, 1936; repr., 1974). A growing interest in the 1970s (often politically influenced) is reflected in a number of scholarly books surveying black music as a whole: Roger D. Abraham's *Positively Black* (Englewood Cliffs, 1970); Hildred M. Roach's *Black Music in America* (Springfield, 1970; repr. as *Black American Music*, Boston, 1973); Eileen Stanza Southern's *The Music of Black Americans* (New York, 1971); and, mainly slanted toward more popular areas, John Storm Roberts' *Black Music of Two Worlds* (New York, 1972; London, 1973).

Moving into the world of folk and popular music, the best historical survey is to be found in Harold Courlander's *Negro Folk Music U.S.A.* (New York, 1963 and 1970). The world of minstrel entertainment is thoroughly covered in Robert C. Toll's *Blacking Up: the Minstrel Show in Nineteenth Century America* (New York, 1974). The cakewalk and other dance forms are dealt with in Marshall & Jean Stearns' *Jazz Dance: the Story of American Vernacular Dance* (New York and London, 1968) and Lynn Fauley Emery's *Black Dance in the United States from 1619 to 1970* (New York, 1972).

The standard book on the rise and development of ragtime remains Rudi Blesh and Harriet Janis's *They All Played Ragtime* (New York, 1971), backed up by William J. Schafer & Johannes Riedel's scholarly study *The Art of Ragtime* (Baton Rouge, 1973). There are now innumerable books on the blues. A good basic study will be found in Paul Oliver's *The Story of the Blues* (London, 1972), and the same author has written several more detailed and reliable books on the subject which may also be seen from the black point of view in Le Roi Jones' *Blues People* (New York, 1965). The influence of black music and the blues on present-day pop music is traced in Michael Haralmbos' *Right On* (London, 1974).

The wider subject of jazz is covered in literally hundreds of volumes. The best concise but comprehensive history is Marshall Stearns' *The Story of Jazz* (New York and London, 2nd ed. 1970), while a smaller historical area is covered in Gunther Schuller's *Early Jazz: its Roots and Musical Development* (New York and London, 1968). Jazz history is led to the modern developments of the 1940s and after in André Hodeir's *Jazz: its Evolution and Essence* (repr. New York, 1975).

PETER GAMMOND

Chapter 40. Music between the Wars (1919–45)

See the bibliography to chap. 38 for general and specific works. Among further general books are:
A. Hodeir, *La musique depuis Debussy* (Paris, 1961; Eng. trans., London, 1961); B. Schwarz, *Music and Musical Life in Soviet Russia 1917–1970* (London, 1972); A. Whittall, *Music since the First World War* (London, 1977).
The literature on individual composers, other than those covered also in chap. 38, includes:

BAX

C. Scott Sutherland, *Arnold Bax* (London, 1973).

BERG

A. Berg, *Briefe an seiner Frau* (Munich and Vienna, 1965; Eng. trans., London, 1971); M. Carner, *Alban Berg* (London, 1975); H. F. Redlich, *Alban Berg* (Vienna, 1957; Eng. trans., London, 1957); W. Reich, *Alban Berg* (Zürich, 1963; Eng. trans., London, 1965).

BRITTEN

D. Mitchell, and H. Keller, (ed.), *Benjamin Britten: a Commentary on his Works from a Group of Specialists* (London, 1952); E. W. White, *Benjamin Britten: his Life and Operas* (London, 1948, 2nd ed. 1970).

COPLAND

A. Berger, *Aaron Copland* (New York, 1953).

GERSHWIN

M. Armitage, *George Gershwin, Man and Legend* (New York, 1958); I. Goldberg, *George Gershwin: a Study in American Music* (New York, revised ed. 1958).

HINDEMITH

P. Hindemith, *Unterweisung im Tonsatz* (Mainz, 1937; Eng. trans., New York, 1941–2); P. Hindemith, *A Composer's World* (Cambridge, Mass., 1952); I. Kemp, *Hindemith* (Oxford Studies of Composers, London, 1970); G. Skelton, *Paul Hindemith: the Man behind the Music* (London, 1976); H. Strobel, *Paul Hindemith* (Mainz, 1948).

HONEGGER

A. Honegger, *Je suis compositeur* (Paris, 1951; Eng. trans., New York, 1966); Roland-Manuel, *Arthur Honegger* (Paris, 1925).

IVES

H. and S. Cowell, *Charles Ives and his Music* (New York, 2nd ed. 1969); H. W. Hitchock, *Ives* (Oxford Studies of Composers, London, 1977); C. Ives, *Essays before a Sonata, The Majority and Other Writings* (ed. H. Boatwright) (London, 1969); C. Ives, *Memos* (ed. J. Kirkpatrick) (London, 1973).

KODÁLY

L. Eösze, *Zoltan Kodály* (Budapest, 1962; Eng. trans., London and Budapest, 1962).

KŘENEK

E. Křenek, *Horizons Circled: Reflections on My Music* (Berkeley, Calif., 1974).

LAMBERT

C. Lambert, *Music Ho!* (London, 1934); R. Shead, *Constant Lambert* (London, 1973).

LUTYENS

E. Lutyens, *A Goldfish Bowl* (London, 1972).

MARTINŮ

R. Layton, *Bohuslav Martinů* (London, 1975); M. Šafránek, *Bohuslav Martinů* (New York, 1944).

MESSIAEN

A. Goléa, *Rencontres avec Olivier Messiaen* (Paris, 1961); R. S. Johnson, *Messiaen* (London, 1975); O. Messiaen, *Technique de mon langage musical* (Paris, 1948; Eng. trans., Paris, 1950); R. Nichols, *Messiaen* (Oxford Studies of Composers, London, 1975); C. Samuel, *Entretiens avec Olivier Messiaen* (Paris, 1967).

MILHAUD

G. Beck, *Darius Milhaud* (Paris, 1949); D. Milhaud, *Notes sans musique* (Paris, 1949; Eng. trans., London, 1952); D. Milhaud, *Entretiens avec Claude Rostand* (Paris, 1952).

POULENC

H. Hell, *Francis Poulenc* (Paris, 1958; Eng. trans., London, 1959); F. Poulenc, *Journal de mes mélodies* (Paris, 1964); F. Poulenc, *Moi et mes amis* (ed. S. Audel) (Paris, 1963); F. Poulenc, *Correspondance 1915–1963* (ed. H. de Wendel) (Paris, 1967).

PROKOFYEV

I. V. Nestyev, *Prokof'yev*, (Moscow, 1957, enlarged edition, 1973; Eng. trans., London, 1961); Shlifsteyn, *S. S. Prokof'yev; materiali dokumenti, vospominaniya* (Moscow, 1956; Eng. trans., Moscow, n.d.).

SATIE

R. Myers, *Erik Satie* (London, 1948); P. D. Templier, *Erik Satie* (Paris, 1932; Eng. trans., London, 1971).

SHOSTAKOVICH

N. Kay, *Shostakovich* (Oxford Studies of Composers, London, 1971); D. Rabinovich, *Dmitry Shostakovich* (Moscow and London, 1959).

TIPPETT

I. Kemp (ed.), *Michael Tippett: a Symposium on his 60th Birthday* (London, 1965); M. Tippett, *Moving into Aquarius* (London, 1959).

VARÈSE

G. Charbonnier, *Entretiens avec Edgard Varèse* (Paris, 1970); H. Jolivet, *Edgard Varèse* (Paris, 1974); F. Ouellette, *Edgard Varèse* (Paris, 1966; Eng. trans.,

Bibliography

London, 1973); L. Varèse, *Varèse: a Looking-Glass Diary* (vol. i, New York, 1972); O. Vivier, *Varèse* (Paris, 1973).

WALTON

Howes, F.: *The Music of William Walton* (London, 2nd ed. 1973).

WEBERN

H. Eimert and K. Stockhausen (ed.), *Anton Webern (=Die Reihe* vol. ii) (Vienna, 1956; Eng. trans., Bryn Mawr, Penn., 1958); D. Irvine (ed.), *Anton von Webern: Perspectives* (Seattle, 1966); W. Kolneder, *Anton Webern* (Rodenkirchen am Rhein, 1961; Eng. trans., London, 1968); A. Webern, *Briefe an Hildegard Jone und Josef Humplik* (Vienna, 1959; Eng. trans., Bryn Mawr, Penn., 1967); A. Webern, *Der Weg zur neuen Musik* (Vienna, 1960; Eng. trans., Bryn Mawr, Penn., 1966); A. Wildgans, *Anton Webern* (London, 1966).

PAUL GRIFFITHS

Chapter 41. Cross-currents after 1945

See the bibliographies to chaps. 38 and 40 for many general and specific works. Among further general books are:
A. P. Basart, *Serial Music: a Classified Bibliography on 12-Tone and Electronic Music* (Berkeley, Calif., 1962); L. Cross, *A Bibliography of Electronic Music* (Toronto, 1967); Walter Gieseler, *Komposition im 20. Jahrhundert* (Celle, 1975); P. H. Lang and N. Broder (ed.), *Contemporary Music in Europe* (New York, 1965); F. Routh, *Contemporary British Music* (London, 1972); R. Smith Brindle, *The New Music. The avant-garde since 1945* (London, 1975). The literature on individual composers, other than those covered also in chapters 38 and 40, includes:

BOULEZ

P. Boulez, *Penser la musique aujourd'hui* (Paris, 1963; Eng. Trans., London, 1971); P. Boulez, *Relevés d'apprenti* (Paris, 1966; Eng. trans., New York, 1968); P. Boulez, *Werkstatt-Texte* (ed. J. Häusler) (Frankfurt and Berlin, 1972); P. Boulez, *Par volonté et par hasard: entretiens avec Célestin Deliège* (Paris, 1975; Eng. trans., London, 1977); P. Griffiths, *Boulez* (Oxford Studies of Composers, London, 1979).

CAGE

J. Cage, *Silence* (Middletown, Conn., 1961); J. Cage, *A Year from Monday* (Middletown, Conn., 1967); R. Kostelanetz, (ed.), *John Cage* (New York, 1970).

CARTER

E. Carter, *Collected Writings* (New York, 1977).

STOCKHAUSEN

J. Cott, *Stockhausen: Conversations with the Composer* (London, 1974); J. Harvey, *The Music of Stockhausen* (London, 1974); R. Maconie, *The Works of Karlheinz Stockhausen* (London, 1976); K. Stockhausen, *Texte* (3 vols., Cologne, 1963, 1964, and 1971); K. H. Wörner, *Stockhausen* (London, 1973).

XENAKIS

I. Xenakis, *Musiques formelles* (Paris, 1963; Eng. trans., Bloomington, Ind., 1971).

PAUL GRIFFITHS

Index

compiled by Frederick Smyth

Dates of birth and death are given wherever possible for all persons named *other than* those authors, editors, etc., who figure principally in the footnotes.

Bold figures indicate the more important references; *italic* figures denote illustrations or their captions; 'q.' stands for 'quoted', *n* for '(foot)note' and 'Ex./Exx.' for '(musical) example(s)'. '*passim*' conveys that references to the subject are scattered throughout the group of pages.

The works of composers and librettists are indexed individually only where the number of entries makes it necessary or to identify a musical example.

a cappella style, the 344–5
Abbāsid dynasty 191
Abbatini, Antonio Maria (*c.* 1595–1677) 345; opera (with Marazzoli), *Dal Male il Bene* (1653) 313, **315–16** (Ex. 102), 323, 361
Abel, Karl Friedrich (1723–87) 491 and *n*, 520
Abélard, Pierre (1079–1142) 92, 93
Abert, Anna Amalie 312–13*nn*, 320*n*
Abert, Hermann 365*n*, 461*nn*, 468*n*, 471*n*, 529*n*, 552*n*
Abraham, Gerald 616*n*, 697*n*, 729*n*, 732*n*, 846*n*
Abraham, Max (1831–1900) 776*n*
Abyngdon, Henry (15th c.) 187
Académie, *see* Paris
Ad organum faciendum (Anon.) 82*n*
Adam (12th c.) 100 and *n*
Adam, Adolphe (1803–56) 698, 705, 720
Adam de La Hale (*c.* 1237–88) 115–16
Adam of Fulda (*c.* 1445–1505) 154, 181, 185
Addison, Joseph (1672–1719) 365*n*, 370 and *n*
Adenès li Roi, *Li Romauns de Cléomadès* (13th c.) 193
Adkins, Cecil 268*n*
Adler, Guido 82*n*, 88*n*, 93*nn*, 95*n*, 139*n*, 322*n*, 342*n*, 345*n*, 348*n*, 426*n*, 447*n*, 465*n*, 511*n*
Adlgasser, Anton Cajetan (1729–77) 552
Adrio, Adam 303*n*, 334*n*, 350*n*
Adson, John, *Courtly Masquing Ayres* (1611) 290
Ady, Endre (1877–1919) 839, 840
aeneatores 42, 48

Aeolian system 29
Aeschylus (525–456 B.C.) 30, 42
Africa, music of 812–16
Agazzari, Agostino 260; *Del suonare sopra il basso . . .* (1607) 252
Agincour, François (1684–1758) 517
Agostini, Paolo (*c.* 1583–1629) 345
Agrell, Johann Joachim (1701–65) 484
Agricola, Alexander (1446–1506) 161, 164, 165*n*, 167, 176, 178
Aichinger, Gregor (1564–1628) 252, 257–8, 290
air de cour 306–8 (Ex. 94), 340
Alaleona, Domenico 364*nn*
Alanus, Johannes (?John Aleyn) (d. 1373/4) 123, 134, 135
'Alas departynge' 149–50
alba 100
Albéniz, Isaac (1860–1909) 804
Albert II (1397–1439), Emperor 139
Albert, Heinrich (1604–51) 304, 306, 325; *Arien* (1638–50) **304–5** (Ex. 92), 307–8, 385
Alberti, Domenico (*c.* 1710–*c.* 1740) 514
Alberti, Max 605*n*
Albertus (d.*c.* 1180) 88
Albinoni, Tomaso (1671–1750) 372, 425, 428*n*; *concerti* 427, 430, 483; opera, *Didone abbandonata* (1725) 446
Albrecht, Hans 212*n*, 497*n*
Albrechtsberger, Johann Georg (1736–1809) 550
Alcaeus (*c.* 600 B.C.) 25, 28, 30
Alcman (*c.* 670–30 B.C.) 28
Alcuin (735–804) 59, 60, 63, 70; *De Musica* 62, 64
aleatory music 821, 855
Alegria, J. A. 345*n*

Alessi, Giovanni d' 249*nn*
Alexander V (Pope 1409–10) 137
Alexander Severus (Emperor 208–35) 47
Alfonso VI (1030–1109) of Castile and Leon 87*n*
Alfonso X (1226–84) of Castile and Leon 98, *99*, 197
Algarotti, Francesco, *Saggio sopra l'opera in musica* (1755) 465
Alia Musica 77
Alkan, Charles-Valentin (1813–88) 761, 762, 764
Allegri, Gregorio (1582–1652) 345
'Alleluia: Now well may we mirthes make' 150
Allen, William F. *et al.*, *136 Slave Songs of the U.S.* (1867) 816
Allison, Richard (*fl.* 1600) 291, 293
Almahide (1710) 370
Altenburg, Johann Ernst (*fl.* 1795) 542*n*
alternatim practice 157
Altmann, Wilhelm 487*n*, 618*n*, 630*n*
Altnikol, Johann Christoph (1719–59) 535
Altwegg, W. 225*n*
Alyabyev, Aleksandr Aleksandrovich (1787–1851); songs 626, 652–3 (Ex. 250), 768; string quartets 626 (Ex. 238), 652
Alypius, *Introduction to Music* (*c.* 350) 34
Amalar of Metz (*c.* 780–*c.* 850) 65, 88; *De ordine Antiphonarii* 59–60
Amalie, Princess 516
Amati family 205
Ambros, A. W. 174*nn*, 178*nn*, 181*n*, 183*n*
Ambrose, St (340–97) 3, 54, 55, *56*, 57
Ameln, Konrad 154*n*, 220*n*, 258–9*nn*, 281*n*
Amerbach, Bonifacius 184
Amerval, Eloy, *Livre de la Deablerie* (1508) 142
Amiot, Joseph (*fl.* 1780) 564
Ammerbach, Elias Nicholas (*c.* 1530–97) 285; *Orgel oder Instrument Tabulatur* (1571) 225
Amon, Blasius (*c.* 1560–90) 257–8
amour courtois 95, 97
Anacreon (6th c. B.C.) 25
anapaestic mode 102
Anchieta, Juan de (1462–1523) 167, 179
Andersen, Hans Christian (1805–75) 791, 831
Anderson, R. D. 15*n*
André, Johann (1741–99) 474*n*; 'Lenore' (1775) 531 and *n*, 643; *Singspiel, Belmont und Constanze* (1781) 474 (Ex. 171)
Andrea, Marc 675*n*
Andrew of Crete, St (*c.* 660–*c.* 740) 65

Andrews, H. K. 263*n*
Andreyev, Leonid Nikolayevich (1871–1919) 798*n*
Andrieu, F. (?Magister Franciscus) (14th–15th c.) 135
Anerio, Felice (1560–1614) 247, 276, 278, 345
Anerio, Giovanni Francesco (*c.* 1567–1630) 247, 334–5; *Teatro armonico spirituale* (1619) 344–5, 346 (Ex. 114)
Anfossi, Pasquale (1727–97) 459, 471, 500*n*; operas 471–2 (Ex. 169), 504
Angeli, Andrea d' 383*n*, 418*n*
angkloeng 572
Anglebert, Jean-Henry d' (1628–91), *Pièces de clavecin* (1689) 435
Anglès, Higini 93*n*, 98*n*, 110*n*, 179*n*, 236*nn*, 283*n*, 345*n*
Anhalt-Cöthen, Prince Leopold of 431, 535
Animuccia, Giovanni (*c.* 1500–71) 246, 247
Anna (d'Ana), Francesco (15th–16th c.) 173
Annegarn, Alfons 294*n*
Annunzio, Gabriele d' (1863–1938) 809
'Anonymous IV', *De mensuris et discantu* (*c.* 1275) 103, 104 and *n*, 108, 115, 135
'Anonymous VII', *De diversis manieribus* . . . 102
Anonymus Vaticanus (9th–10th c.) q. **63**, 85
anqā 195
Anthony, James 388*n*
Antico, Andrea (*fl.* 1517) 173*n*, 178, 204, 215*n*, 227
Antiphonales, from Mont-Blandin and Monza 58, 59, 62
Antiphonarium Tonale Missarum (St Bénigne Abbey, 11th c.) 82, *83*
antiphons, medieval 89
Anyuta (1772) 479
Aosta Codex 145
Apel, Theodor (19th c.) 674
Apel, Willi 80*n*, 87–8*nn*, 112*n*, 118*n*, 119*n*, 122*n*, 135, 136 and *nn*, 137*n*, 158–9*nn*, 183*n*, 186*n*, 241*n*, 285*n*, 337*n*, 338*n*
Apel Codex 181 and *n*
Apollinaire, Guillaume (1880–1918) 828, 857
Appianus (*fl.* 100–40 A.D.) 43
Apt Codex 135
Apukhtin, Aleksey Nikolayevich (1841–93) 783

Aquila (Aquilano), Serafino d'
(1466–1500) 171
Aquitaine, Dukes of: William IX
(1071–1127) 94–5; William X (d. 1137)
87n, 95
Aragon, Kings of, *see* Ferdinand V, John I
Araja, Francesco (1709–c. 1770) 205, 445,
478
Arcadelt, Jakob (c. 1504–after 1567) 202,
230, 232, 234n, 235
Archilei, Vittoria (*fl.* 1589) 271n
Archilochus (7th c. B.C.) 28
Archimedes (c. 287–212 B.C.) 44
Archytas of Tarentum (c. 375 B.C.) 29
Arensky, Antony Stepanovich (1861–1906)
699
arghūl 190, 195
'aria opera' 205, 361–5 (Ex. 121–3)
Arienzo, Nicolo d' 448n
Arie spirituali (Rossi *et al.*, 1640) 300, 301
Ariette (Rossi *et al.*, 1646) 300, 301
Ariosto, Ludovico (1474–1533) 237, 275,
312
Aristides (2nd c. A.D.) 49
Aristophanes (c. 448–c. 380 B.C.) 31, 44
Aristotle (384–322 B.C.) 29, 31, 33, 50
Aristoxenus (*fl.c.* 354 B.C.) 29n, 31, 33–4,
35, 50, 76, 193
Arkwright, G. E. P. 393n
Armenian church music 54
Armstrong, Louis *817*
Arne, Thomas (1710–78) 446, 495, 541;
keyboard sonatas 513 (Ex. 191(ii));
operas 446, 477; oratorios 544
Arnheim, Amalie 387n
Arnim, Ludwig von (1781–1831) 649
Arnold, Denis 249nn, 251–2nn, 266nn
Arnold, Samuel (1740–1802) 477, 544 and
n. 665
Arras, Moniot d' (12th c.) 97
Arresti, Giulio Cesare (1617–92) 398
Arriaga, Juan (1806–26) 611, 626
Ars nova 72, 117–18, 128
Ars novae musicae (Muris, 1319) 72, 117
Artaria 493n, 530n, 532
Artusi, Giovanni (*fl.* 1600) 267 and n
Arvales 42, 47, 51
Ashbee, Andrew 332n
Asola, Giovanni Matteo (c. 1524–1609)
247
Assisi, Ruffino d', *see* Ruffino
Assyrian music 18 21
Aston, Hugh (*fl.* 1510) 186
Astorga, Emanuele d' (1680–c. 1707),
'Stabat Mater' 409

Athanasius of Alexandria, St (d. 313) 55
Athenaeus (c. 230 A.D.) 31, 44, 50
atsimevu 813, *814*
Attaingnant, Pierre (d. 1552) 203, 212,
213n, 214, 215 (Ex. 59), 216, 218, 219,
229, 239n
Attwood, Thomas (1765–1838) 642, 654
aube 100
Auber, Daniel (1782–1871) 584, 585, 720,
754; operas 584, 705, 706, 708, 717, 722n
Aubry, Pierre 100n, 102, 103n, 110n, 112n
Aucassin et Nicolette 118
Auden, W. H. (1907–73) 861
Auer, Joseph 260n
Auer, Max 696n
Augustine, St (354–430) 54, 55, 56, 58, 88
Augustus (63 B.C.–A.D. 14), Emperor 48
Augustus III of Poland (1696–1763) 478,
549
Auletta, Pietro (c. 1698–1771) 456
aulos 2, 22–3, 25–6, *25–7*, 28, 30–1, 32–4,
37, 41, 44
Aurelianus Reomensis (Aurelian of Réomé)
(9th c.) 63, 64, 70, 75, 89
Aurelius Prudentius (d.c. 405) 56
Auric, Georges (b. 1899) 828, 830
Autran, Joseph (1813–77) 682
'Ave miles celestis' 134
'Ave Regina caelorum' 134
'Ave Rex' 134
Adventure du Tancrède en la forest
enchantée (1619) 307
Avison, Charles (1709–70) 487
axatse 813, *814*
ayre, English 278–80
Ayyar, Subrahmanya (*fl.* 1951) q. 562

Babbitt, Milton (b. 1916) 853
Babst, Valentin, *Geystliche Lieder* (1545)
220
Bach, Anna Magdalena (1701–60) 443
Bach, Carl Philipp Emanuel (1714–88)
486, 487, 503, 529, 574, 632; and the
clavichord 524; and Handel's *Messiah*
541; influence on Haydn 521, 524–5,
574, Mozart 527
Abschied von meinem Silbermannischen
Clavier (1781) 574
concertos 487n, 494 and nn
Fantasien (1781) 574
keyboard sonatas 516, 517, 521, 523,
524–5; *Clavier-Sonaten für Kenner und*
Liebhaber (1779–83) 523, 525;
Probestücke 516, 517; *Sonate per*
cembalo (1742, 1744) 486, 511; *Sonaten*

mit veränderten Reprisen (1760) 517
oratorios 541–2 (Ex. 207)
Passions 539
songs 529–30 (Ex. 201)
symphonies 496 and *n*, 499; *Orchester
Sinfonien* (1776, 1780) 499 (Ex. 183(i)),
574
treatise, *Versuch . . . das Clavier zu spielen*
(1753) 516
Bach, Johann Christian (1735–82) 469,
491, 497, 498, 522, 527
  concertos and symphonies 494–5 (Exx.
  179–80), 496*n*, 500, 502, 518; *simphonies
  concertantes* 496
  operas 205, 459; *Alessandro nell' Indie*
  (1762) 459, 460–1 (Ex. 163(ii)), *Amadis
  des Gaules* (1779) 469, *Artaserse* (1761)
  459, *Catone* (1761) 459, *Lucio Silla*
  (1776) 500, *Temistocle* (1772) 500
  oratorio, *Joas* (1770) 544
  sonatas: instrumental 518, 519, 520, 523;
  solo 520
  string quintets 498 (Ex. 182) 502
Bach, Johann Christoph (1642–1703) 409,
442
Bach, Johann Christoph (1671–1721) 442
Bach, Johann Christoph Friedrich
(1732–95) 541
Bach, Johann Sebastian (1685–1750) 205,
430–2, 442, 443; compared with
Graupner 406, A. Scarlatti 399,
Telemann 409; influence on Reger *et
al.* 796; pupils 516, 535, 538–9
  cello suites 431
  church cantatas 92, 222*n*, 387, 407–8,
  534–5
  concertos, orchestral 431, 482
  keyboard music 425, 430 and *n*, 431, 435
  and *n*, 442–4, 509–10, 511, 518
  Masses: BWV 232, in B minor 409,
  535–6, *536*, 664; BWV 233–6 537
  misattributed works 407*n*, 516
  motets 409
  orchestral suites (*ouvertures*) 431, 482
  organ music 443–4, 509, 510
  Passions 403, 539; *St John* 400, 402,
  403, 535; *St Luke* (attrib.) 403; *St
  Mark* 403; *St Matthew* 403, 535, 747
  secular cantatas and *dramme per musica*
  386, 387
  Trio Sonata (BWV 1015) 431
  violin sonatas, etc. 431
  Weihnachts-Oratorium 534–5
Bach, Wilhelm Friedemann (1710–84)
443, 511, 516, 525

church cantatas 538 (Ex. 204)
  polonaises 520 (Ex. 197), 634–5
Bacilly, Bénigne de (d. 1690) 387
bagpipe 3, 44, 45, 47
Bahrām Gūr (King of Persia 420–38) 53
Bahr-Mildenburg, Anna 795*n*
Baïf, Jean Antoine de 203, 204, 279*n*, 284;
  Les Etrènes de poézie fransoêze (1574) 284
Baillot, Pierre (1771–1842) 598, 606, 622–3
Baines, Anthony 44*n*
Baini, Giuseppe, *Memorie . . . di Palestrina*
  (1828) 752*n*
Bajja, Ibn (Avenpace) (*c.* 1090–1139),
  Kitāb al-mūsīqī 197
Bakfark (Greff), Valentin (1507–76) 239,
285
Balakirev, Mily Alekseyevich (1837–1910)
  719, 729, 758; *Islamey* (1869) 776–7;
  orchestral works 689 and *n*, 699; songs
  783–4
Balázs, Béla (b. 1884) 808
Balbastre, Claude (1727–99) 517
Balet comique de la Royne (1581) 322
Balfe, Michael (1808–70) 720
ballad (narrative) 760
ballad opera 450, 477, 528
ballade 100, 115, 116, 123, 151
Ballard 216, 256, 388
ballata 131, 140
ballet d'action 464*n*
ballet de cour 204, 307, 334
Ballet de Madame (1613) 307
Ballet royal de la Nuit (1653) 323
Bamberg Codex 110*n*, 111 (Ex. 21)
Banchieri, Adriano (1567–1634) 251, 268,
288, 350
Bancroft, Richard (1544–1610),
  Archbishop 261
Banester, Gilbert (d. 1487) 187
Bangert, Emilius 434*n*
Banister, John (1630–79) 369, 390
Bank, J. A. 219*n*, 252*n*
bar form 100
barbât 190, 567
Barber, Samuel (b. 1910) 845, 856
Barberini family 301, 313, 322–3
Barbieri, Francisco (1823–94) 741*n*
Barbireau, Jacques (*c.* 1408–91) 188
barbiton (barbitos) 24–5, *25*, 26, 28
Barbour, J. Murray 432*n*
'Barcelona' Mass 125, 126 and *n*
Bardesanes (3rd c.) 56
Bardi, Count Giovanni de' 268, 269;
  Discorso . . . sopra la musica . . . (*c.* 1580)
  268

bareia 61
Bargiel, Woldemar (1828–97) 686
Barini, G. 472*n*
Barley, William, *A New Book of Tablature* (1596) 285
Bärmann, Heinrich (1784–1847) 605, 622
Barnett, John (1802–90) 720 and *n*
Barnett, R. D. 18
Bartha, Dénes 493*n*, 500*n*, 504*n*
Bartholomaeus de Bononia (Bologna) (15th c.) 139
Bartholomew, L. E. 288*n*
Bartholus de Florentia (Frate Bartholino) (14th c.), 'Credo' 133 and *n* (Ex. 29)
Bartók, Béla (1881–1945) 799, 821, 823, 837, **839–40**, 857; *Bagatelles* for piano (1908) 805; Concerto for orchestra (1943) 845; operas 808, 839, 840; Sonata for solo violin 845; *Kossuth* (1903) 799
Bartolino da Padova (15th c.) 131
Bartoš, František 612*n*, 735*n*
baryton 526
Bascom, William R. 812*n*
Basil, St (*c.* 330–79) 55
Bassani, Giovanni Battista (*c.* 1657–1716) 379, 398
Bassano, Giovanni (*fl.* 1591) 266; *Motetti, Madrigali et Canzoni . . .* (1591) 248 (Ex. 70(ii))
basset-horn 504*n*
Bastian, James 251*nn*
Bataille, Gabriel (1575–1630) 322*n*, 357; *Airs de différents autheurs* (1609–15) 306–7
Bataille d'Annezin 94 (Ex. 15)
Bateson, Thomas (*c.* 1570–1630) 278
Batten, Adrian (1591–1637) 356
Battistin (Stuck, Jean-Baptiste, q.v.)
Baudelaire, Charles Pierre (1821–67) 787, 788
Bäuerle, H. 548*n*
Bauldewyn, Noel (d. 1530) 208
Baussnern, F. von 258*n*
Bavaria, rulers of: Albrecht V (*fl.* 1563) 244, 245, 254, 281; Karl Theodor (1724–99), 498; Ludwig I (1786–1868) 753
Bax, Sir Arnold (1883–1953) 810, 824, 825
Baxter, J. H. 104*n*
'Bay Psalm Book' (1640) 357
Bazin, Germain 12*n*
Beat, Janet 347*n*
Beaujoyeulx, Balthasar de (*fl.* 1581) 322

Beaumarchais, Pierre de (1732–99) 470, 475
Beaumont, Cyril 464*n*
Beaumont, Francis (1584–1616) 370
Beccari, Agostino (*c.* 1510–90) 232*n*
Beck, Conrad (b. 1901) 838
Beck, Hermann 232*n*
Beck, J.-B. 101*n*, 102, 103*n*
Beck, Sydney 290*n*
Becker, Heinz 334*n*, 365*n*, 377*n*
Beckmann, Gustav 530*n*
Beckmann, Klaus 338*n*
Bedbrook, G. S. 289*n*
Bede, the Venerable (673–735) 54, 58
Bedford, John, Duke of (1389–1435) 73, 141, 142
Bedingham, John (14th–15th c.) 73, 149, 187
Beechey, Gwilym 500*n*, 513*n*
Beethoven, Ludwig van (1770–1827) 574, 575, 581, 609, 616, 667; and Cherubini 579, 659, 663; compared with: Brahms 694, Clementi 637, Hummel 637, 658, Prince Louis Ferdinand 620; influence on Berlioz 666, 668, Brahms 694, Bruckner 695–6, Clementi 630, Eberl 603, Wagner 675; influenced by J. C. Bach 523, Förster 619, Gaveaux 581, J. Haydn 618, 619, Mozart 619, Sterkel 523; pupils 603–4, 664
ballet, *Die Geschöpfe des Prometheus* 630
cantatas 665
chamber music 486, 617, **618–19**, 620, 621–2, **626–8**, 629, 636–7, 773
Choral Fantasia, op. 80 602*n*, 611
concertos **600–2**, 622
Masses 602*n*, 658, **664**
misattributed work 598 and *n*
operas: *Léonore* (1805) (*Fidelio*, 1814) **581–2** (Ex. 215(ii)), 585, 589, 625, *Macbeth* (projected) 622
oratorio, *Christus am Ölberge* (1803) 662
overtures 600, 602, 606 and *n*
piano music: Bagatelles 630, 633, 637, *Fantaisie*, op. 77 602*n*, sonatas 523–4 (Ex. 200), 619, **629–30**, 631–2, **636–7**, variations 473, 577, 589, 630, 637, 639
songs and concert arias 643–4; 'Ah, perfido' 602*n*, *An die ferne Geliebte* (1816) 645, 677*n*, Irish airs 642*n*, *Lieder von Gellert* (1803) 643, 646
symphonies 609; No. 1 600, 606, 609, No. 2 600, 609, No. 3 **600**, 630, 667, No. 4 601, No. 5 **601–2**, 603, 607, 637, 667, 673, No. 6 **601–2**, 603, 607, No. 7 **603**, 610, 622, 667, 668, 671, 673, 694,

No. 8 **603**, 694, No. 9 **611**, 627, 665,
667–8, 673, 675, 694–6, 885
Beggar's Opera, The, see Pepusch
bel canto, reaction against 383
Beldemandis, Prosdocimus de, *Tractatus de
Contrapuncto* (1412) 142
Bellay, Joachim du (1524–60) 264, 284
Belli, Domenico (*fl.c.* 1616) 296, 311;
Libro dell'arie 297 (Ex. 85)
Bellini, Vincenzo (1801–35) 586, **587**–8,
705, 709, 710; operas 588 (Ex. 219), 709,
711
bells
Assyrian 19
tuned 98, *99*
Belyaev, Viktor 480*n*
Bembo, Pietro, *Prose della Volgar Lingua*
(1525) 226
Benda, Georg (1722–95) **474** and *n*, 480,
739
Bendl, Karel (1838–97) 735
Bendusi, Francesco, *Opera Nova di Balli a
quatro* (1553) 219
Benedict XII (Pope 1334–42) 126
Benedict XIV (Pope 1740–58) 553–4
Benediktbeuren 99–100
Benet, John (*c.* 1575–after 1614) 278
Benevoli, Orazio (1605–72) 410, 413*n*;
Missa Salisburgensis (wrongly attrib.) 345
and *n*
Benham, Hugh 241*n*
Bennett, William Sterndale (1816–75) 672,
764, 766, 767; oratorio, *The Woman of
Samaria* (1867) 756; overtures 672, 673
(Ex. 257), 688
Benoit, Peter (1834–1901) 576, 756
Bent, Ian 141*n*
Bent, Margaret 123*n*, 141*nn*
Benvenuti, Giacomo 286*nn*, 463*n*
Béranger, Pierre Jean de (1780–1857) 770,
784
Berchem, Jachet (early 16th c.) 229*n*
Berezovsky, Maksim Sozontovich
(1745–77) 205, 478, 550*n*
Berg, Alban (1885–1935) 798, 807, 820,
834, **835**; operas: *Lulu* (incompl.) 835,
837, 858, *Wozzeck* (1925) **834** (Ex. 305),
836, 841, 858
Berg (Montanus), Johannes 203, 225
Bergmann, Walter 372*n*, 482*n*
Bergsagel, John D. 240*n*
Berio, Luciano (b. 1923) 853, 854–5
Berkeley, Sir Lennox (b. 1903) 824, 856
Berlin 452, 589*n*
Berlioz, Hector (1803–69) 575, 612, 675,

677, 678, 691; influence on Chabrier
702, Franck 692, Russian composers
689; influenced by Beethoven 666, 668
cantata, *Herminie* (1828) 668
concert overtures 612, 668, 669, 707, 775
Grande Messe des Morts (1837) 748
Marche funèbre pour . . . Hamlet (1848)
669
operas: *Béatrice et Bénédict* (1862) 740,
Benvenuto Cellini (1838) 669, 707–8,
Francs-Juges, Les (incompl.) 612, 668,
669, *Troyens, Les* (1863) 727 and *n*, 740
sacred trilogy, *L'enfance du Christ* (1854)
749, 750
secular oratorio, *La damnation de Faust*
(1846) 746, **750**, 767
songs 767–8
symphonies: *Harold en Italie* (1834) **668**,
671, 689, *Roméo et Juliette* (1839)
668–9, 746, 751, *Symphonie fantastique*
(1830) 578*n*, **667**–8, 669, 762,
Symphonie funèbre et triomphale (1840)
669
'Te Deum' (1855) 748
writings: *Mémoires* 748, *Traité de
l'instrumentation* . . . 581*n*, 706, 707*n*
Bernabei, Ercole (*c.* 1621–87) 345
Bernard, St (d. 1153) 60
Bernart de Ventadorn (*c.* 1125–95) 97–8
Berner, Alfred 540*n*
Berners, Gerald, Lord (1883–1950) 828*n*
Bernier, Nicolas (1664–1734) 388
Bernini, Gianlorenzo (1598–1680) 339
Bernoulli, Eduard 305*n*
Berry, John, Duke of (d. 1416) 135, 136,
138
Berti, Giovanni (d. 1638) 296, 297*n*, 298,
299
Bertin, Louise, *Notre-Dame de Paris*
(1836) 728*n*
Berton, Henri (1767–1844) 577, 579, 584,
589, 655–6
Bertrand, Antoine de (d.*c.* 1581) 283–4
Bertrand, Louis (1807–41) 803–4
Berwald, Franz (1796–1868) 680;
symphonies 680–1 (Ex. 262)
'Besançon' (or 'Sorbonne') Mass 125, 126
and *n*
Besard, Jean Baptiste, *Thesaurus
harmonicus* (1603) 280, **284**–5
Besseler, Heinrich 81*n*, 93*n*, 122, 135*n*,
139–49*nn passim*, 163*n*
Bèze, Théodore de (*fl.* 1544) 220–2, 256–7
Bezecny, Emil B. 183*n*
Bharata, Natyaśastra 558

Bianchi, Angioletta (*fl.* 1717) 386
Bianchi, Lino 301*n*, 397*n*, 399*n*
Biber, Heinrich (1644–1704) 409*n*, 426
bilini 94
Binchois, Gilles (*c.* 1400–60) 139, 142,
  152–3, 160
bint 13
Birnstiel, *Musikalisches Allerley* (1761–3)
  517
Birtwistle, Harrison (b. 1934) 859
Bischoff, Heinz 226*n*
Bishop, Sir Henry (1786–1855) 595
Bittinger, Werner 303–4*nn*
biwa 569, 570, *571*
Bizet, Georges (1838–75) 691, q. 727
  777–8, 786; operas 740, 741
Bjørnson, Bjørnsterne (1832–1910) 791–2
Blacher, Boris (1903–75) 856
bladder-pipe 98
Blamont, François Colin de (1690–1760)
  377–8, 545
Blanchard, Esprit (1696–1770) 545
Blancks, Edward (16th c.) 292
Blancrocher (17th c.) 342 and *n*
Bliss, Sir Arthur (1891–1975) 824
Blitheman, William (*c.* 1525–91) 240, 241,
  293
Bloch, Ernest (1880–1959) 823
Blodek, Vilém (1834–74) 735
Blok, Aleksandr (1880–1921) 844
Blomdahl, Karl-Birger (1916–68) 858
Blondel de Nesle (12th c.) 97, 98
Blow, John (1649–1708) 390–1, 393, 415,
  417; anthems 416, 417; operas 369,
  422*n*; songs and cantatas 393
blues 817–18
Blume, Friedrich 168*n*, 174–5*nn*, 182*n*,
  218*n*, 260*nn*, 294*n*, 354*n*, 511*n*, 520*n*,
  816*n*
Boccaccio, Giovanni (1313–75) 230
Boccherini, Luigi (1743–1805) 206, 498,
  505, 507, 519; String Quartet, Op. 8, No.
  6 507 (Ex. 189)
Boësset, Antoine (1586–1643) 307, 308*n*,
  322*n*, 387
'Boethian' notation 77, 82, *83*
Boethius (*c.* 480–524) 70–1, 76, 93; *De
  Institutione Musica* 61 and *n*, 70
Boetticher, Wolfgang 256*n*
Bohemia, John (1296–1346), King of 123
Böhm, Georg (1661–1733) 435, 441, 442
Böhner, Ludwig (1787–1860) 592*n*
Boieldieu, Adrien (1775–1834) 584, 585,
  643, 655
Boismortier, Josef (1691–1775) 545

Boito, Arrigo (1842–1918); as composer,
  Mefistofele (1868) 727–8; as librettist
  743, 744
Bologna: early composers from, *see*
  Bartholomaeus and Jacopo; San Petronio
  (church) 398, 419
bonang 572
bone flutes, Neolithic 7
Boniface IX (Pope 1389–1404) 137
Bonno, Giuseppe (1711–88) 550
Bononcini, Antonio (1677–1726) 372*n*,
  420
Bononcini, Giovanni Battista (1670–1747)
  205, 370, 371–2, 372*n*, 398 and *n*, 420
Bononcini, Giovanni Maria (1642–78) 420,
  424
Bontempi, Giovanni Andrea (*c.* 1624–1705)
  365
Bordoni, Faustina (1700–81) 445, 447
Boris I (*fl.* 870) of Bulgaria 66
Borneill, Giraut de (12th c.) 97, 103*n*
Borodin, Aleksandr Porfiryevich (1833–87)
  689, 719; chamber music 799; opera,
  Knyaz Igor (incompl.) 691, 732–3, 844;
  songs 786, 788; symphonies 689, 690–1
  (Exx. 266–7), 805; *V Sredney Azii* 699
Borren, Charles van den 139*n*, 141*n*, 145*n*
Borromeo, Carlo (1538–84) 244, 246, 251,
  253
Bortnyansky, Dmitry Stepanovich
  (1751–1825) 205, 478–9, 654
Boschi, Giuseppe (*fl.* 1708) 383
Bosse, Abraham (1602–76) 341
Bossinensis, Franciscus (*fl.* 1509) 184
  and *n*
Bossler, Heinrich Philipp 523
Boston Symphony Orchestra 826*n*
Botstiber, Hugo 313*n*, 427*n*, 440*n*, 442*n*,
  582*n*
Böttger, Adolf 676
Bouffons, Querelle des 205, 456–7, 459
Bouilly, Jean Nicolas 581 and *n*, 582, 585
Boulez, Pierre (b. 1925) 849–51, 855;
  Structures (1st and 2nd books) 849–51
  (Ex. 309)
Bourgeois, Loys (*fl.* 1547) 220, 221 (Ex.
  62(i)), 222 and *n*
Bousset, Jean-Baptiste de (1662–1725) 387
Bouzignac, Guillaume (*fl.* 1634) 355;
  motet, 'Dum silentium' 355 (Ex. 119)
Boyce, William (1710–79) 495, 544 and *n*
Boyvin, Jacques (*c.* 1653–1706) 437
Brabant, Henry III, Duke of 97
Brade, William (1560–1630) 290, 334
Bragard, Anne-Maria 228*n*

Brahms, Johannes (1833–97) 574–5,
685–6, 688, 693, 697–8, 702, 711, 761,
764; on Beethoven q. 667; chamber
music 773, **774–5** (Ex. 294(i)), 780;
choral works **759–60**, 790; concertos
685, 694–5, 697; orchestral works 686,
693–4; organ works 759, 772; piano
works 636, 693–4, **773–4** (Ex. 294(ii)),
775; songs 789–90; symphonies **694–5**,
697, 701
Brandt, Jobst vom (1517–70) 225 and *n*
Brassart, Johannes (early 15th c.) 139
Braun, Werner 258*n*
Brecht, Bertolt (1898–1956) 836
Breitkopf (and Härtel) 600*n*, 614, 686*n*;
Cataloghi delle Sinfonie 489
Brentano, Clemens (1778–1842) 649
Bréton, Tomás (1850–1923) 741*n*
Brett, Philip 275*nn*
Breuning, Stephan von 581
Bridgman, Nanie 20*n*
Britten, Benjamin, Lord (1913–76) 825,
845, 857; operas 845, **859**
Britton, Thomas (1644–1714) 390
Broadwood, Thomas 636
Brockes, Barthold Heinrich (1680–1747)
403; *Der für die Sünden der Welt
ermarterte und sterbende Jesus* 402, 403,
539
Broder, Nathan 498*n*
Brolo, Bartholomeo (early 15th c.) 160,
161
Brook, Barry S. 506*n*
Brown, Alan 292*n*
Brown, David 261*n*, 263*n*, 720*n*, 768*n*
Brown, Howard M. 173*n*, 270*n*, 313*n*,
319*n*, 322*n*, 359*nn*, 361*n*, 363*n*, 371–2*nn*,
446*nn*, 448*nn*, 459*n*, 461*n*
Brown, John (1715–66), *Dissertation on the
Union and Power . . . of Poetry and Music*
(1763) and *The Cure of Saul* 544
Browne, Earl (b. 1926) 853
Browne, John (c. 1426–98) 187
Bruch, Max (1838–1920) 571, 686, 687,
739, 760
Bruck, Arnold von (c. 1490–1554) 223; 'O
du armer Judas' 223–4 (Ex. 63)
Bruck, Friedrich 403*n*
Bruckner, Anton (1824–96) 575, 696, 697,
698, 753; church music 753;
symphonies 687, 693, **695–6**, 701, 753
Brudieu, Joan (c. 1520–91) 283
Bruhns, Nicholas (1665–97) 405 and *n*,
441, 442
Brulé, Gace (12th c.) 97, 101

Brumel, Antoine (c. 1460–c. 1520) 161,
164, 165 and *n*, 176, 177–8, 185, 219
Bruneau, Alfred (1857–1934) 743, 744,
802
Brunold, Paul 341–2*nn*
Brunswick, Court of 260
Bruyant (*fl.* 1417) 138
'Bryd one brere' 99
Bryusov, Valery (1873–1924) 826
Bucer, Martin, *Gesangbuch* (1541) 220
Buchner, Hans (Hans von Constanz)
(1483–1538) 182, 184–5, 225
bucina 42
Bücken, Ernst 459*n*
Buelow, George J. 367*n*
bugaku 569
Bugenhagen, Johann 259
Buhle, Edward 529*n*
Bukofzer, Manfred 109–10*nn*, 134*n*, 141*n*,
143*n*, 145*nn*, 151*n*
Bulgaria 66
Bull, John (c. 1563–1628) 290, **293–4**
Bülow, Hans von (1830–94) 685
Buonamente, Giovanni Battista (*fl.*
1620–37) 330; sonatas **330** (Ex. 108),
331
Buontalenti, Bernardo (*fl.* 1589) 270
Burald, J. 256*n*
Burck, Joachim a (1546–1610) 258
Bürger, Gottfried August (1747–94) 531
and *n*, 643, 661, 692, 789
Burgundy, Dukes of: Charles (the Bold)
(1433–77) 153; Philip (the Good)
(1396–1467) 73, 142, 151–2, 161; their
Chapel 138, 148, 153, 167, 170, 188;
music in 150–1 (Ex. 36), 152–3
Burnacini, Ludovico (1636–1707) 322*n*,
360
Burney, Dr Charles (1726–1814) 321, 493
and *n*, 513, 524*n*, 544*n*
Burns, Robert (1759–96) 792
Burrows, David 302*n*
Burzio, Nicolo, *Musices opusculum* (1487)
162
Busenello, Giovanni Francesco (*fl.* 1641)
319
Bush, Geoffrey 792*n*
Busnois, Antoine (d.c. 1492) **153**, 154,
156, 162, 165, 181
Busoni, Ferruccio (1866–1924) 796, 801,
805, 823, 831; operas 810, 832
Butcher, Vernon 513*n*
Buti, Francesco (1604–82) 323–4
Büttner, Horst 434*n*
Buus, Jakob (d. 1564) 232, 234–5, 286

Buxheim *Orgelbuch* (1460–70) 73–4, **160**
Buxtehude, Dietrich (1637?–1707) 404,
405, 434, 441, 442; church cantatas 405,
408; motet, 'Cantate Domino' 409;
oratorio, *Das allerschröcklichste . . . Ende
der Zeit . . .* 404–5 (Ex. 141); trio sonatas
427
Byrd, William (1543–1623) 254, 261, 276,
290–3 *passim*; church music 261–3 (Ex.
75); fantasies 292; madrigals 203, 276;
Masses 242; *Psalmes, Sonets and Songs
. . .* (1588) 275; *Psalmes, Songs and
Sonnets* (1611) 290; *Songs of sundrie
natures* (1589) 275
Byron, George Gordon, 6th Baron
(1788–1824) 574, 710–11, 634, 669, 770,
784, 799; *Cain* 685; *Childe Harold* 668
and *n*; *Hebrew Melodies* (1815) 649;
Manfred 678
Byttering (15th c.) 141, 143

Cabanilles, Juan (1644–1712) 438
Cabezón, Antonio de (*c.* 1500–66) 236,
241, 338; instrumental music 236–7,
293; *Obras de musica* (1578) 293
caccia (chace) 124, 130
Caccini, Francesca (1587–*c.* 1640) 312
Caccini, Giulio (*c.* 1550–1610) 268, 269,
274, 296, 307
Euridice (1602) 271; *Nuove musiche*
(1602) 274, 280, 'Amarilli' 274, 304,
308; *Nuove musiche e nuova maniera*
(1614) 296, 297
Cadéac, Pierre (*fl.* 1538) 216; chanson, 'Je
suys déshéritée' (attrib.) 212, 245
Caedmon (*fl.* 670) 54
Caffarelli (1710–83) 447
Caffarelli, Filippo 448*n*, 476*n*
Cage, John (b. 1912) 853
cakewalk 817
calamel 125
Caldara, Antonio (1670–1736) 372, 399,
425*n*, 550; 'Crucifixus' 410; opera 445;
Passion 539; *sonate da chiesa* 425
Calder, Alexander (b. 1898) 853
Calderón de la Barca, Pedro (1600–81)
316, 325
Caldwell, John 186*n*, 240*n*
Callcott, John (1766–1821) 665
Calvin, John (1509–64) 220
Calvinist psalms and psalters 219–22, 226
Calzabigi, Ranieri di (1714–95) 464, 465,
466, 471
Cambert, Robert (*c.* 1628–77) 324, 369,
373, 421

Cambini, Giuseppe (1746–1825) 496, 545
Cameron, Francis 293*n*
Cammarono, Salvatore (*fl.* 1847) 710
Campion, Jean 117
Campion, Thomas (1567–1620) 280
Campo, Conrado del (1876–1953) 801
Campra, André (1660–1744) 376–7, 388,
432, 454; ballet, *Le Carnaval de Venise*
(1699) 367*n*, 376*n*; motets 413 and *n*
(Ex. 143), 414; *opéra-ballets* 376, 377, 388;
tragédies lyriques 376–7 (Ex. 129), 469
Cannabich, Christian (1731–98) 491, 494,
496, 498, 522
Cannabich, Rose 522 and *n*
canon 124, 130
Canonici Codex 141, 151*n*, 160*n*
canso 100
'cantata', the earliest uses of the term 296,
297, 303
cantigas 98–9, 99
Cantigas de Amore e de Maldizer 98
Cantigas de Santa Maria 98, 99, 197
canto carnascialescho 171
cantus gestualis (chanson de geste) 94
canzono (canzonetto) a ballo 171, 274
Čapek, Karel (1890–1938) 837
Capell, Richard 648
Capirola, Vincenzo, lute MS (*c.* 1517) 235
and *n*
Cappi and Diabelli 647
Caproli, Carlo (*fl.* 1654) 323
Capua, Rinaldo di (*c.* 1710–after 1770)
453, 457
Cara, Marchetto (late 15th c.) 173
Cardew, Cornelius (b. 1936) 854
Cardoso, Manuel (*c.* 1571–1650) 345
Carey, Henry (*c.* 1687–1743) 393
Carissimi, Giacomo (1605–74) 296, 299,
302*n*, 347, 379, 381, 390; influence on
Purcell 391; pupils 387, 398, 410, 413;
cantatas 301–2 (Ex. 89); church music
345, *348*, 410, 411; oratorios 345, **347**,
395, 420
Carleton, Nicholas (16th c.) 241
Carmina Burana 99–100
Carner, Mosco 835*n*
Carnicer, Ramón (1789–1855) 595
Carniolanus (Jacobus Handl) (1550–91)
254
carnival songs 171–2
Carpentras, *see* Genet
Carr, Benjamin (1768–1831) 595
Carse, Adam 499*n*
Carter, Elliott (b. 1908) 845, **853**
Carver, Anthony F. 232*n*

Carver, Robert (1487–*c.* 1546) 242 and *n*
Casella, Alfredo (1883–1947) 609*n*, 832
Casimiri, Raffaele 246*n*
Cassiodorus (*c.* 485–*c.* 580) 61, 62, 75
castanets: Assyrian 19, Egyptian *16*, 17
Castigliano, Baldassare 170
Catalani, Alfredo (1854–93) 743–4
Catel, Charles-Simon (1773–1830) 577, 579, 592, 655
Catherine II of Russia 453, 478, 480
Cauchie, Maurice 220*n*, 414*n*
caudae 108, 112
Caula, Giacomo 322*n*
Caurroy, *see* Du Caurroy
Cavalieri, Emilio de (*c.* 1550–1602) 269, 270, 271, 273; *Rappresentazione di Anima e di Corpo* (1600) 273–4
Cavalli, Francesco (1602–76) 366; *Musiche sacre* (1656) 349; operas 319–20, 323–4, 358–9, 421, *Artemisia L'* (1656) 320, 359, *Calisto, La* (1651) 320, 420, 421, *Didone, La* (1641) 319, 320*n* (Ex. 103), *Doriclea, La* (1645) 319–20, 320*n*, 420, *Egisto, L'* (1643) 319, 322, *Ercole amante* (1662) 324, 373, 421, *Eritrea, L'* (1652) 359, *Giasone, Il* (1649) 320, 322, 420, *Ipermestra, L'* (1658) 358*n*, *Nozze di Tete e di Peleo, Le* (1639) 319, *Orimonte, L'* (1650) 320, *Ormindo, L'* (1644) 420, *Scipione Africano* (1664) 324, *Xerse, Il* (1654) 320 and *n*, 324, 359, 421
Cavazzoni, Girolamo (*fl.* 1542) 232, 235, 287
Cavazzoni, Marco Antonio (*c.* 1490–*c.* 1559) 232, 235 and *n*, 241*n*
Cavos, Catterino (1776–1840) 589*n*, 594
Cazzati, Maurizio (*c.* 1620–77) 350; instrumental music 419, 425; oratorios 398 and *n*; vocal works 379 and *n*, 411
Čech, Svatopluk (1846–1908) 837
Celtic liturgy, the 4, 57
Ceremoniale parisiense (1662) 436
Certon, Pierre (*fl.* mid-16th c.) 216, 219–22 *passim*
Cesari, Gaetano 137*nn*
Cesti, Pietro (Antonio) (1623–69) 320–2, 329, 360, 366; cantatas 302 and *n* (Ex. 90); operas 359, 422, *Argia, L'* (1655) 322, 421, *Disgrazie d'Amore, Le* (1667) 422, *Dori, La* (1661) 321 (Ex. 104(ii)), 359, 422, *Orontea* (1649) 320–2 (Ex. 104(i)), 359*n*, *Pomo d'Oro, Il* (1667) 322, 360, 422, *Schiava fortunata, La* (with M. A. Ziani, *c.* 1690) 366, 422
cetera (cittern) 270

Chabrier, Emmanuel (1841–94) 575, 702. 778
  operas 741–2 (Ex. 286), 743, 801
chace 124
Chadd, David 242*n*
Chadwick, George (1854–1931) 700
Chailley, Jacques 104*n*, 126*n*
Chaillou de Pestain (14th c.) 118
Chaix, C. 457*n*
Chambers, E. K. 92*n*
Chambonnières, Jacques Champion de (after 1601–*c.* 1671) 340, 341–2, 435, 436
Chamisso, Adalbert von (1781–1838) 770, 791
'Champmeslé, La' (Marie Desmares) (1642–98) 373
Chancun de Guillelme, Gormont et Isembart (11th c.) 94
Chandos, James Brydges, 1st Duke of (1673–1744) 417–18
chang 567
chanson: Burgundian 151–3 (Exx. 36–7), French 213–19 (Exx. 59–61); madrigalian influence and *musique mesurée* in 283–4; Netherland 264–5
chanson courtois 97–9
chanson de geste 94–6
Chanson de Roland (early 12th c.) 71, 94
Chansonnier Cangé (*c.* 1300) 97, 100–1 (Ex. 16), *101*, 113
Chantilly Codex 136, 137, 154
Chapi, Ruperto (1851–1909) 741*n*
Chapman, Roger 334*n*
Char, René (b. 1907), 851
Charlemagne (768–814) 4–5, 59, 70
Charles IV (1316–78), Emperor 130
Charles V (1500–58), Emperor and King of Spain 74, 126, 167, 208, 236, 244
Charles VI (1685–1740), Emperor 550
Charles I (1600–49) of England 300, 308, 333
Charles II (1630–85) of England 415
Charles IX (1550–74) of France 284
Charles X (1757–1836) of France 662
Charles I (of Anjou) (1226–85) of Naples 115, 116
Charles (the Bold) (1433–77), Duke of Burgundy 153
Charlotte (1744–1818), Queen of England 494
Charnasse, Hélène 412*n*
Charpentier, Gustave (1860–1956) 702, 802
Charpentier, Marc-Antoine (1634–1704) 387, 412*n*, 413, 545

Index

Charteris, Richard 290*n*, 332*n*
'Chase de septem temporibus' (14th c.) 124
'Chastelain de Couci' (13th c.) 101, 103*n*
Chausson, Ernest (1855–99) 700–2, 778, 787–8, 802
Chaykovsky, Pyotr Ilyich (1840–93) 575, 689*n*, 690*n*, 719, 780; chamber music 779–80; church music 758–9 (Ex. 290); operas 690, 731–3; orchestral works (including ballet music, concertos and symphonies) 689–90, 698, 701; piano works 773, 776; songs 783
Chekhov, Anton Pavlovich (1860–1904) 733
chelys (lyra) 24
Chemin, du (16th c.) 216
chêng 567, 569
Chernïshevsky, Nikolay Gavrilovich (1828–89) 730
Cherubic Hymn 65, 758–9
Cherubini, Luigi (1760–1842) 470, 508, 606, 612, 655, 662, 706; Masses and other church music 658–60, 663, 664, 748, *Messe solennelle* in D minor 659 (Ex. 254), 664; operas 577–8, 579, 582, *Anacréon* (1803) 580, 673, *Abencérages, Les* (1813) 583, *Démophoon* (1788) 470, *Deux journées, Les* (1800) 578–9, 581, *Eliza ou le Mont St Bernard* (1794) 578, 580, *Faniska* (1805) 578, 580, *Lodoïska* (1791) 470, 577–8, *Médée* (1797) 577, 578, 579, 582, 667, 681; songs 643; String Quartet in E flat 626*n*; Symphony in D (1815) 608–9 (Ex. 231(ii))
Chiarelli, Alessandro 317*n*
Chickering 761
ch'in 565, 567, 569
ching 564
Ch'ing (Manchu) dynasty (1644–1912) 568
Ching Fang (*fl.c.* 40 B.C.) 565
ching-hsi 568
chipendari 813
chittarone 269, 270
Chopin, Fryderyk (1810–49) 575, 588, 761; compared with Liszt 761–3, Schumann 763–4; influences on 616, 641; Cello Sonata 762; songs 769; works for piano and orchestra 616, 761; works for solo piano 635, 641, 761, 762, 763
Choralfantasien 337
Choral-variations *337*
Christian IV (1577–1648) of Denmark 280, 283

Christina (1626–89), Queen of Sweden 300, 322
Chrodegang (8th c.) 58
Chrysander, Friedrich 367–8*nn*, 381*n*, 417
Chrysostom, St (347–407) 3
Ch'un-ch'iu (239 B.C.) 564, 565
Churgin, Bathia 484*n*
Cicero, Marcus Tullius (106–43 B.C.) 47
Cicognini, Giacinto (1606–60) 320–1
Ciconia, Johannes (*c.* 1335–1411) 137, 138, 139, 140–1, 145; 'Doctorum principem' 140 (Ex. 31)
Cima, Gian Paolo (b.*c.* 1570) 328
Cimarosa, Domenico (1749–1801) 469, 473, 478, 577
cinquillo 815
cithara see *kithara*
citharoedus 48, 49
cittern 240*n*, 270
Civitate, Antonius de (early 15th c.) 139, 161
clappers 10, 13, 16–17, 41, 44, 64; Greek (*krotala*) 25, 25, 41
clarinet, the 504 and *n*; *see also* double-clarinet
Clarke, Jeremiah (*c.* 1673–1707) 391, 393
Clarke (-Whitfield), John (1770–1836) 654
Claudel, Paul (1868–1955) 828, 830
Claudius, Matthias (1740–1815), 531, 647
clausulae 103, 108–9, 111
clavecinistes 340–2
clavichord 184, 188
Clayton, Thomas (*c.* 1670–*c.* 1730) 370
Clemens 'non Papa', Jacobus (*c.* 1510–*c.* 1557) 207, 242; chansons 212 (Exx. 57–8), 213–14, 245, 'C'est a grant tort' 216–18 (Ex. 60(ii)); Magnificats 209, 212; Masses 209, 211–13, *Missa Misericorde* 209, 211–12 (Ex. 56); motets 209–11, 232, 'Jerusalem surge' 208–9 (Ex. 54), 'Tulerunt autem' 210–11 (Ex. 55), 'Vox in Rama' 209, 233
Clement VI (Pope 1342–52) 123
Clement VII (Pope 1378–94) 135
Clement VII (Pope 1523–34) 179
Clement IX (Pope 1667–9), see Rospigliosi, Giulio
Clement of Alexandria (*c.* 150–*c.* 220) 52; *Paedagogus* 51
Clementi, Muzio (1752–1832) 206, 508, 523, 598*n*, 604, 632*n*; compared with Beethoven 637; pupils 613, 631; *Gradus ad Parnassum* (1817–26) 637; sonatas 523 (Ex. 199), 630–1, 637; symphonies 609, 611

Clemenza de Tito, La (1747) 477
Cleonides (2nd c.) 49
Clérambault, Louis-Nicolas (1676–1749)
  413*n*, 435, 438; *cantates françaises* 389
  (Ex. 134)
Clercx, Suzanne 140*n*
Cloveshoe, Council of (747) 58
'Club Anthem' ('I will always give thanks',
  Humfrey *et al.*, 1664) 415
Coates, William 290*n*, 332*n*
Coclico, Adrian Petit (16th c.) 175
Cocteau, Jean (1889–1963) 827–30 *passim*
Codex Calixtinus 86, 87*n*, 88
Coelho, Manuel Rodrigues (*c.* 1555–*c.*
  1635) 340
Coeuroy, André 692*n*
Coffey, Charles (d. 1745), *The Devil to
  Pay* 450, 459
Colasse, Pascal (1649–1709) 366, 376
Coleman, Charles (d.*c.* 1664) 326, 369
Colista, Lelio (1629–80) 425
Collegium symphoniacorum 48
Collegium tibicinum Romanorum 48
Colloredo-Waldersee, Hieronymus von
  (1732–1812) 552–4
Collin, Heinrich von (1772–1811) 600
Collins, H. B. 187*n*, 242*n*
Collins, Walter 263*n*
Colonna, Giovanni Paolo (1637–95) 398,
  410, 411
color 119
comedie armoniche 267
comédie-ballet 324–5, 373
comédiens italiens du Roy 450
Comes, Juan Bautista (1568–1643) 345,
  801
commedia dell'arte 267
commedia musicale (1639) 315
Commemoratio brevis de tonis . . . (*c.* 10th
  c., anon.) 86*n*
'Como poden per sas culpas' 99
Compenius, Johann Heinrich (*fl.* 1624)
  337*n*
Compère, Loyset (*c.* 1450–*c.* 1518) 161,
  165, 170, 188, 219; chansons 168–9, 173
  and *n*, 174, 'Venez regretz' 166 (Ex.
  44(ii)), 167*n*; Mass, 'Alles regrets' 167
concert sinfonia 483–4
concertato style 317, 318, **344**
'concerto', the term 249
concerto grosso **423–4** (Ex. 147), 482–3, 487
concertos, the earliest solo 427
conducting, early instances 607*n*
conductus 103, 108–9, 112, 116
conductus-style, English 142–3 (Ex. 32)

conga 815
Congreve, William (1670–1729), *Semele*
  543
Conon de Béthune (12th c.) 97, 98
Conradi, August (1821–73) 681
consort and virginals, English music for
  290–4, *291*
Constance, Council of (1414–18) 138, 141
Constantine (*c.* 288–337), Emperor 50
Constantine V, Emperor (741–75) 59
Contarini collection 319
Conti, Francesco (1682–1732) 399
Cooke, — (d. 1456) 141
Cooke, Henry (*c.* 1616–72) 326, 369
Cooke, Thomas (*c.* 1615–72) **390**, 391, 415
Cooper, James Fenimore (1789–1851) 669
Cooper, Martin 461*n*
Copland, Aaron (b. 1900) 824, 845, 856
Coprario (Cooper), John (*c.* 1575–1626)
  290, 332
Coptic liturgy 6, 13, 54
Coradini, Francesco (*fl.* 1730) 477
Cordier, Baude (?14th–15th c.) 136, 137
Corelli, Arcangelo (1653–1713) 205, 423,
  428, 429, 430, 544; *Concerti grossi*, op. 6
  424; trio sonatas 205, **424–5**, 425–6, 427
cori spezzati 232
Corneille, Pierre (1606–85) 373, 452
Corneille, Thomas (1625–1709) 373
Cornelius, Peter (1824–74) 574, 684–5,
  713, 739, **788–9**
Cornelius Nepos (1st c. B.C.) 23*n*
cornett 249, 251, 252, 253
cornu *41*, 42 and *n*, 46
Cornysh, William (d. before 1502) 187*n*
Cornysh, William (*c.* 1468–1523) 187 and
  n, 188
Correa de Arauxo, Francisco
  (*c.* 1575–1663) 340
Corrette, Michel (1709–95) 518
Corselli, Francesco (d. 1778) 477
Corsi, Jacopo (*fl.* 1592) 271
Costeley, Guillaume (*c.* 1531–1606) 283,
  284
Cöthen: the Court at 430, 431; Prince
  Leopold of (Anhalt-Cöthen) 431, 535
Cotte, Roger 457*n*
Cotto(n), Johannes (*fl.c.* 1100) 82 and *n*
Couperin, François (1668–1733) 414;
  Concerts Royaux (1722) 436*n*; *Leçons de
  ténèbres* (1714) 414 (Ex. 144); *Pièces de
  clavecin* (1713–30) **436**, 517; Masses 414,
  438; sonatas 205, **425–6**
Couperin, Louis (*c.* 1626–61) 334, 340–2
Courant, Maurice 568*n*

courtly song, medieval 98–9, in France and Germany 97–8, its types, forms, and performance 100–2

Cousineau, Georges and Jacques-Georges (latter d. 1824) 528*n*

Coussemaker, Charles de (1805–76) 88*n*, 103, 106*n*, 112*nn*, 142*n*

Coverdale, Miles, *Goostly psalmes and spirituall songes* (1543) 220

Cowell, Henry (1897–1965) 853

Cracoviensis, Nicolaus (Mikolaj z Krakowa) (?15th–16th c.) 226

Cracow: Cathedral 412, Monastery of the Holy Ghost 225–6

Cramer, Johann Baptist (1771–1858) 598*n*, 603, 615, 631, 634

Cranmer, Thomas (1489–1556), Archbishop 207

Crecquillon, Thomas (d.*c.* 1557) 207, 208, 209, 211, 213, 216

Crétin, Guillaume (*fl.* 1497) 161

Croce, Giovanni (*c.* 1557–1609) 251, 252, 267, 278, 280

Crocker, Richard 89

Croft, William (1678–1727) 417

Croll, Gerhard 365*n*

Cromwell, Oliver (1599–1658) 356

Cromwell, Thomas (1485–1540) 241

Crosby, C. Russell 260*n*

Crotch, William (1775–1847) 654, 662

Crotti, Archangelo, *Concerti Ecclesiastici* (1608) 253

Cruz, Ramón de la (*fl.* 1768) 477

Ctesibius of Alexandria (*c.* 250 B.C.) 44–5

Cui, César Antonovich (1835–1918) 731, 786 and *n*

'Cum altre ucele' 129–30 (Ex. 28)

cummedeja in museca 448

Cummings, Edward Estlin (b. 1894) 854

Cure of Saul, The (1763) 544

Curtis, Alan 294*n*

Cuvelier, Jean (14th–15th c.) 135

Cuyler, Louise 183*nn*

Cuzzoni, Francesca (1700–72) 447

'Cyclic' Mass 144–6

cymbals 12, 19, 20, 21, 25, 43, 572

Czerny, Karl (1791–1857) 602, 639

D'Accone, Frank A. 170*n*, 172*n*, 227*n*

Dach, Simon (1605–59) 305

Dadelsen, Georg von 408*n*, 536*n*

Dalayrac, Nicolas-Marie (1753–1809) 471, 473, 579, 584

dalla Libera, Sandro 287*n*, 289*n*

Dallapiccola, Luigi (b. 1904) **833–4**, 853, 858

Damasus I, St (Pope 366–84) 57

Damett, Thomas (d. 1437) 141

Dammonis, Innocentius (before 1508) 173

Damon of Oa (*fl.* 432 B.C.) 31

Danckert, Werner 328*n*, 419*n*

Dandelot, A. 749*n*

Dandrieu, Jean-François (1682–1738) 436

Danjou, Jean-Louis Félix (1812–66) 749

danmono 570–1

Dante Alighieri (1265–1321) 266

Da Ponte, Lorenzo (1749–1838) 470, 475, 476

Daquin, Louis-Claude (1694–1772) 517

darb 191

Dargomïzhsky, Aleksandr Sergeyevich (1813–69), operas **728–30** (Exx. 280–1), 733; songs 768–9, 783, **784–5** (Ex. 247)

Darmstadt *Ferienkurse* 848–9

Dart, Thurston 261*nn*, 263*n*, 275*n*, 279–80*nn*, 290–3*nn*, 308*n*, 332*n*, 513*n*

Darwīsh Muhammad (*fl.* 1900) 198

'daseian' signs 77

Daudet, Alphonse (1840–97) 691

Daumer, Georg Friedrich (1800–75) 789

Dauvergne, Antoine (1713–97) 459

Davaux, Jean-Baptiste (1742–1822) 496

Davenant, Sir William (1606–68) 369, 370; music by H. Lawes *et al.* to his texts 325, 326

David, King of Israel 2, 38–9, 52

David, Félicien (1810–76) 678*n*, 691, 746, 764, 766, 768; opera, *Lalla-Roukh* (1862) 740; oratorio, *Moïse au Sinaï* 750

David, Ferdinand (1810–73) 678

David, Hans 339*n*

David, Jacques-Louis (1748–1825) 577

Davïdov, Stepan Ivanovich (1777–1825) 589*n*

Davies, Peter Maxwell (b. 1934) 859

Davison, Nigel 165*n*, 242*nn*

Davy, Richard (*c.* 1467–*c.* 1516) 187

Dawes, Frank 542*n*

Dean, Winton 542*nn*

Dean-Smith, Margaret 310*n*

Deane, Norma 45*n*

Dearnley, Christopher 416–17*nn*

Deathridge, John 675*n*

Debussy, Claude (1862–1918) 572, 576, 804, 820, 840, 855; influence on Albéniz 804, Bartók 805, Falla 804, Ravel 803; influenced by Wagner 575, 802; ballet, *Jeux* (1912) 809; chamber sonatas 809; *Le Martyre de Saint Sébastien* (1911)

809, 810; *Pelléas et Mélisande* (1902)
802, *803*; orchestral works 802, 803;
piano works 779, 803, 804, 809; songs
788, 804; String Quartet 779, 802
Dedekind, Constantin Christian
(1628–1715) 306
Degen, Dietz 529*n*
Dehmel, Richard (1863–1920) 797
Delibes, Léo (1836–91) 698, 740–1, 786
Delius, Frederick (1862–1934) 805–6, 810,
824
Délivrance de Renaud, La (1619) 307, 322*n*
della Corte, Andrea 381*n*, 399*n*
della Valle, Pietro (*fl.* 1640) 295
Demantius, Christoph (1567–1643) 283,
289, 354
demoeng 572
dengaku 570
Denisov, Edisson (b. 1929) 857
Denmark 280, 283
Dennison, Peter 415*n*
Dent, Edward J. 300*n*, 326*nn*, 364*nn*,
369*nn*, 381–2*nn*
'Deo gracias, Anglia' 150
De organo (?9th–10th c.) 80; 'Benedicta
sit' *79*, 80 (Ex. 10)
Dering, Richard (*c.* 1580–1630) 309*n*, 356
Desmarets, Henri (1662–1741) 376, 413
Desportes, Philippe (16th c.) 356
Destouches, André Cardinal (1672–1749)
376, **377**, 388, 456
Deutsch, Otto Erich 290*n*, 447*n*, 609*n*
Deutsches Evangelisches Kirchen-Gesangbuch
(1854) 752
Dezède, Alexandre (Nicolas) (*c.* 1742–92)
471
Diabelli, Antonio (1781–1858) 637, 639,
640; *see also* Cappi and Diabelli
Diabelli Variations 637, 639
Dialogo di Christo e della Samaritana
(*c.* 1598) 346
Dialogus de musica (11th c.) 82
Dibdin, Charles (1745–1814) 477
Diderot, Denis (1713–84) 465, 502
Dietrich, Sixt (*c.* 1493–1548) 223
Dieudonné, A. 421*n*
diezeugmenon 76
diferencias 236–7
Diletsky, Nikolay (*fl.* 1680) 412*n*
Diomedes Cato (*fl.* 1600) 285
Diruta, Girolamo (1561–after 1625) 285,
286
Discantus positio vulgaris (12th c. treatise)
102 (Ex. 17)
Disertori, Benvenuto 184*n*, 287*n*

dithyramb 28, 30, 31
Dittersdorf, Karl Ditters von (1739–99)
491, 493, 500*n*; concertos 494; operas
476, 631; quintets and quartets 507 (Ex.
188); symphonies 507
Dittmer, Luther 103*n*, 104*n*, 110*n*
divisio modi 103, 105, 114
Dlugoraj, Wojciech (Albert) (*fl.* 1619) 285
Dmitriev, A. N. 732*n*
Dobrokhotov, B. V. 626*n*
Doe, Paul 242*n*
Doernberg, Erwin 695*n*
Dohnányi, Ernö (1877–1960) 806
Doles, Johann Friedrich (1715–97) 538
Dolmetsch, Nathalie 332*n*
Domling, Wolfgang 181*n*
Donati, Ignazio (d. 1638) 349–50, 411
Donato, Baldissera (*c.* 1530–1604) 232
Donatus de Florentia (Donato da Cascia)
(14th c.) 131
Donizetti, Gaetano (1797–1848) 586, 705,
710; operas 588, 708, **709**, 713*n*; string
quartets 626
Dore, Jehan (*fl.* 1429) 138
Dostoevsky, Feodor Mikhaylovich
(1821–81) 837–8
double-clarinet 13, 18
double reed-pipe 2–3, 38: Assyrian 21,
Egyptian 13, 16, *16*, 17, Elamite 20,
Etruscan 40, 41, Greek, see *aulos*,
Indian 561, Mesopotamian 10, 12, 18,
19, *19*, Muslim 190
Dowland, John (1563–1626) **279–80**, *279*,
285, 290–1, *291*, 308, 357
Dowland, Robert (*c.* 1586–1641) 280, 285,
308
Draeseke, Felix (1835–1913) 688, 739, 773
Draghi, Antonio (*c.* 1635–1700) **360–1**,
365, 369, 373–4, 398
Draghi, Carlo (late 18th c.) 360
Draghi, Giovanni Battista (*fl.* 1674) 369,
370
Dresden: Court at 257, 260, 372, 386, 412,
430, 589*n*, Court orchestra 491*n*, Court
theatre 358, Frauenkirche 747,
Hofkirche 663, Landesbibliothek 483
Droz, E. 153*n*
Drummond, Pippa 487*n*
drums 3, 12: African 813, *814*, Assyrian
19, 21, Chinese 564, Egyptian 13, 17,
Elamite 20, frame-drums (tambourines)
10, 11, 13, hand-drum (*tôph*, *duff*) 38,
191, *571*, Japanese 569, 570, pedestal-
drums (Babylonian) 12, Roman 43
Drux, Herbert 542*n*

Dryden, John (1631–1700) 369 and *n*, 370, 384, 391, 393, 542
Du Caurroy, Eustache (1549–1609) 256, 284, 355, 357
Ducis, Benedictus (de Opitiis) (d. 1544) 188, 223
Dufay, Guillaume (*c.* 1400–74) 73, **138**–**9**, 142, **148**–**9**, 151, 156; 169; and Binchois 152–3; and the 'cyclic' Mass 144–6; and proportional notation 146–8; chansons **151**–**2** (Ex. 37), 164, 165, 170; Masses 144, 145, **146**–**8** (Exx. 34–5), 160; motets 141, 144 (Ex. 33)
duff 191
Dufflocq, E. M. 271*n*
Dufourcq, Norbert 435*n*
Dukas, Paul (1865–1935) **804**, 808, 809, 831
Du Mont, Henry (1610–84) 334, 356, 412 and *n*, 413, 754
dūnāy 195
Duni, Egidio-Romoaldo (1709–75) 452, 459, 461, 479; operas **454**, 464, 473
Dunstable, John (d. 1453) 73, **141**–**2**, 145, 146, 149, 160
Duparc, Henri (1848–93) 692, 787
Durante, Francesco (1684–1755) 512, 546, 547, 548; Masses 547–8 (Ex. 210)
Durazzo, Count (*fl.* 1758) 459, 464
Durey, Louis (b. 1888) 828
Dürr, Alfred 408*n*, 535
Dussek, Johann Wenceslaus (1760–1812) 597, 598, 620, 621; piano concertos 599 (Ex. 226), 604, 613, 614, 631; piano sonatas 631–2
Dvořák, Antonin (1841–1904) 576, **696**–**7**, 711, 806; ballad, *The Spectre's Bride* (1884) 760; chamber music 778, **780**–**1**, *Cypřiše* (1887) 781–2 (Ex. 296(ii)); concertos 693, 697; operas **735**–**7** (Ex. 283), 799; oratorio, *Svatá Ludmila* (1886) 756; orchestral works 697, 698; piano works 776; songs 780, 781–2 (Ex. 296), 783; symphonies 687, 693, **696**–**7**, 701, 781
Dyagilev, Sergey (1872–1929) 576, **808**–**9**, 824–7 *passim*, 630, 831
Dzerzhinsky, Ivan (1909–78) 843, 844

East, Michael (*fl.* 1618) 278, 356
East, Thomas (*c.* 1540–1609) 203
Eberl, Anton (1765–1807) 603, 607, 621, 631; Symphony in E flat 601 (Ex. 227)
Eberlin, Johann Ernst (1702–62) 516, 552 and *n*, 553*n*; oratorios 539

Eccard, Johann (1553–1611) 258
Eccles, John (1668–1735) 393
Eckard, Johann Gottfried (1735–1809) 518
Edelmann, Johann Friedrich (1749–94) 545
'Edi beo thu' (13th c.) 115
Edward III (1312–77) of England 120
Edwards, Warwick 291*nn*
Egerton MS. (*c.* 1430) 143 and *n*, 150
Eggebrecht, Hans Heinrich 105*n*, 123*n*
Egidius de Lens (*fl.* 1390) 137
Egyptian music 12–18, 198
Eichendorff, Joseph von (1788–1857) 770, 771, 790
Eichner, Ernst (1740–77) 491
Eimert, Herbert (1897–1972) 851
Einhard (770–840) 70
Einstein, Alfred 173*n*, 174 and *nn*, 215*n*, 229*n*, 230*nn*, 231, 234*nn*, 266–7*nn*, 288*n*, 301*n*, 304*nn*, 383*n*, 425*n*, 465*nn*, 474*n*, 496*n*, 500*n*, 549*n*, 553*n*, 598*n*
Eisenach 432
Eisenstadt 492, 656, 657
Eisenstein, Sergey (1898–1948) 844
Eitner, Robert 223*n*, 320–1*nn*, 361*n*, 420*n*, 422*n*
Eleanor of Aquitaine (d. 1204) 95, 97
electronic music **851**–**2**, 855, 858
Elert, Piotr (d. 1653) 312
Elgar, Sir Edward (1857–1934) 700, **798**, 810, 824
Elizabeth I (1533–1603) 241, 275, 291
Ellerton, John Lodge (1801–73), string quartets 766–7 (Ex. 292)
Ellinwood, Leonard 242*n*
Elliott, Kenneth 242*n*
Elsner, Joseph Xaver (1769–1854) 594, 651; polonaises 635 (Ex. 242)
Elústiza, J. B. 179*n*
Emslie, McD. 308*n*
Encina, Juan del (*c.* 1469–*c.* 1530) 167, 177, 179–80
Enescu, Georg (1881–1955), opera, *Oedipe* (1936) **838**–**9** (Ex. 307)
Engel, Hans 222*n*, 404*n*, 599*n*, 603*n*
Engelmann, Georg (*c.* 1575–1632) 334, 335
Englander, Richard 487*n*, 522*n*
Engyldeo of Regensburg (mid-9th c.) 89*n*
Ephraem (306–73) 55–6
Epstein, Peter 401*n*
Érard, Sébastien (1752–1831) 761
Erbach, Christian (*c.* 1570–1635) 285
Erkel, Ferenc (1810–93), operas 719 (Ex. 278), 734*n*

Erlanger, Baron d' 195*n*, 196*n*
Erlebach, Phillipp Heinrich (1657–1714)
 385, 386
eschiquier 120
Escobar, Pedro (d. 1514) 167, 179
Escorial MS. 155
estampie (stampida) 100, 112
Este family, d', *see* Ferrara, Mantua
Esteve, Pablo (d. 1794) 477
Estocart, Pascal de L' (b.*c*. 1540) 256
Eszterháza 493, 500, 504*n*, 506, 551–2
Eszterházy, Prince Nikolaus (1765–1833)
 658
Eszterházy, Prince Nikolaus Joseph
 (1714–90) 472, 506, 526
Eszterházy, Princess Herminegild (*fl.*
 1808) *661*
Ethelwold, Bishop of Winchester,
 Concordia Regularis (*c*. 970) 91
Etheria (*fl.* 380) 55, 56
Ethiopian church music 54
Eton College Choir book (*c*. 1490–1502)
 186–7, 188, 242
Etruscan music **40–2**, *40–1*
Ett, Caspar (1788–1847) 752
Euclid, *Katatome kanonos* (*c*. 300 B.C.)
 28–9, 193
Eugenius IV (Pope 1431–47) 139
Euripides (480–406 B.C.) 30, 34–5, 42
Eusebius of Caesarea (*c*. 260–*c*. 340)
 39–40, 50, 55
Evans, A. J. 12*n*
Evelyn, John (1620–1706) q. 318, q. 415
Expert, Henry 178*n*, 219*nn*, 239*n*, 256*n*,
 283–4*nn*
Erlebach, Philipp Heinrich (1657–1714)
 662

Faenza Codex 131, **156**–7 (Ex. 40), *157*,
 158
Falla, Manuel de (1876–1946) 804, 830*n*,
 831
Fallersleben, Hoffmann von 783
Fano, Fabio 137*nn*, 183*n*
Fantasie et rechercari a tre voci . . . (1549)
 234
fantasy (fancy) (English) 292, 332
Fārābi, Al (*c*. 870–*c*. 950) 194–5
Farinelli (Carlo Broschi) (1705–82) 447,
 477, 512
Farmer, H. G. 10*n*, 44 and *n*, 190*n*, 192
Farnaby, Giles (*c*. 1566–1640) 291, **293**,
 307
Fasch, Johann Friedrich (1688–1758) 432
Fātimid caliphate (from 909) 195

Fauré, Gabriel (1845–1924) 803, 810, 838;
 chamber music 778–9, 826; piano works
 778; Requiem (1887) 758; songs **787**,
 788
Fauvel MS., see *Roman de Fauvel*
fauxbourdon 144 (Ex. 33)
Favart, Charles-Simon (1710–92) 451,
 454, 458, *458*, 459, 478
Favart, Justine (1727–72) 458, *458*
favola rappresentata (recitata) 311
Fayrfax, Robert (*c*. 1464–1521) 187 and *n*,
 188
'Fayrfax Book' 188
Federhofer, Hellmut 409*n*
Federico, Gennaro (*fl.* 1733) 448
Federlein, Gottlieb (*fl.* 1871) 723*n*
Feininger, Laurence 145*n*, 345*n*
'Felix namque' (*c*. 1400) 186
Fellerer, K. G. 245*n*
Fellowes, E. H. 261*n*, 275*n*, 279–80*nn*,
 292*n*, 308*n*, 415*n*
Feragut, Beltrame (Bertrand) (*fl.* 1416)
 139
Ferand, Ernest T. 185*n*, 234*n*, 287*n*
Ferdinand I (1503–64), Emperor 244, 254
Ferdinand III (1608–57) Emperor 296,
 342
Ferdinand IV (d. 1654) of Bohemia and
 Hungary 342
Ferdinand V (1452–1516) of Aragon 167,
 179
Ferrabosco, Alfonso, the elder (1543–88)
 263, 275, 285; madrigals 276, 277 (Ex.
 80(i))
Ferrabosco, Alfonso, the younger (*c*.
 1575–1628) 292; *Ayres* (1609) 280, 308
 (Ex. 95(i))
Ferrabosco, Domenico (16th c.) 230, 245
Ferrara, Alfonso II d'Este (1533–97),
 Duke of 265
Ferrara, Ercole I d'Este (1431–1505),
 Duke of 170, 182
Ferrara, the 'ladies' of (Tarquinia Molza *et
 al.*) **265**–6, 269
Ferrari, Benedetto (1597–1681) 316 and *n*,
 396
Festa, Costanzo (*c*. 1495–1545) 174,
 228–9, 230, 232
Festa, Sebastiano (before 1530) 228
Fétis, François Joseph (1784–1871) 464*n*,
 469*n*, 470*n*, 667
Feustking, Friedrich Christian (*fl.* 1705)
 367
Fevin, Antoine de (*c*. 1470–*c*. 1512) 177,
 178, 188, 219

Fibich, Zdeněk (1850–1900) 693, 735, 782; operas **737–9** (Ex. 284), 799
Ficino, Marsilio (1433–99) 171
Fiedler, Gottlieb (*fl.* 1695) 366
Field, John (1782–1837) 613, 616, 631, **633–4**, 765; influence on Chopin 616, 641, Kalkbrenner 615; *divertissements* for piano and strings 623; piano concertos 604, **613–15** (Ex. 233); works for solo piano **633–4** (Exx. 240–1), 681
figured bass, earliest works with 309 and *n*
Filmer, Edward, *French Court-Aires . . .* (1629) 308
Filtz, Anton (*c.* 1730–60) 488, 493
Finck, Heinrich (*c.* 1444–1527) 180, 181, 182, 185, 442; 'Festum nunc' (Ascension hymn) 180–1 (Ex. 50)
Findeisen, Nikolay 394*n*
Finscher, Ludwig 167*n*, 181*n*
Fioravanti, Valentino (1770–1837) 585
Fischer, Johann Caspar F. (*c.* 1665–1746) 431 and *n*, 434, 435, 441, 442
Fischer, Kurt von 128*nn*
Fiske, Roger 478*n*
Fitzwilliam Virginal Book (?1609–19) 239*n*, 264*n*, **293, 294,** 307
Flaccus (2nd c. B.C.) 43
Flade, E. 184*n*
Flecha, Mateo (1530–1604) 283
Fleischhauer, Günter 40*n*, 41*n*, 43*n*
Fletcher, John (1579–1625) 370
Flor, Christian (1626–97), *St Matthew Passion* 401 (Ex. 139)
Florence: Accademia degli Immobili 327; carnival singers *172*; early composers from, *see* Bartholus, Donatus, Gherardello, Johannes, Laurentius, Paolo (de Florentia); Teatro della Pergola (1657) 327, 358
Flotow, Friedrich von (1812–83) 713
flute 190, *214*: Chinese 564, 567, 568, Egyptian 13, Indonesian 572, Japanese 569, Neolithic 7, Persian 18, 190, transverse 41, 270, 568
Fock, Gustav 409*n*
Foix, Gaston Phébus, Count of (d. 1391) 135
Folquet de Marseille (12th c.) 98
Fomin, Evstigney Ipatevich (1761–1800) 479*n*, 480; operas 480–1 (Exx. 173, 174(ii))
Fontaine, Pierre (d.*c.* 1450) 138
Fontana, Giovanni Battista (d. 1631) 329
Forbes, Elliot 579*n*
Ford, Anthony 371*n*

Ford, Thomas (*c.* 1580–1648) 356
Formé, Nicolas (1567–1638) 355
Förster, Emanuel Alois (1748–1823) 619
Forster, Georg (*c.* 1510–68) 225; *Ein Ausszug . . . Teutscher Liedlein* (1539) 185 (Ex. 52(i))
Forster, William (*fl.* 1784) 526
Fortner, Wolfgang (b. 1907) 849, 856
Förtsch, Johann Philipp (1652–1732) 366
Fortune, Nigel 81*n*, 279*n*, 298*n*
Foster, Donald H. 413*n*, 545*nn*
Foster, Stephen (1826–64) 817
Foucault, publ. *Cantates françoises* (1703) 388
Foucquet, Pierre-Claude (1694–1772) 517
Fouqué, Friedrich Karl Heinrich de la Motte (1777–1843) 590, 712
'Foweles in the frith' (13th-c. song) 115
Fowkes, Francis (*fl.* 1788) 558
Foxe, John (1516–87) 241 and *n*
Fox Strangways, Arthur (1859–1948) q. 562
frame-drum 10, 11, 18, *19*, 20
Françaix, Jean (b. 1912) 831
Francesco da Milano (1497–1543) 235, 239
Franchois (in the 'Buxheim' book, 1460–70) 160
Francis (of Assisi), St (1182–1226) 99, 836
Francis I (1494–1547) of France 188, 219
Francis II, later Francis I (1768–1835), Emperor 606*n*, 657
Francischiello (cellist) (d.*c.* 1750) 382
Franciscus, Magister (?F. Andrieu) (14th–15th c.) 135
Francisque, Antoine (*c.* 1570–1605) 284
Franck, César (1822–90) 464*n*, 692, 700, 787, 801; chamber music 766, 778; church music 758; operas 801; oratorios 892, 750, **757–8** (Ex. 289); orchestral works 692, 700, 701–2; organ works 773, 778; piano works 778
Franck, Johann Wolfgang (1644–*c.* 1710) 366, 386, 393
Franck, Melchior (*c.* 1580–1639) 283, 289, 334
Franco of Cologne (13th c.) 106; *Ars cantus mensurabilis* (before 1267) 112, 114; notation 114–15
Francoeur, François (1698–1787) 378, 426
Francoeur, Louis (1692–1745) 426
Frankfort, Henri 8*n*, 9*n*, 20*n*, 22*n*
Franklin, P. R. 795*n*
Franus, Jan (*fl.c.* 1505) 180
Franz, Robert (1815–92) 574, **770–1**, 788
Franz Josef (1830–1916) of Austria 754

'Frauenlob' (Heinrich von Meissen, d. 1318) 98
Frederick I (Barbarossa) (1123–90), Emperor 97
Frederick III (1415–93), Emperor 139
Frederick II (the Great) (1712–86) of Prussia 452, 486, 511, 538
Frederick Augustus (d. 1827) of Saxony 663
Frederick William II (1744–97) of Prussia 505, 618
Freiligrath, Ferdinand (1810–76) 763
'French overture', the 376, 421, 422 and *n*, 427, 482
Frescobaldi, Girolamo (1583–1643) 338, 340, 342, 438, 441; *Arie* (1630) 296; keyboard music 338–40 (Ex. 113)
Fricker, Peter Racine (b. 1920) 856
Friebert, Joseph (*fl.c.* 1790) 660
Friedrich von Husen (d. 1190) 98
Froberger, Johann Jakob (1616–67) 338, 340, 341, **342–3**, 434, 441
Fromm, Andreas (1621–83) 404
frottola 74, 171, **173–4** (Ex. 46), 203, 214–15, 226–7, 229, 231
Fry, William Henry (1813–64) 720
Frye, Walter (*fl.c.* 1470) **149**, 156, 160, 169, 187
Fuchs, Robert (1847–1927) 693*n*
Fuenllana, Miguel de 239
Fugger family (Augsburg) 259
Fuller, Loie (1862–1928) 807
Fuller Maitland, J. A. 293*n*, 513*n*
Funck, Heinz 160*n*
Funcke, Friedrich (1642–99) 401
fusa 139*n*
Fux, Johann Josef (1660–1741) 372, 398–9, 550; *Concentus musico-instrumentalis* (1701) 422*n*, 431; *Gradus ad Parnassum* (1725) 409–10; Masses 409, 537; operas 372, 398–9; oratorio, *La fede sacrilega . . .* (1714) 399*n*
Fuzelier, Louis (*fl.* 1735) 451

Gabrieli, Andrea (*c.* 1515–86) 232, **249**, 285, 287, 335, 338; influence on Marenzio 266, and Lassus 255; pupil, Hassler 259; 'Angelus ad pastores' 353; 'Benedicam Dominum' 251; *canzoni alla francese* 286, 287 (Ex. 82); 'Capriccio sopra Il Pass'e mezo Antico' 293; 'Magnificat anima mea' 249, **250** (Ex. 71); *Penitential Psalms* (1583) **248–9**; ricercari on chansons 287; *Sacrae cantiones* (1565) 248

Gabrieli, Giovanni (*c.* 1555–1612) **249**, 251–2, 278, 285, 288, 292; his influence on German music 303, 334; influenced by Lassus 255; his pupils 205, 283; *Canzoni et sonate* (1615) 289, **328**; *Concerti per voci & stromenti . . .* (1587) 249, 252; *Sacrae Symphoniae* (1597, 1615) **252–3**, 260, 288–9 (Ex. 84)
Gabrielli, Domenico (*fl.c.* 1680) 398
Gade, Niels (1817–90) 672, 686, 760, 764, 773, 791; overture, *Efterklang af Ossian* 672–3 (Ex. 256)
Gafurius, Franchinus (1451–1522) 165
gagaku 570 and *nn*, 571
Gagliano, Marco da (*c.* 1575–1642) 274, 296, 311
Gagnebin, Henri 222*n*
Galatea (c. 1630) 312
Galilei, Vincenzo (*c.* 1520–91) **268**, 285 and *n*, 418*n*
Galliard, Johann Ernst (*c.* 1680–1749) 371, 393
Gallican liturgy 4, 57, 58–9
Gallico, C. 252*n*
Gallo, Alberto 103*n*, 128*n*, 139*n*
'Gallus vocatus' *see* Jacobus Handl
Galpin, Francis 8*n*, 10*n*
Galuppi, Baldassare (1706–85) **452–4**, 472, 475*n*, 478, 515, 548; harpsichord sonatas **514** (Exx. 192–3), 515; operas **453** (Ex. 160), 491
gambang 572
gamelan 572, 847
gankogui 813, 814, *814*, 815
García, Manuel (1775–1832) 595
Gardano, Antonio (*fl.* 1577) 251
Garlandia, Johannes de, *De musica mensurabili positio* (*c.* 1240) 102, 103, 106
Gasparini, Francesco (1668–1727) 364, 379, 382
Gassmann, Florian Leopold (1729–74) 472 and *n*, 491, 496*n*, 550; Requiem (incompl.) 550–1 (Ex. 212)
Gastoldi, Giovanni Giacomo (d. 1622) 276, 278, 282
Gastoué, Amédée 58*n*, 109*n*, 135*n*, 356*n*, 412*n*, 426*n*
Gatti, C. 473*n*
Gaudentius (2nd c.) 49
Gaukler (jongleur) 95
Gaultier, Denis (*c.* 1600–72) 340, **341–2**
Gaultier, Ennemond (*c.* 1580–1651) 341 and *n*
Gautier, Théophile (1811–72) 691, 767, 768, 787

Index

Gaveaux, Pierre (1761–1825) 643
  Léonore (1798) 581–2 (Ex. 215(i))
Gay, John (1685–1732) 450, 836
Gazette musicale 748
Gazzaniga, Giuseppe (1743–1818) 473 and
  n, 500*n*
Gebrauchsmusik 835–6, 840
Geering, Arnold 225*n*
Geibel, Emanuel (1815–84), with Paul
  Heyse, *Spanisches Liederbuch* 783, 790
Geiringer, Karl 290*n*, 449*n*
Gelasius, St (Pope 492–6) 57, 59
Gellert, Christian Fürchtegott (1715–69)
  529, 538, 643
Geminiani, Francesco (*c.* 1680–1762) 483,
  487
gender 572
Genet, Elzéar (Carpentras) (*c.* 1470–1548)
  177, 179, 215, 227
Gennrich, Friedrich 94–9*nn passim*, 103*n*,
  108–9*nn*, 112*n*, 123*n*, 129*n*, 136*n*
Gentili, Alberto 361*n*
'Gentille et jeune Lisette, La' 506
George, Stefan (1868–1933) 798, 807
Georgiades, T. G. 105*n*
Gerber, Rudolf 144*n*, 179*n*, 181*n*, 283*n*,
  354*n*, 464*n*
Gerhard, Roberto (1896–1970) 845
Gérold, Théodore 95*nn*
Gershwin, George (1898–1937) 824
Gerstenberg, Walter 232*n*
Gervais, Françoise 454*n*
Gervaise, Claude 218–19, 239*n*
Gesualdo, Carlo, Prince of Venosa
  (*c.* 1562–1613) 253–4, 267, 297
Gevaert, François 464*n*, 469*n*, 470*n*
Gherardello de Florentia (*fl.* 1350) 128,
  131, 133
ghichak 196
Ghiselin, Johannes ('Verbon(n)et') (15th
  c.) 161, 162, 164–5 and *nn*, 170
Ghisi, Federico 173*n*
Ghislanzoni, Alberto 300, 347*n*
Ghizeghem, *see* Hayne van Ghizeghem
Giacobbi, Girolamo (d. 1629) 350
Gianturco, Carolyn 396*nn*
Gibbons, Christopher (1616–76) 326
Gibbons, Orlando (1583–1625) 261, 290,
  292, 356; anthems 263; *Fantasies of
  Three Parts* (*c.* 1620) 292, 332;
  madrigals 278; psalm-settings 357;
  Services 263
Giegling, Franz 329*n*, 428*n*, 483*n*, 632*n*
Giesbert, F. J. 164*nn*, 213*n*, 218*nn*
gigaku 569

Gigault, Nicolas (*c.* 1624–1707) 437
Gilbert, Kenneth 512*n*
Gilbert, Sir William Schwenk (1836–1911)
  740*n*
Gintzler, Simon (*fl.* 1547) 235, 239
Ginzburg, S. L. 394*n*, 479*n*, 550*n*
Giovanni da Cascia (Johannes de
  Florentia) (mid-14th c.) 129 and *n*, 130
Giraut de Borneill (12th c.) 97, 103*n*
Girdlestone, Cuthbert 415*n*, 436*n*, 455*n*
gittern 240*n*
Giustiniani, Leonardo (*c.* 1398–1446) 171;
  'Ayme sospiri' 155–6 (Ex. 39)
Gladkovsky, Arseny (1894–1945) 841–2
Glareanus (Heinrich Loris) 177;
  Dodecachordon (1547) 178, 209, 256
Glasenapp, Carl F. 548*n*
Glazunov, Aleksandr Konstantinovich
  (1865–1936) 699, 732, 780, 841
Glee Club (1787) 665
Gleim, Johann Wilhelm (1719–1803)
  531–2
Glier, Reinhold (1875–1956) 841, 842
Glinka, Mikhail Ivanovich (1804–57) 575,
  689, 728; chamber music 626; operas:
  Ruslan i Lyudmila (1842) 681, 719, 729,
  Zhizn za Tsarya (1856) 718, 733, 759;
  orchestral works 681; piano works 765;
  songs 768
Glogauer Liederbuch (1470 or later) 154,
  156
Glossner, G. A. 409*n*
Gluck, Christoph Willibald (1714–87)
  464–5, 469, 470; Klopstock settings 530;
  operas and other stage works 205, 453,
  464–8 (Exs. 166–7), 476: *Alceste* (1767)
  464, 465, 466, 469, 582, *Armide* (1777)
  467, 468, 469, *Artaserse* (1741) 453, 464,
  Cadi dupé, Le (1761) 459, *Contesa de'
  numi, La* (1749) 466, *Demofoonte* (1742)
  453, *Don Juan* (ballet, 1761) 464, *Ezio*
  (1750) 465*n*, *Iphigénie en Aulide* (1774)
  466, 467, 582, *Iphigénie en Tauride*
  (1779) 466, 468, 582, *Isle de Merlin, L'*
  (1758) 466, *Orfeo ed Euridice* (1762) 459,
  464–5, 466, 471, 492, 683, *Paride ed
  Elena* (1770) 466, *Parnaso confuso* (1765)
  465, *Rencontre imprévue, La (Die
  Pilgrimme von Mecca)* (1764) 465,
  Telemacco (1765) 465, 466, *Trionfo di
  Clelia, Il* (1763) 465
'Go hert hurt with adversite' (15th c.) 150
'God save the King' 597, 611
Godwin, Joscelyn 364*n*
Goethe, Johann Wolfgang von

(1749–1832) 473, 474*n*, q. 501, 643, 650, 663, 770; settings of his poems 531, 532, 625, **644–5**, **647–8**, 665, 666: *Egmont* (1788) 600, *Faust* (1808, 1832) 591, 678, 684, 727–8, *Götz von Berlichingen* (1771) 574, *Harzreise im Winter* 760, *Hermann und Dorothea* (1797) 678, *Iphigenie auf Tauris* (1787) 760, *Meeresstille und Glückliche Fahrt* 665, 672, *Tasso* (1789) 682, *Werther* (1774) 780, *West-östlicher Divan* (1819) 648, *Wilhelm Meister* (1777–1829) 644*n*, 647, 783, 790

Goetz, Hermann (1840–76) 687; *Der widerspenstigen Zähmung* (1874) 739–40 (Ex. 285)

Gogol, Nikolay Vasilyevich (1809–52) 731, 732, 799, 842

Goldmark, Karl (1830–1915) 739; *Ländliche Hochzeit* (1876) 693 (Ex. 268)

Goldoni, Carlo (1707–93), *Buona figliuola, La* 454, 463, 464; libretti set by Galuppi 453

Goldschmidt, Hugo 311–14*nn*, 316*n*, 319*n*, 323*n*, 327*n*, 358–60*nn*, 461*nn*

Golenishchev-Kutuzov, Arseny 785

goliards 71, 92, 93

Göllner, Theodor 154*n*

Gombert, Nicolas (*c.* 1500–*c.* 1556) 207, 208, 209, 242; chansons 213, 216; Masses 211, 212; motets 208 (Ex. 53), 209–10, 232, 236, 253

Gombosi, Otto 164*nn*, 183*n*, 235*nn*, 239*n*

Gomes, Carlos (1836–96) 720*n*

Gomołka, Mikołaj, his Polish psalter (1580) 257

gong 569, 570, 572, 813

Goodchild, A. 309*n*

Gorczycki, Grzegorz (*c.* 1667–1734) 412

Görner, Johann Valentin (1702–62) 529

Gorzanis, Giacomo (*fl.* 1561) 285, 289*n*

Gossec, François-Joseph (1734–1829) 488, 496, 545, 577, 606; festival music **654–5** (Ex. 251(i)); *Messe des morts* (1760) 545

Gostling, John (*fl.* late 17th c.) 393, 416

Göttinger Musenalmanach (1774–5) 530

Gottlieb-Billroth, Otto 780*n*

Gottschalk, Louis (1829–69) 817

Gotwald, Clytus 170*n*

Gotwals, Vernon 408*n*

Goudimel, Claude (*c.* 1514–72) 256; psalm-settings 202–2 (Ex. 62(ii), (iii))

Gounet, Thomas (*fl.* 1830) 767

Gounod, Charles (1818–93) 749; Masses 749, 756; operas **720–1**, 727, 740, 743, 749; oratorios 756–7; songs, **786**, 802

Gozzi, Count Carlo (1720–1806) 705, 826, 832

Grabu, Louis (*fl.* 1674) 369

Gräfe, Johann Friedrich (1711–87) 529

Gran (Esztergom) Cathedral, Hungary 749

Grandi, Alessandro (d. 1630) 296, **348–9**, 350; *Cantade et Arie a voce sola* (1620) 297–8 (Ex. 86), 349; motets 348, 349 (Ex. 116), 353

Grasberger, Franz 492*n*, 521*n*

Gratiosus de Padua (14th c.) 128

Graun, Carl Heinrich (1704?–59) 452, 529, 537, 538 and *n*, 539; *Der Tod Jesu* (1756) 540 (Ex. 206)

Graun, Johann Gottlieb (1703?–71), Mass in E flat 537 (Ex. 203)

Graupner, Christoph (1683–1760) 367, 372, 407, 432; cantatas 406–7 (Ex. 142), 538; Symphony (*c.* 1737) **484–5** (Ex. 175(ii))

Gray, Thomas (1716–71) 528

Greber, Jakob (*fl.* 1705) 370

Greene, Maurice (*c.* 1695–1755) 513, 542 and *n*, 544

'Gregorian' chant **59–60**, 106, **246–7**

Gregory I, St (the Great) (Pope 590–604) 5, **57–8**

Gregory IV (Pope 827–44) 60

Gregory XIII (Pope 1572–85) 246

Greiter, Mathias (*c.* 1490–1550) 220, 222

Grenon, Nicolaus (*fl.* 1385–1427) 138; 'Je suy défait' 151 (Ex. 36)

Grétry, André-Ernest-Modeste (1741–1813) 464, 470, 577, 579, 589; operas 464 and *n*, 469, **470–1**, 476, 478

Grieg, Edvard Hagerup (1843–1907) 576, 688–9; chamber music 776, 779; *Landkjaenning* (1872) 760; orchestral works 689, 791, 792; piano works 773, 775–6, 803; songs **791–2**

Griepenkerl, Robert (*fl.* 1850) 681

Griesinger, Georg August (*fl.* 1810) 492, 521*n*

Grigny, Nicolas de (1672–1703) 441; *Livre* (1699) 437–8 (Ex. 153)

Grillo, Giovanni Battista (*fl.* before 1608) 288

Grillparzer, Franz (1791–1872) 666, 672

Grimani family 317

Grimm, Baron Friedrich Melchior von (1723–1807) 456

Grimm, Hermann (1828–1901) 685

Grindal, Edmund (*c.* 1519–83), Archbishop 261

Grischkat, Hans 403*n*

Grocheo, Johannes de, *De Musica* (*c.*
1300) 94, 117

Grossman, Ludwik (1835–1915) 734

Grout, Donald Jay 320*n*, 363–4*nn*, 446*n*,
720*n*

Grove, Sir George 602*n*

Gruenberg, Louis (1884–1964) 823–4

Grusnick, Bruno 248*n*

Guami, Gioseffo (*c.* 1535–*c.* 1611) 232–3,
288

'Guárdame las vacas' 237 (Ex. 68(i))

Guarini, Giovanni Battista (1537–1612)
265, 273, 304

Guarneri family 205

Gudewill, Kurt 225*nn*

Guédron, Pierre (d. 1621) 307, 308, 322
and *n*
      lute-song, 'Quel espoir de guarir' 307
      (Ex. 94)

Guéranger, Dom Prosper 749

Guerrero, Francisco (*c.* 1527–99) 247

Guglielmi, Pietro (1728–1804) 459, 469,
471, 472, 500*n*

Guglielmi, Pietro Carlo (*c.* 1763–1817) 585

Guidetti, Giovanni (*fl.* 1582) 247

Guido (14th c.) 136

Guido d'Arezzo (b.*c.* 995) 84–5, 93

guilds, musicians', in ancient Rome 48

Guillard, Nicolas-François (*fl.* 1779) 468,
470

Guillemain, Louis-Gabriel (1705–70) 488,
518

Guilmant, Alexandre 340*nn*, 436*n*

Guines, Duc de (*fl.* 1778) 499

Guiot de Provins (12th c.) 98

Guiraud, Albert 807

Guiraud, Ernest (1837–92) 740

guitarra morisca 99, 197

Gülke, Peter 81*n*

Gunther, Ursula 136–7*nn*

Gurilev, Aleksandr Lvovich (1802–56) 768

Gurlitt, Wilibald 153*n*, 261*n*, 404*n*

Gurney, O. R. 10*n*, 22*n*

Gusev, Viktor (1909–44) 842

Gustavus II Adolphus (1594–1632) of
Sweden 300

Gustav III (1746–92) of Sweden 480

Guzman, J. B. 345*n*

Gyrowetz (Jírowec), Adalbert (1763–1850)
589, 597

Haar, James 214*n*

Haas, Robert 85*n*, 304–5*nn*, 317*n*, 358*n*, 364*n*,
398*n*, 427*n*, 472*n*, 474*n*, 518*n*, 539*n*, 589*n*

Hába, Alois (1893–1972) 831

Hába, Karel (b. 1898) 831

Habeneck, François-Antoine (1781–1849)
606, 612

Haberl, F. X. 117*n*, 137*n*, 246*n*, 256*n*

Habert, J. E. 409*n*

Hadrian (76–138), Emperor 48

Hadrian I (Pope 772–95) 60

Hagedorn, Friedrich von (1708–54) 529

Haguka-no-Sammi (918–80) 570

Halde, Jean-Baptiste du (*fl.* 1735) 564*n*

Hálek, Vitěslav 685*n*, 782

Halévy, Fromental (1799–1862) 720;
      Juive, La (1835) 705, **706–7** (Ex. 270),
      728; *Reine de Chypre, La* (1841) 706, 709

Halle, the Moritzkirche 337*n*

Hamburg: *Collegium Musicum* 337, 404;
      Theater am Gänsemarkt 358, 366, 402

Hamm, Charles 142*n*

Hammerschmidt, Andreas (1611–75) 306,
335–6, 351, 404

Hammond, F. F. 112*n*

Händel, Georg Friedrich (George
      Frideric Handel) (1685–1759) 367, 368,
      369, 372, 450, 544; 'borrowings' 371 and
      n, 380, 383; concerts 487–8; influenced
      by Purcell 417, 542
      church music **417–18**
      concertos **482–3**, 487
      Italian cantatas and duets 371 and *n*,
      382–4
      keyboard music 435, 440–1, 510
      masque, *Haman and Mordecai* (*c.* 1720)
      542
      Ode for St Cecilia's Day (1739) 483
      operas 205, 445, 447: *Acis and Galatea*
      (1718) 384, *Admeto* (1727) 372,
      Agrippina (1709) **368**, *Alcina* (1735)
      447, 544 (Ex. 208(i)), *Alessandro
      nell'Indie* (1726) 459–60 (Ex. 163(i)),
      Almira (1705) **367–8** (Ex. 124), 371,
      Amadigi (*c.* 1715) 482, *Ariodante* (1735)
      447, *Deidamia* (1741) 447, *Ezio* (1732)
      447, *Faramondo* (1738) 371*n*, *Giulio
      Cesare* (1724) 372, *Giustino* (1737)
      371*n*, *Nero* (1705) 367, *Orlando* (1733)
      447, *Ottone* (1723) 372, *Poro, re
      dell'Indie* (1731) 446, 447, *Radamisto*
      (1720) 371, *Rinaldo* (1711) 365*n*, **370–1**,
      Rodelinda (1725) 372 and *n*, *Scipione*
      (1726) 372, *Serse* (1738) 371*n*, 447,
      Siroe (1728) 447, *Tamerlano* (1724)
      372, *Tolomeo* (1728) 372
      oratorios, sacred and secular 380, **542–4**,
      660: *Messiah* (1741) 541, 542*nn*, **543**,

747*n*, *Resurezzione*, *La* (1708) 383, 399,
Theodora (1750) 543, 544 (Ex. 208(ii))
Passions: Brockes's Passion (1716) 403,
482, *St John Passion* (1704) 402
Water Music (1715, 1717) 434*n*
Handl, Jacobus ('Gallus vocatus',
'Carniolanus') (1550–91) 254
Handschin, Jacques 63*n*, 89*n*, 100, 101*n*,
107, 171*n*
Hanelle (*fl.* 1417) 138
Hanka, Václav (*fl.* 1820) 651
Hanley, Edwin 397*n*
Hanover: Court opera house (1689) 365,
Electoral Court 370, 383
Harant z Polžic, Kryštof (1564–1621) 254
hardingfele 689
Harich-Schneider, Eta 570*n*
Harleian MS. 978 112, 113; 'In seculum'
112–13 (Ex. 22(i))
Harman, R. Alec 282*n*, 290*n*, 297*n*
harmoniai 29 and *n*, 30–2, 77
Harmonice Musices Odhecaton A (1501) 74
Harmonios (3rd c.) 56
harmony, early three and four-part 106–7
(Exx. 19–20)
Harmosis 15, 16
Harms, Gottlieb 184*n*, 334*n*
Harold, Eduard (*fl.* 1815) 647
harp 2: Arabian 190, Assyrian 19, 21,
Egyptian 13, 14–15, *15*, 16, *16*, Elamite
20, pedal-harp 528*n*, Persian 567, post-
Sumerian *11*, 12, Sumerian 8–9, *8*, 10
Harrer, Johann Gottlob (1703–55) 538;
Passion (1751) 539–40 (Ex. 205)
Harris, Roy (b. 1898) 824, 845
Harrison, Frank Ll. 113, 129*n*, 141, 143*n*
186–7*nn*, 241*n*
Harsdörffer, Georg Philipp (*fl.* 1644) 325
Hartmann, H. 10*n*
Hartmann, Karl Amadeus (1905–63) 848,
856
Hartmann, Viktor A. (1842–73) *777*
Hārun-al-Rashīd (*c.* 766–809), Caliph
191–2
Hasse, Johann Adolph (1699–1783) 446–7,
452, 478 and *n*, 487 and *n*, 491*n*, 549;
Litaniae della Beatissima Virgine (1761)
549 (Ex. 211); operas 205: *Antioco*
(1721) 372, 445, *Artaserse* (1730) 446,
Cleofide (1731) 446, *Ezio* (1731) 447*n*,
Sogno di Scipione, Il (1758) 478, *Trionfo
di Clelia, Il* (1762) 465, *Zenobia* (1761)
478; oratorios 549; Requiem (1763) 549
Hasse, Karl 181*n*
Hassler, Hans Leo (1564–1612) 259–60,

281–3 (Ex. 81), 285, 290
Hassler, Jakob and Kaspar (*fl.c.* 1600) 259
Hässler, Johann Wilhelm (1747–1822)
522–3
Haussmann, Valentin (d.*c.* 1612) 283,
289–90
Hawkes, Jacquetta 7 and *n*, 11*n*, 21*n*
Hawkins, Sir John (1719–89), *General
History of . . . Music* (1776) 544*n*
Haydn, Franz Joseph (1732–1809) 491,
503, 504*n*, 506, 524*n*, 601, *661*; and
C. P. E. Bach 521, 524–5, 574; Burney
on 493; and Cherubini 578; compared
with Stamitz 492; influence on
Beethoven 618, 619, Schubert 609,
Viotti 598, Witte 598; influenced by
Mozart 506
Andante con variazioni for piano 629
baryton trios 526
cantata, *Arianna a Naxos* (1790) 532
concertos 494, 596*n*
keyboard sonatas 495, 520–1 (Ex.
198(ii)), 523, 525, 629
Masses 551–3, 597, 656–7, 658, 660, 753
operas 205, 472: *Anima del filosofo, L'
(Orfeo ed Euridice)* 596, *Fedeltà
premiata, La* (1780) 500, *Mondo della
luna, Il* (1777) 500, *Orlando Paladino*
(1782) 470*n*
oratorios: *Jahreszeiten, Die* (1801) 661–2,
665, *Ritorno di Tobia, Il* (1775) 552,
Schöpfung, Die (1798) 660–1, *661*, 662,
*Sieben Worte des Erlösers am Kreuze,
Die* 545, 552, 660
piano trios 505, 526, 617, 618
songs 532, 642
string quartets 492, 495–6, 500–1 (Exx.
184–5), 502, 505, 506 (Ex. 187), 521,
617–18
Symphonie concertante 597
symphonies: Nos. 1–34 492–3, 495, 496,
631, Nos. 44–72 493, 495–6, 500, 574,
No. 78 499 (Ex. 183(ii)), Nos. 82–7
('Paris') 505–6, 597, No. 92 506, Nos.
93–104 ('London') 596–7, 618, 657
trio sonatas 526
Haydn, Michael (1737–1806) 491, 552,
554, 603, 657; church music 552 and *n*,
553, 554, Masses 657 (Ex. 252); string
quintets 497, 505; symphonies 498, 504
Haym, Niccolò (*fl.* 1728) 447
Hayne van Ghizeghem (d.*c.* 1470) 153,
156, 188; 'Alles regrets' 166 (Ex. 44(i)),
167*n*
Haynes, M. B. 438*n*

Heartz, Daniel 214n, 218n, 468n
Hebbel, Friedrich (1813–63) 789
Hebrew music 37–40, 51
Heine, Heinrich (1797–1856) 647–8, 650,
  731, 770–1, 772n, 782–3, 786, 789, 791
Heinichen, Johann David (1683–1729)
  372, 382, 386, 430
Heinrich von Meissen ('Frauenlob') (d.
  1318) 98
Heiske, W. 225n
Helfert, Vladimir 485n
Heliogabalus (c. 201–22), Emperor 47
Hellendaal, Pieter (1721?–99) 487
Heller, Stephen (1814–88) 764
Hellinck, Lupus (c. 1495–1541) 208, 209,
  223
Helmbold, Ludwig (16th c.) 258
Helmore, Thomas (1811–90) 752
Helms, Siegmund 350n
Henderson, Isobel 35
Hendrie, Gerald 292n
Henestrosa, Luys Venegas de (fl. 1557)
  236, 237
Hennebains, J. P. 234n
Henrici ('Picander') (1700–64) 535
Henricus de Latunna (fl. 1389) 137
Henrietta Maria (1609–69), Queen of
  England 356
Henry VI (1165–97), Emperor 97n
Henry IV (1367–1413) of England 143n
Henry V (1387–1422) of England 141, 143
Henry VI (1421–71) of England 142
Henry VII (1457–1509) of England 74,
  187, 239
Henry VIII (1491–1547) of England 188,
  203, 241
Henry II (1519–59) of France 219
Henry IV (1553–1610) of France 271
Henry III, Duke of Brabant (early 13th
  c.) 97
Henry, Jehan ('Henry le jeune')
  (1560–1635), *Fantaisies* 333 (Ex. 110)
Henselt, Adolph (1814–89) 764–5; Piano
  Concerto in F minor 678, 679–80 (Ex.
  261), 765
Henze, Hans Werner (b. 1926) 856, 858–9,
  Der Prinz von Homburg (1960) 858–9,
  860 (Ex. 312)
Herbert, George (1593–1633) 393
Herder, Johann Gottfried von
  (1744–1803) 532, 541, 646, 649, 683
Hermannus Contractus (1013–54) 82, 85
Hernandez, G. C. 179n
Hero of Alexandria (1st c.) 45, 46
Herodotus (c. 480–c. 425 B.C.) 22, 37

Hérold, Louis-Joseph-Ferdinand
  (1791–1833) 585, 705
Herskovits, Melville J. 812n, 816n
Hertl, Rudolf 623n
Hertzmann, Erich 230–1nn
Herz, Henri (1806–88) 761
Herzog, George 814–15nn
Hesbert, R.-J. 58n
Hesdin of Beauvais (16th c.) 219n
Hess, Willy 600n
heterophony 28, 32, 45, 49, 80
Heuss, Alfred 306n, 330n, 419–20nn,
  422nn
Heuss, Heinz 361n
Hewitt, Helen 153n, 169–70nn
Hewitt, James (1770–1827) 595
Heyden, Reinhold 174n
Heyden, Sebaldus 222
Heyduk, Adolf, poet 782
Heyse, Paul (1830–1914) 790, 791, *see also*
  Geibel and Heyse
hichiriki 569, 570
Hickmann, Hans 13n, 17n
Hidalgo, Juan (d. 1685) 325 and n
Hieronymus de Moravia (c. 1250) 102n,
  103n
Hilarius (12th c.) 92
Hilary of Poitiers, St (d. 366) 56
Hiller, Ferdinand (1811–85) 747, 761
Hiller, Johann Adam (1728–1804) **473**,
  474, 530, 712
Hilton, John, the younger (1599–1657)
  309, 310
Hindemith, Paul (1895–1963) 821, 823,
  833, 834, **835**–7, 840, 849; operas 835,
  836, 837, 840, 856, 857; symphonies 836,
  845, 856, 857; treatise, *Unterweisung im
  Tonsatz* (1937, 1939) 836 and n
Hinnenthal, Johann Philipp 482n
Hintermaier, Ernst 345n
Hita, Rodriguez de (1704–87) 477
Hitchcock, H. Wiley 274n, 413n
Hobohm, Wolf 386n
Hoboken, Anthony van 521n
Hodemont, Léonard (c. 1580–1636) 356
Hofer, Norbert 550n
Hoffman, Ernest Theodor Amadeus
  (1776–1822) 574, 583; *Undine* (1816)
  590–1 (Ex. 222), 712
Hoffmann-Erbrecht, Lothar 183n, 486n,
  489n, 492n, 510n, 513n, 517n, 523n
Hoffmeister, Franz Anton (1754–1812)
  505
Hofhaimer, Paul (1459–1537) 180, 183,
  184, 239, 284n; 'Zucht, eer und lob' 185

(Ex. 52(i))

Hofmann, Leopold (1738–93) 491, 494

Hogwood, Christopher 520*n*

Holborne, Antony (d. 1602), *Pavans, Galliards, Almains* (1599) 290

Hölderlin, Johann Christian (1770–1843) 760

Holmes, William 321*n*

Holschneider, Andreas 81 and *n*

Holst, Gustav (1874–1934) 51–2, 799, 806, 810, 824

Holst, Imogen 799*n*

Hölty, Ludwig (1748–76) 531, 789

Holzbauer, Ignaz (1711–83) 476, 488, 491

Homer (8th c. B.C.) 3, 22–3, 24, 28, 51, 71

Homilius, Gottfried August (1714–85) 538–9

'Homme armé, L'' (Morton) 148, 149, 164; 'L'homme armé' Masses 149, 165, 172–3, 178, 236, 242*n*, 345, 410

Honauer, Leontzi (*c.* 1735–*c.* 1790) 518

Honegger, Arthur (1892–1955) 828, 830–1, 842, 844, 845; operas 830; Symphony 826*n*, 830–1 (Ex. 303)

Hoppin, Richard H. 139–40*nn*

hoquets 110, 119, 124–6, 130

Horace (Quintus Horatius Flaccus) (65–8 B.C.) 93

Hörner, Hans 403*nn*

hornpipe (instrument) 43

Horton, John 594*n*, 626*n*

Hortschansky, Klaus 446*n*

Horwitz, Karl 486–7*nn*

Horwood, William (d. 1484) 187

Hothby, John (d. 1487) 187

Housman, Alfred Edward (1859–1936) 805

Howell, James 323*n*

hsiao 567

Hsüan-tsung, Emperor 567

huang-chung 564

Huberty 488

Hucbald of St Amand (*c.* 840–930) 70, 75–7, 79, 80, 89; *De Institutione Harmonica* 75–7, *75–6* (Exx. 7–8), 89

Hudson, Barton 178*nn*

Hudson, Frederick 253*n*

Hudson, George (*fl.* 1656) 326, 369

Hugh of Cluny (*fl.* 1083) 71

Hughes, Andrew 141*n*

Hughes, Anselm 187*n*

Huglo, Michel 82*n*

Hugo, Victor-Marie (1802–85) 574, 710, 728 and *n*, 767, 768, 786–7; *Angelo* 743; *Feuilles d'automne* 682; *Roi s'amuse, Le*

722*n*; *Ruy Blas* 672

Hulāgū Khan 196

Humanism 202–4, 207

Humfrey, Pelham (1647–74) 369, 390, 415, 416, *417*

Hummel, Johann Nepomuk (1778–1837) 603, 617, 621, 639, 640, 642*n*, 657; compared with Beethoven 637, 658, Voříšek 638; influence on Chopin 616, 641; chamber music 623, 625; *Klavierschule* (1828) q. 615; Masses 657–8 (Ex. 253), 664; piano concertos 605, 613, 615, 616, 637–8; piano sonatas 631, 637–8 (Ex. 244(i)); *Tänze für den Apollosaal* 634

Humperdinck, Engelbert (1854–1921) 740

Hunold, C. F. (1681–1721) 402

Hunt, A. S. 52*n*

Hunt, Edgar 285*n*

Hunter, Anne (1742–1821) 642

Hunter, John (1728–93) 642

Husen, Friedrich von (d. 1190) 98

Husmann, Heinrich 104*nn*, 108–11*nn*, 124*n*, 129–30*nn*

hydraulos 44–5, 46

hymns: early Christian 51–2 (Ex. 5), 55–6 (Ex. 6), 64, 65, medieval 89

Hymns Ancient and Modern (1861) 752

hypate 29, 30

hypate meson 61

hyperhypate 30

hyperteleios 31, 34

'I will always give thanks' ('The Club Anthem', Humfrey *et al.* 1664) 415

iambic mode, the 102

Iamblichus (d.*c.* 330) 21, 50

Ibrāhīm (779–839) Abbasid prince 192

Ibrāhīm al-Mausilī (743–804?) 192

Ibsen, Henrik (1828–1906) 792

Ihan ('Maistre Jan') (?16th c.) 228, 232

Ikuta (1655–1715) 571

Ileborgh, Adam (*fl.* 1448) *158*, 158–9

Ilgner, Gerhard 337*n*

Illey, Hedda 514*n*

Imbert, Hugues 727*n*

India, Sigismondo d' (*c.* 1580–1629) 296–7, 298, 299, 304, 312

Indy, Vincent d' (1851–1931) 801, 802 and *n*, **804**, 828, 830; chamber music 804; operas 802 and *n*, 826; orchestral works 692, 700, 701, 804; piano works 804

Infantas, Fernando de las (*fl.* 1577) 247

Ingegneri, Marc Antonio (*c.* 1547–92) 247,

253, 266, 267
intermedii 268–71 (Ex. 76)
International Society for Contemporary
    Music 824
Ionian *harmonia* 32
Ippolitov-Ivanov, Mikhail (1859–1935)
    841
Irving, Washington (1783–1859) 711
Isaac, Heinrich (Henricus) (*c*. 1450–1517)
    74, 165*n*, 170–1, 181–3, 188; *Choralis
    Constantinus* 183 (Ex. 51); Masses 74,
    174, 182–3; songs 172, 182
Isabella of Portugal (*fl.* 1526) 236
Isfahānī, Al- (897–967) 194; *Kitāb al-
    aghānī al-kabīr* 191, 194
Isḥaq al-Mausilī (767–850) 192–3
Ishimura (*fl.* 16th c.) 570
Isidore of Seville (*c*. 560–636) 62, 75
Ismail (1830–95), Khedive 198
isorhythm 118, 119, 125, 126, 161
Isouard, Nicolò (1775–1818) 584
Ives, Charles (1874–1954) 824
Ives, Simon (1600–62) 333, 334*n*; (with
    W. Lawes) *Triumph of Peace* (1634)
    325–6 (Ex. 106)
Ivrea Codex 124, 126, 134

Jachet of Mantua (before 1550) 230*n*, 232
Jackson, Barbara 388*n*
Jackson, Roland 338*nn*
Jacob de Senleches (Jacomi de Sentluch,
    Jacopinus Selesses) (14th c.) 136
Jacobs, Charles 236*n*, 239*n*
Jacobsen, Jens Peter (1847–85) 797
Jacopo da Bologna (Jacobus de Bononia)
    (mid-14th c.) 129 and *n*, 130, 131 and *n*
Jacquot, Jean 171*n*, 235*n*, 292*n*, 334*n*
Jadin, Emmanuel (1768–1853) 643 and *n*
James I (1566–1625) of England 280
James II (1633–1701) of England (1685–8)
    397
James IV (1473–1513) of Scotland 188
Jammers, Ewald 56
'Jan, Maistre' 228, 232
Janáček, Leoš (1854–1928) 799, 837–8
Jander, Owen 422*n*
Janequin, Clément (*c*. 1475–*c*. 1559) 214,
    216, 219–20, 221, 226, 246, 287
jank 190
Jarecki, Henryk (1846–1918) 734
jati 560
Jaufré Rudel 'de Blaia' (12th c.) 95, 98
jazz 818
Jeanroy, Alfred 95*n*
Jeitteles, Alois 645

Jenkins, John (1592–1678) 332, 333
Jenkins, Newell 486*n*
Jennens, Charles (1700–73) 543
Jensen, Adolf (1837–79), songs 788 (Ex.
    298)
Jeppesen, Knud 173*nn*, 235*n*, 241*n*, 246*n*
Jerome, St (330–420) 54, 57
'Jesu Christes milde moder' (13th c.) 115
jeu parti 100
Joachim, Joseph (1831–1907) 685, 686,
    688
Joaquim, Manuel 345*n*
joculatores, joglar(e)s (jongleurs) 71, 95,
    100
Johannes de Florentia *see* Giovanni da
    Cascia
Johannes Hymmonides (*fl.c.* 872) 59
John XXII (Pope 1316–34) 72; his 'Docta
    Sanctorum' q. 117–18, 126, 202
John I (d. 1395) of Aragon 135, 136
John (of Luxembourg) (1296–1346) of
    Bohemia 123
John II (1319–64) of France 120
John Chrysostom, St (345–407) 54, 55, 65
John of Damascus, St (*c*. 700–60) 64
Johnson, Robert (*c*. 1490–*c*. 1565) 241
Johnson, Robert (*c*. 1580–*c*. 1634) 309
Jolly, Constance 630*n*
Jommelli, Niccolò (1714–74) 452, 461,
    491; operas 453, 457, 461; oratorios
    548; Requiem (1756) 548
Jones, A. M. 812*n*, 814*nn*
Jones, Robert (early 17th c.) 280
Jones, Sir William 558
jongleurs see joculatores
Jonson, Ben (1573?–1637) 280, 308
Joplin, Scott (1869–1917) 817
Joseph II (1741–90), Emperor 553–4
Josephine (1763–1814), Empress 582
Josquin des Prez (*c*. 1440–1521) 74, 161,
    170, 173, 174–7, 180–1, 226; compared
    with Isaac 182, La Rue 168, Obrecht
    169; influence on Lassus 255; pupils
    207; chansons 164, 172, 173*n*, 174, 184*n*,
    235, 236; Masses 165 and *n*, 172–3, 174,
    176–7 (Ex. 48), 248; motets 174, 175
    (Ex. 47), 178, 245; 'Stabat mater' 176,
    223
Journal des Luxus und der Moden (Vienna)
    527
Jouy, Étienne de (*fl.* 1807) 581, 583
Judenkünig, Hans (*c*. 1447–1526) 226
Julius Pollux (*fl.* 2nd c.) 46
Jungmann, A. 60*n*
Justinian I (483–565), Emperor 54, 65

Juvenal (Decimus Junius Juvenalis) (*c.* 60–*c.* 130) 93

Kabalevsky, Dmitry (b. 1904) 842, 843, 844
kabuki 570
Kade, Otto 143*n*, 220*n*
kagan 813
Kagel, Mauricio (b. 1931) 854, 855
Kahl, Willi 430*n*, 432*n*
Kalbeck, Max 667*n*, 686*n*
'Kalenda maya' 100
Kalkbrenner, Friedrich (1785–1849) 615, 616, 631, 639, 641, 761
Kalliwoda, Johann Wenzel (1801–66), symphonies 611–12 (Ex. 232)
Kallman, Chester (b. 1921) 861
kamāncha 195–6
'Kamarinskaya' 633
Kamieński, Maciej (1734–1821) 478
kanon 65
kant 394 (Ex. 135)
Kantionalsatz 226
Kapp, Julius 713*n*
Kapp, Oskar 550*n*
Karl Theodor (1724–99), Elector of Bavaria 498
karnā 190
Karp, Theodore 100*n*
Kassel 484
Kast, Paul 178*n*
Kastner, Santiago 236–7*nn*, 340*nn*, 512*n*
Kathemerinon (4th c.) 56
Kauer, Ferdinand (1751–1831) 589 and *n*, 590, 728
Keats, John (1795–1821) 824
Keiser, Reinhard (1674–1739) 366–7, 368, 371, 372, 376; cantatas 385–6; operas 367, 402; oratorio *Der blutige und sterbende Jesus* (1704) 402; Passions 402–3 (Ex. 140)
Keller, Gottfried (1819–90) 806
Keller, Hans 498*n*, 862*n*
Kellermann, Marshal François (1735–1820) 654
Kellie, Thomas Erskine, Earl of (1732–81) 494–5
Kelway, Joseph (*c.* 1702–82) 513
Kemp, Ian 836*n*
Kempers, K. P. Bernet 207*n*, 210 and *n*, 220*n*
kenanawr 15
Kenney, Sylvia 149*n*
Kerll, Johann Kaspar (1627–93) 325, 365, 438, 441

Kerman, Joseph 276 and *n*, 710*n*, 732
Kerzelli, Iosif (*fl.* 1772) 479 (Ex. 172) and *n*
Khachaturyan, Aram (1903–78) 843, 846, 858
Khrennikov, Tikhon (b. 1913) 843
kidi 813, *814*
Kienzl, Wilhelm (1857–1941) 794
Kiesewetter R. G. 752 and *n*
Kilmer, A. D. 10*n*
Kimmei (*fl.c.* 535), Emperor 569
Kind, Friedrich (*fl.* 1821) 649
Kindermann, Erasmus (1616–55) 335, 336, 337, 351, 404
'King Henry VIII's MS.' 187, 188
Kinkeldey, Otto 234*n*, 266*n*, 285*n*, 385*nn*
kinnāra 190
kinnôr 2, 15, 38, 190
Kirbye, George (d. 1634) 278
Kirchner, Theodor (1823–1903) 776
Kirkendale, Ursula 399*n*
Kirkpatrick, Ralph 512*n*
Kirnberger, Johann Philipp (1721–83) 516, 517, 530, 531
Kitāb al-qānūn 193
kithara (kitharis, cithara) 21–6 *passim*, 27, 31–5 *passim*, 39, 40, *41*, 43, 47, 48, 190
'kitharizing' 22 and *n*
Kittel, Kaspar (1603–39), *Arien und Cantaten* (1638) 304 (Ex. 91), 329
Kjerulf, Halfdan (1815–68) 775, 791
'Klaffers neyden, Des' (*c.* 1452–60) 155 (Ex. 39)
Klafsky, Anton 657*n*
Klebe, Giselher (b. 1925) 856
Kleber, Leonhard (*c.* 1495–1556) 182, 184–5
Kleinecke, Rudolf 590*n*
Kleinmichel, Richard 476*n*
Kleist, Heinrich von (1777–1811) 703, 858
Klingemann, Karl 770
Klinger, Friedrich Maximilian von (1752–1831) 574
Klopstock, Friedrich Gottlieb (1724–1803) 530, 664, 747
Knape, Walter 491*n*
Knapp, Janet 108*n*
Knecht, Justin Heinrich (1752–1817) 602*n*
Knipper, Lev (b. 1898) 842
Knüpfer, Sebastian (1633–76) 405
Köchel, Ludwig von (1800–77), *Verzeichnis . . . Mozarts Werke* (3rd ed., 1947) 527, 528, 553*n*
Koczirc, Adolf 226*n*, 235*n*, 239*n*
Kodály, Zoltán (1882–1967) 839

Koechlin, Charles (1867–1950) 827, 830
Kokoschka, Oskar (b. 1886) 835
Koller, Oswald 154*nn*
Komagaku 570
Kompanevsky, N. 759*n*
komüngo 569
König, Johann Balthasar (1691–1758)
 539*n*
König, Johann Ulrich von (*fl.* 1731) 539
kontakion 65
Koole, Arend 483*n*
Kopelent, Marek (b. 1932) 854
Koran 190–1
Körner, Karl Theodor (1791–1813) 647,
 649
Kosch, Franz 550*n*
Kosegarten, Ludwig (1758–1818) 643, 645,
 665*n*
koto 569, 570, 571
Kotoński, Wlodzimierz (b. 1925) 854
Kotter, Johannes (Hans) (*c.* 1480–1541)
 184–5; 'Zucht, eer und lob' 185 (Ex.
 52(ii))
Kovařovic, Karel (1862–1920) 735
Kozeluch (Koželuh), Leopold (1747–1818)
 531*n*, 532, 642
Kozlov, Ivan Ivanovich 653
Krabbe, W. 529*n*
Krakowa, Mikołaj z (Nicolaus
 Cracoviensis) (?15th–16th c.) 226
'Kralice Bible' 782
Králové Dvůr MS. 782, 783
Krebs, Carl 523*n*
Krebs, Johann Ludwig (1713–80) 516, 517
Kremenliev, Boris A. 197*n*
Křenek, Ernst (b. 1900) 823, 834, **836**–7,
 841, 853
Kretschmar, Hermann 452*n*, 476*n*, 620*nn*
Kreutz, Alfred 524*n*
Kreutzer, Konradin (1780–1849) 593, 661
Kreutzer, Rodolphe (1766–1831) 577*n*,
 598, 619, 620; violin concertos 598–9
 (Ex. 225(i), (ii))
Krickeberg, Dieter 334*n*
Krieger, Adam (1634–66) 306; *Neue Arien*
 (1667, 1676) 306 (Ex. 93), 385
Krieger, Johann (1652–1735) 385, 434–5
Krieger, Johann Philipp (1649–1725) 385,
 405–6, 426–7, 435, 438
Krïlov, Ivan Andreyevich (1768–1844) 783
krotala 25, *25*, 41
Kubilai ('Kubla Khan') (1216–94),
 Emperor 567
Küchelbecker, Wilhelm (1797–1846) 857
Kuffner, Christoph (*fl.* 1808) 602*n*

Kugelmann, Hans (d. 1542) 222
Kuhlau, Friedrich (1786–1832) 594
Kuhn, Max 248*n*
Kuhnau, Johann (1660–1722) 406, 407
 and *n*, q. 439; keyboard works 434,
 439–40 (Ex. 155), 441
Kukolnik, Nestor (1795–1884) 681
kumi 571
k'un-ch'ü 568
Kundera, Ludvik 638*n*
k'ung hou 567
Kunze, Stefan 473*n*
Kupelwieser, Leopold 663
Kurpiński, Karol (1785–1857) 594, 651
Kurtág, György (b. 1926) 854
Kurth, Ernst 465–6*nn*
Kurthen, Wilhelm 552*n*
Kusser, Johann Sigismund (1660–1727)
 366, 376, 386, 393, 426*n*, 431
kymbala 25

La Chevardière, Louis-Balthasar de 488,
 492
Lachner, Franz (1803–90) 693*n*
La Fontaine, Jean de (1621–95) 786*n*
La Guerre, Élisabeth Jacquet de (*c.*
 1664–1729) 388–9, 426, 435
La Guerre, Michel de (*c.* 1605–1679) 324
La Halle, Adam de (*c.* 1237–88) 115–16
Lalande, Michel-Richard de (1657–1726)
 376*n*, 413–14
La Laurencie, Lionel de 194–5*nn*, 198,
 215*n*, 220*n*, 325*nn*, 334*n*, 365*n*, 411*n*,
 518*n*
Lalo, Édouard (1823–92) 692, 700, 702,
 741, 779*n*, 786
Lamartine, Alphonse de (1790–1869) 786
Lambe, Walter (*c.* 1452–*c.* 1500) 187
Lambert, Constant (1905–51) 824, 825
Lambert, Michel (*c.* 1610–1696) 323, 387
Lamennais, Abbé Félicité de (1782–1854)
 748
Lamm, Pavel 729*n*, 731*nn*
Lampe, Johann Friedrich (1703–51) 477
Landi, Stefano (*c.* 1590–*c.* 1655) 296, 299;
 operas: *Morte d'Orfeo, La* (1619) 311,
 314, *Sant' Alassio, Il* (1632) 313–14 (Exx.
 98–9), 420
Landini, Francesco (*c.* 1335–97) 131–3,
 132, 136, 154, 159
'Landini cadence' 131, 152
Landon, H. C. Robbins 492*n*, 500*n*, 597*n*
Landowska, Wanda (1874–1959) 830*n*
Landshoff, Ludwig 483*n*, 494*n*
Lange, Daniel de 572*n*

Lange, Martin 510*n*

Lanier, Nicholas (1588–1666) 308–9, 310, 326; 'Like hermit poor' 308 (Ex. 95(ii))

Lantins, Arnold de (early 15th c.), 139, 145 and *n*, 160

Lantins, Hugo de (early 15th c.) 139

Laodicea, Council of (360–81) 55

Laon Gradual (*c.* 930) *81*

Larsen, Jens Peter 521 and *n*

La Rue, Pierre de ('Perchon') (*c.* 1460–1518) 161, 165, 167–8, 169; chansons 164, 168; Masses 165 and *n*, 167–8 (Ex. 45)

larynx, squeezing the (in singing) 13, *20*, 20*n*

Laskovsky, Ivan Fedorovich (1799–1855) 765; *Pensées fugitives* 765 (Ex. 291)

Lassus (Lasso), Orlandus (*c.* 1532–94) 203, 279*n*, 280; influence on Aichinger 257–8, Lutheran composers 259, 260; pupils 258, 281; church music 213, 218*n*, 245, 246, 254–6 (Ex. 72), 265; secular music 264–5, 276

Laudes Diurnae (1860) 752

laudi spirituali 99, 171, 173, 246, 346

Launay, Denise 334*n*

'Laurencinus Romanus' (16th c.) 285

Laurentius de Florentia (Lorenzo da Firenze) (14th c.) 131, 133

Lavignac, Albert 194–5*nn*, 198, 325*n*, 334*n*, 365*n*

Lawes, Henry (1596–1662) 309–10, 325, 326, 356, 357, 369; *Ayres and Dialogues* (1653–8) 309–10 (Ex. 96)

Lawes, William (1602–45) 309, 310, 325, 332, 333, 356; *Triumph of Peace, The* (with Ives, 1634) 325–6 (Ex. 106)

Layolle, François (*c.* 1475–*c.* 1540) 216

League of Composers (American) 824*n*

Lebègue, Nicolas (1630–1702) 435, 437

Le Cerf de la Viéville, *Comparaison de la musique* (1704–5) 205, 377*n*

Lechner, Leonhard (*c.* 1553–1606) 258, 281; *Das Leiden unsers Herren Jesu Christi* (1594) 259 (Ex. 74)

Leclair, Jean-Marie (1697–1764) 426

Lecocq, Alexandre Charles (1832–1918) 740

Leconte de Lisle, Charles (1818–94) 787

'Le Corbusier' (Charles Jean-Neret) (1887–1965) 855

Le Duc, Simon (*c.* 1745–77) 496, 545

Lefébure-Wély, Louis (1817–70) 773

Lefèvre, Gustave 467*n*, 469–70*nn*

Lefkowitz, Murray 326*n*, 332*n*

le Franc, Martin, *Le Champion des dames* (*c.* 1440) q. 142, 152

Léger, Fernand (1881–1955) *829*

Legouvé, Ernest (1807–1903) 767

Legrant, Guillaume ('Guillermus magnus') (*fl.* 1419) 138 and *n*, 141, 143*n*, 160

Legrenzi, Giovanni (1626–90) 205, 332, 358, 359, 361, 379, 398 and *n*

Le Heurteur, Guillaume (early 16th c.) 219*n*

Le Huray, Peter 263*n*, 356*n*, 415*n*

Leibowitz, René (1913–72) 849 and *n*, 856

Leich 100

Leichtentritt, Hugo 345

Leighton, Sir William, *Teares or Lamentacions* (1614) 291

leimma 29, 192

Leipzig: *Collegium Musicum* 431*n*, 488, *Grosses Concert* 488, Thomaskirche and Thomasschule 222, 303, 334, 405–7, 534, 538–9

Le Jeune, Claude (*c.* 1530–1600) 256, 278, 284, 307

Lekeu, Guillaume (1870–94) 778

Le Maistre, Mattheus (*c.* 1505–77) 257

Lemonnier, Pierre (*fl.* 1761) 459

Lenaerts, René B. 230*n*, 234*n*, 254*n*

'Lenau' (von Strehlenau), Nikolaus (1802–50) 702–3, 770, 771

Lenclos, Henri de (d. 1649), and his daughter, Ninon 341

Leningrad Conservatoire 841

Leo I, St (Pope 440–61) 57, 59

Leo III, St (Pope 795–816) 59

Leo X (Pope 1513–21) 177, 178*n*, 179, 227

Leo, Leonardo (1694–1744) 546; church music 548; operas 445, 451–2: *Amor vuol sofferenze* (1739) 451–2 (Ex. 159), *'Mpeca scoperta, La* (1723) 448, *Olimpiade, L'* (1737) 448*n*, *Pisistrato* (1714) 365; oratorios 546

Leoncavallo, Ruggiero (1858–1919) 744, 801

Leoninus (12th c.) 103, 109*n*; *Magnus liber organi* 104, 108, 'Alleluia' 106 (Ex. 19), 'Judea et Jerusalem' 104–6 (Ex. 18), 108, 113

Leopardi, Giacomo (1798–1837) 833

Leopold I (1640–1705), Emperor 322, 360, 398 and *n*

Leopold II (1747–92), Emperor 554

Leppard, Raymond 349*n*

Lermontov, Mikhail Yurevich (1814–41) 699, 732, 768, 784

Le Roux, Gaspard (*c.* 1660–*c.* 1707) 435

Le Roy, Adrian (*c.* 1520–98) 216, 256, 279*n*
Le Sage, Alain-René (1668–1747) 450–1
L'Escurel, Jehannot de (d. 1303) 115
Leskov, Nikolay Semyonovich (1831–95) 843
Lessing, Gotthold Ephraim (1729–81) 532
Le Sueur, Jean-François (1760–1837) 545–6, 577, 589, 612, 662, 667, 720; festival music 655–6; operas 577, *578*, 579, 580 (Ex. 214)
Lesure, François 216*n*, 219*n*, 220*n*
Levashev, E. M. 480*n*
Leveridge, Richard (*c.* 1670–1758) 393
Levi, Hermann (1839–1900) 667, 694
Levitan, Joseph 162*n*
Lewis, Sir Anthony 369*nn*, 393*n*, 416*n*
Ley, Henry G. 513*n*
Liber Usualis 134, 145, 176*n*, 436*n*, 755*n*
Lichnowsky, Moritz (1771–1837) 600*n*
Liedertafeln 665
ligatures 102–3, 114
Ligeti, György (b. 1923) 854
Liliencron, R. von 284*n*
Limoges, Abbey of St Martial 86–8, 90–4 *passim*, 107, 108
Lindeman, Ludvig Mathias (1812–87) 775
Lindenburg, Cornelius 149*n*
Linley, Thomas (1733–95) 477
Linley, Thomas (1756–78) 477
Lipiński, Karol (1790–1861) 612*n* 'Do Niemna' 651–2 (Ex. 249)
Lipphardt, Walter 65*n*, 258*n*
lira grande 271
Liszt, Franz (1811–86) 574, 575, 639, 681, q. 683, 688, 761–3; on church music q. 748; his protégés 688–90; influence on Russian song 783–4, and Wagner 714*n*; Masses 749–50 (Ex. 287), 753, 754 and *n*; oratorios 753, 754–5, *755*; orchestral works 681–4 (Ex. 264), 701; organ works 772; piano works 761–3, *772*, 773, 775, 776 (Ex. 295); Psalms 13 and 137 749; secular cantata, *Die Glocken des Strassburger Münsters* (1873) 756; songs 770, 771–2, 768, 789
Litolff, Henry (1818–91) 681, 682, 684
liturgical drama 90–2
lituus 41, 42, 43
Litzmann, Berthold 694*n*
liuto grosso 271
Livanova, Tamara 394*n*
Livius Andronicus (*fl.* 240 B.C.) 43
Livy (Titus Livius) (59 B.C.–17 A.D.) 42

Lloyd (Fluyd), John (d. 1523) 187–8
Lloyd-Jones, David 731*n*
Lôbo, Duarte (*c.* 1563–1646) 345
Lobwasser, Ambrosius (*fl.* 1573), translator 222, 256
Locatelli, Pietro (1695–1764) 430, 483 and *n*
Lochamer, Wolflein von, *Liederbuch* (*c.* 1452–60) 154, 159
Lochon, Jacques-François (b.*c.* 1662) 413
Locke, Matthew (*c.* 1630–77) 326, 332, 369 and *n*, 390–1, 415, 425
Lockwood, Lewis 148*n*, 210*n*, 232*n*
Loder, Edward (1813–65) 720
Loewe, Carl (1796–1869) 574, 646, 647, 649; oratorios 746–7; piano works 764; songs and ballads 649–50 (Ex. 248) 768*n*, 769, 770
Löffelholtz, Christoph (1572–1619) 285
Logroscino, Nicola (1698–1765) 452 and *n*
London: All Saints' Church, Margaret St 752, Chapel Royal 141, 187, 390, 415, 752, Italian opera (1705–30) in 370–2, Philharmonic Society 608–9, 611*n*, pleasure gardens 528, public concerts (from the 1670s) in 390, Queen's (King's) Theatre, Haymarket 370, 371, Royal Academy of Music (as an opera enterprise) 371, 372, St Paul's Cathedral 240, 275, Theatre Royal, Covent Garden 369, *708*, Theatre Royal, Drury Lane 370, 450, Westminster Abbey 356, 542*n*
longa imperfecta 114
longa perfecta 105, 114
Longueval (Longaval), Antoine (*fl.c.* 1507) 177 and *n*
Loqueville, Richard (d. 1418) 139, 151
Lorca, Federico García (1899–1936) 857
Lorenz, Alfred 362–3*nn*
Lorenzani, Paolo (1640–1713) 413*n*
Lorenzo da Firenze (Laurentius de Florentia) (14th c.) 131, 133
Lorenzo the Magnificent, *see* Medici, Lorenzo de'
Lorraine, Cardinal Charles de (*fl.* 1550) 230
Lortzing, Albert (1801–51) 712, 713
Lotti, Antonio (1667–1740) 364 and *n*, 365, 372, 379, 386, 410, 548
Louis XI (1423–83) of France 74, 161
Louis XII (1462–1515) of France 170, 176, 178, 219
Louis XIII (1601–43) of France 333
Louis XIV (1638–1715) of France 323, 355, 373, 412

Louis XV (1710–74) of France 457
Louis XVI (1754–93) of France 662
Louis XVIII (1755–1824), of France 662
Louis (d. 1526) of Hungary 190
Louis of Savoy (*fl.* 1434) 139
Louis Ferdinand, Prince (1772–1806) 632;
    chamber music 620–1 (Ex. 235)
Lourié, Arthur (1892–1966) 840, 841
Lowinsky, Eduard 174*n*, 178*n*, 209*n*
Loyola, St Ignatius de (*c.* 1492–1556) 255
Lü Pu-wei, *Ch'un-ch'iu* (239 B.C.) 564, 565
Lübeck: *Abendmusiken*, the 404, 441,
    Marienkirche 338*n*
Lübeck, Vincent (1654–1740) 441, 442
Lublina, Jan z (Ioannis de Lyublyn)
    (*fl.* 1540) 225
Ludford, Nicolas (*c.* 1485–*c.* 1557) 240
Ludus Danielis (Beauvais, *c.* 1230) 92
Ludwig I (1786–1868) of Bavaria 753
Ludwig, Friedrich 123*n*
Lully, Jean-Baptiste (1632–87) 323, 373–5,
    376, 377, 424, 432, 435; compared with
    Purcell 369–70; as a dancer 323, 324;
    influence on Colasse 376, Duni 461,
    Keiser 367, Kusser 366, Muffat 423,
    Rameau 454–6
    motets 412
    operas and other stage works 205, 324–5,
    365, 373, 421, 450, 454: *Achille et
    Polixène* (incompl.) 366, 376, *Acis et
    Galatée* 366, *Alcidiane* (ballet, 1658)
    421, *Amadis* 374 (Ex. 126), *Armide*
    (1686) 375, *375*, 455, 467, *Atys* (1676)
    375, 435, 455, *Bellérophon* (1679) 375,
    Bourgeois gentilhomme, Le (1670) 324,
    Cadmus et Hermione (1673) 369, 373,
    374 (Ex. 125), 376, 421–2 (Ex. 146), 435,
    Festes de l'Amour et de Bacchus, Les
    (pastiche *pastorale*, 1672) 373, 377, *Isis*
    376, *Mariage forcé, Le* (1664) 324,
    Persée (1682) 375, *Phaéton* (1683) 375,
    435, *Proserpine* (1680) 435, *Psyché*
    (1678) 373, *Roland* (1685) 421, 467 (Ex.
    166), *Saisons, Les* (ballet, 1661) 324 (Ex.
    105), 421, *Thésée* 374–5 (Ex. 127),
    Triomphe de Bacchus, Le (ballet, 1666)
    421
Lumsden, David 285*n*
Lunacharsky, Anatoly Vasilyevich
    (1875–1933) 840
Lüneburg, Ratsbibliothek 337
Luntz, Erwin 426*n*
Lupo, Thomas (d. 1628) 290, 292
Lupus (Lupi), Johannes (Jean Leleu) (*c.*
    1506–39) 208, 209, 212, 213*n*, 245

lute 190: Arabian 194, Asiatic 17, in
    Assyria 19, 20, Babylonian *11*, 12, 15,
    Egyptian 15–16, *16*, 17, in France
    340–2, Persian 53, 191, *196*, Roman
    (pandura) 43, theorbo-lute 341
lute ayre 278–80
lute music books (16th–17th c.) 184, 226
    and *n*, 236–9, 284–5
lutenists *214*, 340–2; *see also* Bakfark,
    Bataille, Dowland, Francesco de Milano,
    Galilei, Gintzler, Henry VIII, James IV
    of Scotland, Lambert, Lanier, Neusidler,
    Reys, *et al*
Luther, Martin (1483–1546) 183, 184, 220
Luther Bible *Historiae* 353–4
Lutheran church cantata 395, **405–7** (Ex.
    142)
Lutheran hymn **222–4** (Ex. 63), **257–8**
    (Ex. 73), 350, 352; its organ treatment
    337–8
Lutheran hymn-motet 259–61, 409
Lutheran organ composers 441–3
Lütolf, Max 123*n*, 376*n*
Lutosławski, Witold (b. 1913) 854
Lutyens, Elisabeth (b. 1906) 825
Luython, Charles (*c.* 1557–1620) 254, 285
Luzzaschi, Luzzasco (1545?–1607) **266**,
    288, 296, 338, 339
Lydian system 29, 32, 77
Lymburgia, Johannes de (15th c.) 144,
    145 and *n*
lyra (*chelys*) 24–5, 32–3, 40, *40*
lyra orphica 171
lyre 2: Assyrian 19–20, 21, Bedouin 14,
    14, Egyptian 15, *15*, *16*, 17, Greek 22–4,
    23, 28, 32, Hebrew 38, in Italy, 16th c.
    use 270, Ninevite *19*, post-Sumerian
    11, *11*, 12, Sumerian 9, *9*, 10
Lysander of Sicyon (6th c. B.C.) 30

Maban (before 731) 58
MacArdle, Donald 630*n*
MacClintock, Carol 265*n*, 322*n*
MacCunn, Hamish (1868–1916) 700
Macdonald, Hugh 800*n*
MacDowell, Edward (1861–1908) 700,
    792–3
Macfarren, Sir George (1813–87) 672, 673
McGee, Timothy 91*n*
McGuiness, Rosamond 390*n*
Machaut, Guillaume de (*c.* 1300–*c.* 1372)
    72–3, 118, 120, 130*n*, 131, 135, 136, 156;
    and the polyphonic Mass cycle **125–8**
    (Exx. 25–6), 145; his *Prologue* q. 72;
    secular music 123–4

Machlin, Paul 675*n*

Mackenzie, Sir Alexander (1847–1935) 700

Macourek, Jiří (1815–after 1863) 719

McPeek, Gwynn S. 143*n*

McPhee, Colin 572*n*

Macque, Jean ('Giovanni') de (1551–1614) 265, 299–300, 338

Macran, Henry S. 33*n*

madhyamagrāma (ma-grāma) 559, 560

madriale (mandriale) 129

Madrid: Capilla Real 411, the Court at 445, Teatro de los Caños (1708) 372

madrigal: and Ciconia 140, in Denmark 283, in England 275–8, its influence on the *chanson* 283–4, in Italy 265–8, 379, Netherland composers 264–5, in Poland 283, 16th c. 202–4, **226–8**, **228–31** (Exx. 65–6), **233–4** (Ex. 67), in Spain 283, its transformation 295–7 (Ex. 85), trecento 129–31 (Ex. 28)

madrigale spirituale (from 1581) 246, 346

Madrigali de diversi musici . . . (1530, 1533) 228, 229

Maeterlinck, Maurice (1862–1949) 797, 802, 804, 808

magadis 25

Magalhães, Felipe de (d. 1652) 345

'Maggiolata' 246*n*

Magnard, Albéric (1864–1914) 804

Mahler, Gustav (1860–1911) 796, 798; ballad, *Das klagende Lied* (1880) 760; *Orchesterlieder* 789, **791**, 795, **796**, 810, 857; symphonies **703**, *704*, **795–6**, 798*n*, 806, 810, 841, 855

Mahrenholz, Christhard 335*n*, 337*n*

Mahu, Stephan (*c.* 1485–*c.* 1541) 223, 226

Maillart, Louis (1817–71) 720

Main, Alexander 228*n*

Maione, Ascanio (d. 1627) 338

Mairy, A. 215*n*

Majo, Gian Francesco di (1732–70) 459, 469; operas 459*n*, 461 and *n*, 462 (Ex. 164(ii))

malimba 813, 816

Malines Cathedral 208

Malinowski, Władysław 252*n*

Malipiero, Gian Francesco (1882–1973) 253*n*, 265*n*, 295*n*, 317*n*, 383*n*, 429*n*, 832

Mallarmé, Stéphane (1842–98), poet 741, 802

Malvezzi, Cristoforo (1547–97) 269–70

Ma'mūn, Al- (785–833), Caliph 193

Manchicourt, Pierre de (*c.* 1510–64) 208, 219*n*

Mancini, Francesco (1679–1739) 364–5, 370

mandola, its 16th c. use 270

Mandyczewski, Eusebius 410*n*

Manelli, Francesco (*c.* 1595–1667) 316 and *n*

Mann, Alfred 410*n*

Mannheim orchestra 488, 489, 491, 498, 499*n*, 522

Manniche, Lise 16*n*

Mantica, Francesco 273*n*

Mantua: Court at 265, Isabella d'Este (16th c.), Duchess of 226, Jachet of (before 1550) 230*n*, 232

Manzoni, Alessandro (1785–1873) 348

maqám 191, 197, 198, 560, 812

Marable, Fate (his jazz-band) *817*

Marais, Marin (1656–1728) 376, 435*n*

Marat, Jean Paul (1743–93) 655

Marazzoli, Marco (1619–62) 301, 346 and *n*; operas 313, 314–15 (Exx. 100–1), 315–16, 322, 323, 361

Marbeck, John (*c.* 1510–85) 261, *262*

Marcabru (*fl.* 1130) 95

Marcello, Alessandro (1684–1750) 430

Marcello, Benedetto (1686–1739) 430, 544; *Canzoni madrigaleschi . . .* (1717) 379; operas 383–4 (Ex. 133); oratorios 384; psalms, *Estro Poetico-Armonico* (1724–6) 418*n*; satire, *Il teatro alla moda* (*c.* 1720) 383, 445

Marchand, Louis (1669–1732) 435, 436

Marchettus of Padua (*fl.* 1318) 129 and *n*

Marcus Aurelius (121–80), Emperor 48

Marenzio, Luca (1553–99) 205, 260, 269, 280, 283; madrigals **266–7**, 276, 278

Margaret, Archduchess of Austria (*fl.* 1507) 168–9, 171, 188

Maria Theresia (1717–80), Empress 496, 550

Maria Theresia (d. 1807), Empress of Austria 657 and *n*

Mariazell, pilgrimage church at 552

Marie Antoinette (1753–93), Queen of France 506, 596*n*

Marie Louise (d. 1847), Empress of France 634

Marigny, Enguerrand de (*fl.* 14th c.) 122

marimba 816

Marini, Biagio (1597–1665) 296, 317, **329**, 330, 331, 335

Marino, Giambattista (1569–1625) 296

Mario, Conte di Candia (1808–83) *708*

'Marionette douche' 133, 134

Maritain, Jacques (b. 1882) 830

Marix, J. 148*n*, 152–3*nn*, 160*n*

Marlow, Richard 293*n*

Marmontel, Jean François (1723–99) 467, 469, 470

Marot, Clément (1496–1544) 214, 220–2, 256–7

Marpurg, Friedrich Wilhelm (1718–95) 399*n*, 516*n*, 517, 529

Marrocco, W. T. 124*n*, 129*n*, 130*n*

Marschalk, Max 795*n*

Marschner, Heinrich (1795–1861) 575, 649; choral work, *Klänge aus Osten* 751; operas: *Bäbu, Der* (1838) 712, *Falkners Braut, Des* (1832) 711, *Hans Heiling* (1833) 649, 711–12 (Ex. 273), 747, *Kaiser Adolph von Nassau* (1845) 713, *Schloss am Atna* (1836) 712, *Templer und die Jüdin, Der* (1829) 593–4, 711, *Vampyr, Der* (1828) 593–4, 711, 714; songs **649**, 665, 770

Marshall, Robert L. 535*n*

Martenot, Maurice (b. 1898) 831, 851

Martin I, St (Pope 649–53) 57

Martin V (Pope 1417–31) 73, 138

Martin, E. 256*n*

Martin, Frank (b. 1890) 837 and *n*

Martin y Soler, Vicente (1754–1806) 473, 478, 480, 577

Martinelli, Caterina (d.*c*. 1614) 295

Martini, Aegidius (1741–1816) 528

Martini, ('Padre') Giovanni Battista (1706–84) 550 and *n*; *Sonate per l'organo* . . . 513 (Ex. 191(i))

Martinů, Bohuslav (1890–1959) 823, 831*n*, 838

Martucci, Giuseppe (1856–1909) 801, 832

Marx, Adolf Bernhard (1795–1866) 747

Mary I (1516–58) of England 241, 293

Mary II (1662–94) of England 391

Mascagni, Pietro (1863–1945) 743, 744

Maschera, Florentio (*fl.* 1582) 288

masque (in mid-17th c. England) 325–6 (Ex. 106)

Mass: the 'cyclic' Mass **144–6**, earliest Masses **56–7**, 59, 65, 73, early polyphonic Masses 72–3, 123, **125**, 126–8 (Exx. 25–6), 133 (Ex. 29)

Mass, 'La mort de Saint Gothard' 146

Massaino, Tiburtio (*fl.* before 1608) 288

Massenet, Jules (1842–1912) 702, **743**, 756, 786, 802, 838

Massenkeil, Günther 346*nn*, 397–8*nn*, 540*n*, 542*n*, 545*n*

Masson, Paul-Marie 388*n*

'Master of the female half-lengths' *214*

Masters of the King's (Queen's) Music, etc. 308, 415

Math, Wolfgang 522*n*

Matteis, Nicolà (*fl.* 1672–96) 391, 425

Matteo da Perugia (early 15th c.) 136–7, 139, 151

Mattheson, Johann (1681–1764) **367** and *n*, 386, 403, 510; *Die wol-klingende Finger-Sprache* . . . 510 (Ex. 190)

Matthias Corvinus (1443–90) of Hungary 180

Matthisson, Friedrich von (1761–1831) 643, 645, 649

Mauduit, Jacques (1557–1627) 256, 284, 307, 322*n*

Maugars, André (*c*. 1580–*c*. 1645) 333

Maw, Nicholas (b. 1935) 859

Maximilian I (1459–1519), Emperor 73, 74, 154, 167, 171, 180, 181–2

Maximilian II (1527–76), Emperor 244, 254

Maxton, Willy 405*n*

May, Hans von 247*n*

Mayakovsky, Vladimir (1893–1930) 842

Mayr, Simon (1763–1845) 585–6

Mazarin (Giulio Mazzarini) (1602–61), Cardinal 315, 322–4, 373

Mazzocchi, Domenico (1592–1665) 301 and *n*, 346; opera, *La catena d'Adone* (1626) 311–12 (Ex. 97)

Mazzocchi, Virgilio (1597–1646) 301, 345, 346; opera (with Marazzoli), *Che soffre, speri* (1639) 313, 314–15 (Exx. 100–1), 322, 361

mbira 813

Meane Mass, The 241 and *n*

Meck, Nadezhda von 698, 780*n*

Medici, Cosimo de' (1389–1464) 708*n*

Medici, Ferdinando I de' 268, *270*

Medici, Francesco I de' 268

Medici, Giovanni de' (Pope Leo X) 177, 178*n*, 227

Medici, Lorenzo de' ('the Magnificent') (1448–92) 74, 170, 171, 172, 181

Medici, Maria de' (1573–1642), Queen of France 271

Méhul, Étienne-Nicolas (1763–1817) 577, 579, 581, 584, 585, 592, 643; festival music 655 (Ex. 251(ii)), 656; *Messe solennelle* (1804) 656; operas 577, 579 (Ex. 213), 580, 581 and *n*, 582, **584**; symphonies 606

Mei, Girolamo (16th c.) 204, 268

Meier, Bernhard 210*n*, 233*n*

Meissen, Heinrich von ('Frauenlob') (d. 1318) 98

Melani, Jacopo (1626–76) 327, 358, 361
Melanippides (d. before 413 B.C.) 31
Mele, Giovanni Battista (b. 1701) 477
Mellers, Wilfrid 436n
Melli, Domenico Maria (*fl.* 1602) 308
Mellon Chansonnier 148n
Melodia Germanica, La (*c.* 1755) 489–1
  (Exx. 177–8)
mélodie 767–8, 786–8
Memo, Dionisio (*fl.* 1516) 188, 239
Mendelssohn, Moses (1729–86) 664
Mendelssohn-Bartholdy, Felix (1809–47)
  575, 673, 675; chamber music 612, 617,
  625–6, 628, 765–6; church music 751–2;
  incidental music, *A Midsummer Night's
  Dream* 612, 625, 671, 672; oratorios 747
  and n; organ works 772; overtures 671,
  672, 675; piano concertos 671–2, 677,
  678; piano works (solo) 640–1, 764, 772;
  secular choral work, *Die erste
  Walpurgisnacht* (1832) 751; songs 626,
  770; symphonies 612, 671, 676, 677,
  746; violin concerto 672, 678
Menecrates (1st c.) 48
Ménestrandise, La 436n
Menke, Werner 386n, 403n, 408nn
mensuration of note-values 102–3
Mercadante, Saverio (1795–1870) 586,
  587, 588, 705, 709
Mercer, Frank 493n
Méreaux, Nicolas-Jean (1745–97) 545
Merian, Wilhelm 184n
Merkel, Gustav (1827–85) 773
Mermann, Thomas (*fl.* late 16th c.) 255
Merriam, Alan P. 812–13nn
Merrick, Frank 613n
Merritt, A. Tillman 216n, 219n
Mersenne, Marin (1588–1648), *Harmonie
  universelle* (1636–7) 256n, 333 (Ex. 110),
  341n, 862
Merula, Tarquinio (*c.* 1595–1665) 330, 331
Merulo, Claudio (1533–1604) 249, 251,
  268n, 285, 288, 338, 342, 441; *Canzoni
  ...fatte alla Francese* (1592–1611) 287
  (Ex. 83); Masses 287
Messe de Notre Dame (Machaut) 125,
  126–8 (Exx. 25–6)
Messiaen, Olivier (b. 1908) 572, 831, 844,
  851, 855; *Quatre études de rhythme* 849;
  Turangalîla-Symphonie 846n, 847–8 (Ex.
  308)
Metastasio, Pietro (1698–1782) 445–8,
  451–3, 464–5; letter (1749) to Hasse
  q. 446–7

Adriano in Siria (1734) 448
Alessandro nell' Indie (J. C. Bach, Handel,
  Hasse, di Majo, Piccinni, Vinci) 446,
  459, 467n
Artaserse (Arne, J. C. Bach, Galuppi,
  Gluck, Graun, Hasse, Jommelli, di
  Majo, Vinci) 446, 452, 453, 459, 464,
  465
Attilio Regolo (Hasse) 446–7
Betulia liberata, La (Gassmann,
  Jommelli, Reutter) 548, 550
Catone in Utica (J. C. Bach) 459
Clemenza di Tito, La (Mozart) 469
Demetrio (Caldara) 446
Demofoonte (Berezovsky, Caldara,
  Galuppi, Graun, Traetta) 446, 452, 453,
  459, 470, 478
Didone abbandonata (Albinoni, Sarri,
  Storace, Traetta, Vinci) 446, 448,
  459, 477
Giuseppe riconosciuto (Hasse) 549
Isacco (Jommelli) 548
Joas (J. C. Bach, Reutter) 544, 550
Morte d'Abele, La (Arne, Leo) 544, 546
Olimpiade, L' (Caldara, Duni, Pergolesi,
  Piccinni, Traetta, Vivaldi) 446 and n,
  448, 459, 467n
Parnaso confuso (Gluck) 465
Passione, La (Caldara, Eberlin, Harrer,
  Jommelli, Salieri) 539, 548
Ruggiero (Hasse) 446
Sta Elena al Calvario (Hasse, Leo) 546,
  547
Semiramide (Salieri) 470
Siroe (Vivaldi) 446n, 447
Sogno di Scipione, Il (Hasse) 478
Trionfo di Clelia, Il (Gluck, Hasse) 465
Zenobia (Hasse) 478
Metner, Nikolay (1880–1951) 799
Métru, Nicolas (*fl.* 1642) 334
Metz, *schola cantorum* at 4, 59
Mevlid 191
Mey, Lev Aleksandrovich (1822–62) 783,
  784
Meyer, E. H. 334n
Meyerbeer, Giacomo (Jakob Meyer Beer)
  (1791–1864) 705, 707, 709, 720n, 754;
  operas: *Africaine, L'* (1865) 727,
  Crociata in Egitto, Il (1824) 590n, *Étoile
  du Nord, L'* (1854) 720, *Feldlager in
  Schlesien, Ein* (1844) 720, *Huguenots, Les*
  (1836) 705, 707, 710, 727, *Prophète, Le*
  (1849) 707, 708, 772, *Robert le Diable*
  (1831) 705, 707, *Romilda e Costanza*
  (1817) 590n; overture, *Struensee* (1846)

682 (Ex. 263); songs 768
Mezangeau, René (*fl.* 1639) 341
Miča (Mitscha), František Adam
 (1746–1811) 485*n*
Miča (Mitscha), František Václav
 (1694–1744) 485; serenade, *Operosa
 Terni Colossi Moles* (1735) 485–6 (Ex.
 176)
Michelangelo Buonarroti (1475–1564) 227,
 790
Michna, Adam Václav (*c.* 1600–76) 411
Mickiewicz, Adam Bernard (1798–1855)
 651–2, 698, 762, 769
Mielczewski, Marcin (d. 1651) 345, 412*n*
Migne, J. P. 57*n*, 59*n*, 60*n*
Mikolaj z Radomia (*fl.* 1426) 180
Milan, Luis, *El Maestro* (1535/6) 238, *238*,
 239
Milan Cathedral 136–7, 139, 170, 246
Milanese Court Chapel 170
Milanese liturgy 4, 57, 71
Milanuzzi, Carlo (d. after 1647) 296, 297*n*
Milhaud, Darius (1892–1974) 823, 828,
 829, *829*, 830, 851, 855
Millico, Giuseppe (*fl.* 1762) 465
Milton, John (1608–74) 315, 325, 543,
 660, 760
Minato, Nicolo (*fl.* 1650) 320 and *n*, 324,
 358, 360, 367, 371, 398
Ming dynasty (1368–1644) 568
Miniscalchi, Guglielmo (*fl.c.* 1625) 296
Minnelieder 97, 98, 102
Minnesänger, the 71, 73, 97 and *n*, 98
Minor, Andrew 178*n*
Mirabeau, Gabriel Honoré, Comte de
 (1748–91) 654
Mischiati, Oscar 235*n*, 251*n*, 338*n*
Mishkin, Henry G. 487*n*
Misjaḥ, Ibn (d.*c.* 715) 191
Missa Caput 145
missa parodia 176, 211
Mitchell, William J. 516*n*
Mitjana, Rafael 325*n*
Mitsunobu, Tosa (*fl.* 1744) *571*
Mixolydian mode 77, 128, 341
Mixter, Keith E. 139*n*
Miyoshi, Akira (b. 1933) 571–2
mizmār 195
Mocenigo, Tomaso (d. 1423), Doge 139
Mocquereau, Dom André 749*n*
Modena Codex 136–7, 146
Moderne, Jacques (*fl.* 1532) 203, 213, 216
Modes (church) 64–5
Modes (Greek), *see Harmoniai*
Modes (rhythmic) 102

modus imperfectus and *perfectus* 114, 118
Molière (Jean Baptiste Poquelin)
 (1622–73) 324, 373, 464, 480
Molinet, Jehan (?15th c.) 161
Molza, Tarquinia (*fl.c.* 1580) 265
Mompellio, Federico 296*n*
Mondonville, Jean-Joseph (1711–72) 458,
 459, 518, 545
Moniot d'Arras (12th c.) 97
Moniuszko, Stanisław (1819–72) 733–4,
 786
 operas 733–4 (Ex. 282)
 songs **769** (Ex. 293), 783
Mönlemeyer, Helmut 290*n*, 335*n*
Monmouth, James, Duke of (1649–85) 397
Monn, Mathias Georg (1717–50) 486, 487
 and *n*
monochord 28
monody: instrumental 329, its revival (*c.*
 1580) 268
Monsigny, Pierre-Alexandre (1729–1816)
 459, 464, 470, 479
Montanus (Berg), Johannes 203, 225
Monte, Philipp de (1521–1603) 241, 246,
 247, 254, **265**, 278
Montéclair, Michel Pinolet de
 (1667–1737) 377, 388
Montemezzi, Italo (1875–1952) 810
Monterosso, Raffaele 173*n*, 365*n*
Monteverdi, Claudio (1567–1643) 205,
 296, 309, 348, 353, 832; compared with
 Guédron 307; his *concertato* style 317,
 318, **344**, 353; influence on Cavalli 319,
 Grandi 348; *prima* and *seconda prattica*
 344, 345, 353, 410, 820; pupils 318, 319
 church music **253–4**, 260
 collections: *Scherzi musicale* (1607,
  1632) 303, *Selva Morale* (1640/1) 275,
  344
 madrigals **267**, 275, **295–6**, 297 and *n*,
  303, 309, *Terzo Libro* (1592) 265,
  Quinto Libro (1605) 295, (8th book)
  Madrigali Guerreri (1638) 295, 296, 317
 operas, etc. 311, 316–17, **317–18**: *Adone*
  (1639) 317; *Arianna* (1608) 253, **275**,
  317; *Ballo dell'ingrato, Il* (ballet, 1608)
  275, 295; *Combattimento di Tancredi e
  Clorinda, Il* (1624) 295, **317**, 347;
  Incoronazione di Poppea, L' (1642) 317,
  318, 320 and *n*, 420; *Nozze d'Enea con
  Lavinia, Le* (1641) 317; *Orfeo* (1607)
  204, 253, **274–5**, 297; *Ritorno d'Ulisse in
  patria, Il* (1641) 317, 318, 833; *Tirsi e
  Clori* 395
Montpellier Codex (*c.* 1300) **109–10**, 115,

117, 118, 749
Moore, Thomas (1779–1852) 653 and *n*
729, 751, 767, 770
Morales, Cristóbal (*c.* 1500–53) **236**, 247
Morax, René (1873–1963) 830
Morcourt, Richard de 220*n*
Morehen, John 242*n*
Moreon, Craig 263*n*
Mörike, Eduard (1804–75) 789–91
Morin, Jean-Baptiste (1677–1754) 388,
413
Morlacchi, Francesco (1784–1841) 662
Morlaye, Guillaume (*c.* 1515–60) 186*n*,
220, 239
Morley, Thomas (1557–1602) 261, q. 282,
291, q. 297; church music 263; secular
works **276**, 277–80 *passim*, 290, 291, 293
Moroney, Davitt 342*n*, 513*n*
Mortari, Virgilio 364*n*, 453*n*
Morton, Robert (*fl.* 1457–75) 148 and *n*,
149, 164–5, 187
Moscheles, Ignaz (1794–1870) 636, 639,
684; piano concertos 615 (Ex. 234), 616,
678–9 (Ex. 260)
Moscow, Imperial Theatre 733
Moser, Hans Joachim 183*n*, 225*n*, 303–6*nn*
passim, 353*n*, 365*n*, 367*n*, 529–30*nn*, 532*n*
Mosolov, Aleksandr (1900–73) 842
motet: developments 110–11, 112–13,
early 109 and *n*, 110, instrumental
111–12 (Ex. 21), political and ceremonial
122–3, in the *Roman de Fauvel* 118–19
(Ex. 23), for solo voices 410–11
motet-Passion, *see* Passion
motetus 109, 111, 113, 119, 122–3
Moulinié, Étienne (*c.* 1600–after 1669)
307, 308*n*, 334, 387
Mouret, Jean-Joseph (1682–1738) 377,
451, 454, 545
mousike 26–8, 32
Mouton, Jean (*c.* 1459–1522) 177, 210,
230, 232, 236; 'Non nobis Domine'
178–9 (Ex. 49)
Mozarabic liturgy 4, 57, 81, 87*n*, 190, 197
Mozart, Leopold (1719–87) 491, 502,
529*n*, 552 and *n*, 553, 603
Mozart, Wolfgang Amadeus (1756–91)
compared with C. P. E. Bach 527, J. C.
Bach 522; earliest works 518, 519–20;
his father's *Notenbuch* (1762) 529*n*; and
Freemasonry 476; influence on
Beethoven 619, J. Haydn 506, Schubert
609; influenced by C. P. E. Bach 527,
J. C. Bach 497, 498, 522, Boccherini
498*n*, Gluck 469, Nardini 498,

Sammartini 497; as an instrumental
composer 497–9 (Ex. 181); and the key
of G minor 495; his patron, van
Swieten 660; and the pianoforte 521–2;
his pupils: Attwood 642, Eberl 601,
631, Hummel 603, 615, 631, Süssmayr
469; and Viotti 598
Adagio in B minor (K.540) 574
church music, *see* Masses
Clarinet Concerto 504, 554
Clarinet Quintet 505
epistle sonatas 553
flute concertos and quartets 498, 499
keyboard concertos 497, 498, 499, **502–4**
keyboard sonatas and other works 498,
521–22, 523, 526*n*, 527, 528
keyboard songs 528, **532–3**, 574
Masonic music 554
Masses and other church music **552–3**,
554–5, 753
Oboe Quartet 499
occasional music 498, 505, 506*n*, 526
operas 205, **469**, 473, **474–6**: *Bastien und
Bastienne* (1768) 459*n*, *Clemenza di
Tito, La* (1791) 469, 554, 555, *Cosi fan
tutte* (1790) 475–6, *Don Giovanni*
(1787) 461, 475, 616, *Entführung aus
dem Serail, Die* (1782) **474–5**, 526, *Finta
giardiniera, La* (1775) 471–2 (Ex. 169),
Idomeneo (1781) 469, 500, *Nozze di
Figaro, Le* (1786) **475**, 477, *Zauberflöte,
Die* (1791) **476**, 528, 554, 555, 589
oratorios 553
orchestration of Handel's *Messiah* 542*n*
piano quartets 498, 503*n*, 504, 527, 620
piano trios 505, **526–7**
Piano and Wind Quintet 620*n*
sinfonie concertante 497, 499
string quartets 497–8 (Ex. 181), **501–2**,
504, **505**, 522*n*
string quintets 497, **505**
symphonies 497–8, 499, 502, 504–5 (Ex.
186), 506*n*, 602*n*
violin concertos 498, 502
violin sonatas **522**, 526, 527
mṛdaṅgam 562
Mudaliyar, A. M. Chinnaswami 563*n*
Mudarra, Alonso de (*fl.* 1546) 237, 239;
'Romanesca' 237 (Ex. 68(iii))
Muffat, Georg (1653–1704) 423, 426, 431,
435, 438, 441, 511; *Florilegia* (1695,
1698) 426, **433** (Ex. 151)
Muffat, Gottlieb (1690–1770) 511
mughni 196
Muhammad (571–632) 190

Muhammad Kamel el-Kholay (*fl.* 1900) 198

Müller, Hermann 548*n*

Müller, Wenzel (1767–1835) 476, 589

Müller, Wilhelm (1794–1827) 648

Mulliner, Thomas (*fl.c.* 1550) **240**–1, 292

Mumford, Ivy L. 239*n*

Munajjim, Ibn al- (d. 912), *Risāla fi'l mūsīqī* 191–2, 194

Mundy, John (*c.* 1552–1630) 261

Mundy, William (*c.* 1529–*c.* 1591) 261

Munich: Court 589*n*, Court Chapel 758, Residenztheater (1657) 325, 358

Münzer, Thomas (1491–1525) 207

Muradeli, Vano (1908–70) 846, 857

Muratori, Lodovico Antonio (1672–1750) 447*n*

Muris, Johannes de, *Ars novae musicae* (1319) 72, 117

Murray, Bain 167*n*

Murschhauser, Franz Xaver Anton (1663–1738) 441

Muset, Colin (12th c.) 97

Musica enchiriadis (?9th c.) 70, **77**–**80** (Ex. 9), 85, 89 (Ex. 13)

musica ficta 122, 127 (Ex. 26), 233, 234, 820

musica mensurabilis 102

Musica nova . . . sopra organi . . . (1540) 234

musica plana 102

musica reservata 175 (Ex. 47), 268

Musikalisches Vielerley (Hamburg, 1770) 517

musique concrète 821, 846, 849, 851, 855, 858

musique mesurée à l'antique 203, 256, **284**, 306, 307

Musorgsky, Modest Petrovich (1839–81) 576, 729, 730–1, 733; operas 729, **731**, 732, 844; piano works 776–7, *777*; songs **785**–6, 802

Müthel, Johann Gottfried (1728–88) 516–17

'My Lady Carey's dompe' 186

'My Lady Nevells Booke' (*c.* 1585–90) 292

Myaskovsky, Nikolay (1881–1950) 841, 842, 844, 846

Myers, Rollo H. 827*n*

nacaires 195

Naderman, Jean Henry (*fl.c.* 1780) 528*n*

nafari (nafar) 562

nāgasvaram 562

nagham 191

nakers 195

Nanino, Giovanni Bernardino (*c.* 1560–1623) 247

Nanino, Giovanni Maria (*c.* 1545–1607) 247

Nanteuil, Robert (1623–78) 341

naos-sistrum 13

Napier, William (*fl.* 1792) 642

Naples: dialect comedy and intermezzi at 448–9 (Ex. 157), Spanish viceregal Court at 338, 359

Napoleon I (1769–1821), Emperor 577, 582, 583, 600 and *n*, 655–6

naqqārāt 195

Náray, Canon György, *Lyra Coelestis* (1695) 754

Nardini, Pietro (1722–93) 498

Nares, James (1715–83) 513

Narváez, Luis de (d. after 1555) 236, 239; instrumental works 236–9 *passim* (Ex. 68(ii))

Nathan, Hans 816*n*

Nātyaśāstra 558

nauba 191, 199 and *n*, 567

Naumann, Johann Gottlieb (1741–1801) 594

Nauwach, Johann (*c.* 1595–*c.* 1630) 304

Navarre, Thibaut de Champagne (early 13th c.), King of 97, 101

nāy 18, 190

Nazarene painters 663

nēbel 38

Nebuchadnezzar, King (604–561 B.C.) of Babylon 21

Neefe, Christian Gottlob (1748–98) 474, 523

Nef, Karl 434*n*, 485*n*

Negri, Marc'Antonio (*fl.c.* 1612) 296

Negro music in North America 816–18

Neidhart von Reuental (13th c.) 98

Neighbour, Oliver 766*n*

Nejedlý Zdeněk 133*n*

Nekrasov, Nikolay Alexeyevich (1821–88) 785

Nelson, Horatio, Viscount (1758–1805) 656

Neri, Massimiliano (*c.* 1600–66) 330; sonatas 330, **331** (Ex. 109)

Nero (37–68), Emperor 44, 46, 48

Nerval (Labrunie), Gérard de (1808–55) 750

Ness, Arthur J. 235*n*

Neuber, Ulrich (*fl.* 1542) 203, 225

Neukomm, Sigismund (1778–1858) 747

Neumeister, Erdmann (1671–1756) 385, 406, 407 and *n*, 408

Index

neumes 54, *62*, 62–4, 65, 66, 80–4 *passim*,
81, *83*: 'Aquitanian' 81, 84, 87, 102,
'Beneventan' 81, 'Coislin' 66,
diastematic 93, ekphonetic 66, 'hooked'
94
Neusidler, Hans (*c.* 1510–63) 239
Neusidler, Melchior (1531–*c.* 1590) 239*n*
Newman, 'Master' (before 1550) 241, 292
Newman, William S. 329*n*, 425*n*, 636*n*
Niccolò da Perugia (*fl.c.* 1350) 131
Nichelmann, Christoph (1717–62) 516,
517
Nicholson, Richard 332*n*
Nicolai, Otto (1810–49) 713
Nicolini (Niccoló Grimaldi) (*fl.* 1708) 364
Nicomachus of Gerasa 50
Nielsen, Carl (1865–1931) 801*n*
Nielsen, Hans (*c.* 1580–after 1620) 283
Niemcewicz, Julian Ursyn (*c.* 1757–1841)
652
Nietzsche, Friedrich Wilhelm (1844–1900)
527, 795, 800, 805
Nilsson, Bo (b. 1937) 854
Nirvána 559
Nivers, Guillaume-Gabriel (1632–1714)
412*n*, 413; *Livres d'orgue* (1665–75)
436–7 (Ex. 152)
no 570
Noack, Friedrich 406*n*
Noble, Jeremy 292*n*
Nobutoki, Kiyoshi (1887–1965) 571
Nola, Giovanni Domenico da (*c.* 1510–92)
231*n*
nomos 27–8, 31
Nono, Luigi (b. 1924) 853; *Il canto sospeso*
(1956) 854 (Ex. 311)
Nordraak, Rikard (1842–66) 775
Nörminger, August (*fl.* 1598) 285
North, Hon. Roger (1653–1734) 425
Noske, Frits 296*n*, 308–9*nn*, 387–8*nn*,
393*n*, 643 and *nn*, 768*n*, 786*nn*
Noskowski, Zygmunt (1846–1909) 700,
783
notation (see also *neumes*): 'Boethian' 77,
83, Byzantine 66–7, developments in
80–3, *83*, early 2, 5–6, 10 and *n*, 17, 21,
49 and *n* (Ex. 4), *49*, Egyptian 17, 21,
evidence of 61–2, Franconian 114–15,
Frankish developments in 66, Greek 5,
34–6 (Exx. 1–3), *36*, of the mannerists
136, of note-values 85–6, proportional
146–8 (Exx. 34–5), Roman 47, staff
84–5, Syrian ekphonetic 54, and Vitry's
Ars nova 72, 'white' 139*n*
note-values, mensuration of 102–3

Notker 'Balbulus' (840–912) 82, 85, 89
Nottebohm, Gustav 581*n*, 602*n*, 606*n*,
611*n*, 619*nn*, 622*n*
Novák Vítěslav (1870–1949) 806
'Novalis' (Georg P. F. von Hardenberg)
(1772–1801) 574
Noverre, Jean Georges (1727–1810) 464
and *n*
Nowak-Romanowicz, Alma 478*n*
Nuffel, J. van 254*n*, 265*n*
Nugent, George 228*n*
Nuten, Piet 246*n*
nuzha 196
Nyert, Pierre de (17th c.) 387

Oberdörffer, Fritz 511*n*
Obertello, Alfredo 275*n*
Oboussier, Philippe 414*n*
Obrecht, Jacob (*c.* 1450–1505) 149, 162,
167, **169**, 177*n*, 219; Masses 164, 165
and *n*, 169
Ochsenkun, Sebastian, *Tablaturbuch*
(1558) 285
Ockeghem, Johannes (*c.* 1425–*c.* 1497)
156, 161, 165, 167, 177; Masses 149,
162–4 (Ex. 43), 242; songs **162** (Ex. 42),
164, 176
Odington, Walter (*fl.c.* 1316) 112, 134; *De
speculatione musicae* 112–13 (Ex. 22(ii))
Odo of Cluny (?11th c.) 82
Oehlenschlaeger, Adam Gottlob
(1779–1850) 685, 801
Offenbach, Jacques (1819–80) 740
Offices of the Church, the 56–7, 59, 65,
77, 86*n*
Ogiński, Prince Michal Kleofas
(1765–1835), his polonaises 635
Ohl, John R. 274*n*
Öhlenschläger, *see* Oehlenschlaeger
Oktoechos 64
Old Hall MS. (*c.* 1410–20) 135, 141–2,
143
'Old Roman' chant 59–60
Olleson, Edward 81*n*
Olympus (*c.* 700 B.C.) 27
ondes Martenot 831
Onslow, George (1783–1852) 624, 766;
String Quintet, op. 19 624 (Ex. 237)
opera 204–6; aria opera 205, **361**–5 (Exx.
121–3); earliest operas **271**–3 (Exx.
77–9), 324, 325; early growth 311–27
(Exx. 97–106); *intermedii* 268–71
opéra–ballet 376
opera buffa 205, 450, 451: the first 361,
serious elements in 471–3 (Exx. 168–70)

opéra comique 459, 584: its precursors 450–1 (Ex. 158), sentiment in 463–4
opera-houses, the first 204, **316–17**
opera musicale 311
opera scenica 311
opera *sinfonia*, the 314, **420–2** (Ex. 146)
Opitiis, Benedictus de (*fl.* 1516) 188, 223, 239
Opitz, Martin (1597–1639) 304, 312
Oratorian movement **246**, 347
oratorio: early 346–7 (Exx. 114–15), operatic influence on 395, *oratorio volgare* **395–8** (Exx. 136–7), sources 246
oratorio-Passion, *see* Passion
'orchestral' music, the earliest 423
Ordoñez, Carlos d' (1734–86) 491
Orff, Carl (b. 1895) 836, 840
organ 3, 120, 193: its origins 3, **44–7**, *46*, portative 251
organizatio 75, 80
organo di legno 274
organon hydraulikon **44–5**
organum, early **78–80**, 86, 87*n*, 89 (Ex. 13)
Ortiz, Diego, *Tratado de glosas* (1553) 238
Orto, Marbriano de (?15th c.) 164, 165 and *n*
Osiander, Lucas (1534–1604), *50 Geistliche Lieder* . . . 257 (Ex. 73)
'Ossian' 577, 647
Osterwald, Wilhelm (19th c.) 770
Osthoff, Helmuth 175*n*, 182*n*, 225*n*, 257*n*, 366*n*
Osthoff, Wolfgang 320*n*
Ostrovsky, Aleksandr (1823–86) 689, 731, 732, 837
Othmayr, Caspar (1515–53) 225 and *n*
Ott, Hans (*fl.* 1534) 223–4, 225, 226*n*
Ottoboni, Cardinal Pietro (*fl.* 1708) 382
Overbeck, Johann Friedrich (1789–1869) 663
oxeia 61
Oxford: Cardinal College (*now* Christ Church) 241, Magdalen College 240, New College 133–4

Pacelli, Asprilio (1570–1623) 283, 344
Pachelbel, Johann (1653–1706) 431*n*, 434, 440, **442**
Pacini, Giovanni (1796–1867) 709
Padovano, Annibale (1527–75) 232, 234–5, 286
Padua (Padova): early composers from, *see* Bartolino, Gratiosus; San Antonio's Church 251
Paer, Ferdinando (1771–1839) 585, 720;

operas 585 (Ex. 217); oratorios 662
Paganini, Niccolò (1782–1840) 612, 761*n*, 763, 773
p'ai hsiao 565
paian (paean) 27–8, 31
Paisiello, Giovanni (1740–1816) 459, 478, 500*n*, 548, 577, 656; operas 470*n*, **472–3** (Ex. 170)
Paix, Jacob (*fl.* 1583) 285
pakhavāj 562
Palestrina, Giovanni Pierluigi da (*c.* 1525–94) 203, 246, 264, 275–6, 278, 344, 747; compared with Gabrieli 249; and 'Gregorian' chant 246–7; the 'Palestrina style' 247, **410**, 752; his pupils 247, 344–5; Masses 245–6, **247–8**, 747; motet, 'Benedicta sit Sancta Trinitas' 248 (Ex. 70(i)); *Palestrinas Werke* (1862–1907) 752 and *n*
Palladio, Andrea (1508–80) 249
Pallavicino, Carlo (*c.* 1630–88) 358, 365, 373–4, 379; operas 358, 359, 365, 366, **422**
Palomba, Antonio (*fl.* 1737) 453
pandura 43
Pannain, Guido 381*n*, 399*n*
panpipes 565 (see also *syrinx*)
Pantaleon, H., *Prosopographia* (1565–6) 175
Paoli, Domenico de' 317*n*
Paolo da Firenze (d.*c.* 1419) 133, 139
Papal Chapel: at Avignon 73, 126, at Rome 73, 137, 138, Cappella Giuliana 246
Parabosco, Girolamo (*c.* 1522–57) 232
Paradisi (Paradies), Domenico (*c.* 1710–91) 514–15, 516
paramese 30
paranete 29, 30
parhypate 29
parhypate meson 61
Paris: Académie d'Opéra (1671) 373, Académie de Poésie et de Musique (1570) 203, 204, 284, Académie Royal de Musique (1672) 373, 450, 457, Chapelle Royale, La 412, Comédie italienne 459, *Concert de la Loge olympique* 506, *Concert spirituel* 488, 497, 499*n*, 506, **545**, Conservatoire 577, 579, 606, 612, 668, Dominican Church 545, Foire St Germain 450, 451, 463, Foire St Laurent 450, 454, 459, 463, Notre Dame, Cathedral of **103–6**, 110, 125, 256, 545–6, 749, Opéra, L' (theatre) 378, 470, 705, 721*n*, Opéra Comique, Théâtre

de l' 584, 705, St Antoine's Abbey 256,
Sainte-Chapelle 219*n*, Saints-Innocents,
church of 545, St Louis, church of 413,
St Victor's Abbey 100*n*, 109*n*, 111,
Société des Concerts de Conservatoire
(1828) 612, Société nationale de musique
(1871) 691–2, Théâtre des Champs-
Élysées *829*, Théâtre Feydeau 470
Parker, Horatio (1863–1919) 700, 756, 760
Parma, Philip, Duke of (*fl.* 1754) 454
Parnasse contemporain, Le (review,
1866–76) 787*n*
Parnassiens, les 787
parody (paraphrase) 139, 176
Parrish, Carl 87–8*nn*, 126*n*, 133*n*, 136*n*,
273*n*, 274*n*, 384*n*, 413*n*, 427*n*, 448*n*
Parry, Sir Hubert (1841–1924) 700, 756,
760, 792–3
Pärt, Arvo (b. 1935) 857, 858
Parthenia (1612/13) 204, 290
Parthenia In-Violata (?1614) 332
parthenios (aulos) 31, 34
parts, upper, inter-relation of 112–13
Pascall, Robert 774*n*
Pashchenko, Andrey (b. 1885) 841, 842
Pashkevich, Vasily Alekseyevich (1742–97)
480
Päsler, Karl 435*n*, 439*n*
Pasquini, Bernardo (1637–1710) 379, 380,
397, 438; keyboard works 438 (Ex. 154)
passamezzi antico and *moderna* 240*n*
Passereau (15th–16th c.) 235
Passion music 143 and *n*, 177, 187, 219,
258–9, 354, 397–9, 400–3 (Exx. 139–40),
535, 539–42 (Exx. 205–7)
Pattison, Bruce 284*n*
Patzold, E. 426*n*
Paul, St, and singing 50–1
Paulke, Karl 539*n*
Pauly, Reinhard 383*n*
Paumann, Conrad (*c.* 1415–73) 73,
159–60; *Fundamenta organisandi* 159
(Ex. 41), 160
Paumgartner, Bernhard 512*n*
Pausanias (*fl.* 138–81), *Description of
Greece* 27
Paymer, Marvin 448*n*
Peart, Donald 332*n*
Pedersen, Mogens (*c.* 1585–1623) 283
Pedrell, Felipe (1841–1922) 283*n*, 801
Peerson, Martin (*c.* 1572–1650) 309, 333
Pękiel, Bartłomiej (d.*c.* 1670) 345
'Peking' opera 568
pektis 25, 32
Péladan, Sar (1858–1918) 798*n*

pelog 572
Peñalosa, Francesco de (*c.* 1470–1528)
167, 177, 179
Penderecki, Krzysztof (b. 1933) 854
Pepin the Short (714–68), King of the
Franks 4, 58–9
Pepusch, Johann (1667–1752) 370, 393,
450, 477, 528
Pepys, Samuel (1633–1703) 415
'Per partum virginis' *86*, 87 (Exx. 11–12)
Peranda, Marco Giuseppe (*c.* 1625–75) 365
'Perchon', *see* La Rue, Pierre de
percussion instruments 3, 10: Assyrian
19, Egyptian 17–18, *17*, Greek 25
Perez, Davide (1711–78) 452
perfectio 105, 112, 114
Perger, Lothar Herbert 504*nn*
Pergolesi, Giovanni Battista (1710–36)
546; operas **448–9** (Exx. 156–7), 450,
451, 456, 457, 459; sacred works **546–7**
(Ex. 209), 548
Peri, Jacopo (1561–1633) 269, 273, 274–5,
296, 311; stage works 269 (Ex. 76),
271–3 (Exx. 77–9), 311
Pericles (d. 429 B.C.) 31
Peristephanon (4th c.) 56
Perosi, Dom Lorenzo (1872–1956) 832
Perotinus (*c.* 1183–1236) 103, 104, 106,
108 and *n*, 109*n*, 110, 112; 'Viderunt
omnes' 104, **107** (Ex. 20)
Perrin, Pierre (*fl.* 1669) 373
Perrot, Jean 45*n*, 47*n*
Perti, Giacomo Antonio (1661–1756) 398
and *n*, 410, 411*n*
Perz, Mirosław 257*n*
Pěsantěrin (psalterion) 39
Pesenti, Martino (*c.* 1600–*c.* 1647) 296
Pesenti, Michele (*c.* 1475–after 1521) 173,
174
Peter I (d. 1725), Tsar 394
Petrarch (Francesco Petrarca) (1304–74)
72, 117, 129–30, 151, 226, 264–5, 266;
'Che debb'io far?' 227; 'Crudele acerba'
234; 'Hor che'l ciel e la terra' 174, 226,
296
Petrassi, Goffredo (b. 1904) 833
Petrucci, Ottaviano dei (1466–1539)
165*nn*, 167, 173–4, 178, 182, 184, 188,
202; *Canti B* (1502) 170; *Canti C* (1504)
170, 176; *Harmonice Musices Odhecaton*
(1501) 74, 153*n*, 162, 165, 167, 170, 174,
182*n*; *Intablatura de Lauto* (1507) 184;
Musica di . . . Pisano (1520) 227; *Tenori
e contrabassi intabulati* (1509, 1511) 184,
226*n*

Petrus de Cruce (*fl.* 1298) 115 and *n*, 117
Petzach, Christóph 154*n*
Peurl, Paùl (*c.* 1575–after 1625) 290, 334
Pfeiffer, Karl (?19th c.) 669
Pfitzner, Hans (1869–1949) 794, 798
Phalèse, Pierre (*fl.* 1545) 203, 216
Pherecrates, *Chéiron* (*c.* 430 B.C.) 31
Philidor, Anne-Danican (*fl.* 1725) 488
Philidor, François-André (1726–95) 459,
  464, 469, 470, 473, 479, 545
Philip IV (the Fair) (1268–1314) of
  France 122
Philip II (1527–98) of Spain 208, 236,
  241, 254, 293
Philip V (1683–1746) of Spain 372, 512
Philip, Archduke of Austria (d. 1507) 167,
  168
Philip (the Good) (1396–1467), Duke of
  Burgundy 73, *150*
Philip Neri, St (1515–95) 246
Philippe, chancellor (1218–36) 98, 108,
  109
Philippus (Filipoctus) de Caserta (*fl.c.*
  1380) 136, 137
Philips, Peter (*c.* 1560–1628) 261, 264*n*,
  278, 294
Philo of Alexandria (Judaeus) (b.*c.* 20 B.C.)
  39–40, 50–1
Philo of Byzantium (3rd c. B.C.) 44–5, 46
Philoxenus of Cythera (5th c. B.C.) 31
phorminx 22, 23, 24, *25*, 27, 29
Photian heresy, the 66
Phrygian system, the 29, 32, 77
Phrynicus (*fl.* 511–476 B.C.) 30
Phrynis of Mitylene (5th c. B.C.) 31
piano trios and quartets, prototypes 518
pianoforte, the, its introduction 494
'Picander', *see* Henrici
Picasso, Pablo (1881–1973) 827–8, 829
Piccinni, Niccolò (1728–1800) 205, 459,
  463, 469, 471, 500*n*; operas 461–2 (Ex.
  164(i)), **463** (Ex. 165), **467**–8 (Ex. 167),
  469, 471–2, 475*n*, 477, 542*n*; oratorios
  548
Piccioli, Giuseppe 363*n*
Picken, Laurence 568*n*
Picker, Martin 169*n*
Pidoux, Pierre 220*n*, 286–7*nn*, 293*n*,
  338–9*nn*
Piero, Magister (*fl.c.* 1330–50) 124, 129
  and *n*, 130, 131
Pierront, N. 234*n*
Piersig, F. 225*n*
Pierson, Henry Hugo (Hugh Pearson)
  (1815–73) 688, 752, **792**

pi-li 569
p'i-p'a 567, 568, 569
Pilkington, Francis (*c.* 1562–1638) 278
Pincherle, Marc 429–30*nn*, 518*n*
Pindar (*c.* 522–442 B.C.) 29
Pineau, C. 413*n*
Pinto, George Frederick (1785–1806) 633
pipe 16, 17, *99*; *see also* bagpipe, bladder-
  pipe, double-pipe, panpipe
Pipelare, Matthaeus (?15th c.) 164, 165
Piron, Alexis (*fl.* 1723) 451
Pirro, André 153*n*, 340*n*, 436*n*, 796
Pirrotta, Nino 124*n*, 129*n*, 133*n*
Pisador, Diego (*fl.* 1552) 237
Pisano, Bernardo (1490–1548) 202, 227;
  'Che debb'io far' 227–8 (Ex. 64)
Pisendel, Georg (1687–1755) 430
Pitoni, Giuseppe Ottavio (1657–1743) 410
Pius IV, (Pope 1559–65) 244
Pixis, Johann Peter (1788–1874) 761
Pizzetti, Ildebrando (1880–1968) 832;
  operas 832–3 (Ex. 304)
Plamenac, Dragan 131*n*, 162*n*
Planchart, Alejandro 81*n*
planh 100
Plánický, Josef (1691–1732) 411–12
Plantade, Charles-Henri (1764–1839) 643
Plantinga, Leon 637*n*
Plato (427–347 B.C.) 31–3, 50
Platt, Peter 356*n*
Platt, Richard 495*n*
Platti, Giovanni Benedetto (*c.* 1700–63)
  486, 511
Plautus, Titus Maccius (*c.* 254–184 B.C.)
  43
Playford, Henry (*c.* 1657–*c.* 1706) 393
Playford, John (1623–86/7), 308*n*, **310**,
  356, **390**, 391, 393, 425
Pléiade (16th-c.) 284
Pleshcheyev, Aleksandr (1825–93) 783
Pleyel, Ignaz (1757–1831) 597, 598, 613,
  631, 642, 655
plica 105
Plotinus (205–70) 50
Poglietti, Alessandro (d. 1683) 440
Pohanka, Jaroslav 92*n*, 180*n*, 412*n*
Poliziano, Angelo (1454–94), poet 246*n*
Pollak-Schlaffenberg, Irene 531–2*nn*
Pollarolo, Carlo Francesco (*c.* 1653–1722)
  361 and *n*
Pollin, Alice and Burton 792*n*
Pollonois, Jacques (Jakub Reys) (*c.*
  1545–1605) 285
Polo, Enrico 508*n*
polyphony: early developments 66, 70–1,

75–96, in Masses 72–3, 133 (Ex. 29), organal 72, secular, new forms 226–8 (Ex. 64), suppression advocated 244, words in 169–70

pommer *150*, 152

Ponchielli, Amilcare (1834–86) 743

Ponte, *see* Da Ponte

Pope, Isabel 169*n*

Porphyry (233–304) 50

Porpora, Nicola (1686–1768) 365, 445, 546

Porta, Costanzo (*c*. 1529–1601) 232, 249, 251, 252

Porta, Ercole (d. 1630) 350

Porta, Giovanni (*c*. 1690–1755) 371

Porter, Walter (*c*. 1588–1659) 309, 356

Porter, William V. 271*n*

Portugal, Marcos (1762–1830) 594, 595

Posch, Isaac (d.*c*. 1622) 334

Postel, Christian (*fl*. 1704) 402, 403

Pothier, Dom Joseph 749*n*

Poulenc, Francis (1899–1963) 828, 830, 844

Poultney, David 397*n*, 399*n*

Pouplinière, Alexandre de la (*fl*. 1750) 488

Pousseur, Henri (b. 1929) 854

Power, Leonel (d.*c*. 1445) 73, 142, 145; Sanctus 143 (Ex. 32), 145

Powers, Harold S. 142*n*, 232*n*, 312*n*, 371*n*, 710*n*

Poźniak, Piotr 285*n*, 478*n*

praeambulum 158, *158*

Praetorius, Ernst 428*n*

Praetorius, Hieronymus (1560–1629) 259

Praetorius, Michael (*c*. 1571–1621) 249, 259, 287, 334; church music 260–1, 337, 350; keyboard works 294

Prague: National Theatre 687, Provisional Theatre 733

prelude (earliest known examples) 158

Preston, Thomas (d.*c*. 1564) 240, 293

Prévost d'Exiles, Antoine François (Abbé Prévost) (1697–1763), writer 744

Prez, Josquin des, *see* Josquin

Prieger, Erich 581*n*

primitive music 7

Prioris, Johannes (15th–16th c.) 219 and *n*

Priscus (?5th c.) 54

Procházka, Jan Ludevit (1837–88) 685*n*

Procházka, Rudolph 788*n*

Prod'homme, J. G. 749*n*

Prokofyev, Sergey (1891–1953) 825, 826, 841, 846; ballets 826, 843, 858; cantata, *Alexander Nevsky* (1938) 844; film music, *Poruchik Kizhe* (1934) 843; operas 826, 841, 843, 844, 858; *Simfonicheskaya*

pesn 843; Sinfonia concertante for cello and orchestra 857 and *n*; String Quartet no. 2 844; symphonies 826, 844, 857

Proletarian Musicians, Association of (Russia, 1923) 841

Pronomus of Thebes (*fl*. 5th c. B.C.) 26, 27, 31

proslambanomenos 34 and *n*, 76, 82

Provenzale, Francesco (1627–1704) 361, 364, 379; cantata, 'A che mirarmi o stelle' 381 (Ex. 132); opera, *Schiavo di sua moglie* (1671) 359–60 (Ex. 120)

Provins, Guiot de (12th c.) 98

Prüfer, Arthur 350*n*

Prunières, Henry 302*n*, 322*n*, 323, 387*n*, 412*n*, 421*n*

Psalmes of David in Prose and Meeter (1635) 357

psalm-settings, vernacular (16th–17th c.) 256–7, 356–7

psalm-singing: Christian 3, 54–5, Hebrew 3, 10, 39

psalterion 39

psaltery 55

Ptolemy of Alexandria (2nd c.) 49, 193

Puccini, Giacomo (1858–1924) 575, 743, 744, 801, 832; operas 744, 801, 832

Pujol, Emilio 236–7*nn*

Pujol, Juan Pablo (d. 1626) 345

puncta 103, 108, 112, 113

punctus perfectionis 114

Purcell, Daniel (*c*. 1663–1717) 393

Purcell, Henry (1659–95) *417*, 425, 450, 544; compared with Blow 369, with Lully 369–70; influence on Handel 417, 542; influenced by Lully 376; chamber cantatas 391–3, *392*; *Choice Collection of Lessons* (1696) 434; church music 416; odes 390–1; scena, 'In guilty night' 542*n*; solo songs 393; *Sonnatas of III Parts* (1683) 425; stage works 369–70, 376, 422*n*; trio sonatas 205

Pushkin, Aleksandr (1799–1837) 653, 719, 728, 768, 784, 786 and *n*, 799; *Boris Godunov* (1825) 731; *Evgeny Onegin* 733; *The Stone Guest* 730

Putta (d. 688), Bishop 58

pyknon 30, 33

Pythagoras of Samos (*c*. 570–*c*. 500 B.C.) 30, and early music theory 21, 27, 28–30, 34, 50, 192, 195*n*

qānūn 193, *196*

qaytērōs 21, 39

qeren 21, 38, 190

Quagliati, Paolo (*c.* 1555–1628), *Sfera armoniosa* 298–9 (Ex. 87)
'Quan vei l'aloete' 98
Quantz, Johann Joachim (1697–1773) 399*n*, q. 430, 430*n*
quarter-tone music 831
'Quem queritis in presepe pastores?' 92
'Quem queritis in sepulchro, O Christicole?' 91, 92
Querelle des bouffons 205, 456–7, 459
Questenberg, Count (*fl.* 1730) 485
Quickeberg, Samuel (*fl.* 1565) 175
quilisma 105
Quinault, Philippe (1635–88) 373, 374, 452, 467, 469
Quintilian (Marcus Fabius Quintilianus) (*c.* 35–*c.* 100) 47, 49
Quintilianus (2nd c.) of Alexandria 49
Quittard, Henri 334*nn*, 412–13*nn*
quṣṣāba 190

Raabe, Peter 682*n*
Racek, Jan 82*n*, 379*n*, 612*n*, 623*n*
rabāb (rabel) 99, 195, 197, 562, 572, 812
rabeca 197
Rabelais, François (1494?–1553) 831
Rabl, Walter 183*n*
Racine, Jean (1639–99) 373, 452, 466, 469, 542
Raff, Joachim (1822–82) 682, 685, 693*n*, 700, 703
symphonies 687–8, 693
rāgas 559–63 *passim*
ragtime 817
Raguenet, François, *Parallèle des Italiens et des Français . . .* (1702) 377*n*, 387
Raïmbaut de Vaqueiras (12th c.) 97, 100
Raison, André (d. 1710) 437
Rakhmaninov, Sergey (1873–1943) 799, 810, 823, 845
Raleigh, Sir Walter (1552–1618) 308
Rameau, Jean-Philippe (1683–1764) 454–6, 456–7, 461, 488; cantatas 388; *grands motets* 414–15; keyboard works 435–6, 451, 517, 518, 804*n*; stage works 451, 454–6 (Ex. 161), 464*n*, 466; treatises 454–5, 457
Ramler, Karl Wilhelm (18th c.) 540, 541, 660
Ramsey, Robert (17th c.) 356
Rathaus, Daniel (?19th c.) 783
rattles 3: African 813, *814*, Egyptian 13, Indonesian 572, Roman 43
Raupach, Ernest Benjamin (1784–1852) 673

Rauzzini, Venanzio (1746–1810) 552
Ravel, Maurice (1875–1937) 803–4, 805, 809, 826, 855
Ravenscroft, 'Giovanni' (d.*c.* 1748) 425 and *n*
Ravenscroft, Thomas (*c.* 1590–*c.* 1633) 310, 357
Raverii, Alessandro (*fl.* 1608) 288
Rawsthorne, Alan (1905–71) 824, 825, 856
Rayner, Clare G. 285*n*
Razumovsky, Andrey (1752–1836) 621
Reaney, Gilbert 117*n*, 136*n*, 138–9*nn*, 151*n*
rebab 98, 572
rebec 98, 197
Rebel, François (1701–75) 378
Reber, Henri (1807–80) 768
Rebikov, Vladimir (1866–1920) 800, 838; stage works 798*n* (Ex. 299(ii)), 806, 807, 808*n*
Reckow, Fritz 103*n*
Redel, Kurt 539*nn*
Redford, John (d. 1547) 240, 241
Redlich, Hans F. 253*n*, 502*n*
Reed, John 610*n*
Reese, Gustave 92*n*, 154*n*
Reeser, Eduard 518*n*
Reger, Max (1873–1916) 575, 796, 798, 839
Reggio, Pietro (d. 1685) 369
'Regina caeli laetare' 113
Regino of Prüm (d. 915) 65, 77
Regis, Johannes (*c.* 1430–*c.* 1485) 149
Regnart, Jacob (*c.* 1540–99) 254, 280, 281
Rehm, Wolfgang 153*n*
Reicha, Anton (1770–1836) 606, 623–4, 665*n*; Wind Quintet, op. 100, no. 6 623–4 (Ex. 236)
Reichardt, Johann Friedrich (1752–1814) 531, 589, 648, 663*n*; *Lieder* 531, **644** (Exx. 245, 246(i)), 760
Reichert, G. 303*n*, 335*n*
Reimann, Margarete 337*n*
Reina Codex 131, *132*, 156
Reinach, Theodore 29 and *n*, 30, 34*n*
Reinecke, Carl (1824–1910) 686
Reiner, Stuart 312*n*
Reizenstein, Franz (1911–68) 845
réjong 572
Rellstab, Ludwig (1799–1860) 630, 647, 648
Reni, Guido (1575–1642) 339
Resinarius (Harzer), Balthasar (*c.* 1485–1544) 223
Respighi, Ottorino (1879–1936) 832

Reubke, Julius (1834–58) 773
Reuental, Neidhart von (13th c.) 98
Reusner, Esaias (1636–79) 434
Reutter, Georg, 'the younger' (1708–72) 550
Revue wagnérienne 741
Reyer, Ernest (1823–1909) 691, 741
Reyner (*fl.* 1417) 138
Reys, Jakub (Polak, Jacques Pollonois) (*c.* 1545–1605) 285
Rhaw, Georg (*fl.* 1545) 178, 181, 203; *Newe deudsche geistliche Gesenge* 222–3, 226
Rheims, Guillaume de Trie (*fl.* 1324), Archbishop of 118
Rheinberger, Joseph (1839–1901) 688, 758, 773
Rhétorique des Dieux, La (*c.* 1650) 341
Rhétoriqueurs 161
Rhys, Philip ap (*fl.c.* 1547) 240
rhyton 44
Ricci, Federico (1809–77) 705, 709
Ricci, Luigi (1805–59) 705
Richafort, Jean (*c.* 1480–*c.* 1547) 207, 208, 209, 210, 236
Richard I (1157–99) of England 95, 97
Richard, François, the elder (d. 1650) 307
Richardson, Samuel (1689–1761) 454, 463, 464
Richelieu, Cardinal Armand de (1585–1642) 333
Richter, Franz Xaver (1709–89) 488, 491, 496 and *n*
Richter, Jean Paul (1763–1825) 703, *704*
Ricordi 588*n*
Riedel, Karl 486–7*nn*
Riemann, Hugo 297*n*, 299*n*, 300*nn*, 331–2*nn*, 339*n*, 361*n*, 365*n*, 489*nn*, 496*n*, 518*n*, 527*n*
Ries, Ferdinand (1784–1838) 600*n*, 603–4, 609
  piano concertos 604–5 (Ex. 229)
Rietsch, Heinrich 426*n*, 431*n*
Rifkin, Joshua 535*n*
Rigel, Henri-Joseph (1741–99) 496, 545
Rigveda 558, 559
Rilke, Rainer Maria (1875–1926) 835, 857
Rimbaud, Arthur (1854–91) 845
Rimmer, Joan 9–10*nn*, 19–20*nn*
Rimsky-Korsakov, Nikolay (1844–1908) 575, 719, 729, 758, 847; influenced by Wagner 575; and Musorgsky's operas 731*n*, 732; pupils 780, 809, 832, 841; autobiography, *Letopis moey muzikalnoy zhizni* (5th ed., 1935) q. 784; chamber

music 779; operas 731, 732 and *n*, 733, 784, 799, 806, 808; orchestral works 689, 690, **699**, 809; songs 783, 784
Rinaldi, Mario 429*n*
Ringer, Alexander 606*n*
Ringmann, Heribert 156*n*
Rinuccini, Ottavio (*fl.* 1589) 269, 271, 274, 275, 312
Rinyûgaku 569
Riquier, Guiraut (*c.* 1239–*c.* 1300) 98
Rist, Johann (1607–67) 305–6, 401
Ristori, Giovanni Alberto (1692–1753) 386
Ritter, Alexander (1833–96) 702 and *n*, 703
Ritter, Karl (*fl.* 1853) 685
Riva, Giuseppe (*fl.* 1725) 447 and *n*
Roberday, François (1624–80) 340
Robert (of Anjou) (*fl.* 1318) of Naples 123, 129*n*
Robert II, Count of Artois (*fl.* 1271) 115
Robert, Pierre (*c.* 1618–99) 412
Robertsbridge Codex, the (?1325) 119–22, *120*, 156, 158, 186
Robertus de Sabilone (13th c.) 103
Robinson, Michael F. 320*n*, 446*n*, 464*n*
Roca, Joaquin Martinez de la (*fl.* 1732) 411
Rocchi, A. 473*n*
Rode, Pierre (1774–1830) 598, 601, 606–7; Violin Concerto No. 6 598–9 (Ex. 225(iii))
Roesgen-Champion, Marguerite 435*n*
Roesner, Linda 764*n*
Roger, Estienne (*fl.c.* 1700) 428
Rohloff, E. 94*n*, 117*n*
Rokseth, Yvonne 110*n*, 153*n*, 183, 219*n*
Rolland, Romain (1866–1944) 323*n*, 843
Rolli, Paolo (1687–1765) 447 and *n*
Roman de Fauvel (14th c.) 72, 115, 117, 118–19, *120*, 122–3, and the Robertsbridge Codex 119–20, 122
'Roman style', the 247–8 (Ex. 70)
'Romanesca', the 237, 268, 293, 296
Romani, Felice (*fl.* 1813) 585–6, 588
Romanus, St (5th–6th c.), his *kontakion* 65, 91
Romanus, Antonius (*fl.* 1415) 139
'Romanus' letters, the 82, 85
Romberg, Bernhard (1767–1841) 606
Rombert, Andreas (1767–1821) 606
Rome: Accademia dell'Arcadia (1697) 380, Oratorio del Santissimo Crocefisso 347, *348*, Oratorio della Vallicella 274, 346, St Maria Maggiore 245, St Peter's 344, Teatro delle Quattro Fontane (1632) 313

Römhild, Johann Theodor (1684–1756) 539*n*

Roncaglia, Gino 381*n*

rondeau, 115, 116, 123

rondellus, the English 112, 134

Ronsard, Pierre de (1524–85) 220, 264, 265, 279*n*, 284, 768

Rood, Louise 420n

Rore, Cipriano di (1516–65) 232, 234 and *n*, 266; instrumental works 234; madrigals 233–4 (Ex. 67), 238, 245, 251, 254, 266; Masses and motets 233, 234

Rosa, Salvator (*fl.* 1649) 321

Rose, Bernard 263*n*

Rose, Gloria 301*n*

Roseingrave, Thomas (1690–1766) 513

Rosenmüller, Johann (*c.* 1619–84) 335, 404*n*, 426; *Studenten-Music* (1654) 336 (Ex. 112)

Rospigliosi, Giulio (d. 1669) (Pope, as Clement IX) 313, 315

Rospigliosi, Jacopo (*fl.* 1656) 313

Rosseter, Philip (*c.* 1575–1623) 280, 290, 291

Rossi, Luigi (1598–1653) 296, 299–301, 322, 347, 381, 390, 391; cantata, 'Gelosia' 300–1 (Ex. 88); operas 313, 322–3, *323*; oratorios 346–7 (Ex. 115)

Rossi, Michelangelo (d. after 1670) 313, 340

Rossi, Salamone (*c.* 1570–*c.* 1630) 328, 329, 335; sonatas 328–9 (Ex. 107), 330

Rossi Codex 129 and *n*, 130, 131

Rossini, Gioacchino (1792–1868) 585, 609, 612, 705; church music 664, 754; operas 584, 586–7 (Ex. 218), 592, 641, 703, 705–6; *Sonate a quattro* (1804) 626

Rosthius, Nicolaus (*c.* 1542–1622) 353

Rostropovich, Mstislav (b. 1927) 857

rotrouenge 100

Rouanet, Jules 198

Rouen Cathedral 138, *schola cantorum* 59

Rouget de Lisle, Claude Joseph (1760–1836) 654–5

Roullet, François du (*fl.* 1774) 466

Rousseau, Jean-Baptiste (1670–1741) 545

Rousseau, Jean-Jacques (1712–78) 456, 457, 467, 474*n*, 564*n*; opera, *Le Devin du village* (1752) 457 (Ex. 162), 458, 459, 479 and *n*

Roussel, Albert (1869–1937) 804, 809, 826 and *n*, 838

Rovetta, Giovanni (*c.* 1596–1668) 318, 349, 350

Rozanov, A. S. 478*n*

Różycki, Jacek (*c.* 1634–*c.* 1707) 412

rubāb 195, 562

Rubbra, Edmund (b. 1901) 824, 825, 856

Rubini, Francesco (*fl.* 1656) 395

Rubinstein, Anton (1829–94) 689 and *n*, 690*n*, 766, 773; operas 729, 731–2, 739; songs 783; symphonies 681, 685, 699, 732

Rubinstein, Nikolay (1835–81) 780

Rubio, Samuel 512*n*

Rubsamen, Walter 155*n*

Rückert, Friedrich (1788–1866) 647, 648, 770, 796

Rudel, Jaufré (12th c.) 95, 98

Rudolf II (1552–1612), Emperor 254, 259, 266

Rudolph, Archduke (*fl.* 1811), Archbishop of Olmütz 622, 664

Rufer, Josef 834*n*

Ruffino d'Assisi (*fl.c.* 1524) 232 and *n*, 249

Ruffo, Vincenzo (*c.* 1510–87) 246, 247

'Ruggiero' 237

Ruhnke, Martin 403*n*, 409*n*

rumba 816

Runciman, Sir Steven 95*n*

Rushton, Julian 469*n*

Ruspoli, Marquis (*fl.c.* 1708) 382, 399

Rutini, Giovanni (1723–97) 514, 515; harpsichord sonatas 515–16 (Exx. 194–5)

Ruzitska, József (*fl.* 1822) 594

Ryom, Peter 429*n*

ryuteki 570

Saalfeld, Ralf von 260*n*

saba-saba 815*n*

Sabol, A. J. 326*n*

Sacadas of Argos (*fl.* 586 B.C.) 2, 27, 28

Sacchini, Antonio (1730–86) 459, 469–70; operas 470, 476, 477; oratorios 545, 548

Sachs, Curt 47*n*

Sacrati, Francesco (d. 1650) 316, 322

ṣadjagrāma (sa-grāma) 559, 560

safara 190

Ṣafī al-Dīn (*c.* 1230–94) 196, *196*, 198

Sagan (Silesia), monastery at 158

saibara 569

St Cecilia's Day Odes (1683–97) 390–1, 393, 416, 483

Saint-Exupéry, Antoine de (1900–44) 834

Saint-Foix, Georges de 498

Saint-Georges, Joseph de (1739–99) 496

St Martial, Abbey of, *see* Limoges

St Petersburg: Academy of Arts *777*, Court at 445, 453, Imperial Chapel 758, Imperial Theatre 733

Saint-Saëns, Camille (1835–1921) 415*n*,
518*n*, 691, 778, 787; chamber music 778;
church music 758; operas 740, 743;
oratorio, *Le Déluge* (1876) 757;
orchestral works 691, 692, 693,
Symphony no. 3 in C minor **700–1** (Ex.
269); piano works 777–8; songs 787
St Sophia, Constantinople (Istanbul) 65
St Victor's Abbey, *see* Paris
Salieri, Antonio (1750–1825) 470, 508,
589, 618, *661*; operas 470, 577; oratorio,
Le jugement dernier (1788) 545; *Passion*
(1776) 539
salii 42, 47, 48, 51
Salis, Gaudenz von 643, 652
Salmen, Walter 154*n*, 644*n*
Salomon, Johann Peter (1745–1815) 597
salpinx 23–4, 42 and *n*
Salvador-Daniel, Francesco 198
salyāq 195
Salzburg: *Académies* 497, Archbishop
Colloredo of 552–4, Archiepiscopal
Court at 491, 539, 552–4, Cathedral
345, 539, Peterskirche 553
sāmaveda 559
samba 815
sambyke 195
sāmgīta 559
samisen 569, 570, 571
Sammartini, Giovanni Battista (*c.*
1700–75) 484–8 *passim*, 497
Sammartini, Giuseppe (*c.* 1693–1751) 487
san hsien 567, 568, 569
Sances, Giovanni Felice (*c.* 1600–79) 302
Sandars, N. K. 7 and *n*
Sandberger, Adolf 256*n*, 274*n*, 660*n*
Sandon, Nicholas 242*n*
Sandrin, Pierre (*fl.* before 1538) 216, 219,
226; 'Doulce memoire' 213, 216, 238,
255
Sandys, George (1578–1644) 357
sankangaku 569
sansa 813, 815
Sansovino, Francesco (1521–86) 248
Sanvoisin, Michel 328*n*
Sappho (*fl.c.* 600 B.C.) 25, 28, 30
Saracini, Claudio (1586–after 1649) 296,
297
sāraṅgī 561, 562
Sargeant, Winthrop 817*n*
Śārṅgadeva, *Samgītaratnākara* (*c.*
1200–50) 558, 559, 560
sārod 561, 562
saron 572
Sarri, Domenico (1679–1744) 446, 448

Sarti, Giuseppe (1729–1802) 472, 478, 480
Sarto, Andrea del (1487–1531) 227
Sartorio, Antonio (*c.* 1620–81) 358, 359,
373–4, 422
sarugaku 570
Sarum antiphonal 134
Satie, Erik (1866–1925) 800, 823, **827–9**;
Socrate (1918) 828 (Ex. 302); incidental
music, *Le Fils des étoiles* (1891) 798*n*
(Ex. 299(i))
Savioni, Mario (*c.* 1608–85) 295
Savonarola, Fra Girolamo (1452–98) 171
Sawazumi (*fl.c.* 1600) 570
Saxe-Weimar, Duke Johann Ernst of
(1696–1715) 430
Sayn-Wittgenstein, Princess Carolyne von
(1819–87) 683
scabellum 44, 48
Scacchi, Marco (d.*c.* 1685) 312, 345
scalmuse 125
Scandello, Antonio (1517–80) 258, 353,
354
Scarlatti, Alessandro (1660–1725) 364,
365, 368, 380, 427, 445, 512, 588;
cantatas 379, **381–2**, 391; church music
410, 411, 548*n*; madrigals 379; operas
205, **361–4** (Exx. 121–3), 370, 427, 429
and *n*, 448, 465; oratorios 397, 398,
399–400 (Ex. 138)
Scarlatti, Domenico (1685–1757) 371, **512**,
513, 832
Schaeffer, Pierre (b. 1910) 846
Schatz, Josef 154*nn*
Schedel, Hartmann (15th c.) 154, 156,
225*n*
Scheidemann, Heinrich (*c.* 1596–1663)
337, 338
Scheidt, Samuel (1587–1654) 204, 290,
306, **334–5**, 337*n*, 350–1; church music
350–1 (Ex. 117), **352** (Ex. 118), 353;
instrumental ensemble music 307, 334,
335 (Ex. 111), 336, 405; organ works
337, 352
Schein, Johann Hermann (1586–1630)
290, 334; church music 303, 350;
instrumental ensemble music 334; songs
303
Schelle, Johann (1648–1701) 405, 406
Schenk, Erich 420*n*, 423*n*
Schenk, Johann (1753–1836) 589
Schering, Arnold 273*n*, 396*n*, 398–9*nn*,
405–6*nn*, 430*n*, 487*n*, 492–549*nn passim*,
747*n*
Schiedermair, Ludwig 523 and *n*, 600*n*,
630*n*

Schienerl, Alfred 550*n*

Schikaneder, Emanuel Johann
(1751–1812) 528, 589

Schiller, Johann Christoph Friedrich von
(1759–1805) 574, 643–5, 649, 710, 770;
Braut von Messina, Die (1803) 678, 737;
Don Carlos (1787) 727; 'Gruppe aus dem
Tartarus' 647; 'Huldigung der Künste'
683; *Jungfrau von Orleans, Die* (1801)
732 and *n*; *Kabal und Liebe* (1784) 711;
'Lied an die Freude' (1785) 606 and *n*;
'Ode' (1785) 611 and *n*; *Räuber, Die*
(1781) 574, 685, 710; 'Ritter
Toggenburg' 643; *Turandot* (1809)
564*n*; *Wallenstein* (1799) 692; *Wilhelm
Tell* (1804) 705

Schindler, Anton (1796–1864) 600*n*, 630*n*

Schjelderup-Ebbe, Dag 791*n*

Schlegel, August Wilhelm von
(1767–1845) 574, 644, 647, 663

Schlegel, Friedrich von (1772–1829) 574,
763

Schlick, Arnolt (*c.* 1460–*c.* 1521) 184, 237

Schmelzer, Johann Heinrich (*c.* 1623–80)
360

Schmid, Bernhard, the elder (1535–92)
285

Schmid, Bernhard, the younger
(1567–1625) 285, 286

Schmid, Ernst Fritz 258*n*, 524*n*

Schmid, Otto 504*n*

Schmidt, A. W. 351*n*

Schmidt, Gustav Friedrich 366*n*

Schmidt, Franz (1874–1939) 797

Schmidt, H. 184*n*

Schmidt-Görg, J. 207*n*

Schmieder, Wolfgang 386*n*

Schmitt, Florent (1870–1958) 807, 809

Schmitz, Eugen 298*n*

Schneider, Marius 82*n*, 107*n*

Schneider, Max 238*n*, 252*n*, 367*nn*, 542*n*

Schobert, Johann (*c.* 1740–67) 518, 527;
sonatas 518, 519 (Ex. 196), 527

Schoenberg, Arnold (1874–1951) 576,
797–8, 807–8, 809, 820–1, 823, 837;
chamber music 797–8, 806, 807, 835, 840;
concertos 835, 845; operas 835, 836,
858; orchestral works 797, 806–7,
809–10, 824, 834–5 (Ex. 306), 845; piano
works 807, 808, 835; vocal works 576,
797, 806, 807, 808, 829

scholae cantorum, their establishment 4, 59,
70

Scholes, Percy 524*n*

Scholze, Johann Sigismund (1705–50) 529

Schrade, Leo 118–19*nn*, 122 and *n*, 123*n*,
125–6*nn*, 128*n*, 131*n*, 158*n*, 238*n*, 249*n*

Schreker, Franz (1878–1934) 797, 804,
823, 831; Chamber Symphony 806; *The
Birthday of the Infanta* (1908) 806;
operas 810, 834, 841

Schröder, O. 220*n*

Schröter, Johann Samuel (1752–88) 502
and *n*

Schubert, Franz (1797–1828) 574, 575,
593, 649, 663; cantata, *Lazarus* (1820)
662, 663; chamber music 617, 624–5;
choral works, secular 665, 666; church
music 663–4; concert overtures 609–10,
610*n*; piano works 629*n*, 636, 639–40,
683; songs 531, 625, 639, 645 (Ex.
246(iii)), 647–8; stage works 593, 610
and *n*; symphonies 609–11, 639, 687

Schübler, Georg (*fl.* 1748) 509

Schultz-Hauser, K. 502*n*

Schulz, Johann Abraham Peter
(1747–1800) 531

Schulz, W. 494*n*

Schuman, William (b. 1910) 845

Schumann, Clara Josephine (1819–96)
677, 685, 686, 694

Schumann, Robert (1810–56) 574, 575,
616, 640, 673; chamber music 765–6;
choral works, secular 678, 746, 750–1;
church music 751; concert overtures
675, 678; concertos 675, 677–8; opera,
Genoveva (1848) 678, 813; organ works
772; piano works 763–4, 765, 772; songs
751, 767, 768, 770; symphonies 675,
676–7 (Ex. 259)

Schünemann, Georg 542*n*

Schuppanzigh Quartet 625*n*

Schuster, Joseph (1748–1812) 522 and *n*

Schütz, Heinrich (1585–1672) 205, 304,
335, 350, 352, 365, 478; Bible *historiae*
350, 353–4, 400, 404; church music 303,
350, 351, 353; madrigals 283, 304; opera,
Dafne (1627) 312, 325; *Passions* 354

Schwandt, Erich 388*n*

Schwartz, Rudolf 173*n*, 281*n*

Schwarz, Boris 598*n*

Schweitzer, Albert (1875–1965) 796

Schweitzer, Anton (1735–87) 476

Scotland, James IV (1473–1513), King of
188

Scott, Sir Walter (1771–1832) 574, 584,
586, 642, 647, 770

Scriabin, *see* Skryabin

Scribe, Augustin Eugène (1791–1861) 584,
705, 706, 722 and *n*

sê 565, 567
Seager, Francis (*fl.* 1553) 220
Seay, Albert 178*n*, 213*n*, 215*n*, 230*n*, 332*n*
Sebastiani, Johann (1622–83) 401
Sĕbor, Karel (1843–1903) 735
Sechter, Simon (1788–1867) 753
Sehnal, Jiří 411*n*
Seiber, Mátyás (1905–60) 845
Seidl, J. G. (before 1829) 647
Seiffert, Max: in *DDT* 405–6*nn*, 428*n*, 482*n*, in *DTB*, 434–5*nn*, 442*nn*, in other references 257*n*, 294*n*, 337–8*nn*, 351*n*, 367*n*, 404*n*, 510*n*, 529*n*
Seixas, Carlos (1704–42) 512–13
sekhem 13
Selden MS., the 150
Selfridge-Field, Eleanor 249*n*
Selle, Thomas (1599–1663) 303, 305, 354
selompret 572
semibreve caudatae 118
semiminima 118, 139*n*
semitonum chromaticum (Marchettus) 129
Senaillé (Senallié), Jean Baptiste (*c.* 1687–1730) 426
Seneca (Lucius Annaeus Seneca) (*c.* 5 B.C.–*c.* A.D. 65) 45, 47, 48
Senfl, Ludwig (*c.* 1486–*c.* 1543) 182, 183, 185, 225, 226 and *n*, 235, 284*n*; Lutheran hymns 223; secular song 225
Septimius Severus (146–211), Emperor 48
sequence (ecclesiastical) 70, 72, 89, 90
serialism 833, 834–5, 837, 849–59 *passim*, 862–3
Sermisy, Claudin de (*c.* 1495–1562) 214; chansons 211, 213, *214*, 215–17 (Exx. 59(i), 60(i)), 218 and *n* (Ex. 61), 226, 229; church music 219 and *n*
Serov, Aleksandr Nikolayevich (1820–71) 728, **729–30**, 731, 732
Sert (or Sortes) 126
sesheshet 13
Sessions, Roger (b. 1896) 824, 845, 856
setar 567
Settle, Elkanah (1648–1724) 369*n*
Sforza, Cardinal Ascanio (1455–1505) 170, 171, 176
Sforza, Galleazzo Maria (1442–76), Duke of Milan 170
Sgambati, Giovanni (1841–1914) 699, 801, 832
Shadwell, Thomas (*c.* 1642–92) 369, 370
shahnāi (shannâi) 562, 564
shaipūr 53
Shakespeare, William (1564–1616): *As You Like It* 280, *Julius Caesar* 678, *Macbeth*

710, *Midsummer Night's Dream, A* 370, 477, *Othello* 744, sonnets 792, *Tempest, The* 369, 370, 477, 690, 799
Shaporin, Yury (1887–1966) 842, 844, 857, 858
Shaw, H. Watkins 391*n*, 393*n*, 416*n*
shawm 125, *150*, 152; alto shawm (pommer) *150*, 152; double-shawm 98
Shaydurov, Ivan (late 16th c.) 67
Shchedrin, Rodion (b. 1932) 858
Shebalin, Vissarion (1902–63) 841, 842, 846, 858
Shelley, Percy Bysshe (1792–1822) 792
shêng 565, 568, 569
Sheppard, John (d. 1557) 242
Sherman, C. A. 498*n*
Shiba, Shukehiro 570*n*
Shield, William (1748–1829) 477
Shinohara, Makoto (b. 1931) 854
Shirley, James (1596–1666) 325, 326
Shnitke, Alfred (b. 1934) 858
shō 569, 570
Shokunin Zukushi Uta-awase (1744) *571*
Sholokhov, Mikhail Aleksandrovich (b. 1905) 843
shōphār 38, 190
Shorey, Paul 33*n*
Shostakovich, Dmitry (1906–75) 841, 846, 859; chamber music 843, 857; piano works 842, 843, 857; operas, etc. 842, 843, 846, 858; symphonies 841–4 *passim*, 857
Sibelius, Jan (1865–1957) 575, **805**, 810, 825
Sicher, Fridolin (1490–1546) 225
Sidney, Sir Philip (1554–86) 275, q. 284
Sidow ('Seedo') (d.*c.* 1754) 450
Sieber (*fl.* 1783) 502
Siege of Rhodes, The (1656) 326, 369
Sietz, Reinhold 516*n*
Sigismund (1368–1437), Emperor 138, 139*n*
Sigismund III (1566–1632) of Poland 205, 283
Silbert, Doris 312*n*
Simonetti, Leonardo, publ., *Ghirlanda Sacra* (1625) 349 (Ex. 116)
Simpson, Christopher, *The Division Violist* (1659) 332*n*
Simpson, Thomas (1582–after 1625) 290, 334
Simrock (*fl.* after 1881) 781
Sīnā, Ibn (Avicenna) (980–1037) 195
sinfonia, concert 483–4
sinfonia, opera 319, 320*n*, 483, 484, 491

sinfonia concertante, the 487, **496**–7
Singspiel 450, **473**–5 (Ex. 171), **476**, 575, 589, 590, 712
Sink, Kuldar (b. 1942) 858
sirventès 100
sistrum, the 10, 12, 13, 17
sitar 561, 562, 567
Sitwell, Dame Edith (1887–1964) 825
Sitwell, Sir Sacheverell (b. 1897) 825
Six, Les 828
Skalkottas, Nikos (1904–49) 837
skomorokhi 95
Škroup, František (1801–62) 594, 719
Skryabin, Aleksandr (1872–1915) **799**–**800**, 804, **808**, 809, 820, 839, 840; *Morceaux*, op. 56 800 and *n* (Ex. 300)
Skuherský, František (1830–92) 734, 735
Sleeper, Helen J. 332*n*
slendro 572
slide-trumpet *150*, 152
Slim, Colin 234*n*
Slonimsky, Sergey (b. 1932) 857–8
Small Devotion (Mass by Taverner, adapted) 241 and *n*
Smallman, Basil 177*n*
Smend, Friedrich 402*n*, 431*n*, 536*n*
Smetáček, Václav 623*n*
Smetana, Bedřich (1824–84) 575, 685, 689, 697, 734–5, 757, 765; chamber music 780; operas **734**–5, 739; orchestral works **685**, 693; piano works 764; songs 769, 782
Smijers, Albert 165*n*, 169*n*, 174*n*, 178*n*, 219*n*
Smith, Gertrude 420*n*
Smith, John Christopher (1712–95) 477
Smith, Julian 358*n*
Smitz, Arnold 627*n*
Snelleman, Joh. F. 572*n*
sō 569
so-na 564, 568
soeling 572
sogo 813, *814*
Sokolovsky, Mikhail Matveyevich (*fl.* 1779) 479
Solage (14th c.) 136
Soler, Antonio (1729–83) 512–13
Solerti, Angelo 271*nn*, 274*n*, 295*n*, 311*n*
Somerset, Robert Carr, Earl of (1589–1645) 308
Somfai, László 493*n*, 500*n*, 504*n*
sonata-form, embryonic 485–7 (Ex. 176)
Sonneck, Oscar G. 446*n*, 595*n*
Sonnenleithner, Joseph (*fl.* 1805) 581
Sophocles (496–406 B.C.) 30, 42, 249, 830

Sophronius (7th c.), Patriarch 91
Sorau (Brandenburg), Court at 432
Sørensen, Søren 332*n*
Soriano, Francesco (*c.* 1549–1620) 247
Soto, Francisco de (*c.* 1500–63) 236 and *n*, 239
Souterliedekens (1556–7) 209, 220, 257
Spada, Pietro 611*n*
Spagna, Archangelo (*c.* 1632–after 1720) 395 and *n*
'Spagna, La' 185
Spanke, Hans 100*n*
Sparks, Edgar H. 208*n*
spartitura (sparditura, partidura) 251
Speer, Klaus 235*n*
Spenser, Edmund (*c.* 1552–99) 275
Speyer, Wilhelm (*fl.* 1832) 669
Spinacino, Francesco (*fl.* 1509) 184 and *n*
Spink, Ian 308–9*nn*
Spitta, Philipp 407 and *n*
Spohr, Louis (1784–1859) 575, 592*n*, 606, 607*n*, 609, 610, 616, 678; chamber music 617, 622–3, 624, 625; operas **591**–2 (Ex. 223), 593, 669, 711, 713; oratorios 662 and *n*, 746; songs 646 (Ex. 247), 665; symphonies **607**–8 (Exx. 230, 231(i)), 611, 612, **669**–**71**, 677, *Die Weihe der Töne* (1832) **669**–**70** (Ex. 255), 677; violin concertos 606–7, 613
Sponsus plays 92
Spontini, Gaspar (1774–1851) 582, 612, 705, 707, 717; operas 581, **582**–3 (Ex. 216), 587, 590, 592 and *n*
Spruch 100
Squarcialupi Codex 131*n*, *132*, 159
Squire, W. Barclay 293*n*, 393*n*
śrutis 559, 562
Stäblein, Bruno 88*n*, 90, 93*n*
Stäblein-Harder, Anna 126*n*
Staden, Sigmund Theophil (1607–55) 325
Stadler, Anton (1753–1812) 504*n*
Stadler, Abbé Maximilian (1748–1833) 526 and *n*
Staehelin, Martin 183*n*
Stainer, Sir John F. R. and C. 151*n*
Stamitz, Carl (1745–1801) 491
Stamitz, Johann (1717–57) 456, 488, **489**–**91**, 492–4, 496; symphonies 489–91 (Exx. 177–8)
stampida (estampie) 100
Standfuss, J. C. (d.*c.* 1759) 450
Stanford, Sir Charles Villiers (1852–1924) 548*n*, 700, 740*n*, 760
Stauder, Wilhelm 8*n*
Steele, John 278*n*, 293*n*, 410*n*

Stefani, Andrea 171
Stefani, Jan (*c.* 1747–1829) 478
Steffan (Štěpán), Joseph Anton (1726–97)
531; *Sammlungen deutscher Lieder . . .*
(1778) 531–2 (Ex. 202)
Steffani, Agostino (1654–1728) 366, 367,
376; duets 379, 383; madrigals 379;
operas **365** and *n*, **366**, 422*n*
Steglich, Rudolf 486*n*, 498*n*, 511*n*
Steibelt, Daniel (1765–1823) 598, 603,
611, 631, 660
Steigleder, Johann Ulrich (1593–1635) 337
and *n*
Stein, Fritz 405*n*, 496*n*, 598*n*
Stein, Gertrude (1874–1946) 828*n*
Stein, Johann Andreas (*fl.* 1777) 498
Steinberg, Maximilian (1883–1946) 841,
842
Stephen III (Pope 752–7) 58
Stephenson, Kurt 770*n*, 788*n*
Sterkel, Johann Franz Xaver (1750–1817)
523, 598
Stern, Julius 548*n*
Sternfeld, F. W. 81*n*
Sternhold, Thomas (*fl.* 1556) 220
Stevens, Denis 240*nn*, 242*n*, 317*n*
Stevens, John 150*n*, 187*nn*
Stevens, Richard (1757–1837) 665
Stevenson, Robert 261*n*, 816*n*
stile concertato 248–51 (Ex. 71), 410
stile concitato 317, 318, **344**
Stockhausen, Karlheinz (b. 1928) 849,
851–2, 853, 854, 855, *856*; *Klavierstück
II* 851–2 (Ex. 310)
Stokhem, Johannes (*fl.* late 15th c.) 180
Stoltzer, Thomas (*c.* 1486–1526) 180, 183,
190, 223
Stölzel, Gottfried Heinrich (1690–1749)
537, 538*n*
Storace, Stephen (1763–96) 477, 478, 528,
595
Stradella, Alessandro (1644–82) **361**, 390;
cantatas 379, **380–1** (Exx. 130–1);
instrumental works **423–4** (Ex. 147);
operas 361, 396, 397, **422**; oratorios
395–7 (Exx. 136–7)
Stradivari family 205
Straeten, Pierre Van der (after 1460–1518)
161
strambotto 171, 172
Strauss, Johann, junior (1825–99) 713
Strauss, Richard (1864–1949) 575, 796,
797, 798, 839; ballet, *Josephslegende*
(1914) 809; chamber music 775; operas
794, 806, 809, 810, 834, 855; orchestral

works 702–3; songs 789, 846;
symphonies 702, 794, 795, 797, 809;
tone poems **702–3**, **794**, 795, 797, 799,
805
Stravinsky, Igor (1882–1971) 809, 823,
825–6, 833, 835, 839, 855, **859–63**;
ballets 809, 810, 825, 826, 840; *Cantata*
(1952) 861–2 (Ex. 314); *Histoire du
soldat, L'* (1918) 810, 823, 825; operas
826, 841, 842, **861** (Ex. 313); orchestral
works 825–6, 845; Piano Sonata 840;
Renard (1917) 810; *Symphony of Psalms*
(1930) 826, 827 (Ex. 301)
Striggio, Alessandro (*c.* 1535–*c.* 1595)
251–2, 265, 267, 268*n*, 278
Striggio, Alessandro (*fl.* 1607) 274
Stroud, Peter 280*n*
Strozzi, Piero (*fl.* 1579) 268
Strungk, Delphin (1601–94) 337, 366
Strungk, Nicolaus Adam (1640–1700) 366
Strunk, Oliver 64–590*nn passim* (on 16
pp.)
Strutius, Thomas (*c.* 1621–78) 401
Stuck, Jean-Baptiste (Battistin) (*c.*
1680–1755) 388
Sturgeon, Nicholas (d. 1454) 141
Stuttgart, Ducal Court at 548
Subirá, José 325*n*
Suetonius (Gaius Suetonius Tranquillus)
(*c.* 70–*c.* 160), historian 44
Suffolk, Earl of (*fl.* 1420) 141, 153
Sullivan, Sir Arthur Seymour (1842–1900)
740*n*, 756
Sully Prudhomme, René François
(1839–1907) 787
'Sumer is icumen in' 112, 113, 116, 134
Sumerian music 7–10
Summers, Montague 369*n*
sûmponĕyà 21, 39
Sung dynasty (960–1126) 567
Suppé, Franz von (1819–95) 713
surnāy (surnā) 195, 562, 564
Surrey, Henry Howard, Earl of (*c.*
1517–47) 239
Susato, Tylman (*fl.* 1543) 203, 213 and *n*,
216; *Het derde musyck boexken* 218 (Ex.
61)
Susay, Jehan de (14th c.) 135
Süssmayr, Franx Xaver (1766–1803) 469,
554, 589
Sutherland, Gordon 234*n*
Sutkowski, Adam 330*n*
Sutterfield, John 242*n*
Suvorov, Field-Marshal Aleksandr
(1729–1800) 630

Svendsen, Johan (1840–1911) 689
Sweden, sovereigns of, *see* Christina, Gustavus II, Gustav III
Sweelinck, Jan Pieterszoon (1562–1621) 204, 257, 265, **294**, 307, 334, 337
Swieten, Baron Gottfried van (1730–1803) 660, 661
Swinburne, Algernon Charles (1837–1909) 741
Sylvestre, Paul Armand (1837–1901) 787
symphonia (sûmponëyâ) 39
symphonie concertante 487, **496–7**
symphonos 29
synemmenon 34n, 76, 79
Syrian church music 54, 91
syrinx, 3, 23, 32, 44–5
syrmatike 61, 63
Syrokomla, Władysław 783
Szabolcsi, Bence 239n, 594n, 720n
Székeley, Bertalan 755
Szweykowski, Zygmunt M. 180n, 345n
Szymanowska, Maria (1789–1831) 641, 652
Szymanowski, Karol (1882–1937) 806, **839**

tabl (tabor) 191, 562
tāblā 561, 562
tabor 99, 191
Tacitus, Gaius (?) Cornelius (*c.* 55–*c.* 117) 53
Tagelied 100
Tagliapietra, Gino 435n
Tagliavini, L. F. 435n
T'ai-tsung, Emperor 567
Tailleferre, Germaine (b. 1892) 828, 830
'Talent m'est pris' (14th c.) 124
Tallis, Thomas (*c.* 1505–85) 240, **242–3**, 261, 263 and n
tambourine 17; *see also* frame-drum
tambura 561, 562
tanbūr, see *tunbūr*
Taneyev, Sergey (1856–1915) 780, 799
T'ang dynasty (618–907) 567
tango 816
Tarakanov, Mikhail 858n
Tarr, Edward H. 542n
Tartini, Giuseppe (1692–1770) 205, 483, 487
Tassin (*fl.* 1288) 115
Tasso, Torquato (1544–95) 265, 267, 270, 317
Taubert, Wilhelm (1811–91) 764
Taverner, John (*c.* 1490–1545) 240–1, **241–2**
Tchaikovsky, *see* Chaykovsky

teben 13
teleios 31
Telemann, Georg Philipp (1681–1767) 372, 407, 431 and n, 432, 435, 511; compared with J. S. Bach 409, 432; eclecticism 432–4; pupil, Fasch 432; church cantatas 406, 407 and n, **408–9**, 538; *Concerto grosso* for flutes, oboe, and violin (*c.* 1711) 432–3 (Ex. 150); *dramme per musica* 386; *Getreue Music-Meister, Der* (1728) 529, keyboard works 510–11; Masses 537; *Musique de Table* (1733) 482; operas 372, 476; oratorios and Passions 403, **539**, 541; orchestral overtures 434, 456; songs 529; suites 433, 434
Télémaque (1715) 450–1 (Ex. 158)
Temperley, Nicholas 633n, 792n
tempus perfectum and *imperfectum* 118
Tennyson, Alfred, Lord (1809–92) 792
tenor, the 113, 118–19, 126
Tenorlied 154
tenso 100
Terence (Publius Terentius Afer) (*c.* 190–159 B.C.) 43
Terpander of Lesbos (*fl.* 645 B.C.) 27, 29
Terradellas, Domingo (1713–51) 452, 453
Terry, R. R. 220n
Tertullian (Quintus Tertullianus) (*c.* 160–230) 44
Tessier, André 341nn
tetrachord, the 24, 29, 30, 34 and n, 61
Thaletas (*fl.c.* 665 B.C.) 27
Thayer, Alexander Wheelock (1817–97) 579n, 663n
Theile, Johann (1646–1724) 366, 385
Theodoric (the Great) (455–526), King of the Ostrogoths 61
theogonia 37
'There is no rose' (15th-c.) 150
Therstappen, H. J. 246n
Thibault, G. 153n, 215n
Thibaut, Justus (1774–1840) 752
Thibaut de Champagne (early 13th c.), King of Navarre 97, 101
Thierfelder, Albert 49n (Ex. 4)
Thoene, Walter 523n
Thomas, Ambroise (1811–96) 720, 727, 740, 754
Thomas, Arthur Goring (1850–92) 740n
Thomas, Dylan (1914–53) 862
Thompson, Edward 356n
Thomson, George (*fl.* 1793) 642 and n
Thomson, James (1700–48) 661
Thomson, Virgil (1896–1978) 828n

Thucydides (*fl.* 5th c. B.C.) 26
Thurston, Ethel 104*n*
ti-tzŭ 568
tibia 40, 41, 42, 43, 47
Tieck, Johann Ludwig (1773–1853) 574
Tiersot, Julien 256*n*
Tilmouth, Michael 332*n*, 425*n*
timbila 813
Timotheus of Miletus (*fl.* 5th c. B.C.) 31
Tinctoris, Johannes (*fl.c.* 1474) q. 142,
    154, 156, 165, 186
Tippett, Sir Michael (b. 1905) 824, 825,
    844, 845, 856, 859
Tirabassi, Antonio 165*n*, 311*n*
Tischler, Hans 104*n*
Tishchenko, Boris (b. 1939) 857, 858
Titelouze, Jean (1563–1633), 340
Titov, Nikolay Alekseyevich (1800–75) 652
tjengtjengs 572
Toeschi, Carl Joseph (d. 1788) 491, 492
Tōgaku 567, 569, 570
Tolstoy, Aleksey Konstantinovich
    (1817–75) 783, 786
Tolstoy, Count Leo Nikolayevich
    (1828–1910) 844
Tomášek, Václav (1774–1850) 632, 638*n*,
    639, 644–5, 651; *Eglogues* 632–3 (Ex. 239)
Tomkins, Thomas (1572–1656) 261, 263,
    278, 338*n*, 356, 357
tonadilla escénica 477, 595
tonaria 65
tôph 38, 191
Torchi, Luigi 301*nn*
Torelli, Giacomo (*fl.* 1645) 322, *323*
Torelli, Giuseppe (1658–1709) 427–8, 429,
    483; *Concerti grossi*, op. 8 (1709) 427–8
    (Exx. 148–9)
Torrefranca, Fausto 514*nn*
Torres, José de (1665–1738) 411
'Toulouse' Mass 125, 126 and *n*
'Tournai' Mass 125, 126 and *n*
Touront, Jean (*fl.c.* 1460) 160
Tovey, Sir Donald (1875–1940) 618
Townsend, Douglas 545*n*
Trabaci, Giovanni Maria (*c.* 1575–1647)
    338
Traetta, Tommaso (1727–79) 459, 461,
    471, 472, 478; operas 459, 461, 462 (Ex.
    164(iii)), 471 (Ex. 168); oratorio, *Rex
    Salomone* (1766) 548
tragedia rappresentata 311
tragédie en musique 325, 373–4
tragédie lyrique 376–8, 445, 464
Tregian, Francis (*fl.c.* 1609), see
    Fitzwilliam Virginal Book

Treitschke, Friedrich (*fl.* 1805) 581
Trent, Council of (1551, 1562) 207, 244–6,
    247, 254, 355
trigonon 32
Trionfo di Dori, Il (1592) 278
triplum 110, 111, 113, 119, 122–3, 125
Tritonius, Peter (*fl.* early 16th c.) 284*n*
'Triumphat hodie' (14th-c.) 133, 134
Tromboncino, Bartolomeo (late 15th c.)
    173–4, 226–7; 'Si ben or' 173 (Ex. 46)
trombone, Italian 16th-c. 249, 251–3, 270,
    288–9, 607*n*
trope 72, 77, 87*n*, 88–90, 109, 244
troubadours 71, 94–6, 97–8
trouvères 71, 73, 97–8, 123–4
Trowell, Brian 141*n*
trumpet 3, 11, 98, 125; see also *lituus*;
    Assyrian 20, Egyptian 13, 16, Etruscan
    (*Tyrsenike salpinx*) 42, Greek 23–4,
    Persian 53, 190, Roman 42, slide-
    trumpet *150*, 152, *trompette des
    menestrels* 125
Trutovsky, Vasily (b.*c.* 1740) 480*n*
Tsai-yü, Prince, *Yüeh-lü ch'üan shu* (1606)
    568 and *n*
tuba: Roman (*salpinx*) 42 and *n*, 46,
    Waldhorntube (tenor tuba) 723
Tudway, Thomas (*c.* 1650–1726) 415
Tulpijn, Henricus (*fl.* 1389) 137
tunbūr 191, 194–5, 196, 197, 562
Tunder, Franz (1614–67) 337, 338*n*, 351,
    442
Tunley, David 389*n*
Turina, Joaquin (1882–1949) 806
Türk, Daniel Gottlieb (1750–1813) 523
Turner, William (1651–1740) 391, 415,
    416
Tuttle, Stephen D. 293*n*
twelve-note music 833, 834–5
Tyāgarāja of Tanjore (1767–1842) 563
Tye, Christopher (*c.* 1500–73) 240, 241, 242
tympanum 43

ud 196
'ūgāb 38
Uhland, Johann Ludwig (1787–1862) 649,
    650, 653, 692, 763, 770
Ulaiya (*fl.* 790) Princess 192–3
Umayyad dynasty 191
Umlauff, Ignaz (1746–96) 474, 531
umunaki 813
Unton, Sir Henry (d.*c.* 1596) 291, *291*
Unverricht, Hubert 552*n*
Upmeyer, Walter 496*n*
Urban VIII (Pope 1623–44) 313

Jrrede (Wrede), Johannes (15th–16th c.) 167

Jrsprung, Otto 130n, 245n

Jspensky, V. A. 199n

'aillant, Jean (14th–15th c.) 135, 154

'alderrábano, Enrique de (*fl.c.* 1547) 237

'alle, F. R. 816

'alle de Paz, Giacomo del 235n

'alls, Francisco (1665–1747) 411

an, Guillaume de 125n, 137n

añhal, Jan (Johann Wanhall) (1739–1813) 491

anloo, Charles-André (1705–65) *458*

aqueiras, Raïmbaut de (12th c.) 97, 100

aresco, Giambattista (*fl.* 1781) 46

arèse, Edgard (1885–1965) 823, 824, 853

arlamov, Aleksandr (1801–48) 768

atielli, Francesco 274n

aucelles, Abbey of 115

udevilles 450–1 (Ex. 158)

aughan Williams, Ralph (1872–1958) 805, 806, 810, 825, 844, 856

cchi, Giuseppe 128–9nn

cchi, Orazio (1550–1605) 267–8, 278

limirović, Miloš M. 67n

ndramini, the 317

nice: Biblioteca Marciana 318, 319; Ospedale della Pietà 428, 483–4; St Mark's 249, 862; its *maestri di cappella* 30, 253, 318, 348, 349, musicians 251, 96, 329, organists 234, 330; theatres: Novissimo 316, 318, Santi Apostoli 20–1, San Cassanio 204, 316, 318, Santi Giovanni e Paolo 316, 317, San Moisè 16, 317

ntadorn, Bernart de (*c.* 1125–95) 97–8

nto, Ivo de (d. 1575) 280, 281

racini, Antonio (b. mid 17th c.) 398

racini, Francesco Maria (1690–1768) 98, 832

rbon(n)et', *see* Ghiselin, Johannes

chaly, André 307n

rdelot, Philippe (d.*c.* 1540) 174, 175n, 02, 229–30, 232, 235–6; madrigals 28–30 (Ex. 65), 254

di, Giuseppe (1813–1901) 731, 743; *Messa da Requiem* (1874) 756; operas 5, 709–11 (Exx. 271–2), 721–2, 727, 4–5

haeren, Émile Adolphe (1855–1916), I

laine, Paul (1844–96) 741, 787–8

meulen, M. 373n

mont, Pierre 219n

Veronese, Paolo (1528–88) 248

Verstovsky, Aleksey Nikolayevich (1799–1862) 653; operas 718 (Exx. 276–7), 729

Vetlitsina, I. M. 480n

Viadana, Ludovico (*c.* 1560–1627) 252, 260, 348, 411

Viardot, Pauline (*fl.* 1849) *708*

Vicentino, Michele (late 15th c.) 227

Vicentino, Nicola (1511–76) 233

Vicenza, Teatro Olimpico (1585) 249

Victoria, Tomás Luis de (*c.* 1548–1611) 203, 247, 249, 260; church music 246, 247–8

Vidal, Peire (12th c.) 97

Vide, Jacobus (*fl.* 1420) 139

vielle 95, 98, 111

Vienna: Burgtheater 459, 531, Court Chapel 338, 361, 550, Court musicians 372, 511, 550 and n, *Gesellschaft der Musikfreunde* 647, Karlskirche 749, *Musikalische Sozietät der Witwen und Waisen* (1772) 550, St Stephen's Cathedral 554, Schwarzenberg Palace 660, Theater auf der Wieden 581

Vigilius (Pope 538–55) 65

vihuela de arco 236n, 238

vihuela de mano 197, 236, 238, *238*

Vila, Pedro Alberch (1517–82) 236n

Viletti, Jacobus (early 15th c.) 160, 161

villancico 179, 283, 345

Villiers de l'Isle-Adam, Count Philippe (1840–89) 787

vīṇā 558, 562

Vincenti, Giacomo (*fl.* 1595) 251

Vinci, Leonardo (*c.* 1695?–1730) 546; operas 445–9, 456; oratorios 546

Vinje, Aasmund (*c.* 1818–70) 792

viol, the 240n, 241, 249n, 268, 332–3

Viola, Alfonso della (*c.* 1508–70) 232

violin, the 205: early use 249, 251, 252, 253; family 249n; makers 205; *violino piccolo*, the 249n

Viotti, Giovanni Battista (1755–1824) 205, 597–8, 599, 601; violin concertos 498, 508, 598 (Ex. 224)

virelai 115, 116, 123, 151

Virgil (Publius Virgilius Maro) (70–19 B.C.) 93; *Aeneid* 233, 234, 472

virginals, music for 290–4

Visigothic liturgy, the 57, 190, 197

Vitali, Giovanni Battista (1632–92) 397, 398, 419, 421, 424, 425; instrumental works 419–20 (Ex. 145), 425; oratorios 397

Index

Vitali, Tomaso (1663–1745) 425
Vitellozzi, Vitellozzo (*fl.* 1564) 244, 245
Vitruvius (Marcus Vitruvius Pollio) (*fl.*40
  B.C.) 45, 46
Vitry, Philippe de (*c.* 1291–1361) 72,
  122–3, 129*n*, 136; motets 118–22 (Exx.
  23, 24(i)), *120*; treatise, *Ars Nova* (*c.*
  1320) 72, 117, 118
Vivaldi, Antonio (1678–1741) 205, 372,
  410, 426, 430, 487, 832; concertos,
  sonatas 428–30, 483; operas 445:
  Arsilda, regina di Ponto (1716) 484, *Fida
  nimfa, La* (1732) 365*n*, *Incoronazione di
  Dario, L'* (1717) 484–5 (Ex. 175(i)),
  Olimpiade, L' (1734) 446*n*, *Ottone in
  Villa* (1713) 365, *Siroe* (1727) 446*n*;
  oratorios 398; symphonies 483–4
Vladimir the Great (*fl.* 988) of Russia 66
Vogel, Johann Christoph (1758–88) 470*n*
Vogel, Martin 61*n*
Vogelweide, Walther von der (*c.* 1170–*c.*
  1230) 98
Vogler, Georg Joseph ('Abt' Vogler)
  (1749–1814) 527, 589, 590, 602*n*, 606,
  611
Volkmann, Robert (1815–83) 686–7;
  Symphony in D minor 687 (Ex. 265),
  690
Volkonsky, Andrey (b. 1933) 857
Voltaire, François Marie Arouet de
  (1694–1778) 455, 586
Vořišek (Woržischek), Jan Václav (Hugo)
  (1791–1825) 611, 639; piano works
  638–9 (Ex. 244(ii) and (iii))
Vorobyev, Ivan Ivanovich (1776–1838)
  623

Wackenroder, Wilhelm (1773–98) 663
  and *n*
Waesberghe, J. Smits van 85*n*, 89*n*
Wagenseil, Georg Christoph (1715–77)
  487, 488, 550; harpsichord divertimenti
  520–1 (Ex. 198(i))
Wagner, Peter 63*n*, 82*n*, 85–6*nn*, 89, 106,
  183*nn*, 219*nn*, 252*nn*
Wagner, Richard (1813–83) 575, 627, 673,
  688, 855; and Boito 727*n*; influence on
  Bruckner 695*n*, 696, Chabrier 575,
  Debussy 575, Draeseke 688, Duparc
  692, Franck 692, French opera 741–3,
  Puccini 575, Rimsky-Korsakov 575,
  Sibelius 575; influenced by Auber 717,
  Beethoven 675, Spontini 717; and Liszt
  714*n*; and Loewe 649; and Rossini 706;
  Das Liebesmahl der Apostel (1843) 747–8

operas 713–17, 721–6: *Feen, Die* (1834)
  674, 705, *Fliegende Holländer, Der*
  (1841) 675 and *n*, 686, 713–14, 721,
  Götterdämmerung (1876) 723, 726,
  Liebesverbot, Das (1836) 713, *Lohengrin*
  (1850) 686, 713, 714 and *n*, 715–17
  (Exx. 274–5), 721, 722, 724,
  Meistersinger, Die (1868) 686, 724–6
  (Ex. 279), 799, *Parsifal* (1882) 726,
  Rheingold, Das (1869) 721, 723, 724,
  726, *Rienzi* (1842) 675, 709, 713, 717,
  721, *Siegfried* (1876) 721, 724, 726,
  Siegfrieds Tod (projected) 723,
  Tannhäuser (1845) 686, 713, 714–15,
  721, 728, 799, *Tristan und Isolde* (1865)
  686, 721, 722, 724, 744, 799, *Walküre,
  Die* (1870) 721, 723
overtures 673–4, 675 and *n*; *Christoph
  Columbus* 674, 675; *Polonia* 673–4 (Ex
  258), 675
prose works: *Mein Leben* (1911) 674,
  Mitteilung an meine Freunde, Eine
  (1852) 713*n*, q. 714: *Oper und Drama*
  (1851) 721
songs 768
symphonies 673, 674
wagon 569
Waissar, Alfons 685*n*
Waisselius, Matthäus (*fl.* 1573) 285
Waite, William G. 104*n*, 106*n*
Walcker-Meyer, Werner 47*n*
Waldburg, Cardinal Truchsess von (*fl.*
  1562) 245
Waldhorntube 723
Waldstein, Count Ferdinand von
  (1762–1823) 630 and *n*
Walker, D. P. 171*n*, 269*n*, 306*n*
Walker, Frank 321*n*
Wallace, William Vincent (1812–65) 72c
Wallner, Bertha 160*n*
Walpole, Horace, 4th Earl of Orford
  (1717–97) 464*n*
'Walsingham Consort Books' (*c.* 1591) 2
Walter, Johann (1496–1570) 220, 222, 2
  257, 258, 401
Walter, R. 441*n*
Walther, Johann Gottfried (1684–1748)
  428*n*, 430, 442
Walther, Michael (17th c.?) 405
Walther von der Vogelweide (*c.* 1170–*c.*
  1230) 98
Walton, Sir William (b. 1902) 824, 825
  856, 859
Wanhall, Johann (Jan Vaňhal)
  (1739–1813) 491

966

'Wanley part-books' 241*n*
Ward, John (1571–?1638) 278
Ware 141–2
Warlock, Peter (Philip Heseltine)
(1894–1930) 290*n*, 307*nn*
Warrack, John 613*n*, 634*n*
Warren, Edwin B. 187*n*
Waterman, Richard A. 813*n*, 816
Watkins, Glenn E. 254*n*, 267*n*
Watson, Thomas (?1557–92) 276
Weakland, Rembert 76*n*, 77
Weaver, Robert L. 270*n*
Webbe, Samuel (1740–1816) 665
Weber, Carl Maria von (1786–1826) 575,
592*n*, 610, 615, 617, 624, 641; chamber
music 622; concertos, etc. 604, **605**, **613**,
615, 634; *Kampf und Sieg* (1815) 665;
Masses 663; operas 575, 590 (Ex. 221),
592–3, 606, 607; orchestral works 564*n*,
593, 605–6, 607; piano works 629*n*, 634,
635–6 (Ex. 243)
ebern, Anton von (1883–1945) 183*n*,
798, 806 and *n*, 835, 849, 862
eckerlin, J. B. 373*n*
eckmann, Matthias (1621–74) 335,
36–7, 351, 404
edekind, Frank (1864–1918) 835
edig, Hans Josef 619*n*
elkes, Thomas (*c.* 1575–1623) 261, 263,
77, **278**, 356
erbeke, Gaspar van (*c.* 1440–*c.* 1515)
61, 165 and *n*, 167, 170, 174
gner, Max 8*n*, 11–13*nn*, 15*n*, 19 and *n*,
2–3*nn*
igl, Joseph (1766–1846) 589
igl, Karl 619*n*
ll, Kurt (1900–50) 823, 834, 836, 841
mar, court musicians at 430, 442, 685
nberger, Jaromir (b. 1896) 838
smann, Wilhelm 267*n*
ssenbäck, Andreas 550*n*
ssenfels: Court 405–6; Court opera
5, 405; the Weissenfels poets 385
esz, Egon (1885–1974) 51–2*nn*, 61*n*,
9–20*nn*, 325*n*, 372*n*, 420–1*nn*, 845
ner, Theodor 372*n*, 474*n*
a, Ernst von 431*n*, 435*n*, 441*n*
t, Giaches de (1535–96) 247, 251, 254,
, 266
ey, Samuel (1766–1837) 654, 752
ey, Samuel Sebastian (1810–76) 752
phal, Kurt 173*n*
ron wynde' 242
up, Sir Jack 275*n*, 415*n*, 729*n*
e, Christoph Ernst Friedrich

(1774–1842) 594
White, John R. 225*n*, 340*n*
White, Robert (*c.* 1530–74) 241, 242–3
Whitehill, W. M. 86*n*
Whitgift, John (1530–1604), Archbishop
261
Whitman, Walt (1819–92) 806
Whythorne, Thomas (1528–96) 275
Widmann, Erasmus (1572–1634) 283, 303,
334, 335
Wieland, Christoph Martin (1733–1813)
476
Wieniawski, Henryk (1835–80) 699–700
Wilbye, John (1574–1638), madrigals
277–8 (Ex. 80(ii))
Wilde, Oscar (1856–1900) 794, 806
Wilkin, Ludolf (of Winsum) (*fl.c.* 1431)
158
Wilkins, Nigel 131*n*
Willaert, Adrian (*c.* 1490–1562) 178, 202,
229, 230, 249, 251; church music 230,
232 and *n*, 233, 249; instrumental works
234–5; madrigals 230–1 (Ex. 66); *Musica
nova* (1559) 231*n*, 232
William IX (1071–1127), Duke of
Aquitaine 94–5
William X (d. 1137), Duke of Aquitaine
87*n*, 95
William of York, St 241*n*
Williamson, Malcolm (b. 1931) 859
Wilson, John (1595–1674) 309, 310, 334*n*,
425*n*
Winchester Tropers (11th c.) 63, *83*, 91,
125
Windsor, Chapel Royal at 240
Winschermann, Helmut 403*n*
Winter (*fl.* 1760) 517
Winter, Peter von (1754–1825) 606, 611;
operas 589 (Ex. 220)
Wiora, Walter 230*n*
Wipo (*c.* 995–*c.* 1050) 92
Wise, Michael (*c.* 1648–87) 415, 416
Wither, George (1588–1667) 357
Witte, Friedrich (1770–1837) 598
Witwicki, Stefan (?19th c.) 769
Władysław IV of Poland (1632–48) 312,
313
Wolf, Hugo (1860–1903) 574, 575, 703,
775, 794
songs 789, 790–1
Wolf, Johannes 94*n*, 117*n*, 119*n*, 123*n*,
124*n*, 131*n*, 136*n*, 140*n*, 158*n*, 164*n*, 169*n*,
177*n*, 182*n*, 186*n*, 222*n*, 266*n*, 274*n*, 281*n*,
303*n*, 309*n*
Wolff, Hellmuth Christian 358*n*, 366–7*nn*,

372n, 384n, 446n, 472n
Wolff, Konrad 502n
Wölfl, Joseph (1773–1812) 603, 607, 619;
  piano concertos 603–4 (Ex. 228)
Wolgast, J. 435n
Wolkenstein, Oswald von (d. 1445) 124n,
  138, 154, 159
Wolzogen, Hans von 649n, 717n
Wooldridge, H. E. 112n, 119n
Woolley, Leonard 7n, 11n, 21n
Worcester Antiphonal 134
Worcester Cathedral 356
'Worcester fragments' 113
'Worldes blis' 99
'Worldes blise have god day' (c. 1280) 110
Worms, Diet of (1521) 207
Worsthorne, Simon Towneley 316n,
  318–19nn
Wranitzky (Vranický), Paul (1756–1808)
  476
Wrede, Johannes, see Urrede
Wright, Owen 192 and n
Wulstan, David 10n, 38n, 263n
Würtemberg, Charles Eugene (fl. 1742),
  Duke of 511
Wyatt, Sir Thomas (c. 1503–42) 239
Wyzewa, Théodore de 498

Xenakis, Iannis (b. 1922) 855
xylophone: African 813, Assyrian 19, 19,
  20, Indonesian 572

Yamada, Kosaku (1886–1965) 571
Yamazumi (Yatsuhashi) (1614–85) 570–1
Ya'qūb ibn Isḥāq al-Kindi (Alkindus) (c.
  790–c. 874) 193–4, 565n
Yatsuhashi (Yamazumi) (1614–85) 570–1
Yevtushenko, Yevgeny Aleksandrovich (b.
  1933) 857
Yonge, Nicholas (fl. 1588) 275, 276, 277
Yoshimasa (1435–90) 570
Young, William (d. 1672) 333
Yüan (Tatar) dynasty 567
Yüeh-fu 565

'Zacharias, Magister' (14th c.) 136

Zachow, Friedrich Wilhelm (1663–1712)
  406, 441
zamr 195
Zandonai, Riccardo (1883–1944) 810
Zaragoza (Spain), the Pilar at 411
Zarlino, Gioseffo (1517–90) 170, 178, 233,
  268
zarzuela (burlesca) 477
Zedda, Alberto 398n
Zedlitz, Joseph Christian von (1790–1862)
  768n
Zelenski, Władysław (1837–1921) 734, 783
Zelený, Václav 780n
Zelle, Friedrich 367n, 401n
Zelter, Carl Friedrich (1758–1832) 501n,
  643, 663n, 665; Sämmtliche Lieder . . .
  (1811–12) 644, 645 (Ex. 246(ii))
Zelzer, H. 339n
Zemlinsky, Alexander von (1872–1942)
  797
Zenck, H. 232n, 234n
Zeno, Apostolo (1668–1750) 361n, 364,
  395, 398
Zhukovsky, Vasily Andreyevich
  (1783–1852) 653, 729, 768n
Ziani, Marc'Antonio (c. 1653–1715) 366,
  399, 422
Ziani, Pietro Andrea (c. 1620–84) 358,
  359, 366, 422
Zieleński, Mikołaj (fl. 1611) 252n
Zingarelli, Nicola Antonio (1752–1837)
  585, 586
Zipoli, Domenico (1688–1726) 435, 438
Zirnbauer, Heinz 226n
Ziryāb (fl. 852) 194
zither 19, 19, 20: Chinese types, 564, 5
  567, Japanese, etc., types 569, tube- c
  stick-zithers (Indian, 6th–7th c.) 558
znamenny raspev 67
Zoilo, Annibale (16th c.) 246
Zola, Émile (1840–1902) 743
Zólta szlafmyca (1788) 478
Zschinsky-Troxler, Elsa von 498n
zummârah 18
Zumsteeg, Johann Rudolf (1760–1802)
  574, 589, 643, 645, 648–9, 654